Schroeder's Collectible TOYS
Antique to Modern Price Guide

2004

NINTH EDITION

Edited by
Sharon & Bob Huxford

D1530935

COLLECTOR BOOKS
A Division of Schroeder Publishing Co., Inc.

On the Cover:

Front
  Top: Chein tin windup Seaplane, EX, $250.00 (photo courtesy Dunbar Gallery).
  Center: Robot, Hong Kong, $150.00 (photo courtesy June Moon); Pepsi Batgirl and Robin glass, $2,000.00 (photo courtesy Collector Glass News); American Character Betsy McCall, $250.00, and Sandy McCall, $500.00 (photo courtesy McMaster's Doll Auction).
  Bottom: Hoppy dinnerware set, $225.00; Goebel Dumbo figurine, $60.00 (photo courtesy Joel Cohen); Marx Marine Corp Truck with figurines, MIB, $300.00 (photo courtesy John Turney).
Back
  From top: Steiff dinosaur, $1,250.00; Irwin plastic windup fan, MIB, $95.00 (photo courtesy John Turney); Marx Thunderbolt horse, MIB, $100.00 – 125.00; Garfield toothbrush holder, $14.00.

Editorial Staff:

Editors: Sharon and Bob Huxford
Research and Editorial Assistants: Michael Drollinger, Donna Newnum, Loretta Suiters
Cover Design: Beth Summers
Layout: Terri Hunter

COLLECTOR BOOKS
P.O. Box 3009
Paducah, Kentucky 42002-3009
www.collectorbooks.com

Copyright © 2004 Schroeder Publishing Co., Inc.

Searching For A Publisher?

We are always looking for people knowledgeable within their fields. If you feel that there is a real need for a book on your collectible subject and have a large comprehensive collection, contact Collector Books.

The current values in this book should be used only as a guide. They are not intended to set prices, which vary from one section of the country to another. Auction prices as well as dealer prices vary greatly and are affected by condition as well as demand. Neither the editors nor the publisher assumes responsibility for any losses that might be incurred as a result of consulting this guide.

Introduction

One question on our minds as we readied this edition for the press was 'how is the toy market faring now?' The past decade has been a rollercoaster ride of highs and lows — for our country in general, the economy in particular, and certainly for the toy market. So we polled our advisors for their views. Virtually all had the same opinions.

'Speculators are gone,' says Jim Frugoli (June Moon), 'and now only collectors or the curious ('I remember this' or 'I had one of these when I was a kid') drive the market. They're not spending the big money they once did three or four years ago. The baby boomers are growing older, for one thing, and they have other concerns now. The manic collecting and reviving one's youth phase has passed.'

There's been an obvious shift in the antiques and collectibles market in general; and more than any other influence, eBay is setting the pace. 'How we collect toys, their availability, and their values have changed dramatically with the inception of Internet auctions,' to quote our guns advisor, Bill Hamburg (Happy Memories Collectibles). He goes on to say '[the Internet's] long-term impact has yet to be measured; but one thing is certain, it is a permanent resource for the foreseeable future.'

Not only are thousands of toys offered daily through eBay sales, many dealers who hate to be tied solely to eBay for an online sales outlet are setting up their own 'ecommerce' storefronts. Since we published the first edition of our toy book, besides the drop in the number of toy shows and their poor attendance, we've seen many of the dealers who used to publish catalogs and send out lists completely abandon that approach, finding that even their long-time customer base has virtually evaporated. Bob Wilson (Phoenix Toy Soldiers) had this to say: 'As marketing... was strongly hinting at a transition, I started hitting eBay hard last summer.' He found his total sales about the same as they once were from sending out lists. Ninety-five percent of his buyers were new customers, but curiously some sales were to buyers who had been offered the same merchandise on his last mailing. 'A recent eBay sale was to a customer in my data base who bought a $50.00 item from me that he's been looking for and was happy to have finally found it. That same item was on a list sent to him five months earlier at the same price. The summation is that there's literally an entire customer base out there that I never knew about, and they seem to be available through the Internet only. The tried and proven ways of communicating are quickly drying. Repeat business is falling off dramatically. Glen Ridenour (Fun House Toy Co.) no longer sends out catalogs. He says 'there are still a lot of people out there who don't use computers, or feel intimidated by the one sitting on their desk. The problem is that eBay has changed the shape of the marketplace so that I can't cost-effectively service that dwindling group that isn't online.'

We can't argue the fact; obviously the Internet is where sales are made, and it's great, to a point. Merchandise moves quickly, dealers make a good living without the hassle of setting up at shows, and buyers can select from thousands of toys on any given day. But you can't deny that at best it's very impersonal; and it's this void that keeps the tried and true methods of finding treasures — toy shows, traditional auctions, malls, flea markets, and estate and garage sales — alive, though struggling. 'The Internet will never replace the thrill of discovering and then actually holding that long sought old toy in our hands as we negotiate the price. This one factor alone will keep traditional sources alive and well,' continues Bill Hamburg.

But what can we say about the way the Internet, eBay in particular, has affected values? Again, quoting Bob Wilson, 'The transition to eBay has allowed anyone with a computer and a digital camera to bypass the dealer and sell directly to the general public. Good for them, I'd probably do the same myself. They've realized that while bypassing the dealer they get more (than wholesale) for their product, and the buyer can determine the sales price as well. The sellers seem willing to take a wide range of pricing for their items.' As Cindy Sabulis, our doll advisor, puts it: 'Many collectibles have come out of attics and basements at a faster rate than ever before as more people join the ranks of sellers through online auctions. The supply of vintage items for sale has increased, creating a buyers' market. Some items that used to be considered rare now can be found easily by searching the Internet. Not only can buyers find one example of an item they've been looking for, they can find a great many of them and so can pick and choose which one they want to buy...many items have come down in value because of this increase in supply.' She noted that in particular 'items produced in large quantities have fallen off in value, since so many of them have survived and are now making their way to the resale market.' Bill Hamburg again: 'The soft economy and the Internet have both impacted the value of old toys. The Internet in particular with the increased availability of toys, combined with more sellers and more buyers makes for interesting market dynamics. Once-scarce, old toys aren't so scarce anymore. The quantity exceeds the number of buyers, thereby bringing prices down. On the other hand, the truly rare toys are exposed to more buyers, thereby driving values up. The net effect is some toys have softened in value, and others have skyrocketed.' Jim Frugoli observes that 'eBay has made only the most desirable toys valuable. The others are plentiful and are now worth less in the market.' As Glenn Ridenour says 'There is still interest and still buyers out there. eBay has had impact on supply and in most cases has driven the cost of anything considered ordinary down significantly. Items that are in demand and have cachet of being rare, though, consistently hit record prices realized via eBay.'

How true! eBay results might be relied upon as a standard by which pricing could be determined, but they're very erratic. Here's a good example of what we mean. Quoting from Bob Wilson again, 'I have a dozen or so identical items in stock and put them on eBay regularly. The prices gleaned for this identical item has ranged from $0 (no bids) to $4.00, $5.00, $9.00, $10.00, $13.00, $18.00, $23.00, up to $43.00. The sales were not in that order, but rounded off to the nearest dollar, these were actual numbers.' He continues to say that a Marx Civil War playset that booked for $500.00 sold for only $231.00, a price only slightly above what he normally would expect to pay for one to stock his inventory. Along this line, Glenn Ridenour says 'I've found that eBay is a real hit and miss proposition; on any given day, the same piece graded in like condition will sell for vastly different money. Just depends on who saw the auction and when!'

With the volume of merchandise that passes through Internet auctions on any given day, condition has become an even weightier worth-assessing factor than ever before. Cindy Sabulis reports that 'dolls and toys in played with condition are another group of collectibles that has fallen in value. Collectors can wait and easily locate better examples of the same items in a short period of time. Unless priced reasonably [played-with toys] are passed by more often than they used to be. Mint examples, mint-in-box or never-removed-from-box dolls and toys are still commanding top dollar.' Jim Frugoli goes on to say that 'any old toy in great condition will bring top dollar at shows, in our store, and most of all on eBay or live toy auctions. Everyone wants to own the best, and they are willing to pay for the privilege.'

When you sell on eBay impacts results as well. Cindy Sabulis remarks that 'if a person is looking to weed out or downsize their collection… deciding when to sell can make the difference between getting top dollar, selling at cost, or selling it for less than what was originally paid for it. The [toy] market has become like the stock market with highs and lows changing regularly, based on such things as the economy, the season of the year, and even the weather. During the summer when there are flea markets to attend and other outdoor activities to compete with, selling prices seem to come down.'

On a positive note, Bob Armstrong, our puzzles advisor, feels that 'eBay offers a unique opportunity to develop your market… through invaluable exposure and contacts with collectors and enthusiasts, which can be developed into a customer base.' He feels that 'best results are achieved if the listings are tied in with a well constructed website, through which additional merchandise may be viewed and ordered, a site which is updated and expanded on a regular basis.'

One question we especially asked when we surveyed our advisors was what toys are hot? Which are not? Here are their views: Jim Frugoli: 'Hot toys would include Transformers; boxed or mint toy trucks made of pressed steel such as Marx, Structo, and Smith Miller; Hot Wheels redlines; slot cars; Barbie accessories; anything monster; Western cowboys; super heroes; or any item in a collecting category that is scarce or in limited supply. Lunch boxes, Péz, Star Wars, G.I. Joe, Mego figures have life, but only for [nostalgic] buyers or young children five to eight years of age. '70s and '80s toys are big now. Some toys like Care Bears, Strawberry Shortcake, and My Little Pony are being reproduced.' Concerning special editions, limited editions, packaging vartiations, etc., used by various toy companies to target collectors of vintage toys, he has this to say: 'The companies' attempts to create an artificial market has angered and frustrated collectors, and now they just don't bother with this phoney marketing anymore. A lot of this had to do with perceived investment value which, when it comes to antiques or toys, is not the real or fun way to collect. Beanie Babies are a case in point.' Bob Armstrong, reporting on the puzzles market: 'The effect of eBay has been to boost the value of the best puzzles and devalue the second line puzzles, including nineteenth-century puzzles… map, children's, and cardboard puzzles, unless a highly collectible character is in the scene.' Michael J. Mcquillen, Political Parade: 'High-end politically related toys continue to do well, while mid-range or lower-valued items are moving rather slowly.' Scott Smiles, Antique Toy Information Service: 'I can only speak to the tin toy market. The strongest interest appears to continue to be in the character-related toys — such as Felix, Popeye, Superman, Disney characters, Dick Tracy, etc. — and space-related toys, such as all robots, Flash Gordon, Buck Rogers , etc. Marx, Lehmann, Chein, Wolverine, and Unique Art are some of the more sought after tin toy manufacturers.' Marcia Fanta: 'I am still very satisfied with the [doll] market and can be as busy selling as I want to be.' Bill Campbell: My ads in publications such as the *Toy Shop* have been doing fantastic! I basically can sell all the '60s TV show items that I can get. That includes everything from Universal Monster items to cap guns. On the older items such as radio premiums, sales are more sporadic. I am also doing very well with boxed character watches.' Glen Ridenour: I've seen a significant drop on some of the high-end vintage Star Wars items I have had in storage… when the dotcom bubble burst, a lot of the buying power of those Gen-X'ers went with it, and coupled with waning interest after the new movies hit and market saturation with all the new Star Wars product, we're now seeing prices drop.'

Though it's obvious the venue has shifted and the speculators have switched to some other commodity, there's good news. The toy market is still alive and well; the true collector is still buying for all the right reasons, the most important of which is personal enjoyment. Jim Frugoli comments: 'I would not pass up buying any old toys, and my own toy room is still a pleasant refuge for me.'

So what is the future of toy collecting? Here's where Bill Hamburg sees things going: 'The rarest and highest quality toys will continue to increase in value. The soft end of the market will firm up when that abundance once again diminishes. The basics of vintage toy market values are still in place. Unique old quality toys with intrinsic beauty by nature of their design or manufacture will always be a good investment. As new collectors seek the toys of their youth, many will gravitate to older or newer toys, expanding their collections in both directions outside the parameters of their memories. This foible of human nature will assure the future value of collectible toys. My advice: continue to add high quality toys to your collection. There are some real bargains out there right now. Future values are impossible to predict, but if you buy what you like and the best you can afford, your collections will continue to appreciate over the long term. A good old toy on the shelf is worth far more than money sitting in a bank.' We agree!

In this edition we've tried to bring accurate, up-to-date information concerning market values, but so many of our advisors, experienced though they are, found it impossible to determine fixed prices. We had some advisors who were still reluctant to factor in eBay prices, especially on low-end merchandise, while others gave in to the weight of it and actually lowered values. We left this up to the individual; we have the utmost confidence in their opinions.

Our concept is unique. Though we designed the book first and foremost to be a price guide, we wanted to make it a buying/selling guide as well. So we took many of our descriptions and values from the websites and 'toys for sale' lists of dealers and collectors around the country. In each of those listings we included a dealer's code, so that if you were looking for the particular toy that S5 (for example) had to offer, you'd be able to match his code with his name and address in the Dealer and Collector Codes section and simply drop him a line or call him to see if it were still available. Our experiment has been very successful. Feedback indicates that many of our sellers do very well, making productive contacts with collectors who not only purchase items from them on their initial call but leave requests for other merchandise they are looking for as well.

Each edition contains about 24,000 listings, but even at that we realize that when it comes to the toy market, that only begins to scratch the surface. Our intent is to provide our readers with fresh information, issue after issue. The few categories that are repeated in their entirety in succeeding editions generally are those that were already complete or as nearly complete as we or our advisors could make them. But even those are checked to make sure that values are still current and our information up to date.

Some of our values are auction results; you'll be able to recognize these by the 'A' at the end of the description line. The listings that have neither the 'A' code or the dealer code mentioned above were either sent to us by collectors who specialize in those specific types of toys or were originally dealer coded but altered at the suggestion of an advisor who felt that the stated price might be far enough outside the average market price range to be misleading (in which case, the dealer's code was removed). The bottom line is that there are two factors that determine selling price: the attitude of the individual collector (how strongly he desires to own) and the motivation of the dealer (does he need to turn over his merchandise quickly to replenish and freshen his stock, or can he wait for the most opportune time to turn it over for maximum profit). Where you buy affects prices as well. One of our advisors used this simple analogy: while a soda might cost you $2.50 at the ball park, you can buy the same thing for 39¢ at the corner 7–11. So all we (or anyone) can offer is whatever facts and information we can compile, and ask simply that you arrive at your own evaluations based on the data we've provided, adapted to your personal buying/selling arena.

We hope you enjoy our book and that you'll be able to learn by using it. We don't presume to present it as the last word on toys or their values — there are many specialized books by authors who are able to devote an entire publication to one subject, covering it from 'A' to 'Z,' and when we're aware that such a text book exists, we'll recommend it in our narratives. If you have suggestions that you think will improve our format, let us hear from you — we value your input. Until next time — happy hunting!

— The Editors

Advisory Board

The editors and staff take this opportunity to express our sincere gratitude and appreciation to each person who has contributed their time and knowledge to help us. We've found toys to be *by far* the largest, most involved field of collecting we've ever tried to analyze, but we will have to admit, it's great fun! We've been editing general price guides for twenty years now, and before ever attempting the first one, we realized there was only one way we would presume to publish such a guide — and that would be to first enlist the help of knowledgeable collectors around the country who specialized in specific areas. We now have over fifty toy advisors, and we're still looking for help in several areas. Generally, the advisors are listed following each category's narrative, so if we have mentioned no one and you feel that you are qualified to advise us, have the time and would be willing to help us out with that subject, please contact us. We'd love to have you on our advisory board. (We want to stress that even if an advisor is credited in a category narrative, that person is in no way responsible for errors — those are our responsibility.) Even if we currently list an advisor for your subject, contact us so that we'll have your name on file should that person need to be replaced. This of course happens from time to time due to changing interests or because they find they no longer have the time.

While some advisors sent us listings and prices, others provided background information and photographs, checked printouts or simply answered our questions. All are listed below. Each name is followed by their code, see the section called Dealer and Collector Codes for an explanation of how these are used in the listings.

Matt and Lisa Adams (A7)
Sally and Stan Alekna (A1)
Pamela E. Apkarian-Russell (H9)
Bob Armstrong (A4)
Richard Belyski (B1)
Larry Blodget
Bojo (B3)
Jim Buskirk (B6)
Bill Campbell (C10)
Brad Cassity (C13)
Mark Chase (C2)
Ken Clee (C3)
Joel Cohen (C12)
Cotswold Collectibles (C6)
Marl Davidson (D2)
Donna and Ron Donnelly (D7)
Paul Fink (F3)
Mike and Kurt Fredericks (F4)

Lee Garmon
Bill Hamburg (H1)
George Hardy (H3)
Amy Hopper
Dan Iannotti (I3)
Terri Ivers (I2)
Keith and Donna Kaonis (K6)
David Kolodny-Nagy (K2)
Tom Lastrapes (L4)
John McKenna (M2)
Michael and Polly McQuillen (M11)
Lucky Meisenheimer (M3)
Steven Meltzer (M9)
Gary Mosholder (G1)
Judith Mosholder (M7)
Peter Muldavin (M21)
Dawn Diaz (P2)
Gary Pollastro (P5)

Judy Posner (P6)
John Rammacher (S5)
Jim Rash (R3)
Charlie Reynolds (R5)
Cindy Sabulis (S14)
Scott Smiles (S10)
Carole and Richard Smyth (S22)
Steve Stephenson (S25)
Nate Stoller (S7)
Mark and Lynda Suozzi (S24)
Richard Trautwein (T3)
Judy and Art Turner (H8)
Marci Van Ausdall (V2)
James Watson (W8)
Randy Welch (W4)
Mary Young (Y2)

How to Use This Book

Concept. Our design for this book is two-fold. Primarily it is a market report compiled from many sources, meant to be studied and digested by our readers, who can then better arrive at their own conclusion regarding prices. Were you to ask ten active toy dealers for their opinion as to the value of a specific toy, you would no doubt get ten different answers, and who's to say which is correct? Quite simply, there are too many variables to consider. Where you buy is critical. Condition is certainly subjective, prices vary from one area of the country to another, and probably the most important factor is how badly you want to add the item in question to your collection or at what price you're willing to sell. So use this as a guide along with your own observations.

The second function of this book is to put buyers in touch with sellers who deal in the type of toys they want to purchase. Some of our listings contain a dealer's code, linking that item to a merchant that may have that particular toy in stock. (See the section titled Dealer and Collector Codes in the Directory.) Even though it may have already sold by the time this book is published, many of them tell us that they often get similar or even the same items in over and over, so if you see something listed you're interested in buying, don't hesitate to call any of them. Remember, though, they're not tied down to the price quoted in the book, since their asking price is many times influenced by what they've had to pay to restock their shelves.

Toys are listed by name. Every effort has been made to list a toy by the name as it appears on the original box. There have been very few exceptions made, and then only if the collector-given name is more recognizable. For instance, if we listed 'To-Night Amos 'n Andy in Person' (as the name appears on the box lid), very few would recognize the toy as the Amos 'n Andy Walkers. But these exceptions are few.

Descriptions and sizes may vary. When we were entering data, we often found the same toy had sold through more than one auction gallery or was listed in several dealer lists. So the same toy will often be described in various ways, but we left descriptions just as we found them, since there is usually something to be gleaned from each variation. We chose to leave duplicate lines in when various conditions were represented so that you could better understand the impact of condition on value. Depending on the source and who was doing the measuring, we found that the size of a given toy might vary by an inch or more. Not having the toy to measure ourselves, we had to leave dimensions just as they were given in auction catalogs or dealer lists.

Lines are sometimes coded as to source. Each line that represents an auction-realized price will be coded 'A' at the end, just before the price. Other letter/number codes identify the dealer who sent us that information. These codes are explained later on. Additional sources of like merchandise will be noted under the narratives.

As we said before, collectors have various viewpoints regarding auction results. You will have to decide for yourself. Some feel they're too high to be used to establish prices while others prefer them to 'asking' prices that can sometimes be speculative. But for the most part, auction prices were not far out of line with accepted values. Many times, compared to the general market place, toys in less-than-excellent condition actually sold under 'book.' Because the average auction-consigned toy is in especially good condition and many times even retains its original box, it will naturally bring higher prices than the norm. And auctions often offer the harder-to-find, more unusual items. Unless you take these factors into consideration, prices may seem high, when in reality, they may not be at all. Prices may be driven up by high reserves, but not all galleries have reserves. Whatever your view, you'll be able to recognize and consider the source of the values we quote and factor that into your personal evaluation.

Categories that have priority. Obviously there are thousands of toys that would work as well in one category as they would in another, depending on the preference of the collector. For instance, a Mary Poppins game would appeal to a games collector just as readily as it would to someone who bought character-related toys of all kinds. The same would be true of many other types of toys. We tried to make our decisions sensibly and keep our sorts simple. We'll guide you to those specialized categories with cross-references and 'see alsos.' If all else fails, refer to the index. It's as detailed as we know how to make it.

Price Ranges. Once in awhile, you'll find a listing that gives a price range. These result from our having found varying prices for the same item. We've taken a mid-range — less than the highest, a little over the lowest — if the original range was too wide to really be helpful. If the range is still coded 'A' for auction, all that were averaged were auction-realized prices.

Condition, how it affects value, how to judge it. The importance of condition can't be stressed enough. Unless a toy is exceptionally rare, it must be very good or better to really have much collector value. But here's where the problem comes in: though each step downward on the grading scale drastically decreases a toy's value, as the old saying goes, 'beauty is in the eye of the beholder.' What is acceptable wear and damage to one individual may be regarded by another as entirely too degrading. Criteria used to judge condition even varies from one auction company to the next, so we had to attempt to sort them all out and arrive at some sort of standardization. Please be sure to read and comprehend what the description is telling you about condition; otherwise you can easily be mislead. Auction galleries often describe missing parts, repairs, and paint touch-ups, summing up overall appearance in the condition code. When losses and repairs were noted in the catalog, we noted them as well. Remember that a toy even in mint restored condition is never worth as much as one in mint original condition. And even though a toy may be rated 'otherwise EX' after losses and repairs are noted, it won't be worth as much as one with original paint and parts in excellent condition. Keep this in mind when you use our listings to evaluate your holdings.

These are the conditions codes we have used throughout the book and their definitions as we have applied them:

M — mint. Unplayed with, brand new, flawless.

NM — near mint. Appears brand new except on very close inspection.

EX — excellent. Has minimal wear, very minor chips and rubs, a few light scratches.

VG — very good. Played with, loss of gloss, noticeable problems, several scratches.

G — good. Some rust, considerable wear and paint loss, well used.

P — poor. Generally unacceptable except for a filler.

Because we do not use a three-level pricing structure as many of you are used to and may prefer, we offer this table to help you arrive at values for toys in conditions other than those that we give you. If you know the value of a toy in excellent condition and would like to find an approximate value for it in near mint condition, for instance, just run your finger down the column under 'EX' until you find the approximate price we've listed (or one that easily factors into it), then over to the column headed 'NM.' We'll just go to $100.00, but other values will be easy to figure by addition or multiplication.

G	VG	EX	NM	M
40/50%	55/65%	70/80%	85/90%	100%
5.00	6.00	7.50	9.00	10.00
7.50	9.00	11.00	12.50	15.00
10.00	12.00	15.00	18.00	20.00
12.00	15.00	18.00	22.00	25.00
14.00	18.00	22.50	26.00	30.00
18.00	25.00	30.00	35.00	40.00
22.50	30.00	37.50	45.00	50.00
27.00	35.00	45.00	52.00	60.00
32.00	42.00	52.00	62.00	70.00
34.00	45.00	55.00	65.00	75.00
35.00	48.00	60.00	70.00	80.00
40.00	55.00	68.00	80.00	90.00
45.00	60.00	75.00	90.00	100.00

Condition and value of original boxes and packaging. When no box or packaging is referred to in the line or in the narrative, assume that the quoted price is for the toy only. Please read the narratives! In some categories (Corgi, for instance), all values are given for items mint and in original boxes. Conditions for boxes (etc.) are in parenthesis immediately following the condition code for the toy itself. In fact, any information within parenthesis at that point in the line will refer to packaging. Collector interest in boxes began several years ago, and today many people will pay very high prices for them, depending on scarcity, desirability, and condition. The more colorful, graphically pleasing boxes are favored, and those with images of well-known characters are especially sought-after. Just how valuable is a box? Again, this is very subjective to the individual. We asked this question to several top collectors around the country, and the answers they gave us ranged from 20% to 100% above mint-no-box prices.

Listing of Standard Abbreviations

These abbreviations have been used throughout this book in order to provide you with the most detailed descriptions possible in the limited space available. No periods are used after initials or abbreviations. When two dimensions are given, height is noted first. When only one measurement is given, it will be the greater — height if the toy is vertical, length if it is horizontal. (Remember that in the case of duplicate listings representing various conditions, we found that sizes often varied as much as an inch or more.)

att	attributed to	mk	marked
bl	blue	MOC	mint on card
blk	black	MOT	mint on tree
brn	brown	NM	near mint
bsk	bisque	NOS	new old stock
cb	cardboard	NP	nickel plated
CI	cast iron	NRFB	never removed from box
compo	composition	NRFP	never removed from package
dbl	double	orig	original
dk	dark	o/w	otherwise
dtd	dated	pk	pink
emb	embossed	pkg	package
EX	excellent	pnt	paint, painted
EXIB	excellent in box	pr	pair
EXIC	excellent in container	prof	professional
ft, ftd	feet, foot, footed	rnd	round
G	good	rpl	replaced
GIB	good in box	rpr	repaired
gr	green	rpt	repainted
hdl	handle, handled	rstr	restored
illus	illustrated, illustration	sz	size
inscr	inscribed	turq	turquoise
jtd	jointed	unmk	unmarked
L	long, length	VG	very good
litho	lithographed	VGIB	very good in box
lt	light, lightly	W	width, wingspan
M	mint	wht	white
MBP	mint in bubble pack	w/	with
mc	multicolored	w/up	windup
MIB	mint in box	yel	yellow
MIP	mint in package		

Action Figures

You will find a wide range of asking prices from dealer to dealer, and under the influence of e-Bay buying, prices fluctuate greatly. Be critical of condition! Original packaging is extremely important. In fact, when it comes to recent issues, loose, played-with examples are seldom worth more than a few dollars. When no size is given, assume figures are 3¾" or standard size for that line. Unless otherwise noted, values are for complete accessories or figures.

See also Character, TV, and Movie Collectibles; Dolls, Celebrity; GI Joe; Star Trek; Star Wars.

A-Team, accessory, Command Chopper & Enforcer Van, MIP ..$25.00
A-Team, accessory, Corvette (w/Face figure), Galoob, MIP..$25.00
A-Team, accessory, Headquarters Camp, Galoob, MIP $65.00
A-Team, accessory, helicopter, Galoob, EX......................$20.00
A-Team, accessory, Off Road Attack Cycle, Galoob, MIP..$25.00
A-Team, accessory, Patrol Boat (w/Hannibal figure), Galoob, MIP $28.00
A-Team, accessory, van, removable roof, Galoob, 4½x9½", EX..$35.00
A-Team, figure, Amy Allen, 6½", Galoob, MOC, from $30 to.$40.00
A-Team, figure, BA Baracus, Hannibal, or Murdock, 6½", Galoob, MOC, ea, from $30 to $35.00
A-Team, figure, Cobra, Python, Rattler, or Viper, 6½", Galoob, MOC, ea, from $30 to $40.00
A-Team, figure, Mr T, talking, 12", Galoob, MIB.............$65.00

A-Team, figure, Templeton Peck (Face), Galoob, 1983, MOC, from $30.00 to $35.00.

A-Team, figure set, Bad Guys (Cobra, Python, Rattle, Viper), Galoob, MOC..$60.00
A-Team, figure set, Soldiers of Fortune (BA, Face, Hannibal, Murdock), Galoob, MOC...$70.00
Action Jackson, accessory, Campmobile, Mego, MIB.......$90.00
Action Jackson, accessory, Jungle House, Mego, MIB $90.00
Action Jackson, accessory, Parachute Plunge, Strap-On Helicopter, or Water Scooter, Mego, MIB, ea...................$30.00
Action Jackson, accessory, Scramble Cycle, Mego, MIB ..$45.00
Action Jackson, figure, any color hair or beard, Mego, MIB, ea.$35.00
Action Jackson, figure, Black, Mego, MIB $65.00
Action Jackson, outfit, any, Mego, MIP, ea $15.00

Adventures of Indiana Jones, see Indiana Jones (Adventures of)
Alien, figure, Alien, 18", Kenner, NMIB........................$450.00

Archies, figure, Archie, Betty, Veronica, or Reggie, Marx, 1975, NRFP, each $80.00. (Photo courtesy McMasters Auctions)

Batman, see also Captain Action, Pocket Super Heroes, Super Heroes & Super Powers
Batman (Dark Knight), accessory, Batcopter, Kenner, MIB, from $30 to $35.00
Batman (Dark Knight), accessory, Joker Cycle, Kenner, MIB.$25.00
Batman (Dark Knight), figure, Blast Shield, Claw Climber, Power Wing, Thunder Whip, Kenner, MOC, ea.......$30.00
Batman (Dark Knight), figure, Bruce Wayne, Kenner, MOC.$15.00
Batman (Dark Knight), figure, Crime Attack, Iron Winch, Shadow Wing, or Wall Scaler, Kenner, MOC, ea......$20.00
Batman (Dark Knight), figure, Knockout Joker, Kenner, MOC..$80.00
Batman (Dark Knight), figure, Night Glider, Kenner, MOC ..$40.00
Batman (Dark Knight), figure, Sky Escape Joker, Kenner, MOC.$35.00
Batman (Movie), accessory, Batcave Master Playset, Toy Biz, MIB $75.00
Batman (Movie), accessory, Batmobile (Turbine Sound), Toy Biz, MIB $25.00
Batman (Movie), accessory, Joker Cycle (Detachable Launching Sidecar), Toy Biz, MIB..$20.00
Batman (Movie), figure, Batman (any except sq jaw), Toy Biz, MOC, ea $10.00
Batman (Movie), figure, Batman (sq jaw), Toy Biz, MOC..$20.00
Batman (Movie), figure, Bob (Joker's Goon), Toy Biz, MOC..$25.00
Batman (Movie), figure, Joker (hair curl), Toy Biz, MOC..$25.00
Batman (Movie), figure, Joker (Squirting Orchid), Toy Biz, MOC..$20.00
Batman Crime Squad, accessory, Attack Jet, Kenner, MOC..$18.00
Batman Crime Squad, figure, any, Kenner, MOC, ea $14.00
Batman Forever, figure, any except Talking Riddler, Kenner, MOC, ea from $10 to $15.00
Batman Forever, figure, Talking Riddler, Mego, MIP........$22.00
Batman Returns, accessory, Bat Cave Command Center, Kenner, MIB $80.00
Batman Returns, accessory, Batmissile Batmobile, Kenner, MIB.$140.00
Batman Returns, accessory, Bruce Wayne Custom Coupe (w/figure), Kenner, MIB..$60.00
Batman Returns, figure, any except Bruce Wayne, Catwoman, Penguin, Penguin Commandos, or Robin, Kenner, MOC, ea.$20.00

Batman Returns, figure, Batman, 12", Kenner, MIB.........$80.00

Batman Returns, figure, Bruce Wayne, Kenner, MOC $25.00

Batman Returns, figure, Catwoman, Polar Blast Batman, or Robin, Kenner, MOC, ea..$30.00

Batman Returns, figure, Penguin, Kenner, MOC..............$45.00

Batman Returns, figure, Penguin Commando, Kenner, MOC .$28.00

Battlestar Galactica, accessory, Cyclon Raider or Colonial Viper, Mattel, NRFB, ea from $25 to....................................$30.00

Battlestar Galactica, figure, Colonial Warrior, 12", Mattel, MIP ..$90.00

Battlestar Galactica, figure, Cyclon Centurian, 12", Mattel, EX .$20.00

Battlestar Galactica, figure, Cyclon Centurian, 12", Mattel, MIP.$100.00

Battlestar Galactica (1st Series), figure, any, Mattel, MOC, from $32 to $42.00

Battlestar Galactica (2nd Series), figure, Baltar or Boray, MOC, ea...$80.00

Battlestar Galactica (2nd Series), figure, Cyclon Commander or Lucifer, Mattel, MOC, ea $112.00

Best of the West, accessory, Circle X Ranch, Marx, MIB, from $135 to...$200.00

Best of the West, accessory, Jeep & Horse Trailer, Marx, MIB ..$150.00

Best of the West, accessory, Johnny West Covered Wagon, Marx, MIB, from $100 to $150.00

Best of the West, accessory, Travel Case, Marx, NM $30.00

Best of the West, figure, Bill Buck, Marx, MIB...............$500.00

Best of the West, figure, Captain Maddox, Marx, MIB ..$120.00

Best of the West, figure, Chief Cherokee, Marx, MIB....$175.00

Best of the West, figure, Fighting Eagle, Marx, MIB.......$175.00

Best of the West, figure, General Custer, Marx, loose, M .$115.00

Best of the West, figure, Geronimo, Marx, MIB $125.00

Best of the West, figure, Jaimie West, Marx, loose, M $65.00

Best of the West, figure, Jane West, Marx, loose, M $75.00

Best of the West, figure, Jane West, Marx, MIB $130.00

Best of the West, figure, Janice West, Marx, loose, M $55.00

Best of the West, figure, Jay West, Marx, loose, M $55.00

Best of the West, figure, Jed Gibson, Marx, loose, M $315.00

Best of the West, figure, Johnny West, Marx, loose, EX ...$50.00

Best of the West, figure, Johnny West, Marx, loose, M.....$85.00

Best of the West, figure, Johnny West, Marx, MIB........$150.00

Best of the West, figure, Johnny West (later version w/quick-draw arm), Marx, NMIB..$60.00

Best of the West, figure, Josie West, Marx, NMIB $80.00

Best of the West, figure, Princess Wildflower, Marx, NMIB ..$135.00

Best of the West, figure, Sam Cobra, Marx, loose, M $60.00

Best of the West, figure, Sam Cobra (later version w/quick-draw grip), Marx, MIB..$50.00

Best of the West, figure, Sheriff Garrett, Marx, NMIB...$175.00

Best of the West, figure, Zeb Zachary, Marx, loose, M....$225.00

Best of the West, horse, Comanche, Marx, EXIB $110.00

Best of the West, horse, Flame (palomino), Marx, EXIB ..$110.00

Best of the West, horse, Pancho (palomino w/brn tack), Marx, loose, NM..$45.00

Best of the West, horse, Pancho (sorrel w/blk tack), Marx, EXIB ..$75.00

Best of the West, horse, Thunderbolt, Marx, loose, NM ..$50.00

Best of the West, horse, Thunderbolt, Marx, NMIB.........$75.00

Big Jim, accessory, Baja Beast, Mattel, MIB $25.00

Big Jim, accessory, Boat & Buggy Set, Mattel, MIB $30.00

Big Jim, accessory, Devil River Trip (w/figure & alligator), Mattel, MIB..$32.00

Big Jim, accessory, Jungle Truck, Mattel, MIB $35.00

Big Jim, accessory, Motocross Honda, Mattel, NMIB $25.00

Big Jim, accessory, Rescue Rig, Mattel, MIB $55.00

Big Jim, accessory, Sky Commander, Mattel, MIB............$50.00

Big Jim, accessory, Sport Camper w/Boat, Mattel, MIB....$70.00

Big Jim, figure, Baron Fangg, Mattel, MIB $55.00

Big Jim, figure, Big Jim, Big Jack, Big Jeff, or Big Josh, Mattel, MIB, ea from $25 to..$30.00

Big Jim, figure, Big Jim (Gold Medal Boxer), Mattel, MIB ..$35.00

Big Jim, figure, Dr Steel, Mattel, MIB $35.00

Big Jim, outfit, Dirt Biker, Frogman, Martial Arts, or Ski Patrol (all Double Trouble Disguises), Mattel, MIP, ea.........$15.00

Big Jim, outfit, Eagle Ranger, Mattel, MIP $12.00

Big Jim, outfit, Lifeguard, Mattel, MIP..............................$12.00

Big Jim, outfit, Olympic Uniforms, any, Mattel, MIP, ea ..$12.00

Big Jim's PACK, accessory, Beast, Mattel, MIB..............$110.00

Big Jim's PACK, accessory, Howler, Mattel, MIB............$65.00

Big Jim's PACK, accessory, LazerVette, Mattel, MIB......$110.00

Big Jim's PACK, figure, Big Jim, Mattel, MIB................$100.00

Big Jim's PACK, figure, Buffalo Bill, Mattel, MIB, $100.00.

Big Jim's PACK, figure, Dr Steel, Mattel, MIB $80.00

Big Jim's PACK, figure, Torpedo Fist, Mattel, MIB...........$65.00

Big Jim's PACK, figure, Warpath or The Whip, Mattel, MIB, ea ..$85.00

Big Jim's PACK, figure, Zorack the Enemy, Mattel, MIB..$100.00

Bionic Woman, accessory, Beauty Salon, Kenner, MIB....$75.00

Bionic Woman, accessory, Bubblin' Bath 'n Shower, Kenner, MIB...$150.00

Bionic Woman, accessory, sports car, Kenner, MIB $110.00

Bionic Woman, figure, Fembot, Kenner, MIB $230.00

Bionic Woman, figure, Jaime Sommers (w/purse), Kenner, MIB..$180.00

Bionic Woman, figure, Jaimie Sommers, Kenner, MIB...$155.00

Bionic Woman, outfit, Gold Evening Gown, MIB $15.00

Bionic Woman, outfit, Pant Suit (denim or wht), Kenner, MOC, ea $15.00

Black Hole, figure, Captain Dan Holland, Charles Pizer, Dr Durant, Kate McCrae, or Dr Hans Reinhardt, Mego, MOC, ea .$28.00

Black Hole, figure, Captain Dan Holland, Charles Pizer, Dr Durant, or Dr Hans Reinhardt, 12", Mego, MIB, ea ..$80.00

Black Hole, figure, Captain Harry Booth or Kate McCrae, 12", Mego, MIB, ea $90.00

Black Hole, figure, Humanoid, Mego, MOC $675.00

Black Hole, figure, Old Bob, MOC..............................$225.00

Black Hole, figure, Sentry Robot, Maximilian, or VINCent, Mego, MOC, ea $75.00

Black Hole, figure, STAR, Mego, MOC $375.00
Bonanza, accessory, wagon (4-in-1), Am Character, MIB...$110.00
Bonanza, figure, any w/horse, Am Character, MIB, A....$250.00
Bonanza, figure, Ben, Little Joe, Hoss, or Outlaw, Am Character,
   MIB, ea from $180 to $225.00

**Bonanza, figure set, Hoss and His Horse, Palitoy/NBC, 1966,
unused, NMIB, A, $250.00.** (Photo courtesy New England Auction Gallery)

Bonanza, horse, any, Am Character, MIB, ea.....................$80.00
Buck Rogers, accessory, Land Rover, Mego, NMIB...........$60.00
Buck Rogers, accessory, Star Fighter, Mego, VGIB $40.00
Buck Rogers, figure, Adrella or Killer Kane, Mego, MOC, ea .$18.00
Buck Rogers, figure, any accept Tiger Man, 12", Mego, MIB, ea
   from $50 to...$65.00
Buck Rogers, figure, Buck Rogers, Mego, MOC................$55.00
Buck Rogers, figure, Dr Huer or Draco, Mego, MOC, ea..$22.00
Buck Rogers, figure, Draco, 12", Mego, MIB, from $50 to ..$65.00
Buck Rogers, figure, Draconian Guard, Mego, MOC $22.00
Buck Rogers, figure, Draconian Marauder, Mego, MOC ..$35.00
Buck Rogers, figure, Star Seeker, Mego, MOC $150.00
Buck Rogers, figure, Tiger Man, 12", Mego, MIB $130.00
Buck Rogers, figure, Tiger Man or Wilma Deering, Mego, MOC, ea ..$28.00
Buck Rogers, figure, Twiki, Mego, MOC...........................$50.00
Captain Action, accessory, Action Cave, Ideal, loose, M.$250.00
Captain Action, accessory, Anti-Gravitational Power Pack,
   Ideal, MIB..$275.00
Captain Action, accessory, Directional Communicator, Ideal,
   1966, MIB..$275.00

**Captain Action, acces-
sory, Captain Action
Headquarters, vinyl case
with inner opening door,
14x14x6", EX+, $150.00.**

(Photo courtesy New England Auction Gallery)

Captain Action, accessory, Inter-Galactic Jet Mortar, Ideal, MIB ..$275.00
Captain Action, accessory, Parachute Pack, Ideal, NMIB ..$175.00
Captain Action, accessory, Silver Streak Amphibian Car, Ideal,
   MIB, from $1,500 to...$2,500.00

Captain Action, accessory, Silver Streak Garage, Ideal/Sears,
   loose, complete, 24", NM, from $600 to $675.00
Captain Action, accessory, Survival Kit, Ideal, MIB $250.00
Captain Action, accessory, Weapons Arsenal, Ideal, MIB ..$200.00
Captain Action, figure, Action Boy, Ideal, loose, EX $250.00
Captain Action, figure, Action Boy, Ideal, MIB.............$875.00
Captain Action, figure, Action Boy (space suit), Ideal, MIB.$1,000.00
Captain Action, figure, Dr Evil, Ideal, loose, M $310.00
Captain Action, figure, Dr Evil, Ideal, MIB $1,150.00
Captain Action, figure, Ideal, loose (from box w/parachute
   offer), M..$280.00
Captain Action, figure, Ideal, MIB (from box w/parachute
   offer)..$675.00
Captain Action, figure, Ideal, loose (from Lone Ranger box), M..$210.00
Captain Action, figure, Ideal, MIB (Lone Ranger box) .$475.00
Captain Action, figure, Ideal, loose (from photo box), M.$310.00
Captain Action, figure, Ideal, MIB (photo box).............$875.00
Captain Action, outfit, Aquaman, Ideal, MIB, from $450 to .$550.00
Captain Action, outfit, Aquaman (w/ring), Ideal, MIB .$800.00
Captain Action, outfit, Batman, Ideal, loose, EX $175.00
Captain Action, outfit, Batman, Ideal, MIB...................$675.00
Captain Action, outfit, Batman (w/ring), Ideal, MIB .$1,150.00
Captain Action, outfit, Buck Rogers, Ideal, loose, M $100.00
Captain Action, outfit, Buck Rogers (w/ring), Ideal, EXIB.$1,500.00
Captain Action, outfit, Captain America, Ideal, MIB ...$975.00
Captain Action, outfit, Captain America (w/ring), Ideal, NMIB.$950.00
Captain Action, outfit, Flash Gordon, Ideal, loose, VG.$100.00
Captain Action, outfit, Flash Gordon, Ideal, MIB $625.00
Captain Action, outfit, Flash Gordon (w/ring), Ideal, loose, M .$210.00
Captain Action, outfit, Green Hornet (w/ring), Ideal, loose, M .$1,800.00
Captain Action, outfit, Green Hornet (w/ring), Ideal, MIB.$7,000.00

**Captain Action, outfit,
Lone Ranger, Ideal, 1966,
with flicker ring, MIB, A,
$1,850.00.** (Photo courtesy New England
Auction Gallery)

Captain Action, outfit, Lone Ranger, Ideal, loose, NM .$200.00
Captain Action, outfit, Phantom, Ideal, NMIB..............$500.00
Captain Action, outfit, Robin, Ideal, loose, M $325.00
Captain Action, outfit, Robin, Ideal, MIB $1,150.00
Captain Action, outfit, Steve Canyon, Ideal, loose, M ..$225.00
Captain Action, outfit, Steve Canyon, Ideal, MIB.........$675.00
Captain Action, outfit, Steve Canyon (w/ring), Ideal, loose, M..$230.00
Captain Action, outfit, Steve Canyon (w/ring), Ideal, NMIB.$825.00
Captain Action, outfit, Super Boy, Ideal, NMIB $750.00
Captain Action, outfit, Superman, Ideal, loose, M.........$210.00
Captain Action, outfit, Superman (w/ring), Ideal, NMIB .$850.00

Captain Action, outfit, Tonto (w/ring), Ideal, NMIB $750.00
Captain America, see also Marvel Super Heroes
Charlie's Angels (Movie), figure, any, Jakks Pacific, MIB, ea ..$40.00
Charlie's Angels (TV Series), figure, any, Hasbro, MOC, ea .$80.00
CHiPs, accessory, motorcycle (for 3¾" figures), Mego, MIP.$35.00
CHiPs, accessory, motorcycle (for 8" figures), Mego, MIP.$80.00
CHiPs, accessory, motorcycle w/ramp (for 3¾" figures), Mego, MIP $55.00
CHiPs, figure, Jimmy Squeaks, Mego, MOC....................$16.00
CHiPs, figure, Jon, Mego, MOC..$22.00
CHiPs, figure, Jon, 8", Mego, MOC..................................$52.00
CHiPs, figure, Ponch, Mego, MOC....................................$22.00
CHiPs, figure, Ponch, 8", Mego, MOC $42.00
CHiPs, figure, Sarge, Mego, MOC $32.00
CHiPs, figure, Sarge, 8", Mego, MOC $52.00
CHiPs, figure, Wheels Willie, Mego, MOC.......................$16.00
CHiPs, figure w/motorcycle, Jon or Ponch, Mego, MOC, ea .$30.00
Clash of the Titans, figure, Calibas, Mattel, MOC $60.00
Clash of the Titans, figure, Charon, MIB.........................$80.00
Clash of the Titans, figure, Kraken, Mattel, rare, loose, EX .$80.00
Clash of the Titans, figure, Kraken, Mattel, rare, MOC.$275.00
Clash of the Titans, figure, Pegasus, Mattel, MOC...........$80.00

Clash of the Titans, figure, Perseus, Mattel, MOC, $55.00.

Clash of the Titans, figure, Thallo, Mattel, MOC $55.00
Clash of the Titans, figures, Perseus & Pegasus, Mattel, set of 2, MIP $100.00
Dukes of Hazzard, figure, Bo, Mego, MOC.......................$18.00
Dukes of Hazzard, figure, Bo, 8", Mego, MOC $32.00
Dukes of Hazzard, figure, Boss Hogg, Mego, MOC $22.00
Dukes of Hazzard, figure, Boss Hogg, 8", Mego, MOC......$42.00
Dukes of Hazzard, figure, Cletus, Cooter, Coy, Rosco, Uncle Jesse, or Vance, MOC, ea $32.00
Dukes of Hazzard, figure, Coy (Bo) or Vance (Luke), 8", Mego, MOC, ea $52.00
Dukes of Hazzard, figure, Coy or Vance, Mego, MOC, ea...$32.00
Dukes of Hazzard, figure, Daisy, Mego, MOC $28.00
Dukes of Hazzard, figure, Daisy, 8", Mego, MOC..............$55.00
Dukes of Hazzard, figure, Luke, Mego, MOC $21.00
Dukes of Hazzard, figure, Luke, 8", Mego, MOC..............$32.00
Dukes of Hazzard, figures w/vehicles, Daisy w/Jeep or Bo & Luke w/the General Lee, Mego, MIB, ea $55.00
Girl From UNCLE, figure, April Dancer, 11½", Marx, MIB.$900.00

Grizzly Adams, figures, Grizzly Adams or Nakuma (Nakoma on box), Mattel, 9½", MIB, ea $85.00
Happy Days, accessory, Fonz's Garage, Mego, MIB.........$160.00
Happy Days, accessory, Fonz's Jalopy or Motorcycle, Mego, MIB, ea..$85.00

Happy Days, figures, Ralph, Potsie, and Richie, Mego, 1976, loose, M, each from $25.00 to $30.00; MOC, each $80.00.

Indiana Jones, figure, Indiana, 12", Kenner, NMIB, from $200 to..$275.00
Indiana Jones (Adventures of), accessory, Arabian Horse, Kenner, loose, M...$65.00

Indiana Jones (Adventures of), accessory, Desert Convoy Truck, Kenner, MIB, $100.00.

Indiana Jones (Adventures of), accessory, Map Room, Kenner, MIB (sealed), from $80 to $95.00
Indiana Jones (Adventures of), accessory, Streets of Cairo, Kenner, MIB, from $60 to $75.00
Indiana Jones (Adventures of), accessory, Streets of Cairo, Kenner, loose, EX $30.00
Indiana Jones (Adventures of), figure, Belloq, Kenner, M (in mailing bag) $30.00
Indiana Jones (Adventures of), figure, Belloq, Kenner, MOC..$65.00
Indiana Jones (Adventures of), figure, Cairo Swordsman, Kenner, MOC...$35.00
Indiana Jones (Adventures of), figure, German Mechanic, Kenner, MOC...$50.00
Indiana Jones (Adventures of), figure, Indiana, Kenner, loose, M $120.00
Indiana Jones (Adventures of), figure, Indiana, Kenner, MOC, from $400 to $500.00

Indiana Jones (Adventures of), figure, Indiana (German uniform), Kenner, MOC, from $90 to $100.00

Indiana Jones (Adventures of), figure, Marion Ravenwood, Kenner, loose, M..$95.00

Indiana Jones (Adventures of), figure, Marion Ravenwood, Kenner, MOC, from $300 to...$350.00

Indiana Jones (Adventures of), figure, Sallah, Kenner, loose, M.$35.00

Indiana Jones (Adventures of), figure, Sallah, Kenner, MOC .$100.00

Indiana Jones (Adventures of), figure, Toht, Kenner, MOC ..$35.00

Indiana Jones & the Temple of Doom, figure, Giant Thugee or Mola Ram, LJN, MOC, ea...$75.00

Indiana Jones & the Temple of Doom, figure, Indiana, LJN, MOC...$100.00

James Bond, figure, Bond, Gilbert, MIB.........................$250.00

James Bond, figure, Bond (Pierce Brosnan), Mediacom, MIB .$85.00

James Bond, figure, Oddjob, Gilbert, NMIB...................$225.00

James Bond (Moonraker), figure, Bond, Mego, NM.......$175.00

James Bond (Moonraker), figure, James Bond (in spacesuit with accessories), Mego, MIB, $525.00.

James Bond (Moonraker), figure, Drax or Holly, Mego, MIB, ea $225.00

James Bond (Moonraker), figure, Jaws, Mego, MIB........$525.00

Legend of the Lone Ranger, accessory, Western Town, Gabriel, MIB..$100.00

Legend of the Lone Ranger, figure, Buffalo Bill Cody, Gabriel, MOC...$30.00

Legend of the Lone Ranger, figure, Butch Cavendish, Gabriel, MOC, $25.00.

Legend of the Lone Ranger, figure, Lone Ranger, Gabriel, MOC..$35.00

Legend of the Lone Ranger, figure w/horse, Lone Ranger & Silver, Tonto & Scout, or Butch & Smoke, Gabriel, MOC, ea .$60.00

Legend of the Lone Ranger, horse, Scout, Gabriel, MOC...$22.00

Legend of the Lone Ranger, horse, Silver, Gabriel, MOC...$32.00

Legend of the Lone Ranger, horse, Smoke, Gabriel, MOC..$28.00

Lone Ranger, see also Captain Action

Lone Ranger Rides Again, accessory, Blizzard Adventurer, Gabriel, MIB...$25.00

Lone Ranger Rides Again, accessory, Carson City Bank Robbery, Gabriel, MIB...$55.00

Lone Ranger Rides Again, accessory, Hidden Rattler, Gabriel, MIB $30.00

Lone Ranger Rides Again, accessory, Landslide, Gabriel, MIB.$50.00

Lone Ranger Rides Again, accessory, Prairie Wagon, Gabriel, MIB $40.00

Lone Ranger Rides Again, accessory, Red River Floodwaters, NRFB $30.00

Lone Ranger Rides Again, accessory, Tribal Teepee, Gabriel, EXIB $30.00

Lone Ranger Rides Again, figure, any, Gabriel, MIB, ea from $65 to $80.00

Lone Ranger Rides Again, figure & horse sets, any, Gabriel, MIB, ea from $50 to...$75.00

Lone Ranger Rides Again, horse, any, Gabriel, MIB, ea from $50 to $60.00

Lone Ranger Rides Again, outfit, Indian War, Gabriel, EXOC.$20.00

Lone Ranger Rides Again, outfit, Secret Corral, Gabriel, MOC.$20.00

Lord of the Rings, figure, any, Toy Vault, MOC, ea from $12 to...$18.00

Love Boat, figure, any, Mego, MOC, ea from $20 to $25.00

M*A*S*H, accessory, Ambulance (w/Hawkeye figure), Tri-Star, MIP, from $25 to $35.00

M*A*S*H, accessory, Helicopter (w/Hawkeye figure), Tri-Star, MIP $30.00

M*A*S*H, accessory, Jeep (w/Hawkeye figure), Tri-Star, MIB ..$30.00

M*A*S*H, accessory, Military Base, Tri-Star, MIB..........$50.00

M*A*S*H, figure, BJ, Col Potter, Father Mulcahy, Hawkeye, Klinger, or Winchester, Tri-Star, MOC, ea from $15 to...$20.00

M*A*S*H, figure, BJ, Hawkeye, or Hot Lips, 8", Durham, MOC, ea $75.00

M*A*S*H, figure, Hot Lips, Tri-Star, MOC $25.00

M*A*S*H, figure, Klinger (in dress), Tri-Star, MOC $35.00

Major Matt Mason, accessory, Astro Trac, Mattel, NMIP .$100.00

Major Matt Mason, accessory, Fireball Space Cannon, Mattel, NMIP $75.00

Major Matt Mason, accessory, Gamma Ray Guard, Mattel, MIP .$110.00

Major Matt Mason, accessory, Moon Suit Pak, NMIP......$75.00

Major Matt Mason, accessory, Rocket Launch, Mattel, MIB .$65.00

Major Matt Mason, accessory, Satellite Locker, Mattel, MIP .$75.00

Major Matt Mason, accessory, Space Crawler Action Set (w/figure), Mattel, MIB $100.00

Major Matt Mason, accessory, Space Probe, Mattel, NMIP .$60.00

Major Matt Mason, accessory, Space Station, Mattel, NMIP.$250.00

Major Matt Mason, figure, Callistro, Mattel, loose, EX $75.00

Major Matt Mason, figure, Callistro, Mattel, MOC $225.00

Major Matt Mason, figure, Captain Lazer, 12", Mattel, loose, NM..$100.00

Major Matt Mason, figure, Doug Davis (w/helmet), Mattel, loose, EX $60.00

Major Matt Mason, figure, Doug Davis (w/helmet), Mattel, MOC...$275.00

Major Matt Mason, figure, Jeff Long, Mattel, loose, NM.$100.00

Major Matt Mason, figure, Jeff Long (w/helmet), Mattel, loose, VG $75.00

Major Matt Mason, figure, Matt Mason (on glider w/talking backpack), Mattel, MIB $450.00

Major Matt Mason, figure, Sgt Storm, Mattel, loose, NM .$75.00

Major Matt Mason, figure, Sgt Storm, Mattel, MOC.....$375.00

Major Matt Mason, figure, Scorpio, Mattel, loose, NM .$300.00

Major Matt Mason, figure, Scorpio, Mattel, NMOC......$325.00

Man From UNCLE, figure, Illya Kuryakin, Gilbert, NMIB .$350.00

Man From UNCLE, figure, Napoleon Solo, Gilbert, NMIB ..$275.00

Marvel Super Heroes, accessory, Training Center, Toy Biz, MIB...$25.00

Marvel Super Heroes, figure, Annihilus, Deathlok, Hulk, Human Torch, Mr Fantastic, or Thing, Toy Biz, MOC, ea $18.00

Marvel Super Heroes, figure, Captain America, Toy Biz, MOC..$22.00

Marvel Super Heroes, figure, Daredevil, Toy Biz, loose, M..$18.00

Marvel Super Heroes, figure, Dr Doom or Dr Octopus, Toy Biz, MOC, ea...$26.00

Marvel Super Heroes, figure, Green Goblin (back lever) or Thor (back lever), Toy Biz, MOC, ea...................................$35.00

Marvel Super Heroes, figure, Green Goblin (no lever) or Thor (no lever), Toy Biz, MOC, ea $20.00

Marvel Super Heroes, figure, Invisible Woman (vanishing), Toy Biz, MOC...$125.00

Marvel Super Heroes, figures, Mr. Fantastic (five-way stretch), Toy Biz, MOC, $20.00; Human Torch (fireball flinging action), Toy Biz, MOC, $18.00; Invisible Woman (catapult), MOC, $18.00.

Marvel Super Heroes, figure, Punisher (cap-firing or machine gun sound), Silver Surfer (chrome), Toy Biz, MOC, ea $15.00

Marvel Super Heroes, figure, Spider-Man (ball joints or web tracer), Toy Biz, MOC, ea..$18.00

Marvel Super Heroes, figure, Spider-Man (web climbing or web-shooting), Toy Biz, MOC, ea from $30 to $35.00

Marvel Super Heroes, figure, Venom or Tongue-Flicking Venom, Toy Biz, MOC, ea $20.00

Marvel Super Heroes (Secret Wars), accessory, Doom Copter, Mattel, MIP $30.00

Marvel Super Heroes (Secret Wars), accessory, Doom Copter w/Dr Doom, Mattel, MIP $50.00

Marvel Super Heroes (Secret Wars), accessory, Doom Cycle, Mattel, MIP $18.00

Marvel Super Heroes (Secret Wars), accessory, Doom Cycle w/Dr Doom, Mattel, MIP $35.00

Marvel Super Heroes (Secret Wars), accessory, Doom Roller, Mattel, MIP $18.00

Marvel Super Heroes (Secret Wars), accessory, Freedom Fighter, Mattel, MIP $30.00

Marvel Super Heroes (Secret Wars), accessory, Tower of Doom, Mattel, MIP $30.00

Marvel Super Heroes (Secret Wars), accessory, Training Center, Mattel, MIP $25.00

Marvel Super Heroes (Secret Wars), figure, Baron Zemo or Iron Man, Mattel, MOC, ea...$36.00

Marvel Super Heroes (Secret Wars), figure, Captain America and His Shield, Mattel, MOC, $25.00.

Marvel Super Heroes (Secret Wars), figure, Dr Doom, Dr Octopus, Kang, or Magento, Mattel, MOC, ea...................$22.00

Marvel Super Heroes (Secret Wars), figure, Falcon, Mattel, MOC...$42.00

Marvel Super Heroes (Secret Wars), figure, Hobgoblin, Mattel, MOC...$62.00

Marvel Super Heroes (Secret Wars), figure, Spider-Man (blk outfit), Mattel, MOC..$52.00

Marvel Super Heroes (Secret Wars), figure, Spider-Man (red & bl outfit), Mattel, MOC $42.00

Marvel Super Heroes (Secret Wars), figure, Wolverine (blk claws), Mattel, MOC..$76.00

Marvel Super Heroes (Secret Wars), figure, Wolverine (silver claws), Mattel, MOC..$42.00

Marvel Super Heroes (Talking), figure, any, Toy Biz, MIP,ea...$22.00

Masters of the Universe, accessory, Fright Zone, Mattel, MIB.$130.00

Masters of the Universe, accessory, Jet Sled, Mattel, MIB .$40.00

Masters of the Universe, accessory, Monstroid, Mattel, MIB..$50.00

Masters of the Universe, figure, Battle Armor He-Man or Battle Armor Skeletor, Mattel, MOC, ea $42.00

Masters of the Universe, figure, Beast Man or Blade, Mattel, MOC, ea $75.00

Masters of the Universe, figure, Blast Attack, Buzz-Off, or Buzz-Saw Hordak, Mattel, MOC, ea..............................$42.00

Masters of the Universe, figure, Clamp Champ or Clawful, Mattel, MOC, ea $46.00

Masters of the Universe, figure, Dragstor the Evil Horde, Mattel, MOC..$42.00

Masters of the Universe, figure, Evil-Lyn, Mattel, MOC..$52.00

Masters of the Universe, figure, Extender, Mattel, MOC .$35.00

Masters of the Universe, figure, Faker, Mattel, MOC.....$125.00

Masters of the Universe, figure, Faker II, Mattel, MOC...$75.00

Masters of the Universe, figure, Fisto, Mattel, MOC........$45.00

Masters of the Universe, figure, Grizzlor, Mattel, MOC ...$42.00

Masters of the Universe, figure, Grizzlor (blk), Mattel, MOC..$155.00

Masters of the Universe, figure, Gwilder, Mattel, MOC...$72.00

Masters of the Universe, figure, He-Man, Mattel, MOC, $125.00.

Masters of the Universe, figure, Hordak or Horde Trooper, Mattel, MOC, ea $42.00

Masters of the Universe, figure, Jitsu or King Hiss, Mattel, MOC, ea $48.00

Masters of the Universe, figure, King Randor, Mattel, MOC.$80.00

Masters of the Universe, figure, Leech, Mattel, MOC......$45.00

Masters of the Universe, figure, Man-at-Arms, Mattel, MOC.$42.00

Masters of the Universe, figure, Man-E-Faces, Mattel, MOC..$55.00

Masters of the Universe, figure, Mantenna or Mekaneck, Mattel, MOC, ea $42.00

Masters of the Universe, figure, Mer-Man, Mattel, MOC .$52.00

Masters of the Universe, figure, Modulok, Mattel, MOC.$36.00

Masters of the Universe, figure, Moss Man or Multi-Bot, Mattel, MOC, ea $42.00

Masters of the Universe, figure, Ninjor, Mattel, MOC.....$85.00

Masters of the Universe, figure, Orko, Mattel, MOC $52.00

Masters of the Universe, figure, Prince Adam, Mattel, MOC..$50.00

Masters of the Universe, figure, Ram Man, Mattel, MOC..$75.00

Masters of the Universe, figure, Rattlor, Mattel, MOC $40.00

Masters of the Universe, figure, Rattlor (red neck), Mattel, MOC..$35.00

Masters of the Universe, figure, Rio Blast, Mattel, MOC.$45.00

Masters of the Universe, figure, Roboto, Mattel, MOC....$90.00

Masters of the Universe, figure, Rokkon, Mattel, MOC...$40.00

Masters of the Universe, figure, Rotar, Mattel, MOC.......$75.00

Masters of the Universe, figure, Saurod, Mattel, MOC $75.00

Masters of the Universe, figure, Scare Glow Spector, Mattel, MOC..$80.00

Masters of the Universe, figure, Skeletor, Mattel, MOC .$115.00

Masters of the Universe, figure, Skeletor (Terror Claws), Mattel, loose, NM...$30.00

Masters of the Universe, figure, Snake Face, Mattel, MOC.$50.00

Masters of the Universe, figure, Spikor, Mattel, MOC.....$50.00

Masters of the Universe, figure, Stratos, Mattel, MOC $80.00

Masters of the Universe, figure, Stratos, Mattel, MOC (12 back)..$60.00

Masters of the Universe, figure, Sy-Klone, Mattel, MOC..$75.00

Masters of the Universe, figure, Teela, Mattel, MOC.......$70.00

Masters of the Universe, figure, Teela, Mattel, MOC (new)..$40.00

Masters of the Universe, figure, Teela, Mattel, MOC (12 bk).$12.00

Masters of the Universe, figure, Trap Jaw, Mattel, MOC..$90.00

Masters of the Universe, figure, Tri Klops, Mattel, M (G card, 12 bk)..$40.00

Masters of the Universe, figure, Tung Lasher, Mattel, MOC..$50.00

Masters of the Universe, figure, Twistoid, Mattel, MOC..$80.00

Masters of the Universe, figure, Two-Bad, Mattel, MOC.$32.00

Masters of the Universe, figure, Webstor, Mattel, MOC ..$32.00

Masters of the Universe, figure, Whiplash, Mattel, MOC.$30.00

Masters of the Universe, figure, Zodac, Mattel, MOC......$55.00

Micronauts, accessory, Astro Station, Mego, NMIB.........$30.00

Micronauts, accessory, Battle Cruiser, Mego, MIB............$65.00

Micronauts, accessory, Hornetroid, Mego, NMIB.............$45.00

Micronauts, accessory, Mega City, Mego, NMIB, from $30 to..$40.00

Micronauts, accessory, Microrail City, Mego, NMIB $50.00

Micronauts, accessory, Mobile Exploration Lab, Mego, NMIB..$45.00

Micronauts, accessory, Neon Orbiter, Mego, EXIB...........$35.00

Micronauts, accessory, Rocket Tubes, Mego, NMIB $50.00

Micronauts, accessory, Star Searcher, Mego, MIB.............$75.00

Micronauts, figure, Baron Karza, Mego, EXIB..................$50.00

Micronauts, figure, Biotron, Mego, NMIB $60.00

Micronauts, figure, Force Commander, Mego, NMIB.......$55.00

Micronauts, figure, Kronos, Mego, loose, rare, M $70.00

Micronauts, figure, Lobros, Mego, MOC...........................$75.00

Micronauts, figure, Time Traveler (solid yel or orange), Mego, MOC..$55.00

Micronauts, figure, Time Traveler (translucent yel or orange), Mego, MOC..$30.00

Micronauts, horse, Pegasus, Mego, MIB............................$55.00

Nightmare Warriors (Glow-in-the-Dark), figure, any, MOC, ea, from $10 to...$15.00

Official World's Greatest Super Heroes, see Super Heroes

One Million BC, accessory, Tribal Lair, Mego, MIB.......$125.00

One Million BC, accessory, Tribal Lair Gift Set (w/5 figures), MIB..$200.00

One Million BC, creature, Dimetrodon, Mego, MIB $225.00

One Million BC, creature, Hairy Rhino, Mego, MIB.....$275.00

One Million BC, creature, Tyrannosaur, Mego, MIB $275.00

One Million BC, figure, Grok, Mada, Orm, Trag, or Zon, Mego, MOC, ea $55.00

Planet of the Apes, accessory, Action Stallion, Mego, MIB.$100.00

Planet of the Apes, accessory, Battering Ram, Jail, or Dr Zaius Throne, Mego, MIB, ea $50.00

Planet of the Apes, accessory, Catapult & Wagon, MIB..$165.00

Planet of the Apes, accessory, Forbidden Zone Trap, Fortress, Treehouse (w/5 figures), or Village, Mego, MIB, ea ..$225.00

Planet of the Apes, figure, boxed, any, MIB, ea from $200 to.$250.00

Planet of the Apes, figure, any, MOC, ea from $100 to..$125.00

Pocket Super Heroes, accessory, Batcave, Mego, MIB....$325.00

Pocket Super Heroes, accessory, Batmachine, Mego, MIB..$325.00

Pocket Super Heroes, accessory, Batmobile (w/Batman & Robin), Mego, MIB $225.00

Pocket Super Heroes, accessory, Spider-Car (w/Spider-Man & the Hulk), Mego, MIB.................................$80.00

Pocket Super Heroes, accessory, Spider-Machine, Mego, MIB..$115.00

Pocket Super Heroes, figure, Aquaman, Captain America, or Green Goblin, Mego, MOC, ea $110.00

Pocket Super Heroes, figure, Batman or Robin, Mego, MOC, ea.$45.00

Pocket Super Heroes, figure, General Zod, Mego, MOC..$18.00

Pocket Super Heroes, figure, Incredible Hulk, Mego, MOC (red card) $32.00

Pocket Super Heroes, figure, Incredible Hulk, Mego, MOC (wht card) $42.00

Pocket Super Heroes, figure, Jor-El or Lex Luthor, MOC ...$25.00

Pocket Super Heroes, figure, Robin, Mego, MOC $45.00

Pocket Super Heroes, figure, Spider-Man, Mego, MOC (wht) ..$45.00

Pocket Super Heroes, figure, Superman, Mego, MOC......$35.00

Pocket Super Heroes, figure, Superman, Mego, MOC (red card).$35.00

Pocket Super Heroes, figure, Wonder Woman, Mego, MOC..$50.00

Power Lords, figure, any, MOC, ea from $20 to $30.00

Robocop (Ultra Police), accessory, Robo-Command vehicle, MIB $40.00

Robocop (Ultra Police), accessory, Robo-Jailer vehicle, MIB..$50.00

Robocop (Ultra Police), figure, any, Kenner, 1988-90, MOC, ea, from $15 to..$25.00

Six Million Dollar Man, accessory, Bionic Transport & Repair Station, Kenner, MIB $125.00

Six Million Dollar Man, accessory, Mission Control Center playset, Kenner, MIB..$75.00

Six Million Dollar Man, accessory, OSI Headquarters, Kenner, MIB $90.00

Six Million Dollar Man, accessory, Venus Space Probe, Kenner, MIB $400.00

Six Million Dollar Man, figure, Bionic Bigfoot, Kenner, MIB .$200.00

Six Million Dollar Man, figure, Maskatron, Kenner, MIB .$175.00

Six Million Dollar Man, figure, Oscar Goldman, Kenner, MIB .$125.00

Six Million Dollar Man, figure, Steve Austin, Kenner, MIB.$125.00

Six Million Dollar Man, figure, Steve Austin (w/biosonic arm), Kenner, MIB $325.00

Six Million Dollar Man, figure, Steve Austin (w/engine block), Kenner, MIB $175.00

Six Million Dollar Man, figure, Steve Austin (w/girder), Kenner, MIB...$225.00

Space: 1999, accessory, Moonbase Alpha, Mattel, MIB .$100.00

Space: 1999, figure, any except Zython Alien, Mattel, MOC, ea.$50.00

Space: 1999, figure, Zython Alien, Mattel, MOC $215.00

Stargate, accessory, Winged Glider, MIB, from $15 to......$20.00

Stargate, figure, any, MOC, ea from $6 to.........................$10.00

Starsky & Hutch, accessory, car, Mego, MIB $110.00

Starsky & Hutch, figure, Captain Dobey, Chopper, or Huggy Bear, Mego, MOC, ea from $25 to $35.00

Starsky & Hutch, figure, Starsky or Hutch, Mego, MOC, ea from $25 to...$35.00

Super Heroes, accessory, carrying case, Mego, M $45.00

Super Heroes, figure, Aqualad (Teen Titans), Mego, loose, NM .$150.00

Super Heroes, figure, Aqualad (Teen Titans), Mego, MOC ..$325.00

Super Heroes, figure, Aquaman, Mego, loose, EX............$35.00

Super Heroes, figure, Aquaman, Mego, MIB or MOC, ea .$175.00

Super Heroes, figure, Aquaman (Bend 'n Flex), 5", Mego, MOC.$125.00

Super Heroes, figure, Batgirl, Mego, loose, EX................$85.00

Super Heroes, figure, Batgirl, Mego, MIB $275.00

Super Heroes, figure, Batgirl, Mego, MOC $250.00

Super Heroes, figure, Batgirl (Bend 'n Flex), Mego, MOC .$125.00

Super Heroes, figure, Batman, 12½", magnetic, Mego, MIB.$100.00

Super Heroes, figure, Batman, 12½", Mego, MIB...........$115.00

Super Heroes, figure, Batman (Bend 'n Flex), 5", Mego, MOC..$100.00

Super Heroes, figure, Batman (fist-fighting), Mego, MIB .$325.00

Super Heroes, figure, Batman (fist-fighting), Mego, MOC .$375.00

Super Heroes, figure, Batman (pnt mask), Mego, loose, NM .$65.00

Super Heroes, figure, Batman (pnt mask), Mego, MIB...$175.00

Super Heroes, figure, Batman (removable mask), Mego, MIB.$325.00

Super Heroes, figure, Batman (removable mask), Mego, MOC.$425.00

Super Heroes, figure, Captain America, Mego, MOC....$125.00

Super Heroes, figure, Captain America, 8", Mego, MIB.$175.00

Super Heroes, figure, Captain America, 12½", Mego, MIB .$150.00

Super Heroes, figure, Captain America (Bend 'n Flex), 5", Mego, MOC...$100.00

Super Heroes, figure, Catwoman, Mego, loose, M $125.00

Super Heroes, figure, Catwoman, Mego, MIB $325.00

Super Heroes, figure, Catwoman, Mego, MOC $425.00

Super Heroes, figure, Catwoman (Bend 'n Flex), 5", Mego, MOC..$180.00

Super Heroes, figure, Conan, Mego, MIB $375.00

Super Heroes, figure, Conan, Mego, MOC.....................$475.00

Super Heroes, figure, Falcon, Mego, MIB $150.00

Super Heroes, figure, Falcon, Mego, MOC.....................$425.00

Super Heroes, figure, Green Arrow, Mego, loose, M.........$85.00

Super Heroes, figure, Green Arrow, Mego, MIB.............$400.00

Super Heroes, figure, Green Arrow, Mego, MOC...........$500.00

Super Heroes, figure, Green Goblin, Mego, loose, M $85.00

Super Heroes, figure, Green Goblin, Mego, MIB $250.00

Super Heroes, figure, Green Goblin, Mego, MOC $600.00

Super Heroes, figure, Human Torch, Mego, MIB.............$85.00

Super Heroes, figure, Human Torch, Mego, MOC $45.00

Super Heroes, figure, Incredible Hulk, Mego, loose, M $40.00

Super Heroes, figure, Incredible Hulk, Mego, MOC.........$60.00

Super Heroes, figure, Incredible Hulk, 8", Mego, MIB ...$100.00

Super Heroes, figure, Incredible Hulk, 12½", Mego, MIB...$75.00

Super Heroes, figure, Iron Man, Mego, MIB...................$130.00

Super Heroes, figure, Iron Man, Mego, MOC.................$425.00

Super Heroes, figure, Isis, Mego, MIB $225.00

Super Heroes, figure, Isis, Mego, MOC $100.00

Super Heroes, figure, Joker, (Bend 'n Flex), 5", Mego, MOC .$150.00

Super Heroes, figure, Joker, Mego, MIB or MOC $150.00

Super Heroes, figure, Joker (fist-fighting), Mego, MIB...$375.00

Super Heroes, figure, Kid Flash (Teen Titans), Mego, loose, NM...$150.00

Super Heroes, figure, Kid Flash (Teen Titans), Mego, MOC ..$275.00

Super Heroes, figure, Lizard, Mego, MIB $175.00

Super Heroes, figure, Lizard, Mego, MOC $425.00

Super Heroes, figure, Mr Fantastic, Mego, MIB..............$125.00

Super Heroes, figure, Mr Fantastic, Mego, MOC.............$50.00

Super Heroes, figure, Mr Mxyzptlk (Bend 'n Flex), 5", Mego, MOC..$130.00

Super Heroes, figure, Mr Mxyzptlk (open mouth), Mego, MIB .$80.00

Super Heroes, figure, Mr Mxyzptlk (smirk), Mego, MIB...$150.00

Super Heroes, figure, Penguin, Mego, MIB $125.00

Super Heroes, figure, Penguin, Mego, MOC...................$100.00
Super Heroes, figure, Penguin (Bend 'n Flex), 5", Mego, loose, NM.........................$35.00
Super Heroes, figure, Penguin (Bend 'n Flex), 5", Mego, MOC.$150.00
Super Heroes, figure, Riddler, Mego, MIB $225.00
Super Heroes, figure, Riddler, Mego, MOC....................$375.00
Super Heroes, figure, Riddler (Bend 'n Flex), 5", Mego, MOC.$150.00
Super Heroes, figure, Riddler (fist-fighting), Mego, MIB.$375.00
Super Heroes, figure, Robin (Bend 'n Flex), 5", Mego, MOC .$80.00
Super Heroes, figure, Robin (magnetic), 12½", Mego, MIB..$250.00
Super Heroes, figure, Robin (pnt mask), Mego, loose, M .$60.00
Super Heroes, figure, Robin (pnt mask), Mego, MIB $150.00
Super Heroes, figure, Robin (pnt mask), Mego, MOC ...$100.00
Super Heroes, figure, Robin (removable mask), loose, M .$225.00
Super Heroes, figure, Robin (removable mask), Mego, MIB.$375.00
Super Heroes, figure, Robin (removable mask), Mego, MIB (solid box) $1,450.00
Super Heroes, figure, Shazam, Mego, loose, M.................$65.00
Super Heroes, figure, Shazam, Mego, MIB......................$200.00
Super Heroes, figure, Shazam, Mego, MOC....................$175.00
Super Heroes, figure, Shazam (Bend 'n Flex), 5", Mego, MOC..$130.00
Super Heroes, figure, Speedy (Teen Titans), Mego, loose, NM ..$250.00
Super Heroes, figure, Speedy (Teen Titans), Mego, MOC...$475.00
Super Heroes, figure, Spider-Man, Mego, loose, M $25.00
Super Heroes, figure, Spider-Man, Mego, MIB $100.00

Super Heroes, figures, Spider-Man, Mego, MOC, $50.00; Superman, Mego, MOC, $100.00. (Photo courtesy McMasters Doll Auctions)

Super Heroes, figure, Spider-Man, 12½", Mego, MIB $125.00
Super Heroes, figure, Spider-Man (Bend 'n Flex), Mego, MOC.$75.00
Super Heroes, figure, Supergirl, Mego, loose, NM $250.00
Super Heroes, figure, Supergirl, Mego, MIB or MOC, ea .$425.00
Super Heroes, figure, Supergirl (Bend 'n Flex), 5", Mego, MOC.........................$180.00
Super Heroes, figure, Superman, Mego, loose, M..............$50.00
Super Heroes, figure, Superman, Mego, MIB..................$125.00
Super Heroes, figure, Superman (Bend 'n Flex), 5", Mego, MOC .$80.00
Super Heroes, figure, Tarzan, Mego, MIB......................$125.00
Super Heroes, figure, Tarzan, Mego, MOC $215.00
Super Heroes, figure, Tarzan (Bend 'n Flex), 5", Mego, MOC..$65.00
Super Heroes, figure, Thing, Mego, loose, NM.................$35.00
Super Heroes, figure, Thing, Mego, MIB $160.00
Super Heroes, figure, Thing, Mego, MOC $65.00

Super Heroes, figure, Thor, Mego, loose, NM.................$100.00
Super Heroes, figure, Thor, Mego, MIB or MOC, ea......$275.00
Super Heroes, figure, Wonder Woman, Mego, loose, NM ..$75.00
Super Heroes, figure, Wonder Woman, Mego, MIB $325.00
Super Heroes, figure, Wonder Woman, Mego, MOC.....$425.00
Super Heroes, figure, Wonder Woman (Bend 'n Flex), 5", Mego, MOC.........................$100.00
Super Heroes, figure, Wonder Woman (fly-away action), 12½", Mego, MIB.........................$225.00
Super Heroes, figure, Wondergirl, Mego, loose, M $115.00
Super Heroes, figure, Wondergirl, Mego, MOC.............$375.00
Super Heroes, figure, Wondergirl (Teen Titans), Mego, loose, NM.........................$175.00
Super Heroes, figure, Wondergirl (Teen Titans), Mego, MOC ..$425.00
Super Heroes, see also Pocket Super Heroes
Super Heroes (Superman Movie), figure, General Zod, Jor-El, or Lex Luthor, 12½", Mego, MIB, ea............$75.00
Super Heroes (Superman Movie), figure, Superman, 12½", Mego, MIB.........................$100.00
Super Powers, accessory, Batmobile, Kenner, 1985, MIB, from $80 to $95.00
Super Powers, accessory, carrying case, Kenner, NM, from $28 to $38.00
Super Powers, accessory, Delta Probe One, Kenner, 1984, MIB..$35.00
Super Powers, accessory, Hall of Justice playset, Kenner, MIB..$25.00
Super Powers, accessory, Supermobile, Kenner, MIB........$45.00
Super Powers, figure, Aquaman, Kenner, MOC.............$48.00
Super Powers, figure, Batman, Kenner, MOC..................$80.00
Super Powers, figure, Brainiac, Kenner, MOC................$25.00
Super Powers, figure, Cyborg, Kenner, loose, NM $125.00
Super Powers, figure, Cyborg, Kenner, MOC (unpunched) ..$275.00
Super Powers, figure, Cyclotron, Kenner, loose, M $30.00
Super Powers, figure, Darkseid, Kenner, MOC $30.00
Super Powers, figure, Dr Fate, Kenner, MOC $75.00
Super Powers, figure, Firestorm, Kenner, MOC (unpunched).$30.00
Super Powers, figure, Golden Pharaoh, Kenner, MOC ..$100.00
Super Powers, figure, Green Arrow, Kenner, MOC $50.00
Super Powers, figure, Green Lantern, Kenner, MOC $40.00
Super Powers, figure, Hawkman, Kenner, MOC..............$50.00
Super Powers, figure, Joker, Kenner, MOC $40.00
Super Powers, figure, Lex Luthor, Kenner, MOC.............$15.00
Super Powers, figure, Mantis, Kenner, MOC $32.00

Super Powers, figures, Orion, Kenner, 1986, MOC, $50.00; Plastic Man, Kenner, 1986, MOC, $140.00. (Photo courtesy June Moon)

Super Powers, figure, Mr Freeze, Kenner, MOC................$70.00

Super Powers, figure, Mr Miracle, Kenner, MOC..........$100.00

Super Powers, figure, Penguin, complete w/ID card & comic book, Kenner, loose, NM..$20.00

Super Powers, figure, Penguin, Kenner, MOC $45.00

Super Powers, figure, Red Tornado, Kenner, MOC $50.00

Super Powers, figure, Samurai, Kenner, MOC................$125.00

Super Powers, figure, Shazam, Kenner, MOC $50.00

Super Powers, figure, Steppenwolf, complete w/ID card & comic book, Kenner, loose, NM...............................$15.00

Super Powers, figure, Superman, Kenner, MOC, from $50 to .$60.00

Super Powers, figure, Wonder Woman, Kenner, 1986, MOC, from $32 to..$42.00

Waltons, accessory, barn or country store, Mego, MIB, ea .$100.00

Waltons, accessory, farmhouse (w/6 figures), Mego, MIB ..$275.00

Waltons, accessory, farmhouse (only), Mego, MIB.........$165.00

Waltons, accessory, truck, Mego, MIB.............................$75.00

Waltons, figure set, John Boy & Mary Ellen, Mom & Pop, or Grandma & Grandpa, Mego, MIB, ea set $40.00

Wizard of Oz, accessory, Emerald City (for 8" figures), Mego, MIB..$325.00

Wizard of Oz, accessory, Wizard of Oz & His Emerald City, Mego, MIB, from $100 to......................................$125.00

Wizard of Oz, figure, any 8" except the Wicked Witch or Wizard of Oz, Mego, MIB, ea from $40 to $50.00

Wizard of Oz, figure, Munchkins, any, Mego, MIB, ea from $125 to..$150.00

Wizard of Oz, figure, Wicked Witch, 8", Mego, MIB, from $75 to $100.00

Wizard of Oz, figure, Wizard, 8", Mego, MIB, from $225 to .$250.00

Wonder Woman (TV Series), figure, Queen Hippolyte, Mego, MIB, ea $100.00

Wonder Woman, figures, Wonder Woman, Mego, MIB, $210.00; Steve Trevor, Mego, MIB, $100.00; Nubia, Mego, MOC, $100.00. (Photo courtesy McMasters Doll Auctions)

World's Greatest Super Heroes, or Official World's Greatest Super Heroes, see Super Heroes or Pocket Super Heroes

WWF, figure, Andre the Great, Hasbro, MOC.................$60.00

WWF, figure, Animal (Shotgun Sat Night #1), Jakks, MOC..$10.00

WWF, figure, Bret Hart (Superstars #1), Jakks, MOC......$22.00

WWF, figure, Bret Hart (Superstars #2), Jakks, MOC......$18.00

WWF, figure, Diesel (Superstars #3 reissue), Jakks, MOC ..$18.00

WWF, figure, Dusty Rhodes, Hasbro, EXOC, from $45 to ..$65.00

WWF, figure, Greg The Hammer Valentine, Hasbro, MOC..$15.00

WWF, figure, Hulk Hogan, Hasbro, MOC.......................$15.00

WWF, figure, Hulk Hogan (mail-in), Hasbro, MIP $55.00

WWF, figure, Hulk Hogan (no shirt), Hasbro, MOC $12.00

WWF, figure, Jake 'The Snake' Roberts, Hasbro, MOC ...$15.00

WWF, figure, Jim 'The Anvil' Neidhart, Hasbro, MOC...$10.00

WWF, figure, Jimmy Snuka, Hasbro, MOC $15.00

WWF, figure, Lex Lugar, Hasbro, MOC $18.00

WWF, figure, Macho Man, Hasbro, MOC........................$20.00

WWF, figure, Mr Perfect (w/Perfect Plex), Hasbro, MOC..$20.00

WWF, figure, Nasty Boys, Hasbro, MOC (2-pack) $75.00

WWF, figure, New Age Outlaws (2-Tuff #2), Jakks, MOC..$15.00

WWF, figure, Rick Rude, Hasbro, MOC $28.00

WWF, figure, Rowdy Roddy Piper, Hasbro, MOC $28.00

WWF, figure, Sid Justice, Hasbro, MOC $18.00

WWF, figure, The Warlord, Hasbro, MOC $18.00

WWF, figure, Undertaker, Hasbro, MOC $25.00

WWF, figure, Undertaker (mail-in), Hasbro, MOC $45.00

WWF, figure, Undertaker & Kane (2-Tuff #4), Jakks, MOC..$15.00

WWF, figure, 1-2-3 Kid, Hasbro, MOC $40.00

X-Men, figure, any, Toy Biz, MOC, ea from $10 to...........$25.00

X-Men (Movie), figure, any, Toy Biz, MOC, ea from $10 to ..$15.00

X-Men/X-Force, figure, any, Toy Biz, MOC, ea from $10 to .$25.00

Activity Sets

Activity sets that were once enjoyed by so many as children — Silly Putty, Creepy Crawlers, and Mr. Potato Heads — are finding their way back to some of those same kids, now grown up, more or less. The earlier editions, especially, are carrying pretty respectable price tags when they can be found complete or reasonably so.

The following listings are complete unless noted otherwise.

See also Character, TV, and Movie Collectibles; Coloring, Activity, and Paint Books; Disney; Playsets; and other specific categories.

Adams' Hocus-Pocus Magic Set, SS Adams, 1962, unused, MIB...$85.00

Big Burger Grill, Kenner, 1967, EXIB $35.00

Big Top Cotton Candy Machine, Hasbro, 1960s, unused, MIB .$125.00

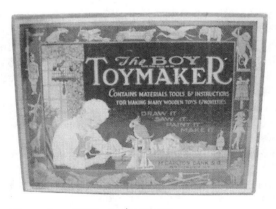

Boy Toymaker, GIB, A, $165.00. (Photo courtesy Randy Inman Auctions)

Boys Union Tool Chest No 500 B, Bliss, wood chest opens to reveal tool set, VG...$250.00

Card Magic, magic tricks to do w/illustrated cards, Ed-U Cards, 1954, NMIB $25.00

Cartoon Charm Set, Prevue, 1954, w/48 celluloid figures of various cartoon characters, NMIB...............................$200.00

Cartoon-O-Graph Sketch Board, features Warner Bros cartoon characters, Moss Mfg Co, 1940s-50s, EXIB.................$75.00

Circus Set, Hasbro, 1962, unused, MIB.............................$75.00

Colorforms Totem Pole Kit, 1958, NMIB $50.00

Creepy Crawlers, 1st issue, Mattel, 1964, EXIB $75.00

Creepy Crawlers Collection Case, Mattel, 1964, NM $50.00

Creepy Crawlers II, Mattel, 1978, NMIB..........................$50.00

Crime Lab, Amsco, 1976, unused, MIB $50.00

David Berglas Conjuring Tricks Magic Set, Kay Ltd/London, 1950s, EXIB, A $100.00

Design-O-Marx Set, Marx, 1960s, scarce, unused, MIB ...$50.00

Drawing Teacher, Milton Bradley, EXIB $100.00

Easy-Bake Oven, Kenner, EXIB, $75.00. (Photo courtesy Martin and Carolyn Berens)

Electrical Workshop, Remco, 1968, unused, MIB $125.00

Freeze Queen Ice Cream Maker, Kenner, 1966, MIB........$75.00

George Pal Eras-O-Board Set, Cobbler & the Elves, MGM/Hasbro, 1963, complete, EX+IB $60.00

Hocus Pocus Magic Set, 1976, NMIB $50.00

Hot Dog Wagon, Ideal, 1950s, plastic, NMIB.................$135.00

Incredible Edibles Gobble-Degoop, Mattel, 1966, MOC .$35.00

Johnny Toymaker Car Molding Set, EXIB $55.00

Lightning Bug Glo-Juice, Kenner, 1960s, EX $30.00

Lite Brite, 1967, NM, N2 ....$50.00

Looney Tunes Cartoon-O-Matic Molding & Coloring Set, Warner Bros, EXIB $100.00

Magic Kit of Tricks & Puzzles, Transogram, 1960s, MIB...$75.00

Magic Set, w/10 tricks, Redhill, 1930s-40s, MIB $50.00

Magician Magic Set, features Bill Bixby, 1974, NMIB......$70.00

Mandrake the Magician Magic Kit, briefcase-style box w/clasp, 1950s, complete, NMIB..$75.00

Martian Magic Tricks, Gilbert, 1963, scarce, NMIB, from $250 to $300.00

Master Magic Set, Sherms, 1930s-40s, set S, EXIB.........$125.00

Mighty Men & Monster Maker Set, 1978, EXIB $30.00

Mister Funny Face Clay & Plastic, 1953, EXIB $100.00

Modelcast N' Color Kit, features Huckleberry Hound & the Flintstones, Standard Toycraft, 1960, unused, MIB..$100.00

Mold Master Combat Set, Kenner, 1963, EXIB................$50.00

Monster Machine, Gabriel, MIB $25.00

Mr Magic Set, Adams, 1960s, NMIB $50.00

Mr Potato Head & Pete the Pepper Set, Hasbro, 1960s, MIB.$30.00

Mr Potato Head In The Parade Set, Hasbro, 1968, MIB ..$35.00

My House Printer Kit, Colorforms, 1962, EXIB................$25.00

Mysto Magic (Exhibition Set), 1920s, NMIB, $500.00.

Picture Maker Hot Birds Skyway Scene, Mattel, 1970s, MIB..$75.00

Play-Doh Fun Factory, 1960s, rare, MIB.............................$50.00

Playstone Funnies Casting Kit, features Little Orphan Annie, Sandy, Skeezix, etc, Allied Mfg, 1936, NMIB $175.00

Power Mite Workshop, Ideal, 1969, EXIB $130.00

Power Shop, Mattel, 1960s, NMIB...................................$50.00

Pre-Flight Trainer Cockpit, Einson, 1942, NMIB.............$50.00

Pretzel Jetzel Factory, Transogram, 1965, EXIB.................$50.00

Rubber Stamp Set, 20 Hanna-Barbera cartoon characters, 1960s, NMIB...$150.00

Sewing Cards, 1950, MIB (image of clown on top), N2...$25.00

Sgt Rock vs the Bad Guys, Remco, 1982, NMIB $85.00

Shaker Maker Bugglies Set, Ideal, 1972, MIB $30.00

Shrink Machine, Wham-O, unused, MIB, $85.00.

Shrinky Dinks, My Little Pony, 1980s, MIP (sealed)........$25.00

Shrunken Head Apple Sculpture, Milton Bradley, 1975, MIB.$75.00

Simple Sewing Cards for Nimble Fingers, Milton Bradley, EXIB $150.00

Sneaky Pete's Broadway Magic Show, Remco, 1960s, unused, MIB $50.00

Space Faces, Pressman, 1950s, unused, NMIB $175.00
Space Scientist Drafting Set, 1950s, EXIB.........................$65.00
Specks & Things Molding Set, MIB $50.00

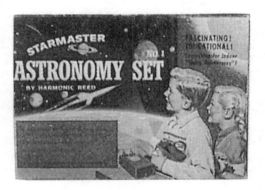

Starmaster
Astronomy
Set, Reed,
1950s, EXIB,
$50.00.

Strange Change Toy (Lost World), Mattel, 1967, NMIB ..$100.00
Sugar Plum Quick Freeze, Hasbro, unused, MIB...............$50.00
Suzy Homemaker Grill, Topper, 1960s, unused, MIB $75.00
Suzy Homemaker Sweet Shoppe Soda Fountain, Topper, 1960s,
    MIB $50.00
Tasket Basket Shape Sorter, Holgate, 1953, NM $35.00
Thingmaker (Triple), Mattel, EXIB $125.00
Thingmaker Featuring Creeple Peeple, Mattel, 1965, MIB .$100.00
Thingmaker Fighting Men Set, Mattel, 1965, EXIB.........$75.00
Thingmaker Fright Factory, Mattel, MIB (sealed)..........$150.00
Thingmaker Fun Flowers Maker Pak, Mattel, 1966, EXIB..$30.00
Thingmaker Giant Creepy Crawlers Maker Pack #2, Mattel,
    1965, EXIB...$75.00
Thingmaker Mini Dragon Maker Pack, Mattel 1967, MIB
    (sealed) $150.00
Tinker Fish, Toy Tinkers, 1927, EXIB.............................$50.00
Tinker Spots, Toy Tinkers, 1930s, EXIB..........................$60.00
Tinkerbeads No 4, Toy Tinkers, 1928, EX (in tin container)...$80.00
Trix Stix, Harry Dearly, 1952, MIP..................................$50.00
Unicorn Fantasy Stamper, Fisher-Price, 1985-86, NM $15.00
Vac-U-Form Playset, Mattel, 1962, NMIB $100.00
Voodini Magic Set, Transogram, 1960, NMIB..................$50.00
Winky Dink Paint Set, Pressman, 1950s, EX $75.00
Wire Puzzle Set, Gilbert, 1930s, MIB (sealed) $75.00
Wood Airplane Kit, Fisher-Price Arts & Crafts, 1982-85, MIB,
    C13..$25.00
Wood Sailboat Kit, Fisher-Price Arts & Crafts, 1982-85, MIB,
    C13..$25.00
Young Magicians Box of Tricks, Saalfield, 1958, NMIB ...$50.00

Advertising

The assortment of advertising memorabilia geared toward
children is vast — plush and cloth dolls, banks, games, puzzles,
trucks, radios, watches, and much, much more. And considering
the popularity of advertising memorabilia in general, when you
add to it the crossover interest from the realm of toys, you have a
real winning combination! Just remember to check for condition
very carefully; signs of play wear are common. Think twice about

investing much money in soiled items, especially cloth or plush
dolls. (Stains are often impossible to remove.)

For more information we recommend *Antique & Contemporary Advertising Memorabilia* by B.J. Summers; *McDonald's Collectibles, 2nd Edition*, by Gary Henriques & Audre DuVall; *Cracker
Jack Toys* and *Cracker Jack, the Unauthorized Guide to Advertising*
both by Larry White; *Pepsi-Cola Collectibles, Vols I, II,* and *III*, by
Bill Vehling and Michael Hunt.

Note: We have used the equal sign (=) in our Pepsi-Cola
listings to indicate the double-dot logo.

Advisors: Jim Rash (R3); Larry White (W7), Cracker Jack

See also Bubble Bath Containers; Buddy L; Cereal Boxes
and Premiums; Character, TV, and Movie Collectibles; Dakin;
Disney; Pin-Back Buttons; Premiums; other specific categories.

A&W Root Beer, bears, bean-stuffed plush, 2 different, 1997-98,
    ea from $15 to $20.00
AC Spark Plugs, figure, AC man w/1 arm extended & other on
    hip, wht & gr w/AC on chest, gr hat, 6", EXIB $160.00
AC Spark Plugs, figure, Sparky the Horse, inflatable vinyl
    w/logo, Ideal, 1960s, 25x15" L, EX..........................$100.00
Alka Seltzer, doll, Speedy, vinyl, 1960s, 8", EX, from $500 to..$600.00
Alka-Seltzer, bank, Speedy figure, pnt soft vinyl, early 1960s,
    5½", VG $135.00
Alka-Seltzer, charm, Speedy, flasher image, glass-covered
    w/frame & mirrored back, 1960s, 1x1", EX $30.00
Allied Van Lines, doll, gr uniform & hat, Lion Uniform Inc, 14",
    MIB, A $1,200.00

Arden Milk,
plastic truck
bank, NM,
A, $60.00.
(Photo courtesy Autopia
Advertising Auctions)

Aunt Jemima, Breakfast Bear, plush, 13", M...................$175.00
Aunt Jemima, doll, Diana, stuffed oilcloth, 1940-50, 8½", EX .$150.00
Aunt Jemima, doll, Uncle Mose, 1940s-50s, stuffed oilcloth, 12",
    EX $100.00
Aunt Jemima, Jr Chef Pancake Set, Argo Industries, 1949, EX .$150.00
Baskin-Robbins, figure, Pinky the Spoon, bendable, 1990s, 5",
    NM+..$6.00
Bazooka Bubble Gum, doll, Bazooka Joe, stuffed print cloth,
    1970s, 19", EX+ $10.00
Bekins Moving & Storage, truck, GMC tandem, litho tin, fric-
    tion, w/3 opening doors, 25", G+, A $275.00
Betty Crocker, doll, stuffed cloth, Kenner, 1974, 13", VG ..$20.00
BF Goodrich, comic book, Magic Shoe Adventure Book, pre-
    mium, 1962, EX $10.00
BF Goodrich Tires, yo-yo, molded plastic tire shape w/emb seal,
    NM..$10.00
Big Boy, bank, ceramic nodder figure holding hamburger, EX .$500.00

Big Boy, bank, plastic figure, red & wht checked overalls, 1973, 9", EX $20.00

Big Boy, figure, Bob on surfboard w/wave, PVC, 1990, 3", EX ..$10.00

Big Boy, kite, Big Boy image on paper, M $100.00

Big Boy, vinyl figure, w/ or w/o hamburger, M, ea $25.00

Big Boy, yo-yo, wood w/die-stamp seal, 1960s, NM+ $10.00

Blue Bonnet Margarine, doll, Blue Bonnet Sue, stuffed cloth w/yel yarn hair, 1980s, NM $5.00

Borden, bank, Beauregard, red plastic figure, Irwin, 1950s, 5", EX $65.00

Borden, Elsie's Funbook Cut-Out Toys & Games, 1940s, EX, P6 ....$65.00

Borden, figure, Elsie the Cow, PVC, 3½", M, from $10 to ..$20.00

Borden, game, Elsie the Cow, Jr Edition, EXIB $125.00

Borden, hand puppet, Elsie's baby, cloth body w/vinyl head, EX .$75.00

Borden, night light, Elsie the Cow head figure, rubber-type composition, 9", NM, $180.00. (Photo courtesy Autopia Advertising Auctions)

Borden, punch-out train, Elsie's Good Food Line, cb, 1940s, 25x37", unpunched, M (EX envelope) $150.00

Borden, push-button puppet, Elsie, wood, EX, A $125.00

Bosco Chocolate, Bosco the Clown, vinyl head on glass container, NM $25.00

Buick, sign, No Parking/Not Even Buicks, lollipop type, pnt tin, 4½", G+, A $175.00

Buick, trash can, Keep Our Streets Beautiful/Drive A Buick, pnt tin w/2-sided slanted top, 3½", VG, A $165.00

Burger Chef, hand puppet, Burger Chef, cloth body & hat w/vinyl head, 1970s, EX $10.00

Burger King, bear, Crayola Christmas, plush, 4 different, 1986, EX, ea $10.00

Burger King, doll, Burger King, stuffed cloth, 1973, 16", NM ..$10.00

Burger King, doll, Burger King, stuffed cloth, 1980, 18", EX ..$10.00

Burger King, doll, Magic King, Knickerbocker, 1980, 20", MIB .$20.00

Buster Brown Shoes, bank, molded plastic ball shape w/busts of Buster & Tige on top, 1960s, 3½" dia $25.00

Buster Brown Shoes, clicker, tin shoe-sole form, bl (Blue Ribbon) lettering on yel, VG, A $20.00

Buster Brown Shoes, clicker, tin w/head image of Buster & Tige, VG, A $20.00

Buster Brown Shoes, doll, Buster, 1974, stuffed cloth, 14", NM $40.00

Buster Brown Shoes, figure, Buster standing w/arms at sides, pnt porcelain, name impressed in back, 3", EX+, A $55.00

Buster Brown Shoes, hobby horse, wood w/pnt advertising as saddle, 28x36", very rare, VG, A $300.00

Buster Brown Shoes, kite, 1940s, NM $40.00

Buster Brown Shoes, shoe box w/Treasure Hunt Game on side, 1930s, unused, from $50 to $75.00

Butterfinger Candy Bar, doll, Butterfinger Bear, plush, 1987, 15", M $25.00

Campbell's Soup, Campbell Kids Cooking Set, 1950s, unused, MIB $200.00

Campbell's Soup, coloring book, A Story of Soup, 1977, EX .$26.00

Campbell's Soup, doll, cheerleader, vinyl, 1967, 8", EX ...$75.00

Campbell's Soup, doll, girl, rubber & vinyl w/cloth outfit, Ideal, 1955, 8", EX, minimum value $125.00

Campbell's Soup, doll, pirate, Home Shopper, 1995, 10", EX (soup can box) $80.00

Campbell's Soup, doll kit, Scottish boy & girl, Douglas Co, 1979, EX, ea $35.00

Campbell's Soup, dolls, boy & girl, pnt vinyl w/movable heads, 1960-70s, 7", NM, pr $65.00

Campbell's Soup, dolls, Paul Revere & Betsy Ross replicas, 1976, 10", M, ea from $45 to $65.00

Campbell's Soup, dolls, rag-type boy & girl, 1970s, MIB ..$75.00

Campbell's Soup, game, Campbell Kids Shopping Game, Parker Bros, 1955, scarce, NMIB $65.00

Campbell's Soup, kaleidoscope, replica of soup can, 1981, EX ..$40.00

Cap'n Crunch, doll, plush, Quaker Oats, 1990, 18", M, $20.00.

Chase & Sanborn Coffee, stake truck, metal, wht sidewall tires, w/6 coffee boxes, Ny-Lint, 1950s, MIB (Ranch Truck), A .$1,150.00

Cheer, doll, Cheer Girl, plastic w/cloth clothes, Proctor & Gamble, 1960, 10", NM $20.00

Cheetos, doll, Chester Cheeta, 18", NM (w/orig tag) $40.00

Chevrolet, mask, Chevrolet Man, See the New 1940... on hat of smiling & winking moon-faced mascot, 1940, NM ...$65.00

Chiquita Bananas, doll, stuffed print cloth, 16", M $30.00

Chiquita Bananas, doll, uncut print cloth, framed, NM, A .$50.00

Chuck-E Cheese Pizza, bank, Chuck-E Cheese vinyl figure, 7", EX $10.00

Cities Service, Fix-All wrecker, plastic, gr & wht, Marx, 11", EXIB, A $100.00

Cities Service/Litchfield Oil Co, tanker truck, cast slush metal w/rubber tires, gr & wht, Nutmeg Models, 4½", EX, A $160.00

Coca-Cola, bang gun, G Man/It's the Real Thing, M $20.00

Coca-Cola, bank, can shape w/repeated red & wht diamond design, NM $85.00

Coca-Cola, bank, pig wearing hat, red plastic w/wht Drink Coca-Cola Sold Everywhere on sides, EX $35.00

Coca-Cola, bear holding Coke bottle, wht plush, 1990s, MIB..$15.00

Coca-Cola, book, Freckles & His Friends, Whitman Better Little Book, premium, 1927, VG+ $35.00

Coca-Cola, bus, VW van, litho tin, friction, Taiyo, 1950s, 7½", VG $235.00

Coca-Cola, car, Ford Taxi, litho tin, friction, Taiyo, 9", MIB...$400.00

Coca-Cola, carousel, metal w/mc C-C graphics, EX.........$50.00

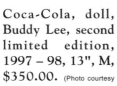

Coca-Cola, doll, Buddy Lee, second limited edition, 1997 – 98, 13", M, $350.00. (Photo courtesy Patsy Moyer)

Coca-Cola, doll, Frozen Coca-Cola mascot, stuffed cloth, 1960s, NM..$150.00

Coca-Cola, game, ball & cup, wooden ball on string attached to cup on hdl w/Coke advertising, 1960s, NM...............$45.00

Coca-Cola, game, Broadsides, Milton Bradley, 1940-50s, VG+ .$150.00

Coca-Cola, game, checkers, metal pegs fit in holes on board w/wave logo, 1970s, NM+ $75.00

Coca-Cola, game, Double-Six Dominos, brn vinyl case w/Sprite Boy logo, 1970s, EX $40.00

Coca-Cola, game set, 12 games (ping-pong, checkers, dominoes, etc), Milton Bradley, 1942, M (w/orig shipping box) $1,900.00

Coca-Cola, jigsaw puzzle, Teenage Party, NMIB.............$100.00

Coca-Cola, truck, Les-Paul, pressed steel, Mack cab w/marque on 2-tier bed, yel w/red, 22½", NM, A $400.00

Coca-Cola, truck, Marx, pressed steel, yellow, with plastic Coke cases, 12½", MIB, A, $1,000.00. (Photo courtesy Bertoia Auctions)

Coca-Cola, truck, Marx #991, pressed steel, stake bed w/Sprite Boy signs, covered wheel wells, yel, 20", G, A.........$135.00

Coca-Cola, truck, Marx #1088, litho tin, stake bed w/Sprite Boy signs, red, yel & bl, NMIB, A $1,300.00

Coca-Cola, truck, Metalcraft, A-frame, metal disk wheels, White grille, red & yel, glass bottles, 1931, 11", VG, A $1,050.00

Coca-Cola, truck, Metalcraft, A-frame, rubber tires, electric lights, red & yel, glass bottles, 1932, 11", EX $1,400.00

Coca-Cola, truck, Metalcraft, A-frame, rubber tires, White grille, red & yel, glass bottles, 1932, 11", VG.......$1,000.00

Coca-Cola, truck, Sanyo, litho tin w/rubber tires, wht, yel & red, 1950s, 13", NMIB, A..$375.00

Coca-Cola, truck, Smith-Miller, metal GMC cab w/wood bed, rubber tires, all red, wood cases, 14", EX, A.............$400.00

Coca-Cola, truck, Smith-Miller, metal GMC cab w/wood bed, rubber tires, red & yel, 16 wood cases, 14", VG, A..$350.00

Coca-Cola, truck, Smith-Miller, metal GMC w/2-tiered bed, rubber tires, yel, cases w/glass bottles, 1950s, 14", NOS, A...$1,540.00

Coca-Cola, truck, Solido, Ford pickup (1936), diecast, 1.18 scale, NM...$35.00

Cracker Jack, bank, metal book shape, W7 ....$275.00

Cracker Jack, baseball card, Cracker Jack Ball Players, image of Edward Collins of the Chicago Americans, 1915, NM, A..............$25.00

Cracker Jack, baseball card, Joe Jackson, 1914, EX, W7..$115.00

Cracker Jack, baseball card, typical (1 of 144), 1914, EX, W7, ea $55.00

Cracker Jack, baseball player, plastic, any of 11, W7, ea.....$9.00

Cracker Jack, baseball score counter, paper, W7.............$125.00

Cracker Jack, book, Animated Jungle Book, pop-up, W7 .$125.00

Cracker Jack, book, Children's Notes, paper, early, 2", W7..$45.00

Cracker Jack, book, Cracker Jack Puzzle Book, paper, series 3, W7 ....$12.50

Cracker Jack, book, Cracker Jack Riddles, jester on cover, W7...$12.50

Cracker Jack, book, Nursery Games, 3", W7 ....$128.00

Cracker Jack, book, Words of Wisdom, 5x3", W7 ....$275.00

Cracker Jack, booklet, Hub-A-Dub, Jack & Jill, etc, W7 .$40.00

Cracker Jack, bookmarks, dog heads, 3 different, metal, NM, ea.$10.00

Cracker Jack, Breakfast Set, agateware in matchbox, W7...$38.00

Cracker Jack, button, US Army Quartermaster, metal w/gold or silver wash, W7, ea $12.00

Cracker Jack, button, Victorian lady, celluloid over metal pinback, W7...$100.00

Cracker Jack, charm, cat, dog, horse, rabbit, etc, W7, ea....$9.50

Cracker Jack, charm, dirigible, metal & celluloid, W7.....$78.50

Cracker Jack, clicker, The Noisy Cracker Jack, metal, 2⅛", VG, A...$8.00

Cracker Jack, compass, paper & metal, 1½" dia, W7........$98.00

Cracker Jack, coupon, The Cracker Jack Embroidery Outfit, W7...$76.00

Cracker Jack, delivery van, The More You Eat the More You Want, 1½x¾", EX, A $30.00

Cracker Jack, dexterity puzzle, A-Maze, plastic & paper, 1" sq, W7...$5.00

Cracker Jack, dexterity puzzle, High Man, cb w/plastic covering, 1950s-60s, EX+ $30.00

Cracker Jack, flip book, Minute Movies, any of 12, W7, ea.$15.00

Cracker Jack, game, Flick-A-Wink, paper, W7.................$35.00

Cracker Jack, game, Ring Toss, paper, Makatoy, W7 ....$24.00

Cracker Jack, game, Send a Message by Dot & Dash, W7 ..$30.00

Cracker Jack, hat, Me for Cracker Jack, paper, W7 ....$295.00

Cracker Jack, horse & wagon, litho tin w/advertising on sides of van wagon, Andelus Marshmallows on reverse, 2x1", NM, A $40.00

Cracker Jack, jigsaw puzzle, dirigible, knights, etc, c 1931, W7.$145.00
Cracker Jack, locomotive, red metal w/yel detail, 2¼", NM, A .$10.00
Cracker Jack, Magicard, paper, D Series #44, any of 15, W7 ..$17.50
Cracker Jack, mechanical toy, boy eating Cracker Jack, paper, 3",
   W7 ....$395.00
Cracker Jack, mechanical toy, frog w/jumping mechanism, paper
   & metal, 3", W7 ....$125.00
Cracker Jack, mechanical toy, Jack at blackboard writes &
   erases, paper, W7 ....$295.00
Cracker Jack, paint book, Birds To Color, paper, W7 ....$75.00
Cracker Jack, paper dolls, Jane & Jimmy Cut Out Twins, W7 ..$145.00
Cracker Jack, pencil holder, paper, 2x4", W7....................$78.00
Cracker Jack, pin, Cracker Jack Air Corps, metal wings, W7..$65.00
Cracker Jack, plastic, 2-tube, any 2-color, 3", W7, ea $3.00
Cracker Jack, pocket peeper, coyote, plastic, 1½", NM, A .$5.00
Cracker Jack, postcard, Cracker Jack Bears, 1908, any of 16, W7,
   ea...$27.50
Cracker Jack, rabbit, pk plastic, 1¼x1¼", NM, A $10.00
Cracker Jack, riddle book, Sailor Jack's Wise Cracks #13, NM,
   A..$10.00

**Cracker Jack, spinners, Always on Top/World's Famous
Confection, 1½" diameter, NM, $25.00; Always on
Top, 1½" diameter, NM, $25.00.** (Photo courtesy Frank's Antiques)

Cracker Jack, spinner, Cracker Jack emb on top, metal
   w/wooden spinner peg, 1½" dia, EX, A $5.00
Cracker Jack, spinner, Fortune Teller, metal w/wooden spinner
   peg, 1½" dia, EX, A $5.00
Cracker Jack, spinner, Jack the Sailor Boy Says To Spell Your
   Name & Read Your Fortune, metal, 1¾" dia, EX, A .$15.00
Cracker Jack, spinner, Two Toppers, metal w/wood spinner, red,
   white & blue, 1½" dia, NM..$20.00
Cracker Jack, spinner, You're It, metal w/finger pointer, W7..$18.00
Cracker Jack, stickers, glow-in-the-dark, 1972, W7............$5.50
Cracker Jack, surrey, metal 2-wheeled cart w/wooden pull rod,
   yel & gr w/name on back, 4¾", EX, A $22.00
Cracker Jack, telescope, Pokemon, plastic, series Cracker Jack
   #20, any of 24, W7, ea $4.50
Cracker Jack, Toonerville Trolley, litho tin, 1¾", EX, A ..$415.00
Cracker Jack, tray, bl metal w/image of product box, 1¼x2", EX,
   A $10.00
Cracker Jack, whistle, metal, airplane shape w/eagle design,
   W7 ....$65.00
Cracker Jack, whistle, metal, Simplex Flute, W7................$6.75
Cracker Jack, whistle, metal, The More You Eat the More You
   Want, oblong, 2½x1", NM, A.................................$25.00
Cracker Jack, whistle, paper, Blow for More, pictures prize box,
   W7 ....$67.50

Cracker Jack, whistle, paper, wolf's head on reverse, 1x2", EX..$10.00
Cracker Jack, zodiac coin, plastic, any of 12, W7, ea $8.75

**Curity, doll, Miss Curity, com-
position with original nurse's
uniform and hat, American,
1940s, 21", VG+, A, $285.00.**

(Photo courtesy Skinner, Inc.)

Dairy Queen, doll, Dairy Queen Kid, stuffed cloth, 1974, EX .$20.00
Dairy Queen, whistle, plastic ice cream cone shape, 2", NM, A .$5.00
Del Monte, doll, Fluffy Lamb, plush, 1984, EX, N2..........$20.00
Del Monte, doll, Lushie Peach, plush, 1982, EX, N2........$20.00
Del Monte, doll, Reddie Tomato, plush, 1982, EX, N2 ....$20.00
Dolly Madison Ice Cream, playing cards, Redi-Slip, 1950s, MIB
   (sealed)..$30.00
Dominos Pizza, doll, Noid, plush, 1988, 19", MIP.............$20.00
Dominos Pizza, yo-yo, Nobody Delivers Faster, plastic,
   Humphrey, NM+...$5.00
DX, game, Getaway Chase, few pcs missing o/w EXIB, T1 .$125.00
Eskimo Pie, doll, Eskimo Pie Doll, stuffed cloth, 1964-74, 15",
   EX, from $15 to..$20.00
Esso, bank, Esso Serviceman, pnt hard plastic, late 1950s-early
   1960s, 5", EX+ $40.00
Esso, tanker truck, litho tin w/plastic hose, Oil Drop man flanks
   name, red light on top of cab, A1/Japan, 18", VG+, A.$300.00
Fig Newtons, doll, balancing cookie on her head & holding lg
   cookie in her hand, plastic, Nabisco, 1980s, 4½", NM.$15.00
Florida Department of Citrus, nodder, Florida Orange Bird, pnt
   plastic, Disney design, WDP, 1970s, 6", M................$55.00
Fruit Stripe Gum, figure, man shaped like gum pack riding
   motorbike, bendable, 1960s, 7½", EX+......................$75.00
General Electric, Radio Man, jtd wood & compo majorette figure,
   red & wht w/gold & blk trim, 1930s, 18½", EX+, A ..$920.00

**Gilmore/Red Lion, tanker truck and accessories, Dorman Prod-
ucts, pressed steel, 26", NM, A, $1,980.00.** (Photo courtesy Bertoia Auctions)

Gilmore/Red Lion, tanker, Smith-Miller, metal, 1949 GMC, red & wht, rubber tires, 22", EX, A $475.00

Goodrich Silvertown Tires Wrecker, 12", G, A $200.00

Gray Dunn & Co Biscuits, limousine, yel litho tin early type w/simulated spoke wheels, roof lifts up, 6", EX, A .$1,760.00

Green Giant, bank, Little Sprout, compo, plays Valley of the Green Giant, 8½", EX $50.00

Green Giant, doll, Little Sprout, talker, MIP....................$55.00

Green Giant, figure, Jolly Green Giant, vinyl, 1970s, 10", EX+..$90.00

Green Giant, figure, Little Sprout, vinyl, 1970s, 6½", EX ..$8.00

Green Giant, jump rope, Little Sprout hdls, MIP $20.00

Green Giant Brands, tractor-trailer, 22", G+, A $200.00

Green Giant Corn, doll, girl dressed in yel & gr dress & hat w/corn motif on purse, vinyl w/rooted hair, 1950s, 17", M........$40.00

Hamburger Helper, figure, Helping Hand, plush, 14", M..$10.00

Hardee's, doll, Gilbert Giddy-Up, stuffed cloth, 1971, EX ..$25.00

Harley-Davidson, doll, Harley Hog, 9", M $25.00

Harley-Davidson, truck, pressed steel, blk doorless cab w/red chassis, yel & gr box van w/ad, disk wheels, 25", EX, A $250.00

Hawaiian Punch, doll, Punchy, stuffed cloth, 20", NM $65.00

Hawaiian Punch, game, Mattel, 1978, NMIB....................$50.00

Heinz, H-57 Rocket Blaster, w/instructions, MIB, C10 ....$15.00

Howard Johnson's, truck, plastic, long-nose cab w/box van, opening doors, Marx, 1950s, 10", EX $125.00

Humble Oil/Exxon, game, Northwest Passage!, Impact, 1969, NMIB..$40.00

Humpty Dumpty Shoes, clicker, image of Humpty Dumpty on walls, VG, A $32.00

Hush Puppies, whistle, plastic dog shape, wht & lt brn, 2", NM, A $10.00

Icee, bank, Icee bear, vinyl figure, 1970s, 8", VG, N2 ......$20.00

Jewel Tea, delivery van, pressed steel & litho tin, 2-tone brn w/sign reading A Better Place To Trade..., 9", G+, A $260.00

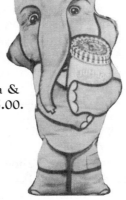

Jumbo Brand Peanut Butter, doll, elephant holding jar, stuffed printed cloth, Frank Tea & Spice Co., 16", EX+, A, $525.00.

(Photo courtesy Wm. Morford)

Kaliko Kat Shoes, clicker, They Last Longer, name & image on wht, VG, A $28.00

Keebler, bank, Ernie the Keebler elf, ceramic, 10", M $50.00

Kellogg's, doll, Bean Bag Bunch, w/tag, MIP....................$10.00

Kellogg's, doll set, Goldilocks & the Three Bears, stuffed printed cloth, 1920s, 10" to 13", assembled but unused, EX+..$200.00

Kellogg's, Friction Powered Mover, Crackle!, plastic, store item, 1984, 2½", NMOC, A...$10.00

Kellogg's, Indoor Bubbles, Snap!, Crackle! & Pop!, Tootsie Toy, unused, MOC, A...$5.00

Kellogg's, push puppet, Pop!, plastic, store item, 1984, 4½", MOC, A...$6.00

Kellogg's, sleeping bag, shows Tony the Tiger & other Kellogg's characters, 1970s, EX...$50.00

Kellogg's Froot Loops, doll, Toucan Sam, vinyl, store item sold w/Rice Krispies Dolls, 1984, 5", NMIB, A $5.00

Kellogg's Rice Krispies, Bath-Tub Toy, Pop! in boat, vinyl, store item, Talbot Toys, 1984, 6x4", NMIB, A $10.00

Kellogg's Rice Krispies, dolls, Snap!, Crackle! & Pop!, vinyl, store items, 1984, 5", MIB, ea.................................$10.00

Kentucky Fried Chicken, bank, Colonel Sanders figure w/cane on sm rnd base, Starling Plastics, 1965, 12½", EX+ $30.00

Kentucky Fried Chicken, coloring book, Favorite Chicken Stores, 1960s, EX $25.00

Kentucky Fried Chicken, hand puppet, Colonel Sanders, plastic, 1960s, EX $20.00

Kentucky Fried Chicken, nodder, Colonel Sanders figure, pnt compo, Chares Products, 1960s, 7", EX....................$65.00

Kiwi Fruit, figures, plush, 1985-90, set of 3, 10½", 11", 17", M, ea..$30.00

Knorr Soup, doll set, boy and girl, hard plastic, in costumes from various countries, Best Foods, 1963 – 64, M, pr, $15.00. (Photo courtesy Carol J. Stover)

Kool-Aid, dispenser, MIB $50.00

Kraft, figures, Cheesasaurus Rex in various sporting poses, PVC, 1990s premiums, M, ea $10.00

Kraft, pull toy, Kraft TV Theatre cameraman, figure seated on rolling camera base, plastic, Velveeta premium, 1954, EX..$110.00

Kraft Macaroni & Cheese, wristwatch, 1980s, M, I1 ....$10.00

Kroger, delivery truck, orange & blk metal w/fold-down gate, disk wheels, Metalcraft, 12", VG, A $330.00

Lifesavers, bank, cb & metal cylinder w/Lifesavers graphics, 1960s, 12", EX, N2..$20.00

Little Caesar's Pizza, doll, Pizza Pizza Man holding slice of pizza, plush, 1990, EX...$5.00

Little Debbie, doll, vinyl w/cloth dress & straw hat, 1980s, 11", NM..$85.00

Log Cabin Syrup, pull toy, Log Cabin Express, NMIB, A ..$900.00

M&Ms, bean bag toys, peanut shape, golfer or witch, 6", ea .$10.00

M&Ms, bean bag toys, plain shape, red, gr, bl, or yel, 6", ea .$5.00

M&Ms, doll, plain shape, plush, 4½" or 8", ea....................$5.00

M&Ms, doll, plain shape, plush, 12" $10.00
M&Ms, figure, peanut shape, bendable arms & legs, 7"....$15.00
M&Ms, pillow, plain-shape figure w/arms & legs, plush, NM..$25.00
M&Ms, wristwatch, several variations, 1980s, M, I1, ea ..$25.00
Magic Chef, bank, Baker Man figure, vinyl, 1990s, 7", EX, N2 .$20.00
McDonald's, action figure, Big Mac, Remco, 1976, NM...$25.00
McDonald's, action figure, Captain Crook, Remco, 1976, 6", NM $25.00
McDonald's, action figure, Grimace, Remco, 1976, NM..$25.00
McDonald's, action figure, Professor, Remco, 1976, 6", NM.$25.00
McDonald's, action figure, Ronald McDonald, Remco, 1976, NM $25.00
McDonald's, bank, Grimace, compo, 1985, NM...............$15.00
McDonald's, bank, Ronald McDonald, ceramic bust, 7½", M..$15.00
McDonald's, bank, Ronald McDonald, plastic, NM $10.00
McDonald's, bop bag, Grimace, 1978, 8", MIP $6.00
McDonald's, doll, French Fries Critter, pillow type, 1987, NM+ $15.00
McDonald's, doll, Fry Girl, stuffed cloth, 1987, 4", M $5.00

McDonald's, doll, Hamburglar, vinyl and cloth, 1980s, 11", NM, $15.00.

McDonald's, doll, Mayor, stuffed cloth, 1970s, 15", NM ..$25.00
McDonald's, doll, McDonald's Girl, stuffed cloth, 1970s, NM..$25.00
McDonald's, doll, Ronald McDonald, Chase Bag Co, 17", EX.$10.00
McDonald's, game, McDonald's, Milton Bradley, 1975, MIB..$25.00
McDonald's, game, Playland Funburst, Parker Bros, 1984, MIB..$20.00
McDonald's, playset, McDonaldland, Remco, 1976, MIB..$125.00
Michelin, doll, Mr Bib holding baby, rubber, 7", EX.......$125.00
Michelin, figure, Mr Bib w/hands on hips, chest banner, wht plastic, 1981, 12", NM.................................$65.00
Michelin, puzzle, Mr Bib on motorcycle, forms figure, MIP .$55.00
Minute Maid, coloring book, features Teddy Snow Crop (polar bear), Saalfield, 1956, unused, scarce, M $45.00
Moxie, auto w/horse & rider, litho tin, red w/blk horse or bl w/wht horse, 8" or 9", EX+, A, ea $2,475.00
Mr Clean, figure, wht-pnt vinyl, Proctor & Gamble, 1961, 8", EX...$50.00
Mr Softee Ice Cream, truck, litho tin, Japan, 1960s, 4½", NM.$65.00
Napa Auto Parts, truck, Ny-Lint, 1988, 10", VG+, N2 ....$25.00
Napa Auto Parts, truck, 1980s, 21", VG+, N2 ....$35.00
National Biscuit Co, semi truck, tin & wood w/celluloid windshield, Rich Toys, 24", EX, A $2,750.00
Nestlé Quik, figure, Quik Bunny, plush w/'Q' on chest, 1970s, 24", EX $30.00

Norge, masks, diecut cb caricature images of Ed Wynn, Danny Thomas, Jimmy Durante & Jack Carson, 1951, EX+.$50.00
Northern Toilet Tissue, doll, Northern Doll, stuffed cloth w/vinyl head & hands, rooted hair, wht outfit, 1980s, 15", M...$10.00
Oscar Mayer, pedal car, Wienermobile, EX, T1 ....$125.00
Oscar Mayer, puppet, Little Oscar, plastic w/printed image, EX+...$6.00
Oscar Mayer, Wienermobile, mechanical, made of Styron, Product Miniature Co, 10", NMIB, A $360.00
Oscar Mayer, whistle, plastic wiener on wheeled base, 2⅛x1¼", NM, A...$15.00
Ovaltine/Bovril, dbl-decker bus, w/up, Tri-Ang/Minic, 1950s, 4x7", EX+...$100.00

Pepsi-Cola, dispenser/bank, battery-operated, Linemar, 1950s, 10", unused, EXIB, A, $350.00. (Photo courtesy Wm. Morford)

Pepsi-Cola, pull toy, puppy w/hot dog wagon, wood, 10", EX.$250.00
Pepsi-Cola, truck, Buddy L, 1970s, metal, Enjoy Pepsi marque on 2-tier open bay w/cases, bl & wht, 16", EXIB, A $100.00
Pepsi-Cola, truck, Buddy-L, wood, gr Railway Express box van w/Pepsi=Cola logo, complete w/accessories, 16", NMIB, A.$1,700.00
Pepsi-Cola, truck, Ny-Lint, metal, 3-part open-sided bays w/Pepsi ads on inside walls, no cart or cases, 16", VG, A $100.00
Pepsi-Cola, truck, Ny-Lint, metal, 3-part open-sided bays w/Pepsi ads on inside walls, w/cart & cases, 17", VGIB, A....$170.00
Pepsi-Cola, truck, Solido, Chevy pickup (1946), diecast, 9½", M, from $15 to $25.00
Pepsi-Cola, whistle, plastic twin bottles, 3x1½", decals missing o/w EX, A...$18.00
Peter Paul Candy, ring, weather w/indicator paper, EX, C10 ..$215.00
Peters Weatherbird Shoes, clicker, dressed bird in ball cap on bl, EX, A $18.00
Peters Weatherbird Shoes, whistle, Happy Days on Healthy Feet, cylindrical, 1¼", EX...$10.00
Peters Weatherbird Shoes, whistle, yel metal w/advertising & mc image of boy on sides of barrel, 1½", EX, A $18.00
Peters Weatherbird Shoes, see also Weatherbird Shoes
PF Flyers, ring, EX, C10...$65.00
Phillips 66, bank, smiling fat gas attendant in uniform & hat, plastic, 5", VG, A $40.00
Pillsbury, doll, Doughboy, wht plush w/hat & scarf, 1970s, VG .$18.00
Pillsbury, doll, Poppin' Fresh, stuffed cloth, 1970s, 11", EX...$20.00
Pillsbury, doll, Poppin' Fresh, stuffed cloth, 1970s, 14", VG..$15.00
Pillsbury, doll, Poppin' Fresh, talker, Mattel, 16", NM ...$100.00

Pillsbury, figure, Poppin' Fresh, rubber, 1970s, 7", NM $20.00
Pillsbury, wristwatch, Doughboy, talker, 1996, M, I1 ....$15.00
Pizza Hut, bank, Pizza Hut Pete, plastic, 1969, 8", EX+ $25.00
Pizza Hut, kite, Garfield, MIP $5.00
Planters, child's dish set, Melmac, 1970s, 3-pc, MIB $20.00
Planters, doll, Mr Peanut, Chase Bag, 1967, 21", EX........$40.00

Planters, Mr. Peanut doll, plush, 1970s, 26", NM, $50.00. (Photo courtesy Patsy Moyer)

Planters, doll, Mr Peanut, wood, jtd, pnt features, 8½", VG+, A.$155.00
Planters, game, Planters Peanut Party, 1930s, complete, uncut & unused, NM $100.00
Planters, nodder, Mr Peanut standing w/ankles crossed & hand on hat on sq base, NM..$150.00
Planters, whistle, Mr Peanut figure, plastic, 2½", EX, A ..$15.00
Poll Parrot Shoes, comic book, 1959, EX, N2 ....$20.00
Poll Parrot Shoes, whistle, yel metal w/advertising & mc image of mascot parrot on sides of barrel, 1¾", NM, A $10.00
Popsicle, Music Maker Truck, plastic, Mattel, Copyright 1954, 11", nonworking, G, A $100.00
Purina, squeak toy, chuck wagon, vinyl, 1975, 8", EX+ $28.00
Raid, figure, Raid Bug, plush, 1989, EX+ $25.00
Raid, figure, remote-control, EX, T1................................$100.00
Raid, wind-up figure, Raid bug, mean expression, 4", EX+ .$45.00

RCA Television Service Truck, plastic, Marx, 8½", EXIB, A, $235.00. (Photo courtesy Collector's Auction Service)

Red Goose, ring, glow-in-the-dark w/secret compartment & photo, EX...$100.00
Red Goose Shoes, Tuck-A-Tub Theatre Play Kit, 1950s premium, complete, unpunched, NM $40.00

Richfield, Mack Bulldog tanker, metal, blk & bl w/cream frame & spoke wheels, Am National, 1920s, 28", EX........$875.00
Salerno, delivery truck, box van, litho tin, wht & bl, Marx, 11", EX+IB...$450.00
Sealtest, clicker, Ask For..., red on wht, EX, A $11.00
Sealtest Dairy Products, bank, delivery truck, plastic, 7", VG (w/cellophane wrap), A..$45.00
Sheffield Farms Co, horse-drawn delivery van wagon, pnt wood, w/glass bottles & carrier, pull string, 20½", VG, A .$770.00
Shell, bank, Shell lettered in red on yel plastic clam shell form, 4x4x2", NM, A $85.00
Shell, tanker truck, tin, friction, red & yel, Japan, 11", EX, A.$150.00
Shoney's, comic book, #184, robot talks to Big Boy, 1972, EX, N2 ....$10.00
Sinclair, Oil Truck Dino Soap, bar of soap in shape of a tanker truck, gr, unused, EXIB, A $25.00
Sinclair, tanker, 1930s, pressed steel, slanted back, wooden disk wheels w/covered wheels wells, gr, 1930s, 18", VG .$750.00
Smile Orange Drink, clicker, mascot w/bow tie reading Drink Smile/It's So Good, bl w/orange & wht, NM, A........$20.00
Snow Crop Frozen Foods, hand puppet, Teddy Snow Crop, fur-like body w/molded face, 1950s, 8", EX......................$30.00
Snow Crop Frozen Foods, van, litho tin w/rubber tires, Teddy mascot on rear, H/Japan, 1950s-60s, 8½", EX+ $125.00
Spaghetti-O's, figure, Wizard of O's, vinyl, 1975, 7½", NM ..$20.00
Sprite, doll, Lucky Lymon, vinyl talker, 1990s, 7½", M....$20.00
Star-Kist Tuna, bank, Charlie Tuna, ceramic, Japan, 10", MIB..$35.00
Star-Kist Tuna, doll, Charlie Tuna, talker, Mattel, 1969, 14", NM, L6..$50.00

Star-Kist Tuna, truck, metal, red, white, and blue, 24", restored, A, $200.00. (Photo courtesy Collector's Auction Service)

Star-Kist Tuna, wristwatch, 25th Anniversary, 1986, MIB $25.00
Taco Bell, dog, bean-filled, w/tags, 1999, M......................$12.00
Taco Bell, yo-yo, Humphrey, plastic, NM............................$2.00
Tastykake Bakery, doll, stuffed print cloth, 1970s, VG $15.00
Terminex, truck, w/ladder, 1960s, G $100.00
Texaco, boat, North Dakota Tanker, red, blk & wht plastic, Wen-Mac Corp/USA, 17", VG+, A $50.00
Texaco, doll, Cheerleader, 1971, 11", NRFB.....................$20.00
Texaco, tanker truck, pressed steel, contemporary sq styling w/plastic windows, red & wht, 24", EX, A $110.00
Texaco Fire Chief, bank, red plastic gas pump w/star logo on rnd wht globe, Ideal, 9", EXIB, A $300.00
Texaco Fire Chief, helmet, plastic, w/speaker on top, Wen-Mac/USA, VG+, A $70.00

Texaco Fire Chief, pencil case, red plastic pump form w/blk rubber gas hose & hinged lid, Hasbro, 8", EX+, A........$180.00
Tropicana, doll, Tropic-Ana, stuffed cloth, 1970s, 17", EX+ ..$18.00
Tru Ade, clicker, Chirp For...Not Carbonated, red & wht, EX, A...$18.00
Twenty Mule Team Borax, Woodburning & Project Kit, complete, vintage, EXIB, T1 ....$45.00
U-Haul, truck set, Ny-Lint #4300, Rental Fleet, MIB, A ..$825.00
US Forest Service, whistle, plastic Smokey the Bear head, tan w/brn details, 3½x2½", NM, A.....................................$20.00
Vlasic Pickles, doll, Stork, plush, Trudy Toys, 1989, 22", NM...$30.00
Weatherbird Shoes, whistle, paper, Crow For..., 2½x1x1¼", EX, A...$5.00
Weatherbird Shoes, see also Peters Weatherbird Shoes
Wendy's, puzzle, Where's the Beef?, 1984, 551 pcs, EX $5.00
Whirlpool, yo-yo, Duncan, 1950s, NM $30.00
Whistle Orange, whistle, Thirsty? Just Whistle, bl metal, NM, A .$10.00
Yellow Cab, whistle, litho tin car shape, 2", NM $22.00

Wrangler Jeans, doll in authentic Wrangler wear, Ertl, 11½", MIB, $125.00.

Advertising Signs, Ads, and Displays

Nowadays, with the intense passion toy buffs pour into their collections, searching for advertising items to complement those collections is a natural extension of their enthusiasm, adding even more diversity to an already multifaceted collecting field.

American Eagle Toy Savings Bank, trade card, shows bank w/extensive instructions, VG, A $110.00

Disneykins by Marx, cardboard and plastic display with 34 permanently attached first series Disneykins, 1960, 16", EX, A, $365.00. (Photo courtesy Collectors Auction Service)

Betty Boop Milk Nut Frappe 5¢, candy box, Schutter-Johnston, 1920s, 8x11", VG, A $350.00
Buffalo Bill Jr for Milky Way Candy, color ad, 1953, 10x13", EX, N2 ....$15.00
Davy Crockett Pocket Knives, display card for 2½" knives (includes 5), shows Fess Parker, Imperial Knives/WDP, EX, A $130.00
Gene Autry & Company With His Famous Horse Champion, diecut cb display w/fold-out image of Gene, 1940s, 14", NM.....$175.00
Gene Autry & Schafer's Bread Adventure Story Trail Map, poster display for labels 1-16, 1950s, 22x17", EX $75.00
Gene Autry/Wrigley Gum, cb standup display, photo of Gene on rearing Champion in belt w/silver buckle frame, 12", EX, A $125.00
HD Lee Co Presents Buddy Lee, display case w/4 dolls, glass & wood w/stenciled glass lid, ca 1923, 20x9x15", EX, A.........$1,700.00
Hopalong Cassidy Rides Again/Read the Knickerbocker News, red cb sign w/blk & wht images, 11x21", EX $250.00
Hopalong Cassidy Rollfast Bicycles, cb stand-up, 20", NM, A..$450.00
Humpty Dumpty Toy Savings Bank, trade card, colorful close-up image, VG, A..$715.00
H2O-Jet Gun, cb display box complete w/48 vinyl water pistols in 4 colors, Hong Kong, 4x9x10", NM, A $135.00
Kellogg's Corn Flakes/Rice Krispies Witch Mask, window display, diecut mask to be cut from cereal boxes, 1950s, 15", M.$65.00
Kernel Nut, sign, Free Halloween Masks (While They Last) With 2-lbs of Brazil Nuts, 8x19", 1950s, EX $85.00
Kilgor's Private Eye Toy Cap Pistol, heavy paper sign w/red & blk graphics & lettering on wht, 14x23", VG+ $100.00
Lone Ranger Western Gun Collection, cb display card w/6 miniature diecast metal brand-name guns, VG card w/EX guns $150.00

Marx, display, featuring ten free figures with purchase of each Mobile Unit, complete, VG, A, $800.00. (Photo courtesy Randy Inman Auctions)

Meccano Motor Car Constructor, diecut cb sign w/litho image of racing car, name across top of yel circle, 9½", NM, A $385.00
Mickey Mouse Club Morning & Night Tooth Brushes, cb display box w/2 brushes ea on 11 cards, DuPont/WDP, 5x6x8", NM, A $165.00
Mickey's Fun Mug, sign, diecut image of Mickey's head w/banners, Drink Up With..., 1960s, 20x17", EX+ $50.00
Munsters Theatre 5¢, cb display box w/24 unopened wax packs, unused, EX, A..$1,250.00

New Haven Character Watches, standup display w/6 watches, 1948-51, NM, C10 ....$2,850.00
Our Gang Hustling To Serve You, poster w/graphics of Our Gang working outside early gas station w/inset, 26x32", EX..$750.00
Pez, molded plastic display head of Pez clown (Peter Pez) holding 6" Pez dispenser, 1960s, 18x18x6", EX+ $1,550.00
Popeye, Official Popeye Pipe display card featuring 5" wooden battery-op pipe, Micro-Lite/Putman Prod, 1958, 9x6", M ..$75.00
Popeye Flashlite, diecut cb standup for displaying 12 flashlite whistle toys (not included), Bantamlite, 1950s, 15", EX.......$65.00
Popsicle Space-Shots, poster, 2 space kids beaming w/Space-Pops, Different Exciting Space Shapes..., 1964, 7x12", NM+ .$65.00
Post Grape-Nuts Flakes/Roy Rogers, window sign, plastic, New!/Crispier!/It's Here!, shows box w/Roy, 24x18", NM, A ..$125.00
Revell Circus, display, complete circus atop electrically-operated box w/turntable, VG to EX, A $700.00
Rin-Tin-Tin Dog Supply Center, display rack, for choker chains, litho tin, Screen Gems, 1956, 8x21", rare, VG........$120.00
Robin Hood Badges, litho cb display w/photo image of Richard Greene as Robin Hood, w/3 of 12 badges, 1950s, 11", EX+ $75.00
Roy Rogers Double R Bar Ranch, cb standup featuring Roy w/lg lasso on rearing Trigger at ranch gate, 20", NM, A .$125.00
Roy Rogers 'Roundup King' Tops, litho cb display box for yo-yos, All Western Plastics, 1950s, 7x5x2½", VG+ $65.00
Santa, cb sign, Gifts That Add Pleasure to His Favorite Sport, 1940s, 22x16", EX..$55.00
Santa, cb sign, They All Want a Wagon!, Santa & children, 1940s, 22x16", EX..$55.00
Santa, litho paper banner w/pointed bottom, Gifts for Christmas Giving, Santa on train, 1940s, 22x16", NM+ $50.00
Santa, litho paper banner w/pointed bottom, Your Christmas Store/Gifts for All, Santa & elves, 1940s, 22x16", NM+ .$50.00
Santa Soaky Bubble Bath, display figural bottle mounted on diecut box bottom, red plastic, Colgate Palmolive, 1960s, NM+ $50.00
Schuco, display sign, red-pnt cast metal trademark name on blk wooden base, 15½" L, EX, A...................................$220.00
Speaking Dog Mechanical Bank, trade card, bank in room setting, EX+, A $450.00

Steiff-Selection, porcelain sign, 6x16", unused new old stock, $400.00. (Photo courtesy Collectors Auction Service)

Stump Speaker Mechanical Bank, trade card, colorful vertical closeup image, M, A $715.00
Superman In Movie Style, display box w/back marque, complete w/3 films, litho cb, Acme, 1947, 5x7½", EX, A........$280.00
Texaco Cheer Leader Doll/2 Fine Toys/23 in Texaco Tank Truck, paper banner w/sewn-in wooden strips, 88x44", NM....$55.00

Texaco New Jet Fuel Truck $4.98, sign, cb, 57x34", EX, A..$110.00
Tonka, sign, red porcelain oval w/wht Tonka lettering, 1960s-70s, 11x23", MIB, A $330.00
Trick Pony Mechanical Bank, trade card, bank in room setting, EX $250.00
Uncle Sam Mechanical Bank, trade card, vertical image, EX, A ...$715.00

Aeronautical

Toy manufacturers seemed to take the cautious approach toward testing the waters with aeronautical toys, and it was well into the second decade of the twentieth century before some of the European toy makers took the initiative. The earlier models were bulky and basically inert, but by the '50s, Japanese manufacturers were turning out battery-operated replicas with wonderful details that advanced with whirling motors and flashing lights.

See also Battery-Operated Toys; Cast Iron, Airplanes; Gasoline-Powered Toys; Model Kits; Pull Toys; Robots & Space Toys; Windups, Friction, and Other Mechanicals.

Air Cruiser, Buddy L, Four Motor #683, wht w/red trim, 27" W, NM+IB...$1,000.00
Air France Super Constellation, France, friction, litho tin, 20" W, VG..$200.00
Air France Super G, Joustra, litho tin, friction, 19" L, G+, A..$250.00
Airport Helicopter, Y, litho tin, battery-op, 13", NMIB, A..$225.00
American Airlines Airliner, Japan, friction, litho tin & plastic, 20" W, G, A $75.00
American Airlines DC-7C, Japan, battery-op, litho tin, 4 props, 24" W, EXIB..$375.00
American Airlines DC-7, Japan, battery-op, litho tin & plastic, 19½" W, G+, A $100.00
American Airlines DC-7, Linemar, friction, litho tin, 19" W, G, A $125.00
American Airlines Electra, Linemar, battery-op, litho tin, 19" W, VG+, A $75.00
American Airlines Flagship NC-EIDO, pressed steel, 27½" W, EX $200.00
American Airlines Jetliner N7501A, Japan, friction, litho tin, 14" W, G $50.00
Army Helicopter, Japan, litho tin, friction, dbl rotors, 17", G.$50.00
Army Scout Plane, Marx, 1930s, pressed steel, 23", G ...$475.00
Army Scout Plane, Steelcraft, Buster Brown advertising on top wing, 22½" W, G, A................................$600.00

Biplane, Distler, wind-up, lithographed tin, 20", EX, A, $2,420.00. (Photo courtesy Randy Inman Auctions)

Army Scout Plane, Steelcraft, 1920s, tri-motor, 22½" W, G+, A...$700.00

Auto-Gyro, Wyandotte, pressed steel w/wooden wheels, 12½" W, EX..$225.00

Biplane, Cor-Cor, 1920s, pressed steel, 17" W, G, A......$275.00

Biplane, Dayton, friction, pnt pressed steel, w/movable stabilizer, 2 applied star insignias on top wing, 15", VG+.......$325.00

Biplane, Meccano, pnt steel, constructed, 18" W, VG, A..$300.00

Biplane, Tipp, litho tin, army gr & yel stripes, 2 full-figure pilots, 19" L, G...$2,000.00

Black Knight BK-02 Fighter Jet, Japan, friction, litho tin, 10" W, VGIB...$125.00

Boeing B-50 Superfortress, Cragstan, 1950s, litho tin, 15" W, NM+...$300.00

Boeing Strato Cruiser, Japan, friction, litho tin, 20 W, G..$175.00

Boeing 733 Supersonic Jet, Japan, battery-op, litho tin, VGIB.$55.00

Bomber, Marx, litho tin w/camo detail, 18½" W, G, A..$275.00

Bomber, pressed steel w/wooden wheels, 2 props, observation cutouts, olive gr fuselage w/yel wings, 27" W, G, A..$385.00

British Caldonian Jetliner, Marx, battery-op, litho tin, 14" W, G, A...$65.00

Capitol Airlines, Linemar, battery-op, litho tin, 14½" W, G..$100.00

Cargo Plane, Orobr, w/up, litho tin, 3 props, simulated wood grain, red trim, 14" W, VG......................................$450.00

Cesnna N5670, Japan, 1960s, friction, litho tin, detachable wings, 16" L, EX+...$100.00

China Clipper, Wyandotte, 1940s, pressed steel, 13" W, unused, NM+IB, A...$725.00

China Clipper, Wyandotte, 1940s, pressed steel, 13" W, G+, A..$110.00

Civilian Bomber, Tipp, wind-up, lithographed tin, 14" long, EX, A, $3,630.00. (Photo courtesy Noel Barrett)

Coast Guard Seaplane, Ohio Art, litho tin, 10", EX, A.$200.00

Cougar Navy Jet Fighter, battery-op, MIB, L4................$325.00

Curtiss Jenny Trainer, Japan, friction, 14" W, EXIB.......$150.00

Douglas DC-7C, battery-op, litho tin, 4 props, 24" W, EXIB.$475.00

Douglas DC-7C, Cragstan, friction, litho tin, 17½" W, EX+IB, A...$250.00

Douglas DC-9, TN, litho tin & plastic, lights flash, attendant & steps come out, 15" L, G+, A.................................$110.00

Douglas Sky Rocket & Tow Car, Bandai, friction jet w/battery-op car, litho tin, 18" plane, EXIB, A........................$360.00

Easter Airlines Super Constellation, Japan, friction, litho tin, 12" W, G+, A...$130.00

Empire Express, American Flyer, pnt sheet metal, silver w/red top wing, red, wht & bl tail, 18" W, VG.................$375.00

Fighter & Bomber Planes Set, Renwal, plastic, 2 fighters & 2 bombers, complete, NMIB, A.................................$450.00

Fighter Jet, Showa, 1950s, piston action, litho tin w/2 pilots under split section canopy, 12½" L, NMIB.............$275.00

Fighter Plane, Marx, pnt pressed steel w/wooden wheels, stars & stripes decals on wings, 15" W, VG, A....................$150.00

Float Plane, Paya, w/up, litho tin, 12" W, G+.................$150.00

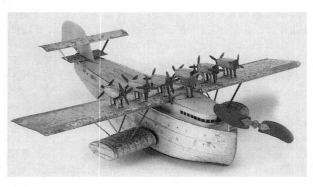

Flying Boat, Fleischmann, wind-up, painted tin, 18" wingspan, G, A, $1,265.00. (Photo courtesy Noel Barrett)

Flying Fortress, Marx, w/up, litho tin, w/sparking wing guns, 18", VG+, A...$275.00

Flying Tiger Line Swing Tail Airplane, Marx, battery-op, litho tin & plastic, 19½", EXIB................................$325.00

Ford Tri-Motor, Kingsbury, 1920s, w/up, pressed steel, rubber tires, 14½", rstr, A...$325.00

G-AMHK N-57 Helicopter, Alps, Japan, remote control, tin, 13" L, nonworking o/w EXIB, A............................$200.00

German D-UDET, Lehmann, litho tin, w/Nazi swastika, 5½" W, EXIB...$165.00

German Heinkel HE111, Lehmann, litho tin, 7" W, EXIB..$225.00

Grasshopper BC-3, Bandai, friction, litho tin, 14½" W, VG+, A...$155.00

Grumman F11-F1 USAF Jet, SSS, 1950s, friction, 5½", NMIB.$100.00

Helicopter, Japan, w/up, litho tin, orange w/stripes, 6" W, G+, A...$230.00

Hughes 500 Helicopter, Japan, battery-op, tin & plastic, 16" L, NMIB, A...$110.00

International 707 Jetliner, Sears, battery-op, litho tin & plastic, 18" W, nonworking o/w EXIB, A............................$135.00

Japan Airlines DC-7, Japan, battery-op, litho tin & plastic, 23½" W, G+, A...$150.00

Japanese Zero Fighter, litho tin & plastic, gr camo, 16" W, EX+, A...$90.00

Lufthansa Talking Viscount Plane, friction with battery-operated voice, lithographed tin and plastic, 18" wingspan, EXIB, $400.00. (Photo courtesy Randy Inman Auctions)

Lockheed Sirus, pnt sheet metal, electric lights, rubber tires enclosed in hub protectors, working prop, 22" W, VG, A $1,650.00

Lockheed Style, Steelcraft, 1930s, gr w/orange wings, 17" W, G+, A..$775.00

Lufthansa Airliner, Schuco, battery-op, litho tin w/plastic cockpit dome, 4 props, 19" W, nonworking o/w VG, A..$145.00

Lufthansa D-ALAK Airliner, Arnold, friction, litho tin w/4 plastic props, 19½" W, G.......................................$225.00

Marine Helicopter, Marx, battery-op, litho tin, 17", G+ ..$50.00

Mercury #107 Helicopter, Marx, 1950s, w/up, litho tin, spinning props & 'tipping' action, EXIB, A $150.00

Monoplane, American Flyer, 1920s, pressed steel, 1 prop, 23½" W, G...$625.00

Monoplane, Buddy L, pressed steel, 10", G+, A $600.00

Monoplane, Chad Valley, w/up, litho tin, w/pilot in open cockpit, 17" W, G+, A...$165.00

Monoplane, Distler, w/up, litho tin, 1-prop, red & yel w/wht & bl bull's-eyes on wings, mk D-19, 14" W, VG $325.00

Monoplane, Distler, w/up, litho tin, 1-prop, yel & red, bl numbers (1422), 10" W, G..$175.00

Monoplane, Distler, w/up, litho tin, 3 props, silver w/red & blk trim, lights mounted atop wings, 16" W, G..............$350.00

Monoplane, early, w/up, tin, open cockpit & frame w/pilot sitting high, articulated wings, 3 spoke wheels, 17", G+, A..$2,200.00

Monoplane, France, w/up, litho tin, yel w/red prop, red, wht & bl graphics & trim, 14" W, VG.............................$225.00

Monoplane, Girard, w/up, litho tin, 3 props, 13" W, VG, A .$550.00

Monoplane, JEP, w/up, litho tin, silver w/red, wht & bl trim, pilot in open cockpit, 15½" W, G+ $225.00

Monoplane, Kingsbury, w/up, pnt tin, rubber tires, 3 props, 15" W, NM $450.00

Monoplane, Mettoy, litho tin w/allover bl stripes on silver & bl bull's-eyes at end of wings, mk K-2010, 17" W, G+, A..$150.00

Monoplane, Steelcraft, 1930s, 1 prop, 23" W, EX, A......$625.00

Monoplane, Steelcraft, 1930s, 1 prop, 23" W, G $250.00

Monoplane, Steelcraft, 1930s, 3 props, 23" W, VG, A ...$300.00

Monoplane, Tipp, w/up, litho tin, yel w/bl trim, mk 1416, 13" W, G $300.00

Monoplane, Wyandotte, pressed steel, 18", G+, A.........$130.00

Monoplane & Hangar, Dayton, 1930s, pressed steel, 16" L, VG, A $350.00

New York Air Vertrol 107 Helicopter, Japan, battery-op, 13½" L, NMIB, A..$85.00

Northwest Airliner, Japan, friction, litho tin, silver w/red & bl trim, 19" W, EXIB..$200.00

Northwest DC-7C, Cragstan, battery-op, litho tin, 24" W, EXIB, A $385.00

Pan Am Air France, France, w/up w/battery-op lights, litho tin, 6 props, 25" W, VG..$700.00

Pan Am Boeing Super Sonic SST Jetliner, Japan, battery-op, litho tin & plastic, 15" W, VGIB, A $75.00

Pan Am Clipper Jet, Japan, battery-op, litho tin, 18" W, G ..$75.00

Pan Am Comet Passenger Jet, Japan, friction, litho tin, 11" W, G $50.00

Pan Am DC-7 Strato Clipper, friction, litho tin, 11" W, G+, A ..$75.00

Pan Am Passenger Plane, Marx, 1940s, pressed steel, 4-prop, 27½" W, G, A..$100.00

Pan Am Sky Taxi, battery-op, MIB, L4..........................$175.00

Pan Am SST 2702, Japan, battery-op, litho tin, 18", EXIB..$125.00

Pan Am Strato Clipper, Gama, friction, battery-op lights, litho tin, 20" W, G...$75.00

Pioneer Express, Marx, litho tin, 25" W, G...................$150.00

Piper N450IP, Tomiyama, friction, litho tin w/clear plastic bubble cockpit, 13½" W, VG...................................$150.00

Piper Sport Plane, Cragstan, friction, litho tin, 20" W, VG+ .$200.00

Police Patrol Helicopter, Japan, 1960s, friction, 12", NMIB, A .$75.00

Pure Oil NC-16113, pressed steel, wht w/bl motor cowling, 18", VG...$1,200.00

Seaplane, Bing, w/up, tin, 2 woodgrain props above wings, 16" W, EX, A...$2,300.00

Seaplane, Guntherman, wind-up, lithographed tin, 21" wingspan, VG, $1,760.00. (Photo courtesy Randy Inman Auctions)

Sikorsky Lines Helicopter, Japan, litho tin, friction, 11½", EXIB, A $100.00

Silver Eagle, Automatic Toy, w/up, aluminum & tin w/wooden wheels, 13" W, NM+IB, A $400.00

Sky Patrol Helicopter, Japan, battery-op, litho tin, 10½" L, NMIB, A...$65.00

Skycruiser, Marx, battery-op, litho tin, 7½" W, nonworking o/w NMIB, A...$100.00

Slick Airways Airliner, Marx, battery-op, litho tin & plastic, 14" W, G, A...$65.00

Spirit of Linemar Biplane, Linemar, 1950s, remote control, litho tin, 11" L, NMIB $450.00

Spirit of St Louis Biplane, Metalcraft, pressed steel, 11½" W, G $75.00

Spirit of St Louis N-X-211, HTC, 1950s, friction, 12" W, NM+...$150.00

Super Copter, Japan, battery-op, plastic, 15" L, NMIB, A .$55.00

Supersonic Jet Liner, Sears, battery-op, litho tin, w/stairs, 19" W, nonworking o/w VGIB, A $350.00

Traffic Control Helicopter, Japan, battery-op, litho tin, 14", G, A $50.00

Transport Plane, Buddy L, pressed steel, 2 props, 26" W, G..$100.00

Transport Plane, Buddy L, pressed steel, 4 props, 26" W, EXIB, A $550.00

Transport Plane, Buddy L, pressed steel, 4 props, 26" W, VG...$250.00

TWA Airliner, w/up, litho tin w/rubber tires, 2 props, 6½" W, VG, A...$110.00

TWA DC-7, Cragstan, battery-op, litho tin, 24" W, EXIB, A...$650.00

TWA Super Jet, Marx, battery-op, litho tin & plastic, 18" W, nonworking o/w EXIB $200.00

TWA 727 Jet, Japan, 1960s, friction, litho tin, 9" L, NMIB...$60.00

Twin Engine Plane, Wyandotte, pressed steel w/skirted wooden wheels, 13", EX...$225.00

United Airlines Super Mainliner Constellation, Wyandotte, pressed steel w/wooden wheels, 13", VG.................$150.00

United Airlines Viscount, Japan, remote control, litho tin, 10" W, EXIB, A...$250.00

United Airlines 727 Jet, Marusyo, 1960s, 3-pc, 18" L, NMIB...$85.00

United Nations C-43, TT, friction, litho tin, bl on wht, 10½" W, EX, A...$100.00

US Army Plane, Marx, litho tin, 2-prop, 18½" W, G+, A..$275.00

US Mail Biplane, Marx, w/up, litho tin w/celluloid props, red w/wht trim, 18" W, NMIB (box mk 4-Motored Biplane), A ..$1,650.00

US Mail Boycraft NX 130, Steelcraft, pressed steel, 22" W, G, A...$300.00

US Mail Plane, Steelcraft, brn & tan, electric lights, 23" W, EX, A...$1,050.00

US Mail Plane, Steelcraft, gr & orange, no electric lights, 23" L, rstr...$300.00

US Mail Plane, Steelcraft, tri-motor, mk Apex (rare), 22½" W, VG, A...$2,200.00

US Marines Monoplane, Girard, w/up, litho tin, 7½" W, EX..$385.00

US Navy 7F7 Biplane, Cragston, 1950s, battery-op, litho tin, 11½" W, EX...$400.00

USAF B-50 Fortress, Yone, friction, litho tin, 19" W, VG+, A..$350.00

USAF BK 250 Bomber, Japan, friction, litho tin, 4 props, 19" W, G...$100.00

USAF B36 Conveyor, Japan, friction, litho tin, 26" W, Fair, A...$230.00

USAF B58 Hustler Jet, Marx, battery-op, litho tin & plastic, 19", L, VGIB...$375.00

USAF Cargo Plane, Modern Toys, battery-operated, lithographed tin, 22½" wingspan, VG, A, $525.00. (Photo courtesy Randy Inman Auctions)

USAF C-120 Pack Plane, Japan, 2-prop, friction, litho tin, 15", G...$125.00

USAF Douglas C-124 Globemaster, Japan, battery-op, litho tin & plastic, 20½" W, VGIB...$425.00

USAF FG-956 Jet Launch, friction, litho tin, 11", VG..$100.00

USAF Fighter Jet, Marx, battery-op, litho tin & plastic, 12" W, VG, A...$165.00

USAF Fighter Jet, TN, 1950s, friction, litho tin, spinning rear exhaust, 14½" L, NMIB...$200.00

USAF FW-707 Fighter Jet w/Jet Plane Base, Japan, battery-op, litho tin, 14" L, G, A...$130.00

USAF FW-707 Fighter Jet w/Jet Plane Base, Japan, battery-op, litho tin, 14" L, MIB, L4...$800.00

USAF F5-059 (Piston Action), Japan, battery-op, litho tin w/open motor compartment, 2 pilots, 12" W, EXIB .$200.00

USAF Grumman F111A Fighter Jet, Japan, battery-op, litho tin & plastic, 16" L, NMIB...$200.00

USAF Helicopter, Japan, remote control, litho tin w/plastic nose, sq shape, 14" L, G+, A...$75.00

USAF Star Fire Jet, Japan, friction, litho tin, 18" W, VG..$225.00

USAF Super Fortress Bomber, friction, litho tin, 14½" W, EX, A...$300.00

USAF Troop Carrier, Bandai, friction, litho tin, red, wht & bl, 17" W, NMIB, A...$300.00

Vertical Liner, Sears, battery-operated, lithographed tin, 18" wingspan, VGIB, $450.00. (Photo courtesy Randy Inman Auctions)

VooDoo F-101A Jet, KO, 1950s, battery-op/friction, litho tin w/pilot under clear dome, 18" L, NMIB...$375.00

Zeppelin, Germany, w/up, pnt tin w/celluloid props, silver w/swastika emblems, 11", EX...$1,000.00

Zeppelin, Marklin, pnt tin, w/2 suspended gondolas, side & rear props, 12", NM...$2,750.00

Zeppelin, Muller & Kadeder, pnt tin, side & rear cb props, trestle observation platform, fins on fuselage, 15", EX.......$1,750.00

Zeppelin (Akron), Steelcraft, 1930s, 31" L, G, A..........$350.00

Zeppelin (GRAF), Steelcraft, 1930s, 26", G+ $350.00

Zeppelin (Shenandoah), Lehmann, w/up, litho tin w/celluloid props, 7", VGIB...$675.00

All American Toy Company

This company was founded in Oregon in 1948 and until 1955 produced toy trucks and heavy duty vehicles. A variety of materials was used, including aluminum, steel, and diecast metal. The company was later purchased by Bill Hellie and now sells parts and makes and sells limited editions from the original molds.

Cargo Liner, 1950s, 38", G, A...$575.00

Cattle Liner, 1950s, 36", G, A...$3,960.00

Delivery Truck, limited ed, w/box van, 24", MIB, A $465.00

Dump Truck, 1950s, hydraulic dump action, Galion decal on bed, US map logo on door, 20", G+, A...$385.00

Dump Truck, 1950s, hydraulic dump action, no decals or logos, 20", G, A...$360.00

Dump Truck & Trailer, limited ed, hydraulic dumping action, 37", MIB, A...$600.00

Flatbed Truck & Trailer, limited ed, 46", M, A.............$470.00

Flatbed Truck & Trailer, 1950s, 35", G w/some rpt, A...$1,430.00

Heavy Hauler, 1950s, 39", G w/some rpt, A $825.00
John Deere Farm Equipment Flatbed Truck, limited ed, 20", M, A $550.00
Kenworth Semi, limited ed, Quality Trucks Since 1923, 23", M, A $500.00
Midget Skagit, 1930s, battery-op, 33", VG, A.............$1,150.00
PIE Kenworth Tandem Tanker, limited ed, 39", M, A....$770.00
Scoop-A-Veyor, 1950s, 14", EX, A $2,200.00
Timber Toter, 1950s, 33", w/lumber load, EX, A.............$630.00
Timber Toter, 1950s, 38", no lumber load o/w VG, A $275.00
Timber Toter Jr, 1950s, w/trailer, 35", lumber load on truck only, no load on trailer, G+, A $2,300.00
Wrecker, limited ed, single crank, 21", MIB, A $690.00

Timber Toter Jr, 1950s, 20", complete, VG+, A, $635.00. (Photo courtesy Randy Inman Auctions)

Automobiles and Other Vehicle Replicas

Listed here are the model vehicles (most of which were made in Japan during the 1950s and 1960s) that were designed to realistically represent the muscle cars, station wagons, convertibles, budget models, and luxury cars that were actually being shown concurrently on showroom floors and dealers' lots all over the country. Most were made of tin, many were friction powered, some were battery operated. In our descriptions, all are tin unless noted otherwise.

See also Promotional Cars; specific manufacturers.

Buick (1950s), ATC, friction, 8½", NMIB (box mk New Buick)...$125.00
Buick Electromobile, M, remote control, electric horn & lights, 8", EXIB, A $165.00
Buick LeSabre (1966), ATC, friction, 19", NM+IB, A ..$850.00

Buick Two-Door (1958), ATC, friction, 14", NMIB, A, $4,675.00. (Photo courtesy Bertoia Auctions)

Buick Sedan (1961), TN, friction, 14", VGIB...............$300.00
Buick Station Wagon (1954), Yonezawa, friction, rear window & gate open, 9", NM, A $125.00
Buick 2-Door (1946), Marusan, battery-op, 7", VG+ $125.00
Buick 2-Door (1955), TN, battery-op, 7½", NM+IB, A .$300.00
Buick 2-Door (1959), TN, friction, 12", EXIB $1,000.00
Buick 2-Door (1962), TN, friction, 12", G $125.00
Cadillac Convertible (1950s), Alps, friction, 11½", MIB, A..$1,150.00
Cadillac Convertible (1950s), Alps, friction, 11½", VG, A.$200.00
Cadillac Convertible (1950s), Gama, friction, 12½", EX.$350.00
Cadillac Fleetwood 75 (1961), SSS, friction, 17", NMIB, A .$2,750.00
Cadillac Fleetwood 75 (1961), SSS, friction, 17", VG+, A .$475.00
Cadillac Sedan (1950), Marusan, battery-op, 12", NMIB, A.$3,300.00
Cadillac Sedan (1950), Marusan, friction, 12", NMIB, A..$1,750.00
Cadillac Sedan (1950), Marusan, friction, 12", VG, A ..$500.00
Cadillac Sedan (1950s), Joustra, friction, 12", VG, A....$225.00
Cadillac Sedan (1960), Bandai, friction, 11", NMIB, A..$500.00
Cadillac Sedan (1960), Marusan, friction, 11", G, A $275.00
Cadillac Sedan (1960), Yonezawa, friction, 18", rstr $475.00
Cadillac Sedan (1961), Yonezawa, friction, 14", EXIB..$650.00

Cadillac Sedan (1964), Yonezawa, friction, 12½", EX, A, $3,300.00. (Photo courtesy Randy Inman Auctions)

Cadillac 2-Door (1954), Marusan, battery-op, 13", VG, A ..$550.00
Cadillac 2-Door (1960), Marusan, friction, 12", G+, A .$300.00
Cadillac 2-Door (1965), ATC, friction, 17", EX, A........$450.00
Chevy Camaro (1967), TN, friction, 14", NMIB, A $400.00
Chevy Camaro (1968), Bandai, battery-op, 13", NMIB, A .$100.00
Chevy Corvair (1962), Yonezawa, friction, 9", EXIB, A..$250.00
Chevy Corvette (1958), Yonezawa, friction, 10", EX, A .$250.00
Chevy Corvette (1964), Ichiko, battery-op, 12", EXIB, A $385.00
Chevy Corvette (1965), Bandai, battery-op, 8", EXIB (box mk Auto-Glide Sports Car Series), A $110.00
Chevy Corvette (1965), Bandai, friction, 8", NMIB, A.$175.00
Chevy Impala (1961), Bandai, battery-op, 11", EX+IB, A..$600.00
Chevy Impala (1962), ATC, friction, yel (scarce), 12", VG.$450.00
Chevy Impala (1962), ATC, friction, 12", VG $350.00
Chevy Impala Convertible (1964), Haji, friction, opening doors, 8½", NMIB (box has 48 states license plates), A $125.00
Chevy Red Cross Ambulance (1950s), Bandai, friction, 10", NMIB, A...$150.00
Chevy 2-Door (1954), Linemar, friction, 11", EX+, A...$850.00
Chevy 2-Door (1954), Linemar, friction, 11", VGIB, A..$1,000.00
Chevy 2-Door (1954), Marusan, friction, 11", NMIB, A..$2,200.00
Chevy 2-Door (1954), Marusan, friction, 11", VG, A....$450.00
Chevy 2-Door (1955), Marusan, battery-op, 11", VGIB..$1,200.00

Chrysler Convertible (1957), Guntherman, friction, 11", EXIB, A $525.00
Chrysler Imperial (1959), Bandai, friction, 8", NMIB, A ..$130.00

Chrysler Imperial (1961), ACT, friction, 16", NMIB, A, $22,000.00. (Photo courtesy Bertoia Auctions)

Chrysler New Yorker (1957), Alps, friction, 14", rstr, A ..$2,420.00
Chrysler Newport (1957), Alps, friction, 14", NMIB, A .$7,150.00
Chrysler Valiant Sedan, Bandai, friction, 8½", NMIB, A .$200.00
Citroen Break Station Wagon, Joustra, friction, 8", EXIB, A .$125.00
Citroen DS-16 Sedan (1960), Bandai, friction, 12", NMIB .$1,000.00
Cunningham C-6R, Ichiko, friction w/siren sounds, 8", EXIB.$450.00
De Soto 2-Door (1950), Asahilo, friction, 7½", EX+, A .$110.00
Electro Hydro Car, Schuco #5720, 10", EX+, A $990.00

Edsel Two-Door (1958), Haji, friction, 11", EXIB, A, $3,025.00. (Photo courtesy Bertoia Auctions)

Ferrari Berlinetta 250 Le Mans #2, ATC, battery-op, 11½", NMIB, A $110.00
Ferrari Gear Shift Car, Bandai, 10½", EXIB, A $260.00
Fiat 1800 (1965), friction, 9½", NMIB, A $200.00
Ford Ambulance (1955), Bandai, friction, 12", G, A $85.00
Ford Convertible (1950s), Hoge, friction, 11½", G........$325.00
Ford Convertible (1955), Bandai, friction, 12", EX, A...$525.00
Ford Convertible (1956), Haji, friction, 12", M, A $1,650.00
Ford Convertible (1956), Haji, friction, 12", rstr (repro box), A .$715.00
Ford Country Sedan Wagon (1956), Cragstan, friction, 10", EXIB, A $600.00
Ford Custom Ranch Wagon, Bandai, friction, 12", NM+IB, A .$475.00
Ford Fairlane Convertible (1957), Bandai, friction, 11½", EXIB, A...$1,200.00
Ford Fairlane Skyliner (1958), Cragstan, battery-op, 10½", NMIB, A $325.00
Ford Fairlane Skyliner (1960), ATC, friction, 14", NMIB, A $1,200.00
Ford Flower Delivery Wagon (1955), Bandai, friction, 12", VG..$200.00
Ford Galaxy (1960), Yonezawa, friction, 10", NMIB, A ..$250.00

Ford Mustang (1965), Bandai, battery-operated, 11", NMIB, A, $250.00. (Photo courtesy Bertoia Auctions)

Ford Mustang Convertible (1965), Bandai, battery-op, gear shift & switch in front seat, 11", NMIB $225.00
Ford Mustang Fastback (1965), ATC, friction, scarce purple color, 11", NM, A $175.00
Ford Mustang Mach I, Taiyo, battery-op, 10", NM, A....$100.00
Ford Mustang w/Slip Action, Bandai, battery-op, 11", NMIB, A $125.00
Ford Pickup (1955), Bandai, elephant decal on door, 12", scarce, NMIB, A $1,650.00
Ford Ranch Wagon (1962), ATC, friction, 12", NMIB..$1,750.00
Ford Ranch Wagon (1962), ATC, friction, 12", VGIB ..$950.00
Ford Ranchero (1957), Bandai, friction, 12", NMIB, A .$900.00
Ford Station Wagon (1955), Bandai, friction, opening rear door & window, 12", EX, A $325.00
Ford Sunliner (1962), friction, 10", NMIB, A $285.00
Ford Taurus 17M, Bandai, friction, mirrors mounted on front fenders, 8", EX+, A $125.00
Ford Thunderbird (1956), TN, friction, removable tinted roof, 8", MIB $250.00
Ford Thunderbird Convertible (1950), Bandai, 7", NMIB, A.$200.00
Ford Thunderbird Sedan (1965), Bandai, friction, 11", EXIB, A..$250.00
Ford Thunderbird w/Retractable Top, Cragstan, remote control, 12", NMIB, A $325.00
Ford Yellow Cab (1954), Marusan, friction, 10", EX+, A.$625.00
Ford 2-Door (1956), Marusan, friction, 13", rstr (repro box), A..$1,320.00
Ford 2-Door (1956), Yonezawa, friction, 13", rstr (repro box), A $525.00
Ford 2-Door (1960), Haji, 11", EXIB, A $300.00
Honda ZGS, TN, friction, 9½", MIB, A $100.00
International Harvester Super Construction Dump Truck (1960s), Bandai, 23", EX+IB, A $2,420.00
Isetta (1960s), Bandai, friction, 6½", NMIB, A $450.00
Jaguar Convertible (1960), Bandai, friction, 9½", VG, A .$100.00
Jaguar XK150 (1960), Bandai, friction, 9½", MIB, A $700.00
Jaguar 3.4 Convertible (1960s), Bandai, friction, 8", EX+IB, A.$360.00
Lincoln Futura, Alps, remote control, 11", EXIB, A ...$2,200.00
Lincoln Mark II (1956), Linemar, friction, electric lights, 11", NMIB, A $8,250.00
Lincoln Mark III (1958), Bandai, friction, 12", EXIB, A.$550.00
Lincoln Sedan (1954), Yonezawa, friction, 12", NMIB, A .$6,050.00
Lincoln Sedan (1956), Ichiko, plastic, friction, 17", EX+, A..$600.00
Lincoln Sedan (1957), Modern Toys, friction, 12½", EXIB, A $4,950.00
Mercedes Benz Sports Car, TN, friction, 8½", NM+IB, A .$200.00

Mercedes Benz 219 Sedan (1960s), Bandai, friction, 8", EX+IB, A $150.00

Mercedes Benz 220, Bandai, friction, 10", NMIB, A $180.00

Mercedes Benz 230 SL (1950s), TN, battery-op, 18", EXIB, A $200.00

Mercedes Benz 230 SL (1960s), Modern Toys, battery-op, 15", EXIB, A $325.00

Mercedes Benz 230 SL (1960s), Yanoman, battery-op, 15", EXIB, A $350.00

Mercedes Benz 250 SE, Ichiko, battery-op, 13", NMIB, A .$250.00

Mercedes Benz 300 SE (1960s), Ichiko, friction, 24", NMIB, A..$125.00

Mercedes Benz 300 SL (1950s), Bandai, battery-op, 8", EXIB, A $215.00

Mercury (Stream Line), Alps, friction, 9½", EXIB, A....$275.00

Mercury Montclair (1958), Yonezawa, friction, 12", EXIB, A $2,750.00

Mercury 2-Door (1954), Rock Valley Toys, battery-op, 10", NMIB, A $275.00

Messerschmitt (1960s 3-Wheeled Hardtop), Bandai #579, friction, 8", EXIB, A $875.00

MG TF (1955), Bandai, friction, 8½", EX, A $120.00

Nash (1950s), MSK, battery-op, 8", NM+IB, A $175.00

Oldsmobile Sedan (1961), Cragstan, friction, 12", EXIB, A, $1,320.00.
(Photo courtesy Bertoia Auctions)

Oldsmobile Toronado, ATC, friction, 15", EXIB, A.......$165.00

Oldsmobile Toronado (1966), Bandai, battery-op, 11", EXIB, A $55.00

Oldsmobile 2-Door (1950s, early), Yonezawa, 12", G+, A .$165.00

Oldsmobile 2-Door (1958), ATC, friction, 12", VG+, A ..$525.00

Oldsmobile 88 Station Wagon, Nakamura, friction, 7", NMIB, A $150.00

Opel Ambulance, Huki, friction, 9", VGIB $165.00

Opel Rekord Coupe, ASC, remote control, opening doors, working turn signals, 12", EX+IB, A $350.00

Packard Sedan (1953), Alps, friction, 16", EX, A, $3,025.00. (Photo courtesy Bertoia Auctions)

Packard Hawk Convertible (1957), Schuco #5700, battery-op, 10", VG+IB, A $350.00

Plymouth Belvedere (1956), Alps, battery-op, 11", NM+ .$475.00

Plymouth Convertible w/Boat & Trailer, friction car & battery-op boat, 23", VG+, A $700.00

Plymouth Fury Convertible (1957), Bandai, friction, 8½", NMIB, A..$575.00

Plymouth Sedan (1959), ATC, friction, 11", EX+, A $575.00

Plymouth 2-Door (1959), Ichiko, friction, 6½", NMIB, A.$185.00

Plymouth 2-Door (1961), Ichiko, friction, 12½", rstr, A.$275.00

Pontiac Firebird (1967), Bandai, battery-op, working windshield wipers, 9½", EX $100.00

Porsche Convertible (1950s), Distler, battery-op, 10", EX+IB, A $600.00

Porsche Convertible (1950s), Distler, battery-op, 10", VG, A ..$250.00

Rambler Rebel Station Wagon, Bandai, friction, 11", VGIB, A $200.00

Rambler Station Wagon (1950s), Marusan, friction, 10", EXIB, A $325.00

Rambler Station Wagon & Shasta Travel Trailer (1960s), Bandai, friction, 22" overall, VG+, A $450.00

Rambler Station Wagon and Shasta Travel Trailer (1960s), Bandai, friction, 22" overall, EX+IB, A, $1,050.00. (Photo courtesy Bertoia Auctions)

Renault Floride, Ichiko, friction, 7½", EXIB, A $250.00

Rolls-Royce Silver Cloud, Bandai, battery-op, electric lights, 12", NMIB $400.00

Saab 93B (1960s), Bandai, friction, 7½", NM, A $200.00

Studebaker Starline (1953), Japan, friction, working windshield wipers, 9", NM+ $275.00

Triumph TR-3 Convertible (1960s), Bandai, battery-op, 8", EXIB, A $200.00

Vespa Cycle (1960s), Bandai, friction, 9", EX, A $225.00

Volkswagen Bug, Japan, friction, oval rear window, VW hubs, 7½", NMIB, A $100.00

Volkswagen Bug (1960s), Bandai, friction, 10", EX+........$60.00

Volkswagen Bug Sedan (1960s), Bandai, battery-op, 7½", NMIB, A..$75.00

Volkswagen Bug w/Visible Engine, Japan, battery-op, 14", EXIB $350.00

Volkswagen Sedan, Cragstan, friction, 8", VGIB, A.........$55.00

Volkswagen Van, Tippco/West Germany, friction, opening side doors, bench seats, 9", VG+, A $450.00

Volvo, Japan, friction, detailed, 8", scarce, NM, A.........$250.00

Banks

The impact of condition on the value of a bank cannot be overrated. Cast-iron banks in near-mint condition with very little paint wear and all original parts are seldom found and might bring twice as much (if the bank is especially rare, up to five times as much) as one in average, very good original condition with no restoration and no repairs. Overpainting and replacement parts (even screws) have a very negative effect on value. Mechanicals dominate the market, and some of the hard-to-find banks in outstanding, near-mint condition may exceed $20,000.00! (Here's a few examples: Girl Skipping Rope, Calamity, and Mikado.) Modern mechanical banks are also included in the collectibles market, including Book of Knowledge and James D. Capron, which are reproductions with full inscriptions stating that the piece is a replica of the original. Still banks are widely collected as well, with more than 3,000 varieties having been documented. Beware of unmarked modern reproductions. All of the banks listed below are cast iron unless noted otherwise.

For more information we recommend *The Dictionary of Still Banks* by Long and Pitman; *The Penny Bank Book* by Moore; *The Bank Book* by Norman; and *Penny Lane* by Davidson. For information on porcelain and ceramic banks we recommend *Collector's Guide to Banks* by Beverly and Jim Mangus and *Ceramic Coin Banks* by Tom and Loretta Stoddard.

Advisor: Dan Iannotti (I3), modern mechanicals

See also Advertising; Battery-Operated; Character, TV, and Movie Collectibles; Disney; Diecast Collector Banks; Political; Reynolds Banks; Robots, Miscellaneous; Rock 'n Roll; Santa; and other specific categories.

Mechanical Banks

Acrobat Bank, J&E Stevens, rpt, A $1,540.00
Administration Building Columbian Exposition 1492-1892,
    Introduction Co, NP, G, A.......................................$200.00
Afghanistan Bank, Mechanical Novelty Works, ca 1885, VG,
    A $3,300.00

Always Did 'Spise a Mule (Boy on Bench), J&E Stevens, G+, A, $875.00; Always Did 'Spise a Mule (Jockey), J&E Stevens, EX+, A, $2,750.00. (Photo courtesy Bertoia Auctions)

Artillery Bank, Book of Knowledge, NM, I3 ....$300.00
Artillery Bank, J&E Stevens, VG+, A........................$1,100.00
Auto, John Wright, limited edition of 250, NM, I3 ....$600.00

Bad Accident, James Capron, M, I3................................$800.00
Bad Accident (Upside Down Lettering), J&E Stevens, G+, A .$1,980.00
Bear & Tree Stump, Judd, VG, A................................$800.00
Betsy Ross, Davidson/Imswiller, bl or yel dress, M, I3, ea .$875.00
Billy Goat Bank, J&E Stevens, overpnt, A $550.00
Bismark Bank, J&E Stevens, VG, A $4,400.00
Bobby Riggs & Billy Jean King, John Wright, limited edition of
    250, scarce, M, I3..$800.00
Bowler's Strike, Richards/Wilton, scarce, NM, I3..........$600.00

Bowling Alley, Kyser & Rex, repainted, A, $16,500.00. (Photo courtesy Bertoia Auctions)

Boy on Trapeze, Barton & Smith, VG $2,500.00
Boy Robbing Bird's Nest, J&E Stevens, EX+, A..........$5,775.00
Boy Robbing Bird's Nest, J&E Stevens, G, A..............$1,870.00
Boy Scout Camp, J&E Stevens, EX+ $7,150.00
Boy Stealing Watermelons, Kyser & Rex, rpt, A............$700.00

Bulldog, England, lithographed tin, EX+, A, $4,950.00.

(Photo courtesy Bertoia Auctions)

Bulldog Bank, J&E Stevens, EX, A..............................$2,750.00
Butting Buffalo, Book of Knowledge, M, I3 ....$350.00
Butting Buffalo, Kyser & Rex, EX, A...........................$5,500.00
Butting Goat, Judd, EX, A..$700.00
Cabin, Book of Knowledge, NM, I3 ....$325.00
Cabin, J&E Stevens, VG, A...$650.00
Calamity, J&E Stevens, VG, A....................................$7,700.00
Calumet Baking Powder Bank, tin or cb, VG, A............$130.00
Cat & Mouse, Book of Knowledge, NM, I3 ....$325.00
Cat & Mouse (Cat Balancing), J&E Stevens, EX $2,500.00
Cat Boat, Richards/Wilton, NM, I3 ....$700.00
Chandlers Bank, National Brass Works, EX, A $600.00
Chief Big Moon, J&E Stevens, EX, A $3,850.00
Chimpanzee Bank, Kyser & Rex, EX+, A $5,500.00
Chinaman Reclining on Log, J&E Stevens, VG, A $2,100.00

Chinaman in Boat, Charles Bailey, lead, EX, A, $25,300.00. (Photo courtesy Randy Inman Auctions)

Cigar Smoker (Monica Lewinsky Bust), Sandman Designs, 1 of 50, unused, M, I3 ....$400.00
Circus Ticket Collector, Judd, EX, A $1,050.00
Clown Bust, Chein, litho tin, EX+, A $130.00
Clown on Globe, J&E Stevens, G+, A........................$1,425.00
Clown on Globe, James Capron, M, I3 ....$775.00
Columbian Magic Savings Bank, Introduction Co, EX, A .$275.00
Cow (Kicking), Book of Knowledge, NM, I3..................$315.00
Creedmore, J&E Stevens, EX, A $700.00
Cross-Legged Minstrel, litho tin, Germany, VG, A........$935.00
Cupola, J&E Stevens, VG, A......................................$4,620.00
Dapper Dan, litho tin, Marx, VG, A $1,540.00
Darktown Battery, J&E Stevens, EX+.........................$6,000.00
Darktown Battery, J&E Stevens, rpl arms, some rpt, A .$1,320.00
Dentist Bank, Book of Knowledge, EX, I3 ....$175.00
Dinah, John Harper, EX+, A.....................................$1,200.00
Dinah (Long Sleeves), John Harper, VG, A $525.00
Dog on Turntable, Judd, G, A $550.00
Eagle & Eaglets, Book of Knowledge, M, I3..................$450.00
Eagle & Eaglets, J&E Stevens, EX, A $1,325.00
Elephant, James Capron, M, I3 ....$250.00
Elephant, John Wright, NM, I3 ....$175.00
Elephant & Howdah (Pull Tail), Hubley, NM, A $1,100.00
Elephant & Howdah (Pull Tail), Hubley, VG, A $275.00
Elephant & Three Clowns, J&E Stevens, VG+, A $775.00
Elephant Sitting Upright on Circus Drum, litho tin, lever action, England, 5¼", VG, A...................................$165.00
Elves (The) Biscuit Penny Machine, litho tin, Huntley Palmer, EX, A $330.00
Flying Saucer HX-268, Duro, NM, I3 ....$525.00
Football Bank, John Harper, EX, A $2,100.00
Frog (Two Frogs), J&E Stevens, VG+, A.....................$3,100.00

Frog (Two Frogs), James Capron, NM, I3 :.....................$625.00
Frog on Rock, Kilgore, EX+, A $935.00
Gem Bank, Judd, EX, A..$935.00
Girl in Victorian Chair, WS Reed, VG, A $3,300.00
Goat, Man & Frog, Mechanical Novelty Works, EX, A..$8,800.00
Halls Excelsior, J&E Stevens, EX+, A............................$700.00
Halls Excelsior, J&E Stevens, rare lead-head version, G, A .$385.00
Halls Lilliput (Tray), J&E Stevens, VG+, A...................$825.00
Hold the Fort (5 Holes), VG, A $5,720.00
Hoopla, John Harper, rpt, A...$875.00
Humpty Dumpty, Book of Knowledge, M, I3..................$325.00
Humpty Dumpty, Shepard Hardware, NM+, A...........$3,075.00
I Have Not Begun To Fight (John Paul Jones), Franklin Mint, 1986, NM, I3 ....$400.00
Independence Hall Tower, Enterprise Mfg, VG, A.........$300.00
Indian Shooting Bear, J&E Stevens, EX $3,800.00
Joe Socko (Joe Palooka Characters), litho tin, Straits Corp, VG, A $385.00
John Deere Anvil, diecast, MIB, I3 ....$125.00
Jolly Clown, Saalheimer & Straus/Germany, ca 1929-33, litho tin, EX, A $1,325.00
Jolly N, S&M (Sydenham & McOustra), lt bl tie & buttons, G, A $200.00
Jolly N, Shepard Hardware, blk face, red shirt w/blk tie, G+, A.$220.00
Jonah & the Whale, Shepard Hardware, EX+, A $3,850.00
Jonah & the Whale, Shepard Hardware, VG, A.........$2,600.00
Kick Inn, Presto Novelty, pnt & paper on wood, 9½", VG..$450.00
Kiltie Bank, John Harper, EX+ $1,650.00
Leap Frog, Book of Knowledge, NM, I3 ....$335.00
Leap Frog, Shepard Hardware, EX $2,650.00
Lion & Monkeys, James Capron, M, I3 ....$875.00
Lion & Monkeys, Kyser & Rex, VG $1,875.00
Lion Hunter, J&E Stevens, VG, A $6,275.00
Lucky Wheel Money Box, Jacob & Co Biscuits, litho tin, EX, A $275.00
Magic Bank, J&E Stevens, NM+, A...........................$3,520.00
Magic Bank, James Capron, MIB, I3............................$650.00
Magician, Book of Knowledge, MIB, I3 ....$325.00
Magician Bank, J&E Stevens, G...............................$2,000.00
Mammy & Child, Kyser & Rex, EX+, A $5,500.00
Mammy & Child, Kyser & Rex, VG, A $3,850.00
Mason Bank, Shepard Hardware, VG, A....................$3,575.00

Girl Skipping Rope, J&E Stevens, EX, A, $57,200.00. (Photo courtesy Bertoia Auctions)

Mickey Mouse (Hands Clasped), Salheimer & Strauss, litho tin, rare, EX+, A, $39,600.00.

(Photo courtesy Bertoia Auctions)

Memorial Money Bank, Enterprise Mfg, VG, A $500.00
Merry-Go-Round, Kyser & Rex, VG, A....................$18,700.00
Milking Cow, Book of Knowledge, NM, I3....................$300.00
Milking Cow, J&E Stevens, EX............................$4,500.00
Minstrel, Saalheimer & Strauss, litho tin, NM, A.........$650.00
Monkey, James Capron, MIB, I3 ....$400.00
Monkey & Parrot, Saalheimer & Strauss, litho tin, VG..$250.00
Monkey Bank, Hubley, EX+, A..............................$500.00
Monkey w/Coconut, J&E Stevens, EX+, A................$3,500.00
Monkey w/Coconut, J&E Stevens, G.....................$1,450.00
Monkey w/Tray, Germany, litho tin, EX+ $350.00
Mule Entering Barn, J&E Stevens, G+ $775.00

Mule Entering Barn, J&E Stevens, NM, A, $2,400.00. (Photo courtesy Bertoia Auctions)

Mule Entering Barn, James Capron, NM, I3..................$500.00
Nation Divided (Lincoln & Confederate Soldier), Sandman
    Designs, M, I3.....................................$750.00
New Bank, J&E Stevens, EX, A..........................$1,200.00
Novelty Bank, J&E Stevens, EX, A.........................$750.00
Organ Bank (Boy & Girl), Book of Knowledge, NM, I3 .$375.00
Organ Bank (Boy & Girl), Kyser & Rex, G, A..............$600.00
Organ Bank (Cat & Dog), Kyser & Rex, EX, A..........$1,050.00
Organ Bank (Miniature w/Monkey), Kyser & Rex, NM+ .$1,750.00
Organ Bank (Miniature w/Monkey), Kyser & Rex, VG, A...$700.00
Organ Bank (Monkey), Kyser & Rex, VG.....................$650.00
Organ Grinder & Performing Bear, Kyser & Rex, NM..$4,500.00
Owl (Slot in Book), Kilgore, EX $530.00
Owl (Turns Head), Book of Knowledge, NM, I3 ....$250.00
Owl (Turns Head), J&E Stevens, VG, A $525.00
Paddy & the Pig, Book of Knowledge, NM, I3 ....$375.00
Paddy & the Pig, J&E Stevens, EX $2,100.00
Peg-Leg Begger, Judd, EX $1,550.00
Pelican (Mammy in Mouth), J&E Stevens, VG+, A ..$2,200.00
Penny Pineapple, Imswiler, 1960, commemorates Hawaii 50th
    state, 1st Run of 500 mk on base, NM, I3 ....$425.00
Penny Pineapple (Hawaii 50th State), Richards/Wilton, NM,
    I3 ....$450.00

Professor Pug Frog's Great Bicycle Feat, J&E Stevens, EX+, A, $12,650.00. (Photo courtesy Randy Inman Auctions)

Piano (Musical), EM Roche Novelty Co, VG $775.00
Pig in Highchair, J&E Stevens, EX $875.00
Presto Bank, Kyser & Rex, EX+ $925.00
Professor Pug Frog's Great Bicycle Feat, James Capron, M, I3 .$850.00
Punch & Judy, Book of Knowledge, NM, I3 ....$325.00
Punch & Judy, Shepard Hardware, EX, A, from $2,500 to ..$3,500.00
Rabbit in Cabbage, Kilgore, VG $325.00
Rabbit Standing (Small), Lockwood Mfg, rnd base, EX .$925.00
Race Course, James Capron, NM, I3........................$575.00
Reagan O'Neill, Miley's, bronze finish, scarce, NM, I3 ..$550.00
Reclining Chinaman, J&E Stevens, rpt hands & face, A .$3,300.00
Ronald Reagan/Tip O'Neill Bank, Miley's, 1983, scarce multi-
    colored version, M, I3..............................$600.00
Rooster, Kyser & Rex, EX, A..............................$700.00
Royal Trick Elephant, Germany, ca 1900, EX+, A......$1,650.00

Sailor (Saluting), Germany, litho tin, NM, A, $2,750.00. (Photo courtesy Bertoia Auctions)

Santa at Chimney, Shepard Hardware, EX, A.............$1,650.00
Santa at Chimney, Shepard Hardware, G $875.00
Shoot a Bear (Davy Crockett), Vacumet, 1950s, NM, I3 .$235.00
Speaking Dog (Red Dress), J&E Stevens, rnd trap, G, A..$1,100.00
Speaking Dog (Red or Maroon Base), Shepard Hardware, G, A.$600.00
Stump Speaker, Shepard Hardware, EX, A................$3,300.00
Tammany Bank, Book of Knowledge, NMIB, I3.............$325.00
Tammany Bank, J&E Stevens, G $325.00
Tammany Bank, J&E Stevens, later version, EX+, A..$1,320.00
Teddy & the Bear, Book of Knowledge, NM, I3 ....$300.00
Teddy & the Bear, J&E Stevens, VG $1,425.00
Thrifty Tom's Jigger Bank, Strauss, litho tin, EX........$2,100.00
Titanic, Sandman Designs, limited edition, M, I3 ....$875.00
Toad on Stump (Dark Green), J&E Stevens, EX, A.......$700.00
Trenton Trust (75th Anniversary), Modern-Mar Roebling, EX+,
    A $825.00
Trick Dog, James Capron, NM, I3 ....$400.00
Trick Dog (Solid Base), Hubley, EX+, A...................$600.00
Trick Dog (6-Part Base), Hubley, VG, A $650.00
Trick Pony, Book of Knowledge, NM, I3....................$350.00
Trick Pony, Shepard Hardware, EX, A....................$1,200.00
Uncle Bugs, Warner Bros, M, I3...........................$200.00
Uncle Remus, Book of Knowledge, M, I3 ....$375.00
Uncle Remus, Kyser & Rex, G, A $1,320.00
Uncle Sam, Richards/Wilton, rear trap, scarce, NM, I3.$450.00
Uncle Sam & Arab, John Wright, 1975, rare, NMIB, I3..$800.00
Uncle Sam Bank, Shepard Hardware, VG+ $2,000.00
Uncle Tom (Star/Lapels), Kyser & Rex, VG $650.00

Uncle Sam, Shepard Hardware, NM, $4,500.00. (Photo courtesy Bertoia Auctions)

Uncle Tom (Star/No Lapels), Kyser & Rex, VG+ $700.00
US & Spain, Book of Knowledge, M, I3 ....$335.00
Washington at Rappahannock, John Wright, scarce, NM, I3 .$550.00
Watch Dog Safe, J&E Stevens, VG, A $600.00
Weeden's Plantation Darky Savings Bank, Weeden, VG .$650.00
Will E Fibb (Bill Clinton Bust), Sandman Designs, 1 of 50,
    unused, M, I3 ....$400.00
William Tell, J&E Stevens, G $325.00
William Tell, J&E Stevens, NM, A $1,650.00
Woodpecker, Gebruder Big & Co, 1890s, sheet metal, musical,
    EX+, A $3,025.00
World's Fair, Book of Knowledge, mc version, NM, I3 ...$450.00
World's Fair, J&E Stevens, overpnt, A $500.00
Y2K the Millennium Bank, Sandman Designs, M, I3.....$475.00
Zoo Bank, Kyser & Rex, NM+ $2,100.00
Zoo Bank, Kyser & Rex, VG+, A $1,050.00

REGISTERING BANKS

Bean Pot, CI, 3", EX $250.00
Beehive Registering Savings Bank, NP CI, 5½", EX $275.00
Bestmaid, tin, 4¾", EX $75.00
Buddy (L) Savings & Recording Bank, sheet metal, 6¼", EX .$125.00

Cash Register Savings Bank, circa 1899, cast iron, 5¼", VG, A, $1,430.00.

(Photo courtesy Bertoia Auctions)

Dandy Self-Registering Savings Bank, tin, 4¾", NM $360.00
Donald Duck Bank, Marx, 1941, litho tin, 4", EX..........$350.00
Keene Savings Bank, Kingsbury, litho tin, 6½", EX, A ..$400.00
Mickey Mouse Dime Register, WDE, 1939, EX, A $300.00
Penny Saver, CI, 5⅛", VG..$80.00
Popeye Daily Dime Bank, KFS, 1956, litho metal, VG, A..$80.00
Prudential Registering Savings Bank (10¢), NP CI, 7¼", EX.$350.00
Pump Registering (Pump & Bucket), CI, takes dimes, VG, A .$1,300.00

Snow White Dime Register, tin, 2½" sq, EX $150.00
Stove (Parlor), Schneider & Trenkamp, gold w/red insert that
    simulates burning, 6", VG, A $200.00
Superman Dime Register Bank, tin, 2½" sq, EX, from $225 to .$250.00
Uncle Sam, sheet steel w/blk & gold, 6¼", EX $80.00
Watch Your Savings Grow, Golliwog & friends, litho tin, EX+ ...$275.00

STILL BANKS

Andy Gump, Arcade, painted cast iron, 4½", VG, A, $770.00. (Photo courtesy Bertoia Auctions)

Alamo, Alamo Iron Works, gold pnt, 2", G, A..............$165.00
Automobile, AC Williams, Hansom type w/spoke wheels, red,
    6", VG, A $450.00
Automobile, AC Williams, long nose, spoke wheels, w/driver &
    passenger, 5½", EX, A $825.00
Bank Building (Crown Top), curved center door, red & yel, 3½",
    EX, A $825.00
Bank Building (Crown Top), 2-story w/5 cut-out windows &
    center door, ftd base, gr w/red trim, 5", G, A $500.00
Bank Building (Cupola), J&E Stevens, 1870s, wht w/red & gr,
    mica trim, 5½", EX, A $700.00
Bank Building (Finial), Keyser & Rex, 5¾", EX+ $875.00
Bank Building (Roof #1), J&E Stevens, japanned w/gold trim,
    5", EX, A $200.00
Bank Building (Roof #2), J&E Stevens, japanned w/gold trim,
    5", EX, A $200.00
Bank Building (1876), Judd, 3", EX, A $110.00
Basket (Puzzle), Automatic Savings Co, rnd basket-weave w/2
    hdls, flat lid w/knob, electroplated, 4" dia, EX, A....$130.00
Battleship Oregon, J&E Stevens, 6", NM, A..............$1,100.00
Bear on Hind Legs Begging, AC Williams, gold, 5", NM .$150.00
Bear Sitting on Log w/Arms & Paws Resting on Belly, 7",
    NM..$1,100.00
Bear Sitting Upright Holding Honey Pot, Hubley, 7", EX ..$400.00
Bear Stealing Beehive, Sydenham & McOustra, England, 1908,
    G $325.00
Billy Can, gold w/red hat, 5", VG $550.00
Black Child w/Nodding Head, Germany, pnt lead head in top hat &
    collar on pnt tin ball-shaped body w/slot, 4½", G, A....$385.00
Bulldog Sitting Upright, silvered lead w/bl ribbon collar, 5",
    VG $250.00
Bullet (Aus Eiferner Zeif), emb tin, eagle on front, 7", NM, A.$450.00
Bus (Double-Decker), US, orange & blk, 3½", VG+, A .$935.00
Buster Brown & Tige, AC Williams, 5½", G, A.............$135.00
Cadet, Hubley, 6", EX, A...$470.00

Caisse Building w/Finial on Copula, lead variation, gray w/red roof, 6", EX, A $165.00

Camel Kneeling w/Trunk on Back, Kyser & Rex, ca 1889, japanned, 2½x5", NM...$500.00

Camel w/Hinged Hump & Heart-Shaped Padlock, Germany, ca 1920, silvered wht metal, 5", EX, A $55.00

Cat Climbing Fruit Basket, Germany, 1900, pnt porcelain, 3", EX+, A $385.00

Cat Sitting Upright w/Large Neck Bow, Germany, pnt lead, 4", NM, A $935.00

Cat Standing w/Long Tail, US, japanned, 4½", EX+, A .$990.00

Century of Progress-Chicago 1934 Building, Arcade, 7" L, EX, A $1,320.00

Chanticleer (Rooster), ca 1911, gold w/wht face, 4½", rare, G, A..$1,200.00

Chicago Bank Building, John Harper, japanned cast iron, 6½", NM+, A, $6,050.00. (Photo courtesy Bertoia Auctions)

Church (Rose Window Church), England, japanned, 2½", EX, A $400.00

Clock (Hall), Arcade, sq w/diamond-shaped pediment atop, rnd dial, swinging pendulum, 5½", VG+, A $385.00

Clock (Hall), Hubley, ornate w/open grille front, top resembles pagoda, paper face, ftd, gold w/red trim, 6", VG, A.$350.00

Clock (Mantel), Judd, movable hands on rnd face w/sm top pediment, ftd base, blk w/NP dial, 4½", rare, VG $250.00

Clock (Street), AC Williams, crown-like decoration atop rnd face w/Grecian-type column, red w/gold face, 6", EX........$425.00

Columbia Bank Building, Kenton, 4½", NM, A $600.00

Columbia Bank Building, Kenton, 6", NM+, A $825.00

Columbia Bank Building, Kenton, 7", EX.....................$775.00

Columbia Bank Building, Kenton, 9", overpnt...............$650.00

Columbia Tower, Grey Iron, 7", VG, A $660.00

Coronation Bank, Sydenham & McOustra, ca 1911, 7", VG.$450.00

Devil's Head (Two-Faced), AC Williams, 4", VG $650.00

Dog Sitting Upright w/Hat in Mouth, Germany, ornate base w/German building, 3½", G, A.................................$300.00

Doghouse w/Dog Lying in Door, Germany, ca 1859, sterling silver w/ornate detail, 4", EX+ $450.00

Dolphin (Boy in Boat), US, gold pnt, 4½", VG, A $385.00

Donkey w/Hinged Saddle, Germany, emb side bag, silvered lead, 5½" L, EX, A $165.00

Dreadnought Bank, Sydenham & McOustra, ca 1915, 7", VG.$325.00

Dresser (Bureau), J&E Stevens, ornate detailing, 3 drawers w/bottom opening for coin retrieval, 6½", VG, A...$385.00

Duck Standing w/Outstretched Wings, Hubley, wht pnt w/orange beak & feet, grassy base, 4¾", EX+, A $275.00

Dutch Boy Standing w/Hands in Pockets, Grey Iron, gold pnt, 6¾", EX, A $550.00

Dutch Girl Standing w/Hands on Hips, Grey Iron, gold pnt, 6½", NM, A..$650.00

Eiffel Tower, Syndenham & McOustra/England, japanned cast iron with gold highlights, 8¾", NM, $2,420.00. (Photo courtesy Bertoia Auctions)

F Wasata U-1909-Z-1902 Bank Building, brass, 6", VG.$275.00

Football Player on Knee Holding Large Football Above Head, Hubley, mc pnt, 5", VG, A $1,320.00

Ford Station Wagon, Gama/Germany, plastic, lt beige w/wht top, key-lock trap, w/key, 8", EXIB..........................$225.00

Fort (John Brown's), gray, 2x2", VG $425.00

Gas Pump, Arcade, red sq pedestal w/gold globe, 6", EX, A.$385.00

Globe w/Eagle Finial, Enterprise Mfg, gold-pnt globe w/red base, 5¾", EX, A $400.00

Goose, Arcade, gold pnt, 3¾", G, A $165.00

Grandpa's Hat, L&SI Co, blk w/gold-pnt lettering, 4", EX.$200.00

Hen on Nest, gold pnt, US, 3", G $650.00

Home Bank, painted cast iron, NM, A, $3,575.00. (Photo courtesy Bertoia Auctions)

Horse w/Fly Net, Arcade, gold pnt, 4½" L, regilded.......$250.00

Horse w/Saddle, Grey Iron, gold pnt, 5½" L, EX............$450.00

Ice Cream Freezer (North Pole Bank-Save Your Money & Freeze It), Grey Iron, NP, 4", EX.......................................$450.00

Independence Hall-Birthplace of America, Enterprise Mfg, ca 1875, 10", EX+, A $1,320.00

Indian Shooting Bear, J&E Stevens, rpr base, A............$935.00

King Midas, Hubley, mc pnt, 4½", EX, A $500.00

Kriegsandenken Bank Building, Germany, 1941, bronzed lead, 4", EX, A $400.00

Liberty Bell (1905), John Harper, lg yoke, gold pnt, 4", EX, A.$300.00

Locomotive on Base (Fernsprech-Gebuhren), Germany, pnt tin on wood base, 9" L, EX, A..$500.00

Mail Box (Pillar Box), England, late 1800s, dome top, 5½", VG $650.00

Mammy w/Laundry Basket, wht metal, bl dress w/wht apron, 5¼", VG, A $130.00

Mascot-American League, Hubley, cast iron, 6", G, A, $1,300.00. (Photo courtesy Bertoia Auctions)

Mermaid (Girl in Boat), US, gold pnt, 4½", EX, A $350.00

Minuteman Statue, Banthrico, ca 1941, tall sq base w/message, 8", EX+, A $200.00

Mosque Bank Building, Grey Iron, 3", NM..................$325.00

Mosque Bank Building, Grey Iron, 4½", VG $100.00

Owl (Be Wise Save Money), AC Williams, gold pnt w/red lettering, 4⅞", EX, A $140.00

Pig Smiling, Wilton, standing w/mouth open, pnt in yel highlights, 5½", EX...$150.00

Polar Bear Sitting Upright Begging, Arcade, wht pnt, 5¼", VG, A $415.00

Policeman Standing w/Arms at Sides, Arcade, bl dbl-breasted uniform, 5½", EX...$650.00

Porky Pig, Hubley, 1930, name on base, 6", EX+, A.......$550.00

Porter w/Suitcase Wiping Face w/Towel, German, pnt porcelain, 4", EX, A $500.00

Potato (Bark), Mary Martin design, ca 1897, 5" L, G, A .$600.00

Professor Pug Frog, AC Williams, gr w/gold highlights, 3¼", EX...$375.00

Put Money in Thy Purse (Coin Purse), ca 1886, blk w/gold trim, 3", G...$425.00

Rabbit Sitting Upright w/Long Ears (1 Up & 1 Out to Side), Germany, collar w/padlock, pnt lead, 5", scarce, EX+, A..$2,750.00

Rhino Standing w/Head Straight, Arcade, gold pnt, 2x5", EX, A $525.00

Rooster, Hubley, gold tone w/red comb & waddle, 4¾", EX, A $175.00

Safe (Boom Safe), Kenton, NP CI & sheet metal, combination lock, 3½", VG, A...$70.00

Safe (Daisy Deposit), Arcade, NP w/open cast detailing, key lock, 3½", EX, A...$330.00

Safe (Home Safe), Grey Iron, 1904, NP CI & sheet metal, combination dial, 3¼", VG, A...$65.00

Safe (Ideal Trust), NP, 7", VG+, A...$95.00

Safe (Rival Bank), Kenton, emb name & star, NP CI & sheet metal, key lock, 3¼", NM $200.00

Safe (Save Your Pennies), Kenton, brass w/extensive detailing, embossed dial, rivet coin retrieval, 3½", NM $450.00

Safe (Security), 3-part combination dial, 8", EX $250.00

Safe (Union Bank), Kenton, NP CI & sheet metal, combination lock, 3¼", EX, A...$140.00

Sailor Boy, Europe, painted lead, 4½", EX+, A, $2,860.00. (Photo courtesy Bertoia Auctions)

Santa Sleeping in Chair, USA, prewar, pnt cast metal gold chair, 8", NM $85.00

Santa Standing Beside Tree, Ives, bronzed figure on base next to gr-flocked tree, 7", EX...$450.00

Santa Standing in Hooded Robe, Wing Mfg, ca 1915, red & wht, 5½", G $450.00

Scotsman w/Nodding Head Standing w/Hands on Lapels, mc wht metal, 8", NM, A...$165.00

Sharecropper Standing w/Hands in Pockets, AC Williams, toes visible, gold shirt & hat, 5½", EX, A $275.00

Shell (Shell Out), J&E Stevens, ca 1882, wht pnt, 5" L, VG, A.$385.00

Side-Wheeler, Arcade, gold pnt, 7½", EX, A $300.00

Soccer Ball on Pedestal Base, Chein, 1970s, litho tin, by Gene Bosch, NM+ $275.00

St Bernard w/Back Pack, AC Williams, 8", EX, A $150.00

State Bank, Kenton, japanned, 4", EX, A $170.00

State Bank, Kenton, japanned, 6", VG, A $165.00

State Bank, Kenton, japanned, 9", VG+, A $550.00

Stork Feeding Young, John Harper, cast iron with copper finish, 10", MIB, $2,100.00. (Photo courtesy Bertoia Auctions)

Stove (York), gold pnt, 4", rpr, A $165.00

Taxi, Arcade, brn & wht, w/driver, 8", EX, A.................$2,750.00

Taxi (Red Top Cab), Arcade, w/driver, 8", rpt.................$450.00

Taxi (Yellow Cab), Arcade, w/driver, 8", EX+.................$1,400.00

Taxi (Zaumstein — Canal 2100), Arcade, blk & orange, metal disk wheels, w/driver, 8", G, A...$470.00

Transvaal Money Box, John Harper, short stout man in top hat,
    bronze finish, 6", EX+ $2,850.00
Trolley (Main Street), AC Williams, gold pnt, 7" L, Fair, A ..$55.00
Trust Bank (Seated Banker), J&E Stevens, 7¼", VG+, A .$2,250.00
Turkey w/Fanned Tail, AC Williams, japanned w/red head, 4",
    EX, A $300.00
White City Puzzle Barrel on Hand Cart, 1894, NP, 5", EX .$425.00
Windmill, England, copper finish, blades revolve, 4½", NM,
    A..$1,870.00

Barbie Doll and Friends

No one could argue the fact that vintage Barbie dolls are
holding their own as one of the hottest areas of toy collecting on
today's market. Barbie was first introduced in 1959, and since
then her face has changed three times. She's been blond and
brunette; her hair has been restyled over and over, and it's varied
in length from above her shoulders to the tips of her toes. She's
worn high-fashion designer clothing and pedal pushers. She's
been everything from astronaut to veterinarian, and no matter
what her changing lifestyle required, Mattel (her 'maker') has
provided it for her.

Though even Barbie doll items from recent years are bought
and sold with fervor, those made before 1970 are the most sought
after. You'll need to do a lot of studying and comparisons to learn
to distinguish one Barbie from another, but it will pay off in terms
of making wise investments. There are several books available; we
recommend them all: *The Story of Barbie, Second Edition*, by Kit-
turah B. Westenhouser; *Barbie Doll Fashion, Vol. 1, 1959 – 1967,
Vol. II, 1968 – 1974, Vol. III, 1975 – 1979*, by Sarah Sink Eames;
Barbie, The First 30 Years, 1959 Through 1989, 2nd Edition, by Ste-
fanie Deutsch; *Collector's Encyclopedia of Barbie Doll Exclusives and
More* by J. Michael Augustyniak; and *The Barbie Years* by Patrick
C. and Joyce L. Olds (all published by Collector Books).

Remember that unless the box is mentioned in the line (orig
box, MIB, MIP, NRFB, etc.), values are given for loose items. As
a general rule, a mint-in-the box doll is worth twice as much (or
there about) as one mint, no box. The same doll, played with and
in only good condition, is worth half as much (or even less).
Never-removed-from-box examples sell at a premium.

Advisor: Marl Davidson (D2)

DOLLS

Allan, 1964, pnt red hair, straight legs, MIB, D2, from $125 to..$150.00
Allan, 1965, bendable legs, NRFB $550.00
Barbie, #1, 1958-59, blond or brunette hair, MIB, D2, ea from
    $5,000 to..$6,500.00
Barbie, #2, 1959, blond or brunette hair, MIB, D2, ea from
    $5,000 to..$6,000.00
Barbie, #3, 1960, blond hair (extra long), orig swimsuit, NM,
    D2 ....$1,100.00
Barbie, #3, 1960, blond or brunette hair, orig swimsuit, NM, D2,
    ea..$950.00
Barbie, #4, 1960, blond or brunette hair, orig swimsuit, M, D2,
    ea from $450 to...$500.00

Barbie, #1, 1958 – 59, blond ponytail, original swimsuit, VGIB, A, $3,400.00. (Photo courtesy McMasters Doll Auctions)

Barbie, #5, 1961, blond hair, MIB, D2, from $550 to $650.00
Barbie, #5, 1961, red hair, orig swimsuit, NM, D2..........$375.00
Barbie, #6, blond hair, orig swimsuit, EX, D2 ....$250.00
Barbie, #6, brunette hair, MIB, D2, from $525 to...........$600.00
Barbie, American Airline Stewardess, 1963, NRFB $700.00
Barbie, American Girl, 1964, blond, brn, or brunette hair,
    NRFB, ea $1,500.00
Barbie, American Girl, 1964, platinum cheek-length hair, orig
    swimsuit, NM, D2..$650.00
Barbie, American Girl, 1964, red hair, replica swimsuit, NM,
    D2..$600.00
Barbie, Angel Lights, 1993, NRFB................................$100.00
Barbie, Angel of Peace, 1999, Timeless Sentiments, NRFB..$50.00
Barbie, Arctic, 1996, Dolls of the World, NRFB $25.00
Barbie, Army Desert Storm (Black or White), 1993, Stars &
    Stripes, NRFB, ea..$30.00
Barbie, Autumn in London, 1999, City Season Collection,
    NRFB $45.00
Barbie, Avon Representative (White or Hispanic), 1999, NRFB,
    ea $50.00
Barbie, Ballerina Barbie on Tour, 1976, NRFB..............$125.00
Barbie, Barbie Celebration, 1987, NRFB $30.00
Barbie, Barbie Sign Language (Black or White), 1999, NRFB,
    ea $20.00
Barbie, Bay Watch (Black or White), 1995, NRFB, ea.....$20.00
Barbie, Brazilian, 1989, Dolls of the World, NRFB, D2....$75.00

Barbie, Bubble Cut, brunette, in kimono, VGIB, A, $900.00.

(Photo courtesy McMasters Doll Auctions)

Barbie, Bubble-Cut, 1961, blond, brunette, or red hair, orig swimsuit, NM, D2, ea $200.00
Barbie, Bubble-Cut, 1962, blond or brunette hair, NRFB, ea .$400.00
Barbie, Bubble-Cut, 1962-64, side part, red hair, orig swimsuit, NM, D2...$500.00
Barbie, Busy Barbie, 1972, NRFB.....................$200.00
Barbie, Calvin Klein, 1996, Bloomingdales, NRFB, D2 ...$65.00
Barbie, Celebration Cake Barbie (any), 1999, NRFB, ea .$20.00
Barbie, Children's Doctor, 2000, NRFB $20.00
Barbie, Chinese, 1993, Dolls of the World, NRFB, D2.....$50.00
Barbie, Coca-Cola Soda Fountain Sweetheart, 1996, NRFB, D2.$300.00
Barbie, Color-Magic, 1966, blond or brunette hair, orig swimsuit hair band & belt, NM, D2, ea $750.00
Barbie, Cool Times, 1989, NRFB $25.00
Barbie, Cut & Style (any), 1995, NRFB, ea......................$20.00
Barbie, Deluxe Quick Curl, 1976, Jergens, NRFB $100.00
Barbie, Deluxe Tropical Barbie, 1986, NRFB....................$40.00
Barbie, Dinner at Eight, 1964, NRFB $600.00
Barbie, Dinner Date, 1998, red hair, NRFB $20.00
Barbie, Dorothy (Wizard of Oz), 1994, Hollywood Legends Series, NRFB $350.00
Barbie, Dorothy (Wizard of Oz), 1996, NRFB $220.00
Barbie, Dramatic Living, 1970, brunette hair, NRFB $250.00
Barbie, Dramatic New Living, 1970, red hair, orig swimsuit & cover-up, NM, D2...$175.00
Barbie, Dream Date, 1983, MIB $45.00
Barbie, Dutch, 1994, Dolls of the World, NRFB...............$65.00
Barbie, Easter Party, 1995, NRFB $20.00
Barbie, Elizabethan, 1994, Great Eras, MIB, D2 ....$50.00
Barbie, Enchanted Evening, 1991, JC Penney, NRFB $75.00
Barbie, Enchanted Princess, 1993, Sears, NRFB...............$50.00
Barbie, Eskimo, 1982, Dolls of the World, NRFB...........$100.00
Barbie, Evening Sparkle, 1990, Hill's, NRFB $35.00
Barbie, Fabulous Fur, 1986, NRFB..................................$65.00

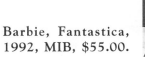

Barbie, Fantastica, 1992, MIB, $55.00.

(Photo courtesy Margo Rana)

Barbie, Fantasy Goddess of Asia, 1998, Bob Mackie, NRFB .$225.00
Barbie, Fantasy Goddess of Asia, 1998, International Beauty, NRFB...$185.00
Barbie, Feelin' Groovy, 1987, NRFB..............................$175.00
Barbie, Fire Fighter, 1995, Toys R Us, NRFB....................$50.00

Barbie, Flower Seller (My Fair Lady), 1995, Hollywood Legend Series, NRFB, D2.......................................$70.00
Barbie, Fountain Mermaid (Black or White), 1993, NRFB, ea..$20.00
Barbie, French Lady, 1997, Great Eras Collection, NRFB.$35.00
Barbie, Gap Barbie (Black or White), 1996, Gap Stores, NRFB, ea $60.00
Barbie, Glinda (Wizard of Oz), 2000, NRFB.................$25.00
Barbie, Goddess of the Sun, 1995, Bob Mackie, NRFB..$180.00
Barbie, Gold Medal Skater or Skier, 1975, NRFB, ea $75.00
Barbie, Grand Premier, 1997, Barbie Collectors Club, NRFB .$110.00
Barbie, Great Shape (Black), 1984, NRFB $25.00

Barbie, Growin' Pretty Hair, 1971, NRFB, A, $475.00.

(Photo courtesy McMasters Doll Auctions)

Barbie, Hawaiian Superstar, 1977, MIB $110.00
Barbie, Holiday, 1988, NRFB, D2, minimum value........$500.00
Barbie, Holiday, 1989, NRFB, D2 ....$250.00
Barbie, Holiday, 1990, NRFB, D2 ....$200.00
Barbie, Holiday, 1991, NRFB, D2 ....$200.00
Barbie, Holiday, 1992, NRFB, D2 ....$150.00
Barbie, Holiday, 1993, NRFB, D2 ....$175.00
Barbie, Holiday, 1994, NRFB, D2 ....$150.00
Barbie, Holiday, 1995, NRFB, D2 ....$75.00
Barbie, Holiday, 1996, NRFB, D2 ....$50.00
Barbie, Holiday, 1997, NRFB, D2 ....$35.00
Barbie, Holiday, 1998, NRFB $25.00
Barbie, Indiana, 1998, University Barbie, NRFB.............$15.00
Barbie, Island Fun, 1988, NRFB.................................$20.00
Barbie, Jamaican, 1992, Dolls of the World, NRFB........$125.00
Barbie, Jewel Essence, 1996, Bob Mackie, NRFB, D2 ....$150.00
Barbie, Kellogg Quick Curl, 1974, Kellogg Co, NRFB $60.00
Barbie, Kenyan, 1994, Dolls of the World, NRFB $50.00
Barbie, Knitting Pretty (pk), 1964, NRFB...................$1,265.00
Barbie, Knitting Pretty (royal bl), 1965, NRFB..............$635.00
Barbie, Lights 'N Lace, 1991, NRFB $30.00
Barbie, Lily, 1997, FAO Schwarz, NRFB $125.00
Barbie, Malibu (Sunset), 1971, NRFB $65.00
Barbie, Malt Shop, 1993, Toys R Us, NRFB $35.00
Barbie, Medieval lady, 1995, Great Eras Collection, NRFB..$60.00
Barbie, Miss America, 1972, Kellogg Co, NRFB $175.00
Barbie, Moon Goddess, 1996, Bob Mackie, NRFB, D2 ..$175.00
Barbie, Moonlight Magic, 1993, Toys R Us, NRFB $85.00
Barbie, My First Barbie, 1981, NRFB $25.00

Barbie, NASCAR 50th Anniversary, 1998, NRFB...........$25.00
Barbie, Native American #2, 1994, Dolls of the World, NRFB, D2...$55.00
Barbie, Neptune Fantasy, 1992, Bob Mackie, NRFB $600.00
Barbie, Nifty Fifties, 2000, Great Fashions of the 20th Century, NRFB $50.00
Barbie, Nutcracker, 1992, Musical Ballet Series, NRFB .$165.00
Barbie, Opening Night, 1993, Classique Collection, NRFB .$80.00
Barbie, Oreo Fun, 1997, NRFB, D2....................................$35.00
Barbie, Paleontologist, 1997, Toys R Us, NRFB $20.00
Barbie, Party in Pink, 1991, Ames, NRFB $30.00
Barbie, Party Sensation, 1990, NRFB...............................$55.00
Barbie, Peach Blossom, 1992, NRFB.................................$40.00
Barbie, Peach Pretty, 1989, K-Mart, MIB.........................$35.00
Barbie, Peaches 'N Cream, 1985, MIB $35.00
Barbie, Pepsi Sensation, 1989, Toys R Us, NRFB $75.00
Barbie, Perfume Party, 1988, NRFB..................................$30.00
Barbie, Phantom of the Opera, 1998, FAO Schwarz, NRFB ..$150.00
Barbie, Picnic Party, 1992, Osco, NRFB $35.00
Barbie, Pilgrim, 1995, American Stories Collection, NRFB .$25.00
Barbie, Pink & Pretty, 1982, MIB.....................................$60.00
Barbie, Pink Sensation, 1990, Winn Dixie, NRFB $25.00
Barbie, Pioneer, 1995 or 1996, American Stories Collection, NRFB, ea...$25.00
Barbie, Plum Royal, 1999, Runway Collection, NRFB...$200.00
Barbie, Police Officer, 1993, Toys R Us, NRFB $75.00
Barbie, Polly Pockets, 1994, Hill's, NRFB........................$20.00
Barbie, Portrait in Blue, 1998, Wal-Mart, NRFB.............$15.00

Barbie, Pretty Hearts, 1991, MIB, $25.00.

(Photo courtesy Margo Rana)

Barbie, Queen of Hearts, 1994, Bob Mackie, NRFB, D2 ..$325.00
Barbie, Queen of Sapphires, 2000, Royal Jewel, NRFB..$100.00
Barbie, Quick Curl Miss America, 1972, orig outfit, EX, D2..$75.00
Barbie, Quick Curl Miss America, 1976, MIB.................$125.00
Barbie, Ralph Lauren, 1997, Bloomingdale's, NRFB $60.00
Barbie, Rising Star Barbie, 1998, Grand Old Opry, NRFB..$85.00
Barbie, Rockettes, 1993, FAO Schwarz, NRFB $120.00
Barbie, Romantic Wedding 2001, 2000, Bridal Collection, NRFB $50.00
Barbie, Russian, 1988, Dolls of the World, NRFB, D2......$50.00
Barbie, Safari, 1998, Disney, NRFB..................................$30.00

Barbie, Sapphire Dreams, 1995, Toys R Us, NRFB...........$50.00
Barbie, Sapphire Sophisticate, 1997, Toys R Us, NRFB ...$30.00
Barbie, Savvy Shopper, 1994, Bloomingdale's, NRFB $50.00
Barbie, School Spirit Barbie, 1993, Toys R Us, NRFB......$25.00
Barbie, Scottish, 1981, Dolls of the World, NRFB $140.00
Barbie, Sea Princess, 1996, Service Merchandise, NRFB .$45.00
Barbie, Sentimental Valentine, 1997, Hallmark, NRFB...$30.00
Barbie, Sheer Illusion #1 or #2, 1998, Designer Collection, NRFB, ea...$80.00
Barbie, Snap 'N Play, 1992, NRFB $20.00
Barbie, Snow Princess, 1994, Enchanted Seasons, blond hair, NRFB $100.00
Barbie, Snow Princess, 1994, Mattel Festival, brunette hair, NRFB $800.00
Barbie, Snow White, 1999, Children's Collector Series, NRFB ..$40.00
Barbie, Something Extra, 1992, Meijer, NRFB $25.00
Barbie, Songbird, 1996, NRFB $25.00
Barbie, Southern Beauty, 1991, Winn Dixie, NRFB.........$25.00
Barbie, Southern Belle, 1994, Great Eras Collection, NRFB .$75.00
Barbie, Sports Star, 1979, NRFB $25.00
Barbie, Standard, 1967, brunette hair, straight legs, NRFB..$600.00
Barbie, Standard, 1967, red hair, straight legs, NRFB .$1,100.00
Barbie, Standard, 1970, blond hair, replica swimsuit, NM, D2..$325.00
Barbie, Starlight Dance, 1996, Classique Collection, NRFB..$45.00
Barbie, Steppin' Out Barbie 1930s, 1999, Great Fashions of the 20th Century, NRFB..$35.00
Barbie, Sugar Plum Fairy, 1997, Classic Ballet Series, NRFB .$30.00
Barbie, Swan Lake Ballerina, 1991, NRFB, D2...............$200.00
Barbie, Swirl Ponytail, 1964, blond or brunette hair, NRFB, ea.$650.00
Barbie, Swirl Ponytail, 1964, blond or brunette hair, orig swimsuit, M, D2, ea from $400 to.....................................$500.00

Barbie, Swirl Ponytail, 1964, brunette, original red swimsuit, NRFB, A, $650.00.

(Photo courtesy McMasters Doll Auctions)

Barbie, Swirl Ponytail, 1964, platinum hair, NRFB.....$1,300.00
Barbie, Talking, 1968, blond, brunette, or red hair, NRFB, ea...$400.00
Barbie, Talking, 1970, blond, brunette, or red hair, NRFB..$300.00
Barbie, Ten Speeder, 1973, NRFB $30.00
Barbie, Thailand, 1998, Dolls of the World, NRFB, D2 ...$25.00
Barbie, Theatre Date, 1964, NRFB $660.00
Barbie, Twirly Curls, 1983, MIB $45.00
Barbie, Twist 'N Turn, 1966, blond hair, MIB, D2 ....$600.00

Barbie, Twist 'N Turn, 1966, brunette hair, orig swimsuit, NM, D2 ....$275.00
Barbie, Twist 'N Turn, 1967, blond or cinnamon hair, orig swimsuit, NM, D2, ea $250.00
Barbie, Twist 'N Turn, 1968, blond hair, MIB, D2 ....$700.00
Barbie, Twist 'N Turn, 1969, lt brn flipped-up hair, NRFB, D2 ....$900.00

Barbie, Twist 'N Turn, 1971, blond flip hair, NRFB, A, $425.00. (Photo courtesy McMasters Doll Auctions)

Barbie, Twist 'N Turn, 1971, brunette hair, NRFB $500.00
Barbie, Unicef, 1989, NRFB.....................................$20.00
Barbie, Winter Fantasy, 1990, FAO Schwarz, NRFB, D2 .$200.00
Barbie, Wonder Woman, 2000, Pop Culture Collection, NRFB $40.00
Barbie, Working Woman (Black or White), 1999, NRFB, ea .$25.00
Barbie, Xavier, 1999, University Barbie, NRFB $16.00
Barbie, Yuletide Romance, 1996, Hallmark, NRFB..........$30.00
Casey, Twist 'N Turn, 1968, blond or brunette hair, NRFB ...$350.00
Chris, 1967, blond hair, orig outfit, NM, D2 ....$125.00
Chris, 1974, auburn hair, orig outfit & shoes, EX, D2 ......$75.00
Christie, Beauty Secrets, 1980, MIB............................$60.00
Christie, Fashion Photo, 1978, MIB..............................$95.00
Christie, Golden Dream, 1980, MIB $50.00
Christie, Kissing, 1979, MIB......................................$65.00
Christie, Pink & Pretty, 1982, NRFB $35.00
Christie, Pretty Reflections, 1979, NRFB $85.00

Christie, Talking, 1969, red hair, NRFB, A, $250.00.

(Photo courtesy McMasters Doll Auctions)

Christie, Sunsational Malibu, 1982, NRFB.....................$30.00
Christie, Superstar, 1977, MIB $95.00
Christie, Talking, 1969, brunette hair, NRFB.................$250.00
Christie, Twist 'N Turn, 1968, red hair, orig swimsuit, NM, D2...$250.00
Francie, Busy, 1972, NRFB..$425.00
Francie, Growin' Pretty Hair, 1970, orig outfit, NM, D2 ..$150.00

Francie, Malibu, 1970s, NRFB, A, $235.00. (Photo courtesy McMasters Doll Auctions)

Francie, Malibu (Japanese), dk brn hair w/side part, orig swimsuit, NM, D2...$2,200.00
Francie, Twist 'N Turn, 1966, blond hair, orig swimsuit, NM, D2...$350.00
Francie, Twist 'N Turn, 1966, brunette hair, orig swimsuit, EX, D2...$150.00
Francie, 30th Anniversary, 1996, NRFB $65.00
Ginger, Growing Up, 1977, MIB..................................$95.00
Jamie, New & Wonderful Walking, blond hair, orig outfit, EX, D2 ....$225.00
Kelly, Quick Curl, 1972, NRFB, D2 ....$175.00
Ken, 1961, flocked blond or brunette hair, straight legs, MIB, D2, ea from $150 to $200.00
Ken, 1962, pnt blond or brunette hair, NRFB, ea..........$175.00
Ken, 1963, pnt blond hair, ¼" shorter, NRFB................$200.00
Ken, 1965, pnt blond hair, bendable legs, NRFB............$650.00
Ken, 1965, pnt blond hair, orig outfit & shoes, bendable legs, M, D2 ....$225.00
Ken, Air Force, 1994, Stars 'N Stripes, NRFB $30.00
Ken, Arabian Nights, 1964, NRFB $420.00
Ken, Army, 1993, Stars 'N Stripes, NRFB.......................$35.00
Ken, Beach Blast, 1989, NRFB....................................$25.00
Ken, Busy, 1972, NRFB...$175.00
Ken, California Dream, 1988, NRFB $30.00
Ken, Crystal, 1984, NRFB $40.00
Ken, Dream Date, 1983, NRFB....................................$30.00
Ken, Earring Magic, 1993, NRFB $40.00
Ken, Fashion Jeans, 1982, MIB....................................$35.00
Ken, Gold Medal Skier, 1975, NRFB.............................$100.00
Ken, Hawaiian, 1979, MIB $45.00
Ken, Henry Higgins, 1996, Hollywood Legends Series, NRFB.$65.00
Ken, In-Line Skating, 1996, FAO Schwarz, NRFB...........$20.00
Ken, Jewel Secrets, 1987, NRFB...................................$40.00
Ken, King Arthur, 1964, NRFB....................................$500.00

Ken, Live Action, 1971, NRFB.....................$100.00
Ken, Marine Corps, 1992, Stars 'N Stripes, NRFB $40.00
Ken, Now Look, 1976, longer or shorter hair, NRFB, ea ..$75.00
Ken, Ocean Friends, 1996, NRFB $20.00
Ken, Party Time, 1977, NRFB $35.00
Ken, Rappin' Rockin', 1992, MIB $25.00
Ken, Rhett Butler, 1994, Hollywood Legend Series, NRFB, D2..$75.00
Ken, Sea Holiday, 1993, FAO Schwarz, NRFB.................$40.00
Ken, Sport & Shave, 1980, MIB $40.00
Ken, Sun Charm, 1989, MIB.....................$25.00
Ken, Sun Lovin' Malibu, 1979, NRFB $35.00
Ken, Superstar, 1977, MIB.....................$95.00

Ken, Talking, 1960s, NRFB, $200.00. (Photo courtesy McMasters Doll Auctions)

Ken, Tin Man, 1995, Hollywood Legends Series, NRFB, D2 .$60.00
Ken, Totally Hair, 1991, NRFB, D2 ....$50.00
Ken, Walk Lively, 1972, MIB $150.00
Ken, Western, 1982, MIB $35.00
Midge, 1963, blond or red hair, bendable legs, MIB, D2, ea.$500.00

Midge, 1963, brunette hair, straight legs, VGIB, A, $225.00. (Photo courtesy McMasters Doll Auctions)

Midge, Cool Times, 1989, NRFB.....................$30.00
Midge, Earring Magic, 1993, NRFB $30.00
Midge, Japanese, brunette hair, straight legs, orig swimsuit, rare, NM, D2 ....$1,250.00
Midge, Ski Fun, 1991, Toys R Us, MIB $30.00
Midge, Winter Sports, 1995, Toys R Us, MIB.....................$40.00
Midge, 30th Anniversary, 1992, porcelain, MIB, D2......$175.00
Nikki, Animal Lovin', 1989, NRFB $30.00

PJ, Deluxe Quick Curl, 1976, MIB.....................$65.00
PJ, Fashion Photo, 1978, MIB $95.00
PJ, Free Moving, 1976, MIB $85.00
PJ, Gold Medal Gymnast, 1975, NRFB.....................$120.00
PJ, Live Action, 1971, orig outfit, M, D2 ....$150.00
PJ, Malibu, 1978, MIB.....................$55.00
PJ, New & Groovy Talking, 1969, orig swimsuit, beads & glasses, NM, D2.....................$150.00
PJ, Sun Lovin' Malibu, 1979, MIB $50.00
PJ, Sunsational Malibu, 1982, MIB $40.00
PJ, Talking, 1970, orig outfit & beads, M, D2, from $175 to .$250.00
Red Velvet Delight Haute Couture, 1994, Barbie Festival, NRFB $350.00

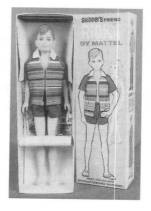

Ricky, 1965, painted red hair, NMIB, A, $150.00. (Photo courtesy McMasters Doll Auctions)

Ricky, 1965, orig outfit & shoes, NM, D2 ....$75.00
Scott, Skipper's boyfriend, 1980, MIB.....................$55.00
Skipper, 1965, blond or red hair, bendable legs, MIB, D2, from $350 to $400.00
Skipper, Deluxe Quick Curl, 1975, NRFB $125.00
Skipper, Dramatic New Living, 1970, orig swimsuit, NM, D2 ..$50.00
Skipper, Dream Date, 1990, NRFB.....................$25.00
Skipper, Growing Up, 1976, MIB.....................$100.00
Skipper, Hollywood Hair, 1993, NRFB $30.00
Skipper, Homecoming Queen, 1989, NRFB $35.00
Skipper, Music Lovin', 1985, NRFB.....................$65.00
Skipper, Pepsi Spirit, 1989, NRFB.....................$70.00
Skipper, Sunsational Malibu, 1982, MIB $40.00
Skipper, Super Teen, 1980, NRFB.....................$35.00
Skipper, Totally Hair, 1991, NRFB.....................$30.00
Skipper, Twist 'N Turn, 1969, blond banana curls, MIB, D2...$400.00
Skipper, Twist 'N Turn, 1969, brn hair, w/certificate of authenticity, MIB, D2 ....$550.00
Skipper, Western, 1982, NRFB.....................$40.00
Skipper, Workout Teen Fun, 1988, NRFB.....................$30.00
Skipper, 30th Anniversary, 1994, porcelain, NRFB........$165.00
Skooter, 1963, brunette hair, orig swimsuit & bows, MIB, D2 ..$175.00
Skooter, 1965, blond hair, bendable legs, MIB, D2.........$225.00
Stacey, Talking, blond or red hair, orig swimsuit, NM, D2, ea from $250 to $350.00
Stacey, Twist 'N Turn, 1968, blond hair, NRFB, D2 ....$900.00
Stacey, Twist 'N Turn, 1968, red hair, orig swimsuit, NM, D2 ...$350.00
Steffie, Walk Lively, 1968, orig outfit & scarf, NM, D2 .$175.00
Teresa, All American, 1991, MIB.....................$25.00
Teresa, California Dream, 1988, MIB.....................$30.00

Teresa, Country Western Star, 1994, NRFB......................$30.00
Teresa, Rappin' Rockin', 1992, NRFB.............................$45.00
Tutti, 1966, brunette hair, orig outfit, NM, D2 ....$85.00
Tutti, 1974, blond hair, orig outfit, EX, D2 ....$60.00
Tutti, Night Night Sleep Tight, 1966, NRFB $275.00
Whitney, Nurse, 1987, NRFB.......................................$80.00
Whitney, Style Magic, 1989, NRFB...............................$35.00

CASES

Barbie, Francie, Casey & Tutti, hard plastic, EX, from $50 to .$75.00
Barbie, Stacey, Francie & Skipper, pk hard plastic, rare, NM,
    from $75 to $100.00
Barbie, 1961, red vinyl, Barbie pictured in 4 different outfits, EX,
    from $30 to $40.00
Barbie, 1963, pk vinyl, Bubble-Cut Barbie wearing Solo in the
    Spotlight, rare, NM, from $75 to...............................$85.00
Barbie, 1967, vinyl, Barbie wearing All That Jazz surrounded by
    flowers, from $30 to $40.00
Barbie & Ken, 1963, blk vinyl, Barbie wearing Party Date &
    Ken wearing Saturday Night Date, EX, D2 ....$65.00
Barbie & Midge, pk vinyl, Barbie wearing Rain Coat & Midge
    wearing Sorority Meeting, NM, from $45 to..............$55.00
Barbie & Stacey, 1967, vinyl, NM, from $65 to...............$75.00
Barbie & Stacey Sleep 'N Keep, 1960s, vinyl, several color varia-
    tions, EX, ea from $55 to $65.00
Barbie Goes Travelin', vinyl, rare, NM $100.00
Barbie on Madison Avenue, FAO Schwarz, 1992, blk back-
    ground, pk hdl, M $40.00
Circus Star Barbie, FAO Schwarz, 1995, M.....................$25.00
Fashion Queen Barbie, 1963, red vinyl, w/mirror & wig stand,
    EX, D2 ....$100.00
Francie & Casey, vinyl, Francie wearing Groovy Get-Up &
    Casey wearing Iced Blue, rare, from $65 to...............$75.00

Ken, green vinyl with plastic handle and closure, 1961, NM, from $30.00 to $40.00. (Photo courtesy Connie Craig Kaplan)

Midge, 1963, bl vinyl, Midge wearing Movie Date, rare, NM,
    from $100 to $125.00
Miss Barbie, 1963, wht vinyl, w/orig wig, wig stand & mirror,
    rare, EX, D2 ....$150.00
Skooter, 1965, bl vinyl, Skooter wearing Country Picnic & chas-
    ing butterflies, rare, from $125 to.........................$175.00
Tutti Play Case, bl or pk vinyl w/various scenes, EX, ea from $30
    to $40.00

CLOTHING AND ACCESSORIES

Barbie, After Five, #934, 1962, NRFP $450.00
Barbie, All Decked Out, #17568, 1997, NRFP $20.00
Barbie, All Turned Out, #4822, 1984, NRFP $20.00
Barbie, Barbie Hot Togs, #1063, NRFP, D2 ....$1,300.00
Barbie, Barbie in Hawaii, #1605, 1964, NRFB...............$175.00
Barbie, Beach Dazzler, #1939, 1981, NRFP.....................$10.00
Barbie, Beautiful Bride, #1698, 1967, complete, M, D2 .$900.00
Barbie, Brunch Time, #1628, 1965, complete, NM, D2 .$125.00
Barbie, Busy Morning, #981, 1960, NRFP $415.00
Barbie, Cinderella, #872, 1964, complete, NM, D2 ....$150.00
Barbie, City Fun, #5717, 1983, NRFP $10.00
Barbie, Cloud Nine, #1489, 1969-70, complete, M........$200.00
Barbie, Club Meeting, #1672, 1966, NRFP $400.00
Barbie, Cotton Casual, #912, 1959, NRFP $125.00
Barbie, Cruise Stripes, #918, 1959, NRFP $150.00
Barbie, Day 'N Night, #1723, 1965, NRFP.....................$75.00
Barbie, Disco Dazzle, #1011, 1979, NRFP $15.00
Barbie, Dog 'N Duds, #1613, 1964, NRFP $275.00
Barbie, Dream Wrap, #1476, 1969-70, complete, M $150.00
Barbie, Drum Majorette, #875, 1964, NRFP..................$225.00
Barbie, Enchanted Evening, #983, complete, EX, D2 ..$195.00
Barbie, Evening Outfit, #2221, 1978, NRFP...................$30.00
Barbie, Evening Splendor (reissue), #961, 1964, NRFP ...$15.00
Barbie, Fashion Bouquet, #1511, 1970, NRFP...............$350.00
Barbie, Fashion Luncheon, #1656, complete, EX, D2 ....$450.00
Barbie, Fashion Matinee, #1640, complete, M, D2 ....$500.00
Barbie, Fashion Shiner, #1691, 1967, NRFP.................$300.00
Barbie, Firelights, #1481, 1969-70, MIP $175.00
Barbie, Floral Petticoat, #921, 1959, NRFP $125.00
Barbie, Flying Colors, #3492, 1972, complete, M...........$300.00
Barbie, Fraternity Dance, #1638, complete, M, D2 ....$400.00
Barbie, Friday Night Date, #979, 1960, NRFP...............$225.00
Barbie, Fun Flakes, #3412, 1971-72, complete, M $175.00
Barbie, Fun Shine, #3480, 1972, complete, M................$250.00
Barbie, Galaxy A Go-Go, #2742, 1986, NRFP................$30.00
Barbie, Glamour Group, #1510, 1970, NRFP $350.00
Barbie, Gold 'N Glamour, #1647, complete, M, D2 ....$800.00
Barbie, Gold Spun, #1957, 1981, NRFP.........................$15.00
Barbie, Golden Glory, #1645, complete, M, D2 ....$250.00
Barbie, Graduation, #945, 1963, NRFP.........................$60.00
Barbie, Great Coat, #1459, 1970, NRFP $90.00
Barbie, Groovin' Gauchos, #1057, 1971, NRFP $300.00
Barbie, Holiday Dance, #1639, 1965, NRFP.................$550.00
Barbie, In the Limelight, #2790, 1979, NRFP.................$15.00
Barbie, Indian Print Separates, #7241, 1975, NRFP.........$35.00
Barbie, Invitation to Tea, #1632, 1965, NRFP.............$575.00
Barbie, Jumpin' Jeans, Pak, 1964, NRFP $85.00
Barbie, Knit Separates, #1602, 1964, NRFP $140.00
Barbie, Lady in Blue, #2303, 1978, NRFP......................$15.00
Barbie, Light 'N Lazy, #3339, 1972, NRFP.....................$75.00
Barbie, Little Bow Pink, #1483, 1969-70, complete, M..$150.00
Barbie, Little Red Riding Hood & the Wolf, #880, 1964, NRFP..$600.00
Barbie, Loop Scoop, #1454, 1970, complete, M $150.00
Barbie, Lunch on the Terrace, #1649, 1966, NRFP $350.00
Barbie, Madras Plaid, #3485, 1972, NRFP $120.00
Barbie, Make Mine Midi, #1861, 1969, NRFP $300.00

Barbie, Midi-Marvelous, #1870, 1969, NRFP $160.00
Barbie, Mood Matchers, #1792, complete, NM, D2 ....$75.00
Barbie, Movie Groovie, #1866, 1969, NRFP $125.00
Barbie, My First Picnic, #5611, 1983, NRFP...................$10.00
Barbie, Now Knit, #1452, 1970, NRFP $100.00
Barbie, Olympic Warm-Ups, #7243, 1975, NRFP $40.00
Barbie, Overall Denim, #3488, 1972, NRFP...................$110.00
Barbie, Pajama Party, #1601, 1964, NRFP $80.00
Barbie, Patio Party, #1708, 1965, NRFP.........................$50.00
Barbie, Peachy Fleecy, #915, complete, NM, D2 ....$100.00
Barbie, Perfectly Pink, #4805, 1984, NRFP $10.00
Barbie, Picnic in the Park, #16077, 1996, NRFP $30.00
Barbie, Plush Pony, #1873, 1969, NRFP $175.00
Barbie, Princess Aurora, #9329, 1976, NRFP...................$40.00
Barbie, Purple Pleasers, #3483, 1972, complete, M $175.00
Barbie, Rainbow Wraps, #1796, complete, NM, D2 ....$135.00
Barbie, Rare Pair, #1462, 1970, NRFP $125.00
Barbie, Reception Line, #1654, 1966, NRFP $600.00
Barbie, Red Flair, #939, 1962, NRFP $175.00
Barbie, Romantic Ruffles, #1871, complete, M, D2........$150.00
Barbie, Royal Ball, #2668, 1979, NRFP $15.00
Barbie, Saturday Matinee, #1615, complete, M, D2 ....$600.00
Barbie, Scene Stealers, #1845, 1968, complete, M $250.00
Barbie, Scuba Do's, #1788, 1970, NRFP.........................$65.00
Barbie, Sea-Worthy, #1872, 1969, NRFP $225.00
Barbie, Shape-Ups, #1782, 1970-71, MIB......................$175.00
Barbie, Sharp Shift, #20, 1970, NRFP $110.00
Barbie, Sheath Sensation, #986, 1961, NRFP $150.00
Barbie, Shimmering Magic, #1664, complete, M, D2.....$900.00
Barbie, Silken Flame, #977, 1960, NRFP.......................$175.00
Barbie, Silver Serenade, #3419, 1971-72, complete, MIP.$300.00
Barbie, Silver Sparkle, #1885, 1969, MIB $200.00
Barbie, Skate Mates, #1793, 1970, NRFP $130.00
Barbie, Ski Party Pink, #5608, 1983, NRFP $10.00
Barbie, Skin Diver, #1608, 1964, NRFP.........................$125.00
Barbie, Slip On Wrap 'N Tie, #1910, 1981, NRFP $10.00
Barbie, Snap Dash, #1824, 1968, NRFP........................$140.00
Barbie, Snug Fuzz, #1813, 1968, NRFP $250.00
Barbie, Sparkle Squares, #1814, 1968-69, complete, M..$300.00
Barbie, Star of the Snow in Golden Glow, #9741, 1977, NRFP..$15.00
Barbie, Stormy Weather, #949, 1964, NRFP $100.00
Barbie, Student Teacher, #1622, 1965, complete, M, D2..$250.00
Barbie, Sugar Plum Fairy, #9326, 1976, NRFP $40.00
Barbie, Sunny Sleep Ins, #3348, 1973, NRFP $50.00
Barbie, Sweetheart Satin, #3361, 1972, complete, M.....$250.00
Barbie, Swinging Easy, #955, 1963, NRFP $200.00
Barbie, Teachers, #9085, 1985, NRFP $5.00
Barbie, Team Ups, #1855, 1968-69, complete, M............$150.00
Barbie, Togetherness, #1842, 1968, NRFP $175.00
Barbie, Topsy Twosider, #4826, 1984, NRFP..................$10.00
Barbie, Tour-Ins, #1515, 1969, NRFP $50.00
Barbie, Trail Blazer, #1846, 1968, NRFP......................$250.00
Barbie, Tropicana, #1460, 1967, NRFP.........................$170.00
Barbie, Twinkle Togs, #1854, 1968-69, complete, M......$150.00
Barbie, Two-Way Tiger, #3402, 1971, NRFP $110.00
Barbie, United Airlines Stewardess, #7703, 1973, NRFP .$75.00
Barbie, Velvet Touch, #2789, 1979, NRFP $15.00
Barbie, Velvet Venture, #1488, 1969-70, complete, M...$250.00

Barbie, Victorian Velvet, #3431, 1971, NRFP $175.00
Barbie, Walking Pretty, Pak, 1971, NRFP......................$130.00
Barbie, White Delight, #3799, 1982, NRFP.....................$15.00
Barbie, Wild 'N Wintery, #3416, complete, M, D2........$300.00

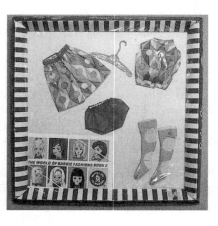

Barbie, Wild 'N Wonderful, #1856, 1968 – 69, NRFB, $200.00. (Photo courtesy Sarah Sink Eames)

Barbie, Wild Things, #3439, 1971, NRFP.....................$250.00
Barbie, Yellow Go, #1816, 1967, NRFP $800.00
Barbie, Zokko!, #1820, 1968, NRFP $200.00
Barbie & Stacey, All the Trimmings Fashion Pak, #0050, 1970, MOC..$75.00
Barbie & Stacey, Foot Lights Fashion Pak, #0040, 1970, MOC..$75.00
Francie, Beach Outfit, #7710, 1973, NRFP $200.00
Francie, Cheerleading Outfit, #7711, 1973, NRFP...........$80.00
Francie, Clam Diggers, #1258, 1966, NRFP...................$185.00
Francie, Dancing Party, #1257, complete, M, D2 ....$150.00
Francie, Far Out, #1262, complete, M, D2.....................$400.00
Francie, First Things First, #1252, 1966, NRFP.............$115.00
Francie, Frosty Fur, #3455, 1971-72 & 1974, complete, M.$150.00
Francie, Furry-Go-Round, #1294, Sears Exclusive, 1967, NRFP.$500.00
Francie, Get-Ups 'N Go Candy Striper, #7709, 1973, MIP..$100.00
Francie, Get-Ups 'N Go Ice Skater, #7845, 1974-75, MIP...$75.00
Francie, Hip Knits, #1265, 1966, NRFB $225.00
Francie, In-Print, #1288, 1967, NRFP $150.00
Francie, Little Knits, #3275, 1972, NRFP $125.00
Francie, Long on Leather, #1769, 1970, NRFP $155.00
Francie, Merry-Go-Rounders, #1230, NRFB, D2 ....$375.00
Francie, Midi Bouquet, #3446, 1971, NRFP $125.00
Francie, Peach Plush, #3461, 1971, NRFP $250.00
Francie, Pretty Frilly, #3366, 1972, MIB $200.00
Francie, Quick Shift, #1266, 1966, NRFP $200.00
Francie, Satin Happenin', #1237, 1970, NRFP $75.00
Francie, Simply Super, #3277, 1972, complete, M..........$175.00
Francie, Slightly Summery Fashion Pak, 1968, NRFP......$95.00
Francie, Striped Types, #1243, 1970, NRFP....................$75.00
Francie, Summer Number, #3454, 1971-72 & 1974, MIP .$175.00
Francie, Sweet 'N Swinging, #1283, complete, NM, D2 .$300.00
Francie, Totally Terrific, #3280, 1972, MIP $225.00
Francie, Two for the Ball, #1232, MOC, D2 ....$225.00
Francie, Wedding Whirl, #1244, 1970-71 & 1974, complete, M.$275.00
Francie, Zig-Zag Zoom, #3445, 1971, NRFP $125.00
Francie & Casey, Cool It! Fashion Pak, 1968, MIP $50.00
Francie & Casey, Corduroy Cape, #1764, 1970-71, MIB..$150.00
Francie & Casey, Culotte-Wot?, #1214, 1968-69, MIB..$300.00
Francie & Casey, Floating In, #1207, 1968-69, MIB $200.00

Francie & Casey, Snooze News, #1226, 1969, complete, M ..$150.00
Francie & Casey, Somethin' Else, #1219, 1969-70, complete, M $150.00
Francie & Casey, Tennis Time, #1221, 1969-70, MIP $150.00
Francie & Casey, Tenterrific, #1211, 1968-69, complete, M...$250.00
Francie & Casey, Victorian Wedding, #1233, 1969-70, MIB..$300.00
Jazzie, Mini Dress, #3781 or #3783, 1989, NRFP, ea $10.00
Julia, Brrr-Furrr, #1752, 1969, NRFP..............................$175.00
Kelly, #24310, 1999, NRFP...$5.00
Ken, Army & Air Force, #797, 1963, NRFP.................$145.00
Ken, Baseball, #9168, 1976, NRFP................................$70.00
Ken, Casual Suit, #9167, 1976, NRFB $70.00
Ken, City Sophisticate, #2801, 1979, NRFP.................$15.00
Ken, Date With Barbie, #5824, 1983, NRFP $10.00
Ken, Evening Elegance, #1415, 1980, NRFP $15.00
Ken, Fun at McDonalds, #4276, 1983, NRFP $15.00
Ken, Fun on Ice, #791, 1963, NRFP $125.00
Ken, Get-Ups 'N Go Doctor, #7705, 1973, MIP..............$75.00
Ken, Going Bowling, #1403, 1964, NRFP $85.00
Ken, Groom, #9596, 1976, NRFP $15.00
Ken, Gym Shorts (bl) & Hooded Jacket, #2795, 1979, NRFP .$60.00
Ken, Hiking Holiday, #1412, 1965, NRFP.....................$260.00
Ken, Jazz Concert, #1420, 1966, NRFP..........................$300.00
Ken, King Arthur, #773, NRFP, D2.................................$400.00
Ken, Midnight Blues, #1719, 1972, NRFP.....................$115.00
Ken, Mr Astronaut, #1415, 1965, NRFP $725.00
Ken, Night Scene, #1496, 1971, NRFP $100.00
Ken, Outdoor Man, #1406, 1980, NRFP $15.00
Ken, Pepsi Outfit, #7761, 1974, NRFP..........................$40.00
Ken, Rain or Shine, #4999, 1984, NRFP........................$10.00
Ken, Running Start, #1404, 1981, NRFP........................$10.00
Ken, Safari, #7706, 1973, NRFP....................................$70.00
Ken, Sea Scene, #1449, 1971, NRFP $60.00

Ken, Shore Lines, #1435, 1970, complete, M, $200.00.

Ken, Ski Champion, #798, 1963, NRFP $100.00
Ken, Special Date, #1401, complete, NM, D2 ....$85.00
Ken, Summer Job, #1422, 1966, NRFP..........................$450.00
Ken, Town Turtle, #1430, 1969-70, complete, M $200.00
Ken, United Airlines Pilot Uniform, #7707, 1973, NRFP .$100.00
Ken, Western Winner, #3378, 1972, NRFP......................$60.00
Ken, White Is Right Fashion Pak, 1964, NRFP $40.00
Ken, Wide Awake Stripes, #3378, 1972, NRFP $60.00
Ken, Yachtsman, #789, complete, NM, D2....................$225.00

Ken & Brad, Sun Fun Fashion Pak, 1971, MIP..............$75.00
Ken & Brad, Way Out West, #1720, 1972, MIP...........$175.00
Midge, Orange Blossom, #987, 1962, NRFP $75.00

Ricky, Saturday Show, #1502, 1965, NRFB, $90.00. (Photo courtesy McMasters Doll Auctions)

Skipper, All Over Felt, #3476, NRFP, D2 ....$150.00
Skipper, Bandanna Print, #9023, 1975, NRFP $36.00
Skipper, Budding Beauty, #1731, 1970, NRFP $70.00
Skipper, Confetti Cutie, #1952, 1968, NRFP $250.00
Skipper, Dressed in Velvet, #3477, 1971, NRFP............$125.00
Skipper, Funtime #1920, 1965, NRFP...........................$140.00
Skipper, Get-Ups 'N Go Flower Girl, #7847, 1974-76, MIP .$100.00
Skipper, Goin' Sleddin', #3475, 1971, NRFP...................$75.00
Skipper, Hearts 'N Flowers, #1945, 1967, NRFB $300.00
Skipper, Ice Cream 'N Cake, #1970, 1969-70, MIB $200.00
Skipper, Ice Skatin', #3470, 1971-72, MIB $150.00
Skipper, Jeepers Creepers, #1966, 1969, NRFP $125.00
Skipper, Little Miss Midi, #3468, 1971, NRFP $70.00
Skipper, Nifty Knickers, #3291, 1972, NRFP.................$85.00
Skipper, Popover, #1943, 1967, NRFP $175.00
Skipper, Posie Party, #1955, 1965, complete, M $200.00

Skipper, Quick Change, #1962, 1968, NRFB, $200.00. (Photo courtesy Sarah Sink Eames)

Skipper, Real Sporty, #1961, 1968, NRFP......................$200.00
Skipper, Rik Rak Rah, #1733, 1970, complete, M..........$150.00
Skipper, Rolla-Scoot, #1940, 1967, NRFP.....................$180.00
Skipper, School's Cool, #1976, 1969-70, MIB $200.00
Skipper, Shoe Parade Fashion Pak, 1965, NRFP...........$45.00
Skipper, Skating Fun, #1908, NRFB, D2 ....$175.00
Skipper, Skimmy Stripes, #1956, 1968, MIP.................$200.00
Skipper, Summer Slacks Fashion Pak, 1970, MIP.........$75.00
Skipper, Sunny Brights, #1408, 1980, NRFP $10.00

Skipper, Tea Party, #1924, 1966, NRFP $250.00
Skipper, Teeter Timers, #3467, 1971-72, complete, M ...$175.00
Skipper, Trim Twosome, #1960, 1968, complete, M $200.00
Skipper, Velvet Blush, #1737, 1970, NRFP.......................$85.00
Skipper & Fluff, Fun Runners, #3372, 1972, MIP............$50.00
Skipper & Fluff, Slumber Party Fashion Pak, 1971, MIP..$65.00
Skipper & Fluff, Some Shoes Fashion Pak, 1971, MOC...$65.00
Skipper & Fluff, Sporty Shorty Fashion Pak, 1971, MOC.$65.00
Skipper & Fluff, Super Snoozers, #3371, 1972, NRFB......$55.00
Stacey, Stripes Are Happening, #1544, 1968, NRFP........$75.00
Tutti, Birthday Beauties, #3617, 1968, NRFP................$160.00
Tutti, Clowning Around, #3606, 1967, NRFP...............$195.00
Tutti & Chris, Sea-Shore Shorties, #3614, 1968-69, complete,
    M..$125.00
Twiggy, Twiggy Turnouts, #1726, 1968, NRFP...............$250.00

Tutti, Pink PJs, #3616, 1968 – 69, complete, M, $125.00. (Photo courtesy Sarah Sink Eames)

FURNITURE, ROOMS, HOUSES, AND SHOPS

Action Sewing Center, 1972, MIB....................................$50.00
Barbie & Ken Little Theatre, 1964, complete, NMIB....$600.00
Barbie & Skipper Deluxe Dream House, Sears Exclusive, 1965,
    MIB, minimum value $175.00
Barbie & Skipper School, 1965, rare, MIB $500.00
Barbie & the Beat Dance Cafe, 1990, MIB.....................$35.00
Barbie & the Rockers Dance Cafe, 1987, MIB $50.00
Barbie & the Rockers Hot Rockin' Stage, 1987, MIB $40.00
Barbie Baby-Sitting Room, Canada, MIB.....................$100.00
Barbie Beauty Boutique, 1976, MIB $40.00
Barbie Cafe, JC Penney Exclusive, 1993, MIB.................$45.00
Barbie Cafe Today, 1971, MIB.......................................$400.00
Barbie Cookin' Fun Kitchen, MIB $50.00
Barbie Deluxe Family House, 1966, complete, VG, D2..$135.00
Barbie Dream Armoire, 1980, NRFB $35.00
Barbie Dream Bath Chest & Commode, 1980, lt pk, MIB .$25.00
Barbie Dream Bed & Nightstand, 1984, pk, MIB $25.00
Barbie Dream Dining Center, 1984, MIB.........................$25.00
Barbie Dream Glow Vanity, 1986, MIB............................$20.00
Barbie Dream House, 1961, 1st edition, complete, NM, D2 .$150.00
Barbie Dream House Bedroom, 1981, MIB $6.00
Barbie Dream House Kitchen Set, 1981, MIB....................$6.00
Barbie Dream Luxury Bathtub, 1984, pk, MIB.................$20.00
Barbie Dream Store Makeup Department, 1983, MIB......$40.00
Barbie Fashion Salon, Sears Exclusive, 1964, MIB........$225.00
Barbie Fashion Wraps Boutique, 1989, MIB $35.00

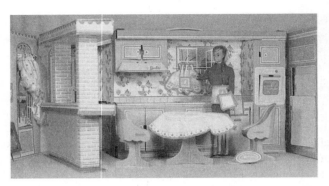

Barbie Dream Kitchen-Dinette #4095, 1964, MIB, $600.00. (Photo courtesy Paris and Susan Manos)

Barbie Glamour Home, 1985, MIB $125.00
Barbie Lively Livin' Room, MIB....................................$50.00
Barbie Mountain Ski Cabin, Sears Exclusive, MIB..........$50.00
Barbie Playhouse Pavilion, Europe, MIB.........................$75.00
Barbie Teen Dream Bedroom, MIB $50.00
Barbie Unique Boutique, Sears Exclusive, 1971, MIB $185.00
Barbie Vanity & Shower, Sears Exclusive, 1975, MIB......$50.00
Barbie's Apartment, 1975, MIB.....................................$140.00

Barbie's Room-fulls Country Kitchen, #7404, 1974, NRFP, $100.00. (Photo courtesy McMasters Doll Auctions)

Barbie's Room-fulls Firelight Living Room, 1974, MIB..$100.00
California Dream Barbie Hot Dog Stand, 1988, NRFB $50.00
Cool Tops Skipper T-Shirt Shop, 1989, complete, MIB ...$25.00
Francie & Casey Housemates, 1966, complete, NM, D2.$200.00
Francie House, 1966, complete, M..................................$150.00
Go-Together Chair, Ottoman & End Table, MIB..........$100.00
Go-Together Chaise Lounge, MIB $75.00
Go-Together Couch, 1964, MIB.....................................$30.00
Go-Together Dining Room, Barbie & Skipper, 1965, MIB .$50.00
Go-Together Lawn Swing & Planter, 1964, complete, MIB, D2 ..$150.00
Go-Together Living Room, Barbie & Skipper, 1965, MIB..$60.00
Ice Capades Skating Rink, 1989, MIB $70.00
Jamie's Penthouse, Sears Exclusive, 1971, MIB $475.00
Living Pretty Cooking Center, 1988, MIB $25.00
Living Pretty Refrigerator/Freezer, 1988, MIB.................$30.00
Magical Mansion, 1989, MIB.......................................$125.00
Movietime Prop Shop, 1989, MIB..................................$50.00

Party Garden Playhouse, 1994, MIB $275.00
Pink Sparkles Armoire, 1990, NRFB......................$25.00

Pink Sparkles, Refrigerator/Freezer #4776, 1988, NRFB, $30.00. (Photo courtesy McMasters Doll Auctions)

Pink Sparkles Starlight Bed, 1990, MIB...........................$30.00
Skipper Dream Room, 1964, MIB $300.00
Skipper's Deluxe Dream House, Sears Exclusive, 1966, MIB..$500.00
Superstar Barbie Beauty Salon, 1977, MIB $55.00
Superstar Barbie Photo Studio, Sears Exclusive, 1977, MIB .$45.00
Surprise House, 1972, MIB..$100.00

Susy Goose: Four Poster Bed Outfit, M, $35.00; Wardrobe, EX, $35.00; Vanity and Bench with Throw Rug, M, $35.00. (Photo courtesy Paris and Susan Manos)

Susy Goose Barbie & Midge Queen Size Chifforobe, NM $100.00
Susy Goose Canopy Bed, 1962, MIB..............................$150.00
Susy Goose Chifforobe, 1964, MIB $275.00
Susy Goose Ken Wardrobe, M...$50.00
Susy Goose Mod-A-Go-Go Bedroom, 1966, NRFB....$2,300.00
Susy Goose Queen Size Bed, Sears Exclusive, 1963, NRFB .$200.00
Susy Goose Skipper's Jeweled Bed, 1965, MIB $150.00
Susy Goose Skipper's Jeweled Vanity, Sears Exclusive, 1965, NRFB..$200.00
Town & Country Market, 1971, MIB $135.00
Tutti Playhouse, 1966, M...$100.00
Workout Center, 1985, MIB...$30.00
World of Barbie House, 1966, MIB $175.00

GIFT SETS

Army Barbie & Ken, 1993, Stars 'N Stripes, MIB $60.00

Ballerina Barbie on Tour, 1976, MIB $175.00
Barbie & Her Horse Dancer, Canada, MIB......................$75.00
Barbie & Ken Campin' Out, 1983, MIB $75.00
Barbie Beautiful Blues, Sears Exclusive, 1967, MIB $3,000.00

Barbie Dance Club Doll and Tape Player Set, #4217, 1989, MIB, $75.00. (Photo courtesy Margo Rana)

Barbie Loves Elvis, 1996, NRFB, D2 ....$75.00
Barbie Snap 'N Play Deluxe Gift Set, JC Penney Exclusive, 1992, MIB...$40.00
Barbie Travel in Style, Sears Exclusive, 1968, MIB.....$1,500.00
Barbie's Olympic Ski Village, MIB $75.00
Barbie's 'Round the Clock Gift Set, 1964, MIB..............$700.00
Barbie's Sparkling Pink Gift Set, 1963, MIB...................$600.00
Barbie's Wedding Party, 1964, MIB $700.00
Beauty Secrets Barbie Pretty Reflections, 1980, NRFB ..$100.00
Birthday Fun at McDonald's, 1994, NRFB.......................$75.00
Bright & Breezy Skipper, Sears Exclusive, 1969, NRFB .$975.00

Cinderella, 1992, NRFP, $125.00. (Photo courtesy Margo Rana)

Dance Magic Barbie & Ken, 1990, NRFB.........................$50.00
Dance Sensation Barbie, 1985, MIB $35.00
Dolls of the World II, 1995, NRFB $100.00
Dramatic New Living Skipper Very Best Velvet, Sears Exclusive, 1970-71, NRFB $1,500.00
Francie & Her Swingin' Separates, Sears Exclusive, 1966, MIB...$600.00
Golden Dreams Glamorous Nights, 1980, NRFB $100.00
Golden Groove Barbie, Sears Exclusive, 1969, NRFB .$2,000.00
Halloween Party Barbie & Ken, Target, 1998, NRFB, D2 .$65.00
Happy Birthday Barbie, 1985, NRFB $50.00
Happy Meal Stacey & Whitney, JC Penney Exclusive, 1994, MIB...$30.00

Hollywood Hair Barbie, #10928, 1993, MIB, $35.00. (Photo courtesy Margo Rana)

Ken Red, White & Wild, Sears Exclusive, 1970, NRFB..$525.00
Live Action PJ Fashion 'N Motion, Sears Exclusive, 1971-72, NRFB..$1,500.00
Living Barbie Action Accents, Sears Exclusive, 1970, MIB.$450.00
Loving You Barbie, 1984, MIB $75.00
Malibu Barbie Beach Party, M (M case)...........................$75.00
Malibu Barbie Fashion Combo, 1978, NRFB...................$80.00
Malibu Ken Surf's Up, Sears Exclusive, 1971, MIB $350.00
New Talking Barbie Dinner Dazzle Set, Sears Exclusive, 1968, MIB...$1,500.00
Night Night Sleep Tight Tutti, NRFB, D2....................$300.00

On Parade With Barbie, Ken, and Midge, #1014, 1964, MIB, $650.00. (Photo courtesy McMasters Doll Auctions)

Pretty Pairs Nan 'N Fran, 1970, NRFB $250.00
Skipper Bright 'N Breezy, Sears Exclusive, 1969, MIB...$2,000.00
Skipper Party Time, 1964, NRFB..................................$500.00
Stacey & Butterfly Pony, 1993, NRFB $30.00
Stacey Nite Lighting, Sears Exclusive, 1969, NRFB ...$2,000.00
Stacey Stripes Are Happening, Sears Exclusive, 1968, MIB.$1,500.00
Sun Sensation Barbie Spray & Play Fun, Wholesale Clubs, 1992, MIB $60.00
Superstar Barbie & Ken, 1978, MIB...............................$175.00
Superstar Barbie Fashion Change-Abouts, 1978, NRFB ..$95.00
Superstar Barbie in the Spotlight, 1977, MIB.................$125.00
Talking Barbie Golden Groove Set, Sears Exclusive, 1969, MIB $1,500.00

Talking Barbie Mad About Plaid, Sears Exclusive, 1970, NRFB...$1,200.00
Talking Barbie Perfectly Plaid, Sears Exclusive, 1971, MIB...$500.00
Travelin' Sisters, 1995, NRFB......................................$70.00
Tutti & Todd Sundae Treat, 1966, NRFB $500.00
Walking Jamie Strollin' in Style, NRFB $450.00
Wedding Party Midge, 1990, NRFB...............................$150.00

VEHICLES

Allan's Roadster, 1964, aqua, MIB $500.00
ATC Cycle, Sears Exclusive, 1972, MIB $65.00
Austin Healy, Irwin, 1962, red & wht, very rare, NRFB, D2 .$3,500.00
Barbie & Ken Dune Buggy, Irwin, 1970, pk, MIB...........$250.00
Barbie & the Rockers Hot Rockin' Van, 1987, MIB.........$60.00
Barbie Silver 'Vette, MIB...$30.00

Barbie's Own Sports Car, NMIB, A, $150.00. (Photo courtesy McMasters Doll Auctions)

Barbie Travelin' Trailer, MIB.......................................$40.00
Beach Buggy for Skipper, Irwin, 1964, rare, MIB, minimum value...$500.00
Beach Bus, 1974, MIB..$45.00
California Dream Beach Taxi, 1988, MIB $35.00
Ken's Classy Corvette, 1976, yel, MIB $75.00
Ken's Dream 'Vette, 1981, dk bl, MIB...........................$100.00
Ken's Hot Rod, Sears Exclusive, 1964, red, MIB $900.00
Snowmobile, Montgomery Ward, 1972, MIB $65.00
Sports Plane, Sears Exclusive, 1964, MIB.....................$3,600.00
Star 'Vette, 1977, red, MIB...$100.00
Starlight Motorhome, 1994, MIB.................................$45.00
Sunsailer, 1975, NRFB, D2...$55.00
Western Star Traveler Motorhome, 1982, MIB $50.00
1957 Belair Chevy, 1989, 1st edition, aqua, MIB $150.00
1957 Belair Chevy, 1990, 2nd edition, pk, MIB $125.00

MISCELLANEOUS

Ballerina Dress-Ups, Colorforms, 1977, complete, EXIB..$15.00
Barbie & Ken Sew Magic Add-Ons, 1973-74, complete, MIB .$55.00
Barbie & the Rockers, purse, vinyl, w/comb & cologne, M .$15.00
Barbie Beauty Kit, 1961, complete, M $125.00
Barbie Cutlery Set, Sears Exclusive, 1962, MIP............$50.00
Barbie Electric Drawing Set, 1970, complete, MIB $75.00
Barbie Electronic Drawing Set, Sears Exclusive, 1963, MIB..$200.00
Barbie Ge-Tar, 1965, M $325.00
Barbie Make-Up Case, 1963, NM $25.00

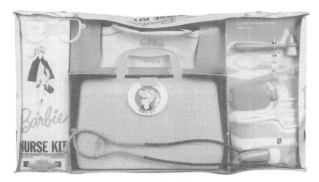

Barbie Nurse Kit, #1694, 1962, complete, NMIB, A, $400.00. (Photo courtesy McMasters Doll Auction)

Barbie Pretty-Up Time Perfume Pretty Bath, 1964, complete, M $150.00
Barbie Queen of the Prom Game, Mattel, 1960, complete, NMIB $50.00
Barbie Sew Magic Fashion Set, 1973-75, complete, MIB .$100.00
Barbie Shrinky Dinks, 1979, MIB $30.00
Barbie Snaps 'N Scraps Scrapbook, several color variations, rare, ea from $200 to...$250.00
Barbie Young Travelers Play Kit, Sears Exclusive, 1964, MIB ...$75.00
Book, Barbie's Fashion Success, Random House, 1962, hardcover, w/dust jacket, NM, D2 ....$50.00
Book, Target's 30th Anniversary Barbie Keep Sake, 1989, hardcover, EX $20.00
Booklet, World of Barbie Fashion, 1968, M, D2 ....$10.00
Christie Quick Curl Beauty Center, Sears Exclusive, 1982, MIB .$35.00
Collector's Club Kit, 1999, M...$40.00
Coloring Book, Barbie & Ken, 1963, unused, NM $50.00

Diary, 1962, black vinyl with metal clasp and key, VG, A, $95.00. (Photo courtesy McMasters Doll Auctions)

Embroidery Set, Barbie & Ken, 1962, complete, rare, NMIB, D2..$150.00
Fashion Designer Set, Mattel, 1969, NM (EX+ box) $50.00
Game, Barbie Queen of the Prom, Mattel, 1962, MIB $80.00
Game, Barbie 35th Anniversary, Golden, 1994, MIB.......$60.00
Game, Barbie's Keys to Fame, Mattel, 1963, NMIB..........$40.00
Ornament, Holiday Barbie, Hallmark, 1993, 1st edition, MIB.$75.00
Paper Dolls, Angel Face Barbie, Golden #1982-45, 1983, uncut, M $20.00
Paper Dolls, Ballerina Barbie, Whitman #1993-1, 1977, uncut, M $30.00

Paper Dolls, Barbie, Whitman #4601, 1963, uncut, M $85.00
Paper Dolls, Barbie & Skipper Campsite at Lucky Lake, Whitman #1836-31, 1980, M, uncut $25.00
Paper Dolls, Barbie Country Camper, Whitman #1990, 1973, uncut, M..$30.00

Paper Dolls, Midge Cut-Outs, Whitman #1962, 1963, uncut, NM, A, $150.00. (Photo courtesy McMasters Doll Auctions)

Picture Maker Designer Fashion Set, Mattel, 1969, NMIB.$40.00
Puzzle, jigsaw; Barbie & Ken, Whitman, 1963, 100 pcs, MIB..$40.00
Puzzle, jigsaw; Nostalgic Barbie, American Publishing, 1989, 550 pcs, MIB $25.00
Puzzle, jigsaw; Skipper & Skooter, 1965, 100 pcs, MIB $30.00
Quick Curl Miss America Beauty Center, Sears Exclusive, 1975, MIB $75.00

Record Tote, 1961, black vinyl with black plastic handles, VG, A, $55.00. (Photo courtesy McMasters Auctions)

Sweet Sixteen Promotional Set, 1974, M $70.00
Tea Set, Barbie, Chilton Globe, 1989, china, 16 pcs, NRFB $30.00
Tea Set, Barbie, Sears Exclusive, 1962, 42 pcs, MIB.......$200.00
Tea Set, Barbie 25th Anniversary, 1984, complete, M ...$150.00
Umbrella, Barbie, 1962, several variations, EX, ea $65.00
Wagon, Camp Barbie, 1995, 34", EX...............................$50.00
Wristwatch, Barbie & Ken, Bradley, 1963, MIB $200.00
Wristwatch, Swirl Ponytail Barbie, 1964, bl or yel band, MIB, ea $400.00
Wristwatch, 30th Anniversary, 1989, MIB $80.00
Yo-yo, Spectra Star, plastic w/paper sticker, MIP $5.00

Battery-Operated Toys

From the standpoint of being visually entertaining, nothing can compare with the battery-operated toy. Most (probably as much as 95%) were made in Japan from the '40s through the '60s, though some were distributed by American companies — Marx, Ideal, and Daisy, for instance — who often sold them under their own names. So even if they're marked, sometimes it's just about impossible to identify the actual manufacturer. Though batteries had been used to power trains and provide simple illumination in earlier toys, the Japanese toys could smoke, walk, talk, drink, play instruments, blow soap bubbles, and do just about anything else humanly possible to dream up and engineer. Generally, the more antics the toy performs, the more collectible it is. Rarity is important as well, but first and foremost to consider is condition. Because of their complex mechanisms, many will no longer work. Children often stopped them in mid-cycle, rubber hoses and bellows aged and cracked, and leaking batteries caused them to corrode, so very few have survived to the present intact and in good enough condition to interest a collector. Though it's sometimes possible to have them repaired, unless you can buy them cheap enough to allow for the extra expense involved, it is probably better to wait on a better example. Original boxes are a definite plus in assessing the value of a battery-op and can sometimes be counted on to add from 30% to 50% (and up), depending on the box's condition, of course, as well as the toy's age and rarity.

We have made every attempt to list these toys by the name as it appears on the original box. Some will sound very similar. Many toys were reissued with only minor changes and subsequently renamed. The number in parenthesis in the line represents the number of actions the toy can perform. For more information we recommend *Collecting Toys* by Richard O'Brien (Books Americana) and *Collecting Battery Toys* by Don Hultzman (Collector Books).

Advisor: Tom Lastrapes (L4)

See also Aeronautical; Automobiles and Other Vehicle Replicas; Boats; Marx; Robots and Space Toys.

Accordion Bear, MST (Flare Toy), 1950s (6), 9", rare, M, L4...**$975.00**
Accordion Player Hobo w/Monkey, Alps, 1950s (6), NMIB, L4 ..**$450.00**

Antique Fire Car, TN, 1950s, six actions, 10", EXIB, $350.00. (Photo courtesy Don Hultzman)

Acro-Chimp Porter, YM, 1960s, 9", NMIB......................**$100.00**
Animated Squirrel, S&E, 1950s (8), 9", MIB, L4...........**$225.00**
Antenna-Car, TN, 1960s (4), 15", EXIB, A **$225.00**
Anti-Aircraft Jeep, K, 1950s (5), 10", NMIB, A **$150.00**
Arctic Sled Explorer, rare, MIB, L4 ....**$1,075.00**
Armored Knights Contest Set, Bandai, 1950s (6), 8", MIB, L4...**$700.00**
Astro Racer, Daiya, 1960s (4), 12", NMIB, A **$975.00**
Atom Motorcycle Racer, see Expert Motor Cyclist
Automatic Toll Gate, Sears, 1955 (6), MIB, L4 ....**$375.00**
Avenue Coach Bus, Yonezawa, 16", VGIB, A **$165.00**
B-Z Rabbit, MT, 1950s, 7" L, NMIB **$125.00**
Baby Bertha the Watering Elephant, Mego, 1960s (3), 10", MIB, L4 ....**$575.00**
Baby TV With Music, rare, MIB, L4..........................**$1,075.00**
Barber Bear, TN/Linemar, 1950s (5), 10", MIB, L4 ....**$675.00**
Barber Bear, TN/Linemar, 1950s (5), 10", VGIB, L4......**$400.00**
Barney's Auto Factory, Remco, 1964, unused, NMIB.....**$300.00**
Batmobile, ASC, 1966, 1st issue (3), 9", NM **$300.00**
Batmobile, ASC, 1972, 2nd issue (3), 12", NMIB..........**$600.00**
Batmobile (Fire-Lighted Engine), ASC, 1970s (3), 11", NMIB.**$750.00**
Big Ring Circus Truck (Circus Parade), MT, 1950s (3), 13", NM, A **$175.00**
Bimbo the Drumming Clown, Alps, 1950s (3), 9", MIB, L4 ..**$575.00**
Bingo Clown, TN, 1950s (3), 13", NM, L4 ....**$475.00**
Blacksmith Bear, A-1, 1950s (6), 10", NMIB, A **$245.00**
Blinky the Clown, Amico, 1950s (5), 11", MIB, L4.......**$575.00**
Broadway Trolley #10430, MT, 1950s (4), 11" L...............**$75.00**

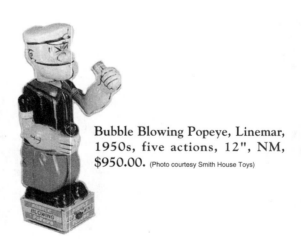

Bubble Blowing Popeye, Linemar, 1950s, five actions, 12", NM, $950.00. (Photo courtesy Smith House Toys)

Bubble Blowing Washing Bear, Y, 1950s (3), 8", MIB, L4....**$475.00**
Bubbling Bull, Linemar, 1950 (5), 8", MIB...................**$350.00**
Busy Secretary, Linemar, 1950s (7), 8x7", M **$200.00**
Cable Car, Alps, 1950s, 7x6", EXIB **$125.00**
Calypso Joe, Linemar, 1950s (4), 10", EX+ **$350.00**
Candy Vending Machine Bank, W Toy Co, 1950s (3), 9", MIB, L4...**$1,450.00**
Cappy the Happy Baggage Porter, Alps, 1960s (4), 12", MIB, L4...**$275.00**
Captain Hook, Marusan, 1950s (3), 11", rare, EX, L4, minimum value...**$750.00**
Captain Kidd Pirate Ship, Yonezawa, 1960s (4), 13", rare, EX, L4...**$200.00**
Captain Kidd Pirate Ship, Yonezawa, 1960s (4), 13", rare, MIB, L4...**$275.00**

Charlie the Funny Clown, Alps, 1960s (3), 9", NMIB, L4 ..$275.00
Chippy the Chipmunk, Alps, 1950s (4), 12", MIB, L4...$125.00
Circus Clown Car Galaxie 500, Rico, 19", EX, L4 ....$650.00
Circus Parade, see Big Ring Circus Truck
Circus Queen (Seal), Kosuge, 1950s (4), 11", rare, MIB, L4...$375.00
Clown the Magician, Alps, 1950s (6), 12", MIB, L4 ......$375.00
Clucking Clara, CK, 1950s (4), NM..................................$130.00
College Jalopy, Linemar, 10", NMIB.................................$375.00
Collie, Alps, 1950s (5), 9", M..$25.00
Coney Island Rocket Ride, Remco, 1950s (4), 14", EXIB, A..$1,100.00
Cragstan Crap Shooting Monkey, Alps, 1950s (3), 9", MIB,
   L4 ....$125.00
Cragstan One-Arm Bandit, Y, 1960s (3), 6", MIB, L4 ...$225.00
Cragstan Playboy, 1960s (5), 13", NMIB, L4, from $225 to...$275.00
Cragstan Rolling Honey Bear, Y, 1950s, 8", NM $125.00
Cragstan Roulette Gambling Man, Y, 1960s (5), 9", NM..$225.00
Cragstan Telly Bear, S&E, 1950s (6), 8", MIB................$475.00
Cragstan Telly Bear, S&E, 1950s (6), 8", NM.................$300.00
Cragstan Tugboat, San, 1950s (3), 13", NM $125.00
Cute Puddle, Y, 1950s (6), 8", M $25.00
Cycling Daddy, Bandai, 1960s (4), 10", NM...................$100.00
Daisy the Jolly Drumming Duck (Cragstan Melody Band), Alps,
   1950s (7), 9", MIB, L4..$275.00
Dalmatian One-Man Band, Alps, 1950s (6), 9", NM.....$125.00
Dancing Merry Chimp, Kuramochi, 1960s (5), 11", NM ..$150.00
Dandy Turtle, DSK, 1950s (4), 8", M................................$150.00
Dennis the Menace Xylophone Player, Rosko, 1950s, 9", MIB,
   L4...$325.00
Dentist Bear, S&E, 1950s, 9" (7), EXIB, A $350.00
Desert Jeep Patrol, MT, 1960s (4), 11", NM...................$125.00
Dilly Dalmatian, Cragstan, 1950s (5), 10", EX $130.00
Dip-ie the Whale, SH, 1960s (3), 13", M $275.00
Disney Acrobats (Donald Duck, Mickey Mouse or Pluto), Line-
   mar, 1950s (4), 11" L, MIB, L4, ea minimum value...$875.00
Disney Fire Engine, Linemar, 1950s (4), 11", VG...........$450.00
Donald Duck Locomotive, MT, 1970 (6), 9", M, L4 .....$225.00
Doxie the Dog, Linemar, 1950s (5), 9", M $75.00
Dozo the Steaming Clown, Rosko, 1960s (5), 10", MIB, L4...$375.00
Dream Car, Linemar, 12", nonworking o/w EX, A..........$360.00
Drinker's Savings Bank, Illfelder, 1960s, 9", MIB, L4 .....$150.00
Drinking Dog, Y, 1950s (4), 7", MIB.................................$225.00
Drinking Licking Cat, TN, 1950s (6), 10", MIB..............$275.00
Drumming Bear, Alps, 1960s (4), 12", MIB, L4, from $100 to..$125.00
Drumming Indian, Bandai, 1950s (5), 10", M $75.00

Drumming Mickey Mouse, Linemar, 1950s, four actions, 10", NMIB, $975.00.

(Photo courtesy New England Auction Gallery)

Drumming Mickey Mouse, Linemar, 1950s (4), 10", nonworking
   o/w EXIB..$575.00
Ducky Duckling, Alps, 1960s (4), 8", M $75.00
Dune Buggy, Bandai, 1970s (3), 10", M $75.00
Electric Chair, Poynter Products, 1950s, 7", MIB...........$250.00
Electric Lucky Car (Renault), MT, 1950s (3), 7", EXIB, A..$225.00
Electric School Bus, MT, 1950s, 10", MIB......................$175.00
Electric School Bus, MT, 1950s, 10", NM......................$100.00
Electricmobile (Buick Model), M, 8", EXIB $200.00
Electro Hydro Car, Schuco #5720, 10", EX+, A.............$990.00
Electro Manic 7500 Porsche Roadster, Distler, 10", NMIB, A..$550.00

Electro Toy Racer #21, Yonezawa, 10", EXIB, $875.00. (Photo courtesy Bertoia Auctions)

Electro Toy Sand Loader, TN, 1950s (4), 11", MIB, L4...$225.00
Expert Motor Cyclist, MT, 1950s (5), 12", EX, A...........$475.00
Fairyland Loco, Daiya, 1950s (4), 9", MIB......................$150.00
Farm Truck, Alps, 1960s (3), 11", MIB $325.00
Farm Truck (John's Farm), TN, 1950s (5), 9", MIB........$350.00
FBI Godfather Car, Bandai, 1970s (3), 10", MIB............$125.00
Feeding Bird Watcher, Linemar, 1950s (5), 9", EX.........$250.00
Ferrari Gear Shift Car, Bandai (4), 11", EXIB, A $260.00
Fido the Xylophone Player, Alps, 1950s (6), 9", MIB, L4 ...$375.00
Fighter (Airplane), KO, 1960s (6), 11" L, MIB $375.00
Fighting Bull, Alps, 1960s (5), 10", MIB $175.00
Fire Boat, MT, 1950s (5), 15", MIB.................................$350.00
Firebird Racer #3, Tomiyama, 1950s, 14", EXIB, A $250.00
Fishing Bear (Forest, Panda or Polar), Alps, 1950s (6), 10", MIB,
   L4 ....$325.00
Fishing Bears (Savings Bank), Wonderful Toy Co, 1950s (6),
   10", M, minimum value $1,200.00
Flexie the Pocket Monkey, Alps, 1960s (3), 12", MIB ...$200.00
Flintstone Yacht, Remco, 1960s, 17", NM $225.00
Flippy the Only Roller Skating Monkey That Skis, Alps, 1950s
   (3), 12", rare, MIB, L4, from $550 to $650.00
Flying Circus, Tomiyama, 1960s (3), 17", rare, MIB, L4...$1,075.00
Flying Dutchman, Remco, 1960s (5), 25" L, MIB $250.00
Ford GT, Bandai, 11", NMIB, A $110.00
Ford Gyron, Ichida, 1960s (3), 11", MIB, L4 ....$600.00
Fordson Industrial Tractor, MIB, L4 ....$400.00
Frankenstein, Poynter Products, 1970s (5), 12", EX.......$100.00
Frankenstein (Name on Base), TN, 1960s, 13", G, A $75.00
Frankie the Roller Skating Monkey, Alps, 1950s (3), 12", MIB,
   L4 ....$250.00
Fred Flintstone's Bedrock Band, Alps, 1962 (4), 10", NM, L4..$350.00

French Cat, Alps, 1950s (5), 10" L, MIB $125.00
Friendly Jocko, Alps, 1950s (5), 8", MIB $275.00
Funland Cup Ride, Sonsco, 1960s, 6", MIB, L4 ....$375.00
Future Fire Car, TN, 1950s (5), 9", VG $225.00
Galloping Cowboy Savings Bank, Y (Cragstan), 1950s, 8x7", MIB, L4 ....$1,275.00
Giant Construction Site, Technofix, #315, NMIB, A $240.00
Girl in Swing, Linemar, 1950s, 9", MIB $400.00
GM Coach Bus (GMC 3113), Y, 16", EX, A $150.00
Godzilla, Bullmark, 1960a (5), 11", MIB $650.00
Godzilla Monster, Marusan, 1970s (3), 12", M $450.00
Gomora Monster, Bullmark, 1960s (4), 8", M $350.00
Gorilla w/Smoking Pipe, NGT (3), remote control, 7", MIB ..$750.00
Grandpa Bear (Rocking Chair), Alps, 1950s (5), 9", NMIB, A ..$150.00
Grasshopper, MT, 1950s (5), 6", M $350.00
Green Caterpillar, Daiya, 1950s (3), 20" L, MIB $350.00
Green Hornet Secret Service Car, ASC, 1960s, 11", EX+..$700.00
Greyhound Bus w/Headlights, Linemar, 1950s (3), 10", MIB..$250.00
Greyhound Scenicruiser (Sonar Guided), Bell Products, plastic, 21", nonworking o/w EXIB, A..................................$220.00
Growling Tiger Trophy Plaque, Cragstan, 1950s (3), 10", EX, L4, from $150 to $200.00
Gypsy Fortune Teller, Ichida, 1950s (5), 12x6x7", M, minimum value $1,800.00
Hamburger Chef, K, 1960s (3), 8", MIB $250.00
Handy-Hank Mystery Tractor, TN, 1950s (4), 9" L, NM....$125.00
Happy 'N Sad Magic Face Clown, Yonezawa, 1960s (5), 10", EXIB...$100.00
Happy Band Trio, MT, 1970s (7), 11", MIB, L4, from $550 to...$600.00
Happy Fiddler Clown, Alps, 1950s (4), 10", MIB...........$475.00
Happy Fiddler Clown, Alps, 1950s (4), 10", NM $275.00
Happy Naughty Chimp, Daishin, 1960s (4), 10", M.........$50.00
Happy Santa, Z Co, 1950 (3), 11", MIB $250.00
Happy Singing Bird, MT, 1950s (3), 3" L, M $75.00
Happy the Clown Puppet Show, Y, 1960s 10" (3), 10", NMIB, L4 ....$500.00
Hasty Chimp, Y, 1960s (4), 9", MIB, L4, from $100 to ..$125.00
Haunted House Mystery Bank, Hong Kong, 1970s, 6", MIB.$225.00
High Jinks at the Circus, TN (6), 1950s, MIB................$375.00
Highway Patrol Car, Bandai, 1960s (5), 11", NMIB.......$175.00
Highway Patrol Motorcycle, MT, 1950s (7), 12", MIB, L4 ..$800.00
Hiller Hornet Helicopter, Alps, 1950s (4), 12" L, MIB..$300.00
Home Washing Machine, Y, 1950s, 6", MIB $100.00
Honda Big Rider Motorbike #34, TPS, 1960s-70s, 10", NMIB...$125.00

Hoop Zing Girl, Linemar, 1950s, minor actions, 12", MIB ..$375.00
Hooty the Happy Owl, Alps, 1960s (6), 9", MIB............$200.00
Hop Up Boat, MT, 1960s (3), 9" L, MIB, L4, from $100 to ..$125.00
Hopalong Cassidy Tiny Television, More Mfg, 1950, scarce, MIB, A...$130.00
Hot Rod 158, TN, 1950s (4), 10", EXIB......................$450.00
Hungry Baby Bear, Y, 1950s (6), 10", MIB...................$225.00
Hungry Cat, Linemar, 1960s (7), 9", MIB.....................$575.00
Hungry Hound Dog, Y, 1950s (6), 10", M.....................$400.00
Hungry Sheep, MT, 1950s (3), 9", M $250.00
Hy-Que Monkey, TN, 1960s (6), 17", MIB $475.00
Ice Cream Baby Bear, MT, 1950s (3), 10", rare, NM $475.00
Indian Signal Choo Choo, Kanto, 1960s (4), 10" L, NM ..$175.00
Indianapolis 500 Racer, Sears/TN, 1950s (7), 15", NMIB, A ..$450.00
Interceptor Target Game, S&E, 1950s (4), MIB, L4 ......$575.00
Interpol Cadillac, MIB, L4 ....$275.00
Jaguar E Type, Tomiyama, 12", EXIB, A $600.00
Jig-Saw-Magic, Z Co, 1950s, 7x5x9", MIB....................$100.00
Jocko the Drinking Monkey, Linemar, 1950s (4), 11", MIB, L4..$275.00
Jocko the Drinking Monkey, Linemar, 1950s (4), 11", VG, L4 ...$75.00
John's Farm Truck, TN, 1950s (7), 9", MIB $275.00
Johnny Speedmobile, Remco, 1960s (3), 15", MIB $350.00
Jolly Bambino, Alps, 1950s (5), 9", M $475.00
Jolly Bambino, Alps, 1950s (5), 9", MIB, L4 ....$750.00
Jolly Daddy (Smoking Elephant), Marusan, 1950s (4), 9", VG..$180.00
Jolly Drummer Chimpy, Alps, 1950s (6), 9", NM...........$180.00
Jolly Pianist, see Pianist (Beethoven...)
Jolly Popcorn Vendor, TN, 1950s (4), 8", MIB..............$375.00

Jolly Santa on Snow, Alps, 1950s, four actions, 12½", EXIB, $225.00.
(Photo courtesy Don Hultzman)

Journey Pup, S&E, 1950s (4), 8" L, M.............................$50.00
Jumbo the Roaring Elephant, Alps, 1960s (5), 10" L, MIB ...$150.00
Jungle Jumbo, B-C Toy, 1950s (6), 10", rare, M..............$650.00
Jungle Trio, Linemar, 1950s (8), 8" dia, MIB, L4............$875.00
Jungle Trio, Linemar, 1950s (8), 8" dia, nonworking o/w EX, A..$385.00
King Size Fire Engine, Bandai, 1960s (3), 13", M...........$150.00
King Zor, Ideal, 1961 (4), 26" L, very rare, M..............$1,000.00
Kissing Couple, Ichido, 1950s (5), 11", MIB $350.00
Knight in Armour Target Game, Japan, 12", EXIB, A....$350.00
Knitting Grandma, TN, 1950s (3), 9", MIB $250.00
Lady Pup Tending Her Garden, Cragstan, 1950s (5), 8", MIB, L4 ....$375.00
Leo The Growling Pet Lion w/Magic Face-Change Action, Tomiyama, 1970s (3), 9", MIB $275.00

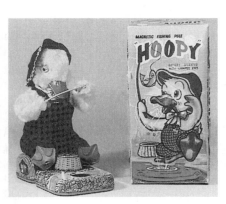

Hoopy the Fishing Duck, Alps, 1950s, seven actions, 10", MIB, $425.00. (Photo courtesy Don Hultzman)

Linemar Hauler, Linemar, 1950s (3), 14", MIB $250.00
Linemar Music Hall, Linemar, 1950s (4), 8x6", MIB $350.00
Little Indian, TN, 1960s (3), 9", rare, NM $175.00
Little Poochie in Coffee Cup, Alps, 1960s (3), 9", M.......$80.00
Lucky Cement Mixer Truck, MT, 1960s (4), 12", M $150.00
Lucky Crane, MT, 1950s (5), 9", M $700.00
M-48 Army Tank, TN, 8", MIB, A...................................$75.00
M-81 Army Tank, Masudaya, 1960s, 9", NMIB................$85.00
M-99 Army Tank, MT, 18", NMIB $150.00
Magic Action Bulldozer, TN, 1950s (3), 10", MIB, L4...$250.00
Main Street, Linemar, 1950s (3), 20", very rare, M, minimum
    value $1,200.00
Major Tooty, Alps, 1960s (3), 14", MIB, L4....................$275.00
Make-Up Bear, MT, 1960s (4), 9", very rare, NM, minimum
    value $1,300.00
Mambo the Jolly Drumming Elephant, Alps, 1950s (6), 10",
    MIB, from $300 to $350.00
Man From UNCLE Headquarters Transmitter, NMIB, L4...$375.00
Man From UNCLE Talking Patrol Car, Rico, 1960s, 19", EXIB .$350.00
Marching Bear, Alps, 1960s (5), 10", NM $200.00
Marvelous Locomotive, 1950s, TN (4), 10", M $100.00
Maxwell Coffee-Loving Bear, TN, 1960s (5), 10", MIB, L4..$300.00
McGregor, TN, 1960s (6), 12", M.................................$125.00
Melody Camping Car, Yonezawa, 1970s (3), 10", NM ...$150.00
Mercedes Convertible (Elektro Phanomenal), Schuco #5503, 9",
    MIB, A...$500.00
Mercedes C111, Schuco #5508, MIB, A.........................$150.00
Mercedes 230SL, Alps, w/driver, 10½", NMIB, A..........$110.00
Merry-Go-Round Truck, TN, 1950s (4), 11", EX, L4.....$475.00
Mickey Mouse, see also Disney Acrobats & Drumming Mickey
    Mouse
Mickey Mouse Locomotive, MT, 1960s (6), 9", NM $175.00
Mickey Mouse on Hand Car, MT, 1960s (3), 8x10", EXIB, A ...$260.00
Mickey Mouse Sand Buggy, MT, 1960s (4), 11", NM.....$350.00
Mickey Mouse Trolley, MT, 1960s (3), 11", M $175.00
Mickey the Magician, Linemar, 1960s (4), 10", rare, MIB, mini-
    mum value $2,000.00
Mischievous Monkey, MT, 1950s (6), 13", MIB, L4........$375.00
Monkee-Mobile, ASC, 1967, 12", NMIB $525.00
Monkey the Shoe Maker, TN, 1950s (3), 9", rare, NMIB...$650.00
Monorail Set, Haji, 1950s, complete, EXIB $175.00
Mother Goose, Yonezawa, MIB, L4, from $200 to $175.00
MP Jeep, TN, 1950s (6), 10", NM $100.00
Mr Al E Gator, Alps, 1950s (5), 12", rare, MIB, L4........$325.00

Mr Fox the Magician, Y, 1960s (5), 9", EXIB $500.00
Mr Magoo Car, Hubley, 1961 (5), 8", NMIB, A $275.00
Mumbo Jumbo Hawaiian Drummer, Alps, 1960s (3), 10", MIB,
    L4...$300.00
Mumbo Jumbo Hawaiian Drummer, Alps, 1960s (3), 10", VG..$150.00
Musical Bulldog, Marusan, 1950s (4), 9", NMIB, A.......$850.00
Musical Comic Jumping Jeep, Alps (5), 12", M, L4........$175.00
Musical Dancing Sweethearts, KO, 1950s, 10", rare, NM..$500.00
Musical Ice Cream Truck, Bandai, 1960s (5), 11", NM...$325.00
Musical Jackal, Linemar, 1950s (6), 10", very rare, MIB ..$1,100.00
Musical Jolly Chimp, CK, 1960s (5), NM......................$50.00
Musical Marching Bear, Alps, 1950s (4), 11", MIB........$575.00
Musical Melody Mixer, Taiyo, 1970s (4), 11", M...........$100.00
Mystery Action Tractor, Japan, 1950s, 7", MIB $150.00
Mystery Police Car, TN, 1960s (3), 10", NM $280.00
Naughty Dog & Buzzing Bee, MT (4), 10" L, M $150.00
Nutty Nibbs, Linemar, 1950s, 12", rare, EX+, A...........$500.00
Ol' Sleepy Head Rip, Y, 1950s (7), 9" L, MIB.................$475.00
Old Fashioned Bus, MT, 13", NMIB, A $85.00
Overland Stagecoach, MT, 1950s (4), 18", MIB.............$325.00
Pat O'Neill, TN, 1960s (6), 12", MIB, L4......................$475.00
Peppy Puppy With Bone, Y, 1950s (7), 7", M $125.00
Pesky Pup the Shoe Stealer, Y, 1950s (4), 8", M $110.00
Pete the Talking Parrot, TN, 1950s (6), 18", M.............$250.00
Pianist (Beethoven...or Jolly Pianist), TN, 1950s (5), MIB...$300.00
Picnic Bunny, Alps, 1950s (4), 11", M $100.00
Piggy Cook, Y, 1950s (5), 10", MIB $275.00
Pinky the Juggling Clown, Alps, 1950s (5), 10", NM, L4..$250.00
Pinocchio Xylophonist, TN (Rosko), 1962 (3), 10", EXIB ..$250.00
Pioneer Covered Wagon, Ichiko, 1960s (4), 15", NM....$175.00
Pipie the Whale, Alps, 1950s, 12", NM $325.00
Playful Puppy w/Caterpillar, MT (4), 5", MIB $250.00
Pleasant Kappa, ATD, 1950s (4), 10", NM, minimum value ..$1,200.00
Pluto, see Disney Acrobats
Police Auto Cycle, Bandai, 1960s (5), 12", EXIB, A......$250.00
Police Cadillac, MIB, L4 ....$250.00

Police Car (1954 Chevy), Marusan, 10", EX, A, $550.00. (Photo courtesy Randy Inman Auctions)

Police Car w/Stick Shift, TM, 1960s, 12", NMIB...........$175.00
Police Patrol, TN, 1950s (4), 10", NMIB......................$300.00
Popcorn Eating Bear, MT, 1950s (5), EX, L4 ....$175.00
Popcorn Vendor (Bear), S&E, 1960s (6), 8", MIB.........$575.00
Popcorn Vendor (Duck), TN, 1950s (5), 8", EX............$300.00
Popeye, see also Smoking Popeye
Popeye & Olive Oyl Tumbling Buggy, Hong Kong, 1981, 7",
    NMIB, A $60.00

Mr. Magoo Car, Hubley, 1961, 8", EXIB, A, $225.00. (New England Auction Gallery)

Popeye in Rowboat, Linemar, 1950s (3), 10", EX $2,420.00
Popeye in Rowboat, Linemar, 1950s (3), 10", EXIB, A ..$7,700.00
Porsche Racer #1, Schuco, plastic, 11", NMIB, A $75.00
Porsche w/Visible Engine, Bandai, 10", NMIB, A $100.00
Quick Draw McGraw Target Car w/Baba Looie, EXIB, T1..$200.00
Rabbits & the Carriage, S&E, 1950s, 8" L, rare, EX.......$225.00
Radicon Bus, MT, 14", EX, A $75.00
Radicon Bus, MT, 14", NMIB, A $250.00
Rambling Ladybug, MT, 1960s, 8", EX.............................$100.00

1397

RCA-NBC Mobile Color TV Truck, Cragstan, 1950s, 9", NMIB, A, $600.00. (Photo courtesy Randy Inman Auctions)

Rembrandt the Monkey Artist, Alps, 1950s (5), 8", rare, M ..$500.00
Return Tram, MT, 1950s (5), 30" L, rare, NM................$350.00
Rex Dog House, Tel-E-Toy, 1950s, 5", M $130.00
Road Roller, MT, 1950s (4), NM+ $150.00
Roaring Gorilla Shooting Gallery, MT, 1950s, 10", EXIB ..$350.00
Robo Tank TR2, TN, 1960s, 6", NM+, A $180.00
Rocky, Linemar, 1960s, 3" dia, MIB, L4.........................$200.00
Romance Car, Modern Toys, 8", EXIB, A.......................$275.00
Sam the Shaving Man, Plaything Toys, 1960s (7), 12", EXIB...$325.00
Sammy Wong the Tea Totaler, TN, 1950s (4), 10", EXIB, A....$375.00
Santa Helicopter, Japan, litho tin & plastic, 9½", EX+IB, A...$130.00
Santa's Express, Adler USA/Hong Kong, 1960s, unused, MIB, A $185.00
Secret Agent's Aston Martin Action Car, Gilbert, 12", NMIB..$375.00
Serpent Charmer, Linemar, 1950s (4), 7", very rare, MIB, L4...$1,450.00
Shutter-Bug, TN, 1950s (5), MIB, L4 ....$875.00
Sight Seeing Bus, Bandai, 1960s (4), 15", EXIB, A $225.00
Siren Patrol Motorcycle, MT, 1960s (3), 12", MIB, L4 ..$475.00
Skipping Monkey, TN, 1960s, 10", NMIB.....................$100.00
Sleeping Baby Bear, Linemar, 1950s (6), 9", MIB..........$475.00
Smokey Bear Jeep, MT, 1950s (4), 10", MIB, L4.........$1,000.00

Smokey Bill on Old Fashioned Car, TN, 1960s, four actions, 9", MIB, $250.00. (Photo courtesy Don Hultzman)

Smoking Bunny, SAN, 1950s (4), 11", NMIB, L4..........$275.00
Smoking Popeye, Linemar, 1950s (5), 9", rare, NM, A....$1,700.00
Sneezing Bear, Linemar, 1950s (5), 9", MIB, L4 ....$350.00
Spanking Bear, Linemar, 1950s (6), 9", EX, L4, from $200 to...$250.00
Speed Challenger #8 (Racer), Japan, 12", EXIB, A $325.00
Speed Control Racer, Daiya, 1960s (4), EX (partial box), A..$175.00
State Trooper Motorcycle, 1950s, 10", rare, MIB, L4 ..$1,675.00
Strutting Sam, Haji, 1950s, 11", VG+ $150.00
Stunt Plane-Spad III, TPS, 1960s (3), 9" L, MIB $275.00
Sunbeam Side Car, Marusan, 1950s (3), 10", very rare, NM, minimum value $1,600.00
Super Susie, Linemar, 1950s (6), 8", rare, NM...............$980.00
Superior Ambulance, Asakusa, 1960s (3), 12", rare, NMIB, A..$110.00

Superman Tank, Linemar, 1950s, three actions, 11", NMIB, A, $3,545.00. (Photo courtesy Don Hultzman)

Surrey Jeep, TN, 1960s (3), 11", M.................................$200.00
Swimming Duck, Bandai, 1950s (4), 8", rare, NM $150.00
Swimming Fish, Koshibe, 1950s, 11", NM......................$125.00
Switchboard Operator, Linemar, 1950s (4), 8", rare, NM ...$720.00
Taxi Cab, Y, 1960s (4), 9", NMIB $175.00
Teddy Balloon Blowing Bear, Alps, 1950s (6), 12", MIB ..$200.00
Teddy Bear Swing, TN, 1950s (3), 17", rare, MIB, L4....$500.00
Teddy the Manager, S&E, 1950s (6), 8", MIB $350.00
Telephone Bear, Linemar, 1950s (6), 8", MIB, L4 ....$300.00
Tinkling Trolley, see Broadway Trolley #10430
Tom & Jerry Auto, Rico/Spain, 1960s (3), 13", very rare, MIB $1,000.00
Tom & Jerry Choo Choo, MT, 1960s (5), 10", M...........$175.00
Tom & Jerry Formula Racing Car, MT, 1960s (3), 11", M ...$225.00

Tom & Jerry Handcar, MT, 1960s, three actions, 10", EXIB, each $350.00. (Photo courtesy Don Hultzman)

Tom Tom Indian, Y, 1960s (4), 11", M............................$75.00
Topo Gigio Xylophone Player, TN, 1960s (3), 11", very rare, M, minimum value $1,200.00
Tractor T-27, Amico, 1950s (5), 12", rare, M $125.00

Trumpet Playing Monkey, Alps, 1950s (4), 9", M...........$380.00
Tumbles the Bear, YM, 1960s, 9", NMIB $150.00
Tumbling Bozo the Clown, Sonsco, 1970s, 8", M $160.00
Tunnel Train, TN, 1950s (4), 18", M..............................$125.00
Turn-O-Matic Gun Jeep (Police), TN, 1960s (5), 10", NMIB...$275.00
Twirly Whirly Rocket Ride, Alps, 1950s (4), 13", NMIB, A...$1,525.00
Union Mountain Monorail, TN, 1950s, MIB, L4...........$225.00
Vertol AirPort Service (Helicopter), Alps, 1950s (5), 13",
    NMIB...$250.00
VIP the Busy Boss, S&E, 1950s (5), 8", VG, A $125.00
VIP the Busy Boss, S&E, 1950s (6), 8", NMIB..............$350.00
Waddles Family Car, Y, 1960s, MIB, L4, from $135 to ...$175.00
Wagon Master, MT, 1960s (4), 18" L, NM $150.00
Walk-Boot Hobo, Tomy, 1960s, 20", NM $100.00

Walking Bear With Xylophone, Linemar, 1950s, seven actions, 10", EXIB, $725.00.
(Photo courtesy Don Hultzman)

Walking Donkey, Linemar, 1950s (3), 9", MIB...............$250.00
Walking Elephant, Linemar, 1950s (3), 9", MIB $250.00
Walking Gorilla, Linemar, 1950s (3), 8", MIB, L4 ....$475.00
Walking Knight in Armour, MT, 1950s (5), rare, NMIB, L4....$3,000.00
Waltzing Matilda, TN, rare, MIB, L4.............................$975.00
Western Style Music Box, 1950s, 5", rare, MIB $575.00
Whirlybird Helicopter, Remco, 1960s (3), 25", NMIB, L4 ..$250.00
Willie the Walking Car, Y, 1960s (6), 9", MIB, L4.........$325.00
Windy the Juggling Elephant, TN, 1950s (3), 11", MIB, L4...$250.00
Wonder Loco, Taiyo Kogyo, 1970s (4), 8", NM..............$100.00

Worried Mother Duck, TN, 1950s, three actions, 7", MIB, $250.00. (Photo courtesy Don Hultzman)

Xylophone, Ace, 1950s, 6" L, NM....................................$60.00
Yo-yo Clown, S&E, 1960s (5), 10", rare, MIB $425.00
Zero Fighter Plane, Bandai, 1950s (3), 13" L, NM $350.00

Beanie Babies

The popularity of Ty Beanie Babies is not as intense and values for them are not as high as during the years 1996 – 2000, when crazed collectors swarmed stores for the newest releases and prices soared for many Beanie Babies. However, collectors will still find value in the rare and exclusive Beanie Babies, as well as some of the retired regular issues. There are many other bean bag animals on the market, many of which are very similar to Ty Beanie Babies, and collectors need to learn the characteristics that distinguish Ty Beanie Babies from counterfeits and/or reproductions.

The most important thing to know is that there are different swing tags (heart-shaped paper tags, usually attached to the animal's ear, but also to arms, legs, or wings) and tush tag styles (sewn into the tush of the animal), and these indicate year of issue. Ty Beanie Babies were introduced in 1994, and the earliest their tags date is 1993.

#1 Swing tag: single heart-shaped tag; comes on Beanie Babies with tush tags dated 1993.
#2 Swing tag: heart-shaped; folded, with information inside; narrow letters; comes on Beanie Babies with tush tags dated 1993.
#3 Swing tag: heart-shaped; folded, with information inside; wider letters; comes on Beanie Babies with tush tags dated 1993 and 1995.

#1 Swing tag

#2 Swing tag

#3 Swing tag

#4 Swing tag

#6 Zodiac variation swing tag

#5 Swing tag

#6 Holiday variation swing tag

#6 Swing tag

#8 Swing tag

#9 Swing tag

#4 Swing tag: heart-shaped; folded, with information inside; wider lettering with no gold outline around the 'ty'; yellow star on front; first tag to include a poem and birth date; comes on Beanie Babies with tush tags dated 1993, 1995, and 1996.

#5 Swing tag: heart-shaped; folded, with information inside; different font on front and inside; birth month spelled out, no style numbers, website listed; comes on Beanie Babies with tush tags dated 1993, 1995, 1996, 1997, 1998, and 1999.

#6 Swing tag: features holographic star with '2000' across star; inside: Ty, Inc., Ty Canada, Ty Europe, and Ty Japan; birthdate, website address, and poem in smaller font than #5; new safety precaution on back, smaller font and UPC; comes on Beanie Babies with tush tags dated 2000.

Variations on #6 Swing tags: The twelve Zodiac Beanie Babies, released in September 2000, have all the characteristics of the sixth generation swing tag with the exception of the word 'Zodiac' on the front of the swing tag, which replaces the star and 2000. The interiors of the three Holiday Beanie Babies' tags released in October 2000 have a blue background and white snowflakes.

#7 Swing tag: identical to #6 tag except 'Beanies' is written across the holographic star instead of '2000.' This tag appears in UK Beanie Babies (photo not available); comes on Beanie Babies with tush tags dated 2000.

#8, Swing tag: shows a ¼" holographic star with the word 'Beanie' and 'Baby' below in fine yellow print. Inside information identical to #6 swing tag; comes on Beanie Babies with tush tags dated 2000 and 2001.

#9 Swing tag: shows five smaller holographic stars above the words 'Beanie Babies' in fine yellow print. Inside information identical to #6 and #7 swing tags; comes on Beanie Babies with tush tags dated 2001 and 2002.

#10 Swing tag

#11 Swing tag

#10 Swing tag: same as #9 tag except inside lists two more locations of Ty, Inc., on left-handed side: Ty Asia and Ty Australia.

#11 Swing tag: a holographic '10' and a white star with 'yrs' inside it appears above the words 'Beanie Babies' on the front of these tags, commemorating the tenth anniversary of Beanie

Babies. First released in December 2002.

Early tush tags (dated 1993 and 1995) do not have the Beanie's name on them; after 1995 Beanie Baby names were printed on both swing tags and tush tags. The earlier Beanie Babies have white tags with black writing with the year of issue, 'Ty Inc,' and manufacturing information on the tag; later tush tags are white with red writing and list the Beanie Baby's name along with manufacturing information.

Removing tags from the more current Beanie Babies or having ripped, creased, or damaged tags decreases the value of the animal. However, most of the rarer 1994, 1995, and 1996 issues are still quite valuable with a damaged tag or even without a swing tag, due to their scarcity.

Remember that Ty produces several other plush lines, some of which are even stuffed with pellets. You need to be able to determine what product you have. Beginning collectors often confuse Teenie Beanie Babies and Beanie Buddies with Beanie Babies. Beanie Babies are approximately 6" to 10" in length/height (though Slither the snake is even longer!). Teenie Beanie Babies debuted in April 1997 as Happy Meal Toys in McDonald's restaurants and are smaller versions of Beanie Babies. Beanie Buddies are larger versions of Beanie Babies and are made of a more plush fabric. Sometimes Ty produced a Beanie Baby, Teenie Beanie Baby, *and* a Beanie Buddy, all with the same name and look, with the exception of the size. It is important to know which type of animal you own! Ty produced Teenie Beanie Baby versions of the rare Beanie Babies in 1999, and these certainly do not have the same values as the rare Beanie Babies by the same names.

Our prices are for mint or near-mint condition Beanie Babies with both swing tag and tush tags intact and in perfect condition. Values for Beanie Babies missing a hang tag decrease by up to 50% and up to 75% if missing both swing and tush tags. For Beanie Babies with a #1, #2, or #3 swing tag, add 30% to 40% to the prices suggested below. Style numbers are the last four digits in the UPC code located on the back of the Beanie Baby's swing tag.

Advisor: Amy Sullivan (See Directory, Beanie Babies)

Key: R — retired   # — style number
       BBOC — Beanie Babies Official Club
       Ty Store — Beanie offered only through the Ty Store
               on Ty's website, www.ty.com

#1 Bear, red w/#1 on chest, issued only to Ty sales reps, 253 made, R, minimum value $5,000.00

Addison, #4362, given to fans at Chicago Cubs vs AZ Diamondbacks game at Wrigley Field, May 20, 2001, R, from $10 to...$15.00

Ally, #4032, alligator, R, minimum value..........................$35.00

Almond, #4246, bear, R, from $5 to $7.00

Amber, #4243, tabby cat, gold, R, from $6 to..................$8.00

America, #4409, bear, wht, R, from $7 to $12.00

America, #4412, bear, red, R, from $10 to $15.00

America, #4506, bear, bl, R, proceeds sent to American Red Cross for relief to victims of September 11, from $9 to..........$12.00

Amigo, dog, Ty Store, from $5 to $8.00

Ants, #4195, anteater, R, from $5 to $7.00

Ariel, #4288, fundraising bear for the Elizabeth Glaser Pediatric AIDS Foundation, R, from $5 to...................................$8.00

Aruba, #4314, angelfish, R, from $5 to...........................$7.00

Asia-Pacific Exclusives, all bears: Ai (Japan), Aussiebear (Australia), Coreana (Korea), Kiwiana (New Zealand), Singabear (Singapore), Wirabear (Malaysia), ea from $10 to......$20.00

Aurora, #4271, polar bear, R, from $5 to........................$7.00

Baby Boy, #4534, It's a Boy, bear, bl, from $6 to..................$8.00

Baby Girl, #4535, It's a Girl, bear, pk, from $6 to...............$8.00

Baldy, #4074, eagle, R, from $6 to $12.00

Bam, #4544, ram, from $6 to $8.00

Bananas, #4316, orangutan, R, from $5 to $7.00

Bandito, #4543, raccoon, grey, from $6 to......................$8.00

Batty, #4035, bat, pk or tie-dyed, R, from $5 to $8.00

BB, #4253, birthday bear, R, from $6 to $8.00

Beak, #4211, kiwi bird, R, from $5 to $7.00

Beani, #4397, cat, gray, R, from $6 to...............................$8.00

Beanie baby of the month, Ty Store, 12 different Beanies offered to members each month of 2003, each from $8 to.....$10.00

Bernie, #4109, St Bernard, R, from $5 to $8.00

Bessie, #4009, cow, brn, R, from $20 to......................$40.00

Birthday bears (2001), named by months, #4370 through #4372; #4386 through #4393; #4547, all R, ea from $5 to.............$7.00

Birthday bears (2002-2003), named by months, w/hats, #4547 through #4558, all R, from $6 to..............................$8.00

Blackie, #4011, bear, R, from $8 to $20.00

Blessed, praying bear, wht w/wings, from $5 to $8.00

The original nine Beanie Babies, clockwise from top: Squealer the pig #4005, from $10.00 to $20.00; Splash the whale, #4022, minimum value $30.00; Patti the platypus, #4025, 2nd issue, purple, from $10.00 to $20.00; Legs the frog, #4020, from $10.00 to $20.00; Pinchers the lobster, #4026, from $8.00 to $15.00. Flash the dolphin, #4021, minimum value $30.00; Spot the dog, #4000, 2nd issue with a spot on his back, from $15.00 to $30.00; Chocolate the moose, #4015, from $8.00 to $12.00; and Cubbie the bear, #4010, from $15.00 to $20.00. (Photo courtesy Amy Sullivan)

Blizzard, #4163, tiger, wht, R, from $9 to $12.00

Bloom #4596, bear, R, from $5 to $7.00

Blue, bear, Ty Store, R, from $7 to $10.00

Bo, #4595, Dalmatian, from $5 to $7.00

Bones, #4001, dog, brn, R, from $10 to $15.00

Bongo, #4067, monkey, 1st issue, brn tail, R, from $20 to .$50.00

Bongo, #4067, monkey, 2nd issue, tan tail, R, from $10 to..$15.00

Bonsai, #4567, chimpanzee, R, from $6 to $8.00

Booties, #4536, kitten, blk, from $6 to $8.00

Bride, #4528, bear, from $7 to $9.00

Brigitte, #4374, poodle, pk, R, from $10 to $12.00

Britannia, #4601, British bear, UK exclusive, R, minimum
    value $40.00

Bronty #4085, bl brontosaurus, R, minimum value $250.00

Brownie, #4010, bear, w/swing tag, R, minimum value.$1,500.00

Bruno, #4183, terrier, R, from $5 to................................$7.00

Bubbles, #4078, fish, yel & blk, R, minimum value $35.00

Buckingham, #4603, bear, UK exclusive, R, minimum value..$60.00

Bumble, #4045, bee, R, minimum value $215.00

Bunga Raya, #4615, Asia-Pacific flower bear, Malaysia exclusive,
    yel, from $15 to $30.00

Bushy, #4285, lion, R, from $5 to $7.00

Butch, #4227, bull terrier, R, from $5 to $7.00

Buzzie, #4354, bee, R, from $5 to $7.00

Buzzy, #4308, buzzard, R, from $6 to $8.00

Cand-e, bear, wht w/candy canes, Ty Store, R, from $5 to..$8.00

Canyon, #4212, cougar, R, from $5 to $8.00

Carnation, #4575, cat, from $7 to $9.00

Carrots, #4512, rabbit, R, from $6 to $8.00

Cashew, #4292, bear, brn, R, from $5 to $7.00

Cassie, #4340, collie, R, from $5 to $8.00

Caw, #4071, crow, R, from $215 to $350.00

Celebrate, #4385, 15-year anniversary bear, R, from $8 to $12.00

Celebrations, #4620, The Queen's Golden Jubilee bear, R, UK, Aus-
    tralia, New Zealand & Canada exclusive, from $15 to....$25.00

Champion, #4408, 32 different versions representing teams in 2002
    World Cup soccer tournament, all R, from $7 to $30.00

Charmer, #4568, unicorn, from $6 to $8.00

Cheddar, #4525, mouse holding cheese, R, from $5 to $8.00

Cheeks, #4250, baboon, R, from $5 to $7.00

Cheery, #4359, Sunshine bear, R, from $6 to $8.00

Cheezer, #4301, mouse, R, from $6 to $10.00

Chickie, #4509, chick, R, from $6 to $8.00

Chilly, #4012, polar bear, R, minimum value..................$550.00

China, #4315, panda bear, R, from $6 to $8.00

Chinook, #4604, bear, Canada exclusive, R, from $20 to $25.00

Chip, #4121, calico cat, R, from $5 to $7.00

Chipper, #4259, chipmunk, R, from $5 to $7.00

Chops, #4019, lamb, R, from $40 to $75.00

Cinders, #4295, bear, blk, R, from $5 to $7.00

Classy, #4373, bear, 'The People's Beanie,' R, from $5 to...........$7.00

Claude, #4083, crab, tie-dyed, R, from $5 to $8.00

Clover, #4503, bear, wht w/shamrocks, R, from $8 to...........$10.00

Clubby, bear, bl, BBOC exclusive, R, from $12 to $20.00

Clubby II, bear, purple, BBOC exclusive, R, from $12 to..........$15.00

Clubby III, #4993, bear, brn, BBOC exclusive, R, from $15 to.$30.00

Clubby IV, #4996, bear, purple, BBOC exclusive, R, from $12
    to $14.00

Clubby V, #4998, bear, pk, BBOC exclusive, from $8 to ..$10.00

Color Me Beanie, #4989, bear that can be decorated by owner,
    R, from $8 to $12.00

Color Me Bunny, #4554, wht, sold w/markers to create your own
    Beanie, from $7 to..$9.00

Colosso, #40002, elephant, from $5 to $8.00

Congo, #4160, gorilla, R, from $5 to $7.00

Coral Casino, bear given to club members only, R, minimum
    value $1,800.00

Coral, #4079, fish, tie-dyed, R, minimum value...............$40.00

Cottonball, #4511, rabbit, R, from $6 to $8.00

Courage, #4515, German Shepherd, all profits donated to NY
    Police & Fire widow's/children's benefit fund, R, from $6
    to..$8.00

Creepers, #4376, skeleton, R, from $6 to $8.00

Crunch, #4130, shark, R, from $5 to $7.00

Cupid, #4502, dog, wht, R, from $7 to $9.00

Curly, #4052, bear, brn, R, from $8 to $10.00

Dad-e 2003, #4421, Father's Day bear, Ty Store, R, from $8
    to..$12.00

Dad-e, #4413, Ty Store, R, from $15 to $30.00

Daffodil, #4624, bear, Ty Europe exclusive, R, from $30 to..$40.00

Daisy, #4006, cow, blk & wht, R, from $10 to..................$30.00

Darling, #4368, dog, R, from $10 to $14.00

Dart, #4352, frog, R, from $5 to......................................$8.00

Dearest, #4350, bear, peach, R, from $7 to....................$10.00

Decade, #4585, 10-year Ty company anniversary bear, lt bl,
    red, royal bl, and wht versions, lt bl version, R, ea from
    $10 to..$15.00

Derby, #4008, horse, 1st issue, fine yarn mane & tail, R, mini-
    mum value $550.00

Derby, #4008, horse, 2nd issue, coarse mane & tail, R, from $10 to..$15.00

Derby, #4008, horse, 3rd issue, wht star on forehead, R, from $5
    to..$8.00

Derby, #4008, horse, 4th issue, wht star on forehead, fur mane &
    tail, R, from $5 to $7.00

Diddley, #4383, dog, green, R, from $6.00 to $8.00. (Photo courtesy Amy Sullivan)

Digger, #4027, crab, 1st issue, orange, R, minimum value..$300.00

Digger, #4027, crab, 2nd issue, red, R, minimum value $25.00

Dinky, #4341, dodo bird, R, from $5 to $8.00

Dippy the bunny, #4582, R, from $5 to $7.00

Dizzy, #4365, dalmatian, R, 5 versions w/different colored ears &
    spots, ea from $6 to $15.00

Doby, #4110, doberman, R, from $6 to..............................$10.00

Doodle, #4171, rooster, tie-dyed, R, from $6 to $10.00

Dotty, #4100, dalmatian, R, from $6 to $8.00

Dublin, #4576, Irish bear, R, from $5 to $8.00

Duck-e, #4425, duck, Ty Store, R, from $5 to $10.00

Dusty, #4702, Chicago Cubs bear, R, minimum value $120.00

Early, #4190, robin, R, from $5 to $7.00

Ears, #4018, rabbit, brn, R, from $10 to $20.00

Echo, #4180, dolphin, R, from $8 to $10.00

Eggbert, #4232, baby chick, R, from $5 to $7.00

Eggs, #4337, Easter bear, pk, R, from $6 to $12.00

Eggs II, #4516, Easter bear, bl, R, from $5 to $8.00

Eggs III, #4581, Easter bear, purple, R, from $5 to.............$8.00

England, #4608, bear, UK exclusive, R, from $15 to $20.00

Erin, #4186, Irish bear, R, from $6 to $8.00

Eucalyptus, #4240, koala, R, from $6 to $8.00

Ewey, #4219, lamb, R, from $5 to $7.00

Fancy, #40003, cat, from $5 to $7.00

Ferny, #4618, Asia-Pacific flower bear, blk, New Zealand exclu-
    sive, R, from $30 to..$40.00

Fetch, #4189, golden retriever, R, from $6 to......................$8.00

Fetcher, #4298, chocolate lab, R, from $5 to $8.00

Fidget, dog, from $5 to $7.00

Filly, #4592, horse, from $5 to..$7.00

Flaky, #4572, bear, w/snowflakes, R, from $6 to $10.00

Flashy, #4339, peacock, R, from $8 to $10.00

Fleece, #4125, lamb, wht w/cream face, R, from $5 to............$8.00

Fleecie, #4279, lamb, cream w/purple neck ribbon, R, from $5
    to...$8.00

Flip, #4012, cat, wht, R, from $15 to.................................$30.00

Flitter, #4255, butterfly, pastel, R, from $6 to......................$8.00

Float, #4343, butterfly, R, from $5 to $8.00

Floppity, #4118, bunny, lilac, R, from $6 to $10.00

Flutter, #4043, butterfly, tie-dyed, R, minimum value.........$300.00

Fortune, #4196, panda bear w/red ribbon around neck, R, from
    $5 to $7.00

Fraidy, #4379, cat, blk & orange, R, from $8 to $10.00

Frankenteddy, #4562, 2002 Halloween bear, R, from $8 to..$10.00

Freckles, #4066, leopard, R, from $5 to $8.00

Freiherr von Schwarz, #4611, bear, Germany exclusive, R, from
    $40 to $55.00

Fridge, #4579, polar bear, from $6 to $9.00

Frigid, #4270, king penguin, R, from $6 to..........................$8.00

Frills, #4367, hornbill bird, R, from $6 to..........................$10.00

Frisco, #4586, cat, from $5 to..$7.00

Frolic, #4519, dog, R, from $7 to $10.00

Frosty, bull, from $5 to $7.00

Fuzz, #4237, bear, R, from $8 to..$11.00

Garcia, #4051, bear, tie-dyed, R, from $80 to $125.00

Germania, #4236, German bear, UK exclusive, R, from $15
    to $20.00

Giganto, #4384, mammoth, R, from $6 to $10.00

Gigi, #4191, poodle, R, from $5 to $7.00

Gizmo, #4541, lemur, R, from $6 to $8.00

Glider, #4574, prehistoric bird, R, from $5 to $10.00

Glory, #4188, American bear w/stars, R, from $15 to $20.00

Glow, #4283, lightning bug, R, from $5 to $7.00

Goatee, #4235, mountain goat, R, from $5 to $7.00

Gobbles, #4034, turkey, R, from $5 to $7.00

Goldie, #4023, goldfish, R, from $15 to $30.00

Goochy, #4230, jellyfish, R, from $5 to $7.00

Grace, #4274, bunny, praying, R, from $5 to........................$8.00

Gracie, #4126, swan, R, from $5 to $8.00

Graf von Rot, #4612, bear, Germany exclusive, R, from $25
    to $40.00

Groom, #4529, bear, from $5 to...$8.00

Groovy, #4256, bear, R, from $5 to $7.00

Grunt, #4092, razorback pig, red, R, minimum value $45.00

Hairy, #4336, spider, brn w/hair, R, from $6 to...................$8.00

Halo, #4208, angel bear, R, from $7 to $10.00

Halo II, #4269, angel bear, R, from $7 to $10.00

Happy, #4061, hippo, 1st issue, gray, R, minimum value .$225.00

Happy, #4061, hippo, 2nd issue, lavender, R, from $15 to .$20.00

Harry, #4546, bear, R, from $7 to $10.00

Haunt, #4377, 2001 Halloween bear, blk, R, from $6 to.....$8.00

Herald, #4570, angel bear, R, from $7 to...........................$10.00

Herder, #4524, sheep dog, R, from $6 to $10.00

Hero, #40012 & #40013, bear supporting USO troops - Aus-
    tralian, UK, and USA versions, Ty Store, Australian & UK
    R, from $7 to..$15.00

Hero, #4351, bear, brn, w/necktie, R, from $6 to $8.00

Herschel, #4700, bear, Crackel Barrel restaurant exclusive, R,
    from $7 to..$15.00

Hippie, #4218, rabbit, tie-dyed, R, from $6 to....................$8.00

Hissy, #4185, coiled snake, R, from $5 to $7.00

Hodge-Podge, #4569, dog, R, from $5 to.............................$9.00

Frisbee, #4508, dog, gray, R, from $6.00 to $8.00. (Photo courtesy Amy Sullivan)

Hippity, #4119, bunny, mint green, R, from $7.00 to $10.00.

(Photo courtesy Amy Sullivan)

Holiday Teddy (1997), #4200, R, from $12 to **$15.00**
Holiday Teddy (1998), #4204, R, from $14 to **$20.00**
Holiday Teddy (1999), #4257, R, from $10 to **$12.00**
Holiday Teddy (2000), #4332, R, from $8 to **$10.00**
Holiday Teddy (2001), #4395, R, from $8 to **$10.00**
Holiday Teddy (2002), #4564, R, from $9 to **$12.00**
Honks, #4258, goose, from $5 to **$7.00**
Hoofer, #4518, Clydesdale horse, from $6 to **$8.00**
Hoot, #4073, owl, R, from $20 to **$30.00**
Hope, #4213, bear, praying, R, from $6 to **$8.00**
Hopper, #4342, rabbit, R, from $6 to.............................**$8.00**
Hoppity, #4117, bunny, pk, R, from $6 to **$10.00**
Hornsly, #4345, triceratops, R, from $5 to....................**$7.00**
Howl, #4310, R, from $5 to **$10.00**
Huggy, #4306, bear, R, from $6 to.................................**$8.00**
Humphrey, #4060, camel, R, minimum value................**$400.00**
Iggy, #4038, iguana, all issues, R, from $6 to **$8.00**
Inch, #4044, worm, felt antenna, R, from $50 to............**$70.00**
Inch, #4044, worm, yarn antenna, R, from $10 to **$15.00**
India, #4291, tiger, R, from $5 to...................................**$10.00**
Inky, #4028, octopus, 1st issue, tan, no mouth, R, minimum value...**$350.00**
Inky, #4028, octopus, 2nd issue, tan, w/mouth, R, minimum value...**$350.00**
Inky, #4028, octopus, 3rd issue, pk, R, from $10 to.............**$20.00**
Issy, #4404, bear, New York City Four Seasons Hotel exclusive to guests, minimum value **$165.00**
Issy, #4404, bear, R, retail stores, from $8 to **$10.00**
Jabber, #4197, parrot, R, from $5 to.................................**$7.00**
Jake, #4199, mallard duck, R, from $5 to **$7.00**
Jester, #4349, clown fish, R, from $6 to............................**$8.00**
Jinglepup, #9394, dog w/Santa cap, R, from $6 to **$15.00**
Jolly, #4082, walrus, R, from $5 to **$7.00**
Kaleidoscope, #4348, cat, rainbow-colored, R, from $6 to **$8.00**
Kanata, #4621, bear, Ty Canada exclusive, inside swing tag has flag of one of the Canadian provinces or territories, from $10 to **$20.00**
Kicks, #4229, soccer bear, R, from $6 to............................**$8.00**
Kirby, #4396, dog, wht, R, from $6 to...............................**$8.00**
Kiss-e, #4419, bear, Ty Store, R, from $7 to **$10.00**
Kissme, #4504, bear w/hearts, R, from $6 to **$10.00**
Kiwi, #4070, toucan, R, minimum value..........................**$55.00**
Knuckles, #4247, pig, R, from $5 to..................................**$7.00**
Kooky, #4357, cat, purple, bl & wht, R, from $10 to **$12.00**
Kuku, #4192, cockatoo, R, from $5 to...............................**$7.00**
L'amore, poodle, wht, from $5 to **$7.00**
Lefty 2000, #4290, donkey, red, wht & bl, R, USA exclusive, from $6 to..**$8.00**
Lefty, #4057, donkey w/American flag, bl-gray, R, minimum value..**$60.00**
Libearty, #4057, bear w/American flag, wht, R, minimum value **$135.00**
Liberty, #4531, American bear, 3 versions, red, wht & blue heads, all R, ea from $10 to **$20.00**
Lightning, #4537, horse, from $6 to **$9.00**
Lips, #4254, fish, R, from $5 to..**$7.00**
Lizzy, #4033, lizard, 1st issue, tie-dyed, R, minimum value **$275.00**
Lizzy, #4033, lizard, 2nd issue, bl, R, from $15 to **$20.00**

Loosy, #4206, Canada goose, R, from $5 to.......................**$7.00**
Luck-e, #0600, Irish bear, Ty Store, R, from $8 to **$10.00**
Lucky, #4040, ladybug, 1st issue, 7 spots, R, minimum value..**$70.00**
Lucky, #4040, ladybug, 2nd issue, 21 spots, R, minimum value ..**$125.00**
Lucky, #4040, ladybug, 3rd issue, 11 spots, R, from $10 to .**$15.00**
Luke, #4214, Labrador puppy, R, from $8 to **$15.00**
Lullaby, #4583, lamb, R, from $5 to.................................**$7.00**
Lumberjack, #40001, beaver, from $5 to **$7.00**
Lurkey, #4309, turkey, R, from $5 to **$8.00**
Mac, #4225, cardinal, R, from $5 to **$7.00**
Magic, #4088, dragon, R, from $30 to **$45.00**
Manny, #4081, manatee, R, minimum value......................**$45.00**
Maple, #4600, bear, Ty Canada exclusive, R, minimum value...**$35.00**
Mattie, #4521, cat, R, from $6 to **$10.00**
MC Beanie, brn bear w/MasterCard logo, R, free w/first use of Ty MasterCard, from $50 to **$80.00**
MC Beanie II, bear, Anniversary edition, from $50 to.......**$75.00**
MC Beanie II, orange bear w/MasterCard logo, free w/first use of Ty MasterCard, from $50 to **$70.00**
Mel, #4162, koala, R, from $5 to **$7.00**
Midnight, #4355, panther, R, from $10 to **$12.00**
Millennium, #4226, bear, R, from $9 to **$12.00**
Mistletoe, #4500, bear, red, R, from $6 to **$8.00**
Mom-e 2003, #4426, Mother's Day bear, Ty Store, R, from $14 to...**$20.00**
Mom-e, #4411, Ty Store, R, minimum value **$30.00**
Mooch, #4224, spider monkey, R, from $5 to....................**$8.00**
Morrie, #4282, eel, R, from $5 to......................................**$7.00**
Mother #4588, 2003 Mother's Day bear, from $9 to **$12.00**
Mr, #4363, groom bear, R, from $5 to **$9.00**
Mrs, #4364, bride bear, R, from $5 to **$9.00**
Muddy, dog, from $5 to **$7.00**
Mugungwha, #4617, Asia-Pacific flower bear, wht, Korea exclusive, R, from $20 to...**$25.00**
Mum, #4517, 2002 Mother's Day bear, pk, R, from $6 to.....**$10.00**
Mystic, #4007, unicorn, 1st issue, soft fine mane & tail, R, minimum value **$100.00**
Mystic, #4007, unicorn, 2nd issue, coarse yarn mane & brn horn, R, from $10 to **$15.00**
Mystic, #4007, unicorn, 3rd issue, iridescent horn, R, from $6 to...**$8.00**
Mystic, #4007, unicorn, 4th issue, iridescent horn, rainbow fur mane & tail, R, from $5 to..**$7.00**
Nana, #4067, 1st issue of Bongo the monkey, R, minimum value...**$1,000.00**
Nanook, #4104, husky dog, R, from $5 to **$7.00**
Nectar, #4361, hummingbird, R, from $30 to **$40.00**
Neon, #4239, sea horse, tie-dyed, R, from $5 to................**$7.00**
Nibbler, #4216, rabbit, cream, R, from $5 to.....................**$7.00**
Nibblies, #4584, bunny, from $6 to..................................**$8.00**
Nibbly, #4217, rabbit, brn, R, from $5 to **$8.00**
Niles, #4284, camel, R, from $5 to **$8.00**
Nip, #4003, cat, 1st issue, gold w/wht face & tummy, R, minimum value **$150.00**
Nip, #4003, cat, 2nd issue, all gold, R, minimum value **$350.00**
Nip, #4003, cat, 3rd issue, gold w/wht paws, R, from $15 to....**$25.00**
Nipponia, #4605, bear, Japan exclusive, R, from $20 to **$30.00**

Nuts, #4114, squirrel, R, from $5 to..................................$7.00
Nutty, #4587, squirrel, from $5 to....................................$7.00
Oats, #4305, horse, R, from $5 to $8.00
Osito, #4244, Mexican bear, USA exclusive, R, from $8 to.......$10.00
Panama, #4520, tree frog, R, from $5 to.........................$10.00
Pappa, #4593, 2003 Father's Day bear, from $7 to..............$9.00
Patriot, #4360, bear, red, wht & bl, 2 versions w/flag on bottom
    of right or left foot, R, ea from $10 to $25.00
Patti, #4025, platypus, 1st issue, maroon, R, minimum value .$285.00
Paul, #4248, walrus, R, from $5 to $7.00

Peace, #4599, tie-dyed bear, embroidered peace sign, R, from $10.00 to $20.00. (Photo courtesy Amy Sullivan)

Peace sign bear, #4053, bl, R, from $9 to..........................$12.00
Peanut, #4062, elephant, lt bl, R, from $7 to $10.00
Peanut, #4062, elephant, royal bl (manufacturing mistake), R,
    minimum value $1,000.00
Pecan, #4251, bear, gold, R, from $5 to $7.00
Peekaboo, #4303, turtle, R, from $5 to $8.00

Pegasus, #4542, winged horse, from $6.00 to $10.00.

(Photo courtesy Amy Sullivan)

Peking, #4013, panda bear, R, minimum value...............$450.00
Pellet, #4313, hamster, R, from $6 to $10.00
Periwinkle, #4400, e-Beanie bear, bl, R, from $7 to..............$10.00
Pierre, #4607, bear, Canada exclusive, R, from $15 to $20.00
Pinky, #4072, flamingo, R, from $8 to..............................$10.00
Pompey, #4625, soccer bear, Ty Europe exclusive, available only
    through the Portsmouth football club, from $25 to ...$50.00
Poofie, #4505, dog, R, from $6 to $8.00
Poopsie, #4381, bear, yel, R, from $7 to $10.00
Pops, #4522, bear w/American flag tie, R, from $6 to............$8.00

Pops, #4522, bear w/British flag tie, UK exclusive, R, from $12
    to $16.00
Pops, #4522, bear w/Canadian flag tie, Canada exclusive, R,
    from $10 to $12.00
Poseidon, #4356, whale shark, from $5 to $8.00
Pouch, #4161, kangaroo, R, from $5 to $7.00
Pounce, #4122, cat, brn, R, from $5 to $7.00
Pounds, #4530, elephant, R, from $5 to $8.00
Prance, #4123, cat, gray stripe, R, $5 to $7.00
Prickles, #4220, hedgehog, R, from $5 to $8.00
Prince, #4312, bullfrog, R, from $5 to $8.00
Princess, #4300, bear, purple, commemorating Diana, Princess of
    Wales, PVC or PE pellets, R, from $10 to....................$15.00
Prinz von Gold, #4613, bear, Germany exclusive, R, from $15
    to $25.00
Propeller, #4366, flying fish, R, from $5 to $7.00
Puffer, #4181, puffin, R, from $5 to $7.00
Pugsly, #4106, pug dog, R, from $5 to $8.00
Pumkin', #4205, pumpkin, R, from $8 to $10.00
Punchers, #4026, 1st issue of Pinchers the lobster, R, minimum
    value $1,500.00
Punxsutawn-e Phil, #4418, groundhog, Ty Store, R, from $7
    to $10.00
Purr, #4346, kitten, gray, R, from $5 to...........................$7.00
Quackers, #4024, duck, 1st issue, no wings, R, minimum value .$750.00
Quackers, #4024, duck, 2nd issue, w/wings, R, from $10 to .$20.00
Radar, #4091, bat, blk, R, minimum value $45.00
Rainbow, #4037, chameleon, 4 versions, R, ea from $5 to.........$10.00
Red, patriotic bear, R, from $10 to $12.00
Red, White & Blue, #40000, bear, R, from $5 to $7.00
Regal, #4358, King Charles spaniel, R, from $6 to $10.00
Rescue, #4514, dalmatian, all profits donated to NY Police & Fire
    widow's & children's benefit fund, R, from $6 to $10.00
Rex, #4086, tyrannosaurus, R, minimum value $300.00
Righty 2000, #4289, elephant, red, wht & bl, R, USA exclusive,
    from $10 to..$12.00
Righty, #4085, elephant w/American flag, gray, R, minimum
    value...$50.00
Ringo, #4014, raccoon, tan, R, from $10 to $15.00
Roam, #4209, buffalo, R, from $5 to.................................$7.00
Roary, #4069, lion, R, from $6 to $8.00
Rocket, #4202, blue jay, R, from $5 to.............................$7.00
Romance, #4398, bear, pk, R, from $7 to $9.00
Rose, #4622, bear, Ty Europe exclusive, from $35 to $50.00
Rover, #4101, dog, red, R, from $10 to.............................$15.00
Roxie, #4334, reindeer, red or blk nose, R, from $7 to..............$10.00
Rufus, #4280, dog, R, from $6 to $8.00
Rumba, tiger, from $5 to $7.00
Runner, #4304, mustelidae, R, from $6 to........................$10.00
Rusty, #4563, red panda, from $5 to $8.00
Sakura, #4602, Japanese bear, Japan exclusive, R, minimum
    value...$70.00
Sakura II, #4619, Asia-Pacific flower bear, pk, Japan exclusive,
    from $10 to..$20.00
Sammy, #4215, bear, tie-dyed, R, from $5 to.....................$7.00
Sampson, #4540, dog, from $6 to $9.00
Santa, #4203, R, from $10 to $12.00
Sarge, #4277, German shepherd, R, from $5 to $7.00

Scaly, #4263, lizard, R, from $5 to $7.00

Scared-e, orange Halloween cat, R, Ty Store, from $9 to .$12.00

Scary, #4378, witch, R, from $5 to $8.00

Scat, #4231, cat, R, from $5 to $7.00

Schnitzel, #4578, dog, from $5 to $8.00

Schweetheart, #4252, orangutan, R, from $6 to.................$8.00

Scoop, #4107, pelican, R, from $5 to.............................$8.00

Scorch, #4210, dragon, R, from $5 to............................$8.00

Scotland, #4609, bear, Scotland exclusive, R, from $20
    to $35.00

Scottie, #4102, Scottish terrier, R, from $7 to $10.00

Scurry, #4281, beetle, R, from $5 to $7.00

Seadog, #4566, Newfoundland dog, from $5 to...................$8.00

Seamore, #4029, seal, wht, R, minimum value $45.00

Seaweed, #4080, otter, brn, R, from $12 to $20.00

Sequoia, #4516, grizzly bear, R, from $5 to $9.00

Serenity, #4533, dove, R, from $7 to $9.00

Shamrock, #4338, bear, R, from $7 to............................$10.00

Sheets, #4260, ghost, R, from $5 to $7.00

Sherbet, #40004, bear, 3 brighter versions, bl, lavender &
    magenta, ea from $7 to..$10.00

Sherbet, #4560, bear, 3 versions, pk, yel or gr, R, ea from $8 to .$12.00

Siam, #4369, Siamese cat, R, from $5 to $8.00

Side-Kick, #4532, dog, from $7 to $10.00

Signature bear (1999), #4228, R, from $8 to...................$10.00

Signature bear (2000), #4266, R, from $8 to...................$12.00

Signature bear (2001), #4375, R, from $8 to...................$12.00

Signature bear (2002), #4565, R, from $5 to...................$10.00

Signature bear (2003), from $5 to $10.00

Silver, #4242, tabby cat, gray, R, from $6 to...................$8.00

Sizzle, #4399, bear, red, R, from $6 to $10.00

Slayer, #4307, frilled dragon, R, from $5 to $7.00

Sledge, #4538, hammerhead shark, R, from $6 to.............$8.00

Slippery, #4222, seal, gray, R, from $5 to $7.00

Slither, #4031, snake, R, minimum value $600.00

Slowpoke, #4261, sloth, R, from $5 to............................$7.00

Sly, #4115, fox, 1st issue, all brn, R, minimum value.............$50.00

Sly, #4115, fox, 2nd issue, brn w/wht belly, R, from $10 to $15.00

Smart, #4353, 2001 graduation owl, R, from $5 to $8.00

Smarter, #4526, 2002 graduation owl, R, from $6 to $10.00

Smartest, #4591, 2003 graduation owl, from $5 to............$7.00

Smitten, #4577, bear, R, from $7 to $15.00

Smooch, #4335, bear, R, from $15 to $20.00

Smoochy, #4039, frog, R, from $5 to $7.00

Sneaky, #4278, leopard, R, from $6 to.............................$8.00

Sniffer, #4299, beagle, R, from $6 to..............................$8.00

Snocap, #4573, fox, from $6 to $9.00

Snort, #4002, bull, red w/cream feet, R, from $7 to $10.00

Snowball, #4201, snowman, R, from $8.00 to $12.00.

(Photo courtesy Amy Sullivan)

Snowgirl, #4333, snowgirl, R, from $8 to $12.00

Soar, #4410, eagle w/American flag wings, Ty Store, R, from $10
    to $15.00

Spangle, #4245, American bear, red, wht or bl face, R, from $8
    to $20.00

Sparky, #4100, dalmatian, R, minimum value.................$30.00

Speckles, #4402, bear, e-Beanie offered through Ty website, R,
    from $10 to..$12.00

Speedy, #4030, turtle, R, from $15 to $18.00

Spike, #4060, rhinoceros, R, from $5 to $7.00

Spinner, #4036, spider, striped, R, from $5 to $7.00

Spooky, #4090, ghost, orange neck ribbon, R, minimum value .$20.00

Sport, #4590, dog, from $5 to $7.00

Spot, #4000, dog, 1st issue, no spot on back, R, minimum value .$675.00

Spring, #4513, bunny, lt bl, R, from $5 to $8.00

Springy, #4272, bunny, lavender, R, from $5 to $7.00

Spunky, #4184, cocker spaniel, R, from $6 to $8.00

Squirmy, #4302, worm, gr, R, from $5 to $8.00

Starlett, #4382, cat, wht, R, from $5 to $7.00

Steg, #4087, stegosaurus, R, minimum value $275.00

Stilts, #4221, stork, R, from $5 to $7.00

Sting, #4077, stingray, R, minimum value.......................$40.00

Stinger, #4193, scorpion, R, from $5 to $7.00

Stinky, #4017, skunk, R, from $10 to $15.00

Stretch, #4182, ostrich, R, from $5 to $7.00

Stripes, #4065, 1st issue, gold tiger w/thin stripes, R, minimum
    value..$100.00

Stripes, #4065, 2nd issue, tiger, caramel, wide stripes, R, from
    $10 to $20.00

Strut, #4171, rooster, R, from $7 to $9.00

Sunny, #4401, e-Beanie bear, yel-orange, R, from $8 to $10.00

Sunray, #4598, manta ray, from $5 to $7.00

Snip, #4120, Siamese cat, R, from $5.00 to $7.00.

(Photo courtesy Amy Sullivan)

Swampy, #4273, alligator, R, from $5 to $8.00
Swirly, #4249, snail, R, from $5 to $7.00
Swoop, #4268, pterodactyl, R, from $5 to $7.00
Tabasco, #4002, bull, red feet, R, minimum value $40.00
Tabs, #4571, cat, from $5 to..$7.00
Tank, #4031, armadillo, 1st issue, no shell, 7 lines, R, minimum
    value..$30.00
Tank, #4031, armadillo, 2nd issue, no shell, 9 lines, R, minimum
    value..$150.00
Tank, #4031, armadillo, 3rd issue, w/shell, R, minimum
    value $60.00
Ted-e, brn bear, Ty Store, R, from $6 to $9.00
Teddy, #4050, bear, brn, new face, R, from $40 to $50.00
Teddy, #4050, bear, brn, old face, R, minimum value $535.00
Teddy, #4051, bear, teal, new face, R, minimum value ...$555.00
Teddy, #4051, bear, teal, old face, R, minimum value.....$535.00
Teddy, #4052, bear, cranberry, new face, R, minimum value .$550.00
Teddy, #4052, bear, cranberry, old face, R, minimum value .$535.00
Teddy, #4055, bear, violet, new face, R, minimum value.$550.00
Teddy, #4055, bear, violet, old face, R, minimum value .$535.00
Teddy, #4056, bear, magenta, new face, R, minimum value .$550.00
Teddy, #4056, bear, magenta, old face, R, minimum value..$535.00
Teddy, #4057, bear, jade, new face, R, minimum value ..$550.00
Teddy, #4057, bear, jade, old face, R, minimum value $535.00
Teddy, #4347, 100th Year Anniversary bear w/gold medal around
    neck, from $5 to $9.00
Thank You bear, given to Ty authorized retailers to display in
    their stores, R, from $175 to $225.00
The Beginning, #4267, bear, wht w/silver stars, R, from $10 to .$15.00
The End, #4265, bear, blk, R, from $10 to $15.00
Thistle, #4623, bear, Ty Europe exclusive, from $40 to $45.00
Tiny, #4234, chihuahua, R, from $6 to $8.00
Tiptoe, #4241, mouse, R, from $5 to................................$7.00
Tooter, #4559, dinosaur, from $7 to $10.00
Toothy, #4523, tyrannosaurus, R, from $6 to.....................$8.00
Tracker, #4198, basset hound, R, from $6 to.....................$8.00
Tracks, #4507, lynx, R, from $6 to $8.00
Tradee, #4403, Ty Store, R, from $8 to $10.00
Trap, #4042, mouse, R, minimum value.........................$465.00
Tricks, #4311, dog, R, from $5 to $8.00
Trumpet, #4276, elephant, R, from $5 to $8.00
Tubbo, #4597, hippo, from $5 to $7.00
Tuffy, #4108, terrier, R, from $5 to.................................$8.00
Turk-e, #4416, turkey, Ty Store, from $8 to $10.00
Tusk, #4076, walrus, R, from $35 to $40.00
Twitterbug, #4580, cicada, R, from $7 to..........................$9.00
Ty Billionaire bear (1998), brn, new face, dollar sign on chest,
    issued only to Ty employees, R, minimum value $700.00
Ty Billionaire II bear (1999), purple, BB on chest, issued only to
    Ty employees, R, minimum value $775.00
Ty Billionaire III bear (2000), orange, issued only to Ty employ-
    ees, R, minimum value $700.00
Ty Billionaire IV bear (2001), brn, issued only to Ty employees,
    R, minimum value $650.00
Ty Billionaire V bear (2002), bl, issued only to Ty employees, R,
    minimum value $650.00
Ty Employee Christmas bear (1997), violet, new face, R, mini-
    mum value $2,600.00

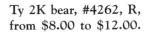

Ty 2K bear, #4262, R, from $8.00 to $12.00.

(Photo courtesy Amy Sullivan)

Unity, #4606, Ty Europe exclusive, R, from $20 to..........$25.00
USA, #4287, American bear, USA exclusive, R, from $7 to .$10.00
Valentina, #4233, bear, fuchsia w/wht heart, R, from $6 to............$8.00
Valentino, #4058, bear, wht w/red heart, R, from $8 to................$12.00
Vanda, #4614, Asia-Pacific flower bear, bl, Singapore exclusive,
    R, from $15 to $30.00
Velvet, #4064, panther, R, from $12 to $20.00
Waddle, #4075, penguin, R, from $10 to.........................$12.00
Wales, #4610, bear, red, Wales exclusive, R, from $18
    to $25.00
Wallace, #4264, bear, gr, R, from $6 to............................$9.00
Wattlie, #4616, Asia-Pacific flower bear, gr, Australia exclusive,
    from $20 to $30.00
Waves, #4084, whale, R, from $6 to $8.00
Web, #4041, spider, blk, R, minimum value $225.00
Weenie, #4013, dachshund, R, from $10 to $15.00
Whiskers, #4317, terrier, R, from $5 to $7.00
Whisper, #4187, deer, R, from $5 to $7.00
Wiggly, #4275, octopus, R, from $5 to $7.00
Wise, #4194, 1998 graduation owl, R, from $6 to $8.00
Wiser, #4238, 1999 graduation owl, R, from $5 to $7.00
Wisest, #4286, 2000 graduation owl, R, from $5 to............$8.00
Wish, #4594, starfish, from $5 to $7.00
Woody, #4539, brn bear, from $5 to $8.00
Wrinkles, #4103, bulldog, R, from $6 to...........................$8.00
Yours Truly, #4701, bear, Hallmark Gold Crown Stores exclu-
    sive, R, from $10 to..$15.00
Zero, #4207, penguin, w/Christmas cap, R, from $5 to..........$7.00
Zeus, #4589, moose, from $5 to $7.00
Ziggy, #4063, zebra, R, from $10 to..................................$15.00
Zip, #4004, cat, 1st issue, blk w/wht face & tummy, R, minimum
    value...$200.00
Zip, #4004, cat, 2nd issue, all blk, R, minimum value $200.00
Zip, #4004, cat, 3rd issue, blk w/wht paws, R, from $8 to $12.00
Zodaic Goat, #4329, R, from $6 to $8.00
Zodaic Horse, #4324, R, from $6 to $8.00
Zodiac Dog, #4326, R, from $6 to $8.00
Zodiac Monkey, #4328, R, from $6 to $8.00
Zodiac Ox, #4319, R, from $6 to $8.00
Zodiac Pig, #4327, R, from $6 to $8.00
Zodiac Rabbit, #4321, R, from $6 to..................................$8.00
Zodiac Rat, #4318, R, from $6 to.......................................$8.00

Zodiac Rooster, #4325, R, from $6 to $8.00
Zodiac Snake, #4323, R, from $6 to $8.00
Zodiac Tiger, #4320, R, from $6 to $8.00
Zoom, #4545, turtle, from $6 to..$8.00

Bicycles, Motorbikes, and Tricycles

The most interesting of the vintage bicycles are those made from the 1920s into the 1960s, though a few even later models are collectible as well. Some from the '50s were very futuristic and styled with sweeping Art Deco lines; others had wonderful features such as built-in radios and brake lights, and some were decked out with saddlebags and holsters to appeal to fans of Hoppy, Gene, and many other western heroes. Watch for reproductions.

Condition is everything when evaluating bicycles, and one worth $2,500.00 in excellent or better condition might be worth as little as $50.00 in unrestored, poor condition. But here are a few values to suggest a range.

Note: A girl's bicycle does not command the price of a boy's bicycle in the same model. The difference can be as much as ½ to ⅓ less.

Advisor: Richard Trautwein (T3)

AMF Jr Rocket, 24", G, from $85 to $135.00
AMF Spiderman Jr Roadmaster, 1978, boy's, EX, A $100.00

Cleveland Racing Bicycle, boy's, 1896, wooden wheels, cork handgrips, leather seat, 38", VG, from $250.00 to $300.00.
(Photo courtesy Copake Auction, Inc.)

Colson Firestone Cruiser, 1930s, girl's, 3-ribbed snap-in tank,
    Delta front fender light, Fair, from $110 to..............$200.00
Colson Firestone Super Cruiser, 1950s, girl's, EX, A $325.00
Columbia Airrider, 1940-41, boy's, EX, A $800.00
Columbia Model #46, 1890s, girl's, wooden rear fender, spoon
    brake, G, A $200.00
Columbia Playbike 3-Speed, 1970s-80s, boy's, VG $75.00
Columbia Superb, 1941, boy's, VG $600.00
Columbia 3-Star Deluxe, 1949-50, girl's, VG, A $100.00
Crescent #12 Pneumatic Safety, 1890s, girl's, G, A $225.00
Dayton Pneumatic Safety, 1915-20, boy's, G, from $125 to...$155.00
Elgin, 1937, girl's, w/rack & headlight, G $400.00
Elgin Blackhawk, 1934, boy's, rstr, A.............................$2,000.00
Elgin Miss America, 1940, girl's, rstr, A......................$1,900.00

Elgin Pneumatic Safety, 1927-28, boy's, VC older rstr, A.$175.00
Garton Falcon, 26", G+, A...$170.00
Hawthorn Zep, ca 1939, boy's, rstr, A $3,000.00

Hendee Indian Electric, 1918, boy's, good older restoration, from $2,600.00 to $3,200.00. (Photo courtesy Copake Auction, Inc.)

Huffman Topflight, 1941, boy's, rare, VG, A...............$1,600.00
Huffy BMX, 1970s, boy's, VG, from $100 to.....................$75.00
Humber Sports Classic 3-Speed, 1960s, boy's, EX, A $100.00

Indian Motorcycle Co., 1930, boy's, VG, from $7,000.00 to $8,000.00. (Photo courtesy Copake Auction, Inc.)

Iver Johnson, 1939, girl's, balloon tires, 26", Fair, A.........$55.00
Iver Johnson Cruiser, 1936, girl's, G, from $70 to...........$100.00
JC Higgins Flow Motion, 1948, girl's, rstr, from $100 to..$150.00
JC Higgins Wonderide Spring Fork, 1950s, boy's, EX, from $800
    to $900.00
John Wanamaker Continent Pneumatic Safety, 1890s, girl's,
    Fair, A $185.00
Meade Crusader, 1920s, boy's, w/'Solar' headlamp, Fair w/some
    rpt, A $150.00
Monarch Firestone Pilot, 1941, boy's, Fair, A $275.00
Monarch Firestone Super Cruiser, 1949, boy's, 26", VG, from
    $550 to $650.00
Monarch Silver King M1, 1937, boy's, VG, A.................$525.00
Montgomery Ward's Hawthorn Cruiser, 1939, girl's, G, A...$50.00
Raleigh Chopper, 1970s, boy's, EX $150.00
Raleigh Space Rider 3-Speed, 1968, boy's, EX, A.............$75.00
Raleigh Sports Classic 3-Speed, 1970s, boy's, EX, A $100.00
Red Indian, 1890-1900, boy's, pneumatic safety w/wooden rims,
    saddle grips, oil lamp, G, A $750.00
Roadmaster Fleet Wing, 1941, girl's, rpt, A.....................$70.00

Schwinn Black Phantom, 1950s, boy's, balloon tires, rstr, from $1,000 to...$1,500.00
Schwinn Black Phantom, 1950s, girl's, balloon tires, rstr, A .$800.00
Schwinn Century Motobike, 1937, boy's, G, from $1,500 to.$2,000.00
Schwinn Collegiate Sport S, 1979, boy's, M, A.............$100.00
Schwinn Corvette, 1964, boy's, EX, A..........................$200.00
Schwinn Debutante, 1950s, girl's, 26", G, A....................$90.00

Schwinn Fleet, 1964, boy's, VG, $230.00. (Photo courtesy Copake Auction, Inc.)

Schwinn Henderson, 1937, girl's, G partially rstr condition, from $500 to...$600.00
Schwinn Hollywood, 1940, girl's, Fair, A......................$100.00
Schwinn Scrambler Phantom BMX, 1970-80, boy's, EX, A..$75.00
Schwinn Spitfire, 1950, girl's, rstr, from $150 to.............$200.00
Schwinn Stingray Pea Picker, 1968, boy's, VG, A..........$525.00
Schwinn Stingray Slik-Chik, 1965, girl's, G, A..............$150.00
Schwinn Stingray 5-Speed, 1970, boy's, EX, from $150 to .$200.00
Sears Free Spirit, 1960s, boy's, 20", EX.........................$90.00
Sears Spaceliner, 1960s, boy's, G, from $100 to.............$150.00
Shelby Traveler, 1938, boy's, G, A $175.00
Westfield Columbia Balloon Cruiser, 1930s, girl's, Fair, A ..$35.00

MOTORBIKES

Elgin Motorbike/Bicycle, G $400.00
Monarch Super-Twin, 1949, EX, A.............................$3,200.00

Speed Cycle, 1930s, with imitation twin-cylinder motor, 46" long, VG, $650.00 to $850.00. (Photo courtesy Randy Inman Auctions)

Whizzer Pontiac Chiefton, 1950s, Fair, A......................$625.00
Whizzer Sportsman, w/windshield, 20", rstr................$3,200.00

TRICYCLES

Anthony Bros Tri-Bike, 1950s, convertible cast aluminum, G, A...$55.00

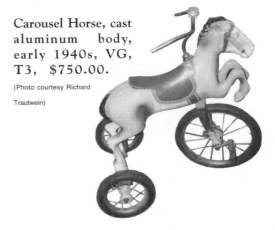

Carousel Horse, cast aluminum body, early 1940s, VG, T3, $750.00.
(Photo courtesy Richard Trautwein)

Colson, 1940s, VG, A...$50.00
Donaldson Jockey Cycle, scooter-type handlebars, 24½x37", rpt, from $350 to $400.00
Early American, 1880-90, blk pnt strap steel fr, leather-covered pan seat, wooden hdl grips, 24" front wheel, G, A ..$325.00
Gendron Pioneer, wide-spoked front wheel, 19½", G $375.00
Good Humor Trike, 1955, chain drive, 36", EX, from $1,000 to $1,400.00
Indland Pinky Lee Sports Trike, 36", G+, A $85.00
Iver Johnson, 1920s-30s, 19" front wheels, VG, A $130.00
Murray Airflow Jr, pnt pressed steel, 17½", G, from $75 to..$125.00
Rocket, prewar, Airflow design, rear wheel steering, needs rstr, from $300 to $400.00

Sky Skipper, Junior Toy Corporation, Hammond, Indiana, 1937, 16" front wheels, fully restored, T3, $1,400.00. (Photo courtesy Richard Trautwein)

Black Americana

Black subjects were commonly depicted in children's toys as long ago as the late 1870s. Among the most widely collected today are the fine windup toys made both here and in Germany.

Early cloth and later composition and vinyl dolls are favorites of many; others enjoy ceramic figurines. Many factors enter into evaluating Black Americana, especially in regard to the hand-made dolls and toys, since quality is subjective to individual standards. Because of this you may find wide ranges in dealers' asking prices.

    Advisor: Judy Posner (P6)

    See also Banks; Battery-Operated Toys; Schoenhut; Windups, Friction, and Other Mechanicals.

Bike Bobber, golliwog figure, spring-mounted, bobs up & down, back & forth, eyes move, 5", MOC, A........................$30.00
Book, Further Adventures of Wongabilla, Australian, hardcover, 50 pgs, EX, A............................$300.00
Book, Jasper & the Watermelons, George Pal 'Puppetoons,' Diamond Publishing, 1945, Pal illus, VG+ (w/dust jacket).$95.00
Book, Jolly Romps, England, prewar, cb cover, 18 pgs of poems & stories, EX............................$65.00
Book, Little Black Sambo, Bannerman, 1948, hardcover, 20 pgs (4 mechanical), NM............................$175.00

Book, Little Black Sambo, Rand McNally, G, $95.00.

Book, Presents Past & Present, Frederick Loeser Co Christmas premium, 1920s, 12 pgs, EX, P6............................$75.00
Book, Sunshine Corner Picture & Story Book, England, 1930s, hardcover, EX............................$75.00
Book, Ten Little 'N' Boys, Great Britain, last edition, 1965, hardcover, 54 pgs, EX+, A............................$125.00
Book, The Story of Little Black Sambo, McLoughlin, 1938, illus by Hildegarde Lupprain, 50 pgs, VG+............................$100.00
Book, The Three Little Black Boys/A Play With Me Book, England, hardcover, 10 pgs, mechanical & pop-out features, M, A............................$80.00
Book, Topsy, McLoughlin, 1880s, diecut hardcover figure of Topsy, 14 pgs, 9", EX+, A............................$425.00
Book, Well Done Noddy!, by Enid Blyton, hardcover, EX...$30.00
Book, You Funny Little Noddy, by Enid Blyton, 1950, EX, P6.$30.00
Candy Container, litho tin egg shape w/image of Black baby hatching from lg egg w/chickens & ducks, Germany, 1890s, EX+............................$250.00
Doll, Dream Baby, compo body w/brn bsk head, open/close eyes, pnt hair, wht gown, Armand Marseille, 1920s, 10", EX, A...$285.00
Doll, girl, brn cloth w/blk-printed features & short blk wig, red & wht striped dress w/wht apron, 15", EX, A.........$275.00

Doll, girl, all bisque with swivel neck, painted features with open eyes, astrakhan wig, jointed, comes with outfit, Kestner/Germany, late 1800s – early 1900s, 6", VG, A, $375.00. (Photo courtesy Skinner, Inc.)

Doll, girl, stuffed brn muslin body covered w/blk stockinette, embroidered features, yarn wig, cloth dress, 20", VG, A............$475.00
Doll, girl toddler, jtd compo body, eyes w/metal lids, open mouth, curly wig, wht dress & underwear, Germany, 18", VG, A............................$350.00
Doll, Golliwog, crocheted yarn body w/crocheted bow at neck, lg eyes, red & yel, England, 1950s, 7", NM, A.........$100.00
Doll, Golliwog, stuffed cloth, mink-like hair, lg facial features, pinstriped pants, jacket & bow tie, prewar, 13", EX...$100.00
Doll, Golliwog, stuffed cloth, Susie Brand/Hong Kong, 8", MIP (sealed), A............................$75.00
Doll, Golliwog Cowboy, ceramic & Bakelite, detailed cloth outfit w/leather chaps, poseable arms, 7", NM.............$150.00
Doll, Mammy, brn cloth w/bl cloth legs, pnt features, sew-on bandanna, cloth dress, pnt shoes, early 20th C, 16", EX, A............................$750.00
Doll, Native, stuffed plush & felt caricature native holding spear, yel 'grass' skirt, leaf on head, 8", NM, A....................$20.00
Doll, shoulder head, cloth body w/papier-mache head & upper body, wooden lower limbs, lacy dress, mid-19th century, 9", EX, A............................$750.00
Doll, stockinette, child, stuffed body w/stitched features, astrakhan wig, shirt, overalls, hat, American, early 1900s,10", EX.$520.00
Doll, stockinette, lady, stuffed body w/embroidered features, astrakhan wig, dress, shoes, American, early 1900s, 21", EX, A...$2,300.00
Doll, stockinette, man, stuffed body w/embroidered features, astrakhan wig, no clothes, w/shoes, American, early 1900s, 21", VG.$980.00
Doll, Topsy-Turvy, stuffed cloth, 4 faces w/embroidered features, cotton dresses w/matching bonnets, late 1900s, 19", EX.....$300.00
Figure, Banjo Player (seated Uncle Remus), pnt CI, Hubley, 1920s, 2½", scarce, EX+............................$125.00

Figure Set, Jazz Band, painted cast iron, tallest approximately 2½", VG, A, $260.00. (Photo courtesy Skinner, Inc.)

Figure, Golliwog musicians, chalkware, Robertsons Marmalade premiums, 3-pc, 3", NM+, A.....................$100.00
Figure, Mammy Clapping, pnt CI, Hubley, 1920s, 3½", VG+, A.....................$60.00
Figure, Sambo Dancing, pnt CI, Hubley, 1920s, 2¼", EX, A..$150.00
Figure, Topsey Seated, pnt CI, Hubley, 1920s, 2", NM, A ..$90.00
Game, Chuck, target, litho cb, Ottman/USA, 1890s, rare, EXIB, A $360.00
Game, Dr Busby, Milton Bradley, 1905, NMIB, A $365.00
Game, Game of Animal, Milton Bradley, 1920s, EX+IB, A .$85.00
Game, Game of Door Jenny (The Mishaps of a Little Donkey), USA, 1929, NMIB, A $220.00
Game, Game of Sambo, ring toss, Parker Bros, 1900s, NM+..$300.00
Game, Game of Snap (Punch & Judy Series), McLoughlin Bros, 1892, EXIB, A $180.00
Game, Happy Party Game/Twenty Little 'N' Boys, England, pre-war, NM $75.00
Game, Jolly Darkie Target Game, McLoughlin Bros, 1890s, complete, EX $575.00
Game, Little Black Sambo, Cadaco-Ellis, 1945, VGIB ..$125.00
Game, Little Black Sambo Target, Wyandotte, w/gun & darts, 23x14", VG, A.....................$150.00
Game, Muffin & Golly Card Game, 45 cards w/Muffin & friends, England, late 1940s, NMIB $100.00
Game, My Black Babies/Shoot the Babies, steel fold-up target game, 22x9x11", VG, A.....................$1,500.00
Game, Poke the Golly, unused, England, 1920s, NM+, A..$35.00

Game, Sambo Target, Wyandotte, litho tin, complete with gun and darts 23x14", VG, $150.00. (Photo courtesy James D. Julia Inc.)

Kobe Toy, acrobat figure swing freely over trapeze bar when knob is turned, wood, 5¼", EX, A, $385.00. (Photo courtesy Bertoia Auctions)

Game, Snakes & Ladders, England, 1940s-50s, NMIB...$160.00
Game, Zulu Native Target, Knickerbocker, 1950s, complete, EX.....................$35.00
Jigger, Jubilee, articulated wood figure in cloth clothes dances atop wooden box w/beveled base, Webb, 1870s, 10", EX, A..$1,150.00
Kobe Toy, figure seated in 3-wheeled cart holds stick in hand, head wobbles, wood, Japan, 7" L, VG, A.....................$240.00
Kobe Toy, figure w/oversized head in top hat holds stick in hand, hat unscrews to be used as container, wood, 4", EX, A........$240.00
Kobe Toy, man seated at block table lifts arms to mouth when side knob is turned, Japan, late 19th century, 4", VG, A $100.00
Mechanical Hand Toy, metal, squeeze & clown w/hammer hits bouncing Golliwog, circus tent behind, prewar, 5½", NM+, A.....................$125.00
Mechanical Toy, Black Man in Rocking Chair, articulated mouth, tin figure w/cloth outfit, tin hat, wire chair, 6", G, A ..$800.00
Mechanical Toy, Black Suffragette, clockwork, cloth-dressed, seated in front of drums atop wooden box, EX, A ..$3,080.00
Mechanical Toy, Boxers, clockwork, 2 cloth-dressed figures w/CI feet atop wooden box, 11", EX, A $10,450.00
Mechanical Toy, Boy on Velocipede, clockwork, cloth-dressed, 3 spoke wheels, Stevens & Brown, Pat 1870, 12", EX, A $3,080.00
Mechanical Toy, Dancers (2), clockwork, cloth dresses w/pnt wht knee socks atop wooden box, Ives, 1890s, 10", EX,A.$880.00
Mechanical Toy, Dancing Couple, clockwork, cloth-dressed, rnd wood stage w/cloth & paper backdrop, 1800s, 10½", EX, A...$4,180.00
Mechanical Toy, Dancing Man, clockwork, cloth-dressed on wire hook on platform, Ives/Charles Hatchkiss, 1886, 12", EX, A.....................$3,300.00
Mechanical Toy, Fiddler, clockwork, cloth-dressed w/tin shoes, glass eyes, seated on wood box, Ives, 1880s, 10", EX, A.....$6,000.00
Mechanical Toy, Happy Joe Dancing Dude, crank-op, litho tin, KW/Germany, 1920s, 3¼", EX.....................$350.00

Mechanical Toy, Jubilee Dancer, articulated wood figure with cloth clothes dances atop wooden box, spring motor, Webb, 1870s, 10", EX, A, $1,150.00. (Photo courtesy Skinner, Inc.)

Mechanical Toy, Microphone Dancer, battery-op, voice or music activated tin & wood figure by lamppost, National, 12", EX $300.00
Mechanical Toy, Native Drummer, rocks back & forth as he plays drum, Marx USA, 8", NM, A $130.00
Mechanical Toy, Negro Preacher, clockwork, cloth-dressed man atop stenciled wooden pulpit, Ives, 1880s, 10½", NMIB, A .$6,600.00

Mechanical Toy, Pango Pango, native spins & dances as head goes back & forth, Japan, 6½", MIB, A $150.00

Mechanical Toy, Preacher at the Pulpit, clockwork, cloth-dressed figure atop wooden box, Ives, 10½", re-dressed, EX, A...$3,080.00

Nodder, barefoot boy seated on box holding chalkboard, bsk, Austria, 1880s, 5½", NM $365.00

Paper Dolls, Oh Susanna! Musical Pack O' Fun, complete, unused, EX, P6...$65.00

Puppet, Golliwog (Jumpelles), pnt wood w/cloth outfit, Pelham, 9", NMIB, A $180.00

Puppet, marionette, minstrel strumming banjo, wood w/cloth outfit, 14", unused, MIB, A $250.00

Puppet Set, Boy, Girl & Baby, molded rubber hand puppets, 3-pc, Child Craft, 1965, EX+, A $60.00

Puppet Set, Mother, Father & Grandparents, molded rubber hand puppets, 4-pc, Child Craft, 1965, 9½", EX, A ..$60.00

Puzzle, jigsaw, Boo Boogey Man, red, wht & bl image of 3 missionaries & 3 natives stranded on an island, 4", NMIB $65.00

Puzzle, jigsaw, carnival scene w/Golly & friends on roller coaster, litho wood, England, prewar, NMIB, A $125.00

Puzzle, jigsaw, Golly & 'Noah' loading train (ark) w/animals, litho wood, very scarce, unused, NMIB, A $100.00

Puzzle, jigsaw, jack-in-the-box scene w/Golly in toy room, litho wood, England, prewar, unused, MIB......................$175.00

Puzzle, jigsaw, snow scene w/Golly & friends & train, litho wood, scarce, NMIB $150.00

Ramp Walker, Mammy, wood figure in cloth dress & headscarf, ca 1900, 4½", NM, A $75.00

Roly Poly Clown, papier-mache body, pointed felt hat with plush brim, white with red trim, 7", VG, A, $150.00.

(Photo courtesy Bertoia Auctions)

Whirligig, Dancing Sam and Dan the Banjo Man, painted wood, Eau Clair Wood Products Company, 12½x20", MIB, A, $1,100.00. (Photo courtesy James D. Julia Inc.)

Roly Poly, man in suit w/cigar in hand, pnt pressed cb, brn face w/eyes encircled w/lt tan, mc clothes, 9½", VG, A .$230.00

Sand Pail, litho tin w/A Present From The Seaside around rim & beach scene w/2 Golliwogs, England, 1920s, 7", EX, A .$200.00

Squeeze Toy, Golliwog figure, pnt rubber, England, 1930s, 6", NM, A..$85.00

Boats

Though some commercially made boats date as far back as the late 1800s, they were produced on a much larger scale during WWI and the decade that followed and again during the years that spanned WWII. Some were scaled-down models of battleships measuring nearly three feet in length. While a few were actually seaworthy, many were designed with small wheels to be pulled along the carpet or out of doors on dry land. Others were motor-driven windups, and later a few were even battery operated. Some of the larger manufacturers were Bing (Germany), Dent (Pennsylvania), Orkin Craft (California), Liberty Playthings (New York), and Arnold (West Germany).

Advisor: Richard Trautwein (T3)

See also Battery-Operated Toys; Cast Iron, Boats; Paper-Lithographed Toys; Tootsietoys; Windups, Friction, and Other Mechanicals; and other specific manufacturers.

Aircraft Carrier, Japan, 1950s, battery-op, wood, bl-gray & red, 13", EX, from $130 to $230.00

Aircraft Carrier, Linemar, 1960s, battery-op, litho tin, w/airplanes, 14", nonworking o/w EX+IB, from $200 to .$250.00

Aircraft Carrier, Ventura/Italy, 1950s, battery-op, plastic, 31", VG $125.00

Battleship, Bing, w/up, pnt tin, 2-tone bl-gray w/red trim, 16", EXIB, A $4,500.00

Battleship, Bing, w/up, tin, 2-tone gray w/blk, red & wht trim, 16", VG+, A...$1,980.00

Battleship, Carette, w/up, pnt tin, bl & gray, 2 planes supported from masts, 15", rstr, A..$1,200.00

Battleship, Carette, w/up, pnt tin, 14", rstr $350.00

Battleship, Dayton, friction, pressed steel, 2-tone gr w/gold guns, masts & trim, 2 red stacks, lifeboats, 18", EX, A $550.00

Battleship, Fleischmann, w/up, pnt tin, 3 stacks & 2 masts, fore & aft flags, deck cannons & swivel guns, 17", rstr, A .$1,500.00

Battleship, Ives, w/up, pnt tin, gray & wht, 14", rstr, A..$750.00

Battleship, Japan, battery-op, pnt wood w/extensive details, cabin lifts up, 31", EX (partial wooden box)............$600.00

Battleship, Orkin, w/up, pnt tin & steel, 38", EX, A...$5,000.00

Battleship, Sutcliff, w/up, pnt steel, 12", unused, NMIB...$100.00

Battleship (Lubeck), contemporary, wht & red, 41", rstr (no motor), A $1,200.00

Battleship (New York), Marklin, w/up, pnt tin, 35", rstr, A ..$20,900.00

Battleship (New York), Orkin, w/up, tin, complete, 25", EX,A..$475.00

Battleship (Taku), Lehmann, w/up, litho tin, 9½", EXIB, A ..$525.00

Battleship (USS Washington), Marx, w/up, litho tin, 15", VG+, A $100.00

Battleship (Yamato), Japan, candle-powered, litho tin, 8", EX+IB, A $60.00

Battleship (Wisconsin), Orkin, 38", restored, $1,550.00. (Photo courtesy Randy Inman Auctions)

Cabin Cruiser, Ito, wood, electric motor, 15½", VGIB ..$225.00
Cabin Cruiser (Sea Queen) #56, Japan, litho tin, 10", G+, A.$110.00
Cabin Cruiser (Vacationer #22), Linemar, 1950s, battery-op,
   litho tin, 12½", NM+IB $325.00

Cabin Cruiser (Deluxe), Orkin, 1932, scale model, white, red, and black with gold cast fittings and trim, 33", EX, from $2,000.00 to $2,800.00. (Photo courtesy Bertoia Auctions)

Cruiser (U.S.S. Marcella), Orkin, pressed steel with nickel-plated deck, 18", EX, $2,100.00. (Photo courtesy Bertoia Auctions)

Dreadnaught (Nevada modeled after USS New Mexico), Orkin,
   w/up, pressed steel, some NP accessories, 22", rstr, A..$2,475.00
Ferry Boat, Keystone, stenciled wood w/metal ramps, w/2 cars &
   tandem trucks, 12", NMIB, A $110.00
Flotilla, Bing, gunboat w/4 smaller boats, attached by rods, pnt
   tin, 27", VG $800.00
Freighter, Fleischmann, pnt tin, red, blk & wht, opening cargo
   lid cover, lifeboats, 15", EX+, A.......................$1,100.00
Gunboat, American, friction, pnt tin, 15", G+, A $325.00
Gunboat, Carette, w/up, pnt tin, red & wht, 11", rstr, A..$360.00
Gunboat, Carette, w/up, pnt tin, 18½", VG, from $850 to .$1,000.00
Gunboat, Carette, w/up, pnt tin, 8", rpt, A.................$55.00
Gunboat, Marklin, w/up, pnt tin, 11½", rstr, A $500.00
Gunboat (Japanese), w/up, pnt tin, 13", Fair, A.............$60.00

Hornby Speedboat (Alcyon), Meccano, w/up, pressed steel, 11",
   EXIB, A $130.00
Hornby Speedboat (Condor), Meccano, w/up, pressed steel, 16",
   G, A $55.00
Hornby Speedboat (Hornby), Meccano, w/up, pressed steel, 16",
   G $60.00
Hornby Speedboat (Racer II), Meccano, w/up, pressed steel, 12",
   VG, A $90.00
Hornby Speedboat (Racer III), Meccano, pressed steel, 16", rstr,
   A $100.00
Hornby Speedboat (Swift), Meccano, w/up, pressed steel, 12",
   NMIB..,.....................................$125.00
Hornby Speedboat (Venture), Meccano, w/up, pressed steel, 16",
   rstr, A $110.00
Hornby Speedboat (Viking), Meccano, w/up, pressed steel,
   16½", EXIB, A............................$165.00
Lackawanna Railroad Ferry, CK, w/up, litho tin, 10", EX, A.$300.00
Launch, Bing, pnt tin, steam engine w/brass boiler, 19", EXIB,
   A $1,760.00
Live Steam Launch, Schoenner, pnt tin, brass burner, 12½", G+,
   A $825.00
Neptune Tug Boat, TM, battery-op, litho tin, 14", NM .$125.00
Ocean Liner, Arnold, w/up, tin, red, blk & wht, 13", EX, A.$450.00
Ocean Liner, Bing, w/up, litho tin, red, blk & wht, 6½", VG..$225.00
Ocean Liner, Bing, w/up, litho tin, red, blk & wht, 10", EX, A..$400.00
Ocean Liner, Bing, w/up, pnt tin, red, blk & wht, 21", rstr, A ..$2,530.00

Ocean Liner, Bing, wind-up, painted tin, 40", restored, A, $3,080.00.

(Photo courtesy Randy Inman Auctions)

Ocean Liner, Carette, w/up, pnt tin, red, wht, blk & gray, 18",
   rstr, A $1,200.00
Ocean Liner, Carette, w/up, pnt tin, red & wht, 12½", rstr, A .$360.00
Ocean Liner, Dayton, friction, pnt tin, wave design around bottom, 12½", G+ $250.00
Ocean Liner, Fleischmann, w/up, pnt tin, red, blk & wht, 2
   stacks, 19", partially rstr, A $1,050.00
Ocean Liner, Fleischmann, w/up, pnt tin, red, blk & wht, 2 yel
   stacks, 10½", EX+, A $600.00
Ocean Liner, Fleischmann, w/up, pnt tin, wht w/bl & red, single
   stack, 20", EX, A...........................$600.00
Ocean Liner, Germany, tin, fly-wheel motor, red, wht & bl
   w/lithoed deck, 8", EXIB $450.00
Ocean Liner, Germany, w/up, pnt tin, red, wht & blk, 13", non-
   working o/w VG, A $250.00
Ocean Liner, Ives, w/up, pnt tin, red, blk, wht & yel, 13", EX+,
   A $1,050.00
Ocean Liner, Ives, w/up, pnt tin, red, blk & wht, 13½", rstr .$750.00

Ocean Liner, Liberty, dual w/up for twin screw engine, mostly wood, 27", Fair, A $385.00

Ocean Liner, Modern Toys, battery-op, litho tin, red, wht & bl, 22", VG, A $65.00

Ocean Liner, Wolverine, w/up, litho tin, 14", NMIB (box mk Luxury Liner) $250.00

Ocean Liner (Queen Mary), Japan, w/up, litho tin, 10", EX, A .$110.00

Ocean Liner (United States), Japan, battery-op, litho tin, red, blk & wht, 18", EX (w/partial box), A $285.00

Ocean Liner (United States), Marusan, friction, pnt tin, red, blk & wht, 16", EX+IB, A $275.00

Ocean Liner w/Circling Planes, Kellerman, w/up, litho tin, 10½", EX, A $650.00

Ocean Liner w/Circling Planes, Kellerman, w/up, litho tin, 10½", EX+IB, A $1,200.00

Oil Tanker, Fleischmann, w/up, pnt tin, red, blk & wht, 20", EX+ $750.00

Patrol Boat, CKO, w/up, litho tin, red sides w/wht deck, 2 figures, 9", EX, A $250.00

Patrol Boat, Japan, w/up, litho tin, red & wht sides, mounted guns, w/figure, 9", EXIB, A $260.00

Patrol Boat (Scout), Ives, w/up, pnt tin, 14", G, A $300.00

Phantom Raider, Ideal, 1960s, changes from freighter to cruiser, 30", NMIB $165.00

Queen of the Sea, MT, battery-op, litho tin, 21½", MIB, L4 ..$575.00

Racing Skull, Issmayer, windup, tin, four-man rowing team, 20½", VG, $4,400.00. (Photo courtesy Randy Inman Auctions)

Riverboat, Carette, w/up, pnt tin, wht & gray w/red & yel trim, 19", rstr, A $1,200.00

Riverboat, Schoenner, live steam, pnt tin, steerable rudder, 8", pnt wear, A $330.00

Riverboat, Ubelacker, w/up, pnt tin, yel & blk w/red trim, 20", rstr, A $1,100.00

Riverboat (Vulcan), Ubelacker, w/up, pnt tin, red & wht w/blk stacks, 24", EX, A $3,850.00

Runnerboat, NKK/Japan, battery-op, wood, bl & red, 9½", MIB, A $60.00

Sailboat, Keystone, wood w/vinyl sail, 16", EX+, A $25.00

Sailboat (Maria), Germany, w/up, litho tin, uniformed pilot controls sail w/rope in hand, 9", EX, A $1,320.00

Sailboat (Squalo), Ventura/Italy, 1950s, plastic, mc, 33", EX, A $175.00

Sea Babe, Fleetline, battery-op, wood, 13", NMIB, from $100 to $160.00

Side-Wheeler, Carette, ca 1900, tin, w/spring motor & smoke key, 8", VG, A $175.00

Side-Wheeler (Atlantic), Althof, Bergman & Co, pnt tin, 10", EX $7,650.00

Side-Wheeler (La Suisse), Fulgurex/Switzerland, painted tin, red and white, 41", EX+, from $3,000.00 to $3,400.00. (Photo courtesy Bertoia Auctions)

Speedboat, Japan, battery-op, wood, dual inboard motors, w/lights & flag, red & blk, uses 4 D-cell batteries, 18", VG $150.00

Speedboat, Lindstrom, w/up, litho tin, gr & red, 14", VG+ .$200.00

Speedboat, Lindstrom, w/up outboard motor, litho tin, red, yel & gr, 21", EX, A $500.00

Speedboat, Lindstrom, w/up outboard motor, litho tin, w/driver, 12", G+ $150.00

Speedboat, Lionel-Craft, w/up, heavy tin, wht & red, 2 figures, 17", NM, A $935.00

Speedboat, Lionel-Craft, w/up, heavy tin, wht & red, 2 figures, 17", VG, A $385.00

Speedboat, Orkin, w/up, masonite, twin cockpit, yel, blk & red, w/driver, 29", VG+, A $775.00

Speedboat (Miss America), Lindstrom, w/up, litho tin, w/driver, 7", G from $35 to $55.00

Speedboat (Miss Canada), steam-powered, pnt tin, gr & red w/brass boiler, British flag, w/funnel & fuel can, 12", VG+, A $400.00

Speedboat (Queen-3), Marusan, 1950, w/up, litho tin, w/driver, 6½", NM+IB, A $150.00

Steam Launch, Bing, live steam, tin, canopied top, 16½", G+, A $880.00

Steam Launch, HE Boucher, speedboat style with twin cylinder motor marked New York U.S.A., complete with fuel and steam tanks, 50", restored, A, $500.00. (Photo courtesy Randy Inman Auctions)

Steam Launch, Schoenner (?), forward canopy w/twin benches, 21", overpnt, from $375 to **$450.00**

Steam Launch (Radiguet), ca 1890, zinc hull w/wood deck, brass boiler & bow gun, twin side wheels, 16", EX, A...**$1,000.00**

Steam Launch Little Pet No 50, Union Toy, brass hull, 12", EX (EX wood box dtd 1885), A...................................**$3,100.00**

Steamboat, Bing, w/up, litho tin, 2 stacks & cabin, railed deck, 6", MIB, A **$550.00**

Submarine, Bing, w/up, pnt tin, lt gray & orange, 13", EX+IB .**$450.00**

Submarine (Barracuda Atomic), Remco, 1960s, EXIB...**$150.00**

Submarine (Diving), Wolverine, w/up, litho tin, 13", EXIB, A .**$175.00**

Submarine (Nautilus 919), Jep, w/up, pnt tin, gray & wht, 17", EXIB, from $175 to...**$200.00**

Submarine (SSN No 25), crank-op friction, litho tin, 10", EXIB..**$200.00**

Torpedo Boat, Japan, 1950s, battery-op, wood, bl-gray & red, very detailed, 17", EX **$300.00**

Torpedo Boat, Japan, 1950s, battery-op, wood, bl-gray & red, very detailed, 32", VG+..**$500.00**

Torpedo Boat PT 107, Linemar, 1950s, battery-op, litho tin, 11", EX+IB, A **$200.00**

Wizard Outboard Motor Boat, Y, friction, litho tin, w/outboard motor & pull string, 11", NMIB, A.........................**$165.00**

Yacht, Carette, 1905, wind-up, painted tin, yellow and red, 18", restored, $1,925.00. (Photo courtesy Bertoia Auctions)

Books

Books have always captured and fired the imagination of children, and today books from every era are being collected. No longer is it just the beautifully illustrated Victorian examples or first editions of books written by well-known children's authors, but more modern books as well.

One of the first classics to achieve unprecedented success was *The Wizard of Oz* by author L. Frank Baum — such success, in fact, that far from his original intentions, it became a series. Even after Baum's death, other authors wrote Oz books until the decade of the 1960s, for a total of more than forty different titles. Other early authors were Beatrix Potter, Kate Greenaway, Palmer Cox (who invented the Brownies), and Johnny Gruelle (creator of Raggedy Ann and Andy). All were accomplished illustrators as well.

Everyone remembers a special series of books they grew up with, the Hardy Boys, Nancy Drew Mysteries, Tarzan — there were countless others. And though these are becoming very collectible today, there were many editions of each, and most are very easy to find. Generally the last few in any series will be most difficult to locate, since fewer were printed than the earlier stories which were likely to have been reprinted many times. As is true of any type of book, first editions or the earliest printing will have more collector value. For more information on series books as well as others, we recommend *Collector's Guide to Children's Books, Volume II*, and *Boys' & Girls' Book Series* by Diane McClure Jones and Rosemary Jones (Collector Books).

Big Little Books came along in 1933 and until edged out by the comic-book format in the mid-1950s sold in huge volumes, first for a dime and never more than 20¢ a copy. They were printed by Whitman, Saalfield, Goldsmith, Van Wiseman, Lynn, and World Syndicate, and all stuck to Whitman's original layout — thick hand-sized sagas of adventure, the right-hand page with an exciting cartoon, well illustrated and contrived so as to bring the text on the left alive. The first hero to be immortalized in this arena was Dick Tracy, but many more were to follow. Some of the more collectible today feature well-known characters like G-Men, Tarzan, Flash Gordon, Little Orphan Annie, Mickey Mouse, and Western heroes by the dozens. (Note: At the present time, the market for these books is fairly stable — values for common titles are actually dropping. Only the rare, character-related titles are increasing.) For more information we recommend *Big Little Books*, by Larry Jacobs (Collector Books).

Little Golden Books were first published in 1942 by Western Publishing Co. Inc. The earliest had spines of blue paper that were later replaced with gold foil. Until the 1970s the books were numbered from 1 to 600, while later books had no numerical order. The most valuable are those with dust jackets from the early '40s or books with paper dolls and activities. The three primary series of books are Regular (1 – 600), Disney (1 – 140), and Activity (1 – 52). Books with the blue or gold paper spine (not foil) often sell at $8.00 to $15.00. Dust jackets alone are worth $20.00 and up in good condition. Paper doll books are generally valued at about $30.00 to $35.00, and stories about TV Western heroes at $12.00 to $18.00. First editions of the 25¢ and 29¢ cover-price books can be identified by a code (either on the title page or the last page); '1/A' indicates a first edition while a 'number/Z' will refer to the twenty-sixth printing. Condition is important but subjective to personal standards. For more information we recommend *Collecting Little Golden Books*, Vols I and II, by Steve Santi. The second edition also includes information on Wonder and Elf books.

Advisors: Ron and Donna Donnelly (D7), Big Little Books

See also Black Americana; Coloring, Activity, and Paint Books; Rock 'n Roll; and other specific categories.

BIG LITTLE BOOKS

Adventures of Huckleberry Finn, Whitman #1422, NM..**$40.00**

Apple Mary & Dennie Fool the Swindlers, Whitman #1130, NM..**$50.00**

Bambi's Children, Whitman #1497, 1943, EX.................**$50.00**

Billy the Kid, Whitman #773, 1935, EX **$35.00**

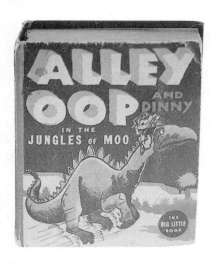

Alley Oop and Dinny in the Jungles of Moo, VG, $25.00.

The Green Hornet, #1453, VG, $60.00.

Blondie & Bouncing Baby Dumpling, Whitman #1476, NM .$40.00
Blondie in Hot Water, Whitman #1410, NM $45.00
Buccaneers (TV Show), 1958, EX+ $15.00
Buck Jones & the Two Gun Kid, Whitman #1404, 1937, EX .$35.00
Buck Rogers & the Doom of Comet, Whitman, 1935, EX .$50.00
Buck Rogers in City of Floating Globes, EX $150.00
Captain Easy Soldier of Fortune, Whitman #1128, NM...$60.00

Hal Hardy in the Lost Land of the Giants, Whitman #1413, EX $25.00
In the Name of the Law, Whitman #1124, VG $24.00
Inspector Charlie Chan in Villany on the High Seas, #1424, EX.$35.00
Jane Withers in Keep Smiling, Whitman #1463, EX........$40.00
Jimmy Allen in the Air Mail Robbery, Whitman #1143, 1936, EX..$35.00
Jungle Jim & the Vampire Woman, Whitman #1139, NM..$75.00
Junior G-Men, Whitman #1442, 1937, EX $30.00
Kayo in the Land of Sunshine, Whitman #1180, EX........$35.00
Ken Maynard in Western Justice, Whitman #1430, EX ...$35.00
Li'l Abner in New York, Whitman #1198, 1936, EX........$60.00
Little Orphan Annie & Chizzler, Whitman #748, EX......$60.00
Little Women, Whitman #757, EX $45.00
Mickey Mouse & the Stolen Jewels, Whitman #1464, NM.$75.00
Mutt & Jeff, Whitman #1113, NM $75.00
Nancy & Sluggo, Whitman #1400, EX $45.00
Once Upon a Time, Whitman #718, EX.........................$35.00
Our Gang on the March, Whitman #1451, NM..............$65.00
Popeye & Queen Olive Oyl, Whitman #1458, EX+.........$40.00
Porky Pig & His Gang, Whitman #1404, VG..................$45.00

Captain Midnight and the Moon Woman, VG, $25.00.

Convoy Patrol, Whitman #1469, NM................................$35.00
Cowboy Lingo, Whitman #1457, 1938, EX $35.00
Dan Dunn & the Border Smugglers, Whitman #1481, 1938, EX $35.00
Dick Tracy & the Tiger Lily Gang, Whitman #1460, 1949, VG...$35.00
Dick Tracy Returns, Whitman #1495, NM $75.00
Donald Duck Gets Fed Up, Whitman #1462, EX.............$50.00
Donald Duck Off the Beam, Whitman #1438, EX............$60.00
Ella Cinders & the Mysterious House, Whitman #1106, NM.$50.00
Felix the Cat, Whitman #1129, 1936, EX.........................$55.00
Frankenstein Jr, Whitman, 1968, NM...............................$20.00
Freckles & the Lost Diamond Mine, Whitman #1164, EX..$35.00
G-Man & the Gun Runners, Whitman #1469, EX+ $35.00
Gene Autry & the Hawk of the Hills, Whitman #1493, NM...$50.00
Goofy in Giant Trouble, Whitman, 1968, NM+ $10.00
Hairbreath Harry in Dept QT, Whitman #1101, EX $35.00

Radio Patrol, #1173, EX, $25.00.

Return of Tarzan, Whitman #1102, EX+ $65.00
Roy Rogers & the Deadly Treasure, Whitman #1473, VG .$40.00
Secret Agent K-7, Saalfield #1191, 1940, EX $35.00
Sir Lancelot, #1649, NM $15.00
Skeezix Goes to War, Whitman #1414, NM.....................$50.00

Sleeping Beauty, Golden All Star, 1967, EX+, N2 ....$15.00
Smokey Stover, Whitman #1413, 1942, EX.....................$35.00
Snow White & the Seven Dwarfs, Golden Star, 1967, VG+,
 N2 ....$15.00
Sombrero Pete, Whitman #1136, VG $25.00
Tarzan & the Golden Lion, Whitman #1448, NM $75.00
Tarzan the Terrible, #1453, EX+ $40.00
Texas Kid, Whitman #1429, EX $25.00
Thumper & the Seven Dwarfs, Whitman #1409, EX $60.00
Two-Gun Montana, Whitman #1104, VG......................$25.00
Uncle Don's Strange Adventures, Whitman #1114, VG .$30.00
Wings of the USA, Whitman #1401, EX+ $25.00
Wyatt Earp, 1958, EX, N2 ....$15.00

DELL FAST ACTION BOOKS BY WHITMAN

Adventures of Andy Panda, NM...............................$75.00
Adventures of Charlie McCarthy & Edgar Bergen, NM ..$85.00
Bugs Bunny & the Secret Storm Island, NM $75.00
Captain Marvel — Return of the Scorpion, NM............$225.00
Dan Dunn Secret Operative 48 & the Zeppelin of Doom, NM.$120.00
Dick Tracy & the Blackmailers, NM...........................$150.00
Dick Tracy & the Chain of Evidence, NM $175.00
Dick Tracy & the Maroon Mask Gang, EX+ $100.00
Dick Tracy Detective & Federal Agent, NM $200.00
Donald Duck & the Ducklings, EX+............................$100.00
Donald Duck Out of Luck, NM.................................$165.00
Donald Duck Takes It on the Chin, NM $165.00
Dumbo the Flying Elephant, NM...............................$125.00
Flash Gordon & the Ape Men of Mor, NM...................$200.00
Flash Gordon Vs the Emperor of Mongo, EX................$85.00
G-Man on Lightning Island, NM $85.00
Gang Busters & Guns of Law, NM $100.00
Gene Autry in Gun Smoke, EX.................................$80.00
Katzenjammer Kids, NM...$90.00

The Katzenjammer Kids,
1942, VG, $40.00.

Little Orphan Annie Under the Big Top, NM $140.00
Lone Ranger & the Lost Valley w/Silver & Tonto, NM ...$90.00
Mickey Mouse & Pluto, NM $90.00
Mickey Mouse the Sheriff of Nugget Gulch, NM...........$175.00
Mickey Mouse w/Goofy & Mickey's Nephews, rare, NM .$225.00
Pinocchio & Jiminy Cricket, NM $100.00

Red Ryder Brings Law to Devil's Hole, NM $80.00
Smilin' Jack & the Border Bandits, EX $60.00
Tailspin Tommy & Flying Aces, NM $100.00
Tailspin Tommy & the Airliner Mystery, NM $100.00
Tarzan & the Avenger, rare, NM...............................$200.00
Terry & the Pirates & the Mystery Ship, NM................$130.00
Tom Mix in the Riding Avenger, NM $90.00
Zane Grey's King of the Royal Mounted Policing the Frozen
 North, NM..$75.00

LITTLE GOLDEN BOOKS

A Day in the Jungle, #18, 1st edition, 1943, VG $30.00
ABC Is for Christmas, #108, 1st edition, 1974, EX............$5.00
Animal Quiz, #396, A edition, 1960, VG $5.00
Big Red, #102, A edition, 1963, G+..............................$8.00
Bugs Bunny, #72, A edition, 1949, VG $12.00
Busy Timmy, #50, A edition, 1948, G+.........................$25.00
Captain Kangaroo, #261, A edition, 1956, EX+, N2 ....$20.00
Captain Kangaroo & the Beaver, #427, A edition, 1972, EX,
 N2 ....$20.00
Captain Kangaroo & the Panda, #278, A edition, 1957, EX..$15.00
Chicken Little, #413, A edition, 1960, NM+ $8.00
Chip 'n' Dale, #D38, A edition, 1954, NM+ $18.00
Christopher & the Columbus, #103, A edition, 1951, EX.$10.00
Cinderella's Friends, #D17, A edition, 1950, NM+ $18.00
Circus Boy, #290, A edition, 1957, EX, N2....................$25.00
Cleo, #287, A edition, 1957, NM+ $15.00
Daniel Boone, #256, A edition, 1956, EX, N2.................$25.00
Day at the Playground, #119, A edition, 1951, VG..........$20.00
Dennis the Menace A Quiet Afternoon, #412, A edition, 1960,
 VG $8.00
Doctor Dan at the Circus, #399, A edition, 1960, EX, N2 .$25.00
Donald Duck & Santa Claus, #D27, A edition, 1952, EX, N2.$25.00
Donald Duck & the Witch, D34, A edition, 1953, VG+, N2.$20.00
Donald Duck in Disneyland, #D86, D edition, 1960, EX, N2.$20.00
Donald Duck Lost & Found, #86, A edition, 1960, EX, N2 .$20.00
Donald Duck's Adventure, #D14, 1950, A edition, VG+, N2 .$20.00
Dumbo, #D3, L edition, 1952, VG $15.00
Frosty the Snowman, #142, L edition, 1951, VG+ $6.00
Funny Book, #74, A edition, 1950, NM+ $15.00
Gene Autry & Champion, #267, A edition, 1956, VG....$20.00
Gunsmoke, #320, A edition, 1958, VG $18.00

The Happy Family, A
edition, #216, EX+,
$18.00. (Photo courtesy Steve Santi)

Helicopters, #357, A edition, 1959, NM+ $10.00
Howdy Doody & Clarabell, #121, A edition, 1951, VG+ .$18.00
Howdy Doody's Circus, #99, A edition, 1950, EX $20.00

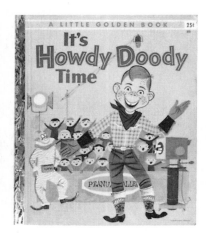

It's Howdy Doody Time, A edition, #223, EX, $25.00.

(Photo courtesy Steve Santi)

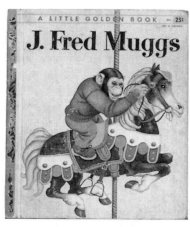

J. Fred Muggs, A edition, #234, EX, $18.00. (Photo courtesy Steve Santi)

Jack & the Beanstalk, #281, A edition, 1957, NM+.........$10.00
Katie the Kitten, #75, A edition, 1949, VG......................$12.00
Laddie & the Little Rabbit, #116, A edition, 1952, EX....$10.00
Little Galoshes, #68, A edition, 1949, VG $18.00
Little Red Hen, #6, M edition, 1952, VG $20.00
Magic Next Door, #106, 1st edition, 1971, EX...................$5.00
Mickey Mouse & His Spaceship, #D29, A edition, 1952, NM+ .$18.00
Mister Rogers' Neighborhood — Henrietta Meets Someone
		New, #133, 1st edition, 1974, VG+ $5.00
My First Book of Bible Stories, #19, 1st edition, 1943, VG.$35.00
National Velvet, #431, A edition, 1961, NM+ $15.00
New Baby, #41, G edition, 1954, VG $12.00
Noah's Ark, #D28, A edition, 1952, VG+ $15.00
Old Yeller, #D65, A edition, 1957, VG...........................$15.00
Party in Shariland, #360, A edition, 1958, NM+ $18.00
Pink Panther in the Haunted House, #140, 1st edition, 1975,
		NM+..$8.00
Quick Draw McGraw, #398, A edition, 1960, VG $15.00
Raggedy Ann & Andy & The Rainy Day Circus, #107-2, 1973,
		NM $5.00
Raggedy Ann & Fido, #585, 1st edition, 1972, NM+ $10.00
Raggedy Ann & The Cookie Snatcher, #107-3, 1976, VG+ .$3.00
Rin Tin Tin, #276, A edition, 1956, NM+.......................$18.00

Roy Rogers & the Mountain Lion, #231, A edition, 1955, NM+..$25.00
Savage Sam, #D104, A edition, 1963, VG+ $10.00
Scooby-Doo & the Pirate Treasure, #126, 1st edition, 1974,
		VG+ $10.00
Sleeping Beauty, #D61, 1957, A edition, EX, N2 ....$18.00
Smokey Bear & the Campers, #423, A edition, 1961, VG .$8.00
Snow White & the Seven Dwarfs, #D4, A edition, 1948, VG.$15.00
Story of Jesus, #27, F edition, 1949, NM+ $20.00
Story of Jonah, #311-61, A edition, 1986, NM+ $5.00
Three Little Kittens, #1, Q edition, 1951, EX+ $22.00
Tommy's Wonderful Rides, #63, A edition, 1948, NM.....$18.00

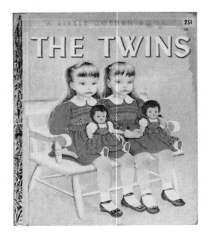

The Twins, A edition, #227, EX+, $80.00.

(Photo courtesy Steve Santi)

Up in the Attic, #53, A edition, 1948, NM......................$20.00
Wagon Train, #326, A edition, 1958, NM+.....................$20.00
What If?, #130, A edition, 1951, VG $10.00
Whistling Wizard, #132, A edition, 1953, VG $15.00
Year on the Farm, #37, 4th edition, 1949, VG.................$12.00
Yogi Bear, #395, A edition, 1960, VG.............................$15.00
Zorro, #D68, D edition, 1965, NM+ $15.00

POP-UP AND MOVABLE BOOKS

Adventures in Oz, Derrydale, 1991, EX $10.00
Alice in Wonderland, Modern Publishers, EX+...............$15.00
Barbie Rockin' Rappin' Dancin' World Tour, Western, 1992, 1st
		edition, EX $20.00
Buck Rogers, Pleasure Books, 1934, EX $600.00
Child's Garden of Verses, Dutton, 1991, EX $15.00
Christmas on Stage, 1950, spiral-bound, EX (orig brn box).$40.00
Christmas Time in Action, Newton, 1949, spiral bound, EX .$50.00
Christmas Time in Action, Walter P Phillips, 1949, spiral spine,
		20 pgs, 5 pop-ups, EX+ $50.00
Cinderella, Blue Ribbon, 1933, NM $425.00
Dick Tracy Captures Boris Arson, 1935, VG $20.00
Dino & the Mouse Who Had Hiccups, 1974, EX.............$25.00
Funny Bunny, by Rachael Learnard, Golden, 1950, VG....$50.00
Hopalong Cassidy & Lucky, EX.....................................$100.00
Hopalong Cassidy Lends a Helping Hand, Bonnie Books, 1950,
		EX..$75.00
Jack & the Beanstalk, Blue Ribbon, 1933, M $150.00
Jolly Jump-Ups Favorite Nursery Story, McLoughlin, 1942, VG..$75.00
Jolly Old St Nicholas, 1992, musical, EX $15.00

Koko's Circus, Animated Book Co, 1942, VG.................$55.00
Mickey Mouse in King Arthur's Court, M.................$1,500.00
My Pop-Up Book of Sleeping Beauty, EX $10.00
New Adventures of Tarzan, Pleasure Books, 1935, NM .$450.00
Popeye w/the Hag of the Seven Seas, 1935, EX.............$450.00
Puss-In-Boots, Blue Ribbon, NM $250.00
Rainbow Round-A-Bout, 1992, EX.................................$15.00
Santa Claus in Storyland, USA, 1950, EX+, A $60.00
Seven Natural Wonders of the World, 1991, EX $15.00
Snow White's Party, Windmill Books & Dutton, 1976, 1st edi-
     tion, EX, P6...$25.00
Tale of Two Mice, 1990, EX...$15.00
Tom & Jerry Book of Numbers, EX $15.00
101 Dalmatians, Belgium, 1972, rare, NM....................$70.00

TELL-A-TALE BY WHITMAN

Alphabet Rhymes, #2400-2, 1956, EX $8.00
Bible Stories, #828, 1947, EX...$8.00
Big Little Kitty, #2515, 1953, VG.................................$10.00
Big Red Pajama Wagon, Top Top Tale #2479, 1949, EX ..$10.00
Bugs Bunny Hangs Around, 1957, NM, N2....................$15.00
Bugs Bunny Keeps a Promise, 1951, EX, N2 ....$10.00
Cinderella, #2552, 1959, EX...$10.00
Cinnamon Bear, #2674, 1961, EX $15.00
Circus Alphabet, #2531, 1974, EX $5.00
Circus Alphabet, 1954, EX, N2.....................................$15.00
Donald Duck & Chip 'n' Dale, 1954, EX, N2 ....$10.00
Donald Duck & the New Birdhouse, #2550, 1956, EX.......$8.00
Donald Duck & the Sticky Secret, 1976, EX, N2 ....$10.00
Donald Duck on Tom Sawyer's Island, #2454-43, 1960, G ..$10.00

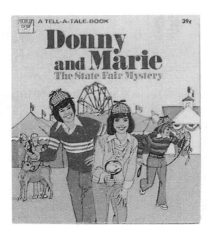

***Donny and Marie —
The State Fair Mystery,***
Whitman, 1977, $5.00.

(Photo courtesy Greg Davis and Bill Morgan)

Ernie the Cave King, #2604, 1975, EX..............................$5.00
Flying Sunbeam, #849, 1950, EX...................................$10.00
Frisker, #2426, 1956, EX $5.00
Fuzzy Duckling, #2673, 1952, EX $20.00
Goofy & the Tiger Hunt, #2612, 1954, EX $10.00
Grandpa's Police Friends, #2544, 1967, NM $8.00
Hey There Yogi Bear, 1964, EX, N2 ....$15.00
Hooray for Lassie, 1964, EX, N2 ....$10.00
In, On, Under & Through, #2601, 1961, EX $6.00
Lassie & the Busy Morning, 1973, EX, N2.....................$10.00
Lassie & the Kittens, 1956, EX, N2................................$15.00

Lassie Finds a Friend, 1960, VG, N2 ....$10.00
Lassie the Busy Morning, #2484, 1973, EX.....................$5.00
Little Black Sambo, 1959, EX, N2.................................$50.00
Little Lulu in Lucky Landlady, 1973, EX, N2.................$20.00
Little Miss Muffet, #2464-33, 1958, EX...........................$5.00
Little Red Riding Hood, #2670, 1960, EX $10.00
Magilla Gorilla, 1965, EX, N2.......................................$12.00
Mother Goose on the Farm, #2587, 1975, EX...................$8.00
Night Before Christmas, #2517, 1969, VG $5.00
Pete's Dragon, #248-3, 1977, EX.....................................$5.00
Peter Pan & the Tiger, #2616, 1976, EX..........................$6.00
Princess Who Never laughed, #2610, 1961, EX $5.00
Quiet Quincy & the Delivery Truck, #2615, 1961, EX.......$5.00
Roy Rogers & the Sure 'Nough Cowpoke, #80115, 1952, VG .$25.00
Roy Rogers' Surprise for Donnie, #943, 1954, EX.............$20.00
Snoozy, #2564, 1944, w/dust jacket, EX $20.00
Snow White & the Seven Dwarfs, 1957, EX, N2 ....$10.00
Surprise for Howdy Doody, #2573, 1950, EX.................$30.00
Three Bears, #2592, 1968, EX..$5.00
Three Little Pigs, #921, 1958, EX....................................$5.00
Try Again Sally, 1969, EX, N2......................................$10.00
Tweety, #2481, 1953, EX...$10.00
Walt Disney Bear Country, #2612, 1954, EX $8.00
Waltons — Elizabeth & the Magic Lamp, 1975, EX, N2 .$15.00
Winnie the Pooh & Eeyore's House, #2620, 1976, EX $15.00

WHITMAN MISCELLANEOUS

Annette in Mystery at Smuggler's Cove, #1574, 1963, EX ..$15.00
Annette in Sierra Summer, 1960, EX, N2.......................$15.00
Annie Oakley in the Ghost Town Secret, 1957, VG+, N2...$25.00
Big Valley, 1966, EX, N2 ....$20.00
Blondie & Dagwood's Secret Service, 1942, EX, N2 ....$25.00
Brenda Starr Girl Reporter, 1943, EX, N2 ....$15.00
Buffy Finds a Star, 1970, EX...$8.00
Bullwinkle's Masterpiece, 1976, NM $6.00
Crusader Rabbit in Bubble Trouble, 1960, NM...............$20.00
Don Winslow of the Navy, 1946, EX, N2 ....$20.00
Donald Duck in Bringing Up the Boys, EX, C10............$15.00
Flipper in the Mystery of the Black Shadow, 1966, NM+..$10.00
Gene Autry in the Ghost Riders, 1955, NM....................$20.00
Gene Autry in the Redwood Pirates, 1946, w/dust jacket, NM .$25.00
Gunsmoke, 1958, slick hardcover, EX, N2......................$25.00
Have Gun Will Travel, 1959, EX $15.00
Hoppity Hooper Vs Skippity Snooper, 1966, EX+...........$10.00
HR Pufnstuf, 1970, EX...$10.00
Indian Mummy Mystery, 1964, slick hardcover, EX, N2...$10.00
Janet Lennon at Camp Calamity, 1962, EX, N2 ....$20.00
John Paul Jones Boy Sailor, 1946, EX, N2......................$15.00
Lassie & the Blackberry Bog, 1956, EX, N2 ....$25.00
Lassie in Bristlecone Pine, 1967, M, N2.........................$25.00
Lassie in the Wild Mountain Trail, 1966, EX, N2............$15.00
Leave It to Beaver, 1962, EX $15.00
Lennon Sisters at Holiday Island, 1960, EX, N2.............$20.00
Liddle Kiddles — A Counting Book, 1966, EX+ $10.00
Little Folks Story of Rin-Tin-Tin, 1927, unused, NM......$55.00
Loopy de Loop Odd Jobber, 1964, EX+ $6.00
Magic Train, 1959, EX, N2..$25.00

Maverick, 1959, slick hardcover, EX, N2 ....$25.00
Munsters in Camera Caper, 1965, EX, N2 ....$15.00

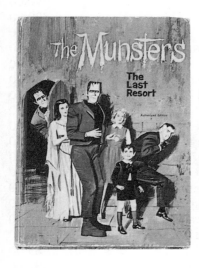

The Munsters — The Last Resort, G, $15.00.

National Velvet, 1962, M $10.00
Patty Duke & Mystery Mansion, 1964, EX+ $6.00
Quick Draw McGraw Badmen Beware, 1960, EX $6.00
Rifleman, 1959, slick hardcover, EX, N2 ....$25.00
Rin-Tin-Tin in One of the Family, 1953, NM+ $12.00
Rin-Tin-Tin's Rinty, 1954, NM+ $10.00
Roy Rogers Favorite Western Stories, 1956, VG (w/box)..$30.00
Roy Rogers in Gopher Creek Gunman, 1945, EX, N2 .....$15.00
Son of the Phantom, 1946, VG, N2 ....$15.00
Spin & Marty, 1956, NM $10.00
Tarzan & the City of Gold, 1954, EX, N2 ....$15.00
Tarzan & the Forbidden City, 1952, EX (w/dust jacket), N2..$35.00
Tarzan & the Forbidden City, 1952, VG, N2 ....$15.00
Tarzan & the Lost Safari, 1957, VG+, N2 ....$15.00
Tom Stetson & the Giant Ants, 1948, VG+, N2 ....$15.00
Tony & His Pals (Tom Mix), 1934, NM (w/dust jacket) ..$75.00
Trixie Belden in Arizona, 1958, VG+, N2 ....$5.00

Wagon Train, Authorized TV Edition, 1959, EX, $15.00.

Walton Boys in Gold in the Snow, 1958, EX, N2 ....$15.00
Wyatt Earp, 1956, EX, N2 ....$25.00
Yogi Bear, 1962, EX+ $15.00

Zorro, 1958, slick hardcover, EX, N2 ....$20.00

WONDER BOOKS

A Horse for Johnny, #754, 1952, EX $5.00
A Puzzle for Raggedy Ann & Andy, 1957, EX $20.00
ABC & Counting Rhymes, #823, EX+ $5.00
Baby Bunny, #545, 1951, EX $12.00
Baby Elephant, #541, 1950, EX $10.00
Billy & His Steam Roller, #537, 1951, EX..........................$5.00
Buzzy the Funny Cow, 1963, EX $15.00
City Boy, Country Boy, #810, 1963, VG $20.00
Counting Book, #692, 1957, EX $8.00
Doll Family, #802, 1962, VG $20.00
Famous Fairy Tales, #505, 1949, EX $10.00
Felix the Cat, #665, 1953, NM......................................$40.00
Flash Gordon & the Baby Animals, 1956, EX $30.00
Goose Who Played the Piano, #567, 1951, VG.............$12.00
Heckle & Jeckle Visit the Farm, 1958, EX $25.00
Hector Heathcote & the Knights, 1965, NM+ $8.00
Hector Heathcote Crosses the River, 1961, EX, N2 ....$20.00
Henry in Lollipop Land, #664, 1953, EX $25.00
Hoppy the Curious Kangaroo, #579, 1952, EX $10.00
Hungry Baby Bunny, #847, 1951, EX $10.00
I Can Do Anything...Almost, #822, 1963, EX $5.00
It's a Lovely Day, #632, 1956, EX $5.00
Jetsons in the Great Pizza Hunt, 1976, EX $6.00
Kewtee Bear's Christmas, #867, 1956, EX $8.00
Let's Give a Birthday Party, #752, 1960, VG $35.00
Little Audrey & the Moon Lady, #759, 1977, EX, N2 ......$10.00
Little Cowboy's Christmas, 1951, EX, N2 ....$20.00
Little Lost Puppy, #528, 1976, EX....................................$6.00
Little Red Caboose That Ran Away, #715, 1952, VG $6.00
Luno the Soaring Stallion, #831, 1964, EX......................$15.00
Make-Believe Book, #634, 1959, VG.............................$15.00
Mighty Mouse in Santa's Helper, 1955, EX, N2...............$25.00
Moppets Surprise Party, #794, 1955, EX+ $15.00
Mr Bear Squash-You-All-Flat, 1950, extremely rare, EX ..$150.00
Nonsense Alphabet, #725, 1959, EX..............................$12.00
Once There Was a House, #842, 1965, EX $8.00
Pelle's New Suit, #803, 1962, EX...................................$12.00
Pony Engine, #626, 1957, EX $8.00
Raggedy Andy's Surprise, #604, 1953, EX $10.00
Raggedy Ann's Merriest Christmas, 1952, NM.................$15.00
Romper Room, 1957, EX, N2 ....$10.00
Runaway Baby Bird, #748, 1960, EX $6.00
Sleepy Time for Everyone, #612, 1954, EX+ $8.00
Snowman's Christmas Present, 1951, EX, N2 ....$20.00
Soupy Sales & the Talking Turtle, #860, 1965, EX...........$10.00
Surprise Doll, #519, 1949, EX..$30.00
This Magic World, #723, 1959, VG $8.00
Trick on Deputy Dawg, 1964, NM....................................$6.00
Twelve Days of Christmas, #651, 1956, EX $8.00
Visit to the Hospital, #690, EX...$5.00
Water Water Everywhere, #607, 1953, EX+ $10.00
What's for Breakfast?, #846, 1950, VG..........................$10.00
Who Goes There?, 1961, EX, N2 ....$10.00
Who Likes Dinner?, #598, 1953, EX+ $10.00

MISCELLANEOUS

A Penny for Candy, Jr Elf, 1946, VG+, N2 ....$10.00

Alice in Wonderland (Movie Edition), Grosset & Dunlop, 1934, hardcover, 297 pgs, EX+ $100.00

Arf! The Life & Hard Times of Little Orphan Annie 1935-1945, by Harold Gray w/Gray bio & intro by Al Capp, 1970, NM+ $30.00

Babes in Toyland, Golden, 1961, Frankie & Annette photo, EX, N2 ....$25.00

Beany & Cecil Captured for the Zoo, 1954, EX+ $5.00

Bozo & His ABC Zoo, Saalfield, 1961, lg paperback, EX .$15.00

Daniel Boone, Hunter, Trapper & Indian Fighter, by Lillian Moore, Random House, 1955, NM $12.00

Dennis the Menace, Holt, 1952, 1st edition, EX+ $15.00

Disney Studio Story, by Richard Holliss & Brian Sibley, Crown, 1988, M (w/dust jacket), M8 ....$65.00

Donald Duck & His Friends, Disney/Heath, 1939, NM, M8 .$50.00

Dr Seuss Yertle the Turtle & Other Stories, Random House, 1958, 1st edition, NM...$30.00

Dr Seuss' Happy Birthday to You, Random House, 1959, 1st edition, NM $30.00

Fun With Ventriloquism, by A Van Rensselaer, Doubleday, 1955, 1st edition, EX+ $50.00

Gene Autry in Redwood Pirate, 1946, EX, N2 ....$20.00

Gene Autry in Golden Ladder Gang, 1950, EX, N2.........$20.00

George Pal Presents Rusty & Al, Diamond Publishing, 1945, scarce, EX (w/dust jacket) $100.00

Gulliver's Travels, Max Fleischer/Sun Dial Press, 1939, M (w/dust jacket) $45.00

Hansel & Gretel, Elf, 1960, EX, N2 ....$10.00

Happy Trails (Roy Rogers & Dale Evans), 1981, photo cover, EX, N2 ....$10.00

Here They Are, Disney/Heath, 1940, NM+, M8 ....$50.00

How the Grinch Stole Christmas, by Dr Seuss, Random House, 1957, 1st printing, NM $20.00

Jack & the Beanstalk, Platt & Munk, 1934, softcover, VG+, N2...$30.00

Jackie Gleason's Funny Book for Boys & Girls, Bonnie Books, 1956, VG+ $65.00

The Land of Oz — Junior Edition, by L. Frank Baum, Rand McNally, $35.00.

Little Pig's Picnic & Other Stories, Disney/Heath, 1939, NM+, M8...$50.00

Little Red Riding Hood, Platt & Munk, 1934, softcover, VG+, N2 ....$30.00

Little Red Riding Hood and The Big Bad Wolf, McKay, 1934, NM, $ 65.00. (Photo courtesy Larry Jacobs)

Little Red Wagon, Jr Elf, 1949, VG+, N2 ....$10.00

Magilla Gorilla Takes a Banana Holiday, 1965, EX+ $6.00

Meet Chitty-Chitty Bang-Bang, Random House, 1968, EX+ .$8.00

Mickey Never Fails, Disney/Heath, 1939, NM+, M8 ....$55.00

Mickey Sees the USA, Disney/Heath, 1944, NM+, M8...$55.00

Mighty Mouse, McGraw Hill, 1964, NM $20.00

Mother Westwind Animal Friends, by Burgess, 1931, VG, N2..$10.00

Mr Big Goes to Town, Max Fleischer, Garden City, 1941, EX+ ..$50.00

My Toys, Jr Elf, 1955, EX, N2 ....$10.00

Palmer Cox Juvenile Budget Book, MA Donahue, 1902, VG.$50.00

Partridge Family, #10, 1972, paperback w/David Cassidy photo cover, VG+, N2...$10.00

Perri, Big Golden Book, 1939, M, M8..............................$22.00

Peter's Treasure, by Clara Judson, 1945, EX, N2 ....$10.00

Popeye's How To Draw Cartoons, 1939, EX+ $40.00

Quick Draw McGraw, Tip Top, VG+, N2 ....$20.00

Raggedy Ann & Andy in The Camel w/the Wrinkled Knees, Bobbs-Merrill, 1960, EX+..$15.00

Raggedy Ann Scratch & Sniff, 1976, EX, N2 ....$25.00

Rin-Tin-Tin in the Hidden Treasure, Golden, 1958, NM+...$18.00

Robin Hood & His Merry Men (British TV Series), Rand McNally, 1955, EX...$10.00

Roy Rogers in Sundown Valley, 1950, EX, N2..................$20.00

School Days in Disneyville, Disney/Heath, 1939, NM, M8.$50.00

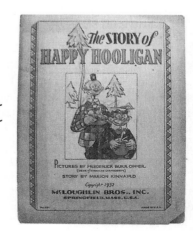

The Story of Happy Hooligan, McLoughlin Brothers, VG, A, $35.00.

Shirley Temple, by J Neatty, Saalfield, 1935, EX $40.00
Steve Canyon in Operation Convoy, by Milton Caniff, Grosset
    & Dunlap, 1959, NM...$8.00
Steve Canyon in Operation Snowflower, by Milton Caniff,
    Grosset & Dunlap, 1959, NM $10.00
Tarzan, Golden, 1964, lg sz, NM...$10.00
Terry & the Pirates, Big Big Book, 1938, EX, N2 ....$250.00
Through the Looking Glass, by Lewis Carroll, Maxton, 1947,
    NM (w/dust jacket) $15.00
Tom Sawyer, Little Big Classic, 1938, EX, N2 ....$25.00
Tom Swift & His Jetmarine, Grosset & Dunlap, 1954, NM..$10.00
Tom Terrific!, Pines #4, 1958, NM $20.00
Tony the Tramp, by Horatio Alger Jr, ca 1915, VG $20.00
True Story of Smokey the Bear, Big Golden Book, 1955, VG+,
    N2 ....$15.00
Tuffy the Tugboat, Tip-Top, 1947, VG, N2 ....$10.00
Valley of the Dinosaurs, T Rand, 1975, NM+ $8.00

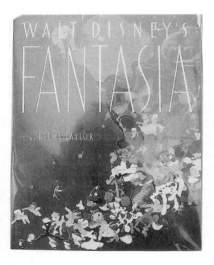

Walt Disney's Fantasia, **by Deems Taylor, Simon & Schuster, 1940, VG (with dust jacket), C12, $475.00.**

(Photo courtesy Joel Cohen)

Walt Disney's World of Fantasy, by Adrian Baily, Gallery Books,
    1930s, NM+ (w/dust jacket), M8 ....$60.00
Water Babies' Circus & Other Stories, Disney/Heath, 1940,
    NM+, M8..$50.00
Welcome to Upsy Downsy Land, Mattel, 1969, NM $30.00
Wild Bill Hickok & Joey, Elf, 1954, VG+, N2 ....$20.00
Wizard of Oz, Random House, 1950, illus by Anton Loeb, NM..$15.00
Zippy the Chimp, Rand McNally, 1956, NM....................$40.00

Breyer

Breyer collecting seems to be growing in popularity, and though the horses dominate the market, the company also made dogs, cats, farm animals, wildlife figures, dolls, and tack and accessories such as barns for their models. They've been in continuous production since the '50s, all strikingly beautiful and lifelike in both modeling and color. Earlier models were glossy, but since 1968 a matt finish has been used, though glossy and semiglossy colors are now being reintroduced, especially in special runs. (A special run of Family Arabians was done in the glossy finish i n 1988.)

One of the hardest things for any model collector is to determine the value of his or her collection. The values listed below are for models in excellent to near mint condition. This means no rubs, no scratches, no chipped paint, and no breaks — nothing that cannot be cleaned off with a rag and little effort. A model which has been altered in any way, including having the paint touched up, is considered a customized model and has an altogether different set of values than one in the original finish. The models listed herein are completely original. For More information we recommend *Breyer Animal Collector's Guide, Third Edition,* by Felicia Browell.

CLASSIC SCALE MODELS

Andalusian Mare (Chaval), 1997, shaded red roan $14.00
Andalusian Mare (Classics Show Award Set), 2002-current, bay
    w/blk mane & tail..$25.00
Andalusian Stallion (Classic Andalusian Family), 1979-93,
    alabaster w/shaded gray points.................................$13.00
Arabian Foal, 1973-82, blk...$10.00
Arabian Foal (Toys R Us/Drinkers of the Wind), 1993, rose gray
    w/darker points $10.00
Arabian Mare (Desert Arabian Family), 1992-94, bay w/blk
    points $12.00
Arabian Stallion (Bedouin Family Gift Set), 1995-96, bay
    w/striped mane & wht-tipped tail $14.00
Black Stallion (King of the Wind Set), 1990-93, red bay w/blk
    points $14.00

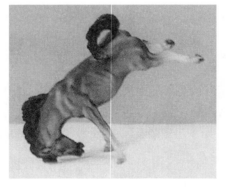

Bucking Bronco, matt gray with darker mane and tail, 1961 – 67, $95.00. (Photo courtesy Felicia Browell)

Bucking Bronco, 1998-99, rose dun w/dk gray or blk
    points $17.00
Charging Mesteno (The Progeny Gift Set), 1995, dk buckskin
    (matt/semigloss) w/dk brn or blk points....................$25.00
Fighting Mesteno (Wal-Mart/Azul & Fausto), 2001, bl roan
    w/blk mane, tail & lower legs $22.00
Ginger (Black Beauty Family), 1980-93, chestnut w/darker
    mane, tail & hooves...$14.00
Hobo (Hobo the Mustang of Lazy Heart Ranch), 1975-80, buck-
    skin...$35.00
Hollywood Dun It, 1998, buckskin w/blk points...............$32.00
Jet Run (US Equestrian Team Gift Set), bay w/blk points & wht
    star..$10.00
Keen (Hanoverian Family), 1992-93, blk w/star & narrow blaze..$14.00
Keen (Sears/German Olympic Set), 1989-90, red bay w/blk
    points $21.00

Kelso, dark bay, 1975 – 90, $20.00. (Photo courtesy Carol Karbowiak Gilbert)

Kelso (QVC/Ladies of the Bluegrass/Genuine Risk), 2002, chestnut $20.00
Kelso (Toys R Us/Geronimo & Cochise), lt bay appaloosa w/darker points $14.00
Lipizzan Stallion (World of Horses), 1993, lightly shaded alabaster $35.00
Man O'War (King), 1993-94, dk chestnut $18.00
Man O'War (Pepe), 1991-92, lt chestnut w/darker mane & tail.$18.00
Merrylegs (A Pony for Keeps), 1990-91, alabaster w/wht mane & tail...$10.00
Mesteno the Foal (Wal-Mart/America's Wild Mustangs/Alona & Damita), 2001, brn dun w/blk points $9.00
Might Tango (A Pony for Keeps), 1990-91, lt dapple gray w/gray points $14.00
Mustang Mare (JC Penney/Breyer Mustang Family), 1992, bay w/blk points..$14.00

Mustang Mare (Mustang Family), matt chestnut pinto with chestnut mane and tail, gray hooves, 1976 – 90, $15.00. (Photo courtesy Felicia Browell)

Mustang Stallion (A Pony for Keeps), 1990-91, chestnut w/flaxen mane & tail, gray to blk lower legs $12.00
Polo Pony (Breyer Show Special/Silver Comet), 1994, dapple gray w/darker points...$25.00
Quarter Horse Mare (JC Penney/Quarter Horse Family), 1991, dk chestnut bay $18.00
Quarter Horse Stallion (Montgomery Ward/Appaloosa Family), 1989, blk appaloosa...$25.00
Rearing Stallion, 1965-85, palomino w/wht mane & tail.$21.00

Rearing Stallion (Mustang), 1998-99, bay roan w/blk points.$15.00
Rojo (Wal-Mart/Adriano & Roano), 2001, chestnut blanket appaloosa..$14.00
Ruffian, 1977-90, dk bay w/blk points $14.00
Ruffian (QVC/Ladies of the Bluegrass/Regret), 2002, brn chestnut $20.00
Sagr (Bay Arabian), 1998, blk points................................$16.00
Silky Sullivan (Andrew), 1993-94, gray w/darker points (or just mane & tail) $18.00
Sombra (BLM Adopt-A-Horse/Runaway/Mustang Kiger), 1997, cocoa dun...$21.00
Swaps (Prince), 1993-94, lt gray w/gray points $18.00
Terrang (Gaucho), 1991-92, red roan w/lt chestnut mane & tail...$18.00
Unicorn (Toys Are Us/Lipizzan Stallion), 1996, blk w/gold accents $21.00
Wahoo King (Calf Roper Set/Western Action Series), 2002-current, bay $30.00

STABLEMATE SCALE

Andalusian, 1998-current, dapple gray w/lighter mane & tail ..$4.00
Appaloosa, 1998-current, buckskin blanket w/blk points ...$4.00
Arabian Mare, 1975-81, alabaster w/lt gray mane & tail ..$11.00
Arabian Mare, 1989-94, alabaster w/gray mane, tail & hooves..$7.00
Arabian Stallion, 1975-76, dapple gray w/darker mane & tail..$42.00
Arabian Stallion, 1975-81, alabaster w/lt gray mane, tail & hooves $14.00
Citation (Standing Thoroughbred), 1991-94, lt bay..........$7.00
Clydesdale (Stablemates Collection/Shire), 1998-2001, matt blk w/blaze & high stockings $7.00
Draft Horse, 1985, red sorrel w/flaxen mane & tail $49.00
Draft Horse, 1995-97, brn bay w/darker mane & tail........$11.00
Morgan Mare, 1976, chestnut...$38.00
Morgan Prancing (Pinto Stallion & Foal), 2000-current, bay pinto w/bi-color mane & tail $6.00
Morgan Stallion, 1976-88, blk...$14.00
Native Dancer (Sears/Stablemate Assortment II), 1990, alabaster w/blk points $11.00
Paso Fino (New Arrival Playset), current, bay w/blk points.$15.00
Quarter Horse Stallion, 1976-87, buckskin w/blk points, no dorsal stripe $11.00
Quarter Horse Stallion (JC Penney/Stablemates Barn), bay roan w/blk points, chestnut-shaded head $16.00
Saddlebred, 1975-76, dapple gray w/darker points, bald face..$35.00
Saddlebred, 1998, lt chestnut pinto....................................$12.00
Scrambling Foal (Stablemates Fun Foals Gift Pack), 2000-current, bay pinto (mostly wht) w/blk upper mane.........$12.00
Scratching Foal (Stablemates Fun Foals Gift Pack), 2002-current, palomino w/wht mane & tail $12.00
Seabiscuit (Running Paint), 1995-97, chestnut pinto w/darker mane & tail $6.00
Shetland Pony (Stablemates Collection), 1998-2001, red roan w/chestnut points..$11.00
Silky Sullivan, 1976-94, dk chestnut w/darker mane & tail..$7.00
Swaps, 1976-94, matt/semigloss chestnut w/darker mane & tail.$7.00
Thoroughbred (Stablemates Collection), 1998-2001, bay w/blk points $9.00
Thoroughbred Lying Foal, 1975-76, blk $14.00

Thoroughbred Mare, 1975-88, red bay w/blk points $11.00
Thoroughbred Standing Foal, 1975-76, blk w/various stockings .$14.00
Trotting Foal (Dude Ranch Play Set), 2001-current, bay semi-leopard appaloosa...$15.00
Warmblood, 1998-current, bay w/blk points $4.00

TRADITIONAL SCALE

Action Stock Horse Foal, 1989-93, chestnut leopard appaloosa w/chestnut mane & tail $16.00
Adios (Clayton Quarter Horse), 1995-96, dapple palomino w/wht mane & tail..$35.00
Adios (Remrock — The Horse Whisper), 1998-99, bay w/blk points $30.00
Amber (Sears/Twin Appaloosa Foals), 1998, bay blanket appaloosa...$21.00
Appaloosa Performance Horse, 1975-80, chestnut roan w/dark brn-blk mane & tail (add 20%-50% for chalky models) $35.00
Aristocrat Champion Hackney, 1995-96, bay w/blk points & 4 socks $28.00
Balking Mule (Black Horse Ranch), 1993, alabaster w/gray points $78.00
Belgian, 1964-67, glossy dapple gray or dapple blk $545.00
Belgian (Montgomery Ward), 1982-83, semigloss blk w/red on yel ribbon $67.00
Big Ben (Appropos), 2001, buckskin appaloosa w/blk points .$360.00
Black Beauty (Sears/Running Horse Family Set), 1984, red bay w/blk points, gray hooves..$58.00
Black Beauty (Sir Wrangler), 1998-99, bay semi-leopard appaloosa w/blk points $28.00
Black Stallion, 1981-88, semigloss blk $39.00
Black Stallion (Majestic Arabian Stallion), 1989-90, leopard appaloosa...$35.00
Buckshot (Cody), 1995, bay pinto w/blk points................$31.00
Buckshot (Mustang), 2000-2001, dun roan w/blk & dk brn points $32.00
Cantering Welsh Pony (Yes I Can 'Sonnet'), lt dapple gray..$34.00
Cedarfarm Wixom (QVC/Equinox), 2002, glossy liver chestnut..$100.00
Cigar Famous Race Horse, 1998, dk bay w/blk points.......$37.00
Clydesdale Foal, 1990-91, lt bay or yel bay w/blk mane & tail, ea $24.00
Clydesdale Foal (Spotted Draft Foal), 1999-2001, blk pinto w/wht mane & blk tail...$18.00
Clydesdale Mare, 1969-89, chestnut w/darker mane & tail .$24.00
Clydesdale Mare (Mail Order), dapple gray w/darker points...$117.00
Clydesdale Stallion, 1961(?)-63, glossy bay w/blk mane & tail .$235.00
Clydesdale Stallion, 1962(?)-65, glossy dapple gray w/darker mane & tail..$175.00
Cody, 1999-2000, bay w/blk points $32.00
El Pastor (Tesoro), 1992-95, palomino w/wht mane & tail..$35.00
Family Arabian Foal (Spot), 1968-71, gray appaloosa w/blk points $24.00
Family Arabian Mare (Dickory), 1961-67, glossy charcoal w/wht mane & tail...$43.00
Family Arabian Mare (Speck), 1961-67, glossy gray appaloosa w/blk points...$32.00
Family Arabian Stallion (Fleck), 1963-67, glossy gray appaloosa w/blk points..$47.00

Fighting Stallion, 1961-67, glossy gray appaloosa w/gray points $136.00
Fighting Stallion (GaWaNi Pony Boy's Mihunka), 1999-2001, dk bay pinto w/wht tail..$32.00

Five-Gaiter, sorrel, 1963 – 86, $45.00.

Five-Gaiter (CH Imperator), 1994-95, glossy dk chestnut.$43.00
Five-Gaiter (Commander), 1962-66, alabaster w/red eyes .$215.00
Five-Gaiter (Rhett), 2001, glossy charcoal $45.00
Foundation Stallion (Toys R Us/Titan Glory), 1996, bay w/blk points $39.00
Friesian, 1992-95, matt blk $47.00
Friesian (Sears/Lots of Spots), 2000, blk leopard appaloosa w/shaded points..$40.00
Fury Prancer (Cowboy & Prancer), 1998, buckskin w/blk points.$50.00
Galiceno (Crillo Pony), 1998-99, yel dun w/darker points .$26.00
Gem Twist, 1998-99, gray semi-leopard appaloosa w/blk points.$34.00
Gem Twist (Monte Thoroughbred), 1996-97, shaded chestnut ..$32.00
Grazing Foal, 1964-76 & 1978-81, bay w/blk points.........$24.00
Grazing Mare, 1961-80, palomino w/wht mane & tail, gray hooves $39.00

Grazing Mare (JC Penney Serenity Set), buckskin, 1995, $25.00.

Haklinger (Scat Cat Children's Pony), 1993-94, bay roan leopard appaloosa w/blk points..$27.00
Halla (Famous Jumper), 1977-85, bay w/blk points, sm star.$39.00

Halla (Noble Jumper), 1990-91, gray w/blk points, hind socks..**$43.00**

Hanoverian (Horses International), 1986, dapple gray w/wht spots **$296.00**

Hanoverian (Your Horse Source), 1987, alabaster w/lt gray mane & tail..**$98.00**

Indian Pony, 1970-72, buckskin (dun) w/brn mane & tail..**$273.00**

Iron Metal Chief (Just About Horses/Fanfare), 2000, glossy gold w/wht mane, tail & stockings......................................**$180.00**

John Henry (Cree Indian Horse/Naytukskie-Kukatos), 1996, dk bay w/gray hooves **$31.00**

Jumping Horse (Starlight), 1994 (limited edition), very dk bay w/blk points..**$47.00**

Justin Morgan (Double Take), 1993-94, dk chestnut w/darker mane & tail **$27.00**

Khemosabi (Arabian Stallion), 1999-2000, rose gray w/darker points, wht dappling **$32.00**

Lady Phase (Just About Horses), 1980, unpnt **$66.00**

Lady Phase (Silky Keno), 2001 (limited edition), semigloss blk & wht pinto **$45.00**

Lady Roxanna (Prancing Arabian Mare), 1988-89, chestnut w/flaxen mane & tail, gray hooves **$31.00**

Legionario (Galant), 1997-98, shaded chestnut w/darker points.**$29.00**

Legionario (Promenade Andalusian), 1995-96, bay w/wht.**$31.00**

Legionario (Toys R Us/Stardust), 1997, dapple gray **$47.00**

Llanarth True Briton Champion Welsh Cob, 1994-96, dk chestnut w/darker mane & tail **$31.00**

Lonesome Glory (QVC/Seattle Slew), 2002, dk bay w/reddish highlights **$55.00**

Lying Down Foal, 1969-73, red roan w/dappling & solid mane & tail **$50.00**

Lying Down Foal (Toys R Us/Unicorn IV/Black Pearl or White Pearl), 1997, gold accents, ea **$28.00**

Man O'War (My Prince Thoroughbred), shaded med brn chestnut w/darker mane & tail **$31.00**

Man O'War (Sears/Race Horse Set), 1990, glossy red chestnut w/darker mane & tail......................................**$58.00**

Marabella (JC Penney/Great Spirit Mare & Foal), 2001, chestnut pinto, mare only **$36.00**

Marabella (Morgan Broodmare), 1997-98, bay w/blk points, 4 wht socks **$33.00**

Midnight Sun (Tennessee Walker), 1988-89, red bay w/blk points, gray hooves, red on wht braids **$50.00**

Midnight Tango, 2000-01, blk pinto w/blk & wht mane & tail ..**$23.00**

Misty (Marguerite Henry's Misty), 1972, palomino pinto w/dbl-eye circles..**$117.00**

Misty's Twilight, chestnut pinto w/wht legs & darker lower half of tail **$31.00**

Misty's Twilight (JC Penney/Sundance & Skipper Set), bay pinto w/darker points..**$39.00**

Morgan (Mid-States Distributing/Stonington), 1998, shaded seal brn w/darker mane & tail **$45.00**

Morgan (Vermont), 1992-93, chocolate sorrel w/flaxen mane & tail **$31.00**

Morganglanz (Black Beauty 1991), 1991-95, blk w/star or stripe w/wht front sock **$23.00**

Mustang Semi-Rearing (Baron), 1996-97, glossy mahogany bay w/blk points..**$39.00**

Mustang Semi-Rearing (Diablo), 1961-66, alabaster w/red eyes..**$195.00**

Mustang Semi-Rearing (Paint American Mustang), 1990-91, bay pinto w/blk points, apron face..............................**$43.00**

Old Timer, 1966-87, glossy dapple gray w/gray mane & tail, w/harness & hat **$43.00**

Pacer (Brenda Breyer & Sulky Set), 1982-87, alabaster w/lt gray points, horse only......................................**$58.00**

Pacer (Laag Standardbred/Commemorative Edition), 1996, lt dapple gray w/shading..**$39.00**

Phar Lap (Famous Race Horse), 1985-88, red chestnut....**$39.00**

Phar Lap (hobo), 1991-92, buckskin w/blk points **$35.00**

Phar Lap (Tonto's Scout), 2001-current, bay pinto w/wht legs, blk mane & tail..**$36.00**

Pluto the Lipizzar, 1991-95, lt gray w/shading...............**$35.00**

Pony of the Americas, 1976-80, chestnut leopard appaloosa, 6-spot variation **$47.00**

Pony of the Americas, 1976-80, chestnut leopard appaloosa w/gray hooves, stenciled spots **$35.00**

Proud Arabian Foal, 1973-80, mahogany bay w/blk & dk gray points & hooves, various socks, ea **$20.00**

Proud Arabian Foal (Joy), 1956-60, glossy alabaster (old mold) w/blk & dk gray mane, tail & hooves......................**$35.00**

Proud Arabian Mare (Just About Horses/Steel Dust), 1994, shaded gray w/darker points **$117.00**

Proud Arabian Mare (QVC/Parade of Breeds), 1995, lt bay w/blk points..**$35.00**

Proud Arabian Stallion, 1983, dapple gray w/blk points ...**$137.00**

Proud Arabian Stallion (Show Special/Kalico), 1999, bay pinto w/blk points..**$42.00**

Quarter Horse Gelding (Two Bits), 1959-66, glossy bay w/blk points **$117.00**

Quarter Horse Gelding (Two Bits), 1961-80, buckskin w/blk points **$39.00**

Quarter Horse Yearling, 1970-80, palomino w/lighter mane & tail **$35.00**

Racehorse, 1956-67, glossy chestnut, w/saddle **$117.00**

Rejoice (National Show Horse), 1999-current, bay pinto w/blk points **$36.00**

Roemer Dutch Warmblood, 1990-93, dk chestnut w/wht blaze, chin & stockings, pk hooves......................................**$31.00**

Roy Belgian Drafter, 1989-90, sorrel/lt chestnut w/flaxen mane & tail & socks, shaded muzzle **$39.00**

Running Mare, red roan, 1971 – 73, $100.00.

Running Foal, 1963-65, glossy Copenhagen w/wht points..**$702.00**

Running Foal, 1963-65, woodgrain **$98.00**

Running Foal (JC Penney/Frisky Foals Set), blk appaloosa w/spotted hind blanket **$39.00**

Running Foal (Little Bub), 1994-95, red bay w/blk points, blk hooves **$23.00**

Running Mare, 1961-87, matt/semigloss bay/chestnut w/blk mane, tail & hooves (add $5 to $10 for wht eyes) **$31.00**

Running Stallion, 1968-71, glossy charcoal w/wht points, bald face **$215.00**

Running Stallion (QVC/Year of the Horse/Jade), 2002, lt gr w/resist design **$53.00**

Running Stallion (Xena's Argo), palomino w/wht mane & tail..**$34.00**

Saddlebred Weanling (Sears/Future Champion Set), 1992, bay pinto w/blk & wht tail **$39.00**

San Domingo (Blanket Appaloosa), 1988-89, dk gray w/darker & blk points, hind blanket w/spots **$39.00**

San Domingo (Toys R Us/TRU Riley), 2000, red roan w/chestnut points & head **$45.00**

Scratching Foal, 1970-71, liver chestnut w/darker or blk mane & tail, various stockings, ea **$98.00**

Sea Star (Scribbles Paint Horse Foal), 1994-95, chestnut pinto w/darker points, stripe & stockings, pk hooves **$16.00**

Secretariat, 1987-95, chestnut w/darker mane & tail **$31.00**

Sham (PetSmart/Seth), 1997, red roan w/speckled roaning, chestnut mane & tail, gray muzzle & hooves **$39.00**

Sham (Prancing Arabian Stallion), 1989-91, palomino w/wht mane & tail, 3 socks (no left hind), gray hooves **$35.00**

Sham (Walter Farley's The Black Stallion), 2002-current, blk .**$36.00**

Sherman Morgan Prancing, 1987-90, chestnut w/darker mane, tail & hooves **$58.00**

Shetland Pony, 1960-72, glossy alabaster w/gray mane, tail & hooves **$35.00**

Shire, 1972-73 & 1975-76, dapple gray w/darker points, wht stockings..**$78.00**

Shire (Montgomery Ward), 1982-83, semigloss gray w/darker points, bald face, stockings **$117.00**

Silver (Mid-Year Release/Skullduggery), 2001, blk appaloosa w/stenciled 'skull' hind blanket **$80.00**

Silver (QVC/Black Beauty), 2001, blk w/right fore sock, gray hooves **$54.00**

Smoky the Cow Horse, 1981-85, med gray w/blk or darker points, wht socks & blaze, gray hooves......................**$46.00**

Stock Horse Foal (Appaloosa), 1983-86, gray w/blanket over barrel & hindquarters, blk mane & tail......................**$23.00**

Stock Horse Foal (Golden Joy Paint), 1997-98, palomino pinto w/wht, mane, tail, blaze & hind socks **$21.00**

Stock Horse Mare (Sorrel Quarter Horse), 1982, flaxen mane & tail, leg up version.......................................**$35.00**

Stormy (Toys R Us/Buckaroo & Skeeter), 1995, bay pinto w/3 socks **$23.00**

Stud Spider (Mister Mister Champion Paint), 1995-96, chestnut pinto..**$32.00**

Stud Spider (Smooth Copper Quarter Horse), 1997-98, shaded bay w/blk points **$28.00**

Touch of Class (Selle Francais), 1991-92, dk chestnut w/darker mane & tail **$32.00**

Trakehner, 1995-96, liver chestnut w/lighter mane & tail ..**$28.00**

Trakehner (Just About Horses), 1987, chestnut w/darker mane & tail **$98.00**

Western Horse, 1950-70(?), glossy palomino, w/snap-girth saddle..**$35.00**

Western Horse, 1951-53, glossy wht w/gray hooves, w/blk snap-girth saddle **$47.00**

Western Horse, 1956-67, glossy palomino or chestnut pinto, w/out saddle, ea **$62.00**

Western Pony, 1956(?), semigloss plum brn, w/out saddle .**$58.00**

Western Pony, 1956(?), semigloss plum brn, w/saddle **$78.00**

Western Pony (Gambler), 1997-98, palomino w/wht mane & tail, w/out saddle **$27.00**

Western Prancer (Vigilante), 1996-97, semigloss blk, w/out saddle..**$20.00**

Western Prancer (Vigilante), 1996-97, semigloss blk, w/saddle .**$32.00**

OTHER ANIMALS

Bear (Bear Family), 1974-76, blk, adult **$45.00**

Bear Cub (Bear Family), 1974-76, blk.............................**$25.00**

Benji, 1978-79, matt/semigloss shaded tan.......................**$63.00**

Brahma Bull, 1968-95, matt/semigloss lt gray w/shading ..**$32.00**

Buffalo (Tatanka), 1992-93, alabaster **$105.00**

Calf (Ayrshire), 1972-73, dk red & wht pinto pattern......**$53.00**

Charolais Bull, 1975-95, alabaster................................**$25.00**

Cow (Jersey), 1972-73, dk tan.....................................**$88.00**

Cutting Calf (Cutting Horse & Calf), 2000-01, calf only ...**$14.00**

Elk, 1968-97, variations, ea **$25.00**

Kitten (Calico), 1966-73 ....**$88.00**

Kitten (Socks), 1995-96, matt/semigloss blk & wht **$21.00**

Labrador (Black, Yellow or Chocolate), 1999-current, ea...**$6.00**

Lassie, 1958-65, semigloss chestnut & wht, w/gold or blk eyes, ea **$56.00**

Mountain Goat, 1998-current, alabaster..........................**$25.00**

Moose, Traditional scale, 1966 – 95, up to $25.00.

Polled Hereford Bull, 1968-current, red-brn & wht..........**$30.00**

Poodle, 1958-68, glossy blk w/collar of various colors.......**$49.00**

Spanish Fighting Bull, 1970-85, blk w/dk-tipped wht horns ..**$70.00**

St Bernard (Brandy), 1995-96, golden brn & wht w/shaded head **$21.00**

Texas Longhorn, 1990-95, dk chestnut pinto....................$28.00
Zebra (Damara), 2000-current...$30.00

Bubble Bath Containers

Since back in the 1960s when the Colgate-Palmolive Company produced the first Soaky, hundreds of different characters and variations have been marketed, bought on demand of the kids who saw these characters day to day on TV by parents willing to try anything that might make bathtime more appealing. Purex made their Bubble Club characters, and Avon and others followed suit. Most Soaky bottles came with detachable heads made of brittle plastic which cracked easily. Purex bottles were made of a softer plastic but tended to loose their paint.

Rising interest in US bubble bath containers has created a collector market for those made in foreign countries, i.e, UK, Canada, Italy, Germany, and Japan. Licensing in other countries creates completely different designs and many characters that are never issued here. Foreign containers are generally larger and are modeled in great detail, reminiscent of the bottles that were made in the US in the '60s. Prices may seem high, considering that some of these are of fairly recent manufacture, but this is due to their limited availability and the costs associated with obtaining them in the United States. We believe these prices are realistic, though many have been reported much higher. Rule of thumb: pay what you feel comfortable with — after all, it's meant to be fun. And remember, value is affected to a great extent by condition. Many of our values are for examples in near-mint to mint condition. Bottles in very good condition are worth only about 60% to 65% of these prices. For slip-over styles, add 100% if the bottle is present.

Advisors: Matt and Lisa Adams (A7)

Alvin (Chipmunks), Colgate-Palmolive, red sweater w/wht A, w/puppet, neck tag & contents, M..............................$50.00
Alvin (Chipmunks), Colgate-Palmolive, wht sweater w/blk A, cap head, NM..$30.00
Alvin (Chipmunks), Ducair Bioescence, holding microphone, w/contents, M..$20.00
Anastasia, Kid Care, 1997, NM...$8.00
Astroniks Robot, Ducair Bioescence, gold buck-toothed robot on red base, EX+...$15.00
Atom Ant, Purex, 1965, NM...$60.00
Auggie Doggie, Purex, orange w/gr shirt, orig tag, EX......$45.00
Baba Looey, Purex, 1960s, brn w/bl scarf & gr hat, NM...$25.00
Baba Looey, Roclar, 1977, NM...$15.00
Baloo Bear, Colgate-Palmolive, 1966, NM......................$20.00
Bambi, Colgate-Palmolive, sitting & smiling, NM...........$25.00
Bamm-Bamm, Purex, blk or gr suspenders, NM, ea..........$35.00
Barney, Kid Care, 1994, yel hat & puppy slippers, NM.......$8.00
Barney Rubble, Milvern (Purex), bl outfit w/yel accents, NM..$35.00
Barney Rubble, Roclar (Purex), brn outfit w/yel accents, MIB..$20.00
Batman, Colgate-Palmolive, 1966, NM...........................$75.00
Batman, Kid Care, 1995, bl & gray w/yel belt, M.............$10.00
Batmobile, Avon, 1978, bl & silver w/decals, EX.............$20.00
Bear, Tubby Time, 1960s, NM..$35.00

Beatles, any character, Colgate-Palmolive, EX, ea from $100 to..$150.00
Beauty & the Beast, Cosrich, orig tag, M, ea from $5 to.....$8.00
Betty Bubbles, Lander, 1960s, NM...................................$15.00
Big Bad Wolf, Tubby Time, cap head, EX........................$35.00
Bobo Bubbles, Lander, 1950s, NM...................................$30.00
Bozo the Clown, Colgate-Palmolive, 1960s, NM.............$30.00
Bozo the Clown, Step Riley, cap head, EX........................$30.00
Broom Hilda, Lander, 1977, EX..$30.00
Brutus (Popeye), Colgate-Palmolive, 1965, red shorts w/red & wht striped shirt, EX...$40.00
Bugs Bunny, Colgate Palmolive, lt bl & wht, NM............$25.00
Bugs Bunny, Colgate-Palmolive, gray, wht & orange w/cap ears, EX...$30.00
Bugs Bunny, Kid Care, in swim trunks w/surfboard, M.......$8.00
Bullwinkle, Colgate-Palmolive, several color variations, NM, ea.$45.00
Bullwinkle, Fuller Brush, 1970s, NM...............................$60.00
Butterfly Princess Barbie, Kid Care, orig tag, M..................$5.00
Care Bear, AGC, 1984, NM...$10.00

Casper the Friendly Ghost, Colgate-Palmolive, 1960s, EX, $30.00.
(Photo courtesy Greg Moore and Joe Pizzo)

Cecil (Beany & Cecil), Purex, 1962, NM........................$40.00
Cement Truck, Colgate-Palmolive, bl & gray w/movable wheels, EX+...$35.00
Charlie Brown, Avon, red baseball outfit, NM.................$20.00
Cinderella, Colgate-Palmolive, 1960s, movable arms, NM..$30.00

Dick Tracy, Colgate-Palmolive, 1965, NM, $50.00.

Creature From the Black Lagoon, Colgate-Palmolive, 1960s, NM..$125.00

Darth Vader, Omni, 1981, NM......................$20.00

Deputy Dawg, Colgate-Palmolive, 1960s, gray, yel & bl w/cap hat, VG (VG box) $30.00

Dino & Pebbles, Cosrich, 1994, NM...............$15.00

Donald Duck, Colgate-Palmolive, 1960s, wht, bl & yel w/cap head, EX..$20.00

Dopey, Colgate-Palmolive, 1960s, purple, yel & red, NM .$20.00

Dum Dum, Purex, 1964, wht w/pk accents, rare, EX, from $75 to $100.00

El Cabong, Knickerbocker (Purex), blk, yel & wht, rare, G to NM..$50.00

Elmer Fudd, Colgate-Palmolive, 1960s, hunting outfit, NM.$25.00

Elmo, Kid Care, 1997, NM $10.00

Ernie (Sesame Street), Minnetonka, holding rubber duckie, orig tag, M $8.00

ET, Avon, 1984, NM....................................$15.00

Felix the Cat, Colgate-Palmolive, 1960s, bl, red or blk, EX .$30.00

Fozzie Bear, Muppet Treasure Island, Calgon, 1996, NM..$10.00

Frankenstein, Colgate-Palmolive, 1963, NM, from $100 to .$125.00

Fred Flintstone, Milvern (Purex), 1960s, red outfit w/blk accents, EX+ $30.00

Garfield, Kid Care, lying in tub, NM $10.00

Genie (Aladdin), Cosrich, M $5.00

GI Joe (Drill Instructor), DuCair Bioescence, 1980s, NM.$15.00

Goofy, Colgate-Palmolive, 1960s, red, wht & blk w/cap head, NM..$20.00

Gravel Truck, Colgate-Palmolive, 1960s, orange & gray w/movable wheels, EX $35.00

Gumby, M&L Creative Packaging, 1987, NM.................$30.00

Harriet Hippo, Merle Norman, in party hat, NM $10.00

Holly Hobbie, Benjamin Ansehl, 1980s, several variations, M, ea..$15.00

Huckleberry Hound, Knickerbocker (Purex), bank, red & blk, orig neck tag, 15", M......................................$60.00

Huckleberry Hound, Secol, 1960s, bl w/yel bow tie, rare, EX.$100.00

Huckleberry Hound & Yogi Bear, Milvern (Purex), 1960s, MIB (sealed)..$75.00

Little Orphan Annie, Lander, 1977, NM, $25.00.

(Photo courtesy Greg Moore and Joe Pizzo)

Hunchback of Notre Dame, Kid Care, in robe w/scepter, M.$5.00

Incredible Hulk, Benjamin Ansehl, standing on rock, M.$25.00

Jasmine (Aladdin), Cosrich, w/bird or mirror, orig tag, M, ea .$6.00

Jiminy Cricket, Colgate-Palmolive, 1960s, gr, blk & red or gr, blk & yel, EX+, ea $30.00

Kermit the Frog, Calgon, Treasure Island outfit, w/tag, M.$8.00

King Louie (Jungle Book), Colgate-Palmolive, slip over, 1960s, NM..$15.00

Lamb Chop (Shari Lewis), Kid Care, holding duck, w/tag, M..$8.00

Lippy the Lion, Purex, 1962, purple vest, rare, EX...........$35.00

Little Mermaid, Kid Care, 1991, tail up, NM...................$10.00

Lucy (Peanuts), Avon, 1970, red dress w/top hat, MIB $20.00

Mad Hatter, Avon, 1970, bronze w/pk hat & clock, EX $20.00

Magilla Gorilla, Purex, 1960s, NM..............................$60.00

Marvin the Martian, Warner Bros, 1996, NM $15.00

Mickey Mouse, Avon, 1969, MIB................................$30.00

Mickey Mouse, Colgate-Palmolive, red shirt & wht pants, cap head, NM..$30.00

Mickey Mouse as Band Leader, Colgate-Palmolive, 1960s, NM .$25.00

Mighty Mouse, Colgate-Palmolive, red and yellow, large head, EX, $25.00.

Miss Piggy, Muppet Treasure Island, Calgon, 1996 ....$10.00

Morocco Mole, Purex, 1966, rare, EX, from $75 to $100.00

Mr Do Bee, Manon Freres, 1960s, w/sticker, rare, NM.........$75.00

Mr Jinks w/Pixie & Dixie, Purex, w/contents, MIB $30.00

Mr Magoo, Colgate-Palmolive, 1960s, red or bl outfit, EX, ea..$25.00

Mr Robottle, Avon, 1971, MIB $20.00

Mummy, Colgate-Palmolive, 1960s, NM, from $100 to .$125.00

Oil Truck, Colgate-Palmolive, gr & gray w/movable wheels, VG $35.00

Pebbles & Dino, Cosrich, Pebbles on Dino's back, M.........$6.00

Pebbles Flintstone, Purex, 1960s, several color variations, EX, ea $35.00

Peter Potamus, Purex, 1960s, purple w/wht or yel shirt, w/contents & orig tag, M, ea..$20.00

Pinocchio, Colgate-Palmolive, 1960s, red & wht or solid brn or red, M, ea..$20.00

Pluto, Colgate-Palmolive, 1960s, orange w/cap head, NM .$20.00

Popeye, Colgate-Palmolive, 1967, wht w/bl accents, w/contents, NMIB..$50.00

Popeye, Colgate-Palmolive, 1977, bl w/wht accents, NM .$35.00

Porky Pig, Colgate-Palmolive, 1960s, red or bl tuxedo, EX+, ea .$25.00
Power Rangers, Kid Care, 1994, any character, M, ea.........$8.00
Punkin' Puss, Purex, 1966, orange w/bl outfit, VG $30.00
Quick Draw McGraw, Purex, 1960s, several variations, NM, ea.$30.00
Race Car, Tidy Toys, several variations w/movable wheels, NMIB, ea $40.00
Raggedy Ann, Lander, 1960s, NM $50.00
Rainbow Brite, Hallmark, 1995, NM $10.00
Ricochet Rabbit, Purex, movable arms, VG $35.00
Robin, Colgate-Palmolive, 1966, EX, from $75 to $100.00
Robocop, Cosway, 1990, NM $15.00
Schoolhouse, Avon, 1968, red, MIB..............................$15.00
Schroeder, Avon, 1970, MIB $25.00

Secret Squirrel, Purex, 1966, MIP, from $75.00 to $85.00.

(Photo courtesy Greg Moore and Joe Pizzo)

Secret Squirrel, Purex, 1966, rare, VG $45.00
Simba, Kid Care, M...$6.00
Simon (Chipmunks), Colgate-Palmolive, 1960s, 3 color variations, w/tag & puppet, M, ea $50.00
Skeletor (Masters of the Universe), Ducair Bioescence, NM.$15.00
Smokey Bear, Colgate-Palmolive, 1960s, NM $25.00
Snaggle Puss, Purex, 1960s, pk w/gr hat, NM....................$50.00
Snoopy & Woodstock, Avon, 1974, on red skis, MIB.........$20.00
Snoopy as Flying Ace, Avon, 1969, MIB $20.00
Snoopy as Flying Ace on Doghouse, Minnetonka, M........$10.00
Snoopy as Joe Cool, Minnetonka, 1996, NM $10.00
Snoopy in Tub of Bubbles, Avon, 1971, MIB....................$20.00
Snow White, Colgate-Palmolive, 1960s, bank, bl & yel, VG..$25.00
Snow White, Colgate-Palmolive, 1960s, movable arms, NM..$35.00
Speedy Gonzales, Colgate-Palmolive, 1960s, EX $25.00
Spider-Man, Benjamin Ansehl, orig tag, M $25.00
Splash Down Space Capsule, Avon, 1970, MIB $20.00
Spouty Whale, Roclar (Purex), bl, orig card, M................$20.00
Squiddly Diddly, Purex, 1960s, purple w/pk shirt, rare, NM..$75.00
Superman, Avon, 1978, complete w/cape, MIB................$35.00
Superman, Colgate-Palmolive, 1965, EX $50.00
Sylvester & Tweety, Ducair Bioescence, 1988, Sylvester holding Tweety, M, from $10 to..$15.00
Sylvester & Tweety, Minnetonka, Tweety standing on Sylvester's head, M $8.00
Sylvester the Cat w/Microphone, Colgate-Palmolive, 1960s, EX..$30.00

Tasmanian Devil in Inner Tube, Kid Care, 1992, EX..........$8.00
Teenage Mutant Ninja Turtles, Kid Care, 1990, any character, M, ea..$8.00
Tennessee Tuxedo, Colgate-Palmolive, 1965, w/ice-cream cone, NM...$25.00
Tex Hex (Brave Starr), Ducair Bioescence, w/tag, M $15.00
Theodore (Chipmunks), Colgate-Palmolive, wht w/bl T or gr w/red sweater & gr T, w/tag & puppet, M, ea.............$50.00
Three Little Pigs, Tubby Time, 1960s, any character, rare, M, ea $40.00
Thumper, Colgate-Palmolive, 1960s, EX $25.00
Tic Toc Tiger, Avon, orange w/yel hands & hat, M $15.00
Tic Toc Turtle, Avon, 1968, gr w/yel face & pk hands, MIB...$20.00
Tommy (Rugrats), Kid Care, 1977, NM $8.00
Top Cat, Colgate-Palmolive, 1963, yel w/bl or red shirt, EX, ea..$30.00
Touche Turtle, Purex, lying on stomach, gr w/pk accents, EX...$30.00
Touche Turtle, Purex, standing, NM $40.00
Tweety on Cage, Colgate-Palmolive, NM.........................$30.00
Wally Gator, Purex, 1963, rare, VG $35.00
Watering Can, Avon, 1962, yel w/flowers, NM $15.00
Wendy the Witch, Colgate-Palmolive, 1960s, NM $30.00
Whitey the Whale, Avon, 1959, EX $15.00
Winkie Blink Clock, Avon, 1975, yel w/bl hands & hat, MIB.$15.00
Winnie the Pooh, Johnson & Johnson, 1997, NM $6.00
Winsome Witch, Purex, 1965, rare, NM...........................$30.00
Wolfman, Colgate-Palmolive, 1963, red pants, NM, from $100 to $125.00
Woodsy Owl, Lander, early 1970s, EX..............................$35.00
Woody Woodpecker, Colgate-Palmolive, 1977, NM........$45.00
Yaaky Doodle Duck, Roclar (Purex), w/contents & neck card, M $20.00
Yoda (Star Wars), Omni, 1981, NM $20.00
Yogi Bear, Milvern (Purex), brn, rare, NM.......................$50.00
Yogi Bear, Purex, powder/bank, gr hat & yel tie, NM..........$30.00
101 Dalmatians, Kid Care, red & blk doghouse w/2 pups, M ..$5.00

Yogi Bear, Purex, 1960s, brown with black hat, NM, $25.00. (Photo courtesy Greg Moore and Joe Pizzo)

FOREIGN

Action Man (Dr X), Rosedew Ltd/UK, 1994, topper, NM .$15.00
Action Man (Night Creeper), Rosedew Ltd/UK, 1994, topper, silver gun, w/suction cups, M...$15.00

Action Man (Space Commando), Rosedew Ltd/UK, 1994, bl & gray combat uniform, M $35.00

Aladdin, Grosvenor/UK, 1994, flying on carpet w/girl & monkey, M $30.00

Alf, PE/Germany, 1980s, NM $40.00

Alice in Wonderland, Aidee Int'l Ltd/UK, 1993, NM $30.00

Aliens, Grosvenor/UK, 1993, topper, M $20.00

Ariel (Little Mermaid), Damascar/Italy, 1995, sitting on purple rock, NM $30.00

Ariel (Little Mermaid), Prelude/UK, 1994, sitting on clear bubbles, NM...$20.00

Baloo (Jungle Book), Boots/England, 1965, NM $70.00

Barney Rubble, Damascar/Italy, 1995, wearing Water Buffalo hat, w/bowling ball, M $35.00

Bart Simpson, Grosvenor, 1991, w/wht towel & soap, NM .$25.00

Bashful, Grumpy & Happy, Grosvenor/UK, 1994, topper, M..$15.00

Batman, Grosvenor/UK, 1992, gray suit & blk cape, NM .$25.00

Batman (Animated), Damascar/Italy, 1995, NM.............$30.00

Batmobile (Batman Forever), Prelude/UK, 1995, blk w/silver wheels, body lifts for bottle, NM $25.00

Beast (Beauty & the Beast), Prelude/UK, 1994, movable arms, comes apart at waist, NM $25.00

Belle (Beauty & the Beast), Prelude/UK, 1994, yel gown, w/hands crossed & head tilted back, NM..................$25.00

Big Bird, Grosvenor/UK, 1995, topper, sitting in bubbles w/teddy bear, M $10.00

Boo Boo Bear, Damascar/Italy, M $35.00

Bubba Saurus, Belvedere/Canada, 1995, bank, pk dinosaur, M..$15.00

Bugs Bunny, Centura/Canada, 1994, in purple robe holding carrot, NM $20.00

Bugs Bunny, Prelude/UK, 1995, cloth hand puppet, slips over bottle, M $20.00

Casper the Ghost, Damascar/Italy, 1995, sitting on pumpkin, glow-in-the-dark, M..$35.00

Casper's Friends, Damascar/Italy, 1995, 3 ghosts sitting on trunk, NM $35.00

Cinderella, Damascar/Italy, 1994, gray & wht gown, NM .$35.00

Cindy Bear, Damascar/Italy, 1995, sitting on purple rock, NM..$35.00

Cookie Monster, Jim Henson/PI/UK, 1995, bl w/wht cloth towel, NM $20.00

Daffy Duck, Prelude/UK, 1994, wearing shark suit, M......$20.00

Daffy Duck, Prelude/UK, 1995, cloth hand puppet, slips over bottle, M $20.00

Darth Vader, Grosvenor/UK, 1995, holding light saber, movable arm, M..$20.00

Dino (Flintstones), Rosedew/UK, 1993, M.............$30.00

Dino (Flintstones), Rosedew/UK, 1993, topper, NM........$15.00

Doc & Dopey, Grosvenor/UK, 1994, topper, NM............$15.00

Donald Duck, Centura/Canada, 1994, standing on red base, NM $20.00

Donald Duck (Mickey & Pals), Centura/Canada, 1995, Donald driving yel boat, NM $20.00

Dopey & Sneezy, Grosvenor/ UK, 1994, NM $30.00

Flipper Riding a Wave, Euromark/England, 1996, NM $20.00

Forever Friends, Grosvenor/England, 1995, NM $20.00

Fred Flintstone, Damascar/Italy, 1994, w/golf club, NM...$35.00

Fred Flintstone, Rosedew/UK, 1994, w/bowling ball, NM.$30.00

Garfield, Grosvenor/England, 1981, NM $25.00

Genie (Aladdin), Centura/Canada, 1994, holding microphone, NM..$20.00

Genie (Aladdin), Damascar/Italy, 1994, released from lamp, real hair, NM $35.00

Goofy, Centura/Canada, 1995, coming out of shower/tub, M .$20.00

Hulk Hogan, Fulford/Canada, 1986, Hulkmania on shirt, NM .$20.00

Jasmin (Aladdin), Damascar/Italy, 1994, in purple dress, head tilted, M $30.00

Joker (Batman), Prelude/UK, 1995, topper, NM $15.00

Jungle Land Boat, Top Care/Canada, 1995, NM $15.00

Magic Princess, Boots/England, 1996, NM $20.00

Matchbox Indy Race Car, Grosvenor/UK, 1995, topper, red w/blk & wht checker flag, NM.................................$15.00

Mickey Mouse, Centura/Canada, 1994, NM $20.00

Mickey Mouse, Disney/Canada, 1994, pie-eyed, traditional outfit, M $25.00

Mickey Mouse, Prelude/UK, 1994, topper, pie-eyed, legs crossed, NM $15.00

Minnie Mouse, Disney World/UK, 1989, red dress, yel shoes, flower & umbrella, NM $30.00

Minnie Mouse, Prelude/UK, 1994, topper, pie-eyed, w/legs crossed, red skirt, NM $15.00

Mr Men, UK, yel & orange hat, M..................................$40.00

Nala (Lion King), Centura/Canada, 1994, sitting on pk base, M $20.00

Noddy, Grosvenor/UK, 1994, topper, sitting w/coffee cup, NM $15.00

Olive Oyl, Damascar/Italy, 1995, sitting w/hands clasped, NM .$35.00

Oscar the Grouch, Grosvenor/UK, 1994, taking a bath in trash can w/I Hate Baths sign, NM $25.00

Paddington Bear, Grosvenor/UK, 1989, topper, EX (EX window box)...$20.00

Papa Smurf, IMPS Brussels/Germany, 1991, bl w/red pants & hat, M..$30.00

Pebbles & Bamm-Bamm, Damascar/Italy, 1995, sitting on sabertooth tiger, M...$35.00

Peter Rabbit, Grosvenor/UK/Canada, 1991, bl coat, NM .$20.00

Piglet (Winnie the Pooh), Prelude/UK, topper, waving, M .$15.00

Pocahontas, Grosvenor/UK, 1995, standing on rock in dive position, NM $20.00

Pocahontas, Grosvenor/UK, 1995, topper, in canoe w/raccoon, NM..$15.00

Popeye, Rosedew Ltd/UK, 1987, on blk base holding spinach can, M..$30.00

Pumbaa (Lion King), Prelude/UK, 1994, M $20.00

Robin, Damascar/Italy, 1995, squatting on eagle head statue, M..$35.00

Rupert Bear, UK, 1995, topper, in yel airplane, M............$20.00

Scooby Doo, Damascar/Italy, 1995, brn, M $35.00

Simba (Lion King), Prelude/UK, 1994, sitting on rock w/paw up, NM..$20.00

Sleeping Beauty, Damascar/Italy, 1994, holding roses, NM..$35.00

Sneezy & Sleepy, Grosvenor/UK, 1994, topper, NM........$15.00

Snow White, Rosedew/UK, 1994, standing w/arms crossed, M .$25.00

Spider-Man, Euromark/UK, 1995, walking over trash can & tire, NM $20.00

Superman, Euromark/UK, 1994, NM..............................$25.00

Superman, Euromark/UK, 1994, topper, kneeling, M $15.00

Spider-Man, Euromark/
England, 1996, M (with
tag), $45.00. (Photo courtesy Greg More
and Joe Pizzo)

Sylvester, Prelude/UK, 1995, cloth hand puppet, slips over bottle, M..$25.00
Tasmanian Devil, Prelude/UK, 1995, mouth wide open, movable arms, M $25.00
Tom & Jerry, Damascar/Italy, 1995, sitting in drum, NM ..$35.00
Tweety Bird, Prelude/UK, 1995, bl robe & wht towel, NM .$35.00
Two-Face (Batman), Prelude/UK, 1995, topper, NM..........$15.00
USS Enterprise (Star Trek), Euromark/UK, 1994, NM $30.00
Wile E Coyote, Prelude/UK, 1995, w/rocket backpack, NM..$35.00
Wilma Flintstone, Damascar/Italy, 1993, standing on turtle shell, M $35.00
Winnie the Pooh, Boots/UK, blk base, M $35.00
Yogi Bear, Damascar/Italy, 1994, standing on gr base w/purple grass, M $35.00
101 Dalmatians, Grosvenor/UK, 1994, father w/pup on head & 1 between legs, NM $35.00
101 Dalmatians, Grosvenor/UK, 1994, topper, pups on pillow w/red sunglasses, M $15.00

Buddy L

First produced in 1921, Buddy L toys have escalated in value over the past few years until now early models in good original condition (or restored, for that matter) often bring prices well into the four figures when they hit the auction block. The business was started by Fred Lundahl, founder of Moline Pressed Steel Co., who at first designed toys for his young son, Buddy. They were advertised as being 'Guaranteed Indestructible,' and indeed they were so sturdy and well built that they just about were. Until wartime caused a shortage, they were made of heavy-gauge pressed steel. Many were based on actual truck models; some were ride-ons, capable of supporting a grownup's weight. Fire trucks with hydraulically activated water towers and hoisting towers that actually worked kept little boys entertained for hours. After the war, the quality of Buddy Ls began to decline, and wood was used to some extent. Condition is everything. Remember that unless the work is done by a professional restorer, over-

painting and amateur repairs do nothing to enhance the value of a toy in poor condition. Professional restorations may be expensive, but they may be viable alternatives when compared to the extremely high prices we're seeing today.

See also Advertising; Aeronautical; Boats; Catalogs.

CARS AND BUSSES

Flivver Coupe, #210B, 1920s, black, 11", EX, A, $1,100.00. (Photo courtesy Randy Inman Auctions)

Flivver Coupe, #210B, 1920s, 11", G, A $385.00
Flivver Roadster, #210A, 1920s, 11", G+, A..................$600.00
Greyhound Bus, automatic door, ringing bell, electric lights, bl & wht, 16", EX $225.00
Greyhound Bus, automatic door, ringing bell, electric lights, bl & wht, 16", NMIB, A $1,100.00
Hot Rod w/Motorcycles on Trailer, bl & wht w/wht-wall tires, wht trailer, 2 plastic motorcycles, 17", NMIB, A.....$500.00
Motor Coach, #208, 1920s, gr w/NP trim, 29", VG, A..$5,500.00
Scarab, #711, 1930s, w/up, red, 11", G............................$150.00

CONSTRUCTION

Cement Mixer, #54, 1930s, 35", G, A.............................$300.00
Cement Mixer, #280A, 1929-31, w/treads, 16", G+, A ..$1,320.00
Cement Mixer, #832, 1940s, 11", NMIB, A $825.00
Dandy Digger, 18", NM, A $275.00
Dandy Digger (Giant), 24", NMIB..................................$625.00
Elevator, wooden wheels, 18", G, A $100.00
Excavation Truck & Steam Shovel, #16, 1930s, 24", VG, A..$3,300.00
Excavation Truck & Steam Shovel, #948, 1940s, 22", NMIB, A $3,630.00
Hoisting Tower, #350, 1929-31, 38", G, A $1,375.00
Jr Excavator, 18", EXIB, A...$300.00
Locomotive Wrecking Crane, w/boiler, long boom w/hook, steel treads w/spring-tension bars, red & blk, 14", rstr, A...$825.00
Mechanical Magnetic Crane, rubber treads, gr & orange, 24", EXIB, A $500.00
Mobile Derrick, #5737, rubber treads, 24", NMIB, A.....$575.00
Mobile Derrick, #5737, 24", no treads, G+ $150.00
Mobile Power Digger, #5847, 1950s, 27", EXIB, A.........$935.00
Mobile Power Digger, #5847, 1950s, 27", VGIB, A........$550.00

Road Roller, #290, 1929 – 31, 18", VG, A, $3,500.00. (Photo courtesy Richard Opfer Auctioneering, Inc.)

Pile Driver, #260, 1920s, 20" L, NM, A $5,500.00
Sand Loader, #230, 1925-31, yel (scarce), 18", EXIB, A.$6,270.00
Sand Screener, #350, 1920s, 22", VG, A $1,100.00
Steam Shovel, #30, 1930s, 18", EXIB, A $550.00
Steam Shovel, #220, 1920s, 19", rstr, G, A $120.00

FIREFIGHTING

Aerial Ladder Truck, #205B, 1920s, 39", EX+, A........$1,760.00
Aerial Ladder Truck, #205B, 1920s, 39", NMIB, A.....$5,720.00
Aerial Ladder Truck, pressed steel & molded plastic, enclosed cab
    w/2 molded lights on roof, 3 wht ladders, 21", VG, A.$325.00
Extension Ladder Trailer Fire Truck, #5751, 1950s, 29", NMIB,
    A $825.00
Fire & Chemical Truck, red w/slanted red & wht nose, wht lad-
    ders, chemical pump, 24", NMIB, A.....................$1,320.00
Fire Department Set, tandem aerial ladder truck w/ladder &
    hose truck, red w/wht-wall tires, NMIB, A...........$1,870.00
Hook & Ladder Truck, #205, 1920s, 29", G, A...............$770.00
Hook & Ladder Truck, #411, 20", EXIB, A $650.00
Hose Truck, #38, 1930s, electric lights, 22", EXIB, A .$1,265.00

Insurance Patrol, 1920s, 26", VG+, A, $6,050.00. (Photo courtesy Randy Inman Auctions)

Ladder Truck, #436, 1930s International, sq cab w/visor, red
    w/wht ladders, 21", NM+IB, A $2,750.00
Ladder Truck, #436, 1930s International, sq cab w/visor, red
    w/yel ladders, 21", VG+, A $630.00

Ladder Truck, 1930s International, curved cab, no visor, red w/2
    silver ladders, 22", NMIB, A $770.00
Pumper Truck, #205A, 1920s, 23", EX+, A $3,960.00
Pumper Truck, #205A, 1920s, 23", G, A $1,320.00
Water Tower Truck, #205D, 1920s, 46", EX+, A........$4,180.00
Water Tower Truck, #205D, 1920s, 46", G, A $2,200.00

OUTDOOR TRAINS

Bottom Dump Car, blk, 22", EX, A............................$3,960.00
Boxcar, red, 20", VG, A..$780.00
Caboose, red, 19", VG, A..$1,150.00
Coal Car, blk, 22", VG, A...$1,200.00
Flatbed Car, blk, 21", G+, A...$700.00

Locomotive and Tender, 1920s, 41", VG+, A, $2,970.00. (Photo courtesy Randy Inman Auctions)

Locomotive & Tender, 41" w/48" track, G+, A...........$1,375.00
Ore Car, blk, side dumping action, 12", EX, A.............$5,500.00
Sand & Gravel Car, blk, w/divider & opening side doors, 22",
    EX+, A..$3,300.00
Stock Car, red, 22", EX, A $1,200.00
Tank Car, red & blk, 17", G+, A......................................$625.00
Tank Car, yel (scarce), 20", Fair+, A $1,100.00
Train Set, 4-6-2 steam locomotive, tender, coal car, stock car, box-
    car, flatbed, 2 tankers, w/18-pc track, VG+, A.......$9,350.00
Train Set (Industrial), 6-pc w/12-pc track, 50", EX.....$2,100.00

RIDERS

Allied Van Lines Truck, #818-B, 29", NMIB, A $4,950.00
Allied Van Lines Truck, #918, 30", G, A......................$900.00
Allied Van Lines Truck, #918, 30", MIB, A $6,600.00

Delivery Truck, 1930s International, 23", NM+IB, A, $4,620.00. (Photo courtesy Randy Inman Auctions)

Allied Van Lines Truck, #918, 30", w/Strombecker doll furniture, 30", VGIB, A $2,750.00

Automatic Tailgate Loader, 1940s, 25", EXIB, A $1,100.00

Baggage Truck, 1935-36, electric lights, 28", EXIB, A..$6,270.00

Buddy L Farms Horse-Drawn Cart, wooden horse pulling steel cart w/seat, 24", NMIB, A......................................$1,650.00

City Special Delivery/Wrigley's Gum & Curtiss Candies, #853, 24", NMIB, A......................................$13,200.00

Coal & Coke Truck, 1940s, rope lift mechanism, 22", EXIB, A..$1,760.00

Deluxe Rider Delivery Stake Truck, 1940s, 23", NMIB, A..$4,620.00

Dump Truck, 1930s International, curved cab, 26", EXIB, A..$5,000.00

Dump Truck, 1930s International, sq cab, electric lights, 25", EX, A..$2,750.00

Dump Truck, 1930s International, sq cab, no electric lights, 25", NMIB, A $4,620.00

Fire Aerial Ladder Truck, 1933 – 34, electric lights, 40", EX, A, $5,280.00. (Photo courtesy Randy Inman Auctions)

Fire Extension Ladder Truck, 1930s, tandem w/enclosed cab, 30", EXIB, A...$1,200.00

Fire Pumper Truck, 1930s, open cab, electric lights, 26", G, A..$2,200.00

Fire Water Tower Truck, 1933, open cab, 41", EX.......$3,600.00

Highway Dept Truck w/Cement Mixer, 1930s, International, 31", very rare, NMIB, A......................................$5,500.00

Ice Truck, 1930s, w/ice & canvas cover, 27", G, A......$1,150.00

Pure Ice Truck, 1930s International, electric lights, 29", VGIB, A..$4,675.00

Saddle Dump Truck, 1920s, NP grille, NMIB, A $3,520.00

Saddle Speedster, #440, 1930s International, electric lights, NMIB, A..$3,400.00

Sand & Gravel Dump Truck, 1940s International, 22", NMIB, A..$1,870.00

Shell Tanker Truck, 1930s International, 29", EXIB, A .$2,200.00

Stake Truck, 1930s International, electric lights, 24", NMIB, A..$4,400.00

Standard Oil of Indiana Tanker, 1934, electric lights, 25", EXIB, A..$19,800.00

Steam Shovel, 1950s, 18", G+, A...................................$50.00

Steam Shovel, 1950s, 18", NMIB, A..............................$550.00

Steam Shovel Truck, 1930s International, sq cab, electric lights, 25", EXIB, A $16,500.00

Steam Shovel Truck, 1930s International, sq cab, no electric lights, 25", GIB, A..$2,530.00

Texaco Locomotive & Tank Car, wood & plastic, w/steering wheel, 35", EX, A..$330.00

Wrecker, Sit-N-Ride decal, w/steering wheel & siren, 25", G+, A..$400.00

Wrecker, 1938 International, 33", G, A $3,190.00

TRUCKS AND VANS

Air Force Supply Truck, w/canvas cover, 15", NMIB, A..$1,150.00

Airway Express Delivery Truck, 1950s, GMC, 15", NMIB, A..$1,600.00

Anti-Aircraft Unit, flatbed truck w/2 mounted marble-shooting guns, rubber tires, 15", EX, A $300.00

Army Combination Set, w/2 Army trucks, searchlight, cannon & accessories, NMIB, A......................................$1,650.00

Army Electric Searchlight Unit, 15", NM+IB, A, $600.00. (Photo courtesy Randy Inman)

Army Half-Track Mobile Artillery Unit, #409, 21", EXIB, A..$415.00

Army Half-Track Mobile Artillery Unit & Howitzer, #3409, 1949, unused, MIB, A $575.00

Army Half-Track Mobile Artillery Unit & Howitzer, #5409, 21", NMIB, A..$550.00

Army Supply Corps Truck, 1950s, w/canvas cover, 15", G, A..$110.00

Army Transport & Trailer, International, w/canvas covers, 32" overall, EXIB, A $650.00

Army Transport w/Cannon, GMC, w/canvas cover, 20", NMIB, A..$550.00

Army Transport w/Cannon, International, w/canvas cover, 21", EX, A..$110.00

Atlas Van Lines Semi, 1950s, w/removable roof & opening rear door, 29", EX+, A..$1,760.00

Baby Ruth Delivery Truck, 29", VG, A..........................$250.00

Auto Carrier, 1950s GMC, with three plastic cars, 27", EXIB, A, $4,500.00. (Photo courtesy Randy Inman Auctions)

Baggage Stake Truck, 1920s, w/accessories, 27", EX+, A ..$6,600.00
Baggage Stake Truck, 1920s, 27", no accessories o/w VG, A .$3,300.00
Baggage Truck, enclosed cab w/streamlined bed, rubber tires, 17½", VG, A $110.00

Bell Telephone Truck, GMC, 16", VG, A, $770.00. (Photo courtesy Randy Inman Auctions)

Boat Transport Tractor-Trailer, w/3 plastic boats, 27", VG, A....$300.00
Borden Delivery Truck, 13", unused, NRFB (sealed), A ...$935.00
Brinks Armored Truck, 1958 GMC, w/accessories, 15", VG, A ..$525.00
Camper Truck, 1960s, 15", NMIB, A $500.00
Cattle Transport, stake bed, w/accessories, 15", NMIB, A..$1,050.00
Cattle Transport, stake bed, 15", no accessories o/w EXIB, A..$770.00
City Dray, 1930s International w/stake bed, 21", NMIB, A..$2,970.00
Coal & Coke Truck, 1950, 24", VG, A $715.00
Coal Truck, #202, 1920s, 25", rstr, A $1,050.00
Coast-To-Coast Stores Stake Truck, 14", NMIB, A $1,540.00
Curtiss Candies/Baby Ruth/Butterfinger Semi, 1950s, 29", EXIB, A...$1,100.00
Dump Truck, #434, 1930s International, electric lights, NMIB, A..$2,970.00
Dump Truck, #434, 1930s International, electric lights, VGIB, A..$1,650.00
Dump Truck, curved dump bed, 17", EXIB, A $525.00
Dump Truck, 1920s, open seat, chain drive, metal disk wheels, 24", G, A $600.00
Electric Emergency Unit, 15", unused, NMIB, A $770.00
Emergency Auto Wrecker, 15", NMIB (unassembled w/parts in sealed bag), A $575.00

Express Line Tandem Truck, 1930s International, electric headlights, 38", EX+, A, $4,950.00. (Photo courtesy Randy Inman Auctions)

Express Line Tandem Truck, 1930s International, 23", VG, A...$525.00
Express Line Van, 1920s, 24", EX+, A $5,500.00
Express Line Van, 1920s, 25", VG, A $2,200.00
Express Truck, 1920s, open bench seat, open bed, spoke wheels, blk w/red trim, 24", EX, A $2,200.00
Farm Supplies Hydraulic Dump Truck, 1940s International, 21", NMIB, A $1,375.00
Farm Supplies Hydraulic Dump Truck & Tandem Trailer, 1950s, 24" overall, NMIB, A...$2,530.00
Fast Freight Semi, open U-shaped trailer, 20", NMIB, A...$650.00
Firestone Wrecker, 25", complete, NMIB, A, from $6,270 to..$7,150.00
Firestone Wrecker, 25", incomplete, VG, A...............$1,100.00
Flivver Delivery Truck, 1920s, 12", EX+, A $1,100.00
Flivver Delivery Truck, 1920s, 12", G, A $525.00
Flivver Dump Cart, 1920s, 13", VG+, A $2,300.00

Flivver Huckster Delivery Truck, 1920s, 14", EX, A, $5,390.00. (Photo courtesy Bertoia Auctions)

Freight Delivery Stake Truck, w/removable sides & chain, 15", EXIB, A $650.00
Heavy Hauling Dump Truck, #5622, 23", NMIB, A.......$600.00
Heavy Machinery Service Truck, 1950s, w/lifting boom, 23", G, A $185.00
Heavy Machinery Service Truck, 1950s, 23", no lifting boom o/w NMIB, A..$330.00
Highway Maintenance Truck & Portable Compressor, 1950s, NMIB, A $770.00
Highway Maintenance Truck w/Steam Shovel on Lowboy Trailer, 1940s International, 31", NMIB, A..........$3,190.00
Hydraulic Dump Truck, #201A, 24", VG, A $770.00
Hydraulic Dump Truck, #5641, 21", EXIB, A.................$275.00
Hydraulic Dump Truck, #5859, 20", NMIB, A.................$525.00
Ice Truck, #207, 1920s, 26", EX, A $1,000.00
Ice Truck, 1930s International, w/tongs & canvas cover, 21½", NMIB, A $1,870.00
IHC Sales & Service Red Baby Express Truck, 24", G, A ..$1,760.00
Jr City Dray Stake Truck, 1930s, 24", VG, A $3,300.00
Jr Dairy Truck, 24", G+, A $1,800.00
Jr Dump Truck, electric lights, 22", G, A $275.00
Jr Milk Delivery, 1930s, 24", G+, A..........................$3,850.00
Load & Dump Truck, 1950s, w/side conveyor, 20", NMIB, A...$825.00
Lumber Truck, #203A, 1920s, no lumber, overpnt, A ..$1,000.00
Medical Corps Truck, wht, 21", no canvas cover o/w NMIB, A $600.00

Lumber Truck, #203A, 1920s, replaced lumber and stakes, 26", VG, $3,300.00. (Photo courtesy Randy Inman Auctions)

Merry-Go-Round Truck, #5429, 13", G+ $200.00
Milk Transport, plastic semi tanker, red & bl, 22", EXIB, A..$770.00
Mobile Repair-It Unit, 1940s International, w/accessories, NMIB, A $2,750.00
Motor Market Truck, 1930s International, 20", missing marque, GIB, A $525.00
One-Ton Express Truck, #212A, 1920s, 14", G+, A ...$1,870.00
Pickup Truck, 1960s, spring suspension, bl w/wht plastic grille guard & mirror, wht-wall tires, 13", NMIB, A $715.00
Pure Ice Truck, 1930s International, 23", NM $700.00
Railroad Transfer Stake Truck, 23", Fair, A.....................$250.00
Railway Express Agency Van, 1930s International, Serve Ice Cream ads on sides, 23", G, A..................................$475.00
Railway Express Agency Van, 1930s International, Wrigley's Gum ad on sides, gr & yel, EXIB, A $17,600.00
Railway Express Line Van, #204A, 1920s, 25", EX, A...$2,750.00
Railway Express Line Van, #204A, 1920s, 25", G, A $725.00
Railway Express Line Van, #204A, 1920s, 25", rstr, A...$1,200.00
REA Express Truck, #5352, 1950s, 13", MIB (unopened), A .$300.00
Red Baby, see IHC Sales & Service
Repair-It Tow Truck, #5560, 1950s, 16", NMIB $450.00
Repair-It Tow Truck, #5560, 1950s, 16", some rpt, A.....$150.00

Riding Academy Horse Truck, 1960s, with two accessory horses, 19", VG, A, $385.00. (Photo courtesy Randy Inman Auctions)

Rival Dog Food Delivery Truck, 15", NM+IB, A $1,870.00
Robotoy Dump Truck, electric lights, w/transformer, 22", EX+, A...................................$1,200.00

Robotoy Dump Truck, electric lights, 22", no transformer o/w GIB $700.00
Sand & Gravel Truck, #202A, 1920s, 15", G, A.........$1,900.00
Sand & Gravel Truck, #202A, 1920s, 25", EX, A $3,025.00
Sand & Stone Dump Truck, 1960s, dbl rear axle, 15", NMIB, A $770.00
Sand & Stone Dump Truck, 1960s, single rear axle, 15", EXIB, A $550.00
Sand Loader & Dump, #810, 1940s International, 23", NMIB, A $1,650.00
Scoop-N-Dump Truck, 18", NMIB, A $500.00
Sheffield Farms Co Tanker, 1930s, 25", VGIB, A $1,320.00
Shell Tanker, 1930s International, 22", NMIB, A.......$3,960.00
Store Door-Delivery Stake Truck, w/food product boxes, 15", EX+, A..................$990.00
Tank Line Truck, #438, 1930s International, GIB, A....$1,760.00
Telephone & Maintenance Truck, #450, w/accessories, 17", NMIB, A..................$650.00
Texaco Tanker, red w/wht name & star decal on doors, 24", EX, A...................$200.00
Tow Truck, 1960s, yel w/blk crane, red light on roof, 14", G, A...................$200.00
Towing Service Truck, 1940s International, 22", EX, A..$200.00
Towing Service Truck, 1940s International, 22", NMIB, A .$1,150.00

US Mail Truck, Buy Defense Bonds decal, 22", NMIB, A, $1,485.00. (Photo courtesy Randy Inman Auctions)

Utility Service Truck, GMC, w/crane, 16", EXIB, A......$575.00
Wild Animal Circus on Wheels Truck, metal & plastic, 26", EX $150.00
Wrecking Truck, #209, 1920s, 28", VG, A $2,200.00
Wrecking Truck, #937, 1930s International, 26", VGIB, A................$1,265.00
Zoo Pickup Truck, 1960s, w/plastic cages & 3 animals, 13", EX+, A................$465.00

WOODEN VEHICLES

Army Tank, 1940s, 12", EX, A....................................$1,100.00
Army Tank, 1940s, 12", G, A..$450.00
Army Truck, 1940s, open bed, 16", no canvas cover o/w VG, A $220.00
Buick Convertible, 1940s, electric lights, 18", EXIB, A .$5,500.00

Aerial Hook and Ladder Truck, 1940s, 33", VG+, A, $1,760.00. (Photo courtesy Randy Inman Auctions)

Buick Station Wagon, 1940s, electric lights, railed top, folding rear gate, 18", VG, A $1,150.00
Fire Truck, 1940s, 16", incomplete, Poor, A $120.00
Greyhound Lines Bus, 1950s, opening door, 18", G+, A ..$990.00
Ladder Truck, 1940s, 23", Fair+, A......................................$75.00
Milk Farms Delivery Truck, 1940s, long nose w/side door, w/bottle carrier, 14", Fair, A $200.00
Milk Farms Delivery Truck, 1940s, snub nose van w/side doors, w/bottle carrier, 13", VG, A $470.00
Moving Van, 1940s, 28", G+, A.......................................$250.00

Pontoon Boat, 1940s, with wind-up motor, 16", EX, A, $2,860.00. (Photo courtesy Randy Inman Auctions)

Pure Ice Truck, 1940s, open bed, w/ice cubes & tongs, 16", VG+, A $400.00
Sky View Taxi Cab, 1940s, celluloid windows, opening doors & sky roof, rubber tires, NM, A $2,750.00
Timber Truck, 1940s, w/logs, 27", G+, A $250.00
Woody Convertible, 1940s, retractable top, 19", EX, A .$1,000.00
Woody Convertible, 1940s, retractable top, 19", G........$225.00
Wrecker, 1940s, 18", G+, A $185.00

MISCELLANEOUS

Gas Pump, motorized plastic pump with magnetic nozzle, 7", EXIB, A, $120.00.

(Photo courtesy Randy Inman Auctions)

Catapult Hangar, w/2 planes, 20", VG, A....................$1,500.00
Catapult Hangar, 8x12", missing airplane, Fair+, A $275.00
Zephyr, 1-car, #121, 30", Fair, A................................$330.00
Zephyr, 1-car, #121, 30", VGIB, A..............................$1,980.00
Zephyr, 3-car, #20-21, EXIB, A $3,300.00

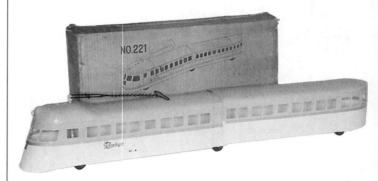

Zephyr, two-car, #221, 50", NMIB, A, $3,960.00. (Photo courtesy Randy Inman Auctions)

Building Blocks and Construction Toys

Toy building sets were popular with children well before television worked its mesmerizing influence on young minds; in fact, some were made as early as the end of the eighteenth century. Important manufacturers include Milton Bradley, Joel Ellis, Charles M. Crandall, William S. Tower, W.S. Read, Ives Manufacturing Corporation, S.L. Hill, Frank Hornby (Meccano), A.C. Gilbert Brothers, The Toy Tinkers, Gebruder Bing, R. Bliss, S.F. Fischer, Carl Brandt Jr., and F. Ad. Richter (see Anchor Stone Building Sets by Richter). Whether made of wood, paper, metal, glass, or 'stone,' these toys are highly prized today for their profusion of historical, educational, artistic, and creative features.

Richter's Anchor (Union) Stone Building Blocks were the most popular building toy at the beginning of the twentieth century. As early as 1880, they were patented in both Germany and the USA. Though the company produced more than six hundred different sets, only their New Series is commonly found today (these are listed below). Their blocks remained popular until WWI, and Anchor sets were one of the first toys to achieve international 'brand name' acceptance. They were produced both as basic sets and supplement sets (identified by letters A, B, C, or D) which increased a basic set to a higher level. There were dozens of stone block competitors, though none were very successful. During WWI the trade name Anchor was lost to A.C. Gilbert (Connecticut) who produced Anchor blocks for a short time. Richter responded by using the new trade name 'Union' or 'Stone Building Blocks,' sets considered today to be Anchor blocks despite the lack of the Richter's Anchor trademark. The A.C. Gilbert Company also produced the famous Erector sets which were made from about 1913 through the late 1950s.

Note: Values for Richter's blocks are for sets in very good condition; (+) at the end of the line indicates these sets are being reproduced today.

Building Blocks and Construction Toys

Advisor: George Hardy (H3), Anchor Stone Building Sets by Richter

Aeroplane Constructor #0, Meccano, EXIB, A $375.00
Aeroplane Constructor #1, Meccano, VGIB, A $350.00
Aeroplane Constructor #2, Meccano, EXIB, A $450.00
American Logs, Halsam, EXIB $50.00
American Model Builder, American Mech Toy Co, EXIB...$150.00
American Plastic Bricks, Halsam, 1950s, EXIC $35.00
American Skyline, Elgo, 1950s, NMIB $35.00
Big Boy Tinkertoy, Spalding, 1950s-60s, EXIC $45.00
Big Tinkertoy Construction Set for Little Hands, Questor, 1976,
    EXIC $25.00
Block City #B-500, Plastic City Block Inc, 1960, EXIC...$50.00
Building Bricks, Auburn Rubber, 1950s, EXIC $40.00
Built-Rite Army Trench w/6 Soldiers, 1940s, MIB, A $100.00
Built-Rite Fort w/Soldiers, 1940s, EXIB, A $130.00
Busy Mechanic Construction Kit, Renwal #375-198, EXIB.$300.00
Construx Action Building System, Fisher-Price, #6331 Mobile
    Missiles, Military Series, NMIB, from $50 to $75.00
Curtain Wall Builder No 640, Spalding, 1959-64, EXIC..$40.00
Dirigible Builder, Schoenhut, EXIB............................$1,000.00
Double Tinkertoy, Toy Tinkers, 1927, EXIC $40.00
Drawbridge Set, Renwal #155, rare, EXIB $250.00

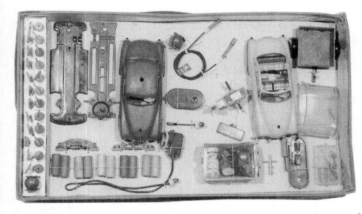

Elektro Champion Deluxe Set, Schuco, lithographed and painted tin, complete, VGIB, A, $325.00. (Photo courtesy Richard Opfer Auctioneering, Ltd.)

Erector Set, Gilbert #1 (Tru Model), EXIB...................$200.00
Erector Set, Gilbert #3, MIB $200.00
Erector Set, Gilbert #4, VGIB $125.00
Erector Set, Gilbert #5½, MIB.....................................$175.00
Erector Set, Gilbert #6½, MIB.....................................$165.00
Erector Set, Gilbert #7, EXIB (wood box) $250.00
Erector Set, Gilbert #7½, EXIB (wood box)..................$350.00
Erector Set, Gilbert #8, EXIB (wood box) $850.00
Erector Set, Gilbert #8½, EXIB (wood box)..................$950.00
Executive Tinkertoy, Spalding, 1966, EXIC....................$35.00
Falcon Building Lumber Set, EXIB (wood box), A $150.00
Fire Alarm Set, Hasbro, NMIB, A $135.00
Giant Tinker, Toy Tinkers, 1926, EXIB........................$225.00
Girder & Panel Constructioneer Set #8, Kenner, EXIB.$100.00
Girder & Panel Hydro-Dynamic Double Set #18, Kenner,
    VGIB..$200.00

Girder & Panel Hydro-Dynamic Single Set #17, Kenner,
    VGIB..$175.00
Girder & Panel International Airport, Kenner, 1977, EXIB.$40.00
Junior Tinkertoy, Spalding, 1963, EXIC.........................$25.00
Major Tinkertoy, Spalding, 1964, EXIC.........................$25.00
Marklin Auto-Baukasten, contemporary reissue of 1930s race
    car, MIB, A $185.00
Mold Master Road Builder, Kenner, 1964, NMIB, J2 .....$125.00
Montage-Mercedes 190SL Kit, Schuco #2097, EX+IB, A.$165.00
Motor Car Constructor #1, Meccano, unassembled, EXIB, A .$350.00

Motor Car Constructor Set #2, Meccano, assembled pressed-steel racer with driver, riveted construction, 12", EX (with original box), A, $420.00. (Photo courtesy Bertoia Auctions)

Motor Car Constructor #2, Meccano, unassembled, MIB, A.$460.00
Motorized Tinkertoy, Toy Tinkers/Spalding, EXIC $60.00
Roadster Constructor, Meccano, EXIB $500.00

Schoenhut's Aeroplane Builder, assembled wood monocoupe, with directions, 15½" wingspan, EX (with original box), A, $250.00. (Photo courtesy Bertoia Auctions)

Schoenhut's Hollywood Home Builder, EXIB, A............$165.00
Special Tinkertoy w/Windlass Drive, Toy Tinkers, 1943, EXIC ..$35.00
Spirit of St Louis Airplanes, Metalcraft, builds over 250 air-
    planes, VGIB, A $450.00
Steel Worker Set, Dayton, VGIB, A...............................$215.00
Super City Heliport Building Set, Ideal, 1968, EX (EX vinyl
    case) $50.00
Super City Skyscraper Building Set, Ideal, 1960s, EXIB...$75.00
Super City Town & Country, Ideal, VGIB.......................$50.00

Teck Tinkertoy, Spalding, 1963, EXIC................$25.00
Tinker Zoo No 717, Spalding, 1970, EXIC................$15.00
Tinker Zoo No 737, Spalding, 1962-70, EXIC................$25.00
Tinkerblox, Toy Tinkers, 1917-20, EXIB................$60.00
Tinkertoy Design Blocks, Questor, EXIC................$30.00
Tinkertoy Giant Engineer, Questor, EXIC................$25.00
Tinkertoy Junior Architect, Questor, EXIC................$25.00
Tinkertoy Little Designer, Questor, EXIC................$25.00
Tinkertoy Locomotive & Driver, Questor, EXIC................$15.00
Tinkertoy Master Builder, Questor, EXIC................$25.00
Tinkertoy No 30040, Gabriel, EXIC................$25.00
Tinkertoy No 30060, Gabriel, motorized, EXIC................$35.00
Tinkertoy Panel Builder #600, Spalding, 1958, EXIC................$30.00
Tinkertoy Panel Builder #800, Spalding, 1958, EXIC................$40.00
Train Kit, Metalcraft, stock car, caboose & trucks, EXIB..$300.00

**Tinkertoy Wonder Builder,
Spalding, 1953 – 54, EXIC,
$30.00.** (Photo courtesy Craig Strange)

ANCHOR STONE BUILDING SETS BY RICHTER

American House & Country Set #206, VG, H3................$600.00
American House & Country Set #208, VG, H3................$600.00
American House & Country Set #210, VG, H3................$700.00
DS Set #E3, w/metal parts & roof stones, VG, H3................$80.00
DS Set #3A, w/metal parts & roof stones, VG, H3................$80.00
DS Set #5, w/metal parts & roof stones, VG, H3................$150.00
DS Set #5A, w/metal parts & roof stones, VG, H3................$150.00
DS Set #7, w/metal parts & roof stones, VG, H3................$270.00
DS Set #7A, w/metal parts & roof stones, VG, H3................$200.00
DS Set #9A, w/metal parts & roof stones, VG, H3................$250.00
DS Set #11, w/metal parts & roof stones, VG, H3................$675.00
DS Set #11A, w/metal parts & roof stones, VG, H3................$300.00
DS Set #13A, w/metal parts & roof stones, VG, H3................$325.00
DS Set #15, w/metal parts & roof stones, VG, H3................$1,500.00
DS Set #15A, w/metal parts & roof stones, VG, H3................$475.00
DS Set #19A, w/metal parts & roof stones, VG, H3................$475.00
DS Set #21A, w/metal parts & roof stones, VG, H3................$975.00
DS Set #23A, w/metal parts & Roof stones, VG, H3................$750.00
DS Set #25A, w/metal parts & roof stones, VG, H3...$1,500.00

DS Set #27, w/metal parts & roof stones, VG, H3................$6,000.00
DS Set #27B, w/metal parts & roof stones, VG, H3....$2,000.00
Fortress Set #402, VG, H3................$100.00
Fortress Set #402A, VG, H3................$130.00
Fortress Set #404, VG, H3................$250.00
Fortress Set #404A, VG, H3................$275.00
Fortress Set #406, VG, H3................$500.00
Fortress Set #406A, VG, H3................$400.00
Fortress Set #408, VG, H3................$1,000.00
Fortress Set #408A, VG, H3................$800.00
Fortress Set #410, VG, H3................$1,800.00
Fortress Set #410A, VG, H3................$1,000.00
Fortress Set #412A, VG, H3................$1,500.00
Fortress Set #414, VG, H3................$5,000.00
German House & Country Set #301, VG, H3................$500.00
German House & Country Set #301A, VG, H3................$500.00
German House & Country Set #303, VG, H3................$1,000.00
German House & Country Set #303A, VG, H3................$2,000.00
German House & Country Set #305, VG, H3................$3,000.00
GK-AF Great-Castle Set, VG, H3................$9,950.00
GK-NF Set #6, VG, H3 (+)................$140.00
GK-NF Set #6A, VG, H3 (+)................$160.00
GK-NF Set #8, VG, H3................$300.00
GK-NF Set #8A, VG, H3 (+)................$180.00
GK-NF Set #10, VG, H3................$480.00
GK-NF Set #10A, VG, H3 (+)................$200.00
GK-NF Set #12, VG, H3................$680.00
GK-NF Set #12A, VG, H3 (+)................$250.00
GK-NF Set #14A, VG, H3................$250.00
GK-NF Set #16, VG, H3................$1,180.00
GK-NF Set #16A, VG, H3................$300.00
GK-NF Set #18A, VG, H3................$400.00
GK-NF Set #20, VG, H3................$2,000.00
GK-NF Set #20A, VG, H3................$500.00
GK-NF Set #22A, VG, H3................$500.00
GK-NF Set #24A, VG, H3................$600.00
GK-NF Set #26A, VG, H3................$1,000.00
GK-NF Set #28, VG, H3................$4,000.00
GK-NF Set #28A, VG, H3................$1,200.00
GK-NF Set #30A, VG, H3................$1,200.00
GK-NF Set #30A, VG, H3................$1,200.00
GK-NF Set #32B, VG, H3................$1,600.00
GK-NF Set #34, VG, H3................$7,000.00
KK-NF Set #5, VG, H3................$110.00
KK-NF Set #5A, VG, H3................$100.00
KK-NF Set #7, VG, H3................$200.00
KK-NF Set #7A, VG, H3................$115.00
KK-NF Set #9A, VG, H3................$120.00
KK-NF Set #11, VG, H3................$315.00
KK-NF Set #11A, VG, H3................$275.00
KK-NF Set #13A, VG, H3................$300.00
KK-NF Set #15A, VG, H3................$450.00
KK-NF Set #17A, VG, H3................$750.00
KK-NF Set #19A, VG, H3................$2,500.00
KK-NF Set #21, VG, H3................$4,500.00
Neue Reihe Set #102, VG, H3................$100.00
Neue Reihe Set #104, VG, H3................$150.00
Neue Reihe Set #106, VG, H3................$200.00

Neue Reihe Set #108, VG, H3.......................................$300.00
Neue Reihe Set #110, VG, H3.......................................$600.00
Neue Reihe Set #112, VG, H3 ....$1,000.00
Neue Reihe Set #114, VG, H3 ....$1,500.00
Neue Reihe Set #116, VG, H3 ....$2,000.00

California Raisins

The California Raisins made their first TV commercials in the fall of 1986. The first four PVC figures were introduced in 1987, the same year Hardee's issued similar but smaller figures, and three 5½" Bendees became available on the retail market. In 1988 twenty-one more Raisins were made for retail as well as promotional efforts in grocery stores. Four were graduates identical to the original four characters except standing on yellow pedestals and wearing blue graduation caps with yellow tassels. Hardee's increased their line by six.

In 1989 they starred in two movies: *Meet the Raisins* and *The California Raisins — Sold Out*, and eight additional characters were joined in figurine production by five of their fruit and vegetable friends from the movies. Hardee's latest release was in 1991, when they added still four more. All Raisins issued for retail sales and promotions in 1987 and 1988 (including Hardee's) are dated with the year of production (usually on the bottom of one foot). Of those released for retail sales in 1989, only the Beach Scene characters are dated, and these are actually dated 1988. Hardee's 1991 series are also undated.

Advisor: Ken Clee (C3)

AC, 'Gimme-5' pose, Meet the Raisins Second Edition, CALRAB-Applause, 1989, M...................................$225.00
Alotta Stile, purple boom box, Hardee's Fourth Promotion/ CALRAB-Applause, 1991, sm, MIP (w/collector's card).$15.00
Anita Break, shopping w/Hardee's bags, Hardee's Fourth Promotion/CALRAB-Applause, 1991, sm, MIP (w/collector's card) ...$15.00
Banana White, yel dress, Meet the Raisins First Edition/Applause-Claymation, 1989, M $20.00
Bass Player, w/gray slippers, Second Commercial Issue/ CALRAB, 1988, M.......................................$8.00
Benny, w/bowling ball & bag, Hardee's Fourth Promotion/ CALRAB-Applause, 1991, sm, MIP (w/collector's card).$15.00

Boy With Surfboard, purple board, brown base, Beach Theme Edition/CALRAB-Applause, 1988, M, $10.00. (Photo courtesy Larry DeAngelo)

Blue Surfboard, board connected to foot, unknown promotion/ CALRAB, 1988, M $35.00
Blue Surfboard, board in right hand (not connected to foot), unknown promo/CALRAB, 1987, M........................$50.00
Boy in Beach Chair, orange glasses, brn base, Beach Theme Edition/CALRAB-Applause, 1988, M $20.00
Boy w/Surfboard, not connected to foot, Beach Theme Edition/CALRAB-Applause, 1988, M $10.00
Captain Toonz, bl boom box, yel glasses & sneakers, Hardee's Second Promotion/Applause, 1988, sm, M, from $1 to $3.00
Cecil Tyme (Carrot), Meet the Raisins Second Promotion/ CALRAB-Applause, 1989, M.................................$250.00

Christmas Issue, with candy cane or red hat, CALRAB, 1988, M, each, $9.00. (Photo courtesy Larry DeAngelo)

Drummer, Second Commercial Issue, CALRAB-Applause, 1988, M..$10.00
FF Strings, bl guitar & orange sneakers, Hardee's Second Promotion/Applause, 1988, sm, M, from $1 to......................$3.00
Girl w/Boom Box, purple glasses, gr shoes, Beach Theme Edition/CALRAB-Applause, 1988, M $20.00
Girl w/Tambourine, gr shoes & bracelet, Beach Theme Edition/CALRAB-Applause, 1988, M $15.00
Girl w/Tambourine (Ms Delicious), yel shoes, Second Commercial Issue/CALRAB-Applause, 1988, M $15.00
Graduate, in sunglasses w/index finger touching face, Graduate Key Chains/CALRAB-Applause, 1988, M, ea..........$85.00
Graduate, saxophone player, Graduate Key Chains/CALRAB-Applause, 1988, M..$85.00
Graduate, saxophone player, yel base, Post Raisin Bran/ CALRAB-Claymation, 1988, from $45 to.................$65.00
Graduate, singer, yel base, Post Raisin Bran Issue/CALRAB-Claymation, 1988, from $45 to $65.00
Graduate, sunglasses, yel base, Post Raisin Bran Issue/CALRAB-Claymation, 1988, from $45 to $65.00
Graduate, yel base, Post Raisin Bran Issue/CALRAB-Claymation, 1988, M, from $45 to $65.00
Guitar, red guitar, First Commercial Issue/CALRAB, 1988, M .$8.00
Hands, left hand points up, right hand points down, Post Raisin Brand Issue/CALRAB, 1987, M $2.00
Hands, pointing up w/thumbs touching head, First Key Chains/CALRAB, 1987, M...$5.00
Hands, pointing up w/thumbs touching head, Hardee's First Promotion/CALRAB, 1987, sm, M $3.00

Hip Band Guitarist (Hendrix), w/headband & yel guitar, Second Key Chains/CALRAB-Applause, 1988, sm, M..........$65.00

Hip Band Guitarist (Jimi Hendrix), with headband and yellow guitar, Third Commercial Issue/CALRAB-Applause, 1988, M, $30.00. (Photo courtesy Larry DeAngelo)

Hitchhiker, see Winky

Hula Girl, gr skirt, yel shoes & bracelet, Beach Theme Edition/CALRAB-Applause, 1988, M $20.00

Lenny Lima Bean, purple shirt, Meet the Raisins Second Promotion/CALRAB-Applause, 1989, M $175.00

Lick Broccoli, gr & blk w/red & orange guitar, Meet the Raisins First Edition/Applause-Claymation, 1989, M $20.00

Michael Raisin, Special Edition/Applause, 1989, M.........$15.00

Microphone, left hand extended w/open palm, Second Key Chains/CALRAB-Applause, 1988, sm, M.................$45.00

Microphone, right hand in fist w/microphone in left hand, Raisin Bran Issue/CALRAB, 1987, M.......................$2.00

Microphone, right hand points up w/microphone in left, First Key Chains/CALRAB, 1987, M..............................$5.00

Microphone, right hand points up w/microphone in left, Hardee's First Promotion/CALRAB, 1987, M $3.00

Microphone (Female), yel shoes & bracelet, Second Key Chains/CALRAB-Applause, 1988, sm, M.................$45.00

Microphone (Female), yel shoes & bracelet, Third Commercial Issue/CALRAB-Applause, 1988, M $12.00

Mom, yel hair, pk apron, Meet the Raisins Second Promotion/CALRAB-Applause, 1989, M, from $150 to...........$200.00

Piano, bl piano, red hair, gr sneakers, Meet the Raisins First Edition/CALRAB-Applause, 1989, M $35.00

Rollin' Rollo, roller skates, yel sneakers & hat mk H, Hardee's Second Promotion/Applause, 1988, sm, M, from $1 to .$3.00

Rudy Bagaman, w/cigar, purple shirt & flipflops, Meet the Raisins First Edition/Applause-Claymation, 1989, M $20.00

Saxophone, blk beret, bl eyelids, Third Commercial Issue/CALRAB-Applause, 1988, M $15.00

Saxophone, gold sax, no hat, First Key Chains/CALRAB, 1987, M..$5.00

Saxophone, gold sax, no hat, Hardee's First Promotion/CALRAB, 1987, M..$3.00

Saxophone, inside of sax pnt red, Post Raisin Bran Issue/CALRAB, 1987, M...$2.00

Saxophone, see also Graduate

SB Stuntz, yel skateboard & bl sneakers, Hardee's Second Promotion/Applause, 1988, sm, M, from $1 to.................$3.00

Singer, microphone in left hand (not touching face), 1st Commercial Issue/CALRAB, 1988, M.................................$6.00

Singer (Female), reddish purple shoes & bracelet, Second Commercial Issue/CALRAB-Applause, 1988, M $12.00

Sunglasses, index finger touching face, First Key Chains/CALRAB, 1987, M.......................................$5.00

Sunglasses, index finger touching face, orange glasses, Hardee's First Promotion/CALRAB, 1987, M......................$3.00

Sunglasses, right hand points up, left hand points down, orange glasses, Post Raisin Bran Issue/CALRAB, 1987, M......$2.00

Sunglasses II, eyes not visible, aqua glasses & sneakers, First Commercial Issue/CALRAB, 1988, M........................$4.00

Sunglasses II, eyes visible, aqua glasses & sneakers, First Commercial Issue/CALRAB, 1988, M..............................$35.00

Sunglasses, see also Graduate

Trumpy Trunote, trumpet & bl sneakers, Hardee's Second promo/Applause, 1988, sm, M, from $1 to $3.00

Valentine Girl and Boy Holding Hearts, Special Lover's Edition/CALRAB-Applause, 1988, M, each $8.00.

Waves Weaver I, yel surfboard connected to foot, Hardee's Second promo/Applause, 1988, sm $5.00

Waves Weaver II, yel surfboard not connected to foot, Hardee's Second Promotion/Applause, 1988, sm, M $2.00

Winky, hitchhiking pose & winking, First Commercial Issue/CALRAB, 1988, M...$5.00

MISCELLANEOUS

Auto Sun Shield, roll-away type, suction cup mounting, 16¾x51", MIP (sealed)...$15.00

Autograph book, rainbow-colored pgs, Autumn Rose/CALRAB 1988, MIP (sealed) $12.00

Bank, figure standing w/Sun-Maid Raisins box, CALRAB, 1987, 7", MIB..$8.00

Beach towel, singer w/3 musicians, bl, 58x29", EX $12.00

Belt, yel w/purple characters, Lee, EX $10.00

Book, California Raisins What's Cool, CALRAB, 1988, 5x8", M.$12.00

California Raisins Board Game, 1987, MIB (sealed) $8.00

Card Game, CALRAB, 1987, MIP...................................$6.00

Cassette Tape, Christmas w/the California Raisins, 1988, M .$15.00

Chalkboard, w/eraser, Rose Art/CALRAB 1988, MIP $20.00

Computer Game, Box Office, MIB (sealed)....................$20.00

Costume, w/white gloves, CALRAB, 1987, 33", EX.........$10.00
Crayon-By-Number Set, Rose Art, 1988, MIB $40.00
Fan Club Kit, w/watch, ID card, button & bumper sticker, M.$35.00
Fingertronic Puppet, male or female, Bendy Toys/CALRAB
    1988, MIB $25.00
Inflatable Figure, vinyl, Imperial Toy, 1987, 42", MIB......$50.00
Lunch Box, yel plastic w/bl scene, w/vacuum bottle, Thermos,
    9x4x8", EX..$10.00
Mad Magazine, California Raisin on front cover, September,
    1988, EX...$12.00
Magnets, Singers, Saxophone Player, Orange Sunglasses & Blue
    Shoes, Applause, 1988, M, ea...................................$50.00
Mug, mc scenes, Applause, 1987, M...................................$5.00
Photo Album, 3-ring binder, 24 pgs, CALRAB 1988, 13x8", M.$20.00

**Pillow Raisin, plush,
17x14" with 12" arms
and legs, EX, $10.00.**

Pinback, California Raisins for President, 1¾" dia, M........$8.00
Pinback, Soft Toys Are Here, Grapevine Tour '88, worn by
    Hardee's employees, 3¾x3", EX $10.00
Poster, California Raisins Tour, cities on bottom w/Sold Out,
    34x22", NM $12.00
Puffy Stick-Ons, 1987, MIP $8.00
Radio, AM/FM, figure w/poseable arms & legs, MIB......$150.00
Record, Heard It Through the Grapevine, 45 rpm, 1987, EX
    (w/sleeve)..$10.00
Record, Rudolph the Red Nosed Reindeer, 45 rpm, Atlantic,
    NM (w/sleeve) $12.00
Record, Signed Sealed Delivered/Same, 45 rpm, Atlantic 1988,
    EX+ (w/sleeve) $15.00
Record, When a Man Loves a Woman/Sweet, Delicious & Mar-
    velous, Buddy Miles lead vocals, NM+ (w/sleeve).....$20.00
Sandwich Stage, slice of bread shaped stage w/3 figurines, Del
    Monte mail-in, EX..$25.00
Sheet, Raisins doing their line dance, cotton, CALRAB 1988,
    64x84", EX $8.00
Sunglasses, child's, MOC $5.00
Suspenders, yel w/purple figures & red I Heard It Through the
    Grapevine, EX $20.00
Valentine Cards, set of 38, Cleo/CALRAB 1988, MIB $4.00
Video, Meet the California Raisins, Atlantic, 1988, NRFB.$8.00

Wall clock, female raisins w/tambourines, battery-op, 8½" dia,
    M $35.00
Watch, figural, Applause, 1988, MIP...................................$5.00
Welcome Mat, purple band members w/yel sun on bl, 18x30",
    EX...$55.00
Windsock, character on bl, Windsicals, 44x27", MIP.......$15.00

Cast Iron

Realistically modeled and carefully detailed cast-iron toys
enjoyed their heyday from about the turn of the twentieth century (some companies began production a little earlier) until
about the 1940s when they were gradually edged out by lighter-
weight toys that were less costly to produce and to ship. (Some
of the cast irons were more than 20" in length and very heavy.)
Many were vehicles faithfully patterned after actual models seen
on city streets at the time. Horse-drawn carriages were phased
out when motorized vehicles came into use.

Some of the larger manufacturers were Arcade (Illinois),
who by the 1920s was recognized as a leader in the industry;
Dent (Pennsylvania); Hubley (Pennsylvania); and Kenton
(Ohio). In the 1940s Kenton came out with a few horse-drawn
toys which are collectible in their own right but naturally much
less valuable than the older ones. In addition to those already
noted, there were many minor makers; you will see them mentioned in the listings.

For more detailed information on these companies, we recommend *Collecting Toys* by Richard O'Brien (Books Americana).
Note: World record prices continue to climb for mint and mint-
in-box examples which are generally found at most larger toy
shows. Prices for rare toys can be absolutely breathtaking. However, prices for common toys are generally stable and have not
changed much. Nearly all of our listings have been gleaned from
the large auction houses that specialize in toy sales. Prices realized at these auctions generally represent the higher end of value
ranges. Although there are generally weaker prices for vintage
toys due to world events, a rebound is certain during the months
and years to come as the economy rebounds.

Advisor: John McKenna (M2)

See also Banks; Dollhouse Furniture; Guns; Pull and Push Toys.

Airplanes

**Friendship Fokker Seaplane, Hubley, 11"
long, EX+, A, $7,700.00.** (Photo courtesy Bertoia Auctions)

DO-X Plane, Hubley, 8" W, rubber tires, very rare, VG, A..$2,300.00
Flying Boat, Kenton, 9" W, NP disk wheels, VG, A....$8,250.00
Friendship Fokker Seaplane, Hubley, 11" L, rpt, A $3,300.00
Lindy, Hubley, 10" W, G...$300.00
Lindy, Hubley, 13" W, VG, A $1,200.00
Lindy Lockheed Sirus NR-211, Ironman Toys, 10", NP pontoons
    & prop, 2 pilots, EX...$225.00
Lucky Boy Tri-Motor, Hubley, 7" W, EX, A.................$1,100.00
Monocoupe, Arcade, 11" W, pressed steel wing, VG, A...$55.00
Monocoupe, Hubley, 5" W, NP wings & prop, wht rubber tires,
    EX, A $130.00
Sea Gull, Kilgore, 8" W, EX, A $1,200.00
Sea Gull, Kilgore, 8" W, G, A $575.00
TAT Passenger Plane, Hubley, 5½" W, NP wings & 2 props, rub-
    ber tires, EX..$50.00
TAT Tri-Motor, Kilgore, 13½" W, EX+, A $3,850.00
UX-166 Monoplane, Hubley, 6" L, G $125.00

BOATS

Adirondack Sidewheeler, Dent, 15", G, A......................$600.00
Baby Outboard, Hubley, 4", w/integral driver, G+, A.....$110.00

**Penn-Yan Speed Boat, Hubley, circa 1939, 14", with driver
and three passengers, EX, $6,500.00.** (Photo courtesy Bertoia Auctions)

Sidewheeler, Wilkens, 10½", articulated action, EX, A .$360.00
Speed Boat (embossed on side), 5", w/integral driver, VG, A.$160.00

CHARACTER

Alphonse & Gaston Auto, Kenton, 8", early open vehicle
    w/wheels, driver on open seat w/facing passengers, G.$950.00
Amos 'N Andy Fresh Air Taxi, Dent, 6", w/2 figures (no dog),
    EX $875.00
Amos 'N Andy Fresh Air Taxi, Dent, 6", w/2 figures & dog, VG,
    A $600.00
Andy Gump Car #348, Arcade, 7", w/figure, VG........$1,250.00
Chester Gump in Horse-Drawn Cart, Arcade, 7", w/figure, VG..$325.00
Happy Hooligan Nodder in Horse-Drawn Cart, Kenton, 11", 2-
    wheeled cart w/Wilkins horse, G, A $275.00
Happy Hooligan Police Patrol Wagon, Kenton, 18", 2 horses, 3
    figures, G, A $2,200.00
Popeye, Olive Oyl & Wimpy Figure Set, Hubley, 3", G .$125.00
Popeye Spinach Cycle, Hubley, 5½", rubber tires, VG+, A .$600.00
Santa in Sleigh, Hubley, 15", 1 reindeer, EX $1,800.00

**Katzenjammers in Mule-Drawn Cart, Kenton,
11", EX+, A, $5,500.00.** (Photo courtesy Bertoia Auctions)

Santa in Sleigh, Hubley, 16", 2 reindeer, EX $2,300.00
Toonerville Trolley, Dent, 6", MIB, A............................$550.00

**Seeing New York #899, Kenton, 10", with five charac-
ter figures, G, $3,350.00.** (Photo courtesy James D. Julia, Inc.)

CIRCUS

Overland Circus Band Wagon, Kenton, 14", 1940s version, w/4
    figures & 2 horses, VG, A $350.00
Overland Circus Band Wagon, Kenton, 16", w/7 figures & 2
    horses, EX, A $450.00
Overland Circus Band Wagon, Kenton, 16", w/7 figures & 2
    horses, M, A $700.00
Overland Circus Cage Truck, Kenton, 9", w/lion, VG ...$450.00
Overland Circus Cage Wagon, Kenton, 14", w/bear, driver & 2
    horses w/riders, EX, A...$350.00

**Royal Circus Band Wagon, 23", with seven figures and four
horses, EX, A, $1,870.00.** (Photo courtesy Noel Barrett Auctions, Inc.)

Overland Circus Cage Wagon, Kenton, 14", w/bear, driver & 2 horses w/riders, M, A $650.00
Overland Circus Calliope Wagon, Kenton, 14", 2 horses w/riders, musician & driver, EX.......................................$250.00
Royal Circus Cage Wagon, Hubley, 9", w/lion, driver & 2 horses, G, A $200.00
Royal Circus Cage Wagon, Hubley, 12", w/bear, driver & 2 horses, Fair, A $200.00
Wagon w/Monkey on Trapeze, Kenton, 12", emb lions flank oval insert, spoke wheels, gr w/2 gold horses & trim, EX .$2,450.00

CONSTRUCTION

Buckeye Ditcher, Kenton, 9", chain drive, G, A $425.00
Buckeye Ditcher, Kenton, 12", chain drive, VG, A........$675.00
Caterpillar Bulldozer, Arcade, 8", metal treads, engine exposed through open sides, NP driver, VG+, A...................$750.00
Elgin Street Sweeper, Hubley, 8½", complete & w/driver, very scarce, EX $5,500.00
Galion Master Road Roller, 7", wooden front roller, NP spoke wheels, movable rear road cleaner, integral driver, EX+, A..........$525.00
General Steam Shovel Truck, Hubley, 8½", rubber tires, EX+, A $650.00
General Steam Shovel Truck, Hubley, 10", rubber tires, NM, A .$700.00
Huber Road Roller, Hubley, 8", w/roof, seated driver, G, A...$250.00

Huber Road Roller, Hubley, 14", no roof, standing driver, EX, A $3,850.00. (Photo courtesy Bertoia Auctions)

International Diesel Bulldozer, Arcade, 7½", rubber treads, NP driver & trim, VG, A $500.00
Jaeger Cement Mixer, Kenton, 6", NP spoke wheels, EX, A.$250.00
Jaeger Cement Mixer, Kenton, 6", wht rubber tires, EX, A..$325.00

Jaeger Cement Mixer Truck, Kenton, 7", rubber tires, NMIB, A, $3,300.00. (Photo courtesy Bertoia Auctions)

Jaeger Cement Mixer Truck, Kenton, 7", NP drum & chain pulley on open bed, rubber tires, no driver, VG, A.......$600.00
Jaeger Cement Mixer Truck, Kenton, 9", NP drum partially enclosed in bed, rubber tires, w/driver, VG $1,500.00
Panama Steam Shovel, Hubley, 9", w/2 figures, VG+ $350.00
Panama Steam Shovel Truck, Hubley, 10", Mack style, rubber tires, w/driver, rstr, A..$700.00
Panama Steam Shovel Truck, Hubley, 12½", rubber tires, no driver, NM, A $4,950.00

FARM TOYS
See also Horse-Drawn.

Allis Chalmers Tractor & Wagon, Arcade, 12", rubber tires, bottom of wagon opens, integral driver, G $125.00
Farmall Tractor, Arcade, 7½", 4-wheeled, rubber tires, NP driver, G, A $250.00
Fordson Tractor, AC Williams (?), 5½", lg flat spoke wheels, w/driver, G, A $200.00
Fordson Tractor w/Front-End Loader, Hubley, 9", spoke wheels, NP driver, VG, A $575.00

Fordson Tractor and Hay Rake, Arcade, 5" to 6", nickel-plated driver, EX, A, $330.00. (Photo courtesy Bertoia Auctions)

John Deere Tractor, Arcade, 7½", 4-wheeled, rubber tires, NP driver, VG+, A $575.00
McCormick-Deering Tractor, Arcade, 7", 4 spoke wheels, NP driver, G...$150.00
McCormick-Deering 2-Bottom Plow, Arcade, 8", 2 spoke wheels, EX+ $425.00
Oliver Plow, Arcade #282, 6½", 2 spoke wheels, EX......$250.00
Tractor, AC Williams #868, 4", NP spoke wheels, w/driver, E X .$325.00
Tractor, Arcade, 12", 4-wheeled, rubber tires, w/driver, VG.$250.00

FIREFIGHTING

Only motor vehicles are listed here; see also Horse-Drawn.

Fire Patrol Truck, Kenton, 9", open seat, railed body, metal disk wheels, no front bumper, 4 figures, VG, A...............$500.00
Ladder Truck, Arcade, 8½", Mack, open, rubber tires, NP trim, w/driver, G $325.00
Ladder Truck, Arcade, 19", NP spoke wheels, w/driver, G+, A.$575.00

Ladder Truck, Hubley, 8½", open seat, rubber tires, red w/silver chassis, NP grille, ladders, 2 figures, EX, A $550.00

Ladder Truck, Hubley, 11", open seat, rubber tires, red w/blk chassis, NP grille, hose reel, 2 figures, VG $375.00

Ladder Truck, Kenton, 9", open frame & seat, metal disk wheels, emb tanks on sides, cast driver, VG $475.00

Ladder Truck, Kenton, 9", open frame & seat, metal spoke wheels, w/driver, VG $225.00

Ladder Truck, Kenton, 12", open frame & seat, metal disk wheels, w/driver, rpt..$150.00

Ladder Truck, Kenton, 17", open frame & seat, metal spoke wheels, w/driver, VG, A $625.00

Ladder Truck, Kenton, 25", open frame & seat, metal spoke wheels, no figures, VG...$450.00

Pumper Truck, Arcade, 8½", open doorless cab, rubber tires, NP trim, 2 NP figures, G, A $200.00

Pumper Truck, Hubley, 8", open frame & seat, rubber tires, all red, orig decal on hood, w/driver, VG, A................$150.00

Pumper Truck, Hubley, 8", open seat, rubber tires, red w/silver chassis, NP grille & pumper top, no driver, G, A $100.00

Pumper Truck, Hubley, 12", open frame & seat, rubber tires w/spoke wheels, NP front, rear figures, VG $300.00

Pumper Truck, Kenton, 6½", open frame & seat, NP spoke wheels, integral driver, VG..$150.00

Pumper Truck, Kenton, 10", open frame & seat, metal disk wheels, integral driver, VG+ $250.00

Pumper Truck, Kenton, 10", open frame & seat, rubber tires, integral drive, G $175.00

Pumper Truck, Kenton, 14½", open frame & seat, metal spoke wheels, NP boiler, no figures, VG, A $300.00

Water Tower Truck, Kenton, 14", open frame & seat, metal disk wheels, no figures, EX..$625.00

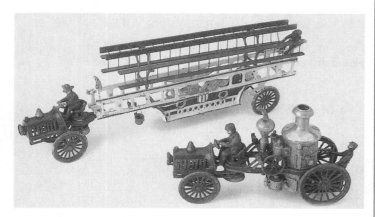

Transitional Ladder Wagon, Hubley, 27½", EX, A, $3,300.00; Transitional Pumper, Hubley, 14", EX, $3,000.00. (Photo courtesy Noel Barrett Auctions, Inc.)

HORSE-DRAWN

Bakery Wagon, Kenton, 13", spoke wheels, 1 horse, no driver, VG, A $300.00

Broadway Car Line #712 Trolley, Wilkins, 18", 1 horse, EX, A .$2,000.00

Brougham, Stanley, 12", 2 horses, NP driver & lady passenger, NMIB..$225.00

Cairo Express Cart (Elephant-Drawn), Kenton, 10", 2 spoke wheels Egyptian driver, overpnt $350.00

Cart, Buffalo, 10", 2 spoke wheels, 1 horse, w/driver, EXIB..$825.00

Cart, Carpenter, 13", 2 spoke wheels, 1 horse, no driver, VG $250.00

Cart, Pratt & Letchworth, 9½", sheet metal cart, 2 spoke wheels, 1 horse, w/driver, EX, A..............................$600.00

Cart, Shimer, 10½", NP, 2 spoke wheels, 1 horse, lady driver, EX+, A..$650.00

Cement Mixer, Kenton, 14", NP drum on wagon w/high bench seat, sm spoke wheels, 1 horse, w/driver, EX.........$1,000.00

Chariot, Hubley, 10½", emb w/musicians & lion's head, 2 spoke wheels, 3 horses, w/standing lady driver, EX, A ...$1,115.00

Chief Wagon, 15½", 1 horse, w/driver, Fair, A $575.00

City Delivery Wagon, Harris, 15", no driver, VG, A, $1,430.00. (Photo courtesy Bertoia Auctions)

Coal & Wood Wagon, Harris, 12", spoke wheels, 1 horse, w/driver, VG, A $700.00

Coal Cart (Mule-Drawn), Ives, 13", solid sides w/slanted back, 2 spoke wheels, 1 mule, w/driver, NM $1,000.00

Contractor's Dump Wagon, Arcade, 14", floor drops down for unloading, spoke wheels, 2 horses, w/driver, EX $475.00

Covered Wagon, Kenton, 15", cloth Conestoga-type cover, 2 horses, no figures, MIB $475.00

Dray Wagon, Dent, 14½", stake bed, spoke wheels, 1 horse, w/driver, G, A $250.00

Dray Wagon, Hubley, 16", spoke wheels, 1 mule, w/driver, VG, A $500.00

Farm Wagon, Arcade, 11", rubber tires, with driver, EX+, $475.00.

Dray Wagon, Kenton, 15", solid sides, spoke wheels, 2 horses, w/driver, Fair+, A $100.00

Dray Wagon, Wilkens, 13½", stake bed, spoke wheels, w/driver, EX, A $650.00

Eagle Milk Wagon, Hubley, 13", spoke wheels, milk bottles, 1 horse, w/driver, EX, A $1,100.00

Farm Wagon, Hubley, 10", open stake sides w/2 spoke wheels, pressed steel seat, 1 mule, w/driver, 10", VG............$325.00

Fire Chief Wagon, Wilkins, 12", sheet metal w/bench seat, spoke wheels spaced far apart, 2 horses, w/driver, VG, A ...$385.00

Fire Chief Wagon, Wilkins, 12", stenciled FD Chief, spoke wheels spaced close together, 1 horse, w/driver, EX, A $1,870.00

Fire Hose & Reel Wagon, Ideal, 21½", open frame w/lg ornate reel, spoke wheels, 2 horses, w/driver, NM $2,400.00

Fire Hose Reel Cart, 10½", reel on 2 spoke wheels, 1 horse, w/driver, G+, A $525.00

Fire Ladder Wagon, Dent, 19", open frame, spoke wheels, 2 horses, 2 figures, VG, A $250.00

Fire Ladder Wagon, Hubley, 19", open frame, spoke wheels, 3 horses, 2 figures, G..$175.00

Fire Patrol Wagon, Carpenter, 16½", railed bed, spoke wheels, 2 horses, w/figures, G+ $1,000.00

Fire Patrol Wagon, Ives, 18½", railed bed, spoke wheels, 1 horse, 4 figures, G, A...$900.00

Fire Patrol Wagon, Ives, 22", railed bed, spoke wheels, 3 horses, 7 figures, VG $1,200.00

Fire Pumper, Hubley, 20", open frame, spoke wheels, 2 horses, 2 figures, EX, A..$525.00

Fire Pumper, Ives, 17½", open frame, spoke wheels, 3 horses, w/driver, G $300.00

Fire Pumper, Ives, 24", open frame, spoke wheels, 2 horses, w/driver, EX, A $3,575.00

Fire Pumper, Kenton, 13", open frame, spoke wheels, 3 horses, w/driver, EX, A $150.00

Fire Pumper, Kenton, 16", open frame, spoke wheels, bronze color, 2 horses, w/driver, EX, A.............................$1,100.00

Fire Pumper, Wilkins, 15", open frame, spoke wheels, 3 horses, integral driver, VG, A $300.00

Fire Pumper, Wilkins, 18½", open frame, spoke wheels, 3 horses, w/driver, EX, A $600.00

Hansom Cab, Pratt & Letchwork, 12", open front, spoke wheels, 1 horse, w/driver, EX+, A...................................$1,200.00

Horse-Drawn Pumper Wagon, Carpenter, 17½", 2 horses, w/driver, VG+...$2,000.00

Ice Wagon, 11½", spoke wheels, 2 horses, no driver, VG+ .$775.00

Landau, Hubley, single horse & driver, 15", EX, A.........$865.00

Landau, Wilkins, 15", opening doors, spoke wheels, 2 horses, 2 figures, VG, A $1,200.00

Log Wagon, Hubley, 15", spoke wheels, 2 oxen, w/driver, G, A.$500.00

Patrol Wagon, Dent, 19½", railed bed, spoke wheels, 2 horses, 2 figures, VG, A...$525.00

Patrol Wagon, Hubley, 20", railed bed, spoke wheels, 2 horses, 5 figures, VG, A...$650.00

Patrol Wagon, Hubley, 20", railed bed, spoke wheels, 3 horses, 7 figures, EX..$1,400.00

Patrol Wagon, Kenton, 14½", railed bed, spoke wheels, 3 horses, 4 figures, VG+, A $600.00

Phoenix Ladder Wagon, Ives, 27", spoke wheels, 2 horses, 2 figures, Poor to Fair, A...$360.00

Plantation Cart (Mule-Drawn), Wilkins, 10", open stake sides, 2 spoke wheels, 1 mule, seated driver, EX, A.............$300.00

Plantation Cart (Ox-Drawn), 11", open stake sides, 2 spoke wheels, standing driver, VG $350.00

Police Patrol Wagon, Dent, 17½", railed bed, spoke wheels, 3 horses, 3 figures, VG...$925.00

Police Patrol Wagon, Hubley, 14", railed bed, spoke wheels, 2 horses, 2 figures, G..$175.00

Police Patrol, Hubley, 21", with six figures, G+, A, $1,200.00. (Photo courtesy Bertoia Auctions)

Pony Cart, Wilkins, 10", 2 spoke wheels, 1 horse, w/driver, EX, A $500.00

Sand & Gravel Wagon, Hubley, 14", floor dumping action, 2 horses, w/driver, G, A...$100.00

Hansom Cab (not to be confused with the commonly found 1940s version), Kenton, 12½", with driver, EX+, $1,500.00.
(Photo courtesy Bertoia Auctions)

Sulky (Mule-Drawn), J&E Stevens, circa 1895, 9", with driver, EX, $885.00. (Photo courtesy Bertoia Auctions)

Sand & Gravel Wagon, Kenton, 10", spoke wheels, 1 horse, w/driver, VG $100.00

Sand & Gravel Wagon, Kenton, 15", spoke wheels, 2 horses, w/driver, EX+ $325.00

Sleigh, Hubley, 15", 2 horses, lady driver, G, A $275.00

Stake Wagon, Hubley, 9", spoke wheels, 1 horse, w/driver, EX, A $200.00

Sulky, Kenton, 7", 1 horse, w/driver, EX, A $100.00

Surrey, Stanley Toys, 11½", cloth fringed top, spoke wheels, 2 horses, w/driver, G+, A $100.00

Transfer Wagon, Kenton, 19", spoke wheels, some goods in wagon bed, 3 horses, w/driver, VG $950.00

MOTOR VEHICLES

Note: Description lines for generic vehicles may simply begin with 'Bus,' 'Coupe,' or 'Motorcycle,' for example. But more busses will be listed as 'Coach Bus,' 'Coast-To-Coast,' 'Greyhound,' 'Interurban,' 'Mack,' or 'Public Service' (and there are other instances); coupes may be listed under 'Ford,' 'Packard,' or some other specific car company; and lines describing motorcycles might be also start 'Armored,' 'Excelsior-Henderson,' 'Delivery,' 'Policeman,' 'Harley-Davidson,' and so on. Look under 'Yellow Cab' or 'Checker Cab' and other cab companies for additional 'Taxi Cab' descriptions. We often gave any lettering or logo on the vehicle priority when we entered descriptions, so with this in mind, you should have a good idea where to look for your particular toy. Body styles (double-decker bus, cape-top roadster, etc.) were also given priority.

Airflow, see also Century of Progress Airflow

Airflow Sedan, Arcade, 6", rubber tires, no rear spare, NP grille, G+, A $250.00

Airflow Sedan, Hubley, 6½", electric lights, rubber tires & rear spare, NP trim, VG $925.00

Airflow Sedan, Hubley, 8", electric lights, rubber tires & rear spare, NP trim, G+, A $600.00

Ambulance, Kenton, 7", nickel-plated driver, EX, A, $1,200.00. (Photo courtesy Bertoia Auctions)

Army Motor Stake Truck, Kenton, 9", metal spoke wheels, G, A $165.00

Austin Car Carrier, see Car Carrier

Auto Express Truck, Kenton, 9", open bed, metal spoke wheels, w/driver, G+ $950.00

Auto Wrecker, Kenton, 10", metal disk wheels, no driver, VG $1,450.00

Auto Wrecker, Kenton, 10", with driver, EX, $3,600.00. (Photo courtesy Randy Inman Auctions)

Aviation Gas Tandem Tanker Truck, Kilgore, 13", metal spoke wheels, very rare, EX $1,700.00

Bell Telephone Truck, Hubley, 3", Mack cab, NP disk wheels & driver, VG $200.00

Bell Telephone Truck, Hubley, 3", Mack cab, rubber tires, no driver, EX, A $250.00

Bell Telephone Truck, Hubley, 4", Mack cab, rubber tires, no driver, EX, A $200.00

Bell Telephone Truck, Hubley, 5", Mack cab, rubber tires, integral driver, EX $250.00

Bell Telephone Truck, Hubley, 7", Mack cab, rubber tires, recast ladders & shovels, integral driver, VG+ $250.00

Bell Telephone Truck, Hubley, 9", Mack cab w/extended flat roof, 2-wheeled trailer & cast accessories, no driver, EX $300.00

Bell Telephone Truck, Hubley, 10", Mack cab, NP spoke wheels, w/driver, Poor to Fair, ...$200.00

Blue Bird Cab, Arcade, 8", rear spare, rubber tires, NP driver, Fair, A $825.00

Borden's Milk Truck, Arcade, 6", milk bottle shape, rubber tires, EX, A $1,300.00

Borden's Milk Truck, Hubley, 6", emb Milk/Cream/110, pnt grille & headlights, rubber tires, G, A $600.00

Borden's Milk Truck, Hubley, 7½", emb Milk/Cream/110, NP grille & headlights, rubber tires, VG, A $1,650.00

Breyer's Ice Cream Truck, Dent, 8½", with driver, EX+, A, $1,600.00.

Buick Coupe, Arcade, 8½", metal tires w/spoke wheels, pnt rear spare, NP grille & driver, rstr, A..................$935.00

Buick Coupe, Arcade, 8½", rubber tires w/metal spoke wheels, pnt rear spare, NP grille & driver, G, A $1,100.00

Buick Deluxe Sedan, Arcade, 8½", 1927 model, rubber tires w/spoke wheels, rear spare, NP driver, rstr, A $700.00

Buick Deluxe Sedan, Arcade, 8½", 1927 model, rubber tires, with nickel-plated driver, EX, $4,600.00. (Photo courtesy Randy Inman Auctions)

C to CC Co Stake Truck, AC Williams, 7", 6-wheel tandem, rubber tires, VG, A..................................$110.00

Car Carrier, AC Williams, 12½", angled bed, metal disk wheels, 3 Austin vehicles, G, A.............................$400.00

Car Carrier, AC Williams, 12½", angled bed, with three Austin vehicles, NMIB, $2,000.00. (Photo courtesy Randy Inman Auctions)

Car Carrier, AC Williams, 14", straight bed, rubber tires, 4 Austin vehicles, G, A..................................$300.00

Car Carrier, Arcade, 11", dbl-decker (1930s), 4 vehicles, G .$450.00

Car Carrier, Arcade, 14", Ford Model A, 3 vehicles, G, A .$385.00

Car Carrier, Arcade, 15½", dbl-decker (1930s), 4 vehicles, G, A $685.00

Car Carrier, Arcade, 19", metal spoke wheels, 3 vehicles, Poor to Fair, A..$1,150.00

Car Carrier, Arcade, 24", metal spoke wheels, 4 vehicles, G, A..$1,300.00

Car Carrier, Hubley, 10", metal disk wheels, 3 vehicles, G, A .$650.00

Car Carrier, Hubley, 10½", cabover, rubber tires, 4 vehicles, VG+, A..$415.00

Century of Progress, see also Greyhound Lines

Century of Progress Airflow, Arcade, 4", rubber tires, no rear spare, VG, A..................................$165.00

Century of Progress Airflow, Hubley, 6", rubber tires, rear spare, G $475.00

Century of Progress Taxi, Arcade, 6½", metal disk wheels, G..$300.00

Century of Progress Taxi, Arcade, 6½", rubber tires, EX.....$1,100.00

Century of Progress Taxi, Arcade, 6½", rubber tires, G $550.00

Checker Cab, Arcade, circa 1925 – 28, with driver, VG, $6,000.00. (Photo courtesy Bertoia Auctions)

Chevy Coupe, Arcade, 8", 1920s model, NP disk wheels, grille & rear spare, EX $1,100.00

Chevy Coupe, Arcade, 8", 1920s model, pnt metal spoke wheels & rear spare, pnt grille, G............................$475.00

Chevy Roadster, Arcade, 7", 1920s model w/top up, rubber tires w/spoke wheels, metal rear spare, VG $450.00

Chevy Sedan, Arcade, 7", 1920s model w/single 'belt line,' metal spoke wheels, NP driver, VG+ $475.00

Chevy Sedan, Arcade, 8½", 1920s model w/dbl 'belt line,' NP disk wheels, no driver, rstr $700.00

Chevy Touring Car, Arcade, 7", 1920s model w/top up, metal spoke wheels, G, A $300.00

Chicago Motor Coach Double-Decker Bus, Arcade, 8", rubber tires, bl (scarce), G, A $550.00

Chrysler Coupe, Hubley, 4½", rubber tires, EX...............$875.00

Coal Truck, Kenton, 6½", open cab & bed, metal spoke wheels, w/driver, EX, A $275.00

Coal Truck, Kenton, 6½", open cab & bed, NP disk wheels, w/driver, VG $200.00

Coal Truck, Kenton, 8½", #844, lever-action dump bed, no driver, G, A $175.00

Coal Truck, Kenton, 8½", #844, lever-action dump bed, w/driver, EX $700.00

Contractors Truck, 8½", open seat, 3 dumping buckets, metal disk wheels, pnt driver, EX+, A $2,200.00

Coupe, Arcade, 6", 1920s model, metal spoke wheels, no rear spare, Fair+, A $175.00

Coupe, Hubley, 6½", take-apart body, rubber tires, no side spares, G+, A $185.00

Coupe, Hubley, 6½", take-apart body, rubber tires, 2 side spares, G+, A $220.00

Coupe, Hubley, 7", 1920s model, metal disk wheels, rear spare, pnt driver, G $250.00

Coupe, Hubley, 9½", 1920s model, metal disk wheels, rear spare, w/driver, G, A $600.00

Coupe, Kenton, 6½", slanted windshield, metal disk wheels, bl & blk, pnt driver, VG, A..$935.00

Coupe, Kenton, 8", slanted windshield, metal disk wheels, rear spare, red & blk, no driver, VG, A.......................$1,430.00

Coupe, Kenton, 8", slanted windshield, metal disk wheels, rear spare, red & blk, NP driver, G, A.........................$1,050.00

Coupe, Kenton, 8½", no driver, G+, $1,300.00. (Photo courtesy Randy Inman Auctions)

Coupe, Kilgore, 5", 1920s model, metal spoke wheels, no driver, VG, A..$220.00

Coupe, Kilgore, 6½", 1920s model, metal spoke wheels, NP driver, G, A..$165.00

Crash Car (Motorcycle), Hubley, 4½", rubber tires, integral driver, Fair..$150.00

De Soto Sedan, Arcade, 6", NP grille & bumper, rubber tires, G, A..$275.00

Dodge Coupe, Arcade, 8½", metal disk wheels & rear spare, rpt, A..$250.00

Dodge Coupe, Arcade, 8½", metal disk wheels & rear spare, G.$450.00

Dodge Coupe, Champion, 7", rubber tires, w/rumble seat, NP grille, no driver, VG, A..$825.00

Double-Decker Bus, Arcade, 8", long nose, rubber tires, 3 NP figures, VG..$350.00

Double-Decker Bus, Arcade, 8", snub-nosed, rubber tires, 5 figures, EX, A..$500.00

Double-Decker Bus, Kenton, 10", long nose, metal disk wheels, 2 figures, VG, A..$475.00

Dump Truck, Hubley, 3¼" (Midget Series), NP bed w/slanted back, rubber tires, NM..$225.00

Double-Decker Bus, Kenton, 10", rubber tires, with five figures, EX+, $1,500.00. (Photo courtesy Bertoia Auctions)

Dump Truck, Hubley, 7½", cabover tractor w/roof shield on dump bed, 3-axle, rubber tires, VG+.....................$250.00

Dump Truck, Kilgore, 8", enclosed cab, tilting bed w/side lever, NP disk wheels, EX..$450.00

Dump Truck, see also International, Mack, State Highway, etc.

Dump Truck & Trailer, Arcade, 13", enclosed cab w/visor, tilting dump trailer, NP spoke wheels, G+, A.................$900.00

Express Truck, AC Williams, 7", simulated wood paneling, open bed, metal spoke wheels, VG......................................$250.00

Faegol Safety Coach, Arcade, 12", NP disk wheels & driver, EX..$775.00

Five (5) Ton Stake Truck, see Stake Truck

Ford Coupe, AC Williams, 6", Model T, metal spoke wheels w/deep treads, 6", EX..$225.00

Ford Coupe, Arcade, 5", Model A, metal spoke wheels, opening rumble seat, w/driver, VG, A.............................$600.00

Ford Coupe, Arcade, 6½", Model A, metal spoke wheels, opening rumble seat, no driver, Fair+..............................$150.00

Ford Coupe, Arcade, 6½", Model A, metal spoke wheels, opening rumble seat, no driver, VG...............................$400.00

Ford Coupe, Arcade, 6½", Model T, metal spoke wheels, all blk, no driver, VG..$225.00

Ford Coupe, Arcade, 6½", Model T, metal spoke wheels, blk w/gold stripe, w/driver, EX+..................................$400.00

Ford Coupe, Arcade, 7", 1927 model, NP spoke wheels & driver, VG..$350.00

Ford Coupe, Tom Seyloff Products, 11", 1930s model, blk w/extensive NP trim, rubber tires w/NP hubs, w/driver, NM, A..$935.00

Ford Sedan, Arcade, 6½", 1924 model w/center door, metal spoke wheels, no driver, EX, A....................................$220.00

Ford Sedan, Arcade, 6½", 1924 model w/center door, metal spoke wheels, w/driver, NM, A......................................$470.00

Ford Touring Car, Arcade, 6½", Model T, top up, rubber tires w/spoke wheels, w/driver, VG, A..............................$250.00

Ford Tudor Sedan, Arcade, 6½", 1928 model, metal spoke wheels, w/driver, G, A..$300.00

Ford Wrecker, Arcade, 6", Model A, NP spoke wheels, G, A...$350.00

Ford Wrecker, Arcade, 8", Model A, NP spoke wheels, EX, A..$525.00

Ford Wrecker, Arcade, 11", Model T, NP spoke wheels, VG, A..$750.00

Gasoline Tank Truck, Hubley, 7", rubber tires, NP grille & front bumper, 7", VG, A..$120.00

General Steam Shovel Truck, see Construction

Great Lakes Exposition, see Greyhound Lines

Greyhound Lines Century of Progress Tandem Bus, Arcade, 5½", rubber tires, unmk, G, A..$100.00

Greyhound Lines Century of Progress Tandem Bus, Arcade, 7½", rubber tires, EX+, A..$250.00

Greyhound Lines Century of Progress Tandem Bus, Arcade, 7½", rubber tires, VG+..$150.00

Greyhound Lines Century of Progress Tandem Bus, Arcade, 10", rubber tires, VG+..$250.00

Greyhound Lines Century of Progress Tandem Bus, Arcade, 11", rubber tires, VG+..$300.00

Greyhound Lines Century of Progress Tandem Bus, Arcade, 14", rubber tires, VG+..$300.00

Greyhound Lines Great Lakes Exposition 1936 Bus, Arcade, 11", rubber tires, EX $625.00

Greyhound Lines NY World's Fair Bus, Arcade, 7", rubber tires, EX, A $300.00

Hanson Auto, Kenton, 6", canopy roof over open cab, cast headlights & lanterns, spoke wheels, w/driver, VG $325.00

Hanson Auto, Kenton, 8", canopy roof over open cab, cast headlights & lanterns, spoke wheels, driver & passenger, EX+ $1,425.00

Harley-Davidson Motorcycle, Hubley, 6", w/sidecar, rubber tires w/spoke wheels, w/driver, EX, A $275.00

Harley-Davidson Hill-Climber Motorcycle, Hubley, 6½", driver hunched forward, VG, $900.00.

(Photo courtesy Randy Inman Auctions)

Harley-Davidson Motorcycle, Hubley, 9", twin cylinder, aluminum handlebars, rubber tires, spoke wheels, no driver, VG, A $500.00

Hathaway Bread-Cake Delivery Truck, see International Delivery Truck

Ice Truck, Arcade, 7", 1928 Studebaker, railed sides, NP grille & headlights, rubber tires, VG, A $350.00

Ice Truck, Kenton, 6", open cab, railed sides, NP disk wheels & driver, G $200.00

Ice Truck, Kenton, 16", early Ford tractor-trailer model w/ICE trailer & stake trailer, metal disk wheels, VG+ $950.00

Indian Motorcycle, Hubley, 9", NP 4-cylinder engine, rubber tires w/spoke wheels, w/driver, yel (scarce), G $875.00

Interchangeable Set, AC Williams, chassis w/3 bodies, EXIB (6x11") $850.00

Interchangeable Set, AC Williams, chassis w/3 car bodies & stake truck, GIB (6x11") $450.00

International Delivery Truck, Arcade, 9½", 1932 model, rubber tires, Hathaway Bread-Cake decal, w/driver, rstr, A .$700.00

International Red Baby Dump Truck, Arcade, 11", rubber tires, NP driver, VG...$650.00

International Red Baby Express Truck, Arcade, 10½", open bed w/slanted back, NP disk wheels & driver, EX, A..$1,320.00

International Red Baby Truck, Arcade, 10", open bed w/straight back, NP disk wheels & driver, VG, A $700.00

International Red Baby Wrecker, Arcade, 10", NP disk wheels & driver, EX, A...$1,050.00

International Stake Truck, Arcade, 11", partially enclosed body w/stake rail, rubber tires, Fair+, A..........................$275.00

International Stake Truck, Arcade, 12", regular stake body, rubber tires, NP driver, rstr, A $725.00

International Van, Arcade, 9½", 1936 model, rubber tires, EX+, A...$4,400.00

International Yellow Cab Express Truck, Arcade, 10", stationary bed, rubber tires, NP driver, rstr, A $525.00

Jaeger Concrete Mixer Truck, see Construction

Lakeshore Lines Fageol Safety Coach Bus, Arcade, 12", NP disk wheels, w/driver, G+, A..................................$750.00

Liberty Cab, Kenton, 6", metal disk wheels, EX+, A......$775.00

Lifesavers Truck, Hubley, 4", 1932 model, VG $650.00

Limousine, Hubley, 7", curved top, metal spoke wheels, G+ .$250.00

Limousine, Kenton, 8", roof extends over open front seat, metal disk wheels, w/driver & lady passenger, Fair, A $650.00

Lincoln Touring Car, AC Williams, 9½", top up, NP spoke wheels, rear spare & grille, VG, A $880.00

Lincoln Zephyr and House Trailer, Hubley, 13½", rubber tires, nickel-plated bumpers and grille, EX, $800.00. (Photo courtesy Randy Inman Auctions)

Live Stock Stake Truck, Kilgore, 8", NP disk wheels, VG, A $500.00

Mack Coal Dump Truck, Arcade, 10½", NP spoke wheels (rear duals), no driver, EX, A..............................$1,265.00

Mack Coal Dump Truck, Arcade, 10½", rubber tires (rear single axle), w/drive, G+, A $700.00

Mack Delivery Truck, 6", enclosed bed w/open grid sides, NP disk wheels, cast driver, EX $200.00

Mack Dump Truck, Arcade, 12", metal spoke wheels, w/driver, EX, A $775.00

Mack Dump Truck, Arcade, 12", metal spoke wheels, w/driver, G+, A $375.00

Mack Dump Truck, Arcade, 12", rubber tires, w/driver, G, A.$400.00

Mack Dump Truck, Champion, 8", slant-sided dump bed, rubber tires, VG, A $100.00

Mack Dump Truck, Hubley, 5", rubber tires, w/driver, EX, A .$185.00

Mack Ice Truck, Arcade, 8½", NP spoke wheels, w/tongs & block of ice, NP driver, VG, A...............................$475.00

Mack Ice Truck, Arcade, 8½", NP spoke wheels, w/tongs & block of ice, no driver, EX, A $700.00

Mack Ice Truck, Arcade, 11", rubber tires, w/tongs & block of ice, w/driver, VG, A...$1,050.00

Mack Stake Truck, Champion, 7½", rubber tires, EX, A.$200.00

Mack Stake Truck, Hubley, 5½", NP disk wheels, EX, A...$165.00

Mack Tanker Truck (Gas & Motor Oil), Champion, 8", rubber tires, VG $150.00

Mack Tanker Truck (Gasoline), Arcade, 5", metal spoke wheels, G, A $100.00

Mack Tanker Truck (Pennsylvania Independent Oil Co), Arcade, 13", rubber tires, w/driver, rpt, A $1,050.00

Mack Wrecker, Arcade, 10½", enclosed cab, rubber tires, w/driver, VG, A $1,200.00

Mack Wrecker, Champion, 8", open cab, rubber tires, VG......$150.00

Mack Tanker Truck (Webaco Oil Co/Fuel Oil), Arcade, 13", nickel-plated driver, VG, $2,100.00. (Photo courtesy Randy Inman Auctions)

Motor Express Tractor-Trailer, Hubley, 7", curved-back trailer, rubber tires, EX, A $100.00

Motorcycle, Champion, 7", rubber tires, integral driver, VG+, A $225.00

Motorcycle, Hubley, 6", electric lights, emb flair design on tank, rubber tires w/wooden hubs, w/driver, G, A.............$275.00

Motorcycle, Hubley, 9", 4-cylinder engine, rubber tires w/spoke wheels, civilian driver w/movable arms, G, A $650.00

Motorcycle, see also Harley-Davidson, Indian, etc.

Motorcycle w/Sidecar, Hubley, 8½", electric light, rubber tires w/spoke wheels, no figures, EX, A $800.00

Nash Sedan, Kenton, 5", NP disk wheels, G+, A........$1,050.00

New York World's Fair, see Greyhound Lines

Nucar Transport, Hubley, 15½", rubber tires, 3 vehicles, NP driver, VG, A $775.00

Packard Gasoline Truck, AC Williams, 7", 1936 model, rubber tires, 7", G, A..$130.00

Packard Sedan, Hubley, 11½", 1929 model, opening doors & hood, metal disk wheels & rear spare, w/driver, VG, A....$13,200.00

Packard Sedan (Shovel Nose), AC Williams, 8½", take-apart model, rubber tires, VG, $1,000.00. (Photo courtesy Randy Inman Auctions)

Panama Steam Shovel Truck, see Construction

Parcel Post Cycle, Hubley, 9½", Harley-Davidson model, rubber tires w/spoke wheels, w/driver, VG, A $1,100.00

Parlor Coach Double-Decker Bus, Arcade, 13", rubber tires, w/spares, NP driver, 13", EX, A $1,650.00

Patrol Motorcycle, Hubley, 6½", rubber tires, integral driver, 6½", EX, A $275.00

Patrol Truck, Hubley, 7½", open seat, railed bed, metal spoke wheels, 4 figures, G+, A $265.00

Patrol Truck, Hubley, 10½", open seat, railed bed, metal disk wheels, 3 figures, VG, A $1,200.00

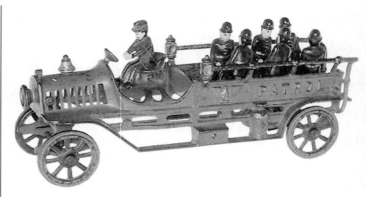

Patrol Truck, Hubley, 15½", with seven figures, G+, A, $2,750.00. (Photo courtesy Randy Inman Auctions)

Patrol Truck, Kenton, 7", open seat, railed back, metal disk wheels, w/driver, EX $450.00

Patrol Truck, Kenton, 9", open seat, railed bed, metal spoke wheels, emb side spare or hose (?), 3 figures, VG.....$700.00

Pennsylvania Independent Oil Co, see Mack Tanker Truck

Pickwick Nite Coach, Kenton, 9½", enclosed double-decker w/NP front end & disk wheels, rpt, A......................$935.00

Pierce-Arrow Station Wagon, Hubley, 5", 1934 model, take-apart body, rubber tires, no side spares, NM, A $935.00

Pierce-Arrow Station Wagon, Hubley, 5", 1934 model, take-apart body, rubber tires, 2 side spares, VG, A $250.00

Plymouth Sedan, Arcade, 4½", rubber tires, promo ad on roof, EX, A $3,080.00

Police Motorcycle, Hubley, 4", blk rubber tires, w/driver, EX, A $140.00

Police Motorcycle w/Sidecar, Hubley, 8", aluminum handlebars, rubber tires w/NP spoke wheels, driver & passenger, EX, A .$650.00

Pontiac Roadster, Kilgore, 10", open, NP disk wheels & trim, VG, A $900.00

Pontiac Sedan, Vindex, 8", thick metal spoke wheels w/rear spare, no driver, VG+..$2,750.00

Pontiac Sedan Pulling Motor Home, Kenton, 10", rubber tires, NP grille, EX $2,850.00

Public Service Bus, Dent, 13½", metal disk wheels w/rear spare, EX+, A $4,675.00

Racer, AC Williams, 7½", early boat tail, metal spoke wheels, w/driver, EX+, A $200.00

Racer, Hubley, 8½", articulated flames, with driver, EX+, A, $1,650.00. (Photo courtesy Randy Inman Auctions)

Racer, AC Williams, 8½", high tail fin, cast cylinders on hood, rubber tires, w/NP driver, EX, A $350.00

Racer, Arcade, 5½", rubber tires, integral driver, NM, A .$330.00

Racer, Champion, 8½", long hood, tail fin, cast cylinders, rubber tires, w/driver, G, A $200.00

Racer, Champion, 8½", long hood, tail fin, no cast cylinders, rubber tires, w/driver, VG+, A $400.00

Racer, Hubley, 6", cast side vents & grille, contoured tail, rubber tires, w/driver, NM, A $1,375.00

Racer, Hubley, 6½", cast cylinders, electric headlights, rubber tires, w/driver, VG, A $220.00

Racer, Hubley, 7", #8, canoe-type rear, rubber tires, w/driver, EX, A $350.00

Racer, Hubley, 8½", articulated flames, tail fin, NP disk wheels, w/driver, G, A $550.00

Racer, Hubley, 9", cast cylinders & radiator, tail fin, NP spoke wheels, w/driver, G, A.......................................$1,375.00

Racer, Hubley, 10", #5, hood opens to reveal engine, metal disk wheels, w/driver, VG, A $900.00

Racer, Hubley, 10", #5, hood opens to reveal engine, rubber tires, w/driver, G, A $700.00

Racer, Hubley, 10½", articulated flames, tail fin, rubber tires w/spoke wheels, w/driver, VG, A $1,050.00

Racer, Vindex, 11", rubber tires w/spoke wheels, no driver, G, A $1,200.00

Racer, see also Stutz Racer

Railway Express Truck, Hubley, 4", NP disk wheels, EX, A..$300.00

Railway Express Truck, Hubley, 5", rubber tires, EX, A ..$550.00

Railway Express Truck, Hubley, 6", rubber tires, EX, A ..$990.00

Red Baby, see International

REO Coupe, Arcade, 7½", opening rumble seat, rubber tires, cast side spares, no driver, G, A $700.00

REO Coupe, Arcade, 9", opening rumble seat, NP spoke wheels, side spares, grille & driver, rstr w/aged patina, A..$1,200.00

REO Coupe, Arcade, 9", opening rumble seat, rubber tires & side spares w/spoke wheels, NP driver, G, A...........$925.00

Roadster, Dent, 6", open w/metal disk wheels, NP driver, G...$200.00

Roadster, Globe, 11", opening rumble seat, metal disk wheels, G $525.00

Roadster, Hubley, 6½", open w/curved bench seat, metal spoke wheels, G+, A $100.00

Roadster, Hubley, 7", C-style roof, metal spoke wheels, VG, A.$775.00

Roadster, Kenton, 7", open rumble seat, no windshield, NP bumpers, grille & running boards, rubber tires, no driver, EX $1,150.00

Roadster, Kenton, 7", open w/high bench seat, metal disk wheels, w/driver, G, A $575.00

Roadster, Kenton, 8½", simulated cloth top extended outward behind driver, metal spoke wheels, G+, A............$1,200.00

Roadster, Kilgore, 6", 1928 model, no windshield, NP disk wheels & driver, VG, A..$275.00

Roadster, Kilgore, 7½", open rumble seat w/sq back, no windshield, metal disk wheels, w/driver, Poor, A............$150.00

Roadster, Kilgore, 8", open rumble seat w/rnd back, no windshield, NP disk wheels, steering wheel & driver, VG, A $525.00

Runabout Auto, Dayton, 7", Hill Climber, w/wood, spoke wheels, lady driver, G+, A....................................$550.00

Runabout Auto, Ives, 5½", tiller steering, front curves upward, metal spoke wheels, w/driver, G, A.........................$200.00

Runabout Auto, Kenton, 5½", tiller steering, front curves upward, metal spoke wheels, w/driver, VG $450.00

Runabout Auto, Kenton, 6½", tiller steering, front curves upward, metal spoke wheels, lady driver, VG $550.00

Sedan, AC Williams, 6", 1920s model w/NP spoke wheels, G+, A...$200.00

Sedan, Arcade, 6½", 1924 2-door model, NP spoke wheels & driver, VG, A $220.00

Sedan, Dent, 7½", later model w/sq doors, NP disk wheels & front bumper, w/driver, VG, A $550.00

Sedan, Dent, 8", earlier model w/curved doors, rear luggage rack, metal disk wheels, w/driver, older rpt, G, A.............$385.00

Sedan, Kenton, 6½", slanted windshield, metal disk wheels, EX $525.00

Sedan, Kenton, 7", 1930s model, enclosed rear wheel wells, NP grille & bumpers, rubber tires, VG..........................$575.00

Sedan, Kenton, 10", slanted windshield, EX, $2,650.00. (Photo courtesy Randy Inman Auctions)

Sedan, Kenton, 12", take-apart model, metal spoke wheels & rear spare emb Stop-1926, w/driver, Sears exclusive, NM+ .$1,400.00

Sedan, Skogland & Olson, 7½", rubber tires, G+, A $825.00

Sedan Pulling Mullen's Trailer, Arcade, 9", rubber tires, G+, A $300.00

Shortline GMC Cross Country Bus, Arcade, 7½", rubber tires, NM, A $1,540.00

Silver Arrow Sedan, Arcade, 7", rubber tires, NP grille, VG.$450.00

Speed Tandem Stake Truck, Kenton, 9", rubber tires, EX..$550.00

Stake Truck, Arcade, 7", 1920s model, enclosed cab, NP spoke wheels, VG, A $275.00

Stake Truck, Hubley, 5", NP curved stake back, rubber tires, EX, A $175.00

Stake Truck, Hubley, 7", NP curved stake back & grille, rubber tires, NM..$775.00

Stake Truck, Hubley, 16", 5 Ton, open cab, spoke wheels, w/driver, Fair+, A $600.00

State Highway Dump Truck, Kenton, 10", International model w/metal disk wheels, scarce, overpnt, A $1,430.00

Streamline Coupe, Hubley, 6½", open wheel wells, rubber tires, G $150.00

Streamline Sedan, Hubley, 8½", covered wheel wells, rubber tires, VG $1,100.00

Studebaker Coupe, Hubley, 6½", NP trim, rubber tires, rpt, A .$165.00

Studebaker Roadster, Hubley, 6½", NP trim, rubber tires, VG+, A $385.00

Studebaker Town Car, Hubley, 6½", open front seat w/enclosed passenger part, NP trim, rubber tires & spare, Fair, A.$300.00

Stutz Racer, Kenton, 7½", lg metal spoke wheels, NP driver, VG, A $525.00

Stutz Roadster, Kilgore, 10½", extensive NP trim, NP disk wheels & rear spare, VG, A $1,760.00

Tanker Truck, see Gasoline Tank Truck, Mack Tanker Truck or Packard Gasoline Truck

Taxi, Arcade, 8", blk & wht w/red top, metal disk wheels, rear spare, G+, A $500.00

Taxi, Arcade, 8", brn & wht, metal disk wheels, rear spare, EX, A $800.00

Taxi, Freidag, 8", #543, metal disk wheels, w/driver, EX+, A .$1,200.00

Taxi, Freidag, 8", #543, metal disk wheels, w/driver, G ..$450.00

Taxi, Hubley, 6", orange, metal disk wheels, w/driver, missing rear spare o/w G, A..$100.00

Taxi, Hubley, 8", blk & gr, metal disk wheels, NP driver, G .$525.00

Taxi, Hubley, 8", blk & gr w/blk & wht checked band, metal disk wheels, rstr, A $470.00

Taxi, Hubley, 8", blk & wht, pnt metal disk wheels, rear spare, w/driver, EX, A $2,300.00

Taxi, Hubley, 8", orange w/blk trim, metal disk wheels, rear spare, w/driver, EX, A $550.00

Texas Centennial (1936) Bowen Motor Coach, Arcade, 11", tandem bus w/rubber tires, 11", VG, A.................$1,200.00

Touring Car, AC Williams, 7", top up, blk w/gold stripe, NP spoke wheels, NM $1,400.00

Touring Car, AC Williams, 9½", top down, gr w/red-pnt metal spoke wheels, VG $225.00

Touring Car, Dent, 9½", top down, simulated spoke wheels, w/driver & lady passenger, VG, A............................$850.00

Touring Car, Dent, 12", top down, metal spoke wheels, w/driver & lady passenger, G+, A...$935.00

Touring Car, Hubley, 6", top up, NP grille, rubber tires & rear spare, EX+ $775.00

Touring Car, Jones & Bixler, 9", stationary top, hood curves downward, metal spoke wheels, driver & lady passenger, G, A $750.00

Touring Car, Jones & Bixler, 9", top up, straight hood, metal spoke wheels, w/driver & lady passenger, VG+, A .$1,050.00

Touring Car, Kenton, 8", open, straight hood, high front seat w/curved single back seat, driver & passenger, NM.$1,750.00

Touring Car, Kenton, 9", open, curved hood, high seats, spoke wheels, w/driver & lady passenger, G, A...................$385.00

Touring Car, Kenton, 10", open, straight hood, high seats, no fenders or running boards, spoke wheels, w/driver, EX $1,200.00

Touring Car, Kenton, 11½", top down, straight hood, regular spoke wheels, w/driver & lady passenger, EX........$1,150.00

Touring Car, Kenton, 12", open, straight hood, high seats, fenders & running boards, w/driver & lady passenger, VG ...$850.00

Traffic Car, Hubley, 8½", Indian 3-wheeled cycle w/stake cart, rubber tires, cast driver, EX, A $825.00

Traffic Car, Hubley, 8½", Indian 3-wheeled cycle w/stake cart, rubber tires, cast driver, G, A $475.00

Truck, Freidag, 4½", 1920s model, open seat & bed, metal disk wheels, NP driver, VG, A...$220.00

US Air Mail Cycle, 9½", rubber tires w/spoke wheels, w/driver, VG $1,400.00

Valley View Farms Milk Truck (Guernsey A Milk), Dent, 8", bus-like w/opening side doors, standing driver, VG, A $900.00

Webaco Oil Co Tanker Truck, see Mack Tanker Truck

White Moving Van, Arcade, 13", USCO. Union Supply Co. decal on side, EX, A, $3,575.00. (Photo courtesy Bertoia Auctions)

White Panel Delivery Truck, Arcade, 9", metal disk wheels, NP driver, EX+ $3,600.00

White Panel Delivery Truck, Arcade, 9", metal disk wheels, NP driver, G $1,750.00

Wrecker, Hubley, 6½", take-apart body, rubber tires, EX ..$325.00

Wrecker, see also Auto Wrecker, Ford, International, Yellow Cab, etc.

Yellow Cab, Arcade, 5", Phone 4-11-44, blk & yel, metal disk wheels, no driver, G...$475.00

Yellow Cab, Arcade, 6½", Pontiac, all yel, NP grille & bumper, rubber tires, no driver, G, A $600.00

Yellow Cab, Arcade, 8", limousine style, blk & yel w/NP headlights, disk wheels & driver, EX, A $3,575.00

Yellow Cab, Arcade, 8", Parmalee, blk & yel w/NP radiator, bumper & headlights, rubber tires, no driver, EX+, A $6,050.00

Yellow Cab, Arcade, 8", 1923 model, blk & orange, metal disk wheels, w/driver, NM...$875.00

Yellow Cab, Arcade, 8", 1923 model, blk & orange, metal disk wheels, w/driver, VG, A $500.00

Yellow Cab, Arcade, 9", Dodge coupe, blk & orange w/wht, metal disk wheels & rear spare, w/driver, rstr, A......$525.00

Touring Car, Kenton, 9½", removable roof, with lady driver, VG, $1,500.00. (Photo courtesy Randy Inman Auctions)

Yellow Cab, Arcade, 9", Main 43, blk & orange, mesh front grille, metal disk wheels, NP driver, EX, A $330.00

Yellow Cab, Arcade, 9", 1927 model, blk & dk orange, metal disk wheels, no driver, G $150.00

Yellow Cab, Arcade, 9½", Phone 386, blk & orange, metal disk wheels, blk & orange, no driver, VG $225.00

Yellow Cab, Freidag, 7½", metal disk wheels, w/driver, G .$200.00

Yellow Cab, Hubley, 5", blk & orange, NP disk wheels, no driver, VG $450.00

Yellow Cab, Hubley, 7", 1936 Lincoln Zephyr, orange w/NP grille & bumper, rubber tires, no driver, rpt, A $600.00

Yellow Cab, Hubley, 8½", 1938 Skyview, orange w/NP grille & bumper, rubber tires, w/driver, EX, A $880.00

Yellow Cab Baggage Express Truck, Arcade, 10", very rare, VG, A, $12,100.00. (Photo courtesy Bertoia Auctions)

Yellow Cab Bus, Arcade, 13", Ride the Yellow Bus/Tel 152 printed on top, metal disk wheels, w/driver, G+, A $1,100.00

Yellow Cab Express, see International Yellow Cab Express

Yellow Cab Wrecker, Arcade, 9", metal spoke wheels, rpt, A.$440.00

Yellow Coach Double-Decker Bus, Arcade, 13½", rubber tires, VG, A...$1,200.00

Yellow Taxi Corp, Arcade, 9", Lenox 2300, metal disk wheels, w/driver, EX, A $880.00

5-Ton Stake Truck, see Stake Truck

TRAINS

Big 6 Freight Set, JP Stevens, locomotive, tender & gondola mk UPRR, 17" overall, Fair+, A $220.00

CRI & PRR Train Set, Arcade, locomotive, tender, 22" overall, Fair+, A $120.00

Derrick Car, Arcade, flat car supports crane w/hoist levers, NP spoke wheels, 11", VG, A.......................................$250.00

Erie Railroad, 6-pc w/locomotive, tender & 4 coaches, 38" overall, VG $325.00

Lake Shore & Michigan Southern Train Set, Kenton, 'camel back' locomotive, 3 coaches, 45" overall, Fair, A $330.00

Lake Shore & Michigan Southern Train Set, Kenton, locomotive, tender, 2 coaches, NP, 33" overall, G+, A $120.00

Locomotive, Welker & Crosby, w/wood boiler, spoke wheels, cow catcher, cast name & Pat date (Nov 10 '85), 12", VG+, A $880.00

Locomotive & Tender, Pratt & Letchworth, tender is sheet metal w/CI wheels, 15" overall, G, A $130.00

LS & MS Caboose, Kenton, 7", VG+, A.....................$130.00

MCRR Train Set, Dent, locomotive, tender, 2 gondolas, caboose, 36" overall, Fair+, A $220.00

MCRR Train Set, Dent, locomotive w/integral-cast tender, gondola, caboose, 18" overall, G, A $300.00

MCRR Train Set, Ideal, locomotive, tender, gondola, 2 coaches, 34" overall, VG+, A $250.00

NPR Train Set, J&E Stevens, locomotive, tender, 2 coaches, 30" overall, G, A $360.00

NY Central & Hudson River Set, Ideal, locomotive, tender & 3 coaches, NP, 53" overall, G, A $200.00

New York Central Hudson River RR, Pratt & Letchworth, locomotive, tender, baggage car, and coach marked Vanderbilt, 60", EX, A, $6,700.00. (Photo courtesy Noel Barrett, Inc.)

Pennsylvania Lines Train Set, Kenton, locomotive, tender, baggage car & 2 coaches, electro-oxidized finish, 40", VG+, A .$220.00

Pennsylvania RR Ivanhoe Train Set, locomotive, tender, 3 coaches, 28½" overall, G, A $160.00

Pennsylvania RR Train Set, Hubley, locomotive, tender & 2 coaches mk Narcissus, 33" overall, Fair+, A $130.00

PRR Co Locomotive & Tender, Dent, 14" overall, G $150.00

Pullman Railplane, Arcade, rubber tires, 1-pc, 5", G+, A..$75.00

Pullman Railplane, Arcade, rubber tires, 2-pc, 16", Fair+, A .$60.00

Train Set, Carpenter, locomotive, tender & 2 gondolas, mk Pat 1880, 20" overall, Fair+, A $250.00

Train Set, Dent, locomotive, tender #152, 2 coaches, 24" overall, Fair+, A $105.00

Train Set, H Wallwork/England, locomotive, tender, boxcar, 2 gondolas, flanged spoke wheels, 30" overall, G, A ..$700.00

Train Set, Pratt & Letchworth, 4-4-0 locomotive, #917 tender, Royal Blue Line #1192 coach & #1193 baggage car, 16", G, A $600.00

Train Set, Wilkens, locomotive, tender, Limited Express Parlor car & Baggage Express-US Mail car, 54", VG+, A ..$745.00

Train Set, Wilkins, locomotive, tender, Smoker US Mail Express Baggage car, coach, 38" overall, G, A $165.00

Train Set, Wilkins, locomotive (mk Pat June 19 '88), tender, 3 coaches, 50" overall, G..$200.00

MISCELLANEOUS

Arcade Service, wht-pnt wood station w/gr stenciling & 3 red ball ornaments on roof, 3 CI pumps, gr lift, 12" L, EX, A..$715.00

Arcade Super Service Station, wht-pnt wood w/red stenciling, 3 red CI pumps, 12" L, NM.....................................$1,650.00

Arcade Super Service Station, wht-pnt wood w/red stenciling, 3 red CI pumps, 12" L, VG...$650.00

Arcade Service Station, wooden model with car ramp, 12" long, NM, A, $1,320.00. (Photo courtesy Bertoia Auctions)

Arcadia Airport, wood w/2 CI planes, 12", VG, A $950.00
Baby Buggy, bl w/NP spoke wheels, hdl & canopy, 5¼", VG..$350.00
Boy Riding Tricycle, Kenton, NP spoke wheels, 4½", NM .$875.00
Coaster Wagon w/Boy Rider, Hubley, NP disk wheels, 3½", VG, A $300.00
Fat Boy Seated on 3-Wheeled Scooter, orange, 3¼", VG, A..$175.00
Gas Pump, Arcade, GAS emb on globe, red w/gold trim, front dial, rope gas hose, 7", EX.......................................$385.00
Gas Pump, Kilgore, GAS emb on globe, red w/gold trim, side crank measures gallons, 6¼", EX, A $330.00
Horse & Jockey, Hubley, removable jockey, 5½", EX $200.00
Jackbilt Fire House, paper litho on cb assembly pc w/graphics of Arcade CI Fire Truck, 15x28", unassembled, M (NOS) .$400.00
Kids Kar, Kilgore, NP spoke wheels, 5", EX, A $525.00

Marble Game, J&E Stevens, three-footed pan shape with multicolored marble wells, spring-lever action, 9½" long, VG, A, $550.00. (Photo courtesy Bertoia Auctions)

Road Sign, Arcade, US 30 shield on post, yel w/blk trim, 3½", VG, A $100.00
Sign, Men Working, 3¾", EX..$60.00
Traffic Light, Obey Traffic Laws/Department Of Police emb on front, yel w/red trim, 9¾", EX $600.00
Windmill, Arcade, pnt CI w/4 pressed-steel blades, 14½", EX, A $550.00

Catalogs

In any area of collecting, old catalogs are a wonderful source for information. Toy collectors value buyers' catalogs, those from toy fairs, and Christmas 'wish books.' Montgomery Ward issued their first Christmas catalog in 1932, and Sears followed a year later. When they can be found, these 'first editions' in excellent condition are valued at a minimum of $200.00 each. Even later issues may sell for upwards of $75.00, since it's those from the '50s and '60s that contain the toys that are now so collectible.

American Flyer, 1949, G..$25.00
Breyer Animal Creations, 1976, EX $20.00

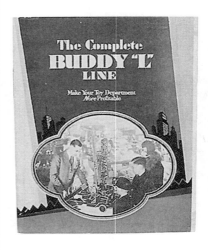

Buddy L (Complete Line), 1929, full color with outdoor railroad fold-out spread, 11x8", EX, A, $4,400.00. (Photo courtesy Randy Inman Auctions)

Buddy L Catalog of Steel Toys 1935, full color w/center spread of Zephyr train, 8x11", VG, A.....................................$575.00
Buddy L Junior (And Here's....There's Only One Buddy L Line), full-color showing complete line of Jr, 6x8", Fair, A.$145.00
Capitol Children's Record Albums, 1950s, 14 pgs w/foldouts, EX+ $40.00
Coleco Toys, 1972, EX..$10.00
Dennison's Hallowe'en Suggestions, 1931, 16 pgs w/products & decorating suggestions, VG+ $50.00
Elastolin, 1980, 60 pgs, EX $25.00
Fisher-Price Toys, 1950, EX $135.00
Galoob, 1973, EX...$30.00
Hasbro Romper Room, 1972, EX....................................$50.00

Keystone Steam Shovels & Trucks, 1925, 6x4", G, A, $130.00.

Kusan Toys, 1968, EX $25.00
Marx, 1975, 48 pgs, EX $50.00

Marx Toyland, 1950, M $40.00
Mattel Toys, 1968, NM...$40.00
Mego Superstars, 1974, EX $250.00
Mickey Mouse Merchandise 1936-37, complete, EX......$500.00
Nylint, 1967, EX $35.00
Ohio Art, 1974, Woody Woodpecker on cover, EX..........$50.00
Parker Bros Games & Toys, 1976, EX $80.00

Roy Rogers & Dale Evans Catalogue & Merchandising Manual, 1953, 82 pages, laser copy (not original), M, A, $100.00. (Photo courtesy Smith House Toys)

Snow White Merchandising Supplement, 1960s, tie-in campaigns featuring various products & companies, 12 pgs, M $50.00
Steiff, 1957, features 150 animals, 15 pgs, M $35.00
Thingmaker, Mattel, 1967, EX $15.00
Tom Mix Straight Shooter Premium Catalog, Ralston, 1935, 6-panel folder, EX+ $40.00
Tonka, 1963, NM..$100.00
Toyland (Large Dept Store), 1950s, lg image of Santa displaying selection of toys, 8 pgs, 15½", M $55.00
Toytown Flyer, Snow White & the Seven Dwarfs Welcomes You to Toytown Miscellaneous 5&10¢ Store, 1938, newsprint, NM, C6..$40.00
Transogram, 1969, EX $75.00
Ventriloquist Figures By Fred Maher, #1, 1950, 16 pgs, EX+.$65.00
Vogue Dolls, 1978, EX $40.00
Walt Disney Character Merchandise 1938-39, complete, VG..$500.00
Western Auto Christmas Gifts, 1968, focusing on toys, 72 pgs, EX+ $30.00
Wolverine Toys, 1973, EX $20.00

Cereal Boxes and Premiums

This is an area of collecting that attracts crossover interest from fans of advertising as well as character-related toys. What makes a cereal box interesting? Look for Batman, Huckleberry Hound, or a well-known sports figure like Larry Bird or Roger Maris on the front or back. Boxes don't have to be old to be collectible, but the basic law of supply and demand dictates that the older ones are going to be expensive! After all, who saved cereal boxes from 1910? By chance if Grandma did, the 1910 Corn Flakes box with a printed-on baseball game could get her $750.00. Unless you're not concerned with bugs, it will probably be best to empty the box and very carefully pull apart the glued

flaps. Then you can store it flat. Be sure to save any prize that might have been packed inside.
      Advisor: Don Goodsell (G2)

General Mills Cap 'n Crunch, 1973, bank offer, EX $125.00
General Mills Cap'n Crunch's Crunch Berries, 1969, Wiggle Figure inside, 10", NM $200.00
General Mills Cheerios, 1958, Annette cut-out doll & 3 outfits on back, 9½", EX...$150.00

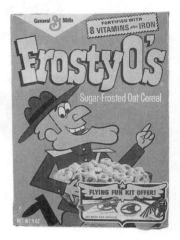

General Mills Frosty O's, 1970, Dudley Do-Right and Flying Fun Kit Offer!, EX, $400.00. (Photo courtesy Scott Bruce)

General Mills Jets, 1958, 10¢ Toy Certificate inside, 8½", EX.$100.00
General Mills Kix, 1964, Rocky & Bullwinkle Ring Toss Game on back, 11", EX $45.00
General Mills Sir Grapefellow, w/biplane glider offer, NM, from $125 to..$200.00
General Mills Sugar Jets, 1956, Mickey Mouse & His Pals Ring inside, 8½", NM $300.00
General Mills Trix, 1955, Tonto belt offer, EX $250.00
General Mills Wheaties, 1940s, w/Paul Bunyon mask, EX .$35.00
General Mills Wheaties, 1950-51, Walt Disney's Fun Masks on back, NM $100.00
General Mills Wheaties, 1957, Big as Life poster offer of the Lone Ranger & Tonto on back, 10¼", EX..............$300.00
General Mills Wheaties, 1962, Bullwinkle's Electric Quiz Fun Game offer, 9½", EX...$100.00

General Mills Wheaties, 1995, Larry Bird Commemorative Edition, M (sealed), $25.00.

Kellogg's All Stars, 1960, Walking Finger Puppet cutout on back, 9¾", NM $100.00

Kellogg's Cocoa Krispies, Snagglepuss with 'New Treat Ideas,' EX, $200.00. (Photo courtesy Scott Bruce)

 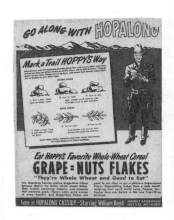

Post Grape-Nuts Flakes, 1950, 'Hopalong Cassidy's Favorite Whole-Wheat Cereal,' 'Mark a Trail Hoppy's Way' on back, EX, $300.00. (Photo courtesy Scott Bruce)

Kellogg's Corn Flakes, 1957-58, Battery-Powered Electric Train offer on back, 9¾", EX $100.00

Kellogg's Corn Flakes, 1962, Yogi Bear Birthday Dell Comic, EX...$300.00

Kellogg's Pep Corn Flakes, 1952, Vote As You Please..., pictures Eisenhower & Stevenson on front, 11½", EX $150.00

Kellogg's Puffa Puffa Rice, 1967, Monkees Flicker Ring inside w/cut-out portraits on back, 9", NM $250.00

Kellogg's Raisin Bran, 1950, Disney Joinies, EX $150.00

Kellogg's Raisin Bran, 1992, Dream Team, NM $15.00

Kellogg's Rice Krispies, 1953, Howdy Doody Doll Offer, EX.$300.00

Kellogg's Rice Krispies, 1954-55, Atom Sub inside, Operating Instructions on back, 10¼", EX $125.00

Kellogg's Rice Krispies, 1967, Woody Woodpecker swimmer toy, NM...$75.00

Kellogg's Sugar Corn Pops, 1952, features Wild Bill Hickok w/cut-out derringer & badge on back, EX...............$100.00

Kellogg's Sugar Frosted Flakes, 1954, Superman Stereo-Pix cutouts on back, 9½", NM $300.00

Kellogg's Sugar Frosted Flakes, 1955, pictures Tony & Tony Jr on tricycle, 20" display box, EX.....................................$150.00

Kellogg's Sugar Smacks, 1964, Quick Draw McGraw, road race game on back, flat, NM $200.00

Nabisco Rice Honeys, 1969, Beatles Rub-Ons Free Inside, NM..$750.00

Nabisco Shredded Wheat, 1956, Rin-Tin-Tin insignia patch offer, NM..$75.00

Nabisco Shredded Wheat Juniors, 1959, Spoonmen graphics w/Spoonman premium inside, EX $400.00

Nabisco Wheat Honeys, 1956, Buffalo Bee hummer toy on back, EX...$50.00

Post Corn Fetti, 1953, peg-leg pirate w/parrot mascot on front, New Improved!, ...Magic Sugar Coat!, 9½", NM $75.00

Post Crispy Critters, 1963, Linus the Lion Stuffed Toy offer, 9¾", NM..$100.00

Post Krinkles, 1951, shows mascot front & back, NM......$65.00

Post Raisin Bran, 1950-51, Hopalong Cassidy Western Badge In This Package!, 8", NM $400.00

Post Raisin Bran, 1988, California Raisin figure offer, EX...$15.00

Post Sugar Crisp, 1957, Mighty Mouse Magic Mystery Picture inside, 10½", NM $100.00

Post Sugar Crisp, 1957, Roy Rogers Jig Saw Puzzle inside, 9½", NM...$150.00

Post Sugar Rice Krinkles, 1955, Flip-Top inside, 9", NM .$45.00

Post Toasties, 1951, Indian Canoe cutouts on back, 9¾", NM.$50.00

Post Toasties, 1966, Billy Bird on back, flat, M.................$50.00

Post Wheat Meal, 1950, Free Sample, image of Hopalong Cassidy on reverse, 4", EX, A $85.00

Quaker Mother's Oats, 1950s, Gabby Hayes comic book offer, lid missing, VG $45.00

Quaker Puffed Rice, 1950, Sgt Preston's Yukon Trail, 1 of 8 different packages w/cut-out & build models on back, EX.$125.00

Quaker Puffed Rice, 1955, Yukon Gold Country Deed-of-Land offer, 9", NM...$150.00

Quaker Puffed Wheat, 1951, Gabby Hayes western gun collection, EX...$200.00

Quaker Puffed Wheat Sparkies, Terry & the Pirates, NM .$100.00

Quaker Quisp, 1968, Spacequaft offer on back, 10", EX.$200.00

Ralston Purina Rice Chex, 1953, Space Patrol Magic Space Pictures inside w/Space Binoculars offer, EX $300.00

Ralston Purina Wheat Chex, 1953, Magic Space Pictures inside w/Space Binoculars offer on back, 9", EX $300.00

PREMIUMS

Sure, the kids liked the taste of the cereal too, but in families with more than one child there was more clamoring over the prize inside than there was over the last bowlful! In addition to the 'freebies' included in the boxes, many other items were made available — rings, decoders, watches, games, books, etc. — often for just mailing in boxtops or coupons. If these premiums weren't free, their prices were minimal. Most of them were easily broken, and children had no qualms about throwing them away, so few survive to the present. Who would have ever thought those kids would be trying again in the '90s to get their hands on those very same prizes, and at considerable more trouble and expense.

Atom Submarine, plastic, Kellogg's, 1954-55, 2½", NM ..$15.00

Bracelet, Kellogg's Pep Self-Starter Club, EX (EX card), A .$8.00

Cap'n Crunch Coloring Book, EX..................$25.00
Cap'n Crunch Hand Puppets, 1966, any character, paper, 9", EX,
    ea...$20.00
Cap'n Crunch Treasure Chest Bank, 1966, 6" L, EX $45.00
Cheerios Airport Airplanes, plastic, General Mills, 1958, 8 dif-
    ferent, 2½" to 3" L, M, ea from $5 to $15.00
Cocoa Puffs Train, locomotive & 3 cars, litho tin w/up, General
    Mills, 1959-61, 12" L, EX $75.00
Disney Fun Masks, cb cutouts, General Mills, 1950-51, EX, ea
    from $15 to..$20.00
Flip Movies (Droopy in Growing Pains), Post Grape-Nuts, 1949,
    EX..$15.00

General Mills Character Figures (Fruit Brute, Frankenberry,
Count Chocula, and Boo Berry), vinyl, 8", EX, each
$125.00.

Howdy Doody Hand Puppets, any character, cloth with vinyl
heads, Kellogg's, 1954, each $25.00. (Photo courtesy Scott Bruce)

Kellie Gro-Pup Dog, stuffed print cloth, Kellogg's, 1948, assem-
    bled, EX orig mailer, A $30.00
License Plates, Wheaties, 1954, MIP, C10 ....$50.00
Lone Ranger or Tonto Big as Life Posters, General Mills, 1957,
    EX, ea...$100.00
Magic Color Cards, Kellogg's Rice Krispies, 1933, complete,
    unused, EX+ (EX+ envelope).....................................$65.00
Mary Poppins, Nabisco Rice Honeys, 1964, 4", MIP $25.00
Melvin Previs Secret Operator's Manual, Post Toasties, 1937,
    EX..$50.00
Post Vehicle, 1954 Ford Ranch Wagon, Glacier Blue, M .$150.00
Post Vehicle, 1954 Ford Sunliner, Cameo Coral, M $45.00
Post Vehicle, 1954 Ford Victoria, Sierra Brown, M $30.00

Post Vehicle, 1954 Mercury XM/Post Vehicle, 1954 Mercury
    Sport Coupe, Torch Red, M $175.00
Post Vehicle, 1955 Ford Country Sedan, Aquatone Blue, no ID
    on roof...$395.00
Post Vehicle, 1955 Ford Crown Victoria, Buckskin Brown,
    M..$25.00
Post Vehicle, 1955 Ford Sunliner, Torch Red, M.............$20.00
Post Vehicle, 1955 Ford Tudor Customline, Goldenrod Yellow,
    M..$15.00
Post Vehicle, 1957 Ford Custom Fordor Highway Patrol, Coral
    Sand, M...$40.00
Post Vehicle, 1966 Mustang Hardtop, Arcadian Blue, M.$10.00
Post Vehicle, 1969 Mercurys, set of, 4 by JVZ Co, M $25.00

Prospector's Pouch 'with 1 oz
of Klondike Land,' EX,
$45.00. (Photo courtesy Scott Bruce)

Ranger Joe Ranch Mug, milk glass w/bright bl graphics, Ranger
    Joe Wheat Honnies, 1950s, 3", NM $10.00
Rin-Tin-Tin Pen, rifle shape, plastic, Nabisco Shredded Wheat,
    5½", NM (EX mailer box)...$50.00
Santa Fe Super Chief Train, battery-op, Kellogg's, 1957-58, com-
    plete, 7" L, M $75.00
Speedy Spaceman, Nabisco, 1960, unused, NM+ $20.00
Tobor the Robot, plastic, Nabisco, 1959, 1¾", M.............$50.00
Tony the Tiger Bank, sitting upright, Kellogg's, 1968, 9", NM+..$60.00
US Army Flying Platform, plastic, Kellogg's, 1957-58, 6", M .$35.00

Character and Promotional Drinking Glasses

    Once given away by fast-food chains and gas stations, a few
years ago you could find these at garage sales everywhere for a
dime or even less. Then, when it became obvious to collectors
that these glass giveaways were being replaced by plastic, as is
always the case when we realize no more (of anything) will be
forthcoming, we all decided we wanted them. Since many were
character-related and part of a series, we felt the need to begin to
organize these garage-sale castaways, building sets and completing series. Out of the thousands available, the better ones are
those with super heroes, sports stars, old movie stars, Star Trek,
and Disney and Walter Lantz cartoon characters. Pass up those
whose colors are worn and faded. Unless another condition or

material is indicated in the description, values are for glass tumblers in mint condition. Cups are plastic unless noted otherwise.

There are some terms used in our listings that may be confusing if you're not familiar with this collecting field. 'Brockway' style tumblers are thick and heavy, and they taper at the bottom. 'Federal' is thinner, and top and diameters are equal. For more information we recommend *Collectible Drinking Glasses, Identification and Values*, by Mark E. Chase and Michael J. Kelly (Collector Books) and *The Collector's Guide to Cartoon and Promotional Drinking Glasses* by John Hervey. See also Clubs, Newsletters, and Other Publications.

Advisor: Mark E. Chase (C2)

Al Capp, Dogpatch USA, ruby glass, oval portraits of Daisy or Li'l Abner, ea from $25 to $30.00
Al Capp, Shmoos, USF, 1949, Federal, 3 different sizes (3½", 4¾", 5¼"), ea from $10 to......................$20.00
Al Capp, 1975, flat bottom, Daisy Mae, Li'l Abner, Mammy, Pappy, Sadie, ea from $50 to......................$70.00
Al Capp, 1975, flat bottom, Joe Btsfplk, from $30 to $50.00
Al Capp, 1975, ftd, Daisy Mae, Li'l Abner, Mammy, Pappy, Sadie, ea from $25 to......................$50.00
Al Capp, 1975, ftd, Joe Btsfplk, from $60 to......................$90.00
Animal Crackers, Chicago Tribune/NY News Syndicate, 1978, Eugene, Gnu, Lana, Lyle Dodo, ea from $7 to $10.00
Animal Crackers, Chicago Tribune/NY News Syndicate, 1978, Louis, scarce......................$25.00
Arby's, Actor Series, 1979, 6 different, smoked-colored glass w/blk & wht images, silver trim, numbered, ea from $3 to......................$5.00
Arby's, Bicentennial Cartoon Characters Series, 1976, 10 different, 5", ea from $8 to......................$15.00
Arby's, Bicentennial Cartoon Characters Series, 1976, 10 different, 6", ea from $10 to......................$20.00
Arby's, see also specific name or series
Archies, Welch's, 1971 & 1973, many variations in ea series, ea from $3 to......................$5.00
Baby Huey & Related Characters, see Harvey Cartoon Characters
Batman & Related Characters, see also Super Heroes
Batman Forever, McDonald's, 1995, various emb glass mugs, ea from $2 to......................$4.00
Battlestar Galactica, Universal Studios, 1979, 4 different, ea from $7 to......................$10.00
Beatles, Dairy Queen/Canada, group photos & signatures in wht starburst, gold trim, ea from $95 to......................$125.00
Beverly Hillbillies, CBS promotion, 1963, rare, NM......$200.00

Burger Chef, Friendly Monster Series, 1977, six different, each from $15.00 to $25.00. (Photo courtesy Mark Chase and Michael Kelly)

Bozo the Clown, Capital Records, 1965, Bozo head image around top w/related character at bottom, ea from $10 to $15.00
Bozo the Clown, Capital Records, 1965, Bozo on 3 sides only, from $8 to......................$10.00
Buffalo Bill, see Western Heroes or Wild West Series
Bugs Bunny & Related Characters, see Warner Bros
Bullwinkle, Rocky & Related Characters, see Warner Bros or PAT Ward
Burger King, Collector Series, 1979, 5 different Burger King characters featuring Burger Thing, etc, ea from $3 to..$5.00
Burger King, Put a Smile in Your Tummy, features Burger King mascot, from $5 to......................$6.00
Burger King, see also specific name or series
California Raisins, Applause, 1989, juice, 12-oz, 16-oz, ea from $4 to......................$6.00
California Raisins, Applause, 1989, 32-oz, from $6 to........$8.00
Captain America, see Super Heroes
Casper the Friendly Ghost & Related Characters, see Arby's Bicentennial or Harvey Cartoon Characters
Charlie McCarthy & Edger Bergen, Libbey, 1930s, set of 8, M (EX illus display box)......................$600.00
Children's Classics, Libbey Glass Co, Alice in Wonderland, Gulliver's Travels, Tom Sawyer, ea from $10 to $15.00
Children's Classics, Libbey Glass Co, Moby Dick, Robin Hood, Three Musketeers, Treasure Island, ea from $10 to....$15.00
Children's Classics, Libbey Glass Co, The Wizard of Oz, from $25 to......................$30.00
Chilly Willy, see Walter Lantz
Chipmunks, Hardee's (no logo on glass), 1985, Alvin, Simon, Theodore, Chipettes, ea from $1 to......................$3.00
Cinderella, Disney/Libbey, 1950s-60s, set of 8................$120.00
Cinderella, see also Disney Collector Series or Disney Film Classics
Clarabell, see Howdy Doody
Daffy Duck, see Warner Bros
Dick Tracy, Domino's Pizza, M, from $75 to..................$100.00
Dick Tracy, 1940s, frosted, 8 different characters, 3" or 5", ea from $50 to......................$75.00
Dilly Dally, see Howdy Doody
Disney, see also Wonderful World of Disney or specific characters

Disney, First Dairy Series, 1930s, Mickey Mouse, 4¾", from $25.00 to $35.00.

Disney Characters, 1936, Clarabelle, Donald, F Bunny, Horace, Mickey, Minnie, Pluto, 4¼" or 4¾", ea from $30 to..$50.00
Disney's All-Star Parade, 1939, 10 different, ea from $25 to.$50.00

Disneyland, 1955, juice, Adventureland/Donald, Fantasyland/Tinker Bell, Frontierland/Mickey, Tomorrowland/Goofy, $20 to .**$30.00**

Donald Duck, Donald Duck Cola, 1960s-70s, from $10 to .**$15.00**

Donald Duck or Daisy, see also Disney or Mickey Mouse (Happy Birthday)

Dynomutt, see Hanna-Barbera

ET, Pepsi/MCA Home Video, 1988, 6 different, ea from $15 to .**$25.00**

ET, Pizza Hut, 1982, ftd, 4 different, ea from $2 to..............**$4.00**

Fantasia, see Disney Film Classics or Mickey Mouse (Through the Years)

Flintstones, see also Hanna-Barbera

Flintstones, Welch's, 1962 (6 different), 1963 (2 different), 1964 (6 different), ea from $4 to **$6.00**

Ghostbusters II, Sunoco/Canada, 1989, 6 different, ea from $3 to..**$5.00**

Goonies, Godfather's Pizza/Warner Bros, 1985, 4 different, ea from $3 to..**$5.00**

Great Muppet Caper, McDonald's, 1981, 4 different, 6", ea..**$2.00**

Green Arrow or Green Lantern, see Super Heroes

Hanna-Barbera, Pepsi, 1977, Dynomutt, Flintstones, Josie & the Pussycats, Mumbly, Scooby, Yogi & Huck, ea from $10 to .**$20.00**

Hanna-Barbera, 1960s, jam glasses featuring Cindy Bear, Flintstones, Huck, Quick Draw, Yogi Bear, rare, ea from $75 to.......**$110.00**

Happy Days, Dr Pepper, 1977, Fonzie, Joanie, Potsie, Ralph, Richie, ea from $6 to **$10.00**

Happy Days, Dr Pepper/Pizza Hut, 1977, any character, ea from $6 to **$10.00**

Harvey Cartoon Characters, Pepsi, 1970s, action pose, Baby Huey, Hot Stuff, Wendy, ea from $8 to **$10.00**

Harvey Cartoon Characters, Pepsi, 1970s, static pose, Baby Huey, Casper, Hot Stuff, Wendy, ea from $12 to **$15.00**

Harvey Cartoon Characters, Pepsi, 1970s, static pose, Richie Rich, from $15 to..**$20.00**

Harvey Cartoon Characters, Pepsi, 1970s, static pose, Sad Sack, scarce, from $25 to..**$30.00**

Harvey Cartoon Characters, see also Arby's Bicentennial Series

He-Man & Related Characters, see Masters of the Universe

Holly Hobbie, American Greetings/Coca-Cola, 1980 Christmas, 4 different: Christmas Is..., Wrap Each..., etc, ea $3 to .**$5.00**

Holly Hobbie, American Greetings/Coca-Cola, 1981 Christmas, 3 different: 'Tis the Season..., A Gift..., etc, ea $2 to ...**$4.00**

Holly Hobbie, American Greetings/Coca-Cola, 1982 Christmas, 3 different: Wishing You..., Share in the Fun..., ea $2 to....**$4.00**

Honey, I Shrunk the Kids, McDonald's, 1989, plastic, 3 different, ea from $1 to..**$2.00**

Hopalong Cassidy, milk glass w/blk graphics, Breakfast Milk, Lunch Milk, Dinner Milk, ea from $15 to **$20.00**

Hopalong Cassidy, milk glass w/red & blk graphics, 3 different, ea from $20 to..**$25.00**

Hopalong Cassidy's Western Series, ea from $25 to **$30.00**

Hot Stuff, see Harvey Cartoon Characters or Arby's Bicentennial

Howard the Duck, see Super Heroes

Howdy Doody, Welch's/Kagran, 1950s, 6 different, emb bottom, ea from $10 to..**$15.00**

Huckleberry Hound, see Hanna-Barbera

Incredible Hulk, see Super Heroes

Indiana Jones & the Temple of Doom, 7-Up (w/4 different sponsors), 1984, set of 4, ea from $8 to............................**$15.00**

James Bond 007, 1985, 4 different, ea from $10 to **$15.00**

Joe Btsfplk, see Al Capp

Joker, see Super Heroes

Jungle Book, Disney/Canada, 1966, 6 different, numbered, 5", ea from $40 to..**$75.00**

Jungle Book, Disney/Canada, 1966, 6 different, numbered, 6½", ea from $30 to..**$60.00**

Jungle Book, Disney/Pepsi, 1970s, Bagheera or Shere Kahn, unmk, ea from $50 to..**$75.00**

Jungle Book, Disney/Pepsi, 1970s, Mowgli, unmk, from $25 to .**$35.00**

Jungle Book, Disney/Pepsi, 1970s, Rama, unmk, from $30 to..**$40.00**

Kellogg's, 1977, Big Yella, Dig 'Em, Snap!, Crackle! & Pop!, Tony, Tony Jr, Toucan Sam, ea from $5 to....................**$7.00**

Laurel & Hardy, see Arby's Actor Series

Leonardo TTV, see also Arby's Bicentennial Series

Leonardo TTV Collector Series, Pepsi, Underdog, Go-Go Gophers, Simon Bar Sinister, Sweet Polly, 6", ea from $10 to.......**$15.00**

Leonardo TTV Collector Series, Pepsi, Underdog, Simon Bar Sinister, Sweet Polly, 5", ea from $6 to......................**$10.00**

Little Mermaid, 1991, 3 different sizes, ea from $6 to.......**$10.00**

Masters of the Universe, Mattel, 1983, He-Man, Man-at-Arms, Skeletor, Teels, ea from $5 to **$10.00**

Masters of the Universe, Mattel, 1986, Battle Cat/He-Man, Man-at-Arms, Orko, Panthor/Skeletor, ea from $3 to .**$5.00**

McDonald's, McDonaldland Action Series or Collector Series, 1970s, 6 different ea series, ea from $2 to....................**$3.00**

MGM Collector Series, Pepsi, 1975, Tom, Jerry, Barney, Droopy, Spike, Tuffy, ea from $5 to...**$10.00**

Mickey Mouse, Happy Birthday, Pepsi, 1978, Clarabelle & Horace or Daisy & Donald, ea from $5 to.................**$10.00**

Mickey Mouse, Happy Birthday, Pepsi, 1978, Donald, Goofy, Mickey, Minnie, Pluto, Uncle Scrooge, ea from $5 to .**$7.00**

Mickey Mouse, Mickey's Christmas Carol, Coca-Cola, 1982, 3 different, ea from $5 to **$7.00**

Mickey Mouse, Pizza Hut, 1980, milk glass mug, Fantasia, MM Club, Steamboat Willie, Today, ea from $2 to **$5.00**

Mickey Mouse, see also Disney Characters

Mickey Mouse, Through the Years, K-Mart, glass mugs w/4 different images (1928, 1937, 1940, 1955), ea from $3 to **$5.00**

Mickey Mouse Club, 4 different w/filmstrip bands top & bottom, ea from $10 to..**$20.00**

Mister Magoo, Polomar Jelly, many different variations & styles, ea from $25 to..**$35.00**

Pac-Man, Arby's Collector Series, 1980, rocks glass, from $20 to...**$4.00**

Pac-Man, Bally Midway MFG/AAFES/Libbey, 1980, Shadow (Blinky), Bashful (Inky), Pokey (Clyde), Speedy (Pinky), ea from $4 to..**$6.00**

Pac-Man, Bally Midway Mfg/Libbey, 1982, 6" flare top, 5⅜" flare top or mug, from $2 to...**$4.00**

PAT Ward, Pepsi, late 1970s, action pose, Bullwinkle w/balloons, Dudley in Canoe, Rocky in circus, 5", ea from $5 to ...**$10.00**

PAT Ward, Pepsi, late 1970s, static pose, Boris, Mr Peabody, Natasha, 5", ea from $10 to **$15.00**

PAT Ward, Pepsi, late 1970s, static pose, Boris & Natasha, 6", from $15 to...**$20.00**

PAT Ward, Pepsi, late 1970s, static pose, Bullwinkle, 5", from $15 to **$20.00**

PAT Ward, Collector Series, Holly Farms Restaurants, 1975, Boris, Bullwinkle, Natasha, Rocky, each from $20.00 to $40.00. (Photo courtesy Mark Chase and Michael Kelly)

PAT Ward, Pepsi, late 1970s, static pose, Bullwinkle (brn lettering/no Pepsi logo), 6", from $15 to $20.00

PAT Ward, Pepsi, late 1970s, static pose, Bullwinkle (wht or blk lettering), 6", from $10 to $15.00

PAT Ward, Pepsi, late 1970s, static pose, Dudley Do-Right, 5", from $10 to..$15.00

PAT Ward, Pepsi, late 1970s, static pose, Dudley Do-Right (blk lettering), 6", from $10 to..$15.00

PAT Ward, Pepsi, late 1970s, static pose, Dudley Do-Right (red lettering/no Pepsi logo), 6", from $10 to $15.00

PAT Ward, Pepsi, late 1970s, static pose, Rocky, 5", from $15 to .$20.00

PAT Ward, Pepsi, late 1970s, static pose, Rocky (brn lettering/no Pepsi logo), 6", from $10 to $15.00

PAT Ward, Pepsi, late 1970s, static pose, Rocky (wht or blk lettering), 6", from $10 to..$15.00

PAT Ward, Pepsi, late 1970s, static pose, Snidley Whiplash, 5", from $8 to..$10.00

PAT Ward, Pepsi, late 1970s, static pose, Snidley Whiplash (wht or blk lettering), 6", from $10 to $15.00

PAT Ward, see also Arby's Bicentennial Series

Peanuts Characters, Dolly Madison Bakery, Snoopy for President or Snoopy Sport Series, 4 different ea series, ea $3 to..$5.00

Peanuts Characters, ftd, Snoopy sitting on lemon or Snoopy sitting on lg red apple, ea from $2 to.................................$3.00

Peanuts Characters, Kraft, 1988, Charlie Brown flying kite, Lucy on swing, Snoopy in pool, Snoopy on surfboard, ea.....$2.00

Peanuts Characters, McDonald's, 1983, Camp Snoopy, wht plastic w/Lucy or Snoopy, ea from $5 to $8.00

Peanuts Characters, milk glass mug, At Times Life Is Pure Joy (Snoopy & Woodstock dancing), from $3 to $5.00

Peanuts Characters, milk glass mug, Snoopy for President, 4 different, numbered & dated, ea from $5 to $8.00

Peanuts Characters, milk glass mug, Snoopy in various poses, from $2 to...$4.00

Peanuts Characters, plastic, I Got It! I Got It!, I Have a Strange Team, Let's Break for Lunch!, ea from $3 to $5.00

Peanuts Characters, Smuckers, 1994, 3 different, ea from $2 to $4.00

Penguin, see Super Heroes

Peter Pan, see Disney Film Classics

Pinocchio, Dairy Promo/Libbey, 1938-40, 12 different, ea from $15 to $25.00

Pinocchio, see also Disney Collector's Series or Wonderful World of Disney

Pluto, see Disney Characters

Pocahontas, Burger King, 1995, 4 different, MIB, ea $3.00

Popeye, Coca-Cola, 1975, Kollect-A-Set, any character, ea from $3 to $5.00

Popeye, Popeye's Famous Fried Chicken, 1978, Sports Scenes, Popeye, from $7 to $10.00

Popeye, Popeye's Famous Fried Chicken, 1978, Sports Scenes, Brutus, Olive Oyl, Swee' Pea, ea from $10 to $15.00

Popeye, Popeye's Famous Fried Chicken, 1979, Pals, 4 different, ea from $10 to $15.00

Popeye, Popeye's Famous Fried Chicken/Pepsi, 1982, 10th Anniversary Series, 4 different, ea from $7 to............$10.00

Quick Draw McGraw, see Hanna-Barbera

Raggedy Ann & Andy, going down slide, skipping rope, stacking blocks, riding in wagon, ea from $5 to $10.00

Rescuers, Pepsi, 1977, Brockway tumblers, Bianca, Brutus, or any character except Madame Medusa or Rufus, 6¼", each from $5.00 to $10.00.

Rescuers, Pepsi, 1977, Brockway tumbler, Madame Medusa or Rufus, ea from $25 to $30.00

Richie Rich, see Harvey Cartoon Characters

Riddler or Robin, see Super Heroes

Roadrunner & Related Characters, see Warner Bros

Rocky & Bullwinkle, see Arby's Bicentennial or PAT Ward

Roy Rogers Restaurant, 1883-1983 logo, from $3 to...........$5.00

Sad Sack, see Harvey Cartoon Characters

Scooby Doo, see Hanna-Barbera

Sleeping Beauty, American, late 1950s, 6 different, ea from $8 to .$15.00

Sleeping Beauty, Canadian, late 1950s, 12 different, ea from $10 to $15.00

Smurfs, Hardee's, 1982 (8 different), 1983 (6 different), ea, from $1 to $3.00

Snidley Whiplash, see PAT Ward

Snoopy & Related Characters, see Peanuts Characters

Snow White & the Seven Dwarfs, Bosco, 1938, ea $20.00

Snow White & the Seven Dwarfs, Libbey, 1930s, verses on back, various colors, 8 different, ea from $15 to $25.00

Snow White & the Seven Dwarfs, see also Disney Collector's Series or Disney Film Classics

Star Trek, Dr Pepper, 1976, 4 different, ea from $15 to **$20.00**

Star Trek, Dr Pepper, 1978, 4 different, ea from $25 to **$30.00**

Star Trek II, The Search for Spock, Taco Bell, 1984, 4 different, ea from $3 to **$5.00**

Star Trek: The Motion Picture, Coca-Cola, 1980, 3 different, ea from $10 to...**$15.00**

Star Wars Trilogy: Empire Strikes Back, Burger King/Coca-Cola, 1980, 4 different, ea from $5 to **$7.00**

Star Wars Trilogy: Return of the Jedi, Burger King/Coca-Cola, 1983, 4 different, ea from $3 to **$5.00**

Star Wars Trilogy: Star Wars, Burger King/Coca-Cola, 1977, 4 different, ea from $8 to **$10.00**

Sunday Funnies, 1976, Brenda Star, Gasoline Alley, Moon Mullins, Orphan Annie, Smilin' Jack, Terry & the Pirates, $5 to ..**$7.00**

Sunday Funnies, 1976, Broom Hilda, from $80 to **$100.00**

Super Heroes, Marvel, 1978, Federal, flat bottom, Captain America, Hulk, Spider-Man, Thor, ea from $50 to....**$75.00**

Super Heroes, Marvel, 1978, Federal, flat bottom, Spider-Woman, from $100 to **$250.00**

Super Heroes, Marvel/7 Eleven, 1977, ftd, Amazing Spider-Man, from $25 to...**$30.00**

Super Heroes, Marvel/7 Eleven, 1977, ftd, Captain America, Fantastic Four, Howard the Duck, Thor, ea from $15 to....**$20.00**

Super Heroes, Marvel/7 Eleven, 1977, ftd, Incredible Hulk, from $15 to **$20.00**

Super Heroes, Pepsi Super (Moon) Series/DC Comics, 1976, Green Arrow, from $20 to **$30.00**

Super Heroes, Pepsi Super (Moon) Series/DC Comics, 1976, Green Lantern, Joker, Penguin, Riddler, ea from $25 to **$30.00**

Super Heroes, Pepsi Super (Moon) Series/DC Comics or NPP, 1976, Batgirl, Batman, Shazam!, ea from $10 to........**$15.00**

Super Heroes, Pepsi Super (Moon) Series/NPP, 1976, Green Lantern, Joker, Penguin, Riddler, ea from $20 to.......**$30.00**

Superman, NPP/M Polanar & Son, 1964, 6 different, various colors, 4¼" or 5¾", ea from $20 to.............................**$25.00**

Sylvester the Cat or Tasmanian Devil, see Warner Bros

Tom & Jerry & Related Characters, see MGM Collector Series

Underdog & Related Characters, see Arby's Bicentennial or Leonardo TTV

Universal Monsters, Universal Studio, 1980, footed, Creature From the Black Lagoon, Dracula, Frankenstein, Mutant, Wolfman, each from $110.00 to $130.00. (Photo courtesy Mark Chase and Michael Kelly)

Walter Lantz, Pepsi, 1970s, Chilly Willy or Wally Walrus, ea from $25 to..**$45.00**

Walter Lantz, Pepsi, 1970s, Cuddles, from $40 to **$60.00**

Walter Lantz, Pepsi, 1970s, Space Mouse, from $125 to.**$200.00**

Walter Lantz, Pepsi, 1970s, Woody Woodpecker, from $7 to .**$15.00**

Walter Lantz, Pepsi, 1970s-80s, Anty/Miranda, Chilly/Smelley, Cuddles/Oswald, Wally/Homer, ea from $20 to.........**$30.00**

Walter Lantz, Pepsi, 1970s-80s, Buzz Buzzard/Space Mouse, from $15 to **$20.00**

Walter Lantz, Pepsi, 1970s-80s, Woody Woodpecker/Knothead & Splinter, from $15 to **$20.00**

Walter Lantz, see also Arby's Bicentennial Series

Warner Bros, Acme Cola, 1993, bell shape, Bugs, Sylvester, Taz, Tweety, ea from $4 to..**$8.00**

Warner Bros, Arby's, 1988, Adventures Series, ftd, Bugs, Daffy, Porky, Sylvester & Tweety, ea from $25 to................**$30.00**

Warner Bros, Marriott's Great America, 1975, 12-oz, 6 different (Bugs & related characters), ea from $20 to...............**$30.00**

Warner Bros, Marriott's Great America, 1989, Bugs, Porky, Sylvester, Taz, ea from $7 to **$10.00**

Warner Bros, Pepsi, 1973, Brockway 12-oz tumbler, Bugs, Porky, Roadrunner, Sylvester, Tweety, ea from $5 to **$10.00**

Warner Bros, Pepsi, 1973, Federal 16-oz tumbler, Bugs Bunny, wht lettering, from $5 to..**$10.00**

Warner Bros, Pepsi, 1973, Federal 16-oz tumbler, Cool Cat, blk lettering, from $5 to...**$10.00**

Warner Bros, Pepsi, 1973, Federal 16-oz tumbler, Elmer Fudd, wht lettering, from $5 to...**$8.00**

Warner Bros, Pepsi, 1973, Federal 16-oz tumbler, Henry Hawk, blk lettering, from $25 to...**$40.00**

Warner Bros, Pepsi, 1973, Federal 16-oz tumbler, Speedy Gonzales, blk lettering, from $6 to **$10.00**

Warner Bros, Pepsi, 1973, wht plastic, 6 different, Bugs, Daffy, Porky, Roadrunner, Sylvester, Tweety, ea from $3 to ...**$5.00**

Warner Bros, Pepsi, 1976, Interaction, Beaky Buzzard & Cool Cat w/kite or Taz & Porky w/fishing pole, ea from $8 to **$10.00**

Warner Bros, Pepsi, 1976, Interaction, Bugs & Yosemite w/cannon, Yosemite & Speedy Gonzales panning gold, ea $10 to..**$15.00**

Warner Bros, Pepsi, 1976, Interaction, Foghorn Leghorn & Henry Hawk, from $10 to...**$15.00**

Warner Bros, Pepsi, 1976, Interaction, others, ea from $5 to .**$10.00**

Warner Bros, Pepsi, 1979, Collector Series, rnd bottom, Bugs, Daffy, Porky, Roadrunner, Sylvester, Tweety, ea $7 to..**$10.00**

Warner Bros, Pepsi, 1980, Collector Series, Bugs, Daffy, Porky, Roadrunner heads on star, names on band, ea from $6 to..........**$10.00**

Warner Bros, Six Flags, 1991, clear, Bugs, Daffy, Sylvester, Wile E Coyote, ea from $5 to **$10.00**

Warner Bros, Six Flags, 1991, clear, Yosemite Sam, from $10 to .**$15.00**

Warner Bros, Welch's, 1974, action poses, 8 different, phrases around top, ea from $2 to...**$4.00**

Warner Bros, Welch's, 1976-77, 8 different, names around bottom, ea from $5 to..**$7.00**

Warner Bros, 1995, Taz's Root Beer/Serious Suds, clear glass mug, from $5 to...**$7.00**

Warner Bros, 1996, 8 different w/ea character against busy background of repeated characters, names below, ea from $4 to..**$6.00**

Warner Bros, 1998, 6 different w/characters against vertically striped background, ea from $4 to **$6.00**

WC Fields, see Arby's Actor Series

Western Heroes, Annie Oakley, Buffalo Bill, Wild Bill Hickok, Wyatt Earp, ea from $8 to..**$12.00**

Western Heroes, Lone Ranger, from $10 to **$15.00**

Western Heroes, Wyatt Earp, fight scene or OK Corral gunfight, name at top, from $12 to $22.00
Wild West Series, Coca-Cola, Buffalo Bill, Calamity Jane, ea from $10 to..$15.00
Wile E Coyote, see Warner Bros
Winnie the Pooh, Sears/WDP, 1970s, 4 different, ea from $7 to .$10.00
Wizard of Oz, Coca-Cola/Krystal, 1989, 50th Anniversary Series, 6 different, ea from $7 to...............................$10.00
Wizard of Oz, Swift's, 1950s-60s, fluted bottom, Emerald City or Flying Monkeys, ea from $8 to $15.00
Wizard of Oz, Swift's, 1950s-60s, fluted bottom, Glinda, from $15 to $25.00
Wizard of Oz, Swift's, 1950s-60s, fluted bottom, Wicked Witch, from $35 to...$50.00
Wizard of Oz, see also Children's Classics
Wonder Woman, see Super Heroes
Wonderful World of Disney, Pepsi, 1980s, Alice, Bambi, Lady & the Tramp, Pinocchio, Snow White, 101 Dalmatians, $15 to .$20.00
Woody Woodpecker & Related Characters, see Arby's Bicentennial or Walter Lantz
Yogi Bear, see Hanna-Barbera
Yosemite Sam, see Warner Bros
Ziggy, Number Series, 1-8, ea from $4 to..............................$8.00
Ziggy, 7-Up Collector Series, 1977, Here's to Good Friends, 4 different, ea from $3 to $5.00

Character Bobbin' Heads

Frequently referred to as nodders, these papier-mache dolls reflect accurate likenesses of the characters they portray and have become popular collectibles. Made in Japan throughout the 1960s, they were sold as souvenirs at Disney, Universal Studios, and Six Flags amusement parks, and they were often available at roadside concessions as well. Papier-mache was was used until the mid-'70s when ceramic composition came into use. They were very susceptible to cracking and breaking, and it's difficult to find mint specimens — little wonder, since these nodders were commonly displayed on car dashboards!

Our values are for nodders in near-mint condition. To calculate values for examples in very good condition, reduce our prices by 25% to 40%.

Advisors: Matt and Lisa Adams (A7)

Andy Griffith, 1992, ceramic, NM, J6 ....$75.00
Barney Fife, 1992, ceramic, NM, J6....................................$75.00
Beetle Bailey, NM, A7, from $150 to...............................$175.00
Bugs Bunny, NM, A7, from $175 to..................................$200.00
Charlie Brown, Japan, ceramic w/gr baseball cap & mitt, NM, A7 ....$50.00
Charlie Brown, sq blk base, NM.......................................$125.00
China Man, Japan, 1960s, compo, NM, J6......................$65.00
Chinese Boy & Girl, 5½", NM, pr $65.00
Colonel Sanders, 2 different styles, NM, A7, ea from $125 to.$150.00
Dagwood, 1950s, compo, Kiss Me on gr rnd base, 6", EX, from $150 to...$200.00
Danny Kaye & Girl, kissing, NM, A7, pr, from $150 to.$200.00

Charlie Brown, Snoopy as Flying Ace, Snoopy as Santa, and Woodstock, 1970s, NM, each $45.00.

Dobie Gillis, NM, A7, from $300 to $400.00
Donald Duck, Walt Disney World, sq wht base, NM, A7..$75.00

Donald Duck, Irwin/WDP, 5", EX, $100.00.

Donald Duck, 1970s, rnd gr base, NM, A7 ....$75.00
Donny Osmond, wht jumpsuit w/microphone, NM, A7, from $100 to..$150.00
Dr Ben Casey, NM, A7, from $125 to $175.00
Dr Kildare, A7, from $125 to $175.00
Dr Kildare, 1960s, compo, rnd wht base, 7", EX, from $100 to..$150.00
Dumbo, rnd red base, NM, A7 ....$100.00
Elmer Fudd, NM, A7, from $175 to $200.00
Foghorn Leghorn, NM, A7, from $175 to.......................$200.00
Goofy, Disneyland, arms at side, sq wht base, NM, A7.....$75.00
Goofy, Walt Disney World, arms folded, sq wht base, NM, A7 .$75.00
Hobo, Japan, 1960s, compo, NM, J6 ....$65.00
Linus, Japan, ceramic, baseball catcher w/gr cap, NM, A7 .$60.00
Linus, Lego, sq blk base, NM, A7, from $100 to............$125.00
Linus (Peanuts), Lego, sq blk base, NM, from $100 to ...$125.00
Linus (Peanuts), Lego/UFS, 1960s, 5½", EX, from $75 to .$100.00
Little Audrey, NM, A7, from $100 to $150.00
Lt Fuzz (Beetle Bailey), NM, A7, from $150 to $175.00
Lucy (Peanuts), Japan, ceramic, gr baseball cap & bat, NM, A7.$50.00
Lucy (Peanuts), Lego, sq blk base, NM, A7, from $100 to.$125.00
Lucy (Peanuts), 1970s, no base, sm, NM, A7 ....$45.00
Mammy (Dogpatch USA), NM, A7 ....$75.00
Mary Poppins, Disneyland, 1960s, wood, w/umbrella & satchel, 5¾", M, from $100 to..$150.00
Maynard Krebs (Dobie Gillis), holds bongos, NM, A7, from $300 to...$400.00

Mickey Mouse, celluloid figure in red shorts on bl tin base, Japan, 7", EX, A..$825.00

Mickey Mouse, Disneyland, red, wht & bl outfit, sq wht base, NM, A7, from $75 to...$100.00

Mickey Mouse, Walt Disney World, bl & shirt & red pants, NM, A7 ....$75.00

Mickey Mouse, yel shirt & red pants, rnd gr base, NM, A7 .$75.00

Mr Peanut, moves at waist, w/cane, NM, A7, from $150 to.$200.00

NY World's Fair Boy & Girl, kissing, NM, A7, from $100 to.$125.00

Oodles the Duck (Bozo the Clown), NM, A7, from $150 to..$200.00

Pappy (Dogpatch USA), NM, A7......................................$75.00

Peppermint Patti, Japan, ceramic, gr baseball cap & bat, NM, A7 ....$50.00

Phantom of the Opera, sq base, rare, NM, A7, from $500 to..$750.00

Phantom of the Opera, Universal Studios of California, gr face, NM, A7, from $150 to..$200.00

Pig Pen, Lego/Japan, 1960s, 6", NM, from $100.00 to $125.00. (Photo courtesy June Moon)

Pluto, 1970s, rnd gr base, NM, A7 ....$75.00

Porky Pig, NM, A7, from $175 to $200.00

Raggedy Andy, bank, mk A Penny Earned, NM, A7........$75.00

Raggedy Ann, bank, mk A Penny Saved, NM, A7...........$75.00

Roy Rogers, Japan, 1962, compo, sq gr base, 6½", M, from $150 to...$200.00

Schroeder (Peanuts), Lego, sq blk base, NM, from $100 to..$125.00

Sgt Snorkel (Beetle Bailey), NM, A7, from $150 to $175.00

Smokey the Bear, w/shovel, rnd base, NM, A7, from $125 to .$200.00

Smokey the Bear, w/shovel, sq base, NM, A7, from $125 to .$200.00

Snoopy, as Joe Cool, 1970s, no base, sm, NM, A7............$45.00

Snoopy, Japan, ceramic, gr baseball cap & mitt, NM, A7..$50.00

Snoopy, Lego, sq blk base, lg, NM, A7, from $100 to.....$125.00

Space Boy, blk space suit & helmet, NM, A7 ....$75.00

Speedy Gonzales, NM, A7, from $175 to.........................$200.00

Three Little Pigs, bl overalls & yel cap, rnd red base, NM, A7, ea, from $100 to...$125.00

Three Stooges, bsk, set of 3, MIB, A7, from $100 to......$150.00

Topo Gigio, Rossini/Japan, 1960s, 9", EX.........................$55.00

Topo Gigio, standing w/apple, orange or pineapple, NM, A7, ea.$75.00

Topo Gigio, standing w/out fruit, NM, A7......................$75.00

Tweety Bird, NM, A7, from $175 to $200.00

Wile E Coyote, NM, A7, from $175 to...........................$200.00

Winnie the Pooh, 1970s, rnd gr base, NM, A7, from $100 to .$150.00

Wolfman, sq base, rare, NM, A7, from $500 to $750.00

Woodstock, Japan, ceramic, w/bat, NM, A7....................$50.00

Woodstock, 1970s, no base, sm, NM, A7.........................$45.00

Yosemite Sam, NM, A7, from $175 to $200.00

Zero (Beetle Bailey), NM, A7, from $150 to $175.00

Character Clocks and Watches

Clocks and watches whose dials depict favorite sports and TV stars have been manufactured with the kids in mind since the 1930s, when Ingersoll made a clock, a wristwatch, and a pocket watch featuring Mickey Mouse. The #1 Mickey wristwatch came in the now-famous orange box commonly known as the 'critter box,' illustrated with a variety of Disney characters. There is also a blue display box from the same time period. The watch itself featured a second hand with three revolving Mickey figures. It was available with either a metal or leather band. Babe Ruth stared on an Exacta Time watch in 1949, and the original box contained not only the watch but a baseball with a facsimile signature.

Collectors prize the boxes about as highly as they do the watches. Many were well illustrated and colorful, but most were promptly thrown away, so they're hard to find today. Be sure you buy only watches in very good condition. Rust, fading, scratches, or other signs of wear sharply devaluate a clock or a watch. Hundreds have been produced, and if you're going to collect them, you'll need to study *Comic Character Clocks and Watches* by Howard S. Brenner (Books Americana) for more information.

Note: Our values are typical of high retail. A watch in exceptional condition, especially an earlier model, may bring even more. Dealers (who will generally pay about half of book when they buy for resale) many times offer discounts on the more pricey items, and package deals involving more than one watch may sometimes be made for as much as a 15% discount.

Advisor: Bill Campbell (C10)

CLOCKS

Bambi Wall Clock, 1970s, yel plastic w/image of Bambi & friends in forest, battery-op, 11x11", NM....................$65.00

Batman & Robin Talking Alarm Clock, Janex, 1974, 3-D image of Batman running behind car at side of clock, EXIB.....$100.00

Beatles Yellow Submarine Alarm Clock, Sheffield, red & yel, EX, A $1,800.00

Bugs Bunny Alarm Clock, Ingraham, Bugs lying down w/carrot, 4x4", EX, from $150 to...$200.00

Bugs Bunny Wall Clock, Seth Thomas, 1970, plastic case, image of Bugs w/carrot, electric, 10" dia, NM $85.00

Cinderella Alarm Clock, Bradley/Japan, image of Cinderella leaving slipper on steps, 3" dia, scarce, MIB $125.00

David Cassidy Wall Clock, 1972, NM $100.00

Davy Crockett Time Pendulum Clock, pressed wood w/image of Davy, lg blk numbers, 7½" dia, EXIB, A................$100.00

Felix the Cat, Bright Ideas, 1989, MIB, C10....................$65.00

Howdy Doody Talking Alarm Clock, Janex, plastic, 7" long, EXIB, $150.00. (Photo courtesy Randy Inman Auctions)

Mickey Mouse & Donald Duck Alarm Clock, Hamilton, plastic & metal, 2 figures hit bell w/hammer, 3-ftd, 7x5", VG, A .$80.00
Mickey Mouse Alarm Clock, Bayard, rnd red metal case, Mickey w/moving head & arms as clock hands, chrome trim, 5", EX..........$100.00
Mickey Mouse Alarm Clock, Ingersoll, Mickey w/tin head & moving arms, gr rnd case & base, chrome trim, 4½", EX....$300.00
Mickey Mouse Alarm Clock, Ingersoll, 1948, Mickey w/illuminating arms on rnd face, plastic dome case, 4½", NMIB, A.....$350.00
Mickey Mouse Talking Alarm Clock, plastic, clock face is front of train engine w/Mickey as engineer, 9", G+, A.......$50.00
Mickey Mouse Wall Clock, Hamilton, 1970s, 10" dia, EX .$75.00
Peanuts Alarm Clock, Japan, 1988, character faces as numbers, silver metal case, 3½" dia, MIB..................$60.00
Pluto Wall Clock, Allied, plastic figure w/clock attached to his chest, hands shaped as dog bones, 8", EXIB.............$300.00

Roy Rogers and Trigger Alarm Clock, Ingraham, desert mountain scene on face, 4½", MIB, A, $600.00. (Photo courtesy Smith House Toys)

Roy Rogers & Trigger Alarm Clock, Ingraham, desert mountain scene, 4½" sq, VG+, A..............................$280.00
Santa Alarm Clock, Bayard, numbered ornaments surround standing Santa figure, 4¾" dia, M, A.........................$85.00
Shmoo Pendulette Alarm Clock, Lux, 1950, plastic figure, 8", EXIB...$275.00
Snoopy & Charlie Brown Talking Alarm Clock, Janex, 1974, 2-D image of Snoopy & Charlie beside clock, plastic, MIB.$135.00

Snoopy Analog Clock, Armitron, 1989, plush figure w/clock in stomach, 9", MIB..............................$35.00
Tweety Bird Talking Alarm Clock, Janex, 1978, battery-op, EX .$75.00
Underdog Alarm Clock, Germany, 1970s, Underdog's hands keep time, yel plastic octagonal case, 3", NM..........$200.00

POCKET WATCHES

Big Bad Wolf, Ingersoll, 1934, EX, C10 ....$950.00
Captain Marvel, Fawcett, 1948, full figure, rnd chrome case, gr plastic strap, EXIB $750.00
Donald Duck, decal on back, EXIB, C10 ....$950.00
Donald Duck, Ingersoll, Donald w/hands on hips, Mickey emb on back, rnd chrome case, G, A..............................$275.00
Hopalong Cassidy, unmk, 1950s, blk dial w/wht numbers surrounding bust image of Hoppy, chrome case, 2" dia, EX..$150.00
Lone Ranger, 1970, Lone Ranger & Silver on face, bl strap, silver chain, NM $100.00
Mary Marvel, Fawcett, 1948, full figure, rnd chrome case, red plastic strap, VG, A $125.00
Mickey Mouse, Bradley, 1970s, red plastic, 2" dia, EX......$50.00

Mickey Mouse, Ingersoll, circa 1935, rare design, NMIB, from $1,100.00 to $1,500.00.

Roy Rogers, Bradley, lg image of Roy w/sm image of Roy & Trigger in background, w/stopwatch feature, EX............$600.00
Superman, New Haven, 3-quarter figure, rectangular chrome case, w/stopwatch feature, EX, A $600.00
Tom Mix, Ingersoll, 1930s, Tom on rearing horse, emb phrase on back, rnd chrome case, EX $3,500.00
Woody (Toy Story), Fossil, 1996, limited edition, M (M box & container) $125.00

WRISTWATCHES

Alice in Wonderland, Ingersoll, image of Alice, fabric strap, EX (EX rnd pk box w/clear plastic teacup), from $250 to.$350.00
Alice in Wonderland, Timex, 1950s, name on rnd face, w/ceramic figure, MIB, A $300.00
Angelique (Dark Shadows), Abbelare, MIB (coffin), C10 .$100.00
Bambi, Ingersoll/US Time, 1949, Birthday Series, rare, NMIB, A..$450.00
Barnabas Collins (Dark Shadows), Abbelare, MIB (coffin), C10.$100.00
Batman, Fossil, 1990, limited edition, complete w/pin, M (M litho tin box), from $150 to $200.00

Batman, 1966, batwings keep time on rnd face encased in blk plastic wings, NMIB $850.00

Bionic Woman, MZ Berger, 1970s, image & lettering on face, vinyl band, NM, from $60 to.....................................$80.00

Blondie & Dagwood, rare, C10 ....$450.00

Bongo, Ingersoll-US Time/WDP, Birthday Series, EXIB, A.$320.00

Bozo the Clown, 1960s, image w/name in red, vinyl band, EX.$50.00

Buffy & Jody, Sheffield, 1969, image & names on face, visible gears, various bands, M, ea $125.00

Buzz Lightyear (Toy Story), Fossil, 1996, complete w/Buzz Lightyear plaque, M (M rnd tin box), M8 ....$75.00

Captain Marvel, Fawcett, 1948, EXIB, $700.00. (Photo courtesy James D. Julia, Inc.)

Charlie Chaplin, Bradley, 1985, Oldies Series, MIB, C10 .$50.00

Cinderella, Timex, 1950s, image on face, w/plastic figure, MIB, A $225.00

Cool Cat, Sheffield, 1960s, full-figure image, VG.............$50.00

Daisy Duck, Ingersoll-US Time/WDP, Birthday Series, EXIB, A..$350.00

Dale Evans, Bradley, 1950s, MIB, $450.00. (Photo courtesy Smith House Toys)

Davy Crockett, WD, 1950s, Davy's image on face, leather strap, w/powder horn, M (EX+ box featuring Fess Parker), A .$400.00

Dick Tracy, New Haven, 1948, Tracy on face, Tracy & Jr on box, NM+IB, A $725.00

Dizzy Dean, Everbrite-Ingersoll, 1933, scarce, M, C10.$1,100.00

Donald Duck, 1947, all orig, EX (EX+ box w/laser insert), C10.$550.00

Dopey, Ingersoll-US Time/WDP, Birthday Series, EXIB, A .$250.00

Dr Seuss' Cat in the Hat, 1972, NM $150.00

Dracula, Fossil, 1990s, w/figure, MIB, C10 ....$265.00

Dukes of Hazzard, 1981, MIB (illus), N2..........................$20.00

Evel Knievel, Bradley, 1976, vinyl band, EX, A..............$150.00

Flipper, ITF/MGM, glow-in-the-dark image, M..............$125.00

Frankenstein (Universal Monsters), 1995, glow-in-the-dark, MOC, C10..$25.00

Gene Autry, New Haven, 1951, Six Shooter, brn leather band, unused, MIB, A $650.00

Gene Autry, Wilane, 1948, Champion, NMIB...............$400.00

Girl From UNCLE, 1960s, pk face w/blk line drawing & numbers, EX $65.00

Green Lantern, MIB, C10 ....$85.00

Hopalong Cassidy, Bradley, 1980s, Oldies Series, M.........$60.00

Hopalong Cassidy, US Time, 1950s, MIB (with saddle display), $500.00. (Photo courtesy James D. Julia, Inc.)

Howdy Doody, Patent Watch Co/Bob Smith, movable eyes, EX (VG box), A $340.00

Joe Carioca, Ingersoll-US Time/WDP, Birthday Series, EXIB .$400.00

Johnny Mack Brown, MIB, C10.......................................$50.00

Josie & the Pussycats, Bradley, 1971, complete w/3 bands, MIB..$350.00

Kaptain Kool & the Kongs, 1977, Kaptain Kool on face, M .$100.00

Lash LaRue, MIB, C10 ....$50.00

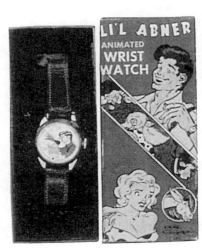

Li'l Abner Animated, New Haven, 1947, rare, MIB, from $600.00 to $800.00.

(Photo courtesy Smith House Toys)

Little Orphan Annie, New Haven, 1948, Orphan Annie Watch w/Annie on rnd face, brn leather band, MIB, A $450.00

Man From UNCLE, Bradley, 1960s, very rare w/box, MIB, C10.$200.00

Mickey Mouse, Bradley, 1977, 50th Birthday, MIP.........$125.00

Mickey Mouse, Ingersoll, 1933, MIB $1,200.00

Mickey Mouse, Ingersoll-US Time, 1947, NM (EX box) .$350.00

Mickey Mouse, Kelton, MIB, C10 ....$700.00

Mickey Mouse, Timex, 1950s, w/plastic figure, MIB, A .$350.00

Minnie Mouse, Timex, 1950s, Minnie on rnd face, w/emb celluloid plaque, MIB, A $300.00

Partridge Family, 1970s, family image on face, NM, from $150 to..$200.00

Pocahontas, Time Works/Disney, 1990s, leather strap, unused, MIB, M8...$75.00

Popeye, New Haven/King Features, 1930s, EXIB, $1,250.00. (Photo courtesy James D. Julia, Inc.)

Popeye, unknown maker, ca 1948, Popeye, Wimpy, Olive Oyl & Swee' Pea on rnd face, 1¼" dia, rare, EXIB, A $575.00

Porky Pig, Ingraham, 1950s, MIB, C10.....................$600.00

Rocky Jones Space Ranger, Ingraham, 1950s, MIB, C10.$750.00

Roy Rogers, Bradley, 1950s, Roy & Trigger on rnd face, brn leather band, MIB, A $400.00

Roy Rogers, metal bracelet band, MIB, C10..................$450.00

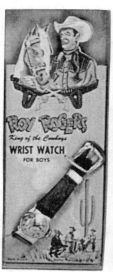

Roy Rogers and Dale Evans, Bradley, 1950s, MIB, each $400.00. (Photo courtesy Smith House Toys)

Smitty, New Haven, 1930s, rectangular face, leather band, VG (VG+ box), A...$430.00

Smokey Bear, Hamilton, 1960s, MIB...........................$150.00

Snoopy, Determined, 1969, dancing Snoopy, gold or silver case, various bands, EX $100.00

Snoopy, Lafayette Watch, 1970s, dancing Snoopy w/Woodstock as second hand, silver case, EX............................$115.00

Superman, Bradley-Ingraham, 1958, NM, from $250 to..$400.00

Superman, Dabbs, NM, C10 ....$100.00

Superman, 1939, all orig, lg sz, NM...........................$450.00

Tarzan, Bradley, MIB, C10...$60.00

Three Little Pigs & the Big Bad Wolf, Ingersoll, 1934, MIB, C10 ....$3,000.00

Tim Holt, MIB, C10 ....$50.00

Tom Corbett Space Patrol, all orig, EX+.....................$350.00

Tom Mix, 1983, 100th Anniversary, EX, C10 ....$200.00

Tom Mix, 1983, 100th Anniversary, M, C10.................$275.00

Wonder Woman, Dabbs, NM, C10..............................$125.00

Woody (Toy Story), Fossil, 1996, complete w/Woody plaque, unused, M (M rnd tin box), M8 ....$75.00

X-Files, Fossil, 2000, M (M see-through cylinder box), C10.$75.00

Zorro, US Time/WDP, 1950s, blk face w/Zorro in red, blk band, EX+ $125.00

Zorro, US Time/WDP, 1957, blk face w/Zorro in red, blk band, unused, NM+ (EX+ hat box), A $350.00

ADVERTISING CHARACTER WATCHES

Big Boy, 1970, MIB...$50.00

Buster Brown, 1970s, red costume, VG, I1........................$75.00

Campbell Kids, 1982, 4 different, MIB, I1, ea..................$35.00

Campbell's Vegetable Soup, 1994, Campbell Kids, M, I1 .$50.00

Charlie Tuna, Star-Kist, 1971 & 1972 versions, MIB, ea..$40.00

Charlie Tuna, Star-Kist, 1986, 25th Anniversary, MIB, I1 .$15.00

Count Chocula, Booberry & Frankenberry, Lafayette Watch Co, MIB, I1...$300.00

Ernie the Keebler Elf, 1970s, photo image, lt bl band, M...$30.00

Goofy Grape, Kool-Aid, 1976, G, I1 ....$200.00

Mr Peanut, Planters, 1966, yel face, VG, I1 ....$50.00

Mr Peanut, Planters, 1967, yel face w/date window, VG, I1..$50.00

Mr Peanut, Planters, 1975, bl face, digital, EX, I1 ....$50.00

Punchy, Hawaiian Punch, 1970s, digital, red strap, VG, I1..$25.00

Raid Bug, 1970s, revolving disk, EX.............................$75.00

Red Goose Shoes, 1960s, G, I1 ....$130.00

Ronald McDonald, McDonald's, 1970s, MIB, I1 ....$25.00

Swiss Miss, 1981, EX, I1 ....$40.00

Tony the Tiger, Kellogg's, 1976, MIB $75.00

Toppie Elephant, 1950s, G, I1 ....$100.00

Twinkie the Brown Shoe Elf, 1920s, G $100.00

Character, TV, and Movie Collectibles

To the baby boomers who grew up glued to the TV set and addicted to Saturday matinees, the faces they saw on the screen were as familiar to them as family. Just about any character you could name has been promoted through retail merchandising to some extent; depending on the popularity they attain, exposure may continue for weeks, months, even years. It's no wonder, then, that the secondary market abounds with these items or that there is such wide-spread collector interest. For more information, we recommend *Collector's Guide to TV Toys and Memorabilia, 1960s & 1970s, 2nd Edition*, by Greg Davis and Bill Morgan; *The World of Raggedy Ann Collectibles* by Kim Avery; *Peanuts Collectibles, Identification and Value Guide*, by Andrea Podley with Derrick Bang.

Note: Though most characters are listed by their own names, some will be found under the title of the group, movie, comic strip, or dominate character they're commonly identified with. The Joker, for instance, will be found in the Batman listings.

All items are complete unless noted otherwise.

Advisors: Lisa Adams, Dr. Dolittle; Trina and Randy Kubeck, The Simpsons

See also Action Figures; Battery-Operated; Books; Chein; Character Clocks and Watches; Coloring, Activity, and Paint Books; Dakin; Disney; Dolls, Celebrity; Fisher-Price; Games; Guns; Halloween Costumes; Lunch Boxes; Marx; Model Kits; Paper Dolls; Pin-Back Buttons; Plastic Figures; Playsets; Puppets; Puzzles; Ramp Walkers; Records; View-Master; Western; Windups, Friction, and Other Mechanicals.

A-Team, Signal Light, 1983, MOC..................................$35.00
Addams Family, bank, Lurch, ceramic, Korea, 1970s, 8", NM.$200.00
Addams Family, doll, Morticia, stuffed cloth, 27", NM $50.00
Addams Family, figure, Morticia, hard plastic w/oversized rubber head, 4", 1964, NM $100.00
Addams Family, figure, Uncle Fester, standing w/frog in hand, plastic w/soft vinyl head, Remco, 1964, 4½", NM+ .$150.00
Alvin & the Chipmunks, bank, Alvin holding harmonica, vinyl, recent, NM..$30.00
Alvin & the Chipmunks, Curtain Call Theater, Ideal, 1984, MIB $50.00
Alvin & the Chipmunks, doll, Alvin, plush, talker, 1983, 22", EX..$25.00
Alvin & the Chipmunks, doll, Alvin, Simon, or Theodore, plush w/vinyl face, Knickerbocker, 1963, 14", NM, ea $50.00
Alvin & the Chipmunks, Stuff & Lace Set, Hasbro, 1950s-60s, NMIB..$75.00
Amos 'N Andy, figure set, jtd wood, Jaymar, 1930s, 6", NM .$300.00

Amos 'N Andy, Amos sparkler, diecut lithographed tin head with cigar in mouth, glass eyes, Germany, 4", NM, A, $420.00.

Andy Panda, bank, pnt compo, name emb on chest, Crown Toy/WLP, 1939, 5", EX...$100.00

Annie (Movie), doll, Annie, Knickerbocker, 6", MIB......$45.00
Annie (Movie), doll, any character except Annie, Knickerbocker, 1982, 7", MIB, ea $35.00
Archies, doll, Archie, stuffed cloth, 1960s, 18", MIP $75.00
Archies, stencil set, 1983, MOC...................................$18.00
Aristocats, Colorforms, 1960s, MIB, N2 ....$50.00
Atom Ant, Play Fun Set, Whitman, 1966, NMIB............$50.00
Baba Looey, see Hanna-Barbera
Banana Splits, guitar, Snorky Elephant, 1960s, 10", EX, N2 .$25.00
Banana Splits, Kut-Up Kit, Larami, 1973, MOC (sealed) .$20.00
Banana Splits, tambourine, plastic & cb, 1973, MIP........$35.00
Barney Google & Spark Plug, figure, Spark Plug, stuffed cloth w/blanket mk Sparky, 10", VG+ $225.00
Barney Google & Spark Plug, figures, both, wood w/pnt features, jtd, cloth clothes, Schoenhut, 7½", VG+, A, pr $715.00

Barney Google and Spark Plug, pull toy, lithographed tin, Nifty/KFS, 1920s, 8", VG, A, $1,700.00. (Photo courtesy Smith House Toys)

Barney Google & Spark Plug, pull toy, Spark Plug, stenciled wood figure on 4 wheels, mk Spark Plug on blanket, 5", VG .$50.00
Barney Google & Spark Plug, pull toy, Spark Plug Wa-Gee Walker, stuffed cloth w/orig blanket mk Spark Plug, 9", EX+ ...$550.00
Batman, bank, waist-length figure w/arms crossed, EX $50.00
Batman, coin set, Transogram, 1966, MIP (sealed)...........$35.00
Batman, Color Pin-Ups, litho cb, various images, 1966, 11x14", NMIB, ea $25.00
Batman, Colorforms Cartoon Kit, 1966, EXIB $40.00
Batman, doll, cloth costume, Toy & Novelty Co, 1966, 16", NM..$175.00

Batman, Give-A-Show Bat Projector, complete, Chad Valley/NPPI, 1966, NMIB, A, $580.00. (Photo courtesy New England Auction Gallery)

Batman, doll, Flying Batman, Transogram, 1966, 13", MIP (sealed) $175.00

Batman, doll, vinyl w/movable arms, Japan, 1960s, 14", EX+..$150.00

Batman, flicker ring, Batman/Captain Action, 1960s, chrome band, NM...$25.00

Batman, helmet & cape, plastic & vinyl, Ideal, 1966, EX+IB, A..$400.00

Batman, lantern, figural, Ahi, 1977, scarce, EX $50.00

Batman, makeup kit, Joker, 1989, MIP.............................$15.00

Batman, Paint-By-Number Set, Hasbro, 1973, NMIB......$30.00

Batman, pencil box, gun shape, 1966, unused, MOC.....$175.00

Batman, playset, Super Batman, Tonka, 1990, MIB $50.00

Batman, playsuit, Ben Cooper, 1974, NMIB....................$50.00

Batman, playsuit, Playset, Ben Cooper, 1965 (pre-TV show), MIB (sealed) $100.00

Batman, Print Putty, 1966, MOC....................................$35.00

Batman, Sparkle Paints, Kenner, 1966, EXIB $75.00

Batman, Stamp & Print Set, AHI, 1966, MOC $100.00

Batman, water gun, lg head, G $30.00

Batman & Robin, Cartoon-A-Rama...Cartoon Paint Set, 1977, MIB $50.00

Batman & Robin, pennant, name & artwork on felt, 1966, 24", NM..$25.00

Batman & Robin, Sip-A-Drink Cup, plastic, w/built-in straw, NPP, 1966, 5", EX+...$30.00

Batman Returns (Movie), bank, vinyl, 1991, 9", EX, N2 .$10.00

Battlestar Galactica, Cruiser, diecast metal, Larami, 1978, 3¼", MOC (unpunched)..$30.00

Beanie & Cecil, bank, Cecil's head, molded plastic, NM .$35.00

Beanie & Cecil, doll, Beanie, stuffed cloth w/vinyl head, cloth outfit, Bob Clampett, ca 1960, NM $200.00

Beany & Cecil, Beany-Copter, Mattel, 1961, NMOC......$75.00

Beany & Cecil, carrying case, rnd vinyl case w/strap, mc image, 1960s, EX $50.00

Beany & Cecil, doll, plush, talker, Mattel, 1961, EXIB, A..$215.00

Beany & Cecil, jack-in-the-box, Mattel, 1961, M..........$250.00

Beany & Cecil, record player, Vanity Fair, 1961, EX+....$125.00

Beauregard Hound, figure, vinyl, 1969, 5", EX, N2..........$15.00

Ben Casey, doctor kit, Transogram, EX $35.00

Ben Casey, Paint-By-Number Set, Transogram, 1962, MIB (sealed) $125.00

Betty Boop, Colorforms Big Dress-Up Set, 1970s, MIB...$45.00

Betty Boop, doll, Ko-Ko the Clown, plush w/rubber head, cloth outfit, Presents, 1987, 12", NM......................$25.00

Betty Boop, figure, Betty, compo w/pnt features, molded hair, jtd, cloth dress, 12", G, A $550.00

Betty Boop, figure, Betty, wood, jtd, pnt red dress, USA, 1931, 4½", VG+ $125.00

Betty Boop, figure, Bimbo, bsk, playing fiddle, Japan, 1930s, 3½", NM $125.00

Betty Boop, figure, Bimbo, wood & compo, jtd, 7", EX, A .$330.00

Betty Boop, figure set, Betty, 5 pnt nesting figures, Russia, 1980s, M..$75.00

Betty Boop, Happy House, celluloid, Occupied Japan, EX .$1,150.00

Betty Boop, quilt, printed cloth w/image of Betty on center panel, mk Fleisher Studios, 1925, 17x13", EX, A $125.00

Betty Boop, tambourine, litho tin, 1930s, 6" dia, EX......$150.00

Beverly Hillbillies, BH Car, plastic w/up w/figures & accessories, Ideal, 1963, 22½", nonworking o/w EXIB, A $500.00

Beverly Hillbillies, Colorforms w/foyer scene, 1963, NMIB .$100.00

Beverly Hillbillies, doll, Ellie May, complete w/wardrobe, Unique Art, 1964, 12", MIB $200.00

Beverly Hillbillies, doll, Jane Hathaway, gr skirt & jacket w/yel blouse, Japan, 1969, 11½", MIB..............................$400.00

Beverly Hills 90210, dolls, any character, Mattel, 1991, 11½", MIB, ea...$50.00

Bewitched, doll, Samantha, red gown & hat, Ideal, 1965, 11½", M...$300.00

Bimbo, see Betty Boop

Bionic Woman, Give-A-Show Projector, Kenner, 1977, MIB..$25.00

Bionic Woman, Paint-By-Number Set, Craftmaster, 1976, MIB..$30.00

Bionic Woman, Play Doh Action Playset, Kenner, 1977, MIB $20.00

Bionic Woman, See-A-Show Viewer, Kenner, 1976, MOC .$15.00

Bionic Woman, Styling Boutique, Kenner, 1977, MIB.....$50.00

Bionic Woman, wallet, pk or bl w/image, Faberge, 1976, MIP..$20.00

Blondie, dog, Daisy, stuffed plush, w/orig tag, 1985, EX, C10.$25.00

Blondie, wallet, EX+, C10..$25.00

Blossom (TV Show), dolls, any character, Tyco, 1993, 9", MIB $35.00

Blues Brothers, dolls, Elwood & Jake, blk cloth suits, hats & sunglasses, Fun 4 All, 1997, 26", MIB, set $200.00

Blues Brothers, dolls, Elwood & Jake, shiny blk suits, hats & sunglasses, w/accessories, Fun 4 All, 1997, 12", MIB, ea ...$30.00

Blues Brothers (2000), dolls, Elwood & Mack, blk cloth suits, hats & sunglasses, Toy Biz, 1997, 12½", MIB, ea.......$25.00

Boo-Boo, see Hanna-Barbera

Bozo the Clown, Decal Decorator Kit, Meyerscord/Capitol Records, 1950s, unused, EX+....................................$50.00

Bozo the Clown, mask, diecut paper litho, Capitol Records, 1950s, 10x13", scarce, VG+ $65.00

Bozo the Clown, puzzle blocks, litho on wood, 10 4-sided blocks w/Bozo's image, Capitol Records, 1950s, 6½x6½", EX .$50.00

Bozo the Clown, record player, Transogram, EX $65.00

Brady Bunch, banjo, Larami, 1973, 15", MIP...................$65.00

Brady Bunch, Brain Twisters, Larami, 1973, MOC...........$25.00

Brady Bunch, Fishin' Fun Set, Larami, 1973, MOC $30.00

Buck Rogers, Communications Outfit, Remco, EXIB, A .$250.00

Buck Rogers, crayon box, Buck Rogers Crayon Box/School Crayons, cb, American Pencil Co #019, 1930s, 5x2x½", EX........$125.00

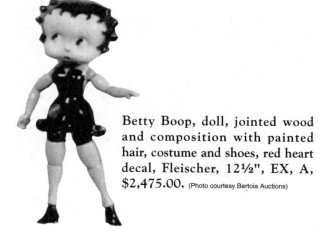

Betty Boop, doll, jointed wood and composition with painted hair, costume and shoes, red heart decal, Fleischer, 12½", EX, A, $2,475.00. (Photo courtesy Bertoia Auctions)

Buck Rogers, flicker ring, Buck Rogers/Captain Action, chrome band, 1960s, NM $20.00
Buck Rogers, gum wrapper, 1979, 5x6", VG+, N2 ....$10.00
Buck Rogers, outfit, gun & holster set, sleeveless shirt w/rnd studded emblem & suede-like leggings, VG, A $700.00
Buck Rogers, pencil box, litho on cb, American Lead Pencil Co, 1936, 5x8½", VG+ $75.00

Buck Rogers, roller skates, pressed steel, streamlined clampons, marked Buck Rogers, Marx, VG+, pair, $2,860.00. (Photo courtesy Bertoia Auctions)

Buck Rogers, Strato-Kite, Aero-Kite Co, 1946, EXIP $100.00
Buffy the Vampire Slayer (TV Show), dolls, any character, Diamond Select, 1999, MIB, ea $30.00
Bugs Bunny, see Looney Tunes
Bullwinkle, see Rocky & Friends
Buster Brown, mask, Froggie the Gremlin, diecut cb, Ed McConnell, 1946, 10x8", EX $75.00
Buster Brown, squeeze doll, Froggy the Gremlin, pnt soft rubber, Rempel, 1948, 10", VG+ $65.00
Buster Brown, see also Advertising category
Captain America, figure, porcelain, standing on wooden base, MIB $50.00
Captain America, Flashmite, Jane X, 1976, MOC $75.00
Captain Kangaroo, Colorforms, GIB.............................$20.00
Captain Kangaroo, doll, Captain Kangaroo, Mattel, 1967, MIB.$150.00
Captain Kangaroo, doll, Mr Green Jeans, stuffed cloth w/yel yarn hair, gr outfit w/red & wht plaid shirt, 1960s, 13", M ...$30.00
Captain Kangaroo, squeak toy, the Captain standing w/hands in pockets, vinyl, 1950s, 8", MIB..............................$65.00
Captain Kangaroo, TV Eras-O-Board Set, Hasbro, 1956, MIB.$30.00
Captain Planet, ring, Light & Sound, 1991, MOC, N2 ...$25.00
Charlie Chaplin, w/up toy, tin body w/felt tuxedo, litho tin head & derby hat, 6½", EXIB, A $770.00
Charlie McCarthy, figure, compo, 12", EX.....................$150.00
Charlie McCarthy, figure, wood, Fun-E-Flex, 1930s, 5½", NM+, A..$250.00
Charlie McCarthy, lapel pin, litho tin figure, England, 4¼", EX+, A..$140.00
Charlie McCarthy, valentine, mechanical, diecut cb image of Charlie in cowboy outfit w/movable mouth, 1930s, 5", NM ...$40.00
Charlie's Angels, wallet, vinyl w/circular image of stars, 1977, MOC...$35.00
Chilly Willie, film, Yukon Have It, 8mm, blk & wht, 1960s, NMIB...$15.00
Ching Chow, see Andy Gump
CHiPs, bicycle siren, 1977, EX, N2 ....$25.00
CHiPs, Colorforms Playset, 1981, unused, MIB...............$45.00

CHiPs, wallet, brn leather w/logo w/whip-stitched edge, Imperial, 1981, MOC (sealed) $20.00
CHiPs, Wind 'N Watch Speedster, Buddy L, 1981, MOC (sealed)...$25.00
Chitty-Chitty Bang-Bang, Automobile, plastic w/opening wings & inflatable raft, 4 figures, Mattel, 1960s, 5", NMIB.$135.00
Clueless, dolls, any character, Mattel, 1996, 11½", MIB, ea .$40.00
Crazy Green-Eyed Monster, figure set, ceramic, dinosaur w/2 cavemen, Kreiss & Co, 1950s, EX+ $75.00
Creature From the Black Lagoon, see Universal Monsters
Daffy Duck, see Looney Tunes
Dennis the Menace, lamp, pnt plaster figures of Dennis & his dog Ruff on drum-shaped base, Hall Syndicate, 1967, NM.$150.00
Dennis the Menace, Mischief Kit, Hasbro, 1955, NMIB..$50.00
Dennis the Menace, paint set, Pressman, 1950s, EXIB.....$50.00
Dennis the Menace, Tiddley Winks, Whitman, 1960s, EX+..$45.00
Dick Tracy, Colorforms Cartoon Kit, 1962, EXIB.............$75.00
Dick Tracy, figure set, Hingees, punch-out & fold-out figures w/movable limbs, diecut litho cb, 5 pcs, EX..............$60.00
Dick Tracy, Handcuffs for Junior, 1940s, NMOC.............$85.00
Dick Tracy, picture slide (7), 1962, EX, N2......................$10.00
Dick Tracy (Movie), Breathless Cosmetic Glamour Set, Cosrich, 1990, MIB $60.00
Dick Tracy (Movie), doll, Tracy, Applause, 1990s, 14", M..$45.00
Dick Tracy (Movie), dolls, any character, Applause, 1990s, 9", M, ea $30.00
Dick Tracy (Movie), dolls, Tracy or Breathless Mahoney, Playmate, 1990, 15", MIB, ea $85.00
Dick Tracy (Movie), pillow, cloth w/4 silkscreened corner images, Tracy & name in the middle, 1990, sq, M.....$30.00
Dick Tracy (Movie), wallet & coin purse set, Breathless Mahoney, red cloth w/head image & name, MIB $35.00
Don Winslow, magic slate & storybook, ...Breaking the Sound Barrier, series #1, Strathmore, 1953, EX....................$40.00
Dr Dolittle, Animal Fist Faces, EXIB $40.00
Dr Dolittle, bank, Dr Dolittle w/monkey & dog at feet, plastic, NM...$50.00
Dr Dolittle, Colorforms Cartoon Kit, 1967, NMIB $30.00
Dr Dolittle, doll, Dr Dolittle, talker, Mattel, 1969, 24", NMIB.$150.00
Dr Dolittle, doll, Pushmi-Pullyu, talker, Mattel, 1967, NM .$125.00
Dr Dolittle, Stich-a-Story, Hasbro, NMIP........................$25.00
Dr Kildare, doll, plastic, 1960s, 11½", rare, MIB $450.00
Dr Seuss, barrettes, The 5000 Fingers of Dr T, pnt metal, Columbia Pictures/Cullen, 1952, NMOC, pr $100.00
Dr Seuss, doll, Gowdy the Dowdy Grackle, MIB, L4......$275.00
Dr Seuss, doll, Grinch, Coleco, 1980s, EX+.....................$75.00
Dr Seuss, doll, Horton, talker, Mattel, 1970, EX+ $125.00
Dr Seuss, Grow Chart, Cat in the Hat, 1977, MIP (sealed) .$20.00
Dr Seuss, jack-in-the-box, Cat in the Hat, Mattel, 1969, EX+ .$125.00
Dracula, doll, cloth outfit, Lincoln Toys, 1975, 8", NM.$375.00
Drew Carey Show, dolls, Drew or Mimi Bobeck, vinyl w/cloth outfits, Creation Entertainment, 1998, 12", MIB, ea.$35.00
Droop-A-Long Coyote, see Magilla Gorilla
Dudley Do-Right, see Rocky & Friends
Dukes of Hazzard, bank, General Lee car, plastic, 1981, 17", G, N2 ....$10.00
Dukes of Hazzard, car, General Lee, plastic, 1980, 10", VG+, N2 ....$25.00

Dukes of Hazzard, car case, vinyl w/cast photo, holds 24 cars, 1981, EX+, N2..$35.00

Dynasty (TV Series), dolls, Alexis Colby or Krystal Carrington, World Doll, 1985, 19", MIB, ea...........................$175.00

Elmer Fudd, see Looney Tunes

Family Affair, doll, Buffy w/ Mrs Beasley, talker, pk dress, shoes & socks, 1960s, 36", rare, MIB.............................$800.00

Family Affair, doll, Buffy w/Mrs Beasley, talker, Mattel, 1969, 10½", MIB..$150.00

Family Affair, makeup & hairstyling set, Buffy, Amsco, 1970s, EX..$50.00

Family Matters (TV Series), doll, Steve Urkle, talker, Hasbro, 1991, 18", MIB, $50.00.
(Photo courtesy David Spurgeon)

Fantastic Four, bubble gum wrapper, 1979, 1x1½", M, N2 .$10.00

Fat Albert, doll, vinyl w/cloth outfit, Remco, 1985, lg, NRFB..$50.00

Fat Albert, figure, vinyl, 1973, 3", VG, N2 ....$10.00

Felix the Cat, figure, stuffed plush w/removable track outfit, name & #7 on chest, 1980s-90s, 10", NM+ $10.00

Felix the Cat, figure, wood, Schoenhut, 4", VG+...........$125.00

Felix the Cat, figure, wood, Schoenhut, 8", EX $225.00

Felix the Cat, pencil box, School Companion, 1939, empty, EX .$75.00

Felix the Cat, Pencil Color-By-Number, Hasbro, MIP (sealed) .$75.00

Felix the Cat, pillow cover, image of Felix serenading lady friend on balcony, Vogue Needlecraft Co #199, 17x15", EX+.....$165.00

Felix the Cat, pull toy, litho tin, Felix & 2 mice on 4-wheeled platform, Nifty/Pat Sullivan, EX $450.00

Felix the Cat, pull toy, pnt wood, Felix in race car, Felix goes up & down, 12", VG+...$375.00

Felix the Cat, sparkler, litho tin, Felix's head w/eyes wide open & open smiling mouth, blk & wht, 5¼", VG, A $165.00

Flash Gordon, Road-Stars Spaceship, diecast metal, 1975, MOC .$30.00

Flash Gordon, Space Outfit, w/goggles, belt & wrist compass, Esquire Novelty, 1951, NMOC...............................$200.00

Flash Gordon, table cover, paper, 1978, 54x88", MIP.......$25.00

Flash Gordon, wrist compass, plastic w/3-D red, wht & bl head portrait, band features space images, FG Inc, 1950s, EX+ ...$65.00

Flintstones, bank, Fred standing next to safe, plastic, MIB.$35.00

Flintstones, bowl & plate, plastic w/Fred, Wilma & Pebbles on plate & Pebbles on bowl, Melmac, 1960s, NM.........$25.00

Flintstones, Colorforms, 1972, NMIB $30.00

Flintstones, doll, Barney, plastic w/movable arms, 1980, 6", EX, N2 ....$15.00

Flintstones, doll, Barney, plush w/vinyl head, fur suit, Knickerbocker, 1962, 11", NM..$60.00

Flintstones, doll, Barney, vinyl, Knickerbocker, 1960s, 10", EX+..$85.00

Flintstones, doll, Barney, vinyl, 1980, 6", EX, N2 ....$20.00

Flintstones, doll, Betty, vinyl, Knickerbocker, 1960s, 10", EX..$100.00

Flintstones, doll, Fred, plush w/vinyl head, fur suit, Knickerbocker, 1960s, 11", EX+......................................$55.00

Flintstones, doll, Fred, talker, Mattel, 1993, 15", MIB......$30.00

Flintstones, doll, Fred, vinyl, Knickerbocker, 1960s, 10", EX+..$75.00

Flintstones, doll, Fred, vinyl, Knickerbocker, 1960s, 15", EX+ ..$100.00

Flintstones, doll, Wilma, vinyl, Knickerbocker, 1960s, 10", EX..$100.00

Flintstones, Give-A-Show Projector, w/112 color slides, Kenner, 1964, NMIB..$100.00

Flintstones, Magic Movies, Embree, 1965, scarce, NMIB..$250.00

Flintstones, see also Hanna-Barbera

Flintstones, Tricky Trapeze, w/Fred figure, Kohner, 1960s, 5", NM..$30.00

Flintstones, wallet, vinyl w/image of Dino, Estelle, 1964, unused, NM+..$50.00

Flipper, magic slate, Lowe, 1960s, EX+ $25.00

Flying Nun, doll, Hasbro, 1967, 4½", rare, MIB.............$175.00

Flying Nun, doll, Hasbro, 1967, 12", rare, MIB, $350.00. (Photo courtesy New England Auction Gallery)

Foodini, birthday card, diecut paper, RC Cox, 1950, 6x5", EX+ $50.00

Foodini, chair, Foodini TV Director w/Foodini, Jolo & Pinhead, canvas on wood frame, RC Cox & Krimstock Bros, 1950s, EX.....$175.00

Frankenstein, see Universal Monsters

Froggie the Gremlin, see Buster Brown

Full House (TV Series), doll, Jesse, vinyl w/cloth outfit, red guitar, Tiger Toys, 1993, 12", MIB.................................$50.00

Full House (TV Series), doll set, Danny's Family, Tiger Toys, 1993, from 3" to 7", MIB $50.00

Full House (TV Series), doll set, Jesse's Family, Tiger Toys, 1993, from 3" to 7", MIB $50.00

Fury, picture slide (7), 1962, VG+, N2.............................$10.00

George Pal Puppetoons, Home Movies, 8mm, various titles, blk & wht, NTA, 1958, EX+, ea..................................$40.00

Get Smart, doll, Agent 99, red dress w/gold belt, Japan, 1967, 11½", rare, MIB..$400.00

Gilligan's Island, doll, Mary Ann, in 2-pc swimsuit, Japan, 1965, 11½", rare, MIB..$400.00

Gilligan's Island, dolls, Gilligan or Skipper, molded vinyl w/jtd arms, Presents, 1990s, 9", M, ea.................................$40.00

Gilligan's Island (Cartoon Series), figure set, Gilligan, Skipper, and Mary Ann, vinyl, Playskool, 1977, NM, $20.00 set.

(Photo courtesy Greg Davis and Bill Morgan)

Good Times, doll, JJ, stuffed cloth w/molded vinyl head, red suit, Shindana, 1975, 15", rare, MIB...............................$150.00

Good Times, doll JJ, talker, stuffed cloth w/Dyn-O-Mite label on chest, Shindana, 21", MIB $125.00

Grease, gum wrapper, 1978, 5x6", VG+, N2 ....$10.00

Green Hornet, Ed-U Cards, 1966, NMIB $75.00

Green Hornet, figure, bendable, Lakeside Toys, 1966, 6", MOC.$175.00

Green Hornet, flicker rings, any of 6, 1966, EX+, ea from $18 to.$25.00

Green Hornet, Official...Mask, set of two marked Green Hornet and Kato, Arlington Hat/Greenway, 1966, NMOC, A, $225.00; Green Hornet, Stardust Touch of Velvet Art By Numbers, Hasbro, 1960s, unused, NMIB (sealed), A, $110.00. (Photo courtesy New England Auction Gallery)

Gremlins, Colorforms Play Set, 1984, unused, MIB $35.00

Groucho Marx, Groucho Goggles, Eldon Mfg, 1955, VG (w/orig display card)...$160.00

Gulliver's Travels, handkerchief, cloth w/mc graphics of Gulliver & other characters, Paramount Pictures, 1939, EX+ .$60.00

Gulliver's Travels, plate & mug set, pnt & glazed china w/character images, gold trim, Hammersley & Co/England, 1939, EX $125.00

Gulliver's Travels, valentine, diecut image of Princess Glory w/movable arm placing heart in flower, Paramount, 1939, EX ..$30.00

Gumby & Pokey, Electric Drawing Set, Lakeside Toys, 1966, EXIB..$30.00

Gumby & Pokey, figure, Gumby seated, w/up, 1966, 4", NM.$25.00

Gumby & Pokey, stick horse, Pokey, VG $65.00

Hanna-Barbera, bank, Baba Looey, vinyl w/plastic head, Knickerbocker, 1960s, 9", EX $35.00

Hanna-Barbera, bank, Huckleberry Hound, plastic figure, 1960, 10", EX, N2 ....$35.00

Hanna-Barbera, bubble pipe, Yogi Bear, plastic figure, 1965, MIP (sealed)..$35.00

Hanna-Barbera, doll, Auggie Doggie, plush w/vinyl face, Knickerbocker, 1959, 10", EX+ $40.00

Hanna-Barbera, doll, Baba Looey, plush w/vinyl head, Knickerbocker, 1959, orig tag, EX+ $50.00

Hanna-Barbera, doll, Cindy Bear, plush w/vinyl face, Knickerbocker, 1959, 16", EXIB............................$75.00

Hanna-Barbera, doll, Dixie, plush w/felt eyes & tie, Knickerbocker, 1959, 13", EX+ $50.00

Hanna-Barbera, doll, Mr Jinks, plush w/vinyl face, Knickerbocker, 1959, 13", EX $50.00

Hanna-Barbera, doll, Quick Draw McGraw, plush w/vinyl face, Knickerbocker, 1960, 16", NM.....................$100.00

Hanna-Barbera, doll, Yogi Bear, Knickerbocker, 1959, 10", EX+ .$75.00

Hanna-Barbera, doll, Yogi Bear, stuffed, 50", EX, N2 .....$200.00

Hanna-Barbera, doll set, Yogi & Boo-Boo, stuffed cloth w/printed images, 1960s, 16" & 11", NM, pr $50.00

Hanna-Barbera, Ed-U-Cards, Huckleberry Hound, 1961, VGIB, N2 ....$15.00

Hanna-Barbera, figure, Birdman, vinyl, Japan, 11", NM .$250.00

Hanna-Barbera, figure, Huckleberry Hound, plastic, 1960s, 7½", VG+, N2 ....$20.00

Hanna-Barbera, figure, Quick Draw McGraw, ceramic, EX, T1..$55.00

Hanna-Barbera, figure, Yogi Bear, plastic, Knickerbocker, 1960s, 9", EX $50.00

Hanna-Barbera, figure, Yogi Bear leaning against sign reading 'Don't Feed the Bears,' Ideas Inc, 1960s, 5½", EX+ ...$50.00

Hanna-Barbera, flicker card set, 3-pc w/Huck playing drum, making a birdhouse, Pixie & Dixie on seesaw, 1960s, 1" sq, M...$10.00

Hanna-Barbera, guitar, Yogi Bear Ge-Tar, Mattel, 1960s, EX.$75.00

Hanna-Barbera, magic slate, Pixie & Dixie, 1960, EX......$25.00

Hanna-Barbera, Modelcast 'N Color Kit, Huckleberry Hound & The Flintstones, Standard Toycraft, 1960, NMIB......$80.00

Hanna-Barbera, Modelcast 'N Color Kit, Quick Draw McGraw, Standard Toycraft, 1960s, EXIB $75.00

Hanna-Barbera, napkins, Happy Birthday, graphics of Huckleberry Hound & gang, 5-pc, 1959, NM $8.00

Hanna-Barbera, Paint 'em Pals Paint-By-Number Set, Yogi, Craft Master, 1970s, complete, EXIB $30.00

Hanna-Barbera, pencil sharpener, Quick Draw McGraw, pnt ceramic figure w/plastic sharpener, China, 1960s, 2", NM+ $20.00

Hanna-Barbera, plate, Jellystone Park, Melmac, 1960s, 8", NM+ .$20.00

Hanna-Barbera, slippers, fur-trimmed w/head image of Yogi on toe, 1961, child-sz, unused, M $35.00

Hanna-Barbera, slippers, vinyl w/color images of Yogi & Huck, Buster Brown Shoes, 1960s, NMIB $50.00

Hanna-Barbera, tumbler, wht plastic w/Huck on unicycle, Melmac, 1960s, 3½", EX+ $12.00

Hanna-Barbera, TV tray, metal w/fold-out legs, shows Huck as William Tell, Yogi w/apple on head..., 1960, 13x18", EX.$30.00

Hanna-Barbera, wall plaques, Huckleberry Hound & Quick Draw McGraw, 1978, 12", pr, EX, N2 ....$50.00

Happy Days, belt, 'Fonz & the Happy Days Gang,' colorful cartoon images, Paramount, 1981, unused, M $15.00

Happy Days, Colorforms Presents the Fonz..., 1976, MIB..$25.00

Happy Days, doll, Fonz, stuffed print cloth, Samet & Wells, 1976, 16", M, $50.00.

Happy Days, Flip-A-Knot, National Marketing, 1977, MIP ..$20.00

Happy Days, Miracle Bubble Shooter, Imperial, 1981, MOC..$15.00

Happy Days, mug, Fonzie, thermo plastic, 1976, EX, N2..$15.00

Happy Days, pins, pnt enamel on gold-tone metal, several different images of Fonz & Gang, Gordy, 1981, EX, ea $12.00

Happy Days, Play Set Featuring the Fonz!, Toy Factory, 1976, EXIB...............................$35.00

Happy Days, Presto Magix Rub-Down Transfer Game, several different, APC, 1981, MIP, ea $20.00

Happy Days, puffy stickers, 6 different sets, Imperial, 1981, unused, MIP, ea............................$10.00

Happy Hooligan, figure set, painted slush metal, nine different characters, 3½", EX, A, $1,150.00. (Photo courtesy Skinner, Inc.)

Happy Days, record player, features the Fonz, Vanity Fair, 1976, EX................................$40.00

Happy Days, wallet, Larami, 1981, MIP $20.00

Happy Hooligan, doll, jtd wood, Schoenhut, 1924, 9", EX.$750.00

Hardy Boys Mysteries, dolls, Frank or Joe, Kenner, 1978, 12", MIB, ea.............................$100.00

Harold Lloyd, sparkler bell toy, litho tin face w/changing expressions attached to bell, 6", G+, A............$220.00

Harry & the Hendersons, doll, Harry, talker, gray fur body w/vinyl face & hands, Galoob, 1990-91, 20", MIB....$60.00

Heckle & Jeckle, film, 8mm, 1962, EXIB, N2.................$35.00

Heckle & Jeckle, pinball game, 7½", EX...........$15.00

Hector Heathcote, Colorforms, 1964, EXIB $40.00

Hello Dolly!, doll, red satin dress & head feathers, Nasco, 1961, 11½", rare, MIB...............................$350.00

Henry, figure, bsk, standing in pk shorts & wht T-shirt, blk shoes, jtd arms, Carl Anderson, 1930s, 7", EX+, A .$130.00

Home Alone (Movie), doll, Kevin, talker, T-HQ, 1991, 17", MIB.....................................$100.00

Honey West, doll, Honey West, Gilbert, 1965, 11½", rare, MIB.$400.00

Honey West, Pet Set, Gilbert, unused, MIB, A $85.00

Honeymooners, dolls, any character, Exclusive Premiere, 1997, 9", MIB, ea.............................$25.00

Honeymooners, dolls, Ralph or Ed, Effanbee, 1986, 16", MIB, ea.$350.00

Howdy Doody, bank, Mr Bluster, plastic w/flocking, Strauss, 1970s, 9", NM+.........................$65.00

Howdy Doody, barrette, Clarabell figure w/legs crossed, molded plastic, 1950s, 1¾x1½", scarce, EX...........$75.00

Howdy Doody, bubble pipe, Howdy, Lido, 1950s, 4", EX+..$175.00

Howdy Doody, canister, Cookie-Go-Round, litho tin, Luce Mfg, 1950s, 7¾", EX $100.00

Howdy Doody, doll, Howdy, as sheriff, squeeze vinyl, 1950s, 13", EX..................................$85.00

Howdy Doody, doll, Howdy, plastic, moving eyes, mouth & limbs, cloth clothes, Beehler Arts/Kagran, 1950s, 8", EX+ ..$125.00

Howdy Doody, doll, Howdy, talker, Ideal, 24", EXIB, A.$350.00

Howdy Doody, doll, Howdy, wood body w/compo head, jtd, name on chest decal, Ideal, 12", VG, A..............$115.00

Howdy Doody, embroidery kit, Summer Fall-Winter Spring, Milton Bradley, 1950s, incomplete o/w VGIB.............$50.00

Howdy Doody, Frosty Snow Spray & Stencils, US Packaging, 1950s, unused, NM+ $125.00

Howdy Doody, lamp base, plastic figure of Howdy seated on rnd base, electric, Nor East Nauticals, 6½", EX, A $165.00

Howdy Doody, Outdoor Sports Box, Adco Liberty/Kagran, 1950s, VG (VG box) $75.00

Howdy Doody, poster, Howdy Doody Fudge Bar, head image of Howdy & ad banner, Doughnut Corp of America, 1950s, 12x9", EX+............................$75.00

Howdy Doody, Put on Your Own Tee Vee Show, plastic, 5 different characters, Tee Vee/Kagran, EXIB, A $110.00

Howdy Doody, sand forms, 4 different molded plastic face molds, of Howdy, Bluster, Clarabell & Flub, Ideal, 1950s, NM $65.00

Howdy Doody, wall light, molded plastic image of Howdy on Santa's lap, Royal Electric, 1950s, 14x10x2½", EX .$100.00

Howdy Doody, washcloth mitt, puppet style, terry cloth, Bernhard Ulmann Co, 1950s, NM+ $50.00

HR Pufnstuf, doll, Witchiepoo, My-Toy, 1970, 19", rare, EX..$450.00

Huckleberry Hound, see Hanna-Barbera

Hulk Hogan, doll, stuffed cloth, Ace Novelty, 1991, 42", EX..**$50.00**

Hulk Hogan, doll, talker, pnt vinyl, Hasbro, 1990s, 13", MIB.**$50.00**

Hulk Hogan, doll, vinyl in cloth outfit & cape, 1980s, 18", MIB..**$100.00**

Hulk Hogan, pillow, Ace Novelty, 1991, 5x5", EX **$5.00**

Hulk Hogan, Sparkle Art, Colorforms, 1991, MIB..........**$15.00**

Hulk Hogan, sticker album w/decoder, Hulk Hogan's Rock 'N Wrestling, 32 pgs, Diamond Publishing, 1986, EX **$20.00**

Humpty Dumpty, figure, wooden bead type w/elastic string coming out of top of head, 4¼", EX, A **$10.00**

I Dream of Jeannie, doll, Jeannie, Libby, 1966, 20", rare, MIB.**$600.00**

I Dream of Jeannie, dolls, good Jeannie & the wicked twin sister Jeannie, Trendmasters, 1996, 11½", MIB, ea **$55.00**

I Dream of Jeannie, knitting & embroidery kit, Harmony, 1975, MOC..............**$30.00**

I Dream of Jeannie, magic slate, Rand McNally, 1975, M .**$30.00**

I Spy, camera/gun, plastic 35mm camera shoots 'bullets,' Ray-Line, 1966, EX+..............**$40.00**

I Spy, Weapons Set, Ray Line, 1966, NMIB **$200.00**

In Living Color (TV Series), doll, Homey the Clown, Acme, 1992, 24", M **$50.00**

Incredible Hulk, Crazy Foam, 1979, w/contents, EX **$25.00**

Incredible Hulk, Flip-it, Tillotson, 1977, MOC..............**$50.00**

Incredible Hulk, TV tray, metal, image of Hulk walking street, 1979, rectangular, EX..............**$25.00**

Jack Benny, TV Bank Safe, hard plastic combination safe w/color portrait of Jack Benny on dial, 1960s, 5x4½x4", EX+ **$80.00**

Jackie Coogan, stick pin doll, pipe cleaner style w/litho head, 1920s, 3¾", EX+ **$40.00**

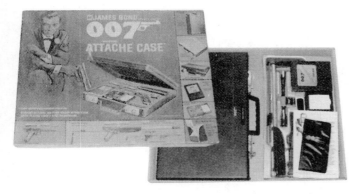

James Bond 007, attache case, Multiple, complete, NMIB, A, $1,050.00. (Photo courtesy New England Auction Gallery)

James Bond 007, bicycle license plate, Agent 007 in wht on blk steel, NM **$28.00**

James Bond 007, Code-O-Matic Secret Coding & Decoding Machine, Multiple, unused, NMIB, A **$290.00**

James Bond 007, doll, Miss Moneypenny, bl dress, Japan, 1963, 11½", rare, MIB..............**$400.00**

James Bond 007, dolls, Bond or Holly Goodhead from Moonraker, Mego, 1979, 12½", MIB, ea **$150.00**

James Bond 007, Electric Drawing Set, Lakeside Toys, 1966, EXIB..............**$100.00**

James Bond 007, ID tags, 1984, MOC, N2..............**$25.00**

James Bond 007, Military Ring & Brooch Set, w/gun-shaped pin, Hong Kong, 1960s, 1½", MIP **$20.00**

James Bond 007, rocket launcher, blk plastic suitcase complete w/launcher, 3 rockets, etc, Multiple Products, EX+, A .**$275.00**

Jeep, see Popeye

Jeffersons, doll, Florence Johnston, Shindana, 1978, 15", MIB.**$100.00**

Jerry Mahoney, key chain, plastic head w/moving eyes & mouth (stick controlled), EXOC **$60.00**

Jet Morgan (Journey Into Space Radio Series), Space Suit, Made in England, complete, EXIB, A **$500.00**

Jetsons, Colorforms, 1960s, EXIB..............**$75.00**

Jetsons, doll, Astro, plush, Nanco, 1989, 10", NM **$10.00**

Jetsons, Slate & Chalk Set, 1960s, unused, MIB **$100.00**

Joan Palooka, doll, Ideal, 1952, 14", EX..............**$135.00**

Joe Palooka Jr, doll, soft molded vinyl w/pnt hair & features (side-glance eyes), cloth outfit, 1960s, 15", NM......**$140.00**

Josie & the Pussycats, chalkboard, 1970s, M, from $50 to .**$75.00**

Josie & the Pussycats, cup, plastic w/color image, 1971, 4", NM.**$15.00**

Josie & the Pussycats, jewelry set, earrings, pin, mirror/comb set, Larami, 1973, MOC (sealed)..............**$15.00**

Josie & the Pussycats, Slicker Ticker Play Watch, Larami, 1973, MOC..............**$25.00**

Josie & the Pussycats, TV Cartoon Tattoos With 1 Stick of Bubblegum, Topp's/Hanna-Barbera, 1971, unused, EX **$75.00**

Josie & the Pussycats, Vanity Set, Larami, 1973, MOC ...**$30.00**

Julia (TV Show), doll, talker or non-talker, any outfit, Mattel, 1969-71, 11½", MIB, ea **$250.00**

Jurassic Park, Colorforms, 1992, EXIB, N2 ....**$20.00**

Katzenjammer Kids, doll, Mama, straw-stuffed w/compo head & arms, cloth dress, squeeze & mouth opens, 10", EX, A .**$175.00**

Kayo, doll, papier-mache like w/pull-string movable talking mouth, pnt clothes & hat, mk Kayo, Williard/FAS, 13", EX, A..**$140.00**

Kayo, figure, jtd & pnt wood, Jaymar, 1938, M..............**$125.00**

Kermit the Frog, see Muppets

King Kong, Colorforms Panoramic Play Set, 1976, EXIB.**$25.00**

King Kong, doll, talker, Mattel, 1966, 12", NM..............**$150.00**

King Kong, Jungle Set With Magnetic Action Hand, Multiple, 1967, complete, NMIB, A, $250.00. (Photo courtesy New England Auction Gallery)

Knight Rider, Colorforms Adventure Set, 1982, MIB **$35.00**

Kojak, doll, Excel Toy Corp, 1976, 8", MOC **$150.00**

Krazy Kat, figure, pnt wood bead type, Chein, 1920s, 7", NM..**$1,250.00**

Krusher, figure, expandable, Mattel, 1970s, 13½", EX......**$65.00**

Land of the Giants, Colorforms, 1968, NMIB $60.00

Land of the Lost, Cosmic Signal, Larami, 1975, MOC.....$40.00

Land of the Lost, Direction Finder, Larami, 1975, MOC .$40.00

Land of the Lost, Explorer's Kit, Larami, 1975, MOC $40.00

Land of the Lost, Give-A-Show Projector, Kenner, 1975, EXIB.$35.00

Land of the Lost, magic slate, Whitman, 1975, unused, M.$40.00

Land of the Lost, Moon Spinners, Larami, 1975, MOC (sealed) .$40.00

Land of the Lost, Safari Shooter Game, Larami, 1975, MIP .$45.00

Land of the Lost, Secret Look Out, Larami, 1975, MOC .$40.00

Land of the Lost, Spark Shooter, Larami, 1975, MIP........$30.00

Lassie, figure, plastic, name emb on her back, 1950s, 9", EX+.$20.00

Lassie, figure, stuffed plush w/vinyl face, metal collar w/name, Knickerbocker, 1966, 24", NM..................................$50.00

Lassie, Trick Trainer Set, Mousley, 1950s, EX+IB..........$150.00

Laugh-In, Button Kit, Schlatter, 1968, EXIB..................$20.00

Laurel & Hardy, figure, Oliver, vinyl, 1950s, 13", VG, N2 .$70.00

Laurel & Hardy, figures, cb, jtd, string activated, 1950s, EX, pr .$50.00

Laurel & Hardy, mug, Stan, ceramic, 1982, 7", EX, N2....$20.00

Laurel & Hardy, pins, plastic resin emb cartoon figures, 1960s, 2¼", unused, M, pr $25.00

Laverne & Shirley, dolls, Laverne & Shirley or Lenny & Squiggy, Mego, 1977, 12", MIB, ea pr $175.00

Linus the Lion-Hearted, doll, talker, Mattel, 1965, NM..$125.00

Little Audrey, Shoulder Bag Leathercraft Kit, Jewel Leather-goods, 1961, EXIB...$75.00

Little House on the Prairie, Colorforms Playset, 1978, MIB .$35.00

Little House on the Prairie, dolls, Laura and Carrie, Knicker-bocker, 1978, MIB, each $35.00. (Photo courtesy Greg Davis and Bill Morgan)

Little Lulu, charm bracelet, Larami, 1973, MOC $15.00

Little Lulu, doll, rubber, 6", MIP $25.00

Little Lulu, doll, stuffed cloth, red dress w/wht bric-a-brac & col-lar, red-print socks & blk shoes, 14", VG, A $35.00

Little Lulu, doll, stuffed cloth, western outfit w/brn fringed skirt & red & wht gun holster, 16", VG, A.....................$275.00

Little Lulu, doll, stuffed cloth w/hair, dress & vinyl purse w/her image & name, Margie, 1944, 16", EX, A................$285.00

Little Orphan Annie, Colorforms, 1968, NMIB...............$30.00

Little Orphan Annie, figure, wood bead type w/elastic string coming out of top of head, 5", EX, A $22.00

Little Orphan Annie, nodder, bsk, standing w/feet together & arms at sides, mk w/name & Germany, 1930s, 3¼", VG+ ...$150.00

Little Orphan Annie, stuffed dog, Sandy, 1982, 25", VG+, N2..$25.00

Little Orphan Annie & Sandy, figures, celluloid, Sandy attached to Annie by string, Japan, prewar, 5", NM, A..........$125.00

Little Rascals, dolls, any character, Effanbee, 1989, 12", MIB, ea $100.00

Little Rascals, see also Our Gang

Little Red Riding Hood, tea set, litho tin w/bl background, Ohio Art, 1920s-30s, 9 pcs, EX+ $350.00

Little Red Riding Hood, tea set, litho tin w/wht background & red border, Ohio Art, 1960s, 11 pcs, NM+ $100.00

Looney Tunes, ball, rubber w/emb images of Porky Pig & friends, 1960s, 6", dia, EX+ $25.00

Looney Tunes, bank, Bugs in barrel of carrots inscribed 'What's Up Doc?,' 13", EX+...$50.00

Looney Tunes, bank, Daffy Duck figure, Applause, 1980s, EX+.$25.00

Looney Tunes, bank, Porky Pig, bsk figure standing w/hands behind back & wearing red jacket, 1930s, EX $175.00

Looney Tunes, bank, Porky Pig standing w/hands on tummy & wearing bl jacket, name on rnd base, 1930s, rare, EX .$300.00

Looney Tunes, bank, Sylvester, vinyl figure, EX $30.00

Looney Tunes, bank (talking), house shape w/Sylvester, fireplace & Tweety in cage, 1978, VG+.................................$35.00

Looney Tunes, Bugs Bunny Cartoon Kit, Colorforms, EXIB.$100.00

Looney Tunes, Cartoon-O-Craft Molding & Coloring Set, Merry Melodies/Warner Bros, EXIB......................$125.00

Looney Tunes, Cartoon-O-Graph Sketch Board, Merrie Melodies/Warner Bros, 1950s, EXIB $150.00

Looney Tunes, doll, Bugs as baseball player, 1950s, rare, NM.$350.00

Looney Tunes, doll, Bugs as Davy Crockett, 1950s, EX..$325.00

Looney Tunes, doll, Bugs Bunny, talker, plush and plastic, Mattel/Warner Brothers, 1971, NMIB, A, $110.00. (New England Auction Gallery)

Looney Tunes, doll, Elmer Fudd, stuffed pillow type, 1970s, 16", EX, N2 ....$20.00

Looney Tunes, doll, Foghorn Leghorn, plush, recent, NM..$35.00

Looney Tunes, doll, Porky Pig, stuffed cloth w/vinyl head, Mat-tel, 1960s, 17", VG+ $25.00

Looney Tunes, Easy-Show Movies, 'It's Magic,' 8mm, Kenner, 1970, EX...$10.00

Looney Tunes, guitar, Bugs Bunny form, eyes & tongue move when played, 1962, EX+..$75.00

Looney Tunes, jack-in-the-box, Bugs Bunny, Mattel, 1962, NM+..$75.00

Looney Tunes, jack-in-the-box, Porky Pig, Mattel, 1960s, EX.$100.00

Looney Tunes, lamp base, Porky Pig figure, painted plaster, early, EX $200.00

Looney Tunes, Magic Rub-Off Pictures, Whitman, 1954, EXIB .$40.00

Looney Tunes, mask, Elmer Fudd, frontal view, Warner Bros, EX...$75.00

Looney Tunes, mug, porcelain, w/Bugs, Road Runner & Wile E Coyote, 1988, M, N2 ....$15.00

Looney Tunes, pull toy, Bugs Bunny on tricycle w/bell wheels, wood, Brice Toys, 1940s, EX..................................$500.00

Looney Tunes, pull toy, Elmer Fudd Fire Chief, wood, Brice Toys, 1940s, 9", rare, NM $200.00

Looney Tunes, squeak toy, Bugs Bunny, soft rubber, beige or gray, 1930s, EX, ea $175.00

Looney Tunes, squeak toy, Porky Pig, Sun Rubber, NM ...$75.00

Looney Tunes, squeak toy, Sylvester the Cat, soft rubber, 1930s, EX $150.00

Looney Tunes, squeak toy, Tweety Bird, soft rubber, Warner Bros, 1940s, EX $100.00

Looney Tunes, Toot-A-Tune, Bugs Bunny, Warner Bros, NMIB.$125.00

Love Boat, Barber Shop, Fleetwood, 1979, MOC (sealed) .$30.00

Love Boat, Doctor's Kit, Imperial, 1983, MOC (sealed)...$30.00

Love Boat, In Port Set, Fleetwood, 1979, MOC (sealed) .$30.00

Love Boat, Pacific Princess Playset, Multi-Toys, 1983, MIB, $100.00. (Photo courtesy Greg Davis and Bill Morgan)

Love Boat, Poster Art Kit, Craft Master, 1978, MIP.........$50.00

Love Boat, Travel Bag, vinyl, Imperial, 1983, MIP...........$25.00

Maggie & Jiggs, figure, Jiggs, wood, Schoenhut, 1924, 7", VG.$400.00

Magilla Gorilla, doll, plush, Ideal, 1960s, 18½", NM+...$100.00

Magilla Gorilla, doll, plush, Nanco, 1990, 13", NM.........$15.00

Magilla Gorilla, doll, plush, Nanco, 1990, 40", NM.........$50.00

Magilla Gorilla, squeeze toy, Droop-A-Long Coyote figure, pnt vinyl, Ideal, 1960s, 7", EX+ $40.00

Mammy & Pappy Yokum, dolls, vinyl w/molded & pnt features, cloth clothes, Baby Barry, 1950s, 12½" & 13½", NM, ea $200.00

Man From UNCLE, flicker ring, silver plastic w/blk & wht photos of, 1960s, EX, ea $20.00

Man From UNCLE, Headquarters Transmitter, battery-op, NMIB, L4...$375.00

Man From UNCLE, Secret Print Putty, Colorforms, 1965, MOC (sealed)...$50.00

Man From UNCLE, Secret Weapon Set, Ideal, 1965, NMIB..$400.00

Man From UNCLE, Thrush Buster Car, EXIB $285.00

Man From UNCLE, see also Action Figures category

Margie, travel case, blk vinyl w/color graphics of Margie dancing, 1962, NM+ $40.00

Marvel Super Heroes, Colorforms, 1983, MIB.................$30.00

Marvel Super Heroes, figure, Thor, w/up, 5", NMIB $125.00

Marvel Super Heroes, Sparkle Paint Set, Kenner, 1967, scarce, MIB (sealed), $400.00. (Photo courtesy New England Auction Gallery)

Marvel Super Heroes, stickers, 49-pc set w/stickers & cards. Topps, 1976, EX to NM $50.00

Masters of the Universe, Magnetix Playset, American Publishing, 1985, MIP (sealed) $20.00

Mighty Mouse, Basketball Game, 1973, MOC, N2 ....$25.00

Mighty Mouse, doll, rubber w/cloth cape, 1955, 10", EX..$75.00

Mighty Mouse, doll, stuffed cloth, Ideal, 1950s, 14", EX+.$75.00

Mighty Mouse, flashlight, figural, Dyno, 1979, 3½", EX+ .$75.00

Moon Mullins, figure, bsk, 1930s, 7½", G.....................$125.00

Mork & Mindy, Colorforms Sets, several different, MIB, ea from $25 to $30.00

Mork & Mindy, doll, Mindy, jeans & red sweater, Mattel, 1979, 8½", MIB $65.00

Mork & Mindy, doll, Mork, red spacesuit w/silver trim, Mattel, 1979, 9", MIB..$45.00

Mork & Mindy, doll, Mork, talker, stuffed cloth, Mattel, 1979, 16", MIB..$55.00

Mork & Mindy, Figurine Painting Set, Milton Bradley, 1979, unused, MOC..$20.00

Mork & Mindy, gum wrapper, 1978, 5x6", VG+, N2........$10.00

Mork & Mindy, Magic Transfer Set, 1979, MIP...............$15.00

Mork & Mindy, Paint-By-Numbers Set, Craft Master, 1979, unused, MIB...$35.00

Mork & Mindy, puffy stickers, several different packages, Aviva, 1979, unused, MOC, ea $5.00

Mork & Mindy, scrapbook, 'The Official...,' Wallaby, 1979, unused, M..$25.00

Mork & Mindy, Shrinky Dinks, Colorforms, 1979, MIB (sealed) $25.00

Mortimer Snerd, doll, compo Flexy figure w/pnt features, cloth outfit, Ideal, 1940, 12", G, A......................................$60.00

Mother Goose, jack-in-the-box, Mattel, 1971, EX+.........$25.00

Mother Goose, tea set, litho tin, Ohio Art, 1930s, 9 pcs, NM.$300.00

Mr Fink, water gun, plastic, Palmer Plastics, 1960s, MOC (sealed) $60.00

Mr Jinks, see Hanna-Barbera

Mr Magoo, doll, Ideal, 1970, 12", EXIB $50.00

Mr T, transfer set, 1984, MIB (sealed)........................$50.00

Munsters, doll, any character, Presents, 1980s, 10½" to 13", MIB, ea..$65.00

Munsters, doll, Baby Herman, Ideal, 1965, NM................$65.00

Munsters, doll, Herman Munster, stuffed cloth w/vinyl head, non-talking version, Mattel, 1964, 20", NM $100.00

Munsters, doll, Herman Munster, talker, Mattel, 1964, 20", rare, MIB..$450.00

Munsters, doll, Lily Munster, Exclusive Premiere, 1997, 9", MIB..$30.00

Munsters, doll, Marilyn Munster, Japan, 1964, orange dress, 11½", rare, MIB..$400.00

Munsters, flicker ring, Lily's name/photo, chrome band, 1960s, NM..$20.00

Munsters, Koach Toy w/Motor Noise, plastic, AMT, EX+IB.$1,100.00

Muppets, bank, Kermit/pirate w/chest, vinyl, 1989, 10", VG+, N2..$20.00

Muppets, bank, Miss Piggy, Sigma, NM........................$50.00

Muppets, doll, Fozzie Bear or Rowlf, Fisher-Price, 1977-81, NM, ea..$10.00

Muppets, Dress-Up Doll, Great Gonzo, Fisher-Price, 1983-83, MIB..$15.00

Muppets, stick puppet, any character, Fisher-Price, 1979, MOC, ea from $5 to..$10.00

My Fair Lady (Broadway Play), doll, plastic w/vinyl hands & head (w/rooted hair), fully dressed, Eegee, 1956, 18", NMIB .$350.00

My Favorite Martian, Magic Tricks Set, Gilbert, 1964, NMIB .$175.00

My Three Sons, doll set, Robbie's Triplets, Remco, 1969, MIB.$350.00

Nanny and the Professor, Colorforms Cartoon Kit, 1971, MIB, $40.00. (Photo courtesy Greg Davis and Bill Morgan)

New Zoo Review, mobile, musical, 1975, MIB................$25.00

New Zoo Revue, doll, Freddie the Frog, plush, Kamar, 1977, w/tag, M..$40.00

New Zoo Revue, doll, Freddie the Frog, plush w/vinyl head, Rushton, 1970s, M..$50.00

New Zoo Revue, doll, Henrietta Hippo, plush, 1977, 17", EX, N2..$60.00

New Zoo Revue, figures, Freddie the Frog, Henrietta Hippo, Charlie Owl, bendable, 1973, 3", M, ea......................$15.00

Nick Carter, Complete Fingerprint Set, NY Toy & Game Co, 1934, EXIB..$85.00

Nightmare on Elm Street, doll, Freddy Kruger, complete w/outfits & various body parts, Matchbox, 1989, 8½", MIB $50.00

Nightmare on Elm Street, doll, Freddy Kruger, talker, Matchbox, 1989, 19", rare (considered violent), MIB $100.00

Nightmare on Elm Street, doll, Freddy Kruger, w/suction cup, The Fourth New Line Heron Venture, 1988, 5", M...$15.00

Oswald the Rabbit, doll, standing w/arms up, stuffed plush w/sewn-on shorts & print cloth shoes, 8½", G, A $75.00

Our Gang, calendar top, shows gang in 'Speerit of 76' parade, Taystee Bread premium/Hal Roach, 1939, 12x10", EX.$65.00

Our Gang, Composition Book, Spanky & Pete on cover w/Our Gang photo on back, MGM/Hal Roach 1930s, 9x7", scarce, G .$30.00

Our Gang, see also Little Rascals

Pac Man, bulletin board, cork, 1980, 17x23", MIB (sealed), N2.$35.00

Pac Man, tray, metal, 1980, 12x17", VG+, N2 ....$15.00

Pagemaster (Movie), doll, Richard Tyler character, yel & bl outfit w/yel helmet, Applause, 1994, 11", MIB............$125.00

Partridge Family, bulletin board, 1970s, 18x24", NM $100.00

Partridge Family, bus, with eight figures, Remco/Columbia, 1973, NMIB, A, $1,950.00. (Photo courtesy New England Auction Gallery)

Partridge Family, doll, Laurie, Remco, 1973, 19", MIB...$325.00

Peanuts, autograph doll, Snoopy, Determined, 1971, 11", unused, MIP..$35.00

Peanuts, bank, Linus as baseball catcher, 7", rare, NM...$125.00

Peanuts, bank, Snoopy on Rainbow, compo, NM.............$25.00

Peanuts, bank, Snoopy on soccer ball, compo, 1966, 5", NM..$45.00

Peanuts, bank, Woodstock, plastic figure, 1972, 6", NM ..$35.00

Peanuts, Camp Kamp Play Set, Child Guidance, 1970s, EXIB.$75.00

Peanuts, Colorforms Happy Birthday Snoopy (Pop-Up), MIB.$35.00

Peanuts, Colorforms Yankee Doodle Snoopy, 1975, EXIB.$40.00

Peanuts, doll, Charlie Brown, vinyl, 1950s, 9", VG..........$75.00

Peanuts, doll, Linus, plush, Determined, 1983, 8", MIB...$25.00

Peanuts, doll, Linus, vinyl, jtd, 1966, 7", VG+, N2..........$25.00

Peanuts, doll, Snoopy, rag-type, Ideal, 7", MIP................$25.00

Peanuts, doll, Snoopy as Rock Star, plush, Ideal, 1977, 14", VG+..$125.00

Peanuts, doll, Snoopy Astronaut, United Features, 1969, 9½", MIB..$425.00

Peanuts, doll, Woodstock as Santa, plush, Applause, 9", MIP.$20.00

Peanuts, drum, Peanuts Marching Band & Good Grief Society w/Five & Frieda, litho tin, Chein, 1963, 5½x11" dia, VG+..........$55.00

Peanuts, hairbrush, Charlie Brown, vinyl, 1971, 6", VG+, N2.$10.00

Peanuts, jack-in-the-box, plastic doghouse, Hasbro/Romper Room, 1980, EX+..$15.00

Peanuts, Mattel-O-Phone, 1968, MIB $125.00

Peanuts, nightlight, Snoopy figure, soft vinyl, EX............$40.00

Peanuts, piano (Schroeder's), Child Guidance, 1970s, EX+ .$100.00

Peanuts, playset, Snoopy Astronaut, Knickerbocker, 1969, EXIB $75.00

Peanuts, pull toy, Snoopy Copter, Romper Room, 1980, MIP.$15.00

Peanuts, punching bag, Charlie Brown, Determined, 1970s, MIP...$50.00

Peanuts, See 'N Say Snoopy Says, Mattel, 1969, EX $75.00

Peanuts, Super (Magic) Slate, backside has 4 to-do activities, Saalfield, 1967, NM+ $20.00

Peanuts, tea set, Chein #208, unused, NMIB, $200.00. (Photo courtesy New England Auction Gallery)

Penelope Pitstop, jewelry/makeup set, w/watch, Larami, 1971, MOC (sealed) $25.00

Pete the Pup, figure, wood & compo, jtd, pnt features & clothes, name on chest, JL Kallus, 10½" (lg), VG, A $40.00

Pete the Pup, figure, wood & compo, jtd, pnt features & clothes, name on chest, JL Kallus, 9" (med), EX, A $40.00

Peter Potamus, movie, Stars on Mars, 8mm, blk & wht, NMIB..$25.00

Peter Rabbit, doll, straw-stuffed cloth body with hand-painted composition head, jointed arms and legs, cloth outfit, England, marked Quaddy Pat. Jan. 30, 1917, 16½", G, A, $1,785.00. (Photo courtesy Bertoia Auctions)

Phantom, dagger set, Larami, 1970s, EXIB $125.00

Phantom, Squirt Camera, Larami, 1976, EXIB...............$125.00

Pink Panther, Cartoonarama, 1970, EXIB $60.00

Pink Panther, doll, stuffed plush w/wire frame for posing, 1970s, 48", EX+...$50.00

Pinky Lee, doll, bl & wht checked jacket & hat, bl pants, squeeze & head pops up, 1950s, 9", MIB.................$200.00

Pinky Lee, doll box, carrying case type, litho on cb, Juro Celebrity, 1950s, 26x9x4½", NM+ $50.00

Pinky Lee, serving tray, tin w/photo image, 1950s, 10x14", EX+.$30.00

Pixie & Dixie, see Hanna-Barbera

Planet of the Apes, Colorforms Play Set, 1967, EXIB $60.00

Pogo, figure, Churchy La Femme holding fishing pole, pnt vinyl, jtd head & arms, 5", scarce, EX+ $85.00

Pogo, figure, Pogo, vinyl, Walt Kelly, 1969, 4", VG+, N2 .$15.00

Pogo, Pogomobile, w/22 different diecut cb Walt Kelly characters & wire hanger, Simon & Schuster, 1954, EX....$150.00

Pollyanna (Movie), doll, red & wht checked dress & bloomers, straw hat, Uneeda, 1960, 30", MIB $200.00

Pollyanna (Movie), doll, red & wht checked dress & bloomers, Uneeda, 1960, 17", MIB...$150.00

Popeye, Balloon Pump (Inflato-Pump), cylindrical w/graphics, Van Dam Rubber/Ideal/KFS, 1957, 12x3" dia, EX+...$50.00

Popeye, bank, head figure w/pipe in mouth, American Bisque, mk USA, scarce, EX $325.00

Popeye, bank, Popeye Knockout Bank, litho tin, Straits MFG/KFS, 1935, EX, A $475.00

Popeye, Beach Boat, 1980, MOC, N2 ....$50.00

Popeye, Bubble Pipe Set, box only, 1936, 5x7", NM $65.00

Popeye, bulletin board, cork, 1980, 16x22", EX, N2.........$25.00

Popeye, Christmas Tree Set, 7 shades depicting Popeye & friends, Mazda, 1930s, unused, MIB, A $400.00

Popeye, Colorforms Popeye the Weatherman, 1959, NMIB.$20.00

Popeye, crayon box, litho tin, images of Popeye, Olive Oyl & Swee' Pea, 1933, empty, NM $20.00

Popeye, doll, Brutus, vinyl w/cloth outfit, w/orig tag, 13", M..$25.00

Popeye, doll, Olive Oyl, vinyl & cloth, 11", MIP $30.00

Popeye, doll, Popeye, compo (hollow), standing w/arms across chest, red & bl, 15", VG+, A $100.00

Popeye, doll, Popeye, plush, 1994, 13, EX, N2.................$10.00

Popeye, doll, Wimpy, 1-pc rubber w/pnt outfit, Schavoir Rubber Co, 1935, NM...$275.00

Popeye, figure, Jeep, composition, 12½", EX, A, $1,980.00; Popeye, figure, wood & composition bead style, 13½", EX, A, $415.00. (Photo courtesy Noel Barrett Auctions)

Popeye, figure, Jeep, compo, jtd, KFS, 1933, 13", G+, A.$750.00

Popeye, figure, Popeye, bsk, dressed in pirate's outfit, eyes & arms move, 1930s, no sz given, EX+, A $500.00

Popeye, figure, Popeye, compo, standing w/arms down & extra long pipe reaching upward, 1930s, 12", EX+ $250.00
Popeye, figure, Popeye, frosted glass w/pnt features, 1930s, 6", NM, A $200.00
Popeye, figure, Popeye, wood & compo bead style, pnt details, ball hands (w/thumbs), 2 buttons, Chein, 1932, 8", EX ...$300.00
Popeye, figure, Popeye, wood & compo bead style, pnt details, ball hands (no thumbs), no buttons, Chein (att), 8", VG.$225.00
Popeye, figure, Popeye, wood bead style, pnt details, string hanger atop head, Jaymar, 6", EX $75.00
Popeye, figure set, Popeye & Olive Oyl, chalkware, 15", EX, A, pr $150.00
Popeye, Funny Face & Mask Set, Jaymar, 1962, NM (EX box) .$50.00
Popeye, Intelligence Test, litho-on-cb dexterity puzzle, w/tin & glass frame, 5x3½", 1930s, NM $75.00
Popeye, jack-in-the-box, litho tin & vinyl, Popeye w/spinach can body, Mattel, 1951-53, 12", EX, A $65.00
Popeye, lantern, litho tin figure w/clear glass dome in belly, battery-op, 7", NMIB...$450.00
Popeye, Modeling Clay, American Crayon Co, 1936, EXIB.$65.00
Popeye, mug, plastic head, thermo liner, 1990s, EX, N2...$20.00
Popeye, pencil, 'Well Blow Me Down This Is What I Call A Marvelusk Pencil,' w/orig leads, Eagle Toys, 1930s, NMIB.$50.00
Popeye, pencil sharpener, litho tin crank-type w/metal mount base, 'A Sharp Pencil Gives You Written Punch,' VG, A....$100.00
Popeye, Photo Printing Kit, MIB, L4 ....$75.00
Popeye, Popeye Pirate Pistol, litho tin clicker gun, 10", EX, A .$415.00
Popeye, Popeye Spinach Can, litho tin & vinyl, makes noise when head pops up, Mattel, 7", EX, A $35.00
Popeye, Presto Paints, Kenner, 1961, VG+.....................$100.00
Popeye, pull toy set, 2 litho paper-on-wood cars & 1 motorcycle w/various characters, 6½" to 15", G to VG, A $465.00
Popeye, soap-on-a-rope, Popeye head, wht w/pnt features, Lester Gaba Design, EX+IB, A $100.00
Popeye, submarine, plastic bathtub sub w/rubber-band w/up motor, Larami, 1973, MOC (sealed) $10.00

Popeye, Thimble Theatre Mystery Playhouse, with three composition figures, Harding/KFS, 1939, NM+IB, A, $2,000.00.

Popeye, TV Eras-O-Board Set, Hasbro, 1957, NMIB $40.00
Popeye, Wimpy's hamburger, soft vinyl w/character graphics & logos, 7", NM $20.00

Porky Pig, see Looney Tunes
Punch & Judy, puppet theater, litho tin figures in front of litho paper ground, spring-activated, 7x8", VGIB, A $60.00
Punky Brewster, doll, Punky, Galoob, 1984, 18", MIB.....$75.00
Puzzy, doll, compo w/pnt hair & features (side-glance eyes), blk & wht cloth outfit w/shoes & socks, 1948, EX $350.00
Raggedy Andy, bank, Play Pal, 1974, 11", EX+.................$25.00
Raggedy Andy, doll, Georgene, 1930s-40s, 13", NM $250.00
Raggedy Andy, doll, musical, Knickerbocker, 12", EX $35.00
Raggedy Andy, planter, papier-mache, 1974, 8", EX, N2..$25.00
Raggedy Ann, bank, Play Pal, 1974, 11", EX+.................$25.00
Raggedy Ann, Colorforms Play Kitchen, 1975, MIB........$25.00
Raggedy Ann, doll, Christmas, 1980s, 13", VG, N2 ....$15.00
Raggedy Ann, doll, Christmas, 1980s, 18", EX, N2 ....$25.00
Raggedy Ann, doll, musical, Knickerbocker, 15", EX+.....$50.00
Raggedy Ann, stove, plastic, 1978, 7x15x20", VG, N2 ....$20.00
Raggedy Ann & Andy, Colorforms Super Deluxe Playhouse, 1988, MIB..$15.00
Raggedy Ann & Andy, crayon box, metal, Chein, 1974, EX+, N2 ....$25.00
Raggedy Ann & Andy, dolls, inflatable vinyl, Ideal/Bobbs-Merrill, 1973, 21" & 22", MIP, ea $50.00
Raggedy Ann & Andy, dolls, sleeping bag, Applause, NM+, ea .$20.00
Raggedy Ann & Andy, tray, metal, 1970s, 13x13", VG+, N2.$25.00
Rambo, knife, steel blade w/compass hdl, fishing line & sharpener in blk leather sheath, MIB................................$30.00
Rat Fink, iron-on transfer, figure playing guitar w/name across bottom, 5", NM (no pkg)......................................$8.00
Ren & Stimpy, dolls, talkers, Mattel, 1992, NRFB, ea......$80.00
Ripcord, parachute toy, 4" plastic figure w/chute, Ray Line, 1961, MOC (sealed)...$20.00
Road Runner, doll, Mighty Star, 1970s, 13", EX+.............$20.00
Rocky (Movie), doll, gray sweat outfit w/name on chest & headband, United Artist, 1985, 18", MIB $100.00
Rocky & Friends, bank, Bullwinkle, plastic, Play Pal, 1970s, 12", EX+ $75.00
Rocky & Friends, Colorforms Cartoon Kit, 1960s, EX+IB .$75.00
Rocky & Friends, doll, Bullwinkle, plush, Ideal, 1960, 20", NM.$75.00
Rocky & Friends, doll, Rocky, plush, 1982, 13", VG+, N2.$20.00
Rocky & Friends, doll, Rocky, plush w/plastic flight helmet & goggles, Nanco, 1991, 24", NM...............................$20.00
Rocky & Friends, figure, Bullwinkle, bendable, 1985, 7", M, N2.$15.00
Rocky & Friends, figure, Dudley Do-Right, bendable, Wham-O, 1970s, 5", EX+ $25.00
Rocky & Friends, figure, Rocky, bendable, 1985, 5", M, N2.$15.00
Rocky & Friends, hat, cloth dome top w/images of characters, visor rim, 1960s, unused, NM..............................$65.00
Rocky & Friends, picture slides (7), 1962, VG+, N2........$10.00
Rocky & Friends, playing cards, Bullwinkle, 1962, VG, N2 .$10.00
Rocky & Friends, Signal Flasher, Bullwinkle, plastic, 1970s, MOC..$25.00
Rocky & Friends, stamp set, Bullwinkle, Larami, 1970, EXIB.$25.00
Rootie Kazootie, magic set, 1950s, NMIB.....................$125.00
Ruff & Reddy, Karbon Kopee Kit, Wonder Art, 1960, EXIB .$75.00
Sabrina the Teenage Witch, doll, Sabrina (in wht outfit w/silver sequins) or Harvey Kinkle, Kenner, 1997, 12", MIB, ea..$45.00
Sabrina the Teenage Witch, doll, Sabrina in red jumper w/wht blouse, Kenner, 1997, 11½", MIB $25.00

Sabrina the Teenage Witch, doll, Sabrina or Harvey Kinkle, Pacific Playthings, 11½" & 12", MIB, ea $30.00

Santa, doll, stuffed red flannel body w/cloth mask face, pnt features, mohair beard & suit trim, musical, 1930s, 28", EX........$250.00

Santa, mechanical toy, Santa in tree, litho tin, depress plunger & tree spins open to reveal Santa, 4½", NMIB, A $65.00

Santa, puppet, diecut figure w/moving eyes & mouth, Happi-Times Toy Town promo for Sears, 1948, 13", NM $30.00

Santa, squeeze doll, vinyl, 1960s, 7", EX, N2 ....$10.00

Saturday Night Live, doll, any character except Killer Bee, Hamilton Gifts, 1990, 10", M, ea $30.00

Saturday Night Live, doll, Ed Grimly, talker, Tyco, 1989, 18", MIB...$125.00

Saturday Night Live, doll, Killer Bee, molded vinyl & plastic, Hamilton Gifts, 1990s, 10", MIB................................$35.00

Saturday Night Live, doll, Roseannadanna, Creation Entertainment, 2000, 11½", MIB.....................................$40.00

Saved by the Bell, doll, any character except Lisa, Tiger Toys, 1992, 11½", MIB, ea......................................$40.00

Saved by the Bell, doll, Lisa, Tiger Toys, 1992, 11½", rare, MIB $75.00

Scooby Doo, figure, sitting, plush, 1997, 11", EX, N2.........$6.00

Scooby Doo, figure, sitting, plush, 1998, 13", EX, N2.........$8.00

Scooby Doo, gumball machine, plastic head, Hasbro, 1968, EX .$25.00

Scrappy, bank, book shape w/leather-like binding on metal, emb image of Scrappy & dog, Columbia, 1930s, 3x3½x1", EX+ $75.00

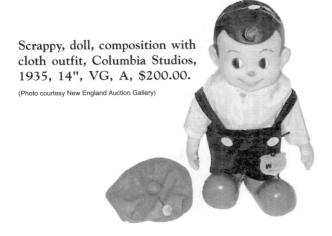

Scrappy, doll, composition with cloth outfit, Columbia Studios, 1935, 14", VG, A, $200.00.

(Photo courtesy New England Auction Gallery)

Scrappy, figure, Marge (Scrappy's girlfriend), pnt bsk, Japan, 1930s, 3½", EX+ $30.00

Sesame Street, doll, Big Bird, talker, Playskool, 1970s, 22", VG $25.00

Sesame Street, figure set, PVC, set of 8, Applause, 1993, M.$20.00

Sesame Street, Lacing Puppets, Big Bird & Ernie, Fisher-Price, 1984, MIP $10.00

Simple Simon, bank, tin book shape, Kirchof, 1930s, EX.$115.00

Simpsons, Activity Pack, Pancake Press, MIP (sealed) $25.00

Simpsons, bank, Bart standing, Street Kids, PVC, 9", M $6.00

Simpsons, Crayon-By-Number, Rose Art, MIB $10.00

Simpsons, doll, any character, rag-type, Dandee, 11", NM, ea $18.00

Simpsons, doll, any character, stuffed w/vinyl limbs, Presents, 9", M, ea $12.00

Simpsons, Fun Dough Model Maker, MIB $45.00

Simpsons, Paint-By-Number, Rose Art, MIB $10.00

Simpsons, pinball game, Jaru, plastic, MOC $5.00

Simpsons, punch ball set, National Latex Products, MIP .$50.00

Simpsons, Stamper Pak, Rubber Stampede, MIP (sealed) .$15.00

Simpsons, Trace 'N Color Drawing Set, Toymax, NMIB..$85.00

Simpsons, Write 'N Wipe, Rose Art, MIB (sealed) $15.00

Simpsons, 3-D Chess Set, MIP (sealed) $35.00

Six Million Dollar Man, Bionic Tattoos & Stickers, Kenner, 1976, unused, MIP..$15.00

Six Million Dollar Man, Play Doh Action Play Set, 1977, MIB (sealed)..$35.00

Six Million Dollar Man, waste can, metal w/lithoed images, 1976, EX...$25.00

Skeezix, School Tablet, red cover w/images of Skeezix & Rachel the Black maid, 1923, 9x5½", unused, NM+, A........$65.00

Smurfs, bank, molded plastic character, Peyo, 1980s, NM.$35.00

Smurfs, Colorforms, EXIB...$35.00

Smurfs, mug, plastic, Peyo, 1980s, M.............................$15.00

Smurfs, pail, plastic, 1-qt, 1981, VG+, N2......................$15.00

Smurfs, phonograph, NMIB...$65.00

Smurfs, sewing cards, MIB (sealed) $25.00

Soupy Sales, pen, plastic w/pnt vinyl head topper, lg polka-dot bow tie, 1960s, NM+ $40.00

Space Patrol, drink shaker, spaceship form, United Plastic Corp, 8½", VGIB, A...$60.00

Spark Plug, see Barney Google

Spider-Man, Action Gumball Machine & Bank, 7" figure, 1984, MIB $20.00

Spider-Man, American Bricks Set, Playskool, 1977, EXIB .$35.00

Spider-Man, Colorforms Adventure Set, 1974, NMIB.....$25.00

Spider-Man, doll, stuffed talker, Mego, 1974, 28", M $50.00

Spider-Man, Presto-Magix Set, rub-on transfers, 1978, NM .$8.00

Spider-Man, roller skates, red, blk & bl plastic, EX $20.00

Spider-Man, skydiving parachute, Ahi, 1973, MOC........$35.00

Spider-Man, Spider Van, Buddy L, 1980, EX, N2 ....$20.00

Spider-Man, squirt gun, plastic head figure, 1974, EX $25.00

Spider-Man, walkie-talkies, plastic, battery-op, Nasta, 1984, MIB $50.00

Starsky & Hutch, AM Wrist Radio, Illco, 1977, MIB....$150.00

Starsky & Hutch, dashboard set, 1976, EX $40.00

Starsky & Hutch, flashlight, Fleetwood, 1976, 7", MOC .$65.00

Starsky & Hutch, Handcuffs & Wallet Set, Fleetwood, 1976, unused, MOC...$30.00

Starsky & Hutch, Poster Put-Ons, Bi-Rite, 1976, unused, MIP, ea..$10.00

Starsky & Hutch, Shoot-Out Target Set, Berwick (European), 1977, MIB $75.00

Steve Canyon, flicker ring, Steve/Captain Action, 1960s, NM.$20.00

Super Powers, Deluxe Talking Storybook, 1985, M, N2...$20.00

Superfriends, wall decorations, set of 4 cb figures of Batman & Robin, Superman, Wonder Woman, Group, 1976, 11x7", NM...$10.00

Superman, Crayon-By-Numbers Set, Transogram, 1954, box only, EX+ $50.00

Superman, Crayon-By-Numbers Set, Transogram, 1954, EXIB..$100.00

Superman, doll, plush, Knickerbocker, 20", EXIB............$30.00

Superman, figure, Justice League, plastic, Ideal, 1966, 3", EX+ .$75.00

Superman, figure, painted wood and composition bead style with chest and belt decals, Ideal/Superman, Inc., 13", EX, A, $2,600.00.

Superman, Flying Superman Toy, molded hollow plastic w/rubber band & launcher, Transogram, 1954, EX $50.00
Superman, horseshoe set, Super Swim Inc, 1950s, EXIB .$100.00
Superman, Krypton Rocket Set, Parks Plastic, 1950s, NMIB.$150.00
Superman, Kryptonite Rock, DC Comics, 1977, NMIB...$30.00
Superman, Paint-By-Numbers Watercolor Set, Transogram, 1954, EXIB...$225.00
Superman, playsuit, Ben Cooper/Superman Inc, NMIB, A .$150.00
Superman, Puncho Bag, package only, red & bl litho tin waxed paper bag, Lee-Tex, 1940s, 7½x5", NM+....................$50.00
Superman, scrapbook, Superman in flight on cover, Saalfield, 1940s, EX+...$425.00
Superman, valentine, diecut cb w/fold-out design, Superman & children by brick wall, Superman Inc, 1940, 5x6", NM+.......$60.00
Superman, wallet, Superman in flight, Croyden, 1950s, EXIB..$175.00
Superman Jr, doll, squeeze vinyl, 1978, 7", EX, N2...........$25.00
Sylvester the Cat & Tweety Bird, see Looney Tunes
Tarzan, flasher ring, Vari-Vue, 1960s, EX+........................$20.00
The Nanny (TV Series), doll, Nanny, talker, Street Players, 11½", MIB $65.00
Three Stooges, Colorforms, 1959, NMIB.......................$120.00
Three Stooges, dolls, any character, Presents, 1988, 14", M, ea .$65.00
Three Stooges, picture slide (7), 1961, VG+, N2 ....$10.00
Tom & Jerry, dolls, stuffed cloth w/linen faces, 1940s, 17" & 7½", VG+, pr...$150.00

Tom Corbett Space Cadet, Molding & Coloring Set, with Tom, Roger, and Astro, Model-Craft, unused, EXIB, A, $100.00.

Tom & Jerry, guitar, character design, musical, Mattel/MGM, 1960s, EX...$150.00
Tom & Jerry, jack-in-the-box, Mattel, 1965, EX..............$45.00
Tom & Jerry, Mattel Music Maker, litho tin, 1960s, NM .$75.00
Tom Corbett Space Cadet, Cosmic Vision Helmet, Rockhill, 1950, MIB, A $285.00
Tom Corbett Space Cadet, flashlight, rocketship w/decals on fin, NM, C10..$250.00
Toonerville Trolley, figure, Skipper, bsk, Japan, 1920s, 3", EX .$125.00
Toonerville Trolley, trolley, bsk, 3½", 1920s, EX+.........$250.00
Toonerville Trolley, trolley, pot metal, cast figures on ea end, yel w/gr & silver trim, gr disk wheels, 3½" T, EX.........$650.00
Top Cat, bank, Top Cat figure standing on trash can, pnt vinyl, 1960s, 10", NM...$50.00
Topo Gigio, bank, nodder figure w/pineapple, M, L4 .....$125.00

Topo Gigio, doll, vinyl with poseable arms, painted detail with realistic hair and cloth bow tie, 1963, 12", EX, A, $50.00.

(Photo courtesy Noel Barrett Auctions)

Ultimate Warrior, kite, WWF/Spectra, 1990, 4½-ft, MIB.$15.00
Universal Monsters, figure, Creature From the Black Lagoon, bendable, Ahi, 1974, 5", NM+................................$100.00
Universal Monsters, figure, Creature From the Black Lagoon, plastic w/jtd arms, 1960s, 13", NM+ $200.00
Universal Monsters, flip movie book, 'Frankenstein in Hiding,' 1960s, 2½", EX+ $18.00
Universal Monsters, Monstress Monster Bisque Figure Paint Set, Wolfman, 12", MIB (sealed).....................................$85.00
Universal Monsters, night lights, set of 4 w/Creature From the Black Lagoon, Frankenstein, Dracula & Wolfman, EX, C10....$50.00
Universal Monsters, pencil sharpener, Wolfman, gr plastic bust, UP Co, 1960s, 3", NM...$25.00
Universal Monsters, valentines, pack of 30, 1991, MIP, N2.$15.00
Universal Monsters, wallet, vinyl w/color images of Creature From the Black Lagoon & Wolfman, 1963, EX+.......$60.00
V (TV Series), Bop Bag, vinyl, 1970s, MIB $30.00
VIP (TV Series), doll, Vallery Irons, Play Along, 2000, 11½", MIB $40.00
Wally Walrus, figure, ceramic, full-length standing pose, 1950s, 5½", NM, A $90.00
Welcome Back Kotter, chalkboard, gray surface w/circular color image & bordering wht images, Board King, 1976, EX .$50.00
Welcome Back Kotter, Classroom Playset, for 10" dolls, Mattel, 1976, EXIB..$50.00

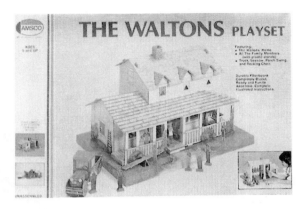

Waltons, Farmhouse Playset, with cardboard figures and accessories, Amsco, 1975, MIB, $75.00. (Photo courtesy Greg Davis and Bill Morgan)

Welcome Back Kotter, Colorforms Set, 1976, MIB $20.00
Welcome Back Kotter, dolls, any character, Mattel, 1976, 9½",
    MOC, ea $75.00
Welcome Back Kotter, magic slate, 2 different, Whitman, 1977,
    unused, M, ea $20.00
Welcome Back Kotter, Paint-By-Number Set, acrylic, 2 different
    sets, 1970s, unused, MIB, ea $30.00
Winky Dink, paint set, Standard Toykraft, 1950s, EXIB ..$85.00
Wizard of Oz, doll, any character, Ideal, 1984-85, 9", MIB, ea..$50.00
Wizard of Oz, doll, any character, Largo, 1989, 14", MIB, ea..$45.00
Wizard of Oz, doll, any character, Multi Toy Corp, 1988, 12",
    MIB, ea...$30.00
Wizard of Oz, picture slide (7), 1961, VG+, N2 ....$10.00
Wizard of Oz, place mat, vinyl, 1989, 12x16", EX, N2 .....$15.00
Wizard of Oz, see also Action Figures category
Wolfman, see Universal Monsters
Wonder Woman, backpack, red or bl canvas w/vinyl lining, M,
    C10...$80.00
Wonder Woman, Color-A-Deck Card Game, MOC, C10..$50.00
Wonder Woman, Flashmite, Jane X, 1976, MOC $75.00
Wonder Woman, iron-on transfers, several different, 1970s, MIP,
    ea..$15.00
Wonder Woman, place mat, vinyl fan shape w/color image of
    Wonder Woman & island, 1977, NM $15.00
Woody Woodpecker, figure, NASCAR beany, 1999, 10", M, N2 .$20.00
Woody Woodpecker, figure, squeeze rubber, Vinfloat, 1960, 8",
    EX+ $50.00
Woody Woodpecker, hat, cloth baseball style w/plastic crest, beak,
    eyes & head feathers, Walter Lantz, 1950s, NM+ $60.00
Woody Woodpecker, Mattel Music Maker, litho tin, 1960s,
    VG $50.00
Woody Woodpecker, movie, 'Witch Crafty,' 8mm, blk & wht,
    1960s, NMIB...$15.00
Woody Woodpecker, mug, porcelain, 1983, 16-oz, MIB, N2..$20.00
Yakky Doodle, see Hanna-Barbera
Yogi Bear, see Hanna-Barbera

Chein

Though the company was founded shortly after the turn of

the century, this New Jersey-based manufacturer is probably best known for the toys it made during the '30s and '40s. Wind-up merry-go-rounds and Ferris wheels as well as many other carnival-type rides were made of beautifully lithographed tin even into the '50s, some in several variations. The company also made banks, a few of which were mechanical and some that were character related. Mechanical, sea-worthy cabin cruisers, space guns, sand toys, and some Disney toys as well were made by this giant company; they continued in production until 1979.

    Advisor: Scott Smiles (S10)

    See also Banks; Character, TV, and Movie Collectibles; Disney; Sand Toys.

WINDUPS, FRICTIONS, AND OTHER MECHANICALS

Aquaplane, 1939, 8½", NM $350.00
Barnacle Bill, 6¼", EX..$325.00
Bass Drummer, 1930s, 9", NM......................................$400.00
Big Top Tent, 1961, 10", EXIB $200.00
Broadway Trolley, 8", EX+..$150.00
Butterfly Sparkler, 1930, celluloid wings, 5", EXIB.........$225.00

Cabin Cruiser, 15", MIB, A, $700.00. (Photo courtesy Bertoia Auctions)

Cabin Cruiser, 15", VG, A $130.00
Cathedral Organ, #130, 9½", NMIB,.............................$225.00
Church Organ, crank-op, 9", EX, A $75.00
Clown Floor Boxer, celluloid boxing bag, 7½", EX $750.00

Dan-Dee Oil Truck, 8½", EXIB, A, $1,100.00; Dan-Dee Roadster, 8½", EXIB, A, $1,200.00. (Photo courtesy Noel Barrett Auctions)

Disneyland Ferris Wheel, 17", EX $500.00
Drummer Boy, 1930s, 6", NM+ $300.00
Easter Bunny Delivery Cart, #98, 1930s, 9½", EX..........$225.00
Fancy Groceries Truck, 6", EX.......................................$300.00

Felix the Cat on Scooter, 7", VG, A, $450.00. (Photo courtesy Bertoia Auctions)

Popeye the Drummer, 7", NM+, $3,100.00. (Photo courtesy Bertoia Auctions)

Ferris Wheel, lithoed base, 1930s, 17"; VG $250.00
Ferris Wheel, rarer non-lithoed base, 16½", EX $375.00
Fish (Mechanical), #55, 1940s, 11" L, NM...................$125.00
Greyhound Coast-to-Coast Bus, disk wheels, 9", VG.....$225.00
Hand-Standing Clown, #158, 5", EX.............................$125.00
Happy Hooligan, name on hat, 6", EX+, A $500.00
Happy Hooligan, no name on hat, 6", EX, A.................$400.00
Junior Truck, 8", EX..$350.00
Musical (Mechanical) Aero Swing, 13", VGIB.............$550.00
Native on Turtle, 1930s, 8", NM $275.00
Navy Frog Man, plastic flippers, 12", NMOC.................$125.00
Pelican, #222, 5", NM, A $150.00
Penguin, #152, 4", NMIB...$125.00
Playland Merry-Go-Round, #385, bl base, 10", EX.........$375.00
Playland Merry-Go-Round, #387, orange base, 10", EX.$450.00
Playland Whip, #340, 20" L, NMIB..............................$950.00
Popeye Floor Puncher, 7", EX+, A.............................$1,350.00

Popeye Waddler, 1932, 6½", VG+ $750.00
Popeye Walker w/Two Parrot Cages, 8½", VGIB, A $500.00
Racer #7 (Emmett Racer or Boat-Tail), 20", VG+ $1,450.00
Racer #52, wooden wheels, EX......................................$200.00
Roadster, #221, 1920s, 8", EX......................................$325.00
Roller Coaster, #275, 1950s, 20", 1930s, 19", NMIB $400.00
Santa Walker, 6", EX $550.00
Santa's Gnome, early mk, 6", MIB $325.00
Seaplane, see Aquaplane
Ski Boy, #157, 8", G, A..$150.00

Popeye Heavy Hitter, 1932, 12", rare, NM, A, $4,000.00.

(Photo courtesy Randy Inman Auctions)

Ski Boy, #157, 8", NMIB, A, $250.00. (Photo courtesy Noel Barrett Auctions)

Ski Ride, #320, 20", MIB...$600.00
Skin Driver, 11½", NMIB $175.00
Surf's Up, 10", NMOC..$100.00
Turtle w/Native Rider (Mechanical), #145, 1930s, 8", EXIB, A..$300.00
US Army Soldier, #153, 5", MOC $150.00
Yellow Taxi, Main 7570, 1920s, 6", NMIB....................$425.00

MISCELLANEOUS

Popeye in Barrel, #258, 1932, 7", NM..........................$850.00
Popeye Overhead Puncher, #255, 1932, 9½", rare, NM .$3,000.00
Popeye Shadow Boxer, #254, 1932, 7", rare, NM........$1,700.00
Popeye Sparkler, litho tin, 6", EXIB..........................$1,250.00

Bank, church, #29, NM $125.00
Bank, clown bust, 5", EX, A $100.00
Bank, elephant on drum, 5", EX...................................$125.00
Bank, monkey, #11, EX...$100.00

Bank, Save for War Bonds & Stamps, dome shape, 4½", NM, A $550.00
Bank, Save for War Bonds & Stamps, shell shape, 6", NM.$225.00
Bank, Uncle Wiggily, #22, 5", M......................................$225.00
Bank, 1939 World's Fair, 12", NM......................................$275.00
Clown Roly Poly, litho tin, 1930s, scarce, NM..............$350.00
Easter Basket, lithoed nursery rhyme characters, 1959, 7½" dia, NM..$125.00
Easter Egg, take-apart w/lithoed scenes, 5", NM...............$75.00
Globe, 10", NMIB...$125.00
Hercules Army Truck, cloth cover, 29", G.....................$300.00

Hercules Coupe, 1920s, green, red, and black, with rumble seat and luggage rack, EX, A, $1,200.00. (Photo courtesy Randy Inman Auctions)

Hercules Coupe, w/rumble seat & luggage rack, 19", G, A.$325.00
Hercules Dump Truck, pressed steel, 20", Fair+, A.........$225.00
Hercules Ferris Wheel, 17", EX, from $300 to $325.00
Hercules Ice Truck, #600, pressed steel, 20", VG............$600.00
Hercules Motor Express Stake Truck, #600, 20", G+......$550.00
Hercules Railway Express Agency Truck, 20", G+..........$425.00
Hercules Roadster, w/rumble seat & luggage rack, 1920s, 18", G+..$900.00
Hercules Roadster, w/rumble seat & luggage rack, 1920s, 18", EXIB, A..$2,300.00
Hercules Royal Blue Line Bus, 18", G............................$750.00
Hercules Stake Truck, w/orig rollers, 14½", EX..............$550.00
Hercules Tow Truck, 18", VG..$600.00
Player Piano, electric, NM $275.00
Pull Toy, cat on 3-wheeled platform, 7½", EX...............$350.00
Sparkler, #95, red, wht & bl, 1930s, 4½", EXIB..............$100.00
Top, w/various images of children's toys, 1930s, NM........$65.00
Train Station, litho tin simulated brick building w/Grove Station sign, 6", EX $75.00

Coloring, Activity, and Paint Books

Coloring and activity books from the early years of the twentieth century are scarce indeed and when found can be expensive if they are tied into another collectibles field such as Black Americana or advertising; but the ones most in demand are those that represent familiar movie and TV stars of the 1950s and 1960s. Condition plays a very important part in assessing worth, and though hard to find, unused examples are the ones that bring top dollar — in fact, as much as 50% to 75% more than one even partially used.

The books in the following listings are unused unless noted otherwise.

Addams Family Coloring Book, Artcraft, 1965, family around Morticia sitting in chair, some coloring, EX $25.00
Addams Family Coloring Book, Artcraft, 1965, family around piano, some coloring, NM $30.00
Alice in Wonderland Coloring Book, Playmore, 1975, M.$15.00
Andy Griffith Show Coloring Book, Artcraft, 1960s, over 200 pgs, some coloring, EX+..$75.00
Archies Coloring & Activity Fun, Whitman, 1969, NM.$15.00
Atom Ant Sticker Book, 1966, used, EX+ $10.00
Bat Masterson, Saalfield, 1959, some coloring, EX+.........$30.00

Batman Coloring Book, Whitman #1002, 1967, NM, $30.00.

Beatles Yellow Submarine Pop-Out Art Book, King Features-Subafilms Ltd, 1968, M..$75.00
Ben-Hur Coloring Book, Lowe #2851, 1959, some coloring, NM.$40.00
Beverly Hillbillies Coloring Book, Whitman, 1960s, Granny chasing kangaroo, some coloring, VG......................$15.00

Bionic Woman Dip Dots Painting Design Book, Kenner, 1977, M, $20.00.

(Photo courtesy Greg Davis and Bill Morgan)

Black Hole Coloring Book, Whitman, 1979, M $15.00
Blondie Sticker Book, 1968, NM $10.00
Bongo, Disney, 1948, some coloring, EX+, N2 ....$25.00

Bozo the Clown Color & Read Book, 1972, some coloring, VG, N2 ....$20.00

Brady Bunch Coloring Book, Whitman, 1973, family camping trip, some coloring, EX+...$25.00

Buck Rogers Coloring & Activity Book, 1979, M $20.00

Buck Rogers Paint Book, Whitman, 1935, NM..............$300.00

Bugs Bunny Coloring Book, Whitman, shows Bugs wearing Indian headdress made of crayons, EX $50.00

Bugs Bunny/Porky Pig Paint Book, 1940s, EX $100.00

Bugs Bunny's Daffy Dots, Whitman, image of Daffy Duck on cover, EX $35.00

Bullwinkle Coloring Book, Whitman, 1971, Bullwinkle in car wearing glasses, some coloring, EX $20.00

Bullwinkle Paintless Paint Book, Whitman, 1960, NM ...$40.00

Cap'n Crunch Coloring Book, Whitman, 1968, some coloring, EX...$25.00

Car 54 Where Are You? Coloring Book, Whitman, 1962, some coloring, NM $40.00

Casper Coloring Book, 1973, 13x11", NM........................$18.00

Cheyenne Coloring Book, Whitman, 1950s, some coloring, EX..$20.00

Chitty-Chitty Bang-Bang Coloring Book, 1968, NM.......$28.00

Cinderella Paint Book, Whitman, 1950, some coloring, NM+ .$25.00

Davy Crockett Frontier Cabin Punchout Book, Whitman/WDP #1943, 1955, M...$75.00

Davy Crockett Stamp Book, 1955, EX $35.00

Disneyland Coloring Book, Golden Books #1136-20, 1983, M.$10.00

Disneyland Sticker Fun, Whitman, 1964, EX+.................$30.00

Donald Duck Coloring Book, Whitman, 1960, image of Donald framed by crayons, some coloring, EX $15.00

Donald Duck Draw & Paint, Whitman, 1936, VG+ $30.00

Dr Kildare Coloring Book, Saalfield, 1963, some coloring, EX.$15.00

Droopy Coloring Book, Whitman, 1957, 7x7", NM........$35.00

Dudley Do-Right Cartoon Color Fun, Whitman, 1972, some coloring, NMIB...$30.00

Dukes of Hazzard Coloring Book, 1981, M $10.00

Dumbo the Elephant Color & Read Book, 1972, some coloring, VG+, N2 ....$20.00

Family Affair Coloring Book, Whitman, 1968, Buffy w/Mrs Beasley surrounded by photo insets of cast, some coloring, EX...$10.00

Family Affair Trace & Color Book, Whitman, 1969, photo insert of family between Buffy & Jody, NM.......................$20.00

Felix the Cat Coloring Book, Saalfield, 1956, NM..........$50.00

First Ladies' Gowns Coloring Book, 1983, M...................$25.00

Flash Gordon Coloring Book, A McWilliams/ King Features #217525, M, $75.00.

Gene Autry Cowboy Paint Book, Merrill, 1940, oversized, some coloring, NM $50.00

Gilligan's Island Coloring Book, Whitman, 1965, Gilligan being chased by sea gulls, NM...$50.00

Good Times With Paint, Pencil, and Crayon, dated 1924, some coloring, G, A, $100.00. (Photo courtesy Randy Inman Auctions)

Goofy Coloring Book, Whitman/Saalfield, 1962, Goofy at easel, some coloring, EX $15.00

Gulliver's Travels Story & Coloring Book, Saalfield, 1939, some coloring, EX+...$50.00

Gumby & Poky Dot Book, Whitman, 1970, some coloring, EX $15.00

Happy Days, 1976, cast photo, some coloring, EX $20.00

Heidi Coloring Book, 1954, some coloring, EX $18.00

Hopalong Cassidy, Lowe, 1950, EX+...............................$65.00

Hot Wheels Coloring Book, 1989, some coloring, EX......$10.00

Elizabeth Taylor Coloring Book, some coloring, EX, $25.00.

Family Affair Color-By-Number, Whitman, 1969, Buffy sitting holding up book, NM $15.00

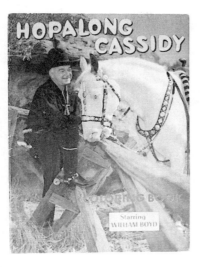

Hopalong Cassidy Coloring Book, Whitman, Authorized Edition, 1951, M, $75.00.

Howdy Doody Puppet Show Punch-Out Book, Whitman, 1952, EX...$85.00

Howdy Doody Sticker Fun to Cut & Paste/Follow the Dots, Whitman, 1951, used, EX+ $25.00

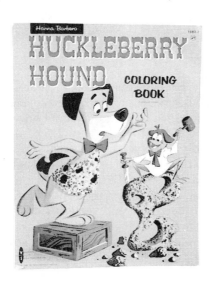

Huckleberry Hound Coloring Book, Western Printing #1883-2, 1962, some coloring, EX, $15.00. (Photo courtesy June Moon)

Jack & the Beanstalk, 1960s, some coloring, NM.............$10.00

Jack Webb's Safety Squad Coloring Book, Samuel Lowe, 1956, some coloring, EX+..$40.00

Jetsons Coloring Book, Whitman, 1963, some coloring, NM...$30.00

Kiddie Dreams Coloring Book, 1965, some coloring, EX..$10.00

Kit Carson, Lowell, 1957, some coloring, NM.................$30.00

Lady & the Tramp Coloring Book, Whitman, 1954, some coloring, EX $25.00

Land of the Lost Coloring & Activity Book, Whitman #1271, 1975, M..$25.00

Laverne & Shirley Coloring & Activity Book, Waldman, 1983, 4 different, M, ea...$10.00

Linus the Lion-Hearted, Whitman, 1965, heavy coloring, EX+ .$20.00

Little Lulu Coloring Book, #1663, some coloring, G........$10.00

Little Orphan Annie's Junior Commandos Coloring Book, Saalfield, 1943, some coloring, EX+ $40.00

Looney Tunes/Merry Melodies Paint Book, c Leon Schlesinger, 1940s, EX $75.00

Magilla Gorilla Sticker Fun Book, Whitman, 1964, used, EX.$20.00

Mickey & Donald Paint Book, Whitman, 1939, M..........$40.00

Millie the Lovable Monster, Artcraft, 1963, some coloring, EX.$25.00

Miss America, 1990, M, N2...$15.00

Mork From Ork — An Outerspace Activity Book, Wonder Books, 1979, M...$15.00

Mrs. Beasley Coloring Book, Whitman #1648, 1975, M, $25.00. (Photo courtesy Greg Davis and Bill Morgan)

My Three Sons Coloring Book, Artcraft, 1971, some coloring, NM...$25.00

Nancy & Sluggo Coloring Book, 1955, some coloring, EX.$35.00

Nanny & the Professor Coloring Book, 1971, NM...........$20.00

New Zoo Revue Coloring Book, Artcraft #5484, 1973, M .$30.00

New Zoo Revue Coloring Book, Saalfield #CO544, 1973, M.$30.00

New Zoo Revue Press-Out & Play Album, Artcraft, 1974, M.$30.00

Partridge Family Coloring Book, Saalfield #3839, 1971, M .$30.00

Partridge Family Pictures to Color, Artcraft, 1970, M $30.00

Partridge Family Pictures to Color, Saalfield #3997, 1971, M..$30.00

Patty Duke Coloring Book, Whitman #1122 or #1141, 1964-1966, M, ea $30.00

Pluto Coloring Book, 1971, some coloring, EX, N2..........$15.00

Pogo Coloring Book, Walt Kelly/Treasure Books, 1964, NM.$85.00

Popeye Coloring Book, 1964, steering ship, some coloring, EX, N2 ....$20.00

Popeye Coloring Book, 1978, some coloring, EX, N2.......$15.00

Porky Pig Paint Book, Looney Tunes/Merry Melodies, early, some coloring, EX $125.00

Prince Valiant Coloring Book, Saalfield, 1957, some coloring, scarce, EX..$30.00

Punky Brewster Coloring Book, 1987, some coloring, EX, N2 .$15.00

Puss 'N Boots Coloring Book, 1970s, M............................$15.00

Raggedy Ann & Andy Dot-to-Dot Book, 1972, some coloring, VG+, N2 ....$15.00

Rescuers, Golden #1224-03, 1977, M..............................$10.00

Rin-Tin-Tin, Whitman, 1956, some coloring, EX+ $25.00

Rita Hayworth Coloring Book, Merrill, 1942, some coloring, EX..$55.00

Road Runner Coloring Book, Whitman, 1968, NM..........$20.00

Rocketeer Coloring Book, Golden #2968, 1991, M............$5.00

Roy Rogers Double R Ranch Activity Book, Whitman & Frontiers Inc, 1955, some coloring, EX+ $50.00

Sabrina the Teenage Witch Coloring Book, Whitman, 1971, featuring the Archie gang, some coloring, NM..........$25.00
Shirley Temple's My Book to Color, Saalfield #1768, 1937, EX.$50.00
Sigmund & the Sea Monsters Coloring Book, Saalfield #C1853, 1974, M..$30.00
Six Million Dollar Man Activity Book, Rand McNally #C2471, 1977, M..$15.00
Six Million Dollar Man Coloring Book, Artcraft #C1832, 1974, M..$15.00
Six Million Dollar Man Coloring Book, Rand McNally #C1520 or #C1868, 1976-77, M, ea................................$15.00
Snagglepuss Sticker Fun Book, Whitman, 1963, EX+ $25.00
Snow White & the Seven Dwarfs Paint Book, Whitman, 1952, some coloring, EX..$25.00
Spider-Man Seeing Double Coloring Book, 1976, some coloring, EX, N2..$15.00
Steve Canyon Coloring Book, Saalfield, 1952, oversized, NM.$50.00
Stingray Coloring Book, Whitman, 1966, some coloring, EX .$30.00

We Land on the Moon Coloring Book, 1969, EX, $15.00.

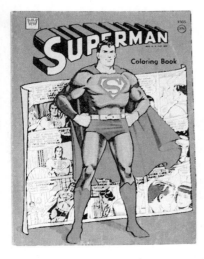

Superman Coloring Book, Whitman #1005, NM, $15.00.

Terry & the Pirates Coloring Book, Saalfield, 1946, NM .$50.00
Thief of Baghdad Coloring Book, Saalfield/UA, 1940, movie edition, some coloring, EX+ $50.00
Three Stooges, Lowe #2965, 1962, some coloring, EX $65.00
Three Stooges Coloring Book, Lowe #2855, 1959-60, some coloring, EX $75.00
Three Stooges Coloring Book, Whitman #1135, 1964, some coloring, VG $30.00
Tom & Jerry, Whitman, 1968, some coloring, EX+ $15.00
Underdog Coloring Book, Whitman, 1972, Underdog above city, some coloring, EX $20.00
Waltons Color & Activity Book, Whitman #1254, 1975, M.$20.00
Waltons Coloring Book, Whitman #1028, 1975, M.........$20.00
Waltons Sticker Book, Whitman #1691, M......................$30.00
Welcome Back Kotter, Whitman #1081, 1977, M............$20.00
Where's Huddles? Coloring Book, Whitman, 1971, some coloring, EX+ $20.00
Wild Bill Hickok, 1958, some coloring, VG, N2 ....$20.00
Woody Wood Pecker Magic Paintless Paint Book, Whitman, 1959, some painting, EX...$15.00
Woody Woodpecker Coloring Book, Watkins-Strathmore, 1956, Woody & Chilly Willy at wall, some coloring, EX $20.00

Woody Woodpecker Sticker Fun Book, Whitman, 1964, NM.$25.00
Woody Woodpecker's Heritage Coloring Book, 1973, some coloring, VG+, N2 ....$15.00
Zorro Coloring Book, Whitman #1586, 1958, some coloring, VG $15.00

Comic Books

For more than a half a century, kids of America raced to the bookstand as soon as the new comics came in for the month and for 10¢ an issue kept up on the adventures of their favorite super heroes, cowboys, space explorers, and cartoon characters. By far most were eventually discarded — after they were traded one friend to another, stacked on closet shelves, and finally confiscated by Mom. Discount the survivors that were torn or otherwise damaged over the years and those about the mundane, and of those remaining, some could be quite valuable. In fact, first editions of high-grade comics books or those showcasing the first appearance of a major character often bring $500.00 and more. Rarity, age, and quality of the artwork are prime factors in determining value, and condition is critical. If you want to seriously collect comic books, you'll need to refer to a good comic book price guide such as Overstreet's.

Our source for comic books is Philip Norman (N2).

Adventures of Mighty Mouse, #149, 1961, VG+, N2.......$20.00
Adventures of the Big Boy, #181, 1972, VG+, N2............$10.00
Alvin & the Chipmunks, #14, 1966, VG+, N2 ....$15.00
Aquaman, #23, 1965, VG, N2......................................$25.00
Aquaman, #30, 1966, VG, N2......................................$20.00
Army War Heroes, #16, 1966, VG, N2 ....$10.00
Batman, #104, 1956, G, N2...$35.00
Batman, #143, 1961, VG+, N2 ....$25.00
Batman, #155, 1963, VG+, N2 ....$50.00
Batman, #171, 1965, VG, N2.......................................$60.00
Batman, #179, 1966, VG+, N2 ....$25.00
Batman, #188, 1966, VG, N2.......................................$15.00
Brave & the Bold (Batman vs Eclipso), #64, 1966, VG+, N2.$25.00
Buffalo Bill Jr, #742, 1956, EX, N2 ....$25.00
Bugs Bunny Halloween Fun, #102, 1965, VG, N2............$10.00

Buster Brown, #39, 1955, VG, N2..........................$15.00
Casper the Friendly Ghost, #23, 1960, VG, N2.............$10.00
Chan Clan, #1, 1973, EX, N2..............................$20.00
Cisco Kid, #14, 1954, EX, N2.............................$25.00
Colt .45, #9, 1961, VG+, N2..............................$25.00
Conan the Barbarian, #7, 1971, VG+, N2...................$20.00
Daffy Duck, #14, 1958, VG+, N2...........................$10.00

Dark Shadows, #15, 1972, EX, $15.00.

Date With Judy, #3, 1948, VG, N2.........................$20.00
Detective Comics, #357, 1966, EX, N2.....................$25.00
Donald Duck, #56, 1957, VG+, N2..........................$10.00
Dude Rancher, #30, 1956, EX, N2..........................$20.00
E-Man, #1, 1973, EX, N2..................................$15.00
Fat Albert, #13, 1976, VG+, N2...........................$15.00
Fight Comics, #30, 1944, Fair, N2........................$15.00
Flintstones, #41, 1967, VG+, N2..........................$10.00
Fox & the Crow, #18, 1954, VG, N2........................$15.00
Funky Phantom, #3, 1974, VG+, N2.........................$10.00
Funny Folks, #8, 1948, VG, N2............................$20.00
Funny Stuff, #63, 1951, VG, N2...........................$15.00
Get Smart, #7, 1967, VG+, N2.............................$20.00
Gorgo, #6, 1962, VG+, N2.................................$25.00
Great Grape Ape, #1, 1976, VG, N2........................$10.00
Green Hornet, #1, 1966, EX, N2...........................$50.00

Invisible Man, #1, 1955, NM, $65.00.

Gunslinger, #1220, 1961, VG+, N2.........................$35.00
Gunsmoke, #12, 1959, VG+, N2.............................$25.00
Hanna-Barbera Laff-a-Lympics, #3, 1978, EX, N2...........$10.00
Hennesey, #1200, 1961, VG+, N2...........................$20.00
Hot Rod Racers, #75, 1965, VG, N2........................$15.00
I Spy, #3, 1967, EX, N2..................................$35.00
Inch High Private Eye, #14, 1974, VG, N2.................$10.00
Incredible Hulk, #243, 1979, EX, N2......................$10.00
Jesse James, #22, 1955, VG+, N2..........................$15.00
Journey Into Mystery w/Thor, #106, 1964, VG, N2..........$15.00
Kid Cowboy, #05, 1951, VG, N2............................$15.00
Krofft Supershow, #2, 1978, VG+, N2......................$15.00
Laff-A-Lympics, #13, 1979, EX, N2........................$10.00
Lawman, #5, 1960, VG+, N2................................$25.00
Life w/Archie, #2, 1964, VG+, N2.........................$10.00
Logan's Run, #1, 1976, VG+, N2...........................$10.00
Lomax NYPD, #1, 1975, VG+, N2............................$15.00
Lost in Space, #39, 1974, VG, N2.........................$10.00
Magilla Gorilla, #4, 1971, VG+, N2.......................$15.00
Magnus Robot Fighter, #2, 1963, VG+, N2..................$35.00
Magnus Robot Fighter, #23, 1968, EX, N2..................$10.00
Man From UNCLE, #9, 1966, VG+, N2........................$20.00
Mandrake the Magician, #5, 1967, VG+, N2.................$10.00
Masters of the Universe, #1, 1986, EX, N2................$10.00

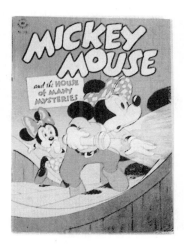

Mickey Mouse and the House of Many Mysteries, #116, 1946, EX, $40.00.

Monkees, #04, 1967, EX, N2...............................$35.00
Nancy & Sluggo, #133, 1956, VG+, N2......................$20.00
Navy Action, #18, 1957, VG, N2...........................$10.00
Nyoka the Jungle Girl, #39, 1950, VG, N2.................$15.00
Occult Files of Dr Spektor, #1, 1973, EX, N2.............$20.00
Oswald the Rabbit, #183, 1948, VG, N2....................$15.00
Outlaw Kid, #1, 1970, VG+, N2............................$10.00
Planet of the Apes, #3, #4, or #5, 1975-76, EX, N2, ea...$15.00
Planet of the Apes, #9, 1976, VG+, N2....................$10.00
Porky Pig, #21, 1968, VG+, N2............................$10.00
Raiders of the Lost Ark, #1, 1981, VG+, N2...............$10.00
Real Screen Comics, #13, 1947, VG, N2....................$20.00
Reptisaurus the Terrible, #3, 1962, VG+, N2..............$15.00
Ripley's Believe It or Not, #1, 1977, 3x6", VG+, N2......$15.00
Roy Rogers, #25, 1950, VG+, N2...........................$25.00
Six Million Dollar Man, #5, 1977, VG+, N2................$15.00
Sleeping Beauty, #564, 1954, VG+, N2.....................$15.00

Spartacus, #1139, 1960, EX, N2 ....$35.00
Speed Buggy, #2, 1975, VG, N2 ....$10.00
Spooky, #38, 1971, VG+, N2 ....$10.00
Star Trek, #26, 1974, VG+, N2 ....$20.00
Star Wars, #16, 1978, EX, N2 ....$10.00
Super Pup, #5, 1954, VG+, N2.................................$20.00
Taffy, #7 (Dane Clark issue), 1947, VG, N2 ....$15.00

Tarzan, #112, 1959, VG, $25.00.

Teen Titans, #50, 1977, NM, N2 ....$25.00
Texas Rangers, #62, 1967, VG+, N2 ....$10.00
Tom Mix, #34, 1950, VG+, N2 ....$25.00
Top Cat, #29, 1970, N2 ....$10.00
Treasure Chest, #20, Vol 17, 1962, VG+, N2 ....$35.00
Twilight Zone, #1, 1977, 6x3", EX, N2 ....$15.00
Uncle Scrooge, #109, 1956, VG+, N2 ....$15.00
V, #3, 1985, EX, N2 ....$10.00

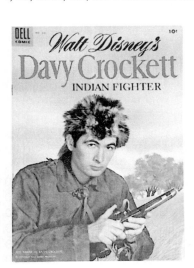

Walt Disney's Davy Crockett, Indian Fighter, #631, EX, $45.00.

Weird Science, #1, 1990, VG+, N2 ....$10.00
Welcome Back Kotter, #2, 1976, EX, N2 ....$15.00
Wild Wild West, #2, 1966, EX, N2 ....$45.00
Woody Woodpecker, #30, 1955, VG, N2 ....$10.00
Wyatt Earp, #07, 1959, VG+, N2 ....$25.00
Zane Grey, #30, 1956, EX, N2 ....$25.00
2001: A Space Odyssey, #1, 1976, VG, N2 ....$15.00

Corgi

The Corgi legacy is a rich one, beginning in 1934 with parent company Mettoy of Swansea, South Wales. In 1956 Mettoy merged with Playcraft Ltd. to form Mettoy Playcraft Ltd. and changed the brand name from Mettoy to Corgi in honor of Queen Elizabeth's beloved Welsh Corgis, which she could regularly be seen taking for walks around Buckingham palace.

In 1993 Mattel bought the Corgi brand and for a short time attempted to maintain the tradition of producing Corgi quality collectible toys. Shortly afterward, employees of the Welsh manufacturing center purchased back the Corgi Collectibles line from Mattel. In July 1999 the brand was purchased again, this time by Zindart, an American-owned company based in Hong Kong, where the Corgi Classics line is now produced.

Some of the most highly prized Corgi toys in today's collectors' market are the character-related vehicles. The assortment includes the cars of secret agent James Bond, including several variations of his Aston-Martin, his Lotus Esprit complete with underwater maneuvering fins, and other 007 vehicles. Batman's Batmobile and Batboat and the Man From U.N.C.L.E.'s Thrushbuster are among the favorites as well.

Our values are for models in new condition in their original package.

Advisor: Dana Johnson (J3)

#50, Massey-Ferguson 50B Tractor $75.00
#50, Massey-Ferguson 65 Tractor $125.00
#51, Massey-Ferguson Tipper Trailer $40.00
#53, Massey-Ferguson Tractor Shovel $125.00
#54, Fordson Half-Track Tractor $175.00
#54, Massey-Ferguson Tractor Shovel $75.00
#55, David Brown Tractor $75.00
#55, Fordson Power Major Tractor $125.00
#56, Plough $35.00
#57, Massey-Ferguson Tractor & Fork...............................$125.00
#58, Beast Carrier $65.00
#60, Fordson Power Major Tractor $120.00
#61, Four-Furrow Plough $35.00
#62, Ford Tipper Trailer $35.00
#64, Conveyor on Jeep $120.00
#66, Massey-Ferguson 165 Tractor.....................................$95.00
#67, Ford 5000 Super Major Tractor $110.00
#69, Massey-Ferguson Tractor Shovel $100.00
#71, Fordson Disc Harrow $40.00
#72, Ford 5000 Tractor & Trencher $130.00
#73, Massey-Ferguson Tractor & Saw $125.00
#74, Ford 5000 Tractor & Scoop...$125.00
#100, Dropside Trailer...$40.00
#101, Platform Trailer..$40.00
#102, Pony Trailer..$40.00
#104, Dolphin Cabin Cruiser $45.00
#107, Batboat & Trailer..$175.00
#109, Pennyburn Trailer $65.00
#112, Rice Horse Box $50.00
#150, Surtees TS9..$60.00

#150, Vanwall, regular $100.00
#151, Lotus XI, regular $100.00
#151, McLaren Yardley M19A $50.00
#152, BRM Racer $100.00
#152, Ferrari 312 B2 ....$50.00
#153, Bluebird Record Car $150.00
#153, Team Surtees $60.00
#154, Ferrari Formula I $60.00
#154, Lotus John Player $55.00
#154, Lotus Texaco Special $55.00
#155, Shadow FI Racer $55.00
#156, Shadow FI, Graham Hill $55.00
#158, Lotus Climax $65.00
#158, Tyrrell-Ford Elf $55.00
#159, Cooper Maserati $65.00
#159, STP Patrick Eagle Racer $60.00
#160, Hesketh Racer $60.00
#161, Elf-Tyrrell Project 34 ....$60.00
#161, Santa Pod Commuter $60.00
#162, Quartermaster Dragster $50.00
#162, Tyrell P34 Racer $55.00
#163, Santa Pod Dragster $55.00
#164, Wild Honey Dragster $55.00
#165, Adams Bros' Dragster $50.00
#166, Ford Mustang $50.00
#167, USA Racing Buggy $45.00
#169, Starfighter Jet Dragster $60.00
#170, John Wolfe's Dragster $60.00
#190, Lotus John Player Special $75.00
#191, McLaren Texaco-Marlboro $75.00
#200, BMC Mini 1000 ....$60.00
#200, Ford Consul, dual colors $200.00
#200, Ford Consul, solid colors $175.00
#200m, Ford Consul, w/motor $200.00
#201, Austin Cambridge $200.00
#201, Saint's Volvo $200.00
#201m, Austin Cambridge $200.00
#201m, Austin Cambridge, w/motor $225.00
#202, Morris Cowley $150.00
#202, Renault 16TS $60.00
#202m, Morris Cowley, w/motor $175.00
#203, Detomaso Mangusta $55.00
#203, Vauxhall Velox, dual colors $200.00
#203, Vauxhall Velox, solid colors $175.00
#203, Vauxhall Velox, w/motor, dual colors $275.00
#203, Vauxhall Velox, w/motor, red or yel, ea $225.00
#204, Morris Mini-Minor, bl $250.00
#204, Rover 90, other colors $200.00
#204, Rover 90, wht & red, 2-tone $250.00
#204m, Rover 90, w/motor $225.00
#205, Riley Pathfinder, bl $175.00
#205, Riley Pathfinder, red $125.00
#205m, Riley Pathfinder, w/motor, bl $175.00
#205m, Riley Pathfinder, w/motor, red $225.00
#206, Hillman Husky, metallic bl & silver $175.00
#206, Hillman Husky Estate, metallic bl & silver, 2-tone $175.00
#206, Hillman Husky Estate, solid colors $150.00
#206m, Hillman Husky Estate, w/motor $175.00

#207, Standard Vanguard $150.00
#207m, Standard Vanguard, w/motor $175.00
#208, Jaguar 2.4 Saloon, no suspension $140.00
#208m, Jaguar 2.4 Saloon, w/motor $180.00
#208s, Jaguar 2.4 Saloon, w/suspension $165.00
#209, Riley Police Car $125.00
#210, Citroen DS19 ....$110.00
#210s, Citroen DS19, w/suspension $120.00
#211, Studebaker Golden Hawk, no suspension $150.00
#211, Studebaker Golden Hawk, w/pnt suspension $175.00
#211m, Studebaker Golden Hawk, w/motor $175.00
#211s, Studebaker Golden Hawk, plated, w/suspension $125.00
#213, Jaguar Fire Chief $175.00
#213s, Jaguar Fire Chief, w/suspension $225.00
#214, Ford Thunderbird, no suspension $140.00
#214m, Ford Thunderbird, w/motor $325.00
#214s, Ford Thunderbird, w/suspension $120.00
#215, Ford Thunderbird Sport, no suspension $140.00
#215s, Ford Thunderbird Sport, w/suspension $125.00
#216, Austin A-40, red & blk $150.00
#216, Austin A-40, 2-tone bl $140.00
#216m, Austin A-40, w/motor $325.00
#217, Fiat 1800 ....$85.00

#218, Aston-Martin DB4 Saloon, $125.00. (From the collection of Al Rapp)

#219, Plymouth Suburban $110.00
#220, Chevrolet Impala $90.00
#221, Chevrolet Impala Taxi $125.00
#222, Renault Floride $110.00
#223, Chevrolet Police $140.00
#224, Bentley Continental $125.00
#225, Austin 7, red $125.00
#225, Austin 7, yel $325.00
#226, Morris Mini-Minor $125.00
#227, Mini-Cooper Rally $275.00
#228, Volvo P-1800 ....$90.00
#229, Chevrolet Corvair $75.00
#230, Mercedes Benz 220SE, blk $140.00
#230, Mercedes Benz 220SE, red $90.00
#231, Triumph Herald $125.00
#232, Fiat 2100 ....$90.00
#233, Heinkel Trojan $90.00

#234, Ford Consul Classic $100.00
#235, Oldsmobile Super 88.................................$95.00
#236, Austin A60, right-hand drive $95.00
#237, Oldsmobile Sheriff's Car............................$120.00
#238, Jaguar MK10, metallic gr or silver $190.00
#238, Jaguar MK10, metallic red or bl..............$125.00
#239, VW Karmann Ghia $90.00
#240, Fiat 600 Jolly...$150.00
#241, Chrysler Ghia...$80.00
#242, Fiat 600 Jolly...$175.00

#245, Buick Riviera, $100.00. (From the collection of Al Rapp)

#246, Chrysler Imperial, metallic turq $265.00
#246, Chrysler Imperial, red $125.00
#247, Mercedes Benz 600 Pullman $90.00
#248, Chevrolet Impala $95.00
#249, Morris Mini-Cooper, wicker $135.00
#251, Hillman Imp $100.00
#252, Rover 2000, metallic bl.............................$95.00
#252, Rover 2000, metallic maroon $195.00
#253, Mercedes Benz 220SE $110.00
#255, Austin A60, left-hand drive $225.00
#256, VW 1200 East Africa Safari $240.00
#258, Saint's Volvo P1800, red hood..................$250.00
#258, Saint's Volvo P1800, wht hood $175.00
#259, Citroen Le Dandy, bl $180.00
#259, Citroen Le Dandy, maroon $120.00
#259, Penguin Mobile...$65.00
#260, Renault R16 ....$65.00
#261, James Bond's Aston Martin DB5................$250.00
#261, Spiderbuggy..$100.00
#262, Capt Marvel's Porsche $65.00
#262, Lincoln Continental Limo, bl $180.00
#262, Lincoln Continental Limo, gold $110.00
#263, Rambler Marlin..$95.00
#264, Incredible Hulk's Mazda Pickup $75.00
#264, Oldsmobile Toronado $110.00
#265, Supermobile $75.00
#266, Chitty-Chitty Bang-Bang, orig..................$395.00
#266, Chitty-Chitty Bang-Bang, replica $130.00
#266, Superbike $75.00
#267, Batmobile, red 'Bat'-hubs $425.00
#267, Batmobile, w/red whizwheels.....................$525.00
#267, Batmobile, w/whizwheels............................$125.00

#268, Batman's Bat Bike $70.00
#268, Green Hornet's Black Beauty $375.00
#269, James Bond's Lotus Esprit $120.00
#270, James Bond's Aston Martin, w/tire slashers, 1/43 scale .$300.00
#270, James Bond's Aston Martin, w/whizwheels, 1/43 scale ...$135.00

#271, Ghia Mangusta de Tomaso, $75.00. (From the collection of Al Rapp)

#271, James Bond's Aston Martin $110.00
#272, James Bond's Citroen 2CV $60.00
#273, Honda Driving School..............................$55.00
#273, Rolls Royce Silver Shadow.......................$110.00
#274, Bentley Mulliner $90.00
#275, Mini Metro, colors other than gold $35.00
#275, Mini Metro, gold......................................$75.00
#275, Rover 2000 TC, gr $85.00
#275, Rover 2000 TC, wht $170.00
#275, Royal Wedding Mini Metro......................$30.00
#276, Oldsmobile Toronado, metallic gold $175.00
#276, Oldsmobile Toronado, metallic red $85.00
#276, Triumph Acclaim.....................................$35.00
#277, Monkeemobile...$320.00
#277, Triumph Driving School $35.00
#279, Rolls Royce Corniche $45.00
#280, Rolls Royce Silver Shadow, colors other than silver .$60.00
#280, Rolls Royce Silver Shadow, silver.............$90.00
#281, Austin Mini..$30.00
#281, Rover 2000 TC..$100.00
#282, Mini Cooper Rally Car $110.00
#283, DAF City Car..$45.00
#284, Citroen SM $60.00
#285, Mercedes Benz 240D.................................$40.00
#286, Jaguar XJ12C $55.00
#287, Citroen Dyane $40.00
#288, Minissima $35.00
#289, VW Polo $35.00
#290, Kojak's Buick, w/hat $85.00
#290, Kojak's Buick, no hat $140.00
#291, AMC Pacer $35.00
#291, Mercedes Benz 240 Rally $45.00
#292, Starsky & Hutch's Ford Torino $95.00
#293, Renault 5TS $30.00
#294, Renault Alpine $30.00

#298, Magnum PI's Ferrari $60.00	#319, Lotus Elan, gr or yel, ea............................$140.00
#299, Ford Sierra 2.3 Ghia.................................$35.00	#319, Lotus Elan, red or bl, ea $100.00
#300, Austin Healey, red or cream $175.00	#320, Saint's Jaguar XJS......................................$85.00
#300, Austin Healey Sports Car, bl $325.00	#321, Monte Carlo Mini Cooper, 1965.............$300.00
#300, Chevrolet Corvette Stingray $110.00	#321, Monte Carlo Mini Cooper, 1966, w/autographs ...$600.00
#300, Ferrari Daytona $35.00	#321, Porsche 924, metallic gr.............................$70.00
#301, Iso Grifo 7 Litre...$75.00	#321, Porsche 924, red $50.00
#301, Lotus Elite $35.00	#322, Rover Monte Carlo....................................$180.00
#301, Triumph TR2 Sports Car $175.00	#323, Citroen DS19 Monte Carlo.......................$150.00
#302, Hillman Hunter Rally, kangaroo $140.00	#323, Ferrari Daytona 365 GTB4.........................$40.00
#302, MGA Sports Car $155.00	#324, Marcos Volvo 1800 GT $80.00
#302, VW Polo $30.00	#325, Chevrolet Caprice......................................$80.00
#303, Mercedes Benz 300SL...............................$125.00	#325, Ford Mustang Competition $95.00
#303, Porsche 924 ....$35.00	#326, Chevrolet Police Car $60.00
#303, Roger Clark's Ford Capri, gold wheels w/red hubs .$250.00	#327, Chevrolet Caprice Cab $60.00
#303, Roger Clark's Ford Capri, w/whizwheels.........$95.00	#327, MGB GT..$140.00
#303s, Mercedes Benz 300SL, w/suspension ...$125.00	#328, Hillman Imp Monte Carlo $140.00
#304, Chevrolet SS350 Camaro............................$75.00	#329, Ford Mustang Rally...................................$60.00
#304, Mercedes Benz 300SL, colors other than yel $125.00	#329, Opel Senator, bl or bronze, ea................$55.00
#304, Mercedes Benz 300SL, yel $450.00	#329, Opel Senator, silver..................................$60.00
#304s, Mercedes Benz 300SL, w/suspension ...$125.00	#330, Porsche Carrera 6, wht & bl $125.00
#305, Mini Marcos GT 850 ....$80.00	#330, Porsche Carrera 6, wht & red $75.00
#305, Triumph TR3 ....$170.00	#331, Ford Capri Rally...$90.00
#306, Fiat X1/9..$45.00	#332, Lancia Fulvia Sport, red or bl, ea............$75.00
#306, Morris Marina $65.00	#332, Lancia Fulvia Sport, yel & blk.................$140.00
#307, Jaguar E Type $150.00	#332, Opel, Doctor's Car $50.00
#307, Renault...$30.00	#334, Ford Escort $35.00
#308, BMW M1 Racer, gold plated $110.00	#334, Mini Magnifique $90.00
#308, BMW M1 Racer, yel $35.00	#335, Jaguar 4.2 Litre E Type............................$150.00
#308, Monte Carlo BMC Mini Cooper S $125.00	#336, James Bond's Toyota 2000GT...................$395.00
#309, Aston Martin DB4......................................$125.00	#337, Chevrolet Stingray.....................................$75.00
#309, Aston Martin DB4, w/spoked hubs $195.00	#338, Chevrolet SS350 Camaro $90.00
#309, VW Polo Turbo...$35.00	#338, Rover 3500 ....$40.00
#310, Chevrolet Corvette, bronze $165.00	#339, Rover 3500 Police Car................................$40.00
#310, Chevrolet Corvette, red or silver, ea $80.00	#339, 1967 Mini Cooper Monte Carlo, w/roof rack $300.00
#310, Porsche 924 ....$35.00	#340, Rover Triplex $35.00
#311, Ford Capri, orange $125.00	#340, 1967 Sunbeam IMP Monte Carlo $135.00
#311, Ford Capri, red $80.00	#341, Chevrolet Caprice Racer $35.00
#311, Ford Capri, w/gold hubs..........................$225.00	#341, Mini Marcos GT850....................................$75.00
#312, Ford Capri S $40.00	#342, Lamborghini P400 GT Miura $75.00
#312, Jaguar E Type $120.00	#342, Professionals Ford Capri $90.00
#312, Marcos Mantis $50.00	#342, Professionals Ford Capri, w/chrome bumpers........$120.00
#313, Ford Cortina, bronze or bl $100.00	#343, Pontiac Firebird, red hubs $120.00
#313, Ford Cortina, yel.......................................$300.00	
#314, Ferrari Berlinetta Le Mans $65.00	
#314, Supercat Jaguar $30.00	
#315, Lotus Elite $35.00	
#315, Simca Sports Car, metallic bl $190.00	
#315, Simca Sports Car, silver $65.00	
#316, Ford GT 70...$50.00	
#316, NSU Sports Prinz.......................................$90.00	
#317, Mini Cooper Monte Carlo $200.00	
#318, Jaguar XJS..$25.00	
#318, Lotus Elan, copper $300.00	
#318, Lotus Elan, metallic bl $110.00	
#318, Lotus Elan, wht...$250.00	
#319, Jaguar XJS..$35.00	
#319, Lamborghini P400 GT Miura....................$35.00	

#345, MGC GT Competition Model, yellow, $150.00. (From the collection of Al Rapp)

#343, Pontiac Firebird, w/whizwheels................................$70.00
#344, Ferrari 206 Dino Sport...$85.00
#345, Honda Prelude $35.00
#345, MGC GT, orange..$320.00
#346, Citroen 2 CV...$25.00
#347, Chevrolet Astro 1, red hubs.................................$120.00
#347, Chevrolet Astro 1, w/whizwheels..........................$50.00
#348, Flower Power Mustang Stock Car $140.00
#348, Pop Art Mustang Stock Car $140.00
#348, Vegas Ford Thunderbird $100.00
#349, Pop Art Morris Mini, from $1600 to................$2,200.00
#350, Thunderbird Guided Missile $125.00
#351, RAF Land Rover..$110.00
#352, RAF Vanguard Staff Car..$110.00
#353, Radar Scanner...$70.00
#354, Commer Military Ambulance $125.00
#355, Commer Military Police $135.00
#356, VW Personnel Carrier $135.00
#357, Land Rover Weapons Carrier $180.00
#358, Oldsmobile Staff Car $140.00
#359, Commer Army Field Kitchen $165.00
#370, Ford Cobra Mustang $35.00
#371, Porsche Carrera..$50.00
#373, Peugeot 505..$35.00
#373, VW Police Car, Polizei...$165.00
#374, Jaguar 4.2 Litre E Type..$110.00
#374, Jaguar 5.3 Litre $90.00
#375, Toyota 2000 GT...$110.00
#376, Chevrolet Stingray Stock Car $55.00
#377, Marcos 3 Litre, wht & gray....................................$120.00
#377, Marcos 3 Litre, yel or bl, ea $75.00
#378, Ferrari 308 GT..$30.00
#378, MGC GT..$160.00
#380, Alfa Romeo P33...$60.00
#380, Beach Buggy..$55.00
#381, Renault Turbo $30.00
#382, Lotus Elite $35.00
#382, Porsche Targa 911S...$65.00
#383, VW 1200, red or orange, ea $70.00
#383, VW 1200, Swiss PTT $140.00
#383, VW 1200, yel ADAC...$200.00
#384, Adams Bros' Probe 15 ....$65.00
#384, Renault 11 GTL, cream $30.00
#384, Renault 11 GTL, maroon $45.00
#384, VW 1200 Rally $75.00
#385, Porsche 917 ....$40.00
#386, Bertone Runabout...$65.00
#387, Chevrolet Corvette Stingray $100.00
#388, Mercedes Benz C111...$55.00
#389, Reliant Bond Bug 700, gr $125.00
#389, Reliant Bond Bug 700 ES, orange $70.00
#391, James Bond's 007 Ford Mustang $250.00
#392, Bertone Shake Buggy $55.00
#393, Mercedes Benz 350 SL, bl......................................$60.00
#393, Mercedes Benz 350 SL, metallic gr.........................$120.00
#393, Mercedes Benz 350 SL, wht..................................$90.00
#394, Datsun 240Z, East African Safari $60.00
#396, Datsun 240Z, US Rally...$60.00

#397, Can Am Porsche Audi...$40.00
#400, VW Driving School, bl...$70.00
#400, VW Driving School, red...$165.00
#401, VW 1200..$65.00
#402, Ford Cortina GXL, wht w/red stripe......................$80.00
#402, Ford Cortina GXL Police, wht $65.00
#402, Ford Cortina GXL Polizei......................................$165.00
#403, Bedford Daily Express $165.00
#403, Thwaites Dumper..$55.00
#403m, Bedford KLG Plugs, w/motor.............................$250.00
#404, Bedford Dormobile, cream, maroon & turq $110.00
#404, Bedford Dormobile, yel & 2-tone bl......................$225.00
#404, Bedford Dormobile, yel w/bl roof $140.00
#404m, Bedford Dormobile, w/motor..............................$175.00
#405, Bedford Utilicon Fire Department, gr $175.00
#405, Bedford Utilicon Fire Department, red $225.00
#405, Chevrolet Superior Ambulance..............................$45.00
#405, Ford Milk Float $35.00
#405m, Bedford Utilicon Fire Tender, w/motor $250.00
#406, Land Rover Pickup..$85.00
#406, Mercedes Ambulance $35.00
#406, Mercedes Benz Unimog $65.00
#407, Karrier Mobile Grocers...$165.00
#408, Bedford AA Road Service $150.00
#409, Allis Chalmers Fork Lift $40.00
#409, Forward Control Jeep FC-150................................$55.00
#409, Mercedes Dumper $60.00
#411, Karrier Lucozade Van..$165.00
#411, Mercedes 240D, orange $80.00
#411, Mercedes 240D Taxi, cream or blk, ea...................$65.00
#411, Mercedes 240D Taxi, orange w/blk roof $50.00
#412, Bedford Ambulance, split windscreen....................$135.00
#412, Bedford Ambulance, 1-pc windscreen....................$265.00
#412, Mercedes Police Car, Police...................................$60.00
#412, Mercedes Police Car, Polizei $45.00
#413, Karrier Bantam Butcher Shop $150.00
#413, Mazda Maintenance Truck $60.00
#413s, Karrier Bantam Butcher Shop, w/suspension.......$225.00
#414, Bedford Military Ambulance $120.00
#414, Coastguard Jaguar $55.00
#415, Mazda Camper $55.00
#416, Buick Police Car $50.00
#416, Radio Rescue Rover, bl..$125.00
#416, Radio Rescue Rover, yel $400.00
#416s, Radio Rescue Rover, w/suspension, bl $125.00
#416s, Radio Rescue Rover, w/suspension, yel $425.00
#417 Land Rover Breakdown $125.00
#417s, Land Rover Breakdown, w/suspension $95.00
#418, Austin Taxi, w/whizwheels $55.00
#419, Ford Zephyr, Rijks Politei $360.00
#419, Ford Zephyr Politei $320.00
#419, Jeep...$45.00
#420, Airbourne Caravan..$100.00
#421, Bedford Evening Standard.....................................$225.00
#422, Bedford Van, Corgi Toys, bl w/yel roof..................$500.00
#422, Bedford Van, Corgi Toys, yel w/bl roof.................$225.00
#422, Riot Police Wagon...$55.00
#423, Rough Rider Van..$55.00

#424, Ford Zephyr Estate Car	$90.00
#424, Security Van	$40.00
#425, London Taxi	$35.00
#426, Chipperfield's Circus Booking Office	$325.00
#426, Pinder's Circus Booking Office	$50.00
#428, Mister Softee's Ice Cream Van	$230.00
#428, Renault Police Car	$35.00
#429, Jaguar Police Car	$50.00
#430, Bermuda Taxi, metallic bl & red	$400.00
#430, Bermuda Taxi, wht	$125.00
#430, Porsche 924 Polizei	$40.00
#431, VW Pickup, metallic gold	$325.00
#431, VW Pickup, yel	$110.00
#432, Vantastic Van	$40.00
#433, VW Delivery Van	$110.00
#434, Charlie's Angels Van	$70.00
#434, VW Kombi	$110.00
#435, Karrier Dairy Van	$150.00
#435, Superman Van	$60.00
#436, Citroen Safari	$110.00
#436, Spider Van	$65.00
#437, Cadillac Ambulance	$110.00
#437, Coca-Cola Van	$55.00
#438, Land Rover, gr	$65.00
#438, Land Rover, Lepra	$400.00
#439, Chevrolet Fire Chief	$125.00
#440, Ford Consul Cortina Super Estate Car, w/golfer & caddy	$160.00
#440, Mazda Pickup	$40.00
#441, Jeep	$35.00
#441, VW Toblerone Van	$135.00
#443, Plymouth US Mail	$125.00
#445, Plymouth Sports Suburban	$100.00
#447, Walls Ice Cream Van	$325.00

#448, Mini Police Van, with dog and handler, $225.00. (From the collection of Al Rapp)

#448, Renegade Jeep	$30.00
#450, Austin Mini Van	$100.00
#450, Austin Mini Van, w/pnt grille	$160.00
#450, Peugeot Taxi	$35.00
#452, Commer Lorry	$145.00
#453, Commer Walls Van	$200.00
#454, Commer Platform Lorry	$140.00
#455, Karrier Bantam 2-Ton, bl	$125.00
#455, Karrier Bantam 2-Ton, red	$325.00
#456, ERF Dropside Lorry	$125.00
#457, ERF Platform Lorry	$115.00

#457, Talbot Matra Rancho, gr or red, ea	$35.00
#457, Talbot Matra Rancho, wht or orange, ea	$55.00
#458, ERF Tipper Dumper	$95.00
#459, ERF Moorhouse Van	$375.00
#459, Raygo Road Roller	$45.00
#460, ERF Cement Tipper	$45.00
#461, Police Vigilant Range Rover, Police	$45.00
#461, Police Vigilant Range Rover, Politie	$80.00
#462, Commer Van, Co-op	$150.00
#462, Commer Van, Hammonds	$170.00
#463, Commer Ambulance	$110.00
#464, Commer Police Van, City Police, minimum value	$325.00
#464, Commer Police Van, County Police, bl	$125.00
#464, Commer Police Van, Police, bl	$125.00
#464, Commer Police Van, Police, gr	$750.00
#464, Commer Police Van, Rijks Politie, bl, minimum value	$325.00
#465, Commer Pickup Truck	$70.00
#466, Commer Milk Float, Co-op	$180.00
#466, Commer Milk Float, wht	$75.00
#467, London Routemaster Bus	$85.00
#468, London Transport Routemaster Bus, Church's Shoes, red	$200.00
#468, London Transport Routemaster Bus, Design Centre, red	$250.00
#468, London Transport Routemaster Bus, Gamages, red	$200.00
#468, London Transport Routemaster Bus, Corgi Toys, brn, gr or cream, ea	$1,000.00
#468, London Transport Routemaster Bus, Corgi Toys, red	$100.00
#468, London Transport Routemaster Bus, Madame Tussand's, red	$200.00
#468, London Transport Routemaster Bus, Outspan, red	$65.00
#470, Disneyland Bus	$45.00
#470, Forward Control Jeep FC-150 Covered Truck	$65.00
#470, Greenline Bus	$30.00
#471, Silver Jubilee Bus	$55.00
#471, Smith's-Karrier Mobile Canteen, Joe's Diner	$155.00
#471, Smith's-Karrier Mobile Canteen, Potato Frittes	$325.00
#471, Woolworth Silver Jubilee Bus	$55.00
#472, Public Address Land Rover	$165.00

#474, Ford Musical Wall's Ice Cream Van, $275.00. (From the collection of Al Rapp)

#475, Citroen Ski Safari	$160.00
#477, Land Rover Breakdown, w/whizwheels	$70.00
#478, Forward Control Jeep, Tower Wagon	$120.00
#479, Mobile Camera Van	$150.00

#480, Chevrolet Impala Cab $95.00
#481, Chevrolet Police Patrol Car $125.00
#482, Chevrolet Fire Chief Car.....................................$100.00
#482, Range Rover Ambulance...$60.00
#483, Dodge Tipper...$65.00
#483, Police Range Rover, Belgian.................................$90.00
#484, AMC Pacer Rescue...$40.00
#484, AMC Pacer Secours...$65.00
#484, Livestock Transporter $70.00
#484, Mini Countryman Surfer, w/silver grille.............$175.00
#485, Mini Countryman Surfer, w/unpnt grille $240.00
#486, Chevrolet Kennel Service $120.00
#487, Chipperfield's Circus Parade...............................$200.00
#489, VW Police Car...$40.00
#490, Touring Caravan $35.00
#490, VW Breakdown Truck..$110.00

#491, Ford Consul Cortina Estate Wagon, $125.00. (From the Collection of Al Rapp)

#492, VW Police Car, Politie $275.00
#492, VW Police Car, Polizei $90.00
#492, VW Police Car, w/gr mudguards............................$300.00
#493, Mazda Pickup $45.00
#494, Bedford Tipper, red & silver $180.00
#494, Bedford Tipper, red & yel.......................................$90.00
#494, Bedford Tipper Truck, red & yel $90.00
#495, Mazda Open Truck $35.00
#497, Man From UNCLE, wht, minimum value $650.00
#497, Man From UNCLE Gun Firing Thrush-Buster.....$300.00
#499, Citroen, 1968 Olympics $225.00
#500, US Army Rover...$450.00
#503, Chipperfield's Circus Giraffe Transporter.............$150.00
#506, Sunbeam Imp Police $140.00
#508, Holiday Minibus $125.00
#509, Porsche Police Car, Polizei.......................................$95.00
#509, Porsche Police Car, Ritjks Politie..........................$165.00
#510, Citroen Tour De France $135.00
#511, Chipperfield's Circus Poodle Pickup $600.00
#513, Alpine Rescue Car...$350.00
#647, Buck Rogers' Starfighter...$75.00
#648, Space Shuttle...$50.00
#649, James Bond's Space Shuttle $90.00
#650, BOAC Concorde, all others (no gold logo on tail)..$65.00
#650, BOAC Concorde, gold logo on tail.......................$100.00
#651, Air France Concorde, all others (no gold tail design) .$65.00

#651, Air France Concorde, gold tail design................$140.00
#651, Japan Air Line Concorde $475.00
#653, Air Canada Concorde $375.00
#681, Stunt Bike..$250.00
#700, Motorway Ambulance...$35.00
#701, Intercity Minibus...$35.00
#703, Breakdown Truck..$35.00
#703, Hi Speed Fire Engine..$35.00
#801, Ford Thunderbird...$40.00
#801, Noddy's Car, blk-face golly...............................$1,200.00
#801, Noddy's Car, other than blk-face golly $475.00
#802, Mercedes Benz 300 Sl...$35.00
#802, Popeye's Paddle Wagon $625.00
#803, Beatle's Yellow Submarine $600.00
#804, Jaguar XK120 Rally $35.00
#804, Jaguar XK120 Rally, w/spats...................................$65.00
#804, Noddy's Car, Noddy only......................................$275.00
#804, Noddy's Car, w/Mr Tubby $350.00
#805, Hardy Boy's Rolls Royce.......................................$320.00
#805, Mercedes Benz 300 SC $35.00
#806, Lunar Bug..$150.00
#806, Mercedes Benz 300 SC $35.00
#807, Dougal's Car..$300.00
#808, Basil Brush's Car...$250.00
#809, Dick Dastardly's Racer $165.00
#810, Ford Thunderbird...$35.00

#811, James Bond's Moon Buggy, $525.00. (Photo courtesy June Moon)

#831, Mercedes Benz 300 SL $35.00
#851, Magic Roundabout Train $425.00
#852, Magic Roundabout Carousel $800.00
#853, Magic Roundabout Playground........................$1,500.00
#859, Mr McHenry's Trike..$275.00
#900, German Tank Tiger Mk I $60.00
#901, British Centurion Mk III $60.00
#902, American Tank M60 A1..$60.00
#903, British Chieftain Tank $60.00
#904, King Tiger Tank $60.00
#905, SU100 Tank Destroyer..$60.00
#906, Saladin Armoured Car..$60.00
#907, German Rocket Launcher $85.00
#908, French Recovery Tank $75.00

#909, Quad Gun Tank, Trailer & Field Gun $65.00
#920, Bell Helicopter $35.00
#921, Hughes Helicopter $35.00
#922, Sikorsky Helicopter $35.00
#923, Sikorsky Helicopter, military $35.00
#925, Batcopter $85.00
#926, Stromberg Helicopter $95.00
#927, Chopper Squad Helicopter $60.00
#928, Spidercopter $90.00
#929, Daily Planet Helicopter $85.00
#930, DRAX Helicopter $85.00
#931, Jet Police Helicopter $55.00

CLASSICS

Daimler 38HP, #9021, red w/4 figures, MIB $85.00
St Mary's County Mack CF Pumper, #52004, MIB $35.00
1915 Ford Model T, #901, MIB $85.00

Thornycroft Van, $35.00.

CORGITRONICS

#1001, Corgitronics Firestreak $90.00
#1002, Corgitronics Roadtrain $65.00
#1003, Ford Torino $50.00
#1004, Corgitronics Beep Beep Bus $50.00
#1005, Police Land Rover $50.00
#1006, Roadshow, Radio $60.00
#1007, Land Rover & Compressor $60.00
#1008, Chevrolet Fire Chief $50.00
#1009, Maestro MG1600 .... $50.00
#1011, Firestreak $40.00

EXPLORATION MODELS

#2022, Scanotron $60.00
#2023, Rocketron $60.00
#2024, Lasertron $60.00
#2025, Magnetron $60.00

GIFT SETS

#1, Car Transporter Set $850.00
#1, Ford Sierra & Caravan $40.00

#1, Ford 500 Tractor & Beast Trailer $160.00
#2, Land Rover & Pony Trailer $180.00
#2, Unimog Dumper $150.00
#3, Batmobile & Batboat, w/'Bat'-hubs $450.00
#3, Batmobile & Batboat, w/whiz wheels $250.00
#3, RAF Land Rover & Missile $250.00
#4, Country Farm Set $75.00
#4, RAF Land Rover & Missile $500.00
#5, Agricultural Set $300.00
#5, Country Farm Set, w/no hay $90.00
#5, Racing Car Set $300.00
#6, Rocket Age Set $1,000.00
#6, VW Transporter & Cooper Maserati $175.00
#7, Daktari Set $150.00
#7, Tractor & Trailer Set $130.00
#8, Combine Harvester Set $400.00
#8, Lions of Longleat $200.00
#9, Corporal Missile & Launcher $600.00
#9, Tractor w/Shovel & Trailer $200.00
#10, Centurion Tank & Transporter $140.00
#10, Jeep & Motorcycle Trailer $40.00
#10, Rambler Marlin, w/kayaks $210.00
#11, ERF Truck & Trailer $200.00
#11, London Set, no Policeman $135.00
#11, London Set, w/Policeman $600.00
#12, Chipperfield's Circus Crane Truck & Cage $300.00
#12, Glider Set $80.00
#12, Grand Prix Set $450.00
#13, Fordson Tractor & Plough $150.00
#13, Peugeot Tour De France $90.00
#13, Renault Tour De France $150.00
#14, Giant Daktari Set $500.00
#14, Tower Wagon $100.00
#15, Land Rover & Horsebox $100.00
#15, Silvertone Set $1,800.00
#16, Ecurie Ecosse Set $500.00
#17, Land Rover & Ferrari $200.00
#17, Military Set $85.00
#18, Emergency Set $80.00
#18, Fordson Tractor & Plough $125.00
#19, Chipperfield's Circus Rover & Elephant Trailer $325.00
#19, Emergency Set $80.00
#19, Flying Club Set $85.00
#20, Car Transporter Set, minimum value $900.00
#20, Emergency Set $70.00
#20, Golden Guinea Set $300.00
#21, Chipperfield's Circus Crane & Trailer, minimum value .$1,600.00
#21, ERF Milk Truck & Trailer $350.00
#21, Superman Set $250.00
#22, James Bond Set $265.00
#23, Chipperfield's Circus Set, w/Booking Office $1,000.00
#23, Spiderman Set $200.00
#24, Constructor Set $150.00
#24, Mercedes & Caravan $50.00
#25, Mantra Rancho & Trailer $50.00
#25, Shell or BP Garage Set, minimum value $1,600.00
#25, VW Transporter & Cooper Maserati $160.00
#26, Beach Bug Set $50.00

#26, Matra Rancho & Racer..............................$75.00
#27, Priestman Shovel Set................................$195.00
#28, Mazda Pickup & Dinghy, w/trailer..........$60.00
#28, Transporter Set $800.00
#29, Ferrari Racing Set $80.00
#29, Jeep & Horsebox.......................................$40.00
#29, Tractor & Trailer.......................................$140.00
#30, Grand Prix Set $285.00
#30, Pinder's Circus Rover & Trailer.............$135.00

#47, Ford 5000 Tractor and Conveyor, $195.00. (From the collection of Al Rapp)

#31, Buick Riviera with Boat, Trailer, and Water Skier, $250.00. (From the collection of Al Rapp)

HUSKIES

Huskies were marketed exclusively through the Woolworth stores from 1965 to 1969. In 1970, Corgi Juniors were introduced. Both lines were sold in blister packs. Models produced up to 1975 (as dated on the package) are valued from $15.00 to $30.00 (MIP), except for the character-related examples listed below.

#31, Safari Set...$100.00
#32, Lotus Racing Set.......................................$110.00
#32, Tractor & Trailer......................................$170.00
#33, Fordson Tractor & Carrier......................$150.00
#35, Chopper Squad $60.00
#35, London Set $175.00
#36, Tarzan Set $250.00
#36, Tornado Set...$250.00
#37, Fiat & Boat..$60.00
#37, Lotus Racing Team $500.00
#38, Jaguar & Powerboat.................................$75.00
#38, Mini Camping Set $100.00
#38, Monte Carlo Set $600.00
#40, Avengers, red & wht vehicles.................$650.00
#40, Batman Set $275.00
#41, Ford Transporter Set $850.00
#41, Silver Jubilee State Landau......................$40.00
#42, Agricultural Set...$80.00
#43, Silo & Conveyor $65.00
#44, Police Rover Set..$65.00
#45, All Winners Set $800.00
#45, Royal Canadian Mounted Police.............$85.00
#46, All Winners Set $600.00
#46, Super Karts $30.00
#47, Pony Club Set..$50.00
#48, Ford Transporter Set $600.00
#48, Jean Richards' Circus Set.........................$200.00
#48, Scammell Transport Set............................$900.00
#49, Flying Club Set $50.00
#3008, Crime Busters Gift Set, scarce, A.........$750.00

#1001A, James Bond's Aston Martin, Husky on base.....$200.00
#1001B, James Bond's Aston Martin, Junior on base......$175.00
#1002A, Batmobile, Husky on base $200.00
#1003A, Bat Boat, Husky on base......................$125.00
#1003B, Bat Boat, Junior on base $85.00
#1004A, Monkeemobile, Husky on base............$200.00
#1004B, Monkeemobile, Junior on base $175.00
#1005A, UNCLE Car, Husky on base................$175.00
#1005B, UNCLE Car, Junior on base $1,500.00
#1006A, Chitty-Chitty Bang-Bang, Husky on base........$200.00
#1006B, Chitty-Chitty Bang-Bang, Junior on base $175.00
#1007, Ironside Police Van...............................$140.00
#1008, Popeye's Paddle Wagon $200.00
#1011, James Bond's Bobsleigh.........................$300.00
#1012, Spectre Bobsleigh $300.00
#1013, Tom's Go-Kart..$75.00
#1014, Jerry's Banger...$75.00
#3008, Crime Busters Gift Set, scarce...............$800.00

MAJOR PACKS

#1100, Carrimore Low Loader, red cab $165.00
#1100, Carrimore Low Loader, yel cab.............$265.00
#1100, Mack Truck..$110.00
#1101, Carrimore Car Transporter, bl cab........$250.00
#1101, Carrimore Car Transporter, red cab......$160.00
#1101, Hydraulic Crane.....................................$65.00
#1102, Crane Fruehauf Dumper $75.00
#1102, Euclid Tractor, gr...................................$160.00
#1102, Euclid Tractor, yel..................................$240.00
#1103, Airport Crash Truck $100.00
#1103, Euclid Crawler Tractor...........................$160.00
#1104, Machinery Carrier $150.00
#1104, Racehorse Transporter $125.00
#1105, Berliet Racehorse Transporter $75.00

#1106, Decca Mobile Radar Van	$185.00
#1107, Berliet Container Truck	$75.00
#1107, Euclid Tractor & Dozer, red	$400.00
#1107, Euclid Tractor & Dozer, orange	$325.00
#1108, Bristol Bloodhound & Launching Ramp	$135.00
#1108, Michelin Container Truck	$50.00
#1109, Bristol Bloodhound & Loading Trolley	$135.00
#1109, Michelin Truck	$65.00
#1110, JCB Crawler Loader	$65.00
#1110, Mobilgas Tanker	$300.00
#1111, Massey-Ferguson Harvester	$225.00
#1112, Corporal Missile on Launching Ramp	$175.00
#1112, David Brown Combine	$120.00
#1113, Corporal Erector & Missile	$375.00
#1113, Hyster	$65.00
#1113, Hyster Sealink	$150.00
#1115, Bloodhound Missile	$120.00
#1116, Bloodhound Missile Platform	$100.00
#1116, Refuse Lorry	$40.00
#1117, Bloodhound Missile Trolley	$75.00
#1117, Faun Street Sweeper	$40.00
#1118, Airport Emergency Tender	$85.00
#1118, International Truck, Dutch Army	$325.00
#1118, International Truck, gr	$150.00
#1118, International Truck, US Army	$275.00
#1119, HDL Hovercraft	$110.00
#1120, Midland Coach	$220.00
#1121, Chipperfield's Circus Crane	$250.00
#1121, Corgimatic Ford Tipper	$60.00
#1123, Chipperfield's Circus Animal Cage	$160.00
#1124, Corporal Missile Launching Ramp	$85.00
#1126, Ecurie Ecosse Transporter	$225.00
#1126, Simon Snorkel Dennis Fire Engine	$70.00
#1127, Simon Snorkel Bedford Fire Engine	$125.00
#1128, Priestman Cub Shovel	$125.00
#1129, Mercedes Truck	$40.00
#1129, Milk Tanker	$325.00
#1130, Chipperfield's Circus Horse Transporter	$295.00
#1130, Mercedes Tanker, Corgi	$35.00
#1131, Carrimore Machinery Carrier	$150.00
#1131, Mercedes Refrigerated Van	$35.00
#1132, Carrimore Low Loader	$275.00
#1132, Scania Truck	$30.00
#1133, Troop Transporter	$265.00
#1134, Army Fuel Tanker	$475.00
#1135, Heavy Equipment Transporter	$475.00
#1137, Ford Tilt Cab w/Trailer	$150.00
#1138, Carrimore Car Transporter, Corgi	$165.00
#1140, Bedford Mobilgas Tanker	$300.00
#1140, Ford Transit Wrecker	$35.00
#1141, Milk Tanker	$425.00
#1143, American LaFrance Rescue Truck	$140.00
#1144, Berliet Wrecker	$80.00
#1144, Chipperfield's Circus Crane Truck	$700.00
#1145, Mercedes Unimog Dumper	$60.00
#1146, Tri-Deck Transporter	$225.00
#1147, Ferrymaster Truck	$140.00
#1148, Carrimore Car Transporter	$175.00

#1142, Holmes Wrecker, $175.00. (From the collection of Al Rapp)

#1150, Mercedes Unimog Snowplough	$70.00
#1151, Scammell Co-op Set	$350.00
#1151, Scammell Co-op Truck	$275.00
#1152, Mack Truck, Esso Tanker	$95.00
#1152, Mack Truck, Exxon Tanker	$160.00
#1153, Priestman Boom Crane	$95.00
#1154, Priestman Crane	$140.00
#1154, Tower Crane	$90.00
#1155, Skyscraper Tower Crane	$75.00
#1156, Volvo Cement Mixer	$65.00
#1157, Ford Esso Tanker	$65.00
#1158, Ford Exxon Tanker	$75.00
#1159, Ford Car Transporter	$110.00
#1160, Ford Gulf Tanker	$65.00
#1161, Ford Aral Tanker	$95.00
#1163, Circus Cannon Truck	$80.00
#1164, Dolphinarium	$160.00
#1169, Ford Guiness Tanker	$125.00
#1170, Ford Car Transporter	$95.00

#1501-1505, Scale Figures, $35.00. (From the collection of Al Rapp)

Dakin

Dakin has been an importer of stuffed toys as far back as 1955, but it wasn't until 1959 that the name of this San Francisco-based company actually appeared on the toy labels. They produced three distinct lines: Dream Pets (1960 – early 1970s), Dream Dolls (1965 – mid-1970s), and licensed characters and advertising figures, starting in 1968. Of them all, the latter series was the most popular and the one that holds most interest for collectors. Originally there were seven Warner Brothers characters. Each was made with a hard plastic body and a soft vinyl head, and all were under 10" tall. All in all, more than fifty cartoon characters were produced, some with several variations. Advertising figures were made as well. Some were extensions of the three already existing lines; others were completely original.

Goofy Grams was a series featuring many of their character figures mounted on a base lettered with a 'goofy' message. They also utilized some of their large stock characters as banks in a series called Cash Catchers. A second bank series consisted of Warner Brothers characters molded in a squatting position and therefore smaller. Other figures made by Dakin include squeeze toys, PVCs, and water squirters.

Advisor: Jim Rash (R3)

Alice in Wonderland, w/Alice, Mad Hatter & White Rabbit, artist Faith Wick, 18", MIB $150.00
Baby Puss, Hanna-Barbera, 1971, NM, R3......................$80.00
Bambi, Disney, 1960s, MIP, R3....................................$35.00
Bamm-Bamm, Hanna-Barbera, w/club, 1970, EX, R3 ......$30.00
Bamm-Bamm (Flintstones Movie), 1993, 8", MIB $15.00
Barney Rubble, Hanna-Barbera, 1970, EX, R3 ....$40.00
Barney Rubble (Flintstones Movie), 1993, 12", MIB........$15.00
Benji, 1978, plush, EX $10.00
Bozo the Clown, Larry Harmon, 1974, EX, R3 ....$30.00
Bugs Bunny, Warner Bros, 1971, MIP, R3 ....$25.00
Bugs Bunny, Warner Bros, 1976, MIB (TV Cartoon Theater box)...$40.00
Bugs Bunny, Warner Bros, 1978, MIP (Fun Farm bag) $20.00
Bullwinkle, Jay Ward, 1976, MIB (TV Cartoon Theater box), R3 ....$60.00
Cool Cat, Warner Bros, w/beret, 1970, EX+, R3 ....$40.00
Daffy Duck, Warner Bros, 1968, EX, R3 ....$30.00
Daffy Duck, Warner Bros, 1976, MIB (TV Cartoon Theater box) $40.00
Deputy Dawg, Terrytoons, 1977, EX, R3 ....$50.00
Dewey Duck, Disney, straight or bent legs, EX, R3 ....$30.00
Dino Dinosaur, Hanna-Barbera, 1970, EX, R3..................$40.00
Donald Duck, Disney, 1960s, straight or bent legs, EX, R3.$20.00
Donald Duck, Disney, 1960s, straight or bent legs, NMIP .$30.00
Dream Pets, Bull Dog, cloth, EX $10.00
Dream Pets, Hawaiian Hound, cloth, w/surfboard & orig tag, EX..$15.00
Dream Pets, Kangaroo, cloth, w/camera, wearing beret, EX.$10.00
Dream Pets, Midnight Mouse, cloth, orig tag, EX.............$15.00

Dream Pets, Seymour Skunk, orig tag, EX, N2 ....$20.00
Dudley Do-Right, Jay Ward, 1976, MIB (TV Cartoon Theater box), R3 ....$75.00
Dumbo, Disney, 1960s, cloth collar, MIB, R3 ....$25.00
Elmer Fudd, Warner Bros, 1968, in tuxedo, EX $30.00
Elmer Fudd, Warner Bros, 1978, MIP (Fun Farm bag), R3 .$60.00
Foghorn Leghorn, Warner Bros, 1970, EX+, R3 ....$75.00
Fred Flintstone, Hanna-Barbera, 1970, EX, R3 ....$40.00
Fred Flintstone (Movie), 1993, 12", MIB........................$15.00
Goofy, Disney, cloth clothes, EX $20.00
Goofy Gram, Bull, I'm Mad About You, EX, R3 ....$25.00
Goofy Gram, Dog, Congratulations Dumm-Dumm, EX, R3.$25.00
Goofy Gram, Frog, Happy Birthday, EX, R3 ....$25.00
Goofy Gram, Kangaroo, World's Greatest Mom, EX, R3..$25.00
Goofy Gram, Pepe Le Pew, You're a Real Stinker, 1971, EX.$40.00
Goofy Gram, Tiger, To a Great Guy, EX, R3 ....$25.00
Hokey Wolf, Hanna-Barbera, 1971, MIP, R3..................$100.00
Hoppy Hopperroo, Hanna-Barbera, 1971, EX+, R3 ....$75.00
Huckleberry Hound, Hanna-Barbera, 1970, EX+, R3 ......$60.00
Huey Duck, Disney, straight or bent legs, EX, R3 ....$30.00
Jack-in-the-Box, bank, 1971, EX, R3 ....$25.00
Lion in Cage, bank, 1971, EX, R3 ....$25.00
Louie Duck, Disney, straight or bent legs, EX, R3............$30.00
Merlin the Magic Mouse, Warner Bros, 1970, EX+ $25.00
Mickey Mouse, Disney, cloth clothes, EX, R3.................$20.00

Mighty Mouse, Terrytoons, 1978, marked Fun Farm, EX, $120.00.

Elmer Fudd, Warner Bros, 1968, in hunting outfit, EX, $125.00.

Minnie Mouse, Disney, 1960s, cloth clothes, EX, R3 ....$20.00
Monkey on a Barrel, bank, 1971, EX, R3 ....$25.00
Olive Oyl, King Features, 1974, cloth clothes, MIP, R3 ...$30.00
Olive Oyl, King Features, 1976, MIB (TV Cartoon Theater box), R3 ....$40.00
Oliver Hardy, Larry Harmon, 1974, EX+, R3...................$30.00
Opus, 1982, cloth, w/tag, EX $20.00
Pebbles (Flintstones Movie), 1993, 8", MIB $65.00
Pebbles Flintstone, Hanna-Barbera, 1970, EX, R3...........$35.00
Pepe Le Pew, Warner Bros, 1971, EX $55.00
Pink Panther, Mirisch-Freleng, 1971, EX+, R3................$50.00
Pink Panther, Mirisch-Freleng, 1976, MIB (TV Cartoon Theater box), R3 ....$50.00
Pinocchio, Disney, 1960s, EX $20.00
Popeye, King Features, 1974, cloth clothes, MIP, R3........$50.00

Popeye, King Features, 1976, MIB (TV Cartoon Theater box), R3, $50.00.

Porky Pig, Warner Bros, 1968, EX, R3 ....$30.00
Porky Pig, Warner Bros, 1976, MIB (TV Cartoon Theater box), R3 ....$40.00
Ren & Stimpy, water squirters, Nickelodeon, 1993, EX, R3 .$10.00
Roadrunner, Warner Bros, 1968, EX, R3 ....$30.00
Roadrunner, Warner Bros, 1976, MIB $45.00
Rocky Squirrel, Jay Ward, 1976, MIB (TV Cartoon Theater box) $60.00
Scooby Doo, Hanna-Barbera, 1980, EX, R3 ....$75.00
Scrappy Doo, Hanna-Barbera, 1982, EX, R3 ....$75.00
Seal on Box, bank, 1971, EX, R3 ....$25.00
Second Banana, Warner Bros, 1970, EX, R3 ....$35.00

Snagglepuss, 1971, EX, $100.00.

Speedy Gonzales, Warner Bros, M $35.00
Speedy Gonzales, Warner Bros, MIB (TV Cartoon Theater box), R3 ....$50.00
Stan Laurel, Larry Harmon, 1974, EX+, R3 ....$30.00
Sylvester, Warner Bros, 1968, EX, R3 ....$20.00
Sylvester, Warner Bros, 1976, MIB (TV Cartoon Theater box), R3 ....$40.00
Sylvester, Warner Bros, 1978, MIP (Fun Farm bag), R3 ...$20.00
Tasmanian Devil, Warner Bros, 1978, rare, NM $300.00
Tiger in Cage, bank, 1971, EX, R3 ....$25.00

Top Banana, Warner Bros, NM, C17 ....$25.00
Tweety Bird, Warner Bros, 1976, MIB (TV Cartoon Theater box), R3 ....$40.00
Underdog, Jay Ward, 1976, MIB (TV Cartoon Theater box), R3 .$150.00
Wile E Coyote, Warner Bros, 1968, MIB, R3 ....$30.00
Wile E Coyote, Warner Bros, 1976, MIB (TV Cartoon Theater box), R3 ....$40.00
Yogi Bear, Hanna-Barbera, 1970, EX, R3 ....$60.00
Yosemite Sam, Warner Bros, 1968, MIB $40.00
Yosemite Sam, Warner Bros, 1976, MIP (Fun Farm bag), R3.$40.00

ADVERTISING

Bay View Bank, 1976, EX+, R3 ....$30.00
Bob's Big Boy, 1974, w/hamburger, EX+, R3 ....$75.00
Buddig Bull, Buddig Meats, 1970s, cloth, EX $10.00
Cocker Spaniel, Crocker National Bank, 1979, cloth, 12", VG..$20.00
Diaperene Baby, Sterling Drug Co, 1980, EX, R3 ....$40.00
Freddie Fast Gas Attendant, 1976, M, P12 ....$75.00
Glamour Kitty, 1977, complete w/crown, EX, R3 ....$200.00
Hobo Joe, bank, Hobo Joe's Restaurant, EX $60.00
Kernal Renk, American Seeds, 1970, rare, EX+, R3 ....$200.00
Li'l Miss Just Rite, 1965, EX+, R3 ....$60.00
Miss Liberty Bell, 1975, MIP, R3 ....$60.00
Quasar Robot, bank, 1975, NM, R3 ....$125.00
Sambo's Boy, 1974, vinyl, EX+, R3 ....$80.00
Sambo's Tiger, 1974, vinyl, EX+, R3 ....$125.00
Smokey the Bear, 1976, M $25.00
St Bernard, Christian Bros Candy, 1982, cloth, VG $10.00
Woodsy Owl, 1974, MIP, R3 ....$60.00

Diecast

Diecast replicas of cars, trucks, planes, trains, etc., represent a huge corner of today's collector market, and their manufacturers see to it that there is no shortage. Back in the 1920s, Tootsietoy had the market virtually by themselves, but one by one other companies had a go at it, some with more success than others. Among them were the American companies of Barclay, Hubley, and Manoil, all of whom are much better known for other types of toys. After the war, Metal Masters, Smith-Miller, and Doepke Ohlsson-Rice (among others) tried the market with varying degrees of success. Some companies were phased out over the years, while many more entered the market with fervor. Today it's those fondly remembered models from the '50s and '60s that many collectors yearn to own. Solido produced well-modeled, detailed little cars; some had dome lights that actually came on when the doors were opened. Politoy's were cleanly molded with good detailing and finishes. Mebetoys, an Italian company that has been bought out by Mattel, produced several; and some of the finest come from Brooklyn.

In 1968 the Topper Toy Company introduced its line of low-friction, high-speed Johnny Lightning cars to be in direct competition with Mattel's Hot Wheels. To gain attention, Topper sponsored Al Unser's winning race car, the 'Johnny Lightning,' in the 1970 Indianapolis 500. Despite the popularity of their cars, the Topper Toy Company went out of business in 1971. Today the Johnny Lightnings are highly sought after, and a new company, Playing Mantis, is reproducing many of the original designs as well as several models that never made it into regular production.

If you're interested in Majorette Toys, we recommend *Collecting Majorette Toys* by Dana Johnson; ordering information is given with Dana's listing under Diecast, in the section called Categories of Special Interest in the back of the book. Dana is also the author of *Toy Car Collector's Guide*, published by Collector Books.

Values are for examples in mint condition and in the original packaging.

Advisor: Dana Johnson (J4)

See also Corgi; Dinky; Diecast Collector Banks; Farm Toys; Hot Wheels; Matchbox; Tekno; Tootsietoys.

Bburago, Chevrolet Corvette (1957), #3024, Bijoux series, $25.00. (Photo courtesy Dana Johnson)

Ahi, Austin A105	$18.00
Ahi, Cadillac	$20.00
Ahi, Dodge Military Ambulance	$15.00
Ahi, Dodge Military Crane Truck	$15.00
Ahi, Dodge Military Lumber Truck	$15.00
Ahi, Ferrari 375 Coupe	$30.00
Ahi, Mercedes-Benz 220SE	$20.00
Ahi, Pontiac	$25.00
Ahi, 1904 Darracq	$15.00
Ahi, 1907 Vauxhall	$15.00
Ahi, 1914 Stutz Bearcat	$15.00
Asahi Model Pet, Datsun Sunny Coupe EX 1400	$55.00
Asahi Model Pet, Nissan Cedric Taxi	$165.00
Asahi Model Pet, Subaru 360	$135.00
Asahi Model Pet, Toyota Toyoace Truck	$165.00
Auto Pilen, Buggi Playero	$50.00
Auto Pilen, Ferrari 512	$60.00
Auto Pilen, Oldsmobile Toronado	$150.00
Bandai, Hato Bus, bl & wht	$20.00
Bandai, Mazda RX7 252	$8.00
Bandai, Tank Lorry JAL	$6.00
Bang, Ferrari 250 SWB, red	$50.00
Bang, Ferrari 250 Tour de France Prova, red	$45.00
Bang, Ford AC Cobra Sebring (1963)	$45.00
Barclay, Army Truck w/Gun, #151	$35.00
Barclay, Auburn Speedster, #58	$40.00
Barclay, Chrysler Airflow	$100.00
Barclay, Renault Tank, #47	$40.00
Barclay, Silver Arrow Race Car	$40.00
Barlux, Ferrari B2	$12.00
Barlux, Fiat Wrecker	$35.00
Barlux, Fiat 697 Fire Truck	$20.00
Barlux, Road Roller	$20.00
BBR, 1938 Alfa Romeo 2900B 8C, maroon	$200.00
BBR, 1952 Ferrari 212 Interpininfarina	$150.00
BBR, 1965 Ferrari 275 GTB	$175.00
BBR, 1994 Ferrari 412 T1 Berger F1 Racer	$225.00
Bburago, Bugatti Atlantic (1936), Bijoux series	$25.00
Bburago, Crane Truck, 1500 series	$30.00
Bburago, Ferrari 312T2 (1976), Formula One series	$55.00
Bburago, Fiat Panda, 4000 series	$12.00

Bburago, Fire Crane Truck, 1500 series	$30.00
Bburago, Jaguar SS 100 (1937), Diamonds series	$35.00
Bburago, Lancia Stratos, 4000 series	$12.00
Bburago, Mercedes SSKL Caracciola (1931), chrome, Diamonds series	$85.00
Bburago, Tyrell 009 (1979), Formula One series	$45.00
BB4, 1949 Alfa Romeo Villa D-Este Coupe, silver	$175.00
Benbros, AEC Box Van	$30.00
Benbros, Austin Champ	$16.00
Benbros, Lorry w/Searchlight	$50.00
Benbros, Royal Mail Land Rover	$30.00
Best Toys of Kansas, Coupe, #96	$45.00
Best Toys of Kansas, Pontiac Sedan, #100	$45.00
Best-Box of Holland, Brabham Formula 1, #2518	$18.00
Best-Box of Holland, Fire Engine, #503 DAF 1400	$27.00
Best-Box of Holland, Saloon, #501 DAF 1400	$27.00
Box Model, AC Cobra 289 Open, alloy wheels, blk, #8411	$24.00
Box Model, Ferrari 250 IM Street, red, #8434	$20.00
Box Model, Jaguar E Coupe (1962), right-hand drive, gr & wht, #8440	$25.00
Brumm, Blitzen Benz Indy (1911), Revival series	$29.00
Brumm, Ferrari 156, GP Belgio '61, 1988 limited edition	$39.00
Brumm, Ferrari 512M Le Mans (1971 NART team), 1998 limited edition	$49.00
Brumm, Fiat F1 Corsa, 1986 limited edition	$39.00
Brumm, Mercedes W154 (1939), Revival series	$29.00
Buccaneer, Chrysler Airflow (1934), #2	$39.00
Buccaneer, La Salle Sedan (1935), #9	$25.00
Budgie, Dump Truck	$24.00
Budgie, Police Car, from $25 to	$32.00
Budgie, Rover Squad Car	$15.00
Chad Valley, Ambulance	$45.00
Chad Valley, Commer Flat Truck	$175.00
Chad Valley, Van	$50.00
Charbens, Alfa Romeo Racer	$120.00
Charbens, Morris Esso Van	$70.00
Charbens, Packard Runabout (1905), Old Crock series	$24.00
Charbens, Standard 6 HP (1903), Old Crock series	$18.00
Chrono, Fiat 24 Spider (1968), red, from $25 to	$39.00
Chrono, Porsche 550 RS (1953), silver, from $25 to	$39.00
Conquest, Buick Super Hard Top (1955), 3-tone	$225.00
Conquest, Chevy Impala Convertible w/Top Down (1960)	$215.00
Conrad, Audi 100	$12.00
Conrad, Volvo Old Timer Fire Engine (1928)	$59.00

Dalia-Solido, Ferrari Testa Rossa, cream, red or wht, ea.**$165.00**

Dalia-Solido, Jaguar D Le Mans, bl, gr or red, ea **$110.00**

Dalia-Tekno, Ford Mustang Hardtop..............................**$75.00**

Dalia-Tekno, Monza GT Coupe **$60.00**

Danbury Mint, Borden's Delivery Truck (1955), wht w/yel top, from $140 to **$150.00**

Danbury Mint, Chevy Apache Pickup (1958), bright bl, from $115 to..**$125.00**

Danbury Mint, Pierce Arrow (1933), silver, from $115 to.**$125.00**

Diapet, Mack Car Carrier, #T54..**$39.00**

Diapet, Nissan Cedric Ultima Station Taxi, #P29 ....**$39.00**

Doepke, Jaguar Convertible, 1950s, 18", G+ **$475.00**

Drudge Bros, Hyster Straddle Truck, #50, 6½", NMIB.**$1,200.00**

Dubuque, Greyhound Bus, 9½" **$400.00**

Dugu, Cord Phaeton (1936), top up, Miniautotoys series, 1968.**$195.00**

Dugu, Fiat 500A (1936), Museo series, 1966 ....**$65.00**

Dugu, OM Dump Truck, Sispla series................................**$95.00**

Durham Classics, Chevy Suburban (1941), Niagara Tours ..**$120.00**

Durham Classics, Ford Pickup (1953), bl **$120.00**

Eagle's Race/Eagle Collectibles, Ford Deluxe Coupe (1940),blk **$25.00**

Eagle's Race/Eagle Collectibles, Ford Hot Rod (1940), any color, from $30 to..**$35.00**

Eagle's Race/Eagle Collectibles, Mustang Mach III, yel, from $18 to **$24.00**

Enchantment Land Coach Builders, Chevy Nomad Wagon (1957) **$125.00**

Enchantment Land Coach Builders, Chrysler Flower Car (1947)..**$125.00**

Enchantment Land Coach Builders, Packard Victoria (1937)..**$95.00**

Ertl, Chevy Bel Air (1957), American Muscle Collection .**$35.00**

Ertl, Chevy Cameo Pickup (1955) **$8.00**

Ertl, Chrysler 300 (1957)...**$16.00**

Ertl, Dodge Challenger (1970), American Muscle Collection .**$35.00**

Ertl, Hawkeye Flatbed (1931), True Value **$24.00**

France Jouets, Tank Truck (Berliet GAK Truck), 100 series, 1962 ....**$80.00**

Franklin Mint, Chevy Corvette (1953) **$95.00**

Franklin Mint, Ford Model A (1930), from $115 to.......**$140.00**

Franklin Mint, Ford Thunderbird (1956), turq, from $85 to.**$130.00**

Franklin Mint, Ford Thunderbird (1962), from $45 to.....**$65.00**

Franklin Mint, Volkswagen Beetle (1967), wht, from $95 to .**$110.00**

Fun Ho!, International Articulated Truck, 1973-82, 5½", from $50 to **$65.00**

Fun Ho!, Land Rover, 1966-78, 1¾", from $40 to **$60.00**

Fun Ho!, Volkswagen Combi Bus, 1964-82, 2⅛", from $55 to .**$65.00**

Gama, BMW 525i Touring Wagon..................................**$20.00**

Gama, Opel Rekord, 1978 ....**$35.00**

Goodee, Ford Police Cruiser, 1953, 6" **$27.00**

Goodee, GMC Pickup Truck (1953), 3" **$18.00**

Hartoy, Hamm's Beer Ford F-7 Freight Truck..................**$35.00**

Hartoy, Hershey's Syrup Tank Trailer, from $15 to **$25.00**

Hartoy, Wrigley's Mack Box Truck **$25.00**

Herpa, Ferrari F40, blk, red or yel, ea **$49.00**

Herpa, Mercedes-Benz E320T Convertible, bl or wht, ea.**$24.00**

Hubley, bulldozer, wood wheels w/rubber treads, 9", G, A .**$40.00**

Hubley, Car Transport, w/4 plastic autos, 14", G+, A.....**$325.00**

Hubley, Corvette Convertible, 1950s, 13", rstr, A **$95.00**

Hubley, Mighty-Metal Dump Truck, Copyright 1969, 12", EXIB, A **$90.00**

Hubley, School Bus, 9½", EX **$70.00**

Hubley Kiddie Toys, Dump Truck, #476 ....**$150.00**

Hubley Kiddie Toys, De Luxe Sports Car, MIB, A, $250.00.

Ertl, John Deere 690C Excavator, MIB, $15.00.

Ertl, Oldsmobile 442 (1970), metallic gold, American Muscle Collection **$20.00**

France Jouets, Ambulance (GMC Truck), 300 series, 1959.**$80.00**

France Jouets, Cement Truck (Pacific Heavy Truck), 200 series, 1966 ....**$135.00**

France Jouets, Dump Truck (Berliet Straidair), 700 series, 1967 .**$80.00**

France Jouets, Fire Truck (Dodge), 400 series, 1966 ....**$80.00**

France Jouets, Police Jeep, 500/600 series, 1965 ....**$70.00**

Johnny Lightning, Custom El Camino (1994), $8.00. (Photo courtesy Dana Johnson)

Hubley Kiddie Toys, Taxi, #5..$35.00
Husky, Man From UNCLE Gull Wing Car, w/2 figures, 1968, 3"..$60.00
Joal, Chevy Monza...$35.00
Joal, Ferrari 512S...$40.00
Johnny Lightning, Custom GTO, MIP $250 o/w from $125 to.$175.00
Johnny Lightning, Jumpin' Jag, MIP $35 o/w from $20 to.$30.00
Johnny Lightning, Mad Maverick, MIP $45 o/w from $20 to .$35.00
Johnny Lightning, Monster, MIP $30 o/w from $15 to.....$25.00
Johnny Lightning, Vulture, MIP $70 o/w from $40 to......$65.00
JRD, Mercedes-Benz 220S Sedan, 1962................................$90.00
JRD, Unic Van Hafa, 1959...$195.00
Kansas Toy & Novelty, Army Truck, #74, 2¼".................$55.00
Kansas Toy & Novelty, Bearcat Racer, #26, 4"..................$90.00
Kansas Toy & Novelty, Indy Racer, #10, 3⅛" $55.00
Kemlows, Armored Car $55.00
Kemlows, Ford Zephyr Mark I $120.00
Kiddie Car Classics, Ford Mustang (1964½), 7" $62.00
Kiddie Car Classics, Garton Delivery Cycle (1950), 6¾".$45.00
Kiddie Car Classics, Steelcraft Lincoln Zephyr (1939), 6¾".$59.00
Kirk, Chevy Monza Spyder...$60.00
Kirk, Saab 99...$70.00
Kyosho, Mazda Miata MX5, top down, Superman, bl, from $40
    to $55.00
Kyosho, MGB Mk-1 (1966), gr, red or wht, from $50 to ..$65.00
Kyosho, Toyota Supra, w/wing, red, from $90 to $105.00
Lansing Slik-Toys, Fastback Sedan, #9600, 7" $45.00
Lansing Slik-Toys, Roadster, #9701, 3½" $45.00

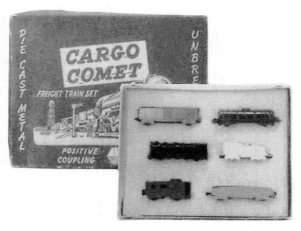

Leslie-Henry, Cargo Comet Freight Train Set, complete, NMIB, $125.00.

Lledo, Bluebird Racer $35.00
Lledo, Volkswagen Cabriolet, red......................................$25.00
Londontoy, Canadian Greyhound Bus, #33, 5".................$55.00
Londontoy, Chevy Master Deluxe Coupe (1941), 6"........$32.00
Lone Star, Cadillac 62 Sedan, 1962, from $65 to.............$85.00
Lone Star, Ford Mustang Fastback, Flyers #39, from $25 to.$40.00
Lone Star, Military Jeep, olive drab, from $65 to $79.00
Maisto, Cadillac Eldorado Biarritz Convertible (1959), pk, red
    or wht..$130.00
Maisto, Jaguar XK8, from $10 to $15.00
Maisto, Porsche 550A Spyder, silver, from $15 to............$22.00
Majorette, Bernard Circus Truck $18.00

Majorette, Camper Truck, orange & wht $15.00
Majorette, Citroen DS..$29.00
Majorette, Formula 1 Racer, chromed or unchromed, ea..$16.00
Majorette, Hotchkiss Jeep w/Cable Carrier.....................$18.00

Majorette, Magic Circus Semi, $12.00. (Photo courtesy Dana Johnson)

Majorette, Mercedes Utility Truck w/Compressor, yel......$16.00
Manoil, Fire Engine, 1945-55 ....$95.00
Manoil, Wrecker, 1935-41 ....$120.00
Manoil, 4 Speedsters Set, #7890, EXIB (6x11"), A $850.00
Master Caster, 1947 Yellow Cab, 7" $225.00
Mebetoys, Fiat 1500 Fire Chief, 1967................................$35.00
Mebetoys, Ford GT Mark II, 1971, from $80 to...............$100.00
Mebetoys, Lotus JPS, 1973, from $65 to..........................$90.00
Mebetoys, Volkswagen 1303, 1974....................................$45.00
Mercury, Alfa Romeo, 1951...$40.00
Mercury, Bentley S Series, 1957 ....$95.00
Mercury, Jack's Demon Dragster, 1969 ....$29.00
Mercury, Lambretta 125 LC, 1952....................................$65.00
Metal Masters, 4-vehicle set, EXIB (12x15").................$750.00
Milton, Chevy Impala Taxi $39.00
Milton, Jaguar 3.8 Saloon $49.00
Milton, Pontiac Firebird $29.00
Mira, Ford Coupe (1949), #6251, red, from $30 to..........$39.00
Mira, GMC Panel Truck (1950), #6212, permanent red, from
    $30 to $39.00
Mira, Renault Espace Ambulance $19.00
Morestone, Daimler Ambulance $120.00
Morestone, Mercedes-Benz Racer.....................................$40.00
National Products, Chrysler New Yorker Sedan (1946), from
    $150 to...$195.00
National Products/Banthrico, Ford F-2 Stake Truck (1952), from
    $350 to...$395.00
Nicky Toys, Daimler Jaguar 3.4 ....$29.00
Nicky Toys, Plymouth Fury Convertible $49.00
Nostalgic, Chevy Corvette (1982) $79.00
Nostalgic, Willys Jeepster (1950) $79.00
Ny-Lint, Ford Lawn & Garden Service Truck, 11", EX+..$59.00
NZG, CAT 627 Scraper...$59.00
NZG, Mercedes 0404 Touring Bus $59.00
NZG, Porsche 911 C2/4 Turbo $29.00
Playart, Jeep, from $6 to...$12.00
Playart, Plymouth Barracuda, from $8 to..........................$12.00
Quiralu, Simca Marly Ambulance, 1957..........................$129.00
Quiralu, Simca Trianon, 1955 ....$95.00
Racing Champions, any, ea from $6 to..............................$12.00

Quiralu, Rolls-Royce Silver Cloud (1958), #17, $125.00.

(Photo courtesy Dana Johnson)

Ralstoy, Chevy Step Van (1982) $24.00
Ralstoy, Dump Truck, 3⅜" $39.00
Ralstoy, Moving Van, any trade name, ea $39.00
Ralstoy, Oldsmobile Sedan $175.00
Rio, any, ea from $25 to $35.00
Road Champs, Ford Crown Victoria (1957), 1998 ....$10.00
Road Champs, Ford Crown Victoria Police Car (1994), Indiana, 1996 license plate, discontinued, from $12 to............$15.00
Road Champs, Ford Woodie (1949), from $16 to $18.00
Schuco, Audi 80 GL, 600 series, 1972 ....$45.00
Schuco, Maserati Grand Prix, Piccolo series, 1958, 2", from $75 to $95.00
Schuco, Micro Racer 101 (1950s Porsche Style), 100 series, 3½" $195.00
Schuco, Porsche 917, 800 series, 1972, 2½"......$25.00
Schuco, Volkswagen Polizei, Piccolo series, 1996, limited edition $40.00
Siku, Ford Granada Fire Command Wagon, 1975-82, from $12 to $18.00
Siku, Jeep w/Trailer, 1964-72 ....$39.00
Siku, Mercedes Esso Tanker, 1980-83, from $35 to..........$49.00
Siku, Pontiac GTO (The Judge), 1972-74 ....$49.00
Siku, Range Rover w/Horse Trailer, 1980-88, from $15 to.$24.00
Solido, Alpine F3 (1965), 1996 reissue $24.00
Solido, Cadillac Eldorado Convertible (1955), top up or down $39.00
Solido, Chevy Camaro Z28 (1983), from $15 to $29.00
Solido, Ford Mustang (1965), 1994......................$24.00

Solido, Peugeot 205 (1984), #1508, M, $18.00. (Photo courtesy Dana Johnson)

Solido, Volkswagen Golf, 1981-82, from $20 to...............$36.00
Spot-On, Austin 1800 ....$120.00
Spot-On, Bentley 4-Door Sports Saloon..............$225.00
Spot-On, BMW Isetta Bubble Car $150.00
Spot-On, Ford Consul Classic $165.00
Spot-On, Volvo P1800 ....$130.00
Tip Top Toy, Coupe, 3½".......................................$39.00
Tip Top Toy, Hupmobile (1935), 3¼".....................$59.00
Tomica, Cadillac Ambulance, #F-2 ....$15.00
Tomica, Datsun Silva Coupe $20.00
Tomica, Isuzu Bonnet Police Bus, #6 ....$19.00
Tomica, Nissan Diesel Dump Truck......................$9.00
Tomica, Toyota Ambulance, #46-40 ....$9.00
Top Gear, Falcon XC Cobra, from $32 to $39.00
Top Gear, Ford Falcon Sedan (1966) $59.00
Tri-Ang, Bentley Sunshine Saloon, 1938 ....$150.00
Tri-Ang, Rolls Royce Sedanca, 1937....................$150.00
Vitesse, any except Vitesse Victoria, ea...............$35.00
Vitesse Victoria, any, ea from $22 to $40.00
Western Models, Buick Electra Convertible (1959), top down..$175.00
Western Models, Buick Riviera (1972)..................$175.00
Western Models, Hudson Sedan (1942) $195.00
Yat Ming, Chevy Bel Air (1957), lt bl or yel, ea from $5 to.$10.00
Yat Ming, Ford Thunderbird (1955), from $25 to............$35.00
Yat Ming, Honda NR Motorcycle, red, from $20 to $30.00
Ziss, Army Jeep, 1968 ....$65.00
Ziss, Ford Ranch Car (1909), 1966.......................$40.00

Diecast Collector Banks

Thousands of banks have been produced since Ertl made its first model in 1981, the 1913 Model T Parcel Post Mail Service #9647. The Ertl company was founded by Fred Ertl, Sr., in Dubuque, Iowa, back in the mid-1940s. Until they made their first diecast banks, most of what they made were farm tractors. Today they specialize in vehicles made to specification and carrying logos of companies as large as Texaco and as small as your hometown bank. The size of each 'run' is dictated by the client and can vary from a few hundred up to several thousand. Some clients will later add a serial number to the vehicle; this is not done by Ertl. Other numbers that appear on the base of each bank are a four-number dating code (the first three indicate the day of the year up to 365 and the fourth number is the last digit of the year, '5' for 1995, for instance). The stock number is shown only on the box, never on the bank, so it is extremely important that you keep them in their original boxes.

Other producers of these banks are Scale Models, incorporated in 1991, First Gear Inc., and Spec-Cast, whose founders at one time all worked for the Ertl company.

In the listings that follow, unless another condition is given, all values are for banks mint and in their original boxes. A (#d) symbol indicates a bank that was numbered by the client, not Ertl.

Advisors: Art and Judy Turner (H8)

Key: JLE — Joseph L. Ertl

ERTL

A-Treat Beverages, 1956 Ford Pickup, #F548 .... $26.00
Alka-Seltzer, 1918 Ford, #9155 .... $50.00
Ben Franklin, 1918 Ford, #1319 .... $35.00
Breyer's Ice Cream, 1905 Ford, #9028 .... $65.00

Orlando Magic, 1918 Ford, #B484 .... $22.00
Pennzoil, 1918 Ford, #7676 .... $30.00
Philgas, 1938 Chevy, #B039 .... $99.00
Quaker Oats, 1925 Kenworth, #B268 .... $95.00
Quality Farm & Fleet, 1932 Ford, #3951 .... $95.00
RCA, 1926 Mack Truck, #9275 .... $45.00
Reese's Pieces, 1950 Chevy, #9809 .... $28.00
Schwan's Ice Cream, 1950 Chevy, #9210 .... $65.00
Sunoco, 1926 Mack Tanker, #9796 .... $50.00
Texaco, 1926 Mack Tanker, #9040 .... $75.00

Campbell's Soup Harvest of Good Foods Produce Truck, #F603, 1987, $30.00.

Cherry Smash, 1905 Ford, #9252 .... $65.00
Dairy Queen, 1950 Chevy, #9178 .... $95.00
Dupont, 1923 Chevy, #1353 .... $75.00
Exxon, P51 Mustang Plane, #47004 .... $45.00
Farmer's Almanac, 1938 Chevy, #3595 .... $25.00
Global Van Lines, 1913 Ford, #1655 .... $45.00
Gulf Oil, 1926 Mack Tanker, #7652 .... $45.00
Hamm's Beer, 1913 Ford, #2145 .... $75.00
Hostess Cupcakes, 1913 Ford, #9422 .... $30.00
Iowa Hawkeyes, 1952 GMC Van, #29-1268 .... $42.00
JC Penney, 1918 Ford, #1328 .... $39.00
Kansas City Chiefs, 1951 GMC, #B838 .... $20.00
Kerr-McGee, 1913 Ford, #9130 .... $55.00

Texaco Petroleum Products Mack Bulldog Tanker, #9238, 1985, M, $250.00.

True Value Mack Bulldog Delivery Truck with Crates, #1362, 1988, $75.00.

Kroger, 1925 Delivery Truck, #3757, $25.00.

Lone Star Beer, 1926 Mack Truck, #9168 .... $55.00
Ludens Candies, 1923 Chevy, #F105 .... $35.00
Marathon Oil, 1929 International Tanker, JLE, #4044 ..... $30.00
NASCAR Racing, Vega Plane, #00312 .... $39.00
NY Fire Dept, Step Van, #H292 .... $35.00

True Value 1930 Diamond 'T' Tanker, #9513, $25.00.

Tonka, 1913 Ford, #9739 ....$35.00
United Parcel Post, 1912 Ford, #9704......................$35.00
United Van Lines, 1925 Kenworth, #B725 ....$36.00
V&S Variety Store, 1905, Ford, #9622......................$45.00
Valvoline, 1937 Ford Semi, #9260 ....$30.00
Winchester, Stearman Plane, #3754..........................$40.00
Wonder Bread, 1913 Ford, #9161.............................$48.00
Yeoman Co, 1931 Hawkeye, #B383...........................$45.00
Yuengling Beer, 1950 Ford, #9176............................$99.00
Zenith Electronics, 1925 Kenworth Semi, #F477 ....$40.00
Zinc Corporation, 1913 Ford, #9670 ....$65.00

FIRST GEAR

AC Gilbert Erector, 1957 International Van, #19-0111 ...$29.00
American Flyer, 1951 Ford Stake Truck, #19-0118...........$50.00
BP Gasoline, Mack B-61 Semi, #19-2006 ....$65.00
Conrock Corporation, B-61 Mack Dump Truck, #19-1956 .$50.00
Cushman Scooters, 1951 Ford DGV, #29-1070 ....$50.00
Daisy Air Rifles, 1952 GMC Van, #10-0126.....................$30.00
Daisy Red Rider, 1957 International, #10-0125................$30.00
Dr Pepper, 1951 Ford Bottle Truck, #19-1700..................$50.00

Eagle Snacks 1951 Ford Dry Goods Van, #19-1121, 1992, $35.00.

Eastern Express, Mack B-61 Semi, #19-1354 ....$115.00
Esso, Mack B-61 Semi, #19-1670 ....$75.00
Firestone Tires, 1957 IHC DGV, #29-1198 ....$45.00
Grapette Soda, Mack B-61 Semi, #19-1619 ....$75.00
Gulf Oil, 1957 IHC Fire Truck, #19-1334....................$45.00
Gulf Oil, 1957 International Wrecker, #19-1336.............$80.00
Hamm's Beer, 1953 Ford, #29-1480............................$35.00
Hershey's Cocoa, 1952 GMC Stake Truck, #19-1273.......$40.00
Humble Oil Co, Mack B-61 Semi, #19-1395.................$175.00
Indian Motorcycle, Mack B-61 Semi, #19-1462 ....$65.00
International Harvester, 1957 International F/T, #19-1289 .$35.00
Iowa Hawkeyes, 1952 GMC Van, #29-1268 ....$42.00
JC Whitney, 1952 GMC Tanker, #10-1215 ....$35.00
Kazam Temple Shrine Circus, 1949 Chevy Panel, #29-1413 .$35.00
Kelly-Springfield Tires, 1955 Diamond T Wrecker, #19-1884.$36.00

Lanser's Garage, 1952 GMC Wrecker, #19-1049 ....$40.00
Lone Star Beer, 1952 GMC Van, #10-1258 ....$32.00
Marathon Oil, 1953 Ford Tanker, #29-1588 ....$34.00
Moxie Cola, 1952 GMC Bottle Truck, #19-0119 ....$55.00
Navajo Freight, 1951 Ford DGV, #19-1030 ....$70.00
Nestle's Crunch, 1931 Hawkeye, #1316......................$32.00
Old Milwaukee Light, 1918 Ford Barrel, #9173............$25.00
Olympic Beer, 1952 GMC, #29-1482..........................$25.00
Pepsi Cola (Santa), 1951 Ford Delivery, #19-1092........$75.00
Pepsi-Cola, 1953 Ford Van, #10-1351........................$30.00
Phillips 66 Pipeline, 1949 Chevy Panel, #19-1831 ....$40.00
Quaker Oats, Buckboard & Horses, #0004...................$65.00
RC Cola, 1951 Ford Bottle, #19-1131.........................$45.00
Red Crown Gasoline, 1951 Ford Tanker, #19-1019.........$40.00
Skelly Oil Co, 1951 Ford Fire Truck, #19-1927 ....$38.00
Slinky 50th Anniversary, 1952 GMC, #19-1315 ....$50.00
Stroh's Beer, 1952 GMC Van, #10-1353 ....$40.00
Texaco Pipeline, 1949 Chevy Panel Truck, #19-1391 ....$125.00
Tollway & Tunnel, 1957 International Wrecker, #19-1439 .$55.00
True Value Hardware, 1953 Ford Van, #19-1490 ....$34.00
Utica Club Beer, Mack B-61 Semi, #18-1697 ....$70.00
Valley Asphalt Co, Mack B-61 Semi, #19-1529 ....$58.00
Vic Irwin Shell, 1956 Ford Stock Car, #19-1425 ....$50.00
Wooster, 1960 B-Mack, #19-1208...............................$180.00
Yellow Freight, 1960 B-Mack, #10-1293 ....$55.00
Zephyr Gasoline, 1957 International DGV, #19-1166......$32.00
Zephyr Petroleums, 1957 International Wrecker, #19-1135 .$32.00

RACING CHAMPIONS

Bojangle/Derrick Cope #98, T-Bird, #424 ....$55.00
Family Channel/Ted Musgrave #16, T-Bird, #2208 ....$30.00

SPEC-CAST

Agway, #11, 1936 Dodge Pickup, #72030 ....$25.00
Brickyard 400, 1955 Chevy Convertible, #0459...............$59.00

Clark's Super Gas Tank Truck, Liberty Classics, #0216, M, $30.00.

Coca-Cola 600, 1929 Ford, #2711 ....$55.00
Diamond Rio, 1940 Ford, #67503 ....$23.00
Ducks Unlimited, 1937 Chevy, #15014 ....$45.00
Essolube Motor Oil, 1936 Dodge, #74003 ....$32.00

Fina Oil, 1929 Ford, #2004 ....$28.00
Gilmore Oil Co, 1940 Ford Tanker, #65504 ....$25.00
Hamm's Beer, 1929 Ford, #1014 ....$29.00
Humble Oil Co, 1936 Dodge Tanker, #72032 ....$27.00
Iola Old Car Show, 1929 Ford, #2535 ....$27.00
JC Penney, 1940 Ford Pickup, #4737 ....$28.00
John Deere, 1936 Dodge Panel Truck, #74042 ....$24.00
K&R Toy Show, Ballys 93, 1955 Chevy, #50028 ....$32.00
Lennox (100th Anniversary), #2, 1940 Ford, #62525 ......$55.00
Little Debbie Snacks, 1929 Ford, #2503 ....$28.00
Mobil Oil, 1940 Ford Tanker, #65506 ....$35.00
Mooseheart Farms, 1916 Studebaker, #22511 ....$25.00
Nabisco, 1929 Ford, #2508 ....$28.00
Neil Bonnett/Citgo #21, 1929 Ford, #0300....................$65.00
Pabst Beer, 1929 Ford, #1512.......................$29.00
Pepsi-Cola, 1936 Dodge Fire Truck, #72034 ....$34.00
Quaker State Racing, 1929 Ford, #0308.............$25.00
Rockingham Raceway, 1929 Ford, #0210.............$65.00
Sentry Hardware, #5, 1955 Chevy, #50030......................$19.00
State Highway Patrol, 1940 Ford Convertible, #60004 ....$23.00

Texaco Model A Ford Roadster, Liberty Classics, #01537, $60.00.

Tractor Supply Co, 1916 Studebaker, #22527 ....$28.00
US Mail, 1916 Studebaker, #25019.................$26.00
Vic Edelbrock Sr, 1931 Roadster, #00236..........................$35.00
Wheaties, 1940 Ford, #67518 ....$23.00
Winchester, Peterbilt Semi, #32509 ....$32.00

Dinky

Dinky diecasts were made by Meccano (Britain) as early as 1933, but high on the list of many of today's collectors are those from the decades of the '50s and '60s. They made commercial vehicles, firefighting equipment, farm toys, and heavy equipment as well as classic cars that were the epitome of high style, such as the #157 Jaguar XK120, produced from the mid-'50s through the early '60s. Some Dinkys were made in France; since 1979 no toys have been produced in Great Britain. Values are for examples mint and in the original packaging unless noted otherwise. For more information see *Toy Car Collector's Guide* by Dana Johnson.
Advisor: Dana Johnson (J4)

#100, Lady Penelope's Fab 1, luminous pk $400.00
#100, Lady Penelope's Fab 1, pk $250.00
#101, Sunbeam Alpine $300.00
#101, Thunderbird II & IV, gr $300.00
#101, Thunderbird II & IV, metallic gr $400.00
#102, Joe's Car $250.00
#102, MG Midget $250.00
#105, Triumph TR2 ....$250.00
#106, Austin Atlantic, bl or blk $200.00
#106, Austin Atlantic, pk $400.00
#106, Prisoner Mini Moke $400.00
#106, Thunderbird II & IV $250.00
#107, Sunbeam Alpine $250.00
#108, MG Midget $250.00
#108, Sam's Car, gold, red or bl $175.00
#108, Sam's Car, silver $175.00
#109, Austin Healey 100 ....$250.00
#109, Gabriel Model T Ford $175.00
#110, Aston Martin DB5 ....$200.00
#111, Cinderella's Coach..........................$125.00
#111, Triumph TR2 ....$175.00
#112, Austin Healey Sprite $125.00
#112, Purdey's Triumph TR7 ....$125.00
#113, MGB $150.00
#114, Triumph Spitfire, gray or gold................$150.00
#114, Triumph Spitfire, purple $175.00

#114, Triumph Spitfire, red, $150.00.

#115, Plymouth Fury..............................$200.00
#116, Volvo 1800S................................$175.00
#117, Four Berth Caravan $150.00
#120, Happy Cab $125.00
#120, Jaguar E-Type $175.00
#121, Goodwood Racing Gift Set $2,000.00
#122, Touring Gift Set $2,000.00
#122, Volvo 265 Estate Car $125.00
#123, Mayfair Gift Set..........................$3,000.00
#123, Princess 2200 HL $175.00
#124, Rolls Royce Phantom V $175.00
#125, Fun A'Hoy Set $325.00
#128, Mercedes Benz 600 ....$175.00
#129, MG Midget................................$1,000.00
#129, VW 1300 Sedan.............................$150.00
#130, Ford Consul Corsair $150.00
#131, Cadillac El Dorado..........................$200.00
#131, Jaguar E-Type, 2+2 ....$150.00

#132, Ford 40-RV	$150.00
#132, Packard Convertible	$200.00
#133, Cunningham C-5R	$175.00
#134, Triumph Vitesse	$150.00
#135, Triumph 2000	$150.00
#136, Vauxhall Viva	$150.00
#137, Plymouth Fury	$150.00
#138, Hillman Imp	$150.00
#139, Ford Cortina	$150.00
#139a, Hudson Commodore Sedan, dual colors	$350.00
#139a, Hudson Commodore Sedan, solid colors	$225.00
#139a, US Army Staff Car	$350.00
#140, Morris 1100	$150.00
#141, Vauxhall Victor	$150.00
#142, Jaguar Mark 10	$150.00
#143, Ford Capri	$150.00
#144, VW 1500	$150.00
#145, Singer Vogue	$150.00
#146, Daimler V8	$175.00
#147, Cadillac 62	$175.00
#148, Ford Fairlane, gr	$175.00
#148, Ford Fairlane, metallic gr	$225.00
#149, Citroen Dyane	$125.00
#149, Sports Car Gift Set	$1,800.00
#150, Rolls Royce Silver Wraith	$175.00
#151, Triumph 1800 Saloon	$200.00
#151, Vauxhall Victor 101	$175.00
#152, Rolls Royce Phantom V	$175.00
#153, Aston Martin DB6	$175.00
#153, Standard Vanguard-Spats	$200.00
#154, Ford Taurus 17M	$175.00
#155, Ford Anglia	$175.00
#156, Mechanized Army Set	$5,000.00
#156, Rover 75, dual colors	$300.00
#156, Rover 75, solid colors	$200.00
#156, Saab 96	$175.00
#157, BMW 2000 Tilux	$175.00
#158, Riley	$200.00
#158, Rolls Royce Silver Shadow	$200.00
#159, Ford Cortina MKII	$150.00
#159, Morris Oxford, dual colors	$300.00
#159, Morris Oxford, solid colors	$200.00
#160, Austin A30	$200.00
#160, Mercedes Benz 250 SE	$175.00
#161, Austin Somerset, dual colors	$300.00
#161, Austin Somerset, solid colors	$200.00
#161, Ford Mustang	$175.00
#162, Ford Zephyr	$200.00
#162, Triumph 1300	$175.00
#163, Bristol 450 Coupe	$150.00
#163, VW 1600 TL, metallic bl	$225.00
#163, VW 1600 TL, red	$75.00
#164, Ford Zodiac MKIV, bronze	$200.00
#164, Ford Zodiac MKIV, silver	$175.00
#164, Vauxhall Cresta	$200.00
#165, Ford Capri	$175.00
#165, Humber Hawk	$225.00
#166, Renault R16	$150.00

#166, Sunbeam Rapier	$200.00
#167, AC Acceca, all cream	$300.00
#167, AC Acceca, dual colors	$225.00
#168, Ford Escort	$150.00
#168, Singer Gazelle	$200.00
#169, Ford Corsair	$150.00
#169, Studebaker Golden Hawk	$225.00
#170, Ford Fordor, dual colors	$300.00
#170, Ford Fordor, solid colors	$200.00
#170, Lincoln Continental	$200.00
#170m, Ford Fordor US Army Staff Car	$350.00
#171, Austin 1800	$150.00
#171, Hudson Commodore, dual colors	$350.00
#172, Fiat 2300 Station Wagon	$150.00
#172, Studebaker Land Cruiser, dual colors	$300.00
#172, Studebaker Land Cruiser, solid colors	$225.00
#173, Nash Rambler	$175.00
#173, Pontiac Parisienne	$150.00
#174, Mercury Cougar	$150.00
#175, Cadillac El Dorado	$150.00
#175, Hillman Minx	$175.00
#176, Austin A105, cream or gray	$200.00
#176, Austin A105, cream w/bl roof, or gray w/red roof	$300.00
#176, Austin A105, gray	$200.00
#176, NSU R80, metallic bl	$175.00
#176, NSU R80, metallic red	$150.00
#177, Opel Kapitan	$150.00
#178, Mini Clubman	$125.00
#178, Plymouth Plaza, bl w/wht roof	$125.00
#178, Plymouth Plaza, pk, gr or 2-tone bl	$200.00
#179, Opel Commodore	$200.00
#179, Studebaker President	$225.00
#180, Rover 3500 Sedan	$125.00

#181, Volkswagen 'Beetle,' $200.00.

#182, Porsche 356A Coupe, cream, red or bl	$250.00
#182, Porsche 356A Coupe, dual colors	$325.00
#183, Fiat 600	$150.00
#183, Morris Mini Minor	$150.00
#184, Volvo 122S, red	$175.00
#184, Volvo 122S, wht	$375.00
#185, Alpha Romeo 1900	$200.00
#186, Mercedes Benz 220SE	$200.00
#187, De Tomaso Mangusta 5000	$150.00
#187, Volkswagen Karmann Ghia Coupe	$225.00
#188, Ford Berth Caravan	$150.00

#188, Jensen FF	$175.00
#189, Lamborghini Marzal	$175.00
#189, Triumph Herald	$175.00
#191, Dodge Royal Sedan, cream w/bl flash	$300.00
#191, Dodge Royal Sedan, cream w/brn flash, or gr w/blk flash	$225.00
#192, Desoto Fireflite	$225.00
#192, Range Rover	$125.00
#193, Rambler Station Wagon	$175.00
#194, Bentley S Coupe	$175.00
#195, Range Rover Fire Chief	$150.00
#196, Holden Special Sedan	$150.00
#197, Austin Countryman, orange	$325.00
#197, Morris Mini Traveller	$150.00
#197, Morris Mini Traveller, dk gr & brn	$400.00
#197, Morris Mini Traveller, lime gr	$300.00
#198, Rolls Royce Phantom V	$175.00
#199, Austin Countryman, bl	$150.00
#200, Matra 630	$150.00
#201, Plymouth Stock Car	$125.00
#201, Racing Car Set	$800.00
#202, Customized Land Rover	$125.00
#202, Fiat Abarth 2000	$50.00
#203, Customized Range Rover	$125.00
#204, Ferrari	$125.00
#205, Talbot Labo, in bubble pkg	$325.00
#206, Customized Corvette Stingray	$150.00
#207, Triumph TR7	$150.00
#208, VW Porsche 914	$125.00
#210, Alfa Romeo 33	$200.00
#210, Vanwall, in bubble pkg	$200.00
#211, Triumph TR7	$125.00
#213, Ford Capri	$125.00
#214, Hillman Imp Rally	$125.00
#215, Ford GT Racing Car	$125.00
#216, Ferrari Dino	$125.00
#217, Alfa Romeo Scarabo	$125.00
#218, Lotus Europa	$125.00
#219, Jaguar XJS Coupe	$125.00
#220, Ferrari P5	$125.00
#221, Corvette Stingray	$150.00
#222, Hesketh Racing Car, dk bl	$125.00
#222, Hesketh Racing Car, Olympus Camera	$150.00
#223, McLaren M8A Can-Am	$125.00
#224, Mercedes Benz C111	$125.00
#225, Lotus Formula 1 Racer	$125.00
#226, Ferrari 312/B2	$125.00
#227, Beach Bunny	$125.00
#228, Super Sprinter	$125.00
#236, Connaught Racer	$175.00
#237, Mercedes Benz Racer	$175.00
#238, Jaguar Type-D Racer	$175.00
#239, Vanwall Racer	$200.00
#240, Cooper Racer	$150.00
#240, Dinky Way Gift Set	$275.00
#241, Lotus Racer	$125.00
#241, Silver Jubilee Taxi	$125.00
#242, Ferrari Racer	$150.00
#243, BRM Racer	$150.00

#243, Volvo Police Racer	$125.00
#244, Plymouth Police Racer	$125.00
#245, Superfast Gift Set	$300.00
#246, International Car Gift Set	$300.00
#249, Racing Car Gift Set	$1,500.00
#249, Racing Car Gift Set, in bubble pkg	$1,800.00
#250, Mini Cooper Police Car	$150.00
#251, USA Police Car, Pontiac	$150.00
#252, RCMP Car, Pontiac	$150.00
#254, Austin Taxi, yel	$200.00
#254, Police Range Rover	$125.00
#255, Ford Zodiac Police Car	$125.00
#255, Mersey Tunnel Police Van	$150.00
#255, Police Mini Clubman	$125.00
#256, Humber Hawk Police Car	$200.00
#257, Nash Rambler Canadian Fire Chief Car	$175.00
#258, USA Police Car, Cadillac, Desoto, Dodge or Ford	$200.00
#259, Bedford Fire Engine	$175.00
#260, Royal Mail Van	$200.00
#260, VW Deutsch Bundepost	$250.00
#261, Ford Taunus Polizei	$325.00
#261, Telephone Service Van	$175.00
#262, VW Swiss Post PTT Car, casting #129	$325.00
#262, VW Swiss Post PTT Car, casting #181, minimum value	$900.00
#263, Airport Fire Rescue Tender	$125.00
#263, Superior Criterion Ambulance	$175.00
#264, RCMP Patrol Car, Cadillac	$200.00
#264, RCMP Patrol Car, Fairlane	$200.00
#265, Plymouth Taxi	$200.00
#266, ERF Fire Tender	$150.00
#266, ERF Fire Tender, Falck	$175.00
#266, Plymouth Taxi, Metro Cab	$200.00
#267, Paramedic Truck	$150.00
#267, Superior Cadillac Ambulance	$150.00
#268, Range Rover Ambulance	$125.00
#268, Renault Dauphine Mini Cab	$175.00
#269, Ford Transit Police Accident Unit	$125.00

#269, Ford Transit Police Accident Unit, Falck Zonen, $125.00.

#269, Jaguar Motorway Police Car	$175.00
#270, AA Motorcycle Patrol	$125.00
#270, Ford Panda Police Car	$125.00

#271, Ford Transit Fire, Appliance $125.00
#271, Ford Transit Fire, Falck $175.00
#271, TS Motorcycle Patrol $300.00
#272, ANWB Motorcycle Patrol $350.00
#272, Police Accident Unit $125.00
#273, RAC Patrol Mini Van $200.00
#274, Ford Transit Ambulance $125.00
#275, Brink's Armoured Car, no bullion $125.00
#275, Brink's Armoured Car, w/gold bullion $200.00
#275, Brink's Armoured Car, w/Mexican bullion $1,000.00
#276, Airport Fire Tender $150.00
#276, Ford Transit Ambulance $125.00
#277, Police Range Rover $125.00
#277, Superior Criterion Ambulance $175.00
#278, Plymouth Yellow Cab $125.00
#278, Vauxhall Victor Ambulance $125.00
#279, Aveling Barford Diesel Roller $125.00
#280, Midland Mobile Bank $150.00
#281, Fiat 2300 Pathe News Camera Car $200.00
#281, Military Hovercraft $125.00
#282, Austin 1800 Taxi $125.00
#282, Land Rover Fire, Appliance $125.00
#282, Land Rover Fire, Falck $135.00
#283, BOAC Coach $150.00
#283, Single-Decker Bus $125.00
#284, London Austin Taxi $125.00
#285, Merryweather Fire Engine $135.00
#285, Merryweather Fire Engine, Falck $150.00
#286, Ford Transit Fire, Falck $160.00
#288, Superior Cadillac Ambulance $150.00
#288, Superior Cadillac Ambulance, Falck $175.00
#289, Routemaster Bus, Esso, purple $750.00
#289, Routemaster Bus, Esso, red $150.00
#289, Routemaster Bus, Festival of London Stores $225.00
#289, Routemaster Bus, Madame Tussaud's $175.00
#289, Routemaster Bus, Silver Jubilee $125.00
#289, Routemaster Bus, Tern Shirts or Schwepps $150.00
#290, Double-Decker Bus $175.00
#290, SRN-6 Hovercraft $125.00
#291, Atlantean City Bus $125.00
#292, Atlantean City Bus, Regent or Ribble $150.00
#293, Swiss Postal Bus $125.00
#295, Atlantean City Bus, Yellow Pages $100.00
#296, Duple Luxury Coach $75.00
#296, Police Accident Unit $175.00
#297, Silver Jubilee Bus, National or Woolworth $125.00
#298, Emergency Services Gift Set, minimum value $1,000.00
#299, Crash Squad Gift Set $150.00
#299, Motorway Services Gift Set, minimum value $1,250.00
#299, Post Office Services Gift Set, minimum value $750.00
#300, London Scene Gift Set $125.00
#302, Emergency Squad Gift Set $125.00
#303, Commando Gift Set $200.00
#304, Fire Rescue Gift Set $175.00
#305, David Brown Tractor $125.00
#308, Leyland 384 Tractor $125.00
#309, Star Trek Gift Set $200.00
#319, Week's Tipping Farm Trailer $125.00

#320, Halesowen Harvest Trailer $125.00
#321, Massey-Harris Manure Spreader $125.00
#322, Disc Harrow $125.00
#323, Triple Gang Mower $125.00
#324, Hay Rake $125.00
#325, David Brown Tractor & Harrow $150.00
#340, Land Rover $150.00
#341, Land Rover Trailer $100.00
#342, Austin Mini Moke $175.00
#342, Moto-Cart $125.00
#344, Estate Car $150.00
#344, Land Rover Pickup $125.00
#350, Tiny's Mini Moke $200.00
#351, UFO Interceptor $175.00
#352, Ed Straker's Car, red $200.00
#352, Ed Straker's Car, yel or gold-plated $225.00
#353, Shado 2 Mobile $275.00
#354, Pink Panther $225.00
#355, Lunar Roving Vehicle $175.00
#357, Klingon Battle Cruiser $175.00
#358, USS Enterprise $175.00
#359, Eagle Transporter $275.00
#360, Eagle Freighter $225.00
#361, Galactic War Chariot $200.00
#362, Trident Star Fighter $225.00
#363, Cosmic Zygon Patroller, for Marks & Spencer $225.00
#364, NASA Space Shuttle, w/booster $225.00
#366, NASA Space Shuttle, no booster $200.00
#367, Space Battle Cruiser $200.00
#368, Zygon Marauder $200.00
#370, Dragster Set $175.00
#371, USS Enterprise, sm version $175.00
#372, Klingon Battle Cruiser, sm version $175.00
#380, Convoy Skip Truck $125.00
#381, Convoy Farm Truck $125.00
#382, Wheelbarrow $100.00
#382 Convoy Dumper $125.00
#383, Convoy NCL Truck $125.00
#384, Convoy Fire Rescue Truck $125.00
#384, Grass Cutter $125.00
#384, Sack Truck $100.00
#385, Convoy Royal Mail Truck $125.00
#386, Lawn Mower $125.00
#389, Med Artillery Tractor $100.00
#390, Customized Transit Van $125.00
#398, Farm Equipment Gift Set $2,000.00
#399, Farm Tractor & Trailer Set $250.00
#400, BEV Electric Truck $125.00
#401, Coventry-Climax Fork Lift, orange $125.00
#401, Coventry-Climax Fork Lift, red $500.00
#402, Bedford Coca-Cola Truck $275.00
#404, Conveyancer Fork Lift $125.00
#405, Universal Jeep $150.00
#406, Commer Articulated Truck $200.00
#407, Ford Transit $125.00
#408, Big Ben Lorry, bl & yel, or bl & orange $350.00
#408, Big Ben Lorry, maroon & fawn $275.00
#408, Big Ben Lorry, pk & cream $2,000.00

#409, Bedford Articulated Lorry $250.00
#410, Bedford Van, Danish Post or Simpsons $175.00
#410, Bedford Van, MJ Hire, Marley or Collectors' Gazette..$150.00
#410, Bedford Van, Royal Mail $125.00
#411, Bedford Truck $175.00
#412, Bedford Van AA $125.00
#413, Austin Covered Wagon, lt & dk bl, or red & tan .$650.00
#413, Austin Covered Wagon, maroon & cream, or med & lt bl $200.00
#413, Austin Covered Wagon, red & gray, or bl or cream .$450.00
#414, Dodge Tipper, all colors other than Royal bl $175.00
#414, Dodge Tipper, Royal bl.......................................$200.00
#416, Ford Transit Van $125.00
#416, Ford Transit Van, 1,000,000 Transits...................$225.00
#417, Ford Transit Van $125.00
#417, Leyland Comet Lorry...$275.00
#419, Leyland Comet Cement Lorry..............................$350.00
#420, Leyland Forward Control Lorry............................$175.00
#421, Hindle-Smart Electric Lorry $175.00
#422, Thames Flat Truck, bright gr $225.00
#422, Thames Flat Truck, dk gr or red $175.00
#425, Bedford TK Coal Lorry $225.00
#428, Trailer, lg $125.00
#429, Trailer..$125.00
#430, Breakdown Lorry, red & gr $1,000.00
#430, Commer Breakdown Lorry, all colors other than tan & gr $1,000.00
#430, Commer Breakdown Lorry, tan & gr....................$200.00
#430, Johnson Dumper $125.00
#432, Foden Tipper $125.00
#432, Guy Warrior Flat Truck $450.00
#433, Guy Flat Truck w/Tailboard................................$525.00
#434, Bedford Crash Truck $175.00
#435, Bedford TK Tipper, gray or yel cab $175.00
#435, Bedford TK Tipper, wht, silver & bl.....................$250.00
#436, Atlas COPCO Compressor Lorry...........................$150.00
#437, Muir Hill Loader $150.00
#438, Ford D 800 Tipper, opening doors $125.00
#439, Ford D 800 Snow Plough & Tipper $150.00
#440, Mobilgas Tanker $175.00
#441, Petrol Tanker, Castrol...$200.00
#442, Land Rover Breakdown Crane $125.00
#442, Land Rover Breakdown Crane, Falck...................$150.00

#442, Petrol Tanker, Esso...$175.00
#443, Petrol Tanker, National Benzole $175.00
#449, Johnson Road Sweeper $125.00
#450, Bedford TK Box Van, Castrol...............................$275.00
#451, Johnston Road Sweeper, opening doors $125.00
#451, Trojan Van, Dunlop..$225.00
#452, Trojan Van, Chivers $250.00
#454, Trojan Van Cydrax $225.00
#455, Trojan Van, Brooke Bond Tea $225.00
#470, Austin Van, Shell-BP $225.00
#475, Ford Model T $175.00
#476, Morris Oxford $175.00
#477, Parsley's Car $175.00
#480, Bedford Van, Kodak...$225.00
#481, Bedford Van, Ovaltine..$225.00
#482, Bedford Van, Dinky Toys $225.00
#485, Ford Model T w/Santa Claus................................$225.00
#486, Morris Oxford, Dinky Beats.................................$175.00
#490, Electric Dairy Van, Express Dairy........................$200.00
#491, Electric Dairy Van, NCB or Job Dairies $200.00
#492, Election Mini Van $350.00
#492, Loudspeaker Van..$175.00
#500, Citroen 2-CV..$175.00
#501, Citroen Police, DS-19 ....$175.00
#501, Foden Diesel Eight-Wheel, 2nd cab.....................$525.00
#501, Foden Diesel 8-Wheel, 2nd cab............................$600.00
#502, Foden Flat Truck, 1st or 2nd cab.......................$1,000.00
#503, Foden Flat Truck, 1st cab..................................$1,200.00
#503, Foden Flat Truck, 2nd cab, bl & orange...............$400.00
#503, Foden Flat Truck, 2nd cab, bl & yel...................$1,200.00
#503, Foden Flat Truck, 2nd cab, 2-tone gr.................$3,000.00
#504, Foden Tanker, red $800.00
#504, Foden Tanker, 1st cab, 2-tone bl $500.00
#504, Foden Tanker, 2nd cab, red $600.00
#504, Foden Tanker, 2nd cab, 2-tone bl......................$3,500.00
#505, Foden Flat Truck w/Chains, 1st cab...................$3,000.00
#505, Foden Flat Truck w/Chains, 2nd cab....................$450.00
#505, Maserati 2000 ....$200.00
#506, Aston Martin $200.00
#509, Fiat 850 ....$175.00
#510, Peugeot 204..$175.00
#511, Guy 4-Ton Lorry, red, gr or brn $900.00
#511, Guy 4-Ton Lorry, 2-tone bl..................................$350.00
#512, Guy Flat Truck, all colors other than bl or red......$750.00
#512, Guy Flat Truck, bl or red $400.00
#512, Lesko Kart..$225.00
#513, Guy Flat Truck w/Tailboard $400.00
#514, Alfa Romeo Giulia..$175.00
#514, Guy Van, Lyons...$2,000.00
#514, Guy Van, Slumberland $600.00
#514, Guy Van, Spratt's $600.00
#515, Ferrari 250 GT $175.00
#517, Renault R8 ....$175.00
#518, Renault 4L $150.00
#519, Simca 100 ....$175.00
#520, Chrysler New Yorker..$275.00
#521, Bedford Articulated Lorry $175.00
#522, Big Bedford Lorry, bl & yel..................................$350.00

#449, Chevrolet El Camino Pickup, $150.00.

#514, Guy Van, Weetabix, $3,500.00.

#563, Blaw-Knox Heavy Tractor, $175.00.

#522, Big Bedford Lorry, maroon & fawn.........................$200.00	
#522, Citroen DS-19 ....$250.00	
#523, Simca 1500 ....$150.00	
#524, Panhard 24-CT $175.00	
#524, Renault Dauphine $175.00	
#525, Peugeot 403-U $225.00	
#526, Mercedes-Benz 190-SL $200.00	
#527, Alfa Romeo 1900..$175.00	
#529, Vespa 2-CV $200.00	
#530, Citroen DS-23 ....$125.00	

#564, Elevator Loader...$150.00
#566, Citroen Police Van..$200.00
#568, Ladder Truck...$225.00
#569, Dump Truck $225.00
#570, Peugeot Van $200.00
#571, Coles Mobile Crane $140.00
#572, Dump Truck, Berliet $225.00
#576, Panhard Tanker, Esso $350.00
#577, Simca Van, Bailly..$300.00
#578, Simca Dump Truck $250.00
#580, Dump Truck $250.00
#581, Container Truck, Bailly $250.00
#581, Horse Box, British Railway...................................$250.00
#581, Horse Box, Express Horse Van $1,000.00
#582, Pullman Car Transporter $175.00
#584, Covered Truck $225.00
#585, Dumper $250.00
#587, Citroen Van, Philips $250.00
#589, Berliet Wrecker $275.00
#590, City Road Signs Set $225.00
#591, AEC Tanker, Shell..$225.00
#591, Country Road Signs Set $225.00
#592, Gas Pumps, Esso..$250.00
#593, Road Signs Set $250.00
#595, Crane $400.00
#595, Traffic Signs Set $175.00
#597, Fork Lift $200.00
#601, Austin Para Moke $225.00
#602, Armoured Command Car....................................$150.00
#603, Army Personnel, box of 12 ....$125.00
#604, Land Rover Bomb Disposal Unit..........................$150.00
#609, 105mm Howitzer & Gun Crew $100.00
#612, Commando Jeep $100.00
#615, US Jeep & 105mm Howitzer $125.00
#616, AEC Articulated Transporter & Tank $175.00
#617, VW KDF w/Antitank Gun...................................$200.00
#618, AEC Articulated Transporter & Helicopter $175.00
#619, Bren Gun Carrier & Antitank Gun $150.00
#620, Berliet Missile Launcher.....................................$175.00
#621, 3-Ton Army Wagon $200.00
#622, Bren Gun Carrier $125.00
#622, 10-Ton Army Truck...$200.00

#531, Leyland Comet Lorry, all colors other than bl or brn .$275.00
#531, Leyland Comet Lorry, bl or brn $600.00
#532, Bedford Comet Lorry w/Tailboard $275.00
#532, Lincoln Premiere $250.00
#533, Leyland Cement Wagon $225.00
#533, Peugeot...$225.00
#534, BMW 1500 ....$200.00
#535, Citroen 2-CV $225.00
#538, Buick Roadmaster $325.00
#538, Renault 16-TX $175.00
#539, Citroen ID-19 ....$225.00
#540, Opel Kadett...$175.00
#541, Simca Versailles $200.00
#542, Simca Taxi $200.00
#543, Renault Floride $175.00
#545, De Soto Diplomat $200.00
#546, Austin-Healey...$225.00
#548, Fiat 1800 Familiare $200.00
#550, Chrysler Saratoga..$325.00
#551, Ford Taunus, Polizei $225.00
#551, Rolls Royce $300.00
#551, Trailer $75.00
#552, Chevrolet Corvair...$225.00
#555, Fire Engine, w/extension ladder $150.00
#555, Ford Thunderbird $250.00
#556, Citroen Ambulance $275.00
#558, Citroen $225.00
#559, Ford Taunus...$225.00
#561, Blaw-Knox Bulldozer $125.00
#561, Blaw-Knox Bulldozer, plastic $600.00
#561, Citroen Van, Gervais $250.00
#561, Renault Mail Car $175.00
#562, Muir-Hill Dumper $80.00
#563, Estafette Pickup $200.00
#564, Armagnac Caravan...$150.00

#623, Army Covered Wagon $200.00	#704, Avro York Airliner..$200.00
#625, 6-Pounder Antitank Gun $125.00	#705, Viking Airliner $175.00
#626, Military Ambulance $175.00	#706, Vickers Viscount Airliner, Air France.............$175.00
#640, Bedford Military Truck $325.00	#708, Vickers Viscount Airliner, BEA $175.00
#641, Army 1-Ton Cargo Truck $175.00	#710, Beechcraft S35 Bonanza $175.00
#642, RAF Pressure Refueller $200.00	#712, US Army T-42A $125.00
#643, Army Water Carrier.....................................$200.00	#715, Beechcraft C-55 Baron $175.00
#650, Light Tank..$225.00	#715, Bristol 173 Helicopter $175.00
#651, Centurion Tank $200.00	#716, Westland Sikorsky Helicopter $90.00
#654, Mobile Gun..$125.00	#717, Boeing 737 ....$85.00
#656, 88mm Gun $125.00	#718, Hawker Hurricane $85.00
#660, Tank Transporter...$200.00	#719, Spitfire MKII..$85.00
#661, Recovery Tractor..$250.00	#721, Junkers Stuka $80.00
#662, Static 88mm Gun & Crew $125.00	#722, Hawker Harrier $80.00
#665, Honest John Missile Erector..........................$275.00	#723, Hawker Executive Jet....................................$60.00
#666, Missile Erector Vehicle w/Corporal Missile & Launching Platform $500.00	#724, Sea King Helicopter $75.00
#667, Armoured Patrol Car $125.00	#725, Phantom II..$100.00
#667, Missile Servicing Platform Vehicle $350.00	#726, Messerschmitt, desert camouflage $100.00
#668, Foden Army Truck.......................................$125.00	#726, Messerschmitt, gray & gr $200.00
#670, Armoured Car $200.00	#727, US Air Force F-4 Phantom II $300.00
#671, MKI Corvette (boat) $125.00	#728, RAF Dominie $80.00
#671, Reconnaissance Car......................................$200.00	#729, Multi-Role Combat Aircraft...........................$75.00
#672, OSA Missile Boat $150.00	#730, US Navy Phantom $100.00
#673, Scout Car $175.00	#731, SEPECAT Jaguar..$80.00
#674, Austin Champ, olive drab $175.00	#731, Twin-Engine Fighter.....................................$60.00
#674, Austin Champ, wht, UN version $500.00	#732, Bell Police Helicopter, M*A*S*H...................$100.00
#674, Coast Guard Missile Launch $175.00	#732, Bell Police Helicopter, wht & bl $60.00
#675, Motor Patrol Boat $150.00	#733, German Phantom II.......................................$200.00
#676, Armoured Personnel Carrier $175.00	#733, Lockhead Shooting Star Fighter $50.00
#676, Daimler Armoured Car, w/speedwheels $150.00	#734, Submarine Swift $60.00
#677, Armoured Command Vehicle $175.00	#735, Glouster Javelin $60.00
#677, Task Force Set $175.00	#736, Bundesmarine Sea King $90.00
#678, Air Sea Rescue $175.00	#736, Hawker Hunter $60.00
#680, Ferret Armoured Car $125.00	#737, P1B Lightning Fighter $90.00
#681, DUKW $175.00	#738, DH110 Sea Vixen Fighter..............................$70.00
#682, Stalwart Load Carrier $175.00	#739, Zero-Sen..$100.00
#683, Chieftain Tank...$175.00	#741, Spitfire MKII..$100.00
#686, 25-Pounder Field Gun $150.00	#749, RAF Avro Vulcan Bomber $3,500.00
#687, Convoy Army Truck $125.00	#750, Call Telephone Box $50.00
#687, Trailer $50.00	#751, Lawn Mower $100.00
#688, Field Artillery Tractor...................................$150.00	#752, Goods Yard Crane $70.00
#690, Mobile Anti-aircraft Gun..............................$175.00	#752, Police Box $50.00
#690, Scorpion Tank...$175.00	#755, Standard Lamp, single arm $30.00
#691, Striker Antitank Vehicle $175.00	#756, Standard Lamp, dbl arm...............................$30.00
#692, Leopard Tank $175.00	#760, Pillar Box..$40.00
#692, 5.5 Med Gun $175.00	#766, British Road Signs, Country Set A $100.00
#693, 7.2 Howitzer..$175.00	#767, British Road Signs, Country Set B $100.00
#694, Hanomag Tank Destroyer $150.00	#768, British Road Signs, Town Set A $100.00
#695, Howitzer & Tractor.......................................$250.00	#769, British Road Signs, Town B $100.00
#696, Leopard Anti-aircraft Tank $175.00	#770, Road Signs, set of 12 ....$150.00
#697, 25-Pounder Field Gun Set............................$225.00	#771, International Road Signs, set of 12 ....$160.00
#698, Tank Transporter & Tank..............................$350.00	#772, British Road Signs, set of 24 ....$200.00
#699, Leopard Recovery Tank $175.00	#773, Traffic Signal $30.00
#699, Military Gift Set $900.00	#777, Belisha Beacon..$30.00
#700, Spitfire MKII RAF Jubilee.............................$175.00	#781, Petrol Pumping Station, Esso $100.00
#701, Shetland Flying Boat $800.00	#782, Petrol Pumping Station, Shell $80.00
#702, DH Comet Jet Airliner..................................$250.00	#784, Dinky Goods Train Set $150.00
	#785, Service Station $300.00

#786, Tire Rack..$150.00

#787, Lighting Kit...$75.00

#796, Healy Sports Boat $175.00

#798, Express Passenger Train $250.00

#801, Mini USS Enterprise $125.00

#802, Mini Klingon Cruiser.................................$125.00

#815, Panhard Armoured Tank $250.00

#817, AMX 13-Ton Tank $225.00

#822, M3 Half-Track $250.00

#893, UNIC Pipe-Line Transporter......................$450.00

#894, UNIC Boilot Car Transporter $400.00

#900, Building Site Gift Set..............................$1,500.00

#901, Foden 8-Wheel Truck...............................$450.00

#902, Foden Flat Truck $450.00

#903, Foden Flat Truck w/Tailboard $750.00

#905, Foden Flat Truck w/Chains $450.00

#911, Guy 4-Ton Lorry $475.00

#912, Guy Flat Truck $475.00

#913, Guy Flat Truck w/Tailboard $625.00

#914, AEC Articulated Lorry $200.00

#915, AEC Flat Trailer $175.00

#917, Guy Van, Spratts..$650.00

#917, Mercedes Benz Truck & Trailer $375.00

#917, Mercedes Benz Truck & Trailer, Munsterland.......$375.00

#918, Guy Van, Ever Ready, $750.00.

#919, Guy Van, Golden Shred.......................................$2,000.00

#920, Guy Warrior Van, Heinz $3,000.00

#921, Bedford Articulated Lorry $325.00

#922, Big Bedford Lorry...$325.00

#923, Big Bedford Van, Heinz Baked Beans can & Heinz 57
    Varieties $750.00

#923, Big Bedford Van, Heinz Ketchup bottle.............$2,000.00

#924, Aveling-Barford Dumper $175.00

#925, Leyland Dump Truck $250.00

#930, Bedford Pallet-Jekta Van, Dinky Toys.................$375.00

#931, Leyland Comet Lorry, all colors other than bl & brn .$275.00

#931, Leyland Comet Lorry, bl & brn $500.00

#932, Leyland Comet Wagon w/Tailboard.....................$275.00

#933, Leyland Cement Truck $300.00

#934, Leyland Octopus Wagon, all colors other than bl & brn.$650.00

#934, Leyland Octopus Wagon, bl & yel $2,000.00

#936, Leyland 8-Wheel Test Chassis............................$225.00

#940, Mercedes Benz Truck...$175.00

#943, Leyland Octopus Tanker, Esso $450.00

#944, Shell-BP Fuel Tanker...$325.00

#944, Shell-BP Fuel Tanker, red wheels $650.00

#945, AEC Fuel Tanker, Esso $200.00

#945, AEC Fuel Tanker, Lucas $250.00

#948, Tractor-Trailer, McLean $400.00

#949, Wayne School Bus $400.00

#950, Foden S20 Fuel Tanker, Burmah $200.00

#950, Foden S20 Fuel Tanker, Shell.............................$200.00

#951, Trailer...$125.00

#952, Vega Major Luxury Coach $200.00

#953, Continental Touring Coach $475.00

#954, Fire Station..$425.00

#954, Vega Major Luxury Coach, no lights.....................$175.00

#955, Fire Engine $200.00

#956, Turntable Fire Escape, Bedford $200.00

#956, Turntable Fire Escape, Berliet $250.00

#957, Fire Services Gift Set $600.00

#958, Snow Plough $325.00

#959, Foden Dump Truck $300.00

#960, Lorry-Mounted Concrete Mixer $200.00

#961, Blaw-Knox Bulldozer $175.00

#961, Vega Major Luxury Coach $350.00

#962, Muir-Hill Dumper $175.00

#963, Blaw-Knox Heavy Tractor $175.00

#963, Road Grader...$150.00

#964, Elevator Loader $175.00

#965, Euclid Rear Dump Truck $200.00

#965, Terex Dump Truck $275.00

#966, Marrel Multi-Bucket Unit $175.00

#967, BBC TV Mobile Control Room $350.00

#967, Muir-Hill Loader & Trencher $150.00

#968, BBC TV Roving Eye Vehicle $350.00

#969, BBC TV Extending Mast Vehicle $350.00

#970, Jones Cantilever Crane $150.00

#971, Coles Mobile Crane...$200.00

#972, Coles 20-Ton Lorry, mounted crane, yel & blk.....$225.00

#972, Coles 20-Ton Lorry, mounted crane, yel & orange .$175.00

#973, Eaton Yale Tractor Shovel $550.00

#973, Goods Yard Crane $200.00

#974, AEC Hoyner Transporter $175.00

#975, Ruston Bucyrus Excavator $375.00

#976, Michigan Tractor Dozer $275.00

#977, Commercial Servicing Platform Vehicle...............$325.00

#977, Shovel Dozer...$200.00

#978, Refuse Wagon $200.00

#979, Racehorse Transporter $625.00

#980, Coles Hydra Truck $225.00

#980, Horse Box, British Railways $375.00

#980, Horse Box Express $800.00

#984, Atlas Digger $200.00

#984, Car Carrier...$475.00

#985, Trailer for Car Carrier..$200.00

#986, Mighty Antar Low Loader w/Propeller $500.00

#987, ABC TV Control Room..$500.00

#988, ABC TV Transmitter Van $500.00

#990, Pullman Car Transporter w/4 Cars....................$2,500.00

#991, AEC Tanker, Shell Chemicals $350.00

#992, Avro Vulcan Delta Wing Bomber........................$3,500.00

#989, Auto Transporters, $2,000.00.

#994, Loading Ramp for #992 ....$100.00
#997, Caravelle, Air France $375.00
#998, Bristol Britannia Canadian Pacific.......................$375.00
#999, DH Comet Jet..$375.00

Disney

Through the magic of the silver screen, Walt Disney's characters have come to life, and it is virtually impossible to imagine a child growing up without the influence of his genius. As each classic film was introduced, toy manufacturers scurried to fill department store shelves with the dolls, games, battery-ops, and windups that carried the likeness of every member of its cast. Though today it is the toys of the 1930s and 1940s that are bringing top prices, later toys are certainly collectible as well, as you'll see in our listings. Even characters as recently introduced as Roger Rabbit already have their own cult following.

Since the advent of the Internet, condition and rarity are even more important than ever when it comes to evaluation. Disney limited editions purchased within the last ten years seldom bring more than 75% of their original purchase price. Vintage items, however, have remained steady in value over the past five years, though down at least 20% from the 1980s.

For more information we recommend *Disneyana* by Cecil Munsey (Hawthorne Books, 1974); *Disneyana* by Robert Heide and John Gilman; *Walt Disney's Mickey Mouse Memorabilia* by Hillier and Shine (Abrams Inc., 1986); *Tomart's Disneyana Update Magazine*; and *Elmer's Price Guide to Toys* by Elmer Duellman (L-W Books).

Advisor: Joel J. Cohen (C12)

See also Battery-Operated; Books; Bubble Bath Containers; Character and Promotional Drinking Glasses; Character Clocks and Watches; Chein; Coloring, Activity, and Paint Books; Dakin; Fisher-Price; Games; Lunch Boxes; Marx; Paper Dolls; Pez Dispensers; Pin-Back Buttons; Plastic Figures; Puppets; Puzzles; Ramp Walkers; Records; Sand Toys; View-Master; Western; Windups, Friction, and Other Mechanicals.

Alice in Wonderland, figure, Cheshire Cat, plush, Disneyland, 1970s, EX $25.00
Alice in Wonderland, figure, Mad Hatter, plush, Gund, 1950s, EX $230.00

Alice in Wonderland, Make-Up Kit, box only, textured bl cb w/metal locking latch & hdl, WDP/Hasbro, 1951, 11x6x4", NM...$50.00
Alice in Wonderland, record player, Bakelite, 1940s, VG .$175.00
Alice in Wonderland, tea set, plastic, cream w/floral trim, 9-pc w/6 utensils, Plasco, 1950s, EX+.................................$65.00
Bambi, bookmark, Prevent Forest Fires, State Forest Service/WDP, 1940s, 6", NM $30.00
Bambi, figure set, Thumper & girlfriend, ceramic, American Pottery, 1940s, 4", pr...$75.00
Cinderella, handkerchief, cloth, 1950s, 8x8", VG+, N2 ..$10.00
Disney, Birthday Party Set, w/cake decorations, baskets, candles, etc, Best Plastics/WDP, 1950s, complete, EXIB, A $85.00
Disney, booklet, Automotive Quiz, features Donald Duck & other characters, 12 pgs, Sunoco Oil premium, 1941, EX $50.00
Disney, Character Lights, 8-character strand of Christmas tree lights, Diamond-Brite, EXIB, A $70.00
Disney, Disney Airliner, wht & red litho tin w/images of Disney characters, 4 metal props, EX, A $340.00
Disney, Disney Castle, clear plastic w/cb & paper base & accessories, no Disneykin figures o/w complete, Marx, EXIB, A.......$100.00
Disney, drum, litho tin w/parade of characters, w/wooden drumsticks, Ohio Art, 9" dia, Fair+, A $230.00
Disney, Mazda Disneylights, strand of 12 bell-shaped lamps decorated w/characters, Thomson Houston Co, 1954, NMIB........$110.00
Disney, top, litho tin w/character band members parading in circle on multicolored bands, 9½" dia, EX, A..............$150.00
Disney, world globe, litho tin w/metal base, characters around base & on globe, WDP, 1950s, 10x9" dia, VG+, A .$120.00
Disney/RCA, placemats, plastic coated w/Disney images & Nipper the RCA dog, 1966, NMIP $45.00
Disneyland, booklet, Sleeping Beauty Castle, 1957, 8 pgs, EX+..$40.00

Disneyland, Melody Player, with five paper rolls, EXIB, A, $265.00. (Photo courtesy Randy Inman Auctions)

Disneyland, Musical Map, cb fold-out map w/5 uncut 78 rpm picture records, Mattel, 1950s, NM............................$75.00
Disneyland, tray, litho tin w/aerial image of park, WDP, 1955, 12½x17", NM..$100.00
Donald Duck, bank, Second National Duck Bank, litho tin w/images of Donald, Mickey & Minnie, Chein, NMIB.................$165.00
Donald Duck, booklet, Automotive Quiz, 12 pgs, Sunoco Oil premium, 1941, EX $50.00
Donald Duck, bread wrapper, Debus brand, waxed paper, 1952, NM, M8 ....$15.00

Donald Duck Camera, plastic, Herbert George/WDP, 1940s, 5", GIB, $150.00. (Photo courtesy James D. Julia, Inc.)

Donald Duck, Dress Buttons, plastic, encircled figures of Donald, set of 3, EX (on Mickey Mouse Dress Buttons card).$100.00
Donald Duck, dump truck, friction, rare, EX, L4 ....$475.00
Donald Duck, figure, bsk, riding scooter, Japan, 1930s, 3½", VG, A $60.00
Donald Duck, figure, bsk, standing holding flag, head turned, side-glance eyes, long bill, sm base, Japan, 3¾", VG, A......$80.00
Donald Duck, figure, bsk, standing holding horn down at side, head turned, long bill, sm base, Japan, 1930s, 3", VG, A........$80.00
Donald Duck, figure, bsk, standing w/hands on belly, head turned, long bill, sm base, Japan, 1930s, 1¾", G, A...$50.00

Donald Duck, figure, bsk, standing w/hands on hips, eyes closed, long bill, no base, Japan, 1930s, 4¼", VG, A $145.00
Donald Duck, figure, bsk, standing w/head turned, jtd arms, no base, Japan, 1930s, 4", VG, A $155.00
Donald Duck, figure, bsk, standing w/head turned, smiling open bill, no base, Japan, 1930s, 3¼", G, A........$35.00
Donald Duck, figure, bsk, strutting w/chest out & bill up, no base, Japan, 1930s, 3¼", VG, A $30.00
Donald Duck, figure, celluloid, long-billed Donald w/movable arms & legs attached by string, Japan, 1930s, 3½", VG, A $90.00
Donald Duck, figure, ceramic, Donald w/fish, airbrushed colors, Leeds Pottery, 6½", EX, A $25.00
Donald Duck, figure, Chatter Chum, 1976, EX+, N2.......$35.00
Donald Duck, figure, plastic, portly, 1970s, 10", VG+, N2 .$15.00
Donald Duck, figure, rubber, w/squeaker, Sun Rubber, 1950s, 11" (scarce sz), EX $30.00
Donald Duck, jack-in-the-box, cb box w/celluloid figure, prewar, 3½", NM, A.........$500.00
Donald Duck, mug, ceramic, wht, shows Donald running w/tray of ice cream cones & picnic basket, Patriot China, 3", EX, A $25.00
Donald Duck, paint box, litho tin, images of Donald, Nephews & Mickey, WDE, 1946, 3¼x8", EX+ $50.00
Donald Duck, pencil sharpener, Donald standing in purple hat & jacket, Japan, 1930s, 2¾", EX, A.........$210.00
Donald Duck, pencil sharpener, winking figure, celluloid, Japan, 1930s, 2½", VG, A...............$110.00
Donald Duck, projector, plastic, complete w/film strip, Stephens Prod, 1950s, 8", EX+, M8 ....$45.00

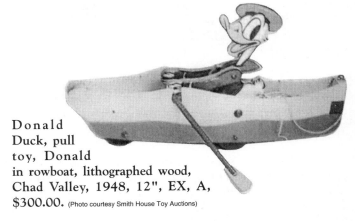

Donald Duck, pull toy, Donald in rowboat, lithographed wood, Chad Valley, 1948, 12", EX, A, $300.00. (Photo courtesy Smith House Toy Auctions)

Donald Duck, record, cereal box premium, 1950s, 5", VG+, N2..$10.00
Donald Duck, slippers, stuffed head on top, Trimfoot/WDP, 1940s-50s, EX.........$65.00
Donald Duck, tea set, lustreware, shows Donald against landscape on wht, tan border, 9-pc, VG, A......$50.00
Donald Duck, wall walker, Kenner, 1971, MOC $40.00
Donald Duck, watering can, litho tin, shows Donald walking along red brick wall, bl top, yel spout, WDE, 1938, 3", VG, A $175.00
Donald Duck & Pluto, toy car, Donald in driver's seat w/Pluto looking on from rear, Sun Rubber, 1930s, EX, A $60.00
Ferdinand the Bull, figure, bsk, seated upright smelling a flower, Japan, prewar, 3", NM, A $20.00

Ferdinand the Bull, figure, compo, Ideal, 9", EX, A........$135.00

Ferdinand the Bull, game, Put the Tail on Ferdinand, WDE/Whitman, 1938, EXIB...................................$125.00

Ferdinand the Bull, soap figure, Kirk Guild, 1938, VGIB, M8..$45.00

Goofy, valentine, mechanical, diecut Goofy w/butterfly net, WDP, 1939, 5", EX...$30.00

Jiminy Cricket, see Pinocchio

Lady & the Tramp, figures, Lady & Tramp, stuffed suede w/felt ears, leather accents, WDP, 1970s, pr.........................$45.00

Lady & the Tramp, roly poly, Lady, plush w/vinyl face, Gund, 1950s, 8", VG+, N2 ....$35.00

Mary Poppins, doll, Mary Poppins, stuffed cloth w/vinyl head, red & wht striped dress w/wht pinafore, 1960s, 19", MIB.$175.00

Mickey Mouse, bank, head form, vinyl, 1971, VG+, N2..$25.00

Mickey Mouse, bank, Mickey w/treasure chest, compo, head swivels, w/key, WD/Crown Toy, 1930s, 6x3½", VG+, A $200.00

Mickey Mouse, bracelet, early rat face on rnd watch-type face w/separated slip-on band, early 1930s, scarce, EX....$200.00

Mickey Mouse, Camera Outfit, plastic camera w/flash attachment & booklet, Ettelson, 1950s, NM+ (EX cb carrying case), A $100.00

Mickey Mouse, child's dish, china with metal warmer, Excello, 6½" diameter, EX, A, $230.00. (Photo courtesy Collector's Auction Services)

Mickey Mouse, child's dish, 3-part, wht ceramic w/blk & wht images of Mickey in ea part, WDE, 7½" dia, VG, A .$100.00

Mickey Mouse, cookie box, litho on cb, National Biscuit Co/WDE, 1937, 1¾x2½x5", scarce, EX $100.00

Mickey Mouse, figure, bsk, playing French horn, Japan, 1930s, 3⅜", VG+, M8...$75.00

Mickey Mouse, figure, bsk, playing saxophone, blk & wht, mk Rosenthal, 3¼", NM $1,200.00

Mickey Mouse, figure, bsk, playing saxophone, blk & wht w/red shoes & silver sax, Japan, 5½", EX, A.....................$100.00

Mickey Mouse, figure, bsk, seated in canoe, Japan, prewar, 4¼", NM, A $900.00

Mickey Mouse, figure, bsk, standing on base w/emb name, jtd arms, Japan, 7¼", EX, A $550.00

Mickey Mouse, figure, bsk, standing on base w/name, jtd arms, Japan/WD, 8¾", EX, A $550.00

Mickey Mouse, figure, bsk, standing w/cane & hand on hip, wearing hat, no base, Japan, 4¼", VG, A $40.00

Mickey Mouse, figure, celluloid, movable arms & head, red shorts, 1930, 7", NM, A $1,150.00

Mickey Mouse, figure, cloth w/pipe cleaner arms, legs & tail, wht & blk, Marshall Field, 1932, EXIB, A...............$550.00

Mickey Mouse, figure, compo, boxer, pie eyes, 10½", EX.$150.00

Mickey Mouse, figure, compo, standing w/hands on hips, blk & wht w/gr base, unmk, 1930s, 5½", EX, A.................$115.00

Mickey Mouse, figure, lead, standing on base w/open mouth, elbows extended out w/hands on hips, blk & wht, 2¼", EX, A $50.00

Mickey Mouse, figure, plush, brn & blk velvet w/felt ears, applied eyes, red velvet pants, Steiff, 1940s, 7", VG, A.........$500.00

Mickey Mouse, figure, plush, Cowboy, print cloth w/compo feet, fur-type chaps, rope, 2 guns, hat, Knickerbocker, 11", VG .$1,500.00

Mickey Mouse, figure, plush, Santa, tag reads Made for the Pepsi Cola Co/WDP, 1950s-60s, 36", VG+, A $45.00

Mickey Mouse, figure, pressed wood w/pipe cleaner tail, blk & wht, rat-faced w/pie eyes, Germany, 2¼", G, A.........$85.00

Mickey Mouse, figure, resin, band leader, 1 of 1200 limited edition, artist signed, WDC, 1993, 13¼", NM, A........$200.00

Mickey Mouse, figure, rubber, standing, w/orig tail, Seiberling Rubber, 1930s, 3¼", NM+, M9...........................$165.00

Mickey Mouse, figure, wood, Fun-E-Flex, Nifty, 3¾", EX, A..$125.00

Mickey Mouse, figure, wood, Fun-E-Flex, rare gr version, Nifty, 7½", G, A $450.00

Mickey Mouse, figure, wood, Fun-E-Flex, red version, Nifty, 7½", VG, A $400.00

Mickey Mouse, figure, wood w/rope arms, leatherette ears, metal tail, red, wht, blk, Walter E Disney, 1928-29, 6", VG, A.......$475.00

Mickey Mouse, fountain pen, figural head on top w/Mickey trim, Inkograph Co, 1930s, 5", rare, NM, M8 ....$225.00

Mickey Mouse, game, Pin the Tail on Mickey, Marks Bros/WDE, 1930s, 22x18", VG, A $115.00

Mickey Mouse, gumball machine, glass bowl w/Mickey Mouse & His Pals decal, CI base, Hamilton, 1938, 16", EX .$1,500.00

Mickey Mouse, Happy Birthday Carousel, tin, WDP/Ross, Japan, 8", NMIB, A $65.00

Mickey Mouse, lamp, chalkware base, S Manegold, 1935, 13", VG+, A, $1,900.00.

Mickey Mouse, lamp base, metal ball shape w/decal of Mickey waving, Soreng-Manegold, 1930s, 6¾", VG, A.........$40.00

Mickey Mouse, Magic Slate Blackboard, Strathmore, 1940s, complete, MIB...$100.00

Mickey Mouse, Mickey Mouse Magazine, Luick Dairy, April 1934, complete, EX, A $175.00

Mickey Mouse, Mickey Mouse Weekly, England, Sept, 1937, complete, EX, A..$85.00

Mickey the Musical Mouse, lithographed tin hand-cranked music box with three animated heads, Germany, 10", EX, $17,600.00. (Photo courtesy Randy Inman Auctions)

Mickey Mouse, Minnie & Pluto, drum, litho metal, yel band w/images of trio in musical scene, Ohio Art, 6½" dia, VG, A $55.00

Mickey Mouse, night light, pnt-glass image of Mickey walking along fence on tin base, England, 8" L, EXIB, A $155.00

Mickey Mouse, nodder, standing w/hands on hips, pnt plastic, hinged at neck, 1940s, 6", EX....................................$40.00

Mickey Mouse Organ Grinder, lithographed tin with Minnie Mouse atop two-wheeled organ, EXIB, A, $24,200.00. (Photo courtesy Randy Inman Auctions)

Mickey Mouse, pencil box, cb, red w/blk & yel trim, Dixon, 1930s, 8½" L, EX, A $50.00

Mickey Mouse, pencil box, Mickey Mouse Parade, complete w/contents, Dixon #2198, 1930s, 11x6x1", EX, M8.$135.00

Mickey Mouse, pencil case, vinyl w/zipper closure, Lunch Money pouch on front w/head image of Mickey, 1950s, 5x8½", M $50.00

Mickey Mouse, pencil holder, compo Mickey figure, blk & wht, WDE/Dixon USA #2925, 5", G, A.........................$125.00

Mickey Mouse, pencil sharpener, Mickey standing w/emb hands on chest, wht, blk & red, Japan, 1930s, 2¾", EX+, A.$210.00

Mickey Mouse Piano, painted wood with lithographed images, Marx Brothers/WDE, 1930s, 10½x9x3", G+, A, $430.00.

Mickey Mouse, pillow cover, image of Mickey picking petals from daisy, Vogue Needlecraft, 1932, 15x17", EX......$75.00

Mickey Mouse, pull toy, diecut wood figure between 2 metal wheels w/cb Mickey images, bell sound, 14", EX, A.$400.00

Mickey Mouse, pull toy, Mickey Mouse Circus, wooden Mickey & Minnie figures on tin 4-wheeled platform, Nifty, 11", G, A $975.00

Mickey Mouse, riding toy, diecut wooden figure w/seat on back attached to 4-wheeled platform, 16x18", VG, A.....$450.00

Mickey Mouse, rocking toy, diecut & pnt wood Mickey on hands & knees w/seat on back attached to base, Triang, 33", EX, A $250.00

Mickey Mouse, scissors, metal w/diecut figure of Mickey running on hdl, WDE, 1930s, 3¼", VG+, A.........................$145.00

Mickey Mouse, sled, wood w/metal runners, name on steering bar & Mickey & Minnie decal, Flyer, WDE, 1930s, 33", EX, A $690.00

Mickey Mouse, Soldier Set, 8 litho cb target figures w/cork gun, Marks Bros/WDE, 18" L, EXIB, A $550.00

Mickey Mouse, sparkler, head figure w/name on bow tie, blk & wht litho tin, 5¾", VG, A $200.00

Mickey Mouse, sprinkler can, litho tin w/image & name, Ohio Art, 6", G, A...$155.00

Mickey Mouse, squeeze toy, red disc w/sm figure of Mickey on top, 5½", VG+, A...$75.00

Mickey Mouse, suitcase, red leather-type w/blk image of Mickey whistling, 6x9", G, A...$150.00

Mickey Mouse, tea set, lustreware, scenes w/Mickey or Mickey & Minnie on wht w/tan borders, 13-pc, complete, EXIB, A $450.00

Mickey Mouse, tea set, wht china outlined in bl w/images of Mickey & other characters, 17-pc, mk Made in France, VG, A...$1,870.00

Mickey Mouse, top, lithographed tin, Mickey and friends parading with musical instruments, 9½" diameter, EXIB, A, $155.00. (Photo courtesy Randy Inman Auctions)

Mickey Mouse, toy chest/child's seat, 1930s, wood, cb & cloth, 36"L, EX..$350.00

Mickey Mouse, tractor toy, rubber, blk & wht Mickey figure on red tractor w/wht tires, Sun Rubber, 1940s, 4½", VG, A.....$30.00

Mickey Mouse, Transfer-O-S, Paas Dye Co, 1930s, unused, EX+ (orig envelope) $65.00

Mickey Mouse, windup crawler, celluloid figure with cloth outfit, scarce, EX, A, $4,620.00.

Mickey Mouse and Donald Duck in a Rowboat, celluloid, Japan, NM, A, $1,775.00.

Mickey Mouse & Donald Duck, car toy, rubber, Mickey driving w/Donald in rear seat, red, WDP/Sun Rubber, 6½", G+, A............$40.00

Mickey Mouse & Donald Duck, figure, celluloid, integral figure of Mickey & Donald dancing, 1935, 3½", rare, NM, A..$2,200.00

Mickey Mouse & Donald Duck, figure set, lead, Mickey & Donald's Garden Set, complete, Salco, 1930s, 4", VGIB, A.......$160.00

Mickey Mouse & Minnie, figure set, bsk, musicians (2 ea), 3½", NMIB...$725.00

Mickey Mouse and Minnie, figure set, bisque, Mickey and Minnie seated at wooden table having tea, with accessories, NMIB, A, $1,200.00.

Mickey Mouse & Minnie, figure set, bsk, shelf sitters, Minnie wearing hat, Japan, 2¾" & 3", VG, A........................$40.00

Mickey Mouse & Minnie, figure set, bsk, standing in nightshirts, Japan, 4", EX, A...$135.00

Mickey Mouse & Minnie, figure set, bsk, standing w/toothy grins, glued to single wood base, 2" & 1¾", VG, A.$180.00

Mickey Mouse & Minnie, figure set, celluloid, World's Fair Century of Progress label, NM, A.................................$400.00

Mickey Mouse & Minnie, figure set, lead, Barrel & Organ Set, complete, Salco, 1930s, 3", EXIB, A........................$150.00

Mickey Mouse & Minnie, figure set, wood, Minnie w/halo of flowers petting lamb & Mickey strolling, Anri/Italy, 6", EX......$350.00

Mickey Mouse & Minnie, fork & spoon, image on ea, mk Fairfield Silverplate, 1930s, EX+.......................................$65.00

Mickey Mouse & Minnie, punch-out figures, 2 diecut cb standup figures w/14 outfit pcs, Saalfield, 1933, VG+..........$225.00

Mickey Mouse & Minnie, purse, wire mesh Deco style w/enameled images of Mickey & Minnie, chain strap, 1930s, 4", G+, A...$200.00

Mickey Mouse & Minnie, tea set, wht china w/decals, 32-pc set, Laveno/Italy, EX, A..$450.00

Mickey Mouse & Minnie, watering can, litho tin, blk & wht figures on bl, red, yel & wht trim, Ohio Art, 3", EX, A.$160.00

Mickey Mouse & Pluto, figure, bsk, Mickey riding Pluto, Borgfeldt/Japan, 2¼", EX, A....................................$70.00

Mickey Mouse & Pluto, figure, bsk, Mickey standing holding leash attached to seated Pluto, prewar, 5½", rare, NM, A..$1,100.00

Mickey Mouse & Pluto, pull toy, stenciled wood Pluto pulling 4-wheeled bell toy w/Mickey figures, Marx Bros/WD, 20", EX...$230.00

Mickey Mouse & Pluto, thermometer, circular image of Mickey standing on Pluto's house, octagonal frame, tin, 3x3", VG, A $200.00

Mickey Mouse Club, coat, wool & leather, 1960s, child's sz, VG+, N2...$35.00

Mickey Mouse Club, harmonica, engraved images, 1960s, 5", NM..$30.00

Mickey Mouse Club, magazine, 1957, NM, M8................$25.00

Mickey Mouse Club, Magic Divider, battery-op, complete, Jaymar, 1950s, EXIB, M8...$60.00

Mickey Mouse Club, magic slate, w/16-pg activity book/storybook inside, Strathmore, 1954, unused, NM+, M8....$45.00

Mickey Mouse Club, Magic Subtractor, battery-op, complete, Jaymar, 1950s, B, M8..$55.00

Mickey Mouse Club, Newsreel, Mattel, complete, EXIB, A .$85.00

Mickey Mouse Club, TV Bulb and Nite-Lite, image of Mickey on bulb, Solar Electric Corporation, 6½", EXIB, A, $80.00.

Minnie Mouse, bank, figural, vinyl, 1980s, 6", VG, N2......$6.00

Minnie Mouse, figure, bsk, hands on hips, Japan, 1930s, 2¾", EX, M8 ....$60.00

Minnie Mouse, figure, bsk, playing mandolin, Japan, 1930s, 3½", EX+, M8..$70.00

Minnie Mouse, figure, bsk, standing w/umbrella hooked over arm, no base, Japan, 4¼", VG, A $45.00

Minnie Mouse, figure, celluloid, bowing w/1 hand on shirt & other pointing to open mouth, red, wht & blk, 2", VG, A ...$160.00

Minnie Mouse, figure, celluloid, standing, jtd head & arms, wearing tall hat, bl skirt w/red bloomers, 1930, 7", NM, A $1,150.00

Minnie Mouse, figure, vinyl, Minnie as baby w/lg head, 1970s, 12", VG+, N2 ....$15.00

Minnie Mouse, figure, wood, Fun-E-Flex, cb ears & cloth dress, Nifty/WDE, 5", EX, A $145.00

Minnie Mouse and Mickey, Helpmates tea set, lithographed tin, seven pieces, Ohio Art, VG+, A, $275.00. (Photo courtesy Randy Inman Auctions)

Minnie Mouse, figure, wood, Fun-E-Flex, WDE, 3¾", VG, A..$85.00

Minnie Mouse, tin, triangular w/colorful image of Minnie admiring flower on yel background, 5", EX, A $200.00

Mouseketeers, mouse ears, blk plastic headband type w/wht emb lettering, Kohner/WDP, 1956, NM+ $40.00

Mouseketeers, vest & mask, vinyl vest, molded plastic half-face mask w/ears, Ben Cooper, 1960s, EXIP (sealed) $35.00

Peter Pan, doll, Peter Pan, Ideal, 1953, 18", EXIB..........$200.00

Peter Pan, figure, Peter Pan, ceramic, sitting on rock, Japan, 1960s-70s, 5", EX+..$40.00

Pinocchio, barrette, celluloid w/pnt image of Pinocchio, 1940s, 2", NM, M8...$30.00

Pinocchio, bottle stopper, silver-plated Pinocchio figure, 1940s, 4½", scarce, NM..$100.00

Pinocchio, brooch, pnt plastic Pinocchio figure, NEMO, 1940, 2", EX (VG card), M8..$40.00

Pinocchio, cup, Jiminy Cricket, plastic w/magic motion eyes, EX, N2 ....$20.00

Pinocchio, figure, Figaro, composition, jointed, white with airbrushing and red painted paws, 6½", VG+, A, $250.00; Pinocchio, figure, Jiminy Cricket, composition with cloth vest, jacket, and hat, jointed, 10", VG, A, $160.00. (Photo courtesy Randy Inman Auctions)

Pinocchio, figure, Geppetto, compo, seated on box, Multi Products, 1940, 5", EX..$60.00

Pinocchio, figure, Gideon, bsk, 1940s, 3", EX+, M8.........$45.00

Pinocchio, figure, Jiminy Cricket, wood, jtd, pnt detail, holding umbrella, mk Shay 3, 8½", EX, A $120.00

Pinocchio, figure, Pinocchio, Bendables, 1960s, MOC $45.00

Pinocchio, figure, Pinocchio, bsk, 1940s, 3", EX+, M8.....$65.00

Pinocchio, figure, Pinocchio, bsk, 1940s, 4", EX+, M8.....$75.00

Pinocchio, figure, Pinocchio, compo, jtd, pnt features, cloth clothes, WDP, 12", EX, A $75.00

Pinocchio, figure, Pinocchio, compo, movable arms, Crown Mfg Co, 1940, 10", EX $165.00

Pinocchio, figure, Pinocchio, compo, name on base, Multi Products, 1940, 2", EX $65.00

Pinocchio, figure, Pinocchio, compo, pnt features, cloth clothes, Knickerbocker, 13", EX, A $300.00

Pinocchio, figure, Pinocchio, porc, Japan, 1940s, 2¾", EX, M8.**$30.00**

Pinocchio, figure, Pinocchio, stuffed cloth w/print striped shirt & bow tie, Knickerbocker, 1963, 13", NM.................**$60.00**

Pinocchio, figure, Pinocchio, wood, feather in cap, Krueger, dated 1939, 16", EX...**$325.00**

Pinocchio, figure, Pinocchio, wood, jtd, felt hat w/feather, cloth bow tie, Ideal, 1940, 10", VG+ **$135.00**

Pinocchio, figure, Pinocchio, wood, standing as to present himself, eyes looking up, rnd base, Anri/Italy, 9¼", EX.**$200.00**

Pinocchio, figure, Pinocchio, wood & compo, jtd, pnt details, cloth hat, Ideal, 20", VG+, A **$525.00**

Pinocchio, figure set, glazed ceramic, seven different characters, National Porcelain Company, 1½" to 3", EX, A, $210.00.

Pinocchio, fork, spoon, knife, Pinocchio & donkey emb on hdls, Duchess Silverplate, 1940s, EX+, M8 ....**$50.00**

Pinocchio, pail, litho tin, straight-sided w/slip lid and bail hdl, red w/blk & wht character images, 1940, 7x5" dia, EX.....**$100.00**

Pinocchio, ring toy, paper litho image of Pinocchio's head on diecut wood w/string-attached ring, ad pc, 1939, EX.**$75.00**

Pinocchio, roly poly, plush w/vinyl face, Gund, 1950s, 8", VG+, N2 ....**$35.00**

Pinocchio, school tablet, pictures Pinocchio & Stromboli, WDP, 1939, some use o/w EX+ **$40.00**

Pinocchio, tumbler, Jiminy Cricket head figure, lt bl plastic w/flicker eyes, WDP, 1950s, 4", NM+ **$30.00**

Pinocchio, valentine, mechanical, diecut cb image of Geppetto, Figaro & Cleo on raft, WDE, 1939, 8x6", EX+..........**$60.00**

Pluto, figure, inflatable vinyl, Ideal, 1960s, 9", MIP **$40.00**

Pluto, figure, plush, Character Novelty Co, 15", G+......**$150.00**

Pluto, lantern, litho tin figure w/clear globe belly, rubber tongue & tail, battery-op, Linemar, 7", NMIB, A.................**$450.00**

Pluto, pull toy, wooden figure on 4-wheeled platform, red w/wht face & blk trim, blk & red platform, 11" L, VG, A....**$50.00**

Pluto, pull toy, wooden figure on 4-wheeled platform, yel figure w/blk outline & name, red platform, 12", EX, A **$145.00**

Pluto the Pup, figure, wood w/rope legs, felt ears, WDE, 3½", VG+, A..**$75.00**

Rocketeer, doll, vinyl, Applause, 1990s, M **$25.00**

Scrooge McDuck, gumball bank, plastic figure standing next to clear gum globe w/$ symbol on base, NM **$40.00**

Silly Symphony, Magic Lantern slide set, Pied Piper, 4 different, Ensign, 1930s, rare, VG+...**$60.00**

Sleeping Beauty, Crib Mobile, plastic, Kenner, 1958, EXIB, M8.**$65.00**

Sleeping Beauty, Magic Bubble Wand, Gardner & Co, 1959, unused, MIP **$40.00**

Snow White & the Seven Dwarfs, bracelet, 8 enamel-on-metal charms, WD, 1938, EX **$65.00**

Snow White & the Seven Dwarfs, bubble toy, Dopey figure, plastic, 1950s, 4x6x3", EX, M8 ....**$20.00**

Snow White & the Seven Dwarfs, Castile Soap Set, 7 figural pcs in storybook box, Lightfoot Schultz Co/WDE, 1938, EX..**$125.00**

Snow White & the Seven Dwarfs, doll, any character, Krueger, 1930s, 12", EX, ea **$175.00**

Snow White & the Seven Dwarfs, doll, Happy, cloth outfit & lantern, Ideal/WDE, 1937, EX **$175.00**

Snow White & the Seven Dwarfs, doll set, Dwarfs, compo, jtd arms, cloth clothes, names on hats, Knickerbocker, 9", EX, A **$935.00**

Snow White & the Seven Dwarfs, doll set, Dwarfs, plush, story's 50th anniversary promo from Sears, 1978, 7", M8...**$100.00**

Snow White & the Seven Dwarfs, figure, Sneezy, ceramic, American Pottery, 6", NM **$125.00**

Snow White & the Seven Dwarfs, figure set, bsk, musicians, 8-pc, Borgfeldt/Japan, 2½" to 3½", VGIB, A..............**$550.00**

Snow White & the Seven Dwarfs, figure set, bsk, 8-pc, Borgfeldt/Japan, 4" to 5¼", VGIB, A.......................**$375.00**

Snow White & the Seven Dwarfs, figure set, bsk, 8-pc, Borgfeldt/Japan, 2½" to 4¼", VGIB, A **$230.00**

Snow White & the Seven Dwarfs, figure set, cast metal, 8-pc, Britains, 1938, scarce, VG..**$475.00**

Snow White & the Seven Dwarfs, figure set, Dwarfs (7), molded rubber, pnt detail, Sieberling, 5½", G, A **$250.00**

Snow White and the Seven Dwarfs, figure set, squeeze rubber with painted detail, marked Diamant, G, A, $130.00. (Photo courtesy Randy Inman Auctions)

Snow White and the Seven Dwarfs, tea set, colorful characters on white ceramic with red border, each with name, twenty-two pieces, Japan, 1937, VG, A, $150.00. (Photo courtesy Collector's Auction Services)

Snow White & the Seven Dwarfs, fork, silver-plated, image on front & back, Roger Bros Co, 1930s, 4¼", scarce, EX+, M8..$30.00
Snow White & the Seven Dwarfs, music box, butterflies fly over wiggling flowers on rnd litho tin base w/graphics, EX+, A ..$300.00
Three Little Pigs, figure set, bsk, playing instruments, #570, #571, #572, Japan, 4½", VG, A $75.00
Three Little Pigs, figure set, bsk, playing instruments, Japan, 3½", VG, A...$40.00

Three Little Pigs and the Big Bad Wolf, figure set, bisque, WDE/Borgfeldt/Japan, 3" to 3½", EXIB, $325.00.

Thumper, see Bambi
Walt Disney, 23 Piece China Tea Set, WDP/Marx #J-9890, complete, EXIB, A $350.00
Who Framed Roger Rabbit, cassette & book, w/12x12" holder, 1988, M, N2...$20.00
Who Framed Roger Rabbit, play money, 1 Zillion Simoleons bill, authentic autograph of creator Gary K Wolf, 1980s, M, M8...$15.00
Willie Whopper, pencil box, cb w/blk, gold & silver litho, w/contents, Eagle Pencil, 1934, scarce oversized version, EX..$75.00
Winnie the Pooh, figure, Chatter Chum, 1976, EX+ $100.00
Winnie the Pooh, figure, stuffed, Gund, 1966, 6½", VG+, N2.$20.00
101 Dalmatians, Colorforms Cartoon Kit, 1961, NMIB...$30.00

Dollhouse Furniture

Back in the '40s and '50s, little girls often spent hour after hour with their dollhouses, keeping house for their imaginary families, cooking on tiny stoves (that sometimes came with scaled-to-fit pots and pans), serving meals in lovely dining rooms, making beds, and rearranging furniture, most of which was plastic, much of which was made by Renwal, Ideal, Marx, Irwin, and Plasco. Jaydon made plastic furniture as well but sadly never marked it. Tootsietoy produced metal items, many in boxed sets.

Of all of these manufacturers, Renwal and Ideal are considered the most collectible. Renwal's furniture was usually detailed; some pieces had moving parts. Many were made in more than one color, often brightened with decals. Besides the furniture, they made accessory items as well as 'dollhouse' dolls of the whole family. Ideal's Petite Princess line was packaged in sets with wonderful detail, accessorized down to the perfume bottles

on the top of the vanity. Ideal furniture and parts are numbered, always with an 'I' prefix. Most Renwal pieces are also numbered.
    Advisor: Judith Mosholder (M7)

Acme/Thomas, carriage, any color, M7, ea $6.00
Acme/Thomas, dog for dog sled, cocker spaniel or dachshund, M7, ea...$8.00
Acme/Thomas, doll, baby in diaper, 1¼", M7.............$3.00
Acme/Thomas, doll, baby in diaper, 1⅛", M7.............$2.00
Acme/Thomas, doll, baby sucking thumb; hard plastic, pk, 1¼", M7...$3.00
Acme/Thomas, doll, Dutch boy or girl, flesh-colored, 2⅜", M7, ea..$5.00
Acme/Thomas, doll, younger boy w/raised hand, M7 ....$3.00
Acme/Thomas, hammock, bl w/red supports, M7.............$20.00
Acme/Thomas, shoofly, dk bl w/yel horse head, M7........$18.00
Allied Pyro, cupboard, corner; aqua, M7.........................$8.00
Allied/Pyro, bed, red w/wht spread, M7 ....$10.00
Allied/Pyro, bedspread, ivory, M7...................................$6.00
Allied/Pyro, chair, dining room or kitchen; pk or red, M7, ea.$3.00
Allied/Pyro, hutch, aqua or red, M7, ea............................$4.00
Allied/Pyro, radio, floor; yel, M7 ....$8.00
Allied/Pyro, refrigerator, ivory, M7 ....$4.00
Allied/Pyro, table, kitchen; wht, M7...............................$4.00
Allied/Pyro, toilet, wht w/red lid, M7.............................$8.00
Arcade, bathtub, wht, G pnt, M7......................................$125.00

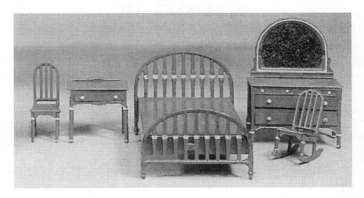

Arcade, bedroom set with chair, table, bed, dresser with pull-out drawers and mirror, and rocker, green painted cast iron, EX, A, $1,430.00.

Ardee, chair, ivory w/brn, M7...$10.00
Ardee, lamp, table; brn base w/red post & ivory shade, M7 .$15.00
Ardee, sofa, ivory w/brn, M7 ....$15.00
Auburn, outdoor set w/red chaise, gr table emb w/tennis rackets, 2 gr chairs, M2 ....$12.00
Banner, crib, pk, M7...$5.00
Best, bunk bed or ladder, bl or pk, M7, ea $5.00
Best, cradle, bl, M7..$4.00
Best, doll, baby sitting; hard plastic, M7.........................$3.00
Best, doll, baby standing; hard plastic, M7 ....$4.00
Blue Box, bed, lt brn w/bl spread, M7.............................$5.00
Blue Box, chair, living room; red w/blk base, M7...........$3.00
Blue Box, chest, 4 drawers, lt brn, M7............................$4.00
Blue Box, piano & stool, M7 ....$15.00

Blue Box, stove, avocado w/silver top, M7 ....$3.00

Blue Box, vanity w/heart-shaped mirror, M7.....................$4.00

Casablanca, vanity, brn, M7 ....$12.00

Cheerio, any hard plastic pc, M7, ea $4.00

Cheerio, any soft plastic pc, M7 ....$2.00

Commonwealth, lamppost w/street sign & mailbox, red, M7..$15.00

Commonwealth, lawn mower, any color, M7, ea $30.00

Commonwealth, rake, any color, M7 ....$4.00

Commonwealth, water can, red or wht, M7, ea $6.00

Donna Lee, chair, kitchen; wht, M7..................................$3.00

Donna Lee, sink, stove or table, kitchen; wht, M7, ea........$4.00

Fisher-Price, chair, dining (brn w/tan seat) or kitchen (wht w/yel); M7, ea...$2.00

Fisher-Price, cradle (wht), dresser w/mirror (wht), refrigerator (wht w/yel) or sink (yel, wht & orange), M7, ea..........$5.00

Fisher-Price, kitchen set, #252, 1978 – 84, M, $15.00. (Photo courtesy Brad Cassity)

Fisher-Price, stove/hood unit, yel, M7 ....$5.00

Fisher-Price, table, kitchen; wht w/red marbled top, M7 ....$3.00

Goldilocks, kitchen set, 6 pcs w/chair, cupboard, stool, stove & table, pnt ivory, M7 ....$175.00

Grand Rapids, chair, living room; club or high back, M7, ea .$12.00

Ideal, bed, w/finials, dk marbleized maroon w/ivory spread or ivory w/bl spread, M7, ea $60.00

Ideal, bird bath (marbleized ivory), lawn bench (bl), M7, ea .$18.00

Ideal, buffet, dk brn or dk marbleized maroon, M7, ea......$10.00

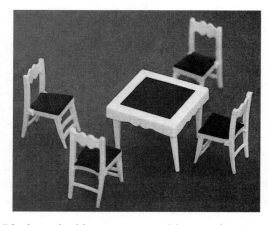

Ideal, card table set, ivory and brown, $125.00.

Ideal, buffet, red, M7...$15.00

Ideal, chair, bedroom; ivory w/bl skirt, M7 ....$30.00

Ideal, chair, dining room; any color, M7, ea......................$10.00

Ideal, chair, high back, red swirl w/brn base, M7 ....$18.00

Ideal, chair, kitchen; ivory w/bl or red seat, M7, ea............$6.00

Ideal, chair, sq back, any color, M7, ea.............................$15.00

Ideal, china closet, red, M7...$20.00

Ideal, cradle, bl or pk, M7, ea...$45.00

Ideal, dishwasher, w/basket, wht w/blk, M7 ....$20.00

Ideal, electric ironer, wht w/blk, M7 ....$18.00

Ideal, fireplace, brn, M7..$35.00

Ideal, highboy, ivory w/bl, M7 ....$18.00

Ideal, highchair, collapsible, bl or pk, M7, ea..................$25.00

Ideal, lamp, table; dk marbleized maroon w/marbleized pk shade or bl shade, M7, ea..$20.00

Ideal, nightstand, brn or dk marbleized maroon, M7 ....$6.00

Ideal, nightstand, ivory w/bl, M7 ....$8.00

Ideal, piano w/bench, caramel swirl or med marbleized brn w/decal & 'sheet music,' M7, ea $35.00

Ideal, radiator, M7..$45.00

Ideal, radio, floor; brn or dk marbleized maroon, M7, ea ..$10.00

Ideal, refrigerator, Deluxe; opening door, cb backing, wht w/blk, M7 ....$30.00

Ideal, refrigerator, ivory w/blk, M7 ....$15.00

Ideal, shopping cart, w/baskets, bl w/wht basket, red w/wht basket or wht w/red basket, M7, ea.............................$40.00

Ideal, sink, bathroom; bl w/yel, M7 ....$10.00

Ideal, sink, bathroom; ivory w/blk, M7 ....$8.00

Ideal, sofa, any color, M7, ea..$22.00

Ideal, stove, deluxe; wht w/blk, M7 ....$25.00

Ideal, stove, ivory w/blk, M7...$15.00

Ideal, table, coffee; brn or dk marbleized maroon, M7, ea..$10.00

Ideal, table, dining room; dk marbleized maroon, M7 ......$20.00

Ideal, table, kitchen; ivory, M7...$6.00

Ideal, table, kitchen; wht, M7...$20.00

Ideal, tub, corner; bl w/yel, M7.......................................$18.00

Ideal, tub, ivory w/blk, M7..$10.00

Ideal, vanity, ivory w/bl, M7..$18.00

Ideal, vanity stool, ivory w/bl seat, M7 ....$6.00

Ideal Petite Princess, accessories, buffet (Royal #4419-B), hearthplace (Regency #4422-2), table (Palace #4431-1), ea...$4.00

Ideal Petite Princess, bench, vanity; #4502-1, M7............$25.00

Ideal Petite Princess, books & bookends, #4428-9, M7, ea.$5.00

Ideal Petite Princess, bottle, wine; #4424-8, M7 ....$5.00

Ideal Petite Princess, boudoir lounge pillow, #4408-1, pk, M7..$5.00

Ideal Petite Princess, Buddha, #4437-0, metal, M7...........$15.00

Ideal Petite Princess, buffet, Royal #4419-8, complete, in orig box, M7 ....$25.00

Ideal Petite Princess, buffet, Royal #4419-8, no accessories, M7 .$10.00

Ideal Petite Princess, cabinet, Treasure Trove #4418-0, M7 .$10.00

Ideal Petite Princess, cabinet, Treasure Trove #4479-2, in orig 1965 box w/cellophane front, M7 ....$12.00

Ideal Petite Princess, candelabra, Fantasia #4438-8, in orig box, M7...$22.00

Ideal Petite Princess, candelabra, Fantasia #4438-8, M7 ..$15.00

Ideal Petite Princess, candelabra, Royal #4439-6, in orig box, M7..$17.00

Ideal Petite Princess, candelabra, Royal #4439-6, M7 ......$15.00

Ideal Petite Princess, chair, drum; Salon #4411-5, gold or gr, in orig box, M7...$17.00

Ideal Petite Princess, chair, guest dining; #4414-9, in orig box, M7...$17.00

Ideal Petite Princess, chair, guest dining; #4414-9, M7.......$8.00

Ideal Petite Princess, chair, host dining, #4413-1 or #4474-3, in orig boxes, M7, ea..$17.00

Ideal Petite Princess, chair, host dining; #4415-6, M7........$8.00

Ideal Petite Princess, chair, kitchen; #4504-7, w/foam cushion, M7...$25.00

Ideal Petite Princess, chair, occasional; #4412-3, w/ottoman, bl, in orig box, M7 ....$22.00

Ideal Petite Princess, chair, wing; Salon #4410-7, gold or red, in orig box, M7, ea..$15.00

Ideal Petite Princess, chest, Palace #4420-6, w/picture, in orig box, M7..$17.00

Ideal Petite Princess, chest, Treasure Trove #4418-0, in orig box, M7..$12.00

Ideal Petite Princess, clock, grandfather; #4423-0, M7.....$15.00

Ideal Petite Princess, grandfather clock, #4423-0, no screen otherwise MIB, $35.00.

Ideal Petite Princess, hamper, #4499-0, M7 ....$25.00

Ideal Petite Princess, hearthplace, Regency #4422-2, w/accessories, no mirror, M7..$18.00

Ideal Petite Princess, piano, Royal Grand #4425-5, w/bench only, M7...$30.00

Ideal Petite Princess, planter, Salon #4440-4, in orig box, M7..$18.00

Ideal Petite Princess, table set, Palace #4431-3, complete, M7 .$25.00

Ideal Petite Princess, table, dining room; #4421-4, in orig box, M7...$22.00

Ideal Petite Princess, table, dining room; #4421-4, M7 ....$15.00

Ideal Petite Princess, table, dressing; #4417-2, w/chair, bl, M7 .$15.00

Ideal Petite Princess, table, kitchen; #4504-7, w/flowerpot, M7 ..$50.00

Ideal Petite Princess, table, occasional; #4437-0, M7 ....$5.00

Ideal Petite Princess, table, Salon; #4433-9, M7 ....$5.00

Ideal Petite Princess, table set, Heirloom #4428-9, occasional #4437-0 or salon coffee #4433-9, w/boxes, M7, ea $27.00

Ideal Petite Princess, tea cart, rolling, #4424-8, no accessories, M7..$10.00

Ideal Petite Princess, telephone set, Fantasy #4432-1, complete, in orig box, M7..$25.00

Ideal Petite Princess, wastebasket, #4501-3, M7 ....$20.00

Ideal Petite Princess, water closet (toilet), #4501-3, complete, M7...$75.00

Ideal Young Decorator, baby bath/basinette, bl w/pk lid, M7 .$55.00

Ideal Young Decorator, carpet sweeper, no rollers, red w/bl hdl, M7...$10.00

Ideal Young Decorator, carpet sweeper, 2 rollers, red w/bl or yel hdl, M7, ea..$30.00

Ideal Young Decorator, chair, dining room; dk marbleized maroon w/yel seat, M7...$12.00

Ideal Young Decorator, chair, kitchen; wht, M7 ....$10.00

Ideal Young Decorator, china closet, dk marbleized maroon, M7...$25.00

Ideal Young Decorator, crib (bl) or playpen (pk), M7, ea.$45.00

Ideal Young Decorator, diaper pail, yel w/bl, M7 ....$25.00

Ideal Young Decorator, highchair, bl or pk, M7, ea...........$45.00

Ideal Young Decorator, night stand, dk marbleized maroon, M7...$15.00

Ideal Young Decorator, sink, bathroom; yel w/bl, M7 ....$45.00

Ideal Young Decorator, sofa, 3 sections w/2 ends & curved center pc, gr, M7..$45.00

Ideal Young Decorator, sofa, 4 sections, rose, M7 ....$60.00

Ideal Young Decorator, stove, wht, M7 ....$55.00

Ideal Young Decorator, table, coffee; dk marbleized maroon, M7...$18.00

Ideal Young Decorator, table, dining; dk marbleized maroon, M7...$35.00

Ideal Young Decorator, television, complete, M7 ....$100.00

Ideal Young Decorator, tub, corner; bl w/yel, M7.............$35.00

Imagination, any pc except lawn set, M7, ea......................$3.00

Imagination, lawn set, 3-pc set w/barbecue, lawn sofa & table w/umbrella, rust, M7 ....$12.00

Irwin, broom, gr or orange hdl, M7, ea............................$10.00

Irwin, dustpan, any color, M7 ....$4.00

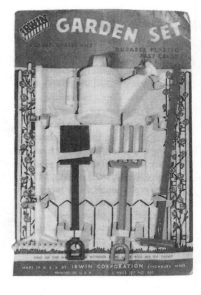

Irwin, Garden Set, MOC, $75.00. (Photo courtesy Marcie Tubbs)

Irwin, water can, orange, M7..$15.00

Irwin Interior Decorator, refrigerator, under counter; yel, M7 .$3.00

Irwin Interior Decorator, refrigerator, yel, M7.....................$5.00
Irwin Interior Decorator, shower curtain, lt gr, M7 ....$4.00
Irwin Interior Decorator, sink or stove, M7, ea $5.00
Irwin Interior Decorator, toilet, towels (2) or tub, lt gr, M7, ea .$5.00
Jaydon, buffet, reddish brn, M7...$4.00
Jaydon, chair, bedroom; bl or pk, M7, ea $6.00
Jaydon, chest, low w/2 opening drawers, reddish brn, M7...$5.00
Jaydon, cupboard, corner; reddish brn swirl, M7 ....$5.00
Jaydon, lamp, table; any color, M7, ea................................$15.00
Jaydon, piano, reddish brn swirl, M7 ....$12.00
Jaydon, piano bench, reddish brn swirl, M7 ....$3.00
Jaydon, sink, bathroom; ivory, M7......................................$10.00
Jaydon, sofa, red w/brn base, M7 ....$18.00
Jaydon, table, dining; reddish brn swirl, M7 ....$5.00
Jaydon, table, end; pk, M7 ....$5.00
Jaydon, toilet, ivory w/red lid, M7 ....$10.00
JP Co, chair, brn, M7 ....$2.00
JP Co, hutch, brn, M7...$4.00
Marx, hard plastic, ½" scale, any pc except barbecue, curved sofa, jukebox, or milk bar, any color, M7, ea from $3 to........$5.00
Marx, hard plastic, ½" scale, barbecue, patio; dk brn, M7 ..$8.00
Marx, hard plastic, ½" scale, curved sofa or milk bar, bright yel or red, M7, ea $15.00
Marx, hard plastic, ½" scale, jukebox, bright yel or red, M7, ea .$20.00
Marx, hard plastic, ¾" scale, any pc except iron, swimming pool or upright sweeper, M7, ea, from $3 to.......$6.00
Marx, hard plastic, ¾" scale, iron, wht, M7 ....$8.00
Marx, hard plastic, ¾" scale, swimming pool (red), upright sweeper (wht), M7, ea.......$10.00
Marx, soft plastic, ¾" scale, any pc except floor lamp, M7, ea from $3 to..................$4.00
Marx, soft plastic, ¾" scale, floor lamp, bright yel or lt yel, M7, ea $6.00
Marx Little Hostess, chair, occasional; yel, M7..................$12.00
Marx Little Hostess, chest, block front, rust, M7 ....$12.00
Marx Little Hostess, dresser, dbl; ivory, M7.....................$8.00
Marx Little Hostess, fireplace, ivory, M7............................$20.00
Marx Little Hostess, piano & bench, rust brn, M7 ....$25.00
Marx Little Hostess, refrigerator, avocado, M7 ....$25.00

Marx Little Hostess, table, coffee; rnd, brn, M7 ....$8.00
Marx Little Hostess, table, gate-leg; rust, M7...................$15.00
Marx Little Hostess, table, tilt-top; blk, M7......................$12.00
Mattel Littles, armoire, M7..$8.00
Mattel Littles, doll, Littles Family (Mr & Mrs Little & baby), in orig box, M7..................$22.00
Mattel Littles, sofa, M7..$8.00
Mattel Littles, sofa & Hedy, in orig box, M7....................$15.00
Mattel Littles, table, drop-leaf; w/cups & 4 plates, in orig box, M7..................$15.00
MPC, any pc, M7, ea...$3.00
Nancy Forbes, bathroom set, 5-pc w/medicine cabinet, scale, sink, tub & vanity w/mirror, ivory, M7.....................$25.00
Nancy Forbes, bathroom sink (wht), bed (walnut) or floor cabinet (walnut), M7, ea..................$4.00
Nancy Forbes, kitchen chair (wht) or nightstand (walnut), M7, ea $2.00
Plasco, bathroom set, 6-pc w/bench, hamper, sink, toilet, tub & vanity, pk, in orig box w/floor plan, M7.....................$55.00
Plasco, bed, brn headboard & footboard w/wht spread, M7 ..$10.00
Plasco, bed, brn headboard w/yel spread, M7.....................$3.00
Plasco, buffet, any color, M7, ea $4.00
Plasco, chair, dining (w/ or w/o arms); brn or marbleized brn, M7, ea..................$3.00
Plasco, chair, dining room; tan w/striped paper seat cover, M7.$4.00
Plasco, chair, kitchen; any color, M7, ea $2.00
Plasco, chair, living room; any color w/brn base, M7, ea ..$15.00
Plasco, chair, living room; no-base style, dk brn or yel, M7, ea.$3.00
Plasco, chairs, patio; any color, M7, ea..............................$3.00
Plasco, clock, grandfather; dk brn or lt brn swirl w/cb face, M7, ea $15.00
Plasco, dining room set, 8-pc w/buffet, table, 4 chairs & 2 side tables, dk marbleized brn, M7..................$25.00
Plasco, doll, baby; M7...$20.00
Plasco, hamper, pk w/gray marbleized lid, M7 ....$6.00
Plasco, highboy, dk marbleized maroon or tan, M7, ea $8.00
Plasco, kitchen set, 4-pc w/refrigerator, sink, stove & table, on-base style, pk, M7..................$15.00
Plasco, nightstand, brn, marbleized med brn or tan, M7, ea.$3.00
Plasco, refrigerator, no-base style, all pk or pk w/blk trim, M7, ea $3.00
Plasco, refrigerator, wht w/bl base, M7 ....$5.00
Plasco, sink, kitchen; no-base style, any color except pk w/blk trim, M7, ea..................$3.00
Plasco, sink, kitchen; no-base style, pk w/blk trim, M7 ......$4.00
Plasco, sofa, no-base style, any color, M7 ....$3.00
Plasco, sofa, w/base, brn, M7 ....$15.00
Plasco, stove, no-base style, lt gr or pk, M7, ea $3.00
Plasco, stove, wht w/bl base, M7 ....$5.00
Plasco, table, coffee; brn, med marbleized brn or tan, M7, ea.$3.00
Plasco, table, coffee; tan w/'leather top,' M7 ....$5.00
Plasco, table, dining room side; tan w/yel, M7 ....$4.00
Plasco, table, kitchen; any color, M7, ea $5.00
Plasco, table, patio; dk gr w/lt gr legs, M7 ....$5.00
Plasco, table, patio; sm, bl w/ivory legs, M7 ....$4.00
Plasco, toilet, pk w/gray marbleized lid & seat or turq w/wht, M7, ea..................$8.00
Plasco, tub, any color, M7, ea $4.00

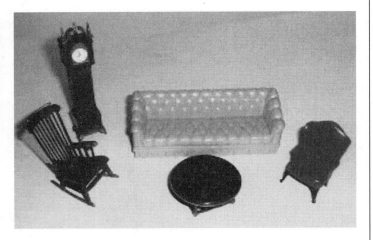

Marx Little Hostess, rocking chair, $12.00; grandfather clock, $18.00; sofa, $10.00; round coffee table, $8.00; wingbacked chair, $12.00. (Photo courtesy Judith Mosholder)

Plasco, vanity, sq-mirror or no-mirror style, any color, M7, ea..$5.00

Plasco, vanity bench, any color, M7.............................$3.00

Pyro, see Allied/Pyro

Reliable, chair, dining room; rust, M7 ....$8.00

Reliable, chair, kitchen; ivory w/bl seat, M7 ....$8.00

Reliable, chair, living room; aqua (1940s), dk bl (1940s) or red (1940s-50s), M7, ea..$10.00

Reliable, chair, living room; red or bl w/rust base, M7, ea..$20.00

Reliable, doll, baby sucking thumb; pk hard plastic, jtd or non-jtd, 2¾", ea...$20.00

Reliable, piano & bench, rust, M7 ....$45.00

Reliable, radio, floor; rust, M7 ....$15.00

Reliable, stove, ivory w/bl trim, M7 ....$20.00

Reliable, table, dining room; rust, M7 ....$25.00

Reliable, table, kitchen; ivory, M7 ....$12.00

Reliable, tub, ivory w/bl trim, M7 ....$25.00

Renwal, baby bath, pk or bl w/decals, M7, ea $15.00

Renwal, broom, metallic bl hdl, M7 ....$75.00

Renwal, buffet, non-opening drawer, brn, M7.................$6.00

Renwal, carpet sweeper, #116, $85.00; mop, #117, $45.00; vacuum cleaner, #37, $25.00.

Renwal, carriage, w/doll insert, all pk, M7 ....$30.00

Renwal, carriage, w/doll insert, bl w/pk wheels, orig box, M7 .$55.00

Renwal, carriage, w/doll insert, bl w/stenciling, M7 ....$35.00

Renwal, chair, barrel; bl w/red base, ivory w/brn base or med bl w/metallic red base, M7, ea from $8 to........................$9.00

Renwal, chair, club; bl or lt bl w/brn base or pk w/red or metallic red base, M7, ea...$8.00

Renwal, chair, club; dk bl base, M7..............................$15.00

Renwal, chair, pk w/bl, M7 ....$18.00

Renwal, chair, teacher's; bl or brn, M7, ea $15.00

Renwal, clock, kitchen; ivory, M7 ....$20.00

Renwal, clock, mantel; ivory or red, M7, ea...................$10.00

Renwal, desk, student; any color, M7, ea $12.00

Renwal, doll, baby; plastic, chubby w/pnt diaper, M7.......$45.00

Renwal, doll, baby; plastic, plain, w/pnt playsuit or pnt diaper, M7, ea...$10.00

Renwal, doll, father; plastic rivets, all tan, M7 ....$25.00

Renwal, doll, father; plastic rivets, brn suit, M7 ....$30.00

Renwal, doll, mother; metal rivets, rose dress, M7...........$30.00

Renwal, doll, sister; plastic rivets, all tan, M7 ....$25.00

Denwal, dresser, simplified style w/mirror, brn w/stenciling, M7..$12.00

Renwal, garbage can, red & yel, M7.............................$15.00

Renwal, hamper, opening lid, lt gr, M7 ....$10.00

Renwal, hamper, opening lid, pk, M7............................$5.00

Renwal, highboy, brn, M7...$6.00

Renwal, highboy, opening drawers, brn, M7 ....$8.00

Renwal, highboy, pk, M7..$12.00

Renwal, ironing board, bl or pk, M7, ea $7.00

Renwal, ironing board w/iron, bl & pk, M7 ....$22.00

Renwal, kiddie car, bl w/red & yel or yel w/bl & red, M7, ea..$55.00

Renwal, lamp, floor; yel w/ivory shade, M7....................$20.00

Renwal, lamp, table; caramel or metallic red w/ivory shade, M7, ea...$12.00

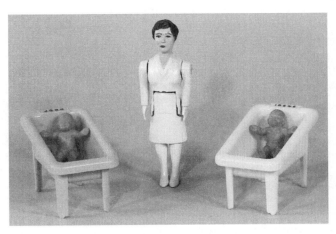

Renwal, nurse, $55.00; nursery cribs, $10.00 each; rubber babies, $4.00 each. (Photo courtesy Judith Mosholder)

Renwal, piano, marbleized brn, M7 ....$35.00

Renwal, playground seesaw, red w/yel, M7 ....$35.00

Renwal, playground slide, bl w/red or yel w/bl, M7, ea $22.00

Renwal, radio, floor; brn, M7......................................$10.00

Renwal, radio, table; brn or red, M7, ea $15.00

Renwal, radio/phonograph, red, M7 ....$20.00

Renwal, rocker, yel w/red, M7.....................................$8.00

Renwal, scale, ivory or red, M7, ea..............................$10.00

Renwal, server, opening door, brn, M7 ....$8.00

Renwal, server, opening drawer, brn, stenciled, M7..........$12.00

Renwal, server, opening drawer, red, M7.......................$15.00

Renwal, server, opening drawer, reddish brn, stenciled, M7.$12.00

Renwal, sewing machine, tabletop; red w/bl base, M7......$85.00

Renwal, sink, bathroom; dk turq w/blk, M7 ....$8.00

Renwal, sink, bathroom; pk w/bl or lt bl or ivory w/blk, M7, ea..$5.00

Renwal, smoking stand, ivory & red, M7 ....$12.00

Renwal, sofa, all red, bright pk w/metallic red base, lt gr w/red base, or pk w/reddish brn base, M7, ea $18.00

Renwal, stool, ivory & red, M7 ....$10.00

Renwal, stove, non-opening door, ivory w/blk or lt turq, M7, ea..$12.00

Renwal, stove, non-opening door, wht w/blk, M7 ....$18.00

Renwal, stove, opening door, ivory w/red, M7 ....$18.00

Renwal, table, cocktail; brn or reddish brn, M7, ea $10.00

Renwal, table, dining room; brn, M7 ....$18.00

Renwal, table, dining room; orange or reddish orange, M7, ea.$15.00

Renwal, table, folding; gold, M7..................................$20.00

Renwal, table, folding; w/4 chairs, metallic gold w/red seats, M7 ....$120.00

Renwal, telephone, red & yel, M7..................................$22.00
Renwal, toilet, ivory w/blk, M7 ....$10.00
Renwal, toilet, no-hdl style, pk, M7 ....$6.00
Renwal, toilet, pk w/lt bl hdl, M7.................................$9.00
Renwal, toilet, pk w/stenciling, M7..............................$15.00
Renwal, toydee, bl, matt bl or pk, M7, ea......................$6.00
Renwal, toydee, bl w/duck stencil, M7, ea...................$15.00
Renwal, tricycle, yel w/bl & red, M7............................$25.00
Renwal, tub, med bl & turq w/blk, M7..........................$12.00
Renwal, tub, pk w/bl or ivory w/blk, M7, ea.....................$7.00

Renwal, twin beds, $8.00 each; nightstand/end table, from $2.00 to $4.00; table lamp, red or brown with ivory shade, $10.00. (Photo courtesy Judith Mosholder)

Renwal, vanity, simplified style w/mirror, brn, M7............$12.00
Renwal, vanity, simplified style w/mirror, brn w/stenciling, M7...$15.00
Renwal, vanity, w/finials & mirror, brn, M7...................$18.00
Renwal, washing machine, bl or pk w/bear decal, M7, ea.$30.00
Strombecker, bed, pk, 1940s, ¾" scale, M7 ....$8.00
Strombecker, bed, walnut, 1936, 1" scale, M7..................$18.00
Strombecker, buffet, opening drawer, walnut, 1930s, 1" scale, M7 ....$30.00
Strombecker, chair, kitchen; red, ¾" scale, M7..................$6.00
Strombecker, chest of drawers, pk, 1930s, ¾" scale, M7 ...$15.00
Strombecker, clock, grandfather; bl or dk peach w/blk, ¾" scale, M7, ea $15.00
Strombecker, clock, lt gr or walnut, ¾" scale, M7, ea.......$10.00
Strombecker, heater, dk bl, ¾" scale, M7 ....$18.00
Strombecker, lamp, floor; unfinished,¾" scale, M7 ....$10.00
Strombecker, lamp, table; gr or yel w/ivory shade, ¾" scale, M7, ea...$15.00
Strombecker, lamp, table; walnut, 1936, 1" scale, M7 ......$18.00
Strombecker, medicine cabinet, dk bl, ¾" scale, M7 ....$18.00
Strombecker, night stand, lt gr or pk, ¾" scale, M7, ea......$6.00
Strombecker, night stand, walnut, 1936, 1" scale, M7 ......$15.00
Strombecker, radio, floor; walnut, 1930s, 1" scale, M7 .....$18.00
Strombecker, refrigerator, wht w/blk, 1950s, ¾" scale, M7, ea.$18.00
Strombecker, scale, bl, dk bl or gr, ¾" scale, M7, ea $15.00
Strombecker, sink, bathroom, aqua or ivory, ¾" scale, M7, ea..$8.00
Strombecker, sink, bathroom; gr w/gold swirl, ¾" scale, M7...$20.00

Strombecker, sink, kitchen; wht w/blk, 1950s, ¾" scale, M7, ea..$18.00
Strombecker, sofa, aqua (1940s), peach (1940s-50s) or red (1940s-50s), ¾" scale, M7, ea...................$10.00
Strombecker, sofa, gr flocked, 1940s, ¾" scale, M7..........$18.00
Strombecker, sofa, gr flocked, 1950s, 1" scale, M7 ....$25.00
Strombecker, stove, ivory or lt gr, 1940s, ¾" scale, M7, ea .$15.00
Strombecker, stove, ivory w/blk trim, 1936, ¾" scale, M7.$20.00
Strombecker, table, coffee; walnut, 1950s, 1" scale, M7 ...$12.00
Strombecker, table, dining room; 1930s, 1" scale, M7 ......$20.00
Strombecker, table, trestle; red, ¾" scale, M7 ....$8.00
Strombecker, tub, any color, ¾" scale, M7, ea $10.00
Strombecker, TV, ivory w/paper screen, ¾" scale, M7......$25.00
Strombecker, vanity & bench, walnut, 1936, 1" scale, M7.$30.00
Strombecker, wastebasket, dk bl, ¾" scale, M7................$15.00
Superior, any soft plastic, sm, M7, ea from $1 to..............$2.00
Superior, bed, any color, ¾"scale, M7, ea $5.00
Superior, chair, dining room; bright bl or dk ivory, ¾" scale, M7, ea $3.00
Superior, chair, kitchen; any color, ¾" scale, M7, ea $3.00
Superior, chair, living room; rnd or sq back, any color, ¾" scale, M7, ea...$4.00
Superior, chest of drawers, low, any color, ¾" scale, M7, ea.$5.00
Superior, crib, bright bl or rust brn, ¾" scale, M7, ea..........$8.00
Superior, hutch, any color, ¾" scale, M7, ea $5.00
Superior, lawn chair (2-seat)/table, no umbrella, yel or gr ,¾" scale, M7, ea...$8.00
Superior, potty chair, bright bl or wht, ¾" scale, M7, ea.....$8.00
Superior, refrigerator, any color, ¾" scale, M7, ea $5.00
Superior, sink, bathroom; ivory or med off-gr, ¾" scale, M7, ea.$5.00
Superior, sink/stove combo, any color, ¾" scale, M7 ....$5.00
Superior, sofa, brn, pale gr or red, ¾" scale, M7, ea.............$5.00
Superior, table, coffee; pale gr or red, ¾" scale, M7, ea.......$8.00
Superior, table, dining room; bright bl or yel, ¾" scale, M7, ea .$8.00
Superior, toilet or tub, any color, ¾" scale, M7, ea.............$5.00
Superior, vanity, any color, ¾" scale, M7.........................$3.00
Superior, vanity w/mirror, red, ¾" scale, M7 ....$5.00
Thomas, see Acme/Thomas
Tomy Smaller Homes, armoire, no hangers, M7 ....$10.00
Tomy Smaller Homes, armoire, w/hangers, M7.................$15.00
Tomy Smaller Homes, bed, canopy; M7 ....$15.00
Tomy Smaller Homes, cabinet, stereo; M7........................$15.00
Tomy Smaller Homes, cabinet w/dbl bowl sink, M7.........$20.00
Tomy Smaller Homes, cabinet w/TV, high wall, M7.........$55.00
Tomy Smaller Homes, chair, kitchen; M7 ....$3.00
Tomy Smaller Homes, mirror, standing, M7 ....$15.00
Tomy Smaller Homes, planter, bathroom; no towels, M7.$10.00
Tomy Smaller Homes, range top w/hood, M7...................$18.00
Tomy Smaller Homes, refrigerator, w/drawers, M7 ....$12.00
Tomy Smaller Homes, scale, bathroom; M7......................$15.00
Tomy Smaller Homes, sink, kitchen; dbl bowls, 1 rack, M7..$3.00
Tomy Smaller Homes, sofa, den; 2-pc, M7 ....$12.00
Tomy Smaller Homes, table, coffee; M7............................$10.00
Tomy Smaller Homes, table, end or kitchen; M7, ea $8.00
Tomy Smaller Homes, toilet, M7....................................$10.00
Tomy Smaller Homes, tub, M7 ....$15.00
Tomy Smaller Homes, TV, M7 ....$50.00
Tomy Smaller Homes, vanity, M7 ....$15.00
Tomy Smaller Homes, vanity stool, M7 ....$6.00

Tomy-Smaller Homes, sink, kitchen; dbl bowls, w/dishwasher, no racks, M7...$8.00
Tootsietoy, bed, w/headboard, footboard & slats, bl or pk, M7..$20.00
Tootsietoy, buffet, w/opening drawer, cocoa brn, M7........$22.00
Tootsietoy, cabinet, medicine; ivory, M7.........................$25.00
Tootsietoy, chair, bedroom; bl or pk, M7 ....$7.00
Tootsietoy, chair, kitchen; ivory, M7 ....$7.00
Tootsietoy, chair, simple back, no arms, M7 ....$7.00
Tootsietoy, chair, simple back w/arms, dk brn, M7............$8.00

Tootsietoy: dining room furniture set, MIB, A, $175.00.

(Photo courtesy Noel Barrett Auctions)

Tootsietoy, chair, tufted look, dk red, M7.........................$20.00
Tootsietoy, chair, XX back, w/ or w/o arms, M7, ea.............$7.00
Tootsietoy, cupboard, non-opening doors, ivory, M7 ....$20.00
Tootsietoy, icebox or stove, non-opening door, ivory, M7, ea.$20.00
Tootsietoy, lamp, table; bl, M7 ....$45.00
Tootsietoy, nightstand, pk, M7 ....$10.00
Tootsietoy, piano bench, yel w/tan seat, M7 ....$15.00
Tootsietoy, rocker, bedroom; bl, M7 ....$12.00
Tootsietoy, rocker, wicker style w/cushion, gold or ivory, M7, ea...$18.00
Tootsietoy, server, non-opening door, dk brn, M7............$22.00
Tootsietoy, sofa, wicker style w/cushion, ivory, M7 ....$20.00
Tootsietoy, table, long, gr crackle, M7..............................$22.00
Tootsietoy, table, rectangular, dk brn, M7 ....$20.00
Tootsietoy, tea cart, dk brn, M7 ....$22.00
Tootsietoy, vanity, bk, M7...$18.00

Tynie Toy, dining room set with drop-leaf table and four chairs, G to EX, $715.00.

Dollhouses

Dollhouses were first made commercially in America in the late 1700s. A century later, Bliss and Schoenhut were making wonderful dollhouses that even yet occasionally turn up on the market, and many were being imported from Germany. During the 1940s and 1950s, American toy makers made a variety of cottages; today they're all collectible.

American, 3-story mansion w/center copula, 9 rooms, arched windows, 2nd & 3rd story bays, 42x29x16", G, A.$2,750.00
Bliss, Garden House, 1-story, paper on wood, simulated brick walls, brass-trimmed, 16x15", VG.........................$1,100.00
Bliss, Wild Rose Cottage, 1-story, paper on wood, full-length arched porch, 11x13x9", EX, A $1,320.00

Bliss, two-story, two rooms, paper lithograph on wood, 17x13x7", EX, A, $1,980.00.

(Photo courtesy Bertoia Auctions)

Bliss, 2-story, 2 rooms, paper on wood, brass trim, full-length porch, upper veranda, w/accessories, 17x12", G, A .$525.00
Bliss, 2-story, 2 rooms, paper on wood, brass trim, full-length porch, upper veranda, 2 dormers, 2 chimneys, 17", G, A $470.00
Bliss, 2-story, 2 rooms, paper on wood, brass trim, full-length porch, upper veranda, 2 dormers, 18x13", EX, A .$2,200.00
Bliss, 2-story, 2 rooms, paper on wood, full-length porch w/oval facade around upper windows, 16x10", VG, A.....$1,750.00
Bliss, 2-story, 2 rooms, paper on wood, full-length porch w/3 arches, upper veranda, front dormer, 20x18", EX, A .$770.00
Bliss, 2-story, 2 rooms, paper on wood, wrap-around front porch, upper veranda, 3 dormers, 24x19", G, A $1,870.00
Christian Hacker, 2-story mansion, 4 rooms w/foyer, pnt wood, lift-off lithoed mansard roof w/2 dormers, 27x22", EX, A $2,420.00
Converse, 2-story, 2 rooms, litho print on wood, full-length porch, red, wht & bl, w/accessories, 18x11x7", EX, A $915.00
Dutch, 2-story mansion, 6 rooms (1 outdoor), elaborate gray & wht facade w/columned porch, filigree trim, 1860, VG+, A $6,050.00

English, 2-story, 4 rooms w/foyer & upper hall, stucco facade w/wood trim, 2 dormers, 2 chimneys, ca 1840, 37x30x26", G, A...$1,870.00

Gottschalk, two-story, two rooms, paper lithograph on wood, 28x17", A, $2,090.00. (Photo courtesy Bertoia Auctions)

Gottschalk, 2-story, 2 rooms, paper on wood, brick facade, arched entry w/lattice trim, w/accessories, 15x9x6", EX, A...$770.00

Gottschalk, 2-story, 2 rooms, paper on wood, steps lead to door w/sm roof, 2nd story balcony, 19x12x8", VG, A......$770.00

Irish, two-story Georgian, painted wood with glass windows, two drawers in base, 1760 – 1780, 26x11x18", VG, A, $8,800.00.

(Photo courtesy Bertoia Auctions)

Marx, ABC Nursery, ½" scale, EX, M7 ....$60.00

Marx, 2-story, plastic bow window, ½" scale soft plastic furniture in orig bags, ca 1968, EX, M7 ....$60.00

McLoughlin Bros, Dolly's Playhouse, 2-story, 2 rooms, paper on wood, arched interior view, 1875-85, 18x14x10", VG, A..........$385.00

Mosher, log cabin, 2-story, paper litho on wood, deer head on side gable, 17x12x10", VG, A $500.00

Schoenhut, bungalow w/porch, 1 room, 'brick & stone,' shingled roof opens to attic, furnished, 11½x14", VG, A......$275.00

Schoenhut, bungalow w/porch, 1 room, pnt exterior w/window box, shingled roof opens to attic, furnished, 9x12", NMIB, A $600.00

Schoenhut, suburban, 1-story, paper on wood, full-length porch, dormer, shuttered windows w/flower boxes, 14", G, A.$600.00

Schoenhut, two-story, six rooms, painted wood, electric lights, completely furnished including dolls, EX, A, $1,320.00. (Photo courtesy Bertoia Auctions)

Schoenhut, 2-story Tudor, 4 rooms, pnt brick & wood siding w/emb red shingle roof, electric, accessories, 19x18", EX, A...$935.00

Silber Fleming, 3-story 19th-C English box type, 6 rooms, pnt brick facade, window awnings, 2 chimneys, 40x22x16", G...$1,760.00

T Cohn, 2-story, ¾" scale, EX, M7.....................................$75.00

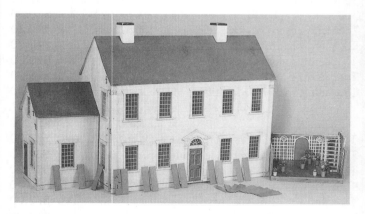

Tynie Toy, New England townhouse and garden, two-story, eight rooms and attic, electric, glazed windows, furnished including dolls, 29x49x17", EX, A, $17,250.00. (Photo courtesy Bertoia Auctions)

Unknown Maker, 'Gutter House,' 2-story, 2 rooms, paper on wood, 1-story turret, dormers, red & gr, 17x13x10", G, A......$825.00

Unknown Maker, bungalow, 1-room, paper on wood, full-length porch, dormer, 1914 Butler Bros catalog, 12x11x8", EX..$550.00

Unknown Maker, 1-story colonial, paper on wood, Dutch-style roof w/columned front entrance, 18x16x10", VG, A .$880.00

Unknown Maker, 2-story, paper on wood, porch across front, chimney, yel & gr, att to Bliss, 18x11x9", G, A.......$440.00

Unknown Maker, 2-story, 6 rooms, wood, hinged gambrel roof w/pasteboard scalloped shingles, w/accessories, 33x28x17", EX $920.00
Unknown Maker, 2-story log cabin, 4 rooms, paper on wood, 1 side of roof extends down to 1st floor, 18x18x10", VG $650.00
Unknown Maker, 4-room fold-down, paper litho on cb, c Jan 30, 1894, 12" sq (unfolded), EX, A $275.00
Whitney Reed, 2-story, 2 rooms, paper on wood, center steeple, 2 chimneys, some accessories, 19", VG, A $1,100.00

SHOPS AND SINGLE ROOMS

Bedroom, Louvre/France, box w/fold-down front displays papered room w/canopy bed & elaborate furniture, 17x9", EX, A $525.00

Butcher Shop, three-sided w/end columns, lithographed meat display on back wall, four pigs on hooks on side walls, with accessories and butcher, EX, A, $5,225.00. (Photo courtesy Bertoia Auctions)

Corner Grocer, Wolverine, litho tin, EX, L4 ....$475.00
Country Store, France, wood & glass open cupboard back w/ornate pediment on base, w/accessories, 17x16", VG, A $550.00
Ecole (School Room), French, paper-litho-on-wood box w/fold-down front, w/furniture & figures, 16x22" (opened), EX, A...$1,760.00

Kitchen, Germany, three-sided with floor, wood with papered walls, with furniture, accessories, and 8½" celluloid doll, 22x29x17", EX, A, $1,380.00. (Photo courtesy Skinner, Inc.)

General Grocery, Durable Toys & Novelty, litho tin w/swing-open doors & cloth awning, 15 cb brand name boxes, 13", VG, A $500.00
German Shop, Germany, wood w/fancy pediment on back wall contains 10 drawers, side shelf w/glass front, w/accessories, G $525.00
Grocery Store, 3-sided shelves w/2 drawers & cloth awning, red-pnt wood w/paper background, product boxes, 16x12", EX, A $220.00
Kitchen, American, pnt tin, 3-sided, integral stove w/hood on back wall, many accessories, 14" L, G, A $200.00
Kitchen, Hoge Play House, 3-sided cb walls w/paper floor, w/4-pc kitchen appliances, EXIB, A $1,540.00

Parlor Room, Gottschalk, circa 1890, wood with blue and white painted walls, gold trim, with accessories and five bisque and china dolls, 15x24x14", VG, A, $3,025.00. (Photo courtesy Bertoia Auctions)

Parlor Room, Victorian, 3-sided box w/dbl doors on back wall, flowered paper, w/accessories & figures, G+, A $330.00
Playskool Pullman, ca 1930, pressed steel, opens from rear to reveal interior of Pullman car, w/accessories, 12x10", EX.......$385.00
Roosevelt Stock Farm, Converse, 1907, wood w/stamped red brick facade, w/compo farm animals, 13x10", EX, A $990.00
Stable, pnt tin w/marquee atop open front, 3 stalls ea w/animal on wheeled base, 2 feeders, 8x7", G, A $110.00
Stable w/Heavy Team, Bliss, paper litho on wood & cb, open front, center copula, w/accessories, 12x15", VG, A...........$1,760.00
Super-Service Market, Wolverine, 1950s, litho tin, 3-sided hinged, service counter, accessories, 14x16", EX $100.00

Dolls and Accessories

Obviously the field of dolls cannot be covered in a price guide such as this, but we wanted to touch on some of the later dolls from the 1950s and 1960s, since so much of the collector interest today is centered on those decades. For in-depth information on dolls of all types, we recommend these lovely doll books, all of which are available from Collector Books: *Doll Values, Antique to Modern*, and *Modern Collectible Dolls*, by Patsy Moyer;

Madame Alexander Collector's Dolls Price Guide and *Madame Alexander Store Exclusives* by Linda Crowsey; *The World of Raggedy Ann Collectibles* by Kim Avery; *Scouting Dolls through the Years* by Sydney Ann Sutton with Patsy Moyer; *Encyclopedia of Bisque Nancy Ann Storybook Dolls* by Elaine M. Pardee and Jackie Robertson; *Small Dolls of the 40s & 50s* by Carol J. Stover; *Collector's Guide to Horsman Dolls* by Don Jenson; and *Dolls of the 1960s and 1970s* by Cindy Sabulis. Other books are referenced in specific subcategories.

See also Action Figures; Barbie Doll and Friends; Character, TV, and Movie Collectibles; GI Joe; and other specific categories.

BABY DOLLS AND OTHER FAVORITES

Remnants of baby dolls have been found in the artifacts of most primitive digs. Some are just sticks or stuffed leather or animal skins.

Dolls teach our young nurturing and caring. Mothering instincts stay with us — and aren't we lucky as doll collectors that we can keep 'mothering' even after the young have 'flown the nest.'

Dolls come in all sizes and mediums: vinyl, plastic, rubber, porcelain, cloth, etc. Almost everyone remembers some doll they had as a child. The return to childhood is such a great trip. Keep looking, and you will find yours.

Advisor: Marcia Fanta (M15)

Baby Cheerful Tearful, Mattel, 1966, 6½", MIB $55.00
Baby First Step, Mattel, 1964, M $50.00
Baby Giggles, Ideal, 1967, 15", MIB $100.00
Baby Kissy, Ideal, 1962, 23", NRFB $185.00
Baby Tender Love, Mattel, 1971, all orig, 16", VG $25.00
Baby Tippee Toes, Mattel, 1967, 16", MIB $100.00
Betsy Wetsy, Ideal, 1954, curly caracul wig, nose runs, complete
   w/accessories, 13½", MIB $100.00
Betsy Wetsy, Ideal, 1954-56, molded or rooted curly hair, 16",
   MIB, ea minimum value $125.00
Cabbage Patch Preemie, Coleco, complete, VG+ $25.00

Gabbigale, Kenner, 1972, 18", MIB, $85.00. (Photo courtesy Cindy Sabulis)

Chatterbox, Madame Alexander, 1961, MIB $250.00
Dancerella, Mattel, 1976, 15", MIB $75.00
Dy-Dee Baby, Effanbee, 1935, w/wardrobe, 11", MIB $425.00
Johnny Playpal, Ideal, 1959, 24", NM $325.00
Lil' Miss Fashion, Deluxe Reading, 1960, 20", MIB $125.00
Magic Baby Tender Love, Mattel, 1978, 14", MIB $30.00

Marjorie, Belle Doll and Toy Company, vinyl, MIB, $125.00. (Photo courtesy Cindy Sabulis)

Miss Ideal the Photographer's Model, includes Play Wave Kit, complete, NMIB, from $250.00 to $300.00. (Photo courtesy McMasters Doll Auctions)

Nancy Nonsense, Kenner, 1968, talker, 17", MIB $115.00
Patti Prays, Ideal, 1957, NM $55.00
Patty Playpal (Nurse), Ideal, 1960s, 36", M $325.00
Pretty Curls, Ideal, 1981-82, all orig, EX $25.00
Rub-A-Dub Dolly in Tugboat Shower, Ideal, 1974-78, 17", MIB .$125.00
Talking Baby Alive, Kenner, 1992, MIB $100.00
Tearful Tender Love, Mattel, 1971, 16", VG+ $50.00
Thumbelina, Ideal, 18", NMIB, from $150 to $200.00
Thumbelina (Tiny), Ideal, 1962-68, 14", MIB $185.00
Tickles, Deluxe Reading, 1963, talker, MIB $100.00
Tiny Baby Tender Love, Mattel, all orig, 11½", VG $35.00
Tiny Tears, American Character, 1950s, all orig, 12", VG .. $125.00

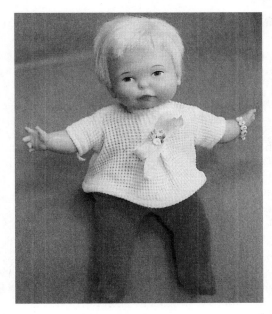

Thumbelina (Newborn), Ideal, 1967, pull string and she wiggles and squirms, 9½", NM, $50.00. (Photo courtesy Cindy Sabulis)

Tiny Tubber, Effanbee, 1976, all orig, 11", MIB $75.00
Upsy Dazy, Ideal, 1973, 15", EX...$40.00
Winnie Walker, Advance, 1957, talker, 24", MIB..........$200.00

BETSY MCCALL

The tiny 8" Betsy McCall doll was manufactured by the American Character Doll Co. from 1957 through 1963. She was made from high-quality hard plastic with a bisque-like finish and hand-painted features. Betsy came in four hair colors — tosca, red, blond, and brunette. She had blue sleep eyes, molded lashes, a winsome smile, and a fully jointed body with bendable knees. On her back there is an identification circle which reads McCall Corp. The basic doll wore a sheer chemise, white taffeta panties, nylon socks, and Maryjane-style shoes and could be purchased for $2.25.

There were two different materials used for tiny Betsy's hair. The first was a soft mohair sewn into fine mesh. Later the rubber skullcap was rooted with saran which was more suitable for washing and combing.

Betsy McCall had an extensive wardrobe with nearly one hundred outfits, each of which could be purchased separately. They were made from wonderful fabrics such as velvet, taffeta, felt, and even real mink. Each ensemble came with the appropriate footwear and was priced under $3.00. Since none of Betsy's clothing was tagged, it is often difficult to identify other than by its square snap closures (although these were used by other companies as well).

Betsy McCall is a highly collectible doll today but is still fairly easy to find at doll shows. Prices remain reasonable for this beautiful clothes horse and her many accessories.

Advisor: Marci Van Ausdall (V2)

Doll, American Character, 8", hard plastic, rooted hair, 1957, EX (in basic chemise) $350.00

Doll, American Character, 14", vinyl w/swivel waist or 1-pc torso, rooted hair, 1958, EX, ea $500.00
Doll, American Character, 19" to 20", vinyl, rooted hair, 1-pc torso, 1959, EX, ea...$500.00
Doll, American Character, 22", vinyl w/jtd limbs & waist, 5 different colors of rooted hair, 1961, EX, ea.................$225.00
Doll, American Character, 29", vinyl w/jtd limbs & waist, 5 different colors of rooted hair, 1961, EX, ea.................$300.00
Doll, American Character, 36", Linda McCall (Betsy's cousin), vinyl w/Betsy face, rooted hair, 1959, EX...............$350.00
Doll, American Character, 36", vinyl w/Patti Playpal-style body, rooted hair, 1959, EX...$325.00
Doll, American Character, 39", Sandy McCall (Betsy's brother), vinyl w/molded hair, red blazer & navy shorts, 1959, EX..........$350.00
Doll, Horsman, 12½", rigid plastic body w/vinyl head, w/extra hairpiece & accessories, 1974, EX $50.00
Doll, Horsman, 29", rigid plastic teen body w/vinyl head, rooted hair w/side part, orig clothing mk BMc, 1974, MIB..$275.00
Doll, Ideal, 14", hard plastic, Toni body, rooted hair, orig outfit, EX $175.00

Doll, McCall, 8", 1957, in riding habit with brown felt pants, green vest, and red and white checked shirt, hard plastic, marked McCall, EX, $200.00. (Photo courtesy Patsy Moyer)

Doll, McCall, 14", 1958, in pink party dress with pink crocheted tam and purse, vinyl, all original, marked McCall, M, $450.00. (Photo courtesy Pat Smith)

Doll, Uneeda, 11½", rigid vinyl body w/rooted hair, wore hip outfits, 1964, EX, minimum value............................$100.00

BLYTHE BY KENNER

Blythe by Kenner is an 11" doll with a slender body and an extra large head. You can change her eye color by pulling a string in the back of her head. She came with different hair colors and had fashions, cases, and wigs that could be purchased separately. She was produced in the early 1970s which accounts for her 'groovy' wardrobe.

Advisor: Dawn Diaz (P2)

Doll, eyes can change to four different colors by pulling string, 11", M, $200.00. (Photo courtesy Cindy Sabulis)

Case, #33241, image of blond-haired doll wearing Pow-Wow Poncho, orange background, vinyl, EX, P2 ....$50.00
Doll, blond hair, MIB $500.00
Doll, brunette hair, MIB $500.00
Doll, brunette hair, wearing Medieval Mood, EX, P2 .....$200.00
Doll, lt red hair, wearing Golden Goddess, EX, P2 ....$200.00
Doll, red hair, wearing Love 'N Lace, EX, P2.................$200.00
Outfit, Aztec Arrival, complete, EX, P2 ....$100.00
Outfit, Golden Goddess, NRFB, P2 ....$150.00
Outfit, Kozy Kape, complete EX, P2 ....$100.00
Outfit, Lounging Lovely, NRFB, P2 ....$150.00
Outfit, Love 'N Lace, NRFB, P2 ....$150.00
Outfit, Pleasant Peasant, missing shoes, EX, P2 ....$75.00
Outfit, Pow-Wow Poncho, complete, EX, P2 ....$100.00
Wig, Lemon, complete w/instructions, M, P2 ....$250.00

CELEBRITY DOLLS

Celebrity dolls have been widely collected for many years. Except for the rarer examples, most of these dolls are still fairly easy to find, and the majority are priced under $100.00.

Condition is a very important worth-assessing factor, and if the doll is still in the original box, so much the better! Should the box be unopened (NRFB), the value is further enhanced. Using

mint as a standard, add 50% for the same doll mint in the box and 75% if it has never been taken out. On the other hand, dolls in only good or poorer condition drop at a rapid pace. For more information see *Collector's Guide to Celebrity Dolls* by David Spurgeon.

For celebrity/character dolls, see also Action Figures; Character, TV, and Movie Collectibles; and Rock 'N Roll.

Abbott & Costello, vinyl in cloth baseball uniforms, w/cassette of the comedy routine 'Who's on First?,' MIB, set ...$250.00
Alan Jackson (Country Music Stars), Exclusive Premiere, 1998, 9", MIB..$30.00
Andy Gibb, Ideal, 1979, 7½", MIB $85.00
Ashley & Mary Kate Olsen, Mattel, 1st issue, Dance & Horseback Riding sets, 9½", MIB, ea......................$30.00
Audrey Hepburn (Breakfast at Tiffany's), Mattel, 1998, 11½", MIB $50.00
Betty Grable, International Doll Co, 1940s, blond Dynel hair, w/tag, 19", NM, minimum value $400.00
Beverly Johnson (Real Model Collection), Matchbox, 1989, 11½", MIB...$50.00
Boy George, LJN, 1984, 11½", rare, MIB $150.00

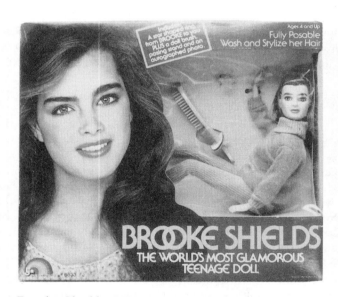

Brooke Shields, LJN, 1982, MIB, $55.00. (Photo courtesy Martin and Carolyn Berens)

Brooke Shields, LJN, 1982, Prom Party, 11½", rare, MIB.$150.00
Brooke Shields, LJN, 1983, suntan doll in yel & wht sun suit, 11½", MIB $65.00
Captain & Tenille, Mego, 1977, 12½", MIB, ea............$125.00
Charlie Chaplin (Little Tramp), Milton Bradley/Bubbles Inc, 1972, 19", MIB $100.00
Cher, Mego, 1976, Growing Hair, 12½", MIB.............$150.00
Cher, Mego, 1976, pk evening gown, 12½", MIB..........$125.00
Cher, Mego, 1981, swimsuit, 12", MIB.....................$50.00
Cheryl Ladd, Mattel, 1978, 11½", MIB.....................$85.00
Cheryl Tiegs (Real Model Collection), Matchbox, 1989, 11½", MIB $50.00
Christy Brinkley (Real Model Collection), Matchbox, 1989, 11½", MIB $50.00

Christy Lane, long red velvet skirt w/wht blouse, 1965-70s, 14", M...$25.00

Danny Kaye (White Christmas), Exclusive Premiere 1998, dressed as Santa, 9", MIB..$45.00

Debbie Boone, Mattel, 1978, 11½", MIB $100.00

Deidre Hall (Days of Our Lives), Mattel, 1999, 11½", MIB..$35.00

Dennis Rodman (Basketball Player), Street Players, 1990s, 12", MIB...$30.00

Diana Ross, Mego, 1977, 12½", MIB, A $150.00

Diana Ross (of the Supremes), Ideal, 1969, 19", rare, MIB.$600.00

Dick Clark, Juro, 1958, 26½", MIB..............................$450.00

Dolly Parton, Goldberger, 1978, red and silver outfit, 11½", MIB, $100.00; Dolly Parton, Goldberger, 1990s, black outfit with silver boots, 12", MIB, $75.00. (Photo courtesy David Spurgeon)

Donny & Marie Osmond, Mattel, 1976, 12", MIB, ea......$85.00

Dorothy Hamill (Olympic Ice Skater), Ideal, 1977, 11½", MIB...$100.00

Dorothy Lamour, Film Star Creations, 1940s-50s, stuffed print cloth w/mohair wig, cloth bathing suit, w/tag, 14", NM.........$135.00

Ekaterina 'Katia' Gordeeva (Olympic Ice Skater), Playmates, 1998, 11½", MIB $25.00

Eleanor Roosevelt, Effanbee, 1985, brn dress, 14½", MIB .$125.00

Elizabeth Taylor (Butterfield 8), Tri-Star, 1982, 11½", MIB..$150.00

Elizabeth Taylor (National Velvet), Madame Alexander, 1990, 12", MIB $100.00

Elvis Presley, Eugene, 1984, issued in 6 different outfits, 12", MIB $75.00

Elvis Presley, Hasbro, 1993, Jailhouse Rock, Teen Idol or '68 Special, numbered edition, 12", MIB, ea....................$50.00

Elvis Presley, World Doll, 1984, Burning Love, 21", MIB.$125.00

Farrah Fawcett-Majors, Mego, 1977, wht jumpsuit, 12½", MIB.$125.00

Farrah Fawcett-Majors, Mego, 1981, swimsuit, 12", MIB .$50.00

Farrah Fawcett-Majors, see also Charlie's Angels in Character, TV & Movies category

Flip Wilson/Geraldine, Shindana, 1970, stuffed reversible talker, 15", MIB...$85.00

Florence Griffith Joyner, LJN, 1989, 11½", MIB $65.00

George Burns, Effanbee, 1996, wearing black tuxedo and holding cigar, 17", MIB, $150.00. (Photo courtesy David Spurgeon)

George Burns, Exclusive Premiere, 1997, w/accessories, 9", MIB...$25.00

Ginger Rogers, World Doll, 1976, limited edition, MIB..$100.00

Grace Kelly (Swan or Mogambo), Tri-Star, 1982, 11½", MIB, ea..$100.00

Groucho Marx, Julius Henry/Effanbee, 1982, 18", MIB .$150.00

Harold Lloyd, 1920s, lithoed stuffed cloth of star standing w/hands in pockets, 12", EX+..................................$100.00

Humphrey Bogart & Ingrid Bergman (Casablanca), Exclusive Premiere, 1998, 9", MIB, ea..$30.00

Humphrey Bogart (Casablanca), Effanbee, 1989, 16", MIB.$150.00

Jaclyn Smith, Mego, 1977, 12½", MIB $200.00

Jaclyn Smith, see also Charlie's Angels in Character, TV & Movies category

James Cagney, Effanbee, 1987, pinstripe suit & hat, 16", MIB.$125.00

James Dean, DSI, 1994, sweater & pants, 12", MIB $55.00

Jerry Springer, Street Players, 1998, 12", MIB...................$50.00

Jimmy Osmond, Mattel, 1978, 10", MIB.........................$125.00

John Travolta (On Stage...Super Star), Chemtoy, 1977, 12", MIB...$100.00

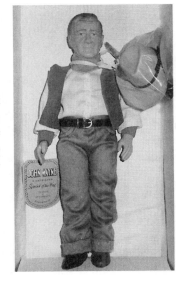

John Wayne (Great Legends), Effanbee, 1981, Symbol of the West (cowboy outfit), 17", MIB, $150.00.

(Photo courtesy Patsy Moyer)

John Wayne (Great Legends), Effanbee, 1982, Guardian of the West (cavalry uniform), 18", MIB..............................$150.00

Kate Jackson, Mattel, 1978, 11½", MIB........................$85.00

Katerina Witt (Olympic Ice Skater), Playmates, 1998, 11½", MIB...$25.00

KISS, Mego, 1978, any from group, 12½", MIB, ea........$350.00

Kristi Yamaguchi (Olympic Ice Skater), Playmates, 1998, 11½", MIB...$25.00

Laurel & Hardy, Goldberger, 1986, denim overalls, 12", MIB, ea $55.00

Laurel & Hardy, Hamilton Gifts, 1991, cloth suits, 16", MIB, ea $65.00

Laurel & Hardy, 1981, cloth bodies w/porcelain heads, cloth suits, 18" & 21", MIB, ea $75.00

Leann Rimes (Country Music Stars), Exclusive Premier, 1998, 9", MIB...$30.00

Leslie Uggams, Madame Alexander, 1966, lt pk dress, 17", MIB.$350.00

Liberace, Effanbee, 1986, glittery blk & silver outfit w/cape, 16½", MIB $250.00

Linda Evans, see Character, TV & Movie category

Louis 'Satchmo' Armstrong, Effanbee, 1984, bl & blk tuxedo, 15½", MIB...$250.00

Lucille Ball, Effanbee, 1985, in blk tails & top hat, 15", MIB.$175.00

Lucille Ball (Hollywood Walk of Fame Collection), CAL-HASCO Inc, 1992, 20", MIB.................................$350.00

Lucille Ball, see also Character, TV, and Movie Collectibles

Mae West, Hamilton Gifts, 1991, 17", M.........................$50.00

Mae West (Great Legends), Effanbee, 1982, 18", MIB...$125.00

Mandy Moore, Play Along, 2000, 11½", MIB $20.00

Marie Osmond (Modeling Doll), Mattel, 1976, 30", MIB.$150.00

Marilyn Monroe, DSI, 1993, blk gown & wht fur stole, 11½", MIB $50.00

Marilyn Monroe, Tri-Star, 1982, pk gown & gloves, 16½", MIB $100.00

Marilyn Monroe, Tri-Star, 1982, 1st issue (same face mold as 16½" doll), 11½", MIB..$75.00

Marilyn Monroe, Tri-Star, 1982, 2nd issue (different face mold), 11½", MIB...$150.00

Marlo Thomas (That Girl), Madame Alexander, 1967, 17", rare, MIB $800.00

Michael Jackson, LJN, 1984, bl & gold outfit holding microphone, 12", MIB $75.00

Muhammad Ali, Hasbro, 1997, 12", MIB $45.00

Muhammad Ali, Mego, 1976, 9", MOC $150.00

New Kids on the Block, dolls, Show Time Kids Rag Dolls, Hasbro, 1990, 5 different, 19", MIB, ea $65.00

New Kids on the Block, Hasbro, In Concert, 5 different, 12", MIB, ea..$50.00

Nicole Boebeck (Olympic Ice Skater), Playmates, 1998, 11½", MIB...$25.00

Patty Duke, Horsman, 1965, 12", rare, MIB $450.00

Penny Marshall or Cindy Williams, see Character, TV & Movie category

Prince William, Goldberg, 1982, christening gown, 18", MIB.$150.00

Prince William, House of Nisbet, 1982, as baby, 18", MIB .$200.00

Princess Diana, Danbury Mint, 1988, pk satin gown, 14", MIB .$125.00

Princess Diana, Effanbee (Fan Club), 1982, wedding dress, 16½", MIB $225.00

Princess Diana, Goldberg, 1983, white gown and boa, 1983, 11½", MIB, $100.00; Prince Charles, Goldberg, 1983, dress uniform, 12", MIB, $100.00.

Princess Diana, Way Out Toys, 1990s, Royal Diana, pk dress, 11½", MIB $20.00

Princess Margaret, Dean's Rag Book Co, 1920s, papier-mache over cloth, mohair wig, cloth coat & hat, 14", unused, M...$350.00

Queen Elizabeth, Effanbee, 1980s, long wht satin gown, 14", MIB $75.00

Queen Elizabeth, Effanbee, 1989, red & wht satin gown, 14", MIB $125.00

Randy Travis (Country Music Stars), Exclusive Premiere, 1998, 9", MIB...$30.00

Red Foxx, Shindana, 1976, 2-sided stuffed print cloth talker, 16", MIB $150.00

Robert Crippen (Astronaut), Kenner, 1997, 12", MIB $45.00

Rosemary Clooney (White Christmas), Exclusive Premiere, 1998, red gown, 8", MIB..$45.00

Rosie O'Donnell, Mattel, 1999, red outfit, 11½", MIB, $30.00.

(Photo courtesy David Spurgeon)

Rosie O'Donnell, Tyco, 1997, The Rosie O'Doll, stuffed cloth w/outfit, 14", MIB $40.00

Selena, Arm Enterprise, 1996, red jumpsuit, 11½", MIB..$85.00

Shari Lewis, Direct Connect International, 1994, rag doll holding Lambchop, 14", MIB $30.00

Shari Lewis, Madame Alexander, 1959, yel sweater w/gr skirt & hat, 21", MIB $450.00

Shirley Temple, Armand Marseille, bsk, jtd, wht & red polka-dot dress, 22", VGIB...$135.00

Shirley Temple, Ideal, 1930s, jointed composition, in blue-dotted dress, 11", EX, A, $750.00; Shirley Temple, Ideal, 1930s, composition, in coat and hat with original photo card, 11", VG, A, $515.00. (Photo courtesy Skinner, Inc.)

Shirley Temple, Ideal, 1973, plastic, wht & red polka-dot dress, 17", MIB, A..$40.00

Sonny Bono, Mego, 1976, 12½", MIB $150.00

Soupy Sales, 1960s, yel sweater & red tie, 11½", MIB ...$250.00

Vanna White, HSC, 1990, gold dress & purple jumpsuit, 11½", MIB $55.00

WC Fields, Effanbee, 1980, blk coat, checked pants & gray top hat, 15½", MIB..$125.00

WC Fields, Knickerbocker, 1972, stuffed print cloth talker, 16", MIB $75.00

Willie Nelson, Catena International Inc, 1989, stuffed cloth w/yarn hair & head bandanna, 16", M $65.00

CHATTY CATHY

Chatty Cathy (made by Mattel) was introduced in the 1960s and came as either a blond or brunette. For five years she sold very well. Much of her success can be attributed to the fact that Chatty Cathy talked. By pulling the string on her back, she could respond with many different phrases. During her five years of fame, Mattel added to the line with Chatty Baby, Tiny Chatty Baby and Tiny Chatty Brother (the twins), Charmin' Chatty, and finally Singin' Chatty. Charmin' Chatty had sixteen interchangeable records. Her voice box was activated in the same manner as

the above-mentioned dolls, by means of a pull string located at the base of her neck. The line was brought back in 1969, smaller and with a restyled face, but it was not well received.

Values are for dolls in excellent talking condition with original outfits unless noted otherwise.

Carrying Case, Chatty Baby, bl or pk, NM, ea $50.00

Carrying Case, Tiny Chatty Baby, bl or pk, NM, ea..........$40.00

Doll, Charmin' Chatty, EX, from $150 to $200.00

Doll, Chatty Baby, EX, from $75 to..............................$100.00

Doll, Chatty Cathy, any style, EX, from $375 to $425.00

Doll, Chatty Cathy, 1970 reissue, MIB, from $75 to $100.00

Doll, Singin' Chatty, blond hair, 1965, M, $250.00. (Photo courtesy Kathy Lewis)

Doll, Tiny Chatty Baby, EX $100.00

Doll, Tiny Chatty Baby (Black), EX $110.00

Doll, Tiny Chatty Baby (Brother), EX $125.00

Outfit, Charmin Chatty, Let's Play Together, MIP $80.00

Outfit, Charmin' Chatty, Let's Go Shopping, MIP $85.00

Outfit, Chatty Baby, Sleeper Set, MIP $60.00

Outfit, Chatty Cathy, Pink Peppermint Stick, MIP $150.00

Outfit, Chatty Cathy, Playtime, MIP $150.00

Outfit, Tiny Chatty Baby, Bye-Bye, MIP........................$75.00

Outfit, Tiny Chatty Baby, Pink Frill, MIP.....................$125.00

CRISSY AND HER FRIENDS

Ideal's 18" Crissy doll with growing hair was very popular with little girls of the early 1970s. She was introduced in 1969 and continued to be sold throughout the 1970s, enjoying a relatively long market life for a doll. During the 1970s, many different versions of Crissy were made. Numerous friends followed her success, all with the growing hair feature like Crissy's. The other Ideal 'grow hair' dolls in the line included Velvet, Cinnamon, Tressy, Dina, Mia, Kerry, Brandi, and Cricket. Crissy is the easiest member in the line to find, followed by her cousin Velvet. The other members are not as common, but like Crissy and Velvet loose examples of these dolls frequently make their appearance at doll shows, flea markets, and even garage sales. Only those examples that are in excellent or better condition and wearing their original outfits and shoes should command book value. Values for the rare Black versions of the dolls in the line are currently on the rise, as demand for them increases while the supply decreases.

Advisor: Cindy Sabulis (S14), author of *Dolls of the 1960s and 1970s*

Baby Crissy, 1973-76, pk dress, EX $65.00
Baby Crissy, 1973-76, pk dress, MIB.............................$125.00
Baby Crissy (Black), 1973-76, pk dress, EX......................$80.00
Brandi (Black), 1972-73, orange swimsuit, EX $125.00
Cinnamon, Curly Ribbons, 1974, EX...............................$45.00
Cinnamon, Curly Ribbons (Black), 1974, EX....................$75.00
Cinnamon, Hairdoodler, 1973, EX....................................$40.00
Cinnamon, Hairdoodler (Black), 1973, EX $75.00
Crissy, Beautiful, 1969, orange lace dress, EX..................$40.00
Crissy, Country Fashion, 1982-83, EX...............................$20.00
Crissy, Country Fashion, 1982-83, MIB............................$45.00
Crissy, Look Around, 1972, EX...$40.00
Crissy, Magic Hair, 1977, EX $30.00

Crissy, Magic Hair, 1977, MIB, from $65.00 to $90.00. (Photo courtesy Cindy Sabulis and Marcia Fanta)

Crissy, Magic Hair, 1977, NRFB......................................$100.00
Crissy, Magic Hair (Black), 1977, EX.............................$100.00
Crissy, Movin' Groovin', 1971, EX....................................$35.00
Crissy, Movin' Groovin' (Black), 1971, EX $100.00
Crissy, Swirla Curla, 1973, EX..$35.00
Crissy, Swirla Curla (Black), 1973, EX...........................$100.00
Crissy, Twirly Beads, 1974, MIB, M15............................$65.00
Dina, 1972-73, purple playsuit, EX...................................$50.00
Kerry, 1971, gr romper, EX...$55.00
Mia, 1971, turq romper, EX $50.00
Tara (Black), 1976, yel gingham outfit, MIB $200.00
Velvet, Beauty Braider, 1973, EX......................................$35.00
Velvet, Look Around, 1972, EX $35.00
Velvet, Look Around (Black), 1972, EX..........................$100.00

Velvet, Movin' Groovin', 1971, EX....................................$35.00
Velvet, reissue, 1982, EX...$30.00
Velvet, Swirly Daisies, 1974, EX.......................................$35.00
Velvet, Swirly Daisies, 1974, MIB $65.00
Velvet, 1st issue, purple dress, 1970, EX............................$55.00

DAWN

Dawn and her friends were made by Deluxe Topper, ca 1970s. They're becoming highly collectible, especially when mint in the box. Dawn was a 6" fashion doll, part of a series sold as the Dawn Model Agency. They were issued in boxes already dressed in clothes of the highest style, or you could buy additional outfits, many complete with matching shoes and accessories.

Advisor: Dawn Diaz (P2)

Accessory, Dawn's Apartment, complete $50.00
Doll, Dancing Angie, NRFB...$50.00
Doll, Dancing Dale, NRFB...$65.00
Doll, Dancing Dawn, NRFB...$50.00
Doll, Dancing Gary, NRFB...$50.00
Doll, Dancing Glori, NRFB..$50.00
Doll, Dancing Jessica, NRFB..$50.00
Doll, Dancing Ron, NRFB..$50.00
Doll, Dancing Van, NRFB..$80.00
Doll, Daphne, Dawn Model Agency, gr & silver dress, NRFB.$100.00

Doll, Dawn Majorette, NRFB, $100.00.

Doll, Denise, NRFB...$100.00
Doll, Dinah, NRFB..$100.00
Doll, Gary, NRFB..$50.00
Doll, Jessica, NRFB...$50.00
Doll, Kip Majorette, NRFB...$65.00
Doll, Longlocks, NRFB..$50.00
Doll, Maureen, Dawn Model Agency, red & gold dress, NRFB..$100.00
Doll, Ron, NRFB $50.00
Outfit, Green Slink, #0716, NRFB....................................$25.00
Outfit, Sheer Delight, #8110, NRFB.................................$25.00

Outfit, Bell Bottom Flounce, #0717, 1969, NRFB, $25.00. (Photo courtesy Pat Smith)

DOLLY DARLINGS BY HASBRO

Dolly Darlings by Hasbro are approximately 4" tall and have molded or rooted hair. The molded-hair dolls were sold in themed hatboxes with small accessories to match. The rooted-hair dolls were sold separately and came with a small brush and comb. There were four plastic playrooms that featured the rooted-hair dolls. Hasbro also produced the Flower Darling series which were 2" dolls in flower corsages. The Dolly Darlings and Flower Darlings were available in the mid to late 1960s.

Advisor: Dawn Diaz (P2)

Beth at the Supermarket, NRFB	$50.00
Cathy Goes to a Party, M (EX case), from $35 to	$45.00
Daisy Darling, complete, EX	$15.00
Flying Nun, MIB, from $50 to	$75.00
Go-Team-Go, doll only, EX, from $25 to	$35.00
Hipster, doll only, EX, from $25 to	$35.00
Honey, NRFB	$50.00

John and His Pets, M (in case), from $35.00 to $55.00. (Photo courtesy Cindy Sabulis)

Lemon Drop, doll only, EX, from $30 to	$50.00
Powder Puff, doll only, EX, from $15 to	$25.00
Rose Darling, NRFB	$50.00
School Days, doll only, EX, from $15 to	$25.00
Shary Takes a Vacation, doll only, EX	$10.00
Slick Set, doll only, EX	$25.00
Slumber Party, doll only, EX	$15.00
Sunny Day, doll only, from $15 to	$25.00
Susie Goes to School, M (EX case), from $35 to	$45.00
Sweetheart, doll only, EX, from $15 to	$25.00
Tea Time, NRFB	$50.00
Teeny Bikini, doll only, EX, from $15 to	$25.00
Violet Darling, doll only, EX	$10.00

FISHER-PRICE

Though this company is more famous for their ruggedly durable, lithographed wooden toys, they made dolls as well. Many of the earlier dolls (circa mid-'70s) had stuffed cloth bodies and vinyl heads, hands, and feet. Some had battery-operated voice boxes. In 1981 they introduced Kermit the Frog and Miss Piggy and a line of clothing for both. For company history, see the Fisher-Price category. For more information, we recommend *Fisher-Price Toys*, by Brad Cassity, our advisor for this category.

See also Advertising; Character, TV, and Movie Collectibles; Disney.

Doll, Audrey, #203, 1974-76, 13", EX	$25.00
Doll, Baby Ann, #204, 1974-76, M	$25.00
Doll, Billie, #242, 1979-80, M	$10.00
Doll, Elizabeth (Black), #205, 1974-76, M	$25.00
Doll, Honey, #208, 1977-80, M	$20.00

Doll, Jenny, #201, 1974 – 76, M, $25.00. (Photo courtesy Brad Cassity)

Doll, Joey, #206, 1975-76, 13", EX	$25.00
Doll, Mandy, #4009, 1985, Happy Birthday, EX	$50.00
Doll, Mary, #200, 1974-77, 13", EX	$25.00
Doll, Mikey, #240, 1979-80, 8", EX	$10.00
Doll, Miss Piggy, #890, Dress-Up Muppet, 1981-84, EX	$12.00
Doll, Muffy, #241, 1979-80, M	$10.00

Doll, My Friend Becky, #218, 1982-84, MIB.....................$20.00
Doll, My Friend Christie, #8120, 1990, EX, from $40 to..$75.00
Doll, My Friend Mandy, #211, 1979-81, EX.....................$20.00

Doll, My Friend Nicky, #206, 1985, MIB, $30.00. (Photo courtesy Brad Cassity)

Doll, Natalie, #202, 1974-76, M..$25.00
Outfit, Aerobics, #4110, 1985, EX $10.00
Outfit, Let's Go Camping, #222, 1978-79, MIB...............$10.00
Outfit, Miss Piggy's Sailor Outfit, #891, 1981-82, EX.......$12.00
Outfit, Rainy Day Slicker, #219, 1978-80, MIB...............$10.00
Outfit, Springtime Party Dress Outfit & Pattern, 1985, EX.$10.00
Outfit, Springtime Tennis, #220, 1978-82, MIB...............$10.00
Outfit, Sunshine Party Dress, #237, 1984, MIB $10.00
Outfit, Valentine Party Dress, #238, 1984-85, EX $10.00

FLATSYS

Flatsy dolls were a product of the Ideal Novelty and Toy Company. They were produced from 1968 until 1970 in 2", 5", and 8" sizes. There was only one boy in the 5" line; all were dressed in 1970s fashions, and not only clothing but accessory items such as bicycles were made as well.

In 1994 Justoys reissued Mini Flatsys. They were sold alone or with accessories such as bikes, rollerblades, and jet skis.

Advisor: Dawn Diaz (P2)

Ali Fashion Flatsy, NRFP, from $45 to $65.00
Bonnie Flatsy, sailing, NRFP $55.00
Candy, Happy Birthday, complete, EX $25.00
Casey Flatsy, MIB..$55.00
Cory Flatsy, print mini-dress, NRFP $60.00
Dale Fashion Flatsy, hot pk maxi, NRFP $60.00
Dewie Flatsy, NRFP $60.00
Dewie Flatsy Locket, NRFP, from $25 to...........................$35.00
Filly Flatsy, complete, EX...$15.00
Grandma Baker, Flatsyville series, complete, M, from $50 to.$75.00
Gwen Fashion Flatsy, NRFP, from $45 to $65.00
Judy Flatsy, complete, NRFP, from $55 to $75.00
Munch Time Flatsy, Mini Flatsy Collection, NRFP, from $50
    to...$85.00

Kookie Flatsy, Flatsyville series, complete in frame, M, from $50.00 to $75.00. (Photo courtesy Cindy Sabulis)

Slumber Time Flatsy, Mini Flatsy Collection, NRFP, from $50
    to $85.00
Spinderella Flatsy, complete, M...$50.00
Summer Mini Flatsy Collection, NRFP $65.00
Susie Flatsy, complete, EX $25.00

GALOOB'S BABY FACE DOLLS

Galoob's Baby Face dolls were first available on the toy market in 1991. By the end of 1992 the short-lived dolls were already being discounted by toy stores. Although they were targeted as play dolls for children, it didn't take long for these adorable dolls to find their way into adult collectors' hearts. The most endearing quality of Baby Face dolls are their expressive faces. Sporting big eyes with long soft eyelashes, cute pug noses, and mouths that are puckered, pouting, smiling, or laughing, these dolls are delightful and fun. The 13" heavy vinyl Baby Face dolls are jointed at the shoulders, elbows, knees, and hips. Their jointed limbs allow for posing them in more positions than the average doll and adds to the fun of displaying or playing with them. Old store stock of Baby Face dolls was plentiful for several years, and since these dolls are still relatively new as collectibles, it isn't difficult to find never-removed-from-box examples.

Advisor: Cindy Sabulis (S14)

Activity Stroller, MIB, S14..$25.00
Asian Versions, NRFB, S14, from $65 to $80.00
Asian Versions, re-dressed, S14, from $20 to $25.00
Bathtub Babies, NRFB, from $40 to $50.00
Bathtub Babies, re-dressed, S14, from $15 to $20.00
Black Versions, NRFB, S14, from $60 to............................$75.00
Black Versions, re-dressed, S14, from $20 to $25.00
Hispanic Versions, NRFB, S14, from $85 to $125.00
Hispanic Versions, re-dressed, S14, from $25 to $40.00
Outfits, NRFB, S14, ea from $20 to $25.00
White Versions, any except So Silly Sally, NRFB, S14, from $50
    to $75.00
White Versions, re-dressed, S14, from $15 to $20.00

GERBER BABIES

The first Gerber Baby dolls were manufactured in 1936. These dolls were made of cloth and produced by an unknown manufacturer. Since that time, six different companies working with leading artists, craftsmen, and designers have attempted to capture the charm of the winsome baby in Dorothy Hope Smith's charcoal drawing of her friend's baby, Ann Turner (Cook). This drawing became known as the Gerber Baby and was adopted as the trademark of the Gerber Products Company, located in Fremont, Michigan. For further information see *Gerber Baby Dolls and Advertising Collectibles* by Joan S. Grubaugh.

Amsco, baby & feeding set, vinyl, 1972-73, complete, 14", NMIB...$85.00
Amsco, baby & feeding set, vinyl, 1972-73, re-dressed, 14", M..$40.00
Amsco, pk & wht rosebud sleeper, vinyl, 1972-73, 10", NM, from $45 to...$55.00
Amsco, pk & wht rosebud sleeper (Black), vinyl, 1972-73, 10", NM, from $60 to...$100.00
Arrow Rubber & Plastic Corp, pk & wht bib & diaper, 1965-67, 14", MIB, from $45 to...$60.00
Arrow Rubber & Plastic Corp, pk & wht bib & diaper, 1965-67, re-dressed, 14", EX...$45.00
Atlanta Novelty, Baby Drink & Wet, 1979-81, 17", complete w/trunk & accessories, M, from $75 to.....................$85.00
Atlanta Novelty, Baby Drink & Wet (Black), 1979-81, 12", complete w/trunk & accessories, M.........................$100.00
Atlanta Novelty, Bathtub Baby, 1985, 12", MIB, from $70 to.$85.00
Atlanta Novelty, bl or rose velour dress w/wht blouse (Black), 1979-81, 17", M, ea from $75 to................................$85.00
Atlanta Novelty, flowered bed jacket w/matching pillow & coverlet, 1979, 17", NRFB, from $75 to..........................$95.00
Atlanta Novelty, mama voice, several different outfits, 1979-81, 17", NRFB, ea from $75 to $85.00
Atlanta Novelty, mama voice (Black), 1979-81, 17", NRFB, from $75 to...$85.00
Atlanta Novelty, porcelain w/soft body, wht eyelet christening gown, limited edition, 1981, 14", NRFB, from $275 to $350.00
Atlanta Novelty, rag doll, pk or bl, 1984, 11½", EX.........$20.00
Atlanta Novelty, snowsuit w/matching hood, 1979, 17", NRFB, from $75 to..$95.00
Atlanta Novelty, snowsuit w/matching hood (Black), 1979-81, 17", NRFB, from $75 to...$85.00
Atlanta Novelty, 50th Anniversary, eyelet skirt & bib, stuffed cloth & vinyl, 1978, 17", NRFB, from $75 to............$95.00
Lucky Ltd, Birthday Party Twins, 1989, 6", NRFB............$40.00
Lucky Ltd, christening gown, cloth & vinyl, 1989, 16", EX.$40.00
Sun Rubber, orig nightgown, 1955-58, M.......................$175.00
Toy Biz, Baby Care Set, 1996, MIB $25.00
Toy Biz, Potty Time Baby, vinyl, 1994-95, 15", NRFB......$25.00

HOLLY HOBBIE

Sometime around 1970 a young homemaker and mother, Holly Hobbie, approached the American Greeting Company with some charming country-styled drawings of children. Her concepts were well received by the company, and since that time over four hundred Holly Hobbie items have been produced, nearly all marked HH, H. Hobbie, or Holly Hobbie.

Doll, Country Fun Holly Hobbie, 1989, 16", NRFB.........$20.00
Doll, Grandma Holly, Knickerbocker, 14", MIB...............$20.00
Doll, Grandma Holly, Knickerbocker, 24", MIB...............$25.00
Doll, Holly Hobbie, Heather, Amy or Carrie, Knickerbocker, 6", MIB, ea..$5.00
Doll, Holly Hobbie, Heather, Amy or Carrie, Knickerbocker, 9", MIB, ea...$10.00
Doll, Holly Hobbie, Heather, Amy or Carrie, Knickerbocker, 16", MIB, ea..$20.00
Doll, Holly Hobbie, Heather, Amy or Carrie, Knickerbocker, 27", MIB, ea..$25.00
Doll, Holly Hobbie, Heather, Amy or Carrie, Knickerbocker, 33", MIB, ea..$35.00
Doll, Holly Hobbie, scented, clear ornament around neck, 1988, 18", NRFB..$30.00
Doll, Holly Hobbie, 25th Anniversary collector's edition, Meritus, 1994, 26", MIB, from $45 to $25.00
Doll, Holly Hobbie Bicentennial, Knickerbocker, 12", MIB ..$25.00
Doll, Holly Hobbie Day 'N Night, Knickerbocker, 14", MIB.$15.00

Toy Biz, Food and Playtime Baby, 1995, MIB, from $25.00 to $35.00.

Plate, 'Start each day in a happy way,' American Greetings Collector's Edition, 10½", $25.00.

Doll, Holly Hobbie Dream Along, Holly, Carrie or Amy, Knickerbocker, 9", MIB, ea..$10.00

Doll, Holly Hobbie Dream Along, Holly, Carrie or Amy, Knickerbocker, cloth, 12", MIB, ea $15.00

Doll, Holly Hobbie Talker, 4 sayings, 16", MIB $25.00

Doll, Little Girl Holly, Knickerbocker, 1980, 15", MIB....$20.00

Doll, Robby, Knickerbocker, 9", MIB.............................$15.00

Doll, Robby, Knickerbocker, 16", MIB...........................$20.00

Dollhouse, M $200.00

Sand Pail, Chein, 1974, 6", EX, N2.............................$25.00

Sewing Machine, Durham, 1975, plastic & metal, battery-op, 5x9", EX $25.00

Sing-A-Long Electric Parlor Player, Vanity Fair, 1970s, complete w/booklet, scarce, NMIB $45.00

Valentine Activity Book, 1978, 5x8", unused, EX, N2 .....$10.00

HONEY HILL BUNCH

In the 1970s, Mattel produced a 'neighborhood' group called the Honey Hill Bunch. These dolls have stuffed bodies and vinyl heads with Velcro sewn into their hands to hold felt accessories or to hold their hands together. Included in the line were accessories such as the 'Club House' or the 'Baskin Robins Ice Cream Store' that helped bring the 'neighborhood' to life.

Accessory, Baskin-Robbins Ice Cream Store, complete, M.$50.00

Accessory, Club House, #9225, complete, MIB $50.00

Accessory, Club House & 4 Dolls, #9373, rare, MIB $85.00

Accessory, Rickety Rig, #9981, MIB, $40.00; Rickety Rig & Six Dolls, #9977, MIB, $65.00. (Photo courtesy J. Michael Augustyniak)

Doll, Battie/Slugger, #9095, MIP, ea.............................$25.00

Doll, Bunny Baskin & Richie Robbins, #9978, MIP, pr....$55.00

Doll, Curly Q, #9713, MIB $30.00

Doll, Darlin', #9099, MIP $25.00

Doll, Hayseed & Chum (dog), #9714, MIB $40.00

Doll, IQ, #9096, MIP..$25.00

Doll, Irish Eyes, #2567, MIB..$40.00

Doll, Li'l Kid, #9097, MIP..$25.00

Doll, Miss Cheevus, #2568, MIB...................................$30.00

Doll, Solo, #9100, MIP...$25.00

Doll, Spunky, #9094, MIP...$25.00

Doll, Sweetlee, #9098, MIP...$25.00

Doll, Sunflower, #2566, scarce, MIP, $35.00. (Photo courtesy J. Michael Augustyniak)

JEM

The glamorous life of Jem mesmerized little girls who watched her Saturday morning cartoons, and she was a natural as a fashion doll. Hasbro saw the potential in 1985 when they introduced the Jem line of 12" dolls representing her, the rock stars from Jem's musical group, the Holograms, and other members of the cast, including the only boy, Rio, Jem's road manager and Jerrica's boyfriend. Each doll was poseable, jointed at the waist, head, and wrists, so that they could be positioned at will with their musical instruments and other accessory items. Their clothing, their makeup, and their hairdos were wonderfully exotic, and their faces were beautifully modeled. The Jem line was discontinued in 1987 after being on the market for only two years.

Accessory, Backstager, M $25.00

Accessory, New Wave Waterbed, M.................................$35.00

Accessory, Star Stage, M..$30.00

Doll, Aja, 1st issue, orig outfit, M..................................$45.00

Doll, Aja, 2nd issue, orig outfit, M $90.00

Doll, Ashley, orig outfit, M..$40.00

Doll, Clash, orig outfit, M..$25.00

Doll, Flash 'N Sizzle Jem, orig outfit, M $60.00

Doll, Glitter 'N Gold Jem, orig outfit, M $60.00

Doll, Jem/Jessica, star earrings, orig outfit, M..................$35.00

Doll, Jem/Jessica, 1st issue, orig outfit, M $30.00

Doll, Jetta, orig outfit, M...$40.00

Doll, Kimber, 1st issue, orig outfit, M.............................$40.00

Doll, Pizzaz, 1st issue, orig outfit, M...............................$50.00

Doll, Raya, orig outfit, M...$150.00
Doll, Stormer, orig outfit, M $45.00
Doll, Synergy, orig outfit, M $45.00

Doll, Video, complete, M, $45.00. (Photo courtesy Lee Garmon)

Outfit, Award Night, MIP $30.00
Outfit, Designing Woman, MIP $35.00
Outfit, Electric Cords, MIP..$25.00
Outfit, Encore, MIP $35.00
Outfit, Friend or Stranger, MIP $50.00
Outfit, Let's Rock This Town, MIP $35.00
Outfit, Moroccan Magic, MIP $75.00
Outfit, Purple Haze, MIP $30.00
Outfit, Rappin', MIP...$45.00
Outfit, She Makes an Impression, MIP $90.00
Outfit, Splashes of Sound, MIP $25.00
Outfit, We're Off & Running, MIP $35.00

LIDDLE KIDDLES

From 1966 to 1971, Mattel produced Liddle Kiddle dolls and accessories, typical of the 'little kid next door.' They were made in sizes ranging from a tiny ¾" up to 4". They were all poseable and had rooted hair that could be restyled. Eventually there were Animiddles and Zoolery Jewelry Kiddles, which were of course animals, and two other series that represented storybook and nursery-rhyme characters. There was a set of extraterrestrials, and lastly in 1979, Sweet Treets dolls were added to the assortment.

In the mid-1970s Mattel reissued Lucky Locket Kiddles. The dolls had names identical to the earlier lockets but were not of the same high quality.

In 1994 – 95 Tyco reissued Liddle Kiddles in strap-on, clip-on, Lovely Locket, Pretty Perfume, and baby bottle collections.

Loose dolls, if complete and with all their original accessories, are worth about 50% less than the same mint in the box. Dressed, loose dolls with no accessories are worth 75% less.

Advisor: Dawn Diaz (P2)
Other Sources: S14

Animiddle Kiddles, #3635 Lucky Lion; #3636 Tiny Tiger, MIP, each $75.00. (Photo courtesy Paris Langford)

Alice in Wonderliddle, complete, NM $175.00
Aqua Funny Bunny, #3532, complete, EX $20.00
Aqua Funny Bunny, #3532, MIP $65.00
Babe Biddle, #3505, complete, M..................................$75.00
Baby Din-Din, #3820, complete, M $50.00
Baby Rockaway, #3819, MIP $100.00
Beach Buggy, #5003, complete, NM...............................$35.00
Beat-A-Diddle, #3510, MIP $500.00
Blue Funny Bunny, #3532, MIP......................................$65.00
Calamity Jiddle, #3506, complete w/high saddle horse, M..$75.00
Chitty-Chitty Bang-Bang Kiddles, #3597, MOC $150.00
Chocolottie's House, #2501, MIP..................................$25.00
Cinderriddle's Palace, #5068, plastic window version, M.$25.00
Cookin' Kiddle, #3846, complete, M $150.00
Dainty Deer, #3637, complete, M...................................$20.00
Florence Niddle, #3507, complete, M $75.00
Flower Charm Bracelet, #3747, MIP...............................$50.00
Flower Pin Kiddle, #3741, MIP $50.00
Flower Ring Kiddle, #3744, MIP $50.00
Frosty Mint Kone, #3653, complete, M..........................$60.00
Greta Grape, #3728, complete, M...................................$50.00
Greta Griddle, #3508, complete, M $85.00
Heart Charm Bracelet Kiddle, #3747, MIP.....................$50.00

Jewelry Kiddles, #3747 Flower Charm Bracelet Kiddle, MIP, $50.00.

Heart Pin Kiddle, #3741, MIP $50.00
Heart Ring Kiddle, #3744, MIP $50.00
Henrietta Horseless Carriage, #3641, complete, M...........$60.00
Hot Dog Stand, #5002, complete, M $25.00
Howard Biff Biddle, #3502, complete, M $75.00
Howard Biff Biddle, #3502, NRFB $300.00
Jewelry Kiddles, #3735 & #5166 Treasure Boxes, M, ea ...$25.00
Kampy Kiddle, #3753, complete, M $150.00
Kiddle & Kars Antique Fair Set, #3806, NRFB.............$300.00
Kiddle Komedy Theatre, #3592, EX $35.00
Kiddle Kolognes, #3704 Honeysuckle, MIP $75.00

Kiddle Kolognes, #3705 Sweet Pea, NRFB, $75.00. (Photo courtesy Cindy Sabulis)

Kiddle Kolognes, #3708 Sweet Three Boutique, NRFB .$300.00
Kiddle Kolognes, #3710 Gardenia, MIP $75.00
Kiddles Sweet Shop, #3807, NRFB $300.00
King & Queen of Hearts, #3784, MIP...........................$150.00
Kleo Kola, #3729, complete, M $50.00
Kola Kiddles Three-Pak, #3734, NRFB...........................$300.00

Kosmic Kiddles, M, each, $150.00. (Photo courtesy Paris Langford)

Lady Crimson, #A3840, NRFB...................................$75.00
Lady Lavendar, #A3840, NRFB...................................$75.00
Laffy Lemon, #3732, MIP $85.00
Larky Locket, #3539, complete, EX.............................$25.00
Lenore Limousine, #3743, complete, M...........................$60.00
Liddle Biddle Peep, #3544, complete, M.......................$125.00
Liddle Diddle, #3503, complete, M...............................$75.00

Liddle Kiddle, complete, M, $75.00. (Photo courtesy Cindy Sabulis)

Liddle Kiddles Kabin, #3591, complete, EX $25.00
Liddle Kiddles Kastle, #3522, complete, M $55.00

Liddle Kiddles Klub, #3301, $20.00. (Photo courtesy Tamela Storm and Debra Van Dyke)

Liddle Kiddles Kolony, #3571, M $25.00
Liddle Kiddles Kottage, #3534, complete, EX $25.00
Liddle Kiddles Open House, #5167, MIB.........................$40.00
Liddle Kiddles Pop-Up Boutique, #5170, complete, M.....$30.00
Liddle Kiddles Pop-Up Playhouse, #3574, complete, M ...$30.00
Liddle Kiddles Talking Townhouse, #5154, MIB $50.00
Liddle Kiddles 3-Story House, complete, M.....................$35.00
Liddle Lion Zoolery, #3661, complete, M $100.00
Liddle Red Riding Hiddle, #3546, complete, M $150.00
Lilac Locket, #3540, MIP $75.00
Limey Lou Spoonfuls, #2815, MIP $25.00
Lois Locket, #3541, complete, M $50.00
Lola Rocket, #3536, MIP...$75.00
Lolli-Grape, #3656, complete, M $60.00
Lolli-Lemon, #3657, MIP...$75.00
Lolli-Mint, #3658, MIP..$75.00
Lorelei Locket, #3717, MIP...$75.00

Lorelei Locket, #3717, 1976 version, MIP $25.00
Lottie Locket, #3679, complete, M $35.00
Lou Locket, #3537, MIP $75.00
Luana Locket, #3680, complete, M $35.00
Luana Locket, #3680, Gold Rush version, MIP $85.00
Lucky Lion, #3635, complete, M $50.00
Lucky Locket Jewel Case, #3542, M.................................$150.00
Lucky Locket Magic Paper Dolls, Whitman, 1968, EXIB.$30.00
Luscious Lime, #3733, complete, M $55.00
Luscious Lime, #3733, glitter version, complete, M..........$75.00

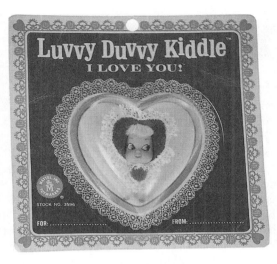

Luvvy Duvvy Kiddle, #3596, MIP, $50.00.

Millie Middle, #3509, complete, M.................................$125.00
Miss Mouse, #3638, MIP..$75.00
Nappytime Baby, #3818, complete, M............................$60.00
Nurse 'N Totsy Outfit, #LK7, MIP $25.00
Olivia Orange Kola Kiddle, #3730, MIP........................$80.00
Peter Pandiddle, #3547, NRFB.......................................$300.00
Pink Funny Bunny, #3532, MIP $65.00
Posies 'N Pink Skediddle Outfit, #3585, MIP $30.00
Rah Rah Skediddle, #3788, complete, M........................$150.00
Rapunzel & the Prince, #3783, MIP $150.00
Robin Hood & Maid Marion, #3785, MIP $150.00
Rolly Twiddle, #3519, complete, M................................$175.00

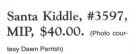

Santa Kiddle, #3597, MIP, $40.00. (Photo courtesy Dawn Parrish)

Romeo & Juliet, #3782, MIP..$150.00
Rosebud Kologne, #3702, MIP $75.00
Rosemary Roadster, #3642, complete, M $60.00
Shirley Skediddle, #3766, MIP $75.00
Shirley Strawberry, #3727, complete, M $50.00
Sizzly Friddle, #3513, complete, M $75.00

Sizzly Friddle, #3513, MIP, $300.00. (Photo courtesy Paris Langford)

Sleep 'N Totsy Outfit, #LK5, MIP $25.00
Sleeping Biddle, #3527, complete, M.............................$100.00
Slipsy Sliddle, #3754, complete, M $125.00
Snap-Happy Bedroom, #5172, complete, M $15.00
Snap-Happy Furniture, #5171, MIP................................$30.00
Snap-Happy Living Room, #5173, NMIP $20.00
Snoopy Skediddler & His Sopwith Camel, M $150.00
Suki Skediddle, #3767, complete, M...............................$25.00
Surfy Skediddle, #3517, complete, M.............................$75.00
Swingy Skediddle, #3789, MIP.......................................$200.00
Teeter Time Baby, #3817, complete, M $60.00
Teresa Touring Car, #3644, complete, M........................$60.00
Tessie Tractor, #3671, complete, NM..............................$150.00
Tiny Tiger, #3636, MIP $75.00
Tracy Trikediddle, #3769, complete, M $50.00
Trikey Triddle, #3515, complete, M $75.00
Vanilla Lilly, #2819, MIP..$25.00
Violet Kologne, #3713, MIP $60.00
Windy Fliddle, #3514, complete, M $85.00
World of the Kiddles Beauty Bazaar, #3586, NRFB $300.00

LITTLECHAPS

In 1964 Remco Industries created a family of four fashion dolls that represented an upper-middle class American family. The Littlechaps family consisted of the father, Dr. John Littlechap, his wife, Lisa, and their two children, Judy and Libby. Their clothing and fashion accessories were made in Japan and are of the finest quality. Because these dolls are not as pretty as other fashion dolls of the era and their size and placement of arms and legs made them awkward to dress, children had little interest in them at the time. This lack of interest during the

1960s has created shortages of them for collectors of today. Mint and complete outfits or outfits never-removed-from-box are especially desirable to Littlechap collectors. Values listed for loose clothing are for ensembles complete with all their small accessories. If only the main pieces of the outfit are available, then the value could go down significantly.

Advisor: Cindy Sabulis (S14)

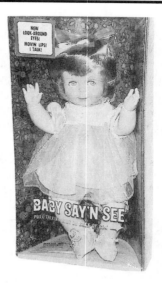

Baby See 'n Say, 1964, MIB, $150.00. (Photo courtesy Cindy Sabulis)

Dr. John Littlechap, MIB, from $65.00 to $70.00. (Photo courtesy Cindy Sabulis)

Carrying Case, EX	$40.00
Doll, Judy, MIB	$70.00
Doll, Libby, MIB	$45.00
Doll, Lisa, MIB	$65.00
Family Room, Bedroom or Doctor John's Office, EX, ea	$125.00
Outfit, Doctor John, EX, from $15 to	$30.00
Outfit, Doctor John, NRFB, from $30 to	$50.00
Outfit, Judy, EX, from $25 to	$40.00
Outfit, Judy, NRFB, from $35 to	$75.00
Outfit, Libby, EX, from $20 to	$35.00
Outfit, Libby, NRFB, from $35 to	$50.00
Outfit, Lisa, EX, from $20 to	$35.00
Outfit, Lisa, NRFB, from $35 to	$75.00

MATTEL TALKING DOLLS

For more information refer to *Talking Toys of the 20th Century* by Kathy and Don Lewis (Collector Books).

See also Character, TV, and Movie Collectibles; Disney.

Baby Beans, EX	$25.00
Baby Cheryl, 1965, 16", MIB	$200.00
Baby Colleen, Sears Exclusive, 1965, 15½", MIB	$100.00
Baby Drowsy, Black, 1968, 15", MIB	$175.00
Baby First Step, 1967, MIB	$225.00
Baby Flip-Flop, JC Penney Exclusive, 1970, MIB	$85.00
Baby Secret, 1966, red hair, 18", EX	$75.00
Baby Sing-A-Song, 1969, 16½", MIB	$150.00
Baby Small Talk, 1968, MIB	$125.00
Baby Teenietalk, 1966, orig dress, 17", VG	$75.00
Baby Whisper, 1968, 17½", MIB	$200.00

Chatty Patty, 1980s, MIB	$50.00
Cheerleader, 1970, several variations, MIB, ea	$75.00
Cynthia, M	$45.00
Drowsy Sleeper-Keeper, 1966, MIB	$125.00
Gramma & Grampa, 1968, MIB, ea	$150.00
Hi Dottie, Black, 1972, complete w/telephone, NM	$75.00
Little Sister Look 'N Say, Sears Exclusive, 18", M	$150.00
Matty the Talking Boy, 1961, MIB	$300.00
Randi Reader, 1968, 19½", MIB	$175.00
Sister Belle, 1961, MIB	$300.00
Sister Small Talk, 1968, blond hair, EX	$55.00
Somersalty, 1970, MIB	$200.00
Tatters, M	$85.00
Teachy Keen, Sears Exclusive, 1966, 16", MIB	$125.00

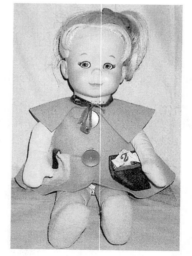

Teachy Keen, Sears Exclusive, 1966, 16", NM, $50.00. (Photo courtesy Cindy Sabulis)

Teachy Talk, 1970, MIB	$50.00
Timey Tell, MIB	$110.00

ROCKFLOWERS

Rockflowers were introduced in the early 1970s as Mattel's answer to Topper's Dawn Dolls. Rockflowers are 6½" tall and have wire articulated bodies that came with mod sunglasses attached to their heads. There were four girls and one boy in the series with eighteen groovy outfits that could be purchased separately. Each doll came with their own 45 rpm record, and the clothing packages were also in the shape of a 45 rpm record.

Advisor: Dawn Diaz (P2)

Case, Rockflowers on Stage, #4993 (3 dolls), vinyl, NM .**$15.00**
Case, Rockflowers, #4991 (single doll), vinyl, NM...........**$10.00**
Doll, Doug, #1177, NRFB, from $40 to.............................**$50.00**

Doll, Heather, NRFB, from $40.00 to $50.00. (Photo courtesy J. Michael Augustyniak)

Doll, Iris, NRFB, from $40 to **$50.00**
Doll, Lilac, #1167, NRFB, from $35 to **$50.00**
Doll, Rosemary, #1168, NRFB....................................**$50.00**
Gift Set, Rockflowers in Concert, w/Heather, Lilac & Rosemary, NRFB **$150.00**
Outfit, Flares 'N Lace, #4057, NRFP..............................**$15.00**
Outfit, Frontier Gingham, #4069, NRFP **$20.00**
Outfit, Jeans in Fringe, NRFP..**$15.00**
Outfit, Long in Fringe, #4050, NRFP..............................**$15.00**
Outfit, Overall Green, #4067, NRFP **$10.00**
Outfit, Tie Dye Maxi, #4053, NRFP................................**$15.00**
Outfit, Topped in Lace, #4058, NRFP.............................**$15.00**

SHANI

Mattel's Shani, Asha, Nichelle, and Jamal came onto the scene in the early '90s. Mattel lists the group as Barbie doll's friends. They came with stylish, colorful fashions and a shiny Corvette.

Accessory, Shani Corvette, #7981, MIB **$60.00**
Doll, Asha, #1752, coral & gold lamé gown, complete, MIB.**$65.00**
Doll, Beach Dazzle Asha, #5777, MIB.............................**$30.00**
Doll, Beach Dazzle Nichelle, #5775, MIB **$25.00**
Doll, Beach Dazzle Shani, #5774, MIB **$25.00**
Doll, Beach Streak Asha, #3457, MIB **$28.00**

Doll, Beach Streak Jamal, #3802, MIB.............................**$20.00**
Doll, Beach Streak Nichelle, #3456, MIB.........................**$20.00**
Doll, Beach Streak Shani, #3428, MIB **$20.00**

Doll, Jamal, #7795, MIB, $40.00. (Photo courtesy J. Michael Augustyniak)

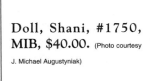

Doll, Jewel & Glitter Shani, #11215, MIB........................**$30.00**
Doll, Nichelle, #1751, pk gown w/yel bodice, MIB **$40.00**

Doll, Shani, #1750, MIB, $40.00. (Photo courtesy J. Michael Augustyniak)

Doll, Soul Train Asha, #10291, MIB................................**$30.00**
Doll, Soul Train Jamal, #10288, MIB **$25.00**
Doll, Soul Train Nichelle, #10290, MIB **$25.00**
Doll, Soul Train Shani, #10289, MIB...............................**$25.00**
Doll, Sun Jewel Shani, #10958 (clear jewels), MIB..........**$15.00**
Doll, Sun Jewel Shani, #10958 (colored jewels), MIB......**$12.00**
Outfit, #1872, wht leathery skirt & jacket w/gold blouse, wht pumps, MIP **$18.00**
Outfit, #1884, yel suit dress w/long skirt, brn suede suitcase & yel pumps, MIP **$18.00**

Outfit, #1896, fringed print jacket w/yel minidress & bl pumps, MIP $18.00

Outfit, #5967, gold lamé belted coat w/long shiny scarf & shoes, MIP $20.00

Outfit, #5968, blk gown w/gold lamé coat & blk shoes, MIP .$20.00

STRAWBERRY SHORTCAKE

It was around 1980 when Strawberry Shortcake came on the market with a bang. The line included everything to attract small girls — swimsuits, bed linens, blankets, anklets, underclothing, coats, shoes, sleeping bags, dolls and accessories, games, and many other delightful items. Strawberry Shortcake and her friends were short lived, lasting only until the middle of the decade.

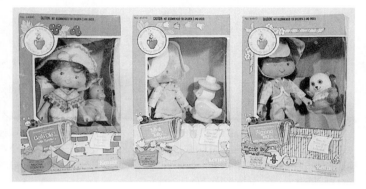

Dolls, Café Olé with Burrito, 6", MIB, $35.00; Mint Tulip with Marsh Mallard, 6", MIB, $25.00; Almond Tea with Marza Panda, 6", MIB, $25.00. (Photo courtesy June Moon)

Big Berry Trolley, 1982, EX $40.00
Doll, Angel Cake, 6", MIB $25.00
Doll, Apple Dumpling, 6", MIB $25.00
Doll, Apricot, 15", NM $35.00
Doll, Baby Needs a Name, 15", NM $35.00
Doll, Berry Baby Orange Blossom, 6", MIB $35.00
Doll, Butter Cookie, 6", MIB $25.00
Doll, Cherry Cuddler, 6", MIB $25.00
Doll, Lime Chiffon, 6", MIB $25.00
Doll, Raspberry Tart, 6", MIB $25.00
Doll, Strawberry Shortcake, 12", NRFB $45.00
Doll, Strawberry Shortcake, 15", NM $35.00
Dollhouse, M $150.00
Dollhouse Furniture, attic, 6-pc, rare, M $150.00
Dollhouse Furniture, bathroom, 5-pc, rare, M $65.00
Dollhouse Furniture, bedroom, 7-pc, rare, M $90.00
Dollhouse Furniture, kitchen, 11-pc, rare, M $100.00
Dollhouse Furniture, living room, 6-pc, rare, M $85.00
Figure, Almond Tea w/Marza Panda, PVC, 1", MOC $15.00
Figure, Cherry Cuddler w/Gooseberry, Strawberryland Miniatures, MIP, from $15 to $20.00
Figure, Lemon Meringue w/Frappe, PVC, 1", MOC $15.00
Figure, Lime Chiffon w/balloons, PVC, 1", MOC $15.00
Figure, Merry Berry Worm, MIB $35.00
Figure, Mint Tulip w/March Mallard, PVC, MOC $15.00

Figure, Purple Pieman w/Berry Bird, poseable, MIB $35.00
Figure, Raspberry Tart w/bowl of cherries, MOC $15.00
Figure, Sour Grapes w/Dregs, Strawberryland Miniatures, MIP, B5, from $15 to $20.00
Ice Skates, EX $35.00
Motorized Bicycle, EX $95.00
Roller Skates, EX $35.00
Sleeping Bag, EX $25.00
Storybook Play Case, M $35.00
Stroller, Coleco, 1981, M $85.00
Telephone, Strawberry Shortcake figure, battery-op, EX ..$85.00

SUNSHINE FAMILY BY MATTEL

The Sunshine Family was produced and sold from 1974 to 1982. The first family consisted of the father, Steve, his wife, Steffie, and their daughter, Baby Sweets. In 1976 Mattel added The Happy Family (an African-American family consisting of mom, dad, and their two children). The line also included grandparents, playsets, vehicles, and a lot of other accessories that made them so much fun to play with.

Camping Craft Kit, 1974, MIP, minimum value $35.00
Craft Store, 1976, MIB, minimum value $70.00
Doll, Little Hon (Black), w/nursery set, 1977, MIB, minimum value $35.00
Doll, Little Sweets, w/nursery set, 1975, MIB, minimum value ..$35.00

Dolls, Steve and Steffie, NM, each from $15.00 to $20.00; New Baby, NM, $15.00; Sister, NM, $20.00. (Photo courtesy Cindy Sabulis)

Doll & Craft Case, Sears Exclusive, 1977, EX, minimum value ..$25.00
Doll Set, Grandparents, 1976, MIB, minimum value $60.00
Doll Set, Happy Family (Black), 1975, MIB, minimum value .$60.00
Doll Set, Steve, Stephie & Baby Sweets, 1976, MIB, minimum value $65.00

Doll Set, Watch 'Em Grow Greenhouse, w/3 dolls, craft kit & seeds, limited edition, 1977, MIB, minimum value .$100.00
Family Farm, 1977, rare, MIB, minimum value $140.00
Kitchen Craft Kit, 1974, MIB, minimum value $35.00
Nursery Craft Kit, 1976, MIP...$25.00
Outfits, several variations, 1975-76, MIP, minimum value, ea.$15.00
Sunshine Family Home, 4 rooms w/furniture, 1974, EX, minimum value...$65.00
Surrey Cycle, 1975, MIB, minimum value $35.00
Van w/Piggyback Shack, 1975, MIB, minimum value $50.00

TAMMY

In 1962 the Ideal Novelty and Toy Company introduced their teenage Tammy doll. Slightly pudgy and not quite as sophisticated looking as some of the teen fashion dolls on the market at the time, Tammy's innocent charm captivated consumers. Her extensive wardrobe and numerous accessories added to her popularity with children. Tammy had a car, a house, and her own catamaran. In addition, a large number of companies obtained licenses to issue products using the 'Tammy' name. Everything from paper dolls to nurse's kits were made with Tammy's image on them. Her success was not confined to the United States; she was also successful in Canada and several other European countries.

Interest in Tammy has risen quite a bit in the past few years according to Cindy Sabulis, co-author of *Tammy, the Ideal Teen* (Collector Books). Values have gone up and supply for quality mint-in-box items is going down. Loose, played-with dolls are still readily available and can be found for as low as $10.00 at doll shows. Values are given for mint-in-box dolls.

Advisor: Cindy Sabulis (S14)

Accessory Pak, baseball bat, catcher's mask, mitt & ball, unknown #, NRFP $35.00
Accessory Pak, electric skillet & frying pan w/lids, unknown #, NRFP $50.00
Accessory Pak, luggage case, airline ticket & camera, #9183-0, NRFP $25.00
Accessory Pak, Misty Hair Color Kit, #9828-5, MIB........$75.00
Accessory Pak, pizza, princess phone, Tammy's Telephone Directory, wht sandals, #9184-80, NRFP $25.00
Accessory Pak, plate of crackers, juice, glasses, sandals & newspaper, #9179-3, NRFP $30.00
Accessory Pak, poodle on leash, red vinyl purse & wht sneakers, #9186-80, NRFP $25.00
Accessory Pak, tennis racket, score book & sneakers, #9188-8, NRFP, S14 ....$15.00
Case, Dodi, gr background, EX, S14.................................$30.00
Case, Misty, Dutch door-type, blk, EX $30.00
Case, Misty, pk & wht, EX..$25.00
Case, Misty & Tammy, dbl telephone, gr or pk, ea $25.00
Case, Misty & Tammy, hatbox style, EX $30.00
Case, Pepper, front snap closure, red or coral, EX $15.00
Case, Pepper, hatbox style, turq, EX.................................$40.00
Case, Pepper, yel or gr, EX $20.00
Case, Pepper & Dodi, front opening, bl, EX $30.00
Case, Pepper & Patti, Montgomery Ward's Exclusive, red, EX.$50.00

Case, Tammy, suitcase type w/doll compartment, closet & accessory compartment, red w/clear see-through front, EX.$50.00

Case, Tammy and Her Friends, pink or green, EX, $30.00. (Photo courtesy Cindy Sabulis)

Case, Tammy Beau & Arrow, hatbox style, bl or red, EX .$40.00
Case, Tammy Evening in Paris, bl, blk or red, EX............$20.00
Case, Tammy Model Miss, hatbox style, bl or blk, EX $30.00
Case, Tammy Model Miss, red or blk, EX.........................$25.00
Case, Tammy Traveller, red or gr, EX $45.00
Doll, Bud, MIB, minimum value $600.00
Doll, Dodi, MIB $75.00
Doll, Glamour Misty the Miss Clairol Doll, MIB $150.00
Doll, Grown Up Tammy, MIB...$85.00
Doll, Grown Up Tammy (Black), MIB $300.00
Doll, Misty, MIB $100.00
Doll, Misty (Black), MIB, minimum value $600.00
Doll, Patti, MIB $200.00
Doll, Pepper, MIB $65.00

Doll, Pos'n Misty and Her Telephone Booth, MIB, $125.00. (Photo courtesy Cindy Sabulis and Susan Weglewski)

Doll, Pepper ('carrot'-colored hair), MIB......................$75.00
Doll, Pepper (Canadian version), MIB $75.00
Doll, Pepper (trimmer body & smaller face), MIB...........$75.00
Doll, Pos'n Dodi, M (decorated box) $150.00
Doll, Pos'n Dodi, M (plain box) $75.00
Doll, Pos'n Pepper, MIB...$75.00
Doll, Pos'n Pete, MIB $125.00
Doll, Pos'n Salty, MIB $125.00
Doll, Pos'n Tammy & Her Telephone Booth, MIB.........$100.00
Doll, Pos'n Ted, MIB $100.00

Doll, Tammy, MIB, $85.00. (Photo courtesy McMasters Doll Auctions)

Doll, Tammy's Dad, MIB...$65.00
Doll, Tammy's Mom, MIB..$75.00
Doll, Ted, MIB $50.00
Outfit, Dad & Ted, blazer & slacks, #9477-1, NRFP $20.00
Outfit, Dad & Ted, pajamas & slippers, #9456-5, MIP $20.00
Outfit, Dad & Ted, sports car coat & cap, #9467-2, NRFP ..$20.00
Outfit, Dad & Ted, sweater, shorts & socks, #9476-3, MIP..$25.00
Outfit, Pepper, After School, #9318-7, complete, M $25.00
Outfit, Pepper, Anchors Away, #9316-1, complete, M $30.00
Outfit, Pepper, Flower Girl, #9332-8, complete, M $45.00
Outfit, Pepper, Happy Holiday, #9317-9, complete, M.....$40.00
Outfit, Pepper, Miss Gadabout, #9331-0, MIP $50.00
Outfit, Pepper & Dodi, Light & Lacy, #9305-4, MIP........$45.00
Outfit, Pepper & Dodi, Sun 'n Surf, #9321-1, MIP...........$50.00
Outfit, Tammy, Beach Party, #9056-3 or #9906-9, complete, M .$45.00
Outfit, Tammy, Career Girl, #9945-7, complete, M..........$75.00
Outfit, Tammy, Cutie Coed, #9132-2 or #9932-5, complete, M..$45.00
Outfit, Tammy, Jet Set, #9155-3 or #9943-2, MIP $55.00
Outfit, Tammy, Knit Knack, #9094-4 or #9917-6, complete, M..$25.00
Outfit, Tammy, Opening Night, #9954-9, MIP.................$75.00
Outfit, Tammy, Private Secretary, #9939-0, MIP $75.00
Outfit, Tammy's Mom, Evening in Paris, #9421-9, complete, M.$40.00
Outfit, Tammy's Mom, Lazy Days, #9418-5, MIP.............$50.00
Pak Clothing, afternoon dress & shoes, #9345-2, NRFP ..$25.00
Pak Clothing, nightgown, sandals & 3-pc fruit set, #9242-9, NRFP $25.00
Pak Clothing, pedal pushers, orange juice, newspaper & hanger, #9224-7, NRFP $25.00

Pak Clothing, sheath dress, blk belt, shoes & hanger, #9243-7, NRFP $30.00
Pak Clothing, short-sleeved blouse, red glasses & hanger, #9231-2, NRFP $15.00
Pak Clothing, skirt, belt, handkerchief, date book & hanger, #9220-5, MIP $30.00
Pak Clothing, skirt, shoes & hanger, #9221-3, NRFP.......$20.00
Pak Clothing, sleeveless blouse, necklace & hanger, #9222-1, NRFP $20.00
Pak Clothing, sweater, scarf & hanger, #9244-5, NRFP ...$25.00
Pepper's Jukebox, M..$65.00
Pepper's Pony, MIB...$250.00
Pepper's Treehouse, MIB..$150.00
Tammy & Ted Catamaran, MIB................................$200.00
Tammy Bubble Bath Set, NRFB.................................$75.00
Tammy Dress-Up Kit, Colorforms, 1964, complete, MIB.$30.00
Tammy Hair Dryer, sq or rnd case, NM.......................$50.00
Tammy's Bed, Dress & Chair, MIB..............................$85.00
Tammy's Car, MIB..$75.00
Tammy's Ideal House, M, minimum value $100.00
Tammy's Jukebox, M $50.00
Tammy's Magic Mirror Fashion Show, Winthrop-Atkins, NRFB.$50.00

TRESSY

American Character's Tressy doll was produced in this country from 1963 to 1967. The unique feature of this 11½" fashion doll was that her hair 'grew' by pushing a button on her stomach. Tressy also had a little (9") sister named Cricket. Numerous fashions and accessories were produced for these two dolls. Never-removed-from-box Tressy and Cricket items are rare, so unless indicated, values listed are for loose, mint items. A never-removed-from-box item's worth is at least double its loose value.

Advisor: Cindy Sabulis (S14)

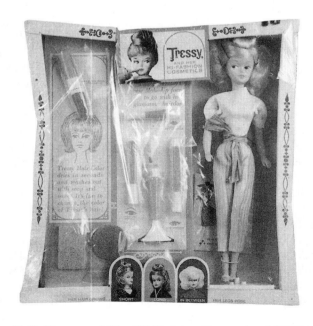

Doll, Tressy and Her Hi-Fashion Cosmetics, NRFB, $145.00. (Photo courtesy McMasters Doll Auctions)

Apartment $250.00
Beauty Salon $200.00
Case, Cricket...$30.00
Case, Tressy..$30.00
Doll, American Character Tressy, MIB $100.00
Doll, Pre-Teen Tressy $60.00
Doll, Tressy in Miss America Character outfit, NM $65.00
Doll, Tressy in orig dress $35.00
Doll, Tressy w/Magic Makeup Face....................$25.00
Doll Clothes Pattern $10.00
Gift Pak w/Doll & Clothing, NRFB, minimum value $100.00
Hair Accessory Pak, NRFB................................$20.00

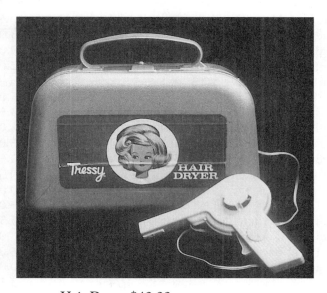

Hair Dryer, $40.00. (Photo courtesy Cindy Sabulis)

Hair or Cosmetic Accessory Kits, ea minimum value $50.00
Millinery $175.00
Outfits, MOC, ea $30.00
Outfits, NRFB, ea minimum value $65.00

UPSY DOWNSY DOLLS BY MATTEL

The Upsy Downsy dolls were made by Mattel during the late 1960s. They were small, 2½" to 3½", made of vinyl and plastic. Some of the group were 'Upsy dolls' that walked on their feet, while others were 'Downsy dolls' that walked or rode fantasy animals while upsidedown.

Advisor: Dawn Diaz (P2)

Baby So-High, #3828, complete, M $50.00
Downy Dilly, #3832, complete, M $50.00
Downy Dilly, #3832, NRFB............................$100.00
Flossy Glossy, #3827, doll & playland, EX.........$25.00
Funny Feeder, #3834, Gooey Chooey only, EX $25.00
Hairy Hurry Downsy Wizzer, #3838, complete, EX.........$100.00
Miss Information, #3831, NRFB $100.00
Mother What Now, #3829, complete, EX $50.00
Pocus Hocus, #3820, complete, M $50.00
Pudgy Fudgy, #3826, NRFB $100.00
Tickle Pinkle & Her Bugabout Car, MIB, from $75 to ...$100.00

Farm Toys

It's entirely probable that more toy tractors have been sold than real ones. They've been made to represent all makes and models, of plastic, cast iron, diecast metal, and even wood. They've been made in at least 1/16th scale, 1/32nd, 1/43rd, and 1/64th. If you buy a 1/16th-scale replica, that small piece of equipment would have to be sixteen times larger to equal the size of the real item. Limited editions (meaning that a specific number will be made and no more) and commemorative editions (made for special events) are usually very popular with collectors. Many models on the market today are being made by the Ertl company.

Advisor: John Rammacher (S5)
See also Cast Iron, Farm; Diecast.

AG Chem Terra Gator Liquid Spreader, Ertl, #12043, 1/64 scale, MIB, S5 ....$8.50
AG Chem 8103 Terra Gator Dry Fertilizer Load, Ertl, #12044, 1/64 scale, MIB, S5 ....$8.50
Agco Allis R-52 Combine, Ertl, #1282, 1/64 scale, MIB, S5..$10.00
Agco Allis 6670 Row Crop, Ertl, #1214, 1/64 scale, MIB, S5 .$3.50
Agco Allis 6690 Tractor w/Duals, Ertl, #1286, 1/64 scale, MIB, S5 ....$3.50
Agco Allis 6690 Tractor w/4 Post ROPS, Ertl, #1239, 1/64 scale, MIB, S5 ....$3.50
Allis-Chalmers Historical Set, Ertl, #13187, 1/64 scale, 4-pc, MIB, S5 ....$15.00
Allis-Chalmers 7060 Tractor w/Cab, Ertl, #13185, 1/16 scale, MIB, S5 ....$35.00
C&J Systems Liquid Fertilizer Spreader, Ertl, #4433, 1/64 scale, MIB, S5 ....$5.00
Case Agriking 970 Tractor, Ertl, #4279, 1/16 scale, MIB, S5..$32.00
Case IH C-90 Tractor (1998 Farm Show), Ertl, #4601, 1/16 scale, MIB, S5 ....$60.00
Case IH Cotton Express Picker, Ertl, #4300, 1/64 scale, MIB, S5.$12.00
Case IH Forge Harvester, Ertl, #201, 1/64 scale, MIB, S5...$2.50
Case IH Hay Rake, Ertl, #210, 1/64 scale, MIB, S5 ....$3.00
Case IH Historical Set, Ertl, #238, 1/64 scale, 2-pc, MIB, S5..$5.50
Case IH Magnum MX180 Tractor, Ertl, #4550, 1/64 scale, MIB, S5 ....$4.00
Case IH Magnum MX240 Tractor (1999 Farm Show), Ertl, #4281NA, 1/64 scale, MIB, S5 ....$10.00
Case IH Maxxum MX100 Tractor w/Loader, Ertl, #4270, 1/64 scale, MIB...$5.00
Case IH Maxxum MX120 Tractor (1997 Farm Show), Ertl, #4487, 1/16 scale, MIB, S5 ....$45.00
Case IH Round Baler, Ertl, #274, 1/64 scale, MIB, S5 ....$3.50
Case IH SPX 4260 Sprayer, Ertl, #1411, 1/64 scale, MIB, S5.$8.00
Case IH Tractor w/Endloader, Ertl, #212, 1/64 scale, MIB, S5..$5.00
Case IH 12-Row 900 Planter, Ertl, #656, 1/64 scale, MIB, S5.$4.50
Case IH 1660 Combine, Ertl, #655, 1/64 scale, MIB, S5 ..$11.00
Case IH 2188 Combine (1995 Farm Show), Ertl, #4607, 1/64 scale, MIB, S5 ....$20.00
Case IH 2366 Axial-Flow Combine, Ertl, #4614, 1/64 scale, MIB, S5 ....$10.00

Case IH 2388 Combine, Ertl, #14176, 1/64 scale, MIB, S5 .**$12.00**

Case IH 5130 Row Crop, Ertl, #229, 1/64 scale, MIB, S5...**$3.00**

Case IH 5130 Row Crop (1991 Farm Show), Ertl, #229, 1/64 scale, MIB, S5 ....**$10.00**

Case IH 7150 FWA (1992 Farm Show), Ertl, #285, 1/64 scale, MIB, S5 ....**$10.00**

Case IH 8212 Mower Conditioner, Ertl, #4362, 1/64 scale, MIB, S5 ....**$4.00**

Case IH 8920 Tractor w/Loader, Ertl, #4289, 1/64 scale, MIB, S5 ....**$4.00**

Case IH 9260 4WD (1993 Farm Show), Ertl, #231, 1/64 scale, MIB, S5 ....**$9.00**

Case STX375 4-Wheel Drive Tractor, Ertl, #14003, 1/16 scale, MIB, S5 ....**$70.00**

Case 090XT Skid Steer Loader, Ertl, #4216, 1/64 scale, MIB, S5......................................**$25.00**

Case 0930 Precision #12 Tractor, Ertl, #4284, 1/16 scale, MIB, S5 ....**$110.00**

Case 1470 Traction King, Ertl, #4332, 1/64 scale, MIB, S5 .**$6.00**

Caterpillar Flotation Liquid Fertilizer Spreader, Ertl, #2324, 1/64 scale, MIB, S5 ....**$5.00**

Caterpillar Flotation VFS50 Tractor w/Gravity Wagon, Ertl, #2326, 1/64 scale, MIB, S5 ....**$5.00**

Chevy Grain Truck (1950), Ertl, #4633, 1/64 scale, MIB, S5..**$6.00**

Deutz-Allis 7085 Tractor (1990 Farm Show), Ertl, #1260, 1/64 scale, MIB, S5 ....**$12.00**

Deutz-Allis 7085 Tractor w/Loader, Ertl, #2233, 1/64 scale, MIB, S5 ....**$5.00**

Deutz-Allis 9150 Tractor (Orlando Show), Ertl, #1280, 1/16 scale, MIB, S5 ....**$200.00**

Farmall A Tractor, Ertl, #14177, 1/16 scale, MIB, S5 ....**$24.00**

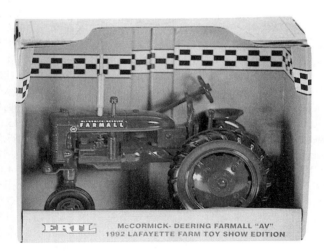

Farmall 'AV' Tractor, Ertl, #25-TA, 1992 Lafayette Farm Toy Show Edition, 1 of 3,000, MIB, $35.00.

Farmall F-20 Precision Tractor, Ertl, #638, 1/16 scale, MIB, S5..**$100.00**

Farmall H Tractor, #4441, 1/16 scale, MIB, S5 ....**$25.00**

Farmall 140 Tractor (1995 Farm Show), Ertl, #4741, 1/16 scale, MIB, S5 ....**$35.00**

Farmall 230 Tractor, Ertl, #14040, 1/16 scale, MIB, S5 ....**$25.00**

Farmall 300 Tractor, Ertl, #14000, 1/16 scale, MIB, S5 ....**$25.00**

Farmall 340 Crawler, Ertl, #4734, 1/67 scale, MIB, S5 .....**$25.00**

Farmall 400 Precision Tractor, Ertl, #14007, 1/16 scale, MIB, S5 ....**$110.00**

Farmall 560 w/Mounted Picker & Wagon, Ertl, #14073, 1/64 scale, MIB, S5 ....**$10.00**

Farmall 856 Tractor, Ertl, #14170, 1/64 scale, MIB, S5.......**$6.00**

Ford F Tractor (Collector's Edition), Ertl, #872, 1/16 scale, MIB, S5 ....**$45.00**

Ford Foxfire NAA Tractor, Ertl, #3074, 1/16 scale, MIB, S5..**$24.00**

Ford Foxfire 771 Tractor, Ertl, #3053, 1/16 scale, MIB, S5 .**$24.00**

Ford New Holland Combine, Ertl, #815, 1/64 scale, MIB, S5 .**$15.00**

Ford New Holland TR97 Combine, Ertl, #815, 1/64 scale, MIB, S5 ....**$10.00**

Ford Pickup w/Horse Trailer, Ertl, #4564, 1/64 scale, MIB, S5 .**$6.00**

Ford Super Major 5000 Tractor, Ertl, #928, 1/64 scale, MIB, S5 .**$3.50**

Ford TW35 Tractor, Ertl, #899, 1/64 scale, MIB, S6..........**$3.00**

Ford 621 Tractor, Ertl, #13529, 1/16 scale, MIB, S5 ....**$22.00**

Ford 640 Tractor, Ertl, #3054, 1/16 scale, MIB, S4 ....**$22.00**

Ford 641 Tractor w/Precision Series Loader, Ertl, #383, 1/16 scale, MIB, S5 ....**$135.00**

Ford 4000 Tractor, Ertl, #3024, 1/64 scale, MIB, S5............**$3.50**

Ford 5000 Tractor, Ertl, #3293, 1/64 scale, MIB, S5............**$4.00**

Ford 5640 Tractor w/Loader, Ertl, #334, 1/64 scale, MIB, S5 .**$5.00**

Ford 6640 Row Crop, Ertl, #332, 1/64 scale, MIB, S5.........**$3.50**

Ford 7740 Row Crop (Collector's Edition), Ertl, #873, 1/16 scale, MIB, S5 ....**$50.00**

Ford 7740 Tractor w/Loader, Ertl, #387, 1/64 scale, MIB, S5 ..**$5.00**

Ford 7840 Tractor, Ertl, #336, 1/64 scale, MIB, S5.............**$3.50**

Ford 7840 Tractor w/Duals, Ertl, #335, 1/64 scale, MIB, S5.**$3.00**

Ford 7840 Tractor w/Loader, Ertl, #3297, 1/64 scale, MIB, S5..**$5.00**

Ford 8 N Tractor, Ertl, #843, 1/16 scale, MIB, S5 ....**$20.00**

Ford 8340 Tractor w/Duals, Ertl, #388, 1/74 scale, MIB, S5.**$3.50**

Ford 8340 Tractor w/4-Wheel Drive (Collector's Edition), Ertl, #877, 1/16 scale, MIB, S5 ....**$50.00**

Ford 901 Power Master Tractor, Ertl, #927, 1/64 scale, MIB, S5 .**$5.00**

Fordson Super Major Tractor, Ertl, #850DO, 1/16 scale, MIB, $30.00.

Fordson Tractor, Ertl, #2526, 1/43 scale, MIB, S5...........**$650.00**

Genesis 8770 Tractor, Ertl, #391, 1/64 scale, MIB, S5 ....**$3.50**

Genesis 8870 Tractor w/4-Wheel Drive, Ertl, #392, 1/64 scale, MIB, S5 ....**$3.50**

Hesston Mower Conditioner, Ertl, #2068, 1/64 scale, MIB, S5...**$3.50**

Hesston SL-30 Skid Steer Loader, Ertl, #2267, 1/64 scale, MIB, S5 ....$4.50

IH I-D9 Tractor (1993 Farm Show), Ertl, #4611, 1/16 scale, MIB, S5 ....$35.00

IH 460 Precision Tractor #11, Ertl, #4355, 1/16 scale, MIB, S5 .$110.00

IH 560 Gas Tractor, Ertl, #4830, 1/64 scale, MIB, S5 ....$4.00

IH 560 Tractor, Ertl, #14035, 1/16 scale, MIB, S5 ....$28.00

IH 560 Tractor w/Precision #14 Corn Picker, Ertl, #14060, 1/16 scale, MIB, S5 ....$175.00

IH 815 Combine, Ertl, #4354, 1/64 scale, MIB, S5...........$10.00

IHC Famous Engine, Ertl, #615, 1/16 scale, MIB, S5 ....$20.00

International 1456 Diesel Tractor w/Cab, Ertl, #2311, 1/16 scale, MIB, S5 ....$30.00

International 756 WF Tractor, Ertl, #2308, 1/16 scale, MIB, S5 .$30.00

John Deere A NF Tractor, Ertl, #539, 1/16 scale, MIB, S5 .$18.00

John Deere BN Tractor, Ertl, #5902, 1/16 scale, MIB, S5.$22.00

John Deere C&J Liquid Fertilizer Spreader, Ertl, #5089, 1/64 scale, MIB, S5 ....$5.00

John Deere Combine, 12½" long, MIB, $330.00. (Photo courtesy Collectors Auction Services)

John Deere Compact Utility Trailer, Ertl, #581, 1/16 scale, MIB, S5 ....$16.00

John Deere CTS II Combine, Ertl, #5172, 1/64 scale, MIB, S5 .$10.00

John Deere CTS Rice Combine, Ertl, #5029, 1/64 scale, MIB, S5 ....$10.00

John Deere D Tractor, Ertl, #5179, 1/16 scale, MIB, S5 ...$25.00

John Deere Field Cultivator, Ertl, #15081, 1/64 scale, MIB, S5.$8.00

John Deere Forage Harvester, Ertl, #566, 1/64 scale, MIB, S5.$3.25

John Deere G Tractor, Ertl, #5104, 1/16 scale, MIB, S5 ...$25.00

John Deere H Tractor, Ertl, #15034, 1/16 scale, MIB, S5 .$22.00

John Deere Historical Set, Ertl, #5523, 1/64 scale, 4-pc, MIB, S5...$10.00

John Deere Hydra-Push Spreader, Ertl, #574, 1/64 scale, MIB, S5 ....$3.25

John Deere Skid Steer Loader, Ertl, #15159, 1/16 scale, MIB, S5 ....$18.00

John Deere Skid Steer Loader, Ertl #569, 1/16 scale, MIB, S5 ..$18.50

John Deere Sprayer, #5752, 1/64 scale, MIB, S5 ....$10.00

John Deere Utility Tractor, Ertl, #15146, 1/16 scale, MIB, S5 ..$15.00

John Deere Vintage Harvesting Set, Ertl, #15014, 1/64 scale, MIB, S5 ....$18.00

John Deere Waterloo Engine, Ertl, #5645, 1/16 scale, MIB, S5 .$20.00

John Deere 40 Crawler, Ertl, #5072, 1/16 scale, MIB, S5 .$26.00

John Deere 60 Narrow Front Tractor, Ertl, #15189, 1/16 scale, MIB, S5..$24.00

John Deere 70 Tractor, Ertl, #5611, 1/16 scale, MIB, S5 ..$20.00

John Deere 83 Tractor, Ertl, #5063, 1/64 scale, MIB, S5.....$4.00

John Deere 95 Combine, #5819, 1/64 scale, MIB, S5.......$10.00

John Deere 338 Rectangular Baler, Ertl, #5646, 1/64 scale, MIB, S5...$3.50

John Deere 430 Crawler, Ertl, #5771, 1/16 scale, MIB, S5.$22.00

John Deere 535 Round Baler, Ertl, #577, 1/64 scale, MIB, S5 ..$3.25

John Deere 0630 Tractor w/Corn Picker & Wagon, Ertl, #15086, 1/64 scale, MIB, S5 ....$10.50

John Deere 720 Precision #18 Tractor, Ertl, #15165, 1/16 scale .$125.00

John Deere 1939 Model B Tractor (Collector's Edition), Ertl, #5822, 1/16 scale, MIB, S5 ....$40.00

John Deere 4010 Diesel Tractor (1996 National Toy Show), Ertl, #5725, 1/43 scale, MIB, S5 ....$25.00

John Deere 4010 Tractor, Ertl, #5716, 1/16 scale, MIB, S5.$25.00

John Deere 4040 Tractor, Ertl, #5133, 1/16 scale, MIB, S5.$30.00

John Deere 4230 Diesel Tractor (1998 Farm Show), Ertl, #5131, 1/43 scale, MIB, S5 ....$28.00

John Deere 4440 Precision #17 Tractor, Ertl, #15077, 1/16 scale, MIB, S5..$120.00

John Deere 4450 Tractor, Ertl, #15160, 1/16 scale, MIB, S5 .$25.00

John Deere 6210 Tractor, Ertl, #5170, 1/64 scale, MIB, S5.$3.50

John Deere 6400 Tractor w/Loader, Ertl #5916, 1/16 scale, MIB, S5 ....$38.00

John Deere 6410 Tractor w/Loader, Ertl, #5069, 1/16 scale, MIB, S5 ....$38.00

John Deere 6410 Tractor w/Loader, Ertl, #5169, 1/64 scale, MIB, S5 ....$5.00

John Deere 7610 Tractor, Ertl, #15128, 1/16 scale, MIB, S5 .$45.00

John Deere 8200 Tractor, Ertl, #5064, 1/64 scale, MIB, S5.$4.00

John Deere 8400T Tractor, Ertl, #5051, 1/64 scale, MIB $6.50

John Deere 9976 Cotton Picker, Ertl, #5765, 1/64 scale, MIB, S5...$10.00

Massey-Ferguson 4-Tractor Historical Set, Ertl, #13192, 1/64 scale, MIB, S5 ....$15.00

Massey-Ferguson 1155 Tractor, Ertl, #13170, 1/16 scale, MIB, S5..$40.00

Massey-Ferguson 3070 Tractor w/Front-Wheel Drive, Ertl, #1107, 1/64 scale, MIB, S5 ....$3.50

Massey-Ferguson 3070 Tractor w/Loader, Ertl, #1109, 1/64 scale, MIB, S5 ....$5.00

Massey-Ferguson 3120 Tractor, Ertl, #1177, 1/64 scale, MIB, S5 .$3.00

Massey-Ferguson 3120 Tractor w/Loader, Ertl, #1109, 1/64 scale, MIB, S5 ....$4.50

Massey-Ferguson 3140 Tractor w/Duals, Ertl, #1176, 1/64 scale, MIB, S5 ....$3.50

Massey-Ferguson 3140 Tractor w/Front-Wheel Drive, Ertl, #1107, 1/64 scale, MIB, S5 ....$3.50

Massey-Ferguson 8280 Tractor w/Duals, Ertl, #13052, 1/64 scale, MIB, S5 ....$6.00

Massey-Harris 55 Tractor (1992 National Farm Toy Show), Ertl, #1131, 1/43 scale, MIB, S5 ....$25.00

Minneapolis-Moline G-750 Tractor (1994 National Show), Ertl, #2291, 1/43 scale, MIB, S5 ....$20.00

New Holland Baler, Ertl #337, 1/64 scale, MIB, S5 ....$2.25

New Holland Box Spreader, Ertl, #308, 1/64 scale, MIB, S5..**$3.00**
New Holland Forage Harvester, Ertl, #372, 1/64 scale, MIB, S5.**$3.50**
New Holland Forage Wagon, #373, 1/64 scale, MIB, S5 ....**$3.00**
New Holland Model 40 w/Forage Blower, Ertl, #343, MIB, S5 .**$3.50**
New Holland Skid Loader, Ertl, #381, 1/64 scale, MIB, S5..**$4.50**
New Holland TM150 Tractor w/4-Wheel Drive, Ertl, #13560,
      1/16 scale, MIB, S5 ....**$40.00**
New Holland TR-98 Combine, Ertl, #13500, 1/64 scale, MIB,
      S5 ....**$10.00**
New Holland Tractor & Implement Set, Ertl, #13558, 1/64
      scale, MIB, S5 ....**$20.00**
New Holland Wing Disk, Ertl, #3049, 1/64 scale, MIB, S5..**$4.00**
New Holland 8260 Tractor (1997 National Farm Show), Ertl,
      #3050, 1/43 scale, MIB, S5 ....**$22.00**
New Holland 8560 Tractor, Ertl, #3032, 1/43 scale, MIB, S5.**$12.00**

Oliver Baler, Slik, #9851, 1952, 10", EX (no box), $255.00; MIB, $500.00.

Oliver Two-Bottom Plow, Slik, #9850, 1952, 9" long, EX (no box), $185.00; MIB, $380.00.

Oliver 1655 Tractor w/Cab, Ertl, #13186, 1/16 scale, MIB, S5 .**$35.00**
Oliver 1655 Tractor w/Wide Front, Ertl, #4472, 1/16 scale, MIB,
      S5 ....**$20.00**
Tractor Set (50th Anniversary), Ertl, #4496, 1/64 scale, MIB,
      S5..**$30.00**

Fisher-Price

In 1930 Herman Fisher, backed by Irving Price, Elbert Hubbard, and Helen Schelle, formed one of the most successful toy companies ever to exist. Located in East Aurora, New York, the company has seen many changes since then, the most notable being the changes in ownership. From 1930 to 1968, it was owned by the individuals mentioned previously and a few stockholders. In 1969 it became an acquisition of Quaker Oats, and in June of 1991 it became independently owned. In Novem-

ber of 1993, one of the biggest sell-outs in the toy industry took place: Fisher-Price became a subdivision of Mattel.

There are a few things to keep in mind when collecting Fisher-Price toys. You should count on a little edge wear as well as some wear and fading to the paint. Pull toys found in mint condition are truly rare and command a much higher value, especially if you find one with its original box. This also applies to playsets; but to command higher prices, they must also be complete, with no chew/teeth marks or plastic fading. Another very important rule to remember is there are no standard colors for pieces that came with a playset. Fisher-Price often substituted a piece of a different color when they ran short. Please note that the dates on the toys indicate their copyright date and not the date they were manufactured.

The company put much time and thought into designing their toys. They took care to operate by their five-point creed: to make toys with (1) intrinsic play value, (2) ingenuity, (3) strong construction, (4) good value for the money, and (5) action. Some of the most sought-after pull toys are those bearing the Walt Disney logo.

The ToyFest limited editions are a series of toys produced in conjunction with ToyFest, an annual weekend of festivities for young and old alike held in East Aurora, New York. It is sponsored by the 'Toy Town USA Museum' and is held every year in August. Fisher-Price produces a limited-edition toy for this event; these are listed at the end of this category. (For more information on ToyFest and the museum, write to Toy Town Museum, P.O. Box 238, East Aurora, NY 14052; see display ad this section.) For more information on Fisher-Price toys we recommend *Fisher-Price, A Historical Rarity Value Guide*, by John J. Murray and Bruce R. Fox; and *Fisher-Price Toys* by our advisor Brad Cassity.

Additional information may be obtained through the Fisher-Price Collectors' Club who publish a quarterly newsletter; their address may be found in their display ad (this section) and in the Directory under Clubs, Newsletters, and Other Publications.

Note: With the ever increasing influence of the Internet it is becoming harder and harder to establish book value. A toy can sell for 100% more than the book value or 75% less on the Internet. The prices we have listed here are derived from dealers, price lists, and toy shows and represent values for very good examples that show little edge and paint wear and minimal fading. Add 20% to 40% for the original box.

Advisor: Brad Cassity (C13)

See also Building Blocks and Construction Toys; Catalogs; Character, TV, and Movie Collectibles; Dollhouse Furniture; Dollhouses; Dolls; Optical Toys; Puppets; and other specific categories.

#5 Bunny Cart, 1948-49, C13 ....**$50.00**
#6 Ducky Cart, 1948-49, C13..**$50.00**
#7 Doggy Racer, 1942-43, C13..**$150.00**
#7 Looky Fire Truck, 1950-53 & Easter 1954, C13...........**$75.00**
#8 Bouncy Racer, 1960-62, C13 ....**$40.00**
#10 Bunny Cart, 1940-42, C13 ....**$65.00**
#11 Ducky Cart, 1940-42, C13..**$50.00**
#12 Bunny Truck, 1941-42, C13 ....**$65.00**
#14 Ducky Daddles, 1941, C13 ....**$85.00**
#15 Bunny Cart, 1946-48, C13 ....**$50.00**

#16 Ducky Cart, 1946-48, C13.................................$50.00

#20 Animal Cutouts, 1942-46, duck, elephant, pony or Scottie dog, C13, ea $50.00

#28 Bunny Egg Cart, 1950, C13 ....$50.00

#50 Bunny Chick Tandem Cart, 1953-54, no number on toy, C13..$75.00

#51 Ducky Cart, 1950, C13 ....$50.00

#52 Rabbit Cart, 1950, C13 ....$50.00

#75 Baby Duck Tandem Cart, 1953-54, no number on toy, C13.$100.00

#100 Dr Doodle, 1931, C13......................................$700.00

#100 Dr Doodle, 1995, Fisher-Price limited edition of 5,000, 1st in series, C13 ....$100.00

#100 Musical Sweeper, 1950-52, plays Whistle While You Work, C13..$75.00

#101 Granny Doodle & Family, 1931-32, C13 ....$800.00

#102 Drummer Bear, 1931, C13 ....$700.00

#102 Drummer Bear, 1932-33, fatter & taller version, C13 .$700.00

#103 Barky Puppy, 1931-33, C13 ....$700.00

#104 Looky Monk, 1931, C13 ....$700.00

#105 Bunny Scoot, 1931, C13..................................$700.00

#107 Music Box Clock Radio, 1971, plays Hickory Dickory Dock $5.00

#109 Lucky Monk, 1932-33, C13..............................$700.00

#110 Chubby Chief, 1932-33, C13 ....$700.00

#110 Puppy Playhouse, 1978-80, C13.......................$10.00

#111 Play Family Merry-Go-Round, 1972-77, plays Skater's Waltz, w/4 figures, C13..$30.00

#112 Picture Disk Camera, 1968-71, w/5 picture disks, C13.$25.00

#114 Music Box TV, 1967-83, plays London Bridge & Row Row Row Your Boat, C13 ....$5.00

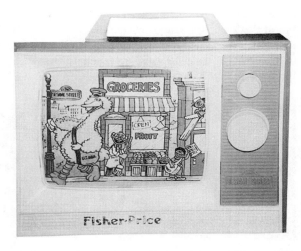

#114 Sesame Street Music Box, 1984 – 87, plays 'People in Your Neighborhood,' $5.00. (Photo courtesy Brad Cassity)

#117, Play Family Barnyard, 1972-74, complete, loose, C13..$8.00

#117, Play Family Farm Barnyard, 1972-74, MOC, C13 ..$25.00

#118 Tumble Tower Game, 1972-75, w/10 marbles, C13 .$10.00

#120 Cackling Hen, 1958-66, wht, C13 ....$35.00

#120 Gabby Goose, 1936-37 & Easter 1938, C13 ....$350.00

#121 Happy Hopper, 1969-76, C13................................$10.00

#122 Bouncing Buggy, 1974-79, 6 wheels, C13...................$2.00
#123 Cackling Hen, 1966-68, red litho, C13...................$35.00
#123 Roller Chime, 1953-60 & Easter 1961, C13 ....$35.00
#124 Roller Chime, 1961-62 & Easter 1963, C13 ....$25.00
#125 Music Box Iron, 1966, aqua w/yel hdl, C13 ....$40.00
#125 Music Box Iron, 1966-69, wht w/red hdl, C13 ....$30.00
#125 Uncle Timmy Turtle, 1956-58, red shell, C13.........$75.00
#130 Wobbles, 1964-67, dog wobbles when pulled, C13 ..$35.00

#131 Milk Wagon, 1964 – 72, truck with bottle carrier, $50.00. (Photo courtesy Brad Cassity)

#131 Toy Wagon, 1951-54, C13......................................$225.00
#132 Dr Doodle, 1957-60, C13 ....$75.00
#132 Molly Moo Cow, 1972-78, C13 ....$15.00
#135 Play Family Animal Circus, 1974-76, complete, C13 .$60.00
#136 Play Family Lacing Shoe, 1965-69, complete, C13..$60.00
#138 Jack-in-the-Box Puppet, 1970-73, C13 ....$25.00
#139 Tuggy Tooter, 1967-73, C13 ....$75.00
#139 Tuggy Turtle, 1959-60 & Easter 1961, C13 ....$75.00
#140 Coaster Boy, 1941, C13 ....$700.00
#140 Katy Kackler, 1954-56 & Easter 1957, C13............$75.00
#141 Snap-Quack, 1947-49, C13 ....$200.00
#142 Three Men in a Tub, 1970-73, w/bell, C13 ....$10.00
#142 Three Men in a Tub, 1974-75, w/flag, C13 ....$5.00
#145 Humpty Dump Truck, 1963-64 & Easter 1965, C13.$40.00
#145 Husky Dump Truck, 1961-62 & Easter 1963, C13...$45.00
#145 Musical Elephant, 1948-50, C13 ....$200.00
#146 Pull-A-Long Lacing Shoe, 1970-73, w/6 figures, C13 .$50.00
#148 Ducky Daddles, 1942, C13 ....$225.00
#148 Jack & Jill TV Radio, 1959 & Easter 1960, C13......$55.00
#149 Dog Cart Donald, 1936-37, C13 ....$700.00
#150 Barky Budd, 1934-35, C13 ....$600.00
#150 Pop-Up-Pal Chime Phone, 1968-78, C13................$25.00
#150 Teddy Tooter, 1940-41, C13 ....$400.00
#150 Timmy Turtle, 1953-55 & Easter 1956, gr shell, C13 .$85.00
#151 Goldilocks & the Three Bears Playhouse, 1967-71, C13.$60.00
#151 Happy Hippo, 1962-63, C13...................................$85.00
#152 Road Roller, 1934-35, C13 ....$700.00
#154 Frisky Frog, 1971-83, squeeze plastic bulb & frog jumps, C13...............$15.00
#154 Pop Goes the Weasel TV-Radio, 1964-67, C13 ....$20.00
#155 Jack & Jill TV Radio, 1968-70, C13 ....$35.00
#155 Moo-oo Cow, 1958-61 & Easter 1962, C13 ....$85.00

#155 Skipper Sam, 1934, C13 ....$850.00
#156 Baa-Baa Black Sheep TV-Radio, 1966-67, C13.......$50.00
#156 Circus Wagon, 1942-44, band leader in wagon, C13 .$400.00
#156 Jiffy Dump Truck, 1971-73, squeeze bulb & dump moves, C13.....................$15.00
#158 Katie Kangaroo, 1976-77, squeeze bulb & she hops, C13..$15.00
#158 Little Boy Blue TV-Radio, 1967, C13 ....$50.00
#159 Ten Little Indians TV-Radio, 1961-65 & Easter 1966, C13.....................$20.00
#160 Donald & Donna Duck, 1937, C13 ....$700.00
#161 Creative Block Wagon, 1961-64, 18 building blocks & 6 wooden dowels fit into pull-along wagon, C13 ....$60.00
#161 Looky Chug-Chug, 1949-52, C13 ....$200.00
#161 Old Woman Who Lived in a Shoe TV-Radio, 1968-70, see-through window on back, C13.....................$30.00
#162 Roly Poly Boats Chime Ball, 1967-69, C13.................$5.00
#164 Chubby Cub, 1969-72, C13....................................$15.00
#164 Mother Goose, 1964-66, C13 ....$30.00
#165 Roly Poly Chime Ball, 1967-85, C13 ....$5.00
#166 Bucky Burro, 1955-57, C13 ....$250.00
#166 Farmer in the Dell TV-Radio, 1963-66, C13............$30.00
#166 Piggy Bank, 1981-82, pk plastic, C13 ....$10.00
#168 Magnetic Chug-Chug, 1964-69, C13 ....$40.00
#168 Snorky Fire Engine, 1960 & Easter 1961, gr litho, C13.$125.00
#169 Snorky Fire Engine, 1961 & Easter 1962, red litho, C13..$100.00
#170 American Airlines Flagship w/Tail Wing, 1941-42, C13..$900.00
#170 Change-A-Tune Carousel, 1981-83, music box w/crank hdl, 3 molded records & 3 figures, C13 ....$20.00
#171 Pull-Along Plane, 1981-88, C13..............................$5.00
#171 Toy Wagon, 1942-47, C13.....................................$275.00
#172 Roly Raccoon, 1980-82, C13 ....$5.00
#175 Gold Star Stagecoach, 1954-55 & Easter 1956, C13 .$250.00
#175 Kicking Donkey, 1937-38, C13 ....$450.00
#175 Winnie the Pooh TV-Radio, 1971-73, Sears only, C13 .$60.00
#177 Donald Duck Xylophone, 1946-52, 2nd version w/'Donald Duck' on hat, C13 ....$275.00
#177 Oscar the Grouch, 1977-84, C13 ....$10.00
#178 What's in My Pocket Cloth Book, 1972-74, boy's version, C13.....................$20.00
#179 What's in My Pocket Cloth Book, 1972-74, girl's version, C13.....................$20.00
#180 Snoopy Sniffer, 1938-55, C13................................$75.00
#183 Play Family Fun Jet, 1970, 1st version, C13 ....$20.00
#185 Donald Duck Xylophone, 1938, mk WDE, C13....$800.00
#189 Looky Chug-Chug, 1958-60, C13 ....$75.00
#189 Pull-A-Tune Blue Bird Music Box, 1969-79, plays Children's Prayer, C13 ....$8.00
#190 Gabby Duck, 1939-40 & Easter 1941, C13............$350.00
#190 Molly Moo-Moo, 1956 & Easter 1957, C13 ....$200.00
#190 Pull-A-Tune Pony Music Box, 1969-72, plays Shubert's Cradle Song, C13 ....$10.00
#191 Golden Gulch Express, 1961 & Easter 1962, C13.$100.00
#192 Playland Express, 1962 & Easter 1963, C13 ....$100.00
#192 School Bus, 1965-69, new version of #990, C13....$125.00
#194 Push Pullet, 1971-72, C13.....................................$15.00
#195 Peek-A-Boo Screen Music Box, 1965-68, plays Mary Had a Little Lamb, C13.....................$25.00
#195 Teddy Bear Parade, 1938, C13................................$600.00

#196 Peek-A-Boo Screen Music Box, 1964, plays Hey Diddle Diddle, C13...$45.00

#198 Band Wagon, 1940-41, C13 ....$350.00

#201 Woodsy-Wee Circus, 1931-32, complete, C13 ......$750.00

#205 Walt Disney's Parade, WDE, 1936-41, C13, ea......$250.00

#205 Woodsy-Wee Zoo, 1931-32, C13 ....$750.00

#207 Walt Disney's Carnival, 1936-38, Mickey, Donald, Pluto or Elmer, complete, C13, ea..$200.00

#207 Woodsy-Wee Pets, 1931, complete w/goat, donkey, cow, pig & cart, C13..$650.00

#208 Donald Duck, 1936-38, C13.................................$175.00

#209 Woodsy-Wee Dog Show, 1932, complete w/5 dogs, C13 .$650.00

#210 Pluto the Pup, 1936-38, C13 ....$150.00

#211 Elmer Elephant, 1936-38, C13.............................$175.00

#215 Fisher-Price Choo-Choo, 1955-57, engine w/3 cars, C13 .$85.00

#225 Wheel Horse, 1935 & Easter 1936, C13................$600.00

#234 Nifty Station Wagon, 1960-62 & Easter 1963, removable roof, C13...$250.00

#237 Riding Horse, 1936, C13.....................................$600.00

#250 Big Performing Circus, 1932-38, C13 ....$950.00

#300 Scoop Loader, 1975-77, C13..................................$15.00

#301 Bunny Basket Cart, 1957-59, C13..........................$40.00

#301 Shovel Digger, 1975-77, C13.................................$25.00

#302 Chick Basket Cart, 1957-59, C13 ....$40.00

#302 Husky Dump Truck, 1978-84, C13 ....$20.00

#303 Adventure People Emergency Rescue Truck, 1975-78, C13...$15.00

#303 Bunny Push Cart, 1957, C13.................................$75.00

#304 Adventure People Wild Safari Set, 1975-78, C13 ...$50.00

#304 Chick Basket Cart, 1960-64, C13 ....$35.00

#304 Running Bunny Cart, 1957, C13............................$60.00

#305 Adventure People Air-Sea Rescue Copter, 1975-80, C13.$10.00

#305 Walking Duck Cart, 1957-64, C13..........................$40.00

#306 Adventure People Daredevil Sport Plane, C13..........$8.00

#306 Bizzy Bunny Cart, 1957-59, C13 ....$40.00

#307 Adventure People Wilderness Patrol, 1975-79, C13.$30.00

#307 Bouncing Bunny Cart, 1961-63 & Easter 1964, C13 .$40.00

#309 Adventure People TV Action Team, 1977-78, C13 .$50.00

#310 Adventure People Sea Explorer, 1975 – 80, $20.00. (Photo courtesy Brad Cassity)

#310 Mickey Mouse Puddle Jumper, 1953-55 & Easter 1956, C13 ....$125.00

#311 Bulldozer, 1976-77, C13..$20.00

#311 Husky Bulldozer, 1978-79, C13 ....$15.00

#312 Adventure People Northwoods Trail Blazer, 1977-82, C13 ....$20.00

#312 Running Bunny Cart, 1960-64, C13 ....$40.00

#313 Husky Roller Grader, 1978-80, C13 ....$15.00

#313 Roller Grader, 1977, C13.......................................$20.00

#314 Husky Boom Crane, 1978-82, C13..........................$25.00

#314 Queen Buzzy Bee, 1956-58, C13............................$30.00

#315 Husky Cement Mixer, 1978-82, C13.......................$20.00

#316 Husky Tow Truck, 1978-80, C13 ....$15.00

#317 Husky Construction Crew, 1978-80, C13 ....$25.00

#318 Adventure People Daredevil Sports Van, 1978-82, C13..$25.00

#319 Husky Hook & Ladder Truck, 1979-85, C13 ....$20.00

#320 Husky Race Car Rig, 1979-82, C13.........................$25.00

#322 Adventure People Dune Buster, 1979-82, C13 ....$10.00

#325 Adventure People Alpha Probe, 1980-84, C13 ....$20.00

#325 Buzzy Bee, 1950-56, 1st version, yel & blk litho, wooden wheels & antenna tips, C13 ....$25.00

#326 Adventure People Alpha Star, 1983-84, C13 ....$25.00

#327 Husky Load Master Dump, 1984, C13 ....$20.00

#328 Husky Highway Dump Truck, 1980-84, C13 ....$20.00

#329 Husky Dozer Loader, 1980-84, C13 ....$15.00

#331 Husky Farm Set, 1981-83, C13..............................$20.00

#333 Butch the Pup, 1951-53 & Easter 1954, C13 ....$55.00

#334 Adventure People Sea Shark, 1981-84, C13............$20.00

#337 Husky Rescue Rig, 1982-83, C13 ....$20.00

#338 Husky Power Tow Truck, 1982-84, C13 ....$25.00

#339 Husky Power & Light Service Rig, 1983-84, C13....$30.00

#344 Copter Rig, 1981-84, C13......................................$10.00

#345 Boat Rig, 1981-84, C13 ....$10.00

#345 Penelope the Performing Penguin, 1935, w/up, C13.$800.00

#347 Little People Indy Racer, 1983-90, C13 ....$8.00

#350 Adventure People Rescue Team, 1976-79, C13.......$18.00

#350 Go 'N Back Mule, 1931-33, w/up, C13 ....$900.00

#351 Adventure People Mountain Climbers, 1976-79, C13..$20.00

#352 Adventure People Construction Workers, 1976-79, C13 .$20.00

#353 Adventure People Scuba Divers, 1976-81, C13.......$15.00

#355 Adventure People White Water Kayak, 1977-80, C13 .$10.00

#355 Go 'N Back Bruno, 1931, C13 ....$800.00

#356 Adventure People Cycle Racing Team, 1977-81, C13.$10.00

#358 Adventure People Deep Sea Diver, 1980-84, C13 ...$10.00

#358 Donald Duck Back-Up, 1936, w/up, C13...............$800.00

#360 Adventure People Alpha Recon, 1982-84, C13 ......$10.00

#360 Go 'N Back Jumbo, 1931-34, w/up, C13................$900.00

#365 Puppy Back-up, 1932-36, w/up, C13 ....$800.00

#367 Adventure People Turbo Hawk, 1982-83, C13........$10.00

#368 Adventure People Alpha Interceptor, 1982-83, C13.$10.00

#375 Adventure People Sky Surfer, 1978, C13.................$25.00

#375 Bruno Back-Up, 1932, C13 ....$800.00

#377 Adventure People Astro Knight, 1979-80, C13.......$15.00

#400 Donald Duck Drum Major, 1946-48, C13..............$275.00

#400 Donald Duck Drum Major Cart, 1946 only, C13...$275.00

#400 Tailspin Tabby, 1931-38, rnd guitar, C13 ....$75.00

#401 Push Bunny Cart, 1942, C13................................$225.00

#402 Duck Cart, 1943, C13..$200.00

#404 Bunny Egg Cart, 1949, C13 ....$75.00

#405 Lofty Lizzy Pop-Up Kritter, 1931-33, C13..............$225.00

#406 Bunny Cart, 1950-53, C13 ....$50.00

#407 Chick Cart, 1950-53, C13.......................................$50.00

#407 Dizzy Dino Pop-Up Kritter, 1931-32, C13 ....$225.00
#410 Stoopy Stork Pop-Up Kritter, 1931-32, C13..........$225.00

#415 Lop-Ear Looie Pop-Up Kritter, 1934, $225.00. (Photo courtesy Brad Cassity)

#415 Super Jet, 1952 & Easter 1953, C13......................$200.00
#420 Sunny Fish, 1955, C13 ....$200.00
#422 Jumbo Jitterbug Pop-Up Kritter, 1940, C13..........$225.00
#423 Jumping Jack Scarecrow, 1979, C13 ....$5.00
#425 Donald Duck Pop-Up, 1938 & Easter 1939, C13 ..$400.00
#433 Dizzy Donkey Pop-Up Kritter, 1939, C13 ....$125.00
#434 Ferdinand the Bull, 1939, C13 ....$600.00
#435 Happy Apple, 1979-84, short stem, C13 ....$3.00
#440 Goofy Gertie Pop-Up Kritter, 1935, C13 ....$225.00
#440 Pluto Pop-Up, 1936, mk WDP, C13.......................$75.00
#444 Fuzzy Fido, 1941-42, C13 ....$225.00
#444 Puffy Engine, 1951-54, C13 ....$75.00
#444 Queen Buzzy Bee, 1959, red litho, C13 ....$30.00
#445 Hot Dog Wagon, 1940-41, C13.............................$250.00
#445 Nosey Pup, 1956-58 & Easter 1959, C13 ....$75.00
#447 Woofy Wagger, 1947-48, C13 ....$85.00
#448 Mini Copter, 1971-84, bl litho, C13 ....$10.00
#450 Donald Duck Choo-Choo, 1941, 8½", C13...........$400.00
#450 Donald Duck Choo-Choo, 1942-45 & Easter 1949, C13..$150.00
#450 Kiltie Dog, 1936, C13..$400.00
#450 Music Box Bear, 1981-83, plays Schubert's Cradle Song, C13...$5.00
#454 Donald Duck Drummer, 1949-50, C13 ....$300.00
#455 Tailspin Tabby Pop-Up Kritter, 1939-42, C13 ....$75.00
#456 Bunny & Container, 1939-40, C13.........................$225.00
#460 Dapper Donald Duck, 1936-37, no number on toy, C13..$600.00
#460 Movie Viewer, 1973-85, crank hdl, C13...................$2.00
#460 Suzie Seal, 1961-63 & Easter 1964, C13 ....$35.00
#461 Duck Cart, 1938-39, C13 ....$225.00
#462 Busy Bunny, 1937, C13..$200.00
#465 Teddy Choo-Choo, 1937, C13 ....$400.00
#466 Busy Bunny Cart, 1941-44, C13.............................$75.00
#469 Donald Cart, 1940, C13 ....$400.00
#469 Rooster Cart, 1938-40, C13 ....$400.00
#470 Tricky Tommy, 1936, C13......................................$350.00
#472 Jingle Giraffe, 1956, C13 ....$225.00
#472 Peter Bunny Cart, 1939-40, C13............................$225.00
#473 Merry Mutt, 1949-54 & Easter 1955, C13 ....$50.00
#474 Bunny Racer, 1942, C13..$225.00

#476 Cookie Pig, 1966-70, C13....................................$50.00
#476 Mickey Mouse Drummer, 1941-45 & Easter 1946, C13..$300.00
#476 Rooster Pop-Up Kritter, 1936, C13......................$350.00
#477 Dr Doodle, 1940-41, C13 ....$225.00
#478 Pudgy Pig, 1962-64 & Easter 1965, C13 ....$45.00
#479 Donald Duck & Nephews, 1941-42, C13 ....$400.00
#479 Peter Pig, 1959-61 & Easter 1962, C13..................$40.00
#480 Leo the Drummer, 1952 & Easter 1953, C13.........$225.00
#480 Teddy Station Wagon, 1942, C13 ....$225.00
#485 Mickey Mouse Choo-Choo, 1949-54, new litho version of #432, C13...$100.00
#488 Popeye Spinach Eater, 1939-40, C13 ....$600.00
#491 Boom-Boom Popeye, C13....................................$425.00
#494 Pinocchio, 1939-40, C13 ....$600.00
#495 Running Bunny Cart, 1941, C13 ....$200.00
#495 Sleepy Sue Turtle, 1962-63 & Easter 1964, C13......$40.00
#499 Kitty Bell, 1950-51, C13.......................................$125.00
#500 Donald Duck Cart, 1937, no number on toy, wheels not painted, C13 ....$700.00
#500 Donald Duck Cart, 1951-53, no baton, gr litho background, C13..$350.00
#500 Donald Duck Cart, 1953, w/baton, yel litho background, C13...$350.00
#500 Pick-Up & Peek Puzzle, 1972-86, C13 ....$10.00
#500 Pushy Pig, 1932-35, C13......................................$500.00
#502 Action Bunny Cart, 1949, C13..............................$200.00
#503 Pick-Up & Peek Wood Puzzle, Occupations, 1972-76, C13..$10.00
#505 Bunny Drummer, 1946, bell on front, C13 ....$225.00
#507 Pushy Doodle, 1933, C13 ....$850.00
#508 Bunny Bell Drummer, 1949-53, C13 ....$85.00
#510 Pick-Up & Peek Wood Puzzle, Nursery Rhymes, 1972-81, C13...$10.00
#510 Strutter Donald Duck, 1941, C13.........................$250.00
#512 Bunny Drummer, 1942, C13..................................$225.00
#515 Pushy Pat, 1933-35, C13......................................$550.00
#517 Choo-Choo Local, 1936, C13 ....$550.00
#517 Pick-Up & Peek Puzzle, Animal Friends, 1977-84, C13.$10.00
#520 Bunny Bell Cart, 1941, C13 ....$225.00

#520 Pick-Up and Peek Puzzle, Three Little Pigs, 1979 – 84, $15.00. (Photo courtesy Brad Cassity)

#525 Cotton Tail Cart, 1940, C13 ....$350.00
#525 Pushy Elephant, 1934-35, C13 ....$550.00
#530 Mickey Mouse Band, 1935-36, C13 ....$800.00
#533 Thumper Bunny, 1942, C13 ....$500.00
#540 Granny Duck, 1939-40, C13 ....$225.00
#544 Donald Duck Cart, 1942-44, C13 ....$300.00
#549 Toy Lunch Kit, 1962-79, red w/barn litho, w/thermos, C13 ....$25.00
#550 Toy Lunch Kit, 1957, red, wht & gr plastic barn shape, no litho, C13 ....$40.00
#552 Basic Hardboard Puzzle, Nature, 1974-75, C13........$15.00
#563 Basic Hardboard Puzzle, Weather, 1975, C13 ....$10.00
#568 Basic Hardboard Puzzle, bear on log, C13 ....$10.00
#569 Basic Hardboard Puzzle, Airport, 1975, C13 ....$10.00
#600 Tailspin Tabby Pop-Up, 1947, C13 ....$250.00
#604 Bunny Bell Cart, 1954-55, C13..............................$100.00
#605 Donald Duck Cart, 1954-56, C13 ....$250.00
#605 Woodsey Major Goodgrub Mole & Book, 1981-82, C13..$15.00
#606 Woodsey Bramble Beaver & Book, 1981-82, 32 pgs, C13.$15.00
#607 Woodsey Very Blue Bird & Book, 1981-82, 32 pgs, C13 .$15.00
#615 Tow Truck, 1960-61 & Easter 1962, C13 ....$65.00
#616 Chuggy Pop-Up, 1955-56, C13 ....$75.00
#617 Prancy Pony, 1965-70, C13 ....$25.00
#621 Suzie Seal, 1965-66, ball on nose, C13....................$30.00
#623 Suzie Seal, 1964-65, umbrella on nose, C13 ....$45.00
#625 Playful Puppy, 1961-62 & Easter 1963, w/shoe, C13.$45.00
#628 Tug-A-Bug, 1975-77, C13......................................$5.00

#616 Patch Pony, 1963 – 64 and Easter 1965, $40.00. (Photo courtesy Brad Cassity)

#629 Fisher-Price Tractor, 1962-68, C13..........................$30.00
#630 Fire Truck, 1959-62, C13..$45.00
#634 Drummer Boy, 1967-69, C13..................................$60.00
#634 Tiny Teddy, 1955-57, C13......................................$75.00
#637 Milk Carrier, 1966-85, C13 ....$15.00
#640 Wiggily Woofer, 1957-58 & Easter 1958, C13 ....$85.00
#641 Toot Toot Engine, 1962-63 & Easter 1964, bl litho, C13..$60.00

Get on board and join the fun!

The Fisher-Price Collector's Club is a rapidly expanding non-profit club organized for the **caring** and **sharing** of Fisher-Price toys. We were organized in 1993 and incorporated in Arizona in 1994. We received notification from the Internal Revenue Service, that effective since 1994, **The Fisher-Price Collector's Club** is recognized as a not-for-profit company under the Internal Revenue Code section 501(c)(3). As such, contributions made to the Fisher-Price Collector's Club are deductible as charitable contributions. Membership fees are not charitable contributions. **The purpose of the corporation** is to study, research, discuss and write about Fisher-Price toys; to preserve and promote the collection of Fisher-Price toys and related items; and to contribute to those activities for which the purposes are charitable, scientific, literary, or educational. The club holds an annual convention in conjunction with ToyFest, in August, in East Aurora, NY, home of Fisher-Price. *The Gabby Goose* newsletter is published quarterly by the club. Material and ads must be submitted one month before the issue dates of March, June, September, and December. Ads are free to members, up to 40 words.

We cordially invite you to join this special toy club. As a member, you will meet the many toy collectors who have already joined our club, exchanging information and sharing experiences about collecting Fisher-Price toys through *The Gabby Goose* newsletter. To become a member, send your name, address and check for $20 ($30 for first class mailing), $25 international, made payable to FPCC for a one year membership to: Jeanne Kennedy, 1442 North Ogden, Mesa, AZ 85205. (The year runs from September to August. Dues are not pro-rated; when you join, you receive all prior newsletters for that year.)

#642 Bob-Along Bear, 1979-84, C13 ....$10.00
#642 Dinky Engine, 1959, blk litho, C13.........................$60.00
#642 Smokie Engine, 1960-61 & Easter 1962, blk litho, C13.$60.00
#649 Stake Truck, 1960-61 & Easter 1962, C13 ....$50.00
#653 Allie Gator, 1960-61 & Easter 1962, C13................$75.00
#654 Tawny Tiger, 1962 & Easter 1963, C13..................$100.00
#656 Bossy Bell, 1960 & Easter 1961, w/bonnet, C13 ......$55.00
#656 Bossy Bell, 1961-63, no bonnet, new litho design, C13.$45.00
#657 Crazy Clown Fire Brigade, 1983-84, C13 ....$45.00
#658 Lady Bug, 1961-62 & Easter 1963, C13 ....$50.00
#659 Puzzle Puppy, 1976-81, C13 ....$5.00
#662 Merry Mousewife, 1962-64 & Easter 1965, C13 ......$45.00
#663 Play Family, 1966-70, blk dog, MIP, C13 ....$120.00
#663 Play Family, 1966-70, tan dog, MIP, C13 ....$170.00
#666 Creative Blocks, 1978-90, C13 ....$10.00
#674 Sports Car, 1958-60, C13 ....$75.00
#677 Picnic Basket, 1975-79, C13 ....$20.00
#678 Kriss Kricket, 1955-57, C13 ....$75.00
#679 Little People Garage Squad, 1984-90, MIP, C13......$15.00
#684 Little Lamb, 1964-65, C13 ....$45.00
#685 Car & Boat, 1968-69, 5 pcs, C13 ....$65.00
#686 Car & Camper, 1968-70, C13 ....$65.00
#686 Perky Pot, 1958-59 & Easter 1960, C13................$50.00
#694 Suzie Seal, 1979-80, C13 ....$15.00
#695 Lady Bug, 1982-84, C13 ....$5.00
#695 Pinky Pig, 1956-57, wooden eyes, C13 ....$75.00
#695 Pinky Pig, 1958, litho eyes, C13 ....$75.00
#698 Talky Parrot, 1963 & Easter 1964, C13 ....$75.00
#700 Cowboy Chime, 1951-53, C13 ....$250.00
#700 Popeye, 1935, C13 ....$700.00
#700 Woofy Wowser, 1940 & Easter 1941, C13 ....$400.00
#703 Bunny Engine, 1954-56, C13 ....$100.00
#703 Popeye the Sailor, 1936, C13 ....$700.00
#705 Mini Snowmobile, 1971-73, C13 ....$45.00
#705 Popeye Cowboy, 1937, C13 ....$700.00
#710 Scotty Dog, 1933, C13 ....$550.00
#711 Cry Baby Bear, 1967-69, C13 ....$25.00
#711 Huckleberry Hound, 1961, Sears only, C13 ....$300.00
#711 Raggedy Ann & Andy, 1941, C13 ....$850.00
#711 Teddy Trucker, 1949-51, C13 ....$225.00
#712 Fred Flintstone Xylophone, 1962, Sears only, C13 .$250.00
#712 Johnny Jumbo, 1933-35, C13 ....$550.00
#712 Teddy Tooter, 1957-58 & Easter 1959, C13 ....$250.00
#714 Mickey Mouse Xylophone, 1963, Sears only, C13.$275.00
#715 Ducky Flip Flap, 1964-65, C13 ....$50.00
#717 Ducky Flip Flap, 1937-39, C13 ....$400.00
#718 Tow Truck & Car, 1969-70, C13 ....$45.00
#719 Busy Bunny Cart, 1936-37, C13...........................$350.00
#719 Cuddly Cub, 1973-77, C13 ....$5.00
#720 Pinocchio Express, 1939-40, C13 ....$500.00
#721 Peter Bunny Engine, 1949-51, C13 ....$200.00
#722 Racing Bunny Cart, 1937, C13 ....$350.00
#722 Running Bunny, 1938-40, C13 ....$225.00
#723 Bouncing Bunny Cart, 1936, C13 ....$350.00
#724 Ding-Dong Ducky, 1949-50, C13 ....$200.00
#724 Jolly Jalopy, 1965, C13.......................................$10.00
#725 Musical Mutt, 1935-36, C13 ....$350.00
#725 Play Family Bath/Utility Room Set, 1972, C13 ....$10.00

#726 Play Family Patio Set, 1970-73, C13.....................$10.00
#727 Bouncing Bunny Wheelbarrow, 1939, C13...........$350.00
#728 Buddy Bullfrog, 1959-60, yel body w/red coat, C13 .$60.00
#728 Pound & Saw Bench, 1966-67, C13......................$25.00
#730 Racing Rowboat, 1952-53, C13 ....$200.00
#732 Happy Hauler, 1968-70, C13 ....$20.00
#732 Happy Whistlers, 1977-79, C13..............................$5.00
#733 Mickey Mouse Safety Patrol, 1956-57, C13 ....$250.00
#734 Teddy Zilo, 1964, no coat, C13 ....$55.00
#734 Teddy Zilo, 1965-66, w/coat, C13 ....$55.00
#735 Juggling Jumbo, 1958-59, C13............................$200.00
#736 Humpty Dumpty, 1972-79, C13............................$4.00
#737 Galloping Horse & Wagon, 1948-49, C13............$250.00
#737 Ziggy Zilo, 1958-59, C13 ....$65.00
#738 Dumbo Circus Racer, 1941 & Easter 1942, C13....$700.00
#738 Shaggy Zilo, 1960-61 & Easter 1962, C13 ....$65.00
#739 Poodle Zilo, 1962-63 & Easter 1964, C13 ....$65.00
#740 Pushcart Pete, 1936-67, C13 ....$600.00
#741 Teddy Zilo, 1967, C13 ....$35.00
#741 Trotting Donald Duck, 1937, C13.........................$800.00
#742 Dashing Dobbin, 1938-40, C13............................$350.00
#744 Doughboy Donald, 1942, C13 ....$600.00
#745 Elsie's Dairy Truck, 1948-49, w/2 bottles, C13.......$700.00
#746 Pocket Radio, 1977-78, It's a Small World, C13......$20.00
#747 Chatter Telephone, 1962-67, wooden wheels, C13 .$30.00
#747 Talk-Back Telephone, 1961 & Easter 1962, C13 .....$75.00
#749 Egg Truck, 1947, C13 ....$225.00
#750 Hot Dog Wagon, 1938, C13 ....$400.00
#750 Space Blazer, 1953-54, C13 ....$300.00
#755 Jumbo Rolo, 1951-52, C13 ....$225.00
#756 Pocket Radio, 1973, 12 Days of Christmas, C13......$25.00
#757 Howdy Bunny, 1939-40, C13 ....$350.00
#757 Humpty Dumpty, 1957 & Easter 1958, C13 ....$175.00
#757 Snappy-Quacky, 1950, C13 ....$225.00
#758 Pocket Radio, 1970-72, Mulberry Bush, C13 ....$15.00
#758 Pony Chime, 1948-50, C13 ....$175.00
#758 Push-Along Clown, 1980-81, C13 ....$10.00
#759 Pocket Radio, 1969-73, Do-Re-Me, C13 ....$15.00
#760 Peek-A-Boo Block, 1970-79, C13 ....$5.00
#760 Racing Ponies, 1936, C13...................................$350.00
#761 Play Family Nursery Set, 1973, C13 ....$10.00
#762 Pocket Radio, 1972-77, Raindrops, C13 ....$20.00
#763 Music Box, 1962, Farmer in the Dell, yel litho, C13.$50.00
#763 Pocket Radio, 1978, I Whistle a Happy Tune, C13 .$15.00
#764 Music Box, 1960-61 & Easter 1962, Farmer in the Dell, red
    litho, C13...$50.00
#764 Pocket Radio, 1975-76, My Name Is Michael, C13.$10.00
#765 Dandy Dobbin, 1941-44, C13 ....$175.00
#765 Talking Donald Duck, 1955-58, C13 ....$125.00
#766 Pocket Radio, 1968-70, Where Has My Little Dog Gone?,
    C13..$20.00
#766 Pocket Radio, 1977-78, I'd Like To Teach the World To
    Sing, C13 ....$15.00
#767 Pocket Radio, 1977, Twinkle Twinkle Little Star, C13..$25.00
#767 Tiny Ding-Dong, 1940, 6 wheels, C13 ....$400.00
#768 Pocket Radio, 1971-76, Happy Birthday, C13 ....$10.00
#770 Doc & Dopey Dwarfs, 1938, C13.......................$1,000.00
#772 Pocket Radio, 1974-76, Jack & Jill, C13 ....$15.00

#773 Tip-Toe Turtle, 1962 – 77, vinyl tail, $10.00.

(Photo courtesy Brad Cassity)

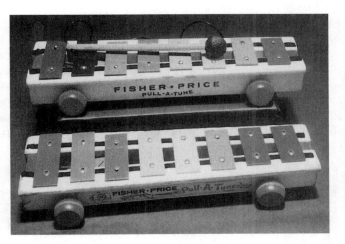

#870 Pull-a-Tune Xylophone, 1957 – 69, with song book, $30.00. (Photo courtesy Brad Cassity)

#775 Gabby Goofies, 1956-59 & Easter 1960, C13 ....$30.00

#775 Pocket Radio, 1967-68, Sing a Song of Six Pence, C13 .$20.00

#775 Pocket Radio, 1973-75, Pop Goes the Weasel, C13..$15.00

#775 Teddy Drummer, 1936, C13 ....$675.00

#777 Pushy Bruno, 1933, C13 ....$725.00

#777 Squeaky the Clown, 1958-59, C13 ....$225.00

#778 Ice Cream Wagon, 1940 & Easter 1941, C13 ....$350.00

#778 Pocket Radio, 1967-68, Frere Jacques, C13 ....$15.00

#779 Pocket Radio, 1976, Yankee Doodle, C13 ....$15.00

#780 Jumbo Xylophone, 1937-38, C13 ....$275.00

#780 Snoopy Sniffer, 1955-57 & Easter 1958, C13 ....$65.00

#784 Mother Goose Music Chart, 1955-56 & Easter 1957, C13..$75.00

#785 Blackie Drummer, 1939, C13 ....$625.00

#785 Corn Popper, 1957-58, red base, C13 ....$60.00

#786 Perky Penguin, 1973-75, C13 ....$15.00

#788 Rock-A-Bye Bunny Cart, 1940-41, C13 ....$300.00

#789 Lift & Load Road Builders, 1978-82, C13 ....$15.00

#791 Tote-A-Tune Music Box Radio, 1979, Let's Go Fly A Kite, C13..$5.00

#792 Tote-A-Tune Music Box Radio, 1980-81, Teddy Bears' Picnic, C13..$5.00

#793 Jolly Jumper, 1963-64 & Easter 1965, C13...............$40.00

#793 Tote-A-Tune Music Box, 1981, When You Wish Upon a Star, C13...$5.00

#794 Big Bill Pelican, 1961-63, w/cb fish, C13 ....$75.00

#794 Tote-A-Tune Music Box, 1981-82, Over the Rainbow, C13..$5.00

#795 Micky Mouse Drummer, 1937, C13 ....$700.00

#795 Musical Duck, 1952-54 & Easter 1955, C13 ....$75.00

#795 Tote-A-Tune Music Box, 1984-91, Toyland, C13 ......$5.00

#798 Chatter Monk, 1957-58 & Easter 1959, C13 ....$75.00

#798 Mickey Mouse Xylophone, 1939, w/hat, C13 ....$400.00

#798 Mickey Mouse Xylophone, 1942, no hat, C13.......$400.00

#799 Duckie Transport, 1937, C13 ....$400.00

#799 Quacky Family, 1940-42, C13 ....$100.00

#800 Hot Diggety, 1934, w/up, C13 ....$800.00

#808 Pop'n Ring, 1956-58 & Easter 1959, C13 ....$75.00

#810 Hot Mammy, 1934, w/up, C13 ....$800.00

#810 Timber Toter, 1957 & Easter 1958, C13..................$85.00

#845 Farm Truck, 1954-55, C13......................................$250.00

#875, Looky Push Car, 1962-65 & Easter 1966, C13........$45.00

#900 Struttin' Donald Duck, 1939 & Easter 1940, C13 .$650.00

#900 This Little Pig, 1956-58 & Easter 1959, C13 ....$55.00

#902 Junior Circus, 1963-70, C13..................................$225.00

#904 Beginners Circus, 1965-68, C13 ....$60.00

#905 This Little Pig, 1959-62, C13 ....$30.00

#909 Play Family Rooms, 1972, Sears only, C13 ....$200.00

#910 Change-A-Tune Piano, 1969-72, Pop Goes the Weasel, This Old Man & The Muffin Man, C13.....................$25.00

#915 Play Family Farm, 1968-79, 1st version w/masonite base, C13...$25.00

#919 Music Box Movie Camera, 1968-70, plays This Old Man, w/5 picture disks, C13...$35.00

#923 Play Family School, 1971-78, 1st version, C13........$20.00

#926 Concrete Mixer, 1959-60 & Easter 1961, C13 ......$200.00

#928 Play Family Fire Station, 1980-82, C13 ....$50.00

#929 Play Family Nursery School, 1978-79, C13............$30.00

#931 Play Family Children's Hospital, 1976-78, C13 .....$115.00

#932 Amusement Park, 1963-65, C13 ....$300.00

#932 Ferry Boat, 1979-80, C13.......................................$30.00

#934 Play Family Western Town, 1982-84, C13 ....$60.00

#935 Tool Box Work Bench, 1969-71, C13 ....$20.00

#937 Play Family Sesame Street Clubhouse, 1977-79, C13 .$70.00

#938 Play Family Sesame Street House, 1975-76, C13.....$75.00

#942 Play Family Lift & Load Depot, 1977-79, C13........$45.00

#943 Lift & Load Railroad, 1978-79, C13......................$45.00

#944 Lift & Load Lumber Yard, 1979-81, C13.................$45.00

#945 Offshore Cargo Base, 1979-80, C13 ....$65.00

#960 Woodsey's Log House, 1979-81, complete, C13.......$20.00

#961 Woodsey's Store, 1980-81, complete, C13 ....$30.00

#962 Woodsey's Airport, 1980-81, complete, C13............$10.00

#969 Musical Ferris Wheel, 1966-72, 1st version w/4 wooden straight-body figures, C13...................................$50.00

#972 Fisher-Price Cash Register, 1960-72, C13 ....$40.00

#979 Dump Truckers Playset, 1965-67, C13 ....$75.00

#982 Hot Rod Roadster, 1983-84, riding toy w/4-pc take-apart engine, C13..$40.00

#983 Safety School Bus, 1959, w/6 figures, Fisher-Price Club logo, C13 ....$225.00

#985 Play Family Houseboat, 1972-76, complete, C13 ....$40.00

#987 Creative Coaster, 1964-82, MIB, C13 ....$40.00
#990 Play Family A-Frame, 1974-76, C13 ....$50.00
#991 Music Box Lacing Shoe, 1964-67, C13 ....$60.00
#991 Play Family Circus Train, 1973-78, w/gondola car, C13 .$15.00
#991 Play Family Circus Train, 1979-86, no gondola car, C13 .$10.00
#992 Play Family Car & Camper, 1980-84, C13 ....$35.00
#993 Play Family Castle, 1974-77, 1st version, C13 ....$100.00
#994 Play Family Camper, 1973-76, C13 ....$50.00

#996 Play Family Airport, 1972 – 76, first version with blue airport and clear lookout tower, $50.00. (Photo courtesy Brad Cassity)

#997 Musical Tick-Tock Clock, 1962-63, C13 ....$30.00
#997 Play Family Village, 1973-77, C13 ....$50.00
#998 Music Box Teaching Clock, 1968-83, C13...............$30.00
#999 Huffy Puffy Train, 1958-62, C13 ....$75.00
#1005 Push Cone, 1937-38, C13....................................$400.00
#1006 Floor Train, 1934-38, C13 ....$600.00
#2155 McDonald's Happy Meal, 1989-90, C13 ....$15.00
#2352 Little People Construction Set, 1985, C13 ....$15.00
#2360 Little People Jetliner, 1986-88, C13 ....$10.00
#2361 Little People Fire Truck, 1989-90, C13 ....$10.00
#2453 Little People Beauty Salon, 1990, C13.................$15.00
#2500 Little People Main Street, 1986-90, C13 ....$30.00
#2501 Little People Farm, 1986-89, C13 ....$15.00
#2504 Little People Garage, 1986, rare, C13 ....$55.00
#2524 Little People Cruise Boat, 1989-90, C13...............$15.00
#2525 Little People Playground, 1986-90, C13 ....$10.00
#2526 Little People Pool, 1986-88, C13 ....$15.00
#2550 Little People School, 1988-89, C13 ....$20.00
#2551 Little People Neighborhood, 1988-90, C13 ....$40.00
#2552 McDonald's Restaurant, 1990, 1st version, C13 ....$65.00
#2552 McDonald's Restaurant, 1991-92, 2nd version, same pcs
    as 1st version but lg-sz figures, C13 ....$40.00
#2580 Little People Little Mart, 1987-89, C13 ....$15.00
#2581 Little People Express Train, 1987-90, C13 ....$10.00
#2582 Little People Floating Marina, 1988-90, C13.........$15.00
#2712 Pick-Up & Peek Puzzle, Haunted House, 1985-88, C13.$15.00
#2720 Pick-Up & Peek Puzzle, Little Bo Peep, 1985-88, C13.$15.00
#4500 Husky Helpers Workmen, 1985-86, 6 different, MOC,
    C13, ea...$15.00
#4520 Highway Dump Truck, 1985-86, C13 ....$15.00
#4521 Dozer Loader, 1985-86, C13 ....$15.00
#4523 Gravel Hauler, 1985-86, C13 ....$15.00

#4550 Chevy S-10 4x4, 1985, $20.00 (add 20% to 40% for the original box). (Photo courtesy Brad Cassity)

#4551 Pontiac Firebird, 1985, C13....................................$20.00
#4552 Jeep CJ-7 Renegade, 1985, C13.............................$20.00
#4580 Power Tow, 1985-86, C13.......................................$20.00
#4581 Power Dump Truck, 1985-86, C13 ....$20.00
#6145 Jingle Elephant, 1993, ToyFest limited edition of 5,000,
    C13 ....$100.00
#6464 Gran'Pa Frog, 1994 ToyFest limited edition of 5,000,
    C13 ....$50.00
#6550 Buzzy Bee, 1987, ToyFest limited edition of 5,000, C13 .$120.00
#6558 Snoopy Sniffer, 1988, ToyFest limited edition of 3,000,
    C13 ....$550.00
#6575 Toot-Toot, 1989, ToyFest limited edition of 4,800, C13 .$65.00
#6588 Snoopy Sniffer, 1990, Fisher-Price Commemorative lim-
    ited edition of 3,500, Ponderosa pine, C13..............$150.00
#6590 Prancing Horses, 1990, ToyFest limited edition of 5,000,
    C13 ....$75.00
#6592 Teddy Bear Parade, 1991, ToyFest limited edition of
    5,000, C13..$50.00
#6593 Squeaky the Clown, 1995, ToyFest limited edition of
    5,000, C13 ....$125.00
#6599 Molly Bell Cow, 1992, ToyFest limited edition of 5,000,
    C13 ....$150.00
#76880 Raggedy Ann & Andy, 1997, ToyFest limited edition of
    5,000, C13 ....$150.00

#7076 Walt Disney Gummi Bear Bubble the Dragon, 1986, came with four-ounce bubble solution, $20.00. (Photo courtesy Brad Cassity)

Games

Early games (those from 1850 to 1910) are very often appreciated more for their wonderful lithographed boxes than their 'playability,' and you'll find collectors displaying them as they would any fine artwork. Many boxes and boards were designed by commercial artists of the day.

Though they were in a decline a few years ago, baby-boomer game prices have leveled off. Some science fiction and rare TV games are still in high demand. Games produced in the Art Deco era between the World Wars have gained in popularity — especially those with great design. Victorian games have become harder to find; their prices have also grown steadily. Condition and rarity are the factors that most influence game prices.

When you buy a game, check to see that all pieces are there. In the listings that follow, assume that all are board games (unless specifically indicated card game, target game, bagatelle, etc.) and that each is complete as issued, unless missing components are mentioned. For further information we recommend *Board Games of the '50s, '60s and '70s* (L-W Book Sales).

Advisor: Paul Fink (F3)

See also Advertising; Black Americana; Barbie; California Raisins; Halloween; Political; Robots and Space Toys; Sporting Collectibles; Tops and Other Spinning Toys.

A-Team, 1984, VGIB...$15.00
Addams Family (Cartoon Series), Milton Bradley, 1974, NMIB...$35.00
Addams Family Card Game, Milton Bradley, 1965, NMIB .$25.00
Adventures of Davy Crockett, Harett-Gilmor, 1955, EXIB .$75.00
Adventures of Lassie, Whiting, 1955, EXIB......................$50.00
Adventures of Rin-Tin-Tin, Transogram, 1955, EXIB $50.00
Adventures of Robin Hood, Bettye-B, 1956, EXIB...........$65.00
Adventures of Superman, Milton Bradley, 1942, EXIB ..$225.00

Adventures of Tom Sawyer and Huck Finn, Stoll & Edwards, VGIB, $125.00. (Photo courtesy Randy Inman Auctions)

Alien, Kenner, 1979, EXIB...$50.00
Allen Sherman's Camp Grenada, EXIB $45.00
Alvin & the Chipmunks Acorn Hunt, Hasbro, 1960, EXIB.$35.00
Amazing Chan & the Chan Clan, Whitman, 1973, NMIB..$20.00
Amazing Spider-Man, Milton Bradley, 1966, EXIB $50.00
American Boy Ten Pins Game, McLoughlin Bros, VGIB..$250.00
American Heritage Battle-Cry Game, Milton Bradley, 1975, NMIB...$45.00
Amusing Game of Kilkenny Cats, Parker Bros, 1890, VGIB $400.00
Annette's Secret Passage Games, Parker Bros, 1958, EXIB.$20.00
Annie Oakley Game, Milton Bradley, 1955, NMIB $45.00
Aquanauts, Transogram, 1961, NMIB..............................$75.00
Around the World in 80 Days, Transogram, 1975, NMIB .$25.00
Arrest & Trial, Transogram, 1963, EXIB $30.00
As the World Turns, Parker Brothers, 1966, NMIB..........$30.00
Astro Launch, Ohio Art, 1960s, NMIB $35.00
Astro The Wizard From Mars Questions & Answers, Peerless Playthings, 1953, EXIB...$35.00
Atom Ant Saves the Day, Transogram, 1966, NMIB........$40.00

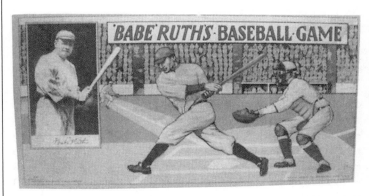

Babe Ruth's Baseball Game, Milton Bradley, EXIB, $500.00.

(Photo courtesy Randy Inman Auctions)

Babes in Toyland, Parker Bros, 1961, EXIB......................$30.00
Bamboozle, Milton Bradley, 1962, NMIB $30.00
Barbie's Keys to Fame, Mattel, 1963, EXIB $35.00
Barnabas Collins Dark Shadows Game, Milton Bradley, 1969, NMIB...$40.00
Barney Google & Spark Plug Game, Milton Bradley, 1932, VGIB, A...$85.00
Baseball Pitching Game, Marx, 1940s, NMIB $225.00
Bash!, Milton Bradley, 1965, NMIB..................................$20.00
Bat Masterson, Lowell, 1958, NMIB $75.00
Batman, Milton Bradley, 1966, NMIB $20.00
Batman & Robin Pinball Game, Marx, 1966, NM $125.00
Batman Pin Ball Game, AHI, 1976, NMIB $100.00
Batman Shooting Arcade, Marx, 1966, NMIB, A..........$535.00
Beany & Cecil Ring Toss, Pressman, 1961, EXIB $50.00
Beatlemania, VGIB...$40.00
Ben Casey, Transogram, 1961, MIB..................................$20.00
Bermuda Triangle, 1976, VG+IB, N2................................$25.00
Betsy Ross Flag Game, Transogram, 1960s, NMIB............$30.00
Beverly Hillbillies, Standard Toycraft, 1963, NMIB.........$50.00
Bewitched Card Game, Milton Bradley, 1965, EXIB........$28.00

Bewitched, T Cohn Inc., 1965, MIB, $85.00.

Big Game, National, 1930s-40s, EXIB $20.00

Big Game (Pinball), Marx, 1950s, NM $60.00

Big Game Hunter, Schoenhut, VG+IB, A......................$275.00

Big Maze, Marx, 1955, MIB $50.00

Bizzy Andy Jr Marble Game, Wolverine, MIB, A............$220.00

Black Ball Express, Schaper, 1957, EXIB.......................$25.00

Blow Football, England, Harlesden Series, VGIB, A $45.00

Blow Your Cool, Whitman, 1969, NMIB.........................$15.00

Bobbsey Twins, Milton Bradley, 1957, NMIB $30.00

Bop the Beetle, Ideal, 1963, EXIB..............................$40.00

Bowling Alley Game, Schoenhut, wooden alley & pins w/steel
    ball, 34½", NM (orig envelope).............................$220.00

Bozo Ed-U Cards, 1972, EXIB $15.00

Bozo the Clown in Circus Land, Transogram, 1960s, NMIB.$25.00

Bradley's Big Tent Peg Game, Milton Bradley, GIB, A $50.00

Brady Bunch, Whitman, 1973, MIB $100.00

Buccaneers, Transogram, 1957, NMIB $45.00

Buck Rogers Adventures on the 25th Century Game, Transo-
    gram, 1965, NMIB...$30.00

Bug-A-Boo, Whitman, 1968, NMIB.............................$25.00

Bugaloos, Milton Bradley, 1971, EXIB $40.00

Bullwinkle & Rocky Magic Dot Game, Transogram, 1962,
    NMIB...$100.00

Bullwinkle Hide 'N Seek Game, Milton Bradley, 1961, EXIB, A.$50.00

Burks Law — Game of Who Killed?..., Transogram, 1963, EXIB.$30.00

Calvin & the Colonel — Game of High Spirits, Milton Bradley,
    1962, NMIB..$35.00

Camp Granada, Milton Bradley, 1965, NMIB $50.00

Candid Camera, Lowell, 1963, NMIB............................$45.00

Candyland, Milton Bradley, 1955, NMIB $20.00

Captain & the Kids, Milton Bradley, 1947, NMIB, A $85.00

Captain America, Milton Bradley, 1977, NMIB...............$20.00

Captain Caveman Card Game, 1979, MIB $8.00

Captain Gallant of the Foreign Legion Adventure Game, Tran-
    sogram, incomplete, NMIB $35.00

Captain Kangaroo TV Lotto, Ideal, 1961, EXIB...............$25.00

Captain Video Space Game, Milton Bradley, 1950s, EXIB.$75.00

Car 54 Where Are You?, Allison, 1963, EXIB.................$150.00

Casper & His Pals Ed-U Cards, 1960s, NMIB $10.00

Casper Target Game, Knickerbocker 1960, EX+ (no box) .$20.00

Cat & Mouse Game, Parker Bros, 1964, NMIB................$18.00

Catching Mice, McLoughlin Bros, c 1888, VGIB (w/paper litho
    image on lid), A...$250.00

Challenge the Chief, Ideal, 1973, NMIB $25.00

Cheyenne, Milton Bradley, 1957, EXIB $30.00

CHiPs, Ideal, 1981, MIB, from $25 to...........................$35.00

Chutes & Ladders, Milton Bradley, 1956, NMIB.............$20.00

Cinderella, Parker Bros, 1964, EXIB $50.00

Combat, Ideal, 1963, NMIB $30.00

Combat Card Game, Milton Bradley, EXIB....................$20.00

Conflict, Parker Bros, 1960, EXIB $70.00

Count Down Space Game, Transogram, 1960, NMIB......$20.00

Countdown, Lowe, 1967, NMIB $55.00

Crazy Clock, Ideal, 1964, NMIB $50.00

Creature From the Black Lagoon, Hasbro, 1963, EXIB ..$250.00

Dangerous World of James Bond 007, Milton Bradley, 1965,
    NMIB...$60.00

Daniel Boone Ed-U Cards, 1965, NMIB........................$40.00

Dark Shadows Mysterious Maze Game, Whitman, 1968, NMIB.$50.00

Dark Tower, Milton Bradley, 1981, NMIB.....................$125.00

Dating Game, Hasbro, 1967, EXIB $30.00

Davy Crockett Ed-U Cards, 1955, EXIB $30.00

Davy Crockett Radar Action, Ewing, 1955, EXIB............$85.00

Davy Crockett Rescue Race, Gabriel, EXIB, from $55 to.$75.00

Dennis the Menace Baseball Game, MTP, 1960, NMIB ..$70.00

Deputy (The), Milton Bradley, 1960, NMIB $75.00

Deputy Dawg, Milton Bradley, 1960, EXIB....................$50.00

Detectives, Transogram, 1961, NMIB $50.00

Dick Tracy, SelRight, 1961, NMIB..............................$40.00

Dick Tracy 'Bagatelle' Pinball, Marx, 1967, EX $65.00

Dick Tracy Card Game, Whitman, 1934, EXIB................$75.00

Dick Tracy Crime Stopper Game, Ideal, 1963, NMIB......$30.00

Dick Tracy Target, Marx, EXIB, A $230.00

Diner's Club Credit Card Game, Ideal, 1961, NMIB........$30.00

Disney's True Life Electric Quiz Game, 1952, VGIB, N2 .$25.00

Disneyland Game, Transogram, 1954, EXIB $50.00

District Messenger Boy, McLoughlin Bros, c 1886, VG (VG 17x9"
    wooden box w/paper litho image of boy in street), A .$350.00

District Messenger Boy, McLoughlin Bros, VG (VG box w/3
    youths on bikes), from $350 to.............................$400.00

Doc Holiday Wild West Game, Transogram, 1960, NMIB.$35.00

Don't Spill the Beans, 1967, EXIB, N2 ....$25.00

Donald Duck's Party Game for Young Folks, WDE/Parker Bros,
    1938, incomplete, VG+IB $65.00

Donkey Kong Board Game, 1982, VG+IB, N2................$25.00

Dr Kildare, Ideal, 1962, NMIB $30.00

Dragnet, Transogram, 1955, NMIB $50.00

Dudley Do-Right's Find Snidley Game, Whitman, 1976,
    NMIB...$30.00

Dukes of Hazzard, Ideal, 1981, EXIB $25.00

Electric Sports Car Race, Tudor, 1959, NMIB $40.00

Electric Target Game, Marx, 1950s, unused, EXIB.........$300.00

Emergency, Milton Bradley, 1973, NMIB.......................$20.00

Ensign O'Toole USS Appleby Game, Hasbro, 1968, NMIB.$30.00

Escort Game of Guys & Gals, Parker Bros, 1955, unused, MIB.$30.00

Excuse Me! A Game of Manners, Parker Bros, EXIB, A ..$25.00

Eye Guess, 1966, EXIB, N2....................................$20.00

Fantastic Voyage, Milton Bradley, 1968, NMIB...............$20.00

Felix the Cat, Milton Bradley, 1960, 1st version, EXIB....$30.00

Felix the Cat Target, Lido, 1960s, EXIB........................$25.00

Felix the Cat's Down on the Farm Game, Built-Rite, 1950s,
    EXIB...$25.00

Fish Pond, McLoughlin Bros, c 1890, VG+ (wood box w/paper litho on lid), A $110.00

Flintstones, Milton Bradley, 1971, NMIB $20.00

Flintstones Brake Ball, Whitman, 1962, EXIB...............$85.00

Flipper Flips, Mattel, 1965, NMIB $40.00

Flug Im Acroplan (Airplane Game), Spear & Son/Germany, VGIB, A $140.00

Flying Nun, Milton Bradley, 1968, NMIB.........................$30.00

Fonz Hanging Out At Arnold's Card Game, Milton Bradley, 1976, MIB $20.00

Foot Ball Game (Popular Edition), Parker Bros, VGIB, A..$175.00

Fugitive, Ideal, 1964, NMIB $75.00

Funny Finger, Ideal, 1968, NMIB.................................$15.00

Game of Famous Men, Parker Bros, VGIB.....................$50.00

Game of Flags, McLoughlin Bros, VGIB, A.....................$75.00

Game of Innocence, Parker Bros, 1888, GIB, A $100.00

Game of Red Riding Hood, Parker Brothers, 1895, VGIB, A, $150.00. (Photo courtesy Skinner, Inc.)

Gee-Wiz Horse Race, Wolverine, EX...............................$100.00

Gene Autry Bandit Trail Game, Kenton, EXIB..............$200.00

George of the Jungle, Parker Bros, 1968, NMIB.............$100.00

Get in That Tub, Hasbro, 1974, unused, NMIB...............$50.00

Get Smart Card Game, Ideal, 1966, EXIB $25.00

Get Smart!, Ideal, 1965, NMIB.....................................$70.00

Gidget, Standard Toycraft, 1965, MIB, from $75 to $100.00

Gil Hodges Pennant Fever, RGJ, 1970, EXIB, A $75.00

Gilligan's Island, Game Gems/T Cohn, 1965, EXIB $225.00

Go Back, Milton Bradley, 1968, EXIB.............................$15.00

Godzilla, Mattel, 1878, EXIB..$40.00

Gomer Pyle, Transogram, 1964, EXIB............................$50.00

Goodbye Mr Chips, Parker Bros, 1969, MIB....................$25.00

Gray Ghost, Transogram, 1958, NMIB $50.00

Great Obstacle Race Game, Spear's, VGIB, A $28.00

Groucho Marx TV Quiz, Pressman, 1950s, VG+IB..........$65.00

Gumby & Poky Playful Trails, 1968, NMIB.....................$25.00

Gunsmoke, Lowell, 1958, NMIB......................................$75.00

Hair Bear Bunch, Milton Bradley, 1971, NMIB...............$30.00

Hang on Harvey, Ideal, 1969, EXIB $15.00

Hardy Boys Treasure, Parker Bros, 1957, VGIB, A $35.00

Hawaiian Eye, Lowell, 1963, EXIB..................................$85.00

Heckle & Jeckle 3-D Target Game, Aldon Industries, 1950s, EXIB...$40.00

Hector Heathcote — The Minute-And-A-Half Man, Transogram, 1963, NMIB...$100.00

Heidi Elevator, Remco, 1965, NMIB $30.00

Higgly Piggly, Cadaco, 1953, NMIB................................$20.00

High Gear, Mattel, 1953, NMIB $40.00

Hippety-Hop, Corey, 1940, EXIB....................................$30.00

Historical Dominoes Card Game, w/historical figures & battle scenes, VG+ (VG wooden box w/paper litho cover), A..............$220.00

Hoopla, Ideal, 1966, NMIB $60.00

Hopalong Canasta Card Game, Pacific, 1950, NM, A...$200.00

Hopalong Cassidy Dominoes Western Style, Milton Bradley, 1950, EXIB, A $100.00

Hopalong Cassidy Target Game, Marx/W Boyd, 1950, EXIB, A.$125.00

Hoppity Hooper, Milton Bradley, 1964, NMIB.................$75.00

Hot Wheels Wipe Out Race Game, Mattel, 1968, NMIB.$50.00

Howdy Doody Bean Bag Game, Parker Bros, 1950s, EXIB.$75.00

Howdy Doody's Own Game, Parker Bros, 1950s, EXIB $75.00

Huckleberry Hound/Piggy Bank Mini Card Games, Whitman, 1967, 2", NMIB...$18.00

I Dream of Jeannie, Milton Bradley, 1965, EXIB $75.00

I Spy, Ideal, 1965, NMIB...$75.00

Improved Game of Fish Pond, McLoughlin Bros, 1890, VGIB.$100.00

Indiana Jones in the Raiders of the Lost Ark, Parker Bros, 1982, NMIB..$20.00

Intrigue, Milton Bradley, 1955, NMIB $40.00

Ipcress File, Milton Bradley, 1966, unused, NMIB...........$40.00

Jack & Jill, Milton Bradley, VGIB, $100.00.

(Photo courtesy Randy Inman Auctions)

James Bond Secret Agent 007, Milton Bradley, 1964, NMIB..$35.00

James Bond 007 Tarot Game, 1973, NMIB.....................$75.00

James Bond 007 Thunderball, Milton Bradley, 1965, NMIB..$45.00

Jan Murray's Charge Account TV Word Game, Lowell, 1961, EXIB..$15.00

Jan Murray's Treasure Hunt, Gardner, 1950s, NMIB $15.00

Jeopardy, Milton Bradley, 1964, VG+IB, N2 ....$25.00

Jeopardy, Milton Bradley, 1972, 10th edition, NMIB.......$15.00

Jerome Park Steeple-Chase, McLoughlin Bros, VGIB....$200.00

Jetsons Fun Pad, Milton Bradley, 1963, NMIB $80.00

Jeu des Cyclistes, France, incomplete, GIB, A...............$600.00

Jocko the Clown Pinball Game, 1960s, 13", VG+, N2.....$25.00

John Drake Secret Agent, Milton Bradley, 1966, EXIB....$30.00

Jerome Park Steeple Chase, McLoughlin Brothers, EXIB, $400.00. (Photo courtesy Randy Inman Auctions)

Jolly Jungleers, Milton Bradley, VGIB, A $100.00
Jonny Quest Card Game, Milton Bradley, 1964, EXIB.....$30.00
Jules Verne's Around the World With Nellie Bly, McLoughlin
    Bros, 1890, EX+IB $200.00
Jungle Book, Parker Bros, 1966, NMIB..........................$45.00
Junior Caster Mold Set, Rapaport, 1950s, EXIB $40.00
King Kong, Milton Bradley, 1966, NMIB.......................$35.00
Knight Rider, Parker Bros, 1983, VG+IB, N2 ....$25.00
Kojak Stake Out Detective Game, Milton Bradley, 1975, MIB
    (sealed)..$85.00
Kojak Stakeout Detective, Milton Bradley, 1975, VGIB, N2.$50.00
Kukla & Ollie, Parker Bros, 1960, EXIB $45.00
Land of the Lost, Milton Bradley, 1975, NMIB $30.00
Last Straw, Schaper, 1966, NMIB....................................$20.00
Legend of Jesse James, Milton Bradley, 1966, NMIB $75.00
Let's Drive, 1969, VGIB, N2 ....$20.00
Let's Face It, Hasbro, 1950s, NMIB $35.00
Li'l Stinker, Schaper, 1956, NMIB $20.00
Lie Detector/Spy Detector, Mattel, 1960, NMIB..............$65.00
Lieutenant Combat Town, Transogram, 1963, NMIB $100.00
Literary Salad, Parker Bros, GIB, A.................................$25.00

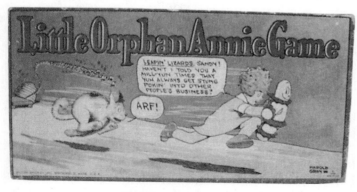

Little Orphan Annie Game, GIB, A, $65.00. (Photo courtesy Randy Inman Auctions)

Little Rascals Clubhouse Bingo, Gabriel, 1958, EXIB $50.00
Little Red Riding Hood, McLoughlin Bros, c 1900, VGIB, A.$190.00

Lone Ranger, Milton Bradley, 1966, NMIB $35.00
Lone Ranger Game, Parker Bros, 1938, EXIB.................$50.00
Lone Ranger Silver Bullets, Whiting, 1956, MIB, A......$165.00
Lone Ranger Target Game, Marx, 1946, NMIB, A $400.00
Looney Tunes, Milton Bradley, 1968, NMIB $50.00
Lost in Space, Milton Bradley, 1965, NMIB...................$75.00
Mad's Spy vs Spy, Milton Bradley, 1986, NMIB...............$40.00
Madame Planchette Horoscope Game, SelRight, 1967, NMIB.$25.00
Magic Magic Magic Game Set, Remco, 1975, NMIB.......$30.00
Magic Robot, J&L Randall Ltd/England, 1950s, NMIB ...$75.00

Magnetic Fish Pond, McLoughlin Brothers, ca 1891, VGIB, $400.00. (Photo courtesy Randy Inman Auctions)

Man From UNCLE Card Game, 1965, NM.....................$35.00
Man From UNCLE Secret Code Wheel Pin Ball Game,
    Sears/MGM, 1966, EXIB, A....................................$450.00
Man From UNCLE The Pinball Affair, Marx/MGM, 1966, EX.$125.00
Man From UNCLE THRUSH Ray Gun Affair 3-D Game, Ideal,
    1965, NMIB..$150.00
Mansion of Happiness, Parker Bros, c 1894, G+ (in box w/paper
    litho lid)...$200.00
Margie The Game of Woopie, Milton Bradley, 1961, NMIB.$20.00
Masquerade Party, Bettye-B, 1955, EXIB $40.00
Match Game, 1963, EXIB, N2 ....$50.00
Matchbox Traffic Game, 1968, EXIB $40.00
McHale's Navy, Transogram, 1962, NMIB......................$50.00
McKeever & the Colonel Bamboozle Game of Hide & Seek,
    Milton Bradley, 1962, NMIB..$30.00
Melvin the Moon Man, Remco, 1959, NMIB $65.00
Merry Game of Fibber McGee & the Wistful Vista Mystery,
    VGIB, A...$55.00
Miami Vice, Pepper Lane, 1984, EXIB............................$25.00
Mickey Mouse Circus, Marks Bros, EXIB.....................$650.00
Mickey Mouse Club Game in Disneyland, Whitman, 1963,
    EXIB..$15.00
Mickey Mouse Kiddy Keno, Jaymar, 1950s-60s, NMIB $20.00
Mickey Mouse Pop Game, Marks Bros, 1930s, EXIB......$650.00
Mighty Comics Super Heroes Game, Transogram, 1966, NMIB.$40.00

Mighty Mouse, Parker Bros, 1964, NMIB $65.00
Mighty Mouse Skill Roll, Pressman/Terrytoons, 1950s, EXIB..$150.00

Military Tenpins, Ives, Pat. 1885, EXIB, A, $1,540.00. (Photo courtesy Bertoia Auctions)

Milton the Monster, Milton Bradley, 1966, EXIB.............$25.00
Mind Maze, Parker Bros, 1970, NMIB $15.00
Mission Impossible, Ideal, 1966, EXIB $75.00
Mister Bug Goes to Town, Milton Bradley, 1956, NMIB..$40.00
Mister Magoo's Maddening Misadventures, Transogram, 1970, NMIB...$40.00
Monday Morning Coach, James De Hart, 1934, VGIB, A .$85.00
Monopoly Deluxe, Parker Bros, 1964, EXIB $35.00
Monster Old Maid, Card Game, Universal Pictures, 1964, EXIB.$85.00
Morton Downey Jr Loudmouth Game, 1988, NMIB $10.00
Movie-Land Keeno, EXIB...$75.00
Moving Picture Game, Milton Bradley, EXIB..................$125.00
Mr Ed, Parker Bros, 1960s, EXIB $65.00
Mr Novak, Transogram, 1963, NMIB................................$25.00
Mr Ree! The Fireside Detective, SelRight, 1957, NMIB..$40.00
Ms Pac Man Board Game, 1982, EXIB, N2 ....$25.00
Murder She Wrote, Warren, VGIB $20.00
My Favorite Martian, Transogram, 1963, VGIB $65.00
Mystery Date, Milton Bradley, 1965, NMIB $100.00
Mystic Skull The Game of Voodoo, Ideal, 1964, NMIB...$50.00
Nancy & Sluggo Game, 1944, rare, NMIB $100.00
Nancy Drew Mystery Game, Parker Bros, 1957, NMIB .$100.00
National Velvet, Transogram, 1961, NMIB $45.00
Neck & Neck, Wolverine, NMIB $200.00
Newlywed Game, Hasbro, 1969, NMIB $20.00

Newport Yacht Race, McLoughlin Brothers, GIB, $450.00.

(Photo courtesy Bertoia Auctions)

No Time for Sergeants, 1964, EXIB..................................$35.00
Nurses, Ideal, 1963, NMIB $40.00
Office Boy — The Good Old Game, Parker Bros, 1889, VGIB, A $140.00
Oh Magoo You've Done It Again, Warren, 1978, NMIB .$30.00
Our Country, ca 1884, VGIB, A $550.00
Our Gang Tipple-Topple Game, All-Fair, c 1930, EXIB..$400.00
Overland Trail, Transogram, 1960, NMIB $75.00
Pac-Man Two Challenging Puzzles Game, Milton Bradley, 1980, NMIB...$30.00
Park & Shop, Milton Bradley, 1960, NMIB....................$75.00
Parlor Croquet, Bliss, GIB, A $150.00
Partridge Family, Milton Bradley, 1971, NMIB................$35.00
Patty Duke Show, Milton Bradley, 1963, NMIB $25.00
Perils of Pauline, Marx, 1964, NMIB $100.00
Perry Mason, Transogram, 1959, NMIB $40.00
Peter Gunn, Parker Bros, 1969, NMIB $40.00
Peter Pan, Transogram, 1953, EXIB $30.00
Peter Potamus & So-So Card Game, 1965, NMIB $20.00
Petticoat Junction, Standard Toycraft, 1963, NMIB.........$60.00
Pin the Hat on Ko-Ko the Clown, All-Fair, 1940, EXIB ..$20.00
Pink Panther, Milton Bradley, 1969, NMIB....................$25.00
Pirate & Traveler, Milton Bradley, 1936, NMIB...............$20.00
Pirates of the Caribbean, Parker Bros, 1967, EXIB $25.00
Play Ball! Game & TV Scorer, Colorforms, 1960s, NMIB .$40.00
Play Sheriff, Milton Bradley, 1958, NMIB $30.00

Playing Department Store, Milton Bradley, VGIB, $400.00.

(Photo courtesy Bertoia Auctions)

Poky the Clown Target Game, Wyandotte, 1950s, EXIB, N2 .$75.00
Pop the Chutes Target Game, NN Hill, NMIB, A $220.00
Pop Yer Top! Game of Suspense, Milton Bradley, 1968, EXIB..$30.00
Pop-A-Puppet Pinball Game, Marx, 1960s, EX, N2 ....$25.00
Popeye Carnival (3 Games in 1), Toymaster, NMIB, A .$190.00
Popeye Clobber Cans, Gardner/KFS, NMIB, A $140.00
Popeye Jet Pilot Target Game, Japan, NM (EX Japanese/English box), A..$160.00
Popeye's Game, Parker Bros/KFS, 1948, unused, NMIB, A..$200.00
Popeye's Good Time/Blow Me Down, Built Rite, 1950s, NMIB .$40.00
Popeye's Sliding Boards & Ladders Game, Built Rite, 1958, NMIB $40.00

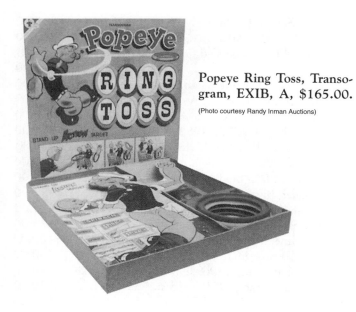

Popeye Ring Toss, Transogram, EXIB, A, $165.00.
(Photo courtesy Randy Inman Auctions)

Price Is Right, Lowell, 1958, 1st edition, EXIB.................$25.00
Prince Valiant, Transogram, 1955, EXIB.......................$45.00
Prisoner of Zelda, Parker Bros, 1896, EXIB, A...............$125.00
PT Boat 109, Ideal, 1963, VGIB $35.00
Puzzle Parties, Gilbert, c 1920, EXIB, A........................$40.00
Quick Draw McGraw Ed-U Cards, 1961, NMIB.....................$10.00
Raggedy Ann's Magic Pebble Game, Milton Bradley/J Gruelle, 1940, VGIB...$75.00
Rawhide, Lowell, 1960, EXIB..$125.00

Red Ryder Target Game, Daisy, VGIB, A, $175.00. (Photo courtesy Randy Inman Auctions)

Restless Gun, Milton Bradley, 1959, EXIB......................$40.00
Rifleman, Milton Bradley, 1959, NMIB.........................$100.00
Rip Van Winkle, Parker Bros, VGIB..............................$125.00
Road Runner, Milton Bradley, 1968, NMIB.....................$40.00
Road Runner Card Game, 1976, NMIB.............................$10.00
Robin Hood, National Games, 1940s, NMIB $50.00
Rocket Race to Saturn, Lido, 1950s, VGIB $50.00
Rocky & His Friends, Milton Bradley, 1960, EXIB...........$75.00
Rondezvous, Create, 1965, NMIB...................................$25.00

Rootie Kazootie Ed-U Cards, 1953, unused, NMIB $25.00
Roulette Wheel, Marx, NMIB, A.....................................$55.00

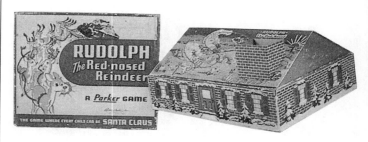

Rudolph the Red-nosed Reindeer, Parker, 1948, EXIB, $200.00. (Photo courtesy Smith House Toy Auctions)

Ruff & Reddy Spelling Game, Hanna-Barbera/Exclusive Playing Card Co, 1958, EXIB..................................$30.00
Scarlett O'Hara — One of Her Problems Marble Game, Marietta Games/MGM, 1939, EXIB $75.00
Scooby Doo Where Are You?, Milton Bradley, 1973, NMIB .$30.00
Scores N' Stripes Bagatelle Game, Marx, 1949, NMIB ..$125.00
Screwball The Mad Mad Mad Game?, Transogram, 1960, NMIB.$75.00
Sea Hunt, Lowell, 1961, EXIB.......................................$75.00
Sea Lab 2020, Milton Bradley, NMIB $20.00
Secret Agent, Milton Bradley, 1966, EXIB $25.00

Shenanigans, Milton Bradley, 1964, EXIB, $50.00. (Photo courtesy Cindy Sabulis)

Shopping at the Supermarket, Whitman, 1955, NMIB....$20.00
Sigmund & the Sea Monsters, Milton Bradley, 1975, NMIB.$40.00
Skittles Game, Art Fabric Mills/Thomas Nast, 9 stuffed cloth bowling-pin type male figures & ball, 10", EX+, A .$1,540.00
Skittles Game, early, swan w/attached wheels & 9 pnt girl figures, compo, 17" L swan, VG, A..........................$1,540.00
Skittles Game, 9 compo girls in Victorian swimwear & hats, w/orig circular inset & ball toss, 6½", EX+, A $2,200.00
Smack-A-Roo Game Set, Mattel, 1964, EXIB.................$40.00
Smokey Bear, Milton Bradley, 1968, unused, NMIB.........$75.00
Snake's Alive, Ideal, 1966, NMIB $30.00
Snoopy & the Red Baron, Milton Bradley, 1970, MIB.....$40.00
Snoopy Card Game, Ideal, 1965, NMIB $25.00
Snoopy Snake Attack, Gabriel, 1980, MIB....................$25.00

Snow White & the Seven Dwarfs, Parker Bros, 1938, EXIB.$150.00
Soldiers on Guard, McLoughlin Bros, VGIB, A $125.00
Space Age Picture Checkers, Common, 1965, NMIB......$15.00
Space Mouse Card Game, Fairchild, 1964, NMIB...........$18.00
Space Pilot, Cadaco-Ellis, 1951, VG+IB.........................$75.00
Space: 1999, Milton Bradley, 1976, NMIB $25.00
Sparky Marble Maze, Built Rite, 1971, NMIB $30.00
Spear's 'Quick Change' Comic Pictures, VGIB, A $65.00
Spot Shot Marble Game, Wolverine, 1930s, NM.............$50.00
Spy Detector, Mattel, 1960, NMIB $75.00
Stagecoach, Milton Bradley, 1958, NMIB.......................$25.00
Stagecoach West Adventure Game, Transogram, 1961, NMIB.$60.00
Star Trek Board Game, 1975, EXIB, N2.........................$50.00
Star Wars Escape From Death Star, Kenner, 1977, NMIB.$25.00
Starsky & Hutch Detective, Milton Bradley, 1977, NMIB.$25.00
Steeple Chase, JH Singer, GIB, A $125.00
Steeple Chase, McLoughlin Bros, VGIB, A $200.00
Steve Canyon Exciting Air Force Game, Lowell, 1950s, NMIB.$50.00
Stop, Milton Bradley, 1950s, NMIB $20.00
Submarine Search, Milton Bradley, 1973, EXIB, N2 ....$40.00
Superman Marble Maze, Hasbro, 1966, EXIB $75.00
Superstition, Milton Bradley, 1977, NMIB $20.00
Surfside 6, Lowell, 1961, unused, MIB $100.00

Table Tennis, McLoughlin Brothers, VGIB, A, $165.00. (Photo courtesy Randy Inman Auctions)

Tales of Wells Fargo, Milton Bradley, 1959, EXIB $50.00
Tennessee Tuxedo, Transogram, 1963, EXIB $135.00
That Girl, Remco, 1969, EXIB.......................................$70.00
Three Little Pigs Game, Einson-Freeman, 1933, game board only, EX...$50.00
Thunderbirds, Parker Bros, 1967, NMIB.......................$80.00
Tic-Tac Dough, Transogram, 1957, EXIB, N2 ....$20.00
Tim Holt Rodeo Dart Games, American Toys, unused, NMIB.$100.00
Tiny Tim Game of Beautiful Things, Parker Bros, 1970, EXIB.$75.00
Tip It, 1965, VGIB...$20.00
To Tell the Truth, Lowell, 1957, EXIB $20.00
Tom & Jerry, Milton Bradley, 1977, EXIB, N2 ....$35.00
Top Cat, Cadaco, 1961, NMIB......................................$45.00
Town & Country Traffic, Ranger Steel, 1940s, EXIB $50.00
Town Hall, Milton Bradley, 1939, NMIB........................$20.00

Touchdown Football Game, Wilder, GIB, $75.00. (Photo Randy Inman Auctions)

Truth or Consequences, Gabriel, 1955, unused, NMIB $20.00
Turn Over, Milton Bradley, EXIB, A $75.00
Twiggy, Milton Bradley, 1967, EXIB..............................$50.00
Uncle Wiggily, Milton Bradley, 1961, NMIB...................$25.00
Unsere 'U-Boofe' (U Boat Game), Germany, EXIB, A $80.00
Untouchables, Transogram, 1961, NMIB........................$60.00
Untouchables Target Game, Marx, 1950s, gun shoots at moving target, tin, NM..$350.00
Virginian, Transogram, 1962, EXIB...............................$85.00
Voodoo, Schaper, 1967, EXIB......................................$25.00
Voyage to the Bottom of the Sea Card Game, Milton Bradley, 1964, NMIB $45.00
Wagon Train, Milton Bradley, 1960, EXIB......................$50.00
Walt Disney's Fantasyland, Parker Bros, 1950, MIB $50.00
Walter Johnson Baseball Game, VGIB, A $200.00
Wanted Dead or Alive, Lowell, 1959, EXIB $85.00
Which Witch?, Milton Bradley, 1970, NMIB $65.00
Who Framed Roger Rabbit?, Milton Bradley, 1987, NMIB .$20.00
Wide World Travel Game, Parker Bros, 1957, NMIB.......$25.00
Wild Bill Hickok's Cavalry & Indians Game, Built Rite, 1950s, NMIB $25.00
Wild World Travel Game, Parker Bros, 1957, NMIB $25.00
Wilder's Football Game, GIB, A $125.00
Wink Tennis, Transogram, 1956, NMIB $15.00
Wonder Woman, Hasbro, 1973, NMIB...........................$50.00
Woody Woodpecker Ring Toss Game, 1958, MIB............$50.00
World's Fair Ed-U Cards, 1965, NMIB...........................$15.00
Wow Pillow Fight Game, Milton Bradley, 1964, NMIB ...$25.00
Wyatt Earp, Transogram, 1958, EXIB............................$50.00
Yogi Bear & Huckleberry Hound Bowling Set, Transogram, 1960, EXIB...$50.00
Yogi Bear Rummy Ed-U Cards, 1961, MIB (sealed) $15.00
Yogi Bear Score-A-Matic Ball Toss, Transogram, EXIB....$65.00
You Don't Say Milton Bradley, 1963, EXIB......................$20.00
Young America Target, Parker Bros, VGIB, A.................$275.00
Zamboola, Norstar, VGIB...$85.00
Zorro, Parker Bros, 1964, EXIB....................................$45.00
$10,000 Pyramid, Milton Bradley, 1972, NMIB................$10.00
$64,000 Dollar Question, Lowell, 1955, EXIB $25.00
10-4 Good Buddy, 1976, VG+IB, N2 ....$25.00

12 O'Clock High, Ideal, 1965, NMIB $70.00
77 Sunset Strip, Lowell, 1960, NMIB $35.00

Zippy Zepps Air Game, All Fair Toys and Games, VGIB, $500.00. (Photo courtesy Bertoia Auctions)

Gasoline-Powered Toys

Two of the largest companies to manufacture gas-powered models are Cox and Wen-Mac. Since the late '50s they have been making faithfully detailed models of airplanes as well as some automobiles and boats. Condition of used models will vary greatly because of the nature of the miniature gas engine and damage resulting from the fuel that has been used. Because of this, 'new in box' gas toys command a premium.

Advisor: Richard Trautwein (T3)

All-American Hot Rod, cast aluminum, 9", VG $250.00
Bremer Whirlwind #02, gr & wht, 1939, 18", NM......$2,900.00
Bremer Whirlwind #08, louvered hood & belly pan, ca 1940, 18", EX...$2,300.00
Bremer Whirlwind #300, red, Brown Jr engine, 1939, VG, A..$1,250.00
Cameron Racer #4, red w/yel flame decals, 8", VG, A ...$275.00

Cameron Rodzy Standard Racer, cast aluminum, rubber tires, 1950s, 8", MIB, A, $500.00. (Photo courtesy Randy Inman Auctions)

Cameron Rodzy Hot Rod Racer, bl, .15 engine, 8", VG, A..$350.00
Cessna UC 78 Bobcat (WWII-era Bamboo Bomber), w/pilot, co-pilot & 2 passengers, 42x57½" W, EX $375.00
Cox AA Fuel Dragster, bl & red, 1968-70, M, from $125 to ..$160.00
Cox Acro-Cub, 1960s, MIB (sealed)............................$85.00
Cox Baja Bug, yel & orange, 1968-73, M....................$65.00
Cox Chopper, MIB...$100.00
Cox Delta F-15, Wing Series, gray, 1981-86, M.............$30.00
Cox E-Z Flyer Comanche, wht, NMIB...........................$35.00
Cox Golden Bee, .49 engine, M..................................$30.00
Cox Marine Helicopter, NM $35.00
Cox ME-109 Airplane, 1994, MIB (sealed) $60.00
Cox Mercedes Benz W196 Racer, red, 1963-65, EX, from $85 to $125.00
Cox Navy Helldiver, 2-tone bl, 1963-66, EX, from $65 to .$80.00
Cox P-51 Bendix Racer, red & yel, molded landing gear, 1963-64, EX, from $65 to...$80.00
Cox Pitts Special Biplane, wht, .20 engine, 1968, EX $50.00
Cox PT-19 Flight Trainer, yel & bl, EX $45.00
Cox QZ PT-19, Quiet Zone Muffler, red & wht, 1966-69, EX..$50.00
Cox RAF Spitfire, dk gr w/camouflage, 1966-69, EX, from $40 to $50.00
Cox Ryan ST-3, w/pilot & co-pilot, wht & bl, .20 ignition power, M $65.00
Cox Sandblaster, brn & tan, 1968-72, M......................$65.00
Cox Shirke Bonneville Special, MIB, from $150 to $200.00
Cox Sky Raider, gray, EXIB $85.00
Cox Sky-Jumper, helicopter w/pilot & parachute, olive, 1989-95, M...$40.00
Cox Skymaster, Sure Flyer Series, orange & blk w/stickers, twin tail, 1976-79, EX..$50.00
Cox Snowmobile, silver, 1968, M $100.00
Cox Stealth Bomber, blk, 1987-89, EX $30.00
Cox Super Sabre F-100, wht & gray, .20 engine, 1958-63, EX, from $60 to..$80.00
Cox Super Stunter, 1974-79, EX, from $30 to $45.00
Cox Thimble Drome Comanche, metal w/plastic wings, .15 engine, 1960s, MIB $75.00
Cox Thimble Drome Prop-Rod, red & yel, 12", EX (worn box), A $200.00
Cox Thimble Drome Prop-Rod, yel plastic w/metal chassis, EX, from $85 to...$130.00
Cox Thimble Drome Racer #92, diecast, 8½", VG $150.00
Cox Thunderbolt, E-Z Flyer Series, blk, w/muffler, 1993-95, M...$30.00
Cox UFO Flying Saucer, Wings Series, wht, 1990-91, M.$25.00
Cub-Kart, Harkimer Tool, 1961, go-kart w/plastic driver, 6½", unused, MIB, A $150.00
Curtiss Jenny Airplane, WWI-era, 65" W/58" L, EX, A.$400.00
Curtiss P-40D Tiger Shark, plastic, Comet Model Hobby Craft, 13½", MIB, from $95 to $135.00
Dooling Bros Arrow Racer #61, mk Yellow Jacket Engineering, 19", EX, A $1,700.00
Dooling Bros F Racer #1, red w/Knoxville Champ logo, 19", EX, from $1,000 to..$1,200.00
Dooling Bros F Racer #3, red, no engine, 1948, 16", EX.$1,000.00
Dooling Bros F Rail Racer #25, gr & yel, McCoy .60 bl-head engine, 16", VG..$1,700.00

Dooling Bros Frog Cabin Streamliner, cast aluminum, Super Cyclone engine, 1939, 16", EX, from $2,600 to ...**$3,200.00**

Dooling Bros. Mercury Racer, cast aluminum, rubber tires, cyclone engine, 1940s, 20", restored, A, $1,265.00. (Photo courtesy Randy Inman Auctions)

Dooling Bros Mercury Racer #59, aluminum w/some pnt detail, Hornet engine, ca 1940, 18½", VG, from $1,800 to **$2,300.00**

Dooling Bros Racer #1, red flat-tail model w/Knoxville Champ logo, 19", EX, from $850 to................................**$1,150.00**

Dooling Bros Racer #4, orange, articulated front end, McCoy engine, rstr, EX, from $1,500 to **$1,650.00**

Dooling Bros Racer #5, red, 16", EX, A **$950.00**

Dooling Bros Racer #6, bl, rear drive w/front drive conversion, Super Cyclone engine, 1941, 18", EX, A.............**$2,300.00**

Dooling Bros Racer #8, Atwood .60 Champion engine, 1939, 19", EX, from $1,500 to......................................**$1,800.00**

Dooling Bros Racer #13, series II, maroon & yel, Super Cyclone engine, 1940, EX **$2,300.00**

Dooling Bros Tether Racing Boat, red w/stepped hull design, .61 engine, 1955, 35", EX, A **$500.00**

Dreyer Special Racer #2, silver w/red seat, 18", NM, from $2,600 to..**$2,800.00**

Deusenberg Racer #5, orange w/louvered 3-pc hood & belly pan, Hornet power, 1939, 21½", EX, from $2,600 to ...**$3,000.00**

England Special Racer #8, gr-pnt aluminum w/leather seats, central clutch, ca 1948, 16", EX.....................................**$825.00**

Fairchild 22 Model Airplane, bl & cream, working shock absorbers in landing gear, 47" W, NM, A.................**$300.00**

Hassad Special Racer #14, tan w/red & gold detail, .60 Hassad Custom engine, 18", EX, A **$2,000.00**

Hiller T Racer #19, yel w/Voit wheels & tires, Hiller .60 engine, 20", EX, A **$1,800.00**

Hiller-Comet Racer #5, red, 1942, 19", EX **$1,800.00**

Hiller-Comet Racer #18, orange w/yel detail, #1082 engine, ca 1940, 18", EX, from $1,000 to...................................**$1,300.00**

Hot Rod Roadster, red, Hornet .60 engine, 15", EX....**$1,200.00**

Korn Meteor #36, mk Vic Felts Powerline Special, wht, Brown Jr engine, 1938, 19", EX, from $1,100 to...................**$1,500.00**

McCoy Invader #1 ('47), bl, 17", rstr, A....................**$1,700.00**

McCoy Invader, cast aluminum, rubber tires, 1940s, 17", restored, A, $1,870.00. (Photo courtesy Randy Inman Auctions)

McCoy Invader #6, yel, McCoy .49 engine, 17", EX, from $1,495 to..**$1,695.00**

McCoy Invader #41, red w/Ed Dowd's racing #300C, White Case .60 engine w/magneto, 1949, 18", EX, from $1,495 to......**$1,695.00**

McCoy Invader #75, red w/cream 75, Hornet engine, factory fuel tank, 17", EX, A **$1,500.00**

McCoy Streamliner, chrome-plated, 1950, 18", EX, from $525 to **$795.00**

McCoy Streamliner, gray, never drilled for an engine, 17", NM, from $475 to **$575.00**

McCoy Streamliner, wht w/red trim, never drilled for an engine, ca 1952, 17", EX, from $475 to **$575.00**

Melcraft Racer, wht w/Champion tires, ignition engine, ca 1948, 16", EX..**$475.00**

Midgetee Racer, cast aluminum, rubber tires, 9½", EXIB, A, $1,485.00. (Photo courtesy Randy Inman Auctions)

Miracle Power Racer #1, blk & yel w/red detail, Dooling engine, 17", EX..**$1,600.00**

Ohlsson & Rice Racer #54, red, modified w/direct O&R marine engine, w/cooling slots, 10", VG, A.......................**$450.00**

Phantom Lady Speedboat, wood, Phantom P-30 engine, 21", EX, A **$650.00**

Railton Champion Racer #12, red & yel, 17", NM, D10.$2,700.00
Reuhl Racer #9, blk, McCoy White .60 engine, 1940, 17",
    EX $2,000.00
Reuhl Racer #39, Bakelite body, grille & seat, .49 McCoy
    engine, 1940, 17", EX................................$2,200.00

Rexner Spl. Racer, cast aluminum, rubber tires, front-wheel drive, 1940s, 19", restored, from $2,800.00 to $3,400.00.

(Photo courtesy Randy Inman Auctions)

Road Runner #143, cast aluminum reproduction, yel, OK Super
    .60 engine, 16", EX, A...............................$800.00
Speed Chief Racer, cast aluminum, Foss engine, 1940s, 21", G,
    from $600 to $800.00
Speed Demon #18, yel-pnt wood, Bunch .60 engine, 1937-38,
    20", EXIB..$5,700.00
Speedboat #37, orange-pnt wood, Apex Skylark engine, ca 1939,
    37", EX..$1,400.00
Spit-Craft Speedboat, plastic, Royal Spitfire engine, 21",
    NMIB $200.00
Testors Avion Mustang Fighter Airplane, NMIB...........$100.00
Testors Cosmic Wind, orange, MIB.............................$50.00
Testors Cosmic Wind, Spirit of '76, M $60.00
Testors OD P-51 Mustang, VG.....................................$30.00
Testors Red Albatross, Fly 'Em series, NM $35.00
Testors Sopwith Camel, Fly 'Em series, NM..................$35.00
Testors Spirite Indy Car, wht, 1966-68, M, from $75 to .$100.00
Trackmaster Tether Racer, hammered aluminum w/CA Racing
    Assoc graphics, Brown Jr engine, 19", rare, EX, A .$2,200.00
Wen-Mac '57 Chevy Racer, orange plastic w/decals, 12", VG.$160.00
Wen-Mac A-24 Army Attack Bomber, 1962-64, EX........$45.00
Wen-Mac Aeromite, blk, Baby Spitfire engine, EX $60.00
Wen-Mac Albatross, Flying Wing Series, red, wht & bl, EX.$40.00
Wen-Mac Basic trainer, bl, blk, red & yel w/chrome detail,
    1962-64, EX $50.00
Wen-Mac Cutlass, blk, blk & yel, 1958-60, EX $50.00
Wen-Mac Falcon, red, wht & blk, 1963-64, EX.............$45.00
Wen-Mac Giant P-40 Flying Tiger, wht, 1959-60, EX......$45.00
Wen-Mac Marine Corsair, red, 1960s, EX.....................$40.00
Wen-Mac Mustang Fast-Back, bl, 1968, EX...................$65.00
Wen-Mac P-63 King Cobra, chrome, 1962-64, EX..........$50.00
Wen-Mac RAF Day Fighter, wht, 1963-64, EX $50.00

Wen-Mac SBD-5 Navy Dive Bomber, 1962-64, EX $50.00
Wen-Mac Turbojet, red & cream w/chrome detail, 1958-64, EX .$45.00
Wen-Mac Yellow Jacket Corsair, yel, 1959-64, EX $40.00
Wen-Max Eagle, Flying Wings series, red, wht & bl, 1963-64,
    EX..$40.00

GI Joe

GI Joe, the most famous action figure of them all, has been made in hundreds of variations since Hasbro introduced him in 1964. The first of these jointed figures was 12" tall; they can be identified today by the mark each carried on his back: GI Joe T.M. (trademark), Copyright 1964. They came with four different hair colors: blond, auburn, black, and brown, each with a scar on his right cheek. They were sold in four basic packages: Action Soldier, Action Sailor, Action Marine, and Action Pilot. A Black figure was also included in the line, and there were representatives of many nations as well — France, Germany, Japan, Russia, etc. These figures did not have scars and are more valuable. Talking GI Joes were issued in 1967 when the only female (the nurse) was introduced. Besides the figures, uniforms, vehicles, guns, and accessories of many varieties were produced. The Adventure Team series, made from 1970 to 1976, included Black Adventurer, Air Adventurer, Talking Astronaut, Sea Adventurer, Talking Team Commander, Land Adventurer, and several variations. In 1974 Joe's hard plastic hands were replaced with kung fu grips, so that he could better grasp his weapons. Assorted playsets allowed young imaginations to run wild; and besides the doll-size items there were wristwatches, foot lockers, toys, walkie-talkies, etc., made for the kids themselves. Due to increased production costs, the large GI Joe was discontinued in 1976.

In 1982 Hasbro brought out the smaller 3¾" GI Joe figures, each with its own descriptive name. Of the first series, some characters were produced with either a swivel or straight arm. Vehicles, weapons, and playsets were available, and some characters could only be had by redeeming flag points from the backs of packages. This small version proved to be the most successful action figure line ever made. Loose items are common; collectors value those still mint in the original packages at two to four times higher.

In 1993 Hasbro reintroduced the 12" line while retaining the 3¾" size. The highlights of the comeback are the thirtieth anniversary collection of six figures which are already selling in the collector's market at above their original price ($29.00).

Production of the 3¾" figures came to an end in December 1994. For more information we recommend *Encyclopedia to GI Joe* and *The 30th Anniversary Salute to GI Joe* both by Vincent San Telmo; *The New Official Identification Guide to G.I. Joe and Accessories, 1964 – 1978,* and *The Official G.I. Joe Collectors Guide to Completing and Collating Your G.I. Joes and Accessories* all by James DeSimone. Note: All items are American issue unless indicated otherwise. (Action Man was made in England by Hasbro circa 1960 into the 1970s.) All listings are complete unless noted.

Advisor: Cotswold Collectibles (C6)

See also Games; Lunch Boxes; Puzzles; Windups, Friction, and Other Mechanicals.

12" GI Joe Figures and Figure Sets

Action Marine, #7700, EXIB $350.00
Action Marine, #7700, MIB....................................$500.00
Action Marine (Talking), #7790, NM $200.00
Action Marine, Beachhead Assault, EX, C6................$295.00
Action Marine, Demolition, EX, C6.........................$325.00
Action Marine, Jungle Fighter, NM $575.00
Action Marine, Medic, NM, C6...............................$325.00
Action Marine, Paratrooper, EX+ $125.00
Action Marine, USMC Dress Blues, EX, C6 ....$215.00
Action Marine, 30th Anniversary, 1994, NRFB.............$50.00
Action Marine Tank Commander, #7731, EX $800.00
Action Nurse, #8060, MIB (sealed)........................$5,000.00
Action Nurse, #8060, nearly complete, EX $1,000.00
Action Pilot, #7800, M (EX box)..............................$400.00
Action Pilot, #7800, NM (EX 2nd issue box w/added sticker
    photo), A...$1,100.00
Action Pilot (Talking), #7890, EX (EX box) $575.00
Action Pilot, USAF Dress Blues, EX, C6......................$185.00
Action Pilot, 30th Anniversary, 1994, NRFB..................$60.00

Action Sailor, NM (EX box), $300.00. (Photo courtesy Cindy Sabulis)

Action Sailor (Talking), #7690, MIB...........................$700.00
Action Sailor (Talking), #7690, VGIB $425.00
Action Sailor, Breeches Buoy Set, EX..........................$200.00
Action Sailor, Breeches Buoy Set, NM..........................$275.00
Action Sailor, Deep Sea Diver, NM, C6 ....$300.00
Action Sailor, Landing Signal Officer, EXIP $375.00
Action Sailor, Landing Signal Officer, NM $200.00
Action Sailor, Navy Attack Set, NM............................$150.00
Action Sailor, 30th Anniversary, 1994, NRFB $60.00
Action Soldier, #7800, MIB, from $275 to $375.00
Action Soldier (Black), #7900, EX $450.00
Action Soldier (Black), #7900, M..............................$900.00

Action Soldier (Talking), #7590, EXIB $450.00
Action Soldier, Army Bivouac Series, #7549.83, M (EX box).$400.00
Action Soldier, Deep Freeze Set, EX...........................$175.00
Action Soldier, Green Beret, EX...............................$115.00
Action Soldier, Heavy Weapons, EX+, C6 ....$475.00
Action Soldier, Military Police, M (EX box), from $350 to .$450.00
Action Soldier, Military Police, VG+ $260.00
Action Soldier, Sabotage, NM, C6..............................$295.00
Action Soldier, Ski Patrol, EX................................$315.00
Action Soldier, Snow Troops, EX, C6...........................$315.00
Action Soldier, West Point Cadet, EX, C6......................$265.00
Action Soldier, West Point Cadet, NM $325.00
Action Soldier, 30th Anniversary, 1994, NRFB $45.00

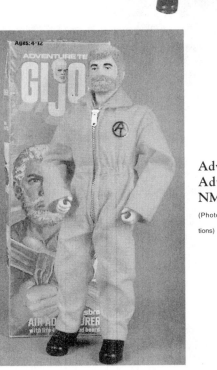

Adventure Team Adventurer (Black), #7404, NMIB, from $250.00 to $300.00. (Photo courtesy Cotswold Collectibles, Inc.)

Adventure Team Air Adventurer, #7282, NMIB, C6, $325.00. (Photo courtesy McMasters Doll Auctions)

Adventure Team Adventurer (Black), #7404, nude, EX, C6 .$80.00

Adventure Team Adventurer (Black), Hidden Treasure, EX, C6 ....$130.00

Adventure Team Adventurer (Black), Trouble at Vulture Pass, EX, C6 ....$310.00

Adventure Team Air Adventurer, #7282, EX, C6 ....$150.00

Adventure Team Air Adventurer, #7282, NM (VG+ French-Canadian box) $275.00

Adventure Team Air Adventurer, #7282, nude, EX $70.00

Adventure Team Air Adventurer, Aerial Recon, EX $175.00

Adventure Team Air Adventurer, Dangerous Climb, EX, C6 .$110.00

Adventure Team Air Adventurer, Fantastic Freefall, VG+, C6 .$325.00

Adventure Team Air Adventurer, White Tiger Hunt, EX, C6 .$125.00

Adventure Team Astronaut (Talking), #7915, EX, from $225 to..$285.00

Adventure Team Astronaut (Talking), #7915, EX (VG box), $400.00. (Photo courtesy Cotswold Collectibles, Inc.)

Adventure Team Astronaut, Hidden Missile Discovery Set, EX $200.00

Adventure Team Bullet Man, #8026, NM, from $250 to .$275.00

Adventure Team Commander (Talking w/Kung Fu Grip), #7290, NMIB..$250.00

Adventure Team Commander (Talking), #7400, EX, C6 .$195.00

Adventure Team Commander (Talking), #7400, nude, VG+, C6 ....$75.00

Adventure Team Eagle Eye Land Commander, #7276, MIP .$80.00

Adventure Team Land Adventurer, #7401, NMIB, from $175 to $235.00

Adventure Team Land Adventurer, #7401, nude, EX, C6 ..$65.00

Adventure Team Land Adventurer, Fight for Survival, EX, C6 .$125.00

Adventure Team Land Adventurer, Secret Rendezvous, EX, C6 ....$125.00

Adventure Team Land Adventurer, Smoke Jumper, near complete, EX $185.00

Adventure Team Land Adventurer, Volcano Jumper, near complete, EX, C6 ....$185.00

Adventure Team Land Adventurer, Winter Rescue, EX, C6 ..$175.00

Adventure Team Land Adventurer (Kung Fu Grip), #1-7280, nude, EX, C6 ....$72.00

Adventure Team Land Adventurer (Kung Fu Grip), Flying Space Adventure, EX $525.00

Adventure Team Machine Gun Emplacement Set, #5931, EX (EX box), from $450 to $500.00

Adventure Team Man of Action, #7500, nude, VG+, C6 ..$65.00

Adventure Team Man of Action, #7500, VGIB.............$200.00

Adventure Team Man of Action (Talking), #7590, NM (EX box)..$285.00

Adventure Team Man of Action, Jungle Survival, EX, C6 .$185.00

Adventure Team Man of Action, Mysterious Explosion, EX, C6...$285.00

Adventure Team Man of Action, Photo Recon, EX, C6 ..$98.00

Adventure Team Mike Power Atomic Man, #8025, complete, MOC, from $80.00 to $100.00.

Adventure Team Sea Adventurer, #7281, EXIB, from $160 to $200.00

Adventure Team Sea Adventurer, #7281, VG+, C6 ....$70.00

Adventure Team Sea Adventurer, Demolition, EX, C6 .$150.00

Adventure Team Sea Adventurer, Jungle Survival, EX, C6 .$185.00

Australian Desert Jeep Driver, EX $165.00

Australian Jungle Fighter, EX $375.00

British Commando, #8104, EX, from $275 to.................$350.00

French Resistance Fighter, #8203, EX+ (EX sm box), C6 .$775.00

French Resistance Fighter, #8203, NM, from $250 to $300.00

German Soldier, near complete, EX $150.00

German Stormtrooper, EX, from $160 to.......................$200.00

Japanese Imperial Soldier, #8101, w/medal, NM, from $500 to ..$550.00

Japanese Imperial Soldier, #8201, EX...........................$300.00
Russian Infantryman, #8102, NM $365.00
State Trooper, M, A...$850.00

ACCESSORIES FOR 12" GI JOE

Boxed and packaged items are listed by name/title just as it appears on the box or card; loose pieces of clothing or equipment are listed by item first, followed by the name of of the series or the character it relates to (for instance 'Jacket & Trousers, Green Beret').

Adventure Team Demolition, #7370, M (EX+ box), C6, $175.00.

(Photo courtesy Cotswold Collectibles, Inc.)

Adventure Team Headquarters, EX (G box) $150.00
Air Force Dress Pants, #7805, M (NM card), C6 ....$175.00
Ammo Box, Tank Commander, gr w/orange US GI Joe stencil, issued for uniform set, NM, A $600.00
Armband, Army Airborne MP, snap connectors (rare), NM..$200.00
Armored Suit, Demolition, EX...$15.00
Army Combat Engineer Set, #7571, 1967, M................$650.00
Astronaut Boots, plastic, VG+, pr, C6 ....$25.00
Astronaut Suit, multi-pocket, w/side tabs, EX $400.00
Belt, Action Man, brn web, EX, C6 ....$3.00
Binoculars, Hurricane Spotter, gray, EX, C6 ....$7.00
Binoculars, red w/string, 1960s, EX, C6 ....$14.00
Bivouac Set, sleeping bag, knife, spoon, fork, mess kit, canteen & cover, rifle, bayonet, belt & army field manual, MIB..$285.00
Boots, Flying Space Adventure, yel, EX, pr......................$32.00
Breeches Buoy, Action Sailor, EX, C6...............................$35.00
Camera, Secret Mission to Spy Island, blk w/elastic strap, EX, C6...$7.00
Canadian Mountie Set, outfit, rifle, ammunition belt, goggles, radio & mess kit, NM $290.00
Canteen & Cover, British, EX, C6....................................$35.00
Cap, Action Pilot, bl, EX, C6...$14.00
Carrying Case/Play Set, Takara, VG+.............................$100.00
Cobra, Search for the Golden Idol, EX, C6 ....$15.00
Combat Field Jacket, 1964, MOC....................................$700.00
Command Post Poncho, Action Soldier, MOC $170.00

Coveralls, Landing Signal Officer, VG, C6.......................$35.00
Crash Crew, Action Pilot, M (EX photo box) $450.00
Crash Crew, Action Pilot, MIP (sealed) $550.00
Crocodile, Adventure Team, EX $15.00

Desert Explorer, Adventure Team, #8205, M (EX card), C6, $65.00. (Photo courtesy Cotswold Collectibles, Inc.)

Diver Belt, 1st issue w/exposed weights & leg strap, EX, C6 ..$25.00
Entrenching Tool, Australian, EX, C6 ....$10.00
Fatigue Pants, Action Marine, #7715, camo, M (NM card), A..$400.00
Fatigue Pants, Action Soldier, #7504, gr, M (NM card), A..$250.00
Fatigue Shirt, Action Marine, #7714, camo, M (EX card)..$400.00
Fatigue Shirt, Action Soldier, #7503, gr, M (NM card), A.$435.00
First Aid Pouch, gr cloth, w/snap closure, EX $50.00
Flag, Army, EX, C6 ....$35.00
Flag, USAF, EX, C6 ....$35.00
Flame Thrower, gr, EX, C6 ....$35.00
Flight Suit, Scramble, w/accessories, MIB $1,000.00
Flight Suit, Scramble, w/accessories, NM $250.00
Geiger Counter, Volcano Jumper, yel, EX, C6....................$7.00
Goggles, Desert Patrol, amber, rpl elastic, EX, A $65.00
Green Beret Set, #7533, M (EX card) $325.00
Green Beret Set, #7533, NM...$250.00

Helmet, A.S. (Air Security), EX, A, $450.00. (Photo courtesy Cotswold Collectibles)

Grenade Launcher, Action Man, EX, C6..........................$15.00
Handgun (.45), Action Man, EX, C6.................................$5.00
Head Gear, Landing Signal Officer, 1960s, EX, C6 ....$60.00
Helmet, British, EX, C6...$18.00
Helmet Set, #7507, M (NM card)....................................$110.00
Helmet Sticker, Soldier Helmet, #7507, EX, C6..............$10.00
High Voltage Escape, 1972, M (EX pkg).........................$120.00
Hunting Rifle, Action Man, C6.......................................$10.00
Jacket & Trousers, Airborne MP, gr, VG, C6 ....$85.00
Jacket & Trousers, Green Beret, VG, C6 ....$40.00
Jackhammer, EX+..$275.00
Jumpsuit, Adventure Team, mesh, EX, C6........................$12.00
Jumpsuit, Radiation Detection, gr, EX, C6.......................$15.00
Life Vest, orange, padded, 1960s, C6...............................$29.00
Map Case & Map, Sandstorm Survival, silver, EX, C6 ....$7.00
Medal, Australian, Victoria Cross, Action Man, EX, C6 .$10.00
Medic Set, Action Marine, #7719, NMIB $250.00
Mountain Troops Set, NMIB...$185.00
Oar, Secret Mission to Spy Island, blk, for dinghy, EX, C6.$6.00
Parachute Pack, Sky Dive to Danger, EX+ $125.00
Pup Tent, Marine, EX $25.00
Pup Tent, White Tiger Hunt, orange/gr (1st version), no poles,
    EX, C6...$15.00

Trousers, Capture of the Pygmy Gorilla, camo, EX, C6 ......$6.00
Tunic & Trouser Set, German, VG, C6 ....$30.00
Uniform, State Trooper, w/accessories, NM...................$500.00
White Tiger Hunt, NMIB...$100.00
Work Shirt, Action Sailor, #7608, MOC, from $200 to.$250.00

VEHICLES FOR 12" GI JOE

Adventure Team Vehicle, NMIB $230.00
Amphibian Duck, M, from $150 to...............................$180.00
ATV, yel, EX, from $50 to...$75.00
Avenger Pursuit Craft, MIB, from $175 to.....................$200.00
Big Trapper, cardboard seat & side panels, EX, from $175 to..$200.00
Capture Copter, #7481, NM (EX box), from $225 to.....$275.00
Combat Jeep Set, #7000, EX $175.00
Combat Jeep Set, #7000, EX (EX box)...........................$265.00
Crash Crew Truck, M..$1,200.00
Crash Crew Truck, MIB, from $2,500 to $3,200.00
Desert Patrol Jeep, #8030, EX+, from $350 to $375.00
Escape Car, #7360, MIB, from $50 to $75.00
Friendship VII Space Capsule, w/astronaut, complete, MIB .$165.00

German Staff Car, Action Man Task Force, M (VG+ box),
$275.00. (Photo courtesy Cotswold Collectibles, Inc.)

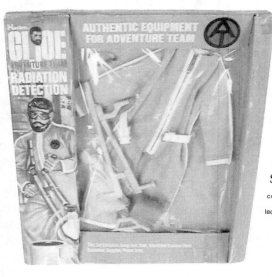

Radiation Detection, #7341A, M (VG+ card), $175.00. (Photo courtesy Cotswold Collectibles, Inc.)

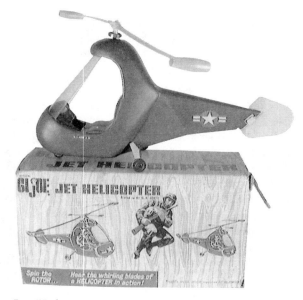

Jet Helicopter, Irwin, #5395, EX (EX box), $175.00. (Photo courtesy Cotswold Collectibles, Inc.)

Radio, Airborne MP, blk, mk Hong Kong, G+ $245.00
Rockblaster, Sonic Blaster, EX, C6 ....$5.00
Scabbard, Annapolis Cadet, w/slings, no sword, EX, C6 .$125.00
Scuba Gear, orange suit, tanks & fins, NM...................$150.00
Scuba Suit, MIP (sealed) $580.00
Scuba Top, Action Man, EX, C6.....................................$12.00
Shirt & Trousers, Japanese, EX, C6 ....$45.00
Shore Patrol Dress Pants, #7614, MOC.........................$250.00
Shore Patrol Jumper Set, #7613, MOC $1,125.00
Shorts, Australian, EX, C6..$27.00
Sleeping Bag, #7515, MOC..$185.00
Space Capsule Collar, inflatable, Sears, EX $115.00
Stethoscope, Medic, EX, C6...$19.00
Survival Life Raft, #7802, MIB $100.00
Tripod, Combat Engineer, w/plumb bob, EX+ $250.00

Helicopter, #7380, EX (G box), C6 ....$200.00
Iron Knight Tank, M $135.00
Iron Knight Tank, VG $35.00
Mobile Support Vehicle, EX.......................................$250.00
Mobile Support Vehicle, EX (EX box), from $300 to $325.00
Motorcycle & Sidecar, Cherilea, gr, near complete, EX, C6 .$50.00
Motorcycle & Sidecar, Irwin, rust colored, w/machine gun, EX.$110.00
Night Raven, w/blueprints, EX....................................$110.00
Panther Jet, EX, C6 ....$400.00
Sandstorm Jeep, gr, EXIB...$275.00
Sea Sled & Frogman, #5957, Sears Exclusive, EX (VG box), C6 .$395.00
Sea Sled & Frogman, #8050, no cave, complete, MIB ...$345.00
Sea Wolf (submarine), EXIB $100.00
Sky Hawk, #7470, MIB, from $80 to.........................$120.00
Space Capsule, VG+, C6 ....$55.00

Space Capsule, Suit, and Record, #8020, EX (VG+ box), C6, $345.00. (Photo courtesy Cotswold Collectibles, Inc.)

Trouble Shooter ATV, orange, w/tracks, EX $210.00
Windboat, #7353, NM (EX box)....................................$80.00

3¾" GI JOE FIGURES

Ace, 1983, EX $15.00
Aero-Viper, 1989, NM $1.10
Airborne, 1983, from Argentina, EXOC........................$10.00
Airtight, 1985, MOC $15.00
Annihilator, 1989, NMOC...$25.00
Astro Viper, 1988, MIP...$30.00
AVAC, 1985, NM+ $35.00
Backblast, 1988, NM $15.00
Banzai, 1993, MOC...$8.00
Barbecue, 1985, EX $15.00
Barbecue, 1985, MOC $50.00
Baroness, 1984, EX...$55.00
Baroness, 1984, MOC..$185.00
Barricade, 1992, MOC..$13.00
BAT, 1986, EX $27.50

BAT, 1990, MOC...$25.00
Bazooka, 1985, EX $11.00
Bazooka, 1985, NMOC..$40.00
Beach Head, 1986, MOC...$30.00
Beach Head, 1986, NM $20.00
Big Boa, 1987, EX $18.50
Blast-Off, 1993, MOC $11.00
Blast-Off, 1993, NM $5.50
Blaster, 1987, NM $8.00
Blizzard, 1988, MOC $25.00
Blocker, 1987, NM $8.00
Blocker, 1988, MOC $15.00
Blowtorch, 1983, MOC, from $150 to $300.00
Breaker, 1982, straight arms, M $25.00
Breaker, 1982, straight arms, MOC $95.00
Breaker, 1982, swivel-arm battle grip, EX $20.00
Budo, 1988, EX $12.00
Bullhorn, 1990, MOC..$3.00
Bushido Shadow, 1993, MOC $10.50
Buzzer, 1985, EX $15.00
Buzzer, 1985, MOC $35.00
Captain Grid Iron, 1990, NM $15.00
Carcass, 1994, MOC..$25.00
Cesspool, 1991, MOC..$20.00
Charbroil, 1989, NM $28.00
Chuckles, 1987, MOC..$30.00
Chuckles, 1987, NM $15.00
Clutch, 1984, tan, NM $27.00
Cobra, 1983, swivel-arm battle grip, M (NM card), from $160
    to $185.00
Cobra Commander, 1982, Mickey Mouse emblem, straight arms,
    EX...$50.00
Cobra Commander, 1984, hooded, NM $25.00
Cobra Commander, 1986, battle armor, MOC $45.00
Cobra HISS Driver, 1983, NM $15.00
Cobra Officer, 1982, MOC...$125.00
Cobra Officer, 1983, swivel arm battle grip, EX $32.50
Cobra Stinger Driver, 1984, NM $25.00
Colonel Courage, 1993, MOC $15.00
Crazylegs, 1987, MOC...$18.50
Crimson Guard, 1985, MOC..$95.00
Crimson Guard Commander, 1993, NM $15.00
Crimson Guard Immortal, 1991, MOC..........................$21.50
Croc Master, 1987, NM $13.50
Cross Country, 1986, NM $8.00
Crystal Ball, 1987, MOC $18.00
Cutter, 1992, NM $12.50
Cyber-Viper, 1993, NM $17.00
Dee-Jay, 1989, NM $15.00
Deep Six, 1984, NM $17.00
Destro, 1983, MOC $35.00
Dial-Tone, 1986, MOC $160.00
Doc-Medic, NM..$30.00
Dodger, 1990, Electronic Battle Sound, MOC................$13.50
Dojo, 1992, MOC...$10.50
Dr Mindbender, 1986, MOC $35.00
Dr Mindbender, 1986, NM $13.50
Drop-Zone, 1990, MOC...$25.00

Deep Six, 1989, MOC, $25.00.

(Photo courtesy Old Tyme Toy Store)

Drop-Zone, 1990, NM	$17.00
Eels, 1985, NM	$25.00
Falcon, 1987, NM	$33.00
Firefly Cobra, MOC (Japanese)	$150.00
Flame Thrower, 1983, NMOC	$320.00
Flint, 1985, MOC	$260.00
Flint, 1985, NM	$25.00
Footloose, 1985, MOC	$27.50
Frag Viper, 1989, MOC	$16.00
Free Fall, 1989, MOC	$37.00
Fridge, 1986, mail-in, NM	$20.00
Frostbite, 1985, MIP	$18.00
General Hawk, 1993, mail-in, MIP	$15.00
Ghostrider, 1988, NM	$16.00
Gnawgahyde, 1989, w/Micro figure, MOC	$15.00
Grunt, 1982, straight arms, NM	$22.50
Gung-Ho, 1983, swivel-arm battle grip, NM	$16.00
Gung-Ho, 1987, Version II, MOC	$50.00
Gyro Viper, 1987, EX	$10.00
Hardball, 1988, NM	$12.00
Hardtop, 1987, NM	$70.00
Heat-Viper, 1989, face camouflage, MOC	$20.00
Iceberg, 1986, NM	$10.00
Interrogator, 1991, NM	$25.00
Jinx, 1987, MOC	$52.50
Ken Masters, 1993, MOC	$10.00
Lady Jaye, 1985, MOC	$80.00
Lady Jaye, 1985, NM	$27.50
Lampery, 1985, NM	$10.00
Law & Order, 1987, NM	$23.50
Leatherneck, 1986, MOC	$60.00
Lobotomaxx, 1994, MOC	$16.50
Low-Light, 1986, NM	$25.00
Mainframe, 1986, NM	$18.00
Major Bludd, 1983, mail-in, MIP	$20.00
Maverick, 1987, NM	$10.00

Mercer, 1987, NM	$18.50
Monstro-Viper, 1993, NM	$10.00
Motor Viper, 1986, NM	$13.00
Mutt & Junkyard, 1984, MOC	$55.00
Nunchuk, 1992, MOC	$11.50
Outback, 1987, white shirt, MOC	$20.00
Outback, 1988, gray shirt, NM	$35.00
Ozone, 1991, MOC	$11.50
Ozone, 1993, MOC (Canadian)	$8.00
Predacon, 1994, MOC	$21.50
Psyche-Out, 1988, NM	$17.00
Quick Kick, 1985, MOC	$310.00
Ranger-Viper, 1990, MOC	$19.00
Raptor, 1987, MOC	$36.00
Recoil, 1989, EX	$10.00
Recondo, 1984, swivel-arm, MOC	$110.00
Red Dog, 1987, NM	$8.00

Repeater, 1988, MOC, $35.00.

Ripcord, Halo Jumper, 1984, NM	$18.50
Ripper, 1985, EX	$12.00
Road Pig, 1988, EX	$18.00
Roadblock, 1984, MOC	$50.00
Roadblock, 1988, NM	$21.00
Robo-Joe, 1993, MOC	$10.00
Rock 'n Roll, 1989, NM	$7.50
Ryu, 1993, MOC	$12.50
Scarlett, 1982, straight arms, MOC	$110.00
Scoop, 1989, MOC	$25.00
Scrap Iron Cobra, 1984, NM	$23.50
Shipwreck, 1985, swivel-arm battle grip, MOC	$515.00
Short-Fuze, 1982, straight arms, NM	$17.00
Slip Stream, 1986, EX	$7.00
Snake Eyes, 1985, NM	$75.00
Snake Eyes, 1985, w/Timber (dog), NMOC	$360.00
Sneak Peek, 1988, NM	$25.00
Snow Job, 1983, MOC	$20.00

Sci-Fi (Directed Energy Expert), 1986, MOC, from $25.00 to $35.00.

(Photo courtesy Old Tyme Toy Store)

Sci-Fi (Laser Expert), 1986, MOC, from $15.00 to $25.00. (Photo courtesy Old Tyme Toy Store)

Snow Serpent, 1985, MOC	$50.00
Snow Serpent, 1985, NM	$25.00
Snow Storm, 1994, MOC	$15.00
Spearhead & Max, 1988, near complete, NM	$13.00
Spirit, 1984, MOC	$85.00
Stalker, 1982, straight arms, MOC	$125.00
Stalker, 1982, straight arms, NM	$35.00
Steeler, 1983, NM	$23.00
Storm Shadow, 1984, NM	$40.00
Storm Shadow, 1984, swivel-arm battle grip, MOC	$190.00
Strato-Viper, 1986, EX	$15.00
Sub-Zero, 1990, Free Command Ring offer, MOC	$22.00
TARGAT, 1989, NM	$10.00
Taurus, 1987, NM	$10.00

Techno-Viper, 1987, MOC	$23.00
Tele-Viper, 1985, MOC	$35.00
Thrasher, 1986, NM	$10.00
Thunder, 1984, NM	$17.50
Tomax & Xamot, 1985, MOC	$210.00
Topside, 1990, NM	$25.00
Torch, 1985, EX	$15.00
Torpedo, 1983, NM	$17.50
Toxo Viper, 1988, w/free Micro figure, MOC	$23.50
Toxo Viper, 1991, NM	$11.50
Tripwire, 1983, swivel-arm battle grip, MOC	$62.50
Tunnel Rat, 1987, MOC	$45.00

Voltar, MOC, $35.00. (Photo courtesy Old Tyme Toy Store)

Wet Suit, 1986, NM	$23.00
Wild Bill, 1983, NM	$15.00
Wild Bill, 1992, MOC	$13.00
Wild Weasel, 1984, NM	$12.50
Zandar, 1986, swivel-arm battle grip, NM	$15.00
Zap, 1982, swivel-arm battle grip, MOC	$57.50
Zarana, 1986, earring, swivel-arm battle grip, MOC	$60.00
Zartan, 1984, NM	$30.00
Zartan w/Swamp Skier, 1984, complete & accessories, NM.	$48.00
Zartan w/Swamp Skier, 1984, sealed packages in VG+ box.	$70.00

VEHICLES AND ACCESSORIES FOR 3¾" GI JOE

Ammo Dump Unit, 1985, EXIP	$20.00
Arctic Blast, 1988, EX	$12.00
Assault Copter Dragonfly, B0627, NM (VG box)	$150.00
Battlefield Robot Radar Rat, 1988, NRFB	$30.00
Bridge Layer (Toss 'N Cross), M (VG box)	$140.00
Cobra Condor Z25 Plane, 1988, MIB, from $65 to	$80.00
Cobra Terror Dome, M (NM box)	$325.00
Cobra Wolf w/Ice Viper, 1985, EX	$18.00
Combat Jet Skystriker XP-14F, 1983, MIB	$250.00

A.G.P. (Anti-Gravity Pod) With Super Trooper Figure, 1988, MIB, $30.00.

Cobra Ferret, NM (VG box), $30.00. (Photo courtesy Old Tyme Toy Store)

Crimson Attack Tank, 1985, MIB...............$325.00
Crusader Space Shuttle, 1988, NRFB $175.00
Devil of the Deep Turbo Swamp Craft, EX (EX box) $130.00
Dreadnok Attack Jeep, EX $150.00
Equalizer, 1989, NMIB............................$165.00
Heavy Artillery Laser w/Grand Slam, 1982, NRFB........$110.00
Hovercraft, 1984 mail-in, MIP $40.00
Hovercraft Killer WHALE, 1984, M (VG box) $265.00
Jet Pack JUMP & Platform, 1982, MIP (Canadian) $50.00
LCV Recon Sled, 1983, EX $5.00
Mauler MBT Tank, 1985, NRFB, H4 ....$80.00
Mobile Command Center, 1987, M (EX box) $235.00
Mobile Command Center, 1987, M (G box) $150.00
Mobile Missile System, EX $45.00
Motorized Battle Wagon, 1991, MIP................$35.00
Mountain Howitzer, 1984, EX $8.00
Phantom X-19 Stealth Fighter, MIB (sealed), from $100 to .$125.00
Polar Battle Bear, 1983 mail-in, MIP $10.00
Q-Force Battle Gear, Action Force, MIP $5.00

SAS Action Hawk & Blades, 1984, EXIB, from $175 to..$200.00
SAS Parachutist Attack, Action Force, MIP $35.00
Sky Raven Sky Patrol Set, MIB (sealed)..............$225.00
Skystriker F-14, w/Ace figure, M....................$120.00
Terror Drome, complete except for bomb, EX $260.00
Tiger Cat w/Frostbite, 1988, EX $20.00
Tiger Force Tiger Shark, 1988, M (sealed packages & VG+ box)..$30.00
Transportable Tactical Battle Platform, 1985, NM $30.00
USS Flagg Aircraft Carrier, 1986, EX, from $250 to $280.00

MISCELLANEOUS

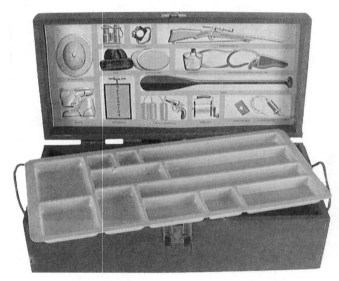

Adventure Locker, red wooden footlocker with removable tray and inner lid illustration, NM, $4,000.00. (Photo courtesy Cotswold Collectibles)

Air Manual, wide, EX, C6.........................$6.00
Backing Card, Takara, Gun Collection Series, EX, C6.....$15.00
Canteen, EX......................................$15.00
Catalog, Palitoy Retailer's, 1970, 34 pages, 10 showing Action Man, EX, A.....................................$335.00
Coloring Book, Scramble, GI Joe Action Pilot, 1965, unused, EX, A $55.00
Coloring Book, Whitman, 1965, Joes in various military garb, some coloring, EX+................................$18.00
Comic Book, America's Movable Fighting Man, 1967, EX, C6..$5.00
Comic Book, Big Trapper Adventure, EX, C6 ....$15.00
Comic Book, Eight Ropes of Danger, EX, C6 ....$16.00
Comic Book, GI Joe, Vol 1 #18, 1952, Ziff-Davis, EX, A .$110.00
Comic Book, Mystery of the Boiling Lagoon, EX, C6 ......$17.00
Comic Book, Secret Mission to Spy Island, EX, C6.........$16.00
Dog Tag w/Chain, NM.............................$20.00
Electric Drawing Set, Lakeside, 1965, NMIB.............$30.00
Flare Gun, EX......................................$8.00
Footlocker, wood, gr w/blank Name, Rank, Serial No fields, NM (EX rpr sleeve), A.............................$250.00
Game, Capture of Hill 79, Hasbro, 1969, EXIB $60.00
Game, Let's Go Joe, Hasbro, 1966, EXIB $55.00
Instructions, Adventure Team Danger of the Depths, EX, C6..$12.00

Instructions, Revenge of Spy Shark Sonar Detector, EX, C6 .$8.00
Knapsack, GI Joe US Army, Hassenfeld Bros/Hasbro, 1964, unused, NM+..$250.00
Manual, Counter-Intelligence, EX, C6 ....$25.00
Manual, Gear & Equipment, EX, C6.................................$3.00
Mess Kit, EX...$10.00
Official ID Bracelet, KMT Inc, 1982, rare, MOC............$10.00
Package Ad Insert, Adventure Team, 1975, EX, C6 ....$8.00
Puzzle, jigsaw, Whitman, 1965, beach landing, NMIB $25.00
Puzzle, jigsaw, Whitman, 1965, Joe in sea battle, NMIB...$25.00

Sticker Book, Man of Action, Figurine Panini, complete with twenty sticker sheets, unused, EX/NM, A, $35.00. (Photo courtesy Cotswold Collectibles)

Sticker Book, Whitman, 1965, used, EX $20.00
Trace & Color Book, Whitman, 1965, unused, NM.........$20.00
Walkie-Talkies, EX...$15.00

Guns

Until WWII, most cap guns were made of cast iron. Some from the 1930s were nickel plated, had fancy plastic grips, and were designed with realistic details like revolving cylinders. After the war, a trend developed toward using cast metal, a less expensive material. These diecast guns were made for two decades, during which time the TV western was born. Kids were offered a dazzling array of toy guns endorsed by stars like the Lone Ranger, Gene, Roy, and Hoppy. Sales of space guns, made popular by Flash Gordon and Tom Corbett, kept pace with the robots coming in from Japan. Some of these early tin lithographed guns were fantastic futuristic styles that spat out rays of sparks when you pulled the trigger. But gradually the space race lost its fervor and westerns ran their course, replaced with detective shows and sitcoms. Since guns were meant to see a lot of action, most will show wear. Learn to be realistic when you assess condition; it's critical when evaluating the value of a gun.

Advisor: Bill Hamburg (H1)

Actoy Pony Boy Cap Guns & Holster Set, w/cuffs, spurs, silver bullets, all w/bronco medallions, NMIB $300.00

Aoki Space Ray Gun, litho tin, 10", NMIB....................$200.00
Clarinda P-38 Cocking Pistol, metal, unused, NM, C10 ..$75.00
Crossman C02 Target Pistol Model #115, EXIB.............$100.00
Daisy Zooka Pop Pistol & Holster, 1930s (?), litho tin & leatherette, 7½", VG, A..$125.00
Halco Texan Double Gun & Holster Set, unused, MIB .$350.00

Hubley Double Gun and Holster Set, EX, $400.00. (Photo courtesy James D. Julia, Inc.)

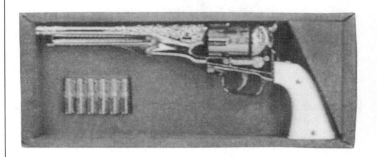

Hubley Colt .45, complete with six cap-loading bullets, unused, MIB, A, $300.00. (Photo courtesy Smith House Toys)

Hubley Panther Pistol, 4", MIB, A, $150.00.

Hubley Dagger Derringer Cap Gun, 1960, NP, 6¾", EX+ .$200.00
Hubley Deputy Pistol, highly scrolled plastic grips, 10", unused, MIB, A...$175.00
Hubley Padlock Cap Gun, 1950s, barrel extends & fires when key is turned, silver finish, NM+............................$100.00
Hubley Texan Guns & Keyston Bros Double Holster Set, wht w/studs & jewels, gold-tone guns w/wht grips, EX+.$450.00
Ives Clown on Powder Keg Cap Pistol, ca 1880, CI, clown seated atop keg on barrel, 3¾", VG, A.................$2,750.00
Ives Hunter Bear Head Cap Pistol, ca 1887, CI, single action, cast bear's head on barrel, 5¼", EX, A.....................$850.00
Ives Hunter Cap Pistol, Pat 1890, CI, single action derringer w/figural wolf's head on barrel, 5¼", EX, A.............$715.00
Ives Lion Cap Pistol, ca 1898, japanned CI, cast lion's head on barrel, 5¼", EX+, A...$850.00

Ives Punch and Judy Cap Pistol, circa 1882, cast iron, cast figures on barrel, 4x4½", EX, A, $1,870.00. (Photo courtesy Bertoia Auctions)

Ives Sambo Cap Pistol, ca 1883, japanned CI, boy somersaults over figure hitting head to explode cap, 5½", EX, A $4,400.00
J&E Stevens America Revolving Cap Pistol, ca 1880, single action, 8¾", EX $150.00
J&E Stevens Caps Exploder, boy & bear w/hammers ready to hit cap on anvil, japanned finish, 13" L $1,850.00
J&E Stevens Cowboy King Pistol, CI w/gold finish, jeweled blk grips, 9", EXIB...$250.00
J&E Stevens Sea Serpent Cap Pistol, early, CI, mouth opens for cap, 4", EX $1,300.00
Japan Astronaut Rocket Gun, 1960s, battery-op, 10", EX+ .$125.00
Japan Atom Rifle, 1950s, litho tin, friction, 19½", EX.....$75.00
Japan Atomic Ray Gun, 1950s, tin w/transparent barrels & rockets, friction, NM $65.00
Japan Double Barrel Space Ray Gun, w/sparking action, litho tin w/plastic gun barrels, 15", NMIB, A $300.00
Japan S-28 Space Gun, 1960s, battery-op, 10", EX+ $125.00
Kenner Gun That Shoots Around the Corner, 1964, 20", unused, NMIB..$60.00
Kenton Cannon Cap Pistol, NP CI, cannon mounted on barrel, single action, 5", VG $450.00

Japan Space Ruler Machine Gun, lithographed tin, battery-operated, 20", EX+IB, $200.00.

Kenton Lightning Express Cap Pistol, CI, locomotive mounted on barrel, 5", VG $450.00
Kenton Magic .22 Derringer, CI w/NP barrel, single action, second trigger tips barrel for loading, 6¼", EX, A $90.00
Keystone Lasso 'Em Bill Single Gun Holster Set, leather holster w/Texas Jr cap pistol, unused, NM $200.00
Kilgore Old West Double Gun & Holster Playset, 1970, MIB, A...$25.00

KO Space Super Jet Gun, lithographed tin, 9", MIB, $250.00.

Lockwood Joker Cap Pistol, ca 1880, CI, single action, 4½", EX, A $275.00
Marklin Coastal Defense Gun, brass & iron w/detailed rack-&-pinion elevating & rotating mechanisim, shoots caps, 6", EX $220.00

Marx Anti-Aircraft Gun, 1930s, crank action, complete with shells, NMIB, A, $350.00.

Marx Automatic Repeater Paper Pop Pistol, 1930, pressed steel, 7", unused, NM+IB..$100.00

Marx Big Game Rifle, unused, MIB, C10 ....$125.00
Marx Cork Shooting Submachine Gun, 1951, MIB.......$250.00

Marx Space Cadet Atomic Pistol (Flashlite), EXIB, A, $250.00.

Marx Security Pistol, MOC..$35.00
Marx Spinner Rifle, NMOC, C10 ....$125.00
Marx Twin Pomp Pom Anti Aircraft Cannon, 1950s, metal & plastic, 20", EX+IB..$30.00
Mattel Little Burp Guerrilla Machine Gun, NMIB, T1 .$125.00
Mattel Shootin' Shell Cap Gun, EXIB $350.00
Mattel Shootin' Shell Scout Rifle, unused, MIB $350.00
McDowell Mac Machine Gun, metal, 12½", VG, A........$80.00

MT Atomic Ray Gun, lithographed tin, battery-operated, 18½", EXIB, $300.00. (Photo courtesy Smith House Toys)

Reliable Toys Ray Gun, 1950s-60s, air-pump, blk w/yel barrel, 8", NM+...$150.00
Russell Cowboy Double Holster Set w/Buck'n Bronc Cap Guns, NMIB..$350.00
Shudo Cosmic Rays Gun, 1960s, litho tin, friction, 13", NMIB..$100.00
Smith's Automatic Machine Gun, w/tripod & accessories, 22", VGIB $200.00
SY Space Machine Gun, 1950s, tin, friction, 12½", NMIB .$150.00
Taiyo Space Pilot Jet Ray Gun, 16", NMIB.......................$60.00
TN Flashy Ray Gun, 1950s, battery-op, 18", NMIB.......$200.00
TN Foxhole Tommy Gun Space Rifle, 1950s, litho tin, battery-op, 17", NMIB $250.00
Topper Toys Multi-Pistol 09, NM+ (in case) $150.00
Wyandotte Double-Barrel Pop Gun, pressed steel w/wood stock, 23", EXIB $100.00
Wyandotte Pump Action Dart Gun, pressed steel w/wood stock, 21", EXIB, A $110.00
Wyandotte Red Ranger Clicker Pistol, pressed steel w/lithoed detail, EX+IB, A $75.00
Wyandotte Single Barrel Pop Gun, pressed steel w/wood stock, 22½", EXIB, A $100.00

CHARACTER

Agent Zero Radio-Rifle, Mattel, 1964, NMIB $80.00

Batman Freeze Ray Gun, Baravelli/Italy, battery-op, plastic, unused, NMIB $200.00
Buck Rogers Atomic Pistol #U-235, Daisy/Dille, 1930s, metal, 9½", EXIB..$850.00
Buck Rogers Disintegrator Combat Set, Daisy, 10", VGIB .$500.00
Buck Rogers Popgun, Daisy, 1930s, pressed steel w/image stamped on grip, 9½", EX+, A $300.00
Buck Rogers XZ-44 Liquid Helium Water Pistol, Daisy, 1936, litho steel, 7½", G..$200.00
Buffalo Bill Repeating Cap Pistol, J&E Stevens, cast metal, emb plastic grip, 8½", VGIB....................................$125.00

Burke's Law Automatic Repeater Cap Pistol, Leslie-Henry, 1964, metal with white grip, 6½", NMOC, A, $50.00. (Photo courtesy Smith House Toys)

Captain America Clicker Gun, Larami, 1974, plastic, MIP (sealed)..$10.00
Captain Gallant Cap Gun & Holster, EX......................$125.00
Dan Dare Planet Guns, Merit Toys, 1950s, complete, NMIB.$150.00
Davy Crockett Cap Gun, Gasque/WDP, 100-shot repeating cap pistol, longhorn steer on grips, 9", unused, NMIB...$150.00
Davy Crockett Cap Gun, Marx, 1950s, pnt marbleized plastic w/working metal 'flintlock' hammer & trigger, 10½", NM+ $75.00
Davy Crockett Cap Guns, Schmidt, metal w/blk grips, 7½", EX, A, pr $250.00
Davy Crockett Clicker Guns, Marx (?), litho tin w/name & image, 8", VG, pr $75.00
Davy Crockett Double Gun & Holster Set, R&S Toys, tan & brn leather w/jeweled buckle, name & image on pockets, NMIB..$250.00

Davy Crockett Frontier Rifle, Marx/WDP, metal, 34", NMIB, A, $225.00. (Photo courtesy Smith House Toys)

Davy Crockett Gun, Latco, NP w/floral bronze-type grips, 10½", unused, NM+ $250.00

Flash Gordon Click Ray Pistol, Marx, litho tin, 10", NMIB, A .$450.00

G-Man Machine Gun, Japan, 1950s, 18", unused, MIB.$125.00

Gene Autry Buzz Henry Cap Gun, Leslie-Henry, 7½", unused, MIB $300.00

Gene Autry Cap Gun, Kenton, CI, blk w/red hdl, 7", EX .$150.00

Gene Autry Cap Gun, Leslie-Henry, NP w/pearl horsehead grips, 9", unused, MIB...$300.00

Gene Autry Cap Gun & Holster Set, Kenton, tan leather single holster w/studs & head image, name in ivory grip, VGIB, A.........$600.00

Gene Autry Champion Cap Gun, Leslie-Henry, gold-tone w/blk grip, 9", unused, NM+ $250.00

Gene Autry Champion Cap Gun, Leslie-Henry, NP w/caramel-colored grips, 9", EX $150.00

Gene Autry Double Gun & Holster Set, blk leather w/silver pockets, Flying A Ranch, 9" cap guns w/horse head grips, NM..$600.00

Gene Autry Double Gun & Holster Set, red leather w/tan pockets, silver-tone studs, Buzz Henry cap guns, unused, NM+ .$250.00

Gene Autry Official Ranch Outfit (Gun & Holster), Leslie-Henry, 1941, blk leather w/star emblem, 7½", EXIB, A $300.00

Gene Autry Repeating Cap Gun, Kenton, CI, wht pearl grips w/name in red script, 7", EX....................................$150.00

Gene Autry Repeating Cap Gun, Kenton, CI, wht pearl grips w/name in red script, 7", unused, MIB $300.00

Hamilton Invaders Monster Science Fiction Grenade Launcher, Remco, 1960s, blk & chrome, 12", unused, MIB (sealed) .$125.00

Hopalong Cassidy Cap Gun, Schmidt, blk grip w/emb wht silhouette bust image, unused, 9½", NM+ $350.00

Hopalong Cassidy Double Gun and Holster Set, black leather with nickel-plated studs, gold-tone guns with black plastic grips, VG, $600.00. (Photo courtesy James D. Julia, Inc.)

Hopalong Cassidy Double Gun & Holster Set, blk leather w/wht medallions & studs, Wyandotte guns w/wht grips, NM .$800.00

Hopalong Cassidy Double Gun Holster Set, blk leather w/silver studs, blk outline head images on wht grips, EXIB ..$650.00

James Bond Attack Pistol, Multiple, 1966, plastic, 8", NM .$40.00

James Bond 007 Goldeneye Pistol, Wicke, 1996, MOC...$20.00

Lone Ranger Official Outfit, Feinburg-Henry, 1938, leather holster w/compo gun, blk mask, red scarf, EXIB, A $200.00

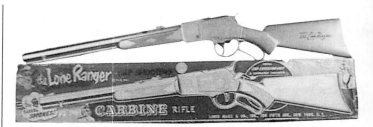

Lone Ranger Carbine Rifle, Leslie-Henry, plastic, shoots caps, 26", NMIB, A, $450.00. (Photo courtesy Smith House Toys)

Lone Ranger Pistol, Kilgore, dk metal w/dk tan grips inscribed Hi-Yo Silver, 8½", EX...$275.00

Lone Ranger Single Gun & Holster Set, Esquire, blk leather w/silver-look trim & red jewels, Pony Boy cap gun, MIB...$300.00

Lone Ranger Sparkling Pop Pistol, Marx, 1938, metal, 7½", EXIB, A $165.00

Lost in Space Roto-Jet Gun, Mattel, 1966, 20", rare, EX+ $300.00

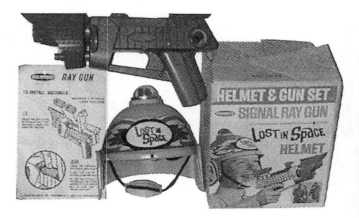

Lost in Space Helmet and Gun Set, Remco, 1966, EX+IB, $900.00. (Photo courtesy New England Auction Gallery)

Man From UNCLE Napoleon Gun Set, Ideal, converts into rifle, complete, NMIB, $1,000.00. (Photo courtesy New England Auction Gallery)

Mirror Man Double Barrel Pop Gun, Takatoku, tin & plastic, 21", NMIB $100.00

Popeye Gun Set, Halco, 1961, complete dbl gun & holster set w/diecut Popeye card, VG $150.00

Popeye Pirate Pistol, Marx, 1935, litho tin, 10", EX.......$200.00

Popeye Pirate Pistol, Marx, 1935, litho tin, 10", NMIB .$500.00

Rin-Tin-Tin Cap Gun, Actoy, copper-colored metal w/wht grips, 9", NM $125.00

Roy Rogers Cap Gun, Schmidt, emb Roy Rogers & RR, copper color metal grips w/red jewel, 9¼", EX $350.00

Roy Rogers Cap Guns, Classy, set of 2 gold-tone cast metal w/emb image of Roy on Trigger on grips, 7½", EX, A.............$350.00

Roy Rogers Double Gun & Holster Set, brn leather w/tooled detail, buckled pocket straps, stud trim, Schmidt guns, EX......$500.00

Roy Rogers Double Gun & Holster Set, Classy, brn & wht leather w/silver pockets, jewels, 10" Schmidt guns, EXIB.......$800.00

Roy Rogers Double Gun & Holster Set, Classy, red & wht leather w/rnd images, Roy mounted on Trigger emb on grips, NM, A...$300.00

Roy Rogers Double Gun & Holster Set, Classy, tan & brn leather w/buckle & stud trim, 10½" guns w/gray grips, NMIB, A...$750.00

Roy Rogers Double Gun and Holster Set, Kilgore, 1955, 9" guns, MIB, A, $3,400.00. (Photo courtesy Smith House Toys)

Roy Rogers Double Gun & Holster Set, Schmidt, 2-tone brn leather w/studs, NP guns w/RR on copper-color grips, EX, A $600.00

Roy Rogers Double Gun & Holster Set, tan leather w/name on strap across brn pockets, plastic guns, VG, A $120.00

Roy Rogers Double Gun & Holster Set, 1958, 3-tone leather holsters w/6" red & bl plastic guns, EX+IB, A $275.00

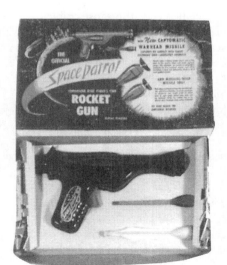

Space Patrol Rocket Gun, US Plastics, complete, 9", NMIB, $300.00.

(Photo courtesy New England Auction Gallery)

Roy Rogers Shootin' Iron, Kilgore, simulated pearl hdl, 9", MIB, A $450.00

Roy Rogers Tuck-Away Gun & Holster, EX, C10............$50.00

Superman Krypton Gun, EX $450.00

Tom Corbett Cadet Space Gun, Marx, litho tin, 10", NMIB (box reads Official Space Pistol) $500.00

Tom Corbett Space Cadet Atomic Pistol Flashlite, Marx, plastic, 7½", NMIB, A..$250.00

Tom Corbett Space Cadet 1507-4 Official Space Gun, Marx, 1950s, tin & plastic, 21", NM+ $350.00

Wild Bill Hickok Cap Guns, Leslie-Henry, Marshall Wild Bill Hickok on grips, 9½", EX, pr $250.00

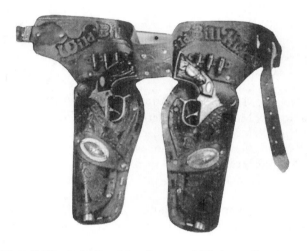

Wild Bill Hickok Double Gun and Holster Set, two-tone brown leather with name in relief, 11" .44 cap guns, EX, $450.00. (Photo courtesy Smith House Toys)

Wilma Deering's Gun & Holster (Buck Rogers), NM, C10 .$1,200.00

Wyatt Earp Double Gun & Holster Set, Esquire, blk leather w/silver-tone medallions & trim, wht grips, MIB $500.00

Zorro Cap Pistol, flintlock style, NM $100.00

BB Guns

Values are for BB guns in excellent condition.
Advisor: Jim Buskirk (B6)

Daisy, Model 21, double barrel, plastic stock, 37", 1968, B6, $400.00. (Photo courtesy Randy Inman Auctions)

Daisy '1,000 Shot Daisy,' lever action, wood stock, B6...$400.00

Daisy '500 Shot Daisy,' lever action, wood stock, B6......$400.00

Daisy Model A, break action, wood stock, B6 ....$350.00

Daisy Model B, lever action, wood stock, B6..................$100.00

Daisy Model B, lever action, wood stock, CI sight, B6....$200.00

Daisy Model C, break action, wood stock, B6.................$300.00
Daisy Model H, lever action, wood stock, B6 ....$125.00
Daisy Model 1938B, 'Christmas Story/Red Ryder,' B6......$90.00
Daisy No 11, Model 29, lever action, wood stock, B6 ......$80.00
Daisy No 12, Model 29, lever action, wood stock, B6 ......$80.00
Daisy No 25, pump action, pistol grip, wood stock, many varia-
      tions, B6, ea $65.00
Daisy No 25, pump action, straight wood stock, many variations,
      B6, ea $75.00
Daisy No 30, lever action, wood stock, B6.....................$100.00
Daisy No 40, 'Military,' lever action, wood stock, B6 .....$200.00
Daisy No 40, 'Military,' lever action, wood stock, w/bayonet, B6..$500.00
Daisy No 50, 'Golden Eagle,' lever action, blk wood stock, B6....$150.00
Daisy No 100, Model 38, break action, wood stock, B6....$80.00
Daisy No 101, Model 33, lever action, wood stock, B6 ....$60.00
Daisy No 101, Model 36, lever action, wood stock, B6 ....$50.00
Daisy No 102, Model 36, lever action, wood stock, B6 ....$50.00
Daisy No 102, Model 36, lever action, wood stock, nickel finish,
      B6..$75.00
Daisy No 103, Model 33, 'Buzz Barton,' nickel finish, B6 ..$250.00
Daisy No 103, Model 33, lever action, wood stock, B6 ..$300.00
Daisy No 104, Model 1938, dbl barrel, wood stock, B6..$650.00
Daisy No 105, 'Junior Pump Gun,' wood stock, B6 ....$250.00
Daisy No 106, break action, wood stock, B6 ....$40.00
Daisy No 107, 'Buck Jones Special,' pump action, wood stock,
      B6..$150.00
Daisy No 107, pump action, plastic stock, B6 ....$30.00
Daisy No 108, Model 39, 'Carbine,' lever action, wood stock,
      B6 ....$90.00
Daisy No 111, Model 40, 'Red Ryder,' aluminum lever, B6..$75.00
Daisy No 111, Model 40, 'Red Ryder,' iron lever, B6........$90.00
Daisy No 111, Model 40, 'Red Ryder,' plastic stock, B6 ...$50.00
Daisy No 140, 'Defender,' lever action, wood stock, B6 .$275.00
Daisy No 195, 'Buzz Burton,' lever action, wood stock, B6 .$100.00
King No 1, break action, wood stock, B6 ....$200.00
King No 2, break action, wood stock, B6 ....$65.00
King No 4, lever action, wood stock, B6 ....$250.00
King No 5, 'Pump Action,' wood stock, B6 ....$150.00
King No 5, lever action, wood stock, B6 ....$200.00
King No 10, break action, wood stock, B6 ....$50.00
King No 17, break action, wood stock, B6 ....$175.00
King No 21, lever action, wood stock, B6 ....$65.00
King No 22, lever action, wood stock, B6 ....$70.00
King No 24, break action, wood stock, B6 ....$225.00
King No 24, lever action, wood stock, B6 ....$75.00
King No 55, lever action, wood stock, B6 ....$85.00
King No 2136, lever action, wood stock, B6 ....$40.00
King No 2236, lever action, wood stock, B6 ....$40.00
King No 5533, lever action, wood stock, B6 ....$35.00
King No 5536, lever action, wood stock, B6 ....$35.00
Markham/King 'Chicago,' break action, all wood, B6 ....$300.00
New King, repeater, break action, wood stock, B6..........$250.00
New King, single shot, break action, wood stock, B6 .....$225.00

RELATED ITEMS AND ACCESSORIES

Box, Hopalong Cassidy Holster Set, mk America's Favorite
      Western Star w/image, Wyandotte, 7x12", VG+.....$300.00

Darts, Wyandotte, complete set of 3, 5", EXOC, A..........$40.00
Holster Set, Buck Rogers, 1930s, tan felt-type material
      w/red images on yel rnd patches, some stud & star trim,
      EX+..$250.00

**Holster Set, Dale Evans Queen of the West, NM+IB,
$900.00.** (Photo courtesy Smith House Toys)

Holster Set, Davy Crockett, Arrow Sales, wht leather w/emb
      medallion, MIB, A...$150.00
Holster Set, Lone Ranger, Smallman & Sons, blk leather w/sil-
      ver-tone studs & jewels, NMIB, A $300.00
Shooting Gallery, Wolverine #151-A, litho tin, complete,
      NMIB $175.00
Shooting Gallery, Wyandotte, litho tin w/up target w/2 plastic
      dart pistols, 11x15", EXIB $175.00
Shooting Gallery ('Posse'), Wyandotte, complete w/litho tin
      w/up target & pistol, 11x15", EXIB.........................$150.00
Spin 'Em Target Game, Wyandotte, litho tin & plastic target
      w/plastic cork gun, 5x12", EXIB, A.........................$40.00

Halloween

Halloween, the most colorful and fantasy-filled of all the holidays, is enjoying a popularity not known since the golden years of 1900 – 1920. Prices have fluctuated greatly because of the tremendous amount of reproductions and the fake pre-WWII items being made in Germany today and being sold as old. The folk art pieces made here in the U.S. have become some of the most desired items because production is so low and demand is great. Artists such as Jack Roads, Debbee Thibault, Ram Pottery, and the Millers cannot sufficiently supply the demand. Vintage pieces have leveled out in price because of so many investors cashing in on the high prices. Collectors will find this a welcome relief. As more collectors continue to discover the artistic as well as nostalgic joys of the holidays, more contemporary, mass-produced items have gone up in value, especially those that are character related. Artist-signed contemporary folk art seems to be the items most coveted by collectors. For more information we recommend *Collectible Halloween; Hal-*

loween: Decorations and Games; and *More Halloween Collectibles* by Pamela E. Apkarian-Russell.

Advisor: Pamela E. Apkarian-Russell, The Halloween Queen (H9)

See also Halloween Costumes.

Balancing Toy, pumpkin man, celluloid, EX $250.00
Book, Boogie Book, Dennison, 1924, hardcover, 36 pgs, VG.$125.00
Book, Games for Halloween, by Mary E Blain, 1912, hardcover, 60 pgs, EX (w/dust jacket) $50.00
Book, Hallowe'en Fun, Willis 'N Bugbee Co, hardcover, 87 pgs, EX+ $50.00

Boxes, round hand-painted wood folk-art pieces, scowling witch with hat lid, $175.00; man-in-the-moon images with a black cat, owl, or bat, each $125.00. (Photo courtesy Pamela Apkarian-Russell)

Cake Decoration Set, plastic figures on picks, orange & blk, 5 different, 1950s, 2½", NM+ $40.00
Candy Container, cat on rnd container, compo & cb, Germany, 2", EX..$200.00

Candy Container, cat sitting upright, black painted paper material, painted features, 7", VG, $75.00. (Photo courtesy Randy Inman Auctions)

Candy Container, cat's head, molded paper material pnt blk w/inserted eyes & pnt nose, bow at neck, 3½", VG, A.$415.00
Candy Container, jack-o'-lantern pirate, compo, Germany, 4½", EX $350.00
Candy Container, skull, mk Germany, 1912, 3", EX, A .$250.00
Candy Container, witch head w/cat body, compo, Germany, 1920, 5½", EX..$700.00
Candy Container, witch on shoe, compo, EX $400.00
Candy Container, witch w/broom on rnd base, compo w/pnt face, cloth costume, mk Germany, 1910, 14", NM $1,200.00

Candy Container, witch with jack-'o lantern head holding broom, bisque and paper, 7", EX, A, $440.00.
(Photo courtesy Randy Inman Auctions)

Candy Display Box, Curtiss Baby Ruth Tricks or 40 Treats, blk & wht on orange w/Halloween graphics, 1958, 7x10x2", EX+ $65.00
Coloring Book, Halloween..., Dell #163, 1957, unused, NM .$40.00
Cookie Cutters, Trick or Treat, tin, set of 6, 1954, EXIB..$25.00
Crepe Paper Roll, witches in pumpkin patch, Dennison, 1920s, 10-ft, NMIP $50.00
Decoration, blk cat or jack-'o-lantern, blk & orange crepe paper diecuts w/long streamers, 1930s-40s, 54x20", EX+, ea.$45.00

Decoration, cat with feet attached to round head, black painted paper material, Germany, 6", G+, $60.00.
(Photo courtesy Randy Inman Auctions)

Decoration, cat, arched back & tail straight up, diecut pressed cb, Germany, 1930s, 9x8", EX+ $40.00

Decoration, cat in dress & apron w/maid's cap, diecut cb, Germany, 1920s, 15½", EX $125.00

Decoration, diecut stand-up, 4 images w/witch, ghost, jack-o'-lantern & blk cat, USA, 1940s, 10x10", EX+ $50.00

Decoration, scarecrow w/jack-o'-lantern head, diecut cb w/string tissue paper arms & legs, Beistle, 1950s, 28", EX+ $30.00

Decoration, witch dancing, cb & crepe paper, HE Luhrs, 1920s, 18", EX, A $125.00

Decoration, witch w/broom, crepe paper, 4", EX $28.00

Decoration, witches, diecuts, Dennison #H-37, 1930s, set of 8, VG (VG envelope) $30.00

Doll, Halloween Witch, cloth, 1981, 8", M, N1 ....$15.00

Fan, blk cat, dbl-sided, Germany, 1920s, 13", EX $100.00

Figure, jack-o'-lantern boy holding parade stick w/pumpkin, compo, Germany, 3", EX $800.00

Figure, owl, pulp, US, 1940s, 7", NM $250.00

Figure, owl on spooky stump, celluloid, 1930s, 6", EX $250.00

Figure, witch, composition with cloth outfit and hat on wooden base, by folk artist Jack Roads, M, $600.00.

(Photo courtesy Pamela Apkarian-Russell)

Figure, witch on rocketship, hard plastic, EX $100.00

Game, Gypsy Fortune Telling Game, McLoughlin Bros, 1890s, VG+ (box top only) $100.00

Game, Phoney Fortunes, punchboard, A Master, 1930s, EX.$25.00

Game, Witzi-Wits the Fortune Teller, Alderman Fairchild Co, 1928, EXIB $100.00

Hand Puppet, goblin type w/striped body, pointy ears & hat, vinyl, 1950s, 10", EX+ $45.00

Hat & Siren Whistle, Clinton Toy Co, 1950s, unused, EX (w/header card) $55.00

Horn, cb cone shape w/lithoed witch & screaming cat, 1921, EX $20.00

Jack-o'-Lantern, plastic, molded & pnt geometric features, battery-op, Miller, 1950s, 6", NMIB $75.00

Jack-o'-Lantern, pulp, cut-out eyes, nose & mouth w/molded accents, gr trim, 1950s, 7x9", VG+ $95.00

Jack-o'-Lantern, pulp, cut-out eyes & mouth w/molded nose & accents, gr trim, wire hdl, 1950s, 6x5", EX...............$95.00

Jack-'o-Lanterns, pulp, 5½", VG+, A, $90.00; 4½", G, A, $45.00. (Photo courtesy Randy Inman Auctions)

Jack-o'-Lantern, pulp, cut-out eyes & mouth w/paper inserts, molded nose w/pnt nostrils, pnt brows, 5½", EX $150.00

Jack-o'-Lantern, pulp, cut-out eyes & mouth w/paper inserts, pnt triangular nose, 4½", EX $150.00

Jack-o'-Lantern, pulp, cut-out eyes & V-shaped mouth, gr stem, wire hdl, 1950s, 5x6", EX $150.00

Jack-o'-Lantern, pulp, pnt features, Atco, 1950s, 4x5", EX.$150.00

Jug, devil figure with large looping arms for handles, high-gloss glaze, by Ryan Miller of Ram Pottery, M, $250.00. (Photo courtesy Pamela Apkarian-Russell)

Lantern, blk cat face on pedestal, pulp, US, 1940s, 5", EX $200.00

Lantern, blk cat head, pulp, cut-out eyes & mouth, molded nose, American, 1940s-50s, 8", NM $375.00

Lantern, devil's head, diecut cb w/pnt features, dbl-sided, wire hdl, American, 1950s, 7½", EX, A $125.00

Lantern, witch, pulp, Germany, 1920s, 18", rare, EX $900.00

Lantern, jack-'o-lantern, painted tin, 1800s, 9", EX, A, $900.00. (Photo courtesy Skinner, Inc.)

Noisemaker, pan knockers, Japan, 1930s, 6", $65.00 each.

Noisemaker, Old Witch Sparkler, litho tin, Range Steel Products, 6", NMIB $85.00
Noisemaker, pumpkin head, pressed cb w/wooden hdl, Germany, 1930, 6", NM $150.00
Noisemaker, ratchet-type, witch, owl & pumpkins motif, US Metal Toy, 1950s, VG+ $30.00
Noisemaker, ratchet-type, woman, devil & clown masqueraders, US Metal Toy, 1950s, 5x4", NM $30.00
Party Favor, girl in pumpkin patch, celluloid & crepe paper, 1930s, 5", EX, A $150.00
Party Favor, jack-'o-lanterns w/gr stems, set of 3, ¾", VG to EX, A $65.00
Pennant, Salem Witch Museum, blk felt w/orange lettering & graphics of witch standing w/broom beside cat, 1950s, EX+.......$40.00

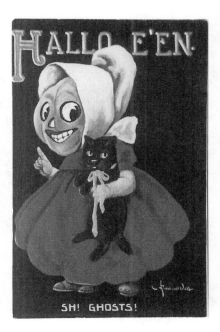

Postcard, 'Hallo e'en/Sh! Ghosts,' jack-o'-lantern girl holding black cat, by Berhardt Wall, ca 1912, EX, $50.00. (Photo courtesy Pamela Apkarian-Russell)

Rattle, witch head, molded pnt plastic on wooden stick, blk & orange, USA, 1950s, 12", EX $40.00
Salt & pepper shakers, ghost figures, wht ceramic w/blk accents, Japan, 1950s, 3¼", NM+, pr..................................$30.00
Sparkler, witch face, litho tin, Hale-Ness, 1950s, 7", NMOC $50.00
Tambourine, litho tin, blk cat face, T Cohn, 1940s, EX ...$95.00
Tambourine, litho tin, kids playing w/lg pumpkin, Chein, 1930s, NM, A...$95.00
Tambourine, litho tin, masquerade party scene, Kirchhof, 1950s, 6" dia, NM $85.00
Toy, Dancing Red Devil, rubber devil w/squeeze blower & air tubing (to make him dance), Japan, 1950s, 3½", EXIB....$50.00
Toy, jack-o'-lantern drummer, crank-op, rnd head w/cloth suit, Germany, EX $1,800.00

Halloween Costumes

During the '50s and '60s Ben Cooper and Collegeville made Halloween costumes representing the popular TV and movie characters of the day. If you can find one in excellent to mint condition and still in its original box, some of the better ones can go for over $100.00. MAD's Alfred E. Neuman (Collegeville, 1959 – 1960) usually carries an asking price of $150.00 to $175.00, and The Green Hornet (Ben Cooper, 1966) around $200.00. Earlier handmade costumes are especially valuable if they are 'Dennison-Made.'

Advisor: Pamela E. Apkarian-Russell, The Halloween Queen (H9)

Admiral Ackbar (Return of the Jedi), 1983, NMIB..........$25.00
Alf, Collegeville, MIB $35.00
Alfred E Neuman, mask only, litho on plastic, Ben Cooper, late 1960s, EX+..$45.00
Aquaman, Ben Cooper, 1967, NMIB...........................$125.00

Archie, Collegeville, 1960, MIB $50.00

Barbarino (Welcome Back Kotter), Collegeville, 1976,
MIB $40.00

Barbie, TV Comic, Collegeville, 1975, MIB, $55.00.

Barbie Super Star Bride, Collegeville, 1975, MIP $60.00

Batgirl, 1977, NMIB $35.00

Batman, Ben Cooper, 1969, NMIB $60.00

Beany & Cecil, Ben Cooper, 1950, NMIB $50.00

Bewitched, Ben Cooper, 1965, MIB................................$125.00

Boss Hogg (Dukes of Hazzard), Ben Cooper, 1982, MIB ..$40.00

Brady Bunch, any character, Collegeville, 1970s, MIB, ea from
$25 to $35.00

C-3PO (Star Wars), Ben Cooper, 1977, MIB..................$45.00

Casper the Friendly Ghost, Collegeville, 1960s, EXIB $45.00

Charlie's Angels, Collegeville, 1976, any character, MIB, $75.00 each. (Photo courtesy Greg Davis and Bill Morgan)

CHiPs, any character, Ben Cooper, 1978, MIB, ea $25.00

Cookie Monster, Ben Cooper, 1989, MIB $30.00

Courageous Cat, Halco, 1950s, NMIB $75.00

Daffy Duck, Collegeville, 1960s, EXIB $25.00

Darth Vader, Ben Cooper, 1977, MIP, N2 ....$25.00

Darth Vader, ESB, 1980, VGIB $35.00

Donny & Marie, Collegeville, 1977, MIB, ea $35.00

Droopy Dog, Collegeville, 1952, EXIB............................$50.00

Electra Woman, Ben Cooper, 1976, MIB........................$60.00

Flipper, Collegeville, 1964, MIB $80.00

GI Joe, Halco, 1960s, EXIB $65.00

Great Grape Ape, Ben Cooper, 1975, EXIB....................$50.00

Green Hornet, Ben Cooper, 1966, NMIB........................$200.00

Gumby, TV Comic, Collegeville, EXIB, $65.00.

Hardy Boys, Collegeville, 1978, MIB, ea..........................$45.00

He-Man, mask only, Mattel, M $10.00

Hong Kong Phooey, 1974, NMIB....................................$20.00

HR Pufnstuf, Collegeville, 1970s, MIB $80.00

Hush Puppy, Shari Lewis Masquerade Costumes, Halco, 1961,
EXIB..$60.00

Impossibles, Ben Cooper, 1967, NMIB............................$50.00

Jeannie, TV Comic, Ben Cooper, 1974, MIB, $95.00. (Photo courtesy Greg Davis and Bill Morgan)

Jimmy Osmond, Collegeville, 1977, MIB.........................$20.00
Joker, vinyl, 1989, MIB...$35.00
King Kong, Ben Cooper, 1976, MIB...............................$75.00
Lambchop, mask only, Halco, 1961, NM $40.00
Land of the Giants, 1968, complete, EX+ $50.00
Laugh-In, Ben Cooper, MIP $40.00

Laverne and Shirley, Collegeville, 1977, MIB, $30.00 each. (Photo courtesy Greg Davis and Bill Morgan)

Li'l Abner, Cooper, 1957, NMIB......................................$45.00
Li'l Tiger, 1960s, VG (VG box), N2.................................$25.00
Little Audrey, Collegeville, 1959, MIB $50.00
Lost in Space, silver flight suit, Ben Cooper, 1965, complete, EX...$60.00

Return of the Jedi, Luke Skywalker, Ben Cooper, EXIB, 125.00.

Mandrake the Magician, Collegeville, 1950s, EXIB $85.00
Marie Osmond, 1977, NMIB...$35.00
Maverick, 1959, complete, EX..$40.00
Miss Kitty (Gunsmoke), Halco, EXIB, A.......................$125.00
Monkees, any member, Bland Charnas, 1967, NMIB, ea .$200.00
Mork (Mork & Mindy), Ben Cooper, complete, NM $35.00
Raggedy Andy, Ben Cooper, 1965, MIB...........................$30.00
Raggedy Ann, Ben Cooper, 1965, MIB $30.00
Rin-Tin-Tin, 1950s, NMIB...$50.00
Sabrina the Teenage Witch, Ben Cooper, 1971, NMIB....$40.00
Sigmund & the Sea Monsters, Ben Cooper, 1970s, MIB..$60.00
Six Million Dollar Man, Ben Cooper, 1965, MIB............$40.00
Space Ghost, Ben Cooper, 1965, MIB, from $75 to $100.00
Space: 1999, Commander Koenig, 1975, EXIB.................$35.00
Steve Canyon, Halco, 1959, NMIB $50.00

Superman, complete with comic book, Ben Cooper, EXIB, A, $225.00.

SWAT, Ben Cooper, 1975, NMIB $35.00
Tattoo (Fantasy Island), Ben Cooper, 1978, MIB $30.00
Top Cat, Ben Cooper, 1965, NMIB..................................$75.00
Underdog, Collegeville, 1974, NMIB $40.00
Witchiepoo, Collegeville, 1971, MIB...............................$75.00
Yoda (Empire Strikes Back), EXIB $35.00

Hartland Plastics, Inc.

Originally known as the Electro Forming Co., Hartland Plastics Inc. was founded in 1941 by Ed and Iola Walters. They first produced heels for military shoes, birdhouses, and ornamental wall decor. It wasn't until the late 1940s that Hartland produced their first horse and rider. Figures were hand painted with an eye for detail. The Western and Historic Horsemen, Miniature Western Series, Authentic Scale Model Horses, Famous Gunfighter Series, and the Hartland Sports Series of Famous Baseball Stars were symbols of the fine workmanship of the '40s, '50s, and '60s. The plastic used was a virgin acetate. Paint was formulated by Bee Chemical Co., Chicago, Illinois, and Wolverine Finishes Corp., Grand Rapids, Michigan. Hartland figures are best known for their uncanny resemblance to the TV Western stars who portrayed characters like the Lone Ranger, Matt Dillon, and Roy Rogers.

Though in today's volatile marketplace, some categories of toys have taken a downward turn, Hartlands have remained strong. For more information we recommend *Hartland Horses and Riders* by Gail Fitch.

Advisor: Howard Cherry (C16)

See also Sporting Collectibles.

Alpine Ike, NM	$150.00
Annie Oakley, NM	$275.00
Bill Longley, NM	$600.00
Brave Eagle, NM	$200.00
Brave Eagle, NMIB	$300.00
Bret Maverick, miniature series	$75.00
Bret Maverick, NMIB	$600.00
Bret Maverick, w/coffeedunn horse, NM	$500.00
Bret Maverick, w/gray horse, rare, NM	$600.00

General George Washington, NM, $125.00.

Buffalo Bill, NM, $300.00. (Photo courtesy Pat Smith)

Bullet, NM	$35.00
Bullet, w/tag, NM	$150.00
Cactus Pete, NM	$150.00
Champ Cowgirl, very rare, NM	$275.00
Cheyenne, miniature series, NM	$75.00
Cheyenne, w/tag, NM	$190.00
Chief Thunderbird, rare shield, NM	$150.00
Cochise, NM	$150.00
Comanche Kid, NM	$150.00
Dale Evans, bl, rare, NM	$500.00
Dale Evans, gr, NM	$175.00
Dale Evans, purple, NM	$250.00
Davy Crockett, NM	$500.00
General Custer, NM	$150.00
General Custer, NMIB	$350.00
General George Washington, NMIB	$175.00

General Robert E Lee, NMIB	$175.00
Gil Favor, prancing, very rare, NM	$1,100.00
Gil Favor, semi-rearing, NM	$550.00
Hoby Gillman, NM	$250.00
Jim Bowie, w/tag, NM	$250.00
Jim Hardy, EX+	$200.00
Jim Hardy, NMIB	$300.00
Jockey, NM	$150.00
Josh Randle, NM	$650.00
Lone Ranger, Champ version, w/chaps, blk breast collar, NM	$125.00
Lone Ranger, miniature series, NM	$75.00
Lone Ranger, NM	$150.00
Lone Ranger, rearing, NMIB	$300.00
Lone Ranger, rearing, w/tag, NMIB	$600.00
Matt Dillon, w/tag, NMIB	$300.00
Paladin, NMIB	$350.00
Rebel, miniature series, NM	$125.00
Rebel, NM	$250.00
Rebel, NMIB	$1,200.00
Rifleman, miniature series, EX	$75.00
Rifleman, NMIB	$350.00
Ronald MacKenzie, NM	$1,200.00
Roy Rogers, semi-rearing, NMIB	$600.00
Roy Rogers, walking, NMIB	$300.00
Seth Adams, NM	$275.00
Sgt Lance O'Rourke, NMIB	$300.00
Sgt Preston, NM	$650.00
Tom Jeffords, NM	$175.00
Tonto, miniature series, NM	$75.00
Tonto, NM	$150.00
Tonto, semi-rearing, rare, NM	$650.00
Warpaint Thunderbird, w/shield, NMIB	$350.00
Wyatt Earp, NMIB	$250.00

STANDING GUNFIGHTERS

Bret Maverick, NM, $350.00.

Horse on 4-Wheeled Platform, real horsehide over straw-stuffed fr, glass eyes, harness, horsehair mane & tail, 31", G .$460.00
Mobo Bronco, 1940s, pedal horse on wheels, 26", rstr, A ..$275.00
Rocking Horse, pnt wood primitive look w/CI stirrups, lg rocking platform, early, 46", G, A $440.00
Rocking Horse, wht fur-covered w/blk mane & tail, leather-like saddle & harness, wooden rockers, 30", G, A $100.00
Rocking Horse, wood w/CI head, leather saddle, wooden rockers w/center platform, early, 40", EX, A........................$220.00
Rocking Horse, wood w/leather ears & saddle, horsehair tail, jtd swing legs, wooden swing base, 34x56", rpt, A $950.00

Bat Masterson, NMIB...$500.00
Chris Colt, NM..$150.00
Clay Holister, NM $200.00
Dan Troop, NM $600.00
Jim Hardy, NM..$150.00
Johnny McKay, NM..$800.00
Paladin, NM..$400.00
Vint Bonner, NMIB..$850.00
Wyatt Earp, NM $150.00

Horses

Horse riding being the order of the day, many children of the nineteenth century had their own horses to ride indoors; some were wooden while others were stuffed, and many had glass eyes and real horsehair tails. There were several ways to construct these horses so as to achieve a galloping action. The most common types had rocker bases or were mounted with a spring on each leg.

Spark Plug Rider, wooden wheeled horse with cloth blanket and leather saddle, painted features, 38", VG, A, $275.00. (Photo courtesy Collectors Auction Services)

Hot Wheels

When introduced in 1968, Hot Wheels were an instant success. Sure, the racy style and flashy custom paint jobs were instant attention-getters, but what the kids loved most was the fact that the cars were fast — fastest on the market! It's estimated that more than two billion Hot Wheels have been sold to date — every model with a little variation, keeping up with the big cars. The line has included futuristic vehicles, muscle cars, trucks, hot rods, racers, and some military vehicles. A lot of these can still be found for very little, but if you want to buy the older models (collectors call them 'Redlines' because of their red sidewall tires), it's going to cost you a little more, though many can still be found for under $25.00. By 1977, black-wall tires had become the standard and by 1978, 'Redlines' were no longer used.

A line of cars with Goodyear tires called Real Riders was made from 1983 until about 1987. (In 1983 the tires had gray hubs with white lettering; in 1984 the hubs were white.) Califor-

Rocking Horse, hide-covered with real horsehair mane and tail, leather saddle, iron supports attached to rockers, 64", VG, A, $1,050.00. (Photo courtesy Bertoia Auctions)

nia Customs were made in 1989 and 1990. These had the Real Rider tires, but they were not lettered 'Good Year' (and some had different wheels entirely).

Chopcycles are similar to Sizzlers in that they have rechargeable batteries. The first series was issued in 1972 in these models: Mighty Zork, Blown Torch, Speed Steed, and Bruiser Cruiser. Generally speaking, these are valued at $35.00 (loose) to $75.00 (MIB). A second series issued in 1973 was made up of Ghost Rider, Rage Coach, Riptide, Sourkraut, and Triking Viking. This series is considerably harder to find and much more expensive today; expect to pay as much as $600.00 to $1,000.00 for a mint-in-package example.

Though recent re-releases have dampened the collector market somewhat, cars mint and in the original packages are holding their values and are still moving well. Near mint examples (no package) are worth about 50% to 60% less than those mint and still in their original package, excellent condition about 65% to 75% less.

For further information we recommend *Hot Wheels, the Ultimate Redline Guide, Vol. 1* and *2*, by Jack Clark and Robert P. Wicker, and *Toy Car Collector's Guide* by Dana Johnson (all from Collector Books).

Advisor: Steve Stephenson (S25)

'35 Classic Caddy, 1989, blk walls, metalflake gray w/pk fenders, MIP $30.00
'56 Flashsider, 1992, blk walls, aqua, MIP $16.00
'56 Hi-Tail Hauler, 1977, blk walls, orange, M...............$30.00
'57 T-Bird, 1990, blk walls, aqua, Park 'n Plates, M $10.00
'93 Camaro, 1997, blk walls, dk bl, MIP...........................$10.00
Alive '55, 1977, redline, chrome, M.................................$45.00
American Hauler, 1976, redline, bl, NM+ $35.00
AMX/2, 1971, redline, magenta, NM $70.00
AMX/2, 1971, redline, purple, EX+ $60.00
Backwoods Bomb, 1975, redline, lt blue, NM+ $55.00
Baja Bruiser, 1974, redline, orange, metal base, NM.........$50.00
Battle Tank, 1984, blk walls, tan, MIP $25.00
Beatnik Bandit, 1968, redline, bl w/wht interior, NM+....$40.00
Beatnik Bandit, 1968, redline, gold w/gold interior, NM..$35.00
Beatnik Bandit, 1968, redline, lt olive w/wht interior, NM+...$60.00
Big Bertha, 1988, blk walls, tan, M.................................$7.00
Blazer 4x4, 1984, blk walls, blk, M $5.00
Boss Hoss, 1971, redline, gr w/gray interior, NM+..........$125.00
Brabham Repco F1, 1969, redline, purple, EX+ $65.00
Brabham Repco F1, 1969, redline, red, NM+ $40.00
Bugeye, 1971, redline, aqua, NM+ $85.00
Buzz Off, 1974, redline, dk bl, NM+................................$80.00
Bye Focal, 1971, redline, bl w/gold interior, NM+..........$225.00
Bywayman, 1990, blk walls, blk, M $15.00
Carabo, 1970, redline, red, NM+ $160.00
Carabo, 1974, redline, lt gr, NM+ $85.00
Cargoyle, 1986, blk walls, orange, M...............................$5.00
CAT Dump Truck, 1982, blk walls, yel, MIP $18.00
Chaparral ZG, 1969, redline, gold w/blk interior, NM+ ...$45.00
Chaparral ZG, 1969, redline, magenta w/blk interior, EX+...$60.00
Chevy Monza 2+2, 1975, redline, orange, EX+ $30.00
Classic '31 Ford Woody, 1969, redline, gold, NM+...........$50.00
Classic '31 Ford Woody, 1969, redline, lt bl, EX+.............$85.00

Classic '32 Ford Vicky, 1968, redline, aqua, EX $30.00
Classic '32 Ford Vicky, 1969, redline, bl w/gold interior, NM ...$45.00

Classic '36 Ford Coupe, 1969, redline, dark olive, NM+, $80.00.

Classic '36 Ford Coupe, 1969, redline, pk, NM+............$360.00
Classic '57 T-Bird, 1969, redline, aqua w/wht interior, NM+ ..$65.00
Classic '57 T-Bird, 1969, redline, gr w/wht, NM $65.00
Classic Nomad, 1970, redline, lt gr, NM+ $100.00
Classic Nomad, 1970, redline, purple, NM+ $145.00
Corvette Stingray, 1977, blk walls, red, NM $22.00
Custom AMX, 1969, redline, magenta, NM+ $140.00
Custom AMX, 1969, redline, pk w/wht interior, EX+....$100.00
Custom Barracuda, 1968, redline, antifreeze w/wht interior, M $450.00
Custom Barracuda, 1968, redline, aqua w/wht interior, VG+..$40.00
Custom Camaro, 1968, redline, yel w/brn interior, EX+..$130.00
Custom Charger, 1969, gr, NM+ $125.00
Custom Continental Mark III, 1969, redline, dk magenta, NM+ $100.00
Custom Continental Mark III, 1969, redline, orange, NM+ ..$65.00
Custom Continental Mark III, 1969, redline, pk, NM+ ...$200.00
Custom Corvette, 1968, redline, aqua w/wht interior, NM+..$125.00
Custom Corvette, 1968, redline, orange w/brn interior, EX+ ..$90.00
Custom Corvette, 1968, redline, purple, EX $100.00
Custom Eldorado, 1968, redline, ice bl w/gold interior, NM+...$225.00
Custom Eldorado, 1968, redline, purple w/wht interior, NM..$100.00
Custom Eldorado, 1968, redline, red w/wht interior, NM+..$110.00
Custom Firebird, 1968, redline, red w/brn interior, EX+ ..$50.00
Custom Fleetside, 1968, redline, brn, Hong Kong, NM+ ..$220.00
Custom Fleetside, 1968, redline, ice bl w/blk interior, EX....$75.00

Custom Volkswagen, 1968, redline, hot pink, EX, $225.00.

Custom Fleetside, 1968, redline, orange w/blk interior, Hong Kong, NM+...$60.00
Custom Mustang, 1968, redline, bl w/gray interior, EX+..$90.00
Custom Mustang, 1968, redline, olive w/gray interior, Hong Kong, NM+ $155.00
Custom T-Bird, 1968, redline, aqua w/wht interior, NM+ ..$100.00
Custom T-Bird, 1968, redline, purple w/gold interior, NM+...$175.00
Custom Volkswagen, 1968, redline, gr w/gold interior, NM+ ..$185.00
Custom Volkswagen, 1968, redline, purple w/brn interior, NM...$165.00
Demon, 1970, redline, lt gr w/blk interior, EX+...............$45.00
Demon, 1970, redline, lt gr w/wht interior, NM+.............$95.00
Deora, 1968, redline, aqua w/gray interior, EX+ $30.00
Deora, 1968, redline, purple w/wht interior, NM+ $80.00
Double Vision, 1973, redline, red, NM+.......................$155.00
Dumpin' A, 1983, blk walls, gray, M $30.00
Dune Daddy, 1973, redline, lt bl w/wht interior, NM $75.00
Dune Daddy, 1973, redline, red, NM.............................$75.00
Dune Daddy, 1975, redline, lt gr, EX+ $45.00
Dune Daddy, 1975, redline, orange, rare color, NM+ $245.00
Emergency Squad, 1975, redline, red, NM+ $20.00
Emergency Squad, 1977, blk walls, red, MIP...................$15.00
Ferrari Testarossa, 1989, blk walls, red, M $3.00
Ferrari 312P, 1970, redline, pk, NM+ $80.00
Ferrari 512P, 1972, redline, magenta, NM+ $100.00
Ferrari 512P, 1973, redline, lt bl, NM.........................$120.00
Flame Stopper, 1988, blk walls, red, MIP $10.00
Ford J-Car, 1969, redline, gold w/blk interior, NM+.........$30.00
Ford Mark IV, 1969, redline, purple, NM+ $40.00
Formula PACK, 1976, redline, blk, NM+ $35.00
Formula PACK, 1978, blk walls, blk, NM+ $14.00
Funny Money, 1972, redline, gray, NM+.........................$75.00
GMC Motor Home, 1977, redline, orange, EX+ $175.00
Grass Hopper, 1971, redline, lt gr, NM+ $55.00
Gulch Stopper, 1987, blk walls, red, M $15.00
Gun Bucket, 1976, redline, olive, M $35.00
Hairy Hauler, 1971, redline, pk, NM $140.00
Heavy Chevy, 1970, redline, aqua w/brn interior, NM $95.00
Heavy Chevy, 1970, redline, red w/gold interior, NM....$100.00
Heavyweight Cement Mixer, 1970, redline, brn, NM+....$50.00

Heavyweight S Cool Bus, 1971, redline, yel, NM+ $180.00
Heavyweight Team Trailer, 1971, redline, red, M...........$110.00
Heavyweight Waste Wagon, 1971, redline, aqua, NM+...$90.00
Hood, 1971, redline, purple w/brn interior, NM+ $110.00

Hot Bird, 1980, black walls, blue, EX+, $35.00. (Photo courtesy June Moon)

Hot Heap, 1968, redline, lavender, NM+ $175.00
Hot Heap, 1968, redline, pk w/wht interior, NM+.........$325.00
Ice T, 1973, redline, lt bl, NM+ $180.00
Indy Eagle, 1969, redline, aqua, NM+............................$35.00
Indy Eagle, 1969, redline, olive, NM+ $50.00
Inferno, 1976, redline, lt yel, M....................................$60.00
Jack Rabbit Special, 1970, redline, wht w/blk interior, NM..$30.00
Jet Threat, 1971, redline, yel, NM+ $75.00
Jet Threat II, 1976, redline, plum, NM+ $30.00
Large Charge, 1976, redline, chrome, M.........................$50.00
Letter Getter, 1977, redline, wht, G+ $75.00
Letter Getter, 1982, blk walls, wht, Frito Lay, MIP.........$225.00
Light My Firebird, 1970, redline, purple w/brn interior, NM+...$90.00
Lola GT70, 1969, redline, bl, Hong Kong, NM+ $25.00
Lola GT70, 1969, redline, dk gr w/blk interior, M...........$30.00
Mantis, 1970, redline, gr w/brn interior, Hong Kong, NM+...$35.00
Mantis, 1970, redline, pk w/brn interior, Hong Kong, NM+..$90.00
Maserati Mistral, 1969, redline, gr w/wht interior, NM+..$95.00

Heavyweight Dump Truck, 1970, redline, MIP, $130.00.

Mighty Maverick, 1970, redline, aqua, MIP, $215.00.

Mazda MX-5 Miata, 1992, blk walls, yel, M $5.00
McLaren M6A, 1969, redline, bl, NM+ $30.00
McLaren M6A, 1969, redline, purple, NM+ $40.00
Mercedes Benz C-111, 1972, redline, lt gr, NM+ $125.00
Mercedes Benz C-111, 1974, redline, red w/gold interior, NM- ..$60.00
Mercedes Benz 280 SL, 1969, redline, brn w/brn interior,
    NM+ $40.00
Mighty Maverick, 1970, redline, gr, NM+ $75.00
Mod Quad, 1970, redline, pk w/brn interior, Hong Kong,
    NM+ $215.00
Mongoose Funny Car, 1970, redline, red, NM+ $95.00

Mongoose Rail Dragster, 1971, redline, blue, NM+, $75.00.

Monte Carlo Stocker, 1979, blk walls, dk bl, EX+ $18.00
Mustang Stocker, 1976, redline, chrome w/bl stars & stripes,
    NM $60.00
Mutt Mobile, 1971, redline, aqua, NM+ $45.00
Mutt Mobile, 1971, redline, bl, NM+ $75.00
Neat Streeter, 1976, redline, lt bl, M..........................$65.00
Nissan 300ZX, 1985, blk walls, red, MIP.........................$12.00

Nissan 300ZX, 1992, purple with ultra gold, NM, $170.00.

(Photo courtesy June Moon)

Nitty Gritty Kitty, 1970, redline, red w/gold interior, NM+ ..$110.00
Noodle Head, 1971, redline, aqua w/gray interior, Hong Kong,
    NM+ $100.00
Olds 442, 1971, redline, rose w/wht interior, NM+ $750.00
P-911, 1975, redline, yel, NM+ $45.00
P-911, 1988, blk walls, blk, NM $4.00
Paramedic Van, 1975, redline, wht, plastic base, NM+ $55.00
Peepin' Bomb, 1970, redline, yel, NM+ $30.00
Peterbilt Cement Mixer, 1980, blk walls, red, M $5.00
Peterbilt Dump Truck, 1983, blk walls, yel, MIP $10.00

Paddy Wagon, 1970, redline, blue with silver lettering, M, $40.00. (Photo courtesy June Moon)

Poison Pinto, 1976, redline, chrome, NM+ $55.00
Porsche 917, 1970, redline, salmon, NM+ $65.00
Porsche 917, 1970, redline, yel w/wht interior, NM+ $45.00
Power Pad, 1970, redline, pk, NM+ $100.00
Prowler, 1973, redline, orange w/wht interior, EX+ $165.00
Prowler, 1974, redline, orange, NM+ $60.00
Python, 1968, redline, red w/gold interior, Hong Kong, EX+ ..$35.00
Quik Trik, 1984, blk walls, metallic magenta, NM+ $5.00
Rash 1, 1974, redline, gr, NM+ $75.00
Rear Engine Snake, 1972, redline, yel, NM $150.00
Red Baron, 1974, redline, red, NM+ $20.00
Red Baron, 1977, blk walls, red, MIP $25.00
Rescue Ranger, 1988, blk walls, red, M $6.00
Rock Buster, 1976, redline, chrome, NM+.....................$45.00
Rocket Bye Baby, 1971, redline, aqua w/wht interior, NM+ ..$65.00
Rocket Bye Baby, 1971, redline, magenta, NM+ $160.00
Sand Drifter, 1975, redline, yel, NM+ $50.00
Seasider, 1970, redline, gr, NM+ $90.00
Second Wind, 1977, redline, wht, NM+ $65.00
Sheriff Patrol, 1989, blk walls, blk, MIP.........................$10.00

Short Order, 1971, redline, dark blue, rare, MIP (unpunched), $250.00.

Short Order, 1971, redline, dk bl, NM+ $90.00
Show Hoss II, 1977, redline, yel, G+ $75.00
Side Kick, 1972, redline, red, NM+ $110.00
Silhouette, 1968, redline, aqua w/wht interior, NM+ $40.00
Silhouette, 1968, redline, magenta w/wht interior, NM+ ..$100.00
Silhouette, 1968, redline, pk w/wht interior, NM+ $300.00
Silver Bullet, 1985, blk walls, metalflake gray, NM+ $8.00
Sir Rodney Roadster, 1974, redline, yel, EX.....................$30.00
Sky Show Fleetside, 1970, redline, lt gr, NM+ $350.00
Snake, 1970, redline, yel, no stickers, NM+ $60.00
Snake II, 1971, redline, wht, M $85.00
Snake Rail Dragster, 1971, redline, wht, NM $75.00
Snorkel, 1971, redline, yel w/brn interior, EX+ $55.00
Special Delivery, 1971, redline, lt bl, NM+ $60.00
Splittin' Image, 1969, redline, lt gr, NM+ $25.00
Steam Roller, 1974, redline, wht, NM+ $40.00
Steam Roller, 1974, redline, wht, 7 star, NM+ $300.00
Sting Rod, 1988, blk walls, olive, MIP $12.00
Street Eater, 1975, redline, yel, NM+..............................$80.00
Street Snorter, 1973, redline, pk, NM+ $250.00

Super Van, 1975, redline, blue with flames, EX+, $450.00.

(Photo courtesy June Moon)

Super Van, 1976, redline, chrome, metal base, NM+ $50.00
Superfine Turbine, 1973, redline, red, NM $400.00
Swingin' Wing, 1973, redline, fluorescent pk, EX $75.00
Swingin' Wing, 1973, redline, lt bl, NM+.........................$90.00
T-4-2, 1971, redline, aqua, M $90.00
Tall Rider, 1985, blk walls, gray, MIP $10.00
Thor, 1979, blk walls, yel, M $12.00
Tough Customer, 1975, redline, olive, NM+ $20.00
Tricar X8, 1988, blk walls, yel, MIP...................................$6.00
Turbo Heater, 1986, blk walls, magenta, MIP $11.00
Turbo Streak, 1988, blk walls, wht, EX.............................$6.00
Turbofire, 1969, redline, aqua w/wht interior, NM+ $25.00
Turbofire, 1969, redline, rose, NM+.................................$40.00
Turismo, 1981, blk walls, red, MIP $8.00
Twinmill, 1969, redline, olive, NM+ $85.00
Twinmill, 1977, blk walls, chrome, M $35.00
Vega Bomb, 1976, redline, orange, NM+ $50.00
Volkswagen, 1974, redline, orange, bug on roof, metal base,
NM...$60.00

Volkswagen, 1980, redline, orange, bug on roof, plastic base,
NM $20.00
VW Beach Bomb, 1969, redline, purple w/wht interior, NM ..$185.00
What 4, 1971, redline, gr, NM+ $90.00
Whip Creamer, 1970, redline, purple, NM+ $95.00
Z Wiz, 1977, blk walls, gray, NM+...................................$14.00

MISCELLANEOUS

Action Command Sto & Go Base, MIB $75.00
Bad to the Bone Watch, 1994, blk, MIB...........................$15.00
Body Swappers Gift Pack, 1985, MIB...............................$30.00
Button, Beatnik Bandit, 1968, metal, M $3.00
Button, Cement Mixer, 1970, metal, M $5.00
Button, Classic '32 Ford Woody, 1969, metal, EX $2.00
Button, Cockney Cab, 1971, plastic, M $10.00
Button, Custom Eldorado, 1968, metal, M........................$4.00
Button, Ferrari 312P, 1970, metal, M.................................$3.00
Button, Mantis, 1970, metal, M..$5.00
Button, Short Order, 1971, plastic, EX...............................$6.00
Button, Snake II, 1971, plastic, M....................................$12.00
Car Carrier, w/cars, MIB $15.00
Cargo Plan, w/cars, MIB $15.00
City Burger Stand, aqua mini truck, MIB $30.00
Color Racers Auto Paint Set, w/cars, MIB.......................$35.00
Crazy Cyberspace Game, 1993, bl, MIB...........................$15.00
Funny Car Gift Pack, 1991, MIB......................................$30.00

Gran Toros, Toyota 2000 GT, blue, MIB, $250.00.

Jigsaw Puzzle, Whitman, 1970s, 100-pieces, MIB, $25.00.

John Andretti Pro Circuit Set, 1992, yel, MIB $375.00
Joiner Pack, MIP...$20.00
Leapin' Demons, MIB...$75.00
Mini Race & Show Gas Station, 1989, MIB....................$20.00
Real Rider, Beach Patrol, 1983, wht, gray hubs, MIP $25.00
Real Rider, Beach Patrol, 1983, wht, wht hubs, MIP........$35.00
Real Rider, Classic Cobra, 1983, bl, gray hubs, MIP........$40.00
Real Rider, Classic Cobra, 1983, bl, wht hubs, MIP $100.00
Real Rider, Jeep CJ-7, 1985, metalflake brn, gray hubs, M .$30.00
Real Rider, Jeep CJ-7, 1985, metalflake brn, wht hubs, M.$45.00
Real Rider, Turbo Streak, 1983, yel, gray hubs, MIP $25.00
Real Rider, Turbo Streak, 1983, yel, wht hubs, MIP $35.00
Shift Kicker's Leap of Flame Stunt Set, NMIB $40.00
Sizzler, Angelino M-70, chrome, NM..............................$45.00
Sizzler, Firebird Trans Am, pk, NM+ $75.00
Sizzler, Straight Scoop, magenta, NM+ $50.00
Snake Mountain Challenge Set, w/cars, MIB $40.00
Speed Buster 4 Car Gift Set, MIB $60.00
Speedometer, MIB $35.00
Sto & Go Baywatch, MIB...$25.00
Sto & Go City Playset, MIB...$15.00
Sto & Go Fix & Fill Center, MIB $25.00
Tune-Up Tower, NM+IB $125.00

Housewares

Back in the dark ages before women's lib and career-minded mothers, little girls emulated mommy's lifestyle, not realizing that by the time they grew up, total evolution would have taken place before their very eyes. They'd sew and bake, sweep, do laundry and iron (gasp!), and imagine what fun it would be when *they* were big like mommy. Those little gadgets they played with are precious collectibles today, and any child-size houseware item is treasured, especially those from the '40s and '50s.

See also Character, TV, and Movie Collectibles; Disney.

CLEANING AND LAUNDRY

Washing Machine, Sunny Suzy, Wolverine #78W, complete, 12", EXIB, $440.00.
(Photo courtesy Randy Inman Auctions)

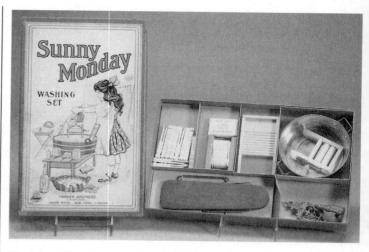

Washing Set, Sunny Monday, Parker Bros, complete, EXIB, A, $400.00. (Photo courtesy Randy Inman Auctions)

Clothes Presser, 1930s, yel & gr tin w/wooden roller, w/up & electric, EX...$85.00
Iron, Wolverine, 1950s, electric, MIB.............................$35.00
Ironing Board, Sunnie Miss, Ohio Art, 1960s, tin, 20", VG .$25.00
Sweeper, Little Queen, Bissel, tin w/wood hdl, functional, 25½", EX...$50.00
Sweeper, Mickey Mouse, WD, 1930s, litho tin over wood w/wood hdl, rolling action rotates sweeping brush, EX..........$400.00
Washboard & Tub, 4-legged wooden tub w/metal bands & hdls, corrugated tin & wooden scrub board, 8" dia, EX.....$125.00
Washing Machine, Pretty Maid, Marx, EX $150.00
Wringer, Thor, Arcade, yel-pnt CI w/NP parts, ftd, 4", VG, A.$300.00

Wringer, Toy Mangle, japanned cast iron, 9½" high, EX+, A, $330.00. (Photo courtesy Bertoia Auctions)

COOKING

Baking Set, Mother's Little Helper, complete, MIB.......$150.00
Canister Set, Wolverine, tin, MIB $150.00

Children's Kitchen Set, Krest, complete, NMIB, $50.00. (Photo courtesy Linda Baker)

Cooking Set, Farberware, Linemar, 1950s, NMIB $275.00
Cooking Set, Graniteware, bl, 8 pcs, EX.........................$275.00
Stove, Acme, Kenton, silver-pnt CI w/ornate details, several
    accessories, 13" L, EX $325.00
Stove, Baby, Ideal, CI w/copper flashing, stovepipe w/ornate top
    shelf, few accessories, 18" L, EX $700.00
Stove, Baby, Ideal, CI w/emb name on front door, plain stovepipe
    (no top shelf), few accessories, 15½", EX.................$450.00
Stove, Beauty, Ideal, NP CI w/ornate details, w/few accessories,
    VG, A $550.00
Stove, Crescent, CI, stovepipe w/ornate shelf, w/accessories &
    coal bucket, 9x10x4", EX, A $80.00
Stove, Eagle, Hubley, NP CI w/emb front door, few accessories,
    5½" L, no stovepipe o/w VG, A $25.00

Stove, Eagle, Hubley, NP CI w/ornate details, several acces-
    sories, 16" L, VG, A...$400.00
Stove, Eagle, Lancaster Brand, NP CI w/ornate details, few
    accessories, EX $250.00
Stove, Ernst Plank/Germany, blk tin w/NP door trim & latches,
    stove pipe to 1 side in back, few accessories, 13", EX..$450.00
Stove, Home, J&E Stevens, NP CI w/emb front door, few acces-
    sories, 8" L, no stovepipe, G, A $65.00
Stove, Little Orphan Annie, Marx, gr & cream tin w/images,
    electric, 9" L, VG..$200.00
Stove, Rival, silver-pnt CI w/ornate details, several accessories,
    14x12" L, VG, A $800.00
Stove, Royal, Kenton, NP CI w/emb front door, few accessories,
    6½" L, no stovepipe o/w VG $75.00
Stove, Royal, Kenton, NP CI w/ornate details, few accessories,
    8½" L, no stovepipe o/w EX, A $150.00
Stove, Royal, NP CI, w/stove pipe & back shelf, few accessories,
    13½", G, A $55.00
Toaster, chrome curved shape on dk metal base, electric, EX ..$50.00
Utensil Set, rolling pin, slotted spoon, spatula, masher, wire soap
    holder, etc, wht-pnt wood hdls, 9 pcs, VG.................$75.00

NURSERY

Carriage, litho tin w/collapsible cloth hood, 4 disk wheels, chrome
    hdl, West Germany (?), 11" (w/hdl), NM, A $100.00
Carriage, surrey w/fringed top, pnt wood seat, gold stenciling,
    wooden spoke wheels, Am, ca 1870, 32x28", VG, A .$350.00
Carriage, wicker, automobile shape w/cloth top & headlights,
    running board over spoke wheels, 36", EX...............$850.00
Carriage, wicker, horse-drawn, wood frame, spoke wheels
    w/rubber treads, rear hdl, late 19th-early 20th century, 53",
    EX $1,350.00
Carriage, wicker, natural w/diamond pattern, clamshell hood,
    steel spoke wheels, Heywood-Wakefield, 30", VG ..$150.00
Carriage, wicker, natural w/horizontal cloth tuffed seat, cloth
    parasol on hook, wood spoke wheels, 30", EX $225.00

Mickey Mouse and Betty Boop Stroller, 10", VG+, A, $2,300.00.
(Photo courtesy Randy Inman Auctions)

Stove, Little Chef, Ohio Art, 1950s, NM, $100.00.

Carriage, wicker w/corduroy interior, w/hood, spoke wheels, straight turned wood hdl grip, 36", EX+ $400.00

Carriage, wood w/3 wood spoke wheels, turned hdl, 12, G+ .$200.00

Cradle, France, blk scrolled wrought iron w/wht lace covering & head drape, 27x19", VG $200.00

Grooming Set, 1920s-30s, comb, brush & rattle w/bl ribbon flowers, pnt celluloid, M (M floral box)...................$125.00

Stroller, Loeminster, 1920s, blk pnt wicker, 26", EX.......$200.00

SEWING

Cutting Machine, Singer, wht plastic w/suction cup ft, 5x6½", EX...$50.00

Sewing Basket, sq wicker basket w/lid & bottom shelf on 4 tall legs, 17x9", EX+ $75.00

Sewing Cabinet, Martha Washington, ca 1930, dk wood w/3 drawers, flip-top side compartments, 18", EX $250.00

Sewing Kit, Victorian girls & Christmas pram illus on lid, w/mirror, needles, thread, thimble & button, MIB $150.00

Sewing Machine, Jaymar, metal w/orange crinkle-pnt finish, battery-op, EX, minimum value.............................$50.00

Sewing Machine, Jr Miss, Sew-Rite/Hasbro, 1960s, NM (NM carrying case), minimum value..................................$55.00

Sewing Machine, Little Miss, Lindstrom, steel & iron, 4-ftd, crank-op, blk, 8" L, EX $100.00

Sewing Machine, Little Mother, Artcraft, 1940s, EX+...$100.00

Sewing Machine, Playskool, 1989, uses markers to make designs on paper & fabric, 9x11", EX............................$25.00

Sewing Machine, Sew Master, LAYanEE, metal, crank-op, 8" L, EXIB, A $100.00

Sewing Machine, Singer, CI w/electric motor, early, 7", G ..$75.00

Sewing Machine, Singer, early, 30", VG+, A, $550.00. (Photo courtesy Noel Barrett Auctions)

Sewing Machine, Singer Featherweight No 221-1, 1941, complete, EX, A $250.00

Sewing Machine, Singer Lockstitch #T-6406, 1987-90, NM ..$50.00

TABLE SERVICE

Castor Set, 4 glass condiment bottles w/stoppers in metal stand, EX $100.00

Decanter Set, brass, service for 6, MIB...........................$50.00

Percolator Set, Tootsietoy, 1920s, samovar, sugar bowl & cream on tray, MIB...$200.00

Silverware Set, Banner Metallone Tableware, 4 place settings w/butter knife & cake server, MIB $75.00

Tea Set, Crown Fairy/Germany, late 19th-early 20th C, porcelain w/emb bl & yel floral pattern, service for 6, EXIB, A .$100.00

Tea Set, France, white china with blue floral motif, gold trim, 15 pieces, EX (with case), A, $300.00. (Photo courtesy Bertoia Auctions)

Tea Set, Little American Maid, Akro Agate, MIB $375.00

Tea Set, Little Hostess, Made in Japan, lustre ware, service for 4, EXIB...$200.00

Tea Set, Noritake, yel & blk Art-Deco motif w/gold trim, service for 4, MIB $375.00

Tea Set, Ohio Art, 1950s, litho tin w/circus animals & clowns on red background, 31 pcs, EX $250.00

Tea Set, Sunnie Miss, Ohio Art, 1976, litho tin, 6 pcs, MOC ..$35.00

MISCELLANEOUS

Crumb Set, Little Miss Muffet.../Little Jack Horner, aluminum, NM...$100.00

Doll Sleigh, wicker w/scrolled metal runners, scrolled metal hdl w/wooden grip, 31", VG $200.00

Doll Wagon, mk American Express Co, paper on wood, wood spoke wheels, bowed oak hdl & rabbit-jtd corners, 17" L, G+, A $400.00

Dresser Set, pitcher & bowl, soap dish, lotion, powder & pin containers, china w/purple & brn flowers, EX $250.00

Dresser Set, 1930s, mirror, brush, comb & hair receiver, celluloid, doll sz, MIB...$200.00

Ice Cream Freezer, Dana-Peerless, wooden barrel w/CI crank,
  bail hdl, 7½", EX, A $125.00
Salt Box, 1920, wood & metal w/blk stenciled letters, 5", M .$85.00
Scale, Arcade, mk Toledo, red-pnt CI, 5", EX, A $600.00
Scale, Kenton, red-pnt CI w/NP balance beam & weights, MIB,
  A $550.00

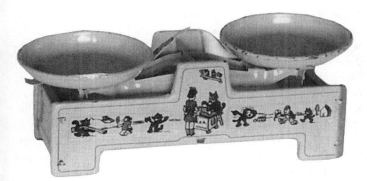

**Scale, lithographed tin with Felix the Cat motif, 7" long, EX,
A, $1,430.00.** (Photo courtesy Randy Inman Auctions)

Spinning Wheel, early, oak, fully functional, 28", EX, A..$260.00
Tool Set, Ideal, 1960s, diecast metal, 5-pc set, MIB..........$15.00
Typewriter, Unique Toy, 1940s-50s, tin w/lithoed keys, alphabet
  wheel, EXIB $50.00

Jack-in-the Boxes

Very early jack-in-the-box toys were often made of papier-
mache and cloth, fragile material to withstand the everyday wear
and tear to which they were subjected, so these vintage German
examples are scarce today and very expensive. But even those
from the '50s and '60s are collectible, especially when they represent well-known TV or storybook characters. Examples with
lithographed space themes are popular as well.

See also Character, TV, and Movie Collectibles; Disney.

Clown in House, Germany, papier-mache & cloth figure in
  paper-covered box pops out of window, 6½", EX.....$475.00
Devil's Head, Germany, 1920s, yel- & red-pnt wood box w/devil
  on spring, EX $875.00
Girl, compo figure w/cloth clothes in paper-covered wooden
  box, EX $300.00
Jesters, paper litho on wood w/2 papier-mache heads, fabric hats
  & fur-lined clothing, 6", G, A $700.00
Jolly Jack, figure w/cloth clothes in tin litho box, EXIB ...$75.00
Man in Red Top Hat, Germany, papier-mache figure w/gray hair
  in paper-covered wood box, w/squeaker, 5", EX.......$450.00
Poodle Wearing Glasses, Germany, papier-mache figure
  w/wht fur trim in wood box w/paper label, w/squeaker, 4"
  sq, EX $300.00
Santa Claus, ca 1910, Santa in cloth suit & fur beard in chimney
  box, 9½", EX..$350.00
Talking Clown in the Box, Mattel, 1971, NM, minimum
  value $100.00

Keystone

Though this Massachusetts company produced a variety of
toys during their years of operation (ca 1920 – late 1950s), their
pressed-steel vehicles are the most collectible. As a rule they
were very large, with some of the riders being 30" in length.

Air Mail Plane NX-263, 24" W, EX+, A $1,425.00
Air Mail Plane NX-263, 24" W, G................................$475.00
Airplane (Rapid Fire Motor), 24" W, G+, A..............$1,540.00

Airplane, rider, 1941, 36" wingspan, EX+, A, $1,540.00.
(Photo courtesy Randy Inman Auctions)

Ambulance (Military), #73, 28", EX............................$1,025.00
Ambulance (Military), #73, 28", rstr, G+, A $425.00
American Railway Express, #43, 26", G, A.....................$525.00
Coast-To-Coast Bus, rider, #84, 32", G+, A $5,720.00
Dump Truck, #41, 27", G+, A $325.00
Dump Truck, rider, electric headlights, 26", EX, A $2,300.00
Fighter Plane, rider, 25", EX, A $500.00
Fire Aerial Ladder Truck, #79, 31", VG, A....................$825.00
Fire Aerial Ladder Truck, rider, 28", G, A.....................$750.00
Fire Aerial Pumper Truck, 31", rpt, G, A $450.00
Fire Chemical Truck, #57, 29", EX, A.........................$3,400.00
Fire Ladder & Hose Truck, #49, 28", VG, A..................$550.00
Fire Ladder Truck, #52, 28", G, A $200.00
Fire Water Tower Truck, #56, 31", VG, A...................$1,100.00
Fire Water Tower Truck, #59, 32", EX, A...................$2,750.00

Hydraulic Dump Truck, 1929, 27", VG+, A, $2,100.00. (Photo
courtesy Bertoia Auctions)

Hydraulic Dump Truck, #62, 28", rstr, A $1,100.00
Keystone Garage, particle board & plastic, w/4 plastic cars, complete & working, VG+, A $175.00
Koaster Flatbed Truck, #54, 25", old rstr, A $350.00

Locomotive, rider, 1920s, 27", EX, A, $880.00. (Photo courtesy Randy Inman Auctions)

Milk Truck, rider, 26", overpnt, A $2,200.00
Police Patrol, #51, 27", G+, A $1,760.00
Pullman Train Car, rider, 25", VG, A $1,150.00
Steam Roller, #60, rider, 20", EX, A $450.00
Steam Roller, #60, rider, 20", G+, A $250.00
Steamshovel, #46, 26" (w/arm extended), G, A $110.00
Train, 4-pc w/locomotive, tender, wrecking car & Pullman, ea car approx 24", Poor to Fair, A $770.00
Truck Loader, #44, 17", G+, A $285.00
US Army Truck, #48, no canvas cover, 27", G, A $275.00

US Army Truck, 1920s, complete, EX, A, $1,430.00. (Photo courtesy Randy Inman Auctions)

US Mail Truck, #45, 27", rstr/rpt, A..............................$525.00
US Mail Truck, #45, 27", VG, A $800.00
Water Tower Truck, rider, 30", VG, A $1,100.00
Wrecker, #78, 28", VG $1,500.00

Lehmann

Lehmann toys were made in Germany as early as 1881. Early on they were sometimes animated by means of an inertia-generated flywheel; later, clockwork mechanisms were used. Some of their best-known turn-of-the-century toys were actually very racist and unflattering to certain ethnic groups. But the wonderful antics they perform and the imagination that went into their conception have made them and all the other Lehmann toys favorites with collectors today. Though the company faltered with the onset of WWI, they were quick to recover and during the war years produced some of their best toys, several of which were copied by their competitors. Business declined after WWI. Lehmann died in 1934, but the company continued for awhile under the direction of Lehmann's partner and cousin, Johannes Richter.

Advisor: Scott Smiles (S10)

Acrobat, VG $750.00
Adam the Porter, 8", NM $1,200.00
Adam the Porter, 8", NMIB $1,350.00
AHA Delivery Van, 8", EX $650.00
Ajax Acrobat, 9", G $1,000.00
Ajax Acrobat, 9", NM $1,600.00
Alabama Coon Jigger, 10", EX $700.00
Alabama Coon Jigger, 10", NMIB $900.00
ALSO Auto, 4", NM $500.00
ALSO Auto, 4", VG, A $350.00
Anxious Bride, 4½", NMIB $2,000.00
Austin Pedal Car, 4", NM (in box mk American Boy) .$1,000.00
Auto Post Delivery Van, 5", EX $1,200.00
Auto-Onkel, 5½", NMIB, A $1,400.00
Autobus #590, 7", EX, A $1,300.00
Autohutte & Galop Racer #1, NM $1,600.00
Baker & Chimney Sweep, 5", NMIB $4,000.00
Balky Mule, 8", NM $650.00
Balky Mule, 8", VG, A $400.00
Berolina Convertible, 7", NM $3,500.00
Bird, tin body w/pasteboard wings, 10" W, EX+ $525.00
Boxer, 4 Chinese men mounted on base throw figure in cloth blanket, 5x5" base, rare, NM, from $5,500 to.......$6,500.00
Bucking Bronco & Cowboy, brn horse, 6½", NM $900.00
Bucking Bronco & Cowboy, wht horse, 6½", EX $800.00
Buster Brown in Auto, 4", NM $2,000.00
Buster Brown in Auto, 4", VG $950.00
Captain of Kopenvil, 7½", NM....................................$2,700.00
Climbing Monkey, 8", NMIB $300.00
Crawling Beetle, 4½", NM $250.00
Crocodile, 9", EX, A $500.00
Crocodile, 9", NMIB $600.00
Dancing Sailor (HMS Dreadnaught), 7½", NM $1,000.00
DUO Rooster w/Rabbit on Egg, unmk, 7½", NM $1,400.00
Echo Motorcycle w/Driver, 8½", EX, A $1,500.00
Echo Motorcycle w/Driver, 8½", NMIB $2,500.00
EHE & CO Truck, 7", VG $500.00
EPL-1 Dirigible, 8", NMIB, A $800.00

EPL-1 Dirigible, 8", VGIB................................$600.00
EPL-11 Zeppelin, 9½", EX..............................$800.00
Express Porter, 6", NM..................................$700.00
Futurus Peace Chime, 5" dia, VG, A.............$650.00
Gala Sedan, bl & wht, rare, 12", VG $750.00
Galop Racer #1, yel & bl stripe, 5½", NMIB, from $1,600 to .$1,500.00
Galop Zebra Cart, 1954 reissue (determined by new color scheme), 7½", NMIB, from $500 to........$550.00
Garage w/Gnome (Series) Racer & Sedan, 4½x4", VG, A..$550.00

Garage With Sedan, 6" long, EX, $600.00. (Photo courtesy Bertoia Auctions)

Going to the Fair, 6", G.................................$1,000.00
Going to the Fair, 6", NM $3,000.00
Gustav the Miller, 18", NM...........................$500.00
Halloh Rider on Cycle, 8", NM $2,400.00
Heavy Swell (Dapper Fella), 8½", G..............$900.00
Heavy Swell (Dapper Fella), 8½", NMIB.........$2,000.00
IHI Meat Van, 6½", EX..................................$1,700.00
Icarus, EXIB...$3,500.00
Icarus, VG+, A $1,100.00
ITO Sedan, 6", VG.......................................$700.00
Jonny Lion, plastic, friction, 3", MIB $50.00
Jonny Sailor Boy, 6", EXIB $200.00

Kadi, 7", EX, $1,700.00. (Photo courtesy Randy Inman Auctions)

Kadi, 7", NMIB...$2,500.00
Kamerun Ostrich Cart, 6", EX......................$850.00
Kimado Family, 7", EX $1,700.00
Lexus Sedan, 12½", VG, A............................$2,475.00
Li La Hansom Cab, 5½", EX..........................$1,500.00
Li La Hansom Cab, 5½", G............................$1,000.00
Li La Hansom Cab, 5½", NMIB $2,000.00
Lo & Li, 8", NM, A.......................................$10,000.00
Lo & Li, 8", VG..$5,000.00
Lo Lo, 4", G, A $500.00
Lo Lo, 4", VG...$750.00
Los Angeles Zeppelin, 9", VG+, A................$470.00
Mandarin, 7", G...$1,500.00
Mandarin, 7", NMIB.....................................$4,000.00
Masuyama, 7", NM $2,000.00
Masuyama, 7", NMIB, A $2,250.00
Mensa Delivery Van, 5", EX..........................$2,200.00
Mice on Spiral Rod, EX.................................$250.00
Military Plane, sold as an 'Assembly Kit,' 6" W, EXIB....$225.00
Minstrel Man, 1906, flat tin, 7½", scarce, EX (in envelope) .$800.00
Miss Blondin, tightrope walker, 10½", EX...................$3,000.00
Mixtum, 4½", EX $1,500.00
Motor Car, 5", EX...$750.00
Motor Car, 5", EXIB......................................$1,000.00
NA-OB Donkey Cart, 6", EX..........................$550.00
Nani Cart, plastic, friction, 3", MIB..............$50.00
Naughty Boy, 5", EX.....................................$1,300.00
Naughty Boy, 5", NMIB $1,800.00
New Century Cycle, 5", NM $900.00
New Century Cycle, 5", VG $600.00
Nu-Nu, 4½", NM (partial box).......................$1,300.00

Oh My, 10", EX, $650.00. (Photo courtesy Bertoia Auctions)

OHO, 4", EX+ $600.00
OHO, 4", G, A $400.00
Ostrich Cart (African), 6", EX........................$600.00
Paak-Paak Quack-Quack Duck Cart, 8", EX..............$500.00

Paddy & the Pig, 5½", NM $2,300.00
Panne Touring Car, 7", EX $1,700.00
Pao-Pao (Peacock), 9", NMIB..............................$650.00
Performing Sea Lion, 7", NMIB $400.00

Pilot Motorcycle with Driver, 8¾" long, VG, $3,500.00. (Photo courtesy Bertoia Auctions)

Primus Roller Skater, 8½", rare, NM, from $6,500 to .$7,000.00
Rad Cycle, NM...$2,000.00
Rigi Cable Car, 4", EX+IB, A.................................$200.00
Roll Mops (Ball), 3" dia, VG.................................$550.00
Royal Mail Van, 7", NM $2,000.00
Sedan #765, 5½", VG...$300.00

Ski Rolf, 7", EX, $3,000.00. (Photo courtesy Bertoia Auctions)

Ski Rolf, 7", VG $2,200.00
Snik-Snak, 8", EXIB..$5,000.00
Stiller Berlin Truck, 6", rare, EX..............................$900.00
Stubborn Donkey, 8", NMIB..................................$650.00

Susu (Realistic Turtle), 5", NMIB, A $90.00
Tap-Tap, 6", EX $700.00
Tap-Tap, 6", NMIB $900.00
Taxi, 7", EX, A..$880.00
Terra Sedan, 10", NM..$1,500.00
Terre Sedan, 10", VG...$800.00
Titania Sedan, electric lights, 10", G $600.00
Titania Sedan, electric lights, 10", NM, A $2,475.00
Tom the Climbing Monkey, plain vest, hand-pnt face, 7½", MIB $400.00
Tom the Climbing Monkey, polka-dot vest, litho tin face, 7½", MIB $650.00
Tut-Tut, 6½", EX..$1,200.00

Tut-Tut, 6½", EX+IB, $1,700.00. (Photo courtesy Randy Inman Auctions)

Tut-Tut, 6½", G, A $600.00
Tyras the Walking Dog, 6", NM $850.00
UHU Amphibious Car, 9", EX $800.00
Velleda Touring Car, 10", G $1,000.00
Vineta Monorail, 9½", EX $850.00
Waltzing Doll, 9", EXIB $1,800.00
Zig-Zag, 4", EX, A $1,400.00
Zig-Zag, 4", EXIB $1,800.00
Zikra Dare Devil, 7", NM $1,200.00
Zikra Dare Devil, 7", VG, A $800.00
Zulu, 7", VG..$650.00

Lunch Boxes

When the lunch box craze began in the mid-1980s, it was only the metal boxes that so quickly soared to sometimes astronomical prices. But today, even the plastic and vinyl ones are collectible. Though most lunch box dealers agree that with few exceptions, prices have become much more reasonable than they were at first, they're still holding their own and values seem to be stabilizing. So pick a genre and have fun. There are literally hundreds to choose from, and just as is true in other areas of character-related collectibles, the more desirable lunch boxes are those with easily recognized, well-known subjects — western heroes; TV, Disney, and other cartoon characters; and famous entertainers. Thermoses are collectible as well. In our listings, values are just for the box unless a bottle (thermos) is mentioned in the description. If you'd like to learn more about them, we recommend *A Pictorial Price Guide to Metal Lunch Boxes and Thermoses* and a companion book *A Pictorial Price Guide to Vinyl and Plastic Lunch Boxes* by Larry Aikins, and *Collector's Guide to Lunchboxes* by Carole Bess White and L.M. White. For more pricing information, Philip R. Norman (Norman's Olde Store) has prepared a listing of hundreds of boxes, thermoses, and their variations. He is listed in the Categories of Special Interest under Lunch Boxes.

Advisor: Terri Ivers (I2)

Other Sources: N2

METAL

Annie Oakley and Tagg, 1955, EX, $250.00.

A-Team, 1983, VG, N2	$20.00
Action Jackson, 1973, w/bottle, EX	$175.00
Adam-12, 1972, VG	$35.00
Addams Family, 1974, EX	$50.00
Animal Friends, 1975, EX, N2	$30.00
Annie, 1981, NM, N2	$35.00
Annie, 1981, w/bottle, M, N2	$50.00
Astronauts, 1969, VG+, N2	$50.00
Atom Ant, 1966, G	$40.00
Auto Race, 1967, w/bottle, EX, N2	$75.00
Back in '76, 1975, w/bottle, EX	$40.00
Batman & Robin, 1966, w/bottle, NM	$200.00
Battle of the Planets, 1979, EX, N2	$30.00
Battlestar Galactica, 1978, w/bottle, NM	$45.00

Beatles, 1966 – 67, with bottle, EX, $500.00.

Betsy Clark, 1975, beige, w/bottle, EX, N2	$25.00
Beverly Hillbillies, 1963, w/bottle, NM	$150.00
Black Hole, 1979, EX	$30.00
Bonanza, 1963, VG+	$50.00
Bond XX Secret Agent, 1966, EX	$80.00
Bozo the Clown, 1963, dome top, w/bottle, NM	$250.00

Archies, 1970 – 71, with bottle, $100.00. (Photo courtesy Joe Hilton and Greg Moore)

Buccaneer, 1957, dome top, EX, $150.00.

Brady Bunch, 1970, w/bottle, EX $150.00
Brave Eagle, 1957, w/bottle, NM $250.00
Buck Rogers, 1979, EX..$28.00
Bullwinkle & Rocky, 1962, bl, NM...........................$600.00
Campbell Kids, 1975, NM $275.00
Campus Queen, 1967, VG, N2...................................$25.00
Captain Astro, 1966, NM...$250.00
Care Bear Cousins, 1985, w/bottle, EX+, N2 ....$20.00
Care Bears, 1983, w/bottle, EX, N2 ....$15.00
Carnival, 1959, EX, N2 ....$350.00
Cartoon Zoo Lunch Chest, 1962, EX $175.00
Casey Jones, 1960, dome top, w/bottle, NM $400.00
Chan Clan, 1973, blk rims, VG+, N2 ....$50.00
Chavo, 1979, M..$100.00
Children at Play, 1930s, gr, 2-hdl, VG, N2 ....$75.00
Chitty-Chitty Bang-Bang, 1968, VG+, N2 ....$75.00
Chuck Wagon, 1958, dome top, w/bottle, NM..............$250.00
Cracker Jack, 1979, EX $35.00
Cyclist, 1979, VG, N2 ....$25.00
Davy Crockett, 1955, gr rim, VG+............................$60.00
Davy Crockett/Kit Carson, 1955, EX, N2................$175.00
Denim Diner, 1975, dome top, VG+ $35.00
Dick Tracy, 1967, w/bottle, NM $200.00
Disney Express, 1979, EX, N2 ....$20.00
Disney on Parade, 1970, VG, N2 ....$25.00
Disney School Bus, 1968, dome top, w/bottle, EX $85.00
Disney World, 1976, w/bottle, EX $28.00
Disney's Magic Kingdom, 1979, w/bottle, EX $28.00
Disney's Wonderful World, 1980, VG, N2......................$10.00
Double-Deckers, 1970, EX, N2................................$60.00
Dr Dolittle, 1967, G, N2...$35.00
Dr Dolittle, 1967, w/bottle, EX, N2 ....$95.00
Dr Seuss, 1970, VG+..$70.00
Duchess, 1960, VG..$30.00
Duchess, 1960, w/bottle, EX $60.00
Dudley Do-Right, 1962, bl rim, NM $1,000.00
Dukes of Hazzard, 1980, EX, N2.............................$35.00
Dukes of Hazzard, 1980, w/bottle, VG, N2 ....$25.00
Dynomutt, 1976, EX $35.00
Elephants, 1980s, 2-hdl, EX, N2..............................$25.00
ET, 1982, EX, N2 ....$25.00
Fall Guy, 1981, VG, N2 ....$15.00
Fall Guy, 1981, w/bottle, EX, N2.............................$35.00
Family Affair, 1969, w/bottle, EX $135.00
Flintstones, 1964, EX, N2...$120.00
Flipper, 1967, EX, N2 ....$100.00
Flying Nun, 1968, EX $60.00
Fraggle Rock, 1984, w/bottle, EX $25.00
Frontier Days, 1957, VG, N2 ....$100.00
Gene Autry Melody Ranch, 1954, w/bottle, NM $500.00
Gentle Ben, 1968, EX..$75.00
Get Smart, 1966, EX...$135.00
Ghostland, 1977, EX..$30.00
Globe-Trotters, 1958, dome top, VG+, N2 ....$175.00
Goober & the Ghost Chasers, 1974, VG+.................$35.00
Goofy, 1984, EX+..$25.00
Great Wild West, 1959, EX, N2...............................$375.00
Green Hornet, 1967, w/bottle, M.............................$500.00

GI Joe, 1982, EX, N2, $25.00.

Gremlins, 1984, w/bottle, NM+ $45.00
Grizzly Adams, 1977, dome top, NM $75.00
Grizzly Adams, 1977, dome top, VG+.............................$50.00
Guns of Will Sonnet, 1968, VG, N2................................$100.00
Gunsmoke, 1959, EX, N2 ....$175.00
Gunsmoke, 1962, w/bottle, VG $80.00
Hair Bear Bunch, 1971, EX $50.00
Hansel & Gretel, 1982, EX...$50.00
Heathcliff, 1982, EX, N2 ....$20.00
Hector Heathcote, 1964, w/bottle, NM $150.00
Hee Haw, 1970, EX..$50.00
Hi-My Lunch, 1977, M, N2..$60.00
Highway Signs, 1968, 1st design, VG+, N2 ....$50.00
Hogan's Heroes, 1966, dome top, w/bottle, EX...............$200.00
Holly Hobbie, 1979, EX+, N2..$20.00
Hopalong Cassidy, 1952, red w/sq decal, w/bottle...........$300.00
How the West Was Won, 1979, w/bottle, VG+, N2.........$35.00
HR Pufnstuf, 1970, w/bottle, NM $185.00
Huckleberry Hound & Friends, 1961, VG, N2 ....$75.00
Incredible Hulk, 1978, EX, N2 ....$40.00

Jetsons, 1963, dome top, with bottle, EX, from $900.00 to $1,200.00.

Incredible Hulk, 1978, w/bottle, EX..................$50.00
Indiana Jones & the Temple of Doom, 1984, VG+ $25.00
Jet Patrol, 1957, VG+................................$100.00
Jetsons, 1963, dome top, G+ $170.00
Johnny Lightning, 1970, VG+..........................$35.00
Jr Miss, 1966, girl w/bird, VG+......................$25.00
Jr Miss, 1970, 3 girls & a duck, EX+.................$25.00
Jr Miss, 1973, attic scene, EX, N2...................$25.00
Jr Miss, 1978, basset hound, VG+.....................$20.00
Knight Rider, 1983, EX...............................$20.00
Korg, 1974, EX, N2...................................$35.00
Krofft Supershow, 1976, VG, N2.......................$50.00
Lance Link Secret Chimp, 1971, VG....................$60.00
Land of the Giants, 1968, VG, N2.....................$75.00

Munsters, 1965, VG, $200.00.

Land of the Giants, 1969 – 70, with bottle, NM, $200.00.

Lassie, 1978, VG.....................................$35.00
Laugh-In, 1970, tricycle, VG.........................$75.00
Lawman, 1961, VG.....................................$45.00
Little Dutch Miss, 1959, VG, N2......................$75.00
Little Dutch Miss, 1959, w/metal bottle, EX+ $225.00
Little Orphan Annie, 1981, EX+ $28.00
Lone Ranger, 1980, VG, N2............................$20.00
Lost in Space, reproduction, dome top, M $40.00
Lost in Space, 1967, dome top, w/bottle, EX+, A......$385.00
Marvel Super Heroes, 1976, VG+, N2...................$25.00
Masters of the Universe, 1983, w/bottle, M (w/hang tags), N2.$60.00
Mickey Mouse Club, 1962, EX, N2......................$65.00
Mickey Mouse Club, 1976, yel, EX $45.00
Mickey Mouse Club, 1977, red, VG, N2.................$20.00
Miss America, 1972, VG+, N2..........................$40.00
Monkees, 1997, M (sealed), N2 ....$40.00
Monroes, 1967, EX $150.00
Mork & Mindy, 1979, VG+..............................$25.00
Mr Merlin, 1981, VG..................................$25.00
Muppet Babies, 1985, EX, N2..........................$10.00
Muppets, 1979, VG, N2................................$15.00
Nancy Drew Mysteries, 1977, VG, N2...................$35.00

NFL Quarterback, 1964, EX $90.00
Pac Man, 1980, VG, N2................................$15.00
Pac Man, 1980, 2 swing hdls, 1980, NM+ $30.00
Pathfinder, 1959, VG+ $200.00
Peanuts, 1966, G, N2.................................$10.00
Peanuts, 1973, EX, N2................................$25.00
Peanuts, 1976, w/bottle, EX, N2......................$35.00
Peanuts, 1980, G, N2.................................$10.00
Peke (Japanese), 1970s, EX, N2 ....$75.00
Pele, 1975, EX, N2...................................$60.00
Pete's Dragon, 1978, EX, N2..........................$35.00
Pigs in Space, 1978, dome top, EX, N2 ....$35.00
Pit Stop, 1968, EX+, N2..............................$175.00
Planet of the Apes, 1974, VG, N2 ....$60.00
Play Ball, 1969, VG+.................................$35.00
Polly Pal, 1974, w/bottle, EX $25.00
Popeye, 1980, EX $40.00
Pro Sports, 1962, EX, N2.............................$45.00
Raggedy Ann & Andy, 1973, VG+, N2....................$25.00

Robin Hood, 1965, with bottle, $150.00. (Photo courtesy Scott Bruce)

Raggedy Ann & Andy, 1973, w/bottle, EX, N2 ....$40.00
Rambo, 1985, NM+ $25.00
Rambo, 1985, w/bottle, VG, N2 ....$15.00
Return of the Jedi, 1983, VG+, N2 ....$30.00
Road Runner, 1970, VG, N2 ....$55.00
Ronald McDonald, 1982, w/bottle, M............................$55.00
Roscoe Recycle, 1990, EX $50.00
Rose Petal Place, 1983, EX $25.00

Roy Rogers and Dale Evans, 1957, with bottle, EX, $200.00.

Satellite, 1958, EX $70.00
School Days, 1960, VG+ $60.00
Secret Agent T, 1968, VG $50.00
Secret of Nimh, 1982, w/bottle, M $50.00
Secret Wars, 1984, VG, N2 ....$15.00
See America, 1972, EX $40.00
Sesame Street, 1979, w/bottle, EX, N2............................$20.00
Skateboarder, 1978, EX...$45.00
Snow White, 1975, G, N2 ....$20.00
Snow White, 1977, same on both sides, EX $40.00
Space Shuttle Orbiter Enterprise, 1977, VG, N2.............$40.00
Space: 1999, w/bottle, VG+ $40.00
Sport Goofy, 1984, EX, N2 ....$25.00
Sport Skwirts, 1972, basketball, M $80.00
Star Trek The Motion Picture, 1979, EX+ $60.00

Star Wars, 1977, with bottle, VG/NM bottle, $65.00.

Star Wars, 1977, characters on band, G, N2 ....$20.00
Strawberry Shortcake, 1980, w/bottle, EX, N2 ....$25.00
Submarine, 1960, VG, N2 ....$50.00
Sunnie Miss, 1972, VG+, N2 ....$45.00
Super Friends, 1976, w/bottle, EX, N2 ....$50.00
Super Powers, 1983, VG+, N2 ....$25.00

Superman, 1967, EX, $150.00.

Superman, 1967, G, N2 ....$65.00
Superman, 1978, w/bottle, VG, N2 ....$25.00
Three Little Pigs, 1982, EX...$80.00
Thundercats, 1985, VG, N2 ....$15.00
Thundercats, 1985, w/bottle, EX, N2 ....$25.00
Tom Corbett, 1954, VG, N2 ....$200.00
Train, 1970, NM, N2 ....$45.00
Transformers, 1986, w/bottle, EX, N2 ....$25.00
Treasure Chest, 1960, dome top, VG+, N2.....................$325.00
UFO, 1973, NM, N2...$75.00

Underdog, 1974, NM, $1,500.00.

UFO, 1973, VG, N2 ....$35.00
US Mail/Mr Zipp, 1969, dome top, w/bottle, EX+............$50.00
Wagon Train, 1964, VG, N2 ....$88.00
Wags 'N Whiskers, 1978, w/bottle, EX, N2......................$25.00
Weave Pattern, 1972, M $40.00
Wee Pals Kid Power, 1973, w/bottle, EX, N2 ....$35.00
Wild Frontier, 1977, EX, N2..$40.00
Yankee Doodle, 1975, w/bottle, EX, N2 ....$25.00

PLASTIC

A-Team, 1985, EX, $13.00.

Astrokids, 1988, w/robot bottle, M, N2 ....$25.00
Barbie, 1990, w/bottle, EX $8.00
Barney Baby Bop, 1992, w/bottle, EX...................................$5.00
Benji, 1974, EX, N2 ....$15.00
Cabbage Patch Kids, 1983, EX $10.00
Casper the Friendly Ghost, 1996, w/bottle, M, N2 ....$15.00
Chiclets Chewing Gum, 1987, w/bottle, M, N2 ....$50.00
Chip 'n Dale, 1980s, w/bottle, EX $5.00
Chuck E Cheese, 1996, w/bottle, NM, N2........................$30.00
Crest Toothpaste, 1980, tubular, w/bottle, EX, N2 ....$50.00
Dick Tracy, 1990, red, w/bottle, M $15.00
Disney School Bus, 1990, complete, M (sealed) $35.00
Dr Seuss, 1996, EX, N2 ....$15.00
Fat Albert, 1973, dome top, G+, N2 ....$15.00
Flintstones, 1992, red, EX, N2..$10.00

Flintstones (A Day at the Zoo), 1989, NM, $20.00.

Garfield, 1980s, red, EX, N2..$15.00
Holly Hobbie, 1989, pk, w/bottle, M, N2.........................$25.00
Hot Wheels, 1997, w/bottle, M, N2 ....$20.00
Incredible Hulk, 1980, dome top, w/bottle, EX................$40.00
Jabberjaw, 1977, EX $30.00

Jem, ca 1987, with bottle, NM, $10.00.

Jif Peanut Butter, 1980s, EX, N2 ....$20.00
Jurassic Park, 1992, w/recalled bottle, EX, N2 ....$25.00
Keebler Cookies, 1987, w/bottle, M, N2 ....$50.00
Kermit the Frog, 1981, dome top, EX, N2.........................$25.00
Little Orphan Annie, 1973, dome top, w/bottle, NM $30.00
Looney Tunes, 1977, EX, N2 ....$10.00
Lucy Luncheonette, 1981, dome top, EX $18.00
Mickey Mouse, 1988, head form, w/bottle, M..................$30.00
Mickey Mouse & Donald Duck, 1984, w/bottle, EX.........$10.00
Mighty Mouse, 1979, EX, N2 ....$20.00
Minnie Mouse, 1988, head form, w/bottle, VG+, N2.......$25.00
Muppet Babies, 1986, pk, w/plastic bottle, EX, N2..........$15.00
Muppets, 1990s, w/bottle, M $15.00
Nestle Quik, 1980, NM, N2 ....$25.00
New Kids on the Block, 1990, w/bottle, EX, N2 ....$15.00
Nosey Bears, 1988, w/bottle, EX..$10.00
Pee Wee Herman, 1987, w/red generic bottle, EX+..........$20.00
Pepsi, 1980s, EX, N2 ....$25.00
Popeye, 1979, plastic dome, EX $30.00
Rap It Up, 1992, EX, N2 ....$15.00
Robot Man, 1984, EX $15.00
Rocky Roughneck, 1977, EX $20.00
Rover Dangerfield, 1990, w/bottle, EX, N2.........................$20.00
Shadow, 1994, w/bottle, M $20.00
Smurfs, 1983, dome top, w/bottle, EX $20.00
Snoopy & Woodstock, 1970, dome top, w/bottle, EX $20.00
Snoopy as Joe Cool, 1971, w/bottle, M, N2 ....$25.00
Star Trek The Next Generation, 1989, w/bottle, M $20.00
Star Wars Ewoks, 1983, EX, N2..$15.00
Sunnie Miss, 1972, VG+, N2 ....$45.00
Superman, 1986, phone booth scene, EX, N2..................$25.00

SWAT, 1975, dome top, w/bottle, EX.................................$30.00
The Tick, 1995, w/bottle, M (w/hang tag), N2 ....$50.00
Tom & Jerry, 1992, w/bottle, M, N2 ....$20.00
Train Engine #7, 1990, EX, N2 ....$10.00
Winnie the Pooh, 1990s, w/bottle, M, N2 ....$25.00
Yogi Bear, 1990, 5x8", EX, N2 ....$10.00
Young Astronauts, 1986, M, N2 ....$15.00

VINYL

Annie, 1981, EX, N2 ....$45.00
Barbie, 1972, pk, w/bottle, VG+, N2 ....$60.00

Barbie Lunch Kit, 1962, with bottle, EX, $300.00.

Casper the Friendly Ghost, 1966, EX, $350.00.

Batman, 1995, EX, N2 ....$10.00
Denim, 1970, w/bottle, M, N2..$65.00
Deputy Dawg, 1961, EX..$325.00
Donny & Marie, 1977, w/bottle, EX $80.00
Fire Station Engine Co #1, 1975, EX, N2 ....$100.00
Holly Hobbie, 1972, w/bottle, EX, N2 ....$50.00
Jr Deb, 1960, EX, N2 ....$100.00
Li'l Jodie, 1985, EX $40.00
Lion in the Van, 1978, NM $40.00
Little Old Schoolhouse, 1974, EX $40.00
Mardi Gras, 1971, w/bottle, EX, N2.................................$100.00
Mary Poppins, 1973, VG, N2 ....$50.00
Pac Man, 1980, EX $30.00

Monkees, 1967, EX, $275.00.

Pepsi-Cola, 1980, yel, EX, N2 ....$50.00
Pink Panther, 1980, EX..$65.00
Pretty Miss, 1979, snap-on bag, EX, N2 ....$35.00
Psychedelic Blue, 1970, EX..$35.00
Ringling Bros & Barnum & Bailey Circus, 1970, VG+ ..$170.00
Ronald McDonald, 1988, lunch bag, EX..........................$15.00
Snoopy, 1977, brunch bag, w/bottle, EX, N2 ....$75.00
Snoopy at Mailbox, 1969, red, EX, N2.............................$60.00

Soupy Sales, 1966, NM, $300.00.

Speedy Turtle, 1978, drawstring bag, M, N2 ....$25.00
The Sophisticate, 1970, brunch bag, w/bottle, EX...........$50.00
Tic-Tac-Toe, 1970s, EX, N2..$50.00
Wizard in the Van, 1978, orange, VG+.............................$60.00
Wonder Woman, 1977, w/bottle, EX, N2 ....$100.00
World of Barbie, 1971, EX, N2 ....$50.00
World Traveler, 1961, brunch bag, w/metal bottle, M $60.00
Ziggy, 1979, EX $50.00

VACUUM BOTTLES

ABC Wide World of Sports, 1976, metal, 13", EX, N2 ....$35.00

Beverly Hillbillies, 1963,
EX, $45.00.

Boating, 1959, metal, EX, N2 ....$75.00
Campbell Soup, 1968, metal, EX...........................$50.00
Casey Jones, 1960, EX, N2 ....$100.00
Casper the Friendly Ghost, 1966, metal, EX, N2.............$95.00
CB'er, 1976, plastic, 12", M, N2 ....$35.00
Davy Crockett, 1955, metal, unused, M (EX box), A $200.00
Dukes of Hazzard, 1980, plastic, VG+, N2 ....$10.00
Fireball XL-5, metal, EX, N2 ....$50.00
Flintstones, 1964, metal, EX, N2 ....$50.00
Fonz, 1976, metal, NM+, N2 ....$50.00
Greyhound, 1970, plastic/glass, EX, N2 ....$35.00
Hopalong Cassidy, 1950, metal, EX+, N2 ....$55.00
Hopalong Cassidy, 1950, metal, unused, M (G box), A .$200.00
Johnny Lightning, 1970, plastic, EX..........................$20.00
Jonathan Livingston Seagull, 1973, plastic, EX, N2 ....$15.00
Jr Miss, 1966, plastic, EX $15.00
Jr Miss, 1966, metal, EX, N2................................$25.00
Kewtie Pie, 1964, metal, M, N2 ....$60.00
Kewtie Pie, 1964, metal, VG+, N2 ....$25.00
King Kong, 1977, plastic, EX...............................$15.00
Major League Baseball, 1968, metal, M, N2 ....$50.00
NFL Quarterback, 1964, metal, EX, N2 ....$60.00
Osmonds, 1973, plastic, M...................................$30.00
Outdoor Sports, 1960, metal, EX, N2.......................$45.00
Peanuts, 1966, metal, EX, N2 ....$25.00
Peter Pan, 1976, plastic, EX.................................$20.00
Pets & Pals (Lassie & Black Beauty), 1961, metal, EX, N2..$25.00
Play Ball, 1969, metal, NM+ $40.00
Punky Brewster, 1984, plastic, EX, N2 ....$15.00
Satellite, 1958, metal, EX, N2 ....$40.00
Secret Agent T, 1968, metal, EX, N2 ....$35.00
Spalding Tennis Balls, 1960s, metal, 13", EX, N2.............$45.00
Spider-Man/Incredible Hulk, 1983, plastic, EX $15.00
Street Hawk, 1984, plastic, EX $25.00
Super Friends, 1976, plastic, EX $15.00
Superman, 1967, metal, EX $50.00
Tim Hortons Donuts, 1970s, plastic/glass, 13", EX, N2 ....$35.00
Transformers, 1986, plastic, M..............................$10.00

US Mail, 1969, metal (for dome box), EX, N2 ....$25.00
Wild Bill Hickok & Jingles, 1955, metal, EX...................$40.00
Wonder Woman, 1977, plastic, bl or yel, EX, ea..............$25.00

Yellow Submarine, 1968,
EX, $200.00.

Yogi Bear, 1963, metal, EX+ $55.00
Ziggy, 1979, plastic, EX......................................$15.00
Zorro, 1958, metal, EX.......................................$50.00

Marbles

Antique marbles are divided into several classifications: 1) Transparent Swirl (Solid Core, Latticinio Core, Divided Core, Ribbon Core, Lobed Core, and Coreless); 2) Lutz or Lutz-type (with bands having copper flecks which alternate with colored or clear bands; 3) Peppermint Swirl (made of red, white, and blue opaque glass); 4) Indian Swirl (black with multicolored surface swirls); 5) Banded Swirl (wide swirling bands on opaque or transparent glass); 6) Onionskin (having an overall mottled appearance due to its spotted, swirling lines or lobes: 7) End-of-Day (single pontil, allover spots, either two-colored or multicolored); 8) Clambroth (evenly spaced, swirled lines on opaque glass); 9) Mica (transparent color with mica flakes added); 10) Sulfide (nearly always clear, colored examples are rare, containing figures). Besides glass marbles, some were made of clay, pottery, china, steel, and even semiprecious stones.

Most machine-made marbles are still very reasonable, but some of the better examples may sell for $50.00 and up, depending on the colors that were used and how they are defined. Guineas (Christensen agates with small multicolored specks instead of swirls) sometimes go for as much as $200.00. Mt. Peltier comic character marbles often bring prices of $100.00 and more with Betty Boop, Moon Mullins, and Kayo being the rarest and most valuable.

From the nature of their use, mint-condition marbles are extremely rare and may be worth as much as three to five times more than one that is near-mint, while chipped and cracked marbles may be worth half or less. The same is true of one that has been polished, regardless of how successful the polishing was. If you'd like to learn more, Everett Grist has written three books on the subject that you will find helpful: *Antique and Collectible Marbles*, *Machine Made and Contemporary Marbles*, and *Everett Grist's Big Book of Marbles*. Also refer to MCSA's *Marble Identification and Price Guide*, recently re-written by Robert Block (Schiffer Publishing).

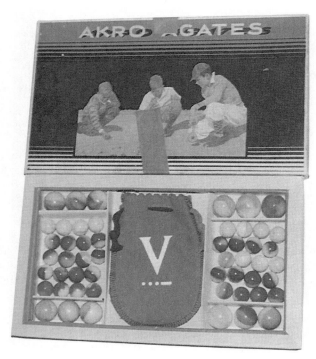

Akro Agate, 'V' (for Victory) set, early 1940s, EXIB, $500.00. (Photo courtesy Everett Grist/Roy Katskee)

Artist-Made, angelfish or sea horse, David Salaxar, 1⅜", M..$100.00
Artist-Made, end-of-day w/lutz or mica, Bill Burchfield, 1½", M $75.00
Artist-Made, end-of-day w/lutz or mica, Mark Mathews, ⅝" to ¾", M $50.00
Artist-Made, swirl w/lutz or mica, Bill Burchfield, 1½", M, ea $75.00
Artist-Made, 1 flower or 3 flowers, Harry Boyer, 1½", M, ea ..$50.00
Clambroth Swirl, any color variation, 1½" to ⅞", M, ea .$250.00
Comic, Andy Gump, Peltier Glass, M $125.00
Comic, Annie, Peltier Glass, M $150.00
Comic, Betty Boop, Peltier Glass, M............................$200.00
Comic, Emma, Peltier Glass, M....................................$75.00
Comic, Herbie, Peltier Glass, M....................................$150.00
Comic, Kayo, Peltier Glass, M $450.00
Comic, Koko, Peltier Glass, M $125.00
Comic, Moon Mullins, Peltier Glass, M $300.00
Comic, Skeezix, Peltier Glass, M..................................$150.00
Comic, Smitty, Peltier Glass, M....................................$125.00
Comic, Tom Mix, Peltier, Glass, minimum value $500.00
Divided Core Swirl, peewee, any variation, ⅜" to ½", M, ea .$25.00
Divided Core Swirl, 4 yel outer bands w/3 mc inner bands, 1¹⁄₁₆", NM, A $100.00

End-of Day, red & wht, 1½", NM $225.00
End-of-Day, clear w/gr, red & bl pattern, polished pontil, 2⅛", VG, A..$275.00
End-of-Day, peewee, any color, ⅜" to ½", M, ea.............$50.00
End-of-Day, red & wht, 1½", NM $225.00
End-of-Day, single pontil cloud w/mica, mc, 1⅝", NM $55.00

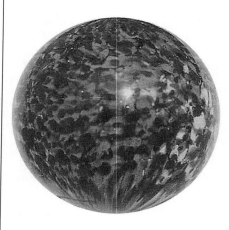

End-of-Day, single pontil, 2¹⁄₁₆", $1,800.00. (Photo courtesy Everett Grist/Lloyd Huffer)

Indian Swirl, any color variation, ½" to ⅞", ea $125.00
Indian Swirl, Colonial Blue, 1¾"................................$1,750.00
Indian Swirl, Colonial Blue, ⅝" $85.00
Joseph's Coat, transparent bl base w/mc swirl, 1⁵⁄₁₆", VG, A..$65.00
Joseph's Coat, transparent clear base w/mc swirl, shrunken core w/aventurine, M, A $165.00
Latticinio Core, lt bl transparent base w/4 mc outer bands, gr core, 1⁹⁄₁₆", EX, A $125.00
Latticinio Core, red, wht & bl outer bands w/yel core, 1¾", M.$250.00
Latticinio Swirl, peewee, any color, ⅜" to ½", M $25.00
Latticinio Swirl, 6 red & wht outer bands, yel core, 1⅝", NM.$150.00
Lucky Boy Marble Set, 28 tiger-eyes, MIB, A $300.00
Lutz, banded colored glass, any color, ½" to ⅞", M $200.00
Lutz, banded opaque, any color, ½" to ⅞", M $400.00

Lutz, clear with bright blue and white-bordered gold-color surface swirls, ⅝", $125.00; 1¾", $900.00. (Photo courtesy Everett Grist/Bucky Zeleski)

Machine-Made, Akro Agate, 1930s, set of 100 tri-colors, MIB.$500.00
Machine-Made, brn slag, MF Christensen, 1³⁄₁₆", NM $75.00
Machine-Made, limeade corkscrew or swirl, Akro Agate, ⁹⁄₁₆" to ¹¹⁄₁₆", M, ea...$20.00
Machine-Made, limeade oxblood, Akro Agate, ⁹⁄₁₆" to ¹¹⁄₁₆", M, ea...$100.00

Machine-Made, National Line Rainbo, Superman, 9/16 to 11/16", M, ea $125.00
Machine-Made, National Line Rainbo, tiger, Peltier Glass, 9/16" to 11/16", M, ea....$20.00
Machine-Made, opaque swirl, Christensen Agate, 2-color, 9/16" to 11/16", M, ea....$15.00
Machine-Made, opaque swirl, Christensen Agate, 3-color, 9/16" to 11/16", M, ea....$35.00
Machine-Made, Popeye corkscrew, Akro Agate, purple & yel or red & bl, 9/16" to 11/16", M, ea....$65.00
Machine-Made, tiger eye, Master Marble, 9/16" to 11/16", M .$20.00
Machine-Made, yel swirl, lt bl base, MF Christensen, 1 9/16", NM, A $25.00

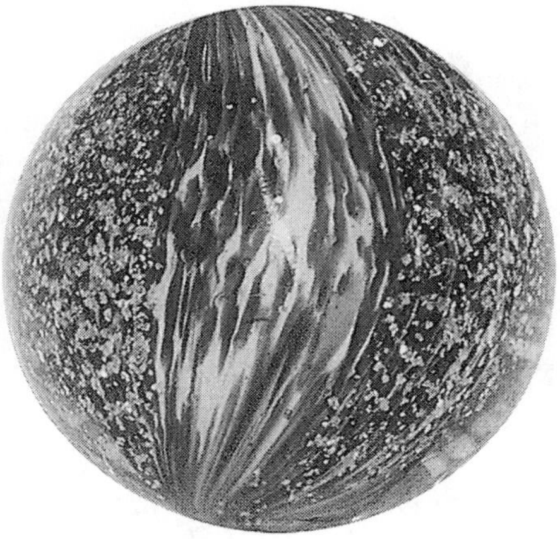

Onionskin, red, white, and blue with three panels of thick mica, 1 3/4", $600.00. (Photo courtesy Everett Grist/Bucky Zeleski)

Onionskin, wht base w/2 transparent pk, 1 bl & 1 gr panel, 1 5/8", NM, A $350.00
Ribbon Core Swirl, any color, 1/2" to 7/8", M, ea $150.00
Ribbon Core Swirl w/Lutz, opaque emerald gr w/gold swirl, 1 3/4", M, minimum value....$1,000.00
Solid Core Swirl, peewee, any color, 3/8" to 1/2", M, ea $50.00
Solid Core Swirl, wht & bl outer bands, red & wht core surrounded by yel bands, 5/8", M....$60.00
Solid Mica, clear, amber, bl, gr or red, 1 3/4", M, ea....$650.00
Solid Mica, clear, amber, gr or red, 1 3/4", M, ea....$650.00
Solid Opaque, bl, blk, gr, pk or wht, 5/8", M, ea....$35.00
Solid Opaque, bl, blk, gr, pk or wht, 1 3/4", M, ea....$800.00

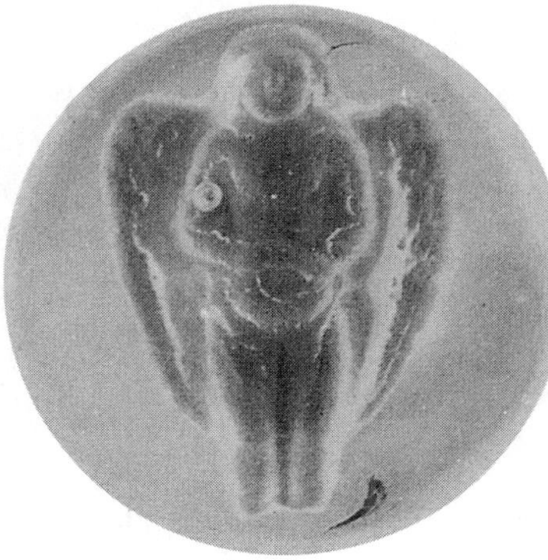

Sulfide, angel holding wreath, 1 3/4", $600.00. (Photo courtesy Everett Grist)

Sulfide, #1, 1 3/4", M....$400.00
Sulfide, #7, pnt gr, sm bubble, 1 5/8", EX....$975.00
Sulfide, alligator, 1 3/4", M....$200.00
Sulfide, angel kneeling w/lyre, 1 5/8", EX....$210.00
Sulfide, baby in basket, 1 3/4", M....$800.00
Sulfide, bear, 1 3/4", M....$200.00
Sulfide, bear standing, 1 5/16", VG, A....$145.00
Sulfide, buffalo, 1 3/4", M....$300.00
Sulfide, camel (1 hump), standing on mound of grass, 1 1/2", NM....$200.00
Sulfide, cat lying down, 2 1/8", EX....$55.00
Sulfide, cherub, 1 3/4", M....$1,000.00
Sulfide, chicken standing, 1 13/16", VG, A....$115.00
Sulfide, child w/hammer, 1 3/4", M....$600.00
Sulfide, child w/sailboat, 1 3/4", M....$650.00
Sulfide, clown, 1 3/4", M....$100.00
Sulfide, cow standing, bubble around figure, 1 11/16", VG, A .$145.00
Sulfide, cow standing, 2 1/4", EX, A....$55.00
Sulfide, crucifix, 1 3/4", M....$650.00
Sulfide, dog (Nipper), 1 3/4", EX....$350.00
Sulfide, dog standing, 2", EX....$55.00
Sulfide, dog standing (curly tail), 1 3/4", M, A....$115.00
Sulfide, dog standing (shepherd), amber, 1 1/4", NM, A ..$745.00
Sulfide, dog w/bird, 1 3/4", NM....$1,100.00
Sulfide, dog w/bushy tail, 1 1/4", EX....$110.00
Sulfide, dove, 1 5/8", M....$165.00
Sulfide, fish, 1 5/8", EX....$180.00
Sulfide, frog leaping, 1 3/4", EX, A....$165.00
Sulfide, frog sitting, bubble around figure, 1 13/16", VG....$200.00
Sulfide, girl sitting in chair, bubble around figure, 1 9/16", VG, A....$260.00
Sulfide, goat, lt amethyst, 2", EX....$150.00
Sulfide, hen standing, 1 3/4", VG, A....$115.00
Sulfide, horse grazing, 1 5/8", NM....$200.00
Sulfide, horse standing, 1 3/4", G, A....$85.00
Sulfide, horse standing, 2 1/8", EX, A....$110.00
Sulfide, Jenny Lind, 1 1/2", NM....$750.00
Sulfide, lion, 1 7/8", VG, A....$110.00
Sulfide, lion preparing to pounce, 1 5/8", NM....$180.00
Sulfide, lion standing on mound of grass, 2", NM....$125.00
Sulfide, Little Boy Blue, 1 3/4", M....$750.00
Sulfide, man (politician) standing on stump, 1 1/4", VG..$450.00

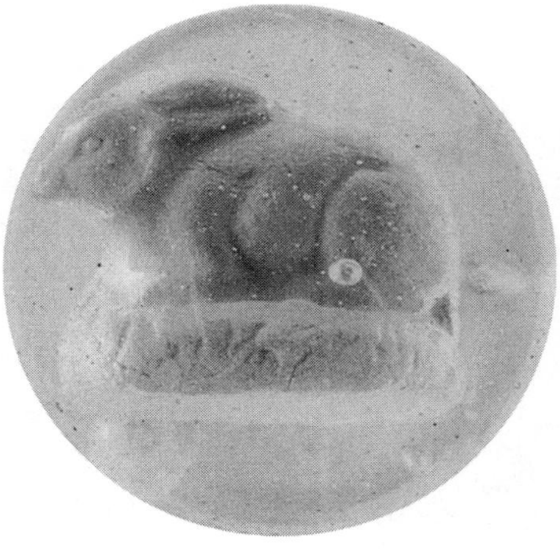

Sulfide, rabbit crouching, 1 3/4", $250.00. (Photo courtesy Everett Grist)

Sulfide, man seated on potty, 1½", NM......................$2,000.00
Sulfide, owl, 1¾", M..$350.00
Sulfide, papoose, 1¾", M..$700.00
Sulfide, parrot on perch, 1⅞", VG...........................$140.00
Sulfide, parrot, 1½", EX, A....................................$100.00
Sulfide, peasant boy on stump w/legs crossed, 1½", NM..$400.00
Sulfide, pony running in field of grass, 1¾", M...........$200.00
Sulfide, rabbit sprinting over grass, 1⅞", NM...............$150.00
Sulfide, ram, 2", very rare, NM, A...........................$2,200.00
Sulfide, ram standing, 2⅛", EX, A............................$55.00
Sulfide, Santa Claus, 1¾", M..................................$1,300.00
Sulfide, sheep, honey amber, 2⅛", EX........................$900.00
Sulfide, sheep lying down, 2", EX.............................$88.00
Sulfide, sheep standing, bubble around figure, 2³⁄₁₆", VG...$175.00
Sulfide, squirrel sitting holding nut, 1½", VG, A...........$145.00
Sulfide, squirrel w/nut, 2", EX................................$200.00
Sulfide, Victorian boy sailor w/sailboat, 1⅞", EX...........$260.00
Sulfide, wild boar, 2½", EX, A................................$220.00
Sulfide, woman (Kate Greenaway), 1½", NM................$450.00

Marx

Louis Marx founded his company in New York in the 1920s. He was a genius not only at designing toys but also marketing them. His business grew until it became one of the largest toy companies ever to exist, eventually expanding to include several factories in the United States as well as other countries. Marx sold his company in the early 1970s; he died in 1982. Though toys of every description were produced, collectors today admire his mechanical toys above all others. For more information on Marx battery-operated toys, refer to *Collector's Guide to Battery-Operated Toys* by Don Hultzman.

Advisors: Scott Smiles (S10), windups; Tom Lastrapes (L4), battery-ops

See also Advertising; Banks; Character, TV, and Movie Collectibles; Dollhouse Furniture; Games; Guns; Plastic Figures; Playsets; and other categories. For toys made by Linemar (Marx's subsidiary in Japan), see Battery-Operated Toys; Windups, Frictions, and Other Mechanicals.

BATTERY-OPERATED

Alley the Roaring Stalking Alligator, 1960s, 18", EXIB.$350.00
Armored Attack Set, battery-op tank & jeep w/plug-in controller, MIB...........$300.00
Barking Boxer Dog, 1950s, 7", EX..........................$25.00
Barking Spaniel Dog, 1950s, 7", EX........................$25.00
Barnyard Rooster, 1950s, 10", EX..........................$75.00
Big Bruiser Highway Service Truck, 1960s, 23", EX......$175.00
Big Parade, plastic, 1963, 15" L, NMIB...................$200.00
Colonel Hap Hazard, 1968, 11", EX........................$700.00
Coupe w/Cuday Advertising, battery-op lights, VG, A..$660.00
Forrestal Aircraft Carrier, 1950s, 14", NM+.............$325.00
Frankenstein's Monster Robot, 1950, 12", VG+.........$900.00

Great Garloo, remote control, 23½", NM+IB, A, $500.00.
(Photo courtesy Smith House Toys)

Hootin' Hollow Haunted House, 1960s, 11", NM+.......$750.00
Jetspeed Racer #7, w/driver, 17", EXIB, A.................$475.00
Mickey Mouse Krazy Kar, plastic, 7", EXIB................$125.00
Mickey Mouse Little Big Wheel, 10", nonworking o/w EXIB, A...$75.00
Mighty Kong Big Mouth Ball Blowing Game, 1950s, MIB, L4...$675.00

Buttons (The Puppy With a Brain), MIB, L4, $375.00.
(Photo courtesy Don Hultzman)

Mighty Kong, plush with shackled hands, 1950s, 11", MIB, $700.00. (Photo courtesy Don Hultzman)

Nutty Mad Indian, 1960s, MIB, L4 ....$250.00
Penny the Poodle, remote control, 1960, NMIB $125.00
Race a Cart, 1960s, 10½", EX $150.00
Walking (Esso) Tiger, plush, 11½", NM+IB, A $575.00
Whistling Spooky Kooky Tree, 1960s, 14", EX...........$1,250.00
Yeti the Abominable Snowman, 1950s, 11", NMIB.......$975.00

PRESSED STEEL

A&P Super Markets Local Delivery Truck, w/rear plastic mesh
   door, silver & red, 19", EXIB, A.............................$450.00
Apex Construction Crane Truck, wooden wheels, 15½", G, A .$200.00
Barrel Stake Truck, red & bl, w/orig insert & 4 wooden flour bar-
   rels & handcart, 11", EX, A $600.00
City Sanitation Truck, w/litho tin, 13", G, A $150.00
Coupe, w/rear luggage compartment, red w/silver grille, lights &
   bumper, 1930s, 9", G, A $130.00
Cunningham's Drug Store Stake Truck, enclosed wheel covers,
   gr & yel w/yel wht-wall tires, 13", EX+ $200.00
Deluxe Delivery Truck, rider, 1940s, EX+, A..................$600.00
Dept of Street Cleaning Truck, silver, w/broom & shovel, 10",
   NM, A $600.00
Dump Truck, bl & red, open wheel wells (none in back), horns
   on roof, 18", EX+, A...$130.00
Dump Truck, blk & orange, rear dual axle, lever action, 1950s,
   20", VGIB, A $230.00
Dump Truck, red & dk bl-gray, covered wheel wells (front &
   back), 13½", EX+, A $60.00
Earth Hauler, 18", EX+, A $80.00
Emergency Searchlight Dept Truck, 18½", VG, A.........$250.00
Fire Hook & Ladder Truck, mk VFD #9, 40½", MIB, A .$550.00
Fire Ladder Hose & Reel Truck, 1930s, 15", NM, A ...$1,020.00

**Fire Hook and Ladder Truck, ride-on, red with yellow seat
and side ladders, bell on hood, 1950s, 31", NMIB, A,
$2,100.00.** (Photo courtesy Randy Inman Auctions)

Fire Truck w/Searchlight, battery-op lights, 13", G, A ...$220.00
G-Man Pursuit Car, w/up, 14", VG, A $385.00
Garden (Stake) Truck, red w/bl stake bed, orig insert w/rake, hoe
   & shovel, 10½", NM $650.00
HD Staff Coupe/Army Headquarters Staff Coupe, w/up, driver
   w/gun, rubber tires, 14½", NMIB, A $4,675.00
Hi-Lift Loader, 1950s, 19", Fair (w/box), A $50.00
Hydraulic Dump Truck, 19½", EX, A $175.00

Ice Truck, red w/yel bed, rear platform, orig insert w/ice tongs &
   bucket, 11", NM, A $1,430.00
La Salle Coupe, red w/Berks County Trust-Low Rates advertis-
   ing, 11", very rare, VG, A $520.00
La Salle Town Car, red w/bl roof, silver-trimmed windshield,
   grille & hood molding, 11", EX, A $520.00
Lumar Coal Co Truck, red w/bl open bed, orig insert w/bucket, chute
   & shovel, from Warehouse Collection, 11", NM, A $1,430.00
Lumar Utility Truck #18, 1950s, 22", complete, G+, A .$200.00
Lumar Van Lines Truck, red & yel w/bl top, 19", EXIB, A..$800.00
Meadow Brook Dairy Stake Truck, wht, w/orig insert & 2 glass
   milk bottles w/lids, 10", NM...............................$650.00
Motor Market Stake Truck, 1939, 14", EX.....................$275.00
Mystery Car, friction, 9", G+, A..................................$120.00
Nelly Belle Jeep, 1950, EXIB......................................$275.00
Nite/Day Service Truck, 1950s, 20", NM......................$350.00
Power Grader, 17", MIB (mk Road Grader), A $145.00
Powerhouse Heavy Duty Dump Truck, #2528, 19", NMIB, A.$300.00

**Railway Express Agency, movable tailgate, 20", EXIB, A,
$600.00.** (Photo courtesy Richard Opfer Auctioneering, Inc.)

Roadster Convertible, red streamlined styling w/silver wind-
   shield, grille, lights & bumper, 1940s, 11", EX, A ...$825.00
Sand & Gravel Dump Truck w/Dump Bucket, 16", VG, A .$110.00
Sand Dump Truck, litho tin & steel, 10", G+, A..............$70.00

Siren Fire Chief Car, wind-up, 14", NM+IB, A, $1850.00.

Siren Fire Chief Car, w/up, 14", VG, A $250.00
Siren Police Patrol #1, friction, electric lights, 15", G+, A.$275.00
Steam Shovel Truck, w/loading ramp, 1940s, 18", G, A.$175.00

Sunshine Trucking Service Truck, 14", NMIB, A..........$375.00

Taxi, yel w/NP grille & hood trim, rear spare, wooden wheels, 10", G..$45.00

Tow Truck, covered wheel wells, NP grille & headlights, 1940s, 18", G+, A...$130.00

US Army Jeep (Willys) w/Searchlight Trailer, plastic battery-op searchlight trailer, 24" overall, NMIB, A.................$360.00

US Army Truck, simulated stake bed, 1950s, 19", no canvas cover or supports o/w VG, A.......................................$40.00

US Army Truck & Searchlight Trailer, w/canvas cover, 1950s, 32", EX, A...$130.00

US Mail Semi, red, wht & bl, 1950s, 25", Fair+, A..........$75.00

Willys Jeep, 1950s, 11", EXIB, A, $275.00. (Photo courtesy Randy Inman Auctions)

WINDUPS, FRICTIONS, AND OTHER MECHANICALS

Aero Oil Company Tanker Truck, friction, 5½", EX, A.$575.00

American Railroad Express Agency Van, litho tin, rear hinged door, w/hand cart, 9½", NM, A............................$2,090.00

Amos 'N Andy Fresh Air Taxi, 1930, G.......................$375.00

Amos 'N Andy Fresh Air Taxi, 1930, VGIB..................$875.00

Animal Express, 1930s, 14½", MIB...........................$750.00

Amos 'N Andy Walkers, 11½", G, pair, $900.00.

(Photo courtesy Richard Opfer Auctioneering, Inc.)

Army Staff Car, electric lights, 1940s, EXIB, A............$450.00

Ballet Dancer, friction, 6", EX+IB, A.........................$325.00

Barney Rubble on Dino, 8½", VG..............................$200.00

Be-Bop Jigger, 11", EX...$200.00

Bear Cyclist, 6", EXIB, A..$300.00

Beat It!! Komikal Kop, 7", EXIB................................$775.00

Big Aerial Acrobats, 11", EXIB, A..............................$300.00

Big Load Van Company Truck, 13", Fair+, A...............$175.00

Big Parade, 24", VG...$475.00

Big Show Circus Wagon, 9", VG+, A..........................$500.00

Big Silver Mack Dump Truck, 1920s, 20", Poor to Fair..$200.00

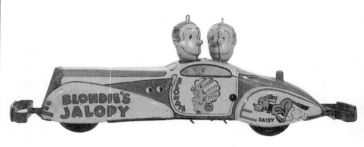

Blondie's Jalopy, 16", G, $950.00. (Photo courtesy Richard Opfer Auctioneering, Inc.)

BO Plenty, 1930s, 8", EXIB, A..................................$300.00

BO Plenty, 1930s, 8", VG, A.....................................$150.00

Buck Rogers 25th Century Rocket Ship, 12", EX+IB, $2,000.00. (Photo courtesy Skinner, Inc.)

Busy Bridge, 24" L, EX..$525.00

Busy Miners, 1930s, 16", NMIB................................$375.00

Busy Miners, 1930s, 16", VG....................................$200.00

Butter & Egg Man, 1930s, 8", EX..............................$700.00

Butter & Egg Man, 1930s, 8", VG.............................$500.00

Cadillac, blk & yel, w/driver, 12", EX, A.....................$575.00

Captain America Car, friction, 1960s, EX+..................$150.00

Charleston Trio, dtd 1921, 10", NMIB........................$950.00

Charlie McCarthy & Mortimer Snerd Private Car, 15", NM.$2,100.00

Charlie McCarthy & Mortimer Snerd Private Car, 15", NMIB...$4,000.00

Charlie McCarthy & Mortimer Snerd Private Car, 15", VG.$1,500.00

Charlie McCarthy Benzine Mobile, 1930s, 7", EXIB, A.$700.00
Charlie McCarthy Benzine Mobile, 1930s, 7", G+, A....$350.00
Charlie McCarthy Drummer Boy, 8", EXIB, A............$1,750.00
Charlie McCarthy Walker, 9", VG, A $250.00
Climbing Bulldozer Tractor, rubber treads, w/driver, 8", EXIB, A .$150.00
Climbing Fireman, 22", VG+...$225.00
Climbing Tractor #5, w/driver, 8", NMIB $225.00
Coast Defense, 1920s, 9" dia, EX, A..............................$750.00
College Jalopy, 6", EX, A..$250.00
Coo Coo Car, 8", G+..$300.00
Coupe, electric lights, simulated spoke wheels, 1920s, 8", VG, A $450.00

Dagwood Aeroplane, 1935, 9", EX, A, $800.00.

Dagwood the Driver, 1935, 9", NMIB $1,600.00
Dare Devil Flyer, 1930, 13", Fair+, A.............................$350.00

Dare Devil Flyer, 1930, 13", EX+IB, $1,750.00.

Dare Devil Motor Drome, 4", unused, MIB $225.00
Deco Coupe, red w/NP trim, disk wheels, 15", G $300.00
Delivery Cycle, 3-wheeled cycle w/driver, 9½", G+, A ..$225.00
Dick Tracy Police Car, battery-op light on roof, gr, 1950s, 11", EXIB (box mk Siren Squad Car), A........................$300.00

Dick Tracy Police Car, lithoed light on roof, gr, 1950s, 7", EX+, A $200.00
Dick Tracy Sparkling Riot Car, bl, 7", NMIB, A $275.00
Dick Tracy Squad Car (Convertible), friction w/battery-op siren, 20", VG+, A $325.00
Disney Parade Roadster, w/4 plastic characters, 12", NMIB, A..$1,150.00
Disney Parade Roadster, w/4 plastic characters, 12", EX, A .$700.00
Disneyland Jeep, 10", EXIB, A $250.00
Donald Duck Dipsy Car, 6", EXIB, A.............................$650.00
Donald Duck Dipsy Car, 6", VG, A.................................$350.00
Donald Duck Drummer, nonworking o/w G+, A $200.00
Donald Duck Duet, 11", EX $450.00
Donald Duck Duet, 11", NMIB......................................$975.00
Donald the Skier, plastic, 1960s, 11", EXIB, A $250.00
Dopey Walker, WDE, 1930s, 8", EX, A..........................$400.00
Doughboy Tank, 1940s, 10", EX+.................................$325.00
Drive-Ur-Self Car, 14", EX $375.00
Drive-Ur-Self Car, 14", NMIB $500.00
Ferdinand the Bull, w/flower, 1930s, 7", VG.................$275.00
Fire Chief Car, plastic, friction, 10", VG, A....................$80.00
Flash Gordon Rocket Fighter, 12", EX+.........................$725.00
Flash Gordon Rocket Fighter, 12", NM+IB.................$1,750.00
Flintstone Car (Fred), 1960s, 4", EX+IB, A....................$450.00
Flintstone Car (Wilma), 1960s, 4", EX+IB, A $400.00
Flintstone Flivver (Fred), friction, 7", G+, A $275.00
Flintstone Pals on Dino (Fred), 9", EX, A $250.00
Flintstone Pals on Dino (Fred), 9", VGIB, A.................$325.00
Funny Flivver, 1920s, 7", VG+, A.................................$400.00
Gang Buster Police Car, litho tin, 15", EX....................$500.00
George the Drummer Boy, 1930s, moving eyes, 9", EX ..$225.00
George the Drummer Boy, 1930s, stationary eyes, 9", NM .$225.00
Giant King Racer #711, w/driver, 12", rare, EX $250.00
Giant Reversing Tractor Truck, 14", NMIB....................$300.00
Golden Goose, 1930s, 9", EX $150.00
Goofy the Walking Gardner, 9x8", EX...........................$350.00
Gorilla, plush, in shackles & chains, 8", MIB.................$450.00
Harold Lloyd Funny Face Walker, 1929, 10", EX, A $475.00
Harold Lloyd Funny Face Walker, 1929, 10", G+, A......$250.00
Hee-Haw the Balky Mule, 9", EXIB...............................$375.00
Hee-Haw the Balky Mule, 9", G $175.00
Hey! Hey! the Chicken Snatcher, 1926, 9", NMIB, A.$1,250.00
Hey! Hey! the Chicken Snatcher, 1926, 9", VG $650.00
Hi-Yo Silver the Lone Ranger, no base, 7", G................$150.00
Hi-Yo Silver the Lone Ranger, rocker base, 1939, 9", EXIB .$675.00
Honey-Moon Express, 1930s, 10" dia, NMIB $250.00
Hop-In Jalopy, 7", EX $100.00
Hopalong Cassidy, rocker base, 10", EX+IB...................$475.00
Hopalong Cassidy, rocker base, 10", VG+, A $350.00
HQ Staff Car, 14", G, A..$400.00
Indian Motorcycle w/Sidecar, 6", VG, A $350.00
Joe Penner & His Duck Goo Goo, 1930s, 9", NMIB ..$1,100.00
Joe Penner & His Duck Goo Goo, 1930s, 9", VG, A $300.00
Joy Rider, 1929, 8", EX, A..$350.00
Jumpin' Jeep, 6", VG+, A...$120.00
Knockout Champs, 7" sq, NM, A...................................$275.00
Komical Kop, see Beat It! Komical Kop
Little Orphan Annie Skipping Rope & Sandy, VG+, A, pr..$550.00
Lizzie of the Valley, 7", EX $75.00

Looping Plane, 1930s, 8", NMIB....................................$300.00
Looping Plane, 1930s, 8", VG $100.00
Mack Army Truck, w/canvas cover, friction, 5", EX, A..$200.00
Mack Tow Truck, 10", VG+ $350.00
Main Street, 1929, 24" L, VG, A $275.00
Marxie Marx on Bell Trike, 1950s, 5", NM....................$100.00
Merry Makers, conductor on piano, no marque, 1930s,
    NMIB $1,200.00
Merry Makers, conductor on piano, w/marque, 1930s,
    NM+IB $1,500.00

Merry Makers, violinist on piano, with marque, 1930s, NMIB, $1,400.00. (Photo courtesy Randy Inman Auctions)

Mickey Mouse Dipsy Car, 7", NM+IB............................$700.00
Mickey Mouse Dipsy Car, 7", VG, A $350.00
Mickey Mouse Express, 1950s, 9" dia, NMIB.................$900.00

Moon Mullins and Kayo Handcar, DeLuxe version, 7", G, A, $350.00; 'Dynamite' box version, 6½", EX, A, $600.00. (Photo courtesy Richard Opfer Auctioneering, Inc.)

Mickey Mouse Go Cart, friction, 6", EX $150.00
Mickey Mouse Meteor Train, 1950s, 40" L, EXIB, A ..$1,100.00
Mickey Mouse the Driver, 7", NM, A $500.00
Mickey the Musician (Xylophone Player), 11", NMIB ..$475.00
Milton Berle Crazy Car, 6", EX+IB, A $575.00
Milton Berle Crazy Car, 6", VG $225.00
Monkey Cyclist, 1930s, 6", NMIB.................................$200.00
Moon Mullins & Kayo Handcar, Dynamite box version, 1930s,
    7", NMIB, A $1,200.00
Mortimer Snerd Drummer Boy, 1939, 8", NMIB, A....$1,600.00
Mortimer Snerd Tricky Auto, 1939, 8", VG, A $400.00
Mortimer Snerd Walker, 1939, 9", NMIB, A.................$725.00
Mortimer Snerd Walker, 1939, 9", VG, A $275.00
Mountain Climber, 13", EXIB......................................$175.00
Musical Pluto, 9", VG...$175.00
Mystic Motorcycle, 5", EXIB.......................................$300.00
Nutty Mad Indian, 7", EXIB..$100.00
Party Pluto, soft plastic w/rubber tail & ears, 10", NM ...$800.00
Peter Rabbit Eccentric Car, plastic w/tin wheels, 6", EX+ .$475.00

Pinocchio and His Famous Pet Figaro, WDE, 1939, NMIB, $1,000.00.

Pinocchio the Acrobat, WDP, 1939, 17", VG, A $300.00
Pinocchio Walker, WDE, 1939, 9", EX $450.00
Pinocchio Walker, WDE, 1939, 9", NMIB, A $600.00
Pluto the Drum Major, 1940s, 7", EX, A $250.00
Police Motorcycle, red w/bl tires, 9", EX $325.00
Police Motorcycle, red w/gray tires, mk PD on gas tank, 9",
    NMIB...$425.00
Police Motorcycle w/Sidecar, wooden wheels, 1930s, 4", NM.$250.00
Police Squad Motorcycle w/Sidecar, 9", G $300.00
Police Squad Motorcycle w/Sidecar, 9", NMIB..............$500.00
Poor Fish, 8", EXIB $525.00
Popeye & Olive Oyl Jiggers, 1930s, 9", EXIB $1,750.00
Popeye Express (Train), 9" dia, EXIB, A.....................$1,250.00
Popeye Express (Wheelbarrow & Parrot), 9", EX, A $750.00
Popeye Handcar (w/Olive Oyl), EXIB.........................$1,000.00
Popeye Handcar (w/Olive Oyl), VG+ $450.00
Popeye Jigger & Olive Oyl Playing Accordion on Roof, 1930s,
    10", G, A..$650.00

Popeye Jigger on Roof, 9", G+, A..................$500.00
Popeye the Champ, 2 figures in boxing ring, 8" sq, NM+IB.$2,500.00
Popeye the Champ, 2 figures in boxing ring, 8" sq, VGIB..$1,750.00
Popeye the Pilot (Popeye Eccentric Airplane), 8", VG, A .$825.00
Popeye w/Parrot Cages, 1930s, 9", EXIB..................$650.00
Popeye w/Parrot Cages, 1930s, 9", VG, A..................$375.00
Porky Pig w/Lasso, 8", EXIB, A $550.00
Porky Pig w/Umbrella, 8", VGIB..................$425.00
Porter, see Walking Porter
Racer #1, 6", EXIB..................$300.00
Racer #3, 5", EX..................$225.00
Racer #12, w/driver, 1940s, 16", EX $375.00
Racer #27, w/driver, 11", G+ $225.00
Racer #27, w/driver, 11", MIB $375.00
Racer #410, w/driver, 11", EX, A..................$325.00
Range Rider (Lone Ranger), 9", NMIB..................$425.00
Ranger Rider (Cowboy), 11" L, EX..................$350.00
Red Cap Porter, see also Walking Porter
Red Cap Porter Pushing Trunk on Cart, 6", VG..........$550.00
Reversible Coupe (The Marvel Car), 16", NMIB $2,000.00
Reversible Coupe (The Marvel Car), 16", VG, A $250.00
Ring-A-Ling Circus, 1925, 8" dia, VG, A..................$500.00

Rocket Racer, 1930s, 16", EX+, $400.00.

Sam the City, Gardener, 8", VG+, A $100.00
Siren Police Patrol, rubber tires, electric lights, 15", EX, A..$450.00
Sky Flyer, earlier version w/brick tower & extra plane, 9", G+..$150.00
Skybird Flyer Control Tower, EX, A $450.00

Snoopy and Gus Hook and Ladder Truck, 9", NM+, $2,000.00.

(Photo courtesy Randy Inman Auctions)

Ring-A-Ling Circus, 1925, 8" diameter, VGIB, $1,200.00.

(Photo courtesy Randy Inman Auctions)

Rocket Fighter, w/sparking action, 12", unused, NM+IB, A.$1,200.00
Rocket Police Patrol, 12" L, VG, A..................$440.00
Roll-Over Plane, 5", NMIB..................$300.00
Roll-Over Pluto, 1939, 9", EXIB, A..................$325.00
Rookie Cop Motorcycle, 9", VG, A..................$225.00
Rookie Pilot, 1938, 7", NM..................$475.00
Royal Bus Line Bus, w/passengers & roof storage rack, friction, 10", EX+..................$550.00
Royal Van Co Truck, 9", Fair..................$100.00
Sabre Car, plastic, friction, 1950s, 10", NMIB..................$200.00
Safe Driving School Car #1, 7", G $75.00

Snoopy & Gus Hook & Ladder Truck, 1920s, 9", VG....$800.00
Son of Garloo, 1960s, 6", EX+ $250.00
Sparkling Climbing Fighting Tank, 10", NM+IB $250.00
Sparkling Climbing Tractor Set, w/plastic plow, 1950s, 15", NMIB..................$225.00
Sparkling Hot Rod Racer, plastic body w/metal chassis, rubber tires, 6", NMIB $100.00
Sparkling Mountain Climber, 42x22" (assembled), NMIB, A..$200.00
Sparkling Soldier Motorcycle, 1940, 8", NMIB..................$600.00
Sparkling Tank, gr w/red stripe on yel, 10", EXIB, A......$200.00
Sparkling US Army Airplane, 7", G $125.00
Sparkling US Army Airplane, 7", NM+IB, A $325.00
Speed Boy Delivery Cycle, no lights, 1930s, 10", VG $300.00
Speed Boy Delivery Cycle, w/lights, 1930s, 10", NMIB .$650.00
Streamline Speedway, 13x18", VG+IB $175.00
Super Hero Express, 1960s, 12", EX+..................$650.00
Superman Turnover Plane, bl/yel, 1940, 6", VG+ $700.00
Superman Turnover Plane, gold/silver, 1940, 6", EX+..$1,100.00
Superman Turnover Plane, red/yel, 1940, 6", EX..........$800.00
Superman Turnover Tank, 1940, 4", EX+IB $500.00
Tank (WWI), soldier appears firing rifle, 10", VG, A $150.00
Thor on Tricycle, 1960s, NM $200.00
Tidy Tim Street Sweeper, 1930s, 8", EX $575.00
Tidy Tim Street Sweeper, 1930s, 8", G..................$350.00

Tidy Tim Street Sweeper, 1930s, 8", NM+, $750.00. (Photo courtesy Bertoia Auctions)

Toddler, boy in bl sleeper, plastic, 1950s, NMIB.............$300.00
Tom Corbett Sparkling Space Ship, 12", NMIB, A $1,500.00
Tom Corbett Sparkling Space Ship, 12", VGIB, A $650.00
Toyland's Farm Products Horse-Drawn Wagon, 10", G ..$250.00
Toytown Dairy Horse-Drawn Wagon, 11", EX...............$275.00
Tricky Taxi, 5", EX+IB...$225.00
Tricky Taxis on Busy Street, 6x10" base w/2 4½" cars, NMIB..$400.00
Tricky Taxis on Busy Street, 6x10" base w/5 4½" cars, EX.$300.00
Tumbling Monkey, 5", VG+...$175.00
Turn-Over Tank, 4", MIB $225.00
Turnover Tank, w/rubber treads, 9", EXIB $300.00
Uncle Wiggily Car, 1935, 8", EX..................................$700.00
Uncle Wiggily Car, 1935, 8", EXIB...............................$850.00
US Army Tank Corps Roll-Over Tank, 8", EX, A..........$175.00

US Army Tank No 3, 8", G, A, $150.00. (Photo courtesy Randy Inman Auctions)

US Tank Division Tank, w/rubber treads, 7½", EX $175.00
US Trucking Co Truck #7, 1920s, 9", G+ $150.00
Wacky Taxi #77, friction, 8", G+ $150.00
Walking Pinocchio, see Pinocchio Walker

Walking Porter, w/suitcases, 8", EXIB $550.00
Walt Disney's Television Car, friction, 7", G+, A..........$150.00
Walt Disney's Television Car, friction, 7", NMIB..........$500.00

Whee-Whiz Auto Racer, 1930s, 13" diameter, EX+IB, A, $825.00. (Photo courtesy Randy Inman Auctions)

Whoopee Cowboy Car, 1932, 8" L, VG, A $300.00
Wilma Flintstone on Bell Trike, 1960s, 4", EX+.............$350.00
Wise Pluto, WDP, 1939, 8", NMIB, A $525.00
Wonder Cyclist, 1930s, 9", VG+..................................$250.00
Yellow Cab Co Taxi, lithoed driver & passengers, rubber tires,
    11", EX $225.00

MISCELLANEOUS

Acme Markets Semi, litho tin, 25", EX+ (Fair box), A..$470.00
Best of the West Fighting Eagle Water Gun, 1970s, scarce,
    NMOC...$125.00
Brightlite Filling Station, EXIB, A...............................$775.00
City Airport, litho tin, electric lights, no planes, 11x17",
    VG+..$300.00
Day & Night Service Station, litho tin, electric light, 12",
    VG..$200.00

City Airport, electric lights, with two planes, 11x17", M (with box sleeve), $1,000.00. (Photo courtesy Bertoia Auctions)

East-West Coast Fast Freight Semi, plastic tractor w/tin trailer, bl & yel, 17", EXIB..$400.00

Gas Pump Set, litho tin w/electric glob lights, w/oil pump accessories, 9", EX..$400.00

Glendale Depot, litho tin, 10x13", few pcs missing o/w NM+, A..$250.00

Gyro-Zip Flying Top, Montgomery Ward premium, ca 1930s, 5", MIB, A..$250.00

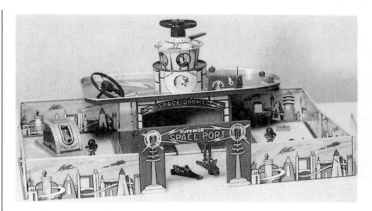

Superior Space Port, lithograph tin, with figures and autos, 16½" long, NM, $500.00. (Photo courtesy Bertoia Auctions)

Universal Freight Station, litho tin, 7x12", NMIB, A....$650.00

USMC Troop Carrier, w/canvas cover, 20½", VG+, A ..$175.00

Utility Service Truck & Cable Trailer, litho tin, 1950s, 19", G+ $100.00

Lincoln Highway, Electric Lighted Service Station, NMIB, $1,800.00. (Photo courtesy Randy Inman Auctions)

Midtown Service Station, unused & unassembled, MIB .$400.00

Penny the Poodle, pull toy, 1963, 16", NMIB................$100.00

Roadside Cafe & Service Station, litho tin, complete, 10x13", EX $900.00

Roadside Rest Service Station, litho tin, electric lights, complete, 10x12", G, A..$250.00

Roadside Rest Service Station, litho tin, electric lights, complete, 10x12", VG, A...$450.00

Soldiers of Fortune Set, 8 litho tin figures w/cannon that shoots wooden bullets, NMIB $250.00

Telescope, w/Marx Brothers Co label, 14", GIB...............$50.00

Universal Bus Terminal, litho tin, 7x12", scarce, NM+IB .$425.00

Matchbox

The Matchbox series of English and American-made autos, trucks, taxis, Pepsi-Cola trucks, steamrollers, Greyhound buses, etc., was very extensive. By the late 1970s, the company was cranking out more than five million cars every week, and while those days may be over, Matchbox still produces about seventy-five million vehicles on a yearly basis.

Introduced in 1953, the Matchbox Miniatures series has always been the mainstay of the company. There were seventy-five models in all but with enough variations to make collecting them a real challenge. Larger, more detailed models were introduced in 1957; this series, called Major Pack, was replaced a few years later by a similar line called King Size. To compete with Hot Wheels, Matchbox converted most models over to a line called SuperFast that sported thinner, low-friction axles and wheels. (These are much more readily available than the original 'regular wheels,' the last of which were made in 1969.) At about the same time, the King Size series became known as Speed Kings; in 1977 the line was reintroduced under the name Super Kings.

In the early '70s, Lesney started to put dates on the baseplates of their toy cars. The name 'Lesney' was coined from the first names of the company's founders, Leslie and Rodney Smith. The last Matchbox toys that carried the Lesney mark were made in 1982. Today many models can be bought for less than $10.00, though a few are priced much much higher.

In 1988, to celebrate the company's fortieth anniversary, Matchbox issued a limited set of five models that except for minor variations were exact replicas of the originals. These five were repackaged in 1991 and sold under the name Matchbox Originals. In 1993 a second series expanded the line of reproductions.

Another line that's become very popular is their Models of Yesteryear. These are slightly larger replicas of antique and vin-

Sunny Side Service Station, 10x14", complete, G, A, $225.00; Roadside Rest Service Station, electric lights, complete, 10x12", NM, $700.00; Gas Station Island, complete, G, A, $225.00. (Photo courtesy Noel Barrett Auctions)

tage vehicles. Values of $20.00 to $60.00 for mint-in-box examples are average, though a few sell for even more.

Sky Busters are small-scale aircraft measuring an average of 3½" in length. They were introduced in 1973. Models currently being produced sell for about $4.00 each.

The Matchbox brand has changed hands several times, first to David Yeh and Universal Toy Company in 1982, then to Tyco Toys in 1992, and finally to Mattel, who purchased Tyco, and along with it, Matchbox, Dinky, and several other Tyco subsidiaries such as Fisher-Price, Milton Bradley, and View Master.

To learn more, we recommend *Matchbox Toys, 1947 to 1998* and *Toy Car Collector's Guide* by Dana Johnson.

To determine values of examples in conditions other than given in our listings, based on MIP prices, deduct a minimum of 10% if the original container is missing, 30% if the condition is excellent, and as much as 70% for a toy graded only very good.

Advisor: Dana Johnson

Key:
LW — Laser Wheels (introduced in 1987)
reg — regular wheels (Matchbox Miniatures)
SF — SuperFast

1-75 Series

1-A, Diesel Road Roller, 1953, dk gr, MIP, from $100 to ...$130.00
1-A, Diesel Road Roller, 1953, lt gr, MIP, from $180 to ...$220.00
1-B, Road Roller, gr w/lt or dk tan driver, MIP, from $80 to $100.00
1-D, Aveling Barford Road Roller, 1962, gr w/red plastic rollers, MIP, from $30 to $40.00
1-H, Dodge Challenger, 1976, hood grilles, no scoop, red w/silver interior, MIP, from $5 to $10.00

1-J, Toyman Dodge Challenger, 1983, MIP, from $3.00 to $5.00. (Photo courtesy Dana Johnson)

2-A, Dumper, 1953, gr metal wheels, MIP, from $180 to ...$220.00
2-A, Dumper, 1953, unpnt metal wheels, MIP, from $65 to ...$80.00
2-E, Mercedes Trailer, 1969, SF, metallic gold w/orange canopy, MIP, from $20 to $25.00
2-F, Jeep Hot Rod, 1971, pk or red, from $15 to $20.00
2-I, Pontiac Fiero, 1985, blk over red w/2 Dog Racing Team decal, MIP, from $10 to $15.00
3-A, Cement Mixer, 1953, bl w/gray plastic wheels, MIP, from $80 to $100.00

3-A, Cement Mixer, 1953, bl w/orange metal wheels, MIP, from $60 to $80.00

3-C, Mercedes Benz Ambulance, 1968, opening rear hatch, MIP, $20.00. (Photo courtesy Dana Johnson)

3-E, Monteverdi Hai #6, 1973, orange w/blk base, MIP, from $15 to $20.00
3-F, Porsche 911 Turbo, 1978, metallic brn w/unpnt base, MIP, from $45 to......$55.00
3-F, Porsche 911 Turbo, 1978, red w/opaque windows, MIP, from $5 to $10.00
4-A, Massey-Harris Tractor, 1954, w/fenders, MIP, from $75 to....$95.00
4-B, Massey Harris Tractor, 1957, no fenders, MIP, from $60 to ...$80.00
4-E, Dodge Stake Truck, 1970, SF, MIP, from $20 to $25.00
4-F Gruesome Twosome, 1971, gold w/amber windows, MIP, from $10 to $15.00
4-H, '57 Chevy Bel Air, 1979, metallic maganta, MIP, from $5 to $10.00
4-K, '97 Corvette, 1997, metallic bl, MIP, from $2 to $4.00
5-A, London Bus, 1954, red, MIP, from $75 to $95.00
5-A, London Bus, 1954, red w/Buy Matchbox Series decal, metal wheels, MIP, from $75 to $95.00
5-E, Lotus Europa, 1969, SF, blk, MIP, from $16 to......$20.00
5-E, Lotus Europa, 1969, SF, pk, unpnt base, MIP, from $12 to....$16.00
6-A, 6-Wheel Quarry Truck, 1954, metal wheels, MIP, from $65 to $80.00
6-C, Euclid Quarry Truck, 1964, yel, MIP, from $20 to $25.00
7-A, Horse-Drawn Milk Float, 1955, orange w/gray plastic wheels, MIP, from $140 to......$160.00
7-C, Ford Refuse Truck, 1966, blk plastic wheels, MIP, from $12 to $16.00

7-B, Ford Anglia, 1961, black plastic wheels, MIP, from $35.00 to $45.00. (Photo courtesy Dana Johnson)

7-D, Ford Refuse Truck, 1970, SF, MIP, from $30 to $40.00

7-F, Volkswagen Rabbit, 1976, yel w/red interior, rack & surfboards, MIP, from $6 to...$10.00

8-A, Caterpillar Tractor, 1955, orange w/orange driver, no blade, MIP, from $175 to...$225.00

8-B, Caterpillar Tractor, 1959, yel w/metal rollers, MIP, from $85 to..$100.00

8-C, Caterpillar Tractor, 1961, silver plastic rollers, MIP, from $85 to...$100.00

8-E, Ford Mustang Fastback, 1966, orange, MIP, from $360 to $400.00

8-G, Ford Mustang Wildcat Dragster, 1970, MIP, from $20 to $30.00

9-A, Dennis Fire Escape, 1955, no front bumper, no number cast, MIP, from $85 to..$100.00

9-C, Merryweather Marquis Fire Engine, 1959, red w/gold ladder, gray plastic wheels, MIP, from $65 to $80.00

9-E, AMX Javelin, 1971, red w/blk hood scoop, doors don't open, MIP, from $35 to..$50.00

10-A, Mechanical Horse & Trailer, 1955, red cab w/gray trailer, metal wheels, MIP, from $75 to $90.00

10-G, Plymouth Grand Fury Police, 1979, wht w/Metro tampos, MIP, from $3 to..$6.00

11-A, Road Tanker, 1955, yel w/metal wheels, MIP, from $110 to $130.00

11-E, Scaffolding Truck, 1970, SF, silver, complete, M, from $25 to $35.00

11-F, Flying Bug, 1972, MIP, from $15 to $20.00

12-A, Land Rover, 1955, olive gr, metal wheels, w/driver, MIP, from $65 to...$80.00

12-D, Safari Land Rover, SF, 1970, bright bl, luggage on roof, MIP, from $900 to $1,200.00

12-E, Setra Coach, 1970, metallic gold w/tan roof, MIP, from $20 to $25.00

12-F, Big Bull Bulldozer, 1975, orange rollers, MIP, from $5 to..$10.00

13-A, Bedford Wreck Truck, 1955, tan w/gray plastic wheels, MIP, from $85 to...$100.00

13-A, Bedford Wreck Truck, 1955, tan w/metal wheels, MIP, from $75 to..$90.00

13-C, Ford Thames Trader Wreck Truck, 1961, gray wheels, from $100 to $120.00

13-F, Baja Dune Buggy, 1971, lt metallic gr w/police shields decal, MIP, from $30 to..$45.00

13-F, Dodge BP Wreck Truck, 1970, SF, MIP, from $55 to.$70.00

14-A, Daimler Ambulance, 1956, MIP, from $65 to.........$85.00

14-B, Daimler Ambulance, 1956, gray plastic wheels, MIP, from $80 to $100.00

14-C, Bedford Lomas Ambulance, 1962, silver plastic wheels, MIP, from $275 to...$350.00

15-A, Prime Mover Truck Tractor, 1956, yel w/metal wheels, MIP, from $1,000 to $1,250.00

15-C, Dennis Refuse Truck, 1963, dk bl w/gray container, porthole in rear hatch, MIP, from $25 to $40.00

15-E, Volkswagen 1500 Saloon, 1970, SF, metallic red, MIP, from $25 to...$40.00

15-J, Saab 9000, 1988, LW, metallic bl, MIP, from $8 to ..$12.00

16-B, Atlantic Trailer, 1957, tan w/tan towbar, gray plastic wheels, MIP, from $95 to...$115.00

16-C, Scammell Mountaineer Dump Truck, 1964, gray plastic wheels, MIP, from $80.00 to $90.00; black plastic wheels, MIP, from $175.00 to $200.00. (Photo courtesy Dana Johnson)

16-D, Case Bulldozer, 1969, blk treads, MIP, from $35 to.$50.00

16-E, Badger Exploration Truck, 1974, Rolomatic radar, metallic orange-red, MIP, from $6 to.....................................$10.00

17-A, Bedford 'Matchbox Removal' Van, 1956, maroon body, MIP, from $350 to..$425.00

17-C, Hoveringham Tipper, 1963, red cab, orange tipper, MIP, from $25 to...$40.00

14-F, Rallye Royale, 1973, MIP, from $8.00 to $12.00. (Photo courtesy Dana Johnson)

17-D, Ergomatic Cab Horse Box, 1969, with two horses, 2¾", MIP, from $25.00 to $30.00. (Photo courtesy Dana Johnson)

17-E, AEC Ergomatic Horse Box, 1970, SF, MIP, from $25 to..**$40.00**

18-A, Caterpillar DB Bulldozer, 1956, yel w/red blade, MIP, from $80 to..**$100.00**

18-C, Caterpillar Bulldozer, 1961, silver plastic rollers, MIP, from $175 to...**$225.00**

18-E, Field Car, 1969, gr plastic hubs, MIP, from $800 to .**$1,000.00**

19-A, MG Midget Sports Car, 1956, cream, w/driver, MIP, from $80 to..**$100.00**

19-A, MG Midget Sports Car, 1956, wht w/driver, MIP, from $160 to..**$200.00**

19-B, MGA Sports Car, 1958, wht w/gold grille, metal wheels, MIP, from $375 to...**$475.00**

19-C, Aston Martin Racer, #3 decal, 1961, gray or wht driver, MIP...**$210.00**

19-C, Aston Martin Racer, #5, #41 or #52 decal, 1961, gray or wht driver, MIP...**$160.00**

19-C, Aston Martin Racer, #19 decal, 1961, gray or wht driver, MIP...**$80.00**

19-F, Road Dragster, 1970, red, MIP, from $16 to............**$20.00**

21-E, Foden Concrete Truck, 1970, SF, MIP, from $25 to.**$40.00**

22-C, Pontiac Grand Prix, 1964, blk plastic wheels, MIP, from $20 to..**$30.00**

23-A, Berkeley Cavalier Travel Trailer, 1956, lime gr, MIP, from $100 to..**$125.00**

23-A, Berkeley Cavalier Travel Trailer, 1956, pale bl, MIP, from $20 to..**$30.00**

23-D, Volkswagen Camper, 1970, turq, opening roof, M, from $18 to..**$20.00**

23-F, Mustang GT350, 1979, MIP, from $10 to................**$15.00**

23-H, Honda ATC, 1985, red, MIP, from $9 to **$12.00**

26-A, Foden Ready Mix, silver grille, metal wheels, MIP, from $60.00 to $80.00. (Photo courtesy Dana Johnson)

29-E, Racing Mini, 1970, orange, MIP, from $10 to **$15.00**

30-E, Beach Buggy, 1970, SF, lavender, EX+, from $16 to .**$20.00**

31-B, Ford Fairlane Station Wagon, 1960, gr w/pk roof, silver or gray plastic wheels, MIP, ea from $60 to....................**$80.00**

31-B, Ford Fairlane Station Wagon, 1960, yel w/silver plastic wheels, MIP, from $275 to.......................................**$325.00**

31-D, Lincoln Continental, 1970, SF, gr-gold, NM+, from $50 to...**$65.00**

32-B, Jaguar XKE, 1961, metallic red w/gray plastic wheels, clear windows, MIP, from $100 to...............................**$120.00**

32-B, Jaguar XKE, 1961, red w/gray plastic wheels, gr windows, MIP, from $80 to..**$110.00**

33-A, Ford Zodiac Mk II Sedan, 1957, lt bl, lt bl-gr or dk gr, no windows, metal wheels, MIP, ea from $100 to........**$120.00**

33-A, Ford Zodiac Mk II Sedan, 1957, silver-gray & orange, no windows, gray plastic wheels, MIP, from $160 to.....**$180.00**

40-C, Hay Trailer, 1967, beige (rare color), from $160 to.**$220.00**

40-C, Hay Trailer, 1967, common color, MIP, from $5 to.**$10.00**

42-C, Iron Fairy Crane, 1969, MIP, from $12 to **$16.00**

42-E, Tyre Fryer Jaffa Mobile, 1972, bl, MIP, from $90 to.**$120.00**

42-G, 1957 T-Bird, 1982, red, MIP, from $4 to **$8.00**

44-C, GMC Refrigerator Truck, 1967, MIP, from $12 to..**$16.00**

45-C, Ford Group 6, 1970, SF, dk gr, MIP, from $900 to.**$1,200.00**

45-C, Ford Group 6, 1970, SF, metallic gr, MIP, from $12 to..**$16.00**

45-C, Ford Group 6, 1970, SF, purple, MIP, from $10 to ..**$15.00**

47-D, DAF Tipper Truck, 1970, SF, silver & yel, M, from $30 to...**$40.00**

47-F, Pannier Tank Locomotive, 1979, MIP, from $5 to ...**$10.00**

48-C, Dodge Dump Truck, 1966, MIP, from $10 to **$15.00**

49-E, Crane Truck, 1976, red, MIP, from $60 to **$80.00**

49-E, Crane Truck, 1976, yel, MIP, from $6 to.................**$12.00**

49-G, Dune Man Volkswagen Beetle, 1984, from $4 to......**$5.00**

50-A, Commer Pickup, 1958, lt or dk tan w/metal or plastic wheels, MIP, ea from $65 to.......................................**$95.00**

51-C, Eight-Wheel Tipper Truck, 1969, Pointer decal, MIP, from $30.00 to $45.00. (Photo courtesy Dana Johnson)

52-A, Maserati 4CL T/1948 Racer, red w/blk plastic wheels, MIP, from $65 to...**$85.00**

54-D, Ford Capri, 1971, MIP, from $10 to........................**$15.00**

55-C, Ford Galaxie Police Car, 1966, bl dome light, MIP, from $225 to..**$265.00**

55-C, Ford Galaxie Police Car, 1966, red dome light, MIP, from $40 to..**$60.00**

58-C, DAF Girder Truck, 1968, MIP, from $10 to **$16.00**

58-D, DAF Girder Truck, 1960, pale metallic gr, SF, MIP, from $25 to..**$35.00**

58-D, DAF Girder Truck, 1970, cream, SF, MIP, from $70 to...**$90.00**

52-A, Maserati 4CL T/1948 Racer, 1958, yellow with black tires, MIP, from $120.00 to $135.00. (Photo courtesy Dana Johnson)

59-H, T-Bird Turbo Coupe, 1988, LW, metallic gold w/Motorcraft decal, MIP, from $5 to $10.00

63-C, Dodge Crane Truck, 1968, yel, M, from $15 to......$20.00

66-F, Ford Transit, 1977, orange, no tab on base, MIP, from $5 to...$10.00

66-F, Ford Transit, 1977, orange, tab on base, MIP, from $40 to..$55.00

68-A, Austin Mk 2 Radio Truck, 1959, olive w/blk plastic wheels, MIP, from $70 to..$90.00

69-E, Wells Fargo Armored Truck, 1978, red with clear windows, MIP, from $30.00 to $40.00; red with blue windows, MIP, from $4.00 to $8.00. (Photo courtesy Dana Johnson)

71-E, Jumbo Jet Motorcycle, 1973, MIP, from $15 to $20.00

72-B, Standard Jeep CJ5, 1966, red interior, MIP, from $15 to .$20.00

72-B, Standard Jeep CJ5, 1966, wht interior, MIP, from $900 to $1,200.00

72-C, Standard Jeep CJ5, 1970, SF, MIP, from $30 to.......$40.00

75-D, Alfa Carabo, 1971, M, from $15 to $20.00

75-E, Seasprite Helicopter, reg, 1977, dk gr or dr cream, MIP, ea from $275 to $325.00

CONVOY, HIGHWAY EXPRESS, SUPER RIGS

CY-1-A, Kenworth Car Transporter, 1982, red w/beige ramp, wht stripes, MIP...$12.00

CY-2-A, Kenworth Rocket Transporter, 1982, silver-gray w/wht plastic rocket, MIP...$12.00

CY-6-A, Blue Grass Farms Kenworth Horse Box Transporter, 1982, gr cab, MIP...$12.00

CY-9-A, Midnight X-Press Kenworth Box Truck, 1982, blk, England cast, MIP, from $40 to..............................$55.00

CY-12-B, DARTS Kenworth Aircraft Transporter, 1984, wht & bl w/dk gr or brn tampos, bl plane, England cast, MIP, ea.$18.00

CY-13-A, Peterbilt Fire Engine, 1984, red w/8/Fire Dept decals, Macau cast, MIP $12.00

CY-13-A, Peterbilt Fire Engine, 1984, fluorescent orange w/City Fire Dept 15 decals, Thailand cast, MIP.....................$9.00

CY-13-A, Peterbilt Fire Engine, 1984, red w/8/Fire Dept decals, Thailand cast, MIP $8.00

CY-14-A, Kenworth COE Power Launch Transporter, wht w/wht boat, MIP $12.00

CY-15-B, Peterbilt MBVT News Remote Truck, blue, MIP, from $12.00 to $15.00; CY-3-A, Peterbilt Conventional Double Container Truck, white with Federal Express decals, MIP, from $12.00 to $15.00. (Photo courtesy Dana Johnson)

CY-15-B, Peterbilt MBTV News Remote Truck, 1989, olive w/Strike Team/LS2009 decal, MIP, from $20 to.........$30.00

CY-17-A, Scania Petrol Transporter, 1985, wht w/FEOSO decal, MIP $50.00

CY-18-A, Scania Container Truck, 1986, bl w/blk interior, Varta Batteries decal, MIP, from $35 to $45.00

CY-18-A, Scania Container Truck, 1986, bl w/gray interior, Varta Batteries decal, MIP...$20.00

CY-21-A, DAF Aircraft Transporter, 1987, wht w/Airtrainer decal, MIP..$12.00

CY-23-A, Scania Covered Truck, 1988, yel w/Michelin decal, MIP $12.00

CY-24-A, DAF Box Truck, 1988, orange & red w/Parcel Post decal, MIP...$15.00

CY-32-A, Mack Shovel Transporter, 1992, orange & yel w/29-F Shovel Nose tractor, MIP $9.00

CY-104-A, Kenworth Superstar Transporter, 1989, any Indy 500 version except K-Mart/Havoline, MIP, ea..................$12.00

CY-104-A, Kenworth Superstar Transporter, 1989, Indy 500 version, wht w/K-Mart/Havoline decal, MIP $18.00

CY-109-A, Ford Aeromax Superstar Transporter, 1991, red w/Melling Performance or Motorcraft decal, MIP, ea .$18.00

KING SIZE, SPEED KINGS, AND SUPER KINGS

K-1C, O&K Excavator, 1970, MIP.....................................$24.00
K-2-B, KW Dart Dump Truck, 1964, MIP, from $25 to $50.00
K-3-A, Caterpillar Bulldozer, 1960, MIP............................$50.00
K-5-B, Racing Car Transporter, 1967, MIP......................$45.00
K-5-C, Muir Hill Tractor-Trailer, 1972, yel, MIP............$30.00
K-6-A, Allis-Chalmers Earth Scraper, 1961, MIP............$50.00
K-6-D, Motorcycle Transporter, 1975, MIP.....................$20.00
K-7-A, Curtiss-Wright Rear Dumper, 1961......................$45.00
K-7-B, refuse truck, 1967, blk wheels, MIP....................$40.00
K-10-B, Pipe Truck, 1967, w/4 orig pipes, EX $30.00
K-10-C, Auto Transport, 1976 ....$25.00
K-11-C, Breakdown Tow Truck, 1976, red, MIP.............$60.00
K-14-A, Taylor Jumbo Crane, 1964, yel weight box (scarce),
    MIP $45.00

**K-15-A, Merryweather Fire Engine, 1964, MIP, from
$65.00 to $75.00.** (Photo courtesy Dana Johnson)

K-15-B, Londoner Bus, The Royal Wedding 1981, M $35.00
K-16-B, Petrol Tanker, 1974, Total decal, MIP................$35.00
K-18-A, Articulated Horse Box, 1967, complete, NM+...$50.00
K-19-A, Scammell Tipper Truck, 1967, MIP $45.00
K-19-B, Security Truck, 1979, MIP $20.00
K-21A, Mercury Cougar, 1968, red interior, MIP $45.00
K-22-A, Dodge Charger, 1969, MIP.................................$25.00
K-22-C, Seaspeed SRN6 Hovercraft, 1974, bl & wht, NM .$3.00
K-24-A, Lamborghini Miura, 1969, bronze, mag wheels, NM+.$15.00
K-24-B, Michelin Scammell Container Truck, 1977, MIP .$30.00
K-27-B, Power Boat & Transport, 1978, MIP $30.00
K-29-A, Miura Seaburst Set, 1971, MIP $45.00
K-32-A, Shovel Nose Custom Car, 1972, MIP $25.00
K-33-B, Cargo Hauler, 1978, MIP $30.00
K-34-A, Thunderclap Racer, 1972, MIP $20.00
K-38-A, Gus' Gulper, 1973, pk w/yel interior, roll bar, MIP..$15.00
K-39-B, ERF Simon Snorkel Fire Engine, 1980 ....$30.00
K-40-B, Pepsi Delivery Truck, 1980, wht, MIP................$30.00
K-41-A, Fuzzy Buggy, 1973, MIP.....................................$20.00
K-45-A, Marauder Racer, 1973, MIP................................$20.00
K-60-A, Ford Mustang, 1976, MIP...................................$20.00
K-80-A, Dodge Custom Van, 1980 ....$20.00
K-90-A, Matra Rancho, 1982, MIP...................................$20.00

MODELS OF YESTERYEAR

Y-01-A, 1926 Allchin Traction Machine, 1956, diagonal unpnt
    treads, silver boiler door, MIP $200.00
Y-1-B, 1911 Ford Model T, 1965, cream, MIP..................$25.00
Y-1-C, 1936 Jaguar SS 100, lt yel w/wht-wall tires, England cast,
    MIP $125.00
Y-2-B, 1911 Renault 2-Seater, 1963, silver-plated, MIP ...$75.00
Y-2-C, 1914 Prince Henry Vauxhall, 1970, bl w/wht
    seats...$30.00
Y-3-B, 1910 Benz Limousine, 1966, lt gr w/pale lime gr roof,
    MIP..$50.00
Y-3-C, 1934 Riley MPH, 1974, lt metallic red w/red 12-spoke
    wheels...$45.00
Y-3-D, 1912 Ford Model T Tanker, 1982, gr & wht roof & tank,
    gold spoke wheels, Zerolene decal, MIP.................$125.00
Y-4-B, Shand-Mason Horse-Drawn Fire Engine, 1960, Kent, gray
    horses, MIP..$400.00
Y-4-D, 1930 Deusenberg Model J Town Car, 1876, brn & beige,
    lt bl or silver & bl (Macau cast), MIP, ea $25.00
Y-5-A, 1929 Lemans Bentley, 1958, gr tonneau, MIP.......$95.00
Y-5-C, 1907 Peugeot, 1969, yel w/clear windows, blk rook,
    MIP $85.00
Y-5-D, 1927 Talbot Van, 1978, bl w/blk roof, Frasers decal,
    MIP..$425.00
Y-6-B, 1923 Type 35 Bugatti, 1961, red & wht dash & floor,
    MIP..$65.00
Y-6-C, 1913 Cadillac, 1967, gold-plated, MIP...............$250.00
Y-7-A, 4-Ton Leyland Van, 1957, 2 lines of text, cream roof,
    metal wheels, MIP, from $1,200 to $1,500.00
Y-8-B, Sunbeam Motorcycle & Milford, 1962, dk gr sidecar seat,
    MIP $60.00

**Y-8-D, 1945 MG TC, 1978, cream with tan top, MIP,
$15.00.** (Photo courtesy Dana Johnson)

Y-11-B, 1912 Packard Landaulet, 1964, beige & brn, MIP .$30.00
Y-11-C, 1938 Lagonda Drophead Coupe, 1973, plum w/blk inte-
    rior...$30.00
Y-11-D, 1932 Bugatti Type 35, 1987, MIP $25.00
Y-12-A, 1899 Horse-Drawn London Bus, 1959, beige driver &
    seats, MIP..$125.00
Y-12-C, 1912 Ford Model T Truck, 1979, cream w/blk roof, sil-
    ver wheels, Coca-Cola decal, MIP $80.00

Y-16-B, 1928 Mercedes Benz SS Coupe, 1972, metallic gray w/red chassis, blk roof, MIP......................$80.00
Y-16-C, 1957 Ferrari Dino 246/V12, 1986, MIP $25.00
Y-16-D, 1922 Scania Vabis Postbus, MIP $35.00
Y-19-A, 1933 Auburn 851 Boattail Speedster, 1080, beige & cream w/chrome spoke wheels, MIP.....................$30.00
Y-20-A, 1937 Mercedes Benz 540K, 1981, metallic gray w/red disc or spoke wheels, MIP......................$45.00
Y-23-B, 1930 Mack Tanker, 1989, MIP $20.00
Y-24-A, 1927 Bugatti T44, 1983, gray w/tan interior & plum accents, MIP $30.00
Y-26-A, 1918 Crossley Beer Lorry, 1984, any color & decal, MIP, ea.................$25.00
Y-39-A, 1820 Horse-Drawn Royal Mail Coach, 1990, MIP.$75.00
Y-43-A, 1905 Busch Steam Fire Engine, 1991, MIP $75.00
Y-61-A, 1933 Cadillac Fire Engine, 1992, MIP.................$30.00

SKYBUSTERS

SB-1-A, Learjet, 1973, red w/Datapost decal, MIP...........$10.00
SB-3-B, NASA Space Shuttle, 1980, wht & gray, MIP....$10.00
SB-4-A, Mirage F1, 1973, red w/bull's-eye on wings, MIP ...$15.00
SB-8-A, Spitfire, 1873, dk brn & gold, MIP $20.00
SB-12-B, Pitts Special Biplane, 1980, any, MIP................$15.00
SB-15-A, Marine Phantom F4E, 1975, pk, MIP $8.00
SB-19-A, Piper Comanche, 1977, beige & dk bl, Macau cast, MIP..................$8.00

SB-19, Piper Commanche, red and white, MIP, from $10.00 to $15.00; SB-1 US Air Force Learjet, white with black detail, MIP, $8.00. (Photo courtesy Dana Johnson)

SB-20-A, Army Helicopter, 1977, olive, MIP...................$12.00
SB-22-A, Tornado, 1978, lt gray & wht, dk gray & wht or red & wht, MIP, ea $10.00
SB-22-A, Tornado, 1978, lt purple & wht, MIP.................$8.00
SB-23-A, Heinz 57 SST Super Sonic Transport, 1979, wht, MIP.................$30.00
SB-24-A, F-16, 1979, any, MIP $10.00
SB-25-A, 007 Rescue Helicopter, 1979, red & wht, MIP .$12.00
SB-26-A, James Bond Cessna 210 Float Plane, 1981, wht, MIP $12.00
SB-31-A, Boeing 747-400, 1990, any, MIP $8.00
SB-35-A, MiL M24 Hind-D Chopper, 1990, any, MIP, ea..$6.00
SB-36-A, Lockheed F-117A Stealth, 1991, wht, no markings, MIP.................$8.00
SB-39-A, Circus-Circus Boeing Stearman Biplane, 1992, wht, MIP.................$6.00

Model Kits

Though model kits were popular with kids of the '50s who enjoyed the challenge of assembling a classic car or two or a Musketeer figure now and then, when the monster series hit in the early 1960s, sales shot through the ceiling. Made popular by all the monster movies of that decade, ghouls like Vampirella, Frankenstein, and the Wolfman were eagerly built up by kids everywhere. They could (if their parents didn't object too strongly) even construct an actual working guillotine. Aurora had other successful series of figure kits, too, based on characters from comic strips and TV shows as well as a line of sports stars.

But the vast majority of model kits were vehicles. They varied in complexity, some requiring much more dexterity on the part of the model builder than others, and they came in several scales, from 1/8 (which might be as large as 20" to 24") down to 1/43 (generally about 3" to 4"), but the most popular scale was 1/25 (usually between 6" to 8"). Some of the largest producers of vehicle kits were AMT, MPC, and IMC. Though production obviously waned during the late 1970s and early 1980s, with the intensity of today's collector market, companies like Ertl (who now is producing 1/25 scale vehicles using some of the old AMT dies) are proving that model kits still sell very well.

As a rule of thumb, assembled kits (built-ups) are priced at about 25% to 50% of the price range for a boxed kit, but this is not always true on the higher-priced kits. One mint in the box with the factory seal intact will often sell for up to 15% more than if the seal were broken, though depending on the kit, a sealed perfect box may add as much $100.00. Condition of the box is crucial. Last but not least, one must factor in Internet sales, which could cause some values to go down considerably.

For more information, we recommend *Collectible Figure Kits of the '50s, '60s, and '70s*, by Gordy Dutt.

Advisors: Mike and Kurt Fredericks (F4)

See also Plasticville.

Adams, Around the World in 80 Days Balloon, 1960, MIB................$325.00

Addar, Planet of the Apes, General Ursus, 1973, MIB (sealed), $50.00.

Adams, Hawk Missile Battery, 1958, MIB.........................$70.00
Addar, Evel Knievel's Ramp Jump, 1974, assembled, EX..$50.00
Addar, Evil Knievel's Wheelie, 1974, MIB $125.00
Addar, Planet of the Apes, Caesar, Dr Zaius, Dr Zira or Gen
    Aldo, 1973-74, MIB, ea $50.00
Addar, Planet of the Apes, Cornelius, 1973, MIB (sealed) ..$90.00
Addar, Planet of the Apes, Stallion & Soldier, 1974, MIB.$85.00
Addar, Super Scenes, Jaws, 1975, MIB............................$75.00
Addar, Super Scenes, Spirit in a Bottle, 1975, MIB.........$50.00
Airfix, Bristol Bloodhound, 1992, MIB............................$15.00
Airfix, Corythosaus, 1970, MIB (sealed) $30.00
Airfix, Sam-2 Missile, 1973, MIB...................................$40.00
Airfix, Yeoman of the Guard, 1978, MIB (sealed) $25.00
AMT, Farrah's Foxy Vet, 1970s, MIB $50.00
AMT, Get Smart Sunbeam Car, 1967, MIB (sealed) $100.00

AMT, Grave Yard Ghoul Duo With the Overtaker and Body-
snatcher, 1970, MIB, $125.00.

AMT, KISS Custom Chevy Van, 1977, MIB $70.00
AMT, Laurel & Hardy, '27 Touring Car, 1976, MIB.........$60.00
AMT, My Mother the Car, 1965, MIB.............................$50.00
AMT, Sonny & Cher Mustang, 1960s, MIB...................$225.00
AMT, Star Trek, Klingon Battle Cruiser, 1968, MIB (sealed)..$125.00
AMT, Star Trek, Romulan Bird of Prey, 1975, EXIB $75.00
AMT, Star Trek, Spock, 1967, MIB (sealed)......................$75.00
AMT, Star Trek, USS Enterprise Command Bridge, 1975, MIB.$75.00
AMT, Wackie Woodie Krazy Kar, 1960s, MIB (sealed) $85.00
AMT/Ertl, A-Team Van, 1983, MIB $30.00
AMT/Ertl, Back to the Future, Delorian, 1991, MIB (sealed).$35.00
AMT/Ertl, Batman (movie), Batman Cocoon, 1989, MIB.$20.00
AMT/Ertl, Batman (movie), Batwing, 1990, MIB (sealed) .$30.00
AMT/Ertl, Monkeemobile, 1990, MIB (sealed) $100.00
AMT/Ertl, Peterbilt 359 Truck, MIB................................$35.00
AMT/Ertl, Robocop 2, Robo 1 Police Car, 1990, MIB.....$25.00
AMT/Ertl, Star Trek (TV), Kirk, 1994, MIB (sealed) $25.00
AMT/Ertl, Star Trek (TV), McCoy, 1994, MIB (sealed)..$25.00
AMT/Ertl, Star Trek: Deep Space Nine, Defiant, 1996, MIB..$20.00
AMT/Ertl, Star Trek: TNG, USS Enterprise, 1988, MIB.$30.00
ANT/Ertl, Star Wars, Cut-Away Millennium Falcon, 1996,
    MIB $25.00
Anubis, Jonny Quest, Robot Spy, 1992, MIB...................$60.00

Anubis, Jonny Quest, Turu the Terrible, 1992, MIB.........$60.00
Arii, Orguss Flier, MIB...$15.00
Arii, Regult Missile Carrier, MIB $25.00
Arii, Southern Cross, NAD-Jun Yamashita, MIB $25.00
Arii-Macross, Valkyrie VF-1J, MIB $20.00
Aurora, Alfred E Neuman, 1965, EXIB (unused) $120.00
Aurora, Archie's Car, 1969, MIB (sealed).....................$125.00
Aurora, Banana Splits Banana Buggy, 1969, MIB..........$450.00
Aurora, Batman, 1964, MIB (sealed) $300.00
Aurora, Big Frankie (Frankenstein), 1964, assembled, 19", EX.$325.00
Aurora, Bloodthirsty Pirates, Blackbeard, 1965, MIB.....$250.00
Aurora, Bride of Frankenstein, 1965, MIB.....................$600.00
Aurora, Captain Action, 1966, MIB................................$300.00
Aurora, Captain America, 1966, MIB $300.00
Aurora, Castle Creatures, Vampire, 1966, MIB $250.00
Aurora, Chitty-Chitty Bang-Bang, 1965, assembled, EX..$40.00
Aurora, Comic Scenes, Superboy, 1974, MIB (sealed)...$100.00
Aurora, Comic Scenes, Tonto, assembled, EX $20.00

Aurora, The Creature,
1963, MIB, $250.00.

Aurora, Creature From the Black Lagoon, 1969, glow-in-the-
    dark, MIB...$200.00
Aurora, Dick Tracy Space Coupe, 1967, MIB.................$125.00
Aurora, Dr Dolittle & Pushmi-Pullyu, 1968, MIB $75.00
Aurora, Dr Jekyll as Mr Hyde, 1964, MIB......................$350.00
Aurora, Dr Jekyll as Mr Hyde, 1969, glow-in-the-dark, MIB
    (sealed) $225.00
Aurora, Dracula, 1962, MIB...$300.00
Aurora, Famous Fighters, Gladiator w/Trident, 1958, MIB.$200.00
Aurora, Famous Fighters, Gold Knight of Nice, 1957, MIB.$325.00
Aurora, Famous Fighters, Steve Canyon, 1958, MIB $200.00
Aurora, Famous Fighters, Viking, 1958, MIB.................$250.00
Aurora, Flying Sub, 1968, MIB (sealed) $250.00
Aurora, Forged Foil Buffalo, 1969, MIB $40.00
Aurora, Forgotten Prisoner, 1966, MIB (sealed)............$425.00
Aurora, Forgotten Prisoner (Frightening Lightning), 1969,
    MIB...$450.00

Aurora, Frankenstein, #423-98, MIB, $125.00.

Aurora, George Washington, 1965, MIB (sealed) $150.00
Aurora, Godzilla, 1969, glow-in-the-dark, MIB (sealed) .$250.00
Aurora, Godzilla's Go-Cart, 1966, assembled, EX $675.00
Aurora, Godzilla's Go-Cart, 1966, MIB.......................$3,000.00
Aurora, Green Beret, 1966, MIB...............................$225.00
Aurora, Green Hornet's Black Beauty, 1967, MIB..........$500.00
Aurora, Gruesome Goodies, Monster Scenes, 1971, MIB (sealed) $125.00
Aurora, Guys & Gals, Caballero, 1959, MIB.................$100.00
Aurora, Guys & Gals, Indian Chief, 1957, MIB (sealed) .$150.00
Aurora, Hunchback of Notre Dame, 1969, glow-in-the-dark, MIB (sealed) $200.00
Aurora, Hunchback of Notre Dame (Anthony Quinn), 1964, MIB (sealed) $350.00
Aurora, Incredible Hulk, 1966, MIB...........................$300.00
Aurora, Invaders, Flying Saucer, 1975, MIB $100.00
Aurora, James Bond 007, 1966, MIB..........................$250.00
Aurora, John F Kennedy, 1965, MIB (sealed).................$165.00
Aurora, King Kong, 1964, MIB $500.00
Aurora, King Kong, 1969, glow-in-the-dark, MIB (sealed).$350.00
Aurora, Land of the Giants, Snake Scene, 1968, MIB ...$500.00
Aurora, Lone Ranger, 1967, MIB $200.00
Aurora, Lone Ranger, 1967, MIB (sealed) $250.00
Aurora, Man From UNCLE, Napoleon Solo, 1966, MIB.$275.00
Aurora, Monster Scenes, Gruesome Goodies, 1971, MIB..$100.00
Aurora, Monster Scenes, Pendulum, 1971, MIB $100.00
Aurora, Monsters of the Movies, Dracula, 1975, MIB....$250.00
Aurora, Monsters of the Movies, Ghidrah, 1975, MIB...$275.00
Aurora, Monsters of the Movies, Rodan, 1975, rare, MIB.$375.00
Aurora, Mummy, 1963, MIB $350.00
Aurora, Mummy, 1969, glow-in-the-dark, MIB (sealed) .$200.00
Aurora, Mummy's Chariot, 1965, MIB $500.00
Aurora, Odd Job, 1966, MIB (sealed) $400.00
Aurora, Phantom of the Opera, 1969, glow-in-the-dark, MIB (sealed) $200.00

Aurora, Prehistoric Scenes, Cro-Magnon Man, 1971, MIB ...$75.00
Aurora, Prehistoric Scenes, Tar Pit, 1971, MIB (sealed) .$200.00
Aurora, Rat Patrol, 1967, partially assembled, EXIB $85.00
Aurora, Prince Valiant, 1959, MIB $200.00

Aurora, Robin the Boy Wonder, 1966, MIB (sealed), $125.00.

Aurora, Spider-Man, 1966, MIB $300.00
Aurora, Spider-Man, 1974, MIB (sealed).......................$150.00
Aurora, Superboy, 1964, MIB....................................$300.00
Aurora, Superman, 1963, MIB (sealed) $350.00
Aurora, Tonto, 1967, MIB (sealed) $275.00
Aurora, US Army Infantryman, 1959, MIB....................$75.00
Aurora, USB Sealab III, 1969, MIB $300.00
Aurora, Voyager (Fantastic Voyage), 1969, MIB $500.00
Aurora, Whoosis?, Alfalfa, 1968, MIB $75.00
Aurora, Whoosis?, Denty, 1966, MIB............................$75.00
Aurora, Whoosis?, Suzie, 1966, NMIB..........................$75.00
Aurora, Witch, 1965, assembled, EX............................$100.00
Aurora, Witch, 1965, MIB $350.00
Aurora, Witch, 1969, glow-in-the-dark, MIB (sealed) ...$250.00
Aurora, Wolfman, 1969, glow-in-the-dark, MIB (sealed).$200.00
Aurora, Wonder Woman, 1965, MIB (sealed)................$600.00
Aurora, 12 O'Clock High, B17 Bomber Formation, 1965, MIB..$250.00
Aurora, 12 O'Clock High, P51 Mustang, 1965, MIB $150.00
Bachmann, Animals of the World, Cow & Calf, 1959, MIB .$60.00
Bachmann, Animals of the World, Lion, 1959, MIB........$50.00
Bachmann, Birds of the World, Meadowlark, 1950s, MIB.$30.00
Bachmann, Birds of the World, Scarlet Tanager, 1990, MIB..$20.00
Bachmann, Birds of the World, Screech Owl, 1950s, MIB.$45.00
Bachmann, Dogs of the World, Basset Hound, 1960s, MIB.$30.00
Bachmann, Dogs of the World, Dalmatian, 1960s, MIB...$30.00
Bachmann, Fisher Boy, 1962, MIB $80.00
Bandai, Godzilla, 1984, MIB $50.00
Bandai, Gundman, Amuro Ray, 1980, MIB....................$15.00
Bandai, Kinggidrah, 1984, MIB..................................$50.00

Bandai, Kinggidrah, 1990, MIB..............................$40.00
Bandai, Pegila, 1990, MIB....................................$15.00
Bandai, Thunderbird, 1984, MIB............................$40.00
Billiken, Frankenstein, MIB.................................$150.00
Billiken, Invasion of the Saucerman, Saucerman, vinyl, MIB.$50.00
Billiken, Laser Blast Alien, 1988, vinyl, MIB $100.00
Billiken, Mummy, 1990, vinyl, MIB........................$175.00
Billiken, She-Creature, 1989, vinyl, MIB $65.00
Billiken, War of Colossal Beasts, 1986, vinyl, MIB..........$50.00
Dark Horse, King Kong, 1992, vinyl, MIB $75.00
Dark Horse, Mummy, 1995, MIB $150.00
Dark Horse, Predator II, 1994, MIB $175.00
Dark Horse, Ray Harryhausen's King Kong, MIB $100.00
Dimensional Designs, Mad Doctor, 1992, NMIB...........$75.00
Eldon, Matador Missile & Launcher, 1960, MIB $75.00
Eldon, Pink Panther, 1970s, MIB $75.00
Entex, Message From Space, Comet Fire, 1978, MIB $25.00
Fujimi Mokei, Mad Police, Venus Car #3, 1980s, MIB.....$50.00
Fundimensions, Space: 1999, Alien, 1976, MIB.............$40.00
Geometric Design, Boris Karloff as The Mummy, MIB.....$50.00
Geometric Design, Lon Chaney Jr as the Wolfman, MIB.$50.00
Hawk, Bobcat Roadster, 1962, MIB $30.00
Hawk, Cherokee Sports Roadster, 1962, MIB.................$35.00
Hawk, Cobra II, 1950s, MIB..................................$75.00
Hawk, Indian Totem Poles, Thunderbird, 1966, MIB.......$50.00
Hawk, Monte Carlo Sports Roadster, 1962, MIB.............$75.00
Hawk, Silly Surfers, Woodie on a Surfari, 1964, MIB.....$100.00
Hawk, Weird-Ohs, Francis the Foul, 1963, MIB.............$50.00

Hawk, Weird-Ohs, Huey's Hut Rod #583, 1963, MIB, $50.00.

Horizon, Bram Stoker's Dracula (Bat-Type), 1992, MIB ..$50.00
Horizon, Bram Stoker's Dracula (Wolf-Type), 1992, MIB .$35.00
Horizon, Bride of Frankenstein, MIB $75.00
Horizon, Dracula (Bela Lugosi), MIB...........................$50.00
Horizon, Frankenstein, MIB...................................$125.00
Horizon, Invisible Man, MIB....................................$50.00
Horizon, Marvel Universe, Cyclops, 1993, MIB (sealed) .$50.00
Horizon, Marvel Universe, Dr Doom, 1991, MIB............$45.00
Horizon, Marvel Universe, Incredible Hulk, 1990, MIB ..$40.00
Horizon, Marvel Universe, Punisher, 1988, MIB.............$50.00
Horizon, Marvel Universe, Spider-Man, 1988, MIB........$40.00
Horizon, Marvel Universe, Thing, 1991, MIB.................$50.00
Horizon, Mole People, MIB.....................................$50.00
Horizon, Mole People, Mole Man #2, 1988, MIB.............$75.00

Horizon, Robocop, ED-209, 1989, MIB $70.00
Horizon, Robocop, Robocop #30, 1992, MIB $70.00

Hubley, Model A Roadster, metal, MIB, $60.00.

Imai, Captain Blue, 1982, MIB.......................................$15.00
Imai, Orguss, Cable, 1994, MIB....................................$40.00
Imai, Orguss, Incredible Hulk, 1990, MIB $45.00
Imai, Orguss, Spider-Man, 1994, new pose, MIB $30.00
ITC, Dog Champions, German Shepherd, 1959, MIB $35.00
ITC, Neanderthal Man, 1959, MIB $50.00
Janus, Bela Lugosi as Dracula, MIB $50.00
Kaiyodo, Angurus, 1991, vinyl, NMIB.........................$50.00
KGB, Space Ghost (TV), MIB....................................$35.00
Life-Like, Ankylosaurus, 1968, MIB............................$35.00
Life-Like, Corythosaurus, 1970s, MIB $20.00
Life-Like, Roman Chariot, 1970s, MIB.........................$20.00
Lindberg, Coo Coo Clock, 1965, MIB $40.00
Lindberg, Douglas X-3 Supersonic Stiletto, 1950s, MIB...$60.00
Lindberg, flying saucer, 1952, MIB................................$200.00
Lindberg, Lindy Loonys, Scuttle Bucket, 1965, MIB......$100.00

Lindberg, Star Probe Space Base #1148, 1976, MIB, $40.00.

Lindberg, SST Continental, 1958, MIB.........................$175.00
Lindberg, Tyrannosaurus, 1987, MIB.............................$15.00

Lindberg, US Space Station, 1958, MIB.........................$200.00
Lindberg, Winnie Mae, 1950s, MIB $75.00
Lunar Models, Angry Red Planet, Giant Amoeba, MIB .$100.00
Lunar Models, Lost in Space, Space Pod, MIB $125.00
Lunar Models, Pumpkinhead (movie), 1989, MIB (sealed) .$150.00
Monogram, Bad Machine, 1970s, MIB..............................$60.00
Monogram, Bathtub Buggy, 1960s, MIB (sealed)............$100.00
Monogram, Blue Thunder Helicopter, 1984, MIB............$30.00
Monogram, Boss A Bone, 1969, assembled, EX $25.00
Monogram, Buck Rogers, Starfighter, 1979, MIB $75.00
Monogram, Dracula, 1983, MIB (sealed) $50.00
Monogram, Elvira Macabre Mobile, 1988, MIB $25.00
Monogram, Flying Reptile, 1987 (Aurora reissue), MIB
    (sealed) $35.00

Monogram, Fred Flogger as Flip Out!, 1965, MIB, $160.00.

Monogram, Godzilla, 1978, glow-in-the-dark, MIB $100.00
Monogram, Giraffes, 1961, MIB.......................................$50.00
Monogram, Invaders UFO (Aurora reissue), 1978, MIB ..$35.00
Monogram, Missile Arsenal, 1959, MIB $200.00
Monogram, NASA Space Shuttle, 1986, MIB $25.00
Monogram, Sand Crab, 1969, MIB $50.00
Monogram, Snoopy & His Bugatti Race Car, 1971, MIB.$30.00
Monogram, Snoopy on the Highwire, 1972, MIB.............$35.00
Monogram, Space Buggy, 1969, MIB $100.00
Monogram, TV Orbiter, 1959, MIB $150.00
Monogram, Tyrannosaurus Rex, 1987, MIB.....................$25.00
Monogram, Voyage to the Bottom of the Sea Flying Sub, 1968,
    MIB...$175.00
Monogram, Wolfman, 1983, MIB (sealed).......................$60.00
Monogram, Young Astronauts, Mercury/Gemini Capsules, 1987,
    MIB (sealed) $50.00
Monogram, Young Astronauts, X-15 Experimental Aircraft,
    1987, MIB $35.00
MPC, Alien, 1979, MIB (sealed) $75.00

MPC, Barnabas, 1968, MIB...$400.00
MPC, Barnabas Vampire Van, 1969, MIB.......................$250.00
MPC, Batman, 1984, MIB (sealed) $50.00
MPC, Beverly Hillbillies TV Truck, 1968, MIB $200.00
MPC, Bionic Woman Bionic Repair, MIB (sealed) $50.00
MPC, Duke of Hazzard, Daisy's Jeep, 1980, MIB $40.00
MPC, Dukes of Hazzard, Rosco's Police Car, 1982, MIB ..$30.00
MPC, Fonz Dream Rod, 1976, MIB....................................$50.00
MPC, Hogan's Heroes Jeep, 1968, MIB $125.00
MPC, Hulk, 1978, MIB (sealed)..$50.00
MPC, Incredible Hulk Van, 1977, MIB $20.00
MPC, Magic Bubble Radar Mast Patrol Boat, 1950s, MIB .$60.00
MPC, Mannix Roadster, 1968, MIB.....................................$75.00
MPC, Pilgrim Space Station, 1970, MIB $50.00
MPC, Pirates of the Caribbean, Freed in the Nick of Time, 1973,
    MIB...$100.00
MPC, Road Runner & the Beep-Beep T, 1972, MIB........$75.00
MPC, Space: 1999, Alien Creature & Vehicle, 1976, MIB .$50.00
MPC, Space: 1999, Eagle 1 Transporter, 1975, MIB.......$100.00
MPC, Space: 1999, Hawk Spaceship, 1977, MIB (sealed).$165.00
MPC, Spider-Man, 1978, MIB (sealed)...............................$50.00
MPC, Star Wars, AT-AT, 1981, MIB (sealed)...................$35.00
MPC, Star Wars, Boba Fett's Slave I, 1982, MIB (sealed) .$35.00
MPC, Star Wars, Darth Vader TIE Fighter, 1978, MIB $35.00
MPC, Star Wars, R2-D2, 1978, MIB...................................$50.00
MPC, Star Wars, Shuttle Tydirium, 1983, MIB (sealed) ..$25.00
MPC, Strange Changing Time Machine, 1974, MIB $60.00
MPC, Strange Changing Vampire, 1974, MIB..................$60.00

MPC, Sweathogs Dream Machine, 1976, MIB, $50.00.

MPC, Wacky Races Pussycat, 1969, MIB, from $100 to.$125.00
Nitto, Crusher Joe, BMW-A795 Air Car, MIB.................$20.00
Nitto, Crusher Joe, Dongo Mabot, MIB............................$15.00
Omai, Orguss, Cyclops, 1993, MIB $45.00
Palmer, African Tribal Mask, 1950s, MIB $75.00
Palmer, US Navy Vanguard Missile, 1958, MIB $225.00
Precision, American Bald Eagle, 1957, assembled, EX $25.00
Precision, Cap'n Kidd Pirate, 1959, MIB $75.00
Precision, US Navy Frogman, 1958, MIB $40.00

Pyro, Gladiator Sho Cycle, 1970, MIB.............................$50.00
Pyro, Indian Warrior, 1960s, MIB...................................$50.00
Pyro, Peacemaker 45, 1960, MIB (sealed).....................$100.00
Pyro, Prehistoric Monsters Gift Set, 1950s, MIB............$125.00
Pyro, Restless Gun Deputy Sheriff, 1958, MIB................$75.00
Pyro, Surf's Up!, 1970, MIB...$50.00
Remco, Flintstones Motorized Sports Car & Trailer, 1961, MIB.$175.00
Revell, Alien Invader, 1979, w/lights, MIB (sealed).........$50.00
Revell, Amazing Moon Mixer, 1970, MIB $35.00
Revell, Apollo Astronaut on Moon, 1970, MIB.............$125.00
Revell, Apollo Columbia/Eagle, 1969, MIB (sealed)......$150.00
Revell, Ariane 4 Rocket, 1985, MIB...............................$35.00
Revell, Baja Humbug, 1971, MIB....................................$85.00
Revell, Beatles, any member, 1964, MIB, ea from $200 to.$250.00

Revell, California Highway Patrol Harley-Davidson Patrol Bike, 1976, MIB, $75.00.

Revell, Cat in the Hat, 1960, MIB...................................$150.00
Revell, CHiPs, Helicopter, 1980, MIB.............................$35.00
Revell, CHiPs, Jon's Chevy 4x4, MIB...............................$35.00
Revell, CHiPs, Kawasaki Motorcycle, 1980, MIB.............$35.00
Revell, CHiPs, Ponch's Firebird, 1981, MIB (sealed) $40.00
Revell, Code Red, Fire Chief's Car, 1981, MIB $20.00
Revell, Disney's Love Bug Rides Again, 1974, MIB $100.00
Revell, Disney's Robin Hood Set #1, 1974, MIB (sealed)..$100.00

Revell, Drag Nut, 1963, MIB, $85.00.

Revell, Dr Seuss Zoo Set #1 (Tingo, Norval & Gowdy), 1960,
    assembled, EX $225.00
Revell, Dune, Ornithopter, 1985, MIB (sealed)...............$60.00
Revell, Dune, Sand Worm, 1985, MIB (sealed)................$75.00
Revell, Ed 'Big Daddy' Roth, Angel Fink, 1965, MIB $175.00
Revell, Ed 'Big Daddy' Roth, Fink Eliminator, 1990, MIB.$200.00
Revell, Endangered Animals, Gorilla, 1991, MIB $30.00
Revell, Flipper, 1965, assembled, EX $65.00
Revell, Friskie the Beagle Puppy, 1958, MIB...................$55.00
Revell, Gemini Capsule, 1967, MIB.................................$75.00
Revell, History Makers, Jupitor C, 1983, MIB (sealed) $60.00
Revell, Love Bug, 1970s, MIB $50.00
Revell, Lunar Spacecraft, 1970, MIB..............................$125.00
Revell, Magnum PI, TC's Helicopter, 1981, MIB (sealed).$60.00
Revell, Magnum PI, 308 GTS Ferrari, 1982, MIB (sealed).$60.00
Revell, Moonraker Space Shuttle, 1979, MIB $25.00
Revell, Moon Ship, 1957, MIB $225.00
Revell, Penny Pincher VW Bug, 1980, MIB....................$35.00
Revell, Peter Pan Pirate Ship, 1960s, MIB (sealed)........$125.00
Revell, Rif Raf & His Spitfire, 1971, MIB........................$45.00
Revell, Robotech, Commando, 1984, MIB (sealed) $50.00
Revell, Robotech, VF-1J Fighter, 1985, MIB (sealed) $50.00
Revell, Space Explorer Solaris, 1969, MIB $125.00
Revell, Terrier Missile, 1958, MIB $200.00
Revell, US Army Nike Hercules, 1958, MIB $60.00
Revell, USN Bendix Talos Missile, 1957, MIB $85.00
Screamin', Contemplating Conquest, 1995, MIB (sealed) .$50.00
Screamin', Friday the 13th's Jason, MIB $125.00
Screamin', Mars Attacks, Target Earth, assembled, NM...$30.00
Screamin', Mary Shelly's Frankenstein, 1994, assembled, EX.$30.00
Screamin', Star Wars, Stormtrooper, 1993, MIB..............$45.00
Screamin', Werewolf, MIB $100.00
Strombecker, Disneyland Stagecoach, 1950s, MIB.........$200.00
Strombecker, Interplanetary Vehicle, 1959, MIB $175.00
Strombecker, Walt Disney's Spaceship, 1958, MIB $300.00
Superior, Beating Heart, 1959, MIB................................$35.00
Superior, Seeing Eye, 1959, MIB $35.00
Testors, Davey the Cyclist, 1993, MIB (sealed) $15.00
Testors, Weird-Ohs, Endsville Eddie, 1993, MIB (sealed) .$35.00
Toy Biz, Ghost Rider, 1996, MIB, from $25 to................$30.00
Toy Biz, Storm, 1996, MIB (sealed)................................$30.00
Toy Biz, Thing, 1996, MIB, from $25 to..........................$30.00
Toy Biz, Wolverine, 1996, NMIB, from $25 to $30.00
Tsukuda, Creature From the Black Lagoon, MIB............$150.00
Tsukuda, Frankenstein, 1985, MIB.................................$100.00
Tsukuda, Ghostbusters, Stay Puft Man (sm), 1984, MIB..$40.00
Tsukuda, Ghostbusters Terror Dog, MIB........................$125.00
Tsukuda, Giant Frankenstein, MIB $135.00
Tsukuda, Metaluna Mutant, MIB....................................$100.00
Tsukuda, Mummy, MIB...$100.00
Tsukuda, Wolfman, MIB..$100.00

Movie Posters and Lobby Cards

This field is a natural extension of the interest in character collectibles, and one where there is a great deal of activity.

There are tradepapers that deal exclusively with movie memorabilia, and some of the larger auction galleries hold cataloged sales on a regular basis.

Abbott & Costello Meet Frankenstein, title card, 1948, rare, EX $550.00

Alice in Wonderland, window card, Disney animation, 1951, 17x14", VG $35.00

Babes in Toyland, insert, 1961, 36x14", VG+ $40.00

Bandit of Sherwood Forest, Cornel Wilde as Robin Hood, 1946, ½-sheet, 28x22", EX $50.00

Batman, lobby card, Catwoman, 20th Century Fox, 1966, 11x14", NM+ $75.00

Beach Ball, insert, Edd Byrnes w/the Supremes, Four Seasons, etc, 1965, 36x14", EX $50.00

Blackbeard's Ghost, 1968, 1-sheet, 41x27", EX $35.00

Blue Hawaii, Elvis, 1961, 3-sheet, 72x48", EX $225.00

Brain From Planet Arous, lobby card set, John Agar, 1957, 14x11" ea, EX $150.00

Cinderella, insert, Disney animation, 1957 (reissue), 36x14", EX $65.00

Commando Cody in Satan's Satellites, Republic, 1958, 1-sheet, 41x27", NM $150.00

Daniel Boone Frontier Rider, insert, Fess Parker, Ed Ames & Patricia Blair, 20th Century Fox, 1966, 36x14", NM..$65.00

Daughter of Dr Jekyll, insert, John Agar, 1957, 36x14", EX.$65.00

Doc Savage, Ron Ely, 1975, 1-sheet, 41x27", EX $25.00

Godzilla King of the Monsters!, Embassy Pictures, 1956, ½-sheet, 28 x22", NM, A, $175.00. (Photo courtesy Butterfields)

Godzilla vs The Thing, American International Pictures, 1964, 3-sheet, 81x41", EX+, A $350.00

Green Hornet, 1977, 1-sheet, 41x27", NM $100.00

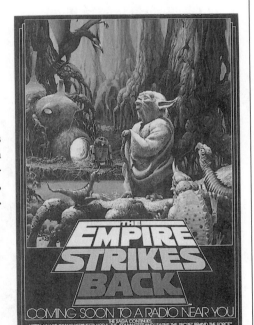

Empire Strikes Back, Lucasfilm Ltd, 1980, ½-sheet, 28x17", NM, A, $ 500.00.

(Photo courtesy Butterfields)

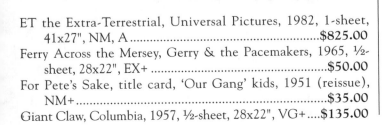

Gulliver's Travels, Paramount, 1939, ½-sheet, 41x27", NM, A, $1,175.00.

(Photo courtesy Butterfields)

ET the Extra-Terrestrial, Universal Pictures, 1982, 1-sheet, 41x27", NM, A $825.00

Ferry Across the Mersey, Gerry & the Pacemakers, 1965, ½-sheet, 28x22", EX+ $50.00

For Pete's Sake, title card, 'Our Gang' kids, 1951 (reissue), NM+ $35.00

Giant Claw, Columbia, 1957, ½-sheet, 28x22", VG+ $135.00

Heart of the Rockies, Roy Rogers, 1951, 1-sheet, 41x27", NM $150.00

Hills of Home, insert, Lassie, 1948, 36x14", EX $50.00

Jack the Giant Killer, window card, 1962, 17x14", EX $35.00

Jason & the Argonauts, insert, Ray Harryhausen, Columbia, 1963, 36x14", EX+ $125.00

King Kong, 1976, 1-sheet, 41x27", NM $40.00

Li'l Abner, lobby card set, w/cast, 1948 (reissue), 11x14" ea, NM $50.00

Little Rascals in Fish Hooky, Monogram, 1952, 1-sheet, 41x27", EX $125.00

King Kong, RKO Radion Pictures, 1960s (reissue), 55x39", EX+, A, $400.00. (Photo courtesy Butterfields)

Pete's Dragon, lobby card set of 9, 1977, 14x11", EX (w/envelope) $50.00

Pinocchio in Outer Space, animation, 1965, 1-sheet, 41x27", EX $50.00

Prince Valiant, window card, 1954, 14x11", EX $65.00

Rainbow Over Texas, Roy Rogers, 1954 (reissue), 1-sheet, EX.$50.00

Range War, Hopalong Cassidy, 1940, 3-sheet, 72x48", Fair .$150.00

Return of Captain Marvel, 1966 (reissue), 1-sheet, 41x27", EX ..$65.00

Snow White & the Seven Dwarfs, lobby card, 1950s, 14x11", EX $75.00

Son of Zorro, lobby card set, Republic Serial in 13 Chapters, 1947, set of 4, 14x11", EX................................$85.00

Song of the South, 1956 (reissue), ½-sheet, 22x14", EX ..$85.00

Space Children, window card, Paramount, 1958, 22x14", NM .$75.00

Springtime in the Rockies, lobby card, Gene Autry, 1937, 14x11", NM..$125.00

Looney Tunes, Vitaphone, 1940 – 41, 1-sheet, EX+, A, $1,300.00. (Photo courtesy Butterfields)

Stan Laurel and Oliver Hardy in Pardon Us, Metro-Goldwyn-Mayer, 1931, 1-sheet, 41x27", NM, $3,000.00.

(Photo courtesy Butterfields)

Lone Ranger Rides Again, lobby card, 1939, 14x11", from $250 to $300.00

Lost Canyon, Hopalong Cassidy, United Artists, 1942, ½-sheet, 22x14", NM, A $135.00

Magic Carpet, window card, Lucille Ball, Columbia, 1951, 17x14", EX+..$50.00

McHale's Navy, 1964, 1-sheet, 41x27", EX+....................$60.00

Moon-Spinners, Hayley Mills, Buena Vista/WDP, 1964, 1-sheet, 41x27", NM+ $30.00

Munster Go Home, lobby card, Universal, 1966, 14x11", EX $45.00

Munster Go Home, Universal, 1966, 3-sheet, 72x48", EX..$150.00

Painted Hills, Lassie, MGM, 1951, 1-sheet, 41x27", EX...$50.00

You Only Live Twice, United Artist, 1967, 30x40", NM, A, $825.00. (Photo courtesy Butterfields)

The Shadow 'Behind the Mask,' lobby card, Monogram, 1946, 14x11", M $150.00
Three Stooges in Have Rocket Will Travel, Columbia Pictures, ½-sheet, 28x22", VG+ $120.00
Three Worlds of Gulliver, 1960, 1-sheet, 41x27", EX.......$65.00
Walt Disney's Melody Time (Once Upon a Wintertime), lobby card, RKO, 1948, 14x11", NM+..............................$60.00
Zorro Rides Again, 1959, 1-sheet, 41x27", EX.................$75.00
2001: A Space Odyssey, Metro-Goldwyn-Mayer, 1968, 1-sheet, 41x27", NM, A $825.00

Musical Toys

Whether meant to soothe, entertain, or inspire, musical toys were part of our growing-up years. Some were as simple as a windup music box, others as elaborate as a lacquered French baby grand piano.

See also Character, TV, and Movie Collectibles; Disney; Rock 'n Roll; Western.

Church Organ, Chein, lithographed tin, hand crank, 9", EX, A, $75.00. (Photo courtesy Randy Inman Auctions)

Accordion, Hohner, 2-octave, leatherette case, 10", NM ..$250.00
Drum, Chein, circus graphics, litho tin w/paper heads, spring-tension body, wooden sticks, 11" dia, EX+, A $110.00
Drum, Chein, 1970s, Revolutionary graphics, tin w/cb insert, designed by Gene Bosch, NM+...................................$425.00
Drum, Chein/Paramount, 1939, Gulliver's Travels, litho tin w/mesh & paper, 6" dia, VG+, A $85.00
Drum, Chein/Paramount/Max Fleischer, 1939, Gulliver's Travels, litho tin, w/wooden sticks, 13" dia, EX..............$165.00
Drum, Ohio Art, Mickey, Minnie & Pluto playing & conducting music, litho tin, w/2 wooden drum sticks, 6" dia, G, A.$165.00
Drum, Ohio Art, Noah's Ark, litho tin, NM $150.00
Drum, Santa Claus Band, litho tin, spring-tension body, wooden sticks, 8" dia, VG, A...$275.00
Farmer-in-the-Dell Music Maker, Mattel, 1950s, litho tin, crank-op, EX $125.00
Golden Banjo, Emenee, 1960s, NMIB..........................$125.00
Harmonica, Strauss, 1925, detachable horn, EXIB, A $150.00

Kiddyphone Record Player, tin, wind-up, 7½" dia, G+, A, $300.00. (Photo courtesy Randy Inman Auctions)

Piano, Bliss, grand style w/internal xylophone, 16", EX, A.$115.00
Piano, Bliss, litho front, 9½", VG, A $115.00
Piano, Chein, Electric Player Piano, NM, L4 ....$325.00
Piano, Marx, 1930s, Play-A-Way, tin w/12 keys, w/book, rare, EXIB, A $150.00
Piano, Schoenhut, gilt cast legs, 16", G, A $60.00
Piano, Schoenhut, upright, EX......................................$115.00
Pigmyphone, Bing, litho tin, VG, A $250.00
Tambourine, T Cohn, litho tin w/clown face, 8" dia, NM, A $100.00
Victrola, Germany, 1920s, red litho tin 4-ftd base, lever action, w/record, 5½" dia, EX, A...$200.00

Optical Toys

Compared to the bulky viewers of years ago, contrary to the usual course of advancement, optical toys of more recent years have tended to become more simplified in concept.

See also Character, TV, and Movie Collectibles; Disney; View-Master and Tru-View; Western.

Easy Show Projector, Kenner, 1971, features Superman, hand-operated, MIB, $75.00.

Automatic Space Viewer, Stephens, 1950s, EX $175.00
Easy Show Projector, Kenner, 1971, Wacky Races/Scooby Doo, hand-op, EXIB $50.00
Flashy Flickers Magic Picture Gun, Marx, EXIB.............$125.00
Give-A-Show Projector, Kenner, 1964, 112 color slides featuring the Flintstones, NMIB...$100.00
Kaleidoscope, Bush, cb tube w/brass element housing, impressed logo, 4-ftd wood base, 14", EX...................................$500.00
Magic Lantern, Bing, tin, w/orig glass slides & instructions, 6½x6½", EX (in cb box), A $80.00
Magic Lantern, Bing, tin & brass, w/orig glass slides, 6½x9½", G+ (in cb box), A...$90.00
Magic Lantern, Ernst Plank, barrel shape on platform, w/3 circular & 8 straight slides, G (w/12" fitted wood box), A .$70.00
Magic Lantern, Ernst Plank, box shape w/all orig components, 9 lg slides, G (in fitted box), A $110.00
Magic Lantern, Ernst Plank, pnt tin, w/unusual illusion wheel, orig glass slides, 9x13½", VG+ (EX cb box), A.......$175.00
Magic Lantern, Ernst Plank, tin & brass, w/orig glass slides, 11x6½", G+ (in wood box), A................................$155.00
Magic Lantern, Ernst Plank, tin & brass, w/orig glass slides, 7½x10½", VG (in cb box w/hinged lid), A.............$100.00
Magic Lantern, Falk, tin, w/orig glass slides, 8x12", VG+ (in cb box), A...$80.00

Magic Lantern, McAllister, complete with catalog (dated 1881) and several glass film slides, VG, A, $230.00. (Photo courtesy Randy Inman Auctions)

Magic Mirror, McLoughlin Bros, paper litho image appears on mercury glass tube, EX (in wooden box), A $1,500.00
Movie Machine, crank-op flip movie viewer, sheet metal, w/3 different cartoons, Peco, 6", EX, A............................$40.00
Movie Projector, Pathex, early, 13", incomplete, G, A.....$90.00
Movieland Drive-In Theatre, Remco, complete, EXIB ..$225.00
Optical Illusions Science Kit, Remco, 1961, NM (orig can).$25.00
Picture Projector, Remington-Morse, 7½x8", VG (in cb litho box), A..$50.00
Play 'N Show Phono Projector, Kenner, 1969, complete, MIB.$35.00
Projector, Keystone, electric, blk, G+IB, A.......................$55.00
Starmaster Astronomy Set, complete w/projector & early space film, Reed, 1950s, EX+IB, A $45.00

Paper Dolls

Turn-of-the-century paper dolls are seldom found today and when they are, they're very expensive. Advertising companies used them to promote their products, and some were printed on the pages of leading ladies' magazines. By the late 1920s most paper dolls were being made in book form — the doll on the cover, the clothes on the inside pages. Because they were so inexpensive, paper dolls survived the Depression and went on to peak in the 1940s. Though the advent of television caused sales to decline, paper doll companies were able to hang on by making paper dolls representing Hollywood celebrities and TV stars. These are some of the most collectible today. Even celebrity dolls from more recent years like the Brady Bunch or the Waltons are popular. Remember, condition is very important; if they've been cut out, even when they're still in fine condition and have all their original accessories, they're worth only about half as much as an uncut book or box set. Our values are for mint and uncut dolls unless noted otherwise.

For more information, refer to *Price Guide to Lowe and Whitman Paper Dolls* and *Price Guide to Saalfield and Merrill Paper Dolls* by Mary Young, and *Collecting Toys* by Richard O'Brien.

Advisor: Mary Young (Y2)

Alice Faye, Merrill #4800, 1941 ....$300.00
Annie Oakley, Whitman #1960, 1956, from $65 to $85.00
Archies Girls, Lowe #2764, 1964 ....$50.00

Ava Gardner, Whitman #965, 1949, $175.00.

Baby Show, Lowe #1021, 1940 ....$100.00
Baby-Sitter, Saalfield #2747, 1956 ....$35.00
Badgett Quadruplets, Saalfield #2348, 1941 ....$150.00
Barbara Britton, Saalfield #4318, 1954, from $85 to $150.00

Bette Davis, Merrill #4816, 1942, from $175 to $300.00
Betty Grable, Whitman #989, 1941 ....$300.00
Bewitched, Magic Wand #114, 1965, boxed set...............$75.00
Blondie, Saalfield #4434, 1968 ....$40.00
Blue Feather Indian, Lowe #1044, 1944...........................$65.00
Bob Hope & Dorothy Lamour, Whitman #976, 1942 ....$300.00
Brady Bunch, Whitman #4784, 1972 ....$45.00
Bride Doll, Lowe #1043, 1946 ....$60.00
Cabbage Patch Deluxe Paper Dolls, Avalon #640, 1983 ..$10.00
Career Girls, Lowe #1045, 1042 ....$75.00
Carmen Miranda, Whitman #995, 1942 ....$200.00
Children in the Shoe, Merrill #1562, 1949 ....$40.00
Chitty-Chitty Bang-Bang, Whitman #1982, 1968 ....$40.00
Cinderella Steps Out, Lowe #1242, 1948....................$60.00
Claudette Colbert, Saalfield #322, 1943 ....$75.00
Cowboys & Cowgirls, Lowe #1286, 1950......................$25.00
Cradle Tots, Merrill #3455, 1945, from $65 to.................$80.00
Deanna Durbin, Merrill #3480, 1940 ....$150.00
Debbie Reynolds, Whitman #1955, 1955 ....$100.00
Dinah Shore, Whitman #977, 1943, from $100 to $200.00
Dionne Quints, Whitman #998, 1935 ....$125.00
Dodie, Saalfield #6044, 1971 ....$32.00
Donna Reed, Artcraft #4412, 1959 ....$90.00
Donny & Marie, Whitman #1991, 1977......................$35.00
Doris Day, Whitman #1179, 1954..........................$125.00
Dr Kildare Play Book, Lowe #955, ca 1963 ....$30.00
Dude Ranch, Lowe #1026, 1943............................$35.00
Edgar Bergman's Charlie McCarthy, Whitman #995, 1938 .$250.00
Elizabeth Taylor, Whitman #968, 1949......................$175.00
Evelyn Rudie, Saalfield #4425, 1958 ....$60.00
Fairy Princess, Merrill #1548, 1951/1958 ....$35.00
Fairy Tale Princess, Lowe #2787, 1962 ....$45.00
Farmer Fred, Lowe #523, 1943.............................$25.00
Faye Emerson, Saalfield #2722, 1952 ....$85.00
Finger Ding Paper Dolls, Whitman #1993, 1971 ....$15.00
Flossy Fair & Peter Fair, Whitman #981, 1933 ....$75.00

Flying Nun, Saalfield #1317, 1969, $60.00. (Photo courtesy Greg Davis and Bill Morgan)

Gabby Hayes, Lowe #4171, 1954....................................$50.00
Gene Autry, Merrill #3482, 1940................................$100.00
Gene Autry's Melody Ranch, Whitman #990, 1950 ......$100.00

Gidget Magic Paper Doll, Standard Toykraft #601, 1965, $75.00. (Photo courtesy Greg Davis and Bill Morgan)

Gigi Perreau, Saalfield #2605, 1951 ....$75.00
Gisele MacKenzie, Saalfield #4421, 1957 ....$100.00
Glenn Miller-Marion Hutton, Lowe #1041, 1942 ....$400.00
Goldilocks & the Three Bears, Lowe #2561, 1955 ....$35.00
Gone With the Wind, Merrill #3404, 1940....................$350.00

Green Acres, Whitman #4773, 1968, $55.00. (Photo courtesy Greg Davis and Bill Morgan)

Hayley Mills Summer Magic Cutouts, Whitman #1966, 1963 ....$50.00
Hedy Lamar, Saalfield #1538, 1951 ....$100.00

Heidi & Peter, Saalfield #4424, 1961 ....$25.00
Henrietta Hippo for Miss America (New Zoo Revue), Saalfield
    #D411, 1974, uncut, MIB................$25.00
Hollywood Personalities, Lowe #1049, 1941..............$400.00
Honeymooners, Lowe #2560, 1956 ....$250.00
In Our Backyard, Lowe #1027, 1941 ....$60.00
It's a Small World, Whitman #1981, 1966 ....$30.00
Jane Withers, Whitman #989, 1940...............$125.00
Janie & Her Doll, Lowe #523, 1943 ....$25.00
Joanne Woodward, Saalfield #4436, 1958............$90.00
Julie Andrews, Saalfield #4424, 1958................$100.00
Junior Prom, Lowe #1042, 1942 ....$50.00
King of Swing & Queen of Song, Lowe #1040, 1942 .....$400.00
Lana Turner, Whitman #964, 1947 ....$200.00
Let's Play House, Lowe #1248, ca 1949 ....$30.00
Little Cousins, Lowe #521, 1940 ....$50.00
Little Lulu, Whitman #1970, 1971............$35.00
Little Women, Lowe #1030, 1941 ....$75.00
Lollypop Crowd, Lowe #1049, 1945..........$50.00

**Lucille Ball/Desi Arnaz With Little Ricky, Whitman
#2116, 1953, $100.00.** (Photo courtesy Rick Wyman)

Margaret O'Brien, Whitman #963, 1946 ....$125.00
Mary Martin, Saalfield #287, 1943.............$125.00
Movie Stars Paper Dolls, Whitman #905, 1931............$250.00
Munsters, Whitman #1959, 1966..............$100.00
My Fair Lady, Ottenheimer #2961, 1965.............$50.00
Nancy & Sluggo, Whitman #1979, 1974..............$35.00
National Velvet, Whitman #1948, 1962 ....$60.00
Nurses, Whitman #1975, 1963 ....$50.00
Oklahoma!, Whitman #1954, 1956 ....$100.00
Our Gang, Whitman #900, 1931 ....$200.00
Ozzie & Harriet, Saalfield #4319, 1954 ....$100.00
Partridge Family, Artcraft #5137, 1971 ....$50.00

**Partridge Family, Saalfield #6157, 1972,
$50.00.** (Photo courtesy Greg Davis and Bill Morgan)

Pat Boone, Whitman #1968, 1959 ....$65.00
Patty Duke, Whitman #1991, 1964.............$35.00
Petticoat Junction, Whitman #1954, 1964 ....$100.00
Playhouse Kiddles, Whitman #1954, 1971.............$40.00
Playhouse Paper Dolls, Lowe #1057, 1947 ....$25.00
Playtime Pals, Lowe #1045, 1946 ....$25.00
Pollyanna, Whitman #995, 1941.............$90.00
Portrait Girls, Whitman #966, 1947 ....$75.00
Princess Diana, Whitman #1530, 1985............$40.00
Prom Home Permanent, Lowe #1253, 1952............$40.00
Raggedy Ann & Andy, Saalfield #2754, 1957..........$45.00
Ricky Nelson, Whitman #2081, 1959.............$100.00
Robin Hood & Maid Marian, Saalfield #2748, 1956......$75.00
Rock Hudson, Whitman #2087, 1957.............$65.00
Rosemary Clooney, Lowe #2569, 1956..............$125.00
Roy Rogers & Dale Evans, Whitman #1172, 1952.........$100.00
Sally & Dick, Bob & Jane, Lowe #1023, 1940 ....$60.00
Sandra Dee, Saalfield #4417, 1959 ....$65.00
School Girl, Saalfield #2400, 1942.............$40.00
Shirley Temple, Saalfield #1715, 1935............$200.00
Sonja Henie, Merrill #3418, 1941.............$250.00
Sparkle Plenty, Saalfield #5160, 1948 ....$65.00
Square Dance, Lowe #968, 1950 ....$25.00
Sugar & Spice, Saalfield #3961, 1969 ....$12.00
Sunshine Family, Whitman #4337, 1974 ....$25.00
Susan Dey as Laurie/The Partridge Family, Artcraft #4218,
    1971 ....$40.00
Tammy & Her Family, Whitman #1997, 1964 ....$60.00
Teen Shop, Saalfield #2701, 1948 ....$25.00
Ten Little Playmates, Lowe #145, 1944.............$20.00
Tricia Nixon, Saalfield #1248, 1970...........$40.00
Trixie, Lowe #3920, 1961 ....$35.00

Shirley Temple, Saalfield #2112, 1934, $250.00.

Tuesday Weld, Saalfield #5112, 1960 ....$60.00
Virginia Mayo, Saalfield #4422, 1957 ....$125.00
Walt Disney's Pinocchio, Whitman #935, 1939 ....$250.00
Walt Disney's Sleeping Beauty, Whitman #1981, 1959 ....$60.00
Walter Lantz Cartoon Stars, Saalfield #1344, 1963 ....$30.00
Waltons (Children), Whitman #1995, 1975....................$50.00
Winnie the Pooh, Whitman #947, 1935......................$100.00
Wonder Woman, Whitman #1398, 1979 ....$25.00

Paper-Lithographed Toys

Following the development of color lithography, early toy makers soon recognized the possibility of using this technology in their own field. By the 1800s, both here and abroad, toys ranging from soldiers to involved dioramas of entire villages were being produced of wood with colorful and well detailed paper lithographed surfaces. Some of the best known manufactures were Crandell, Bliss, Reed, and McLoughlin. This style of toy remained popular until well after the turn of the century.

Advisors: Mark and Lynda Suozzi (S24)

See also Black Americana; Boats; Dollhouses; Games; Puzzles; Schoenhut.

ABC & 123 Picture Blocks, 32-pc set w/images, numbers & letters, VGIB, A...$415.00
ABC Little Word Blocks, 6-pc, McLoughlin Bros, EXIB, A .$300.00
American/European Menagerie, Bliss, ca 1893, pull toy w/3 circus cages & diecut animals on wheeled bases, 27", VG $1,050.00
Aunt Louisa's Cube Puzzles/Visit of St Nicholas, McLoughlin Bros, 30-pc set, EXIB, A................................$750.00

Battleship, red, wht & bl graphics of flag, guns & waves, 2 guns & stack on deck, wheeled, 13", EX $500.00
Battleship Picture Puzzle Cubes, McLoughlin, 6 battleship images, 20-pc, G+IB, A..$415.00
Brownie Blocks, McLoughlin Bros/Palmer Cox, 1891, set of 20, w/illustration booklet, EXIB (wood w/litho lid) ...$1,050.00
Centennial Exhibition 1876 Puzzle Blocks, set of 15 depicting 6 Philadelphia buildings, EXIB, A $450.00
Chicago Limited Train, Bliss, ca 1891, 48", VG, A.....$1,425.00
Church Building Block Set, Bliss, forms church w/steeple, includes 23 blocks w/bible phrases & scenes, 12x9", EX, A...$3,575.00
Cinderella Puzzles, McLoughlin Bros, 4 different, VG+ (w/paper litho-on-wood box), A..$500.00
Fire Co No 9 Firehouse, Schoenhut, w/3 wooden fire vehicles, 8x8", EX+IB, A...$475.00
Fort, multi-level w/ramp entry, many towers w/castle appearance, pnt bark trim on base, 14x22x20", EX, A ...$1,750.00
Fort Sumter Box Set, Reed, unfolds to reveal facade of fort under attack, w/diecut soldiers & accessories, 22x18", EX.$2,475.00

House That Jack Built, Bliss, Pat 1895, with horse-drawn dray, figures, and animals, 20x15", EX+, $2,400.00. (Photo courtesy Bertoia Auctions)

Jackson Park Horse-Drawn Trolley, Bliss, 28", G, A....$1,325.00
Locomotive Picture Puzzle, McLoughlin Bros, ca 1887, VGIB $150.00
Military Tenpins, Ives, Pat 1885, complete, 10", EX ...$1,550.00
New York Tug Boat Co & New York Canal Barge, Reed, 22", EX, A...$1,325.00
Noah's Ark Play Box, Spears, GIB, A $225.00
Palmer Cox Picture Blocks, 20-pc, 10x13", VGIB, A.....$220.00
Picture Blocks, Gilmour & Co, 1910, 2-sided, 6-pc, 13x4½", EXIB, A $220.00
Picture Blocks, multiple images such as peasant woman & girl at cottage window, 48-pc, VGIB (hinged lid)..............$415.00
Pretty Village Set, McLoughlin Bros, 1897, EXIB $300.00
Providence Side-Wheeler, 1890s, w/wheels, detailed graphics, 20", VG, A...$250.00

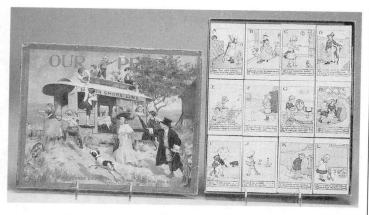

Our Pets Picture Blocks, Parker Bros., VGIB, $400.00. (Photo courtesy Skinner, Inc.)

Pull Toy, boy on horse on wooden platform w/4 metal spoke wheels, 8", VG, A...................................$200.00

Pull Toy, sea horse motif on box w/2 pop-up heads, CI spoke wheels & bell, 6", VG+, A.........................$600.00

Roller Chimes, Pat 1884, rolling barrel w/wire pull hdl, 26½", VG..$250.00

Roosevelt Stock Farm, barn w/removable roof, sliding doors, 6 stalls, 6 prs of farm animals, 19½", VG.........$700.00

Sailing Ship, 3 masts w/string rigging, wooden wheels, shows fisherman catching fish, 36", VG...............$350.00

Soldiers on Parade Set #3, McLoughlin, complete, NMIB, A...$300.00

Target Game, Schoenhut, 6-pc jungle animal set & cannon, VG to EX, A...$220.00

The Flyer Train, Milton Bradley, 1880s, features the Hercules locomotive, tender, and passenger coach, 47", EX, $3,250.00. (Photo courtesy Bertoia Auctions)

The-Royal-Blue-Line Passenger Car, Bliss, 22", VG.......$275.00

Theatre, France, Ombres Chinoises (Chinese Men), 15x21", EXIB...$550.00

Thetis Sailboat, Reed, ca 1901, paper sails, graphic images of waves, 15x18", VG, A...........................$220.00

Train, Reed, locomotive & passenger coach, 33", EX .$1,200.00

Trinity Chimes, Bliss, musical box w/pictorial view on church below & bell tower above, 18½x10", working, VG.$350.00

Western Express Wagon, Bliss, paper-lithoed sides, plain & pnt wooden wheels, filled w/plain wooden blocks, 23", VG+, A..$300.00

World's Columbian Exposition Trolley, Bliss, 18", EX.$1,200.00

Yellow Cab, photo-real image of 1920s cab, 5", G+, A ..$175.00

Pedal Cars and Other Wheeled Goods

Just like daddy, all little boys (and girls as well) are thrilled and happy to drive a brand new shiny car. Today both generations search through flea markets and auto swap meets for cars, boats, fire engines, tractors, and trains that run not on gas but pedal power. Some of the largest manufacturers of wheeled goods were AMF (American Machine and Foundry Company), Murray, and Garton. Values depend to a very large extent on condition, and those that have been restored may sell for $1,000.00 or more, depending on the year and model. The following listings are in original condition unless noted otherwise.

Advisor: Nate Stoller (S7)

American Airlines Jet Flight Crew Car, Murray, 1970, 40", rstr, A..$300.00

Atomic Missile, Murray, chain drive, 1950s, EX restoration, $1,750.00. (Photo courtesy Collectors Auction Services)

Auburn Roadster, Steelcraft, 1930s, padded seat, side spare, 44", rstr...................................$1,300.00

Austin Convertible, Wales, Austin Co, electric horn & lights, padded seat, 58", rstr, A..............$550.00

BMC Hook & Ladder Truck, wooden ladders, 37", G, A ..$110.00

BMC Knee Action Tractor, 38", VG, A $100.00

Bugatti Roadster, Eureka, boat-tail styling, chrome detail, 46", rstr, A....................................$550.00

Buick, Steelcraft, 1920s, full-fendered, disk wheels, 35", rstr, A.$1,100.00

Buick Sky Lark, see Sky Lark

Cadillac, Boy Craft/Steelcraft, 1920s, w/airplane hood ornament, 38", VG+.....................................$5,000.00

Cadillac, Gendron, very early model w/steel body on wood frame, metal spoke wheels, 42", Fair+, A $1,100.00

Castelli Tractor, 29", G, A.....................................$100.00

Caterpillar D6 Dozer, 1950s, 41", Fair......................$1,400.00

Caterpillar Service Tow Truck w/Bulldozer on Trailer, Steelcraft, 93" overall, rstr, A..................$4,500.00

Champion Ball Bearing Car, Murray, 1949-50, 34", G, A .$150.00

Champion Ball Bearing Car, Murray, 1949-50, 34", rstr, A.$475.00

Champion Royal Deluxe, Murray 1950s, rear spare, 36", rstr, A..$750.00

Champion 610 Jet Flow Drive, Murray, 1949-50, 34", rstr, A .$500.00
Champion 81 Pioneer, Gendron, 37", EX, A $2,300.00
Charger, Murray, 1970, w/plastic open engine, 32", rstr, A .$325.00
Checker Cab, AMF, 1970s, yel w/blk & wht detail, 34", rstr, A.$275.00
Chevrolet, Steelcraft, 1930s, 38", old rpt, A....................$600.00
Chief of Police Car, Steelcraft, 35", G (partial rstr), A .$1,700.00
Chrysler, Steelcraft, 1941, bl & silver (rare), 39", VG+..$2,000.00
Chrysler, Steelcraft, 1941, maroon & wht, 37", G+, A .$1,050.00
Chrysler, Steelcraft, 1941, maroon & wht, 37", rstr, A.$2,200.00
Chrysler, Steelcraft, 1941, maroon & wht, 37", VG+ .$1,500.00
Chrysler Airflow, Skippy, 1937, 46", G.....................$10,000.00

Dick Tracy Car, Garton, 35", restored, A, $500.00. (Photo courtesy Collectors Auctions Services)

Chrysler Convertible, Skippy, 1930s, balloon white-wall disc wheels, 46", restored, A, $2,500.00. (Photo courtesy Randy Inman Auctions)

City Fire Dept Ladder Truck, Murray, 'sad-face' grille, w/2 wooden ladders, 42", rstr, A......................................$425.00

Dodge, Steelcraft, bell on hood, 36", old rpt $1,300.00
Dodge Car, Steelcraft, 1939, 34", rstr, A......................$2,000.00
DPW Dump Truck, AMF, pnt steel, 38", Fair+, A..........$185.00
Earth Mover Car, Murray, 1960s, w/working dump body, 46", rstr $400.00
Fiat Sports Car, Murray, 1961, w/music box radio in plastic dashboard, 34", rstr, A $275.00
Fire Chief Car (Oldsmobile), Steelcraft, 1939, 41", old rpt.$1,400.00
Fire Chief Car (1941 Chrysler), Steelcraft, 39", EX $1,750.00
Fire Chief Car #503, AMF, 34", rstr, A $350.00
Fire Chief Car #6, Gendron, early open wood frame, 42", VG, A $2,600.00
Fire Dept Ladder Company Truck, Garton, 1950s, complete, 46", VG+ $500.00

Columbia 6, Gendron, glass windshield, unused, NM, A, $22,000.00. (Photo courtesy Randy Inman Auctions)

Fire Hose and Ladder Truck, American National, wood fram and body with steel hood, 50", VG, $5,000.00. (Photo courtesy F Inman Auctions)

Comet, Murray, 1950s, 40", rstr..$400.00
Comet Super Sport, Murray, 1949-50, 38", rstr, A..........$950.00
Comet V12 Super Drive, Murray, 37", rstr, A.................$600.00
Commando Biplane, Gendron, trimotor, 36" W, G ..$10,000.00
Corvette (1957), Eska, plastic w/2-speed shaft-drive steel frame, wht w/red trim, 50", VG, A......................................$550.00

Fire Ladder Truck, 1910, open bench seat & curved h open frame, spoke wheels, wood ladders, 80", EX..$3
Ford, Steelcraft, 1930s, w/hood ornament, 36", rstr.......
Franklin, Steelcraft, 54", EX ....$
G-A-R-T-O-N Chain Drive Tractor, 38", rstr, A........
G-Man Radio Cruiser Car, Murray, 35", rstr, A ....
Good Humor Ice Cream Cycle, Murray, 36", rstr, A
Good Humor Ice Cream Cycle, Murray, 36", VG A

Graham, Skippy, gear drive, pneumatic tires, 52", VG original paint with some restoration, $8,500.00. (Photo courtesy Randy Inman Auctions)

Racer, Steelcraft, with electric lights and pontoon wheel covers, 37", restored, $2,500.00. (Photo courtesy Randy Inman Auctions)

Hot Rod, Garton, 35", NM $1,000.00
Hot Rod, Garton, 35", rstr, A $850.00
Indy Racer #3, AMF, 1970s, Apache & Indy decals, 42", rstr, A $350.00
Jolly Roger Boat, Murray, 1962, w/plastic battery-op outboard motor, 38", rstr, A $700.00
Jr Streamliner (1937), Steelcraft, 40", G $1,800.00
Kidillac, Garton, 1952, 45", rstr, A $900.00
LaSalle (1927), American National, EX $5,000.00
Leeway Flyer Train, wood & steel, 44", VG $400.00
Lincoln Zephyr, Steelcraft, 1940s, w/lights, hood ornament & bumper, 43", G $1,000.00
Looney Tunes Cartoon Car, rstr, A $300.00
Mack Fire Truck, Steelcraft, complete, 45", rpt, A $500.00
Mack Playboy Trucking Co Dump Truck, Steelcraft, 46", older rpt...$350.00
Mack Playboy Trucking Co Dump Truck, Steelcraft, 46", rstr, A $1,265.00
Murray Diesel 2 Ton Trac, 40", G+, A $75.00
Navy Patrol Plane, Murray-Otto Mfg Co, 50", G+, A....$850.00
Oldsmobile (1939), Steelcraft, 42", VG, A $2,750.00
Oldsmobile see also Fire Chief Car
Packard, American National, 1920s, 45", rstr $2,500.00
Packard, contemporary model fashioned after the 1920s-30s American National, opening trunk & driver's door, 64", New, A $2,860.00
Packard, Gendron, EX, A $12,650.00
Packard, Gendron, VG, A $7,700.00
Pierce-Arrow, Steelcraft, 1930s, 43", Fair, A $1,320.00
Pioneer Willy's Knight Car, Gendron, 1920s, 48", G, A..$7,700.00
Playboy Trucking Co, see Mack Playboy Trucking Co.
Police Radar Patrol Cycle, Murray, chain drive, 36", G, A...$415.00
Pontiac, Murray, 1949, 36", rstr, A $650.00
Pontiac, Steelcraft, 1941, bl & wht w/red hubs (rare), 37", EX, A...$1,320.00
Pontiac, Steelcraft, 1941, maroon & wht w/wht hubs, 37", VG+ A...$600.00
Pursuit Army Airplane, Murray, 1949-50, 45", rstr, A..$2,200.00
Racer, American National, 34", VG $775.00

Racer, Tri-Ang, barrel-back styling w/detailed side exhaust, 48", G, A $360.00
Racer #35, BMC, 1940s, 40", rstr, A $1,500.00
Racer #6 (Ferrari Style), Strombecker, plastic w/chrome trim, 41", rstr, A $470.00
Racer #8, Steelcraft, boat-tail styling w/exhaust graphics on sides, 45", rstr, A $600.00
Roadster, Chandler, 1926, pnt steel, 46", VG+ (rstr)..$1,500.00
Roadster, Garton, 1950s, full-fendered, artillery wheels, 34", old rpt, A $190.00
Roadster, Steelcraft, 44", rstr, A $775.00
Safari Car, AMF, 1970s, 40", VG+, A $330.00
Sand & Gravel Dump Truck, Murray, 1949-50, rstr, A ..$425.00
Skippy Racer, contemporary 1930s styling w/pontoon fenders, 45", New, A $1,155.00
Sky Lark (Buick), Garton, AMF, 33", rstr, A $425.00
Speedway Pace Car, Murray, 1960s, 34", rstr, A............$500.00
Studebaker Lark NYC Checker Cab, 35", rstr, A $260.00
Tee Bird, Murray, 1960s, 31", rstr, A $350.00

Studebaker, American National, with hood ornament and spot light mounted to running board, unusual cowl moldings, 54", G+, $12,000.00. (Photo courtesy Randy Inman Auctions)

Tin Lizzie, Garton, 1950s, 34", rstr, A $650.00
Torpedo, Murray, 1940s, 39", Fair+, A $415.00
Tow-All 24 Hour Service Tow Truck, AMF, 1970s, 42", rstr,
    A...$275.00
US Mail/Air Mail GMC Truck No 7, AMF, 1959, 41", rstr,
    A...$800.00
USAF Jeep, Garton, 1965, 40", EX, A $350.00
Westcott, American National, full-fendered, CI hood ornament,
    brake lever & opening trunk, 48", G $4,600.00
Western Flyer Chain Drive Tractor, 35", rstr, A $275.00

Woody, Garton, 1930s, 48", restored, $3,500.00. (Photo courtesy Frank's Antiques)

ELECTRIC CARS

Ferrari 250 GT Testora (1960s), hammered aluminum body, rub-
    ber spoke wheels, 84", rstr, A $1,100.00
Grand Prix Racer (1920s-30s), Salmson, rubber tires w/spoke
    wheels, 77", old rstr, A $17,600.00

**Packard Roadster, American National, 1920s, with original
canvas top, complete and working, 70", EX, $39,000.00.** (Photo courtesy Randy Inman Auctions)

Power Drivers Batmobile, SLM Inc, 1992, steel chassis w/blk
    plastic body, 54", unassembled, MIB (NOS), A $120.00
4.5 Liter Lower Bently, scalloped windshield, orig blk pnt,
    #1 decal & British flag on door, spoke wheels, 80",
    VG+, A $6,050.00

GAS POWERED

**Mustang Convertible, go-cart type gas engine, fiberglass body
with pneumatic tires, two fold-down front seats, 72", VG+,
$1,500.00.** (Photo courtesy Noel Barrett Auctions)

WAGONS

Buckboard Wagon, mk Acme Milk Co, tin & wood w/spoke
    wheels, 36", w/hdl, G, A...$460.00
Buckboard Wagon, Weber, pnt wood w/bench seat, 2 lg back spoke
    wheels w/2 sm front wheels, pull hdl, 41" L, EX, A ..$1,200.00
Express Wagon, pnt tin w/Express stenciled on sides, 2 sm
    front spoke wheels & 2 lg back spoke wheels, wood hdl,
    32", EX...$300.00
Good-Will Soap, wood w/blk stenciling & red trim, wood
    spoke wheels w/metal rims, 16x18x33" (not counting
    hdl), EX, A $1,000.00

Hy-Speed Wagon, with wheel covers, 24", EX, $500.00. (Photo courtesy Collectors Auction Services)

Katy Flyer, red-pnt wood w/decals, rubber tires w/spoke wheels,
    wood hdl, 36", VG, A..$400.00
Spee-Dee Air Flo, rstr, A $275.00
Streak-O-Lite, 1940s, pressed steel, Air-Flo styling w/headlights,
    41", Fair+, A..$120.00
The Boss, wood w/stamped name, spoke wheels, hdl, ca 1915,
    10x14½x21", VG+ $275.00
Thunderbolt, pnt pressed steel, wht lettering on red, rubber tires,
    36", EX, A $80.00

Walt Disney's Dry Gulch Western Prairie Wagon, tin w/plastic cover, 29", G, A $110.00
Ward's Flyer, w/handrails & front bumper, 39", rstr, A ...$185.00

MISCELLANEOUS

Auto Wheel Scooter, 1920s, straight grip hdl, support stand on back wheel, 29", G+, A $65.00
Bronco, Mobo, 1940s, saddled horse, 26", rstr, A $275.00

Gas Pump, JWK Industries, unpainted pressed steel with Texaco Sky Chief label, 30", VG, $360.00; Go/Stop Traffic Sign, Gendron, pressed steel, free-standing with round base, 34", VG+, $750.00. (Photo courtesy Randy Inman Auctions)

Horse-Drawn Cart, Mobo, 1940s, metal w/wooden slats, 35", rstr, A $275.00
Horse-Drawn Chariot, Mobo, 1940s, 34", orig pnt, VG, A..$150.00
Merri-Go-Galloper, pnt wood & steel, 26", G, A $375.00
Scooter, 1920s, wooden grip hdl & footrest, foot-op brake, rpt, 38" L, A $120.00
Traffic Sign, Stop/Go on pole w/rnd base, pressed steel, 34", VG+ $750.00
Trigger (Horse) Riding Toy, wooden horse head w/image of Trigger on wooden arched board w/seat & 4 wheels, 42", Fair+, A $75.00
V-Room X-15 3-Wheeler, Mattel, 34", orig pnt, VG, A..$110.00

Penny Toys

Penny toys were around as early as the late 1800s and as late as the 1920s. Many were made in Germany, but some were made in France as well. With few exceptions, they ranged in size from 5" on down; some had moving parts, and a few had clockwork

mechanisms. Though many were unmarked, you'll sometimes find them signed 'Kellermann,' 'Meier,' 'Fischer,' or 'Distler,' or carrying an embossed company logo such as the 'dog and cart' emblem. They were made of lithographed tin with exquisite detailing — imagine an entire carousel less than 2½" tall. Because of a recent surge in collector interest, many have been crossing the auction block of some of the country's large galleries. Our values are prices realized at several of these auctions.

Airplane, Kellermann, open cockpit w/pilot, 4½", EX+, A .$700.00
Airplane Spiral Toy, Einfalt/Germany, 6½", EX, A $440.00
Auto w/Driver, Meier, early open style w/top down, 2 lg & 2 sm spoke wheels, 3½", VG+, A $500.00
Billiards Player, Kellermann, man dressed in tails w/cue stick ready to play at table, 4", VG, A $100.00
Bleriotplane (Tip Top Series), Distler, 3", G+, A $500.00
Boat w/Cabin & Sailor at Wheel, Meier, w/flag & disk wheels, 4½", EX, A $300.00

Boxers (Two) on Rectangular Base, Meier, 4" long, VG+, A, $1,320.00. (Photo courtesy Noel Barrett Auctions)

Boy & Rabbit in Rocking Chair, Meier, 2¾", VG, A.....$465.00
Boy on Rocking Horse, Meier, 3¼", EX, A....................$825.00
Butterfly on Toadstool, Meier, 1¾", VG, A $360.00

Clowns Playing Wheelbarrow, Meier, 3", VG+, A, $2,300.00.

(Photo courtesy Noel Barrett Auctions)

Butterfly on Toadstool w/Boy Golfer, Fischer, 4", VG+, A .$580.00
Carousel, Meier, riders on horses, 2½", EX, A $520.00
Child in Highchair, Fischer, foldable chair & table w/wheels, 4", EX+, A...$350.00
Circus Elephant, clicker, 2½", EX+, A $330.00
Cito Tricar, Kellermann, 3¾", EX, A.............................$575.00
Clock Under Glass Dome, 2", G, A $60.00
Clown & Lady on Mule, 3½", EX, A $550.00
Clown Beating Golliwog, clicker, 3¾", EX, A...............$110.00
Coppers (2) w/Barrel, dual action, 4", EX, A.................$250.00
Cow on Wheeled Platform, Meier, 3¼", EX, A..............$300.00
Delivery Van #GF 91, enclosed w/open windows, spoke wheels, w/driver, 5⅛", VG, A $275.00
Delivery Van #245, Fischer, roof over open front w/driver, spoke wheels, 3½", EX, A...$385.00
Dirigible, Meier, w/2 top props, 4½", VG+, A $500.00
Dog (Lg) on Wheeled Platform, Meier, 3¼", EX, A.......$360.00
Dog (Sm) on Wheeled Platform, Meier, 3", EX, A.........$275.00
Equestrians (3), Meier, 4" L, VG+, A $415.00
Express Cycle w/Driver, Meier, 3", A $880.00
Felix the Cat Dancer, Distler, 3½", EX, A...................$3,520.00
Felix the Cat Music Box, rnd, plink-plunk music, 2", EX, A...$330.00
Fire Hose Reel Truck, Meier, w/3 figures, 3½", VG+, A..$155.00
Fire Ladder Truck, Meier, 3½", VG+, A $175.00
Fire Ladder Truck, open w/overhead ladder, NP bumpers & fenders, w/5 seated firemen, clockwork, 4¼", VG, A $130.00
Fire Pumper Truck, Meier, #P-208, 3½", VG, A.............$130.00
Fire Water Tank Truck, Meier, 3½", VG+, A $165.00
Flying Hollander, Meier, 3¼", EX, A $875.00
Flying Swing Ride, Distler, ftd base, 3¼", VG+, A.........$165.00
Frog w/Butterfly on Box, Fischer, 3", EX, A................$1,540.00
Girl & Doll in Rocking Chair, Meier, 3", G+, A $200.00
Girl at School Desk, Meier, 2½", EXIB, A $700.00
Gnome on Egg w/Rabbit, Meier, 3", VG+, A...............$1,760.00
Gondola, inertia drive, 4½", G, A $660.00

Helicopter, open cockpit w/pilot, overhead props & nose prop, clockwork, 3¼", EX, A...$600.00
Horse-Drawn Carriage, Meier, driver on high open seat w/facing passenger seats, spoke wheels, single horse, 5", EX, A...$300.00
Horse-Drawn Express Wagon, w/driver, 4½", VG+, A...$140.00
Horse-Drawn Military Postal Van, Meier, spoke wheels, soldier mounted on 1 of 2 horses, 4½", EX, A.....................$250.00
Horse-Drawn 2-Wheeled Cart w/Driver, Meier, 3¾", EX, A...$300.00
Limousine, roof over open front w/driver, enclosed passenger cab w/cut-out windows, spoke wheels, 4", EX, A $220.00
Luxury Coupe, Fischer, simulated soft top w/cut-out windows, extended bumpers, disk wheels, 5½", EX, A............$415.00
Man in Sailboat, Meier, on platform w/4 lg metal spoke wheels, articulated action, 3", NM, A.................................$1,200.00
Merry-Go-Round, Meier, 2 figures on carousel animals under canopy on ftd base, 3x2", G, A.................................$450.00
Meteor Launch w/Pilot, Meier, 4¾", VG, A...................$325.00
Monkey Climbing Pole, Distler, 1921, driven by internal lead weight, 7", EX $235.00
Motorcycle w/Enclosed Sidecar, passenger behind driver (not in sidecar), gun in sidecar window, 3¼", EX, A...........$300.00
Motorcycle w/Sidecar, Driver & Passenger, Distler, 3¼", VG, A..$1,100.00
Motorcycle w/Sidecar & Driver, Kellermann, w/up & sparkling action, 3¾", EX, A...$330.00
Noah's Ark, roof opens, 4¾", very scarce, EX, A $1,375.00
Ocean Liner, Fischer, 2 stacks, 2 spoke wheels w/sm front wheel, 4½", EX, A $200.00
Passenger Ship, Distler, 5", VG, A $175.00
Passenger Ship, Fischer, 4½", VG+, A...........................$200.00
Passenger Ship, Meier, 4½", G+, A...............................$165.00
Punch & Judy Candy Box, 3", VG, A............................$520.00
Rabbit on Egg on 4-wheeled Platform, Meier, 3", G+, A...$550.00
Rabbits (2) Riding Mother Rabbit, Meier, rocks back & forth on ftd base, 3½", EX, A $875.00

Lady Pushing Child in Sled, 3" long, VG+, A, $1,760.00.
(Photo courtesy Noel Barrett Auctions)

Rabbits (Two) Riding Mother Rabbit, Meier, on four-wheeled base, 2¾", EX, A, $1,150.00. (Photo courtesy Noel Barrett Auctions)

Race Car #10 w/Driver, Distler, 4", VG+, A $800.00
Race Car w/Driver, Distler, 2½", EX, A $935.00
Race Car w/Driver, JVF, red, 3½", EX+, A $1,050.00
Removing & Warehousing Wagon, Meier, 3½", VG+,
    A $200.00
Runabout, open w/drivers in 2 front seats, spoke wheels, rear fly
    wheel, 4", VG, A $220.00
Saloon Car, Fischer, roof over open front w/driver, spoke wheels,
    4⅛", EX, A $165.00
Speedboat w/Lady Driver, Meier, 5", VG+, A $600.00
Stake Truck, Fischer, roof over open cab w/driver, lithoed stake
    bed, spoke wheels, 4", EX, A $250.00
Stake Truck, Meier, open w/driver at center steering wheel,
    spoke wheels, 3¼", EX, A $220.00
Steer on Wheeled Platform, Meier, w/bell collar, 3¼", EX, A .$330.00
Sulky w/Horse & Driver, 4", VG+, A $250.00
Sulky w/Ostrich & Driver, 3½", VG+, A $415.00
Swiss Chalet Barometer Bank, 2¼", EX, A $550.00
Tanker Truck, Gely/Germany, NP running boards &
    bumpers, driver lithoed in door window, disk wheels,
    5¼", VG, A $275.00
Taxi, Rossignol/France, open front w/driver, enclosed passenger
    compartment, spoke wheels, fly wheel, 3½", EX, A .$440.00
Taxi Coach, Meier, driver on open bench seat, enclosed passen-
    ger cab w/lithoed door window, 3¼", EX, A $550.00
Touring Car, open w/full running boards, spoke wheels, w/driver,
    Kellermann, 5", EX, A $935.00
Train, celebrates Nürnberg Line 1835-1935, rnd lithoed
    base, box unfolds to reveal village, w/up, KB, 3" dia,
    EXIB, A $880.00

Triumph Motorcycle, Meier, 2¾", EX, A, $1,200.00. (Photo cour-
tesy Noel Barrett Auctions)

Trolley, Kellermann, electric trolley wire on top, windows
    w/lithoed passengers, 3⅛", EX, A $550.00
Velocette Motorcycle, Paya, 4", VG+, A $470.00
Wall Telephone, Meier, 4¾", EX, A $165.00
Zeppelin in Hangar, Meier, lever action, 2¾", VG+,
    A $2,420.00

Pez Dispensers

Pez was originally designed as a breath mint for smokers, but
by the '50s kids were the target market, and the candies were
packaged in the dispensers that we all know and love today.
There is already more than three hundred variations to collect,
and more arrive on the supermarket shelves every day. Though
early on collectors seemed to prefer the dispensers without feet,
that attitude has changed, and now it's the character head they
concentrate on. Feet were added in 1987, so if you were to limit
yourself to only 'feetless' dispensers, your collection would be far
from complete. Some dispensers have variations in color and
design that can influence their values. Don't buy any that are
damaged, incomplete, or that have been tampered with in any
way; those are nearly worthless. For more information refer to *A
Pictorial Guide to Plastic Candy Dispensers Featuring Pez* by David
Welch and *Collecting Toys #6* by Richard O'Brien. Values are for
mint-condition dispensers unless noted otherwise.

Advisor: Richard Belyski (B1)

Aardvark, w/ft $5.00
Angel, no ft $50.00
Arlene, w/ft, pk, from $3 to $5.00
Asterix Line, Asterix, Obelix, Roman or Getafix, ea from $4
    to $6.00
Baloo, w/ft $20.00
Bambi, no ft $50.00
Barney Bear, no ft $40.00
Barney Bear, w/ft $30.00
Baseball Glove, no ft $150.00
Batgirl, no ft, soft head $125.00
Batman, no ft $10.00
Batman, no ft, w/cape $100.00
Batman, w/ft, bl or blk, ea from $3 to $5.00
Betsy Ross, no ft $150.00
Bouncer Beagle, w/ft $6.00
Boy, w/ft, brn hair $3.00
Bozo, no ft, diecut $175.00
Bubble Man, w/ft $5.00
Bubble Man, w/ft, neon hat $6.00
Bugs Bunny, no ft $15.00
Bugs Bunny, w/ft, from $1 to $3.00
Bullwinkle, no ft $275.00
Candy Shooter, red & wht, w/candy & gun license, unused .$125.00
Captain America, no ft $100.00
Captain Hook, no ft $85.00
Casper, no ft $175.00
Charlie Brown, w/ft, from $1 to $3.00
Charlie Brown, w/ft & tongue $20.00
Chicago Cubs 2000, Charlie Brown in pkg w/commemorative card .$30.00
Chick, w/ft, from $1 to $3.00
Chick in Egg, no ft $15.00
Chick in Egg, no ft, w/hair $125.00
Chip, w/ft $45.00
Clown, w/ft, whistle head $6.00
Clown w/Collar, no ft $65.00

Donald Duck, no feet, from $10.00 to $15.00; Mickey Mouse, no feet, removable nose or cast nose, each from $10.00 to $15.00.

Cockatoo, no ft, bl face, red beak $60.00
Cool Cat, w/ft $75.00
Cow (A or B), no ft, bl, ea, from $80 to $90.00
Creature From the Black Lagoon, no ft......................$275.00
Crocodile, no ft...$95.00
Crystal Hearts, eBay, limited edition, set of 4, ea............$10.00
Daffy Duck, no ft...$15.00
Daffy Duck, w/ft, from $1 to $3.00
Dalmatian Pup, w/ft...$50.00
Daniel Boone, no ft $175.00
Dino, w/ft, purple, from $1 to $3.00
Dinosaur, w/ft, 4 different, ea from $1 to $3.00
Doctor, no ft..$200.00
Donald Duck, no ft, diecut $150.00
Donald Duck, no ft, from $10 to $15.00
Donald Duck's Nephew, no ft $30.00
Donald Duck's Nephew, w/ft, gr, bl or red hat, ea $10.00
Donkey, w/ft, whistle head..$6.00
Droopy Dog (A), no ft, plastic swivel ears $25.00
Droopy Dog (B), w/ft, pnt ears, MIP...............................$6.00
Duck Tales, any character, w/ft, ea................................$6.00
Dumbo, w/ft, bl head..$25.00

Eerie Spectres, Air Spirit, Diabolic, or Zombie (not shown), no feet, each $200.00.

Elephant, no ft, orange & bl, flat hat $85.00
Fat-Ears Rabbit, no ft, pk head $20.00
Fat-Ears Rabbit, no ft, yel head......................................$15.00
Fireman, no ft..$95.00
Fishman, no ft, gr $185.00
Foghorn Leghorn, w/ft $65.00
Football Player $175.00
Fozzie Bear, w/ft, from $1 to $3.00
Frankenstein, no ft..$250.00
Fred Flintstone, w/ft, from $1 to $3.00

Frog, w/ft, whistle head..$40.00
Garfield, w/ft, orange w/gr hat, from $1 to $3.00
Garfield, w/ft, teeth, from $1 to $3.00
Garfield, w/ft, visor, from $1 to $3.00
Gargamel, w/ft..$5.00
Ghosts (Glowing), Happy Henry, Naughty Neil or Slimy Sid,
    ea..$1.00
Ghosts (Non-Glowing), Happy Henry, Naughty Neil or Slimy
    Sid, ea...$2.00
Girl, w/ft, yel hair..$3.00
Gonzo, w/ft, from $1 to $3.00
Goofy, no ft, ea..$10.00
Gorilla, no ft, blk head...$80.00
Green Hornet, 1960s, from $200 to $250.00
Gyro Gearloose, w/ft...$6.00
Henry Hawk, no ft...$65.00
Hulk, no ft, dk gr..$60.00
Hulk, no ft, lt gr, remake..$3.00
Indian, w/ft, whistle head......................................$20.00
Indian Brave, no ft, reddish..................................$115.00
Indian Chief, no ft, yel headdress..........................$90.00
Indian Maiden, no ft..$140.00
Inspector Clouseau, w/ft...$5.00
Jerry Mouse, w/ft, plastic face $15.00
Jerry Mouse, w/ft, pnt face $6.00
Jiminy Cricket, no ft..$175.00
Joker (Batman), no ft, soft head...........................$200.00
Jungle Mission, interactive dispenser........................$3.00
Kermit the Frog, w/ft, red, from $1 to $3.00
Knight, no ft..$250.00
Koala, w/ft, whistle head.......................................$40.00
Krazy Animals, Blinky Bill, Lion, Hippo, Elephant or Gator, ea,
    from $4 to $6.00
Lamb, no ft..$15.00
Lamb, w/ft, from $1 to $3.00
Lamb, w/ft, whistle head..$20.00
Lazy Garfield, w/ft...$5.00
Li'l Bad Wolf, w/ft..$20.00
Lion w/Crown, no ft...$100.00
Lion's Club Lion, minimum value........................$2,000.00
Lucy, w/ft, from $1 to $3.00
Make-A-Face, works like Mr Potato Head $2,500.00
Mary Poppins, no ft...$700.00
Merlin Mouse, w/ft...$15.00
Merry Melody Makers, rhino, donkey, panda, parrot, clown, tiger
    or penguin, w/ft, MOC, ea................................$6.00
Mexican, no ft..$250.00
Mickey Mouse, w/ft, from $1 to $3.00
Mimic Monkey (monkey w/ball cap), no ft, several colors, ea.$40.00
Miss Piggy, w/ft, ea from $1 to................................$3.00
Miss Piggy, w/ft, eyelashes....................................$15.00
Monkey Sailor, no ft, w/wht cap.............................$50.00
Mowgli, w/ft...$15.00
Mr Ugly, no ft..$45.00
Muscle Mouse (gray Jerry), w/ft, plastic nose $15.00
Nermal, w/ft, gray..$3.00
Nintendo, Diddy Dong, Koopa Trooper, Mario, Yoshi, ea from
    $4 to $6.00

Nurse, no ft, brn hair...$175.00
Octopus, no ft, blk...$85.00
Odie, w/ft..$5.00
Olive Oyl, no ft...$175.00
Panda, no ft, diecut eyes.......................................$20.00
Panda, w/ft, remake, from $1 to $3.00
Panda, w/ft, whistle head..$6.00
Papa Smurf, w/ft, red..$6.00
Parrot, w/ft, whistle head...$6.00
Pebbles Flintstone, w/ft, from $1 to $3.00
Penguin, w/ft, whistle head......................................$6.00
Penguin (Batman), no ft, soft head........................$175.00
Peter Pez (A), no ft...$65.00
Peter Pez (B & C), w/ft, from $1 to $3.00
Pilgrim, no ft..$150.00
Pink Panther, w/ft...$5.00
Pinocchio, no ft..$150.00
Pirate, no ft..$50.00
Pluto, no ft..$10.00
Pluto, no ft, red..$10.00
Pluto, w/ft, from $1 to $3.00
Pokemon (non-US), Kottins, Meowth, Mew, Pikachu or Psy-
    duck, ea from $5 to $10.00
Policeman, no ft..$55.00
Popeye (B), no ft...$115.00
Popeye (C), no ft, w/removable pipe......................$110.00
Practical Pig (B), no ft..$30.00
Psychedelic Eye, no ft..$250.00
Psychedelic Eye, remake, blk or pk, MOC, ea............$20.00
Psychedelic Flower, no ft......................................$300.00
Pumpkin (A), no ft, from $10 to $15.00
Pumpkin (B), w/ft, from $1 to..................................$3.00
Raven, no ft, yel beak...$70.00
Rhino, w/ft, whistle head...$6.00
Ringmaster, no ft...$275.00
Road Runner, no ft...$20.00
Road Runner, w/ft...$15.00
Rooster, w/ft, whistle head.....................................$35.00
Rooster, w/ft, wht or yel head, ea...........................$30.00
Rudolph, no ft..$50.00
Santa Claus, w/ft, from $1 to $3.00
Santa Claus (A), no ft, steel pin............................$125.00
Santa Claus (B), no ft..$125.00
Santa Claus (C), no ft, from $5 to..........................$15.00
Santa Claus (C), w/ft, B1, from $1 to $3.00
Scrooge McDuck (A), no ft....................................$35.00
Scrooge McDuck (B), w/ft..$6.00
Sheik, no ft..$55.00
Skull (A), no ft, from $5 to $10.00
Skull (B), w/ft, from $1 to $3.00
Smurf, w/ft...$5.00
Smurfette, w/ft...$5.00
Snoopy, w/ft, from $1 to $3.00
Snow White, no ft..$175.00
Snowman (A), no ft...$10.00
Snowman (B), w/ft, from $1 to $5.00
Space Trooper Robot, no ft, full body....................$250.00
Spaceman, no ft..$200.00

Speedy Gonzales (A), w/ft..$15.00
Speedy Gonzales (B), no ft, from $1 to.....................$3.00
Spider-Man, no ft, from $10 to.................................$15.00
Spider-Man, w/ft, from $1 to.....................................$3.00
Spike, w/ft, B1...$6.00
Star Wars, Boba Fett, Ewok, Luke Skywalker or Princess Leia, ea
    from $1 to..$3.00
Star Wars, C3PO, Chewbacca, Darth Vader or Stormtrooper, ea
    from $1 to..$3.00
Sylvester (A), w/ft, cream or wht whiskers, ea...................$5.00
Sylvester (B), w/ft, from $1 to.................................$3.00
Teenage Mutant Ninja Turtles, 8 different, w/ft, ea from $1
    to..$3.00
Thor, no ft..$275.00
Thumper, w/ft, no copyright..................................$45.00
Tiger, w/ft, whistle head $6.00
Tinkerbell, no ft...$275.00
Tom, no ft..$35.00
Tom, w/ft, plastic face...$15.00
Tom, w/ft, pnt face..$6.00
Truck, many variations, ea, minimum value...................$1.00
Tweety Bird, no ft..$10.00
Tweety Bird, w/ft, from $1 to...................................$3.00
Tyke, w/ft..$15.00

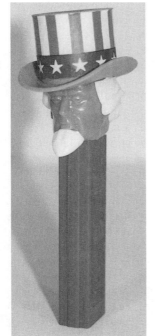

Uncle Sam, no feet, $175.00.

Valentine Heart, B1, from $1 to...$3.00
Wal-Mart Smiley Pez, ea from $1 to....................................$2.00
Whistle, w/ft, from $1 to...$3.00
Wile E Coyote, w/ft..$60.00
Winnie the Pooh (A), w/ft...$75.00
Winnie the Pooh (B), Eeyore, Piglet, Pooh or Tigger, ea from $1
    to $2.00
Witch, 3-pc, no ft..$10.00
Wolfman, no ft...$300.00
Wonder Woman, no ft, soft head $175.00

Wonder Woman, w/ft, from $1 to...$3.00
Woodstock, w/ft, from $1 to...$3.00
Woodstock, w/ft, pnt feathers...$15.00
Yappy Dog, no ft, orange or gr, ea.....................................$70.00
Yosemite Sam, w/ft, from $1 to...$3.00
Zorro...$75.00

MISCELLANEOUS

Bank, truck #1, metal $200.00
Bank, truck #2, metal...$40.00
Body Parts, fit over stem of dispenser & make it look like a per-
    son, many variations, ea..$1.00
Bracelet, pk..$5.00
Bubble Wand..$6.00
Clicker, US Zone Germany, 1950, litho tin, 3½", NM ..$300.00
Clicker, 1960s, metal, 2", EX, N2.......................................$45.00
Coin Plate...$15.00
Coloring Book, Safety #2, non-English, B1.......................$15.00
Power Pez, rnd mechanical dispenser, B1 ....$5.00
Puzzle, Ceaco, 550 pcs, MIB..$30.00
Puzzle, Springbok/Hallmark, 500 pcs................................$15.00
Refrigerator Magnet Set..$10.00
Snow Dome, Bride & Groom, 4½", M.................................$20.00
Snow Dome, ringmaster & elephant, M.............................$20.00
Tin, Pez Specials, stars & lines on checked background, gold col-
    ors, 2½x4½", rare, EX $225.00
Toy Car, Johnny Lightning Psychedelic Eye racer $20.00
Toy Car, Johnny Lightning Racing Dreams PEZ racer......$10.00
Watch, pk face w/yel band or yel face w/bl band, ea.........$10.00
Watch, Psychedelic Hand..$10.00
Yo-yo, 1950s, litho metal w/peppermint pkg, rare, NM..$300.00

Pin-Back Buttons

Pin-back buttons produced up to the early 1920s were made with a celluloid covering. After that time, a large number of buttons were lithographed on tin; these are referred to as tin 'lithos.'

Character and toy-related buttons represent a popular collecting field. There are countless categories to base a collection on. Buttons were given out at stores and theatres, offered as premiums, attached to dolls or received with a club membership.

In the late '40s and into the '50s, some cereal companies packed one in each box of their product. Quaker Puffed Oats offered a series of movie star pin-backs, but probably the best known are Kellogg's Pep Pins. There were eighty-six in all, so theoretically if you wanted the whole series as Kellogg hoped you would, you'd have to buy at least that many boxes of their cereal. Pep pins came in five sets, the first in 1945, three more in 1946, and the last in 1947. They were printed with full-color lithographs of comic characters licensed by King Features and Famous Artists — Maggie and Jiggs, the Winkles, and Dagwood and Blondie, for instance. Superman, the only D.C. Comics character, was included in each set. Most Pep pins range in value from $12.00 to $25.00 in NM/M condition, but some sell for much more.

Nearly all pin-backs are collectible. Be sure that you buy only buttons with well-centered designs, well-aligned colors, no fading or yellowing, no spots or stains, and no cracks, splits, or dents. In the listings that follow, sizes are approximate.

Advisors: Michael and Polly McQuillen (M11)

Other Sources: C10, M8, N2

See also Political; Premiums; Sporting Collectibles.

Always Yours Elvis, image & lettering on red, 7/8", NM....$25.00
Breathless Mahoney, image & lettering on red, M...........$15.00
Buck Rogers in the 25th Century, EX, C10 ....$115.00
Buck Rogers/Buffalo Evening News, contest button w/number & Buck Rogers image, Allied Printing, 1930s, 1¼", EX .$175.00
Buster Brown Bread, Buster & Tige flanking bread ad encircled by name, paper ad on back, 1920s, 1½", NM+ $50.00
Captain Marvel Club, shows Captain Marvel facing left w/chest out, VG, C10 ....$60.00
Captain Marvel Club, shows Captain Marvel throwing plane, EX, C10 ....$175.00
Circus Fantasy '86 (Disneyland), 3", M, M8 ....$6.00
Clutch Cargo Adventure Club/Batterwhipped Sunbeam Bread, name-tag center, red & wht litho, 1950s-60s, 2¼", rare, EX+ $65.00
Dale Evans, blk & wht photo on gr, 1950s, 1½" dia, EX ..$40.00
Dick Tracy Chicago Tribune, EX, C10 ....$15.00
Electrical Parade/Farewell Season (Disney), red lights flash around logo, 1996, 3½", MIP $10.00
Huckleberry Hound for President, lettering around head image on yel, 3", EX $25.00
I Am a Purple People Eater, lettering around character & musical notes, metal, purple on wht, 1950s, 3½", NM+ ...$30.00

I Like the Beatles, flashes to head images, EX+, $35.00.

I'm Bugs About the Beatles, 3½", rare, NM.....................$35.00
Lion King, 1993, rectangular, NM.................................$4.00
Mickey Mouse Globe Trotters Member/I Eat Peter Pan Bread, standing figure w/suitcase in center, 1930s, 1¼", NM+ .$60.00
Monkees, cartoon image on wht, 1967, 1", M...................$10.00
Official Batman Club, yel w/bat symbol in center, oval, 2½", NM+..$8.00

Mickey Mouse Club, black and white on orange, 1928 – 30, 1¼", M, $100.00.

Penney's Back to School Days With Popeye, image of Popeye w/school books, 1935, 1", VG $15.00
Roy Rogers King of the Cowboys, head image encircled by name & phrase, Post Grape-Nuts, 1953, EX.....................$15.00
Saturday Chicago American/10 Pages of Comics, head image of Buck Rogers in center, Greenback Co, 1934, 1⅛", VG.$165.00
Sky King/Safety Is No Accident, lettering around bust image, 1950s, 1¼", EX $50.00
Space Rangers, half-image of Space Ranger waving, NM, A .$42.00
Space Rangers, 3 space figures on deck of spacecraft, NM, A.$18.00
Spider-Man/Official Member Super Hero Club, Button World, 1966, 3", MIP..$50.00
Sputnik Space Dog, image of dog w/wearing space helmet, EX, A $12.00
Superman Muscle Building Club, 1½" dia, G, C10 ....$75.00
Superman-Tim, profile image, red, wht & bl, EX, A........$15.00

Tarzan Club, 1¾" oval, NM, $100.00.

Teenage Mutant Ninja Turtles, 1990, 6", EX, N2 ....$10.00
Yogi Bear for President, red, wht & bl, 1964, 3", EX........$50.00
30th Year Official Birthday Party (Disneyland), 1985, 3", M, M8 ....$5.00

KELLOGG'S PEP PINS

BO Plenty, NM $30.00
Corky, NM $16.00
Dagwood, NM $30.00
Dick Tracy, NM..$30.00
Fat Stuff, NM $15.00
Felix the Cat, NM...$60.00
Flash Gordon, NM $25.00
Flat Top, NM $23.00
Goofy, NM $10.00
Gravel Gertie, NM $15.00
Harold Teen, NM $15.00
Inspector, NM $12.50
Jiggs, NM...$25.00
Judy, NM $10.00

Kayo, NM, $12.00.

Little King, NM $15.00
Little Moose, NM $15.00
Maggie, NM $25.00
Mama De Stross, NM..$30.00
Mama Katzenjammer, NM..................................$25.00
Mamie, NM...$15.00
Moon Mullins, NM $6.00
Olive Oyl, NM $18.00
Orphan Annie, NM $25.00
Pat Patton, NM..$10.00
Perry Winkle, NM $15.00
Phantom, NM $60.00
Pop Jenks, NM $15.00
Popeye, NM $30.00
Rip Winkle, NM $20.00
Skeezix, NM...$15.00
Superman, NM $25.00
Toots, NM $15.00
Uncle Walt, NM $20.00
Uncle Willie, NM $12.50
Winkle Twins, NM $25.00
Winnie Winkle, NM..$15.00

Plastic Figures

Plastic figures were made by many toy companies. They were first boxed with playsets, but in the early '50s, some became available individually. Marx was the first company to offer single figures (at 10¢ each), and even some cereal companies included one in boxes of their product. (Kellogg offered a series of 16 54mm Historic Warriors, and Nabisco had a line of ten dinosaurs in marbleized, primary colors.) Virtually every type of man and beast has been modeled in plastic; today some have become very collectible and expensive. There are a lot of factors you'll need to be aware of to be a wise buyer. For instance, Marx made cowboys during the mid-'60s in a flat finish, and these are much harder to find and more valuable than the later figures with a waxy finish. Marvel Super Heroes in the fluorescent hues are worth about half as much as the earlier, light gray issue. Beware that Internet sales may cause values to change greatly.

Because of limited space, it isn't possible to evaluate more than a representative few of these plastic figures in a general price guide, so if you would like to learn more about them, we recommend *Geppert's Guide* by Tim Geppert.

See also Clubs, Newsletters, and Other Publications for information concerning *Prehistoric Times* magazine for dinosaur figure collectors, published by Mike Fredericks.

Note: All listings below are figures by Marx unless noted otherwise.

Advisor: Mike Fredericks (F4)

See also Playsets.

ACTION AND ADVENTURE

Apollo Astronaut Explorers, set of 8 in 7 poses, 54mm, orange, NM..$33.00
Apollo Astronaut Moon Walking, 6", lt bl, EX..................$6.50
Apollo Astronaut w/American Flag, 6", wht, NM............$14.50
Ben Hur, set of 16, 54mm, NM......................................$70.00
Captain Video, various poses and colors, 4", Lido, 1950s, ea.$25.00
Deep Sea Diver, Ideal, 3" $35.00
Fox Hunt, fox running, 60mm, NM $10.00
Fox Hunt, hound sniffing, 60mm, NM.............................$10.00
Man From UNCLE, Alexander Waverly, 6", steel bl, NM, from $12 to $20.00

Man From UNCLE, THRUSH Officer, 5", NM, $18.00.

Man From UNCLE, Illya Kuryakin, 6", steel bl, NM, from $12 to $20.00

Man From UNCLE, Illya Kuryakin or Napoleon Solo, 6", lt gray, NM (Watch for Mexican copies in near exact gray), ea .$25.00

Man From UNCLE, Napoleon Solo, 6", steel bl, NM, from $12 to $20.00

Royal Canadian Police, Dulcop, NM $5.00

Space Patrol, driver seated, 45mm, tan & orange, NM, ea .$15.00

Spacemen, 3", various poses & colors, Premier, ea..............$5.00

Spacemen, 45mm, metallic bl or yel, NM, ea.....................$5.00

Spacemen, 4", silver and dark metallic blue, NM, ea, $55.00.

(Photo courtesy June Moon)

Sports, baseball player with hands up, 6", gray, NM, $4.00.

Sports, bowler, boxer, figure skater, golfer, or runner, 60mm, wht, NM, ea from $2.50 to...$3.00

Sports, hockey player, 60mm, matt lt bl, NM $12.00

Untouchables, 54mm, NM, ea..$15.00

ANIMALS

Champion Dogs, any, 84mm, NM, ea................................$6.50

Circus Animals, elephant w/howdah, NM.......................$10.00

Circus Animals, giraffe, tan, NM $10.00

Circus Animals, gorilla, NM..$3.00

Farm Stock, any, 60mm, NM, ea from $2 to.....................$5.00

Farm Stock, any from 2nd issue, NM, ea $2.00

Ice-Age Mammals, any, NM, from $10 to $20.00

Prehistoric Dinosaurs, Dimetrodon, marbled gray, NM, from $5 to $10.00

Prehistoric Dinosaurs, Parasaurolophus, brn, NM, from $5 to .$10.00

Prehistoric Dinosaurs, Plateosaurus, lt gr, NM, ea.............$5.00

Prehistoric Dinosaurs, Styacosaurus, tan, NM, from $10 to .$14.00

Prehistoric Dinosaurs, Trachodon, marbled gray, NM, from $5 to $10.00

Prehistoric Dinosaurs, Tyrannosaurus Rex, brn, NM $12.50

Ranch & Rodeo, Bronco bucking, 60mm, reddish brn, NM, from $4 to...$6.00

Ranch & Rodeo, Indian Pony running, 54mm, various colors, EX...$3.50

Ranch & Rodeo, longhorn steer halting, 60mm, reddish brn, NM, from $5 to...$10.00

CAMPUS CUTIES AND AMERICAN BEAUTIES

American Beauties, ballerina, 1955, NM $20.00

American Beauties, hula dancer, NM $20.00

American Beauties, reclining nude, M...............................$40.00

Campus Cuties, any, M, ea..$8.00

COMIC, DISNEY, AND NURSERY CHARACTERS

Disneykids, Wendy, M $35.00

Disneykings, Donald Duck, MIB $20.00

Disneykings, Goofy, MIB $20.00

Disneykins, Alice in Wonderland, M $10.00

Disneykins, Brer Rabbit, gold label, NM.........................$15.00

Disneykins, Daisy Duck, M...$10.00

Disneykins, Dumbo, NM $10.00

Disneykins, King Louie, rare, MIB $45.00

Disneykins, Peter Pan, NM..$15.00

Disneykins, Snow White and the Seven Dwarfs, seven-piece set, MOC (unopened), A, $55.00. (Photo courtesy Collectors Auction Services)

Disneykins, Timothy Mouse, NM.....................................$12.50
Fairykins, set of 21, w/book, EXIB, A............................$125.00
Fun on Wheels, set of 5 Disney characters, 1950s, VG+ to NM .$75.00
Nursery Rhymes, Humpty Dumpty, 60mm, gr or pk, NM, ea.$5.00
Nursery Rhymes, Humpty Dumpty, 60mm, matt gr, NM..$12.50
Nursery Rhymes, Humpty Dumpty, 70mm, NM $12.50
Nursery Rhymes, Little Jack Horner, 70mm, NM.............$10.00
Nursery Rhymes, Little Miss Muffet, 70mm, NM $12.50
Nursery Rhymes, Simple Simon, 60mm, NM $4.00
Oz-Kins, set of 10 different characters, Aurora/MGM, 1967, unused, NMOC, A $100.00
Rolykins, Donald Duck or Pluto, NM, ea from $10 to......$15.00
Tinykins, Benny, NM..$20.00
Tinykins, Flintstones, Barney, NMIB $30.00
Tinykins, Hoky Wolf, NM...$18.00
Tinykins, Jinx, NM..$18.00
Tinykins, Officer Dibble, NM...$20.00
Tinykins, Peter Pan, any character, NM, ea $15.00
Tinykins, Spook, NM..$20.00
Tinykins, Yogi Bear, NM..$18.00

FAMOUS PEOPLE AND CIVILIANS

Civilians & Workman, railroad station people, 45mm, cream, set of 5, NM...$20.00
Civilians & Workmen, racetrack pit crewman, 54mm, cream, NM...$10.00
International VIPs, Prince Charles, 60mm, wht, NM $20.00
International VIPs, Princess Anne, 60mm, wht, NM.......$20.00
International VIPs, Princess Margaret, 60mm, wht, NM .$20.00
International VIPs, Queen Elizabeth II, 60mm, wht, NM .$30.00
Politicians, Adlai Stevenson, NM....................................$50.00
Religious Leaders, Cardinal Spellman, NM $20.00
US Presidents, Eisenhower, 60mm, NM...........................$6.50
US Presidents, Lincoln, 60mm, NM.................................$6.50
US Presidents, Nixon, 60mm, NM.................................$12.50
US Presidents, Roosevelt, 60mm, NM $12.50
US Presidents, Washington, 60mm, NM $8.00

MILITARY AND WARRIORS

American Heroes, Gen Arnold, 60mm, wht, P11.............$20.00
American Heroes, Gen Bradley, 60mm, wht, NM, P11....$20.00
American Heroes, Gen Eisenhower, 60mm, wht, NM, P11.$20.00
American Heroes, Gen Grant, 60mm, pnt, NM, P11.......$15.00
American Heroes, Gen Grant, 60mm, wht, NM, P11......$30.00
American Heroes, Gen Gruenther, 60mm, wht, NM, P11.$15.00
American Heroes, Gen Jackson, 60mm, wht, NM, P11 ...$40.00
American Heroes, Gen Lee, 60mm, wht, rpt, P11............$15.00
American Heroes, Gen Lemay, 60mm, wht, flat face, P11 .$10.00
American Heroes, Gen MacArthur, 60mm, wht, NM, P11.$20.00
American Heroes, Gen Marshall, 60mm, wht, NM, P11 .$20.00
American Heroes, Gen Pershing, 60mm, wht, NM, P11..$40.00
American Heroes, Gen Pickett, 60mm, wht, P11 ....$50.00
American Heroes, Gen Ridgeway, 60mm, wht, NM, P11..$25.00
American Heroes, Gen Sheridan, 60mm, wht, NM, P11.$40.00
American Heroes, Gen Spaatz, 60mm, wht, NM, P11 .....$20.00
American Heroes, Gen Taylor, 60mm, wht, NM, P11......$40.00

American Heroes, Gen Washington, 60mm, wht, NM, P11..$25.00
Civil War, Confederate officer mounted, Andy Guard, NM, P11...$4.00
Civil War, Confederate soldier bayonetting, Andy Guard, NM, P11 ....$3.00
Civil War, Confederate soldier being shot, Andy Guard, NM, P11 ....$3.00
Civil War, Confederate soldier clubbing, Andy Guard, NM, P11..$3.00
Civil War, Confederate soldier kneeling & firing, Andy Guard, NM, P11..$4.00
Civil War, Confederate soldier lying dead, Andy Guard, NM, P11..$3.00
Civil War, Confederate soldier prone & firing, Andy Guard, NM, P11..$4.00
Civil War, Confederate soldier standing & firing, Andy Guard, NM, P11..$4.00
Civil War, Confederate soldier w/ramrod & pistol, Andy Guard, NM, P11..$3.00
Civil War, Union officer mounted, Andy Guard, NM, P11.$8.00
Civil War, Union soldier advancing, Andy Guard, NM, P11 .$6.00
Civil War, Union soldier bayonetting, Andy Guard, NM, P11 .$6.00
Civil War, Union soldier being shot, Andy Guard, NM, P11 .$6.00
Civil War, Union soldier clubbing, Andy Guard, NM, P11.$6.00
Civil War, Union soldier kneeling & firing, Andy Guard, NM, P11 ....$8.00
Civil War, Union soldier lying dead, Andy Guard, NM, P11..$6.00
Civil War, Union soldier prone & firing, Andy Guard, NM, P11..$8.00
Civil War, Union soldier standing & firing, Andy Guard, NM, P11 ....$8.00
Civil War, Union soldier w/ramrod & pistol, Andy Guard, NM, P11..$6.00
Plastic Toys, bugler, EX, A1..$6.00
Plastic Toys, hand grenade thrower, M, A1 ....$8.00
Plastic Toys, machine gunner kneeling, some pnt, EX, A1.$6.00
Plastic Toys, soldier in gas mask w/rifle, some pnt, EX, A1.$6.00
Plastic Toys, soldier standing firing rifle, some pnt, EX, A1.$6.00
Plastic Toys, soldier standing firing rifle, some pnt, M, A1.$8.00

WWII Soldier, rocket launcher, 4½", Tim-Mee, M, $5.00.

Warriors of the World, Cadets, set of 6, NMIB, A..........$120.00
Warriors of the World, US Combat Soldiers, set of 6, NMIB, A .$120.00
Warriors of the World, Viking, EXIB, A $45.00

NUTTY MADS

All Heart Hogan, pk w/cream swirl, NM $20.00
Bull Pen Boo Boo, dk gr, NM $30.00
Dippy the Sea Diver, cobalt, 1st issue, EX.......................$10.00
End Zone Football Player, dk gr, 1st issue, NM, from $15 to .$20.00
Lost Teepee, fluorescent red, NM, from $15 to $20.00
Manny the Wreckless Mariner, lime gr, NM.....................$20.00
Manny the Wreckless Mariner, lt gr, 1st issue, NM $35.00
Rocko the Champ, lime gr, 1st issue, NM, from $15 to $20.00
Rocko the Champ, pk, NM......................................$16.50
Roddy the Hotrod, chartreuse gr, 1st issue, NM...............$35.00
Suburban Sidney, dk gr, 1st issue, NM...........................$32.00
The Thinker, dk gr, NM $35.00
Waldo the Weight Lifter, pk, 1st issue, NM $25.00

WESTERN AND FRONTIER HEROES

Buffalo Bill, Atlantic #1202, MIP (sealed)......................$50.00
Buffalo Bill, 60mm, beige, EX $5.00
Cavalry (7th), mounted, 60mm, ea $18.00
Cowboy, mounted w/rifle, 45mm, NM $27.00
Cowboy, mounted w/rope, 45mm, NM $36.00
Cowboys, 6", Crescent, NM, ea.................................$10.00
Dale Evans, 60mm, cream, NM................................$22.00
Davy Crockett, 50mm, cream, NM $25.00
High Chaparral, 42-pc set, ½", Airfix, unused, MIB $25.00

Indian Brave Throwing Spear, 5½", orange, 1960s, NM, $4.00.

Indian Chief, w/club, 54mm, NM $10.00
Lone Ranger & Tonto, 54mm, NM $65.00
Pioneer, clubbing, 60mm, NM $5.00

Ranch Hand, walking, 60mm, NM $60.00
Rough Rider, mounted, 60mm, NM $18.00
Roy Rogers, hands on hips, NM $27.00
Roy Rogers on Trigger, 5", Ideal, M...........................$150.00
Sky King or Sheriff, NM, ea $18.00
Tonto, cream, 60mm, NM $22.00
Town Cowboys, 19-pc matched set, 60mm, NM $110.00
Wagon Driver, cream, 6", NM $5.00
Zorro w/Horse Tornado, NM $60.00

Plastic Toys

During the 1940s and into the 1960s, plastic was often the material of choice for consumer goods ranging from dinnerware and kitchenware items to jewelry and even high-heel shoes. Toy companies used brightly colored plastic to produce cars, dolls, pull toys, banks, games, and thousands of other types of products. Of the more imaginative toys, those that have survived in good collectible condition are beginning to attract a considerable amount of interest, especially items made by major companies.

Boom Truck, red, yellow, and blue, Tico, 11½", unused, MIB, A, $55.00. (Photo courtesy Collectors Auctions Services)

Bunny Rabbit on Scooter w/Sidecar, Canada, 1940s-50s, 5" L, NM..$40.00
Dump Truck w/Boom, Tico, 11½", unused, MIB (box mk Tico Toy Truck), A $55.00
Li'l Beep Bus, beeps when squeezed, w/pull string, Arrow, 1960s, 11", EX $20.00
Magic Hat Novelty Toy, wht gloves turn on blk top hat to expose rabbit, Commonwealth Plastics, 1940s-50s, NM $65.00
Mayflower Moving Van, Con-Cor, 1.87 scale, MIB..........$15.00
Pull Toy, chicken on a cart pecks for food when pulled, Ideal, 1950, 4½", EX..$25.00

Revell Plumbing Service Truck, Revell, complete, 9½", unused, MIB, A $90.00

Roadster, red, Ideal, 1950s, 9", EX $15.00

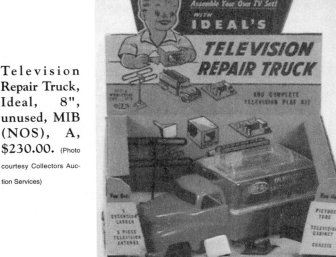

Television Repair Truck, Ideal, 8", unused, MIB (NOS), A, $230.00. (Photo courtesy Collectors Auction Services)

Terrier, eyed open & close, w/squeaker, 9", EX $15.00

Timberjack Log Skidder, Debardeur, 18", EXIB, A $90.00

Witch on Rocket, 1950s-60s, 4", NM+ $175.00

XP-1960 Dream Car, Mattel, 1960, 8", NMIB................$150.00

Plasticville

From the 1940s through the 1960s, Bachmann Brothers produced plastic accessories for train layouts such as buildings, fences, trees, and animals. Buildings often included several smaller pieces — for instance, ladders, railings, windsocks, etc. — everything you could ever need to play out just about any scenario. Beware of reissues.

Advisor: Gary Mosholder, Gary's Trains (G1)

Barbecue, red, 1950s – 60s, $125.00.

Airport Administration Building, #AD-4, EX (EX box), G1 .$55.00
Bank, #BK-1, EX (EX box), G1.....................................$18.00
Bank, #1801, EX (EX box), G1 ....$28.00
Barn, #BN-1, wht w/red roof, chrome silo top & cupola, EX (EX box), G1...$33.00
Barn, #BN-1, wht w/red roof, EX (EX box), G1 ....$15.00
Bridge (Trestle), #BR-2, EX (VG box), G1......................$18.00
Bridge & Pond, #BL-2, EX (EX box), G1 ....$12.00
Church, #CC-9, EX (EX box), G1..................................$12.00
Church, #1600, EX (EX box), G1 ....$15.00
Church, #1818, MIB, G1..$14.00
Colonial House (2-Story), #LH-4, tan w/brn trim, red roof, EX (EX box), G1...$15.00
Colonial House (2-Story), #1700, red w/wht trim, gray roof, EX (EX box), G1...$18.00
Crossing Signals & Gates, #1937, MIB, G1 ....$4.00
Dairy Barn, #1622, red, EX (EX box), G1 ....$20.00
Diner, #DE-7, yel, EX (EX box), G1 ....$22.00
Fence (Picket), #FG-12, 12-pc set, EX (G box), G1.........$10.00

Figures, rare complete set of sixteen, 1950s – 60s, from $110.00 to $120.00.

Firehouse, #FH-4, w/hollow siren, EX (EX box), G1 ....$25.00
Firehouse, #1607, EX (VG box), G1 ....$15.00
Firehouse w/2 Fire Trucks, #1921, EX (EX box), G1 ....$19.00
Five & Ten Cent Store, #CS-5, EX (EX box), G1 ....$15.00
Freight Station, #LM-3, EX (EX box), G1 ....$8.00
Frosty Bar, wht & salmon, EX, G1 ....$18.00
Gas Station, #1800, w/lg auto, EX (EX box), G1..............$25.00
Gas Station, sm, EX, G1 ....$10.00
Hardware & Pharmacy, #DH-2, EX (G box), G1 ....$17.00
Hospital, #HS-6, w/furniture, EX (EX box), G1 ....$35.00
Hospital, #HS-6, w/o furniture, EX (VG box), G1 ....$22.00
Lionel Figure Set, #953, EX (VG box), G1 ....$65.00
Log Cabin, #LC-2, w/chimney & rustic fence, EX (VG box), G1..$18.00
Motel, #1621, salmon w/wht roof & base, EX (EX box), G1..$15.00
Playground, #1406, EX (VG box), G1 ....$30.00
Police Department, #PD-3, dk gray, EX (EX box), G1 .....$25.00
Police Department, #PD-3, lt gray, EX (EX box), G1 ....$20.00
Railroad Accessories, #5605, complete, EX (VG box), G1..$65.00
Railroad Accessories Kit, #RA-6, EX (EX box), G1 ....$18.00
Ranch, #1852, bl w/wht trim, gray roof, EX (EX box), G1 .$15.00
Ranch House, #RH-1, gr w/wht roof & trim, EX (EX box), G1..$28.00
Ranch House, #RH-1, wht w/bl roof & trim, EX (EX box), G1..$15.00
Ranch House, #1603, gr w/wht roof & trim, EX (EX box), G1..$19.00
Ranch House, #1603, turq w/wht roof & trim, EX (EX box), G1...$22.00

Ranch House, #1603, wht sides w/lt bl roof & trim, EX (EX box), G1 ....$15.00
School, #SC-2, EX (EX box), G1 ....$18.00
Signal Bridge, #1403, EX (EX box), G1 ....$9.00
Station Platform, #1200, gr roof, EX (G box), G1 ....$8.00
Suburban Station, #RS-8, brn platform, EX (G box), G1..$10.00
Suburban Station, EX, G1 ....$8.00
Watchman's Shanty, EX, G1 ....$7.00
Windmill, EX, G1 ....$20.00

Playsets

Louis Marx is given credit for developing the modern-age playset and during the '50s and '60s produced hundreds of boxed sets, each with the buildings, figures, and accessories that when combined with a child's imagination could bring any scenario alive, from the days of Ben Hur to medieval battles, through the cowboy and Indian era, and on up to Cape Canaveral. Marx's prices were kept low by mass marketing (through retail giants such as Sears and Montgomery Wards) and overseas production. But on today's market, playsets are anything but low priced; some mint-in-box examples sell for upwards of $1,000.00. Just remember that a set that shows wear or has even a few minor pieces missing quickly drops in value. The listings below are for complete examples unless noted otherwise.

See the Clubs, Newsletters, and Other Publications for information on how to order *Prehistoric Times* by Mike and Kurt Fredericks, and *Playset Magazine*, published six times a year.

Advisors: Mike and Kurt Fredericks (F4)

African Warrior's Canoe, Multiple Toys, 1950s, MIP $75.00
Alamo, Marx #3543, Series 2000, 1960s, EXIB $750.00
Alaska Frontier, Marx #3708, 1959, EXIB $550.00
Alaska Frontier, Marx #3708, 1959, MIB $900.00
Anzio Beach, Aurora, HO scale, VGIB........................$50.00
Arctic Explorer, Marx #3702, Series 2000, 1960, MIB...$800.00
Battle of the Blue & Gray, Marx #4658, Series 2000, 1963, EXIB..$750.00
Battleground, Marx #4204, EXIB..............................$150.00
Battleground, Marx #4749, 1959, NMIB $300.00
Battleground, Marx #4756, 1968, EXIB.......................$200.00
Ben-Hur, Marx #4701, Series 5000, EXIB $1,200.00
Ben-Hur, Marx #4702, Series 2000, 1959, EXIB............$900.00
Big Inch Pipeline, Marx #6008, 1963, EXIB................$600.00
Bonanza/Hoss & His Horse, Palitoy/NBC, 1966, unused, NMIB (sealed), A $250.00
Cape Canaveral, Marx/Sears #5963, 1959, EXIB $325.00
Cape Canaveral Missile Set, Marx #4526, 1958, EXIB ..$250.00
Captain Gallant, Marx #4730, EXIB..............................$700.00
Captain Space Solar Academy, Marx #7018, 1954, EXIB .$275.00
Castle, Elastolin #9756, EXIB $300.00
Castle & Dungeon, Britains #7706, 1990s, unused, MIB..$75.00
Cattle Drive, Marx #3983, 1970s, EXIB $350.00
Civil War Centennial, Marx #5929, 1961, EXIB $1,500.00
Construction Camp, Marx/Wards #4444, EXIB $450.00
Cowboy & Indian Camp, Marx #3950, 1953, VG+IB ...$200.00

Daktari, Marx #3717, 1967, MIB $550.00
Daniel Boone Wilderness Scout, Marx #0631, 1964, EXIB .$275.00
Davy Crockett at the Alamo, Marx #3544, 1955, EXIB.$600.00
Disneyland, Marx #5996, EXIB................................$625.00
Evel Knievel Stunt World, Ideal, 1975, NMIB $125.00
Farm Set, Marx #3948, Series 2000, 1958, EXIB............$300.00
Fighting Aces (WWI Biplane Set), Remco, MIP $325.00
Flintstones, Marx, 1994, MIB................................$100.00

Fort Apache, Marx, Series 500, unused, MIB (unopened), $450.00. (Photo courtesy John Turney)

Flintstones, Marx #4672, 1961-62, EXIB......................$275.00
Fort Apache, Marx/Sears #6063, 1965, EXIB $325.00
Fort Apache Stockade, Marx #3660, Series 2000, 1960, EXIB .$250.00
Fort Cheyenne, Brumberger #848, 1970s, unused, VGIB .$60.00
Fort Dearborn, Marx #3514, EXIB $175.00
Fort Mohawk, Marx #3751, EXIB $350.00
Fort Pitt, Marx #3741, Series 750, 1959, EXIB..............$300.00
Fort Pitt, Marx #3742, Series 1000, 1959, EXIB...........$325.00
Galaxy Command, Marx #4206, 1976, EXIB $100.00

Gun Emplacement Assault Set, Airfix, HO-OO scale, EXIB, $50.00.

Gunsmoke, MPC #1117, EXIB...............................$250.00
Gunsmoke Dodge City, Marx #4268, Series 2000, 1960, EXIB..$1,500.00
Happitime Irrigated Farm Set, Marx #5971, EXIB $500.00
Have Gun Will Travel/Gold Mine, Multiple Products/CBS, 1959, EXIB..$200.00
History in the Pacific, Marx #4164, 1972, EXIB............$300.00
History in the Pacific, Marx #4164, 1972, MIB...........$500.00

Have Gun Will Travel/Gold Mine, Multiple Products/CBS, 1959, EXIB, A, $200.00. (Photo courtesy Smith House Toys)

Indian Warfare, Marx #4778, Series 2000, EXIB $300.00
International Jet Port, Marx #4810, EXIB $175.00
Iwo Jima Mountain, Marx, 1977, EXIB..........................$300.00
Jungle Jim, Marx #3706, Series 1000, 1957, MIB........$1,500.00
Knight & Vikings, Marx #4733, 1973, VGIB $100.00
Legend of the Lone Ranger, MPC, later issue, MIB (sealed).$75.00
Lifelike Farm Set, Ohio Art #195, 1959, MIB $100.00
Lone Ranger Ranch, Marx #3969, Series 500, 1957, EXIB.$300.00
Lone Ranger Rodeo Set, Marx #3696, 1953, EXIB........$125.00
Mars Landing, Marx, MIB $500.00
McDonaldland, Remco, 1976, unused, MIB...................$135.00
Medieval Castle Fort, Marx #4710, 1953, EXIB $150.00
Mobile Army Battlefront, MPC #3501, EXIB $150.00
Modern Farm Set, Marx #3938, VGIB...........................$150.00
Modern Farm Set, Marx #3940, EXIB............................$250.00
Monster Lab, Ideal, 1960s, EXIB...................................$375.00
Mountain Assault Set, Atlantic #202, unused, MIB $175.00
Navarone Mountain Battleground, Marx #3412, 1976, EXIB.$125.00

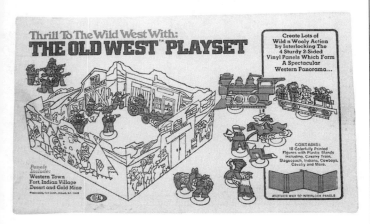

Old West Playset, Ideal, EXIB, $75.00. (Photo courtesy Martin and Carolyn Berens)

One Million BC, Marx #59842, 1970s, EXIB $175.00
Operation Moonbase, Marx #4654, 1962, EXIB.............$600.00
Operation X500, Deluxe Reading USA, 1950s-60s, NMIB.$500.00
Pet Shop, Marx #4209 or #4210, 1950s, MIB, ea $375.00
Pirate's Canoe, Multiple Toys, 1950s, MIP $100.00
Planet of the Apes, MPC, unused, MIB..........................$125.00
Polar Queen, Ideal, M (no box) $200.00
Prairie Rocket, Timpo #244, NMIB $600.00
Prehistoric Dinosaur Playset, Marx #4208, 1978, EXIB..$125.00
Prehistoric Times, Marx #3390, Series 1000, 1957, EXIB.$250.00

Prince Valiant Castle, Marx #4705, 1955, EXIB.............$300.00
Prince Valiant Castle, Marx #4706, 1955, EXIB.............$350.00
Rin-Tin-Tin at Fort Apache, Marx #3628, Series 500, 1956, EXIB..$500.00
Rin-Tin-Tin at Fort Apache, Marx #3658, Series 1000, NMIB .$500.00
Rin-Tin-Tin at Fort Apache, Marx #3686R, Series 5000, 1956, EXIB..$750.00
Rio Bravo, Atlantic #514, unused, MIB.........................$100.00
Robin Hood Castle, Marx #4717, MIB $650.00
Robin Hood Castle, Marx #4718, 1958, MIB $550.00
Roy Rogers Double R Bar Ranch, Marx 3982, 1962, EXIB.$350.00
Roy Rogers Rodeo Ranch, Marx #4259, Series 5000, EXIB.$300.00
Roy Rogers Western Town, Marx #4258, 1952, EXIB $700.00
Royal Canadian Mounted Police, Ideal, NMIB $650.00

Sgt. Rock vs The Bad Guys, Remco, 1980s, EXIB, $85.00. (Photo courtesy June Moon)

Skyscraper, Marx #5449 or #5450, EXIB, ea $850.00
Sons of Liberty, Marx, 1970s, MIB $600.00

Super Circus, Marx #4320, 1952, EXIB, A, $300.00. (Photo courtesy Bertoia Auctions)

Tales of Wells Fargo, Marx #4264, Series 1000, EXIB $500.00
Tales of Wells Fargo Train Set, Marx #54762, EXIB.......$900.00
Tom Corbett, Marx #4444, EXIB $375.00
Turnpike Service Center, Marx #3460, 1960s, MIB $550.00

Undersea Attack, Atlantic #206, EXIB $100.00
US Armed Forces Training Center, Marx #4149, Series 500,
    1955, EXIB..$250.00

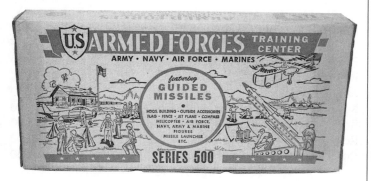

US Armed Forces Training Center, Marx #4149, Series 500, 1955, unused, MIB, $450.00. (Photo courtesy John Turney)

Viking Ship, Eldon, 1960s, 18" L, unused, MIP (sealed) .$125.00
Village Set, Built-Rite #556, VGIB................................$175.00
Western Frontier Town, Ideal #3298, EXIB....................$475.00
Western Set, Auburn #963, EXIB $175.00
Wyatt Earp Dodge City, Marx #4228, Series 1000, EXIB .$1,200.00
Yogi Bear Jellystone Playset, Marx #4364, EXIB............$375.00
Zorro, Marx #3753, Series 500, 1958, EXIB....................$550.00
Zorro, Marx #3758, Series 1000, 1958, EXIB.................$750.00

Political

    As far back as the nineteenth century, children's toys with a political message were on the market. One of the most familiar was the 'Tammany Bank' patented by J. & E. Stevens in 1873. The message was obvious — a coin placed in the man's hand was deposited in his pocket, representing the kickbacks William Tweed was suspected of pocketing when he was the head of Tammany Hall in New York during the 1860s.

    Advisors: Michael and Polly McQuillen (M11)

Bush, George; doll, stuffed cloth w/vinyl caricature head,
    blk jacket, striped shirt & pants, red tie, 1990s, 9½",
    M...$20.00
Carter, Amy; coloring book, 1977, unused, EX.................$15.00
Carter, Jimmy; bank, plastic peanut shape, Plains Georgia,
    1970s, 6", EX, N2..$15.00
Carter, Jimmy; radio, peanut shape, transistor, MIB $75.00
Carter, Jimmy; ring, peanut, EX....................................$15.00
Clinton, Bill; doll, Draft Evader, MIB $15.00
Clinton, Hillary; doll, Dr Hillcare, Tradewinds, MIB $15.00
Goldwater, Barry; board game, 1964 Presidential Election,
    MOC..$30.00
Goldwater, Berry; doll, bobbing head, vinyl, Remco, 1964, 5½",
    MIB $80.00
Gorbachev, doll, Dreamworks, 1990, 11", MIB................$45.00
Hussein, Saddam; doll, Beast of Baghdad/'You Do' Voo Doo
    Doll, stuffed print cloth, Laid Back, 1990, 10", MIB .$25.00

Jackson, Andrew; doll, in military uniform, Effanbee, 1990, 16",
    MIB...$125.00
Kennedy, John; playing cards, Kennedy Kards, red, wht & bl
    w/cartoon images, 1960s, EXIB $20.00
McArthur, Gen Douglas; doll, compo, lt brn cloth uniform, Freundlich Novelty, 1940s, 18", MIB..........................$475.00
Nixon, Richard; hand puppet, cloth body w/plastic head, 1968,
    NM...$35.00
Powell, Gen Colin; figure, American Heroes series, In Time
    Products, 1991, 6", MIB..$40.00
Reagan, Ronald; doll, in suit & tie, Horsman, 1987, 17", MIB .$100.00
Reagan, Ronald; doll, stuffed print cloth (Reaganomics), Dots
    Okay, 1982, 10", MIB $25.00
Schwarzkoph, Gen Norman; figure, American Heroes series, In
    Time Products, 1991, 6", MIB $40.00
Truman, Harry S; doll, in suit & hat w/red bow tie, Effanbee,
    1988, 16", MIB $125.00
Wilson, Woodrow; puzzle, diecut profile, w/envelope, EX .$75.00

Washington, George; candy container, cloth-dressed figure and horse with wooden boots and hooves, painted face, 11x9", NM+, A, $1,900.00. (Photo courtesy Buffalo Bay Auctions)

Premiums

    Those of us from the pre-boomer era remember waiting in anticipation for our silver bullet ring, secret membership kit, decoder pin, coloring book, or whatever other wonderful item we'd seen advertised in our favorite comic book or heard about on the Tom Mix show. Tom wasn't the only one to have these exciting premiums, though, just about any top character-oriented show from the 1930s through the 1940s made similar offers, and even through the 1950s some were still being distributed. Often they could be had free for a cereal boxtop or an Ovaltine inner seal, and if any money was involved, it was usually only a dime. Not especially durable and often made in somewhat limited amounts, few have survived to the present. Today some of these are bringing fantastic prices, but the market at present is very volatile. Note: Those trademark/logo characters created to specifically represent a cereal product or company (for example Cap'n Crunch) are listed in the Cereal Boxes and Premiums category.

Condition is very important in assessing value; items in pristine condition bring premium prices.

Advisor: Bill Campbell (C10)

See also Advertising; Cereal Boxes and Premiums; Pin-back Buttons.

Amos 'N Andy, map, Weber City, 1930s, NM $50.00
Andy Pafko, ring, baseball scorekeeper, EX, C10 ....$215.00
Annie, cup, plastic Beetleware, EX, C10 ....$25.00
Annie, decoder, 1935, EX, C10 ....$35.00
Annie, decoder, 1936, EX, C10 ....$40.00
Annie, decoder, 1937 or 1938, EX, C10, ea $50.00
Annie, decoder, 1939, EX, C10 ....$55.00
Annie, decoder, 1940, EX, C10 ....$75.00
Annie, manual & badge, Secret Society, EX (orig mailer), C10 .$75.00
Annie, mask, diecut paper, Ovaltine, 1933, EX+ $40.00

Annie, mug, Shake-Up, 1931, ivory with orange top, EX, C10, $50.00.

Annie, mug, Shake-Up, 1935, beige w/orange top, EX C10 .$75.00
Annie, mug, Shake-Up, 1938, aqua w/orange top, EX, C10 .$175.00
Annie, mug, Shake-Up, 1939, brn w/orange top, EX, C10 .$150.00
Annie, mug, Shake-Up, 1940, gr w/red top, EX, C10 .....$150.00
Annie, mug, 50th Anniversary, ceramic, EX, C10 ....$25.00
Annie, ring, face, NM+, C10 ....$100.00
Annie, ring, initial, EX, C10 ....$125.00
Annie, ring, Mystic Eye, w/instructions, EX, C10 ....$200.00
Annie, ring, secret message, EX, C10 ....$250.00
Annie, ring, silver star, EX, C10 ....$350.00
Annie, stationery, 5 sheets w/images of gang, NM (w/orig mailer), C10 ....$15.00
Annie, watch, Miracle Compass, NM+, C10 ....$60.00
Babe Ruth, ring, Baseball Club, EX, C10 ....$165.00
Batman, ring, Nestle, M, C10 ....$90.00
Buck Rogers, badge, Solar Scouts Chief Explorer, burgundy, EX, C10 ....$260.00
Buck Rogers, badge/whistle, Space Commander, NM, C10 .$325.00

Buck Rogers, book, City of Floating Globes, Big Little Books, Cocomalt, EX+, C10 ....$175.00
Buck Rogers, Cut-Out Adventure Book, Cocomalt, 1933, unused, VG $375.00

Buck Rogers, Flying Saucer, heavy cardboard disc with steel rim, 1939, 6¼" diameter, NM, $100.00.

Buck Rogers, helmet, Lightning Bolt, Goodyear, 1935, EX+ $450.00
Buck Rogers, manual, Solar Scouts, Cream of Wheat, 1936, EX w/mailer $300.00
Buck Rogers, Penny Card, American Amoco Gas, 3x3", any number, A, ea $275.00
Buck Rogers, pocketknife, Cream of Wheat/Camillus Cutlery, 1935, 3", EX, A $970.00
Buck Rogers, pop gun, XZ-31, Cocomalt, 1934, EX $350.00
Buck Rogers, ring, birthstone, EX, C10 ....$565.00
Buck Rogers, ring, Saturn, NM+, C10 ....$600.00
Buck Rogers, Space Ranger Kit, Sylvania TV, 1952, unused, NM+ (in sealed envelope), A $150.00
Bullwinkle, Electric Quiz Fun Game, General Mills, 1961, 11x11", EX $50.00
Capt America, badge, Sentinels of Liberty Membership, EX $700.00
Capt Marvel, key ring, Capt Marvel Club, EX, C10 ....$75.00
Capt Marvel, Magic Flute, MOC $100.00
Capt Marvel, Magic Whistle, EX, C10 ....$50.00
Capt Marvel, patch, Capt Marvel Club, rectangular, red, wht & bl, EX, C10 ....$225.00

Captain Midnight, badge, Secret Squadron Decoder, brass-plated tin, 2¼", EX, $125.00.

Capt Midnight, badge, Mysto-Magic Weather Forecasting Wings, w/litmus paper, Skelly Oil, 1939, EX, C10.....$50.00

Capt Midnight, badge, pilot's wings, 24k gold-finished brass, 1943, EX, C10 ....$225.00

Capt Midnight, cup, red plastic w/decal, EX, C10 ....$35.00

Capt Midnight, decoder, 1941, Code-O-Graph, EX, C10 .$100.00

Capt Midnight, decoder, 1945, EX, C10......................$125.00

Capt Midnight, decoder, 1946, EX, C10......................$100.00

Capt Midnight, decoder, 1947, whistle, EX, C10.............$75.00

Capt Midnight, decoder, 1948, EX, C10........................$70.00

Capt Midnight, decoder, 1949, Key-O-Matic, w/key, EX, C10..$225.00

Capt Midnight, decoder, 1955, EX, C10......................$175.00

Capt Midnight, decoder, 1955, w/membership card & manual, EX, C10 ....$300.00

Capt Midnight, decoder, 1957, badge w/tailfin, EX, C10...$200.00

Capt Midnight, manual, 1942, NM+, C10 ....$105.00

Capt Midnight, manual, 1945, EX, C10.........................$75.00

Capt Midnight, manual, 1946, NM+, C10 ....$90.00

Capt Midnight, manual, 1947, EX, C10.........................$75.00

Capt Midnight, manual, 1948, NM, C10.......................$100.00

Capt Midnight, manual, 1955-56, w/code book, EX, C10 .$200.00

Captain Midnight, manual, 1957, EX (with mailer), C10, $100.00.

Capt Midnight, manual, 1957, G, C10 ....$75.00

Capt Midnight, manual, 1957, w/letter, EX (w/mailer), C10..$150.00

Capt Midnight, membership kit, 1957, complete, EX, C10 .$575.00

Capt Midnight, mug, Shake-Up, 1955, orange w/bl top, EX, C10...$225.00

Capt Midnight, mug, Shake-Up, 1957, red w/bl top, EX, C10..$100.00

Capt Midnight, ring, Flight Commander, EX, C10 ....$495.00

Capt Midnight, ring, Marine Corps, EX, C10.................$400.00

Capt Midnight, ring, Mystic Sun God, EX $1,200.00

Capt Midnight, ring, secret compartment, EX, C10.......$140.00

Capt Midnight, ring, Whirlwind Siren, EX, C10 ....$400.00

Capt Video, ring, photo, EX, C10 ....$325.00

Charlie McCarthy, Radio Party Game, complete, VG+ (w/orig mailing envelope) $65.00

Cisco Kid, membership card & letter, Triple S, EX, C10..$25.00

Cisco Kid, ring, saddle, EX, C10 ....$500.00

Clarabelle, see Howdy Doody

David Harding Counter Spy, badge, w/secret compartment, EX, C10..$50.00

Davy Adams, ring, siren, rare, EX $600.00

Davy Crockett, ring, compass, w/expansion band, EX, C10.$175.00

Davy Crockett, ring, TV flicker, M, C10 ....$150.00

Dick Tracy, decoder, paper, Post, 1957, 3½", NM............$15.00

Dick Tracy, hat, Dick Tracy Official Hat, DT Detective Club patch & premiums promo tag, Miller Hat Co, 1940s, scarce, NM..$100.00

Dick Tracy, manual, Jr Detective, style B version, EX, C10 .$50.00

Dick Tracy, ring, hat, EX $200.00

Dick Tracy, ring, secret compartment, EX.....................$200.00

Dragnet, badge, Sergeant 714, brass-plated tin, NM, $25.00.

Farfel, mug, litho on ceramic, Nestle's Quik, 1950s, 3", EX+ $40.00

Fibber McGee, party game, Fibber McGee & the Wistful Mystery, Milton Bradley/NBC, 1940, EXIB......................$40.00

Flash Gordon, ring, Post Toasties, MIP, C10 ....$75.00

Flintstones, comic book, March of Comics #243, 1963, NM .$15.00

Flintstones, March of Comics #243, 1963, sm size premium book, NM+ $18.00

Frank Buck, ring, initial, ivory, EX................................$300.00

Gabby Hayes, ring, cannon, EX $250.00

Gene Autry, Pop Pistol, diecut cb w/Gene Autry Show insert, 1950s, 9", NM...$40.00

Gene Autry, ring, flag, NM+, C10 ....$105.00

Green Hornet, ring, rubber stamp seal, EX $100.00

Green Hornet, ring, seal/secret compartment, EX, C10 .$850.00

Green Lantern, ring, FX, brass or silver, w/instructions, M (in pouch), C10, ea $100.00

Green Lantern, ring, FX, solid gr metal w/gr stone, EX, C10 .$85.00

Green Lantern, ring, glow-in-the-dark, gr plastic, DC, EX, C10 ....$15.00

Hopalong Cassidy, Savings Rodeo, complete w/bank (bust), badges, pamphlet, membership card & letter, NM (EX mailer), A $225.00

Hopalong Cassidy, Western Badges, metal, 12 different, Post's Raisin Bran, 1950-51, 1", ea from $15 to $20.00

Howdy Doody, ring, Clarabelle horn, EX, C10..............$385.00

Huckleberry Hound, ring, plastic, NM+, C10 ....$65.00

Jack Armstrong, flashlight, torpedo, steel & cb, 1940s, 4½", EX $20.00

Jack Armstrong, pedometer, EX, C10..............................$25.00

Jack Armstrong, ring, crocodile, w/instructions, EX+ (w/mailer), C10 ....$1,200.00

Jack Armstrong, ring, Egyptian siren, NM+, C10...........$125.00

Jack Armstrong, Secret Bomb Sight, 1942, complete & unused, MIB...$300.00

Jack Armstrong, Sound Effects Kit, Wheaties, 1940, complete, unused, NM+IB, A $175.00

Justice League of America, membership card, plastic, 1982, 2x3", M, N2...$10.00

Lassie, ring, friendship, EX, C10 ....$150.00

Lassie, wallet & Get-Up-And Go card, brn vinyl w/Lassie portrait, Campbell's Soup, 1950s, EX+ $50.00

Little Orphan Annie, see Annie

Lone Ranger, badge, star shape, Bond Bread, EX, C10 .....$25.00

Lone Ranger, belt, glow-in-the-dark, EX, C10..................$25.00

Lone Ranger, collector card, Merita Bread, 1950s, EX, N2.$20.00

Lone Ranger, decoder, Cryptograph, Weber's Bread, 1943, NM+...$275.00

Lone Ranger, flashlight gun, plastic, w/horseshoe logo & secret compartment, Morton's Salt, 6", M, A......................$75.00

Lone Ranger, Hike-O-Meter, General Mills Wheaties, 1957, NMIB, $25.00.

Lone Ranger, membership kit, Merita Bread, 1939, complete, EX (orig mailer) $75.00

Lone Ranger, pedometer, w/ankle strap, EX, C10 ....$25.00

Lone Ranger, pin, gardenia, glow-in-the-dark, EXOC, C10..$25.00

Lone Ranger, punch-out card, w/Lone Ranger, Tonto, Silver, cactus, wagon, fence, etc, Merita Bread, 1947, 12x18", VG+, A.$90.00

Lone Ranger, ring, atomic bomb, EX, C10 ....$215.00

Lone Ranger, ring, flashlight, complete, w/instructions, EX, C10 ....$150.00

Lone Ranger, ring, gold ore/meteorite, EX.................$2,000.00

Lone Ranger, ring, Marine Corps secret compartment, complete w/pictures of Silver & Lone Ranger, EX $700.00

Lone Ranger, ring, Movie Film, w/Marine Corps color film, Cheerios, EX, C10...$180.00

Lone Ranger, ring, Movie Film, w/Marine Corps film, Cheerios, NM+ (w/mailer box), A $200.00

Lone Ranger, ring, saddle, w/film, EX, C10 ....$155.00

Lone Ranger, ring, Six Shooter, 1947, EX......................$150.00

Lone Ranger, ring, weather, w/orig litmus paper, NM, C10..$150.00

Lone Wolf, badge & membership card, 1932, EX, C10 ....$50.00

Melvin Pervis, manual, Secret Operator's, Post Toasties, 1937, EX...$50.00

Melvin Pervis, ring, Jr G-Men Corps, EX, C10................$85.00

Melvin Pervis, ring, Secret Operator, EX, C10 ....$110.00

Mickey Mouse & Pals, rings, plastic, heads on shields w/names on banners, 8 different, General Mills, 1956, ea $25 to $45.00

Mighty Mouse, Magic Mystery Picture, paper, Post, 1957, 5½", M, from $25 to $35.00

Mighty Mouse, Merry-Pack Punch-Outs, Post premium, CBS-TV Ent, 1956, complete, EX+ (w/envelope) $85.00

Mr Ed, comic book, March of Comics, #260, Hahn Shoes/KK Publishing, 1964, EX+...$30.00

Phantom, ring, skull, brass w/red eyes, 1950s, EX $800.00

Popeye, mask, Comedy Club, Juicy Fruit Gum/Einson-Freeman, 1930s, 11x9", VG+ $60.00

Popeye, membership card, Theatre Club, blk & wht, WSOC TV, 1958, EX, A...$30.00

Popeye, puzzle game, Popeye to the Rescue, Thom McAn Shoes/Einson-Freeman & Funland, 1934, scarce, G+ (w/mailer) $65.00

Radio Orphan Annie, see Annie

Red Skelton, mask set, 3 different molded plastic faces, Pet Milk Co/mk Red Skelton 1960, VGIB $150.00

Rin-Tin-Tin, ballpoint pen, rifle shape, Nabisco Shredded Wheat, 5½", MIP, C10 ....$50.00

Rin-Tin-Tin, pin, Name the Puppy Contest, complete w/paperwork, EX (w/mailer), C10..$25.00

Rin-Tin-Tin, ring, magic, w/pencil, EX, C10..................$550.00

Rin-Tin-Tin, stereo cards & viewer, set of 24, EX (orig mailer), C10 ....$75.00

Rin-Tin-Tin, sticker, image of dog, Nabisco, 1958, 2" sq, EX.$8.00

Rin-Tin-Tin, sticker, image of Major Swanson, Nabisco, 1958, EX...$8.00

Rocky & Bullwinkle, ring toss, constructed from cereal box, General Mills, 1964, EX $10.00

Roger Wilco, ring, Flying Tiger, w/whistle & glow top, EX, C10.$325.00

Roger Wilco, ring, MagniRay glow-in-the-dark, 1940s, EX, C10 ....$80.00

Roy Rogers, badge & membership card, star w/compartments, EX, C10..$85.00

Roy Rogers, calendar, Nestle's Quik, 1960, complete, 8x7", EX $110.00

Roy Rogers, cup, figural, Quaker Oats, NM, C10 ....$40.00

Roy Rogers, ring, branding iron w/cap (XX brand), EX, C10.$225.00

Roy Rogers, ring, microscope, EX, C10............................$125.00

Roy Rogers, ring, oval w/Roy on Trigger, sterling silver, EX.$350.00

Roy Rogers, ring, saddle, silver, EX $350.00

Sgt Preston, Klondike Land Prospector's Pouch, chamois cloth, Quaker, 1955, 4½", NM $125.00

Sgt Preston, pedometer, 1952, EX, C10 ....$25.00

Sgt Preston, Sgt Preston's Yukon Trail, complete set of cut-out models, Quaker, 1950, EX, from $100 to $150.00

Sgt Preston, Yukon Gold Country Deed of Land, Quaker, 1955, NM..$15.00

Shadow, ink blotter, Blue Coal, EX, C10 ....$25.00

Shadow, photo, blk & wht, facsimile signature, Blue Coal, EX, C10 ....$100.00

Shadow, ring, Blue Coal, EX, C10.............................$650.00

Shadow, ring, bust, EX, C10.......................................$150.00

Shadow, ring, Carey Salt Crocodile, glow-in-the-dark, EX, C10 ....$900.00

Shadow, ring, Diamond Co, EX, C10..........................$200.00

Shadow, ring, Secret Agent, MIB, C10........................$250.00

Sky King, Detecto Writer, aluminum or brass, EX, C10, ea .$125.00

Sky King, Detecto-Microscope, 1950s, complete, NM (EX mailer), $225.00.

Sky King, ring, Aztec, EX, C10 ....$650.00

Sky King, ring, Magic Picture, no photo or disc o/w EX ...$50.00

Sky King, ring, MagniGlo Writing, EX, C10 ....$115.00

Sky King, ring, Navajo Treasure, EX, C10 ....$125.00

Sky King, ring, radar, EX, C10 ....$125.00

Sky King, ring, Teleblinger, EX, C10 ....$255.00

Sky King, ring, TV, w/4 pictures & instructions, EX, C10 .$385.00

Sky King, Secret Signal Scope, EX, C10.........................$100.00

Smokey the Bear, badge, Junior Forest Ranger, 1960s, 2", NM $25.00

Smokey the Bear, Jr Forest Ranger Kit, US Dept of Agriculture, 1956-57, complete, EX+ (w/mailer), A.....................$65.00

Space Patrol, binoculars, Ralston, 1953, 5", NM............$150.00

Space Patrol, Buzz Cory Color Book, Ralston, 1953, 12 pgs, 11x9", some coloring, EX+ $65.00

Space Patrol, decoder belt buckle w/belt, glow-in-the-dark, Ralston, 1950s, EX, C10 ....$235.00

Space Patrol, mobile, diecut cb, Ralston, 1953, 27" $500.00

Space Patrol, ring, Hydrogen Ray Gun, Wheat Chex, 1950s, EX, C10 ....$250.00

Spider-Man, comic book, #1, Giant Food Store giveaway, 1991, M, N2 ....$10.00

Spy Smasher, membership card, very rare, EX $175.00

Straight Arrow, Puppet Theatre Punchouts, Nabisco, EX, C10 ....$15.00

Straight Arrow, ring, arrow, gold, EX, C10....................$50.00

Straight Arrow, ring, face, EX, C10...............................$70.00

Straight Arrow, ring, Nugget Cave w/photo, EX, C10 ...$275.00

Straight Arrow, trading cards, 10 different, Nabisco Shredded Wheat, 1949, 7x4", NM $20.00

Superman, comic, Supershow of Metropolis, Sugar Smacks, 1955, NM+, C10 ....$100.00

Superman, comic, The Superman Time Capsule, Sugar Smacks, NM+ $100.00

Superman, ring, airplane, Kellogg's Pep, EX, C10 ....$200.00

Superman, ring, Crusader, EX, C10...............................$235.00

Superman, ring, F-187 jet plane, blk, Kellogg's Corn Flakes, EX, C10 ....$250.00

Superman, ring, FX, silver, w/membership papers, M (in tin), C10 ....$200.00

Superman, Stereo Pix, Kellogg's, 1954, 8", NM, ea from $10 to..$15.00

Tennessee Jed, ring, Look-Around, NM+, C10 ....$500.00

Tennessee Jed, ring, magnet, EX................................$850.00

Terry & the Pirates, ring, gold detector, EX, C10 ....$125.00

Tom Corbett, patch, Space Cadet (part of Member Kit), stitched cloth chevron w/spaceship, Kellogg's, 1951, NM+ $50.00

Tom Corbett, ring, face, EX, C10................................$125.00

Tom Corbett, ring, rocket, w/expansion band, unused, M, C10 ....$475.00

Tom Corbett, spinner, Good Luck, complete w/1935 premium catalog, EX (w/mailer), C10................................$150.00

Tom Mix, badge, Deputy Sheriff of Dobie County whistler, w/papers, EX, C10..$75.00

Tom Mix, badge, Straight Shooter, MOC (w/catalog & mailer), C10 ....$150.00

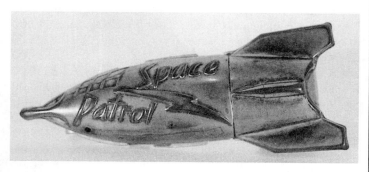

Space Patrol, decoder belt buckle, brass and aluminum, Ralston, 1950s, EX, $185.00.

Tom Mix, puzzle, 125-piece jigsaw, Rexall, 1920s, complete, NM (with envelope), $150.00.

Tom Mix, badge, Straight Shooter, silver, EX, C10 ....$60.00
Tom Mix, compass, glow gun & whistle (arrowhead), w/papers, M (worn mailer), C10 ....$100.00
Tom Mix, compass/magnifier, brass, NM+, C10 ....$30.00
Tom Mix, gun, wood, w/revolving cylinder, early premium, EX, C10 ....$400.00
Tom Mix, periscope, Straight Shooters, Ralston 1939, 9", NM+ $55.00
Tom Mix, ring, Look Around, EX, C10 ....$125.00
Tom Mix, ring, Lucky Initial Signet, EX, C10 ....$200.00
Tom Mix, ring, Magic Tiger Eye, w/burgundy TV set & instructions, EX (w/mailer), C10 ....$425.00
Tom Mix, ring, magnet, M, C10.................................$125.00
Tom Mix, ring, Marlin, EX, C10 ....$300.00
Tom Mix, ring, siren, EX+, C10 ....$150.00
Tom Mix, ring, Straight Shooter, EX, C10 ....$100.00
Tom Mix, ring, whistle, NM, C10..............................$135.00
Tom Mix, Straight Shooter News Vol 1 #2, Life of Tom Mix in Pictures, Ralston, EX, C10 ....$25.00
Tom Mix, Western Movie, Ralston, 1935, cb, turn dials to view story of Tom Mix, 7x4", EX, A.......................$250.00
Wild Bill Hickok, Colt 6-Shooter Pistol, Sugar Pops, 1958, 10", MIB...$300.00

Wild Bill Hickok, Secret Treasure Guide and Map, Kelloggs, NM+ (with envelope), $50.00.

Wizard of Oz, puppet, Toto, Proctor & Gamble Detergent, 1960s, EX $20.00
Wonder Woman, ring, Nestle, 1977, EX, C10...............$110.00
Woody Woodpecker, ring, Club Stamp, EX, C10..........$150.00
Zorro, ring, silver plastic w/logo on blk top, EX, C10 ....$60.00

Pressed Steel

Many companies were involved in the manufacture of pressed steel automotive toys which were often faithfully modeled after actual vehicles in production at the time they were made. Because they were so sturdy, some from as early as the 1920s have survived to the present, and those that are still in good condition are bringing very respectable prices at toy auctions around the country. Some of the better-known manufacturers are listed in other sections.

See also Aeronautical; Buddy L; Keystone; Marx; Pedal Cars and Other Wheeled Goods; Structo; Tonka; Wyandotte.

Alfa Romeo P2 Grand Prix Racer, CIJ/France, 1924, windup, large rubber tires with spoke wheels, opening hood caps, 21", EX, A, $2,650.00. (Photo courtesy Bertoia Auctions)

Armored Car, Dayton, friction, enclosed & windowless cab w/gun porthole, metal spoke wheels, 7½", VG, A...$225.00
Auto-Dux Racer, Germany, w/up, coiled exhaust pipes, celluloid windshield, rubber tires, 16", NM, A....................$1,200.00
Bluebird Cab (Chrysler Airflow), New Era Creations, wht rubber tires, 14", EX, A.......................................$400.00
Brougham, Kingsbury, 1927 model w/#343 license plate, w/up, rubber tires, 13", G, A $350.00
Brougham, Kingsbury, 1927 model w/343 license plate, w/up, rubber tires, 13", NM+, A $2,400.00
Cabriolet, Kingsbury, 1927 model, w/up, open driver's compartment, wht rubber tires, 14", rstr, A.........................$350.00
Chrysler Airflow Sedan, Kingsbury, 1934 model, w/up, electric lights, rubber tires, 14", VG, A $350.00
Chrysler Airflow Sedan, Kingsbury, 1936 model, w/up, electric lights, musical, rubber tires, 14", EX....................$1,000.00

Chrysler Skyroof Sedan, Kingsbury, 1937, windup, white rubber tires, 14", VG+, A, $1,100.00. (Photo courtesy Randy Inman Auctions)

Citroen B14 Sedan, Brepsomy Toys/France, retractable windows, rubber tires, rear spare, 21", NM+, A $1,050.00
Coupe, Dayton, friction, disk wheels, 18½", G, A $200.00
Coupe, Dayton, friction, rubber tires, 13", VG, A..........$350.00
Coupe, Girard, w/up, hood up, electric lights, 14", rstr, VG+, A.$110.00
Coupe, Japan, w/up, Deco style w/height of nose even w/roof, covered wheel wells, red w/NP grille, 12½", G, A...$200.00

Coupe, Kingsbury, w/up, front wire bumper, blk w/red hubs, wht rubber tires, 10½", G, A...$225.00

Coupe, Kingsbury, w/up, 1924 bl & tan model, electric lights, rumble seat, rubber tires, 13", G, A.......................$350.00

Coupe, Kingsbury, w/up, 1924 bl & tan model, electric lights, rumble seat, rubber tires, 13", VG, A.....................$650.00

Coupe, Kingsbury, w/up, 1924 2-tone purple model, electric lights, rumble seat, rubber tires, #544 plate, 13", EX, A.....$1,000.00

Coupe, Marklin, w/up, 'VW Beetle' body type w/long nose, running boards, differential & drive shaft, 15", EX+, A.........$1,760.00

Coupe, Ny-Lint, w/up, turns corners & turns in reverse, 13½", EX $250.00

Coupe, Schieble, friction, long hood & flat roof, rubber tires w/perforated disk wheels, rear spare, 18", G, A........$150.00

DeSoto Sedan, Kingsbury, 1939 model w/sliding moon roof, NP bumper, grille & hood accents, rubber tires, 14", EX, A..$500.00

Flivver Center Door Sedan, Cowdery Toy Works, enclosed cab w/operating steering wheel, spoke wheels, 11", NM, A .$550.00

Golden Arrow Racer, Kingsbury, 1920s, w/up, w/driver, 20", EX, A $600.00

Graham Sedan, NP grille, rubber tires, 19½", rpt, A......$825.00

Hansom Cab, friction Hill Climber, w/wood, close-set spoke wheels, 2 CI figures, 11", VG, A $400.00

Hudson, Cor-Cor, 20½", restored, VG+, A, $550.00. (Photo courtesy Richard Opfer Auctioneering, Inc.)

Limousine, Marklin, 2-door w/3 side windows, rear spare, chrome trim, riveted construction, M, A.................$350.00

Limousine, Schieble, friction, enclosed cab w/driver, metal spoke wheels, 12, VG, A $275.00

Mercedes Racer, Marklin, w/up, sleek styling, rubber tires w/emb simulated spoke wheels, 12", EX, A $110.00

Oldsmobile Runabout, Acme, w/up, upholstered bench, wooden steering hdl, rubber tires w/spoke wheels, 11", VG, A.$525.00

Phaeton, Kingsbury, w/up, spoke wheels, ringing bell mechanism, CI lady driver, 10", VG, A...............................$475.00

Phaeton, Wilkens, w/up, spoke wheels, lady driver, 9", VG, A...$385.00

Police Patrol, friction Hill Climber, slant front w/railed open rear, close-set spoke wheels, 2 CI figures, 9", G, A ..$250.00

Racer, Dayton, friction, 2 open bench seats, long hood, slanted rear, metal spoke wheels, 11½", overpnt, A...............$75.00

Racer, see also Golden Arrow & Sunbeam

Racer, Wilkens, side-by-side 2-seater, w/up, CI spoke wheel, w/driver, 8½", G, A $200.00

Roadster, Clark, friction, angular hood, spoke wheels, CI driver, 11", G, A...$300.00

Roadster, Clark, spring-driven, 6-sided radiator, running boards, metal spoke wheels, CI driver, 10½", Fair, A...........$225.00

Roadster, Dayton, inertia drive, metal spoke wheels, w/orig driver, 7", G, A...$225.00

Roadster, Kingsbury, w/up, electric lights, rubber tires, w/windshield, rumble seat, tan & red, 13", EX, A...............$850.00

Roadster, Kingsbury, w/up, electric lights, rubber tires, w/windshield, rumble seat, tan & red, 13", G, A.................$200.00

Roadster, Meccano, w/up, 2-seater, NP grille & headlights, celluloid windshield, wht rubber tires, 8½", EXIB, A.....$600.00

Roadster, Republic, friction, w/fenders & running boards, metal spoke wheels, no windshield, CI driver, 10", VG, A.$150.00

Roadster, Schieble, friction, open, curved back, emb hood vents, metal spoke wheels, no driver, 12½", VG, A...........$150.00

Roadster, Schieble, friction, open, sq slant back, open hood vents, metal spoke wheels, CI driver, 11½", G, A...$200.00

Roadster, Schieble, friction, open, triangular back, open hood vents, metal spoke wheels, 2 CI figures, 11", G, A ..$250.00

Roadster, Schieble, friction, top down, with windshield, rear spare, 18", no driving mechanism, G, A, $580.00. (Photo courtesy Noel Barrett Auctions)

Roadster, Schieble, friction, top up, no windshield, metal spoke wheels, rear spare, 18", VG+, A.............................$450.00

Roadster, Schieble, friction, top up, no windshield, rubber tires w/perforated disk wheels, rear spare, 18", VG, A.....$350.00

Runabout, friction Hill Climber, w/wood, slant front & back, close-set spoke wheels, CI driver, 7", G, A $330.00

Sedan, Marklin, w/up, 2-door w/spare on curved back, running boards, rubber tires w/disk wheels, drive axle, 16", EX, A.............$880.00

Sedan, Neff-Moon, early-type w/sq cab, full running boards, metal disk wheels, 12", VG, A $100.00

Sedan, Schieble, friction, 3 cut-out side windows, perforated disk wheels, 17½", G, A $220.00

Sunbeam Racer, Kingsbury, w/up, w/driver, 18", EX, A ..$2,700.00

Touring Car, Clark, friction, top down, 2-seater, 6-sided radiator, metal spoke wheels, w/driver, 10", VG, A $275.00

Touring Car, Clark, friction, top extending over open sides, full running boards, spoke wheels, 2 CI figures, 13", G, A.$165.00

Touring Car, friction Hill Climber, bonnet model w/high seats, spoke wheels, 2 CI figures, 12½", VG, A.................$275.00

Touring Car, friction Hill Climber, hood w/open side vents, close-set spoke wheels, 2 CI figures, 7", VG, A $200.00

Touring Car, friction Hill Climber, hood w/slant front, metal spoke wheels, 3 CI figures, 9", Fair, A $150.00

Touring Car, friction Hill Climber, tapered flat-sided hood, metal spoke wheels, 3 CI figures, 8", G, A...............$250.00

Touring Car, friction Hill Climber, wavy frame w/high seats, close-set spoke wheels, 3 CI figures, 8", VG, A $300.00
Touring Car, friction Hill Climber, 2 driver's seats & passenger bench, metal spoke wheels, 11", VG, A.................$225.00
Touring Car, Republic, friction, top up, running boards, metal spoke wheels, 12", VG+, A $200.00
Touring Car, Schieble, friction, top down, hood lamps, circle on radiator, metal spoke wheels, w/driver, 12", VG, A.$450.00
Touring Car, Schieble, friction, top up, full running boards, metal disk wheels, w/driver, 12½", Fair, A $85.00
Town Car, Dayton, spring-driven w/hand brake, roof extends over open front, sm metal spoke wheels, 13", VG+, A......$275.00
Town Car, Schieble, friction, resembles early van w/cut-out windows & opening doors, bench seat, spoke wheels, 12", G, A..$175.00
Yellow Cab, Dayton, friction, blk & orange, pnt metal spoke wheels, tin driver, 11", G+, A $250.00
Yellow Cab, Republic, friction, blk & orange, pnt metal spoke wheels, tin driver, 10½", VG+, A $330.00
Zephyr Sedan, Kingsbury, w/up, rubber tires, 12", rstr, A.$200.00

CONSTRUCTION

Adams Road Grader, Doepke, 1940s-50s, 27", VG, A....$165.00
Barber-Greene Bucket Loader & Conveyor, Doepke, 1950s, 23", VG+, A...$325.00
Bottom Dump, Doepke, 26", Fair, A $55.00
Bucket Loader, Doepke #2001, crank-op, steel treads, 13", G+, A...$125.00
Caterpillar 'Little Jim' Tractor, w/up, 7½", G+, A..........$100.00
Cement Mixer Truck, Lincoln Toys (Elwood Metal Products), mc pnt w/decals, 12½", MIB, A $715.00
Crane Truck, Lumar, 1950s, 33", VG, A $175.00
Euclid, Doepke, 1950s, 27", rstr, A $165.00
Euclid, Doepke, 1950s, 27", some rpt (w/box), A $300.00
Hi-Liner Construction Scraper, Doepke, 1950s, 30", EXIB, A...$385.00
Hi-Liner Construction Scraper, Doepke, 1950s, 30", G, A.$200.00
Hi-Liner Grader, Doepke, 29", G+, A...........................$125.00
Hydraulic Dumper, Ny-Lint #4600, 1960s, 23", EXIB, A.$200.00

Jaeger Cement Mixer, Doepke, 1950s, 12" long, A, $225.00.
(Photo courtesy Randy Inman Auctions)

Michigan Crane, Ny-Lint, 1960s, 20", VG+, A $125.00
Motor Grader, Doepke, 26", G+, A.............................$80.00
Panama Earth Mover, Kingsbury, w/up, open seat, 13½", VG+, A $180.00
Payloader, Ny-Lint, 1950s, open seat, rubber tires, 17", VG, A.$200.00
Payloader, Ny-Lint, 1960s, enclosed cab, rubber treads, 17", EX, A $385.00
Pettibone Speed Swing, Ny-Lint, 1960s, 18", EX, A $500.00
Pile Liner, Doepke, 1950s, 29", rstr, A $200.00
Sand Loader, Doepke, 18", G, A $110.00
Steam Shovel, Turner, 1930s, 4-wheeled, 19", EX.........$150.00
Telescoping Crane, Ny-Lint, w/plastic driver, 20", VG, A.$100.00
Tournahauler, Ny-Lint, 1960s, 32", G, A.....................$65.00
Travel Loader, Ny-Lint, 29", G, A..............................$30.00
Unit Crane, Doepke, 1950s, 24", EX+, A $325.00
Unit Crane, Doepke, 1950s, 24", G+, A $100.00

Woolridge Bottom Dump, Doepke, 1950s, 26", EX, A, $300.00. (Photo courtesy Randy Inman Auctions)

FIREFIGHTING

Aerial Ladder Truck, Clark, friction, open seat w/high cut-out sides, spoke wheels, steel ladders, 2 figures, 19", VG, A..........$525.00
Aerial Ladder Truck, Doepke, 1950s, replica of the American LaFrance, 34", complete, VG+, A $300.00

Aerial Ladder Truck, Kingsbury, windup, white rubber tires, complete, 30", Fair, A, $700.00. (Photo courtesy Richard Opfer Auctioneering, Inc.)

Aerial Ladder Truck, Kingsbury, w/up, open frame wagon w/front steering, spoke wheels, wood ladders, w/driver, 18", G, A $385.00
Aerial Ladder Truck, Kingsbury, w/up, solid frame & open seat, full running boards, wht rubber tires, w/ladders, 34", VG ..$900.00
Aerial Ladder Truck, Turner, friction, open seat, metal disk wheels, 3 metal ladders, 13", G, A $475.00

Big Boy Ladder Truck, Kelmet, open w/metal disk wheels, 3 wooden ladders, 36", VG, A.....................................$550.00

Chemical & Ladder Truck, Kingsbury, #359, w/up, open seat, railed bed, wht rubber tires, 2 wood ladders, 14", G, A..........$450.00

Chemical & Ladder Truck, Kingsbury, w/up, open seat, wht rubber tires, 3 steel ladders, 34", G, A........................$1,870.00

City Fire Dept Truck, Steelcraft, open w/low body, rubber tires, side ladders & hose reel, bell on hood, 26", VG, A.$1,425.00

City Fire Dept Truck, Steelcraft, pickup-type truck, rubber tires, 20", VG, A..$250.00

Fire Chief's Car, Girard, w/up, electric lights, rubber tires, 14", NMIB, A $2,300.00

Fire Chief's Car, Girard, w/up, electric lights, rubber tires, 14", VG, A $250.00

Fire Chief's Car, Hoge, windup, electric lights and siren, rubber tires, 14", EX, A, $450.00. (Photo courtesy Bertoia Auctions)

Fire Chief's Car, Kingsbury, w/up, open w/wire bumper, no windshield, rubber tires, 11", VG, A.................................$400.00

Fire Chief's Car, Kingsbury #341, w/up, open w/NP bumpers & radiator, wht rubber tires, 12", G, A.........................$225.00

Fire Patrol Truck, Clark, friction Hill Climber, open seat, metal spoke wheels, 2 CI figures, 11", VG, A $600.00

Fire Station & Aerial Ladder Truck, Kingsbury, w/up, CI driver on open frame w/rubber tires on metal hubs, 19", EX+, A.$2,200.00

Fire Station #8 & Pumper Wagon, Kingsbury, w/up, pumper w/metal spoke wheels, driver, 13", VG, A $475.00

Fire Truck, Clark, friction, open cab w/rear platform, metal spoke wheels, 2 short ladders, 2 CI figures, 14½", VG, A ...$775.00

Hook & Ladder Truck, Oh Boy, 1920s, open seat w/ladders on open bed, metal disk wheels, 20", G+, A.................$500.00

Hose Reel Truck, friction Hill Climber, metal spoke wheels, wooden reel, 2 CI figures, 10", G+, A......................$350.00

Ladder & Hose Truck, Doepke, mk Rossmoyne, 19", VG+, A.$300.00

Ladder Truck, Dayton, 1920s, open frame & seat, metal disk wheels, red w/gr radiator & seat, 3 ladders, 18", VG+, A...........$165.00

Ladder Truck, Dayton, 1930s, topless cab w/doors, NP disk wheels, 19", VG, A..$200.00

Ladder Truck, Kelmet, 1920s, open bench seat, fire extinguisher & bell, wooden ladders, 35", G, A $875.00

Ladder Truck, Kingsbury, w/up, open frame, metal disk wheels, 2 wooden ladders, CI driver, 11", EX, A $350.00

Ladder Truck, Kingsbury #258, w/up, open cab, electric lights, wht rubber tires, NP ladders, 13½", VG..............$1,000.00

Ladder Truck, Republic, friction, open w/cut-out sides, metal disk wheels, 3 steel ladders, tin driver, 17", EX, A...$525.00

Ladder Truck, Schieble, friction, open w/cut-out sides, metal spoke wheels, 3 wooden ladders, tin driver, 21", G, A $225.00

Ladder Truck, Schieble, friction, open w/cut-out sides, perforated disk wheels, w/extension ladder, 20", VG, A..$350.00

Ladder Truck, Turner, open cab w/doors, 24", Fair, A.....$130.00

Ladder Wagon, Schieble, friction, open frame w/high bench seat, spoke wheels, 3 wooden ladders, tin driver, 18", G, A.$275.00

Mack Fire Truck, Steelcraft, 1930s, marked City Fire Dept, 24", G, A, $935.00. (Photo courtesy Randy Inman Auctions)

Pumper Truck, Clark, friction, open frame wagon w/suspended boiler, metal spoke wheels, w/driver, 11", VG, A $250.00

Pumper Truck, Clark, friction, open w/rear platform, metal spoke wheels, 14½", VG, A $250.00

Pumper Truck, Dayton, friction, open seat, wire-railed back, rubber tires w/disk wheels, 15", VG, A.........................$325.00

Pumper Truck, friction Hill Climber, open frame w/bench seat, 2 lg & 2 sm metal spoke wheels, CI driver, 11", G, A .$330.00

Pumper Truck, friction Hill Climber, wood & pressed steel, slant front w/close-set spoke wheels, CI driver, 10", VG, A $500.00

Pumper Truck, Kingsbury, w/up, open frame wagon w/front steering, spoke wheels, w/driver, 11", VG, A $250.00

Pumper Truck, Republic, friction, open w/curved high-back seat, metal disk wheels, tin driver, 12", EX, A $385.00

Pumper Truck, Republic, friction, open w/rear platform, metal spoke wheels w/side spares, 2 firemen, 14", Fair.......$150.00

Pumper Truck, Schieble, friction, open w/circular cutouts, wood & tin boilers, spoke wheels, CI driver, 14", VG, A .$275.00

Pumper Truck, Schieble, open w/cut-out sides, full running boards, metal wheels, red w/gold, wht & gr trim, 20", EX, A...$350.00

Pumper Truck, Sturditoy #7, 26½", Fair+, A, $800.00. (Photo courtesy Richard Opfer Auctioneering, Inc.)

Pumper Truck, Turner, w/2 ladders & hose reel, rubber tires, 27", rpt, A $400.00

Pumper Truck, Wilkens, w/up, open frame wagon w/front steering, metal spoke wheels, w/driver, 10", G, A $165.00

Pumper Wagon, Wilkens/Kingsbury, open frame, CI driver & 3 horses, 17", VG, A..................................$225.00

Siren Fire Car, Gerard, 1930s, w/up, electric lights, 15", EXIB, A $700.00

Water Tower Truck, Clark, friction, open w/metal spoke wheels, tin driver, 19", Fair, A...........................$225.00

Water Tower Truck, Republic, friction, ladders missing, 20", Fair, A $50.00

Water Tower Truck, Schieble, friction, open w/metal spoke wheels, 11", G, A..................................$150.00

TRAINS

Locomotive & Tender, Clark, friction Hill Climber, pressed steel & wood, w/cow catcher, spoke wheels, 19½", EX, A.$350.00

Locomotive & Tender, Converse, mk 999, w/wood, 27" overall, G, A $130.00

Locomotive and Tender, Steelcraft, 1930s, rider, 22", EX, A, $250.00. (Photo courtesy Randy Inman Auctions)

TROLLEYS AND BUSSES

Bus, Cor-Cor, long nose w/2 side spares, cut-out windows, 24", Fair+, A $200.00

Bus, Cowdery Toy Works, with interior bench seating, 16", NM, A, $1,870.00. (Photo courtesy Bertoia Auctions)

Bus, Kingsbury, snub nose w/cut-out windows, roof lights above windshield, 18", Fair.....................$150.00

Bus, Schieble, friction, long hood, orig tires, 20", VG+, A.$635.00

Bus (American Deluxe), Dayton, friction, 26", VG, A ..$700.00

Bus (Greyhound), Kingsbury, w/up, rubber tires, 18", EX, A.$450.00

Bus (Inter-City), Steelcraft, 1930s, metal disk wheels w/side spares, 25", G, A..................................$300.00

Trolley, Dayton, friction, enclosed ends, cut-out windows, metal spoke wheels, yel & red, 15", VG, A.......................$110.00

Trolley, friction, bench seats with reversible backrests, metal spoke wheels, red and yellow, with driver, 14", EX+, A, $1,100.00. (Photo courtesy Bertoia Auctions)

Trolley, Kingsbury, #782, enclosed ends, cut-out windows, yel-orange, 9", VG, A.....................................$125.00

Trolley, Kingsbury, #784, w/up, enclosed ends, center doors, EX+, A...$300.00

Trolley, Republic, friction, enclosed ends, cut-out windows, 16", G, A $75.00

Trolley (City Hall), Converse, w/up, 16", VG+, A.........$525.00

Trolley (Pay as You Enter), yel w/red roof, 23", VG+, A .$225.00

Trolley (Rapid Transit), Schieble, friction Hill Climber, metal disk wheels, 21", G+, A.............................$250.00

TRUCKS AND VANS

ABC Sports TV Truck (Semi), Ny-Lint, wht, 22", EXIB, A.$100.00

Ambulance, Sturditoy, rubber tires, 26", EX, A, $16,500.00. (Photo courtesy Randy Inman Auctions)

Ambulance, Sturditoy, van roof extends over open cab, rubber tires, cream w/Red Cross emblem, 26", G+, A $6,600.00

Armored Truck, Clark, friction, spoke wheels, 10½", VG, A $325.00

Army Truck, see Cannon Truck, Mack Army Truck or Son-ny Army Truck

Artillery Truck, Kingsbury, w/up, rubber tires, w/orig wooden wheels, 15", EX, A $75.00

Artillery Truck, Schieble, friction, open w/bench seat, cannon enclosed w/side rails, metal spoke wheels, driver, VG.$450.00

Borden Delivery Truck, Kingsbury, doorless sides, silver w/red lettering, 9", VG, A $325.00

Brink's Security Truck/Bank, Ny-Lint, pressed steel & plastic, wht w/red & blk trim, slot on side, 16", NMIB, A $55.00

Bulldog Trucks, see Mack

Canadian Pacific Express Tractor-Trailer, Lincoln/Canada, U-shaped trailer w/stake sides & open rear, 18½", EX, A...........$1,750.00

Cannon Truck, Dayton, friction, open bench seat, sm rear mounted cannon, metal spoke wheels, khaki & red, 11", VG, A $300.00

Cannon Truck, Kingsbury, 1940s, w/up, w/accessory missiles, 15½", VG, A $150.00

Cannon Truck, Ny-Lint, 1960s, license plate reads N-2400, army gr, lg deep-tread tires, 23", VGIB, A $100.00

Cannon Truck, see also Artillery Truck

Car Carrier, Lincoln/Canada, tractor w/2-tier trailer containing 4 plastic cars, 24½", EX, A $1,650.00

City Milk Co Delivery Van, Steelcraft, open windows & side doors, rubber tires, 18", rstr, A................................$200.00

Coal & Coke Dump Truck, Lincoln Toys/Canada, opening tailgate, 16", VG, A $775.00

Coal Truck, see also Mack Coal Truck

Coal Truck, Sturditoy, 1920s, doorless cab, side-dump bed w/deep sides, rubber tires w/disk wheels, orange, 26", G, A.$2,300.00

Coal Truck, Sturditoy, 1920s, doorless cab, slant bed w/side chute, rubber tires w/disk wheels, blk & red, 27", rstr, A....$1,050.00

Crane Truck, Turner, 1930s, truck-mounted crane, red, yel & gr, 21", EX, A..$450.00

CW Brand Coffee Delivery Van, Metalcraft, 1920s, metal disk wheels, blk & gr, 11", G+, A $500.00

Delivery Truck, Kingsbury, w/up, roof extends over open seat, open bed, wht rubber tires, w/bell, 9½", G, A $175.00

Delivery Truck, Republic, friction Hill Climber, open stake bed, metal spoke wheels, cast metal driver, 13", VG, A ..$400.00

Delivery Van, Clark, friction, roof extends over open front, metal spoke wheels, CI driver, 10", VG+, A............$325.00

Delivery Van, Dayton, 1911, friction, roof extends over open front, short running boards, spoke wheels, w/driver, VG, A ..$110.00

Delivery Van, Republic, friction, doorless cab, metal spoke wheels, litho tin driver, 11½", G, A $125.00

Delivery Van, see also specific names such as Groceries, Hoosier, Jr Milk, etc

Department of Highways Dump Truck, Lincoln Toys/Canada, opening tailgate, bl cab w/orange dump bed, 19½", EX, A $1,050.00

Dray, Wilkens/Kingsbury, w/up, C-cab (no hood) w/top over open-sided bed, metal spoke wheels, CI driver, 10", VG+, A $525.00

Dray, Wilkens/Kingsbury, w/up, wagon-type w/open seat, metal spoke wheels, CI driver, 9", EX, A $165.00

Dump Truck, Dayton, friction Hill Climber, open cab w/driver, metal spoke wheels, 13", G, A.............................$75.00

Dump Truck, Kingsbury, w/up, enclosed cab w/slanted dump bed, rubber tires, w/bell, 10½", G, A $150.00

Dump Truck, Kingsbury, w/up, long hood w/emb side vents, visor, tailgate chain, metal disk wheels, 13½", VG+, A......$325.00

Dump Truck, Kingsbury, w/up, open frame & seat w/slanted dump bed, rubber tires, CI driver, 9", G, A..............$125.00

Dump Truck, Kingsbury, w/up, open frame & seat w/straight bed, electric lights, rubber tires, CI driver, 9", G+, A $175.00

Dump Truck, Neff-Moon, open cab w/bench seat, side-lever tilting action, metal disk wheels, 13½", EX, A.............$130.00

Dump Truck, Republic, friction, doorless cab, metal disk wheels, litho tin driver, red, 20", G, A................................$175.00

Dump Truck, Republic, friction, enclosed cab w/visor, metal disk wheels, yel & blk, 13½", G, A $130.00

Dump Truck, see also specific names such as GMC, Mack, Junior, etc.

Dump Truck, Schieble, 1920s, flywheel motor, 20", EX, A, $1,150.00. (Photo courtesy Randy Inman Auctions)

Dump Truck, Steelcraft, 1930s, enclosed cab w/slanted dump bed, rubber tires, yel & aqua, 23", VG+, A..............$385.00

Dump Truck, Steelcraft, 1930s, enclosed cab w/straight dump bed, metal disk wheels, red & blk, 22", G, A...........$100.00

Dump Truck, Sturditoy, 1920s, doorless cab, ratchet dump action, 27", Poor, A $275.00

Dump Truck, Sturditoy, 1920s, doorless cab, ratchet dump action, 27", VG+, A $675.00

Dump Truck, Tri-Ang, enclosed cab w/flat roof, front fenders w/short running boards, thick blk tires, orange, 20", G, A..........$200.00

Dump Truck, Turner, 1940s, enclosed cab, long dump bed w/curved ends, rear dual axle, yel, gr & red, 26", G+, A...$200.00

Electronic Cannon Truck, Ny-Lint #2400, 1960s, 22", VGIB, A $150.00

Express Stake Truck, Clark, friction, open seat, metal spoke wheels, CI driver, gr w/gold trim, 13", G+, A..........$185.00

Express Stake Truck, Dayton, friction, open seat, metal spoke wheels, no driver, blk w/gold trim, 14½", VG+, A..$225.00

Express Stake Truck, Metalcraft, 1920s, electric lights, rubber tires, bl w/NP radiator, 12", G, A $250.00

Express Tractor-Trailer, Kingsbury, w/up, cabover w/open U-shaped stake trailer, rubber tires, red & yel, 20", G, A $100.00

Express Truck, Republic, friction, doorless enclosed cab, short running boards, spoke wheels, tin driver, 12½", G+, A ..$325.00

Express Truck, Schieble, friction, open cab & bed, metal spoke wheels, tin driver, 10", VG+, A $325.00

Ford Huckster One-Ton Delivery Van, enclosed cab w/extended roof over open-sided bed w/posts, spoke wheels, 14", VG, A $1,870.00

GMC Dump Truck, Steelcraft, open cab, side-lever dump action, rubber tires w/disk wheels, 26½", G, A $175.00

Groceries Van, Kingsbury, C-style roof extends over open front (no hood), wht rubber tires, gr w/red trim, 7", VG+, A $350.00

Heinz Truck, Metalcraft, electric lights, wht w/decals, rubber tires, 12", NMIB $1,000.00

Heinz Truck, Metalcraft, electric lights, wht w/decals, rubber tires, 12", G, A $300.00

Hi-Way Emergency Tow Truck, Ny-Lint, red & wht, 16", G+ $100.00

Hoosier Delivery Van, Metalcraft, opening tailgate, blk & red w/disk wheels, 11", very rare, EX $2,500.00

Hoosier Dump Truck, Metalcraft, lever-action dump bed, blk & red w/disk wheels, approximately 11", VG, A $1,650.00

Huckster Pick-up Truck, Kingsbury, w/up, gr w/gold trim, rubber tires, 14", VG $650.00

Ice Truck, Lincoln Toys, open bed w/orig cubes & tongs, red & yel, 13", MIB, A $3,025.00

IH Dump Truck, Eska, hydraulic action, orange, 15", VG, A .$400.00

Interchangeable Truck, Neff Moon, five different interchangeable parts in various colors, EXIB, A, $2,000.00. (Photo courtesy Bertoia Auctions)

Interchangeable Truck, Neff-Moon, 1920s, friction, w/3 different interchangeable parts, 12", Fair+, A $150.00

Jordan Marsh Delivery Van, Steelcraft, ca 1934, electric lights, rubber tires, gr & gray, 19", EX, A $2,970.00

Krug's Delivery Truck, Metalcraft, w/van box, 11½", G, A $130.00

Lincoln Hi-Dump Truck, Lincoln Toys/Canada, 20", VG, A.$110.00

Lincoln Self-Loading Dump Truck, Elwood Metal Products, scoop attached to front of cab, 15½", MIB, A $990.00

Lincoln Van Lines, Lincoln/Canada, tractor w/van trailer, 22½", EX, A $4,125.00

Little Jim Dump Truck, Steelcraft, 1930s, 23", VG $450.00

Machinery Hauler, Metalcraft, electric lights, carries No 4 steam shovel, rubber tires, 12", VG, A $400.00

Mack Army Truck, Steelcraft, open seat, no windshield, open bed, disk wheels, gold w/red, 22", Fair+, A $135.00

Mack Army Truck, Steelcraft, 1930s, open bed (missing canvas top), disk wheels, gold w/red trim, 23", G+, A $325.00

Mack Army Truck, Steelcraft, 1930s, w/canvas Conestoga-style top, disk wheels, 23", EX, A...................................$1,200.00

Mack Coal Truck, American National, 1920s, rubber tires, crank noisemaker, pull cord, red and black, 26", VG, A, $9,020.00. (Photo courtesy Randy Inman Auctions)

Mack Dump Truck, Steelcraft, 1920s, C-style cab, disk wheels, 25½", G+ $385.00

Mack Dump Truck, Steelcraft, 1930s, sq cab, 25", rstr, A ..$250.00

Mack Dump Truck, Toledo, 1920s, doorless C-style cab, rubber tires w/disk wheels, blk & orange, 27", rstr, EX, A .$1,450.00

Mack Dump Truck, Toledo, 1920s, doorless C-style cab, rubber tires w/disk wheels, red & blk, 27", EX+, A $5,170.00

Mack Dump Truck, Turner, 1930s, tandem rear axles, 26", G..$250.00

Mack Express Truck, Toledo, 1926, screened van w/roof extending over open seat, disk wheels, blk & tan w/red, 26", VG, A...$2,750.00

Mack Ice Truck, Steelcraft/Les-Paul Collector's edition, w/canvas cover, rubber tires w/spoke wheels, 24½", EX....$475.00

Mack Railway Express Truck, Steelcraft, disk wheels, red and green, 25", VG, A, $4,125.00. (Photo courtesy Bertoia Auctions)

Mack Stake Truck, Master Metal Products, electric lights, rubber tires, 20½", VG, A $400.00

Mail Truck, Dayton, friction, 1920s, open bucket seats w/open nose, 1-pc fenders over spoke wheels, 13", VG+, A .$350.00

Marklin Delivery Truck, early model w/enclosed cab, name printed on canvas top, M, A $275.00

Metalcraft Express Stake Truck, 1920s, electric lights, rubber tires, red & bl, 12", G, A $415.00

Metalcraft St Louis Delivery Truck, enclosed van, metal disk wheels, 12", VG, A $200.00

Minic Garages Tow Truck, Tri-Ang, friction, electric searchlight, 8", VG+, A $150.00

Moving Van, Steelcraft, 1920s, GMC w/roof extending over open seat, opening gate, disk wheels, 25", Poor, A ..$385.00

Ogilvie All Purpose Flour Stake Truck, Lincoln Toys, 1940s, red & wht, EX+, A $1,265.00

Packard Dump Truck, Turner, 1925, full running boards, rubber tires, 28", VG $475.00

Panama Dump Wagon, Kingsbury, w/up, front steering, metal spoke wheels, CI driver, 13", G, A $125.00

Panama Dump Wagon, Kingsbury, w/up, front steering, rubber tires, CI driver, 13", VG, A $250.00

Parcel Post Delivery Van, Wilkens/Kingsbury, w/up, extended roof over open front, spoke wheels, CI driver, bell, 7", VG.$250.00

Pickup Truck, Schieble, friction, long hood w/emb vents, oval side windows, solid disk wheels, 19", NM, A........$1,200.00

Pickup Truck, Schieble, friction, long hood w/emb vents, oval side windows, perforated disk wheels, 19", VG, A...$450.00

Playboy Trucking Co Delivery Truck, Steelcraft, 1930s, truck w/4-wheeled trailer, disk wheels, 24", VG $1,050.00

Playboy Trucking Co Mack Dump Truck, Steelcraft, 1930s, red & gr, 25", VG, A $825.00

Plee-Zing Dump Truck, Metalcraft, lever-action dump bed w/opening tailgate, disk wheels, 11", G, A $150.00

Police Patrol Truck, Clark, friction, open, metal spoke wheels, CI driver, 14", Fair+, A $200.00

Power & Light Co Truck, Ny-Lint, 1960s, complete, 20", EX, A $250.00

R Grocer/Rite-Way Food Stores, metal disk wheels, 1920s, 11", VG $1,600.00

Rold Gold Pretzels Delivery Truck, Metalcraft, enclosed cab, working tailgate, disk wheels, 11", EX, A $1,325.00

Royal Mail Truck, Bing, 1920s, side ladder leading to railed roof, metal disk wheels, red & blk w/orange hubs, 22", VG .$2,000.00

Royal Mail Van, Tri-Ang, 1930s, metal disk wheels, red & blk, 20", VG, A $1,430.00

Sand & Gravel Truck, Metalcraft, 1920s, metal disk wheels, red & blk, 12", VG, A $385.00

Sand Truck, Schieble, friction Hill Climber, hinged tailgate, metal disk wheels, 17½", rstr, A $225.00

Schuster's Milwaukee Delivery Van, Steelcraft, 1930s, electric lights, steering hdl, brn, 19", EX+, A....................$4,125.00

Sheffield Farms Co Delivery Van, Steelcraft, electric lights, red w/red hubs, NP grille, 20", G, A........................$835.00

Sheffield Farms Co Delivery Van, Steelcraft, electric lights, red w/yel hubs, NP grille, 20", VG+, A $1,320.00

Sheffield Farms Co Stake Truck, Steelcraft, 1930s, Mack cab, red w/yel hubs, 22", EX, A $3,575.00

Shell Motor Oil Stake Truck, Metalcraft, electric lights, w/accessories, 12", VG, A $600.00

Son-ny Army Truck, doorless C-cab, canvas bed topper, rubber tires, 26½", EX, A..$1,760.00

Son-ny Army Truck, open seat & bed w/mounted cannon, 24", Poor, A..$275.00

Son-ny Dump Truck, open bench seat, metal disk wheels, blk w/red hubs, 26½", rpt, A $175.00

Son-ny Dump Truck, open bench seat, metal disk wheels, yel, 26½", G+, A $360.00

Son-ny Moving Van, roof extends over open bench seat, metal disk wheels, blk & red, 26", VG, A $1,000.00

Son-ny Moving Van, roof extends over open seat, metal disk wheels, blk & red, 26", rstr, A...............................$1,050.00

Son-ny Parcel Post Truck, screened van w/roof extending over open seat, metal disk wheels, blk & gr w/red, 26", G, A $935.00

Stake Truck, Cor-Cor, 1930s, extra long hood, rear step platform, metal disk wheels, blk & gray w/yel hubs, 24", G+, A..$225.00

Stake Truck, Dayton, friction, open cab, metal spoke wheels, 13", G..$150.00

Stake Truck, Kingsbury, w/up, no fenders or running boards, rubber tires, blk w/NP radiator & red hubs, 11", VG, A .$250.00

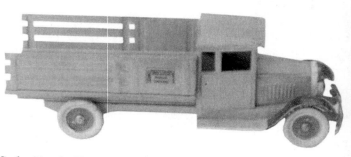

Stake Truck, Kingsbury #349, motor-driven clockwork, rubber tires, yellow, 15½", EX, A, $7,700.00. (Photo courtesy Noel Barrett Auctions)

Standard Tanker Truck, Marklin, w/up, red cab & tank w/bl outer frame, running boards, drive axle, 17", EX+, A......$3,025.00

Street Sprinkler, Ny-Lint, Ford tilt cab, 16", EX+ $150.00

Sturditoy Construction Co Dump Truck, doorless enclosed cab, rubber tires w/disk wheels, VG, A $1,200.00

Rossmoyne Searchlight Truck, 1950s, white, 19", restored, A, $900.00. (Photo courtesy Randy Inman Auctions)

Sunshine Biscuits Delivery Van, Metalcraft, 1920s, electric lights, yel, 13", EX, A....................................$1,265.00

Sunshine Biscuits Stake Truck, Metalcraft, 1920s, metal disk wheels, 12", VG, A..$600.00

Tanker Truck, see Standard Tanker Truck or White Tanker Truck

Tow Truck, Kingsbury, 1930s, w/up, sq cab w/curved front bumper, metal disk wheels, red w/NP trim, 11", VG $350.00

Tow Truck, Schieble, friction, early vented long-nose hood, disk wheels, 20", VG, A.......................................$580.00

Towing & Repairs Tow Truck, Metalcraft, NP disk wheels, blk & yel-orange, 10", G, A......................................$350.00

Towing — Repairs Tow Truck, Metalcraft, NP disk wheels, blk & yel, 10", EX+, A..$715.00

Turnahauler, Ny-Lint #1700, 1950s, tractor w/lowboy trailer, 32", VG, A..$150.00

U-Haul Truck Pulling Trailer, Ny-Lint, enclosed, 30", G+, A.$60.00

US Mail Delivery Van, Kingsbury/Wilkens, w/up, roof extends over open seat, rubber tires, spoke wheels, driver, 7", G..$200.00

US Mail Delivery Van, Schieble, friction, roof extends over open seat, metal spoke wheels, 12", no driver o/w EX, A..$385.00

US Mail Delivery Van, Sturditoy, roof extends over open seat, screened sides, rubber tires w/disk wheels, 26", VG, A...$2,900.00

US Mail Snowcrawler, Cowdery Toy Works, front blade runners, rear wheels w/traction chain, 11½", NM, A........$2,200.00

Weston's English Quality Biscuits Stake Truck, Metalcraft, 1920s, rubber tires, red & bl, 12", G+, A.................$770.00

White Dump Truck, Burdett-Murray, doorless cab, spoke wheels, 26", G+, A..$1,350.00

White Dump Truck, Kelmet, 1920s, doorless cab, metal spoke wheels, blk & red, 26", VG, A...............................$1,150.00

White Dump Truck, Kelmet, 1920s, open bench seat, metal disk wheels, blk & red, 25", G, A..............................$525.00

White Dump Truck, Steelcraft, enclosed cab, side crank dumping action, rubber tires, 24", VG, A........................$155.00

White King Express Stake Truck, Metalcraft, disk wheels, 12", VG, A...$600.00

White Tanker Truck, Kelmet, black and red with white rubber tires on spoke wheels, 26", EX, A, $1,300.00. (Photo courtesy Richard Opfer Auctioneering)

Woodward's (Dept Store) Semi, Lincoln Toys, 1950s, rubber tires, bl w/wht lettering, 28", EX+, A..................$1,200.00

Wrecker, see Tow Truck

Yuengling Dairy Products Delivery Van, Steelcraft, doorless sides, gr & wht, 18", G+, A..............................$1,320.00

Circus Cage Wagon, Republic, friction, cast metal driver & 2 animals, 12", Fair+, A.....................................$125.00

Circus Cage Wagon, Schieble, friction, metal spoke wheels, CI driver, paper litho animals, 14", Fair+, A...............$300.00

Garage, Turner (?), yel w/red roof & door, side cut-out windows, 14" L, G...$150.00

Garage w/2 Roadsters, Turner, friction, 8x8½" garage, VG, A.$230.00

Gas Station, Gibbs, litho paper on tin building w/pressed steel roof, single pump under canopy, 15", G, A...............$165.00

Graf Zeppelin, Steelcraft, 32", restored, EX, A, $375.00. (Photo courtesy Richard Opfer Auctioneering)

Horse-Drawn Dray, Wilkens/Kingsbury, w/up, roof extending over open front, CI spoke wheels, driver & 2 horses, 17", G, A..$740.00

Lawn Mower, Webb, reel-type, 27", EX (G box), A, $500.00.

(Photo courtesy Randy Inman Auctions)

Missile Launcher, Ny-Lint, 21", G+, A............................$80.00

Tank, Clark, friction, 12", VG, A.................................$330.00

Tank, Dayton, early, friction, 12½", G+, A.......................$220.00

Promotional Vehicles

Miniature Model T Fords were made by Tootsietoy during the 1920s, and a few of these were handed out by Ford dealers to promote the new models. In 1932 Tootsietoy was contacted by Graham-Paige to produce a model of their car. These 4" Grahams were sold in boxes as sales promotions by car dealerships, and some were sold through the toy company's catalog. But it wasn't until after WWII that distribution of 1/25 scale promotional models and kits became commonplace. Early models were of cast metal, but during the 1950s, manufacturers turned to plastic. Not only was the material less costly to use, but it could be molded in the color desired, thereby saving the time and expense previously involved in painting the metal. Though the early plastic cars were prone to warp easily, by the early '60s they had become more durable. Some were friction powered, others battery-operated. Advertising extolling some of the model's features was often embossed on the underside. Among the toy manufacturers involved in making promotionals were National Products, Product Miniature, AMT, MPC, and Jo-Han. Interest in '50s and '60s models is intense, and the muscle cars from the '60s and early '70s are especially collectible. The more popularity the life-size models attain, the more popular the promotional is with collectors.

Check the model for damage, warping, and amateur alterations. The original box can increase the value by as much as 100%. Jo-Han has reissued some of their 1950s and 1960s Mopar and Cadillac models as well as Chrysler's Turbine Car. These are usually priced between $20.00 and $30.00.

Nothing affects values of promos more than color, and the difference can be substantial.

If you'd like more information we recommend *The Little Ones Sell the Big Ones!* by Larry Blodget.

Advisor: Larry Blodget

Chevy El Camino, 1960, pale green, 8", EX+, $150.00.

Buick Electra 225, 1962, wht w/chrome trim, AMT, NM..$240.00
Buick Roadmaster, 1954, wht w/red top, remote control, Aluminum Model Toys, EXIB $85.00
Buick Roadmaster, 1958, Polar Mist, EX........................$135.00
Buick Skylark, 1954, lt bl w/painted-on chrome trim, EX .$125.00
Buick Skylark Convertible, 1954, gray w/red & wht interior, VG+..$110.00
Cadillac De Ville Hardtop, 1964, red, Jo-Han, EX $160.00
Cadillac Fleetwood, 1962, yel w/yel interior, Jo-Han, EX ..$110.00
Chevy Belair, 1956, wht over bl, bank, 8", EX..................$85.00
Chevy Camaro Rally Sport SS, 1968, cream, NM..........$250.00
Chevy Camaro Rally Sport SS Convertible (Indy Pace Car), 1967, wht w/bl interior, M......................................$740.00
Chevy Camaro Rally Sport 350, 1973, metallic orange, NMIB.$100.00
Chevy Caprice, 1973, rust, EX $95.00
Chevy Caprice, 1974, bl, EX $80.00
Chevy Corvair, 1965, red, VG..$95.00
Chevy Corvette, 1962, red, EX $750.00
Chevy Corvette, 1976, wht, NMIB....................................$85.00
Chevy Corvette, 1984, silver, MIB....................................$25.00
Chevy Corvette, 1993, metallic burgundy, M $25.00

Chevy Corvette Stingray, 1975, orange, M......................$90.00
Chevy Custom 10 Pickup Truck, 1966, med red, VG.....$275.00
Chevy El Camino, 1964, Saddle Tan $125.00
Chevy Impala, 1963, wht, 409 insignia on side, EX $100.00
Chevy Impala, 1970, yel, AMT, EX $95.00
Chevy Impala, 1972, metallic turq, EX $80.00
Chevy Impala Convertible, 1966, red w/red interior, AMT, EX.$210.00
Chevy Impala Fire Chief Car, 1960, red w/siren $75.00
Chevy Impala SS, 1963, beige, friction, EX....................$100.00
Chevy Monza 2+2, 1976, NM...$15.00
Chrysler New Yorker, 1960, wht over bl, EX $100.00
Chrysler Turbine Car, red w/blk roof, red interior, EXIB.....$135.00
Chrysler 300 Convertible, 1963, metallic turq w/beige interior, Jo-Han, MIB $375.00
Corvette Convertible, 1959, red & silver, friction, M $350.00
Dodge Coronet, 1950, 4-door, pot-metal Banthrico promo, lt gr, 70% paint $145.00
Dodge Coronet, 1969, olive gr, NMIB............................$450.00
Dodge Phoenix, 1960, beige w/lt bl top, Jo-Han, EXIB..$105.00
Dodge Royal Lancer, 1955, rose over beige w/blk roof, EX.$90.00
Dodge Viper Coupe, 1994, yel, MIB................................$25.00
Edsel Convertible, 1960, blk, friction, NM.....................$275.00
Edsel Convertible, 1960, gr, nonfriction version, MIB...$550.00
Ford Chicago Police Car, 1940s, Master Caster Chicago, VG.$135.00
Ford Country Sedan, 1957, bank, bright yel, PMC $175.00
Ford Country Sedan Station Wagon, 1958, bl & wht, EX.$175.00
Ford Country Sedan station wagon, 1962, Sandstone Beige, M..$50.00
Ford Custom, 1949, Seamist Green, EX $75.00
Ford F-100 Pickup Truck, 1960, gr w/wht top, friction, NM .$150.00
Ford Fairlane, 1958, yel & wht w/gold trim, EX $130.00

Ford Galaxie Convertible With Top Up, 1962, light blue with white top, 8¼", EX, $200.00.

Ford Galaxie, 1962, red w/red interior, MIB $550.00
Ford Galaxie, 1962, yel w/wht top & interior, MIB........$210.00
Ford Galaxie, 1963, turq, EX $20.00
Ford Galaxie Starliner, 1960, blk w/blk & wht interior, M.$160.00
Ford Model A Roadster, 1903, AMT (1953), MIB.........$750.00
Ford Mustang Coupe, 1965, lt bl, EX $65.00
Ford Mustang Coupe, 1965, red, EX...............................$75.00
Ford Mustang Mach I, 1972, metallic pewter, EX..........$350.00
Ford Starliner, 1960, wht over bronze metallic, friction ...$65.00
Ford Sunliner w/Coronado Deck, 1953, Seafoam Green, EX.$200.00
Ford Thunderbird, 1955, blk, EX $350.00
Ford Thunderbird, 1955, lt aqua Sky Haze Green w/matching interior $295.00
Ford Thunderbird, 1957, bronze, EX $375.00
Ford Thunderbird, 1961, pale gr w/gold trim, EX $100.00
Ford Thunderbird Convertible, 1962, lt bl, friction, EX..$200.00

Ford Tractor, 1950s, gray and red, 9", EX (G box), $300.00.

Ford Victoria, 1955, wht & purple, EX $170.00
Ford Victoria, 1956, mauve & wht w/red & wht interior, friction, EX..$210.00
Ford Victoria, 1956, Peacock Blue & wht, EX+ $240.00
Ford ½ Mustang (Indy Pace Car), 1964, wht, NM.........$160.00
Ford 4-Door Sedan, 1950, mirrored windows, w/up, EX.$125.00
GMC Jimmy, 1996, blk, MIB...$25.00
Hudson, 1949, 2-tone gr, plastic, VG.............................$450.00
Hudson Commodore, 1949, deep maroon & ruby red, EX..$750.00
Imperial Crown, 1962, wht, EX......................................$375.00
Imperial Crown hardtop, 1963, off wht, missing hood ornament $350.00
Javelin 390 SST, 1969, yel w/red stripes, EX $90.00
Mercury Meteor, 1962, wht, EX $250.00
Mercury Park Lane 2-Door Hardtop, 1960, EX..............$110.00
Mercury Park Lane, 1964, silver, MIB............................$750.00
Mercury Sedan, 1940, stamp dispenser, Mandarin Maroon, 90% paint...$125.00
Nash Airflyte, 1949, brn, National Products, MIB.........$500.00
Oldsmobile Ninety-Eight, 1960, cranberry red, EX $80.00
Opel GT, 1969, red, AMT, EX $100.00
Plymouth Belvedere, 1957, red w/gray top & stripe, friction, Jo-Han, EX $85.00
Plymouth Cuda, 1970, red, NM $275.00
Plymouth Fury, 1962, yel w/wht seat trim, friction, Jo-Jan, EX+..$100.00
Plymouth Savoy 2-Door Sedan, 1956, turq, EX..............$225.00
Pontiac Bonneville, 1958, wht over pk, EX $150.00
Pontiac Bonneville, 1958, 2-tone gr, tin bottom, EX $185.00
Pontiac Grand Prix, 1965, gold, NMIB..........................$410.00
Pontiac Grand Prix, 1970, blk, EX $160.00
Pontiac Grand Prix SJ, 1969, gray w/bl top, EX...............$85.00
Pontiac GTO, 1965, metallic gr, NMIP $400.00
Pontiac GTO, 1965, turq, NM.......................................$265.00
Pontiac GTO, 1966, silver w/silver interior, EX+...........$240.00
Pontiac GTO, 1970, red, plastic, EX..............................$100.00
Pontiac GTO Convertible, 1967, ivory, NM $400.00
Pontiac Silver Streak, 1949, gold, EX $135.00
Pontiac Star Chief, 1957, 2-tone gr, no interior as original, M .$95.00

Thunderbird Sports Roadster, 1962, Corinthian White w/red interior, M...$450.00
Volkswagen Bug, 1959, coral, friction, no interior, EX $75.00

Pull and Push Toys

Pull and push toys from the 1800s often were made of cast iron with bells that were activated as they moved along on wheeled platforms or frames. Hide and cloth animals with glass or shoe-button eyes were also popular, and some were made of wood.

See also Character, TV, and Movie Collectibles; Disney; Fisher-Price; etc.

Alderney Dairy Milk & Cream Wagon, Schoenhut, cloth-covered horse on 4-wheeled platform pulls wooden wagon, EX, A...$2,530.00
America Airplane, Hubley, pnt CI & aluminum, w/clacker & working props, 2 seated figures, 17" W, G, A $2,800.00
American Transfer Co No 7 Wagon, 2 felt-covered horses on wheeled platforms pulling pnt-wood wagon, 16", EX .$450.00
Bear (Growler), Germany, mohair w/muzzle & pull chain, 4 spoke wheels attached to feet, 7x13", NM...............$350.00
Bear on 3-Wheeled Cycle (No Handlebars) Bell Toy, gold-pnt CI, 4", G, A $140.00
Black Figures (2) Bell Toy, 1880s, NP CI, ea figure hits bells on platform w/2 heart-spoke wheels, 7", scarce, EX, A.$450.00
Boy Fishing Bell Toy, J&E Stevens, boy attempting to pull fish out of water on base w/4 spoke wheels, 8", VG, A........$1,200.00
Boy on Sled, Clark (?), pnt pressed steel, figure lying on stomach on sled, flywheel mechanism, 9", EX, A $900.00
Boy Performing on Platform, Germany, pnt bsk head w/cloth outfit, wheeled wooden platform w/articulated axles, 13", EX $770.00
Buffalo on Platform, American, pnt tin w/4 CI spoke wheels, 4½", EX, A $550.00
Buttercup & Spareribs, Nifty, litho tin, 8", G+, A..........$825.00
Car Carrier, Hustler Toy Co, ca 1927, wood, tractor w/4 cars on flatbed trailer, 20½" L, EX+, A $300.00
Circus Animals on Platform, litho tin, seal balances ball & bear rings bell, 10", G, A...$130.00
Cow on Platform, American, pnt tin w/4 CI spoke wheels, 9", VG+, A..$550.00
Cow on Platform, reddish brn felt-covered, wooden platform, steel spoke wheels, 8", G $150.00
Daisy Bell Toy, Gong Bell, CI, girl w/doll under blanket & horse head on front of ornate wheeled frame, 8", VG, A..$880.00
Ding Dong Bell Toy, Gong Bell, pnt CI, depicts Johnny Green & Tommy Stout w/cat that is dropped down well, 9", EX+, A $1,870.00
Dog Chasing Boy on Platform, Clark, pressed steel, friction, 10½", VG $450.00
Duck, Hubley, pnt CI, waddles & opens mouth when pulled, 9", EX, A $1,200.00
Duck Nodder on Integral Wheeled Base, Bunty Toy/England, pnt papier-mache, 15", EX, A $180.00

Duck on Wheels, Clark, pnt pressed steel, red & yel w/gr head, friction, 8", VG+, A $250.00

Duck on Wheels, Clark, pnt pressed steel, yel w/red head, friction, 7", G+, A $125.00

Elephant & Rider on 4-Wheeled Beveled Platform, pnt tin, 2-D form, 4 sm spoke wheels, 4½", Poor, A $65.00

Elephant on Platform, pnt papier-mache on wooden 4-wheeled platform, paper-fringed velvet blanket, 14" L, EX, A..$210.00

Elephant on Platform, Republic, pnt pressed steel, friction, 9", EX, A $165.00

Elephant on 4-Wheeled Platform, pnt tin w/wood platform, 4 sm spoke wheels, 5", Fair+, A $65.00

Fairmont Park Puzzle Blocks, Brett Litho Co, 2 scenes, 11x4", EXIB, A $275.00

Franz the Dog on Platform, metal & metal, articulated, 8", VG+ $200.00

Girl on Duck, Clark, pnt pressed steel, friction, 9", G, A.$275.00

Girl Riding Donkey, CI, girl moves up & down, spoke wheels attached to donkey's feet, 6" L, G, A $350.00

Girl Swinging, early, girl in lacy dress swings from bar on three-wheeled round lace-trimmed wooden platform, 9½", EX, A, $1,870.00. (Photo courtesy Bertoia Auctions)

Goat on Platform, De Camps/France, wht rabbit fur w/glass eyes, baahs when head is pushed down, 10½x14½", EX+, A $720.00

Grasshopper, Hubley, pnt CI w/articulated legs, 12", EX+, A $1,050.00

Harrison Circus Wagon, litho tin, w/2 horses, 11", G, A.$170.00

Hen w/Chicks in Crate, pnt CI, 3 spoke wheels, 7½", VG, A...$500.00

Horse & Chariot on Platform, Clark, pnt pressed steel, friction, 10½", G, A...$110.00

Horse & Jockey, Globe, 1931, pnt CI, 7" L, wheels missing o/w EX, A $250.00

Horse & Jockey, Wilkins, pnt CI w/2 star spoke wheels, w/push stick, G, A...$80.00

Horse on Platform, blk felt-covered w/wht mane & tail, reins & saddle, wood platform, metal wheels, 15", Fair, A ...$155.00

Horse on Platform, early American style, wood w/cloth blanket, metal spoke wheels, 18" T, Fair+, A...........................$75.00

Horse on Platform, Germany, cloth-covered with hair mane and tail, saddle and reins, wooden platform with four spoke wheels, 13", EX, A, $325.00. (Photo courtesy Noel Barrett Auctions)

Horse on Platform, gray & wht pnt w/reins & saddle, wooden platform w/CI spoke wheels, 15", Fair, A $155.00

Horse on Platform w/Driver, Clark, pnt pressed steel & tin, 2-D horse on wheeled platform w/driver on box, 11", EX, A $630.00

Horse Race Bell Toy, gold-pnt CI, jockey on horse on ornate 4-wheeled platform, 7", Fair $130.00

Horse Race Bell Toy, gold-pnt CI, 2 figures on horses on 4-bell plank w/4 wheels, 11", G+, A $200.00

Horse Trotting on Platform, pnt tin, 4 spoke wheels, 9½", rstr, A $250.00

Horse w/Boy Rider, paper-litho-on-wood horse w/litho tin boy, 2 lg metal spoke wheels, wooden push hdl, 28", VG, A $500.00

Grasshopper, Hubley, painted cast iron with articulated legs, front disk wheels, 12", VG, A, $600.00. (Photo courtesy Richard Opfer Auctioneering, Inc.)

Horse-Drawn Bell Toy, pnt CI figure on wire frame w/bell & 2 lg spoke wheels, NP horse, 8", EX, A............$440.00

Horse-Drawn Cart, American, pnt tin w/2 CI spoke wheels, high back w/curved sides, 8", G, A....................$150.00

Horse-Drawn Covered Cart, pnt tin, 2 spoke wheels, 7½", Fair pnt..$100.00

Horse-Drawn Covered Van Cart, American, pnt tin w/2 CI spoke wheels, 10", EX, A.................................$550.00

Horse-Drawn Dray Wagon w/Driver, pnt tin, horse on single-wheeled platform, 9½" L, EX+, A............................$225.00

Horse-Drawn Streetcar, American, pnt & stained tin, 2 horses, 11", G, A...$125.00

Horse-Drawn Van Wagon, Fallows, tin w/paper litho image of children on sides, 4 sm spoke wheels, 2 horses, 11", VG, A...$700.00

Horse-Drawn Wagon, Gibbs, 2 articulated paper-on-wood horses w/wood slatted wagon, spoke wheels, 18", G+, A....$130.00

Indian Riding Horse on Platform Bell Toy, NP CI, bells attached to 2 lg spoke wheels, 7", VG, A $100.00

Jonah and the Whale Bell Toy, NH Hill Brass Co., cast iron with four spoke wheels, 6", EX, A, $1,050.00. (Photo courtesy Bertoia Auctions)

Kiddie Circus, 3 animals on wheeled platforms followed by cage wagon, stenciled wood, VG+, A $80.00

Landing of Columbus Bell Toy, Gong Bell, gold-finished CI, 7", EX $350.00

Landing of Columbus Bell Toy, J&E Stevens, CI boat & figures w/3 spoke wheels, 7¼", overpnt, A..........................$275.00

Locomotive, Walker & Crosby, pnt CI & wood, spoke wheels, front cowcatcher, w/figure, 11½", VG, A.............$1,100.00

Milk Wagon, Converse, litho tin, horse-drawn, spoke wheels, 17½", G, A $425.00

Monkey on Velocipede Bell Toy, japanned CI w/gold trim, red cap, J&E Stevens, 7½" L, EX, A............................$3,080.00

Mule-Drawn Cart w/Girl, Germany, pnt tin w/detailed railed seat back, 2 lg spoked wheels, 8¾", EX+, A.........$6,500.00

Mygeia Ice Wagon, Converse (?), litho tin, horse-drawn, 13½", G, A...$250.00

Pathfinder Airplane, Katz Toy, litho tin, props turn, 22" W, Fair, A $175.00

Pony Cart, Gibbs, paper-on-wood horse, stained tin cart w/2 CI spoke wheels, 7", G, A..................................$45.00

Pony Circus, Gibbs, paper litho on wood & tin, 2 articulated horses, spoke wheels, 13½", Fair+, A.................$200.00

Puppy Town Fire Dept Fire Engine, Gong Bell, EX........$110.00

RR Transfer Wagon, tin, horse-drawn slanted wagon bed w/curved top supports, spoke wheels, 21", G, A $900.00

Sand & Gravel Truck, Nonpareil, litho tin, C-style open cab, button-look disk wheels, 9½", G+, A.....................$120.00

Seal Balancing Ball & Bear Ringing Bell on Wheeled Platform, litho tin w/circus animal graphics, 10", VG+, A $200.00

Seashore Bell Toy, paper litho on wood w/articulated action on base, CI spoke wheels, 6x6", VG.............................$600.00

Steamboat Bell Toy, pnt tin, w/2 side wheels & walking beam engine, 12", rare, G, A $500.00

Sunny Andy Street Railway, litho tin, w/bell, 13", EX, A .$220.00

The Right Plane, pnt tin, single prop turns, 27" W, G+, A..$550.00

Toyland Moving Van, Cass (?), pnt & stenciled wood van w/roof extending over open cab, wooden wheels, 17" L, G+, A...$465.00

Train, American, locomotive & 2 cars, pnt tin w/CI spoke wheels, 17", G, A...$330.00

Train, Toy Tinkers, locomotive & passenger car, pnt wood & metal, 12", EX, A..$190.00

Train (Military), French, locomotive & 3 cars, litho tin, spoke wheels, 12", A..$385.00

Train (Skip), American Tin, locomotive, 2 coaches & caboose, spoke wheels, rpt, 32", A...$110.00

Train Engine (America), American, pnt tin w/CI spoke wheels, 11", Fair+, A...$300.00

Train Engine (Venus), American, pnt tin w/CI spoke wheels, 6½", Fair+, A...$440.00

Trick Pony Bell Toy, mk #39, CI, ornate 4-wheeled platform, 8", G, A $700.00

Troop Carrier (Mack Truck), Chein, litho tin w/6 slush-cast soldiers, disk wheels, 8½", EX+, A $470.00

Union Pacific Floor Train, stamped Pat July 24, 1877, wood Panama locomotive and two dumping cars, 16" locomotive, EX, A, $1,600.00. (Photo courtesy Skinner Inc.)

Whoa There Caesar, CI, boy on burro w/bell on tail tries to jump fence on 4-wheeled platform (spoke wheels), 6", rpt, A $360.00

Wild Jack Mule Bell Toy, J&E Stevens, pnt CI, rider on mule, 2 spoke wheels, 8", VG, A..$385.00

Woman & Duck on Platform, Clark, pnt pressed steel, friction, 10½", G+, A...$350.00

Zeppelin, litho tin, props turn when pulled, 28", Fair, A .$375.00

Puppets

Though many collectible puppets and the smaller scale marionettes were made commercially, others were handmade and are today considered fine examples of folk art which sometimes sell for several hundred dollars. Some of the most collectible today are character-related puppets representing well-known television stars.

Advisor: Steven Meltzer (M9), marionettes and ventriloquist dolls

See also Advertising; Black Americana; Political.

FINGER PUPPETS

Adventure Boy & His Skymobile, Remco, 1970, MIB $65.00
Alf, plush, Coleco, 1987, MIB................................$15.00
Barney Rubble, Knickerbocker, 1972, MOC...................$15.00
Howdy Doody, Clarabelle, Dilly & Buster, rubber, 5", EX..$100.00
Huckleberry Hound, hard plastic head w/cloth body, 9", EX..$15.00
Monkees, Remco, 1970, EX, ea $35.00
New Zoo Revue, Rushton, 1970s, any character, NM, ea from $25 to $30.00
Peanuts, set of 6 characters, Ideal/Determined, MIB, from $30 to $40.00
Ruff 'N Reddy, vinyl, 1959, 3", EX $200.00
Spider-Man, 1970, NM..$15.00
Thor, vinyl, Imperial, 1978, EX $20.00

HAND PUPPETS

Batman and Superman, National Periodicals Pubs., Inc./Ideal, 1965 – 66, EX, $150.00 each. (Photo courtesy Judith Izen)

Batman, cloth w/vinyl head, Ideal, 1965, MIP $100.00
Bozo, cloth w/rubber head, yarn hair, Mattel, 1963, NM.$150.00
Bugs Bunny, grinning likeness w/jiggle eyes & long ears, 1950s, EX...$25.00
Captain America, Ideal, 1966, 11", NM $100.00
Captain Hook (Peter Pan), Gund, 1950s, NM $75.00
Cat in the Hat, plush, 1970, lg, EX $40.00
Cecil (Beany & Cecil), talker, EX, C10....................$50.00
Clarabell (Howdy Doody), cloth w/vinyl head, Bob Smith, 1950s, EX+ $30.00
Dean Martin, cloth w/vinyl head, 1950s, NM $25.00

Hopalong Cassidy, 1950s, scarce, NM, $200.00.

Addams Family, Fester, Gomez, and Morticia, Ideal, 1965, EX, $75.00 each. (Photo courtesy Judith Izen)

Donald Duck, 1st version, Gund, 1950s, G.......................$15.00

Dopey (Snow White & the Seven Dwarfs), cloth w/vinyl head, Ivory Snow premium, 1960s, MIB..........................$100.00

Droop-A-Long (Magilla Gorilla), cloth w/vinyl head, Ideal, EX+ $50.00

Elmer Fudd, cloth w/rubber head, Zany, 1940s, NM.........$75.00

Flash Gordon, cloth w/vinyl head, KFS, 1950s, scarce, EX ..$75.00

Foghorn Leghorn, cloth w/rubber head, Zany, 1940s, EX+ .$60.00

Foghorn Leghorn, plush, Warner Bros, 1970s, M..............$35.00

Howdy Doody, cloth w/vinyl head, Bob Smith, 1950s, EX+ .$30.00

Illya Kuryakin (Man From UNCLE), vinyl, Gilbert, 1960s, NM $175.00

Jiminy Cricket, 1st version, Gund, 1950s, EX+ $50.00

Jiminy Cricket, 2nd version, Gund, 1960s, VG $25.00

Johnny Ringo's Girlfriend Laura, cloth w/vinyl head, felt hands, Tops in Toys, 1959-60, 10", EX+ $40.00

Mad Hatter (Alice in Wonderland), cloth w/vinyl head, 1960s, EX+ $30.00

Mickey and Minnie Mouse, Gund, EX, $25.00 each.

Miss Piggy, Fisher-Price, 1978, MIB $35.00

Mr Magoo, cloth w/vinyl head, 1960s, EX+......................$75.00

Odd Job (Goldfinger), vinyl, AC Gilbert, 1965, 11½", MIB..$200.00

Odd Job (Goldfinger), vinyl, Ideal, 1960s, 13", EX+ $150.00

Pinocchio, Gund, 1950s, EX+ $60.00

Pinocchio, Gund, 1950s, G $25.00

Pinocchio, Knickerbocker, 1962, EX+ $50.00

Pluto, WDP, 1970s, G, A..$10.00

Popeye, cloth & felt w/rubber head, 1930s, 11", EX $75.00

Porky Pig, jiggle eyes, 1950s, NM...................................$30.00

Road Runner, cloth w/vinyl head, Japan, 1970s, MIB $15.00

Santa, Hasbro, MIB $90.00

Spider-Man, plastic body w/vinyl head, Imperial, 1976, EX+.$30.00

Superman, cloth w/vinyl head, Ideal, 1966, EX+ $50.00

Swee' Pea, Gund, 1950s, NM, $50.00.
(Photo courtesy Bill Bruegman)

Sylvester the Cat, Zany, 1940s, EX+ $75.00

Three Little Pigs, set of 3, printed cloth w/compo heads (open mouth smiles), 9", EXIB, A $250.00

Three Stooges, any of 3, cloth w/vinyl head, 1950s, NM, ea.$50.00

Tinkerbell, Gund, 1950s, G $25.00

Tom (Tom & Jerry), cloth w/vinyl head, Mattel/MGM, ca 1960, NM...$75.00

Tweety Bird, Zany, 1940s, EX+ $75.00

Umbriago (Jimmy Durante's Pal), cloth body w/pnt ceramic head, American Merchandise, 1940s, NM+IB $75.00

Wile E Coyote, cloth w/vinyl head, Japan, 1970s, MIB....$15.00

Woody Woodpecker, cloth w/vinyl head, talker, Mattel, 1960s, NM...$75.00

Yogi Bear, Knickerbocker, EX+.......................................$35.00

MARIONETTES

Davy Crockett, composition with cloth outfit, guitar, and gun, Peter Puppet Playthings, 14", EX, $150.00. (Photo courtesy Randy Inman Auctions)

Alice (in Wonderland), Peter Puppet Playthings, MIB (2 different boxes) $225.00

Clarabell (Howdy Doody), Peter Puppet Playthings, 1950s, EXIB..$225.00

Davy Crockett, talker, Hazelle's, 15", M (EX+ box) $350.00

Donny & Marie Osmond, in bl show outfits, Osbro Productions, 1978, 12", MIB, ea..$100.00

Dopey (Snow White), wood w/pnt compo head, cloth & felt clothes, Peter Puppet Playthings, 1950s, 12", VG $95.00

Flub-A-Dub (Howdy Doody), Kagran, unused, MIB, $375.00. (Photo courtesy McMasters Doll Auctions)

Flub-A-Dub (Howdy Doody), Peter Puppet Playthings, 1950s, EXIB..$225.00

Howdy Doody, Peter Puppet Playthings, 1950s, NMIB ..$175.00

Jiminy Cricket, Pelham, 1950s, 10", EXIB......................$250.00

Mad Hatter (Alice in Wonderland), Peter Puppet, 1950s, MIB.$150.00

Minnie Mouse, wood & compo w/cloth & felt clothes, Peter Puppet Playthings, 1950s, 12", VG $65.00

Papa & Mama Bear, wood w/pnt features, hands & feet, cloth outfits, articulated limbs, Germany, 1940s, 10", EX, A, pr .$230.00

Peter Pan, wood w/pnt compo head, cloth clothes, Peter Puppet Playthings, 1952, 15", EX+..$250.00

Princess Summerfall-Winterspring (Howdy Doody), bsk head w/cloth outfit, 13", G+IB, A $110.00

Snoopy, Pelham, 1979, 27", EX...................................$450.00

Soupy Sales, stuffed body w/vinyl head, Knickerbocker, 1966, 13", EX $75.00

Soupy Sales, stuffed body w/vinyl head, Knickerbocker, 1966, 13", MIB $200.00

PUSH-BUTTON PUPPETS

Batman, Kohner/NPPI, 1969, NM $225.00

Boxers, Kohner, 1950s, NMIB (box reads Press Action Toys).$60.00

Casper the Friendly Ghost, Kohner, 1960s, EX+ $25.00

Danger Dog, 1960s, 4", EX, N2 ....$15.00

Dino, Kohner, 1960s, NM+ $30.00

Fred Flintstone, Kohner, EX $85.00

Hoppy (Flintstones), Kohner, 1960s, NM+ $25.00

Howdy Doody, at microphone, wood & plastic w/felt bandanna, Kohner, 1950s, EX+IB...$165.00

Lucy (Peanuts), Ideal, 1977, EX+ $40.00

Bambi, Kohner, 1960s, EX, $40.00. (Photo courtesy Bill Bruegman)

Lone Ranger, Press Action Toys, 1939, NMIB, from $125.00 to $175.00. (Photo courtesy Lee Felbinger)

Magilla Gorilla, Kohner, 1960s, EX...............................$15.00

Pebbles (Flintstones), Kohner, 1960s, EX $25.00

Pinocchio, Kohner, 1960s, EX+......................................$30.00

Popeye and Olive Oyl, Kohner, 1949, NM+IB, A, $130.00. (Photo courtesy Smith House Toys)

Pinocchio & Jiminy Cricket Duet Show Time, Marx/WDP, 1950s, plastic, MIB, A $175.00

Pluto, wood w/oilcloth ears & beaded tail, Fisher-Price Pop-Up Critter, 1930, 5", EX+..$150.00

Snoopy as Joe Cool, Ideal, 1977, EX $40.00

Snoopy as Magician, Ideal, 1977, EX+ $35.00

Snoopy as Sheriff, Ideal, 1977, MIP $40.00

Snoopy as the Flying Ace, Ideal, 1977, EX+ $35.00

Superman & Supergirl Set, Kohner, 1960s, EXIB..........$175.00

Terry Tiger, Kohner, EX $35.00

Yogi Bear & Cindy Bear Set, Kohner, 1960s, EX+ $100.00

VENTRILOQUIST DOLLS

Ventriloquist dolls have pull-strings from the back of the neck for mouth movement. Dummies have a hollow body, with the head mounted on a pole controlled through an opening in the back of the body. Charlie McCarthy was produced in doll or hand puppet form by Ideal, Juro, and Goldberger (currently). Jerry Mahoney was produced by Juro and later by Paul Winchell's own company. Vinyl-headed ventriloquist dolls are still being produced by Goldberger and include licensed versions of Charlie McCarthy, Mortimer Snerd, Bozo, Emmett Kelly, Laurel and Hardy, Howdy Doody, Danny O'Day, WC Fields, and Groucho.

Groucho Marx, Eegee, first made in 1981, NM, $50.00.

Emmett Kelly Jr, Horsman, 1978, MIB.............................$50.00

Jerry Mahoney, head mk Paul Winchell, 1966, 22", MIB ..$350.00

Jerry Mahoney, Juro, 1950s, 25", complete, NMIB $250.00

Knucklehead Smiff, vinyl head & hands w/cloth outfit, Juro, 1960s, 24", NM..$350.00

McGruff the Crime Dog, Puppet Prod, 28", EX..............$125.00

Mickey Mouse, Horsman, 1973, NM $75.00

Mortimer Snerd, Juro, 1968, 30½", EX $50.00

Pee-Wee Herman, Matchbox, 1989, 24", MIB................$125.00

Stan Laurel & Oliver Hardy, Goldberger/Eegee, 1983, 25", MIB, ea...$50.00

Puzzles

Jigsaw puzzles have been around almost as long as games. The first examples were handcrafted from wood, and they are extremely difficult to find. Most of the early examples featured moral subjects and offered insight into the social atmosphere of their time. By the 1900s jigsaw puzzles had become a major form of home entertainment. Cube puzzles or blocks were often made by the same companies as board games. Early examples display lithography of the finest quality. While all subjects are collectible, some (such as Santa blocks) often command prices higher than games of the same period.

Because TV and personality-related puzzles have become so popular, they're now regarded as a field all their own apart from character collectibles in general, and these are listed here as well, under the subtitle 'Character.'

Note: All puzzles are complete unless indicated otherwise.

Advisor: Bob Armstrong (A4), non-character related

See also Advertising; Barbie; Black Americana; Paper-Lithographed Toys; Political.

American Homestead-Autumn, Currier & Ives/Roland Chesley, 1960s, plywood, 181 pcs, 12x9", EXIB, A4 ....$35.00

Ann Hathaway's Cottage, plywood, 566 pieces, 1930s, 16x20", with original box, $75.00. (Photo courtesy Bob Armstrong)

Autumn, WM Thompson, 1910-20, plywood, 100 crooked-line pcs, partly strip-cut, 10x12", EXIB, A4 ....$25.00

Autumnal Beauty, Milton Bradley/Buckingham, 1930s, cb, 250 pcs, 10x14", EXIB, A4 ....$10.00

Battle of Lake Erie (War of 1812), JLG Ferris, 1930s, plywood, 204 pcs, 16x11", EXIB, A4 ....$50.00

Beach Snipe Shooting, Currier & Ives/RH Barbour, 1980, plywood, 177 pcs, 13x10", EXIB, A4 ....$35.00

Betsy Ross Presenting the Flag, Parker Bros/Pastime, 1933, plywood, 546 pcs, 22x16", EXIB, A4 ....$240.00

Birch Glade, D Shirrin/Atlantic/Kingsbridge, 1940-60, plywood, 300 pcs, 13x10", EXIB, A4 ....$25.00

Birth of Old Glory, Madmar/Interlox, 1930s, plywood, 210 pcs, 12x10", EXIB, A4 ....$50.00

Blown Up Steamboat, Peter Thompson, paper lithograph, 5½x6½", EXIB, A, $525.00. (Photo courtesy Randy Inman Auctions)

Canal in Venice, Parker Bros/Pastime, 1931, plywood, 303 pcs, 10x19", VGIB, A4 ....$100.00

Canyon Terrace, Vernal H Brown, 1930s, plywood, 123 pcs, 8x9", EXIB $15.00

Cavalier (Portrait), Chad Valley (?), 1930s, plywood, 16x20", 710 pcs, EX (rpl box) $150.00

Champions of the Field (Dogs), Rosseau/Madmar/Interlox, 1930s, plywood, 1,000 pcs, 23x17", EXIB, A4 ....$250.00

Chieftain's Daughter, Leisure Hour, 1909, 363 pcs, 12x16", EXIB, A4 ....$150.00

Children & Swan, Red Seal Jig, 1930s, plywood, 545 pcs, 16x20", EXIB, A4 ....$190.00

Clan on Ramparts, FLK/Parker Bros/Pastime, 1910s, plywood, 150 pcs, 13x9", EXIB, A4 ....$70.00

Corner of Bryce Canyon, Whitman, 1950s, cb, 304 pcs, 18x16", EXIB, A4 ....$10.00

Cottage of Mary Arden, Parker Bros/Pastime, 1920-30, plywood, 71 pcs, 8x6", EX (rpl box), A4 ....$35.00

Covered Bridge (Winter Town), Roland Chesley, 1950-60, plywood, 299 pcs, 12x9", EXIB, A4 ....$60.00

Day Break & the Hunt Is On, Busy Bee/Novelty, 1930s, plywood, 523 pcs, 20x16", EXIB, A4 ....$150.00

Dissected Map of the United States, McLoughlin, paper litho, 8x10", VGIB, A $25.00

Divinely Fair (Woman), Parker Bros/Pastime, 1929, plywood, 7x13", EXIB, A4 ....$75.00

Dovecot (Cottage/Garden), 1930s, plywood, 150 pcs, 10x8", EXIB, A4 ....$50.00

Dreamland, R Atkinson Fox, 1930s, plywood, 486 pcs, 22x14", EX (rpl box), A4 ....$200.00

Dreams of Long Ago, Randolph, 1930s, plywood, 162 pcs, 10x12", EXIB, A4 ....$55.00

Dutch Boy & Geese (Farm Scene), Parker Bros/Pastime, 1912-11, plywood, 139 pcs, 6x14", EXIB, A4 ....$55.00

Dutch Scene, H Cassiers, 1909, wood, 224 pcs, 10x13", EX (rpl box), A4 ....$90.00

Dutch Windmill, 'Little Imp,' 1930s, plywood, 100 pcs, 6x8", EXIB, A4 ....$25.00

Eastern Getaway (Mediterranean Town), David Malcom/AVN Jones, 1930s, plywood, 600 pcs, 15x23", EXIB, A4 .$120.00

English Home, Hayter Publishing/Teaser, 1930s, cb, 336 pcs, 12x16", EXIB, A4 ....$12.00

Fire Department Puzzle Box, Milton Bradley, paper lithograph, set of three, 10x16", VGIB, A, $350.00. (Photo courtesy Randy Inman Auctions)

Fire-Engine Scroll Puzzle, McLoughlin Bros, 2 puzzles, 17x10", VGIB, A $165.00

Fishing Scene (Untitled), Parker Bros/Pastime, 1920-30, plywood, 414 pcs, 16x21", EXIB, A4 ....$180.00

Flower Market in Holland, 1930s, plywood, 646 pcs, 21x16", 21x16", EX (rpl box), A4 ....$125.00

Found (Winter Scene w/Dog), Cam-Mack Interlocking, 1930s, plywood, 150 pcs, 12x9", EXIB, A4 ....$35.00

Frederick the Great & the Miller, R Caton Woodville/Miller's Pharmacy/Lending, 1930s, plywood, 146 pcs, 8x10", EXIB, A4 ....$30.00

Fromentin's Falconer, J McGregor/Jim's Jig Saw, 1960s, plywood, 513 pcs, 14x16", EXIB, A4 ....$115.00

Gloucester Harbor Massachusetts, Charles Russell, 1940-50, plywood, 358 pcs, 13x10", EXIB, A4 ....$125.00

Golden Memories, N Briganti, 1930s, plywood, 162 pcs, 10x7", EX (rpl box), A4 ....$35.00

Gone to Ground (Fox Hunt), S Willis/Tuck/Zag-Zaw, 1930s, plywood, 250 pcs, 18x9", EXIB, A4 ....$85.00

Harbor of Venice, Milton Bradley/Perfection, 1908-11, wood, 108 pcs, EXIB, A4 ....$30.00

Hide & Seek, 1909, wood, 106 pcs, 7x8", VGIB, A4 ....$40.00

Home Life of Lincoln (Darkness Before Dawn), Percy Moran (?)/RH Mettit/Delta, 1930s, plywood, 398 pcs, 15x11", EXIB, A4 ....$125.00

Hunt Scene (Start of the Hunt w/Tudor Building), F Bennett/Parker Bros/Pastime, 1920-30, plywood, 400 pcs, 18x14", EXIB $200.00

Important Question (Courtship), University, 1932-33, cb, 300 pcs, 10x13", EXIB, A4 ....$12.00

In a Fix, 1900s, pressed board, 20 pieces, 8½x11", replaced box, $20.00. (Photo courtesy Bob Armstrong)

Independence Square, JLG Ferris/Personal Book Shop, 1930s, plywood, 575 pcs, 22x16", VGIB, A4 ....$150.00

Indian Love Calls, Consolidated Paper Box/Perfect, 1930s, cb, 250 pcs, 14x11", EXIB, A4 ....$15.00

Irish Setters (Family), Osthaus/Jigwood Co, 1930s, plywood, 330 pcs, 20x15", EXIB, A4 ....$80.00

Ironsides (Warship), 1930s, plywood, 245 pcs, 12x17", EX (rpl box), A4 ....$60.00

Joy of Spring, H Clements/Parker Bros/Pastime, 1922, plywood, 118 pcs, 10x7", EXIB, A4 ....$50.00

King of the Desert (Lion), 1920s, plywood, 288 pcs, 12x16", EXIB, A4 ....$80.00

Lake Lugano, Parker Bros/Pastime, 1930-40, plywood, 102 pcs, 9x7", EXIB, A4 ....$50.00

Land of Lake & Mountain, Tuck/Multiple Zag-Zaw, 1910-20, plywood, 300 pcs, 12x16", EXIB, A4 ....$25.00

Landlord's Brew, Dovaston/Hayter/Victory/Artistic, 1950-60, plywood, 800 pcs, 24x18", EXIB, A4 ....$120.00

Last Change In (Coaching), Parker Bros/Pastime, 1931-33, plywood, 1012 pcs, 33x22", EX (rpl box), A4 ....$450.00

Light in the Window, Thompson/HE Hamlen/Little Cut-up, 1930s, plywood, 384 pcs, 16x12", EXIB, A4 ....$60.00

Locomotive in Train Station, McLoughlin, stone litho, interlocking pcs, 20x27" (approx), EX, A $110.00

Lovely Summertime, Detroit Gask, 1930s, plywood, 200 pcs, 12x10", VGIB, A4 ....$70.00

Main Street (Christmas Town), Tuco Workshops, 1940s, cb, 200 pcs, 15x11", EXIB, A4 ....$14.00

Mill in the Woods, Milton Bradley, 1930s, cb, 465 pcs, 26x19", EXIB, A4 ....$12.00

Moonlight Night in Sunny Spain, Parker Bros/Pastime, 1930, plywood, 525 pcs, EX (rpl box), A4 ....$220.00

Noon Hour (Farm Scene), EL Ramsdell/Parker Bros/Pastime, 1910s, cb, 111 pcs, 11x9", EXIB, A4 ....$45.00

Ocean w/Rocks (4 Figures), J Stuart, 1909, wood, 175 pcs, 16x10", EX (rpl box), A4 ....$65.00

Old Fort Antigua, Lowell, 1920-30, plywood, 116 pcs, 9x8", EXIB, A4 ....$35.00

Old Voyager, R Atkinson Fox/Leisure Moment, 1930s, masonite, 392 pcs, 12x16", EXIB, A4 ....$60.00

Outward Bound, FJ Aldredge/GS Wesby Jr, 1910-20, plywood, 423 pcs, 16x12", EXIB, A $120.00

Peaceful Waters, Joseph Straus, 1950s, plywood, 100 pcs, 7x10", EXIB, A4 ....$10.00

Peacham Vermont (Winter Village), Roland Chesley, 1950s, plywood, 485 pcs, 15x15", EXIB, A4 ....$95.00

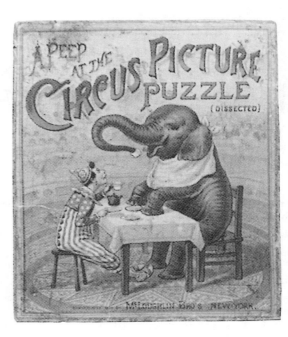

Peep at the Circus Picture Puzzle, McLoughlin Bros, 1887, 12x10", VGIB, A, $175.00. (Photo courtesy Randy Inman Auctions)

Peter Pumpkin Eater, ML Kirk/Leisure Hour, 1909, wood, 50 pcs, 6x8", EX (rpl box), A4 ....$25.00

Picturesque Cottage, Hayter/Victory/Popular, 1950-60, plywood, 250 pcs, 15x10", EXIB, A4 ....$25.00

Pinkie (Woman), Tuco Workshops, 1930s, cb, 180 pcs, 11x15", EXIB, A4 ....$14.00

Poppyfield By the Brook, A Boost (?)/Parker Bros/Pastime, 1929, plywood, 272 pcs, 10x16", EXIB, A4 ....$110.00

Red Rock Canyon (Wagon Train), F Gr Sayre/Clarence Schreiner, 1940s, plywood, 650 pcs, EX (rpl box), A4 ...$200.00

Restful Moments, Parker Bros/Pastime, 1920-30, EX (rpl box), A4 ....$300.00

Rhapsody of Fall (River Scene), Spear/Hayter/Victory Gold Box, 1970-80, plywood, 1000 pcs, 36x18", EXIB, A4 ....$135.00

River in Autumn, D Sherria (?)/AVN Jones, 1930s, plywood, 350 pcs, 20x13", G (rpl box), A4 ....$40.00

Rose of Brittany (Dutch Farm Girl), 1909, wood, 245 pcs, 9x12", EX (rpl box), A4......................$100.00

Setters on Point, GB Fox, 1930s, plywood, 805 pcs, 22x16", EX (rpl box), A4......................$220.00

Shattered Hopes, H Hintermeister/Milton Bradley, 1930s, plywood, 202 pcs, 14x10", EXIB, A4 ....$60.00

Sparkling Raiment (Parade), Par Co, 1940-50, plywood, 860 pcs, 24x17", EXIB, A4......................$1,000.00

Springtime (Woman), Parker Bros/Pastime, 1917, plywood, 81 pcs, EXIB, A4......................$35.00

Steamship Puzzle, Parker Brothers, paper lithograph, has been assembled and framed, 11x17", VG+ with Fair box, $110.00.

(Photo courtesy Randy Inman Auctions)

Strolling Players on Winter Day (Elizabethan), 1909, wood, 153 pcs, 9x12", EXIB, A4 ....$60.00

Sunshine & Shadows (Countryside), R Weber/Joseph Straus, 1940-50, plywood, 750 pcs, 24x18", EXIB, A4........$100.00

Taj Mahal, Chad Valley, 1930s, plywood, 525 pcs, 20x15", VG (rpl box), A4......................$110.00

Tea Time (Untitled), V De Beauvoir Ward/Joseph Straus, 1950-60, plywood, 500 pcs, 20x15", EXIB, A4....................$60.00

That Glorious Song of Old, Jewel Puzzle Co, 1930s, plywood, 150 pcs, 11x7", EXIB, A4 ....$30.00

The Farm, 1910s, plywood, 219 pcs, 16x11", EX (rpl box), A4......................$80.00

The Oaks (Autumn/House), Enneking/1930s, plywood, 155 pcs, 10x8", EXIB, A4 ....$30.00

Tranquil Mountain Waters, Farchild Corp/Fairco E, 1930-40, cb, 350 pcs, 13x19", EXIB, A4 ....$80.00

Village Road Paved w/Pearl, Thompson (?), 1930s, plywood, 16x12", EXIB, A4 ....$65.00

Village Square in Spain, Spear/Hayter/Victory Gold Box, 1970-80, plywood, 1000 pcs, 30x20", EXIB, A4 ....$130.00

Washington Crossing the Delaware, 1930s, plywood, 339 pcs, 16x12", EX (rpl box), A4 ....$80.00

Winter on the Farm (Sleigh Ride), Moe V Lee/Joseph Straus, 1940-50, plywood, 500 pcs, 20x16", EXIB, A4 ....$60.00

Winter on the Spreewald (Winter Countryside), 1910, plywood, 631 pcs, 24x18", EXIB, A4......................$300.00

Wintry Waters, Consolidated Paper Box/Perfect, 1940-50, cb, 375 pcs, 16x20", EXIB, A4 ....$12.00

Woman Writing Before Statue (Untitled), Parker Bros/Pastime, 1930-40, plywood, 314 pcs, EX (rpl box), A4..........$150.00

CHARACTER

Aristocats, fr-tray, 1970s or 1980s, image around chair, MIP, N2......................$15.00

Beetle Bailey, jigsaw, Jay, 1960s, NMIB......................$15.00

Beverly Hillbillies, jigsaw, 1963, image of cast on stairs, VG+IB......................$45.00

Blondie, jigsaw, Jaymar, 1960s, Dagwood's in Trouble, NMIB.$15.00

Bobbsey Twins, fr-tray, 1958, w/pitchfork, 12x9", EX, N2 .$20.00

Bozo the Clown, jigsaw, Whitman, 1969, Bozo walking the high wire, NMIB......................$15.00

Broken Arrow, jigsaw, Built-Rite, 1958, white man & Indian talking w/group of Indians on horseback, NMIB $30.00

Buffalo Bill Jr, fr-tray, Built-Rite, 1956, image of Buffalo Bill & young female co-star, NM+ $10.00

Bullwinkle & Rocky, fr-tray, Whitman, 1960, Rocky & the Moon Men balancing themselves on top of Bullwinkle, VG+......................$15.00

Casey at the Bat, jigsaw, 1960s, EXIB, N2......................$15.00

Casper the Friendly Ghost, fr-tray, 1992, 8x11", EX, N2..$10.00

Charlie's Angels in Action, jigsaw, 1977, EXIB, N2 ....$35.00

Cheyenne, jigsaw, Milton Bradley, 1957, set of 3, EXIB...$40.00

Cinderella, fr-tray, 1960s, Cinderella kneeling by open trunk, EX+ $8.00

Columbo, jigsaw, 1989, MIB, N2......................$15.00

Combat, jigsaw, Jaymar, 1966, MIB (sealed) $18.00

Cracker Jack, jigsaw, 1977, VG+IB, N2 ....$25.00

Daniel Boone, jigsaw, Jaymar, 1961, The Shawnees Attack, NMIB......................$20.00

Dark Shadows, jigsaw, Barnabas in Graveyard, MIB.........$75.00

Deputy Dawg, jigsaw, Whitman, 1972, Deputy Dawg on bucking rocking horse, NM......................$15.00

Disney Movie Classics, Jaymar #105, Bambi scene, 100 pieces, 13x18", EXIB, $10.00.

Donald Duck, fr-tray, 1960, dancing w/senorita, EX, N2 ..$15.00
Donald Duck, fr-tray (2-sided), 1985, Hornet's Nest, EX, N2 .$10.00
Flash Gordon, fr-tray, Milton Bradley, 1951, set of 3, EXIB .$65.00
Flintstones, fr-tray, Whitman, 1963, Pebbles on top of stuffed
    Dino, NM+ $18.00
Flintstones, jigsaw, 1975, Bedrock Postal Service, EXIB...$15.00
Flip the Frog, fr-tray, Celebrity Prod/Saalfield, 1932, Flip eating
    watermelon, 1 from set of 4, 5¾x8", rare, EX+........$110.00
Flipper, jigsaw, Whitman, 1965, Flipper & Porter Ricks playing
    in water, NMIB...$20.00
GI, jigsaw, 1985, Battle 1 or Battle 2, EXIB, N2, ea..........$15.00
Gulliver's Travels Picture Puzzles Set, jigsaw, Saalfield/Para-
    mount, 1939, 2 different, EXIB $100.00
Gunsmoke, jigsaw, Whitman, 1950s, Matt Dillon drawing gun,
    63 pcs, NMIB...$30.00
Hey Diddle Diddle the Cat & the Fiddle, fr-tray, 1957, 10x14",
    EX, N2 ....$15.00

Land of the Lost, Whitman #4609, 1975, NMIB, $20.00. (Photo courtesy Greg Davis and Bill Morgan)

Linus the Lion-Hearted, fr-tray, Whitman, 1966, Linus & Sugar
    Bear watching stage play, EX $25.00

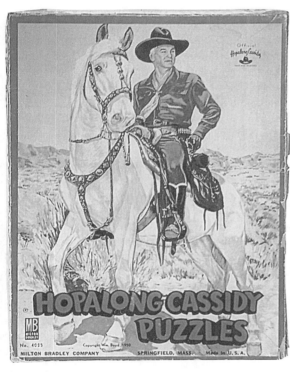

Hopalong Cassidy, Milton Bradley #4025, 1950s, NMIB, $125.00.

Little Bo Peep, Milton Bradley, 7½x13", VGIB, A, $100.00. (Photo courtesy Randy Inman Auctions)

Hoppity Hooper, fr-tray, Whitman, 1965, EX+.................$15.00
Howdy Doody, fr-tray, Whitman, 1954, Clarabell getting haircut
    from Flub-A-Dub, EX+ $8.00
Impossibles, fr-tray, Whitman, 1967, fight scene, EX+ $25.00
Incredible Hulk, jigsaw, 1988, saves bus, EXIB, N2 ....$10.00
James Bond 007/Goldfinger, jigsaw, Milton Bradley, 1965, image
    of Bond, Goldfinger & Golden Girl, NMIB $60.00
King Kong, jigsaw, Giant, 1976, MIB, N2.....................$45.00
Land of the Giants, jigsaw, Whitman, 1969, cartoon art of gang
    being attack by giant kitty, rnd, NMIB $40.00
Laverne & Shirley, jigsaw, HG Toys, 1976, 3 different, 150 pcs,
    unused, MIB, ea $15.00

Lone Ranger, fr-tray, Jaymar, 1947, Lone Ranger & Tonto escort-
    ing stage to town, NM $25.00
Looney Tune Characters, fr-tray (2-sided), 1985, EX, N2..$10.00
Marlin Perkins Wild Kingdom, jigsaw, 1971, Sparrow Hawk,
    VGIB, N2...$15.00
Marx Bros, jigsaw, 1970s, The Late Show, NMIB.............$12.00
Mary Poppins, fr-tray, Whitman, 1966, kids sliding down banis-
    ter, VG+ $10.00

Mary Poppins, jigsaw, 1964, flying kites, VGIB, N2 ....$15.00

Mickey Mouse Club, fr-tray, Whitman, 1956, photo image of 11
members & Jimmy Dodd singing, EX+ $40.00

Mighty Heroes, fr-tray, Whitman, 1967, NM+ $28.00

Mister Bug, fr-tray, Milton Bradley, 1955, EX $20.00

Mod Squad, jigsaw, Milton Bradley #4089, 1969, EXIB ...$30.00

Monkees, jigsaw, Fairchild, 1967, On Stage, NMIB $50.00

Monkees, jigsaw, Fairchild, 1967, Speed Boat, NMIB $50.00

Movie-Land Cutups Set, jigsaw, Wilder Mfg Co, 1930, Noah's
Ark, No No Nanette, Lone Star Ranger, Why Bring That
Up?, EX...$135.00

Mr Jinks, fr-tray, Whitman, 1961, Mr Jinks w/Pixie & Dixie on
high wire, EX+ $15.00

Munsters, jigsaw, Whitman, 1965, shows family in laboratory,
VG+ $40.00

Patty Duke, Jr Jigsaw/Whitman, 1963, 100 pcs, EX $30.00

Perils of Penelope Pitstop, fr-tray, Whitman, 1969, Sylvester
Sneekly giving Penelope a flower, EX $8.00

Peter Pan, fr-tray, Whitman, 1952, closeup images of Captain
Hook, Snee & Tinker Bell, EX+.................................$30.00

Pink Panther Playing Violin, jigsaw, 1979, VGIB, N2......$15.00

Pinocchio Picture Puzzles Set, Whitman, 1939, set of 2, EXIB.$50.00

Pitfall Harry, jigsaw, Playskool, 1983, EXIB, N2 ....$20.00

Punky Bruster, jigsaw, 1984, EXIB, N2 ....$20.00

Raggedy Ann & Andy, fr-tray, Milton Bradley, 1955, picnic
scene, EX+ $15.00

Rin-Tin-Tin, fr-tray, Whitman, 1956, Indians chasing Rin
w/glove in mouth, VG $6.00

Rin-Tin-Tin, jigsaw, Jaymar, 1957, Rusty holding pups, NMIB.$25.00

Road Runner, fr-tray, 1973, EX, N2 ....$10.00

Robin Hood, fr-tray, Built Rite, 1950s, set of 3 w/images of
Richard Greene portrait, aiming bow & arrow, Merry Men,
EX+ $40.00

Rocketeer, fr-tray, #4510F-51, 1991, MIP.............................$5.00

Rootie Kazootie, fr-tray, EE Fairchild, 1950s, set of 3, VGIB..$30.00

Santa, fr-tray, Milton Bradley, 1910, Santa entertaining children
by Christmas tree, NM+, A..$200.00

Santa, fr-tray, Milton Bradley, 1910, Santa in open car loaded
w/toys, house in distance, NM, A $180.00

Santa's Workshop, fr-tray, 1950s, Santa standing next to ice
'North Pole' w/reindeer, EX+ $30.00

Sheriff Bear & Slim Jones, fr-tray, 1960s, EX, N2 ....$20.00

Shotgun Slade, jigsaw, Milton Bradley, 1960, NMIB........$30.00

Sky Hawks, fr-tray, Whitman, 1970, NM+ $20.00

Sleeping Beauty, fr-tray, Whitman, 1958, 3 fairies blessing Sleeping Beauty, NM...$15.00

Snagglepuss, jigsaw, Whitman, 1962, Snagglepuss having tea
w/Yakky Doodle & Chopper, NMIB...........................$30.00

Super Dome Sunday, jigsaw, 1980s, EXIB, N2 ....$10.00

Super Six, jigsaw, Whitman, 1969, NMIB $30.00

Superman, jigsaw, Whitman, 1965, Superman rescuing Lois &
Jimmy in submarine, NMIB.......................................$30.00

Superman, jigsaw, Whitman, 1966, Superman soaring into space
after spaceship, NMIB $30.00

Sword in the Stone, fr-tray, Whitman #4456, 1963, G+ ..$10.00

Tennessee Tuxedo, jigsaw, Fairchild, 1971, NMIB............$40.00

Top Cat, fr-tray, Whitman, 1961, Chopper finds Top Cat under
his welcome mat, NM...$25.00

**Superman the Man of Tomorrow, Saalfield #1505, 300
pieces, EXIB, A, $300.00.** (Photo courtesy New England Auction Gallery)

Wacky Races, fr-tray, Whitman, 1969, car on 'One Way' street,
EX..$25.00

Welcome Back Kotter, fr-tray, Whitman, 1977, closeup image of
Mr Kotter or TV cast, unused, M (sealed), ea............$15.00

Welcome Back Kotter, jigsaw, HG Toys, 1976, several different,
150 pcs, unused, MIB, ea $20.00

Wild Bill Hickok, jigsaw, Built-Rite, 1955, Guy Madison &
Indian, NMIB $30.00

Wizard of Oz, fr-tray, 1988, photo image, EX, N2 ....$15.00

Woody Woodpecker, fr-tray, Whitman, 1976, Woody climbing
cliff w/baby eagles harassing him, NM $10.00

Woody Woodpecker, fr-tray, 1979, Woody building doghouse,
VG+, N2 ....$10.00

Woody Woodpecker, jigsaw, 1970s, w/shark, VG+IB, N2 .$10.00

Zorro, fr-tray, Whitman, 1957, portrait photo of Zorro in court-
yard, NM+ $40.00

101 Dalmatians, fr-tray, Jaymar, 1960, dalmatian family around
TV watching dog on screen, NM+..............................$18.00

101 Dalmatians, fr-tray, Jaymar, 1960, Pongo next to clock,
NM $15.00

101 Dalmatians, fr-tray, Jaymar, 1960, puppies in kitchen
w/cook, NM $15.00

Radios, Novelty

Many novelty radios are made to resemble a commercial
product box or can, and with the crossover interest into the
advertising field, some of the more collectible, even though of
recent vintage, are often seen carrying very respectable price
tags. Likenesses of famous personalities such as Elvis or characters like Charlie Tuna house transistors in cases made of plastic
that scarcely hint at their actual function. Others represent
items ranging from baseball caps to Cadillacs.

Annie w/Sandie, 1980s, red & wht plastic, AM, MIB......$75.00

Big Bird, yel plastic head form, AM, EX $15.00

Bozo the Clown, 1970s, head & shoulders form, AM, EX .$50.00

Bugs Bunny, w/sing-along microphone, finger points to dial, AM, VG......$50.00
Bumble Lion Wuzzle, AM, EX......$35.00
Cabbage Patch Kids, Playtime Prod, 1980s, purse style, EX .$25.00

Lone Ranger, Airline, 1950, white plastic with colorful molded image of the Lone Ranger on Silver, red dial, NM+, A, $1,100.00.

Charlie McCarthy, Majestic, 1930s, brown Bakelite with Charlie seated on front, EX, A, $500.00. (Photo courtesy Bertoia Auctions)

Charlie Tuna, 1970s, w/clamp for handlebar, AM, EX $65.00
Dick Tracy, Creative Creations, 1970s, wristband type, AM, EX.$225.00
Donald Duck, head form, speaker in back, AM, VG $30.00
Dukes of Hazzard, Warner Bros, 1980s, plastic w/paper decal, EX $65.00
Fonz Jukebox, AM, G $20.00
Hamburger Helper's Helping Hand, lg wht hand w/face, NM.$75.00

Mickey Mouse, stuffed figure with red shorts and yellow feet, NM, $25.00. (Photo courtesy Marty Bunis and Robert Breed)

Hopalong Cassidy, Arvin, red metal with silver foil cover, EX, A, $375.00.

M&M Candy Guy, w/head phones, belt clip & wrist band, AM/FM, MIP $35.00
McDonald's Big Mac, GE, AM, EX $60.00

Mork From Ork Eggship, Concept 2000, 1979, MIB $35.00
Mr T, 1980s, photo front as BA Baracus, EX......$60.00
Nestle Crunch Candy Bar, strap hdl, EX+ $60.00
Pac Man, w/headphones, NM......$50.00
Pinball Wizard, Astra, 1980s, AM, MIB $175.00
Pinocchio, Philgee International/WD/Hong Kong, AM, VG......$50.00
Pound Puppy, 1980s, dog atop AM radio, EX......$20.00
Punchy the Hawaiian Punch Guy, Proctor & Gamble, 1970s, figural transistor w/carry strap, 6", NM $50.00
Raid Bug, 1980s, figural clock-radio, NM $200.00
R2-D2 Robot, Kenner, figural, AM, MIB......$150.00

Pink Panther, decaled image on two-dimensional plastic form, 9", NM, $125.00. (Photo courtesy Marty Bunis and Robert Breed)

Sesame Street, Concepts 2000, 1970s, sing-along w/microphone, NM..$50.00
Smurf, 1980s, head form, EX $50.00
Snoopy & Woodstock Doghouse, Determined, 1970s, NM.$50.00
Sonic Radio Man, robot form, MIB.................................$75.00
Spider-Man, Janex/Marvel, 1970s, wristwatch style, AM, EX.$70.00

Ramp Walkers

Ramp walkers date back to at least 1873 when Ives produced two versions of a cast-iron elephant walker. Wood and composition ramp walkers were made in Czechoslovakia and the U.S.A. from the 1930s through the 1950s. The most common were made by John Wilson of Pennsylvania and were sold worldwide. These became known as 'Wilson Walkies.' Most are two-legged and stand approximately 4½" tall. While some of the Wilson Walkies were made of a composite material with wood legs (for instance, Donald, Wimpy, Popeye, and Olive Oyl), most are made with cardboard thread-cone bodies with wood legs and head. The walkers made in Czechoslovakia are similar but they are generally made of wood.

Plastic ramp walkers were primarily manufactured by the Louis Marx Co. and were made from the early 1950s through the mid-1960s. The majority were produced in Hong Kong, but some were made in the United States and sold under the Marx logo or by the Charmore Co., which was a subsidiary of the Marx Co. Some walkers are still being produced today as fast-food premiums.

The three common sizes are (1) small, about 1½" x 2"; (2) medium, about 2¾" x 3"; and (3) large, about 4"x 5". Most of the small walkers are unpainted while the medium or large sizes were either spray painted or painted by hand. Several of the

walking toys were sold with wooden plastic or colorful lithographed tin ramps.

Advisor: Randy Welch (W4)

ADVERTISING

Captain Flint, Long John Silver's, 1989, w/plastic coin weight.$15.00
Choo-Choo Cherry, Funny Face drink mix, w/plastic coin weight...$60.00
Flash Turtle, Long John Silver's, 1989, w/plastic coin weight.$15.00
Goofy Grape, Funny Face drink mix, w/plastic coin weight..$60.00
Jolly Ollie Orange, Funny Face drink mix, w/plastic coin weight...$60.00
Quinn Penguin, Long John Silver's, 1989, w/plastic coin weight..$15.00
Root'n Toot'n Raspberry, Funny Face drink mix, w/plastic coin weight...$60.00
Sydney Dinosaur, Long John Silver's, 1989, yel & purple, w/plastic coin weight $15.00
Sylvia Dinosaur, Long John Silver's, 1989, lavender & pk, w/plastic coin weight $15.00

CZECHOSLOVAKIAN

Bird...$35.00
Bird (lg, store display)..$200.00
Chicago World's Fair (1933), wood, G..........................$100.00
Cow..$35.00
Dog...$30.00
Dutch Girl..$60.00
Man w/Carved Wood Hat..$45.00
Monkey $45.00
Pig...$30.00
Policeman...$60.00

DISNEY CHARACTERS

Unless another manufacturer is noted within the descriptions, all of the following Disney ramp walkers were made by the Marx company.

Donald Duck and Goofy Riding Go-Cart, $40.00. (Photo courtesy Randy Welch)

Big Bad Wolf & Mason Pig $50.00
Big Bad Wolf & Three Little Pigs $150.00
Donald Duck Pulling Nephews in Wagon.........................$35.00
Donald Duck Pushing Wheelbarrow, all plastic $25.00
Donald Duck Pushing Wheelbarrow, plastic w/metal legs, sm.$25.00
Donald's Trio, France, Huey, Louie & Dewey dressed as Indian
    Chief, cowboy & 1 carrying flowers, NMOC, A $150.00
Fiddler & Fifer Pigs $50.00
Figaro the Cat w/Ball $30.00
Goofy, riding hippo $45.00
Jiminy Cricket, w/cello $30.00
Mad Hatter w/March Hare $50.00
Mickey Mouse & Donald Duck Riding Alligator $40.00
Mickey Mouse & Minnie, plastic w/metal legs, sm $40.00
Mickey Mouse & Pluto Hunting $40.00
Mickey Mouse Pushing Lawn Roller $35.00
Minnie Mouse Pushing Baby Stroller..........................$35.00
Pluto, plastic w/metal legs, sm $35.00

HANNA-BARBERA, KING FEATURES & OTHER CHARACTERS BY MARX

Astro $150.00
Astro & George Jetson $75.00

Astro & Rosey, $75.00. (Photo courtesy Randy Welch)

Bonnie Braids' Nursemaid $50.00
Chilly Willy, penguin on sled pulled by parent $25.00
Fred & Wilma Flintstone on Dino $60.00
Fred Flintstone & Barney Rubble $40.00
Fred Flintstone on Dino..$75.00
Hap & Hop Soldiers $25.00
Little King & Guard $60.00
Pebbles on Dino..$75.00
Popeye, Irwin, celluloid, lg $60.00
Popeye & Wimpy, heads on springs, MIB $85.00
Popeye Pushing Spinach Can Wheelbarrow $30.00
Santa, w/gold sack...$45.00

Santa, w/wht sack $40.00
Santa, w/yel sack $40.00
Santa & Mrs Claus, faces on both sides........................$50.00
Santa & Snowman, faces on both sides.........................$50.00
Spark Plug $200.00
Top Cat & Benny..$65.00
Yogi Bear & Huckleberry Hound................................$50.00

MARX ANIMALS WITH RIDERS SERIES

Ankylosaurus w/Clown $40.00
Bison w/Native..$40.00
Brontosaurus w/Monkey $40.00
Hippo w/Native...$40.00
Lion w/Clown $40.00
Stegosaurus w/Black Caveman $40.00
Triceratops w/Native...$40.00
Zebra w/Native..$40.00

PLASTIC

Baby Walk-A-Way, lg $40.00
Bear $20.00
Boy & Girl Dancing..$45.00
Bull $20.00
Bunnies Carrying Carrot..$35.00
Bunny on Back of Dog $50.00
Bunny Pushing Cart..$60.00
Camel w/2 Humps, head bobs....................................$20.00
Chicks Carrying Easter Egg.......................................$35.00
Chinese Men w/Duck in Basket $30.00
Chipmunks Carrying Acorns......................................$35.00
Chipmunks Marching Band w/Drum & Horn $35.00
Cow, w/metal legs, sm $20.00
Cowboy on Horse, w/metal legs, sm $30.00
Dachshund $20.00
Dairy Cow $20.00
Dog, Pluto look-alike w/metal legs, sm........................$20.00

Frontiersman with Dog, $95.00. (Photo courtesy Randy Welch)

Double Walking Doll, boy behind girl, lg $60.00
Duck $20.00
Dutch Boy & Girl $40.00
Elephant $20.00
Elephant, w/metal legs, sm $30.00
Farmer Pushing Wheelbarrow $30.00
Firemen $35.00
Goat $20.00
Horse, circus style $20.00
Horse, lg $30.00
Horse, yel w/rubber ears & string tail, lg $30.00
Horse w/English Rider, lg $50.00
Indian Woman Pulling Baby on Travois $95.00
Kangaroo w/Baby in Pouch $30.00
Mama Duck w/3 Ducklings $35.00
Marty's Market Lady Pushing Shopping Cart $65.00
Mexican Cowboy on Horse, w/metal legs, sm $30.00
Milking Cow, lg $40.00
Monkeys Carrying Bananas $60.00

Slugger the Walking Bat Boy, with ramp and box, $250.00.
(Photo courtesy Randy Welch)

WILSON

Little Red Riding Hood, $40.00; Clown, $30.00; Nurse, $30.00. (Photo courtesy Randy Welch)

Mother Goose, $45.00. (Photo courtesy Randy Welch)

Nursemaid Pushing Baby Stroller $20.00
Pig $20.00
Pigs, 2 carrying 1 in basket $40.00
Pumpkin Head Man & Woman, faces both sides $100.00
Reindeer $45.00
Sailors SS Shoreleave $25.00
Sheriff Facing Outlaw $65.00
Teeny Toddler, walking baby girl, Dolls Inc, lg $40.00
Tin Man Robot Pushing Cart $150.00
Walking Baby, in Canadian Mountie uniform, lg $50.00
Walking Baby, w/moving eyes & cloth dress, lg $40.00
Wiz Walker Milking Cow, Charmore, lg $40.00

Donald Duck $175.00
Elephant $30.00
Eskimo $100.00
Indian Chief $70.00
Mammy $40.00
Olive Oyl $175.00
Penguin $25.00
Pig $40.00
Pinocchio $200.00
Popeye $200.00
Rabbit $75.00
Sailor $30.00
Santa Claus $90.00
Soldier $30.00
Wimpy $175.00

Records

Most of the records listed here are related to TV shows and movies, and all are specifically geared toward children. The more successful the show, the more collectible the record. But condition is critical as well, and unless the record is excellent or better, its value is lowered very dramatically. The presence of the original sleeve or cover is crucial to establishing collectibility.

Advisor: Peter Muldavin (M21) 45 rpm, 78 rpm, and Kiddie Picture Disks

33⅓ RPM RECORDS

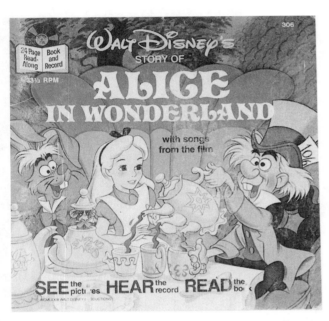

Alice in Wonderland (With Songs From the Film), Disneyland Records #306, 1979, book with record, EX, $15.00.

All in the Family, 1971, w/book, EX (w/sleeve), N2.........$25.00
Alvin Show, 1961, NM (w/sleeve) $25.00
America on Parade (Disney), #AOP2112, 1975, VG (w/sleeve) .$75.00
Aristocats, 1970, w/book, VG+, N2..................................$10.00
At Home With the Munsters, Golden Records #LP-139, EX
    (w/sleeve) $55.00
Battlestar Galactica, 1978, soundtrack, EX (w/sleeve), N2..$20.00
Bedknobs & Broomsticks, #STER-1326, 1971, VG (w/sleeve) .$10.00
Benji, 1976, EX (w/sleeve), N2 ....$15.00
Bozo the Clown Christmas, 1973, w/punchouts, M (w/sleeve),
    N2 ....$25.00
Bozo the Clown on the Farm, 1975, NM (w/sleeve), N2 .$20.00
Bugs Bunny Holly Daze, 1974, VG+ (w/sleeve), N2 ....$15.00
Captain Kangaroo, 1950s, VG+ (w/sleeve), N2 ....$25.00
Charlie Brown, 1966, NM, N2..$20.00
Disneyland Great Moments With Mr Lincoln, #STER 3981,
    1964, w/book, NM (w/sleeve) $75.00
Dumbo, #DQ1204, 1963, sound track, VG (w/sleeve) $10.00
Enchanted Tiki Room (Disney), #ST 3966, 1968, EX (w/sleeve)..$60.00

Everything Archies/The Archies, Kirshner, 1968, NM
    (w/sleeve) $25.00
Flash Gordon, 1980, soundtrack, EX, N2.........................$15.00
Flintstones Time Machine, 1966, EX (w/sleeve)...............$20.00

Get Along Gang and the Big Bully, American Greetings #272, 1984, book with record, EX, $10.00.

Green Hornet, 1973, EX (w/photo sleeve), N2 ....$35.00
Hansel & Gretel, Disney, 1964, M, N2 ....$20.00
Happy Birthday/Halloween, Disney, 1964, NM, N2........$20.00
Hefti in Gotham City (Batman), RCA, 1966, NM (w/sleeve).$30.00
Huckleberry Hound for President, 1960, VG, N2.............$15.00
I Spy, 1966, soundtrack, EX (w/sleeve) $25.00
Indiana Jones & the Last Crusade, 1989, NM (w/sleeve), N2.$15.00
Indiana Jones & the Temple of Doom, 1984, NM, N2 .....$15.00
It's a Mad Mad Mad Mad World (Jonathan Winters), Verve,
    1963, M (sealed sleeve) $20.00
It's a Small World, #ST-3925, 1970s, MIP $20.00
Jiminy Cricket (Tales of...), 1960s, VG+ (w/sleeve), N2..$10.00
Jiminy Cricket Add & Subtract, 1969, VG+ (w/sleeve), N2 .$15.00
Jiminy Cricket Multiply & Divide, 1963, G (w/sleeve), N2 .$5.00
Jungle Book Colonel Hathi's March & Trust Me, Disneyland
    Records #DQ-1304, 1967, EX (w/sleeve), M21 ....$20.00
King Kong, 1977, EX (w/sleeve), N2................................$20.00
Lady & the Tramp, Decca, 1955, EX (w/sleeve) $40.00
Lone Ranger Authentic Story & Song, 1980, EX (w/sleeve),
    N2..$45.00
Magoo in Hi-Fi Mother Magoo Suite, UPA/RAC Victor LPM-
    1362, 1956, EX (w/sleeve)..$30.00
Merry Christmas, Hanna-Barbera, 1965, 12 Christmas songs,
    NM (w/sleeve) $30.00
Mickey Mouse Club, 1975, VG+ (w/sleeve), N2..............$10.00
Mister Ed, 1962, soundtrack, EX (w/sleeve).....................$40.00
Nikki the Wild Dog of the North, 1961, VG+ (w/sleeve), N2.$15.00
Paddington Bear & Friends, 1982, M, N2.........................$20.00

Patty Duke TV's Teen Star, 1967, NM (w/sleeve) $18.00

Pete's Dragon, 1977, EX (w/colorful picture sleeve), N2 ..$20.00

Pirates of the Caribbean, #3937, 1970s, no book, MIP.....$40.00

Popeye, 1980, EX (sleeve w/Robin Williams photo), N2 .$15.00

Raggedy & Andy Birthday Party, 1980, M (w/sleeve), N2 .$35.00

Raggedy Ann & Andy Birthday Party, 1980, EX (w/sleeve), N2..$25.00

Raiders of the Lost Ark, 1981, NM (w/sleeve), N2 ....$15.00

Reluctant Dragon (Touché Turtle), 1965, G (w/sleeve) $5.00

Robin Hood, #DQ-1249 (non-animated), 1964, VG (w/sleeve) .$15.00

Romper Room Activity Songs, 1974, VG, N2.................$10.00

Rudolph the Red Nosed Reindeer & Other Christmas Favorites With Gene Autry, 1960s, NM (w/sleeve) $20.00

Ruff & Reddy Adventures in Space, Col-pix, 1958, EX (w/sleeve) $25.00

Scooby Doo Christmas Stories, 1978, EX, N2 ....$25.00

Shadow, 1980, M (w/sleeve), N2.................................$35.00

Shirley Temple Tells the Story of Walt Disney's Dumbo, 1960, EX (w/sleeve) $20.00

Songs From Annette, Disneyland Records #MM-24, 1950s, EX+ (w/photo sleeve) $50.00

Songs From Dr Dolittle, 1967, VG+ (w/sleeve), N2.........$15.00

Space: 1999, 1975, 3 stories, EX, N2.............................$25.00

Spider-Man & Friends, 1974, 3 stories, VG (w/sleeve), N2.$15.00

Star Trek, 1979, M (w/sleeve), N2 ....$35.00

Star Trek The Motion Picture, 1979, NM (w/sleeve), N2 .$20.00

Story of Dumbo, 1960s, G (w/sleeve), N2 ....$6.00

Story of Star Trek, 1977, w/book, EX+ (w/sleeve), N2 .....$20.00

Strawberry Shortcake Exercise, 1981, w/chart, EX (w/sleeve), N2..$25.00

Strawberry Shortcake Let's Dance, 1982, NM (w/sleeve), N2.$20.00

Strawberry Shortcake Sweet Songs, 1980, VG+ (w/sleeve), N2 .$10.00

Superman Four New Adventures, 1978, VG (w/sleeve), N2 .$10.00

Tarzan, 1983, M (w/sleeve showing boy riding on back of a gorilla), N2..$20.00

Walt Disney Song Fest (Mouseketeers), 1960s, NM (w/sleeve).$20.00

Wonder Woman, 1975, VG, N2....................................$10.00

Yogi Bear & Boo Boo Tell Stories of Little Red Riding Hood & Jack & the Beanstalk, EX (w/sleeve)...........................$20.00

45 RPM RECORDS

Jungle Book 'Colonel Hathi's March' and 'Trust Me,' Disneyland Records #DQ-1304, 1967, EX (w/sleeve), $20.00.

Barbie (Busy Buzz/My First Date), 1961, NM (w/sleeve) ..$10.00

Barbie/Ken (Nobody Taught Me), 1961, EX (w/sleeve) $8.00

Golliwogg's Cake Walk, 1950s, red, EX (w/sleeve), N2....$10.00

Happy Mother Goose (Kukla, Fran & Ollie), 1950, 2-record set, NM (fold-out sleeve) $20.00

Hillbilly Bears Featuring Blue Tail Fly/I've Got a Pony, 1966, NM (w/sleeve) $20.00

Jumbo's Lullaby, 1950s, red, EX (w/sleeve), N2 ....$10.00

Mary Poppins (Super Cali), 1964, EX (w/sleeve), N2 ......$20.00

Mother Goose Hey Diddle Diddle, 1950s, extended play, M (w/sleeve), N2..$10.00

Mother Goose Twinkle Twinkle Little Star, 1950s, extended play, M (w/sleeve), N2..$10.00

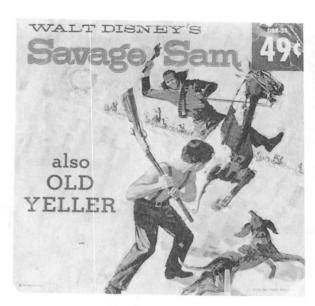

Savage Sam/Old Yeller (Walt Disney's), DBR-23, 1963, EX (w/sleeve), $15.00.

Walt Disney Presents It's a Small World, #LG-775, 1966, EX (w/sleeve)..$15.00

War of the Worlds, 1978, EX (w/sleeve), N2 ....$10.00

78 RPM PICTURE AND NON-PICTURE RECORDS

Annie Oakley Sings Ten Gallon Hat & I Gotta Crow, Golden, 1950s, EX+ (w/sleeve) $10.00

Art Carney Santa & the Doodle-Li Boop/'Twas the Night Before Christmas, Columbia #40400, 1950s, NM (w/sleeve) $30.00

Daffy Duck Meets Yosemite Sam, Capitol, 1940s, EX+ (w/sleeve)..$15.00

Davy Crockett at the Alamo, Columbia #C-518, 1950s, 2-record set, EX (w/photo sleeve) $30.00

Dennis the Menace, Playtime, 1954, NM (w/sleeve) $15.00

Foodini Goes a Huntin', Caravan, 1949, VG+ (w/sleeve).$50.00

Happy Trails/Roy Rogers & Dale Evans, RCA Victor Blue Bird Series #BY-65, EX+ (w/sleeve) $40.00

Hopalong Cassidy & the Two-Legged Wolf, Capitol #CAS 3109, VG+ (w/sleeve) $60.00

Ballad of Davy Crockett/Green Grow the Lilacs, Peter Pan Peanut Butter premium, EX (with sleeve and mailer envelope), $25.00; $10.00 (without sleeve). (Photo courtesy Peter Muldavin)

Hopalong Cassidy and The Story of Topper, Capitol #CAS-3110, 1952, EX (with sleeve), M21, from $50.00 to $75.00.

(Photo courtesy Peter Muldavin)

Howdy Doody and the Air-O-Doodle, RCA Victor Little Nipper Series #Y-397, 1949, EX+ (with sleeve), from $35.00 to $50.00. (Photo courtesy Peter Muldavin)

Huckleberry Hound Presents Mr Jinks & Boo Boo Bear, Golden, 1959, EX (w/sleeve) $15.00
Huckleberry Hound w/Hokey Wolf & Ding-A-Ling — A Wolf's Work Is Never Done, Golden, 1961, NM (w/sleeve) .$20.00

Little Orley Told by Uncle Lumpy, Decca #CUS-7, 1948, EX+ (with sleeve), $25.00. (Photo courtesy Peter Muldavin)

Lone Ranger He Finds Silver (The Adventures of), Decca Children's Set #K-30, 1951, No 2 of Series, EX (with sleeve), from $20.00 to $30.00. (Photo courtesy Peter Muldavin)

Pinocchio, RCA-Victor #349, 1940, VG (w/sleeve) $65.00
Rocky & His Friends: I Was Born To Be Airborne (Rocky)/I'm Rocky's Pal (Bullwinkle), Golden, 1961, NM (w/sleeve)...$20.00
Ruff & Reddy, Golden, 1959, EX+ (w/sleeve) $15.00
Tales of Uncle Remus, Capitol, 1947, 3 records, EX (w/sleeve).$30.00
Willie the Whale, Columbia, 1946, 3 records, EX (w/sleeve) .$30.00
Wizard of Oz, MGM #L-9, 1940s, jacket opens to 'Haunted Forest' scene, EX+ $50.00

Superman in 'The Magic Ring' and 'The Flying Train,' Musette, 1947, rare book sets with two records each, EX, A, $150.00 for both. (Photo courtesy Smith House Toys)

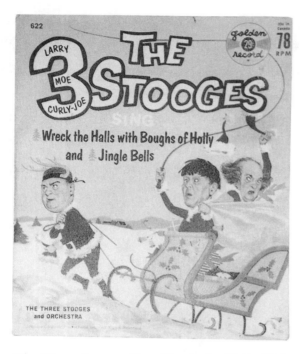

The Three Stooges Sing Wreck the Halls With Boughs of Holly and Jingle Bells, Golden #622, 1960, EX, $20.00. (Photo courtesy Peter Muldavin)

Woody Woodpecker Song/Woodpecker Dance, Golden 1951, NM (w/sleeve) $10.00

KIDDIE PICTURE DISKS

Listed here is a representative sampling of kiddie picture disks that were produced through the 1940s. Most are 6" to 7" in diameter and are made of cardboard with plastic-laminated grooves. They are very colorful and seldom seen with original sleeves. Value ranges are for items in very good to near-mint condition. Ultimately, the value of any collectible is what a buyer is willing to pay, and prices tend to fluctuate. Our values are for records only (no sleeves except where noted). Unlike other records, the value of a picture disk is not diminished if there is no original sleeve.

A Birthday Song to You, Voco #35215, 1948, 5" sq, NM (no mailer envelope), M21 ....$25.00
A Birthday Song to You, Voco #35215, 1948, 5" sq, NM (w/mailer envelope), M21, from $40 to $45.00
Alice in Wonderland, Toy Toon Records, 1952, NM, M21, from $10 to $15.00

Bunny Easter Party, Voco #EB-1, 1948, EX, $20.00.
(Photo courtesy Peter Muldavin)

Cinderella, Toy Toon Records, 1952, NM, M21, from $10 to $15.00
Disneyland Main Street Electrical Parade, 1973, 7", VG+ $60.00

Flash Gordon 'City of Sea Caves' Part I, Record Guild of America/King Features, 1948, EX, $50.00.

Flash Gordon 'City of Caves,' Record Guild of America, 1948, scarce, NM, M21 ....$75.00

Jack & the Beanstalk, Toy Toon Records, 1952, NM, M21, from $10 to $15.00

Kitty Cat, Vovo, ca 1948, 7", EX/NM, from $4 to..............$8.00

Laugh Laugh Phonograph, Voco, 1948, 6" (rare), NM, M21, from $20 to...$25.00

Lionel Train Sound Effects, 1951, NM, M21, from $40 to.$60.00

Red River Valley, Record Guild of America #2002P, 1949, EX (EX rare sleeve), from $15 to....................................$25.00

Shepherd Boy, Bible Storytime, 1948, NM, M21, from $10 to $15.00

Songs From Mother Goose, Toy Toon Records, 1952, NM, M21, from $10 to...$15.00

Ten Little Indians, Voco, 1948, 7", NM, M21, from $4 to ..$8.00

Ten Little Indians, Voco, 1948, 16", NM, M21, from $15 to..$25.00

Three Bears With Uncle Henry, Kidisks, KD-77A, 1948, rare, NM, M21, from $50 to $75.00

Winnie the Pooh and Christopher Robin Songs, RCA Victor, 1933, very rare, NM, M21, from $300.00 to $500.00. (Photo courtesy Peter Muldavin)

Swing Your Partner, Picture Play Records #PR11A/Record Guild of America, 1948, NM, M21, from $100.00 to $150.00. (Photo courtesy Peter Muldavin)

Reynolds Banks

Reynolds Toys began production in 1964, at first making large copies of early tin toys for window displays, though some were sold to collectors as well. These toys included trains, horse-drawn vehicles, boats, a steam toy, and several sizes of Toonerville trolleys. In the early 1970s, they designed and produced six animated cap guns. Finding the market limited, by 1971 they had switched to a line of banks they call 'New Original Limited Numbered Editions (10 – 50) of Mechanical Penny Banks.' Still banks were added to their line in 1980 and figural bottle openers in 1988. Each bank design is original; no reproductions are produced. Reynolds' banks are in the White House and the Smithsonian as well as many of the country's major private collections. *The Penny Bank Book* by Andy and Susan Moore (Schiffer Publishing, 1984) shows and describes the first twelve still banks Reynolds produced. Values are given for mint-condition banks.

Advisor: Charlie Reynolds (R5)

MECHANICAL BANKS

Uncataloged, elephant (conversion), 1970, edition of 4 .$100.00

1M, Train Man, 1971, edition of 30 ....$350.00

2M, Trolley, 1971, edition of 30 ....$450.00

3M, Drive-In, 1971, edition of 10 ....$1,000.00

4M, Pirate, 1972, edition of 10................................... $725.00

5M, Blackbeard, 1972, edition of 10 ....$650.00

6M, Frog & Fly, 1972, edition of 10 ....$1,200.00

Trial of 'Bumble' the Bee Part I, Vogue #R-745, 1947, 10", EX, from $50.00 to $60.00. (Photo courtesy Peter Muldavin)

7M, Toy Collector, 1972, unlimited edition $650.00
8M, Balancing Bank, 1972, edition of 10........................$725.00
9M, Save the Girl, 1972, edition of 10 ....$2,000.00
10M, Father Christmas, 1972, 1 made ea year at Christmas..$850.00
11M, Gump on a Stump, 1973, edition of 10..............$1,100.00
12M, Trick Bank, 1973, edition of 10.........................$1,000.00
13M, Kid Savings, 1973, edition of 10........................$1,200.00
14M, Christmas Tree, 1973, edition of 10.....................$725.00
15M, Foxy Grandpa, 1974, edition of 10 ....$975.00
16M, Happy Hooligan, 1974, edition of 10.................$1,075.00
17M, Chester's Fishing, 1974, edition of 10.................$900.00
18M, Gloomy Gus, 1974, edition of 10 ....$2,800.00
19M, Kids' Prank, 1974, edition of 10 ....$1,100.00
20M, Mary & Her Little Lamb, 1974, edition of 20 ....$850.00
21M, Spook, 1974, edition of 10 ....$800.00
22M, Decoy, 1974, edition of 10 ....$600.00
23M, Decoy Hen, 1974, edition of 10 ....$600.00
24M, Comedy Bank, 1974, edition of 10.......................$975.00
25M, Bozo, 1974, edition of 10 ....$950.00
26M, Reynolds Foundry, 1974, edition of 15 ....$3,400.00
27M, Toonerville, 1974, edition of 10 ....$1,200.00
28M, Bank of Reynolds Toys, 1974, edition of 10 ....$425.00
29M, Simple Simon, 1975, edition of 10 ....$925.00
30M, Humpty Dumpty, 1975, edition of 20................$1,250.00
31M, Three Blind Mice, 1975, edition of 15 ....$1,100.00
32M, Clubhouse, 1975, edition of 10.........................$1,100.00
33M, Boat, 1975, edition of 10 ....$1,500.00
34M, St Nicholas, 1975, edition of 50 ....$775.00
35M, Forging America, 1976, edition of 13................$1,200.00
36M, Suitcase, 1979, edition of 22 ....$825.00
37M, North Wind, 1980, edition of 23......................$1,100.00

42M, Miss Liberty, 1986, edition of 36 ....$1,300.00
42M, Miss Liberty on a Pedestal, 1986, edition of 4....$1,600.00
43M, Auto Giant, 1987, edition of 30........................$2,250.00
45M, Campaign '88, 1988, edition of 50 ....$3,000.00
46M, Hollywood, 1989, edition of 35 ....$825.00
47M, Buffalos Revenge, 1990, edition of 35 ....$900.00
48M, Williamsburg, 1991, edition of 35.......................$850.00
49M, Duel at the Dome, 1992, edition of 50..............$1,000.00
50M, '92 Vote, 1992, edition of 50 ....$3,000.00
51M, Oregon Trail, 1993, edition of 50 ....$800.00
52M, Norway (Lillehammer), 1994, edition of 50..........$825.00
53M, Shoe House, 1994, edition of 50.........................$950.00
54M, J&E Stevens Co, 1995, edition of 50 ....$1,850.00

55M, Hyakutake (The Comet), 1996, edition of 50, $625.00. (Photo courtesy Charlie Reynolds)

39M, Quarter Century, 1984, edition of 25, $4,000.00.

40M, Columbia, 1984, edition of 25 ....$1,350.00
41M, Whirligig, 1985, edition of 30 ....$1,300.00

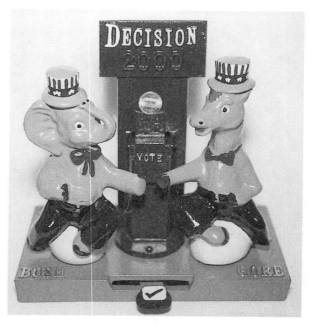

64M, Decision 2000, Bush/Gore, edition of 50, $600.00. (Photo courtesy Charlie Reynolds)

56M, '96 Political Wish, 1996, edition of 50 ....$900.00
58M, Uncle Louie, 1997, edition of 50 ....$350.00
59M, Friar's Favorite, 1997, edition of 50 ....$1,100.00
60M, Wall Street, 1998, edition of 98..............................$750.00
61M, De Bug (Y2K Bug), 1999, edition of 50.................$500.00
65M, The Lawyer, 2001, edition of 50 ....$600.00
66M, Bank of Uncle Sam, 2002, edition of 60................$600.00

STILL BANKS

1S, Amish Man, 1980, edition of 50, $135.00.

2S, Santa, 1980, edition of 50 ....$95.00
3S, Deco Dog, 1981, edition of 50.....................................$85.00
4S, Jelly Bean King, 1981, edition of 100 ....$265.00
5S, Hag, 1981, edition of 50..$160.00
6S, Snowman, 1981, edition of 50......................................$110.00
7S, Mark Twain, 1982, edition of 50 ....$200.00
8S, Santa, 1982, edition of 50...$125.00
9S, Anniversary, 1982, special edition $200.00
10S, Redskins Hog, 1983, edition of 50 ....$125.00
11S, Lock-Up Savings, 1983, edition of 50.......................$55.00
12S, Miniature Bank Building, 1983, edition of 50 ....$195.00
13S, Santa in Chimney, 1983, edition of 50 ....$90.00
14S, Santa w/Tree (bank & doorstop), 1983, edition of 25.$325.00
15S, Redskins NFC Champs, 1983, edition of 35...........$185.00
16S, Chick, 1984, edition of 50...$80.00
17S, Ty-Up, 1984, edition of 35 ....$225.00
18S, Tiniest Elephant, 1984, edition of 50......................$110.00
19S, Baltimore Town Crier, 1984, edition of 50 ....$75.00
20S, Father Christmas Comes to America, July 4th, 1984, edition of 25 ....$325.00
21S, Campaign '84, edition of 100 ....$250.00
22S, Santa, 1984, edition of 50 ....$100.00
23S, Reagan '85, 1985, edition of 100..............................$310.00
24S, Columbus Ohio, 1985, edition of 50.........................$60.00
25S, Austrian Santa (bank & doorstop), 1985, edition of 25.$350.00
26S, Halloween, 1985, edition of 50 ....$210.00

27S, 1893 Kriss Kringle, 1985, edition of 20 ....$2,000.00
27S, 1893 Kriss Kringle (w/tree & candle decorations), 1985, edition of 20 ....$2,400.00
28S, Santa Coming to a Child, 1985, edition of 50........$165.00
29S, Halley's Comet, 1986, edition of 50.........................$190.00
30S, 20th Anniversary, 1986, edition of 86 ....$165.00
31S, Father Christmas (bank & doorstop), gr, edition of 25..$280.00
32S, Santa & the Reindeer, 1986, edition of 50 ....$185.00
33S, Charlie O'Conner, 1987, edition of 50 ....$90.00
34S, Chocolate Rabbit, 1987, edition of 50.....................$110.00
35S, St Louis River Boat, 1987, edition of 60 ....$75.00
36S, German Santa (bank & doorstop), 1987, edition of 25.$275.00
37S, Graduation, 1987, special edition $200.00

38S, Old Stump Halloween, 1987, edition of 50, $95.00.

39S, Santa in Race Car, 1987, edition of 100 ....$130.00
40S, Technology Education, edition of 88 ....$65.00
41S, Super Bowl XXII Redskins, 1988, edition of 50........$90.00
42S, Easter Rabbit, 1988, edition of 50 ....$55.00

43S, Florida Safe, 1988, edition of 75, $90.00.

44S, Father Christmas w/Lantern (bank & doorstop), 1988, edition of 35 ....$260.00

45S, Halloween Spook, 1988, edition of 50 ....$90.00

46S, NCRPBC (National Capitol Region Club), 1988, edition of 20 ....$300.00

47S, Santa on Polar Bear, 1988, edition of 75 ....$110.00

48S, Bush-Quayle, 1989, edition of 100........................$260.00

49S, Shuffle Off to Buffalo, 1989, edition of 75 ....$70.00

50S, Pocket Pigs, 1989, edition of 75 ....$125.00

51S, Regal Santa (bank & doorstop), 1989, edition of 35 .$275.00

52S, Tiniest Snowman, 1989, edition of 75 ....$85.00

53S, Santa on Motorcycle, 1989, edition of 75...............$150.00

54S, Rabbit w/Mammy, 1990, edition of 75....................$225.00

55S, Antique Row Sign Post, 1990, edition of 75............$70.00

56S, Duck w/Puppy & Bee, 1990, edition of 75.............$110.00

57S, 1895 Santa w/Wreath, 1990, edition of 35 ....$250.00

58S, Santa on a Pig, 1990, edition of 75 ....$140.00

59S, St Louis Sally, 1991, edition of 55 ....$85.00

60S, Santa w/Wassail Bowl, 1991, edition of 35 ....$250.00

61S, Santa Express, 1991, edition of 55 ....$125.00

62S, Pig on Sled, 1992, edition of 55 ....$85.00

63S, Santa About To Leave, 1992, edition of 25 ....$290.00

64S, Jack-O'-Lantern, 1992, edition of 60 ....$80.00

65S, Santa in Zeppelin, 1992, edition of 100.................$145.00

66S, Clinton, 1993, edition of 100................................$310.00

67S, Windy City (Chicago Convention), 1993, edition of 60..$85.00

68S, Santa & the Bad Boy (Summer Santa), 1993, edition of 50..$225.00

69S, Arkansas President, 1994, edition of 100...............$325.00

70S, Santa & the Good Kids, 1994, edition of 35 ....$260.00

71S, Penny Santa, 1994, edition of 60, $125.00. (Photo courtesy Charlie Reynolds)

72S, School Days, 1995, edition of 100 ....$110.00

73S, 1880 Snow Santa, 1995, edition of 50 ....$220.00

75S, Santa on Donkey, 1995, edition of 50....................$110.00

76S, Clinton/Dole '96 (SBCCA '96), 1996, edition of 100 .$280.00

77S, Foxy Grandpa & Egelhoff Safe, 1997, edition of 60 .$200.00

78S, Halloween Witch, 1997, edition of 50....................$95.00

79S, Christmas Time, 1997, edition of 50......................$110.00

80S, Portland Chicks, 1998, edition of 20, pr...............$155.00

81S, Old St Nicholas, 1998, edition of 20 ....$450.00

82S, Little League Home Bank, 1999, edition of 50.......$145.00

83S, Santa's Last Check, 1999, edition of 30.................$200.00

84S, Presidential 2000 Campaign Bank, edition of 60 ...$150.00

85S, See Your Savings, 2001, edition of 50....................$150.00

86S, The Conventioneer, 2002, edition of 50 ....$135.00

Robots and Space Toys

Space is a genre that anyone who grew up in the '60s can relate to, but whether you're from that generation or not, chances are the fantastic robots, space vehicles, and rocket launchers from that era are fascinating to you as well. Some emitted beams of colored light and eerie sounds and suggested technology the secrets of which were still locked away in the future. To a collector, the stranger, the better. Some were made of lithographed tin, but even plastic toys (Atom Robot, for example) are high on the want list of many serious buyers. Condition is extremely important, both in general appearance and internal workings. Mint-in-box examples may be worth twice as much as one mint-no-box, since the package art was often just as awesome as the toy itself.

Because of the high prices these toys now command, many have been reproduced. Beware!

See also Marx; Guns.

Answer Game Robot, battery-op, MIB, L4 ....$800.00

Apollo Lunar Module, Japan, battery-op, tin & plastic, 7½", MIB, L4..$700.00

Apollo Super Space Capsule, SH, 1960s, battery-op, 9", NMIB..$225.00

Astro Space Dog, Japan, 1950s, rare remote control version, 6", nonworking o/w EX, A $385.00

Astronaut w/Gun, Haji, w/up, litho tin, yel & bl w/brn ft, face seen through silver helmet, 7", nonworking, G, A..$350.00

Atom Jet #58, Yonezawa, friction, litho tin, 27", EX, A .$3,700.00

Atom Robot, KO, 1950s, crank-action, litho tin, 1st version, 7", EX+ $350.00

Atom Rocket 7, Japan, 1950s, battery-op, litho tin, w/astronaut pilot, 10", EX+, A...$100.00

Atom Rocket 7, Modern Toys, 1960s, friction, litho tin, 13", NM..$125.00

Atomic Fire Car, TN, 1950s, battery-op, litho tin, NM+ .$250.00

Atomic Rocket Launcher, Ideal, 1955, plastic, 12", EX..$100.00

Attacking Martian, SH, battery-op, litho tin & plastic, 9½", NMIB, A..$125.00

Busy Cart Robot, Japan, battery-op, litho tin body w/plastic wheelbarrow, 11½", EXIB, A $880.00

Atomic Robot Man, Japan, 1950s, wind-up, lithograph tin, 6", EXIB, A, $700.00. (Photo courtesy Randy Inman Auctions)

Captain Astro Space Man, Mego, 1960s, w/up, tin & plastic, 6", NM+IB $225.00

Car From Space, Mormac, 1950s, battery-op, plastic, 8", NMIB...$100.00

Change Man Robot (Alien Creature), Japan, 1960s, battery-op, litho tin, 12", EX+, A....................$4,400.00

Change Man Robot (Boy Astronaut), Japan, 1960s, battery-op, litho tin & plastic, 14", NM, A $6,500.00

Chief Robot Man, KO, 1950s, battery-op, litho tin, silver w/red, gr & yel trim, 12", NM+, A $1,050.00

Cragstan Astronaut, Y, crank action, litho tin, 10", VG+, A .$775.00

Cragstan Great Astronaut, Japan, battery-op, litho tin, 14", EX, A $950.00

Cragstan Missile Launcher, Japan, 1950s, litho tin w/cb rocket scene, NMIB, A.....................................$450.00

Cragstan Mr. Atomic, Y, 1950s, battery-operated, lithograph tin with rubber hands and plastic helmet, 9", EXIB, A, $9,350.00.

Cragstan Moon Man, Cobor, 1960s, friction, 6", MOC .$200.00

Cragstan Mr Atomic, Y, 1950s, battery-op, litho tin w/rubber hands & plastic helmet, 9", VG, A.....................$1,430.00

Cragstan Mr Atomic, 1950s reproduction, battery-op, litho tin w/rubber hands & plastic helmet, 9", NMIB, A $470.00

Cragstan Mr Robot, Japan, 1950s, battery-op, litho tin, 10", VG+, A..$400.00

Cragstan Mr Robot, Japan, 1960s, battery-op, litho tin, 10", NMIB, A $1,320.00

Cragstan Ranger Robot, NGS, battery-op, plastic, 11", nonworking, GIB, A...$1,050.00

Cragstan Robot, battery-op, tin, 14", VG, A $550.00

Cragstan Satellite, 1950s, battery-op, litho tin, 8" dia, VG+, A $150.00

Cragstan Space Conqueror, Daiya, 1950s-60s, battery-op, litho tin, 12", NM $875.00

Cragstan Talking Robot, Japan, battery-op & friction, litho tin, 12", EXIB, A...$1,700.00

Delta Bird Space Ship, Japan, battery-op, plastic, 8", NMIB, A..$75.00

Dino Robot, SH, battery-op, tin, head opens to show monster, 11", NMIB, A...$800.00

Directional Robot, Yonezawa, 1950s, battery-op, tin, 11", nonworking, Fair+, A $500.00

Dragon Robot, Japan, 1960s, remote control, lithograph tin and plastic, dragon head opens to reveal astronaut, EX+IB, A, $2,860.00. (Photo courtesy Randy Inman Auctions)

Dux Astroman, West Germany, battery-op, plastic, 12", NMIB, A $880.00

Dux Astroman, West Germany, battery-op, plastic, 12", nonworking o/w EXIB, A...............................$350.00

Excavator Robot, Japan, 1960s, battery-op, plastic & tin, 10", NMIB, A $275.00

Explorer Space Tank, battery-op, litho tin, rare, EX, L4..$975.00

Fighting Robot, Japan, battery-op, litho tin, 11½", nonworking o/w VG+, A $65.00

Fighting Robot, Japan, battery-op, plastic, 10", nonworking, G+IB, A $165.00

Fire Man, SY, w/up, litho tin, 7", very rare, EX, A $750.00

Flash Gordon Strat-O Wagon, Wyandotte, 1940s, litho tin, 6", NMIB...$250.00

Flash Space Patrol, Japan, battery-op, plastic, 8", NMIB, A $220.00

Flashy Jim, Japan, w/up, litho tin, 7½", EX, A..............$580.00

Flying Saucer 101-Z, England, 1950s, litho tin, 7", EX, A.$215.00

Flying Saucer 8, Haji, friction, litho tin, 7" dia, working, EXIB, A $100.00

Machine Man, Japan, 1950s, battery-operated, lithograph tin, 15", G+, A, $27,500.00. (Photo courtesy Randy Inman Auctions)

Friendship-7 Space Capsule, Japan, friction, lithograph tin, 6½", EXIB, A, $150.00. (Photo courtesy Randy Inman Auctions)

Gemini Space Capsule, Lone Star, 1960, plastic, 4", NMIB $100.00

Giant Sonic Robot, Masudaya, 1950s, battery-op, litho tin, 16", VG+, A $2,970.00

Golden Sonic, Tigrett Industries, battery-op, plastic, 18", G+IB, A $100.00

High Wheel Robot, KO, w/up, tin, blk w/red hands & feet, see-through chest shows colored gears, 10", EX, A $175.00

Hysterical Robot, Japan, battery-op, plastic, 13", EXIB, A .$185.00

Interplanetary Explorer Robot, Japan, 1950s, w/up, litho tin, 8", VG+, A $1,000.00

Jet Oto Spaceship, India, 1960s, friction, litho tin w/pilot under clear dome, 7", NMIB...$150.00

Journey to the Moon Space Station, Japan, 1960s, battery-op, plastic & tin, complete, NMIB $100.00

Jupiter Robot, Japan, w/up, plastic, 7½", NMIB, A $110.00

Jupiter Rocket, Japan, friction, litho tin, 9½", EXIB, A.$130.00

Krome Dome Robot, Japan, battery-op, plastic, 11", EXIB, A.$275.00

Laser 008 Robot, Diaya, litho tin, friction, NMIB, A.....$700.00

Lavender Robot, see Nonstop Robot

Looping Space Tank, Daiya, 1950s, battery-op, NMIB...$300.00

Lost in Space Robot, Remco, 1966, battery-op, 12", NMIB.$800.00

Lost in Space Robot (Official), Hong Kong, 1977, battery-op, plastic, MIB, A $400.00

Lunar Expedition, Technofix, tin & plastic, 11x16", NMIB, A.$75.00

Lunar Exploration Vehicle, Gorgo/Argentina, friction, plastic, 14", NMIB, A $150.00

M-18 Space Tank, Modern Toys, 1950s, battery-op, litho tin, 8¼", NMIB...$375.00

Man From Mars, Irwin, 1950s, w/up, 11", NMIB............$600.00

Mars-107 Space Patrol, TN, 1950s, battery-op, litho tin, 13½", EX+ $550.00

Martian, see Walking Martian

Marvel Us Mike Tractor, Saunders, battery-op, plastic robot on pressed-steel dozer, 13", EXIB, A............................$385.00

Mat the Astronaut, Bullmark, w/up, tin w/vinyl head, 9½", NM+IB, A $500.00

Mechanical Robby Robot, Yonezawa, w/up, tin body w/wrench arms, 8", EX, A $1,050.00

Mechanized Robot (Robby-Type), Nomura, battery-op, tin, 13", EXIB, A $2,200.00

Mercury Explorer, TPS, 1960s, battery-op, 8", NMIB $250.00

Mercury X-1 Space Saucer, Japan, battery-op, tin & plastic, 8" dia, NMIB, A $120.00

Mighty Explorer Space Tank, battery-op, MIB, L4.........$475.00

Mighty Robot, Japan, w/up, litho tin, 5½", EXIB, A......$120.00

Miniature Robot, Hong Kong, 1960, plastic, silver, 3", MIB, A.$65.00

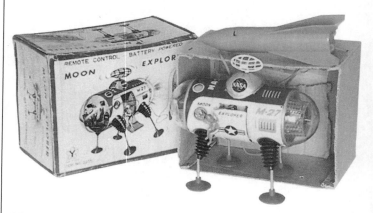

Moon Explorer M-27, Yonezawa, remote control, tin and plastic, 9", EX+IB, A, $935.00. (Photo courtesy Randy Inman Auctions)

Mirror Man Space Rocket, w/up, MIB, L4......................$475.00
Mobile Space TV Unit, battery-op, rare, NM, L4.......$1,800.00
Moon City Playset, Cragstan, 1970, battery-op, MIB (NOS).$200.00
Moon Detector M-27, Yonezawa, 1950s, battery-op, litho tin, 11", EX, A..$300.00
Moon Explorer, Japan, remote control, tin & plastic, 7", EXIB, A..$375.00
Moon Explorer, Japan, 1950s, friction, litho tin, 7", EX+IB, A.$500.00
Moon Explorer, TT Toys, 1960s, w/up, litho tin, 6", NMIB.$150.00
Moon Explorer Robot, Japan, battery-op, tin & plastic, 17", EX, A..$1,900.00
Moon Patrol Space Division No 3 (Moon Car), Japan, 1950s, battery-op, litho tin, 12½", EXIB, A $2,420.00
Moon Rocket Spaceship w/Flying Astronaut, Japan, battery-op, litho tin, 9½", NMIB, A $200.00
Moon Space Ship (Moon Car), Nomura, 1950s, battery-op, litho tin, 13" L, EXIB, A..........................$2,200.00
Moon Traveler Apollo-Z, Japan, battery-op, tin & plastic, 12", EXIB, A $110.00
Moonlight Man, Bullmark, w/up, litho tin w/vinyl head, 9", NMIB, A $1,770.00
Mr Atomic, see also Cragstan
Mr Atomic Robot, w/up, litho tin, 5", EX, A $400.00
Mr Brain, Remco, 1970, battery-op, plastic, NMIB........$100.00
Mr Mercury Robot, Linemar, 1960s, remote control, tin & plastic, 13", VG, A $350.00
Mr Mercury Robot, Marx, 1950s, remote control, tin, 14", G, A $330.00

NASA Space Patrol, MT, friction, litho tin, astronaut under clear dome, 7", NM (in Space Sight Seeing Bus box), A $500.00
NASA Space Station, Japan, 1950s, battery-op, litho tin, 12" dia, nonworking o/w EX, A $300.00
Nonstop Robot (Lavender Robot), Masudaya, 1950s, battery-op, litho tin, 15½", G+, A $1,200.00
Nonstop Robot (Lavender Robot), Masudaya, 1950s, battery-op, litho tin, 15½", NM, A $4,300.00
Official Space Patrol Rocket, Ray-O-Vac, 1950s, metal, 12", NMIB..........................$500.00
Outer Space Robot, Japan, battery-op, plastic, 10", EXIB, A..$155.00
Pegasus 1 Air Car, Japan, litho tin, 9", EXIB, A.............$240.00
Pioneer Space Radar Scout, Japan, friction, tin & plastic, 7", NMIB, A..........................$220.00

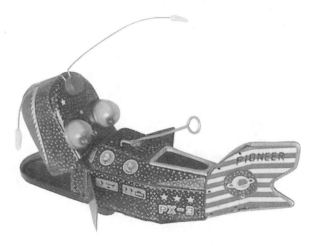

Pioneer Space Whale, Japan, 1950s, lithograph tin, 9½", EX+, A, $250.00. (Photo courtesy Randy Inman Auctions)

Musical Drummer Robot (R-57), Japan, 1950s, remote control, 9", EX+IB, A, $16,500.00. (Photo courtesy Randy Inman Auctions)

NASA Apollo Space Craft, Japan, 1960s, battery-op, mostly tin, 10", EX..........................$100.00
NASA Space Patrol, Aoshin, w/up, plastic, 4", NM+IB, A.$200.00

Radar Robot, TN, battery-operated, tin with plastic arms and disk antenna for ears, 12", NM+IB, A, $23,000.00. (Photo courtesy Smith House Toys)

Piston Action Robot (Pug Robbie), Japan, 1950s, remote control, litho tin, 9", EX+IB, A $1,375.00

Planet Robot, KO, w/up, litho tin, 9", MIB $300.00

Planet Saturn Space Radar Tank, Japan, 1950s-60s, battery-op, litho tin, EX+ $150.00

R-35 Robot, battery-op, litho tin, light-up eyes, 7½", nonworking o/w EXIB, A...$660.00

R-57, see Musical Drummer Robot

Radar Robot, Japan, 1950s, remote control, litho tin, 10", G+, A $575.00

Radicon Robot, Japan, 1950s, wireless remote control, tin, 15", EX+, A, $6,820.00. (Photo courtesy Randy Inman Auctions)

Ratchet Robot, TN, 1950s, w/up, 8", EX $325.00

REX Mars X-1 Planet Patrol, Marx, 1950s, w/up, litho tin, NM $435.00

Robby, see also Mechanized Robot

Robby Robot w/Sparkling Action, Yonezawa, 1950s, w/up, litho tin, 9", EX+IB, A...$2,200.00

Robby Space Patrol, Japan, 1950s, battery-op, litho tin, VG+, A $2,420.00

Robert the Robot, Ideal, 1950s, battery-op, light on top, 13", NMIB..$225.00

Robot, see also Walking Robot

Robot (Control), Linemar #R35, battery-op, litho tin, 8", VGIB (box reads Electric Remote Control...Robot), A.....$660.00

Robot (Domed Easel Back), Linemar, 1950s, remote control, litho tin w/clear plastic dome helmet, 7", NMIB, A $2,530.00

Robot (Easel Back), Linemar, 1950s, w/up, litho tin, silver w/red trim, sq head w/coil antenna, 6½", NM, A..............$215.00

Robot in Mercedes, Cragstan, 1950s, friction, tin, 8", EX+..$475.00

Robot on Road Roller, battery-op, rare, EX, L4..........$1,275.00

Robot on Tractor, Japan, 1950s, remote control, tin w/rubber treads, 10", nonworking, Fair, A.............................$250.00

Robot With Lantern (Powder), Linemar, 1950s, remote control, lithograph tin, 8", EX+IB, A, $7,920.00. (Photo courtesy Randy Inman Auctions)

Rocket Fighter, Marx, w/up, litho tin, 12", unused, NM+IB, A..$1,200.00

Rocket Fighter, see also Flash Gordon Rocket Fighter

Rocket Jeep, Japan, friction, litho tin, 6½", working, VG, A.$55.00

Rocket Launching Pad, Yonezawa, 1950s, battery-op, litho tin, NMIB..$375.00

Rocket Police Patrol, Marx, 12", VG, A.......................$450.00

Rosco Astronaut, Nomura, 1950s, litho tin, 13", VG+, A $1,150.00

Rudy the Robot, Remco, 1960s, battery-op, plastic, 16", NM.$50.00

Satellite Interceptor, Linemar, 1950s, battery-op, litho tin & plastic, MIB, L4 ....$575.00

Satellite Launching Truck, Japan, w/up & friction, litho tin, 12", NMIB, A...$220.00

Sky Patrol Saucer, K-O, 1950s, 7½" dia, MIB, L4 ....$475.00

Sky Patrol Spaceship, Japan, battery-op, tin & plastic, 13", NMIB, A...$275.00

Sky View Observatory, 1950s, litho tin, NMIB...............$100.00

Smoking Engine Robot, SH, battery-op, plastic, 10", MIB, A.$100.00

Smoking Robot, Alps, 1950s, battery-op, litho tin, 12", EXIB, A $2,200.00

Smoking Spaceman, Linemar, 1950s, battery-op, litho tin, rare gr version, 12", EXIB, A......................................$3,300.00

Smoking Spaceman, Linemar, 1950s, battery-op, litho tin, silver version, 12", EXIB, A...$1,650.00

Solar-X Space Rocket, Japan, battery-op, tin & plastic, 15", working, EXIB, A $130.00

Space Bus, Bandai, battery-op, litho tin, 14", EXIB, A ..$200.00

Space Bus, Japan, friction, litho tin w/lithoed robot driver, passengers & space scenes, 14½", EXIB, A................$1,700.00

Space Capsule, Japan, battery-op, litho tin w/plastic astronauts, 6½", working, NMIB, A..$120.00

Space Car, Yonezawa, battery-op, litho tin, w/tail fins, clear dome top, seated driver, 12", EX, A $200.00

Space Car SX-10, Modern Toys, 1960s, battery-op, litho tin, 9", NMIB..$600.00

Space Commander Space Station, Japan, battery-op, litho tin w/plastic dome, 9" dia, nonworking o/w EXIB, A....$100.00

Space Explorer, Japan, battery-op, litho tin, transforms from TV set to robot, 8", EX, A $1,225.00

Space Explorer Ship X-8, Japan, battery-op, litho tin, 10" dia, NMIB, A..$175.00

Space Explorer Tank w/Figure, Japan, friction, litho tin, 7", VG, A $50.00

Space Fighter Rocket Ship, Japan, 1950s, friction, litho tin w/twin pilots under plastic dome, 19", VG+, A ...$1,760.00

Space Frontier Apollo 12 Rocket, Japan, battery-op, tin & plastic, 18", EXIB, A...$150.00

Space Man (Space Commando), Japan, remote control, litho tin, 8", EX+IB, A...$2,650.00

Space Man Robot, Japan, battery-op, litho tin, silver body w/red arms & legs, human face shows through helmet, 10", G, A.....$475.00

Space Patrol, ATC, 1950s, friction, litho tin Mercedes-style car w/laser gun on hood, robot driver, 9", NMIB, A ..$1,870.00

Space Patrol Car With Astronaut, Japan, 1950s, friction with shooting gun on hood, lithograph tin, 8", VG, A, $1,980.00.

(Photo courtesy Randy Inman Auctions)

Space Patrol Super Cycle, Bandai, friction, lithograph tin with rubber driver, 12", extremely scarce, missing radar screen otherwise VG+IB, A, $9,900.00. (Photo courtesy Randy Inman Auctions)

Space Patrol, ATC, 1950s, friction, litho tin Mercedes-style car w/laser gun on hood, robot driver, 9", G, A $300.00

Space Patrol Car R-10, Japan, battery-op, litho tin w/VW emblem on hood & hubcaps, seated driver, 12", NM+IB, A..$6,500.00

Space Patrol Super Cycle, Bandai, friction, litho tin, 12", missing radar screen o/w EXIB, A $9,900.00

Space Patrol Vehicle, Sankei, battery-op, litho tin, astronaut under clear dome, rubber treads, celluloid screen, 9", G $575.00

Space Patrol w/Snoopy Astronaut, Japan, battery-op, tin & plastic, 11", NMIB, A $415.00

Space Patrol Z-206, Japan, battery-op, litho tin, 8", EX, A ..$65.00

Space Patrol 3 Flying Saucer, Japan, KO, battery-op, litho tin w/astronaut under plastic dome, 8" dia, NMIB, A...$450.00

Space Patrol/Space Tank, Indian Head/Japan, friction, litho tin, astronaut at controls, 5", NM+IB, A $600.00

Space Refuel Station, Japan, 1950s, battery-op, 13", nonworking o/w VG+, A..$1,430.00

Space Robot X-70 (Tulip Head), TN, 1960s, battery-op, tin w/plastic arms, head opens to camera & TV, 13", EX, A $660.00

Space Robot X-70 (Tulip Head), TN, 1960s, battery-op, tin w/plastic arms, head opens to camera & TV, 13", NMIB, A......$2,400.00

Space Rotor (Mysterious UFO), Taiwan, 1960s, battery-op, tin & plastic, 7" dia, NMIB.....................................$175.00

Space Saucer, Japan, 1950s, friction, litho tin, rnd w/single fin, pilot under clear dome, 7" dia, NM+ $150.00

Space Scooter, Modern Toys, 1960s, battery-op, tin & plastic, w/boy astronaut rider, 9½", NM $150.00

Space Ship, Japan, battery-op, litho tin, red, wht & bl, 12" dia, EX, A $265.00

Space Ship X-5, Japan, battery-op, litho tin, 8" dia, EXIB, A..$200.00

Space Shuttle Columbia, Japan, battery-op, litho tin & plastic, 10" L, NMIB, A $65.00

Space Tank w/Robot Driver, Japan, friction, litho tin, 6", NMIB, A $170.00

Space Trooper (Man w/Ray Gun), w/up, litho tin, 6½", EX, A $600.00

Space Trooper Robot (Robby Style), Japan, crank-op friction, blk tin, 7", EX, A $500.00

Space Vehicle w/Floating Satellite, Japan, battery-op, tin litho, 8½", working, NMIB, A...$360.00

Sparkling Space Tank, Marx, w/up, litho tin, 10", EX+IB, A..$440.00

Sparky Robot, KO, 1950s, w/up, litho tin, bl version, 8", VG $925.00

Sparky Robot, KO, 1950s, w/up, litho tin, gold version, 8", EX+, A..$1,300.00

Speedboat w/Robot Driver, Japan, friction, litho tin, 13", working, EX, A $650.00

SS-18 Space Car, S&E, 1960s, friction, litho tin, 9", NM .$150.00

ST-1 Robot, West Germany, 1950s, w/up, 8", NMIB......$600.00

Super Cycle (Flying Spaceman), Bandai, 1950s, friction, litho tin, unauthorized Superman driver, 12", G+IB, A.$1,320.00

Super Cycle Space Patron, Bandai, friction, litho tin cycle w/rubber driver, 12", EXIB, A $9,900.00

Super Jet V-7, TN, 1950s, battery-op, litho tin, 12" L, EX, L4.$975.00

Super Moon Patroller, Junior/Japan, battery-op, litho tin, w/NASA symbols, 9", EXIB, A $450.00

Super Space Giant, Japan, battery-op, tin & plastic, 18", NMIB, A $385.00

Swinging Baby Robot, Japan, w/up, litho tin, 12", NMIB, A $440.00

Talking Sound Robot, Japan, 1960s, battery-op, 11", NM+ .$750.00

Target Robot, Japan, 1950s, battery-op, litho tin, 15", EX+, A $7,700.00

Television Spaceman, Alps, 1950s, battery-op, tin & plastic, NMIB, A $600.00

Television Spaceman, Alps, 1950s, w/up, litho tin, 6½", EXIB, A $330.00

Tetsujin 28 Saucer, TN, friction, litho tin, 8½" dia, VG, A .$950.00

Three Stage Rocket (US Air Force), Japan, battery-op, litho tin, 21", EXIB, A $500.00

Titan the Tumbler Robot, battery-op, MIB, L4...............$500.00

Tom Corbett Space Cadet Spaceship, Marx, w/up w/sparking action, litho tin, 12", EX+IB, A $660.00

Train Robot, see Giant Sonic Robot

TV Robot, Japan, 1960s, battery-op, tin & plastic, lg screen in sq chest, 10", VG+, A $175.00

TV Space Patrol Car, Japan, friction, litho tin car w/tail fins, astronaut under clear plastic dome top, 8", EX, A.$1,050.00

TV Space Tank, KO, 1950s, w/up, NM.........................$275.00

Two-Stage Earth Satellite, Linemar, 1950s, w/up, litho tin, 10½", NMIB $425.00

USAF Gemini (USA-NASA Gemini) w/Flying Astronaut, Japan, battery-op, litho tin, 9½", NMIB, A.............$165.00

USAF Three-Stage Rocket, TN, battery-op, litho tin, 21", EX+IB, A...$1,450.00

Walking Robot, Linemar, w/up, litho tin, 6", VG+, A ...$265.00

Wheel-A-Gear Robot, KO, 1950s, w/up, tin, 10", VG+, A.$275.00

Wheel-A-Gear Robot, Taiyo, battery-op, tin & plastic, 15", EXIB, A $770.00

X-10 Space Tank, Japan, 1950s, battery-op, w/camera & box, 12", NMIB $600.00

X-15 Flying Saucer, 1950s, crank w/up, litho tin, scarce gr version, 6" dia, EX+ $250.00

XB115 Rocket, Japan, friction, tin & plastic, 11½", NMIB, A.$150.00

Zoomer Robot, TN, battery-op, tin, scarce dk gray & red version, 8½", EX, A $550.00

MISCELLANEOUS

Astro Ray Flashlight Target Gun, plastic dart shooting gun w/13x13" target board, EXIB, A..........................$110.00

Astronaut Space Helmet & Ear Phones, RCA, w/records, MIB, L4 ....$175.00

Bubble Gun, Japan, 1950s, litho tin w/space design, plastic turret, fan blade turns to blow bubbles, NMIB $75.00

Color Space Gun, Ideal, 1950s-60s, battery-op, 9", NM..$135.00

Floating Satellite Target Game, Japan, battery-operated, complete, NMIB, A, $80.00. (Photo courtesy Randy Inman Auctions)

Gumball Machine, rocket shape w/clear plastic center, solid color cone top w/astronaut decal, EX........................$75.00

Lost in Space Helmet & Ray Gun Set, Remco, 1966, EX+IB, A...$1,800.00

Pencil Sharpener, spaceship, 1960s, 2½", MIP (sealed)....$10.00

Planet Patrol Saucer Gun, Park Plastics, 1960s, complete, NMIB $50.00

Rattle, Japan, litho tin, rnd top w/image of astronaut holding space gun, whistle at end of hdl, 6½", EX+, A $110.00

Rocket Radio, Japan, 1950s, 4", complete, NMIP............$75.00

Space Faces, Pressman, 1950s, unused, NMIB...............$175.00

Space Nik Satellite Helmet, 1950s, plastic, EX $125.00

Space Ship Telescope, tin w/paper graphics, Japan, 1950s, 5", NM...$30.00

Space Suit, Jet Morgan from Journey Into Space radio series, Made in England, complete, EXIB, A....................$500.00

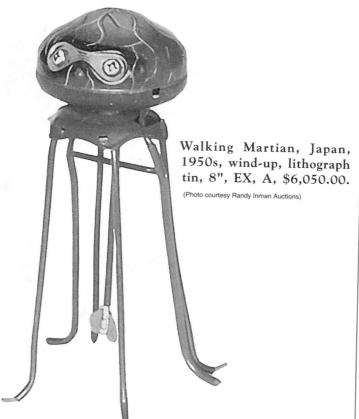

Walking Martian, Japan, 1950s, wind-up, lithograph tin, 8", EX, A, $6,050.00.
(Photo courtesy Randy Inman Auctions)

Space Model QX-2 Electronic Walkie Talkies, Remco, plastic, works with magnetic power, EX+IB, A, $50.00. (Photo courtesy Randy Inman Auctions)

Space War Beany, 1950s, felt w/metal spinning props atop spinning coil, EX+...$125.00

Spinner Toy, lithograph cardboard with space graphics, push lever and astronaut spins and stops on a planet, Japan, 2½" diameter, M, $25.00. (Photo courtesy New England Auction Gallery)

Rock 'n Roll

From the '50s on, rock 'n roll music has been an enjoyable part of many of our lives, and the performers themselves have often been venerated as icons. Today some of the all-time great artists such as Elvis, the Beatles, KISS, and the Monkees, for instance, have fans that not only continue to appreciate their music but actively search for the ticket stubs, concert posters, photographs, and autographs of their favorites. More easily found, through, are the items that sold through retail stores at the height of their careers — dolls, games, toys, books, magazines, etc. In recent years, some of the larger auction galleries have sold personal items such as guitars, jewelry, costumes, automobiles, contracts, and other one-of-a-kind items that realized astronomical prices. If you're an Elvis fan, we recommend *Elvis Collectibles* and *Best of Elvis Collectibles* by Rosalind Cranor (Overmountain Press).

Advisor: Bob Gottuso, BOJO (B3), Beatles, KISS, Monkees.
See also Action Figures; Bubble Bath Containers; Character and Promotional Drinking Glasses; Coloring, Activity, and Paint Books; Lunch Boxes; Model Kits; Paper Dolls; Pin-Back Buttons; Puppets.

Andy Gibb, doll, Ideal, 1979, wht suit & red vest, 7½", MIB .$85.00
Andy Gibb, gum wrapper, 1978, 5x6", EX, N2 ....$10.00
Andy Gibb, poster, image of Andy singing, 1978, 15x10", EX...$10.00
Beatles, badge, I've Got My Beatles Movie Ticket Have You? w/center portrait, cb w/string, 1964, 3¾" dia, EX+....$40.00
Beatles, bank, John, papier-mache half-figure, Pride Creations, VG+, B3 ....$680.00
Beatles, bulletin board, Stamp Out Fun!, puffy cb, unused, VG+ (sealed), B3 ....$120.00
Beatles, charm bracelet, blk & wht photo discs of ea member, Nicky Byrne/Nems Ent Ltd, NMOC $175.00
Beatles, Colorforms Cartoon Kit, 1966, complete, MIB ..$1,000.00
Beatles, doll set, Sgt Pepper Costumes, Applause, 1988, complete w/cb stage & 4 stands, 22", M, B3 ....$450.00
Beatles, drum, blk outline of Ringo's head, hand & signature, w/stand, New Beat, 14" dia, EX, B3 ....$675.00
Beatles, figure, Ringo seated at drums w/The Beatles emb on front, rubber, King Features, 6", rare, EX $600.00

Beatles, Ford Galaxy Convertible Yes/Yes, lithographed tin, battery-operated, push button emits sound, with four figures, unlicensed item by Rico (Spain), 19", NMIB, $1,750.00. (Photo courtesy Bertoia Auctions)

Beatles, guitar, Four Pop, head images of group & name, NM, B3 ....$650.00
Beatles, guitar, New Beat, circle image of group, NMIB, B3 ....$1,050.00
Beatles, guitar, New Sound, head images of group, EX, B3...$420.00
Beatles, hand puppet, Ringo image on wht plastic, World Candies promo, rare, VG+ $600.00
Beatles, harmonica, Hohner, 1964, MOC $1,000.00
Beatles, nodders, Swingers Music Set, 4", MOC............$150.00
Beatles, pencil case, oversized, beige leather w/cloth fringe across top, name & group w/instruments, 5x12", EX, B3 ...$280.00

Beatles, pinback, I'm a Beatles Fan, 4 head shots w/center banner, blk & wht on red, Nems Ent Ltd/Green Duck, 4", EX+ .$30.00

Beatles, Pop Stickles, Dal, unused, MIP (sealed), B3........$90.00

Beatles, poster put-ons, Yellow Submarine, unused, MIP .$225.00

Beatles, punch-out portraits, Whitman, complete & unused, NM, B3 ....$190.00

Beatles, purse, sq w/cutout brass-trimmed hdl, beige w/names/ group name & bust images of group, EX, B3 ....$520.00

Beatles, record player, inside lid displays group w/instruments, 1964, VG, B3 ....$4,700.00

Beatles, Spatter Toy, rare, unused, MIP, B3....................$380.00

Beatles, stationary, Yellow Submarine, complete w/20 sheets & envelopes, NMIB, B3 ....$100.00

Beatles, wallet, red, vinyl w/blk & wht group portrait & signatures, Standard Plastic, 1964, EX+ $90.00

Beatles, wallet, red vinyl w/blk & wht group portrait & signatures, Standard Plastic, 1964, EX+ w/comb, mirror, etc $180.00

Beatles, watercolor set, Yellow Submarine, Craftmaster, complete, MIB, B3 ....$150.00

Bee Gees, Sing-Along Am Radio w/Microphone, EXIB, T1.$65.00

Bobby Sherman, ring, Love & Peace, M $25.00

Boy George, doll, LJN, 1984, 11½", rare, MIB $150.00

Boy George & Culture Club, puffy stickers, set of 6, 1984, M...$15.00

Captain & Tennille, Captain doll, Mego, 1977, 12½", MIB .$125.00

Cher, doll, Mego, 1976, Growing Hair, 12½", MIB........$150.00

Cher, doll, Mego, 1976, pk evening gown, 12½", MIB ..$125.00

Cher, doll, Mego, 1981, swimsuit, 12", MIB.....................$50.00

Chubby Checker, party game, Limbo Under the Bar, Wham-O, 1961, complete, NM....................................$100.00

Dave Clark Five, doll set, Remco, NMIB.......................$550.00

David Cassidy, Colorforms Dress-Up Set, 1972, complete, MIB.$50.00

David Cassidy, guitar, plastic, Carnival Toys, 1970s, MIB..$100.00

David Cassidy, slide-tile puzzle, 1970s, M.......................$35.00

Diana Ross, doll, Mego, 1977, 12½", MIB, A $150.00

Dick Clark, diary, vinyl, 1958, 4x4", EX $125.00

Donny & Marie, guitar, w/photo image, 1977, 29", VG+, N2 ....$75.00

Donny & Marie, microphone, LJN, 1977, MIB $35.00

Elvis, autograph book, EPE, 1956, EX, minimum value .$500.00

Elvis, balloon, King Galahad punching bag type w/feet, unused, EX $100.00

Elvis, earrings, Loving You..., gold-fr portraits w/pierced backs, MIP $225.00

Elvis, flasher ring, 1957, EX, minimum value $100.00

Elvis, guitar, Lapin, 1984, MOC (sealed) $75.00

Elvis, hat, cotton floppy style w/color litho band, Magnet Hat & Cap/EPE, 1956, EX+ $160.00

Elvis, Hound Dog, stuffed plush w/Elvis lettered on wht neck ribbon, Smile Toy Co, NM.................................$250.00

Elvis, key chain, soft wht plastic record shape w/head image in center, Holsom Bread/Action Line, 1960s, EX+........$50.00

Elvis, overnight case, sq w/top hdl, latch closure, simulated leather w/images of Elvis & signatures, EPE, 1956, EX $750.00

Elvis, pillow, Love Me Tender, print of Elvis singing & playing guitar & faux signature, EPE, 1956, sq, NM $400.00

Elvis, poster, Las Vegas, 1976, 36x24", M (sealed), N2.....$15.00

Herman's Hermits, doll, Peter Noone, Show Biz Babies, NMIB..$250.00

Jackson Five, record, cb cutout from cereal box, photo image on front, M..$15.00

KISS, Colorforms, 1979, complete, MIB...........................$85.00

KISS, doll, Mego, 1978, any from group, 12½", MIB, ea.$250.00

KISS, wastebasket, metal cylinder w/lithoed concert images & name, Aucoin, 1977, M...................................$225.00

KISS, Your Face Makeup, Remco, 1978, MIB (sealed)...$200.00

KISS, 3-Function Van, radio controlled, 1979, unused, MIB $600.00

Mamas & the Papas, dolls, Show Biz Babies, any, Hasbro, 1967, 4", MOC, ea..$225.00

Mandy Moore, doll, Play Along, 2000, 11½", MIB $20.00

MC Hammer, Rap Mike, Impact Toys, 1991, MIB $25.00

Donny and Marie, Poster Pen Set, Craft House, 1977, with color poster on back, unused, MIP, $20.00.

(Photo courtesy Greg Davis and Bill Morgan)

Marie Osmond, Marie's Vanity Set, Standard Pyroxoloid Corp., 1977, MOC, $25.00. (Photo courtesy McMasters Doll Auctions)

Michael Jackson, belt, red cloth w/wht stitched name & gloved hand, blk trim, disc buckle w/photo image, US, 1984, M $30.00

Michael Jackson, Colorforms Puzzleforms, 1984, MIB (sealed) .$20.00

Michael Jackson, stamp sets, various, St Vincent, unused, MIP, ea $30.00

Monkees, charm bracelet, rnd disc charms w/photo head images, gold-tone chain-link band, Raybert, 1967, MOC......$90.00

Monkees, finger puppets, Remco, 1970, 5", MIB, ea.........$70.00

Monkees, guitar, plastic, w/up, Mattel, 1966, 14", NM ..$150.00

Monkees, oil paint set, Monkeemania, Art Award, 1967, MIB.$250.00

Monkees, record case, vinyl covered w/plastic hdl, image of group in car w/name in shape of guitar, Raybert, 1966, M...$200.00

Monkees, tambourine, circle images of group w/name in shape of guitar & Tambourine lettered on front, NM............$125.00

New Kids on the Block, Colorforms, 1991, complete, MIB .$15.00

New Kids on the Block, dolls, In Concert, 5 different, Hasbro, 12", MIB, ea $45.00

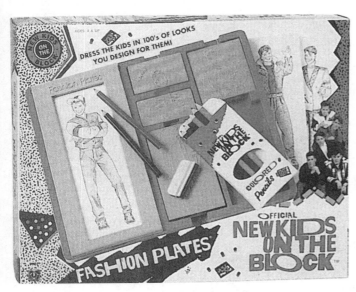

New Kids on the Block, Fashion Plates, Hasbro, 1990, unused, MIB, $35.00. (Photo courtesy Joe Hilton and Greg Moore)

Osmonds, frisbee, The Osmonds Zoom-O, group image in center, 1970s, EX $35.00

Rolling Stones, dolls, Play Pals, 1963, rare, M, ea $125.00

Rolling Stones, Rad-A-Tattoos, Brockham, 1991, MOC .$15.00

Rolling Stones, sticker album, Stanley, 1983, NM+ $20.00

Shaun Cassidy, guitar, Carnival Toys, 1978, MIP $100.00

Van Halen, binoculars, VH logo, NM $20.00

Vanilla Ice, Rap Microphone, THQ, 1991, MIB $25.00

Village People, guitar, plastic w/photo image, Carnival Toys, 1978, 36", MOC $150.00

ZZ Top, mirror, 1980s, 6x6", M...$10.00

Roly Polys

Popular toys with children around the turn of the century, roly polys were designed with a weighted base that caused the toy to automatically right itself after being kicked or knocked over. Their popularity faded to some extent, but they continued to be produced until WWI and beyond. Most were made of papier-mache, though some Japanese toy makers used celluloid later on. Schoenhut made some that are especially collectible today in a variety of sizes — up to almost a foot in height. They represented clowns, animals, and children, as well as some well known story book characters.

All listings are papier-mache unless noted otherwise.

Austrian Boy and Girl, 8", musical, colorful ethnic costumes with real feathers in caps, EX, A, pair, $225.00.

(Photo courtesy Bertoia Auctions)

Baby Boy, 11½", movable head, hands on belly, orange outfit w/wht shirt, yel & red trim, Schoenhut, VG, A $300.00

Boy, 6½", holding suspenders, wht shirt w/red tie, bl hat, tan base, Schoenhut, G, A...$75.00

Boy, 9", hands on belly, wearing baseball-type hat, red, yel & bl, Schoenhut, EX, A...$550.00

Buster Brown, 2¼", Schoenhut, EX, A $165.00

Child Soldier, 4½", holding gun, long blk hair, red uniform & helmet w/yel trim, VG, A..$60.00

Chinese Boy, 4½", hands in pockets, curious look on face, VG, A $40.00

Chinese Clown, 4½", hands on belly, cone hat, red, blk & brn, Schoenhut, EX+, A...$140.00

Clown, 4½", hands on belly, red, wht & bl, Schoenhut, G, A..$100.00

Clown, 5", hands on belly, red pompon button between hands, wht & lt violet suit, EX+, A.......................................$40.00

Clown, 6½", hands on belly, cone hat, pointed collar, red & yel, Schoenhut, EX, A $165.00

Clown, 6½", hands on belly, plume in brimmed yel hat, bl w/wht ruffled collar, 4 buttons, blk trim, EX, A.................$170.00

Clown, 7", hands on belly, cone hat, open jacket w/ruffled collar, red, wht & bl, Germany, VG, A................................$85.00

Clown, 7½", cigar in mouth, rosy cheeks, top hat & bow tie, emb pig on back w/other emb figures, G, A...............$75.00

Clown, 7½", hands clasped on belly, cone hat, bow tie on ruffled collar, red, yel & wht, Noma, EXIB, A....................$200.00

Clown, 8", holding animals, pointed hairdo, red suit w/gr ruffled collar, Schoenhut, VG, A..$115.00

Clown, 9", hands on belly, cone hat w/single pompon, jacket w/vest & bow tie, red, bl & yel, EX, A.....................$115.00

Clown, 9", hands on belly, pointed hairdo, gr & wht suit w/gr ruffled collar, Schoenhut, G, A....................................$75.00

Clown, 9", musical, hands in pockets, fabric tassel on hat, orange, EX, A...$155.00

Clown, 9½", musical, top hat, detailed face w/arched brows, ruffled collar, lime, brn & red, EX, A...........................$170.00

Clown, 10", holding animals, pointed hairdo, yel & red suit w/gr ruffled collar, Schoenhut, EX+, A...........................$440.00

Clown, 11½", hands in front pockets, fabric collar, 6 buttons on band down front, mc, Germany, VG, A...................$150.00

Clown, 15", hands on belly, cone hat w/2 pompons, eyes move, Rolly Toys/Germany, EX, A......................................$215.00

Clown, 15", movable head, blue and white with red stripes, yellow belt, red trim, EX, A, $1,760.00. (Photo courtesy Bertoia Auctions)

Drummer Boy, 4½", holding drum sticks, long hair, bl uniform, wht hat, VG, A...$100.00

Duck, 6", dressed in suit w/hands clasping lapels, yel w/red bill & vest, bl jacket, Germany, EX, A..............................$170.00

Foxy Grandpa, 8¼", glass eyes, bl suit w/yel vest & red tie, some repair, A...$250.00

Girl, 4⅛", hooded, wht w/red trim, gr base, Schoenhut, EX, A .$60.00

Girl Clown, 7", hands on belly, red hat, lime ruffled collar, pk outfit w/yel trim, VG, A..$30.00

Golliwog, 4", gray suit, Schoenhut, EX, A........................$85.00

Happy Hooligan, 4", hands in pockets, exaggerated face w/arched eyebrows & lg eyes, gr & red, EX, A.........$200.00

Happy Hooligan, 4", hands on belly, clown face, bl body w/red jacket & hat, EX, A..$55.00

Happy Hooligan, 11", hands on belly, head cocked, dbl-breasted jacket, red, bl & yel, Schoenhut, EX, A.................$155.00

Indian Baby, 4", painted markings on face, yel outfit w/red trim, wht hood, Schoenhut, G, A......................................$85.00

Keystone Cop, 5", hands on belly, bl single-breasted jacket & hat, detailed face w/mustache, EX, A.......................$125.00

Keystone Cop, 5½", gloved hands on belly, med bl dbl-breasted jacket w/red belt & hat band, no mustache, EX+, A.$165.00

Keystone Cop, 7", hands w/fingers spread on belly, bl dbl-breasted uniform w/blk collar & hat band, mustache, EX, A...$230.00

Keystone Cop, 7", hands w/fingers spread on belly, bl single-breasted overlapping jacket w/buttons to 1 side, VG, A..............$140.00

Keystone Cop, 10", musical, hands on belly, bl single-breasted jacket w/lg buttons, blk belt & hat band, mustache, VG, A.....$165.00

Lady in Man's Suit, 14", movable head, hands on belly, bl suit w/yel vest, hat & hair, red tie, Schoenhut, VG, A ..$385.00

Man, 4½", whimsical w/blk hair & mustache, brn pointed hat, red coat, Schoenhut, EX, A.......................................$60.00

Max & Moritz, 5¼", amusing expressions w/lg bulbous noses, side-glance eyes, mc outfits, Germany, EX, pr $155.00

Mother Goose, 8½", holding goose, bl & wht w/red trim, Schoenhut, EX, A $165.00

Pig Playing Horn, 7½", pk w/gray horn, gr base, Schoenhut, EX, A $275.00

Popeye, 5", celluloid figure w/hands on hips & pipe in mouth standing on filled base, mk CSA, rare, NM, A........$300.00

Rooster Crowing, 9", mc, Schoenhut, G, A....................$110.00

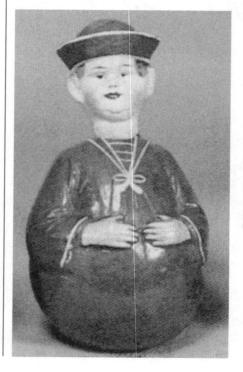

Sailor Boy, 9¼", blue suit and hat with white trim, Schoenhut, EX, A, $525.00. (Photo courtesy Bertoia Auctions)

Sailor Girl, 4½", hands on belly, bl w/wht hat, Schoenhut, VG $150.00
Santa Claus, 5", hands on stomach, red w/wht fur-trimmed hat, long wht beard, NM, A $360.00
Santa Claus, 5", toy bag over shoulder, red suit & hat w/orange & gr trim, long wht beard, NM, A $360.00
Santa Claus, 6", toy bag over shoulder, red suit w/pointed hat, blk belt & cuffs, long wht beard, EX, A $230.00
Santa Claus, 7", hands holding suspenders, red suit & hat w/wht trim, long wht beard, Schoenhut, EX, A $500.00
Santa Claus, 7", toy bag over shoulder, red suit w/wht cuffs, long wht beard, EX, A $500.00
Santa Claus, 7½", holding toys in arms, red suit w/wht buttons, gr bag, long gray beard, Schoenhut, EX, A $600.00
Santa Claus, 9½", toy bag over shoulder, red suit & pointed hat w/blk belt, wht beard, Schoenhut, EX, A $275.00

Santa Claus, 9", pressed cardboard, red with white and black trim, Schoenhut, NM, A, $1,650.00; Santa Claus, 11", musical, felt hat and suit, long white cotton beard, EX, A, $250.00. (Photo courtesy Bertoia Auctions)

Sand Toys and Pails

By 1900 companies were developing all sorts of sand toys, including free-standing models. The Sand Toy Company of Pittsburgh patented and made 'Sandy Andy' from 1909 onward. The company was later bought by the Wolverine Supply & Manufacturing Co. and continued to produce variations of the toy until the 1970s.

Today if you mention sand toys, people think of pails, spades, sifters, and molds.

We have a rich heritage of lithographed tin pails with such wonderful manufacturers as J. Chein & Co., T. Cohn Inc., Morton Converse, Kirchoff Patent Co., Marx Toy Co., Ohio Art

Co., etc, plus the small jobbing companies who neglected to sign their wares. Sand pails have really come into their own and are now recognized for their beautiful graphics and designs. The following listings are lithographed or painted tin. For more information we recommend *Pails by Comparison, Sand Pails and Other Sand Toys, A Study and Price Guide*, by Carole and Richard Smyth.

Advisors: Carole and Richard Smyth

Bowler Andy Mill, Wolverine #57A, 20", NMIB, A, $440.00. (Photo courtesy Bertoia Auctions)

Crane, Wolverine #20, 17½", MIB, A, $385.00. (Photo courtesy Bertoia Auctions)

Captain Sandy Andy, Wolverine #63C, 13½", MIB, A .$385.00

Coal Loader, Wolverine, elevator & crane, 11", MIB, A.$400.00

Crane, Wolverine #103, 13½", VG+IB, A $55.00

Dandy Sandy Andy, Wolverine, 11", Fair+, A.................$75.00

Dutch Mill, Mac #26, 12", VG, A....................................$90.00

Mold & Sifter Set, fish & frog mold, scoop & shovel, Ohio Art, 1950, MOC..$75.00

Pail, boy & girl w/teddy bear & children building castles, 5", EX...$400.00

Pail, carnival scenes w/kids, Chein, 4", NM.....................$65.00

Pail, children in boat fishing, 6", VG, A $30.00

Pail, cowboys & Indians, Ohio Art, 1950s, EX..............$100.00

Pail, farm animals in clothes, 1940s, 8", NM $125.00

Pail, Humpty Dumpty, Ohio Art, 1950s, 8", EX, N2 ....$50.00

Pail, Mickey Mouse leading parade w/cityscape & bl sky in background, w/shovel, 6", VG, A $175.00

Pails, Mother Goose characters on square tapered pails with landscape backgrounds, Chein, 6", VG, A, $125.00; G, A, $65.00. (Photo courtesy Bertoia Auctions)

Pail, Three Cheers For the Red, White and Blue, children parading on red w/bl & wht diamond pattern at base, 8", G, A $40.00

Pail, Treasure Island, Ohio Art, 4½", VG......................$350.00

Pail, Victorian w/2 scenes of children at the beach, floral border, 5½", EX..$350.00

Sand Loader, Wolverine, elevator w/crane, 11", MIB, A.$410.00

Sand Toy (mk Sand Toy), seesaw w/2 children on horse seats, 10½", Poor to Fair, A.......................................$55.00

Sandy Andy Merry Miller Mill, 12", Fair, A $75.00

Sandy Andy Sand Loader (Large Can), Wolverine #50, w/seated figure, 13½", EX, A...$30.00

Sandy Andy Sand Loader (Small Can), Wolverine, VGIB, A.$30.00

Schoenhut

Albert Schoenhut & Co. was located in Philadelphia, Pennsylvania. From as early as 1872 they produced toys of many types including dolls, pianos and other musical instruments, games, and a good assortment of roly polys (which they called

Rolly Dollys). In 1902 – 1903 they were granted patents that were the basis for toy animals and performers that Schoenhut designated the 'Humpty Dumpty Circus.' It was made up of circus animals, ringmasters, acrobats, lion tamers, and the like, and the concept proved to be so successful that it continued in production until the company closed in 1935. During the nearly thirty-five years they were made, the figures were continually altered either in size or by construction methods, and these variations can greatly affect their values today. Besides the figures themselves, many accessories were produced to go along with the circus theme — tents, cages, tubs, ladders, and wagons, just to mention a few. Teddy Roosevelt's 1909 African safari adventures inspired the company to design a line that included not only Teddy and the animals he was apt to encounter in Africa but native tribesmen as well. A third line in the 1920s featured comic characters of the day, all with the same type of jointed wood construction, many dressed in cotton and felt clothing. There were several, among them were Felix the Cat, Maggie and Jiggs, Barney Google and Spark Plug, and Happy Hooligan. (See Character, TV, and Movie Collectibles.)

Several factors come into play when evaluating Schoenhut figures. Foremost is condition. Since most found on the market today show signs of heavy wear, anything above a very good rating commands a premium price (the following value ranges are for good to very good). Missing parts and retouched paint sharply reduce a figure's value, though a well-done restoration is usually acceptable. The earlier examples had glass eyes; by 1920 eyes were painted. In the early 1920s the company began to make their animals in a reduced size. While some of the earlier figures had bisque heads or carved wooden heads, by the '20s, pressed wood heads were the norm. Full-size examples with glass eyes and bisque or carved heads are generally more desirable and more valuable, though rarity must be considered as well.

During the 1950s, some of the figures and animals were produced by the Delvan Company, who had purchased the manufacturing rights.

For more information we recommend *Schoenhut Toy Price Guide* in full color by Keith Kaonis and Andrew Yaffee. Mr. Kaonis is listed in the Directory under Schoenhut.

Advisors: Keith and Donna Kaonis (K6)

See also Character, TV, and Movie Collectibles; Pull and Push Toys; Roly Polys.

Humpty Dumpty Circus Animals

Humpty Dumpty Circus animals with glass eyes, circa 1903 – 1914, are more desirable and can demand much higher prices than the later painted-eye versions. As a general rule, a glass-eye version is 30% to 40% more than a painted-eye version. (There are exceptions.) The following list suggests values for both glass eye and painted eye versions and reflects a low painted eye price to a high glass eye price.

There are other variations and nuances of certain figures: Bulldog — white with black spots or brindle (brown); open-and closed-mouth zebras and giraffes; ball necks and hemispherical necks on some animals such as the pig, leopard, and tiger, to name a few. These points can affect the price and should be judged individually.

Alligator, PE/GE, from $250 to $750.00
Arabian Camel, 1 hump, PE/GE, from $250 to $750.00
Bactrian Camel, 2 humps, PE/GE, from $200 to $1,200.00
Brown Bear, PE/GE, from $200 to $800.00
Buffalo, cloth mane, PE/GE, from $300 to.......................$900.00
Buffalo, cvd mane, PE/GE, from $200 to $1,200.00

Bulldog, from $400.00 to $1,500.00; Cats, rare, from $500.00 to $3,000.00 each; Teeter Totter, from $350.00 to $500.00. (Photo courtesy Keith and Donna Kaonis)

Burro (made for farm set, no harness), PE/GE, from $300 to..$800.00
Burro (made to go w/chariot & clown), PE/GE, from $200 to..$700.00
Cow, PE/GE, from $300 to $1,200.00
Deer, PE/GE, from $300 to..$1,500.00
Donkey, PE/GE, from $75 to $300.00
Donkey w/Blanket, PE/GE, from $100 to.......................$600.00
Elephant, PE/GE, from $75 to $300.00
Elephant w/Blanket & Head Tapestry, PE/GE, from $200 to..$600.00
Gazelle, PE/GE, rare, from $500 to $2,750.00
Giraffe, PE/GE, from $200 to $900.00
Goat, PE/GE, from $150 to $400.00
Goose, PE only, from $200 to $900.00
Gorilla, PE only, from $1,500 to $4,000.00
Hippo, PE/GE, from $200 to $900.00
Horse, brn, saddle & stirrups, PE/GE, from $250 to $500.00

Lion, cloth mane, from $500.00 to $1,200.00. (Photo courtesy Keith and Donna Kaonis)

Horse, wht, platform, PE/GE, from $150 to $450.00
Hyena, PE/GE, rare, from $1,000 to $6,000.00
Kangaroo, PE/GE, from $200 to $1,500.00
Leopard, PE/GE, from $300 to $1,400.00
Lion, cvd mane, PE/GE, from $200 to $1,400.00
Monkey, 1-part head, PE only, from $200 to...................$600.00
Monkey, 2-part head, wht face, from $300 to $1,000.00
Ostrich, PE/GE, from $200 to $900.00
Pig, 5 versions, PE/GE, from $200 to $800.00
Polar Bear, PE/GE, from $200 to..................................$2,000.00
Poodle, cloth mane, GE only, from $150 to $450.00
Poodle, cvd mane, GE, from $400 to $1,200.00
Poodle, PE, from $100 to $300.00
Rabbit, PE/GE, rare, from $500 to $3,500.00
Rhino, PE/GE, from $250 to $800.00
Sea Lion, PE/GE, from $400 to $1,500.00
Sheep (lamb) w/bell, PE/GE, from $200 to....................$700.00
Tiger, PE/GE, from $250 to $1,200.00
Wolf, PE/GE, rare, from $500 to $5,000.00
Zebra, PE/GE, from $250 to $1,200.00
Zebu, PE/GE, rare, from $500 to $3,000.00

HUMPTY DUMPTY CIRCUS CLOWNS AND OTHER PERSONNEL

Clowns with two-part heads (a cast face applied to a wooden head) were made from 1903 to 1916 and are most desirable — condition is always important. There have been nine distinct styles in fourteen different costumes recorded. Only eight costume styles apply to the two-part headed clowns. The later clowns, ca. 1920, had one-part heads whose features were pressed, and the costumes were no longer tied at the wrists and ankles.

Note: Use the low end of the value range for items in only fair condition. Those in good to very good condition (having very minor scratches and wear, good original finish, no splits or chips, no excessive paint wear or cracked eyes and, of course, complete) may be evaluated by the high end.

Black Dude, reduced sz, from $100 to $375.00
Black Dude, 1-part head, purple coat, from $250 to $700.00

Gent Acrobat, bisque head, circa 1906 – 1916, rare, from $300.00 to $750.00 each. (Photo courtesy Keith and Donna Kaonis)

Black Dude, 2-part head, blk coat, from $400 to $850.00
Chinese Acrobat, 1-part head, from $200 to $800.00
Chinese Acrobat, 2-part head, rare, from $400 to.......$1,400.00
Clown, early, 2-part head, G, from $150 to....................$600.00
Clown, reduced sz, from $75 to $125.00

Hobo, reduced sz, from $200 to......................................$375.00
Hobo, 1-part head, from $200 to.....................................$400.00
Hobo, 2-part head, curved-up toes, blk coat, from $500
    to $1,200.00
Lady Acrobat, bsk head, from $300 to $750.00
Lady Acrobat, 1-part head, from $150 to.......................$400.00
Lady Rider, bsk head, from $250 to $550.00
Lady Rider, 1-part head, from $150 to...........................$400.00
Lady Rider, 2-part head, very rare, from $500 to.........$1,800.00
Lion Tamer, 1-part head, from $150 to $700.00
Lion Tamer, 2-part head, early, very rare, from $700 to.$1,800.00
Ringmaster, bsk, from $300 to $800.00
Ringmaster, 1-part head, from $200 to..........................$450.00
Ringmaster, 2-part head, very rare, from $800 to...........$1,800.00

HUMPTY DUMPTY CIRCUS ACCESSORIES

There are many accessories: wagons, tents, ladders, chairs, pedestals, tight ropes, weights, and various other items.

Circus Cage Wagon, 1920, red w/Schoenhut's...Greatest
    Show on Earth stenciled in yel, 10" & 12", from $300
    to...$1,200.00
Menagerie Tent, early, ca 1904, from $1,500 to..........$3,000.00
Menagerie Tent, later, 1914-20, from $1,200 to $2,000.00
Sideshow Panels, 1926, pr, from $2,000 to $5,000.00

Hobo, two-part head, facet toe feet, from
$400.00 to $900.00. (Photo courtesy Keith and Donna Kaonis)

Oval Lithographed Tent, 1926, complete with figures, animals, and accessories, 44" long, from $4,000.00 to $10,000.00.

Lion   Tamer,
bisque   head,
rare,   from
$175.00   to
$850.00. (Photo
courtesy Keith and Donna Kaonis)

Schuco

A German company noted for both mechanical toys as well as the teddy bears and stuffed animals we've listed here, Schuco operated from the 1930s well into the 1950s. Items were either marked Germany or US Zone, Germany.

See also Aeronautical; Battery-Operated; Character, TV, and Movie Collectibles; Diecast; Disney; Windups, Friction, and Other Mechanicals.

Bear, 2½", cream, metal eyes, tan nose & mouth, 1920s, VG $150.00

Bear, 2½", pale gold, metal eyes, paper label, 1950s, NM ...$225.00

Bear, 3½", brn cinnamon ears, orig ribbon, 1950s, NM .$165.00

Bear, 3½", cinnamon, metal eyes, orig ribbon, 1950s, M.$200.00

Bear, 3½", orange, metal eyes, shaved muzzle, 1950s, NM ...$275.00

Bear, 3½", tan, orig red ribbon, 1950s, NM $150.00

Bear, 12", yel, metal eyes, 1920s, VG $350.00

Bigo-Bello Dog, 14", orig clothes, NM $150.00

Black Scottie, 3", Noah's Ark, 1950s, MIB $225.00

Blackbird, 3", Noah's Ark, 1950s, MIB $200.00

Bottle Bear, 3½", pk, NM, minimum value $1,000.00

Dalmatian, 2½", Noah's Ark, rare, M $375.00

Duck Mascot, 3½", bl & wht striped outfit w/red shoes, 1950s, NMIB...$125.00

Elephant, 2½", Noah's Ark, 1950s, NM $125.00

Fox, 2½", Noah's Ark, MIB..$225.00

Janus Bear, 3½", 2 faces (goggly & bear), cinnamon, 1950s, M.$750.00

Janus Bear, 3½", 2 faces (goggly & bear), tan, 1950s, EX .$550.00

Lion, 3½", Noah's Ark, EX..$100.00

Monkey, 2½", cinnamon w/felt hands & feet, NM.........$150.00

Mouse, 6¼", multicolored dress with green shoes, EX, $185.00.

Orangutan, 3", Noah's Ark, 1950s, rare, MIB.................$300.00

Owl, 3", Noah's Arks, 1950s, M..$75.00

Panda Bear, 2½", blk metal bead eyes, 1950s, M $225.00

Perfume Bear, 3½", gold, 1920s, no bottle o/w VG, A ...$145.00

Perfume Bear, 5", bright gold, orig bottle, 1920-30, NM.$650.00

Perfume Bellboy Monkey, 4¾", all orig, EX $650.00

Perfume Monkey, 5", cinnamon, rpl bottle, 1930s, VG..$200.00

Raccoon, 3½", Noah's Ark, 1950s, M $200.00

Squirrel, 2½", Noah's Ark, 1950s, M $150.00

Tiger, 3½", Noah's Ark, EX $125.00

Turtle, 3", Noah's Ark, NM $110.00

Yes/No Bear, 5", blk, glass eyes, 1950s, rare, EX.............$900.00

Yes/No Bear, 5", caramel, glass eyes, 1950s, NM............$450.00

Yes/No Bear, 5, chocolate, glass eyes, yel ribbon, 1950s, rare, NM...$900.00

Yes/No Bear on Wheels, 11½", ginger, steel frame w/CI wheels, 1920s, EX...$375.00

Yes/No Bellboy Monkey, 13½", 1920s, NM $950.00

Yes/No Bulldog, 7", cream & brn, glass eyes, 1930s, NM.$1,200.00

Yes/No Cat, 5", M...$650.00

Yes/No Charlie Dog, cream & rust, 1920-30, rare, NM..$550.00

Yes/No Donkey, 5", felt ears, orig collar & ribbon, 1950s, NM..$475.00

Yes/No Elephant, 5", felt tusks & ears, US Zone cloth tag, 1948, EX...$400.00

Yes/No Fox, 13", tan & cream, faceted jewel eyes, metal glasses fit into head, 1920s, NM................................$1,200.00

Yes/No Monkey, 12½", gray, orig shirt, jacket & handkerchief, 1920s, rare, NM...$750.00

Yes/No Monkey, 18", Tricky Monkey (limited edition replica), glass eyes, NM...$200.00

Yes/No Orangutan, 8", orig FAO Schwarz tag, 1948, rare, NMIB $700.00

Yes/No Panda, 3½", glass eyes, 1950s, NM.................$1,000.00

Yes/No Panda, 5", orig pk bow, 1950s, MIB $900.00

Yes/No Panda, 8", 1940-50, rare, EX $850.00

Yes/No Panda, 13", orig red ribbon, 1948, rare, NM ...$1,200.00

Yes/No Parrot, 11", gr, yel & red, glass eyes, 1926, rare, NM.$650.00

Yes/No Rabbit, 5", NM..$650.00

Yes/No Rooster, 12", felt beak, comb, waddle & tail, glass eyes, cloth clothes, 1950s, NM $350.00

Yes/No Tricky Bear, 8", gold, glass eyes, red plastic medallion, 1950, NM...$950.00

Yes/No Tricky Bear, 13", tan, orig red ribbon & US Zone tag, 1948, M $1,200.00

Yes/No Tricky Elephant, felt ears & tusks, glass eyes, 1940-50, NM..$425.00

Yes/No Tricky Monkey, 10½", orig ribbon, 1948, EX $300.00

Yes/No Tricky Monkey, 14", orig ribbon & tag, NM $450.00

Yes/No Tricky Orangutan, 8", glass eyes, NM $375.00

Yes/No Tricky Orangutan, 14", cinnamon, glass eyes, NM .$950.00

Slot Cars

Slot cars first became popular in the early 1960s. Electric raceways set up in retail storefront windows were commonplace. Huge commercial tracks with eight to ten lanes were located in hobby store and raceways throughout the United States. Large corporations such as Aurora, Revell, Monogram, and Cox, many of which were already manufacturing toys and hobby items, jumped on the bandwagon to produce slot cars and race sets. By the end of the early 1970s, people were loosing interest in slot racing, and its popularity diminished. Today the same baby boomers that raced slot cars in earlier days are revitalizing the sport. The popularity of the Internet has stabilized the pricing of collectible slots. It can confirm prices of common items, while escalating the price of the 'rare' item to new levels. As the Internet grows in popularity, the accessibility of information on slots also grows. This should make the once hard-to-find slot cars more readily available for all to enjoy. Slot cars were generally well used, so finding vintage cars and race sets in like-new or mint condition is difficult. Slot cars replicating the 'muscle' cars from the '60s and '70s are extremely sought after, and clubs and organizations devoted to these collectibles are becoming more and more commonplace. Large toy companies such as Tomy and Tyco still produce some slots today, but not in the quality, quantity or variety of years past.

Aurora produced several types of slots: Screachers (5700 and 5800 number series, valued at $5.00 to $20.00); the AC-powered Vibrators (1500 number series, valued at $20.00 to $150.00); DC-powered Thunderjets (1300 and 1400 number series, valued at $20.00 to $150.00); and the last-made AFX SP1000 (1900 number series, valued at $15.00 to $75.00).

Advisor: Gary Pollastro (P5)

COMPLETE SETS

AMT, Cobra Racing Set, NMIB $185.00
Atlas, Racing Set #1000, HO scale, GIB.................$100.00
Aurora, Home Raceway by Sears #79N9513C, VG $195.00
Aurora, Jackie Stewart Oval 8, VGIB.........................$85.00
Aurora AFX, Jackie Stewart Challenger Raceway, NMIB.$75.00
Aurora AFX, Jackie Stewart Day & Night Enduro, EXIB..$75.00
Aurora AFX, Revamatic Slot Car Set, EXIB $75.00
Aurora AFX, Ultra 5, EXIB...$75.00
Cox, Baja Raceway, Super Scale, NMIB, P5 ....$150.00
Cox, Ontario 8 #3070, w/Eagle & McLaren, GIB............$75.00
Eldon, Challenge Cup Sport & Stock, 1/32 scale, NMIB.$195.00
Eldon, Gold Cup Road Race, 1962, 1/32 scale, EXIB.....$150.00
Eldon, Raceway 24, 1/24 scale, VGIB.........................$195.00
Eldon, Sky High Triple Road Race, w/Ferrari Lotus, Stingray & Porsche, GIB...$75.00

Ideal, Dukes of Hazzard Racing Set, complete, MIB, $85.00.

Gilbert, Miniature Race Set #19041, VGIB.....................$95.00
Ideal, Alcon Highway Torture Track, 1968, MIB.............$50.00
Ideal, Mini-Motorific Set #4939-5, EX $85.00
Marx, Race & Road Cross-Over Trestles, w/Corvette & Thunderbird, NMIB $195.00
Remco, Mighty Mike Action Track, NMIB.....................$75.00
Revell, HiBank Raceway Set #49-9503, w/Cougar GTR & Pontiac Firebird, EXIB...$150.00
Scaletrex, Electric Motor Racing Set, Officially Approved by Jim Clark, made in England, NMIB.......................$400.00
Strombecker, Competition '8' Road Racing Set, VGIB (Sears Allstate)...$125.00
Strombecker, Plymouth Barracuda, 1/32 scale set, MIB .$250.00
Strombecker, Plymouth Barracuda, 1/32 scale set, used, EXIB...$150.00

Strombecker, Thunderbolt Monza, VGIB (Montgomery Ward), $150.00. (Photo courtesy Gary Pollastro)

Strombecker, 4 Lane Mark IV Race Set, VGIB.............$250.00
Tyco, Collector Edition #6994, Petty '92 STP Special #43 & Petty '70 Superbird #43, bl, MIP (twin pack) $48.00
Tyco, International Pro Racing Set #930086, EXIB.......$125.00

SLOT CARS ONLY

Aurora, Ford Baja Bronco, #1909, red, EX.....................$15.00
Aurora, Ford Street Van, #1943, lt bl & brn, NM $15.00
Aurora, Green Hornet's Black Beauty, #1384, unused, NMIB, from $150 to $200.00
Aurora, Javelin, red, wht & bl, NM $30.00
Aurora, Snowmobile, #1485-400, yel w/bl figure, MIB.....$55.00
Aurora AFX, 1929 Model A Woodie, yel & brn, M.........$15.00
Aurora AFX, Autoworld Beamer #5, wht w/bl stripes, NM.$12.00
Aurora AFX, Autoworld McLaren XIR, #1752, bl & wht, EX $14.00
Aurora AFX, Aztec Dragster, #1963, red, EX...................$20.00
Aurora AFX, Blazer, #1917, bl & wht, VG $12.00
Aurora AFX, Camaro Z-28, #1901, red, wht & bl, EX.......$20.00
Aurora AFX, Chevy Chevelle #29, red, wht & bl, EX $30.00
Aurora AFX, Chevy Nomad ('57), orange w/bl pipes, EX..$40.00
Aurora AFX, Datsun Baja Pickup, #1745, bl & blk, EX ...$20.00

Aurora AFX, Dodge Challenger #11, red, wht & bl, EX ..$25.00
Aurora AFX, Dodge Challenger, #1773, lime & bl, NM ..$35.00
Aurora AFX, Dodge Daytona #7, orange, bl & silver, no lights, EX $50.00
Aurora AFX, Dodge Fever Dragster, wht & yel, EX.........$15.00
Aurora AFX, Dodge Rescue Van, red, gold & wht, EX.....$15.00
Aurora AFX, Dodge Street Van, orange & red, MIB........$40.00
Aurora AFX, Dragster, from $15 to $20.00
Aurora AFX, Ferrari 512M, #1763, wht & bl, MIB $25.00
Aurora AFX, Firebird, #1965, blk & gold, EX $15.00
Aurora AFX, Ford Escort #46, blk, red & gr, EX..............$25.00
Aurora AFX, Ford Thunderbird Stock Car, NMIB...........$25.00
Aurora AFX, Javelin #5, bl & blk, EX..............................$20.00
Aurora AFX, Jeep CJ-7 Flamethrower, #1987, orange & red, NM...$18.00
Aurora AFX, Magnatraction, from $15 to $20.00
Aurora AFX, Mario Andretti NGK Indy Car, blk, M.......$35.00
Aurora AFX, Matador GT, red & butterscotch, NM........$25.00
Aurora AFX, Matador Stock Car #5, #1930, orange, blk & red, EX $18.00
Aurora AFX, Matador Taxi, wht, EX $20.00
Aurora AFX, Peace Tank, gr, EX $15.00
Aurora AFX, Peterbilt Lighted Rig, #1156, red & yel, EX.$20.00
Aurora AFX, Plymouth Roadrunner #43, #1762, bl & wht, EX $20.00
Aurora AFX, Plymouth Roadrunner Stock Car, #1762, bl & wht, EX $30.00
Aurora AFX, Pontiac Firebird #9, wht, bl & blk, EX........$25.00
Aurora AFX, Pontiac Firebird, blk & gold, EX $25.00
Aurora AFX, Porsche 510-K, #1786, gold, chrome & orange stripe, EX..$16.00
Aurora AFX, Porsche 917, wht & bl, MIB.......................$40.00
Aurora AFX, Rallye Ford Escort, #1737, gr & bl, EX $15.00
Aurora AFX, Roarin' Rolls Golden Ghost, #1781, yel & bl or wht & blk, EX, ea $18.00
Aurora AFX, Shadow Cam Racer, blk, EX........................$20.00
Aurora AFX, Speed Beamer #11, red, wht & bl, NM.......$15.00
Aurora AFX, Turbo Turn On, #1755, orange, yel & purple, EX $15.00
Aurora AFX, Ultra Shadow #5, #3007, type A, wht, red, orange & yel, M, from $15 to......................................$20.00
Aurora AFX, Vega Van Gasser, #1754, yel & red, EX $15.00

Aurora Cigarbox, Dino Ferrari, red, EX $20.00
Aurora Cigarbox, Ford GT, wht w/bl stripe, NM..............$20.00
Aurora G-Plus, Amrac Cam Am, yel & blk w/wht stripe, EX $15.00
Aurora G-Plus, Capri, wht w/gr & bl stripe, EX...............$15.00
Aurora G-Plus, Corvette, #1954, orange, red & silver, EX .$12.00
Aurora G-Plus, Indy Valvoline, blk, VG...........................$12.00
Aurora G-Plus, Lotus F1, #1783, blk & gold, EX.............$20.00
Aurora G-Plus, NASCAR Camaro, #76, wht, orange & gold, EX $12.00
Aurora G-Plus, Rallye Ford Escort, #1737, gr & bl, EX $15.00
Aurora T-Jet, Hot Rod Coupe, #1554-298, gr, VG $50.00
Aurora T-Jet, Hot Rod Coupe, #1554-298, yel, EX $50.00
Aurora T-Jet, Volkswagen, #1404, wht w/Flower Power, EX.$30.00
Aurora Thunderjet, Alfa Romeo Type 33, #1409, yel, EX.$25.00
Aurora Thunderjet, AMX #5, red, wht & bl, EX..............$25.00
Aurora Thunderjet, Batmobile, EX $150.00
Aurora Thunderjet, Chaparral 2F#7, #1410, lime & bl, EX.$25.00
Aurora Thunderjet, Cheetah, #1403, gr, EX...................$35.00
Aurora Thunderjet, Cobra GT, yel & blk, EX...................$30.00
Aurora Thunderjet, Cobra, #1375, yel w/blk stripe, VG ..$30.00
Aurora Thunderjet, Corvette ('63), #1356, yel, EX..........$50.00
Aurora Thunderjet, Cougar, #1389, wht, EX...................$40.00
Aurora Thunderjet, Dino Ferrari #3, red, wht & gr, EX ...$30.00
Aurora Thunderjet, Dune Buggy Roadster, #1398, bl & blk, EX $35.00
Aurora Thunderjet, Dune Buggy, wht w/red striped roof, EX.$30.00
Aurora Thunderjet, Duster ('73), EX...............................$30.00
Aurora Thunderjet, Ferrari 250, red & wht, EX $50.00
Aurora Thunderjet, Ford 'J,' #1382, wht & bl, VG...........$35.00
Aurora Thunderjet, Ford GT 40, #1374, red w/blk stripe, EX $25.00
Aurora Thunderjet, Ford Lola GT, #1378, dk gr w/wht stripe, VG $30.00
Aurora Thunderjet, Hod Rod Roadster, tan, NM............$35.00
Aurora Thunderjet, Hot Rod Coupe, #1554-298, gr, VGIB.$50.00
Aurora Thunderjet, Hot Rod Coupe, red, VG..................$25.00
Aurora Thunderjet, Int'l Tow Truck, wht w/blk stripe, NM, from $150 to..$200.00
Aurora Thunderjet, Jaguar, red, VG...............................$30.00
Aurora Thunderjet, Lola GT, #1378, turq & wht w/bl stripe, VG..$25.00
Aurora Thunderjet, Mangusta Mongoose, #1400, yel, EX.$45.00
Aurora Thunderjet, McLaren Elva Flamethrower, #1400, yel, EX..$20.00

Aurora AFX, Volkswagen Bug, lime with lime and blue tanks, EX, from $25.00 to $30.00.

Eldon, 1966 Dodge Charger (from set #48), 1/32 scale, red, $30.00.

Aurora Thunderjet, Sand Van Dune Buggy, #1483, pk & wht, EX..$25.00

Aurora Vibrator, Hot Rod Coupe, #1554, bl, VG............$50.00

Aurora Vibrator, Hot Rod Roadster, #1533, bl, yel or gr, EX, ea...$75.00

Aurora Vibrator, Mercedes 300 SL, #1542, wht, EX........$60.00

Aurora Vibrator, Mercedes 300 SL, #1542, yel, EX..........$50.00

Aurora Vibrator, Van Body Trailer, #1586, gray, G...........$35.00

Cox, Javelin, superscale road race car...............................$50.00

Monogram, Cooper Ford w/Tiger 100 Motor, SR-3204-598, red, 1/32 scale, VG..$80.00

Palmer Toys, Sting Ray Corvette, MOC..........................$95.00

Revell, Model Race, Carroll Shelby's Cobra Ford, #R3100-600, w/SP 500 motor, 1/32 scale, G+ $80.00

Screecher, Cuda Funny Car, wht, red & orange, EX.........$20.00

Strombecker, Jaguar SKE, #9220-595, red, MIB $50.00

Strombecker, Pontiac Bonneville, EX $40.00

TCR, Jam Car, yel & blk, EX $15.00

TCR, Mack Truck, EX $15.00

TCR, Maintenance Van, red & wht, EX..........................$15.00

TCR, Mercury Stock Car, purple & chrome, VG $15.00

Tomy, Camaro GT #88 Auto Tech, M, from $10 to $20.00

Tomy, Thunderbird #11 (Bill Elliot sgn), red & wht, EX..$25.00

Tyco, A-Team Van, blk & red, EX..................................$20.00

Tyco, Bandit Pickup, blk & red, EX $12.00

Tyco, Blackbird Firebird, #6914, blk & gold, EX $12.00

Tyco, Camaro Funny Car, silver, gr & blk, EX $40.00

Tyco, Caterpillar #96, blk & yel, EX $20.00

Tyco, Chaparral 2G #66, #8504, VG.............................$14.00

Tyco, Chevy ('57), red & orange w/yel stripes, EX $20.00

Tyco, Chevy Pro Stock ('57), red, orange & yel w/gray bumper, EX..$20.00

Tyco, Corvette, glow-in-the dark, any color, EX, ea $10.00

Tyco, Corvette ('79), silver, bl & orange, EX..................$30.00

Tyco, Corvette ('97), yel, EX..$15.00

Tyco, Corvette #12, wht & red w/bl stripes, EX...............$12.00

Tyco, Corvette Challenge ('83) #33, silver & yel, EX $25.00

Tyco, Corvette Curvehanger, chrome w/flames, EX $15.00

Tyco, Firebird, #6914, cream & red, VG $12.00

Tyco, Firebird Turbo #12, blk & gold, EX $10.00

Tyco, Ford Coupe (1940), #8534, blk w/flames, NM $20.00

Tyco, Funny Mustang, orange w/yel flames, EX...............$25.00

Tyco, GM Aerocoupe #43, bl & fluorescent red, EX $65.00

Tyco, Highway Patrol #56, blk & wht, w/sound, EX.........$16.00

Tyco, Lamborghini, red, VG...$12.00

Tyco, Lamborghini, silver, EX......................................$20.00

Tyco, Lighted Porsche #2, silver w/red nose, EX $20.00

Tyco, Lighted Super American, #8525, red, wht & bl, EX..$20.00

Tyco, Lola 260, #8514, red, wht & bl, EX $14.00

Tyco, Military Police #45, wht & bl, EX $30.00

Tyco, Mustang #1, orange w/yel flames, EX $20.00

Tyco, Oldsmobile #88, yel & bl, EX $25.00

Tyco, Pinto Funny Car Goodyear, red & yel, EX $20.00

Tyco, Porsche Carrea, #8527, yel & blk, EX $25.00

Tyco, Porsche 908, red, wht & bl, EX.............................$20.00

Tyco, Pro #8833, Superbird, candy apple red, VG $45.00

Tyco, Silverstreak Pickup, silver w/pk & orange stripes, EX $15.00

Tyco, Skoal Bandit #33, EX, $40.00.

Tyco, Silverstreak Racing Vette, #8556, silver & pk w/orange stripe, VG..$15.00

Tyco, Thunderbird #15, red & yel, VG $10.00

Tyco, Turbo Firebird, blk & gold, NM...........................$12.00

Tyco, Turbo Hopper #27, red, EX $12.00

Tyco, Valvoline Thunderbird #6, bl & wht, EX $20.00

Tyco, Volvo 850 #3, wht & bl, EX $20.00

Tyco, VW Bug, gold & red, EX......................................$40.00

ACCESSORIES

AMT Service Parts Kit #2000, VG, from $50 to $65.00

Aurora AFX Carrying Case, blk, 2-level, EX $15.00

Aurora AFX Catalog, 1971, color, VG............................$20.00

Aurora AFX Pit Kit, G $15.00

Aurora AFX Speed Steer Breakout Wall #6056, MIB $18.00

Aurora AFX Speed Steer Intersection Overpass #6055, MIB..$20.00

Aurora AFX 45 OHM Hand Controller w/Brakes, EXIB .$15.00

Aurora Layout and Service Manual for Model Motoring in HO Scale, 1961, VG, $10.00. (Photo courtesy Gary Pollastro)

Aurora Model Motoring, 1969, color, EX $30.00
Aurora Model Motoring Auto Starter #1507, EXIB $15.00
Aurora Model Motoring Hill Track, 9", EX $10.00
Aurora Model Motoring Loop the Loop Track Set #1504,
    EXIB..$20.00
Aurora Model Motoring Steering Wheel Controller, EX .$10.00
Aurora Model Motoring Y Turn-Off Track w/Switch, EX .$20.00
Aurora Model Motoring 4-Way Stop Track, 9", EX..........$15.00
Aurora Modeling Motoring Banked Curve #1467, EXIB .$20.00
Aurora Speedline Finish Set, 1968, MOC $25.00
Aurora Speedline Slingslot Starter, 1968, MOC $25.00
Aurora Thunderjet Carrying Case, butterscotch, VG $15.00
Aurora Thunderjet Country Bridge Roadway, EXIB.........$20.00
Aurora Thunderjet Speed Control Steering Wheel Stile,
    EX $20.00
Aurora Thunderjet Transformer, VG $20.00
Books, 'Here Is Your Hobby Slot Car Racing' & 'Complete Book
    of Model Raceways & Roadways,' VG, ea...................$50.00
Eldon Curve Track, MOC $10.00
Eldon Power Track, MOC $10.00
Gilbert Automatic Lap Counter, #19339, MIB................$35.00
Gilbert Autorama Fly Over Chicane Kit #19342, MIB $40.00
Gilbert Autorama Grand Stand #19340, MIB $25.00
Gilbert Autorama Lap Counter #19339, MIB..................$40.00
Monogram Lane Change Track, MIB...............................$20.00
Monogram Tapered Chicane Track, MIB..........................$20.00
Strombecker Grandstand #9399, EX $25.00
Strombecker Scale Lap Counter, 1/32 scale, MIB............$25.00
Thunderjet Hop Up Kit, from $15 to $20.00
Tyco Stick Shift 4-Speed Controller, EX........................$10.00
Tyco Trigger Controller, orange, EX $8.00

Smith-Miller

    Smith-Miller (Los Angeles, California) made toy trucks from 1944 until 1955. During that time they used four basic cab designs, and most of their trucks sold for about $15.00 each. Over the past several years, these toys have become very popular, especially the Mack trucks which today sell at premium prices. The company made a few other types of toys as well, such as the train toy box and the 'Long, Long Trailer.'

    See also Advertising.

Army Materials Truck, L Mack, complete, 20", VG, A, $575.00. (Photo courtesy Richard Opfer Auctioneering, Inc.)

Army Personnel Carrier, L Mack, 19", VG.....................$350.00
Bank of America Armored Truck, GMC, 14", EX+, A ..$625.00
Bank of America Armored Truck, GMC, 14", VG, A..$425.00
Bekins Van Lines Semi, L Mack, 28", rstr, A $800.00
Blue Diamond Dump Truck, L Mack, orange, 19", rstr, VG, A.$525.00
Blue Diamond Dump Truck, L Mack, wht, 19", NM, A.$825.00
Blue Diamond Dump Truck, L Mack, wht, 19", VG+, A .$600.00
Dump Truck, GMC, crank action, 12", G, A..................$150.00
Dump Truck, GMC, crank action, 12", VG+, A $375.00
Dump Truck, Mack, hydraulic, mk MIC, orange, 17", G, A .$275.00
Emergency Towing Service, GMC, 13", NM, A..............$325.00
Fire Aerial Ladder Truck, Mack, mk LAFD, 26", MIB .$1,500.00

Fire Aerial Ladder Truck, Mack, 37", MIB, $1,500.00. (Photo courtesy Randy Inman Auctions)

Fire Aerial Ladder Truck, Mack, mk SMFD, 37", VG+, A .$600.00
Goodrich Silvertown Tires Wrecker, 12", EX, A $650.00
Hi-Way Freighter, GMC, 24", G, A................................$220.00
Hollywood Film-Ad Searchlight Trailer, 4-wheeled, battery-op,
    14", NM, A $300.00
Hollywood Film-Ad Truck & Searchlight Trailer, GMC, 27",
    NM, A $725.00

International Paper Company Semi, red and white, 1940s, 28", restored, A, $700.00. (Photo courtesy Randy Inman Auctions)

Kraft Delivery Truck, 14", G, A $450.00
Lift-O-Matic Stake Truck, Mack, mk MIC, 18", G+, A.$475.00
Lift-O-Matic Stake Truck, Mack, mk MIC, 18", rstr, EX, A .$850.00
Lumber Truck, Mack, single rear axle, w/lumber, 20", VG+,
    A $450.00
Lumber Truck & Trailer, Mack, dbl rear axle, w/lumber, 37"
    overall, VG, A $550.00
Lumber Truck & Trailer, Mack, single rear axle, no lumber, 37"
    overall, G $350.00
Lumber Truck & Trailer, Mack, single rear axle, w/lumber, 37"
    overall, VG+, A..$650.00

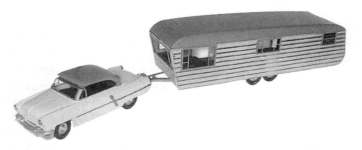

Lincoln Two-Door Hard Top Pulling House Trailer, blue and white, 38", restored, A, $1,150.00. (Photo courtesy Randy Inman Auctions)

Lyon Van Lines Truck, GMC, 22", G, A $500.00
Machinery Hauler, GMC, 26", VG, A $325.00
Materials Truck, GMC, complete, 14", G, A $275.00
Mobilgas Semi Tanker, GMC, red, 22", EX, A $300.00
Mobilgas/Mobiloil Tandem Tanker, Mack, red, 37", VG,
     A $975.00
Mobiloil Tanker, GMC, red, 22", G, A $250.00

Mobiloil Tanker, Mack, red, 1950s, 19", EX, A, $600.00.

(Photo courtesy Collectors Auction Services)

Official Tow Car, Mack, mk MIC, wht, 6", G, A............$650.00
PIE Semi, GMC, 25", G, A $300.00

PIE Semi, Mack, 27", EX, A, $500.00. (Photo courtesy Bertoia Auctions)

PIE Semi, Mack, 27", G, A...$325.00
Red Diamond Dump Truck, Mack, 19", very rare, EX, A .$1,450.00
Searchlight Truck No 1, w/4 battery-op lights on railed bed, 19",
     EX+, A..$880.00
Semi, Mack, mk MIC, red w/silver van trailer, 27", VG, A..$400.00
Silver Streak Semi, GMC, 24", G, A $325.00
Teamsters Union Service Semi, mk MIC, 28", EX, A $650.00
Texaco Tanker, B Mack, #3006, 40", EX, A....................$750.00
Trans-Continental Freighter, GMC, 24", VG, A...........$350.00
Triton Oil Truck, GMC, 14", VG, A $325.00

West Coast Fast Freight, L Mack, 1940s, 20", restored, $775.00. (Photo courtesy Randy Inman Auctions)

Soldiers and Accessories

'Dimestore' soldiers were made from the 1920s until sometime in the 1960s. Some of the better-known companies who made these small-scale figures and vehicles were Barclay, Manoil, and American Metal Toys, formerly known as Jones (hollow cast lead); Grey Iron (cast iron); and Auburn Rubber. They are 3" to 3½" high and were sold in Woolworth's Kresge's, and other 5 & 10 stores for a nickel or a dime, hence the name 'Dimestore.' Marx made tin soldiers for use in target gun games; these sell for about $8.00 to $20.00. Condition is most important as these soldiers saw a lot of action. They are most often found with much of the paint worn off and with some serious 'battle wounds' such as missing arms or rifle tips. Nearly two thousand different figures were made by the major manufacturers, plus a number of others by minor makers such as Tommy Toy and All-Nu.

Another very popular line of toy soldiers has been made by Britains of England since 1893. They are smaller and usually more detailed than 'Dimestores,' and variants number in the thousands. Serious collectors should refer to *Collecting American Made Toy Soldiers* for 'Dimestore' soldiers, and *Collecting Foreign-Made Toy Soldiers* for Britains and others not made in America. Both books are by Richard O'Brien (1997).

You'll notice that in addition to the soldiers, many of our descriptions and values are for the vehicles, cannons, animals, and cowboys and Indians made and sold by the same manufacturers. Note: Percentages in the description lines refer to the amount of original paint remaining, a most important evaluation factor.

Advisors: Sally and Stan Alekna (A1) 'Dimestore'
See also Dinky; Plastic Figures.

Alymer, Alard Monch Von Basel Set #BF-47, M (M box),
     A $45.00
Alymer, American Revolution British Grenadiers Set #AB-75,
     6-pc, EX (EX box), A $70.00
Alymer, American Revolution Pennsylvania Battalion Set #AB-
     74, 6-pc, EX (EX box), A $70.00

Alymer, Colonel Knox's Artillery Regime Set #AB-78, 5-pc, M (M box), A..$80.00

Alymer, English Bowmen Set #BF-50, 2-pc, EX (EX box), A .$60.00

Alymer, Enrique Bastard of Castile Set #BF-63, M (M box), A $60.00

Alymer, Gaelics Set #AB-86, 6-pc, M (M box), A...........$80.00

Alymer, Hall's Delewargt Set #AB-88, 6-pc, M (M box), A .$80.00

Alymer, Jean de Clermont Set #BF-61, EX (EX box), A ..$60.00

Alymer, King Jean's Spearmen Set #BF-56, 2-pc, M (M box), A $60.00

Alymer, King of Bohemia Set #BF-46, M (M box), A $45.00

Alymer, Lancers Zulu War Set #AB-1-R, 3-pc, EX (EX box), A $60.00

Alymer, Lancers Zulu War Set #AB-2-R, 3-pc, EX (EX box), A $70.00

Alymer, Ludwig Von Concibras Set #BF-57, M (box), A .$45.00

Alymer, Montacute Archers Set #BF-60, 2-pc, M (M box), A.$60.00

Alymer, Rainar Von Ouhar Set #55, M (M box), A $45.00

Alymer, Royal Regiment OS Artillery Set #AB-79, 5-pc, EX (EX box), A $80.00

Alymer, Samurai Warriors Set #AB-91, 2-pc, EX (EX box), A..$35.00

Alymer, Sir Eustace D'Abrichecourt (Banners Forward) Set #BF-58, EX (EX box), A, $60.00.

Alymer, Sir John of Hainault (Banners Forward) Set #BF-53, M (M box), A...$45.00

Alymer, Sir Walter Woodland Set #BF-62, EX (M box), A.$60.00

Alymer, Wermacht WWII Set #AB-80, 6-pc, EX (EX box), A..$90.00

American Metal Toys, calf, 99%, A1 ....$19.00

American Metal Toys, camel, M, A1 ....$20.00

American Metal Toys, cow lying, gray & wht, 99%, A1 ..$19.00

American Metal Toys, cow standing, brn, M $20.00

American Metal Toys, dog, brn, sm, scarce, 95%, A1......$23.00

American Metal Toys, donkey, 99%, A1...........................$19.00

American Metal Toys, farmer, 99%, A1 ....$20.00

American Metal Toys, farmer's wife, 96%, A1 ....$17.00

American Metal Toys, horse, blk, sm 99%, A1 ....$18.00

American Metal Toys, horse, wht & blk, sm, 99%, A1 ....$19.00

American Metal Toys, machine gunner on stump, khaki, scarce, 97%, A1 ....$115.00

American Metal Toys, machine gunner prone, khaki, scarce, 98%, A1..$100.00

American Metal Toys, officer in greatcoat w/pistol, khaki, very scarce, 98%, A1 ....$325.00

American Metal Toys, soldier, AA gunner, khaki, scarce, 98%, A1 ....$115.00

American Metal Toys, soldier AA gun, silver, scarce, NM, A1 .$95.00

American Metal Toys, soldier kneeling w/searchlight, khaki, scarce, 99%, A $133.00

American Metal Toys, soldier standing firing, khaki, scarce, 97%, A $156.00

American Metal Toys, soldier wounded, prone, khaki, scarce, 97%, A1 ....$125.00

Auburn Rubber, baseball base runner, wht w/bl trim, scarce, 99%, A1 ....$61.00

Auburn Rubber, baseball batter, gray w/red trim, scarce, 99%, A1 ....$70.00

Auburn Rubber, baseball catcher, scarce, NM, A1 ....$70.00

Auburn Rubber, baseball fielder/baseman, 99%, A1........$62.00

Auburn Rubber, baseball pitcher, scarce, NM, A1...........$70.00

Auburn Rubber, calf, lg, early, 98%, A1 ....$12.00

Auburn Rubber, calf, sm, later version, 98%, A1............$12.00

Auburn Rubber, collie, lg, 95%, A1 ....$18.00

Auburn Rubber, collie, sm, 98%, A1................................$14.00

Auburn Rubber, cow looking to right, 97%, A1 ....$12.00

Auburn Rubber, farmer's wife (milkmaid), 99%, A1 ....$29.00

Auburn Rubber, football backfieldman, scarce, 98%, A1 .$60.00

Auburn Rubber, football lineman, scarce, 97%, A1 ....$59.00

Auburn Rubber, guard officer, yel w/red trim, scarce, 99%, A1.$40.00

Auburn Rubber, infantry private, yel, scarce, 98%, A1 ....$22.00

Auburn Rubber, marine marching, port arms, bl, 2nd version, scarce, 97%, A1 ....$16.00

Auburn Rubber, observer w/binoculars, 97%, A1 ....$25.00

Auburn Rubber, officer on horse, scarce, 98%, A1 ....$51.00

Auburn Rubber, signalman, khaki, very scarce, flag tip broken, 95%, A1 ....$45.00

Auburn Rubber, soldier bomb thrower, khaki, scarce, 97%, A1.$57.00

Auburn Rubber, soldier bugler, khaki, 95%, A1 ....$20.00

Auburn Rubber, soldier charging w/tommy gun, 2nd version, khaki, 97%, A1 ....$26.00

Auburn Rubber, soldier marching port arms, khaki, early, NM, A1 ....$21.00

Auburn Rubber, soldier standing by searchlight, 97%, A1 .$46.00

Auburn Rubber, soldier wounded, prone, 96%, A1 ....$46.00

Auburn Rubber, US Officer, bl, scarce, 97%, A1..............$31.00

Auburn Rubber, White Guard officer, yel w/red trim, 92-94%, A1 ....$18.00

Barclay, aviator, 95%, A1 ....$28.00

Barclay, boy skater, M, A1 ....$20.00

Barclay, bride, 98%, A1 ....$27.00

Barclay, cavalryman, 1930s, 2¼", 95%............................$33.00

Barclay, couple on bench in winter garb, 99%, A1 ....$43.00

Barclay, couple on horse-drawn sleigh w/metal harness & (red tape) blanket, 98%, A1 ....$102.00

Barclay, cow grazing, 98%, A1..$17.00

Barclay, cowboy in mask w/pistol on horse, 99%, A1 ....$52.00

Barclay, cowboy w/lasso (no lasso), brn, 98%, A1............$24.00

Barclay, cowboy w/lasso (no lasso), gray, 95%, A1...........$21.00

Barclay, cowboy w/neckerchief over face & lasso, wht w/blk trim, scarce, 93-95%, A1 ....$23.00

Barclay, American Legionnaire (made for the 1937 Legion convention), NM, $975.00. (Photo courtesy Bertoia Auctions)

Barclay, Indian w/rifle, midi podfoot, scarce, 99%, A1 .....$82.00
Barclay, Indian w/spear & knife, 97%, A1 ....$19.00

Barclay, Italian soldier with rifle in stride, NM, $345.00. (Photo courtesy Bertoia Auctions)

Barclay, cowboy w/pistol on horse, 1930s, scarce, 96%.....$61.00
Barclay, cowboy w/rifle, 99%, A1 ....$22.00
Barclay, cowboy w/2 pistols, gr & red, 96%, A1 ....$24.00
Barclay, detective, bl suit, very scarce, 97%, A1 ....$178.00
Barclay, doctor, wht, 80-85%, A1..$14.00
Barclay, fireman w/axe, 98%, A1...$42.00
Barclay, fireman w/hose, 98%, A1.......................................$37.00
Barclay, flamethrower, gr, 98%, A1....................................$23.00
Barclay, girl figure skater, M, A1..$23.00
Barclay, girl in rocker, bl, 95%, A1.....................................$20.00
Barclay, girl in rocker, red, 99%, A1....................................$24.00
Barclay, girl on skis, NM, A1...$29.00
Barclay, girl on sled, NM, A1 ....$28.00
Barclay, girl skater, 98%, A1..$18.00
Barclay, groom, 98%, A1 ....$27.00
Barclay, HO conductor, 97%, A1 ....$9.00
Barclay, HO engineer, 99%, A1..$11.00
Barclay, HO groom, scarce, NM, A1 ....$26.00
Barclay, HO hobo, 99%, A1...$11.00
Barclay, HO lady w/baby, scarce, 97%, A1 ....$97.00
Barclay, HO man, 99%, A1 ....$11.00
Barclay, HO newsboy, 99%, A1...$11.00
Barclay, HO oiler, M, A1..$12.00
Barclay, HO peg-legged gateman, very scarce, 99%, A1...$24.00
Barclay, HO policeman, NM, A1..$12.00
Barclay, HO porter, 99%, A1..$11.00
Barclay, HO redcap, 99%, A1...$11.00
Barclay, HO woman in red, no dog, 99%, A1 ....$11.00
Barclay, Indian chief w/tomahawk & shield, 99%, A1 .....$25.00
Barclay, Indian on horse w/rifle, 1930s, 95%, A1 ....$48.00
Barclay, Indian w/bow & arrow, M, A1 ....$22.00
Barclay, Indian w/bow & arrow, sm, scarce, 95%, A1 ......$27.00
Barclay, Indian w/bow & arrow kneeling, 99%, A1 ....$25.00
Barclay, Indian w/hatchet & shield, 99%, A1 ....$18.00

Barclay, jockey on gold horse, #4, NM, A1 ....$37.00
Barclay, knight w/pennant, 99%, A1.................................$27.00
Barclay, knight w/shield, blk w/red & bl shield, 97%, A1.$40.00
Barclay, knight w/sword across chest, 98%, A1 ....$40.00
Barclay, knight w/sword across waist, bl & red shield, 97%,
    A1 ....$38.00
Barclay, knight w/sword over right shoulder, orange & blk shield,
    99%, A1 ....$42.00
Barclay, mailman, NM, A1..$22.00
Barclay, man on skis, 99%, A1 ....$28.00
Barclay, man on sled, 99%, A1 ....$27.00
Barclay, man pulling kids on sled, metallic yel, scarce, NM,
    A1 ....$65.00
Barclay, man speed skater, gr, 99%, A1 ....$21.00
Barclay, marine, long stride, bl uniform & cap, NM, A1 ..$40.00
Barclay, minister holding hat, 98%, A1 ....$27.00
Barclay, minister walking, scarce, 97%, A1......................$80.00
Barclay, naval officer, long stride, wht, 96%, A1 ....$29.00
Barclay, newsboy, M, A1...$22.00
Barclay, nurse, blk hair, scarce, 96%, A1 ....$41.00
Barclay, nurse w/hand on hip, 85%, A1 ....$15.00
Barclay, officer, khaki, 98%, A1 ....$19.00
Barclay, officer w/binoculars, midi podfoot, gr, very scarce, M,
    A1 ....$135.00
Barclay, officer w/sword, gr pot helmet, 99%, A1 ....$32.00
Barclay, officer w/sword, long stride, tin helmet, 90-92%,
    A1 ....$24.00
Barclay, officer w/sword, short stride, tin helmet, 95%, A1..$31.00
Barclay, pirate, bl, scarce, 93-95%, A1 ....$32.00
Barclay, pirate, red, scarce, 93-95%, A1 ....$32.00
Barclay, policeman, 99%, A1...$24.00

Barclay, sailor, wht, 99%, A1 ....$27.00
Barclay, sailor marching, long stride, bl, 97%, A1 ....$29.00
Barclay, Santa on sled, 98%, A1.................................$52.00
Barclay, sentry in overcoat, 95%, A1 ....$29.00
Barclay, signalman w/flags, 97%, A1 ....$38.00
Barclay, soldier AA gunner, cast helmet, plow base, 97%,
    A1 ....$32.00
Barclay, soldier AA gunner, cast helmet, 99%, A1 ....$34.00
Barclay, soldier AA gunner, gr pot helmet, 93%, A1........$28.00
Barclay, soldier AA gunner, khaki, 99%, A1 ....$23.00
Barclay, soldier advancing w/raised rifle, tin helmet, 99%, A1 .$34.00
Barclay, soldier at attention, 98%, A1.........................$27.00
Barclay, soldier at order arms, gr pot helmet, 98%, A1 .....$29.00
Barclay, soldier at port arms, tin helmet, 99%, A1............$30.00
Barclay, soldier bomb thrower, rifle off ground, gr cast helmet,
    96%, A1 ....$44.00
Barclay, soldier bomb thrower, tin helmet, 99%, A1 ....$30.00
Barclay, soldier bugler, long stride, tin helmet, 98%, A1 ..$30.00
Barclay, soldier bugler, short stride, tin helmet, NM, A1..$28.00
Barclay, soldier charging, khaki, 99%, A1.....................$19.00
Barclay, soldier charging, pod foot, gr, M, A1 ....$24.00
Barclay, soldier charging, short stride, tin helmet, 97%, A1.$31.00
Barclay, soldier charging w/gas mask & rifle, 99%, A1 .....$33.00
Barclay, soldier charging w/machine gun, tin helmet, 98%,
    A1 ....$26.00
Barclay, soldier crawling w/rifle, tin helmet, 92-94%, A1.$25.00
Barclay, soldier crawling w/rifle, 95%, A1 ....$27.00
Barclay, soldier dispatcher w/dog, scarce, 97%, A1 ....$95.00

Barclay, soldier driving motorcycle with soldier in side-car ready to shoot machine gun, NM, A, $165.00. (Photo courtesy Bertoia Auctions)

Barclay, soldier drummer, tin helmet, 98%, A1 ....$31.00
Barclay, soldier flagbearer, long stride, cast helmet, 98%, A1 .$32.00
Barclay, soldier flagbearer, short stride, tin helmet, 98%, A1..$38.00
Barclay, soldier flamethrower, midi pod foot, gr, very scarce,
    99%, A1...$129.00
Barclay, soldier kneeling at anti-tank gun, 96%, A1........$32.00
Barclay, soldier kneeling firing rifle, pod foot, gr, scarce, 99%,
    A1 ....$28.00

Barclay, soldier machine gunner, prone, tin helmet, 98%,
    A1 ....$30.00
Barclay, soldier machine gunner charging, cast helmet, 94%,
    A1 ....$42.00
Barclay, soldier machine gunner kneeling, 98%, A1.........$25.00
Barclay, soldier machine gunner prone, pod foot, khaki, 97%,
    A1 ....$20.00
Barclay, soldier marching, pod foot, khaki, 99%, A1........$21.00
Barclay, soldier marching at shoulder arms, short stride, tin hel-
    met, M, A1...$29.00
Barclay, soldier marching w/pack, cast helmet, scarce, 98%,
    A1 ....$43.00
Barclay, soldier marching w/slung rifle, cast helmet, 98%,
    A1...$42.00
Barclay, soldier marching w/slung rifle, gr pot helmet, 97%,
    A1 ....$27.00
Barclay, soldier on parade, long stride, 99%, A1 ....$25.00

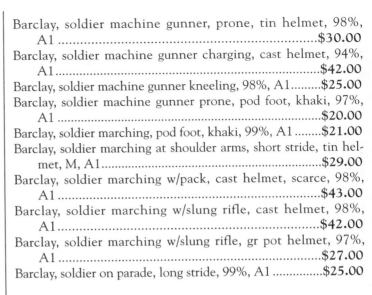

Barclay, soldier, pigeon dispatcher, tin helmet, 98%, A1, $38.00. (Photo courtesy Bertoia Auctions)

Barclay, soldier prone w/binoculars, 97%, A1 ....$50.00
Barclay, soldier running looking up, pod foot, gr, 97%, A1 ..$19.00
Barclay, soldier running looking up, pod foot, khaki, 99%,
    A1...$20.00
Barclay, soldier running w/rifle, tin helmet, 95%, A1.......$32.00
Barclay, soldier shell loader, 94%, A1.............................$21.00

Barclay, soldier telephone operator, 98%, A1, $30.00. (Photo courtesy Bertoia Auctions)

Barclay, soldier sniper kneeling, short stride, tin helmet, 98%, A...$25.00

Barclay, soldier standing at searchlight, high seat, no rivets in front of left foot, 96%, A1 ....$64.00

Barclay, soldier stretcher bearer, closed hand, 95%, A1....$28.00

Barclay, soldier throwing grenade, rifle on ground, tin helmet, 94%, A1 ....$26.00

Barclay, soldier w/range finder, 95%, A1 ....$29.00

Barclay, soldier wireless operator w/separate antenna, 98%, A1 ....$58.00

Barclay, soldier wounded (head & arm), pod foot, khaki, scarce, 90-92%, A1..$36.00

Barclay, soldiers (2) at AA gun, pod foot, 98%, A1.........$42.00

Barclay, soldiers (2) in boat, scarce, NM, A1 ....$99.00

Barclay, surgeon w/soldier, 98%, A1..............................$120.00

Barclay, train conductor, NM, A1 ....$21.00

Barclay, train engineer, 86%, A1 ....$19.00

Barclay, train passenger (boy), 99%, A1...........................$17.00

Barclay, train passenger (elderly man w/cane), 98%, A1 ..$18.00

Barclay, train passenger (elderly woman), pk outfit, 99%, A1.$21.00

Barclay, train passenger (girl), NM, A1 ....$21.00

Barclay, train passenger (man w/overcoat), 98%, A1 ....$21.00

Barclay, train passenger (minister walking), scarce, 99%, A1.$82.00

Barclay, train passenger (woman in bl w/dog), 98%, A1...$21.00

Barclay, train porter w/whisk broom, 99%, A1 ....$27.00

Barclay, train redcap w/bags, 98%, A1 ....$30.00

Barclay, typist, w/table & typewriter, scarce, 93%, A1......$99.00

Britains, Arabs of the Desert Set #193, 1938, 1st version, EX (EX box), A, $1,750.00. (Photo courtesy Bertoia Auctions)

Barclay, tubist, wht helmet, scarce, 93%, A1 ....$69.00

Barclay, West Point cadet officer, short stride, 99%, A1...$30.00

Britains, African Zulu Warriors Set #147, 8-pc, 1935, 3rd version, NM (NM box), A...$550.00

Britains, African Zulu Warriors Set #9190, 7-pc, 1962, M (M box), A...$175.00

Britains, Aircraft Series (Aeroplane, Pilot & Hangar) Set #433, complete, 1937, 2nd version, NM (NM box), A .$3,025.00

Britains, Aircraft Series (Monoplane & Hangar) Set #433, complete, EX (NM box), A...................................$2,100.00

Britains, Aircraft Series (RAF Biplane & Hangar) Set #1521, complete, 1938, 1st version, EX+ (EX+ box), A..$3,300.00

Britains, Aircraft Series (US Biplane & Hangar) Set #1525, complete, 1938, 1st version, NM (NM box), A ...$3,300.00

Britains, Ambulance With Medics Set #1897, 18-pc, 1955, M (EX box), A..$1,325.00

Britains, Anti-Aircraft Gun Set #1522, 1-pc, 1939, 1st version, EX (EX box), A $450.00

Britains, Anti-Aircraft Units Spotting Chair Set #1731, 2-pc, 1950s, EX (G box), A..$25.00

Britains, Arab Display With Trees Set #224, 11-pc, 1950s, MIB (unopened) $465.00

Britains, Arabs on Foot Set #187, 8-pc, 1930s, G, A......$115.00

Britains, Arabs on Horseback & Foot Set #223, 13-pc, 1932, 2nd version, NM (EX+ box), A $500.00

Britains, Arabs on Horseback Set #164, 5-pc, 1950s, G, A ...$100.00

Britains, Arabs on Horseback Set #2046, 12-pc, 1955, G, A..$300.00

Britains, Argentine Cavalry Set #127, 4-pc, 1955, G, A ...$175.00

Britains, Argentine Cavalry Set #217, 4-pc, 1955, M (NM box), A $350.00

Britains, Argentine Infantry (Infanteria Argentina) Set #216, 8-pc, movable arms, 1935, 1st version, NM (EX box), A $500.00

Britains, Armoured Car Set #1321, 1-pc, 1938, 1st version, NM (EX+ box), A...$550.00

Britains, Army Ambulance Set #1512, 3-pc, 1959, M (NM box), A $500.00

Britains, Army Ambulance Set #1512, 4-pc, 1937, 1st version, EX+ (VG box), A...$775.00

Britains, Army Band (Yellow) Set #2110, 25-pc, G, A .$1,500.00

Britains, Army Lorry Set #1335, 2-pc, 1950s, M (NM box), A..$300.00

Britains, Army Service Corps (Horse-Drawn Wagon) Set #1460, 5-pc, 1937, 2nd version, EX-M (NM box), A $415.00

Britains, Army Staff Car With Two Officers Set #1413, 1938, 1st version, NM (EX+ box), A $600.00

Britains, Army Staff Car With Two Officers Set #1448, 1937, 1st version, NM (VG box), A.....................................$650.00

Britains, Australian Infantry (Colonial Army) Set #1544, 8-pc, 1941, 1st version, M (NM box), A $330.00

Britains, Australian Infantry (Colonial Army) Set #1545, 8-pc, 1937, 1st version, NM-M (EX box), A.................$2,100.00

Britains, Austrian Infantry Battledress Set #2031, 8-pc, 1959, G, A $60.00

Britains, Austro-Hungarian Army Lancers Set #175, 4-pc, M (NM box), A...$1,050.00

Britains, Bahamas Police Band Limited Edition Set #5187, 11-pc, 1987, M (M box & orig mailer), A $150.00

Britains, Bahamas Police Band Set #2/228 (2184), 26-pc, 1961, M (NM box), A $5,225.00

Britains, Band of the First Life Guards (Khaki) Set #101, 1934, 4th version, NM (NM box), A $650.00

Britains, Band of the Line Set #27, 12-pc, 1900, 1st version, Fair-G, A...$265.00

Britains, Band of the Line Set #27, 12-pc, 1900, 1st version, G-EX (VG box), A $875.00

Britains, Band of the..., see also specific listings such as Air Force Band Set #2166, etc.

Britains, Beetle Lorry, see British Beetle Lorry

Britains, Belgian Army 'Le Regiment des Grenadiers' Set #2009, 8-pc, 1957, EX (EX box), A $100.00

Britains, Belgian Infantry Marching Set #1389, 8-pc, 1936, 1st version, NM, A...$330.00

Britains, Belgian Infantry Set #189, 8-pc, 1935, 1st version, G, A $80.00

Britains, Belgian Infantry Set #189, 8-pc, 1935, 1st version, M (EX box), A $650.00

Britains, Bengal Cavalry (1st) Set #47, 5-pc, 1896, 1st version, G-EX (EX box), A $715.00

Britains, Bengal Infantry (7th) Set #1342, 8-pc, 1935, 1st version, NM $450.00

Britains, Bengal Lancers (10th) Set #63, 10-pc, 1916, EX-M (EX box), A $1,000.00

Britains, Bodyguard of the Emperor of Abyssinia Set #1424, 8-pc, 1936, 1st version, NM (EX box), A $650.00

Britains, Bodyguard of the Emperor of Ethiopia Set #1424, 8-pc, G (G box), A...$250.00

Britains, Boer Cavalry Set #6, 5-pc, 1901, 1st version (extremely rare), EX (VG box), A $4,125.00

Britains, Boer Infantry Set #26, 8-pc, 1900, 1st version, EX-M (VG box), A $3,025.00

Britains, Bombay Grenadiers Set #68, 8-pc, 1930s, NM (EX+ box), A $775.00

Britains, Bombay Native Infantry (2nd) Set #68, 8-pc, 1896, 1st version, G-EX (EX box), A $825.00

Britains, Bombay Native Infantry (2nd) Set #68, 8-pc, 1930s, NM (on inner box card), A..$500.00

Britains, British Army Presentation Set #131, 275-pc, 1908, 1st version, extremely rare, Fair-G (G box), A........$35,200.00

Britains, British Army Set #21, 30-pc, 1895, 1st version, EX (VG box), A..$4,125.00

Britains, British Army Set #73, 67-pc, 1935, M (EX box), A..$3,850.00

Britains, British Army Set #93, 72-pc, 1937, G (G box), A..$1,600.00

Britains, British Army Set #129, 70-pc, 1930, NM (NM box), A..$5,390.00

Britains, British Army Set #130, 118-pc, 1936, M (NM box), A..$3,575.00

Britains, British Beetle Lorry, 1955, 2nd version, M (NM box), A, $250.00. (Photo courtesy Bertoia Auctions)

Britains, British Infantry Set #195, 8-pc, 1950s, G, A $60.00

Britains, British Infantry Set #258, 8-pc, G (box), A $75.00

Britains, British Infantry Set #1294, 8-pc, 1939, G, A ...$230.00

Britains, British Infantry Set #1515, 8-pc, 1950s, EX (EX Roan box), A...$75.00

Britains, British Infantry Set #1612, 8-pc, EX-M (EX box), A...$80.00

Britains, British Infantry Set #1898, 8-pc, 1950s, EX (EX Roan box)...$100.00

Britains, British Infantry Set #8803, 6-pc, M (M box), A ..$50.00

Britains, British Life Guards (1st) Set #1, 5-pc, 1895, 1st version, EX (EX box) $2,100.00

Britains, British Military Band in Service Dress Set #1287, 21-pc, 1935, 2nd version, NM (EX box), A $1,100.00

Britains, British Navy in Action Set #1613, 7-pc, 1955, EX (EX box), A $75.00

Britains, British Sailors Set #1510, 8-pc, 1950s, Fair, A ...$80.00

Britains, Bulgarian Infantry Set #172, 8-pc, 1935, 2nd version, NM (VG box), A $800.00

Britains, Cameron Highlanders Set #114, 8-pc, 1902, 2nd version, NM (EX box), A $3,575.00

Britains, Boy Scouts Set #161, 1930, 2nd version, NM (EX box), A, $1,750.00. (Photo courtesy Bertoia Auctions)

Britains, Boy Scouts Signallers Set #163, 5-pc, 1950s, M (G box), A...$375.00

Britains, British Army Medical Service Set #137, 24-pc, 1935, 2nd version, EX+ (VG box), A $1,750.00

Britains, Cameron Highlanders Set #2025, 18-pc, 1955, 1st version, M (M box), A $775.00

Britains, Changing of the Guard Set #1555, 83-pc, 1950, EX, A $875.00

Britains, Changing of the Guard Set #9424, 83-pc, 1963, M (NM box), A $1,550.00

Britains, Chasseurs A Cheual Set #139, 5-pc, 1935, 2nd version, NM (NM box), A $775.00

Britains, Chinese Infantry Set #241, 8-pc, 1935, 1st version, G, A $150.00

Britains, Chinese Infantry Set #241, 8-pc, 1935, 1st version, NM (NM box), A $2,750.00

Britains, Circus (Mammoth) Set #1539, 23-pc, 1950s, M (M box), A $1,750.00

Britains, Circus (Mammoth) Set #2054, 12-pc, 1955, M (M box), A $825.00

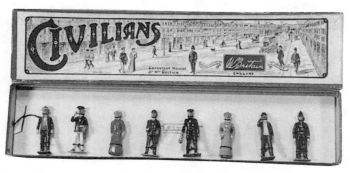

Britains, Civilians Set #168, extremely rare, NM (NM box), A, $3,025.00. (Photo courtesy Bertoia Auctions)

Britains, Coldstream Guards Band Set #27, 21-pc, 1930s, NM (EX box), A...$1,650.00

Britains, Coldstream Guards Band Set #37, 21-pc, 1950s, EX (G box), A...$250.00

Britains, Coldstream Guards Drum & Fife Band Set #322, 25-pc, 1938, rare, NM (NM box), A $2,475.00

Britains, Coldstream Guards Set #90, 24-pc, 1950s, 6th version, NM (NM box), A...$715.00

Britains, Coldstream Guards Set #90, 30-pc, 1910, G (Poor box), A...$450.00

Britains, Coldstream Guards Set #205, 7-pc, 1937, 2nd version, NM (EX box), A $415.00

Britains, Coldstream Guards Set #8880, 6-pc, M (M box), A $25.00

Britains, Colour Party Grenadier Guards Set #460, 7-pc, 1940, 3rd version, NM (EX box), A $2,475.00

Britains, Colour Party of the Black Watch Set #2111, 6-pc, 1959, M (M box), A....................................$525.00

Britains, Colour Party of the Scots Guards Set #2084, 6-pc, M (M box), A $500.00

Britains, Colours & Pioneers of the Scots Guards Set #82, 7-pc, 1957, M (EX box), A..$150.00

Britains, Colours & Pioneers of the Scots Guards Set #82, 8-pc, 1902, 1st version, NM (EX box), A.................$2,100.00

Britains, Confederate Cavalry Set #2055, 5-pc, 1955, G (Fair Roan box), A..$125.00

Britains, Confederate Infantry Set #2060, 7-pc, 1950s, EX (G Roan box), A...$125.00

Britains, Cowboys & North American Indians Set #2061, 90-pc, 1955, 1st version, M (NM box), A....................$8,800.00

Britains, Danish Army Set #2018, 8-pc, EX (Poor box), A...$750.00

Britains, Danish Guard Hussar Regiment Set #2019, 6-pc, 1956, 1st version, M (M box), A $415.00

Britains, Devonshire Regiment Set #110, 8-pc, 1901, 1st version, G-EX (EX box), A.............................$1,430.00

Britains, Dispatch Rider Set #1991, NM+ $100.00

Britains, Dragoon Guards (2nd) Set #44, 5-pc, 1952, G (Fair box), A..$125.00

Britains, Dragoon Guards (5th Royal Inniskilling) Set #2087, 8-pc, 1956, M (NM box), A............................$225.00

Britains, Dragoons (6th Inniskilling) Set #108, 5-pc, 1910, 1st version, G, A $250.00

Britains, Dragoons (6th Inniskilling) Set #108, 5-pc, 1940, EX (EX box), A $600.00

Britains, Dublin Fusiliers Set #109, 8-pc, 1939, Fair-G (G box), A..$175.00

Britains, Duke of Cornwall's Infantry Set #1569, 8-pc, 1936, 1st version, EX (VG box) $1,000.00

Britains, East Kent Buffs (3rd Foot Regiment) Set #16, 10-pc, 1894, 1st version, EX (VG box), A $1,550.00

Britains, East Kent Buffs (3rd Foot Regiment) Set #16, 1900, 2nd version (extremely rare), EX (VG box), A, $6,050.00.
(Photo courtesy Bertoia Auctions)

Britains, Egyptian Camel Corps Set #48, 3-pc, G, A......$125.00

Britains, Egyptian Camel Corps Set #48, 6-pc, 1930s, NM (EX box), A...$1,325.00

Britains, Egyptian Camel Corps Set #9265, 6-pc, 1960s, Fair (Poor box), A..$100.00

Britains, Egyptian Infantry Set #117, 8-pc, 1901, 1st version, EX-M (EX+ box), A.......................................$1,200.00

Britains, Egyptian Infantry Set #117, 8-pc, 1930, G, A ..$150.00

Britains, Egyptian Infantry Set #117, 8-pc, 1957, EX (EX box) $150.00

Britains, Eleventh Hussars (Dismounted) Set #182, 8-pc, 1930, 2nd version, NM (EX+ box) $450.00

Britains, Empress of India's (21st) Lancers Set #100, 5-pc, 1905, 2nd version, EX (G box), A $880.00

Britains, Fifth..., see specific listings such as Dragoon Guards (5th Royal Inniskilling), etc.

Britains, Foreign Service 21st Lancers Set #94, mounted, 5-pc, 1920s, G, A..$160.00

Britains, Fort Henry Guards (Canada) Set #2148, 7-pc, 1959, G, A..$60.00

Britains, Fort Henry Guards (Canada) Set #2148, 7-pc, 1959, M (M box), A...$250.00

Britains, French Cuirassiers Review Order Set #138, 5-pc, 1953, 3rd version, G (G box), A.........................$125.00

Britains, French Cuirassiers Review Order Set #138, 5-pc, 1953, 3rd version, NM (NM box), A....................$450.00

Britains, French Dragons (sic) Set #140, 5-pc, 1935, 3rd version, M (NM box), A..$925.00

Britains, French Foreign Legion Set #1711, 7-pc, 1938, 1st version, NM (EX box), A...............................$525.00

Britains, French Foreign Legion Set #1711, 7-pc, 1950s, EX (Fair box), A...$125.00

Britains, French Foreign Legion Set #1711, 7-pc, 1950s, G, A..$90.00

Britains, French Foreign Legion Set #1712, 15-pc, 1940s, EX (G box), A...$300.00

Britains, French Infantry (Turcos & Dragoons) Set #1388, 21-pc, 1938, M (EX box), A $2,475.00

Britains, French Infantry Set #125, 14-pc, 1930s, G (Fair box), A..$335.00

Britains, French Line Infantry Set #141, 10-pc, 1920s, Fair-G, A...$115.00

Britains, French Turcos Set #191, 8-pc, 1932, 1st version, NM (NM box), A..$775.00

Britains, French Zouaves With Officer Set #142, 7-pc, 1950s, M (NM box), A...$450.00

Britains, Fusiliers/Highlanders/Sussex Set #1323, 23-pc, 1950s, M (EX box), A $1,000.00

Britains, General Service Limbered Wagon (Active Service Order) Set #1331, 4-pc, 1935, 1st version, NM (EX box), A $600.00

Britains, General Service Limbered Wagon Set #1330, 4-pc, 1950s, M (M box), A....................................$650.00

Britains, German Army Set #432, 8-pc, 1950s, EX (EX box), A..$200.00

Britains, Gloucestershire Regiment Set #2089, 8-pc, 1954, M (M box), A..$650.00

Britains, Gordon Highlanders Set #77, 6-pc, EX-M (G box), A $80.00

Britains, Gordon Highlanders Set #77, 8-pc, 1904, 2nd version, NM (EX box), A $935.00

Britains, Greek Cavalry Set #170, 5-pc, 1935, 2nd version, NM, A...$600.00

Britains, Greek Evzones Set #196, 8-pc, 1925 or 1935, 1st version, NM (VG box), ea $500.00

Britains, Greek Evzones Set #196, 8-pc, 1950s, G (G box), A..$160.00

Britains, Grenadier Guards Band Set #2113, 25-pc, 1956, M (EX box), A $1,430.00

Britains, Grenadier Guards Set #8810, 6-pc, 1992, M (M box), A $35.00

Britains, Guards Infantry Set #2027, 8-pc, 1950s, EX-M (G Roan box), A...$115.00

Britains, Gun Detachment Set #1730, 8-pc, 1950s, EX, A .$160.00

Britains, Gurkha Rifles Set #197, 8-pc, 1930s, EX (G box), A..$230.00

Britains, Highland Light Infantry Set #213, 8-pc, 1935, 1st version, EX-M (EX box), A................................$600.00

Britains, Highlanders 42nd Black Watch Set #11, 7-pc, EX (VG box), A $3,025.00

Britains, Horse Guards Set #1343, 5-pc, G (G box), A..$175.00

Britains, Household Cavalry Musical Ride Set #2085, 23-pc, 1959, M (M box), A...$1,550.00

Britains, Howitzer (18" Heavy) With 10-Horse Team Set #211, 12-pc, 1932, 1st version, EX (EX box), A $3,025.00

Britains, Hungarian Infantry Set #178, 8-pc, 1935, EX (EX box), A..$230.00

Britains, Hunt Set #234, 8-pc, G, A $175.00

Britains, Hunt Set #9656, 19-pc, 1960s, G, A $400.00

Britains, Hussars Set #182, 8-pc, 1950s, M (EX+ box), A .$275.00

Britains, Imperial Yeomanry Set #105, 5-pc, 1910, 1st version, EX (EX box), A...$550.00

Britains, Indian (7th) Light Cavalry Set #45, 5-pc, 1920s, M (EX box), A...$775.00

Britains, Indian Army Mounted Set #066, 5-pc, EX (G box), A...$200.00

Britains, Indian Army Service Corps Set #1893, 7-pc, 1959, G (G box), A...$160.00

Britains, Indian Army Set #197, 8-pc, EX (VG box), A ..$90.00

Britains, Infantry in Action Set #1625, 8-pc, G (G box), A.$70.00

Britains, Irish Free State Set #1603, 8-pc, 1950s, G, A $80.00

Britains, Irish Guards Set #2978, 7-pc, 1950s, M (M box), A..$275.00

Britains, Irish Guards Set #8805, 6-pc, 1992, M (M box), A .$35.00

Britains, Irish Lancers (5th Royal) Set #23, 5-pc, 1894, 1st version, EX (G box), A......................................$2,475.00

Britains, Isle of Mann Royal Artillery (Special Paint), 13-pc, 1936, very rare, EX, A..$9,075.00

Britains, Italian Bersagliere Set #169, 8-pc, 1935, 2nd version, EX (EX box) $350.00

Britains, Italian Bersagliere Set #169, 8-pc, 1935, 2nd version, EX $150.00

Britains, Italian Bersagliere Set #169, 8-pc, 1950s, M (NM box), A..$275.00

Britains, Italian Carabinieri, 7-pc, 1950s, NM (EX box), A.$360.00

Britains, Italian Infantry Set #166, 8-pc, 1935, VG (VG box), A...$250.00

Britains, Italian Infantry Set #1435, 8-pc, 1955, EX, A..$115.00

Britains, Italian Infantry Set #1436, 8-pc, 1938, 1st version, NM (NM box), A...$660.00

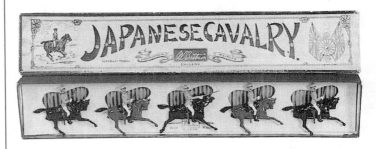

Britains, Japanese Cavalry Set #135, 1935, 2nd version, NM (NM Whisstock box), A, $2,090.00. (Photo courtesy Bertoia Auctions)

Britains, Italian Infantry Set #1437, 8-pc, 1939, 1st version, M (M box), A $300.00

Britains, Japanese Cavalry/Infantry Set #95, 13-pc, 1934, 2nd version, M (NM box), A..........................$4,400.00

Britains, Japanese Infantry Set #134, 8-pc, 1934, 2nd version, NM (EX box), A...................................$660.00

Britains, King George's Own (1st) Gurkha Rifles Set #197, 1955, G (G box), A $80.00

Britains, King George's Own (1st) Gurkha Rifles (Malaun Reg) Set #197, 8-pc, 1936, 1st version, M (NM Whisstock box), A $600.00

Britains, King's African Rifles Set #225, 8-pc, 1930s, G, A $100.00

Britains, King's Own Regiment Limited Edition Set #5292, M (M boxes), A $80.00

Britains, King's Own Scottish Borders Set #1395, 8-pc, 1940, 1st version, EX-M (VG box), A $660.00

Britains, King's Own Scottish Borders Set #1395, 8-pc, 1960s, G, A $70.00

Britains, King's Royal Rifle Corps Set #98, 8-pc, 1900, 1st version, EX-M (EX box), A $1,320.00

Britains, King's Royal Rifle Corps Set #98, 8-pc, 1935, M (NM Whisstock box), A $385.00

Britains, King's Troop Royal Horse Artillery Set #39, Fair (not orig box), A $300.00

Britains, Knights in Armour Set #1258, 6-pc, 1935, 1st version, NM (EX box), A $1,100.00

Britains, Knights of Agincourt Set #1659, 1-pc, 1954, 1st version, M (M box), A $165.00

Britains, Knights of Agincourt Set #1661, 1-pc, G, A $70.00

Britains, Knights of Agincourt Set #1662, 1-pc, 1953, M (M box), A.......................................$385.00

Britains, Knights of Agincourt Set #1662, 1-pc, 1953, VG (G+ box), A $125.00

Britains, Knights of Agincourt Set #1663, 1-pc, G, A $70.00

Britains, Knights of Agincourt Set #1663, 1950s, M (M box), A $385.00

Britains, Knights of Agincourt Set #1664, 5-pc, 1954, 1st version, G, A $100.00

Britains, Knights of Agincourt Set #1664, 5-pc, 1954, 1st version, M (NM box), A $875.00

Britains, Lancers, Territorial Yoemanry, Territorial Infantry, Etc Set #1407, 72-pc, 1935, 1st version, EX-M (VG box), A...$3,300.00

Britains, Life Guards (Mounted) Set #1, 5-pc, 1910, G, A .$185.00

Britains, Life Guards (1837-1897) Set #72, 12-pc, 1900, 1st version, EX-M (G box), A $10,450.00

Britains, Life Guards Band (Band) Set #101, 12-pc, 1905, very rare, EX, A $3,575.00

Britains, Life Guards Band (Khaki) Set #101, 1955, 5th version, M (NM box), A..$600.00

Britains, Life Guards Band (Red) Set #101, 12-pc, 1900, 1st version, EX-M, A $1,320.00

Britains, Line Infantry Set #118, EX (EX box), A $200.00

Britains, Madras Native (1st) Infantry Set #67, 8-pc, 1901, 1st version, EX-M, A.......................................$300.00

Britains, Marine Band (Winter Dress) Set #2014, 21-pc, 1955, G, A...$1,150.00

Britains, Mexican Infantry (Los Rurales de la Federacion) Set #186, 8-pc, 1935, 1st version (brn & gray), NM (NM box), A $600.00

Britains, Mexican Infantry (Los Rurales de la Federacion) Set #186, 8-pc, 1935, 1st version (bl & red), NM (NM box), A $1,050.00

Britains, Middlesex Imperial Yeomanary Set #83, 5-pc, 1939, M (EX Whisstock box), A..................................$1,760.00

Britains, Middlesex Regiment Set #76, 7-pc, 1950s, G (G box), A $60.00

Britains, Middlesex Regiment Set #76, 8-pc, 1897, 1st version, VG (VG box), A $1,320.00

Britains, Middlesex Regiment Set #76, 8-pc, 1897, 2nd version, G-EX, A..$880.00

Britains, Middlesex Yeomanry Cavalry Set #83, 5-pc, 1898, 1st version, NM (EX box), A $4,400.00

Britains, Model Farm Set #120F, 14-pc w/animals, EX (EX box), A $275.00

Britains, Model Fortress (w/Garrison of Soldiers) Set #1394, complete, NM (VG+ box), A............................$3,300.00

Britains, Model Home Farm Set #62F, 23-pc w/animals & figures, NM (VG box), A..................................$525.00

Britains, Montenegrin Infantry Set #174, 8-pc, 1935, 2nd version, NM (NM box), A..................................$1,050.00

Britains, Motorcycle Dispatch Riders Set #200, 4-pc, 1935, 1st version, NM+, A...$550.00

Britains, Mountain Artillery With Mule Team & Quick Firing Gun Set #28, 12-pc, 1938, 3rd version, NM, A.......$650.00

Britains, Mountain Artillery With Mule Team & Quick Firing Gun Set #28, 12-pc, 1898, 1st version, EX (EX box), A ..$2,200.00

Britains, Naval Gun (4.7") Set #1264, 1-pc, 1959, 7", M (EX+ box), A.......................................$140.00

Britains, Oxford & Buckinghamshire Light Infantry Set #1570, 8-pc, 1st version, NM (EX+ box), A $1,050.00

Britains, Painters & Ladder Set #1495, 4-pc, NM (NM box), A $700.00

Britains, Parachute Regiment ('Red Devils') Set #2010, 8-pc, 1950s, G, A...$115.00

Britains, Parachute Regiment Set #2092, 8-pc, 1954, M (NM box), A.......................................$440.00

Britains, Police (Mounted) Set #1511, 5-pc, 1937, 1st version, EX-M (EX box), A $660.00

Britains, Pontoon Section (Royal Engineers) Set #0203, 1925, 2nd version, NM+ (EX box), A........................$2,475.00

Britains, Pontoon Section (Royal Engineers) Set #1254, 1936, 2nd version, NM (EX box), A $1,100.00

Britains, Prairie Schooner Set #2034, 7-pc, 1952, 1st version, (EX box), A $660.00

Britains, Prince Albert's Own 11th Hussars Set #12, 5-pc, EX-NM (EX box), A $3,850.00

Britains, Prussian Hussars Set #153, 5-pc, 1935, 2nd version, G, A $320.00

Britains, Prussian Hussars Set #153, 5-pc, 1935, 2nd version, NM (EX box), A $880.00

Britains, Prussian Infantry of the Line Set #154, 8-pc, 1930, 3rd version, G, A $175.00

Britains, Prussian Infantry of the Line Set #154, 8-pc, 1930, 3rd version, NM (EX box), A................................$550.00

Britains, Queen's (9th) Royal Lancers Set #24, 5-pc, 1955, EX (EX Battle Honors box), A $200.00

Britains, Queen's Own (4th) Hussars (Movable Arms) Set #8, 5-pc, 1896, 1st version, NM (EX box), A $3,575.00

Britains, Queen's Own Cameron Highlanders Set #114, 8-pc, 1940, M (M Whisstock box), A $660.00

Britains, Railway Station Set #158, 1925, 1st version (rare), NM (NM box), A, $2,750.00. (Photo courtesy Bertoia Auctions)

Britains, Red Army Set #2032, 8-pc, 1950s, EX (G box), A .$175.00

Britains, Road Signs & Traffic Lights Set #1427, 8-pc, 1938, 1st version, EX-M (VG box), A $660.00

Britains, Rodeo Set #2043, 12-pc, 1950s, G (G box), A .$500.00

Britains, Royal Air Force Band Set #2166, 12-pc, 1956, 1st version, M (M box), A $715.00

Britains, Royal Air Force Firefighters Set #1758, 8-pc, G (G box), A...$200.00

Britains, Royal Air Force Set #0240, 8-pc, G (G Whisstock box), A...$115.00

Britains, Royal Air Force Set #2073, 8-pc, 1950s, G, A ...$70.00

Britains, Royal Army Medical Corps (Red Cross Ambulance) Set #1450, 7-pc, 1932, 2nd version, NM (VG box), A ..$660.00

Britains, Royal Army Medical Corps (Red Cross Ambulance) Set #1450, 7-pc, 1940, 3rd version (very rare), NM (EX+ box), A $5,225.00

Britains, Royal Army Service Corps Horse-Drawn Wagon (Steel Helmet) Set #1460, 1941, 3rd version (rare), NM (EX box), A..$3,025.00

Britains, Royal Army Service Corps Wagon (ASO) Set #1460, 5-pc, 1937, 2nd version, EX+, A............................$330.00

Britains, Royal Artillery Set #313, 4-pc, G, A $115.00

Britains, Royal Artillery (Service Dress) Set #1440, 9-pc, 1934, 4th version, EX-M (EX box), A............................$1,430.00

Britains, Royal Artillery (Steel Helmet) Set #1440, 9-pc, 1940, 5th version (extremely rare), EX+ (EX+ box), A..$4,400.00

Britains, Royal Artillery Howitzer (4-5") Set #1725, 1-pc, 1950s, M (M box) $65.00

Britains, Royal Artillery Set #144, 9-pc, 1940, 4th version, NM (NM box), A...$880.00

Britains, Royal Artillery Set #1201, 1-pc, 1950s, M (M box), A...$65.00

Britains, Royal Artillery Set #1289, 8-pc, 1936, 1st version, NM (NM box), A...$500.00

Britains, Royal Artillery Set #1292, 1-pc, 1935, 1st version, NM (EX box), A...$110.00

Britains, Royal Berkshire Regiment Band Set #2093, 25-pc, 1954, M (NM box), A $2,200.00

Britains, Royal Canadian Mounted Police Set #1349, 5-pc, EX (G box), A...$140.00

Britains, Royal Canadian Police Marching Set #1554, 8-pc, 1950s, G, A...$100.00

Britains, Royal Corps Signals Set #1791, 4-pc, 1955, EX (EX Roan box), A...$185.00

Britains, Royal Dragoons (1st) Set #31, 5-pc, Fair-G, A..$115.00

Britains, Royal Engineer General Service Wagon Set #1331, 4-pc, 1930s, G, A...$300.00

Britains, Royal Fusiliers (7th) Set #7, 8-pc, 1899, 2nd version, G-EX (EX box), A...$600.00

Britains, Royal Horse Artillery Set #39, 13-pc, 1896, 1st version, NM (VG box), A...$6,600.00

Britains, Royal Horse Artillery Set #39, 13-pc, 1916, 2nd version, NM (VG box), A...$3,300.00

Britains, Royal Horse Artillery Set #39, 13-pc, 1925, 3rd version, EX, A...$1,200.00

Britains, Royal Horse Artillery Set #39, 13-pc, 1946, NM (NM box), A...$5,225.00

Britains, Royal Horse Artillery Set #39, 13-pc, 1950, G (Poor Roan box), A...$400.00

Britains, Royal Horse Artillery Set #1339, 9-pc w/vehicle, 1940, 4th version, EX (EX+ box), A $4,400.00

Britains, Royal Horse Artillery Set #316, 1935, 2nd version, EX – NM, A, $2,100.00. (Photo courtesy Bertoia Auctions)

Britains, Royal Horse Artillery Set #2077, 1955, EX, A.**$460.00**

Britains, Royal Horse Guards, 4th Hussers, Grenadier Guards Set #53, 20-pc, 1930s, G (Fair box), A....................**$635.00**

Britains, Royal Horse Guards (The Blues) Set #2, 5-pc, 1899, 2nd version, G (G box), A..**$100.00**

Britains, Royal Horse Guards (The Blues) Set #2, 5-pc, 1899, 2nd version, NM (NM box), A.................................**$825.00**

Britains, Royal Hussars (10th) Set #315, 5-pc, G (Fair Whisstock box), A...**$220.00**

Britains, Royal Irish Fusiliers Set #2090, 8-pc, 1950s, G (G box), A..**$115.00**

Britains, Royal Lancers (9th/12th) Limited Edition Set #53 92, 9-pc, M (M box), A..**$95.00**

Britains, Royal Mail Van Set #1552, 1-pc, 1937, 1st version, very rare, EX (EX box), A...**$6,050.00**

Britains, Royal Marine Light Infantry Set #97, 8-pc, 1908, 3rd version, EX (EX box), A **$880.00**

Britains, Royal Marines Artillery Set #35, 8-pc, 1902, 1st version, EX (EX box), A...**$2,475.00**

Britains, Royal Marines Set #1288, 21-pc, 1933, 2nd version, NM (EX+ box), A..**$1,320.00**

Britains, Royal Marines Set #1291, 12-pc, 1930s, EX (G box), A **$460.00**

Britains, Royal Marines Set #2071, 7-pc, 1950s, EX (EX box), A **$80.00**

Britains, Royal Marines Set #5289, 10-pc, 1993, limited edition, M (EX box), A..**$45.00**

Britains, Royal Navy Blue Jackets Set #78, 8-pc, EX......**$300.00**

Britains, Royal Navy Blue Jackets Set #78, 8-pc, G (EX Whisstock Flowers box) **$400.00**

Britains, Royal Navy Landing Party Set #70, 11-pc, 1910, 2nd version, M (M box), A **$825.00**

Britains, Royal Navy Landing Party Set #79, 11-pc, 1955, 3rd version, G, A **$265.00**

Britains, Royal Navy Landing Party Set #79, 11-pc, 1955, 3rd version), M (M box), A...**$440.00**

Britains, Royal Navy Marching at Slope Set #2080, 8-pc, 1955, M (NM box) **$450.00**

Britains, Royal Navy Officers & Petty Officers Set #207, 8-pc, 8-pc, M (NM box), A **$935.00**

Britains, Royal Navy White Jackets Set #80, 8-pc, 1898, 1st version, EX (VG box), A **$660.00**

Britains, Royal Rifle Corps Set #98, 8-pc, 1950s, G, A **$70.00**

Britains, Royal Scots Grey Band Set #1720, 7-pc, 1955, 2nd version, NM (EX box), A...**$650.00**

Britains, Royal Scots Greys, 3rd Hussars, 16th Lancers Set #55, 15-pc, 1905, 2nd version, EX (VG+ box), A **$1,200.00**

Britains, Royal Scots Greys Band Set #1720, 7-pc, 1940, 1st version, NM (EX+ box), A **$990.00**

Britains, Royal Scots Set #212, 8-pc, 1935, 1st version, EX-M (EX box), A **$330.00**

Britains, Royal Scottish Archers Set #9301, 14-pc, EX, A..**$240.00**

Britains, Royal Sussex Set #36, 7-pc, 1910, 2nd version, EX (EX box), A...**$770.00**

Britains, Royal Sussex Set #990, 7-pc, 1938, 1st version, NM (EX box), A...**$990.00**

Britains, Royal Tank Corps Set #1250, 7-pc, 1937, EX-M (G Flowers box), A **$115.00**

Britains, Royal Tank Corps Tank Set #1203, 3-pc, 1940, 3rd version, EX+ (EX+ box), A..**$270.00**

Britains, Royal West Surrey Set #0121, 10-pc, 1908, EX (G box), A...**$550.00**

Britains, Royal Welsh Fusiliers Set #74, 8-pc, 1899, 1st version, EX-M (EX box), A **$825.00**

Britains, Royal West Surrey Set #2086, 16-pc, 1959, G, A.**$125.00**

Britains, Russian Infantry Set #133, 8-pc, 1936, NM (EX Whisstock box), A...**$600.00**

Britains, Salvation Army Band (Red Jackets) Set #1317, 24-pc, 1934, rare, EX-M, A..**$6,050.00**

Britains, Scots Guards & 1st Life Guards Set #49, 13-pc, 1950s, M (G box), A **$600.00**

Britains, Scots Guards Pipers Set #69, 7-pc, 1896, 1st version, EX-M (EX box), A **$3,300.00**

Britains, Scots Guards Set #75, 8-pc, 1897, 2nd version, G-EX (VG box), A...**$1,430.00**

Britains, Seaforth Highlanders Set #2062, 17-pc, 1959, M (NM box), A...**$770.00**

Britains, Seventeenth Lancers (Mounted) Set #8806, 4-pc, M (M box), A..**$80.00**

Britains, Sherwood Foresters Set #1594, 8-pc, 1937, 1st version, NM (EX box), A...**$1,050.00**

Britains, Ski Troops Set #2017, 4-pc, 1955, 1st version, M (M box), A...**$715.00**

Britains, Skinner's Horse Set #47, 4-pc, G, A................**$140.00**

Britains, Skinner's Horse Set #47, 4-pc, M (NM box), A..**$250.00**

Britains, Soldiers That Will Shoot Set #25, 4-pc, 1896, 1st version, EX (EX box), A **$2,475.00**

Britains, Soudanese Infantry Set #116, 8-pc, 1936, NM (EX+ box), A...**$660.00**

Britains, South African Mounted Infantry Set #38, 5-pc, rare 2nd version, EX (VG box), A **$400.00**

Britains, South Australian Lancers Set #49, 5-pc, 1896, 1st version, G-EX (VG box), A......................................**$5,225.00**

Britains, South Australian Lancers Set #49, 5-pc, 1930s, VG (VG box), A...**$1,200.00**

Britains, Sovereign's Escort (Coronation of Queen Elizabeth) Set #2081, 200-pc, 1953, EX-M (G box), A **$13,200.00**

Britains, Sovereign's Standard Set #2067, 7-pc, 1950s, EX-M (G box), A...**$200.00**

Britains, Spanish Cavalry (Caballeria Espanola) Set #218, 5-c, M (EX box), A **$1,050.00**

Britains, Spanish Infantry (Infanteria Espanola) Set #92, 8-pc, NM (NM box), A..**$525.00**

Britains, State Coach Set #1476, 28-pc, 1955, G, A **$200.00**

Britains, State Coach Set #1476, 29-pc, 1930s, EX (Fair box), A **$400.00**

Britains, State Open Landau Set #2094, 11-pc, 1958, EX, A **$330.00**

Britains, Sudanese Infantry Set #116, 8-pc, 1935, G (G Flowers box), A...**$265.00**

Britains, Togo Land Warriors Set #202, 8-pc, G (G box), A.**$80.00**

Britains, Turkish Cavalry Set #71, 4-pc, 1930s, M (EX+ Whisstock box), A...**$990.00**

Britains, Twenty-First Lancers (Heroes of Omdurman & Khartoom) Set #94, 5-pc, 1898, 1st version, EX-M (EX box), A **$2,200.00**

Britains, Turkish Infantry Set #167, 1935, 2nd version, NM (EX+ box), A, $775.00. (Photo courtesy Bertoia Auctions)

Britains, UN Infantry Set #2155, 8-pc, 1959, VG, A $140.00

Britains, Union Cavalry & Infantry Set #2069, 1960, NM (M box), A...$525.00

Britains, Union Cavalry Set #2056, 5-pc, EX (G box), A .$110.00

Britains, Uruguayan Army Cadets Set #2051, 8-pc, 1950s, G (G box), A...$150.00

Britains, Uruguayan Cavalry Set #220, 4-pc, 1950s, Fair, A.$115.00

Britains, Uruguayan Infantry (Alumnos de la Escuela) Set #221, 8-pc, 1975, 1st version, NM (NM box), A $600.00

Britains, Uruguayan Infantry (Infanteria de la RO del Uruguay) Set #222, 8-pc, 1938, 1st version, NM (EX box), A.$440.00

Britains, Uruguayan Military Cadets Set #2051, 8-pc, 1950s, M (M box), A $300.00

Britains, US Air Corp Set #2044, 8-pc, G (G box), A $80.00

Britains, US Army Band (Limited Edition) Set #5391, 10-pc, M (M box), A $125.00

Britains, US Army Band (Yellow) Set #9478, 25-pc, 1963, M (EX+ box), A $1,870.00

Britains, US Army Band Set #2217, 12-pc, 1956, M (NM box), A...$1,750.00

Britains, US Army Set #2033, 8-pc, 1950, G, A...............$70.00

Britains, US Aviation in Overcoats Set #331, 8-pc, 1935, 1st version, NM, A...$250.00

Britains, US Civil War Troops & Artillery Set #9485, 30-pc, 1964, M (EX box), A $2,475.00

Britains, US Forces Set #232, 29-pc, 1932, 1st version, M (G box), A...$715.00

Britains, US Forces Set #267, 13-pc, 1934, 1st version, NM (EX+ box), A...$550.00

Britains, US Infantry Set #91, 8-pc, 1900, 1st version, EX (VG+ box), A...$2,475.00

Britains, US Infantry Set #91, 8-pc, 1930, NM (NM box), A.$880.00

Britains, US Landing Party w/Field Gun Set #1306, 11-pc, 1934, 1st version (extremely rare), EX (EX Whisstock box), A...$3,025.00

Britains, US Marine Corps Band Set #2112, 25-pc, 1957, rare, M (EX box), A $3,080.00

Britains, US Marine Corps Review Set #2014, 21-pc, 1952, 1st version, M (EX box), A $1,650.00

Britains, US Marines (Service Dress) Set #399, 8-pc, 1938, 1st version, NM (EX box), A $1,100.00

Britains, US Marines Set #228, 8-pc, EX (EX Whisstock box), A...$200.00

Britains, US Forces Set #233, 1932, NM (EX box), A, $4,400.00. (Photo courtesy Bertoia Auctions)

Britains, US Military Band Set #1301, 12-pc, 1935, 1st version, NM (EX box), A $770.00

Britains, US Military Band Set #1301, 12-pc, 1948, G, A ..$230.00

Britains, US Military Police Set #2021, 8-pc, 1952-60, M (G Roan box), A $80.00

Britains, US Sailors Set #9184, 7-pc, 1962, M (Fair box), A .$90.00

Britains, USSR Cavalry Set #2028, 5-pc, 1955, G-EX, A .$70.00

Britains, Venezuelan Cadets Set #2098, 7-pc, 1955, M (M box), A $385.00

Britains, Welch Fusiliers Set #1323, 23-pc, 1960s, G, A ..$250.00

Britains, Welsh Guard Drums & Fifes Set #2108, 12-pc, 1959, M (M box), A $600.00

Britains, West India Regiment Set #19, 7-pc, 1930s, NM (EX box), A...$935.00

Britains, West Point Cadets (Summer Dress) Set #299, 8-pc, 1936, 1st version, NM (NM Whisstock box), A $660.00

Britains, West Point Cadets Set #226, 8-pc, early, EX (Fair Whisstock box), A $100.00

Britains, Worcestershire Infantry Set #18, 9-pc, Fair-G, A .$90.00

Britains, Zoo Set #112, 11-pc w/animals, M (M box), A .$300.00

Britains, Zouaves Charging Set #142, 7-pc, G, A $90.00

Ducal, Gordon Highland Band Set #186, 12-pc, EX, A .$100.00

Ducal, King's Own Band Set #301, 12-pc, EX, A $115.00

Ducal, Line Regiment Set #315, 12-pc, EX, A.................$90.00

Ducal, Middlesex Set #64, 6-pc, EX, A $45.00

Ducal, Royal Air Force Band, 12-pc, EX, A.....................$90.00

Ducal, Royal Canadian Regiment Set #151, 12-pc, EX, A .$100.00

Ducal, Thirteenth Canadian Light Infantry Band Set #231, 12-pc, EX, A $100.00

Grey Iron, aviator, orange harness, very scarce, 97%, A1.$93.00

Grey Iron, bandit surrendering, very scarce, 97%, A1....$155.00

Grey Iron, black cook, scarce, 99%, A1 ....$36.00

Grey Iron, black man digging, scarce, 96%, A1 ....$32.00

Grey Iron, black man sitting, scarce, 99%, A1..................$33.00

Grey Iron, boy flying kite (w/orig paper kite & wire 'string'), scarce, NM, A1..$35.00

Grey Iron, boy in traveling suit, gray, NM, A1 ....$18.00

Grey Iron, boy in wht swimsuit, very scarce, 98%, A1 .....$70.00

Grey Iron, Boy Scout walking, bl or red scarf, 99%, A1 ...$40.00

Grey Iron, boy w/life preserver, very scarce, 97%, A1.......$69.00

Grey Iron, cadet, bl, 96%, A1...$35.00

Grey Iron, cadet, gray jacket & cap, prewar, 95%, A1......$32.00

Grey Iron, cadet, lt bl jacket & cap, early version, 96%, A1.$33.00

Grey Iron, cavalry officer, wht, 96%, A1..........................$36.00

Grey Iron, colonial officer mounted, 96%, A1.................$49.00

Grey Iron, colt ranch scene, blk, very scarce, 90-93%, A1 .$63.00

Grey Iron, cowboy, 90-92%, A1 ....$19.00

Grey Iron, cowboy on horse, 97%, A1 ....$57.00

Grey Iron, cowboy squatting, very scarce, 99%, A1.........$71.00

Grey Iron, cowboy w/lasso (no lasso), postwar, scarce, M, A1.$49.00

Grey Iron, cowboy w/lasso (no lasso), very scarce, 97%, A1.$70.00

Grey Iron, cowgirl on horse, very scarce, 97%, A1 ....$70.00

Grey Iron, doctor (Red Cross) in wht, scarce, 96%, A1 ...$43.00

Grey Iron, elderly couple on park bench, 3-pc, 97%, A1 .$40.00

Grey Iron, elderly man or woman sitting, 99%, A1, ea $16.00

Grey Iron, Ethiopian chief, scarce, 98%, A1....................$77.00

Grey Iron, Ethiopian soldier charging, scarce, 93-95%, A1 .$78.00

Grey Iron, Ethiopian tribesman, scarce, 99%, A1.............$78.00

Grey Iron, farmer, 97%, A1 ....$19.00

Grey Iron, garage man, gr, postwar, 95%, A1 ....$18.00

Grey Iron, girl in riding suit, very scarce, 96%, A1...........$68.00

Grey Iron, girl in traveling suit, 99%, A1 ....$16.00

Grey Iron, girl kneeling w/sand pail, very scarce, 98%, A1.$70.00

Grey Iron, cavalry officer, brown horse, NM, A, $45.00. (Photo courtesy Bertoia Auctions)

Grey Iron, Greek Euzone, NM, A, $135.00. (Photo courtesy Bertoia Auctions)

Grey Iron, cowboy on bucking horse, scarce, 97%, A1, $86.00. (Photo courtesy Bertoia Auctions)

Grey Iron, hired hand digging, 98%, A1 ....$23.00

Grey Iron, holdup man in blk (Hoppy), M, A1 ....$51.00

Grey Iron, horse, brn, 98%, A1 ....$17.00

Grey Iron, Indian attacking w/tomahawk & knife, very scarce, 96%, A1...$121.00

Grey Iron, Indian brave shielding eyes, 98%, A1 ....$39.00

Grey Iron, Indian chief w/knife, 97%, A1........................$33.00

Grey Iron, Indian lying on horse w/rifle, scarce, 97%, A1 .$70.00

Grey Iron, Indian mounted, 98%, A1 ....$56.00
Grey Iron, Indian w/hatchet, 95%, A1 ....$19.00
Grey Iron, knight in armor, NM, A1 ....$45.00
Grey Iron, Legion bugler, 97%, A1 ....$30.00
Grey Iron, Legion color bearer, 97%, A1 ....$41.00
Grey Iron, Legion drum major, prewar, scarce, 98%, A1 ..$52.00
Grey Iron, mailman, 98%, A1 ....$16.00
Grey Iron, man in traveling suit, 95%, A1 ....$13.00
Grey Iron, man lying under newspaper, very scarce, 88-90%, A1 ....$61.00
Grey Iron, man w/watering can, 94%, A1 ....$15.00
Grey Iron, milkman, tan, scarce, 98%, A1 ....$26.00
Grey Iron, naval officer in lt bl, 97%, A1 ....$27.00
Grey Iron, newsboy, 99%, A1 ....$17.00
Grey Iron, nurse (Red Cross), 97%, A1 ....$38.00
Grey Iron, officer charging w/pistol raised, 95%, A1 ....$25.00
Grey Iron, pig, cream w/blk spots, 98%, A1 ....$17.00
Grey Iron, pirate boy 'Jim,' scarce, 96%, A1 ....$41.00
Grey Iron, pirate chief in red, 98%, A1 ....$43.00
Grey Iron, pirate w/dagger, bl, 97%, A1 ....$39.00
Grey Iron, pirate w/hook, 94%, A1 ....$34.00
Grey Iron, pirate w/sword, gr, 98%, A1 ....$38.00
Grey Iron, policeman, aluminum, bl, scarce, 98%, A1 .....$17.00
Grey Iron, policeman, 99%, A1 ....$17.00
Grey Iron, porter, 98%, A1 ....$19.00
Grey Iron, postman, 98%, A1 ....$16.00
Grey Iron, preacher, M, A1 ....$19.00
Grey Iron, Royal Canadian Mounted Police standing at port arms, 96%, A1 ....$50.00
Grey Iron, ski trooper, 99%, A1 ....$60.00
Grey Iron, soldier ammo carrier, postwar, very scarce, 93-95%, A1 ....$125.00
Grey Iron, soldier radio operator, scarce, 98%, A1 ....$89.00
Grey Iron, soldier w/rifle at attention, 99%, A1 ....$20.00
Grey Iron, soldier w/rifle charging, 97%, A1 ....$18.00
Grey Iron, soldier wounded (on crutches), scarce, 96%, A1 .$75.00
Grey Iron, stretcher bearer, scarce, 94%, A1 ....$45.00
Grey Iron, train conductor, 99%, A1 ....$17.00
Grey Iron, train engineer, 99%, A1 ....$17.00
Grey Iron, train porter, 98%, A1 ....$19.00
Grey Iron, US cavalry officer, 95%, A1 ....$49.00
Grey Iron, US cavalryman, 96%, A1 ....$44.00

Grey Iron, US doughboy bomber crawling, postwar, 97%, A1 .$32.00
Grey Iron, US doughboy charging, 98%, A1 ....$26.00
Grey Iron, US doughboy combat trooper, 93%, A1 ....$33.00
Grey Iron, US doughboy grenade thrower, postwar, 98%, A1 .$57.00
Grey Iron, US doughboy helping wounded soldier, very scarce, 93%, A1 ....$275.00
Grey Iron, US doughboy machine gunner, 97%, A1 ....$21.00
Grey Iron, US doughboy officer, 95%, A1 ....$21.00
Grey Iron, US doughboy plunging rifle w/bayonet downward, scarce, 96%, A1 ....$39.00
Grey Iron, US doughboy port arms, 94%, A1 ....$19.00
Grey Iron, US doughboy sentry, 90%, A1 ....$29.00
Grey Iron, US doughboy sharpshooter, scarce, 80-85%, A1 .$17.00
Grey Iron, US doughboy signaling, postwar, 98%, A1 ......$43.00
Grey Iron, US doughboy w/range finder, scarce, 95%, A1 .$95.00
Grey Iron, US infantry officer, 95%, A1 ....$22.00
Grey Iron, US infantry port arms, 97%, A1 ....$22.00
Grey Iron, US infantry w/shoulder arms, 99%, A1 ....$22.00
Grey Iron, US marine, NM, A1 ....$33.00
Grey Iron, US sailor in bl, 93-95%, A1 ....$23.00
Grey Iron, US sailor signalman, scarce, 97%, A1 ....$45.00
Grey Iron, woman in traveling suit, 98%, A1 ....$16.00
Grey Iron, woman w/basket, 97%, A1 ....$18.00
Grey Iron (Greyklip), bugler charging, EX, A1 ....$7.00
Grey Iron (Greyklip), drummer running, EX, A1 ....$6.00
Grey Iron (Greyklip), officer charging, EX, A1 ....$7.00
Grey Iron (Greyklip), rifleman charging, VG, A $3.00
Jones, British Guardsman (1921), 54mm, scarce, 99%, A1 .$22.00
Jones, British Marine of 1775 firing musket at an angle, 54mm, scarce, 94%, A1 ....$25.00
Jones, German charging w/bayonet, 54mm, scarce, NM, A1 .$40.00

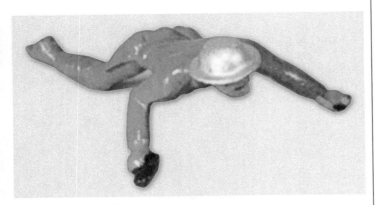

Grey Iron, US doughboy bomber crawling, NM, A, $65.00.

Jones, cowboy on rearing horse shooting gun while looking back, NM, $325.00.

Jones, Midshipmen of 1928, #544, set of 8, M (EX+ box), A1 ....$250.00
Jones, Scots Highlander of 1814, 54mm, scarce, 98%, A1.**$29.00**

Jones, soldier wire cutter crawling, NM, $475.00. (Photo courtesy Bertoia Auctions)

Jones, soldier wounded lying face up, NM, A, $165.00.

(Photo courtesy Bertoia Auctions)

Jones, US Infantry Set #5413, 8-pc, M (EX+ box), A1 ..$250.00
Jones, US Marines of 1809 Set #5436, 7-pc, M (EX+ box), A1 ....$250.00
Jones, Waynes Legion soldier on guard w/bayonet, 54mm, very scarce, M, A1 ....$34.00
Lincoln Log, caveman (Big Tooth) w/bow, scarce, 96%, A1.**$68.00**
Lincoln Log, caveman (OG), scarce, 99%, A1 ....$71.00
Lincoln Log, cave woman (NADA), scarce, 96%, A1 .....$70.00
Lincoln Log, conductor, thin base, 94%, A1.....................$14.00
Lincoln Log, cowboy firing pistol, 97%, A1 ....$18.00
Lincoln Log, cowboy w/lasso, 98%, A1 ....$18.00
Lincoln Log, dinosaur (for cave people), very scarce, 85-88%, A1 ....$68.00
Lincoln Log, engineer, NM, A1 ....$19.00
Lincoln Log, farmer, 99%, A1 ....$22.00
Lincoln Log, foot soldier (1812), scarce, NM, A1 ....$29.00
Lincoln Log, Indian brave w/1 feather & rifle, 97%, A1 ..$19.00
Lincoln Log, Indian brave w/1 feather standing w/bow & arrow, scarce, 88-90%, A1 ....$29.00
Lincoln Log, Indian chief w/bow & arrow looking straight ahead, 99%, A1 ....$19.00
Lincoln Log, Indian in war bonnet w/rifle, 98%, A1 ....$18.00

Lincoln Log, machine gunner prone, concave base, scarce, 99%, A1 ....$22.00
Lincoln Log, officer in 1918 uniform on horse, 97%, A1 .**$39.00**
Lincoln Log, pioneer, skinny version, 95%, A1 ....$18.00
Lincoln Log, pioneer, 98%, A1...$19.00
Lincoln Log, redcap, 98%, A1 ....$18.00
Lincoln Log, sailor at attention w/rifle, scarce, 97%, A1..**$30.00**
Lincoln Log, telegraph messenger, dk bl, scarce, 98%, A1.**$19.00**
Lincoln Log, telegraph messenger, tan, NM, A1..............$19.00
Lincoln Log, traveling man, brn or gray, 98%, A1, ea $17.00
Lucotte, Baron Lejeune Mounted, EX, A $125.00
Lucotte, General Bessiere Mounted, NM (M box), A....$125.00
Lucotte, General de Beauharnais Mounted, EX, A...........$60.00
Lucotte, General Junot Mounted, NM (M box), A........$140.00

Lucotte, General Lassale Mounted, EX (M box), A, $150.00. (Photo courtesy Bertoia Auctions)

Lucotte, Marshall Poiniatowski Mounted, EX, A, $160.00.

Lucotte, General Lepic Mounted, NM (M box), A........$105.00
Lucotte, General Marbot Mounted, 1980s, EX, A............$70.00
Lucotte, Kettle Drummers Mounted, 8-pc, EX, A.........$920.00
Lucotte, Marshall Berthier Mounted, EX, A...................$115.00
Lucotte, Marshall Murat Mounted, EX, A.....................$125.00
Lucotte, Marshall Yourion St Cyn Mounted, EX, A.........$80.00

Lucotte, Napoleon Mounted, EX, A, $70.00.

Lucotte, Polish Lancers of the Guard Mounted, 6-pc, VG-EX,
A $275.00
Manoil, action cannon, camouflaged, later version, 97%, A1.$23.00
Manoil, action cannon w/rod to hold 2 halves together, silver,
early version, scarce, 97%, A1...................................$35.00

Manoil, aviator mechanic with propeller away from head, NM, A, $660.00; aviation mechanic with propeller against head, NM, A, $190.00. (Photo courtesy Bertoia Auctions)

Manoil, aviator holding bomb, 97%, A1.........................$39.00
Manoil, bicycle dispatch rider, 98%, A1 ....$52.00
Manoil, black boy eating watermelon, scarce, 95%, A1.$100.00
Manoil, blacksmith making horseshoes, 97%, A1 ....$28.00
Manoil, blacksmith w/wheel, full pnt, 97%, A1 ....$28.00
Manoil, boy carrying wood, 94%, A1...............................$25.00
Manoil, brahma bull, 98%, A1 ....$28.00
Manoil, bull w/head turned, 97%, A1 ....$24.00
Manoil, calf bawling, 99%, A1...$19.00
Manoil, carpenter carrying door, scarce, 95%, A1 ....$69.00
Manoil, carpenter sawing lumber, 98%, A1 ....$28.00
Manoil, carpenter w/square, very scarce, 98%, A1.........$75.00
Manoil, cobbler making shoes, scarce, 98%, A1..............$42.00
Manoil, colt, maroon, M, A1..$32.00
Manoil, colt, tan, 98%, A1 ....$29.00
Manoil, couple sitting on park bench, 99%, A1 ....$41.00
Manoil, cow feeding, 99%, A1 ....$26.00
Manoil, cowboy on horse, bl & red, 95%, A1...................$26.00

Manoil, cowboy with hands raised, 97%, A1, $35.00; Manoil, cowboy with pistol in air, hollow base, 93 – 95%, A1, $49.00. (Photo courtesy Bertoia Auctions)

Manoil, firefighter (Hot Papa), white, scarce, A, $155.00.

(Photo courtesy Bertoia Auctions)

Manoil, cowgirl on horse, yel & red, 97%, A1 ....$28.00
Manoil, doctor in khaki, 98%, A1.................................$40.00
Manoil, doctor in wht, 93%, A1 ....$27.00
Manoil, ensign in wht, 93%, A1 ....$27.00
Manoil, farmer at water pump, 99%, A1 ....$30.00
Manoil, farmer carrying pumpkin, 99%, A1 ....$30.00
Manoil, farmer cutting corn, 99%, A1 ....$30.00
Manoil, farmer pitching sheaves, 97%, A1 ....$27.00
Manoil, farmer sharpening scythe, 96%, A1 ....$27.00
Manoil, farmer sowing grain, 97%, A1.........................$28.00
Manoil, flag bearer, 97%, A1 ....$47.00

Manoil, shepherd w/flute, very scarce, 97%, A1 ....$71.00
Manoil, sniper camouflaged, 97%, A1 ....$37.00
Manoil, soldier AA gun w/ranger finder, 93%, A1 ....$27.00
Manoil, soldier AA gunner, compo, scarce, 97%, A1 ......$81.00
Manoil, soldier at attention, present arms, wht helmet, 97%, A1...$42.00
Manoil, soldier bullet feeder, 97%, A1..........................$30.00

Manoil, general saluting at podium, NM, $250.00. (Photo courtesy Bertoia Auctions)

Manoil, soldier cannon loader, 97%, A, $30.00. (Photo courtesy Bertoia Auctions)

Manoil, girl picking berries, blk hair, early version, scarce, 92%, A1 ....$63.00
Manoil, girl picking berries, blond hair, later version, scarce, 95%, A1 ....$66.00
Manoil, girl watering flowers, 97%, A1 ....$28.00
Manoil, hod carrier w/bricks, 98%, A1 ....$43.00
Manoil, horse for cowboy or cowgirl, 98%, A1 ....$27.00
Manoil, hound, 97%, A1 ....$28.00
Manoil, Indian chief w/knives, NM, A1 ....$35.00
Manoil, man carrying sack on back, 98%, A1 ....$29.00
Manoil, man chopping wood, 97%, A1.............................$28.00
Manoil, man dumping wheelbarrow, cream, early version, 98%, A1 ....$32.00
Manoil, man planting tree, scarce, 97%, A1 ....$64.00
Manoil, man w/barrel of apples, dk gray, scarce, 96%, A1 .$73.00
Manoil, mason laying bricks, cream, early version, 98%, A1 .$43.00
Manoil, nurse, 97%, A1...$30.00
Manoil, officer lying down firing pistol, scarce, 93-95%, A1 ..$85.00
Manoil, officer w/sword, 98%, A1 ....$31.00
Manoil, policeman, 97%, A1...$29.00
Manoil, policeman w/nightstick, 94%, A1.......................$26.00
Manoil, scarecrow in straw hat, 99%, A1........................$30.00
Manoil, scarecrow in top hat, 98%, A1............................$29.00

Manoil, soldier machine gunner seated, compo, 97%, A1.$81.00
Manoil, soldier machine gunner seated, 98%, A1 ....$32.00
Manoil, soldier machine gunner w/pack on back, prone, 96%, A1 ....$32.00
Manoil, soldier marching w/pack & slung rifle, 99%, A1.$38.00
Manoil, soldier marching w/shoulder arms, 97%, A1 ....$23.00
Manoil, soldier tommy gunner, 1st version, 94%, A1.......$46.00

Marlborough, US Naval Color Guard Set #A12, EX, A, $90.00. (Photo courtesy Bertoia Auctions)

Manoil, soldier tommy gunner (skinny), 93-95%, A1 ......$37.00

Manoil, soldier w/M-1 rifle, 99%, A1................................$49.00

Manoil, soldier wounded, lying down, 98%, A1 ....$12.00

Manoil, woman lifting hen from nest, 97%, A1 ....$29.00

Manoil, woman lying out wash, 99%, A1 ....$30.00

Manoil, woman sweeping w/broom, 99%, A1...................$28.00

Manoil, woman w/butter churn, 95%, A1.........................$26.00

Meguel, 15th Century Historics, 8-pc, 1980s, G, A $200.00

Mignot, Ax Israeli Army Set #113, 18-pc, 1980s, EX, A.$210.00

Mignot, Conseques a L'Attaque Set #236, 6-pc, VG-EX, A.$150.00

Mignot, Farewell at Fountain Blue, 15-pc, ca 1980, EX-M, A $350.00

Mignot, First Hussars Set #224, 5-pc, EX (EX box), A...$220.00

Mignot, Gauls, 5-pc, 1950, G, A $90.00

Mignot, Honor Guards Set #213, 5-pc, 1980s, VG-EX, A.$210.00

Mignot, Israeli Infantry (Winter Uniforms) Set #113, 12-pc, 1987, M (M box), A..$200.00

Mignot, Napoleon & His Marshalls (Mounted), 5-pc, EX, A $250.00

Mignot, Sanciers de la Vistuls Set #230, 5-pc, VG-EX, A .$220.00

Mignot, Standard Bearers, wooden bases, 3-pc, 1 base missing, some rprs, A..$100.00

Mignot, Standard Bearers, wooden bases, 4-pc, 1 base missing, G, A...$300.00

Miller Plaster, General McArthur, M, A1.........................$60.00

Miller Plaster, soldier advancing w/orig rifle, 98%, A1.....$41.00

Miller Plaster, soldier flag bearer (no flag), 99%, A1........$48.00

Miller Plaster, soldier prone firing orig rifle, 99%, A1 ......$33.00

Miller Plaster, soldier wounded, w/stretcher, 99%, A1 .....$46.00

Miller Plaster, stretcher bearer, 99%, A1.........................$31.00

Reeves International, American Civil War Series, 31-pc, G-M, A $175.00

Reeves International, American Revolutionary War Series, 23-pc, EX (G-EX boxes), A...$125.00

Sporting Collectibles

Baseball — the great American pastime — has given us hundreds of real-life sports heroes plus a great amount of collectible memorabilia. Baseball gloves, bats, game-worn uniforms, ephemera of many types, even games and character watches are among the many items being sought out today. And there are fans of basketball, football, and hockey that are just as avid in their collecting.

As you can see, many of our listings describe Hartland and Kenner's Starting Lineup figures. If you are going to collect them, be critical of condition.

Advisor: James Watson (W8) Hartland Figures

See also Cereal Boxes and Premiums; Character and Promotional Drinking Glasses; Character Clocks and Watches; Dolls, Celebrity; Games; Pin-Back Buttons; and other specific categories.

Bill Dickey, windup toy, celluloid, 1940s, NM................$150.00

Dale Earnhardt, bank, car w/dark windows & yel tires, 1996 Atlanta Olympics, 1/24 scale, M.............................$100.00

Detroit Tigers, doll, printed stuffed cloth, 12", NM..........$45.00

Don Drysdale, baseball glove, Spaulding, 1960s, VG, N2..$25.00

Jack Dempsy, boxing gloves set, early, 4-pc, unused, MIB.$225.00

Jeff Gordon, pedal car, molded plastic w/tube steel frame, Pepsi advertising, 48", M $215.00

Joe Dimaggio, wallet, leather w/cartoon image & facsimile signature, zipper closure, 1950s, EX...................................$300.00

Joe Montana, doll, stuffed printed cloth in San Francisco 49ers #16 uniform, Ace Novelty, NM, $30.00. (Photo courtesy Patricia Smith)

Joe Namath, doll, stuffed cloth in 49ers uniform, 25", EX .$40.00

Joe Namath, figure launching footballs, battery-op, removable helmet & launcher, w/3 footballs, 1970s, 24", NM..$275.00

LA Dodgers, doll, stuffed cloth w/plastic eyes & nose, 1960s, 12", EX, minimum value..$35.00

Louisville Slugger, bank, red plastic stand holds 10 baseball bats w/various league logos, 1970s, EX $35.00

Mark Balenger, baseball glove, old, VG, N2 ....$25.00

Mickey Mantle, Paint-A-Player, complete w/several other players, 1950s, EXIB...$200.00

Mickey Mantle & Willie Mays, Pitch-Up Practice Batter, Transogram, 1960s, complete, rare, EXIB.........................$425.00

Muhammad Ali, Boxing Ring, MIB, L4.........................$475.00

New York Nicks, bear, Good Stuff, plush w/uniform & ball, 1991, 6", M $25.00

NFL Players, footlocker toy chest, features Dick Butkus, Daryl Lamonica, etc, EX $100.00

Philadelphia Flyers, doll, stuffed cloth, EX, minimum value ..$25.00

Roberto Clemente, key chain, shows 1960 Topps card, M.$15.00

Roger Maris, Batter Up Home Run Arcade, 1962, rare, VG.$600.00

Ty Cobb, doll, compo head & hands w/stuffed cloth body & limbs, Ideal, 1911, MIB $400.00

San Diego Padres, baseball radio, plastic, Made in China, 3" diameter, $35.00. (Photo courtesy Marty Bunis & Robert F. Breed)

HARTLAND FIGURES

Babe Ruth, 1960s, NM, from $125 to $175.00
Batboy, 25th Anniversary, NM.................................$50.00
Dick Groat, w/bat, 1960s, NM, minimum value............$900.00
Dick Groat, 25th Anniversary, MIB.........................$45.00

Don Drysdale, 1960s, EX, $225.00; Duke Snyder, 1960s, EX, from $300.00 to $350.00; Luis Aparicio, 1960s, NM, from $250.00 to $300.00.

Eddie Mathews, 1960s, NM......................................$125.00
Ernie Banks, 1960s, EX...$275.00
Ernie Banks, 25th Anniversary, MIB............................$40.00
Hank Aaron, 1960s, EX...$190.00
Hank Aaron, 25th Anniversary, MIB.............................$45.00
Harmon Killebrew, NM..$350.00
Harmon Killebrew, 25th Anniversary, MIB......................$45.00
Little Leaguer, 4", EX, from $50 to $75.00
Lou Gehrig, 1960s, NMIB..$150.00
Luis Aparicio, 25th Anniversary, MIB............................$32.00
Mickey Mantle, 1960s, MIB......................................$535.00
Mickey Mantle, 1960s, NM......................................$200.00

Mickey Mantle, 25th Anniversary, MIB $55.00
Nellie Fox, 1960s, EX, from $150 to $175.00
Rocky Colavito, 1960s, NM, from $375 to $500.00
Roger Maris, 1960s, NM, from $250 to $300.00
Roger Maris, 25th Anniversary, MIB $55.00
Stan Musial, 1960s, NM..$175.00
Ted Williams, 1960s, EX..$200.00
Ted Williams, 25th Anniversary, MIB............................$50.00
Washington Redskins, 1960s, EX $310.00
Willie Mays, dk face version, 1962, M...........................$250.00
Willie Mays, NM..$175.00
Willie Mays, 25th Anniversary, MIB..............................$45.00
Yogi Berra, no mask, NM...$125.00
Yogi Berra, w/mask, NM, from $175 to $250.00
Yogi Berra, w/mask, 25th Anniversary, MIB $40.00

KENNER STARTING LINEUP FIGURES

Babe Ruth & Lou Gehrig, 1989, MIP $45.00
Barry Bonds, 1989, MIP..$50.00
Brett Favre, 1995, MIP $35.00
Charles Barkley, 1995, MIP $15.00
Charles Mann, 1989, MIP...$50.00
Chris Miller, 1989, MIP...$50.00
Cy Young, Cooperstown, NM.....................................$20.00
Dale Earnhardt, 1998, MIP..$22.00
Dave Justice, 1992, MIP...$12.00
Deion Sanders, 1993, MIP..$20.00
Don Mattingly, 1988, MIP..$30.00
Don Mattingly Vs Wade Boggs, One on One, 1989, MIP .$40.00
Duane Bickett, 1989, MIP..$65.00
George Brett, 1988, MIP..$75.00

Irving Fryar, 1995; MIP, $30.00.

Jeff Gordon, Pepsi logo, Winner Circle, 1997, MIP..........$25.00
Jim Harbaugh, 1990, MIP..$60.00
Jim Kelly, 1988, MIP...$150.00
Joe Montana, 1989, MIP..$100.00
John Elway, 1989, MIP...$175.00
Johnny Bench & Pete Rose, 1989, MIP............................$45.00
Kareem Abdul-Jabbar, 1988, MIP, from $85 to...............$100.00
Larry Bird, Slam Dunk, 1988-89, MIP (red)...................$165.00
Larry Johnson, 1993, MIP..$15.00
Magic Johnson, 1988, MIP...$50.00
Michael Jordon, Olympic Dream Team, 1992, M.............$30.00
Michael Jordon, 1993, NMIP..$40.00
Michael Jordon Vs Isiah Thomas, One on One, 1989, MIP..$275.00
Reggie Jackson, Cooperstown, 1994, MIP.........................$25.00
Rickey Waters, Gridiron Greats, 1997, MIP.....................$15.00
Roger Staubach, Heisman, 1998, MIP...............................$15.00
Roy Green, 1988, MIP..$75.00
Ryne Sandberg, 1989, MIP...$65.00
Scottie Pippen, 1988, MIP..$145.00
Shaquille O'Neal, 1993, MIP..$45.00
Steve Sax, w/Rookie of the Year collector card, 1989, MIP .$75.00
Steve Young, 1989, MIP..$275.00
Terry Bradshaw, Legends, 1989, MIP...............................$50.00
Tim Hardaway, 1992, MIP..$25.00
Tony Gwynn, 1988, MIP...$125.00
Wally Joyner, 1988, MIP..$15.00
Wilt Chamberlain, MIP...$40.00

Star Trek

The Star Trek concept was introduced to the public in the mid-1960s via a TV series which continued for many years in syndication. The impact it had on American culture has spanned two generations of loyal fans through its animated TV cartoon series (1977), six major motion pictures, Fox network's 1987 TV show, 'Star Trek, The Next Generation,' and two other television series, 'Deep Space 9' and 'Voyager.' As a result of its success, vast amounts of merchandise (both licensed and unlicensed) has been marketed in a wide variety of items including jewelry, clothing, calendars, collector plates, comics, costumes, games, greeting and gum cards, party goods, magazines, model kits, posters, puzzles, records and tapes, school supplies, and toys. Packaging is very important; an item mint and in its original box is generally worth 75% to 100% more than one rated excellent.

See also Character and Promotional Drinking Glasses; Comic Books; Halloween Costumes; Lunch Boxes; Model Kits.

FIGURES

Galoob, STNG, Antican, 3¾", MOC...............................$20.00
Galoob, STNG, Data, bl face, 1988-89, 3¾", MIP..........$25.00
Galoob, STNG, Data, spotted face (error), 3¾", rare, MIP ..$20.00
Galoob, STNG, Ferengi, 3¾", M.....................................$20.00
Galoob, STNG, Ferengi, 3¾", MOC.................................$30.00
Galoob, Final Frontier, Kirk, Klaa, McCoy, Spock or Sybok,
    3¾", MOC, ea...$30.00

Galoob, STNG, LaForge, Lt Worf, Picard or Riker, 3¾", MOC,
    ea...$5.00
Mego, 3¾", Kirk, Spock, McCoy, Scotty, Decker or Ilia, 1980-
    81, MIP, ea...$40.00
Mego, 3¾", Megarite, MOC...$90.00
Mego, 3¾", Zatanite, 1980-81, rare, MOC....................$100.00
Mego, 8", Andorian, 1970s, EX.....................................$200.00
Mego, 8", Capt Kirk, 1970s, MOC, from $65 to..............$75.00
Mego, 8", Cheron, 1960s, M..$60.00
Mego, 8", Cheron, 1970s, MOC, from $135 to...............$175.00
Mego, 8", Dr McCoy, 1970s, MOC, from $75 to...........$125.00
Mego, 8", Klingon, 1970s, MOC, from $35 to.................$55.00

Mego, 8", Lieutenant Uhura, 1970s, MOC, from $75.00 to $90.00.

Mego, 8", Mr Scott, 1970s, M..$35.00
Mego, 8", Mr Scott, 1970s, MOC, from $65 to................$90.00
Mego, 8", Mr Spock, 1970s, MOC...................................$60.00
Mego, 8", Mugato, 1970s, MOC.....................................$600.00
Mego, 8", Neptunian, 1960s, M..$60.00
Mego, 8", Talos, 1970s, MOC, from $350 to..................$400.00
Mego, 8", The Gorn, 1970s, M, from $75 to...................$100.00
Mego, 8", The Gorn, 1970s, MOC, from $275 to...........$300.00
Mego, 8", The Keeper, 1070s, M......................................$55.00
Mego, 8", The Keeper, 1970s, MOC, from $225 to........$275.00
Mego, 12½", Arcturian, 1979, MIP.................................$100.00
Mego, 12½", Decker, 1979, MIP.....................................$125.00
Mego, 12½", Ilia, 1979, MIP..$50.00
Mego, 12½", Klingon, 1979, MIP...................................$125.00
Mego, 12½", Mr Spock, 1979, MIP.................................$100.00
Playmates, First Contact, 1996, 9", any, MIP, ea from $20 to .$25.00
Playmates, STNG, Insurrection Series, Deanna Troi, 1998, 9",
    MIB..$30.00
Playmates, STNG, 1st series, Commander Riker, 1992, MIP .$20.00

Mego, 12½", Captain Kirk, 1979, MIP, $100.00.

Playmates, STNG, 1st series, Deanna Troi, 1992, MIP.....$35.00
Playmates, STNG, 1st series, Ferengi, La Forge or Gowron, 1992, MIP, ea $30.00
Playmates, STNG, 2nd series, any, 1993, MIP, ea from $12 to $18.00
Playmates, STNG, 3rd series, any except Data in Redemption costume, 1994, MIP, ea $15.00
Playmates, Voyager, Capt Janeway or B'Elanna Torres, 1995-96, 5", MIP, ea $30.00
Playmates, Voyager, Chakotay, Kazon, Lt Carey, Neelix, Seska, Tom Paris, Torres as Klingon, Tuvok or Vidian, 5", MIP, ea $10.00
Playmates, Voyager, Chakotay as Maquis, Doctor or Harry Kim, 1995-96, 5", MIP, ea....................................$15.00

PLAYSETS AND ACCESSORIES

Command Communications Console, Mego, 1976, MIB, from $125 to..$150.00
Communications Set, Mego, 1974, MIB........................$150.00
Engineering, Generations Movie, Playmates, MIB $35.00
Mission to Gamma VI, Mego, 1975, rare, MIB...............$400.00
Telescreen Console, Mego, 1975, MIB..........................$125.00
Transporter Room, Mego, 1975, MIB.............................$125.00
USS Enterprise Bridge, Mego, 1975, complete w/3 figures, EX..$80.00
USS Enterprise Bridge, Mego, 1975, MIB......................$130.00
USS Enterprise Bridge, STNG, Playmates, 1991, MIB.....$50.00

VEHICLES

Borg Ship (sphere), Playmates, MIB $60.00
Ferengi Fighter, STNG, Galoob, 1989, NRFB................$75.00
Klingon Bird of Prey, STNG, Playmates, 1995, MIB........$80.00
Klingon Cruiser, Mego, 1980, 8" L, MIB........................$70.00
Klingon Warship, Star Trek II, Corgi #149, MOC............$30.00
Romulan Warbird, Playmates, MIB $50.00

Shuttlecraft Galileo, Star Trek the Next Generation, Galoob, 1989, MIP, $75.00.

USS Defiant Starship, Playmates, MIB..........................$110.00
USS Enterprise, Star Trek II, Corgi, 1982, MOC, from $25 to.$30.00
USS Enterprise B, Motion Picture, Playmates, M............$65.00
USS Enterprise E, Motion Picture, Playmates, NMIB....$135.00
Voyager Starship, Playmates, MIB................................$135.00

MISCELLANEOUS

Action Toy Book, Motion Picture, 1976, unpunched, EX.$30.00
Bank, Spock, plastic, Play Pal, 1975, 12", MIB................$60.00
Belt Buckle, marked 200th Anniversary USS Enterprise on back, 3½", M..$15.00
Book, Star Trek Pop-Up, Motion Picture, 1977, EX.........$25.00
Book, Where No One Has Gone Before, a History in Pictures, Dillard, M (sealed)..$25.00

Bop Bag, Spock, 1975, MIB..............................$80.00
Classic Science Tricorder, Playmates, MIB $65.00
Colorforms Adventure Set, MIB (sealed) $35.00
Comic Book, Gold Key #1, 1967, EX..........................$75.00
Comic Book, Gold Key #1, 1967, M $215.00

Communicators, blue plastic, Mego, 1979, MIB, $175.00.

Decanter, Mr Spock bust, ceramic, M $40.00
Flashlight Gun, plastic, 1968, NM $50.00
Kite, Spock, Hi-Flyer, 1975, unused, MIP $35.00
Metal Detector, Jetco, 1976, EX....................................$150.00
Mix 'n Mold Casting Set, Kirk, Spock or McCoy, MIB,
    ea $65.00
Model kit, Romulan Scoutship, resin, Amaquest, MIB $50.00
Patch, America 1977 Convention, M $40.00
Patch, command insignia, w/instructions for uniform, M .$25.00
Patch, Motion Picture, Kirk or Spock, M..........................$35.00
Pennant, Spock Lives, blk, red & yel on wht, Image Products,
    1982, 30", M $15.00
Phaser Battle, Mego, 1976, NMIB $200.00
Phaser Ray Gun, clicking flashlight effect, 1976, MOC...$75.00
Phaser Water Gun, Motion Picture, 1976, MOC $55.00
Starfleet Phaser, Motion Picture, Playmates, MIB..........$150.00
Tricorder, Mego, 1976, tape recorder, EXIB...................$125.00
Utility Belt, Remco, 1975, M $55.00
Wastebasket, Motion Picture, M $35.00
Water Gun, Motion Picture, Azrak Hamway Int'l, 1976,
    MOC..$50.00

Star Wars

The original 'Star Wars' movie was a phenomenal box office hit of the late 1970s, no doubt due to its ever-popular space travel theme and fantastic special effects. A sequel called 'Empire Strikes Back' (1980) and a third hit called 'Return of the Jedi' (1983) did just as well. Interest has been sustained through the release of two more films, 'Episode I, The Phantom Menace' and 'Episode II, Attack of the Clones.' As a result, an enormous amount of related merchandise was released — most of which was made by the Kenner Company. Palitoy of London supplied England and other overseas countries with Kenner's products and also made some toys that were never distributed in America. Until 1980 the logo of the Twentieth Century Fox studios (under whom the toys were licensed) appeared on each item; just before the second movie, 'Star Wars' creator, George Lucas, regained control of the merchandise rights, and items inspired by the last two films can be identified by his own Lucasfilm logo. Since 1987 Lucasfilm, Ltd., has operated shops in conjunction with the Star Tours at Disneyland theme parks.

The first action figures to be introduced were Luke Skywalker, Princess Leia, R2-D2, and Chewbacca. Because of delays in production that prevented Kenner from getting them on the market in time for Christmas, the company issued 'early bird' certificates so that they could be ordered by mail when they became available. In all, more than ninety action figures were designed. The 'Power of the Force' figures came with a collector coin on each card.

Original packaging is very important in assessing a toy's worth. As each movie was released, packaging was updated, making approximate dating relatively simple. A figure on an original 'Star Wars' card is worth more than the same character on an 'Empire Strikes Back' card, etc.; and the same 'Star Wars' figure valued at $50.00 in mint-on-card condition might be worth as little as $5.00 'loose.'

Especially prized are the original 12-back Star Wars cards (meaning twelve figures were shown on the back). Second issue cards showed eight more, and so on. Unpunched cards tend to be valued at about 15% to 20% more than punched cards, and naturally if the proof of purchase has been removed, the value of the card is less. (These could be mailed in to receive newly introduced figures before they appeared on the market. Remember, pricing is not a science — it hinges on many factors.)

The following 'MOC' and 'MIB' listings are for mint items in mint packaging. 'Loose' items listed are complete and mint unless noted otherwise. Because of the vast amount of Star Wars collectibles, listings are of vintage Kenner items only, including 'Power of the Force.' For more information about current and vintage Star Wars collectibles of all types we recommend *Star Wars Super Collector's Wish Book Identification & Values*, 2nd Edition, by Geoffrey T. Carlton (Collector Books).

See also Character and Promotional Drinking Glasses; Halloween Costumes; Lunch Boxes; Model Kits.

Key: ESB — Empire Strikes Back
    POTF — Power of the Force

ROTJ — Return of the Jedi
SW — Star Wars

FIGURES

A-Wing Pilot, Droids, loose.................................$35.00
A-Wing Pilot, Droids, MOC...............................$200.00
A-Wing Pilot, POTF, loose................................$40.00

A-Wing Pilot, POTF, MOC, $150.00. (Photo courtesy Martin and Carolyn Berens)

Admiral Ackbar, ROTJ, loose $10.00
Admiral Ackbar, ROTJ, MOC.............................$40.00

Barada, POTF, MOC, $110.00.

Amanaman, POTF, MOC..$300.00
Anakin Skywalker, M (in sealed mailer bag) $40.00
Anakin Skywalker, POTF, loose....................................$25.00
Anakin Skywalker, POTF, MOC...............................$1,850.00
AT-AT Commander, ESB, MOC...................................$75.00
AT-AT Commander, loose...$12.00
AT-AT Commander, ROTJ, MOC.................................$50.00
AT-AT Driver, ESB, MOC $80.00
AT-AT Driver, loose..$15.00
AT-AT Driver, ROTJ, MOC...$45.00
AT-ST Driver, loose..$8.00
AT-ST Driver, POTF, MOC..$65.00
AT-ST Driver, ROTJ, MOC..$42.00
B-Wing Pilot, loose $8.00
B-Wing Pilot, POTF, MOC..$42.00
B-Wing Pilot, ROTJ, MOC..$38.00
Barada, loose $35.00
Ben (Obi-Wan) Kenobi, ESB, MOC $115.00
Ben (Obi-Wan) Kenobi, loose, gray hair........................$25.00
Ben (Obi-Wan) Kenobi, loose, wht hair.........................$30.00
Ben (Obi-Wan) Kenobi, POTF, gray hair, MOC...........$105.00
Ben (Obi-Wan) Kenobi, POTF, wht hair, MOC $115.00
Ben (Obi-Wan) Kenobi, ROTJ, gray or wht hair, MOC (tri-
  logo), ea $65.00
Ben (Obi-Wan) Kenobi, ROTJ, gray or wht hair, MOC, ea .$55.00
Ben (Obi-Wan) Kenobi, SW, 12", MIB....................$375.00
Ben (Obi-Wan) Kenobi, SW, gray hair, MOC (12-back) ..$310.00
Ben (Obi-Wan) Kenobi, SW, gray hair, MOC (21-back) ..$175.00

Ben (Obi-Wan) Kenobi, SW, white hair, MOC (12-back), $325.00.

(Photo courtesy June Moon)

Ben (Obi-Wan) Kenobi, SW, wht hair, MOC (21-back) ..$165.00
Bespin Security Guard, ESB, Black, MOC......................$65.00
Bespin Security Guard, ESB, MOC................................$60.00
Bespin Security Guard, loose $10.00
Bespin Security Guard, loose, Black $15.00
Bespin Security Guard, ROTJ, Black, MOC....................$55.00

Bespin Security Guard, ROTJ, MOC.............$45.00
Bib Fortuna, loose $10.00
Bib Fortuna, ROTJ, MOC.................................$35.00
Biker Scout, loose $15.00
Biker Scout, POTF, MOC.................................$90.00
Biker Scout, ROTJ, MOC.................................$45.00
Boba Fett, Droids, loose.................................$100.00
Boba Fett, Droids, MOC...............................$1,090.00
Boba Fett, ESB, 12", MIB..............................$625.00
Boba Fett, ESB, MOC.....................................$425.00
Boba Fett, loose...$45.00
Boba Fett, ROTJ, MOC (desert scene)..........$325.00
Boba Fett, ROTJ, MOC (fireball)...................$365.00
Boba Fett, ROTJ, MOC (tri-logo)..................$635.00
Boba Fett, SW, 12", MIB................................$575.00

Boba Fett, SW, MOC (21-back), $425.00.

(Photo courtesy June Moon)

Bossk, ESB, MOC...$140.00
Bossk, loose $25.00
Bossk, ROTJ, MOC $65.00
C-3PO, Droids, MOC.....................................$115.00
C-3PO, ESB, removable limbs, MOC............$100.00
C-3PO, loose $20.00
C-3PO, loose, removable limbs $15.00
C-3PO, POTF, removable limbs, MOC $90.00
C-3PO, ROTJ, removable limbs, MOC............$50.00
C-3PO, SW, 12", MIB....................................$200.00
C-3PO, SW, MOC (12-back)..........................$275.00
C-3PO, SW, MOC (21-back)..........................$130.00
Chewbacca, ESB, MOC..................................$110.00
Chewbacca, loose..$15.00
Chewbacca, POTF, MOC................................$135.00
Chewbacca, ROTJ, MOC..................................$45.00

Chewbacca, ROTJ, MOC (Endor photo) $50.00
Chewbacca, SW, 12", MIB.............................$215.00
Chewbacca, SW, MOC (12-back) $300.00
Chewbacca, SW, MOC (21-back) $200.00
Chief Chirpa, ROTJ, loose...............................$12.00
Chief Chirpa, ROTJ, MOC..............................$35.00
Cloud Car Pilot, ESB, MOC............................$85.00
Cloud Car Pilot, loose.....................................$24.00
Cloud Car Pilot, ROTJ, MOC $45.00
Darth Vader, ESB, MOC................................$100.00
Darth Vader, loose...$30.00
Darth Vader, POTF, MOC..............................$130.00
Darth Vader, POTF, MOC (pointing)...............$65.00
Darth Vader, ROTJ, MOC (light saber drawn)....$75.00
Darth Vader, ROTJ, MOC (tri-logo).................$80.00
Darth Vader, SW, 12", MIB...........................$275.00

Darth Vader, SW, MOC (12-back), $350.00. (Photo courtesy Geoffrey T. Carlton)

Darth Vader, SW, MOC (21-back) $235.00
Death Squad Commander, ESB, MOC.............$110.00
Death Squad Commander, loose $35.00
Death Squad Commander, SW, MOC (12-back)...........$275.00
Death Squad Commander, SW, MOC (21-back)...........$165.00
Death Star Droid, ESB, MOC.........................$150.00
Death Star Droid, ROTJ, MOC.........................$80.00
Death Star Droid, SW, MOC (21-back).........$175.00
Dengar, ESB, MOC...$70.00
Dengar, loose...$20.00
Dengar, ROTJ, MOC..$48.00
Dulok Scout, Ewoks, loose..............................$10.00
Dulok Scout, Ewoks, MOC..............................$28.00
Dulok Shaman, Ewoks, loose...........................$10.00
Dulok Shaman, Ewoks, MOC...........................$28.00
Emperor's Royal Guard, POTF, loose...............$15.00

Emperor's Royal Guard, ROTJ, MOC..................$55.00
Emperor, loose...$14.00
Emperor, POTF, MOC..$80.00
Emperor, ROTJ, MOC..$25.00
EV-9D9, POTF, loose...$45.00
EV-909, POTF, MOC...$180.00
FX-7, ESB, MOC..$65.00
FX-7, loose..$10.00
FX-7, ROTJ, MOC..$50.00
Gammorrean Guard, loose....................................$15.00

Gammorrean Guard, ROTJ, MOC........................$38.00
General Madine, loose, M.....................................$10.00
General Madine, ROTJ, MOC...............................$45.00
Greedo, ESB, MOC...$125.00
Greedo, loose...$18.00
Greedo, SW, MOC (21-back card)......................$170.00
Hammerhead, ESB, MOC.....................................$135.00
Hammerhead, loose..$18.00
Hammerhead, ROTJ, MOC...................................$75.00
Hammerhead, SW, MOC (21-back)......................$195.00
Han Solo, ESB, Bespin outfit, loose......................$22.00
Han Solo, ESB, Bespin outfit, MOC....................$150.00
Han Solo, ESB, lg head, loose..............................$45.00
Han Solo, ESB, lg head, MOC............................$260.00
Han Solo, ESB, sm head, loose.............................$35.00
Han Solo, ESB, sm head, MOC...........................$315.00
Han Solo, POTF, Carbonite, loose.........................$95.00
Han Solo, POTF, Carbonite, MOC......................$280.00
Han Solo, POTF, trench coat, loose.......................$15.00
Han Solo, POTF, trench coat, MOC.....................$400.00
Han Solo, ROTJ, Bespin outfit, MOC..................$100.00
Han Solo, ROTJ, Hoth gear, loose.........................$15.00
Han Solo, ROTJ, Hoth gear, MOC........................$75.00
Han Solo, ROTJ, lg head, MOC (Death Star)......$175.00
Han Solo, ROTJ, lg head, MOC (Mos Eisley).....$185.00
Han Solo, ROTJ, lg head, MOC (tri-logo)...........$185.00
Han Solo, ROTJ, trench coat, MOC......................$48.00
Han Solo, SW, 12", MIB.....................................$550.00
Han Solo, SW, lg head, MOC (12-back)..............$525.00
Han Solo, SW, lg head, MOC (21-back)..............$525.00

Garmorrean Guard, POTF, MOC, $235.00.

(Photo courtesy Geoffrey T. Carlton)

Greedo, ROTJ, MOC, $65.00.

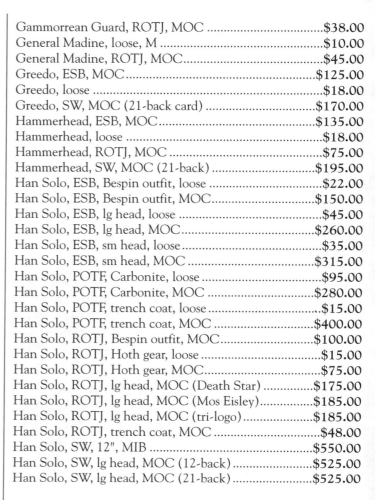

Han Solo, SW, small head, MOC (12-back), $670.00. (Photo courtesy Geoffrey T. Carlton)

IG-88, ESB, 12", MIB...$750.00
IG-88, ESB, MOC...$155.00

IG-88, ROTJ, MOC $78.00
Imperial Commander, ESB, MOC........................$65.00
Imperial Commander, loose................................$10.00
Imperial Commander, ROTJ, MOC......................$40.00
Imperial Dignitary, POTF, loose $35.00
Imperial Dignitary, POTF, MOC.........................$132.00
Imperial Gunner, POTF, loose, M $65.00
Imperial Gunner, POTF, MOC............................$180.00
Imperial Stormtrooper, ESB, Hoth weather gear, MOC...$90.00
Imperial Stormtrooper, Hoth weather gear, loose $22.00
Imperial Stormtrooper, ROTJ, Hoth weather gear, MOC .$54.00
Jann Tosh, Droids, loose $10.00
Jann Tosh, Droids, MOC.....................................$32.00
Jawa, ESB, MOC $112.00
Jawa, POTF, MOC...$125.00
Jawa, ROTJ, MOC...$70.00
Jawa, SW, 12", MIB $265.00

Jawa, SW, MOC (12-back), $265.00; Jawa, SW, plastic cape, MOC (12-back), $2,750.00. (Photo courtesy Geoffrey T. Carlton)

Jawa, SW, loose $28.00
Jawa, SW, MOC (21-back)..................................$185.00
Jawa, SW, plastic cape, loose $85.00
Jord Dusat, Droids, loose $10.00
Jord Dusat, Droids, MOC $30.00
Kea Moll, Droids, loose $10.00
Kea Moll, Droids, MOC $32.00
Kez-Iban, Droids, loose $10.00
Kez-Iban, Droids, MOC $30.00
King Gorneesh, Ewoks, loose............................$10.00
King Gorneesh, Ewoks, MOC $28.00
Klaatu, ROTJ, Palace outfit, loose.....................$12.00
Klaatu, ROTJ, Palace outfit, MOC $45.00
Klaatu, ROTJ, Skiff outfit, loose........................$15.00
Klaatu, ROTJ, Skiff outfit, MOC $45.00
Lady Ugrah Gorneesh, Ewoks, loose $10.00
Lady Ugrah Gorneesh, Ewoks, MOC $30.00
Lando Calrissian, ESB, MOC..............................$80.00
Lando Calrissian, ESB, no teeth, loose...............$16.00
Lando Calrissian, ESB, no teeth, MOC $68.00

Lando Calrissian, POTF, General Pilot, loose.................$42.00
Lando Calrissian, POTF, General Pilot, MOC $125.00
Lando Calrissian, ROTJ, MOC.............................$45.00
Lando Calrissian, ROTJ, Skiff outfit, loose...............$18.00
Lando Calrissian, ROTJ, Skiff outfit, MOC...............$60.00
Lobot, ESB, MOC..$55.00
Lobot, loose $12.00
Lobot, ROTJ, MOC..$42.00
Logray, Ewoks, loose..$10.00
Logray, Ewoks, MOC $28.00
Logray, ROTJ, loose $12.00
Logray, ROTJ, MOC...$36.00
Luke Skywalker, ESB, Bespin fatigues, blond hair, loose....$35.00
Luke Skywalker, ESB, Bespin fatigues, blond hair, MOC (looking)...................................$160.00
Luke Skywalker, ESB, Bespin fatigues, blond hair, MOC (walking)..................................$210.00
Luke Skywalker, ESB, Bespin fatigues, brn hair, loose $20.00
Luke Skywalker, ESB, Bespin fatigues, brn hair, MOC (looking)...................................$120.00
Luke Skywalker, ESB, Bespin fatigues, brn hair, MOC (walking).................................$175.00
Luke Skywalker, ESB, blond hair, MOC.............$200.00
Luke Skywalker, ESB, brn hair, MOC.................$235.00
Luke Skywalker, ESB, Hoth battle gear, MOC $95.00
Luke Skywalker, ESB, X-Wing Pilot, MOC...................$135.00
Luke Skywalker, POTF, battle poncho, loose $35.00
Luke Skywalker, POTF, battle poncho, MOC $138.00
Luke Skywalker, POTF, gr light saber, MOC $245.00
Luke Skywalker, POTF, Stormtrooper outfit, loose.........$145.00
Luke Skywalker, POTF, Stormtrooper outfit, MOC $480.00
Luke Skywalker, POTF, X-Wing Pilot, MOC $118.00

Luke Skywalker, SW, blond hair, MOC (12-back), $475.00. (Photo courtesy June Moon)

Luke Skywalker, ROTJ, Bespin fatigues, blond hair, MOC (looking)..$100.00
Luke Skywalker, ROTJ, bl light saber, loose......................$60.00
Luke Skywalker, ROTJ, bl light saber, MOC.................$175.00
Luke Skywalker, ROTJ, blond hair, loose..........................$40.00
Luke Skywalker, ROTJ, blond hair, MOC (Falcon Gunwell) $190.00
Luke Skywalker, ROTJ, blond hair, MOC (Tatooine) ...$175.00
Luke Skywalker, ROTJ, brn hair, loose $35.00
Luke Skywalker, ROTJ, brn hair, MOC..........................$125.00
Luke Skywalker, ROTJ, gr light saber, loose......................$28.00
Luke Skywalker, ROTJ, gr light saber, MOC.................$100.00
Luke Skywalker, ROTJ, Hoth battle gear, loose................$18.00
Luke Skywalker, ROTJ, Hoth battle gear, MOC $42.00
Luke Skywalker, ROTJ, X-Wing Pilot outfit, MOC (tri-logo) $125.00
Luke Skywalker, ROTJ, X-Wing Pilot, loose $20.00
Luke Skywalker, ROTJ, X-Wing Pilot, MOC $65.00
Luke Skywalker, SW, blond hair, MOC (21-back) $265.00
Luke Skywalker, SW, telescoping saber, loose................$240.00
Luke Skywalker, SW, telescoping saber, MOC (12-back).$3,200.00
Luke Skywalker, SW, X-Wing Pilot, MOC (21-back)....$180.00

Luke Skywalker, SW, 12", MIB, $400.00.

Lumat, loose...$20.00
Lumat, POTF, MOC...$55.00
Lumat, ROTJ, MOC...$50.00
Nien Nunb, loose...$10.00
Nien Nunb, M (in sealed mailer bag)....................................$20.00
Nien Nunb, ROTJ, MOC...$35.00
Nikto, loose,..$12.00
Nikto, POTF, MOC...$575.00
Nikto, ROTJ, MOC..$40.00

Paploo, loose $16.00
Paploo, POTF, MOC $48.00
Paploo, ROTJ, MOC $50.00
Power Droid, ESB, MOC..$115.00
Power Droid, loose $25.00
Power Droid, ROTJ, MOC..$70.00
Power Droid, SW, MOC (21-back).......................................$170.00
Princess Leia, Boushh outfit, M (in sealed mailer bag) $28.00
Princess Leia, ESB, Bespin crew neck, loose $28.00
Princess Leia, ESB, Bespin crew neck, MOC (front view).$170.00
Princess Leia, ESB, Bespin turtleneck, loose $36.00
Princess Leia, ESB, Bespin turtleneck, MOC (front view) .$185.00
Princess Leia, ESB, Bespin turtleneck, MOC (profile)...$170.00
Princess Leia, ESB, Hoth outfit, loose $26.00
Princess Leia, ESB, Hoth outfit, MOC $160.00
Princess Leia, ESB, MOC..$290.00
Princess Leia, POTF, combat poncho, loose.........................$21.00
Princess Leia, POTF, combat poncho, MOC.......................$120.00
Princess Leia, ROTJ, Bespin crew neck, MOC (front view).$90.00
Princess Leia, ROTJ, Bespin turtleneck, MOC (front view) ..$90.00
Princess Leia, ROTJ, Boushh outfit, loose...........................$18.00
Princess Leia, ROTJ, Boushh outfit, MOC $62.00
Princess Leia, ROTJ, combat poncho, MOC.......................$60.00
Princess Leia, ROTJ, Hoth outfit, MOC.............................$95.00
Princess Leia, ROTJ, MOC..$465.00
Princess Leia, ROTJ, MOC (tri-logo) $185.00

Princess Leia, SW, MOC (12-back), $425.00.

(Photo courtesy June Moon)

Princess Leia, SW, MOC (21-back) $265.00
Princess Leia, SW, 12", MIB...$400.00
Pruneface, M (in sealed mailer bag) $28.00

Pruneface, ROTJ, loose.......................................$15.00
Pruneface, ROTJ, MOC......................................$36.00
R2-D2, Droids, loose...$30.00
R2-D2, Droids, MOC...$125.00
R2-D2, ESB, loose..$18.00
R2-D2, ESB, MOC..$85.00
R2-D2, ESB, w/sensorscope, loose.....................$12.00
R2-D2, ESB, w/sensorscope, MOC.....................$80.00
R2-D2, MOC (12-back)......................................$245.00
R2-D2, MOC (21-back)......................................$150.00
R2-D2, POTF, pop-up light saber, MOC...............$215.00
R2-D2, POTF, w/pop-up light saber, loose $65.00
R2-D2, ROTJ, w/pop-up light saber, MOC (tri-logo) $165.00
R2-D2, ROTJ, w/sensorscope, MOC.....................$52.00
R2-D2, SW, 12", MIB...$165.00
R2-D2, w/sensorscope, M (in sealed mailer bag)..............$20.00
R5-D4, ESB, MOC...$160.00
R5-D4, loose...$28.00
R5-D4, ROTJ, MOC...$72.00
R5-D4, SW, MOC...$135.00
Rancor Keeper, ROTJ, loose...............................$12.00
Rancor Keeper, ROTJ, MOC...............................$35.00
Rebel Commander, ESB, MOC............................$72.00
Rebel Commander, loose $10.00
Rebel Commander, ROTJ, MOC..........................$38.00
Rebel Commando, loose....................................$10.00
Rebel Commando, ROTJ, MOC...........................$32.00
Rebel Soldier, ESB, MOC $78.00
Rebel Soldier, loose..$15.00
Rebel Soldier, ROTJ, MOC................................$45.00
Ree-Yees, loose...$12.00
Ree-Yees, ROTJ, MOC.......................................$35.00
Romba, loose..$22.00
Sandpeople, ESB, MOC.....................................$100.00

Sandpeople, loose...$22.00
Sandpeople, SW, MOC (12-back).......................$265.00
Sandpeople, SW, MOC (21-back).......................$155.00
Sise Fromm, Droids, loose.................................$35.00
Sise Fromm, Droids, MOC.................................$110.00
Snaggletooth, ESB, MOC..................................$135.00
Snaggletooth, loose..$16.00
Snaggletooth, loose, bl body.............................$190.00
Snaggletooth, ROTJ, MOC................................$60.00
Snaggletooth, SW, MOC (21-back).....................$185.00
Squidhead, ROTJ, loose....................................$12.00
Squidhead, ROTJ, MOC....................................$40.00
Star Destroyer Commander, ESB, MOC..............$135.00
Star Destroyer Commander, ROTJ, MOC.............$60.00

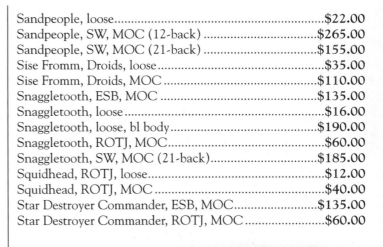

Stormtrooper, SW, MOC (12-back) (unpunched), $325.00. (Photo courtesy June Moon)

Romba, POTF, MOC, $60.00.

Stormtrooper, SW, 12", MIB, $350.00. (Photo courtesy Geoffrey T. Carlton)

Stormtrooper, ESB, MOC $100.00
Stormtrooper, loose..$20.00
Stormtrooper, POTF, MOC...$275.00
Stormtrooper, ROTJ, MOC..$70.00
Stormtrooper, SW, MOC (21-back)............................$178.00

Sy Snootles and the Rebo Band, ROTJ, MIB, $150.00. (Photo courtesy June Moon)

Sy Snootles & the Max Rebo Band, ROTJ, 3-pc, loose....$65.00
Teebo, loose...$14.00
Teebo, POTF, MOC..$185.00
Teebo, ROTJ, MOC $52.00
Thall Joben, Droids, loose..$10.00
Thall Joben, Droids, MOC..$32.00
TIE Fighter Pilot, ESB, MOC.......................................$92.00
TIE Fighter Pilot, loose $18.00
TIE Fighter Pilot, ROTJ, MOC....................................$65.00
Tig Fromm, Droids, loose $24.00
Tig Fromm, Droids, MOC...$75.00
Tusken Raider, ROTJ, MOC $75.00
Ugnaught, ESB, MOC...$45.00
Ugnaught, loose $12.00
Ugnaught, ROTJ, MOC...$40.00
Uncle Gundy, Droids, loose $10.00
Uncle Gundy, Droids, MOC $30.00
Walrus Man, loose...$18.00
Warok, POTF, loose $26.00
Warok, POTF, MOC..$75.00
Weequay, ROTJ, loose $10.00
Weequay, ROTJ, MOC...$32.00
Wicket Warrick, loose...$16.00
Wicket Warrick, POTF, MOC $185.00

Walrus Man, SW, MOC (21-back), $160.00; Walrus Man, ESB, MOC, $135.00; Walrus Man, ROTJ, MOC, $68.00.

(Photo courtesy Geoffrey T. Carlton)

Wicket Warrick, ROTJ, MOC $50.00
Wicket, Ewoks, loose $12.00
Wicket, Ewoks, MOC..$32.00
Yak Face, POTF, w/o weapon, loose $160.00
Yak Face, POTF, w/o weapon, MOC..........................$2,000.00
Yak Face, POTF, w/weapon, MOC.............................$2,180.00
Yoda, ESB, brn snake, MOC $275.00
Yoda, ESB, orange snake, loose....................................$35.00
Yoda, ESB, orange snake, MOC...................................$135.00
Yoda, POTF, brn snake, MOC......................................$465.00
Yoda, ROTJ, brn snake, MOC.......................................$90.00
Zuckuss, ESB, MOC $95.00
Zuckuss, loose...$18.00
Zuckuss, ROTJ, MOC..$55.00

PLAYSETS AND ACCESSORIES

Cantina Adventure Set, SW, loose $175.00
Cantina Adventure Set, SW, MIB $575.00
Cloud City, ESB, loose...$135.00
Cloud City, ESB, MIB $400.00

Creature Cantina, SW, loose, $75.00. (Photo courtesy Linda Baker)

Creature Cantina, SW, MIB...$165.00
Dagobah, ESB, loose $25.00
Dagobah, ESB, MIB...$80.00

Darth Vader's Star Destroyer, ESB, MIB, $200.00. (Photo courtesy Linda Baker)

Death Star Space Station, SW, loose	$115.00
Death Star Space Station, SW, MIB	$285.00
Droid Factory, ESB, loose	$60.00
Droid Factory, ESB, MIB	$170.00
Droid Factory, SW, MIB	$160.00
Ewok Village, ROTJ, loose	$35.00
Ewok Village, ROTJ, MIB	$90.00
Hoth Ice Planet, ESB, loose	$60.00
Hoth Ice Planet, ESB, MIB	$180.00
Imperial Attack Base, ESB, loose	$40.00
Imperial Attack Base, ESB, MIB	$110.00
Jabba the Hutt Dungeon w/8D8, ROTJ, loose	$55.00
Jabba the Hutt Dungeon w/8D8, ROTJ, MIB	$160.00
Jabba the Hutt Dungeon w/Amanaman, ROTJ, loose	$135.00
Jabba the Hutt Dungeon w/Amanaman, ROTJ, MIB	$350.00
Jabba the Hutt, ROTJ, loose	$20.00
Jabba the Hutt, ROTJ, MIB	$70.00
Jabba the Hutt, ROTJ, MIB (Sears)	$75.00
Land of the Jawas, SW, loose	$55.00
Land of the Jawas, SW, MIB	$185.00
Rebel Command Center, ESB, loose	$80.00
Rebel Command Center, ESB, MIB	$240.00
Turret & Probot, ESB, loose	$35.00
Turret & Probot, ESB, MIB	$165.00

VEHICLES

A-Wing Fighter, Droids, loose	$175.00
A-Wing Fighter, Droids, MIB	$525.00
All Terrain Attack Transport (AT-AT), ESB, MIB	$290.00
All Terrain Attack Transport (AT-AT), ROTJ, MIB	$225.00
All Terrain Attack Transport, loose	$90.00
Armored Sentinel Transport (AST-5), ROTJ, loose	$6.00
Armored Sentinel Transport (AST-5), ROTJ, MIB	$25.00
ATL Interceptor, Droids, loose	$25.00

ATL Interceptor, Droids, MIB	$62.00
B-Wing Fighter, ROTJ, loose	$65.00
B-Wing Fighter, ROTJ, MIB	$135.00
Captivator (CAP-2), ESB, MIB	$30.00
Captivator (CAP-2), loose	$10.00
Captivator (CAP-2), ROTJ, MIB	$20.00
Darth Vader's TIE Fighter, SW, loose	$55.00
Darth Vader's TIE Fighter, SW, MIB	$140.00
Darth Vader's TIE Fighter, SW, MIB (w/collector series sticker)	$225.00
Desert Skiff, ROTJ, loose	$12.00
Desert Skiff, ROTJ, MIB	$25.00
Endor Forest Ranger, ROTJ, loose	$12.00
Endor Forest Ranger, ROTJ, MIB	$40.00
Ewok Battle Wagon, POTF, loose	$60.00
Ewok Battle Wagon, POTF, MIB	$160.00
Imperial Cruiser, ESB, loose	$50.00
Imperial Cruiser, ESB, MIB	$150.00
Imperial Shuttle Pod (ISP-6), ROTJ, loose	$10.00
Imperial Shuttle Pod (ISP-6), ROTJ, MIB	$30.00
Imperial Shuttle, ROTJ, loose	$100.00
Imperial Shuttle, ROTJ, MIB	$365.00
Imperial Sniper, POTF, loose	$30.00
Imperial Sniper, POTF, MIB	$85.00
Imperial Troop Transport, ESB, MIB	$128.00
Imperial Troop Transport, loose	$48.00
Imperial Troop Transport, SW, MIB	$155.00
Interceptor (INT-4), ESB, MIB	$30.00
Interceptor (INT-4), loose	$10.00

Interceptor (INT-4), ROTJ, MIB, $25.00. (Photo courtesy June Moon)

Landspeeder, Sonic, SW, loose	$185.00
Landspeeder, Sonic, SW, MIB	$575.00
Landspeeder, SW, loose	$20.00
Landspeeder, SW, MIB	$85.00
Millennium Falcon, ESB, MIB	$255.00
Millennium Falcon, ROTJ, MIB	$185.00
Millennium Falcon, SW, MIB	$375.00
Mobile Laser Cannon (MLC-3), ESB, MIB	$35.00
Mobile Laser Cannon (MLC-3), loose	$10.00

Millennium Falcon, loose, $100.00. (Photo courtesy Linda Baker)

Mobile Laser Cannon (MLC-3), ROTJ, MIB $30.00
Multi-Terrain Vehicle (MTV-7), ESB, MIB.....................$35.00
Multi-Terrain Vehicle (MTV-7), loose............................$10.00
Multi-Terrain Vehicle (MTV-7), ROTJ, MIB................$30.00
One-Man Skimmer, POTF, loose....................................$38.00
One-Man Skimmer, POTF, MIB $100.00
Personnel Deployment Transport (PDT-8), ESB, MIB $30.00
Personnel Deployment Transport (PDT-8), loose $10.00
Personnel Deployment Transport (PDT-8), ROTJ, MIB ..$25.00
Rebel Armored Snowspeeder, ESB, loose..........................$50.00
Rebel Armored Snowspeeder, ESB, MIB $110.00
Rebel Transport, ESB, loose..$45.00
Rebel Transport, ESB, MIB $140.00
Sandcrawler, radio-controlled, ESB, MIB $500.00
Sandcrawler, radio-controlled, loose $175.00
Sandcrawler, radio-controlled, SW, MIB $665.00

Scout Walker (AT-ST), ESB, MIB...............................$100.00
Scout Walker (AT-ST), loose $35.00
Security Scout, POTF, loose $25.00
Security Scout, POTF, MIB $85.00
Side Gunner, Droids, loose $25.00
Side Gunner, Droids, MIB $85.00
Slave I, ESB, loose $60.00
Slave I, ESB, MIB..$185.00
Speeder Bike, ROTJ, loose $15.00
Speeder Bike, ROTJ, MIB $45.00
Tatooine Skiff, POTF, loose..$250.00
Tatooine Skiff, POTF, MIB..$580.00
TIE Fighter (Battle Damage), ESB, MIB $165.00
TIE Fighter (Battle Damage), ROTJ, loose.....................$45.00
TIE Fighter (Battle Damage), ROTJ, MIB......................$135.00
TIE Fighter, ESB, MIB..$210.00
TIE Fighter, loose $75.00
TIE Fighter, SW, MIB..$200.00
TIE Fighter, SW, MIB (Free Figures Inside)...................$385.00
TIE Interceptor, ROTJ, loose $55.00
TIE Interceptor, ROTJ, MIB...$140.00
Twin-Pod Cloud Car, ESB, loose $45.00
Twin-Pod Cloud Car, ESB, MIB.....................................$100.00
X-Wing Fighter (Battle Damage), ESB, MIB...................$160.00
X-Wing Fighter (Battle Damage), loose $40.00
X-Wing Fighter (Battle Damage), ROTJ, MIB..............$120.00
X-Wing Fighter, ESB, MIB $240.00
X-Wing Fighter, loose $65.00
X-Wing Fighter, SW, MIB $165.00
Y-Wing Fighter, ROTJ, loose $60.00
Y-Wing Fighter, ROTJ, MIB...$165.00

MISCELLANEOUS

Bank, C3-PO, Roman Ceramics, M $75.00
Bank, Chewbacca (kneeling), Sigma, M..........................$75.00
Bank, R2-D2, Roman Ceramics, M...............................$200.00
Bank, Yoda, SW, Sigma, M...$150.00
Book, Empire Strikes Back, pop-up, M...........................$15.00
Bop Bag, Darth Vader, MIB...$125.00
Bop Bag, Jawa, MIB $200.00
Card Game, Return of the Jedi, Parker Bros, 1983, MIB (sealed).$10.00

Scout Walker (AT-ST), ROTJ, MIB, $80.00. (Photo courtesy June Moon)

Chewbacca Bandolier Strap, ROTJ, MIB, $40.00. (Photo courtesy June Moon)

Case, Darth Vader, EX $15.00
Chewbacca Bandolier Strap, ROTJ, EXIB $25.00
Color 'N Clean Machine, Craftmaster, M.................$50.00
Doll, Chewbacca, Kenner, 1978-79, synthetic fur w/plastic eyes & nose, 20", EX $25.00
Doll, Latara the Ewok, plush, 1984, 16", MIB, N2............$50.00
Doll, Paploo the Ewok, ROTJ, plush, MIB $135.00
Doll, R2-D2, Kenner, 1978-79, stuffed cloth, w/speaker, 10", EX $25.00
Eraser & Sharpener, Ewok, 1983, MOC, N2 ....$15.00
Erasers, ROTJ, 3-pc, 1983, MOC, N2 ....$10.00
Game, Destroy Death Star, VG $20.00
Game, ESB Yoda Jedi Master, Kenner, 1981, NMIB.........$25.00
Game, Escape From Death Star, Kenner, 1977, NMIB.....$25.00
Game, Laser Battle, SW, MIB................................$75.00
Give-A-Show Projector, ESB, Kenner, complete, NM $75.00
Gum Wrapper, 1977, 5x6", VG+, N2.......................$10.00
Laser Pistol, SW, Kenner, 1978-83, plastic, battery-op, 18½", EX $40.00
Laser Rifle, ESB, Kenner, 1980, plastic, battery-op, 18½", EX ..$75.00
Magnets, ROTJ, set of 4, MOC, B5 ....$25.00
Movie Viewer, SW, Kenner, 1978-79, plastic w/snap-in cartridge, 7", EX $35.00
Paint Kit, Craftmaster, Luke Skywalker or Han Solo, MOC, ea...$15.00
Pencil, ROTJ, 1983, 7½", MOC, N2 ....$6.00
Poster Set, Craftmaster, 1979, w/2 posters, MIB (sealed) .$30.00
Presto Magix Transfer Set, ROTJ, Battle on Endor, NRFB..$15.00
Puppet, Yoda, Kenner, 1981, hollow vinyl, 10", EX $25.00
Radio Watch, Lucasfilm/Bradley, 1982, R2-D2 & C-3PO on face, MIB...$50.00
Ruler, ROTJ, shows 8 characters, 1983, 12", EX, N2........$10.00
Scissors, ROTJ, MOC, N2....................................$10.00
Sew 'N Show Cards, Wicket & Friends, MIB $18.00
Sit 'N Spin, Ewoks, MIB......................................$80.00
Speaker Phone, Darth Vader, MIB, P12...................$145.00
Stick Pin, Darth Vader's mask, diecast metal, 1977, MOC.$25.00
Stickers, ROTJ, 12-pc, 1983, MOC, N2 ....$10.00
Talking Telephone, Ewoks, MIB............................$50.00
Yo-yo, Darth Vader, Dairy Queen promo, Humphrey, 1970s, rare, NM...$25.00
Yo-yo, Stormtrooper, Spectra Star, sculpted plastic, MIP....$5.00

Steam Powered

During the early part of the century until about 1930, though not employed to any great extent, live steam power was used to activate toys such as large boats, novelty toys, and model engines.
See also Boats; Trains.

Accessory, airplane runabout, WK, planes suspended from canopy w/2 flags, round base, 10½", EX, A.............$325.00
Accessory, bandsaw, CI, 6¾", VG, A $470.00
Accessory, butcher at chopping block, Bing, pnt tin, beveled base, 5" L, VG, A...$85.00

Accessory, artist with palette and paint brush standing at easel with landscape painting, painted tin, 5", VG, A, $1,100.00. (Photo courtesy Noel Barrett Auctions)

Accessory, clown acrobat, pnt tin, 5½", G+, A $165.00
Accessory, coal miners, Germany, pnt tin, 1 chips away while the other turns roofed crank, oblong base, 9¼", VG, A .$300.00

Accessory, cottages on mountain, painted tin, heated water runs down slope onto footed square pan-shaped base, 7", VG, A, $550.00. (Photo courtesy Bertoia Auctions)

Accessory, Cyclone Pump, tin windmill w/electric motor on base, 16½", VG+, A $375.00
Accessory, dirigible ride, pnt tin, dbl wheels on trestle tower w/gondolas under hot air dirigibles, 12", VG, A $775.00

Accessory, drill press, Bing, 9", EX, A $500.00
Accessory, Ferris wheel, Doll, tin, 6 gondolas w/compo figures, hand-op or steam-powered, 17", VG, A $1,975.00

Accessory, Ferris wheel, Doll, tin with composition figures, wheel between two trestle towers on base, hand-powered or steam-powered, 27x22", EX, A, $22,000.00. (Photo courtesy Bertoia Auctions)

Accessory, fountain, Germany, sq ftd base w/railing at 4 corners, side flywheel, 8" sq, GIB, A......................................$110.00
Accessory, fountain, Marklin, rnd tin dish w/cherub-like figure on pedestal center, w/twin piston pump, 9x17", rstr, A ..$900.00
Accessory, grindstone, CI, 6", VG, A..............................$325.00
Accessory, lathe, CI, 8", VG, A.......................................$475.00
Accessory, roundabout, Doll, 4 compo figures in open chairs suspended from canopy, pulley on side of base, 9", EX, A.$415.00
Accessory, roundabout, MK/Germany, tin, 3 riders in open chairs on trestle tower on base housing steam pulley, 9", EX, A $275.00
Accessory, sled ride, Doll, tiny figure on sled rides down slope, chain driven, 5", G+, A..$110.00
Accessory, stamping machine, Bing, VG, A $475.00
Accessory, Village Blacksmith, Ives, diecut paper litho figures of 2 blacksmiths working, 9x10", EXIB, A....................$500.00
Accessory, water bucket tower, pnt tin w/decaled detail, litho tin American flag atop, 15", Fair, A.............................$175.00
Accessory, well, Germany, pnt tin w/corrugated roof over rnd well w/crank & pulley system, beveled base, 12", G+, A....$130.00
Accessory, whimsical depiction of people working & rabbits riding horses, Ives, ca 1870, 22", EXIB, A $650.00
Accessory, workshop, Weeden #65, complete, VG, A....$100.00

Accessory, windmill, painted tin, beveled base, 18", EX, A1, $125.00.

Steam Car, pressed steel & CI, early type w/open bench seat, spoke wheels, 15½", VG+, A $180.00
Steam Engine, Bing #10/111/4, overtype, VG, A $300.00
Steam Engine, Bing #130/272, overtype, VG+, A..........$875.00
Steam Engine, Doll #320/4, vertical, CI base & whistle, water glass & burner, 14½", VG, A $200.00
Steam Engine, Doll #365, dbl cylinder, horizontal, VG, A ...$300.00
Steam Engine, Ernst Plank #420, Rapid Boch, VG, A ...$250.00
Steam Engine, Jenson #70, horizontal, electric w/marine engine, EXIB, A...$75.00
Steam Engine, Marklin, mk Union, w/pinstriping & litho tile base, rare, VG, A..$1,750.00
Steam Engine, Marklin #4098/8, w/water glass, steam gauge, water pump, burner & governor, no dynamo, ftd base, VG, A $1,050.00
Steam Engine, Marklin #4106/7, mk ABC, vertical, 16", VG, A $600.00
Steam Engine, Marklin #4140/5½, horizontal, 13¾" w/11½x13" base, incomplete o/w VG, A $1,650.00
Steam Engine, Marx, vertical, w/3 of 8 accessories, VGIB, A..$125.00
Steam Engine, Marx Linemar, w/orig plastic accessories, 7x9" base, VGIB, A $100.00
Steam Engine, Schoenner, vertical, 19½", EX, A $1,265.00
Steam Engine, Schoenner #112/2 'Vulkan,' ca 1900, horizontal, VG, A $325.00
Steam Engine, Weeden #2, vertical, G (w/orig wooden box), A $150.00
Steam Engine, Weeden #38 Walking Beam, w/wooden base & engine platform, G (w/orig wooden box), A...........$135.00
Steam Engine, Weeden #7, VG (w/orig wooden box), A.$250.00

Steam Engine, Marklin #4112/14, 21½" tall with 15x16" base, complete, EX, A, $4,500.00. (Photo courtesy Randy Inman Auctions)

Steam Plant, Bing #10/110/3, w/6" flywheel, VG, A...**$2,100.00**
Steam Plant, Jensen, electrically fired boiler powers dynamo & electric light, wood base, 9½x15", EX, A **$325.00**
Steam Plant, Marklin, horizontal brass boiler on pnt tin 'brick' burner, engine on cast base, 14" sq, VGIB, A..........**$450.00**
Steam Plant, Marklin, mk Tandem-Verbund Machine Patent Steurer Modell 1905, beveled base, 35x24" sq, EX, A...........**$25,300.00**
Steam Roller, Bing, traction engine, 9", VG, A..............**$550.00**
Steam Roller, Bing #130/740, w/reversing gear & whistle, 6¾", VG, A **$350.00**
Steam Roller, Doll, w/steam gauge, whistle & waterglass, 12½" L, VG, A **$450.00**
Steam Roller, Fleischmann #155/1, incomplete o/w VG, A..**$200.00**
Steam Roller, Mamod #SR 1, 9¾", G (w/orig cb box), A.**$125.00**
Steam Roller, Weeden #644, 10½", G+, A......................**$450.00**
Steam Roller, Weeden #646, VG, A **$150.00**
Steam Wagon, Mamod, pressed steel & CI, 16", G+, A.**$100.00**
Tractor, brass & steel, early model w/roof over driver's seat, spoke wheels, 12½", Fair+, A....................................**$125.00**

Steiff

Margaret Steiff made the first of her felt toys in 1880, stuffing them with lamb's wool. Later followed toys of velvet, plush, and wool; and in addition to the lamb's wool stuffing, she used felt scraps, excelsior, and kapok as well. In 1897 and 1898 her trademark was a paper label printed with an elephant; from 1900 to 1905 her toys carried a circular tag with an elephant logo that was different than the one she had previously used. The most famous 'button in ear' trademark was registered on December 20, 1904. In 1904 and 1905 the button with an elephant (extremely rare) and the blank button (which is also rare) were used. The button with Steiff and the underscored or trailing 'F' was used until 1948, and the raised script button is from the 1950s.

Steiff teddy bears, perhaps the favorite of collectors everywhere, are characterized by their long thin arms with curved wrists and paws that extend below their hips. Buyer beware: The Steiff company is now making many replicas of their old bears. For more information about Steiff's buttons, chest tags, and stock tags as well as the inspirational life of Margaret Steiff and the fascinating history of Steiff toys, we recommend *Button in Ear Book* and *The Steiff Book of Teddy Bears*, both by Jurgen and Marianne Cieslik; *Teddy Bears and Steiff Animals, 2nd* and *3rd Series*, by Margaret Fox Mandel; *Teddy Bear Treasury, Volume II*, by Ken Yenke; *4th Teddy Bear and Friends Price Guide* by Linda Mullins; *Collectible German Animals Value Guide* by Dee Hockenberry; and *Steiff Sortiment 1947 – 1995* by Gunther Pefiffer. (This book is in German; however, the reader can discern the size of the item, year of production, and price estimation.)

Note: The following listings are auction prices.

See also Character, TV, and Movie Collectibles; Disney.

Bear, 14", 1905, blond mohair, shoe-button eyes, VG, A, $2,070.00; Bear, 8½", 1915, gold mohair, shoe-button eyes, no ID, EX, A, $1,380.00; Bear, 20", 1905, gold long mohair, shoe-button eyes, EX, A, $8,900.00. (Photo courtesy Skinner, Inc.)

Bear, 3½", 1950s, honey blond mohair, blk bead eyes, no-pad style, jtd, no ID, VG, A **$100.00**
Bear, 4", 1905, blond mohair, shoe-button eyes, no-pad style, jtd, ear button, EX+, A **$750.00**
Bear, 5", 1910, blond mohair, shoe-button eyes, no-pad style, jtd, working rattle, no ID, EX, A **$400.00**
Bear, 5", 1910, blond mohair, shoe-button eyes, no-pad style, jtd, ear button, G, A **$375.00**
Bear, 5½", 1930, blond mohair, glass eyes, no-pad style, dressed in outfit, EX, A **$350.00**

Horse on Wheels, 21x17", white mohair with brown spots, glass eyes, ear button, VG, A, $200.00; Bear, 14", 1905, gold mohair, shoe-button eyes, squeaker, ear button, VG, A, $1,950.00; Bear, 17", 1905, gold mohair, shoe-button eyes, VG, A, $4,885.00. (Photo courtesy Skinner, Inc.)

Bear, 8", 1905, blond mohair, shoe-button eyes, no ID, VG, A $690.00
Bear, 9½", 1910, blond mohair, shoe-button eyes, pads, jtd, no ID, VG, A...$635.00
Bear, 10", 1905, gold mohair, shoe-button eyes pads, jtd, no ID, VG, A $435.00

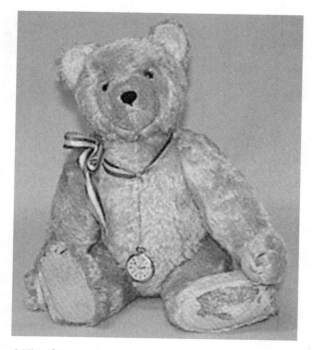

Bear, 20", white mohair, glass eyes, red, white, and blue neck ribbon with stop watch, EX, A, $770.00. (Photo courtesy Bertoia Auctions)

Bear, 12", 1930s, tan mohair, glass eyes, pads, jtd, no ID, VG, A...$490.00
Bear, 12½", 1905, lt apricot mohair, shoe-button eyes, pads, jtd, ear button, VG, A $1,600.00
Bear, 12½", 1950s, yel mohair, glass eyes, pads, jtd, ear button, EX, A...$550.00
Bear, 13", 1908, blond mohair, shoe-button eyes, pads, jtd, leather muzzle over snout, underscored FF button, EX, A..$1,950.00
Bear, 13", 1915, blond mohair, shoe-button eyes, long snout, pads, jtd, underscored button, VG, A $350.00
Bear, 13", 1930s, blond mohair, glass eyes, pads, jtd, ear button, VG, A...$150.00
Bear, 15½", 1905, gold mohair, shoe-button eyes, pads, jtd, ear button, G, A...$1,840.00
Bear, 16", 1905, gold mohair, shoe-button eyes, pads, jtd, blank ear button, fragments of wht tag, VG, A $4,465.00
Bear, 17", 100th Anniversary certificate #3834, gold mohair, plastic eyes, pads, jtd, ear button, EXIB, A $230.00
Bear, 20", 1906, wht curly mohair, shoe-button eyes, pads, jtd, underscored FF button, EX, A $12,650.00
Bear, 20", 1910, yel curly mohair, shoe-button eyes, pads, jtd, VG, A...$4,025.00
Bear, 30", 1940s-50s, blond mohair, glass eyes, pads, jtd, script ear button, VG, A $1,950.00
Bear on All Fours, 5½", 1930s, cream mohair, brn eyes, underscored button, partial tag, VG, A..........................$650.00
Bear on All Fours, 9x14", 1950s, lt mohair w/airbrushed details, brn eyes, no ID, EX, A..$200.00

Bear on Wheels, 21" long, light brown with shoe-button eyes, cast-iron spoke wheels on metal frame, G, A, $230.00. (Photo courtesy Noel Barrett Auctions)

Cow on Wheels, 12", brn & wht, bell around neck, w/growler, CI wheels, VG, A $600.00
Dinosaur (Brosus), 12½", 1960s, beige & yel mohair, goggle-eyed, no ID, EX, A $230.00
Dinosaur (Brosus), 26", 1960s, multi-colored mohair, goggle-eyed, no ID, EX, A $400.00

Camel, 10½", wooly-like fur and felt, EX, A, $250.00. (Photo courtesy Randy Inman Auctions)

Dinosaur (Stegosaurus Dinos), 12", 1960s, mc mohair w/yel underbody, bony backbone, goggle-eyed, no ID, EX, A $230.00
Dinosaur (T-Rex Tysus), 8", 1960s, yel & tan mohair, goggle-eyed, jtd arms, no ID, EX, A $200.00
Dinosaur (T-Rex Tysus), 17", 1960s, yel & tan mohair w/gr felt backbone, goggle-eyed, jtd arms, no ID, VG, A $230.00

School Kids, 10½", stuffed felt with blond mohair hair, fully clothed, VG, A, pair, $1,600.00; Puck the Dwarf, 8", 1914, stuffed felt with mohair beard and hat, glass eyes, jointed neck and shoulders, VG+, $290.00. (Photo courtesy Skinner, Inc.)

Elephant, 14", 1950s, beige mohair w/airbrushed details, glass eyes, red felt blanket, EX, A $120.00
Horse, 9", with mohair w/brn spots, blk nose & tail, tongue sticking out, G, A $145.00
Horse, 10½", gold silky plush, brn eyes, airbrushed facial features, brn hooves, underscored button, stock tag, EX, A $90.00
Lion on Wheels, CI wheels, w/growler, G, A..................$470.00
Santa Bear, 14", 1960s, standing upright in red & wht Santa suit holding toy bag, gold button, yel stock tag, EX, A ..$120.00
Stork, 6½", 1940s, wht & blk felt, glass eyes, celluloid beak, metal feet, EX, A $120.00

Strauss

Imaginative, high-quality, tin windup toys were made by Ferdinand Strauss (New York, later New Jersey) from the onset of World War I until the 1940s. For about fifteen years prior to his becoming a toy maker, he was a distributor of toys he imported from Germany. Though hard to find in good working order, his toys are highly prized by today's collectors, and when found in even very good to excellent condition, many are in the $500.00 and up range.

Advisor: Scott Smiles (S10)

Auto Dump Cart, VG+, A, $300.00. (Photo courtesy Randy Inman Auctions)

Air Devil, w/pilot, EX, from $500 to...............................$550.00
Big Show Circus Truck, VG $900.00
Boob McNutt, flat-hat version, Fair...............................$250.00
Boob McNutt, flat-hat version, VG $600.00
Bus De Luxe, w/driver, G...$500.00
Dandy Jim Clown Dancer, EX...$700.00
Dizzy Lizzy, NMIB..$500.00
Emergency Tow Car #74, nonworking o/w G+ $400.00
Emergency Tow Car #74, VG $1,200.00
Flying Airship, NMIB...$800.00
Graf Zeppelin Jr #2, EXIB, from $600 to.........................$750.00
Ham 'N Sam, EX $850.00
Inter-State Double-Decker Bus, 10", EX........................$750.00
Inter-State Double-Decker Bus, 10", VGIB................$1,000.00

Ham 'N Sam, NMIB, $1,250.00.

(Photo courtesy Richard Opfer Auctioneering, Inc.)

Play Golf (Just Like Daddy) No. 110, EXIB, A, $825.00.

(Photo courtesy Bertoia Auctions)

Jackie the Hornpipe Dancer, 9", EXIB.........................$1,150.00
Jazzbo Jim, EX...$600.00
Jazzbo Jim, EXIB, A...$700.00
Jenny the Balky Mule, EX..$450.00
Jenny the Balky Mule, EXIB..$550.00
Jitney Bus, EX...$425.00
Jolly Pals, EX..$475.00
Knock Out Prize Fighters, VG.......................................$350.00
Kraka Jack Irish Mail Car, EX.......................................$450.00
Leaping Lena Car, EX, from $450 to.................................$550.00

Spirit of St Louis, 7" W, VG..........................$325.00
Standard Oil Truck #73, NM..........................$500.00
Thrifty Tom's Jigger Bank, EX.......................$2,100.00
Timber Truck, VG....................................$500.00
Tip Top Dump Truck, NM.............................$1,000.00
Tip Top Porter, EXIB.................................$350.00

Long Haulage Truck #71, G+, $350.00. (Photo courtesy Richard Opfer Auctioneering, Inc.)

Lumber Tractor-Trailer, no lumber, G.........................$375.00
Porter Pushing Pup in Trunk, VG, A............................$600.00
Red Flash Racer #31, EX, from $700 to.........................$750.00
Rollo-Chair, litho tin, NMIB...................................$1,200.00
Santee Claus in Sleigh, EXIB..................................$1,750.00
Sparko, 5", EXIB..$300.00

Tombo Alabama Coon Jigger, EX, A, $775.00. (Photo courtesy Bertoia Auctions)

Tombo Alabama Coon Jigger, G..........................$400.00
Trackless Trolley/Twin Trolleys, VG....................$250.00

Travelchiks Boxcar, EX...$550.00
Travelchiks Boxcar, EXIB, A.................................$725.00
Trik Auto, no driver, VG..$300.00
Trik Auto, w/driver, EX...$450.00

Cement Truck, 1950s, opening hood, turquoise, black, and red, 22", NMIB, A, $465.00. (Photo courtesy Bertoia Auctions)

Water Sprinkler Truck #72, VG, $675.00. (Photo courtesy Richard Opfer Auctioneering, Inc)

What's It?, Fair...$275.00
What's It?, NMIB..$900.00
Wildfire, EXIB $350.00
Yell-O-Taxi, EX+ $700.00

Bulldozer, 1960s, red & yel, rubber treads, 11", G, A........$40.00
Cement Truck, 1960s, metal & plastic, from Thunderbolt fleet,
       13½", unused, MIB, A...$50.00
Delivery Truck, 1920s, electric lights, bl, 22", VG, A $100.00
Delivery Truck, 1930s, dk gr, 22", VG, A.....................$100.00

Structo

Pressed steel vehicles were made by Structo (Illinois) as early as 1920. They continued in business well into the 1960s, producing several army toys, trucks of all types, and firefighting and construction equipment.

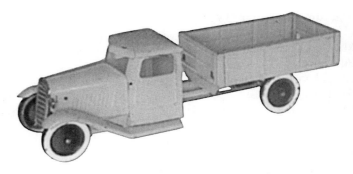

Delivery Truck, 1930s, light aqua, 21", EX, $775.00. (Photo courtesy Randy Inman Auctions)

Airport Mail Truck, 1920s, green with red hubs, 24", G, A, $3,520.00. (Photo courtesy Randy Inman Auctions)

Army Truck, 1930s, opening hood, 21", missing canvas top o/w
       VG, A $130.00
Auto Builder Dump Truck, w/up, 17", VG, A.................$250.00
Auto Builder Racer, w/up, 12", VG, A..........................$275.00
Auto Builder Roadster, w/up, 16", VG, A......................$485.00
Auto Builder Tractor, w/up, 11½", G, A.........................$155.00
Barrel Truck, w/up, 13", G, A..$65.00
Bearcat Racer, wing-nut wound spring motor, CI spoke wheels,
       Structo emb on radiator, 14", G $200.00

Dump Truck, metallic bl & orange w/red light on cab roof, 20",
       NMIB, A..$325.00
Dump Truck, 1920s, electric headlights & spotlight, unusual gr
       color, 23", VG, A..$465.00
Dump Truck, 1920s, electric lights, open bench seat w/slanted
       back on dump bed, disk wheels, 18", VG+ $275.00
Dump Truck, 1935, enclosed cab, side lever dump action, rubber
       tires, red & yel, 21", VG+, A $300.00
Dump Truck, 1950s, hydraulic, opening hood, 21", G+, A.$125.00
Dump Truck, 1960s, w/up, Toyland, 12", G+, A $40.00
Dump Truck, 1970s, mk Structo 22, Typhoon Fleet #303-2, yel,
       13", NRFB, A $135.00
Fire Aerial Ladder Truck, 1950s, mk SFD, 35", VG, A ..$130.00
Fire Dept Emergency Patrol, box van w/red light atop cab, 12",
       G, A $85.00
Fire Ladder Truck, w/top ladder & 2 side ladders, 28½", VG,
       A $150.00

Fire Pumper Truck, mk SFD, opening hood, w/ladders & hydrant, 23", EX+IB, A..................................$275.00

Fire Pumper Truck, mk SFD, opening hood, w/ladders & hydrant, 23", VG, A.....................................$175.00

Fix It Tow Truck, 12", NMIB, A $250.00

Jeep, rider, marked USAF on hood, fold-down windshield, open under-seat storage compartment, 25", EX, A, $275.00.

(Photo courtesy Noel Barrett Auctions)

Machinery Hauler, 1930s, flat bed w/chain pulley, 23", NM $300.00

Mobile Communications Truck, 1950s, 20", EXIB, A $165.00

Pile Driver, 11", G+, A $50.00

Police Patrol Van, 1920s, 17", EX $800.00

Sand Loader, 1920s, 12", G+, A $50.00

Sanitation Dept Truck, 18", G+, A...............................$100.00

Steam Shovel Truck, 1950s, opening hood, orange, 20", VG, $175.00. (Photo courtesy Randy Inman Auctions)

Stake Truck, 1930s, hinged sides, rubber tires, 22", EX ..$450.00

Tanker Truck, 1950s, mk Structo 66, w/up motor, all red, 13½", VG, A..$175.00

Tractor Pulling Trailers, 1920s, 8" tractor w/3 5" trailers, w/up, no tracks, G, A..................................$145.00

Truck Pulling Trailer, w/up, open cab, spoke wheels, 25", G, A $425.00

Truck w/Crane on Flatbed Trailer, 32", G, A $110.00

US Mail Truck, C-style cab w/screened box van, 16", G, A..$350.00

Vista Dome Horse Van, 22", EXIB, A $100.00

Teddy Bears

The history of old teddy bears goes way back to about 1902 – 1903. Today's collectors often find it difficult to determine exactly what company produced many of these early bears, but fortunately for them, there are many excellent books now available that contain a wealth of information on those early makers.

Interest in teddy bears has been increasing at a fast pace, and there are more and more collectors entering the market. This has lead to an escalation in the values of the early bears. Because most teddies were cherished childhood toys and were usually very well loved, many that survive are well worn, so an early bear in mint condition can be very valuable.

We would like to direct your attention to the books on the market that are the most helpful on the detailed history and identification of teddies. *A Collectors History of the Teddy Bear* by Patricia Schoonmaker; *Teddy Bears Past and Present (Volumes I and II)* and *American Teddy Bear Encyclopedia* by Linda Mullins; *Teddy Bears — A Complete Guide to History, Collecting, and Care,* by Sue Pearson and Dottie Ayers; *Teddy Bear Encyclopedia* and *Ultimate Teddy Bear Book* by Pauline Cockrill; *Teddy Bear Treasury, Volume II*, by Ken Yenke; and *Big Bear Book* by Dee Hockenberry. The reader can easily see that a wealth of information exists and that it is impossible in a short column such as this to give any kind of a definitive background. If you intend to be a knowledgeable teddy bear collector, it is essential that you spend time in study. Many of these books will be available at your local library or through dealers who specialize in bears.

See also Schuco; Steiff.

4½", 1940s, gold mohair w/lg glass eyes, EX.....................$75.00

8½", USA, deep golden mohair w/blk faceted shoe-button eyes, fully jtd, EX...$220.00

10", ca 1905, gold mohair w/felt pads, embroidered nose & mouth, brn claws, excelsior stuffing, EX $750.00

12", USA, 1920-30, gold mohair w/glass eyes, fully jtd, straw stuffing, EX $500.00

14½", USA, gold mohair w/brn & blk glass eyes, stitched nose, mouth & claws, padded paws, fully jtd, swivel head, EX $440.00

15", Merrythought, 1930s, curly cream mohair w/glass eyes, embroidered nose, mouth & claws, shaved muzzle, fully jtd, EX $600.00

17", Germany, deep golden mohair w/glass eyes, stitched snout & claws, fully jtd, EX, A...$550.00

17", JK Farnell, off white curly mohair with glass eyes, clipped and stitched snout and claws, padded paws, fully jointed, EX, A, $1,100.00. (Photo courtesy Bertoia Auctions)

17", USA, 1920s, gray mohair w/glass eyes, embroidered features, velveteen pads, fully jtd, VG, A.............................$150.00

18", pre-1915, tan mohair w/glass eyes, rpl pads & nose, VG, from $2400 to...$2,800.00

23", USA, short golden mohair with black button eyes, stitched snout and claws, fully jointed, hump on back, EX, A, $140.00.

(Photo courtesy Bertoia Auctions)

19", Herman, early 1900s, gold mohair w/shoe-button eyes, fabric nose, embroidered mouth, fully jtd, Herman, VG $175.00

20", Knickerbocker (?), 1950s, wht plush w/brn eyes, embroidered nose & mouth, shaved snout, wht velvet pads, EX, A $440.00

21", USA, mid-20th C, brn-tipped blond mohair, glass eyes, embroidered features, shaved muzzle, felt pads, crier, VG, A...$175.00

21", 1920s, beige mohair, blk shoe-button eyes, embroidered mouth & claws, long arms & lg feet, fully jtd, EX, A.............$1,175.00

21½", 1930s-40s, lt mohair, glass eyes, embroidered nose & claws, fully jtd, excelsior stuffing, G, A.....................$85.00

22", 1920s-30s, aqua rayon mohair w/glass eyes, embroidered nose & mouth, fully jtd, excelsior stuffing, VG, A ..$200.00

24", USA, ca 1920, blk mohair, brn glass eyes, embroidered features, velveteen pads, fully jtd, NM, A.................$1,600.00

25", Germany, golden mohair with glass eyes, clipped and stitched snout and claws, padded paws, fully jointed, EX, A, $600.00. (Photo courtesy Bertoia Auctions)

30", Ideal (?), 1920s, honey beige mohair, lg amber eyes, embroidered nose & mouth, jtd, G, A $325.00

34", Ideal, 1919, blond mohair w/glass eyes, embroidered features, fully jtd, NM...$2,500.00

Telephones

Novelty phones representing a well-known advertising or cartoon character are proving to be the focus of a lot of collector activity — the more recognizable the character the better. Telephones modeled after a product container are collectible too, and with the intense interest currently being shown in anything advertising related, competition is sometimes stiff and values are rising.

Bart Simpson, Columbia, 1990s, MIB, $40.00.

Alvin (Alvin & the Chipmunks), 1984, MIB.................$50.00
Batmobile, Columbia, 1990, MIB, from $25 to.................$35.00
Bugs Bunny, Warner Exclusive, MIB, from $60 to............$70.00
Darth Vader, 1983, MIB.....................................$200.00
Garfield, MIB..$50.00
Ghostbusters, Remco, 1987, MIB..............................$30.00
Kermit the Frog, Henson Associates/AT&T, 1983, EX+IB.$125.00
Mickey Mouse, Western Electric, 1976, MIB.................$200.00
Poppin' Fresh, Pillsbury, 1984, MIB........................$100.00
Power Rangers, MIP..$30.00
Raggedy Ann & Andy, Pan Phone, 1983, MIB.................$75.00
Roy Rogers, 1950s, plastic wall type, MIB.................$100.00
R2-D2 (Star Wars), head spins, 12", MIB....................$100.00
Snoopy as Joe Cool, 1980s, MIB..............................$50.00
Spider-Man, REC Sound, 1994, MIB............................$30.00
Star Trek Enterprise, 1993, MIB.............................$50.00
Strawberry Shortcake, MIB...................................$75.00
Superman, early rotary dial, M.............................$500.00
Ziggy, 1989, MIB..$75.00

Tonka

Since the mid-'40s, the Tonka Company (Minnesota) has produced an extensive variety of high-quality painted metal trucks, heavy equipment, tractors, and vans.

Our values are for items with the original paint. A repainted item is worth much less.

Aerial Ladder Truck and other Fire Trucks, see TFD
Airport Baggage Train, see Tonka Airlines
Allied Van Lines Semi, cabover, orange & blk, 22", VG+, A $125.00
Allied Van Lines Semi, slant-front cab w/plastic windows, orange w/blk & wht trim, 16", NM $50.00
Ambulance, 1960s, w/gurney & 5 figures, 19", G $75.00

Army Bulldozer GR-2-243, 1960s, rubber treads, 12", VG, $100.00. (Photo courtesy Richard Opfer Auctioneering, Inc.)

Army Troop Carrier GR-2-243, 1960s, 14", EXIB, $125.00.

(Photo courtesy Richard Opfer Auctioneering, Inc.)

Backhoe Truck, 1960s, EX...............................$200.00
Bottom Dump, 1960s, NMIB $350.00
Bulldozer, orange, rubber treads, 9", VG, A $75.00
Camper Pickup, #530, 1960s, NMIB.......................$325.00
Car Carrier, 1960s, NMIB $300.00

Golf Club Tractor, 12", G, A, $50.00. (Photo courtesy Richard Opfer Auctioneering, Inc.)

Car Carrier, 1970s, VG $50.00
Cargo King, 1950s, aluminum trailer, 24", VG $125.00
Cement Truck, 1960s, 15", G, A $50.00
Cement Truck, 1960s, 15", NMIB $175.00
Cross Country Freight Truck, 1950s, 23", G, A $200.00
Dragline, 1960s, NMIB....................................$300.00
Gambles Pickup, 1960s, 13", G $75.00
Gambles Semi, 1950s, EX+, A $1,875.00
Gasoline Tanker, 1950s, 15", EX, A $300.00
Gasoline Tanker, 1950s, 15", G, A $175.00
Grain Hauler, #550, 1952, 23", VG......................$150.00
Hydraulic Dump Truck, 1960s, 13", G, A $35.00
Jeep Pumper, 1960s, complete, 11", NMIB $230.00
Jeepster, 1960s, simulated cloth top up, wht sidewalls, 13", VG+,
    A $75.00
Livestock Semi, 1950s, cabover, 22", EX $300.00
Livestock Semi, 1950s, long-nose, 24", VG+, A...........$175.00

Lumber Truck, interchangeable body, with lumber, 19", EX, $400.00. (Photo courtesy Randy Inman Auctions)

Marshall Field & Co Semi, 1940s, 22", NMIB, A $1,475.00
Mighty Dozer & Scraper, 1970s, plastic wheels, 33", VGIB,
    A...$250.00
Mobil Clam, 1960s, 21", EX $225.00
Parcel Delivery Van, 1950s, 12", NM $400.00
Pickup Truck, 1950s, 13", G $75.00
Pickup Truck & Trailer, 1960s, 22" overall, G $75.00
Platform Stake Truck, 1950s, open sides w/stakes, 16½", G, A .$140.00
Power Boom Loader Truck, 1960s, 17", EX....................$325.00
Ramp Hoist Truck, 1960s, 19", VG......................$175.00
Rescue Squad, 1960s, 13", NM, A.........................$525.00
Rescue Squad, 1960s, 13", VG, A........................$200.00
Sanitary System Garbage Truck, 1950s, w/hydraulic front loader,
    17", EX, A $350.00
Semi w/Flat-Bed Trailer, 1950s, wood trailer, EX...........$300.00
Serv-I-Car, 1960s, 9", EX+ $100.00
Sportsman Pickup, 1960s, 13", G, A $65.00
Sportsman Pickup w/Boat on Top, 1960s, VG+ $125.00
Sportsman Pickup w/Boat on Trailer, 1960s, VG+ $125.00
State Hi-Way Dept Big Mike Hydraulic Dump Truck, 1950s,
    15", EX, A $450.00
State Hi-Way Dept Dump Truck w/Snow Plow, 1950s, straight
    plow, 15", VG $200.00
State Hi-Way Dept Dump Truck w/Snow Plow, 1960s, V-shaped
    plow, 18", G, A $175.00
State Hi-Way Dept Pickup Truck, 1950s, 13", EX+, A ..$100.00

State Hi-Way Dept Road Grader, 1950s, 17", G+, A $55.00
State Hi-Way Dept Truck w/Dragline on Low-Boy Trailer,
    cream, 32", VG $150.00
State Hi-Way Dept Truck w/Steam Shovel on Low-Boy Trailer,
    1950s, red, 26", EX, A $275.00
Steel Carrier, cabover, 9½", G..........................$150.00
Steel Carrier, long-nose, 24", G........................$125.00
Suburban Pumper Truck, 1950s, red, 17", NMIB...........$400.00
Suburban Pumper Truck, 1950s, red, 17", VG, A $150.00
Suburban Pumper Truck, 1960s, wht, 18", VG, A $125.00
TFD Aerial Ladder Truck, 1959, wht, EX $500.00
TFD Hydraulic Aerial Ladder Truck, 1960s, red, 32", VG, A ..$110.00
TFD Tanker, 1960s, 15", G, A............................$200.00

Tonka Airlines Baggage Train, 1960s, three-piece with plastic luggage, VG, $150.00. (Photo courtesy Randy Inman Auctions)

Tonka Airlines Baggage Train, 1960s, 6-pc w/plastic luggage, EX,
    A $175.00
Tonka Airlines Baggage Train, 1960s, 6-pc w/plastic luggage,
    NMIB...$600.00
Tonka Farms Horse Van, 1960s, w/2 plastic horses, 13", VG+,
    A $150.00
Tonka Farms Livestock Truck, 1960s, 17", VG, A $150.00
Tonka Farms Stake Truck, 1950s, 14", NM................$300.00
Tonka Farms Stake Truck, 1950s, 14", VG, A $100.00
Tonka Farms Stake Truck & Horse Trailer, 1960s, 23" overall,
    G+ $125.00
Tonka Service Van, 1960s, 13", NM+ $500.00
Tonka Service Van, 1960s, 13", VG $125.00
Tonka Tanker, 1960s, plastic trailer tank, 28", EX, A $300.00
Utility Truck, 1950s, stake bed, EX $275.00

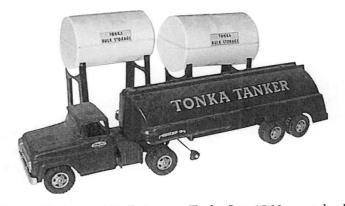

Tonka Tanker and Bulk Storage Tanks Set, 1960s, metal cab with plastic tank trailer and two storage tanks, 28" truck and 11" tall tanks, VG, $400.00. (Photo courtesy Randy Inman Auctions)

Wagoneer w/Snowmobile on Trailer, 1960s, MIB..........$200.00
Wild Animal Circus Semi, 1960s, 26", VG, A $175.00

Contractor Set, #0191, 1933 – 41, NMIB, A, $600.00. (Photo courtesy Randy Inman Auctions)

Winnebago Motor Home, metal and plastic, 23", GIB, A, $100.00. (Photo courtesy Richard Opfer Auctioneering, Inc.)

Delta Jet, 1954-55, silver, NM $35.00
DeSoto Airflow, #0118, 1935-39, lt bl, NM.................$60.00
Farm Set, #6800, 1958, complete, MIB.......................$475.00
Ferrari Racer, 1956, gr w/gold driver, 6", NM..............$40.00
Ford, 1950, yel, 3", VG+, N2 ....$25.00

Wrecker, 1960s, curved bed, wht, 12", G, A $100.00
Wrecker, 1960s, straight bed, wht w/red crane, EX.........$175.00
Wrecker, 1960s, straight bed, wht w/red crane, NMIB...$300.00

Ford Coupe (The New Ford), 2½", EXIB, A, $110.00. (Photo courtesy Randy Inman Auctions)

Tootsietoy

The first diecast Tootsietoys were made by the Samuel Dowst Company in 1906 when they reproduced the Model T Ford in miniature. Dowst merged with Cosmo Manufacturing in 1926 to form the Dowst Manufacturing Company and continued to turn out replicas of the full-scale vehicles in actual use at the time. After another merger in 1961, the company became known as the Stombecker Corporation. Over the years, many types of wheels and hubs were utilized, varying in both style and material. The last all-metal car was made in 1969; recent Tootsietoys mix plastic components with the metal and have soft plastic wheels. Early prewar mint-in-box toys are scarce and command high prices on today's market.

Aero-Dawn, #4660, 1934, red, NM.................................$70.00
Airplane Set, 12-pc, EX+IB $415.00
Autogyro, #4859, 1934, early wheel type, NM $135.00
Biplane, #4650, 1926, NM $115.00
Bleriot Plane, #4482, 1910, NM....................................$120.00
Box Truck, #234, 1942-47, 3", M...................................$25.00
Buck Rogers Flash Blast Attack Ship, 1930s, 4½", EX+IB..$300.00
Buick Coupe (1927), #6003, bl & blk, EX+.....................$85.00
Buick Series 50 Coupe (1924), #4636, 1924, 3", EX.........$90.00
Buick Touring Sedan, #4641, 1925, 78mm, VG $200.00
Carrier, #1036, NM..$35.00
Chevy Coupe, #231, 1940-41, med aqua, NM.................$40.00

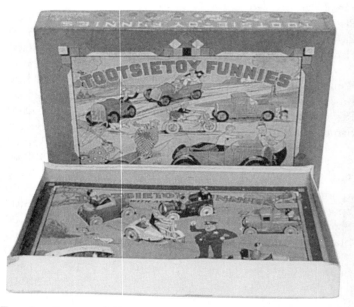

Funnies Set, six different vehicles with comic figures, very rare, EXIB, A, $1,430.00. (Photo courtesy Randy Inman Auctions)

Ford LTD, 1969, bl, 4½", EX, N2 ....$25.00
Ford Model A Sedan (1929), #6665, orange, EX+ $60.00
Ford Station Wagon, 1963, 6", VG+, N2.......................$25.00

Greyhound GMC Scenicruiser, 1950s, 7", EXIB, $100.00.

(Photo courtesy Randy Inman Auctions)

High-Wing Plane, #107, 1932, NM $80.00
Highway Set, #4700, 1949, complete, MIB $450.00
Huber Star Farm Tractor, #4654, no tow loop, NM+ $175.00
Insurance Patrol Car, #104, 1932-34, red, NM $35.00
Jeepster, 1949-52, yel, 3", NM....................................$30.00
Jumbo Coupe, #1017, 1942-46, red w/wht top, EX...........$40.00
Libby's Frozen Food Truckload Sale Tractor-Trailer, 9½", EX (in
    box mk Tootsietoy Van), A..................................$240.00
Los Angeles Zeppelin, 5", G+, A..................................$60.00
Mack Anti-Aircraft Gun, #4643, 1931, NM.....................$65.00
Motorcycle w/Sidecar, yel w/spoke wheels, w/driver & passenger,
    3⅛", VG, A..$275.00
Motors Set, 8-pc 4¼" vehicle set, NMIB, A..................$200.00

Speedway Set, eight-piece set with cars numbered 1 – 8, complete, EXIB, $2,300.00. (Photo courtesy Noel Barrett Auctions)

Motors Set, 9-pc w/plane & 8 vehicles, 4¼", NMIB, A ...$50.00
Oldsmobile 88 Convertible, 1960-68, lt gr, 6", NM..........$30.00
Open Touring Car, #232, 1940-41, gr, NM $55.00
Pan American Airport Set, 12-pc, NMIB......................$750.00
Playtime Toys Miniature Set, #7005, 1933, 10-pc, rare, EXIB ..$1,000.00
Racer #23, 1927, w/driver, sm, rare, NM $85.00
RC 190 Machinery Hauler, 1963-66, NM.........................$65.00
Rescue Helicopter, #2552, 1975-79, red & wht w/bl blades,
    NM $10.00
Seaplane, #4660, purple, NM $100.00

Taxicabs Set, four sedans and one tow truck, EXIB, A, $1,430.00. (Photo courtesy Randy Inman Auctions)

Thunderbird Coupe, 1955-60, 3", NM............................$25.00
Tow Truck, #2485, 1960s, wht w/red trim, NM $45.00
Train Set (Passenger or Freight), #4626 or #4647, 1925, EX, ea
    set $90.00
US Army Airplane, #119, 1936, NM $75.00
Waco Dive Bomber, #718, 1937, NM $130.00
Zephyr Railcar, #117, 1935, gr, 4", rare, NM.................$125.00

Tops and Other Spinning Toys

    Tops are among the oldest toys in human history. Homer in *The Iliad*, Plato in the *Republic*, and Virgil in *The Aeneid* mention tops. They are found in nearly all cultures, ancient and modern.

    There are seven major categories: 1) The twirler — spun by the twisting action of fingers upon the axis. Examples are Teetotums, Dreidels, advertising spinners, and Tippe Tops. 2) The supported top — started with a string while the top is supported upright. These include 'recuperative,' having a string that automatically rewinds (Namurs); 'separative,' with a top that detaches from the launcher; 'spring launched,' which is spun using a wound spring; 'pump' or 'helix,' whereby a twisted rod is pumped to spin the top; and 'flywheel-' or 'inertia wheel-powered.' 3) The peg top — spun by winding a string around the peg of the top which is then thrown. 4) The whip top — which is kept spinning by the use of a whip. 5) The Yo-yo or return top. 6) The gyroscope. 7) The Diavuolo or Diablo.

See also Character, TV, and Movie Collectibles; Chein, Miscellaneous; Political; Yo-yos.

Air-Powered, Cracker Jack, red, wht & bl, Dowsy, Chicago, M...$16.00
Air-Powered, Poll Parrot Shoes, yel, NM.......................$16.00
Aladdin Ball & Top, helix rod-powered, early 1900s, EXIB...$550.00
Archimeds Flying Top Mars (advertised as New Boomerang), 5 blades propel on swivel bar, Lehmann, 8½", EX......$200.00
Autogyro Horse Race, lead & wire, flywheel mechanism w/4 jockeys on horses, Britains, 11" L, EX..................$1,000.00
Circus Horse & Rider, lead w/wire & tin, horse & female rider on rods attached to base, 7", VG.............................$375.00
Dancing Couple w/Arms Entwined, japanned & polychromed CI, she in lead bell-shaped skirt, Ives, 3½", EX.......$135.00
Disk, maroon & red wood flat-top w/natural wood holder, 3½" dia, EX...$45.00
Disk, red & natural wood w/gr stripes, w/hdl, 4" dia, EX ..$75.00
Game, Big Top, battery-op, plastic, Marx, MIB...............$35.00
Game, Brownie Kick-In, litho tin, MH Miller, VGIB......$50.00
Game, Double Diablos, Parker Bros, 1930s, EXIB............$60.00

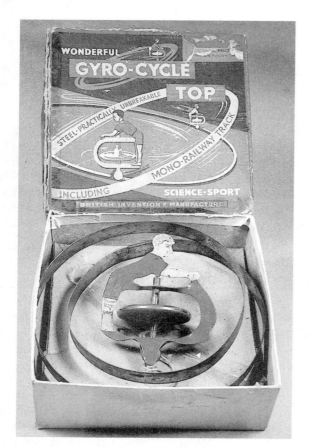

Gyro-Cycle Top, boy rides circular track, British, EXIB, $600.00. (Photo courtesy Bruce Middleton)

Game, Voyage Around the World Gyro-Aero, France, EXIB...$500.00
Hummer, inverted wood beehive shape w/mc stripes, 2½" dia, VG...$415.00
Hummer, litho tin, clown-head knob w/wooden hat, German, 8", VG...$575.00
Hummer, wht celluloid ball w/mc stripes, 7", EX............$415.00

Magic Blossom Top (Blumen Kreisal), litho tin with clear plastic globe, crank-lever action, EX+IB, A, $165.00.

Manur, wooden ball w/brass string housing, EX...............$20.00
Merry-Go-Round, 2 figures spiral down rod, tin & wood, 12", EX...$200.00
Peg Top, Chicago Twister, wood, Duncan, #329, MIP......$20.00
Peg Top, Helix Road Launcher, advertises Kinney Shoes, VG .$15.00
Peg Top, Tournament, wood Duncan #349, MIP.............$20.00
Peg Top, Twin Spin, wood, Duncan #310, MIP $20.00
Peg Top, Whistler, wood, Duncan #320, MIP..................$20.00
Ratchet Ballerina, litho tin, Marx, NM, from $125 to ...$150.00
Recuperative, natural wood w/pnt stripes, wood string housing, EX, from $75 to $100.00
Recuperative, wood, 6-sided string housing over ovoid body, G $85.00
Spinner, Bakelite, Alemite Motor Oil/Keep Your Car Running Like a Top, NM...$25.00
Spinner, Buster Brown/Brown-Bilt Shoes, blk & red lettering on yel w/red trim, EX $45.00
Spinner, Cracker Jack, M, from $45 to.........................$75.00
Spinner, Heads I Win/Tails You Lose, shaped like a pointing spaniel, NM...$25.00
Spinner, litho tin, man w/beer mug, Hvem Betaler on hat, spin to see who pays, NM...$85.00
Spinner, Nolde's American Made Breads & Cakes, red & wht, NM...$30.00
Spinner, Robin Hood Shoes, M, from $45 to...................$75.00
Spinner, Tastybake Cakes & Pies, M, from $45 to...........$75.00
Spinner, Tip Top Bread, plastic, NM..........................$10.00
Supported, pressed board disc w/graphics of boy shooting a toy gun, M...$60.00
Tip Tray, Canada Dry, dimple in center to spin, G............$20.00
Tip Tray, SS Pierce, Wine & Spirits Merchants..., dimple in center on which to spin, M...$60.00

Trains

Some of the earliest trains (from ca 1860) were made of tin or cast iron, smaller versions of the full-scale steam-powered trains that transversed America from the east to the west. Most were made to simply be pushed or pulled along, though some had clockwork motors. Electric trains were produced as early as the late nineteenth century. Three of the largest manufacturers were Lionel, Ives, and American Flyer.

Lionel trains have been made since 1900. Until 1915 they produced only standard gauge models (measuring 2½" between the rails). The smaller O gauge (1¼") they introduced at that time proved to be highly successful, and the company grew until by 1955 it had become the largest producer of toys in the world. Until discontinued in 1940, standard gauge trains were produced on a limited scale, but O and 027 gauge models dominated the market. Production dwindled and nearly stopped in the mid-1960s, but the company was purchased by General Mills in 1969, and they continue to produce a very limited number of trains today.

The Ives company had been a major producer of toys since 1896. They were the first to initiate manufacture of the O gauge train and at first used only clockwork motors to propel them. Their first electric trains (in both O and #1 gauge) were made in 1910, but because electricity was not yet a common commodity in many areas, clockwork production continued for several years. By 1920, #1 gauge was phased out in favor of standard gauge. The company continued to prosper until the late 1920s when it floundered and was bought jointly by American Flyer and Lionel. American Flyer soon turned their interest over to Lionel, who continued to make Ives trains until 1933.

The American Flyer company had produced trains for several years, but it wasn't until it was bought by AC Gilbert in 1937 that it became successful enough to be considered a competitor of Lionel. They're best noted for their conversion from the standard (wide gauge) three-rail system to the two-rail S gauge (⅞") and the high-quality locomotives, passenger, and freight cars they produced in the 1950s. Interest in toy trains waned during the space-age decade of the 1960s. As a result, sales declined, and in 1966 the company was purchased by Lionel. Today both American Flyer and Lionel trains are being made from the original dies by Lionel Trains Inc., privately owned.

For more information we recommend *Collecting Toy Trains, An Identification and Value Guide*, by Richard O'Brien.

Advisors: Gary Mosholder (G1); Greg Stout

See also Buddy L (for that company's Outdoor Railroad); Cast Iron, Trains; Paper-Lithographed Toys.

AMERICAN FLYER

Accessory, #257 talking station, VGIB $525.00
Accessory, #268 remote control switch, MIB (sealed) $75.00
Accessory, #593 signal tower, NMIB................................$500.00
Accessory, #709 talking station, EXIB $450.00
Accessory, #764 Express Office, MIB...............................$500.00

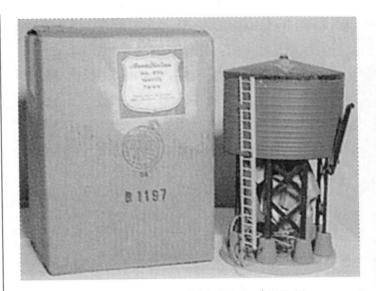

Accessory, #596 water tower, NM+IB, A, $300.00. (Photo courtesy Stout Auctions)

Accessory, #769A aircraft beacon, NMIB.....................$200.00
Accessory, #772 checkerboard water tower, EXIB $200.00
Accessory, #779 oil drum loader, MIB............................$825.00
Accessory, #23780 Gabe the Lamplighter, NMIB.......$1,500.00
Accessory, #35764 accessory kit, EX+IB $500.00
Car, #201 Pacific Fruit Express metal reefer, burgundy, VGIB...$125.00
Car, #715 unloading car, w/auto, controller, track section, paperwork & wrapper, NMIB.......................................$190.00
Car, #910 Gilbert Chemicals tank car, EXIB.................$325.00
Car, #2461 transformer car, red transformer, no lettering, VG+IB $475.00

Car, #4011 caboose, EXIB, A, $1,350.00. (Photo courtesy Stout Auctions)

Car, #24016 MKT boxcar, VG $550.00
Car, #24319 Penn Salt Chemicals tank car, EXIB..........$675.00
Car, #24323 Baker's Chocolate tank car, gray ends, VGIB .$425.00
Car, #24409 Northern Pacific boxcar, EX+IB $1,250.00
Car, #24422 Great Northern reefer, gr, M....................$250.00

Car, #24536 Monon flatcar, w/2 American Flyer trailers, EX $1,300.00

Car, #24557 US Navy Jeep transport flatcar, w/2 orig jeeps, EXIB...$350.00

Car, #24577 Illinois Central jet engine transport flatcar, knuckle couplers, EXIB $250.00

Car, #25057 Exploding TNT boxcar w/button, contact rail & instructions, VG+IB.....................................$250.00

Car, #25515 rocket sled car, NMIB $500.00

Car, #33812 rocket launcher car, w/rocket, controller, track section & inserts, EXIB $150.00

Loco, #70 GP, NMIB...$525.00

Loco, #234 Chesapeake & Ohio GP7, short step variation, EX...$425.00

Loco, #372 Union Pacific GP, Gilbert variation, EX+ ...$400.00

Loco, #499 New Haven EP-5, EX $375.00

Loco, #2338 Milwaukee Road GP, NMIB.....................$600.00

Loco, #2349 Northern Pacific GP, gold lettering, NMIB.$1,500.00

Loco & Tender, #112 Hudson, EXIB.............................$525.00

Loco & Tender, #151 NYC, MIB (sealed) $400.00

Loco & Tender, #314A W Pennsylvania 4-6-2 & tender, whistle inside, retrofitted w/knuckle coupler, VG+ $175.00

Loco & Tender, #332 Union Pacific 4-8-4 steam engine, EX.$375.00

Loco & Tender, #336 4-8-4 steam engine & tender, VG+.$450.00

Loco & Tender, #429 0-6-0 steam engine & tender, VG+.$500.00

Locomotive and tender, #4692 steam engine and #4671 tender with 'Golden State' plates, EX+IB, A, $2,000.00. (Photo courtesy Stout Auctions)

Loco & Tender, #21004 Pennsylvania 0-6-0 & tender, NMIB..$475.00

Loco & Tender, #31004 PRR 0-6-0, w/smoke cartridge, NMIB $350.00

Loco Set, #374/375 AFL lettered Texas & Pacific GP7s, VG+.$550.00

Loco Set, #21918 & #21918-1 Seaboard Baldwin diesels, EXIB $600.00

Loco Set, #48130 Santa Fe Alco PA A-A powered/dummy, MIB $300.00

Set, #12, engine, tender, baggage car & 2 passenger cars, G.$130.00

Set, #13, loco, tender & 2 cars, early, EXIB....................$225.00

Set, #100 Tru-Model Freight, loco, tender & 3 cars, VGIB..$175.00

Set, #101 Tru-Model Freight, loco, tender & 7 cars, VGIB..$250.00

Set, #140 Tru-Model Freight, loco, tender & 3 cars, EXIB .$250.00

Set, #141 Tru-Model Freight, loco & 2 cars, EXIB.........$500.00

Set, #148 steam freight, loco, tender & 3 cars, VGIB $400.00

Set, #501TR freight, loco, tender & 3 cars, NMIB.........$225.00

Set, #805 loco & 2 coaches, w/track, EXIB....................$230.00

Set, #841T, #643 Hiawatha loco, tender & 4 cars, VGIB .$2,000.00

Set, #1097 loco, 2 #1120 coaches, #1108 baggage car, G .$250.00

Set, #3015 Illini, four-piece, O gauge, with instructions, EXIB, A, $1,200.00. (Photo courtesy Noel Barrett Auctions)

Set, #3115 loco, 2 #3281 passenger cars & 1 #3282 passenger car, EX...$825.00

Set, #4000 loco, #4040 baggage car & Pleasant View coach, G $300.00

Set, #5510T New Mountaineer Freight, loco, tender & 3 cars, EXIB..$250.00

Set, #20251 Special, loco, tender & 3 cars including a #2001 Post Cereal operating boxcar, NMIB $450.00

Set, #21925/21925-1 PA, w/4 cars, VG+ $1,250.00

Set, #30030 Chesapeake & Ohio Freight, w/5 cars, EXIB .$800.00

Set, #30415 Southern Pacific Passenger, w/3 cars, NMIB..$900.00

Set, #30505 Dispatcher Freight, loco & 3 cars, EXIB.....$175.00

Set, #30515 Merchandiser, loco, tender & 3 cars, EX+IB.$200.00

Set, #30517 Cannon Ball Freight, w/3 cars, EX+IB..........$55.00

Set, #30705 Reliable Freight, loco & 3 cars, EXIB $150.00

Set, #30710 Rambler Freight, loco, tender & 2 cars, VGIB.$275.00

Set, #30743 Old Smokey Freight, loco, tender & 6 cars, EX+IB $700.00

Set, #35099 Frontiersman, loco, tender & 2 cars, EX+IB.$950.00

Set, #49602 Northern Pacific Passenger, MIB $425.00

Set, #49606 Silver Flash Passenger, MIB $375.00

LIONEL PREWAR

Accessory, #71 telegraph set, NMIB..............................$700.00

Accessory, #86 telegraph set, NMIB $1,300.00
Accessory, #96 coal elevator, EXIB $475.00

Accessory, #98 coal tipple, VGIB, A, $500.00. (Photo courtesy Stout Auctions)

Accessory, #116 station, EX+IB $3,100.00
Accessory, #116 station, VG $1,600.00
Accessory, #123 tunnel, EX+IB.......................................$925.00

Accessory, #134 Lionel City station, EXIB, A, $500.00. (Photo courtesy Noel Barrett Auctions)

Accessory, #140L tunnel, metal, EX $1,950.00
Accessory, #165 magnetic crane, Gray Years variation, 1940-42, EXIB..$575.00

Accessory, #436 power station, NM+IB $6,000.00
Accessory, #438 signal tower, EXIB $1,025.00
Accessory, #439 panel board, EXIB..............................$400.00
Accessory, #550 figure set, 6 pnt figures, 1932-36, EXIB .$675.00
Accessory, #840 power station, base, smokestacks & steps, VG $2,500.00
Accessory, #911 country estate w/#191 villa, EX+ $1,150.00
Accessory, #913 landscape bungalow, base & house, EX .$1,150.00
Accessory, #921 layout, Scenic Park, VG+..................$7,000.00

Locomotive, #54 0-4-4-0 twin-motor engine, brass, fixed doors, G, A, $1,550.00. (Photo courtesy Stout Auctions)

Locomotive and Tender, #225E engine and #2265T tender, NMIB, A, $1,500.00. (Photo courtesy Stout Auctions)

Loco & Tender, #226E engine & #2226W tender, NMIB .$5,500.00
Loco & Tender, #226E engine & #2226W tender, VG+ .$725.00
Loco & Tender, #228 0-6-0 switcher & #2228B tender, NMIB $2,100.00
Loco & Tender, #265E Commodore Vanderbilt Blue Streak & #265WX tender, EX $1,200.00
Loco & Tender, #265E streamliner & tender, EX $375.00
Loco & Tender, #763 steam Hudson & #2226WX tender, EXIB...$4,900.00
Loco & Tender, #8976 0-6-0 switcher & #2228B tender, VGIB $1,100.00

Set, #262E China Blue Streamliner, tender & 3 cars, VG+ .$1,450.00

Set, #265E Silver Streak, loco, tender & 2 cars, 1935 only, EX $2,250.00

Set, #400E steam engine, #400T tender, 3 cars, rstr, EX+ $1,250.00

Set, #402 Mohave Passenger, three-piece, G, A, $1,050.00.
(Photo courtesy Noel Barrett Auctions)

Set, #1700 loco, #1701 tender & #1702 caboose, yel & brn, VG+ $1,750.00

Set, Lionel Jr Streamline Passenger car set, 3 cars, VG+ .$375.00

Tender, #217, orange & maroon, EX+IB......................$900.00

Tender, #1835T, EX+IB $525.00

Tender, #2226W, gray frame version, EX+....................$5,500.00

Tender, #2817, red, EX $225.00

Tender, #2817, red, NMIB..$400.00

LIONEL POSTWAR

Accessory, #68 track inspection car, red and white, complete, NMIB, A , $575.00. (Photo courtesy Stout Auctions)

Accessory, #58 Great Northern rotary snowplow, EX.....$600.00

Accessory, #97 coal elevator, EX+IB.............................$575.00

Accessory, #115 station, VG+ $450.00

Accessory, #164 lumber loader, NMIB $675.00

Accessory, #193 blinking water tower, MIB...................$375.00

Accessory, #197 rotating radar antenna, MIB................$375.00

Accessory, #334 dispatch board, VG+ $2,800.00

Accessory, #350 transfer table, MIB..............................$625.00

Accessory, #352 ice station, MIB $850.00

Accessory, #356 freight station, NMIB $625.00

Accessory, #375 motorized turntable, MIB $625.00

Accessory, #419 heliport (no helicopter), EX+..............$350.00

Accessory, #442 diner, EX $525.00

Accessory, #448 missile firing range, NMIB..................$300.00

Accessory, #455 oil derrick, EXIB $750.00

Accessory, #465 sound dispatch station w/inserts, microphone & packet, EXIB...$300.00

Accessory, #909 smoke fluid, full master carton (12 bottles), EXIB $3,700.00

Accessory, #972 tree assortment, NMIB......................$1,050.00

Accessory, #973 landscape set, EXIB............................$925.00

Accessory, #3330-100 operating submarine kit, NMIB ..$600.00

Accessory, #3360 Burro crane, EXIB $275.00

Accessory, track car, plastic station wagon w/flashing light on roof, red & wht, 7", EX+, A $165.00

Car, #X4454 PRR Baby Ruth boxcar, NMIB $200.00

Car, #44 US Army motorized launcher, NMIB..............$950.00

Car, #55 tie jector, EXIB..$125.00

Car, #69 motorized track maintenance car, EX+IB.........$500.00

Car, #1130-T-500 tender (girl's set), NMIB...................$225.00

Car, #2855 Sunoco tank car, blk w/yel decals, NMIB.....$600.00

Car, #3413 capsule launch car, NM+ $425.00

Car, #3435 aquarium car, rubber stamp variation, EXIB.$375.00

Car, #3474 Western Pacific boxcar, EX+IB $150.00

Car, #3494-625 Soo Line boxcar, NM $475.00

Car, #3666 Minuteman boxcar EX $1,000.00

Car, #5459 dump car, EXIB $475.00

Car, #6262 wheel car, VG+..$1,150.00

Car, #6315 tank car, orange, Blt-56 under ladders, NM+IB.$375.00

Car, #6343 barrel ramp car, blk top, NM $500.00

Car, #6357-50 AT&SF caboose (father & son set), EX ...$925.00

Car, #6414 auto-loader, numbers-to-the-left variation, MIB..$1,050.00

Car, #6414 auto-loader, 4 red autos w/gray bumpers, EX .$175.00

Car, #6427-500 PRR caboose (girl's set), NMIB............$550.00

Car, #6429 work caboose, lt gray, VG+IB......................$150.00

Car, #6436 LV hopper, red, VG....................................$150.00

Car, #6436-500 hopper (girl's set), spreader bar variation, VGIB...$450.00

Car, #6464-150 MP boxcar, type IIb body, solid yel door w/eagle to the left, EXIB..$325.00

Car, #6464-225 Southern Pacific boxcar, type IIa body, NMIB $275.00

Car, #6464-250 Western Pacific boxcar, type IV body, NMIB $300.00

Car, #6464-515 MKT boxcar (girl's set), type IIb body, VGIB, A, $675.00. (Photo courtesy Stout Auctions)

Car, #6464-300 Rutland boxcar, EXIB...................$325.00
Car, #6464-350 MKT boxcar, EXIB $500.00
Car, #6464-500 Timken boxcar, type IIb body, NMIB....$225.00
Car, #6464-650 Rio Grande boxcar, type IIb body, VGIB...$125.00
Car, #6464-725 New Haven boxcar, NMIB...................$425.00
Car, #6517 bay-window caboose, EXIB.....................$700.00
Car, #6672 ATSF reefer car, VGIB........................$400.00
Car, #6844 missile-carrying flatcar, blk holder, EX........$325.00
Loco, #57 AEC switcher, NM $1,700.00
Loco, #59 USAF Minuteman switcher, EX....................$750.00
Loco, #212 USMC Alco, NMIB $400.00
Loco, #218 Santa Fe AA Alco units, silver & red, NMIB.$650.00
Loco, #221 Santa Fe Alco, olive drab, EX..................$825.00
Loco, #225 C&O Alco A unit, MIB $250.00
Loco, #230P Alco, MIB..................................$400.00
Loco, #231P Rock Island A unit, MIB (sealed).............$400.00
Loco, #499 New Haven EP-5, EX $375.00
Loco, #622 Santa Fe switch engine, EX+IB.................$525.00
Loco, #2243 Santa Fe power unit, VG+ $225.00
Loco, #2245 Texas Special F3 AB units, EX $750.00
Loco, #2328 Burlington GP, silver, EX+ $475.00

Locomotive, #2329 Virginian, VG, A, $600.00. (Photo courtesy Stout Auctions)

Loco, #2338 Milwaukee Road GP, EX....................$375.00
Loco, #2339 Wabash GP, EX $400.00
Loco, #2346 Boston & Maine GP, EX....................$675.00
Loco, #2348 M&StL GP, EX+............................$600.00
Loco, #2349 Northern Pacific GP, EX+ $700.00
Loco, #2358 Great Northern, electric, VG...............$400.00
Loco, #2368 Baltimore & Ohio F3 AB units, EX........$3,100.00
Loco, #6250 Seaboard switcher, VG+....................$225.00
Loco & Tender, #736 Berkshire steam engine & #736W tender, NMIB..$500.00
Loco & Tender, #746 N&W J engine & tender (short stripe version), EXIB................................$1,400.00
Loco & Tender, #746 Norfolk & Western steam engine & tender (short stripe version), EX $725.00
Loco & Tender, #773 Hudson & #2426W tender, VG...$900.00
Loco & Tender, #2046 steam engine & #2046W tender, EX...$275.00
Loco set, #229 M & StL AS Alco units, NMIB............$500.00
Loco set, #2031 Rock Island Alco AA units, VG+ $325.00
Loco set, #2245 Texas Special F3 A-B units, EXIB $1,350.00
Tender, #773W NY Central, NMIB.......................$300.00

Set, #1800 The General Frontier Pack, five-piece, with instructions, NMIB, A, $400.00. (Photo courtesy Skinner, Inc.)

Set, Girl's with #2037-500 engine, #1130T tender, #6464-510 boxcar, #6464-515 boxcar, #6462-500 canister, G to EX (with three boxes), A, $2,900.00. (Photo courtesy Stout Auctions)

LIONEL MODERN ERA 1970 – 1996

Car, #9400 Christmas car, 1985, MIB $850.00
Car, #9739 Rio Grande boxcar, yel w/no stripe, EX+ $275.00
Loco, #11724 Great Northern F3 A-B-A, w/RailSounds, MIB.$725.00
Loco & Tender, #18018 Southern 2-8-2 Mikado '4501' & tender, w/RailSounds, MIB..$550.00
Set, #11724 Great Northern F3A-B-A, w/RailSounds, MIB (sealed) $725.00

Locomotive and tender, #18002 New York Central 4-6-4 Hudson '785' and tender, MIB, A, $600.00. (Photo courtesy Stout Auctions)

Locomotive and tender, #18011 Chessie System T1 4-4 engine and #2101 tender, with smoke and RailSounds, MIB, A, $575.00. (Photo courtesy Stout Auctions)

Set, #11726 Erie Lackawanna, MIB (sealed), A, $200.00.
(Photo courtesy Stout Auctions)

Set, #11779 CSX Freight Train, MIB...........................$275.00

Set, Lionel Classics SG Green State, with #12102 1-381E locomotive and four cars, NMIB, A, $1,700.00. (Photo courtesy Stout Auctions)

MISCELLANEOUS

American Beggs, loco & passenger car, #2-4-0 steam loco w/orig burner & 8-wheeled coach, VG (w/orig wooden box), A..........$2,090.00
Bassett-Lowke, accessory, watchman's tower, wood w/litho tin advertising sign, side door & steps, EX, A $175.00
Bing, accessory, bridge, 2 center sections w/high half-circle 'iron-work' sides on 2 ramps w/'brickwork,' #1 gauge, G, A .$175.00
Bing, accessory, crossing plot, w/gates, house & signal, VG, A..$190.00
Bing, accessory, Freight Station, litho tin, O gauge, VG+, A .$250.00
Bing, accessory, lamppost, Broadway & 42nd, rpt, A......$130.00
Bing, accessory, lamppost, hand-pnt trestle pole w/2 chain-suspended glass globes w/NP tops, 16", EX, A..............$440.00
Bing, accessory, lamppost, ornate pole w/scroll wire top, wht glass globe w/electric bulb, 15", NM, A $330.00
Bing, accessory, lamppost (oil), red & gold, VGIB, A $220.00
Bing, accessory, newspaper stand (ml Zeitungen), w/orig newspapers, #1 gauge, G, A $165.00

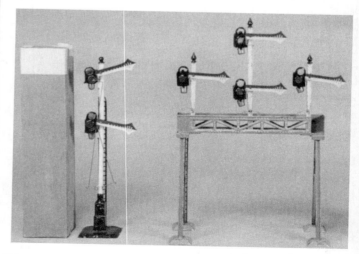

Bing, accessory, semaphore, two signal lights with pole ladder, 14½", NMIB, A, $420.00; Bing, accessory, signal bridge, trestle tower with three semaphores, 18", EX, A, $420.00.
(Photo courtesy Bertoia Auctions)

Bing, accessory, station, building with central walkway flanked by two canopied platforms, painted and lithographed tin, 14½", EX, A, $700.00. (Photo courtesy Bertoia Auctions)

Bing, accessory, station, litho tin w/emb brickwork & rail around telegraph pole on shingled dome roof, 10", EX, A...$550.00

Bing, accessory, station, 2-story w/4-sided slanted roof, 4 opening doors, sq base, 8" L, VG, A......................................$100.00

Bing, accessory, station clock w/destination signs, pedestal w/sq base, G+, A..$250.00

Bing, accessory, tower, 4-sided w/3 portholes on ea side, rnd stepped base, O gauge, VG, A $35.00

Bing, accessory, track-side house w/bell signal, litho tin, w/up, bell activated by passing train, 10" L, VG+, A........$190.00

Bing, baggage car, 8-wheeled, hinged roof, O gauge, Fair+, A.$70.00

Bing, boxcar, gr & orange, #2 gauge, G+, A $140.00

Bing, floor train, loco & tender w/2 PS RR coaches, clockwork w/key, O gauge, working, VG (w/orig box), A.........$600.00

Bing, freight car, Central Railroad of New Jersey, litho tin, maroon w/simulated wood planking, blk top, 9¼", EX, A $140.00

Bing, gondola, open, 4-wheeled, #1 gauge, G+, A.............$45.00

Bing, loco, #0-2-2 tank, w/early tin tag & decorative boiler front, #1 gauge, G+, A...$550.00

Bing, loco, w/up, #1 gauge, 12", G+, A $660.00

Bing, loco & tender, #3768 loco w/6-wheeled tender, clockwork, blk w/red litho, O gauge, G, A $385.00

Bing, loco & tender, 0-4-0 loco w/6-wheeled tender, blk w/gold & red trim, #1 gauge, rstr, A......................................$275.00

Bing, loco & tender, 4-4-0 loco w/4-wheeled tender, blk, VG, A $330.00

Bing, passenger car, #2, gr w/yel trim, #1 gauge, G+, A $90.00

Bing, passenger car, brn & beige, O gauge, Fair, A $55.00

Bing, set, Bing loco, NYC&RR tender, #1207 & #1250 coaches, G, A...$1,100.00

Bing, set, loco, baggage car, 2 passenger cars (1 w/rear railed platform), CI, electric, G, A $180.00

Bing, set, loco, tender, baggage car, 2 passenger cars (1 w/rear railed platform), w/up, G, A......................................$330.00

Bing, set, loco, tender, 2 reefer cars w/latched doors, caboose, electric, VG, A $275.00

Bing, set, NYC Lines passenger car & baggage car, gr, #1 gauge, VG, A $300.00

Bing, signal tower, twin w/orig oil pots, 16", VG, A.......$250.00

Bing, stock car, gr & orange, #2 gauge, G, A $75.00

Bing, set, locomotive and tender with two LNER coaches, track, and implements, live steam, O gauge, complete, VGIB, A, $1,265.00. (Photo courtesy Randy Inman Auctions)

Bing, trolley car #101, bl & cream, O gauge, VG+, A....$770.00

Boucher, loco & tender, #1200, Fair, A $2,090.00

Boucher, loco & tender, #2500, G, A $2,970.00

Bowman, coach, model #550, Tuscan #10153 LMS w/8 wheels & 12 operating doors, O gauge, 16" L, VG+, A $230.00

Bowman, loco & tender, live steam, 4-4-0 loco w/6-wheeled LNDR #4472 tender, gr, O gauge, VG, A................$415.00

Carette, locomotive and tender, 4-2-0 engine with six-wheeled tender, live steam, #3 gauge, scarce, VG, A, $2,500.00. (Photo courtesy Randy Inman Auctions)

Carette, refrigerator freight car, mk LNWR, wht w/blk, Fair+, A..$40.00

Carette, set, loco & tender w/3 coaches, steam, blk w/red trim & cowcatcher, O gauge, G, A......................................$900.00

Carette, set, loco & tenderlock w/baggage car & 2 coaches, #1 gauge, EXIB, A $770.00

Carette, set, 0-2-2 loco & tender w/2 coaches, steam, #1 gauge, VG, A $770.00

Carlisle & Finch, car, Electric Railway Inter Urban, G, A.$4,620.00

Carlisle & Finch, set, #131 loco, #131 tender, PPR gondola, Fair, A $990.00

Carlisle & Finch, set, #171 loco, #683 tender & coach, EX, A $2,090.00

Carlisle & Finch, set, #171 loco, tender & PRR gondola, G, A ..$1,100.00

Carlisle & Finch, set, #171 loco, tender & 4 freight cars, G, A $1,430.00

Carlisle & Finch, set, #171 loco & tender, VG, A $1,100.00

Carlisle & Finch, trolley, Electric Railway, G, A $960.00

Electoy, set, loco, tender, coal car, cattle car, boxcar & caboose, G+, A $2,640.00

Electoy, set, loco (blk), tender (blk), #2518 combination (red) & coach (red), VG, A $1,540.00

Electoy, set, loco (brass color & blk), tender (brass color), #2518 combination (orange) & coach (orange), G, A ...$3,080.00

Electoy, set, PA Line, loco, tender, boxcar, gondola & caboose, G, A $2,530.00

Ernst Plank, floor loco, open seat w/4 spoke wheels, live steam, VG, A $800.00

Ernst Plank, set, loco, tender & passenger car, live steam, #2 gauge, overpnt, A $1,020.00

Ernst Plank, set, Vulkan dribbler loco, tender & baggage car, #32 gauge, rpt, A $935.00

Fandor, boxcar, mk New York, New Haven & Hartford, 4-wheeled, VG, A $100.00

Fandor, set, loco, tender & 5 boxcars, VG, A $990.00

Fandor, set, 2 passenger car & 1 baggage car, hinged roofs, #1 gauge, rstr, A $300.00

Fischer, set, 0-4-0 loco, tender, 2 Pullman cars, litho tin, w/up, NMIB, A $500.00

Fleischmann, loco, New Haven #1215, electric, red, wht & blk, VG, A $240.00

Germany, set, 0-4-0 loco (mk R-4031) & tender, passenger car w/opening roof & doors, pnt tin, 23" L, EX, A $1,870.00

Gilbert, #30320 Pennsylvania steam freight w/#433 0-6-9 tender, 3 cars, track & instruction book, NMIB $300.00

Hafner, set, loco, boxcar, tanker, coal car, caboose, litho tin, w/up, A $210.00

Hafner, set, loco, tender, boxcar, 2 gondolas, caboose, litho tin, w/up, EX, A $470.00

Hafner, set, loco, tender, boxcar, 2 passenger cars, litho tin, w/up, G, A $120.00

Hafner, set, Overland Flyer, loco, tender, freight car & passenger car, CI & litho tin, w/up, G..$175.00

Hafner, set, Overland Flyer, loco, tender, 3 passenger cars, CI & litho tin, w/up, EX $200.00

Hafner, set, Sunshine Special, loco, tender & 2 passenger cars, CI & litho tin, w/up, G, A $120.00

Hafner, set, Sunshine Special, loco, tender & 3 passenger cars, CI & litho tin, w/up, EX, A $300.00

Hafner, set, Sunshine Special, loco, tender & 4 passenger cars, CI & litho tin, w/up, VG, A $225.00

Henry Katz 515 LTD, set, electric profile loco & 2 passenger cars, litho tin, w/up, VG, A $200.00

Hornby, accessory, station, #2, side ramps w/back fencing, litho exterior, EXIB, A $300.00

Issmayer, set, 2-4-0 red & gold loco & tender w/2 gr & yel 4-wheeled clerestory coaches, ca 1900, VG, A $1,050.00

Ives, accessory, station, single story, litho tin, no accessories, 21" L, VG+, A $300.00

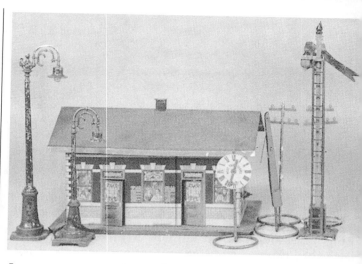

Ives, accessory, station with seven-piece light and semaphore set, litho tin, 13" long, VG+, A, $385.00. (Photo courtesy Bertoia Auctions)

Ives, accessory, Union Station, w/glass-domed canopy platform, VG, A $1,430.00

Ives, car set, #184 baggage car, #185 coach, #196 observation car, VG, A $210.00

Ives, loco, #3217, CI, electric, EX $150.00

Ives, loco, Union, pnt tin, 1870s, rpt, A $990.00

Ives, set, #1071 with #3236 engine, three-piece, EXIB, A, $1,750.00. (Photo courtesy Noel Barrett Auctions)

Ives, ticket office, litho tin, lady lithoed on window, opening doors, w/base, 11½" L, EX, A $55.00

Jep, rail car, Automotrice, pressed steel, 2 cars emb NORD, electric, 27", EXIB, A $550.00

KBN, loco & tender, 0-4-0 loco w/4-wheeled tender, gr w/red & gold trim, #1 gauge, G+, A $330.00

KTM, set, Electric Locomotive, 2 train engines, metal, M (box mk Katsumi Model Hobby Shop), A $110.00

Leland Detroit Mfg, monorail, power car w/2 coaches, tracks & supports, VG, A $1,540.00

Leland Detroit Mfg, monorail 2000 power car & 3 coaches, red & yel, rstr, A $415.00

Marklin, accessory, baggage handcart, no drawer, hdls, driver's platform, NM (partial box), A $220.00

Marklin, accessory, baggage handcart, pullout drawer, hdls, driver's platform, pnt tin, 8¼", EX, A $385.00

Marklin, accessory, direction stand w/canopy roof, contains destination boards suspended on bar, pnt tin, 7", NM, A .$550.00

Marklin, accessory, English country station, #2846, side ramps w/back fencing, 2 signs, VG+, A $6,600.00

Marklin, accessory, freight building w/stepped platform, opening doors, simulated brick, NM, A $1,870.00

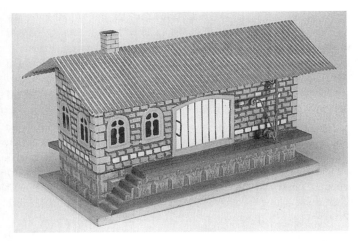

Marklin, accessory, goods station #2047, painted tin with corrugated roof, twin cranes, platforms, and sliding doors, 1906, 15", EX, A, $4,600.00. (Photo courtesy Skinner, Inc.)

Marklin, accessory, station, Central-Bahnof, double towers with central arched walkway, canopied platform, painted tin, EX, A, $5,280.00. (Photo courtesy Bertoia Auctions)

Marklin, accessory, kiosk, back opens for insertion of tickets into slots w/different destinations, enameled tin, VG+, A.$385.00

Marklin, accessory, passenger gate w/destination flags of European cities, enameled tin, 10½", VG+, A $1,980.00

Marklin, accessory, sign & signal bell, Ankunft/Abfahrt, enameled tin sign on gate-type base, crank-op bell, 7", VG+, A ..$660.00

Marklin, accessory, station, 2-story w/etched & stained glass windows, 4 opening doors, furnished interior, 14x9", EX, A...$4,620.00

Marklin, accessory, ticket booth, flanked by swinging turnstiles on platform, hand-pnt, 7" L, EX, A $1,100.00

Marklin, accessory, ticket dispenser, mk Koln-Bonner/Bahnhof, w/ornate gold pediment, 8", NM (contemporary), A .$90.00

Marklin, accessory, ticket rack, pnt & stenciled w/city destinations, slots contain cb tickets, 7½", NM, A.............$500.00

Marklin, accessory destination sign, Next Train To..., pedestal w/sq base $175.00

Marklin, baggage car, #1728, gr & orange, O gauge, G+, A $45.00

Marklin, boxcar, 4-wheeled, curved top, blk & brn, #1 gauge, VG, A $55.00

Marklin, brake & luggage car, L&NWR, litho tin w/wht-pnt roof, #1 gauge, 16¼", VG, A...............................$200.00

Marklin, brake car, Midland, litho tin, #1 gauge, 12¼", EX, A .$220.00

Marklin, coach, Mitropa, 8-wheeled, O gauge, G+, A $80.00

Marklin, coach, Mitropa #342, maroon & gold, HO gauge, VG+, A..$45.00

Marklin, dining car, Mitropa #1888, full interior, VG+, A.$155.00

Marklin, electric rail zeppelin #SZ1297, G, A $800.00

Marklin, flat car w/Gargoyle, BP Standard & BXV barrels, VG, A $330.00

Marklin, freight car #1929, w/guardhouse, brn, VG $150.00

Marklin, freight car #1968, mk Lowenbrau, O gauge, G, A .$100.00

Marklin, freight car #1969, curved roof, O gauge, G+, A.$35.00

Marklin, freight car #1987, mk Kuhlwagen, w/guardhouse, VG, A $275.00

Marklin, freight car #1991, mk Seefishe, w/guardhouse, wht w/red, VG, A $330.00

Marklin, gondola, cloth-covered top mk Marklin, VG, A..$55.00

Marklin, gondola, open, gr & orange, #2 gauge, G+, A .$175.00

Marklin, gondola, open w/brakeman's hut, 4-wheeled, brn w/blk trim, #1 gauge, VG, A $90.00

Marklin, gondola #1763, w/cloth cover mk Marklin, O gauge, VG+IB, A...$250.00

Marklin, gondola #1918 & #1963, 1 is open w/platform & the other is cloth-covered, G to VG, A, pr $70.00

Marklin, loco, #1802, clockwork, #1 gauge, VG+, A $630.00

Marklin, loco, TNM 65/1302, #1 gauge, VG, A.............$465.00

Marklin, loco, 0-4-0, mk RU890, electric, 7", NM (partial box), A $350.00

Marklin, loco, 2-4-0 LMS, electric, rstr, A.....................$550.00

Marklin, loco & tender, 0-40 loco w/4-wheeled tender, blk & gr w/red striping, clockwork, #1 gauge, G+, A.............$770.00

Marklin, loco & tender, 4-4-0 Queen Mary loco w/6-wheeled tender #E1304, electric, VG+, A $935.00

Marklin, log carrier car, w/logs, #1 gauge, G+, A............$140.00

Marklin, mail van, gr-pnt tin w/orange trim, blk roof, brn interior, 6½", NM $1,200.00

Marklin, locomotive and tender, #E-1-20 PLM 'Coupe Vent,' clockwork, green and black with red and gold trim, rare, VG, A, $11,220.00. (Photo courtesy Randy Inman Auctions)

Marklin, passenger car, II-22-I, bl-pnt tin w/orange trim, blk roof, brn interior, 6½", NM.....................$530.00

Marklin, passenger car #17510, gr w/yel trim, hinged roof, O gauge, VG, A $65.00

Marklin, passenger car #1888, hinged roof, VG+, A $275.00

Marklin, passenger car #1892, maroon & blk, #1 gauge, Fair, A $60.00

Marklin, postal car w/passenger compartment, #1895, hinged roof, 3 compo figures, #1 gauge, G+, A....................$220.00

Marklin, set, #E3020 4-4-0 loco w/6-wheeled LMS tender, #2879 Midland baggage car & 3 #2875 LMS coaches, O gauge, VG, A...$1,100.00

Marklin, set, #HR 66/12920, loco & tender w/#19440 baggage car, #19210 coach, #19420 sleeper & #19410 dining car, G+, A $2,200.00

Marklin, set, scale model of 1835 passenger steam train of Eisenbahn Germany, electric, 5-pc, MIB, A....................$935.00

Marx, set, #05944 'Happi-Time' Santa Fe Freight/Passenger, VGIB, A $200.00

Marx, set, #27150 Illinois Central Gulf Yardmaster, VGIB..$200.00

Marx, set, #44464 Western Pacific Passenger, six-piece, complete, MIB, A, $600.00. (Photo courtesy Stout Auctions)

Marx, set, #35250 NY Central Passenger, 5-pc, VGIB, A..$200.00

Marx, set, #40352 NY Central Freight, 5-pc, VGIB.......$150.00

Marx, set, #40845 Rock Island Freight, 7-pc, VGIB......$125.00

Marx, set, #4417 NY Central Wreck Train, 8-pc, w/accessories, EXIB, A $550.00

Marx, set, #44544 Santa Fe Passenger, 6-pc, VGIB........$225.00

Marx, set, #5235 NY Central Freight/Passenger, 9-pc, VGIB, A..$800.00

Marx, set, #9632 Allstate Western Pacific, 6-pc, VGIB, A.$575.00

Marx, set, Empire Express, litho tin, w/up, 4-pc, EXIB, A.$220.00

Marx, set, Joy Line w/red 0-4-0 loco, blk tender, bl Venice gondola, gold & orange Everful tank & Eagle Eye caboose, VG...$250.00

Marx, set, Pacific Stream Liner, 6-pc w/12-pc track, litho tin, w/up, VG, A $155.00

Marx, set, Western Pacific Electric Train #44464, 6-pc, w/transformer, VGIB...$600.00

Meccano, set, loco, coal tender, 2 LMS open cars, tin, w/up, 22" L, VG, A $400.00

Unique Art, set, loco, tender, boxcar, coal car & caboose, VG, A $110.00

Weeden, loco, live steam, 12", VG, A $165.00

Weeden, passenger car & tender, emb tin, Fair, A.........$250.00

Weeden, set, loco, tender & coach, live steam, G+, A...$825.00

Wilag/Fulgerex, passenger car, First Class Saloon, w/seats & tables, stamped steel, blk over maroon, 25", NM, A.$100.00

Transformers

Made by the Hasbro Company, Transformers were introduced in the United States in 1984. Originally there were twenty-eight figures — eighteen cars known as Autobots and ten Decepticons, evil robots capable of becoming such things as a jet or a handgun. Eventually the line was expanded to more than two hundred different models. Some were remakes of earlier Japanese robots that had been produced by Takara in the 1970s. (These can be identified through color differences and in the case of the Diaclone series, the absence of the small driver or pilot figures.)

The story of the Transformers and their epic adventures were told through several different comic books and animated series as well as a highly successful movie. Their popularity was reflected internationally and eventually made its way back to Japan. There the American Transformer animated series was translated into Japanese and soon inspired several parallel series of the toys which were again produced by Takara. These new Transformers were sold in the U.S. until the line was discontinued in 1990.

In 1993 Hasbro reintroduced the line with Transformers: Generation 2. Transformers once again had their own comic book, and the old animated series was brought back in revamped format. In 1996 Hasbro reinvented the series by introducing Beast Wars that transform from robot to animal. Now Transformers have returned to their roots with the Armada series that transforms from robot to vehicle. Sustained interest in them has spawned a number of fan clubs with chapters worldwide.

Because Transformers came in a number of sizes, you'll find a wide range of pricing. Our values are for Transformers that are mint in mint or nearly mint original boxes. One that has been used is worth much less — about 25% to 75%, depending on whether it has all its parts (weapons, instruction book, tech specks, etc.), and what its condition is — whether decals are well applied or if it is worn. A loose Transformer complete and in near-mint condition is worth only about half as much as one mint in the box.

Advisor: David Kolodny-Nagy (K2)

SERIES 1, 1984

Autobot Car, Bluestreak (Datsun), bl $350.00
Autobot Car, Bluestreak (Datsun), silver....................$300.00
Autobot Car, Camshaft (car), silver, mail-in $40.00
Autobot Car, Downshaft (car), wht, mail-in..................$40.00
Autobot Car, Hound (jeep), MIB $235.00
Autobot Car, Jazz (Porsche) $300.00
Autobot Car, Mirage (Indy car) $235.00
Autobot Car, Overdrive (car), red, mail-in...................$40.00
Autobot Car, Powerdasher #1 (jet), mail-in..................$20.00
Autobot Car, Powerdasher #2 (car), mail-in..................$20.00
Autobot Car, Powerdasher #3 (drill), mail-in $40.00
Autobot Car, Prowl (police car)..............................$400.00
Autobot Car, Ratchet (ambulance) $200.00
Autobot Car, Sunstreak (Countach), yel......................$300.00
Autobot Car, Trailbreaker (camper) $235.00
Autobot Car, Wheeljack (Maserati) $335.00
Autobot Commander, Optimus Primus w/Roller (semi)..$350.00
Cassette, Frenzy & Lazerbreak $50.00
Cassette, Ravage & Rumble $50.00
Collector's Case...$15.00
Collector's Case, red 3-D version $25.00
Collector's Showcase...$15.00
Decepticon Communicator, Soundwave & Buzzsaw, w/tape
    player & gold condor $250.00
Decepticon Communicator, Soundwave w/Buzzsaw & Rumble,
    Japanese edition w/headphones............................$350.00
Decepticon Jet, Skywrap, blk $225.00
Decepticon Jet, Starcream, gray, MIB $150.00
Decepticon Jet, Thundercracker, bl $230.00
Decepticon Leader, Megatron, Walther P-38 ....$350.00
Minicar, Brawn (jeep), gr......................................$35.00
Minicar, Bumblebee (VW Bug), red...........................$25.00
Minicar, Bumblebee (VW Bug), w/minispy, yel...............$40.00
Minicar, Bumblejumper (Bumblebee card) $40.00
Minicar, Bumblejumper (Cliffjumper card)....................$50.00
Minicar, Cliffjumper (race car), gr or yel, ea $35.00
Minicar, Gears (truck), bl.....................................$35.00
Minicar, Huffer (semi), orange cab...........................$35.00
Minicar, Windcharger (Firebird), red $35.00
Watch, Time Warrior, w/Autobot insignia, mail-in $80.00

SERIES 2, 1985

Autobot, Red Alert (fire chief) $250.00
Autobot Air Guardian, Jetfire (F-14 jet) $400.00
Autobot Car, Grapple (crane) $250.00

Autobot Car, Hoist (tow truck) $200.00
Autobot Car, Inferno (fire engine)...........................$250.00
Autobot Car, Skids (Le Car) $250.00
Autobot Car, Smokescreen (Datsun), red, wht & bl $250.00
Autobot Car, Tracks (Corvette)...............................$250.00
Autobot Car, Tracks (Corvette), red..........................$400.00
Autobot Commander, Blaster (radio/tape player) $145.00
Autobot Scientist, Perceptor (microscope).....................$60.00
Constructicon, Bonecrusher (1) $60.00
Constructicon, Devastator, gift set $300.00
Constructicon, Hook (4) $50.00
Constructicon, Long Haul (5) $50.00
Constructicon, Mixmaster (6) $50.00
Constructicon, Scavenger (2) $50.00
Constructicon, Scrapper (3) $50.00
Decepticon Jet, Dirge $110.00
Decepticon Jet, Ramjet...$110.00
Decepticon Jet, Thrust, maroon $120.00
Decepticon Military Operations Commander, Shockwave (laser
    gun)..$200.00
Deluxe Insecticon, Beno (bee) $90.00
Deluxe Insecticon, Chop Chop (beetle) $90.00
Deluxe Insecticon, Ransack (grasshopper) $125.00
Deluxe Vehicle, Roadster (off-road vehicle) $60.00
Deluxe Vehicle, Whirl (helicopter), lt bl.....................$70.00
Dinobot, Grimlock (Tynnosaurus) $250.00
Dinobot, Slag (Triceratops) $125.00
Dinobot, Sludge (Brontosaurus)..............................$175.00
Dinobot, Snarl (Stegosaurus) $175.00
Insecticon, Bombshell..$50.00
Insecticon, Kickback...$50.00
Insecticon, Shrapnel...$50.00
Insecticon, Venom..$50.00
Jumpstarter, Topspin $45.00
Jumpstarter, Twin Twist (drill tank) $50.00
Minicar, Beachcomber (dune buggy)...........................$30.00
Minicar, Brawn (jeep), gr......................................$40.00
Minicar, Bumblebee (VW Bug), red............................$45.00
Minicar, Bumblebee (VW Bug), w/minispy, red...............$30.00
Minicar, Bumblebee (VW Bug), yel $50.00
Minicar, Cliffjumper (race car), red or yel, ea $45.00
Minicar, Cliffjumper (race car), w/minispy, red or yel, ea.$50.00
Minicar, Cosmos (spaceship) $30.00
Minicar, Gears (truck), bl $35.00
Minicar, Gears (truck), w/minispy..............................$35.00
Minicar, Huffer (semi), orange cab............................$45.00
Minicar, Huffer (semi), w/minispy..............................$50.00
Minicar, Powerglide (plane) $25.00
Minicar, Seaspray (hovercraft) $25.00
Minicar, Warpath (tank) $30.00
Minicar, Windcharger (Firebird), red $45.00
Minicar, Windcharger (Firebird), w/minispy...................$50.00
Motorized Autobit Defense Base, Omega Supreme $300.00
Triple Charger, Astrotrain (shuttle/train) $80.00
Triple Charger, Blitzwing (tank/plane)........................$80.00
Watch, Autoceptor, Kronofrom (watch car)....................$25.00
Watch, Deceptor, Kronoform (watch jet) $25.00
Watch, Listen 'N Fun, w/tape & yel Cliffjumper $35.00

SERIES 3, 1986

Aerialbot, Air Raid (1) $25.00
Aerialbot, Fireflight (3) $25.00
Aerialbot, Silverbot (5) $50.00
Aerialbot, Skydive (2) $25.00
Aerialbot, Superion, gift set $275.00
Autobot Car, Blurr (futuristic car) $90.00
Autobot Car, Hot Rod (race car), red $375.00

Autobot Car, Kup, $100.00. (Photo courtesy Old Tyme Toy Shop)

Autobot City Commander, Reflector, Spectro, Viewfinder &
   Spyglass into camera, mail-in $225.00
Autobot City Commander, STARS Control Center, mail-
   in $225.00

Combaticon, Onslaught (5), $40.00. (Photo courtesy Old Tyme Toy Shop)

Autobot City Commander, Ultra Magnus (car carrier) ..$135.00
Battlecharger, Runabout (Trans Am) $30.00
Battlecharger, Runamuck (Corvette) $35.00
Cassette, Ramhorn & Eject (robot & rhino), gold weapons .$65.00
Cassette, Ratbat & Frenzy (robot & bat), bl $60.00
Cassette, Rewind & Steeljaw (robot & lion), gold weapons .$60.00
Cassette, Rewind & Steeljaw (robot & lion), silver weapons ..$65.00
Combaticon, Blast Off (3) $30.00
Combaticon, Brawl (1) $35.00
Combaticon, Bruticus, gift set $450.00
Combaticon, Swindle (3) $40.00
Combaticon, Vortex (4) $35.00
Decepticon City Commander, Galvatron $225.00
Heroes, Rodimus Prime (futuristic RV) $150.00
Heroes, Wreck-Car (futuristic motorcycle) $125.00
Jet, Cyclous Space Jet $175.00
Jet, Scrouge (hovercraft) $125.00
Minicar, Hubcap (race car), yel $35.00
Minicar, Outback (jeep), brn $35.00
Minicar, Pipes (semi), bl cab $35.00
Minicar, Swerve (truck), red $35.00
Minicar, Tailgate (Firebird), wht $35.00
Minicar, Wheelie (futuristic car) $35.00
Motorized Autobot Space Shuttle, Sky Lynz $135.00
Motorized Decepticon City/Battle Station, Trypticon $225.00
Predacon, Gnaw (futuristic shark) $70.00
Predacon, Divebomb (3) $70.00
Predacon, Headstrong (5) $70.00
Predacon, Rampage (2) $70.00
Predacon, Razorclaw (1) $70.00
Predacon, Tantrum (4) $70.00
Stunticon, Breakdown (2) $30.00
Stunticon, Dead End (1) $30.00
Stunticon, Drag Strip (4) $30.00
Stunticon, Menasor, gift set $450.00
Stunticon, Motormaster (semi) $75.00
Stunticon, Wildrider (Ferrari) $30.00
Triple Charger, Broadside (aircraft carrier/plane) $100.00
Triple Charger, Octane (tanker truck/jumbo jet) $85.00
Triple Charger, Sandstorm (dune buggy/helicopter) $100.00
Triple Charger, Springer (armored car/copter) $150.00

SERIES 4, 1987

Cassette, Slugfest & Overkill (Stegasaurus & Tyrannosaurus).$25.00
Clone, Fastlane & Cloudraker (dragster & spaceship) $65.00
Clone, Pounce & Wingspan (puma & eagle) $45.00
Double Spy, Punch-Counterpunch (Fiero) $75.00
Duocon, Battlestap (jeep/copter) $50.00
Duocon, Flywheels (jet/tank) $25.00
Headmaster Autobot, Brainstorm w/Arcana (jet) $75.00
Headmaster Autobot, Chromedome w/Stylor (futuristic car) ..$200.00
Headmaster Autobot, Hardhead w/Duros (tank) $120.00
Headmaster Autobot, Highbrow w/Gort (copter) $120.00
Headmaster Base, Fortress Maxiumus w/Cerebros & Spike, Gas-
   ket, Grommet (battle station/city) $800.00
Headmaster Base, Scorponok w/Lord Zarak & Fastrack .$225.00
Headmaster Decepticon, Mindwipe w/Vorath (bat) $70.00

Headmaster Decepticon, Skullrunner w/Grax (alligator) .$70.00
Headmaster Decepticon, Weirdwolf w/Monzo (wolf) $80.00
Headmaster Horrorcon, Apeface w/Spasma (jet/ape).....$100.00
Headmaster Horrorcon, Snapdragon w/Krunk (jet/dinosaur).$100.00
Monsterbot, Doublecross (2-headed dragon) $40.00
Monsterbot, Grotusque (tiger) $50.00
Monsterbot, Repugnus (insect) $90.00
Sixchanger, Sixshot (starfighter jet, winged wolf, laser pistol, armored carrier, tank) $75.00
Targetmaster Autobot, Blurr w/Haywire (futuristic car & gun) .$90.00
Targetmaster Autobot, Crosshairs w/Pinpointer (truck & gun).$30.00
Targetmaster Autobot, Hot Rod & Firebolt (race car & gun).$150.00
Targetmaster Autobot, Kup & Recoil (pickup truck & gun)..$60.00
Targetmaster Autobot, Pointblank w/Peacemaker (race car w/gun) $30.00
Targetmaster Autobot, Sureshot w/Spoilsport (off-road buggy & gun) $30.00
Targetmaster Decepticon, Misfire w/Aimless (spaceship & gun)..$60.00
Targetmaster Decepticon, Scrouge w/Fracas (hovercraft & gun) $125.00
Targetmaster Decepticon, Slugslinger w/Caliburts (twin jet & gun) $50.00
Technobot, Afterburner, w/decoy $30.00
Technobot, Afterburner (1)..$25.00
Technobot, Lightspeed, w/decoy $25.00
Technobot, Lightspeed (4) $20.00
Technobot, Nosecone, w/decoy $30.00
Technobot, Nosecone (2) $25.00
Technobot, Scattershot (5)..$40.00
Technobot, State, w/decoy..$30.00
Technobot, State (3)..$20.00
Terrocon, Blot (monster), w/decoy $30.00
Terrocon, Blot (4)..$25.00
Terrocon, Cutthroat (Vulture), w/decoy $30.00
Terrocon, Cutthroat (3)..$25.00
Terrocon, Hun-gr (5) $40.00
Terrocon, Ripperspapper (1) $25.00
Terrocon, Rippersapper, w/decoy $30.00
Terrocon, Sinnertwin (2) $25.00
Terrocon, Sinnertwin, w/decoy......................................$20.00
Throttlebot, Chase (Ferrari) $12.00
Throttlebot, Chase (Ferrari), w/decoy............................$18.00
Throttlebot, Freeway (Corvette) $15.00
Throttlebot, Freeway (Corvette), w/decoy......................$20.00
Throttlebot, Goldbug (VW bug) $15.00
Throttlebot, Rollbar (jeep)..$15.00
Throttlebot, Rollbar (jeep), w/decoy..............................$20.00
Throttlebot, Searchlight (race car) $15.00
Throttlebot, Searchlight (race car), w/decoy $20.00
Throttlebot, Wideload (dump truck) $15.00
Throttlebot, Wideload (dump truck), w/decoy $20.00

SERIES 5, 1988

Cassette, Grand Slam & Raindance (tank & jet) $40.00
Cassette, Squawkalk & Beastbox (hawk & gorilla) $40.00
Firecon, Cindersaur (dinosaur)......................................$10.00
Firecon, Flamefeather (monster bird)..............................$10.00

Firecon, Sparkstalker (monster) $10.00
Headmaster Autobot, Hosehead w/Lug (fire engine) $40.00
Headmaster Autobot, Nightbeat w/Muzzle (race car).......$40.00
Headmaster Autobot, Siren w/Quig (fire chief car)..........$50.00
Headmaster Decepticon, Fangry w/Brisko (winged wolf) .$40.00
Headmaster Decepticon, Horri-Bull w/Kreb (bull).........$40.00
Headmaster Decepticon, Squeezeplay w/Lokos (crab)......$40.00
Powermaster Autobot, Getaway w/Rev (Mr2)................$50.00
Powermaster Autobot, Joyride w/Hotwire (off-road buggy) .$70.00
Powermaster Autobot, Slapdash w/Lube (Indy car)..........$70.00
Powermaster Autobot Leader, Optimus Prime w/HiQ (semi), minimum value..$200.00
Powermaster Decepticon, Darkwing w/Throttle (jet), dk gray..$60.00
Powermaster Decepticon, Dreadwing w/Hi-Test (jet), lt gray..$60.00
Powermaster Mercenary, Doubledealer w/Knok & Skar (missile launcher)..$75.00
Pretender, Bomb-burst (spaceship), w/shell $60.00
Pretender, Cloudburst (jet), w/shell $60.00
Pretender, Finback (sea skimmer), w/shell $25.00
Pretender, Groundbreaker (race car), w/shell $40.00
Pretender, Iguanus (motorcycle), w/shell $40.00
Pretender, Landmine (race car), w/shell.........................$60.00
Pretender, Skullgrin (tank), w/shell $40.00
Pretender, Sky High (jet), w/shell $40.00
Pretender, Splashdown (sea skimmer), w/shell $40.00
Pretender, Submarauder (submarine), w/shell.................$60.00
Pretender, Waverider (submarine), w/shell $40.00
Pretender Beast, Carnivac (wolf), w/shell.......................$30.00
Pretender Beast, Catilla (sabertooth tiger), w/shell $30.00
Pretender Beast, Chainclaw (bear, w/shell $30.00
Pretender Beast, Snarler (boar), w/shell $30.00
Pretender Vehicle, Gunrunner (jet) w/vehicle shell, red..$40.00
Pretender Vehicle, Roadgrabber (jet) w/vehicle shell, purple.$40.00
Seacon, Nautilator (3) $15.00
Seacon, Overbite (1) $15.00
Seacon, Piracon, gift set, minimum value $200.00
Seacon, Seawing (2) $15.00
Seacon, Skalor (4) $15.00
Seacon, Snaptrap (6) $35.00
Seacon, Tenakil (5) $15.00
Sparkbot, Fizzle (off-road buggy) $10.00
Sparkbot, Guzzle (tank) $10.00
Sparkbot, Sizzle (funny car)..$10.00
Targetmaster Autobot, Landfill w/Flintlock & Silencer (dump truck & 2 guns) $35.00
Targetmaster Autobot, Quickmix w/Boomer & Ricochet (cement mixer & 2 guns) $30.00
Targetmaster Autobot, Scoop w/Tracer & Holepunch (front-end loader & 2 guns) $35.00
Targetmaster Decepticon, Needlenose w/Sunbeam & Zigzag (jet & 2 guns) $50.00
Targetmaster Decepticon, Quaker w/Tiptop & Heater (tank & 2 guns)..$30.00
Targetmaster Decepticon, Spinster & Singe & Hairsplitter (heli-copter & 2 guns) $40.00
Tiggerbot, Backstreet (race car).....................................$15.00
Tiggerbot, Override (motorcycle)....................................$15.00
Triggercon, Crankcase (jeep)..$15.00

Triggercon, Rucus (dune buggy) $15.00
Triggercon, Windsweeper (B-1 bomber) $15.00

SERIES 6, 1989

Legends (K-Mart Exclusive), Bumblebee (VW bug) $35.00
Legends (K-Mart Exclusive), Grimlock (dinosaur)...........$35.00
Legends (K-Mart Exclusive), Jazz (Porsche)....................$35.00
Legends (K-Mart Exclusive), Starscream (jet) $40.00
Mega Pretender, Crossblades (copter w/shell)...................$35.00
Mega Pretender, Thunderwing (jet w/shell)....................$35.00
Mega Pretender, Vroom (dragster w/shell) $35.00
Micromaster Base, Countdown (Rocket Base & Micromaster Lunar Box)..$50.00
Micromaster Base, Groundbreaker & Micromaster (self-propelled cannon & stealth fighter) $35.00
Micromaster Base, Skyhopper w/Micromaster (copter & F-15) $50.00
Micromaster Base, Skystalker (Space Shuttle Base & Micromaster Porsche)..$55.00
Micromaster Patrol, Battle Patrol Series, 4 different, ea ...$30.00
Micromaster Patrol, Off-Road Series, 4 different, ea $25.00
Micromaster Patrol, Sports Car Patrol Series, 4 different, ea..$25.00
Micromaster Station, Greasepit, pickup w/gas station $20.00
Micromaster Station, Ironworks (semi w/construction site)..$20.00
Micromaster Transport, Flattop (aircraft carrier) $20.00
Micromaster Transport, Overload (car carrier) $20.00
Micromaster Transport, Roughstuff (military transport)...$20.00
Pretender, Bludgeon (tank), w/shell..............................$125.00
Pretender, Doubleheader (twin jet), w/shell $45.00
Pretender, Longtooth (hovercraft), w/shell.......................$35.00
Pretender, Pincher (scorpion), w/shell $35.00
Pretender, Stanglehold (rhino), w/shell $35.00
Pretender Classic, Bumblebee (VW bug), w/shell $50.00
Pretender Classic, Grimlock (dinosaur), w/shell...............$50.00
Pretender Classic, Jazz (Porsche, w/shell $40.00
Pretender Classic, Starscream (jet), w/shell $50.00
Pretender Monster, Icepick (1).......................................$12.00
Pretender Monster, Wildfly (3) $12.00
Ultra Pretender, Roadblock (tank w/figure & vehicle).....$40.00
Ultra Pretender, Skyhammer (race car w/figure & vehicle) ..$40.00

SERIES 7, 1990

Action Master, Blaster: Blaster, Flight-Pack (jet pack).....$25.00
Action Master, Devastator: Devastator, Scorpulator (scorpion) $25.00
Action Master, Grimlock: Grimlock, Anti-Tank Cannon (tank gun) $15.00
Action Master, Gutcruncher: Stratotronic Jet $50.00
Action Master, Inferno: Inferno, Hydro-Pack (laser backpack) .$25.00
Action Master, Optimus Prime: Optimus Prime, Armored Convoy $100.00
Action Master, Over-Run: Over-Run, Attack Copter $40.00
Action Master, Prowl: Prowl, Turbo Cycle.....................$60.00
Action Master, Rad: Rad, Lionizer (lion)..........................$15.00
Action Master, Shockwave: Shockwave, Fistfight (mini-robot) $25.00

Action Master, Skyfall: Skyfall, Top-Heavy Rhino..........$30.00
Action Master, Soundwave: Soundwave Wingthing $15.00
Action Master, Wheeljack: Wheeljack, Turbo Racer $70.00
Micromaster Combiner, Anti-Aircraft Base: Anti-Aircraft Base, Blackout & Spaceshot $25.00
Micromaster Combiner, Battle Squad: Meltdown, Half-Track, Direct Hit, Power Punch, Fireshot & Vanguish.........$25.00
Micromaster Combiner, Metro Squad: Wheel Blaze, Road Runner, Oiler, Slide, Power Run & Strike Down $25.00
Micromaster Combiner, Missile Launcher: Missile Launcher, Retro Surge $25.00
Micromaster Combiner, Tanker Truck: Tanker Truck, Pipeline & Gusher..$30.00
Micromaster Patrol, Air Patrol: Thread Bolt, Eagle Eye, Sky High & Blaze Master $10.00
Micromaster Patrol, Hot Rod Patrol: Big Daddy Trip-Up, Greaser & Hubs $10.00
Micromaster Patrol, Military Patrol: Bombshock, Tracer, Dropshot & Growl $10.00
Micromaster Patrol, Race Track Patrol: Barricade, Roller Force, Ground Hog Motorhead $10.00

BEAST WARS

Maximal, Airrazor, loose, M $25.00
Maximal, Blackarachina, 1996, MOC $85.00
Maximal, Cheeter, MOC...$18.00
Maximal, Depth Charge, MIB.......................................$20.00
Maximal, Optimus Primal (Gorilla), MIB......................$110.00
Maximal, Polar Claw, 1995, MIB $15.00
Maximal, Rattrap, MOC...$100.00
Predacon, Dinobot, 1995, MOC....................................$110.00
Predacon, Inferno, 1996, MIB $35.00
Predacon, Megatron (Dragon), Transmetal II, MIB.........$20.00
Predacon, Megatron (T-Rex), MIB $110.00
Predacon, Scorponok, dk purple/bl, MIB (Japanese) $85.00
Predacon, Shokaract, BotCon 2000 exclusive, MIB.........$70.00
Predacon, Terroraur, MOC $90.00
Predacon, Tripedacus, w/instructions, loose, M...............$60.00
Predacon, Waspinator, rare, MOC $110.00

GENERATION 2, SERIES 1, 1992 – 93

Autobot Car, Inferno (fire truck) $30.00
Autobot Car, Jazz (Porsche)..$35.00
Autobot Leader, Optimus Prime w/Roller (semi w/electronic sound effect box) $150.00
Autobot Minicar, Bumble (VW bug), metallic...............$30.00
Autobot Minicar, Hubcap, metallic $20.00
Autobot Minicar, Seaspray (hovercraft), metallic $15.00
Autobot Obliterator (Europe only), Spark.....................$45.00
Color Change Transformer, Deluge $20.00
Color Change Transformer, Gobots...............................$20.00
Constructicon, Bonecrusher (1), orange $12.00
Constructicon, Bonecrusher (1), yel $10.00
Constructicon, Long Haul (5), orange $12.00
Constructicon, Long Haul (5), yel $10.00
Constructicon, Scrapper (3), orange $12.00

Constructicon, Scrapper (3), yel $10.00
Decepticon, Mixmaster, MOC $15.00
Decepticon Jet, Starscream (jet w/electronic light & sound
    effect box), gray $30.00
Decepticon Leader, Megatron (tank w/electronic sound-effect
    treads) $45.00
Decepticon Obliterator (Europe only), Colossus $75.00
Dinobot, Grimlock (Tyrannosaurus), bl $25.00
Dinobot, Grimlock (Tyrannosaurus), turq $90.00
Dinobot, Snarl (Stegosaurus), gray or bl, ea...................$50.00
Small Autobot Car, Skram $15.00
Small Autobot Car, Turbofire $15.00
Small Decepticon Jet, Afterburner................................$15.00
Small Decepticon Jet, Eagle Eye..................................$15.00
Small Decepticon Jet, Terredive $15.00
Small Decepticon Jet, Windrazor $15.00

GENERATION 2, SERIES 2, 1994

Aerialbot, Fireflight (3) $10.00
Aerialbot, Silverbot (5) $25.00
Aerialbot, Skydive (1) $15.00

Aerialbot, Superion, $225.00.

Combaticon, Blast Off (3) $10.00
Combaticon, Brawl (1) $10.00
Combaticon, Onslaught (5) $25.00
Heroes, Autobot Hero Optimus Prime............................$20.00
Heroes, Autobot Hero Optimus Prime, Japanese box.......$35.00
Heroes, Decepticon Hero Megatron................................$20.00
Laser Rod Transformer, Electro......................................$15.00
Laser Rod Transformer, Electro, Japanese box..................$20.00
Laser Rod Transformer, Jolt $15.00
Laser Rod Transformer, Jolt, Japanese box $20.00
Lead Force, Leadfoot, Manta Ray, or Ransack, ea..............$7.00
Rotor Force, Leadfoot..$7.00
Stunticon, Breakdown (2), BotCon '94 Exclusive.............$100.00
Watch, Superion, Ultra Magnus, or Scorpia, ea...............$12.00

JAPANESE REMAKES

Blot, MIB, $70.00. (Photo courtesy Old Tyme Toy Shop)

GodGinrai, MIB (sealed), K2 ....$70.00
Hot Rod, MIB, K2...$60.00
Jazz, MIB (sealed)...$35.00
Megatron, MIB...$90.00
Optimus Prime, New Year's edition.................................$150.00
Prowl, MIB (sealed), K2...$35.00
Ratchet, MIB (sealed)..$50.00
Red Alert, MIB (sealed) $90.00
Rodimus Prime, MIB (sealed), K2 ....$60.00
Sixshot, MIB (sealed) $60.00
Skids, MIB (sealed), K2..$35.00
Skywrap, MIB (sealed), K2..$120.00
Tracks, MIB (sealed)..$35.00
Ultra Magnus, NRFB, K2 ....$80.00

Trolls

The first trolls to come to the United States were modeled after a 1952 design by Marti and Helena Kuuskoski of Tampere, Finland. The first trolls to be mass produced in America were molded from wood carvings made by Thomas Dam of Denmark. As the demand for these trolls increased, several US manufacturers were licensed to produce them. The most noteworthy of these were Uneeda Doll Company's Wishnik line and Inga Scandia House True Trolls. Thomas Dam continued to import his Dam Things line.

The troll craze from the '60s spawned many items other than dolls such as wall plaques, salt and pepper shakers, pins, squirt guns, rings, clay trolls, lamps, Halloween costumes, animals, lawn ornaments, coat racks, notebooks, folders, and even a car.

In the '70s, '80s, and '90s, new trolls were produced. While these trolls are collectible, the avid troll collector still prefers those produced in the '60s. Remember, trolls must be in mint condition to receive top dollar.

Batman, Uneeda Wishnik, 1966, felt outfit, 3", NM, $35.00.

Astronaut, Dam, 1964, 11", EX....................................$125.00
Boy in Raincoat, Dam, 1964, bank, 12", NM, from $115 to...$155.00
Bride & Groom, Uneeda Wishnik, 1970s, 6", EX, pr........$35.00
Cave Girl, Dam, leopard-skin outfit, 3", NM, from $20 to .$25.00
Cow, Dam, wht hair & brn eyes, 3½", EX.........................$45.00

Cowboy, Uneeda Wishnik, red hat, red print shirt & bl pants, 3½", NM...$15.00
Cowgirl bank, Creative Mfg, 1978, molded outfit, 8½", NM...$30.00
Donkey, Dam, 1964, blond hair & amber eyes, 3", NM....$35.00
Eskimo, Dam, 1965, pnt-on clothes, 5½", EX...................$75.00
Fire Chief, Treasure Trolls, bl hair & eyes, 4", M.............$12.00
Goo-Goo Baby, Russ Trolls, 1990s, 9", NM.....................$13.00
Good-Luck-Nik, Uneeda Wishnik, 1970s, M (orig tube).$30.00
Graduate, Uneeda Wishnik, 1970s, w/robe & hat, 6", EX .$25.00
Hunt-Nik, Totsy Wishnik, w/rifle, NM, from $20 to........$25.00
Koko Monkey, Norfin's Ark/Dam, 2½", NM.....................$4.00
Leprechaun Couple, Scandia House, 1960s, stuffed bodies, 10", EX $175.00
Little Red Riding Hood, Russ Storybook, 4½", NM.........$14.00
Lucky Shnook Nodder, Japan, 4½", NM, from $30 to......$40.00
Monkey, Dam, sailor suit, 12", rare, NM.........................$300.00
Neanderthal Man, Bijou Toy Inc, 1963, 7½", EX.............$35.00
No-Good-Nik, Uneeda Wishnik, 1980s, 5", NM...............$15.00
Norfin Seal, Dam, 1984, amber eyes, 6½", NM $50.00
Norfin Turtle, Dam, 1984, amber eyes, 4", NM $50.00
Nurse-Nik, Uneeda Wishnik, 1970s, 6", MOC.................$50.00
Pik-Nik, Uneeda Wishnik, 1970s, bendabel, 5", MOC $40.00
Rock-Nik, Uneeda Wishnik, bendable, w/guitar, 5", EX ..$25.00

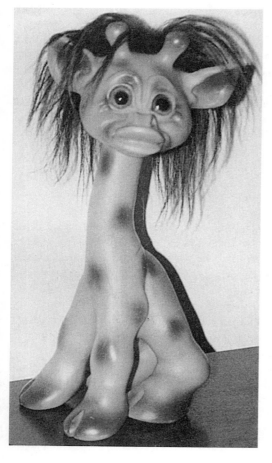

Griaffe, Dam, sitting, jointed neck, 12", NM, $75.00.

Santa Bank, Dam, felt outfit, 9", NM, $65.00.

Seal, Norfin Pets/Dam, 1984, 6½", NM..........................$50.00
Short Order Cook, Russ China, #18582, 4½", NM $8.00
Sock-It-To-Me, Uneeda Wishnik, 6", NM........................$50.00
Superman, Uneeda Wishnik, felt costume, 5", EX.............$75.00
Werewolf Monster, 1980, 3", NM....................................$25.00
Wizard, Treasure Trolls, lt purple hair, bl eyes, 4", M........$15.00

MISCELLANEOUS

Carrying Case, Ideal, w/molded waterfall, M $25.00
Christmas Stocking, Adopt a Norfin Troll, lg vinyl head, M..$25.00
Magnet Toy, Smethport, 1967, colorful illus on 10x14" board,
 EX...$50.00
Outfit, any style, MIP, ea $15.00
Playhouse (Wishnik Mini Trolls), Ideal, 1960s, EX $25.00
Stik-Shack, vinyl, EX...$30.00
Troll Party, Marx, rare, MIB..$50.00
Troll Village, EXIB..$175.00

View-Master and Tru-Vue

View-Master, the invention of William Gruber, was introduced to the public at the 1939 – 1940 New York World's Fair and the Golden Gate Exposition in California. Since then, View-Master reels, packets, and viewers have been produced by five different companies — the original Sawyers Company, G.A.F (1966), View-Master International (1981), Ideal Toys, and Tyco Toys (the present owners). Because none of the non-cartoon single reels and three-reel packets have been made since 1980, these have become collectors' items. Also highly sought after are the three-reel sets featuring popular TV and cartoon characters. The market is divided between those who simply collect View-Master as a field all its own and collectors of character-related memorabilia who will often pay much higher prices for reels about Barbie, Batman, The Addams Family, etc. Our values tend to follow the more conservative approach.

The first single reels were dark blue with a gold sticker and came in attractive gold-colored envelopes. They appeared to have handwritten letters. These were followed by tan reels with a blue circular stamp. Because these were produced for the most part after 1945 and paper supplies were short during WWII, they came in a variety of front and back color combinations, tan with blue, tan with white, and some were marbleized. Since print runs were low during the war, these early singles are much more desirable than the printed white ones that were produced by the millions from 1946 until 1957. Three-reel packets, many containing story books, were introduced in 1955, and single reels were phased out. Nearly all viewers are very common and have little value except for the very early ones, such as the Model A and Model B. Blue and brown versions of the Model B are especially rare. Another desirable viewer, unique in that it is the only focusing model ever made, is the Model D. For more information we recommend *View-Master Single Reels, Volume I*, by Roger Nazeley. Unless noted otherwise, values are for reels complete with cover and book.

A-Team, #4045, MIP (sealed) $15.00
Aladdin, #3088, MIP $5.00
Annie Oakley, #B-470, MIP $26.00
Archie, #B-574, MIP $10.00
Aristocats, #B-365, MIP...$8.00
Bad News Bears, #H-77, MIP $10.00
Banana Splits, #B-502, MIP $22.00

Barbie & the Rockers, #4071, MIP (sealed).....................$12.00
Batman, #BB-492, MIP (sealed) $18.00
Beauty & the Beast, #3079, MIP $5.00
Beetlejuice, #1074, MIP (sealed) $8.00
Big Blue Marble, #B-587, MIP (sealed)...........................$15.00
Black Hole, #K-35, MIP $15.00
Bonanza, #B-471, MIP (sealed) $25.00
Brady Bunch, #B-568, MIP $22.00
Buck Rogers, #L-15, MIP $10.00
Buffalo Bill Jr, #965abc, MIP..$26.00
Bugs Bunny, #B-549, MIP $8.00
Captain America, #H-43, MIP (sealed) $10.00
Casper the Friendly Ghost, #B-533, MIP (sealed) $10.00
Cat From Outer Space, #J-22, MIP (sealed) $10.00
Charlotte's Web, #B-321, MIP $8.00
Chilly Willy, #823, MIP...$4.00
Chip 'N Dale, #3075, MIP $6.00
CHiPs, #L-14, MIP $15.00
Cinderella, #B-318, MIP $12.00
Daktari, #B-498, MIP (sealed)..$18.00
Dale Evans, #B-463, MIP (sealed)...................................$35.00
Daniel Boone, #B-479, MIP $22.00
Dennis the Menace, #B-539, MIP (sealed) $10.00
Dinosaurs (TV Show), #4138, MIP $8.00
Donald Duck, #B-525, MIP $10.00
Eight Is Enough, #K-76, MIP (sealed) $18.00
Fangface, #K-66, MIP (sealed) $10.00
Fantastic Voyage, #B-546, MIP.......................................$18.00
Fat Albert, #B-554, MIP $8.00
Flash Gordon, #B-583, MIP $20.00
Flintstones, #L-6, MIP $10.00
Flipper (Movie), #4162, MIP...$10.00

Flying Nun, #B-495, MIP, $35.00. (Photo courtesy Greg Davis and Bill Morgan)

Godzilla, #J-23, MIP (sealed) $20.00
Goldilocks & the Three Bears, #B-317, MIP $18.00

Green Hornet, #B-488, MIP.................................$65.00
Happy Days, #J-13, MIP $10.00
Hardy Boys, #B-547, MIP $15.00
Holly Hobbie, #B-344, MIP (sealed) $18.00
Howard the Duck, #4073, MIP (sealed) $12.00
Jack & the Beanstalk, #FT-3, MIP (sealed) $4.00
Jetsons, #L-27, MIP..$7.00
John Travolta, #K-79, MIP (sealed) $15.00

KISS, Special Subjects, MIP, $75.00. (Photo courtesy June Moon)

Knight Rider, #4054, MIP..................................$7.00
Kung Fu, #B-598, MIP (sealed) $20.00
Land of the Giants, #B-494, MIP $45.00
Lassie & Timmy, #B-472, MIP $18.00
Laverne & Shirley, #J-20, MIP $10.00
Little Mermaid, #3078, MIP $5.00
Love Bug, #B-501, MIP (sealed).....................$12.00
Mary Poppins, #B-376, MIP $10.00
Mary Poppins, #B-3762, MIP............................$2.00
Mickey Mouse, #B-528, MIP $12.00
Mickey's Trailer, #3-54, MIP..............................$2.00
Mighty Mouse, #BB-526, MIP...........................$6.00
Mission Impossible, #B-505, MIP $20.00
Mod Squad, #B-478, MIP $22.00
Monkees, #B-493, MIP $28.00
Muppet Movie, #K-4005, MIP (sealed).............$8.00
Nanny & the Professor, #B-573, MIP...............$32.00
Partridge Family, #B-569, MIP.........................$22.00

Pete's Dragon, #H-38, MIP (sealed) $10.00
Pink Panther, #BJ-12, MIP $6.00
Planet of the Apes, #BB-507, MIP (sealed) $40.00
Popeye, #B-516, MIP $10.00
Punky Brewster, #4068, MIP (sealed) $10.00
Ren & Stimpy, #1084, MIP (sealed) $8.00
Rescuers, #H-26, MIP $8.00
Return From Witch Mountain, #J-25, MIP $8.00
Rin-Tin-Tin, #B-467, MIP $16.00
Robin Hood, #B-373, MIP (sealed) $25.00
Rocketeer, #4115, MIP (sealed) $10.00
Rocky & Bullwinkle, #B-515, MIP $15.00
Romper Room, #K-20, MIP (sealed) $10.00
Rookies, #B-452, MIP (sealed) $20.00
Roy Rogers, #475, MIP $26.00
Run Joe Run, #B-594, MIP $16.00
Scooby Doo, #1079, MIP (sealed) $5.00
Secret Valley, #BD-208, MIP (sealed) $15.00
Shaggy DA, #B-368, MIP (sealed) $15.00
Sigmund & the Seamonsters, #B-595, MIP $20.00
Six Million Dollar Man, #B-556, MIP $18.00
Sleeping Beauty, #B-308, MIP $6.00
Snoopy & the Red Baron, #B-544, MIP (sealed).............$12.00
Snow White & the Seven Dwarfs, #FT-4, MIP...............$5.00
Spider-Man vs Dr Octopus, #K-31, MIP $12.00
Star Trek, #B-555, MIP.....................................$12.00
Tarzan Rescues Cheetah, #975, single, MIP $7.00
Teenage Mutant Ninja Turtles, #1073, MIP (sealed) $5.00
Time Tunnel, #B-491, MIP (sealed) $40.00
Tom & Jerry, #810, MIP $4.00
Tom Corbett, #B-581, MIP................................$30.00
Top Cat, #BB-513, MIP $16.00
Waltons, #B-596, MIP $15.00
Welcome Back Kotter, #J-19, MIP (sealed) $18.00
Who Framed Roger Rabbit?, #4086, MIP.........$18.00
Wind in the Willows, #4084, MIP $12.00
Winnie the Pooh, #B-3622, MIP.........................$3.00
Woody Woodpecker, #1011, MIP $10.00
Wrestling Superstars, #4067, MIP (sealed) $12.00
X-Men Captive Hearts, #1085, MIP $15.00
Zorro, #B-469, MIP (sealed) $45.00

Western

No friend was ever more true, no brother more faithful, no acquaintance more real to us than our favorite cowboys of radio, TV, and the silver screen. They were upright, strictly moral, extremely polite, and tireless in their pursuit of law and order in the American West. How unfortunate that such role models are practically extinct nowadays.

For more information and some wonderful pictures, we recommend *Roy Rogers and Dale Evans Toys & Memorabilia* by P. Allan Coyle; *Guide to Cowboy Character Collectibles* by Ted Hake; and *The W.F. Cody Buffalo Bill Collector's Guide* by James W. Wojtowicz. With the exception of Hake's, all are published by Collector Books.

Advisors: Donna and Ron Donnelly (D7)

See also Advertising Signs, Ads, and Displays; Books; Cereal Boxes and Premiums; Character and Promotional Drinking Glasses; Character Clocks and Watches; Coloring, Activity, and Paint Books; Guns; Lunch Boxes; Premiums; Puzzles and Picture Blocks; Radios; Telephones; Windups, Friction, and Other Mechanicals.

Bat Masterson, cane, chrome-covered plastic hdl w/name emb across top, 1958, EX+ $35.00
Bat Masterson, outfit, w/shirt, pants & tie, Gene Barry labels, Kaynee, MIB, A...$160.00
Cisco Kid, belt, blk leather w/brn embellishments & name tags, 1950s, NM, A $55.00

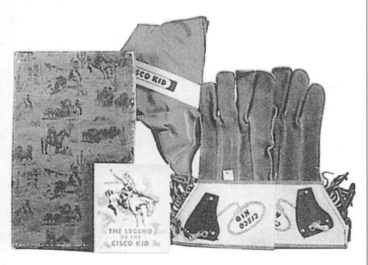

Cisco Kid, gloves and scarf set, The Legend of the Cisco Kid, leather, gloves have small holsters with removable guns, NMIB, A, $250.00. (Photo courtesy Smith House Toys)

Cisco Kid, hat & scarf, yel felt hat w/brn whipstitching on brim, The Cisco Kid silk-screened on yel scarf, NM, A $75.00
Cisco Kid, outfit, w/shirt & hat, hat band reads The Cisco Kid & Pancho Like Sugardale Meats, NM, A $100.00
Dale Evans, bathrobe, chenille w/image of Dale & Buttermilk, Roy Rogers Polly Prentiss label, girl's sz, NM+ $175.00

Dale Evans, hat, felt, Dale Evans Queen of the West on band, Lancaster Hat Co., NM+, A, $100.00. (Photo courtesy Smith House Toys)

Dale Evans, outfit, blk & red denim jacket & pants w/Dale Evans snap & patch on pockets, EX, A $125.00
Dale Evans, washcloth mitt, terry cloth w/color image of Dale & inscribed name & Queen of the West, EX, A $25.00
Daniel Boone, coonskin cap, lifelike fur w/gold Fess Parker image on brn vinyl top, American Tradition, 1964, EX+.......$90.00
Daniel Boone, figure, pnt plastic w/vinyl head, fur-like coonskin cap, powder horn, American Tradition, 1964, 5½", NM.........$75.00
Davy Crockett, bath towel, wht terry w/color litho Fess Parker bust image, WDP/Cannon, 1950s, 37x20", unused, NM+ $60.00
Davy Crockett, belt buckle, molded metal w/framed image of emb gun & powder horn, 1950s, 3¼", EX+, M8........$50.00
Davy Crockett, binoculars, plastic, Harrison, MIB, A....$175.00

Davy Crockett, book bag, cloth and plastic saddle type with fringe, image of Davy on horse, unused, M, A, 250.00. (Photo courtesy Smith House Toys)

Davy Crockett, book bag, leather saddle type w/scenes on sky bl background, brn trim, NM+, A.................................$115.00
Davy Crockett, boots, Indian Fighter, leather w/fringe, simulated coonskins on boot pulls, Trimfoot/WDP, NMIB, A.$370.00
Davy Crockett, breakfast set, w/plate, bowl & mug, wht china w/sepia Davy scenes, Royal China, 1955, unused, MIB.$175.00
Davy Crockett, chair, lithoed image of Davy on vinyl back & seat w/steel rod frame, child-sz, USA, 1950s, EX+, A $200.00
Davy Crockett, dart gun set, MIB, C10............................$50.00
Davy Crockett, Dart Gun Target, Knickerbocker, unused, MIB, A $80.00
Davy Crockett, doll, in frontier costume, Mattel, 1994, 12", MIB $165.00
Davy Crockett, figure, Davy (w/removable hat) on horse, plastic, Ideal, 6", NM+ (in box mk Davy Crockett & His Horse), A $250.00
Davy Crockett, Fix-It Stagecoach, plastic, Ideal, 14", NMIB, A.$85.00
Davy Crockett, Frontier Kit, leather pouch & powder horn on belt, Industrial Safety Belt, NM+IB, A $135.00
Davy Crockett, guitar, plastic, Emenee, 15", NMIB, A ..$100.00
Davy Crockett, guitar, wood & paperboard, yel w/blk graphics & Davy Crockett of Tennessee on front, 31", VG $135.00

Davy Crockett, hat, coonskin type, Weathermac/WD, M (in Official...Indian Fighter Hat Box)............$300.00

Davy Crockett, Huntin' Glasses, blk plastic w/wht lettering & image, Powerscope/W Germany, 4", NMIB, A........$100.00

Davy Crockett, lamp, ceramic figures of Davy & bear by tree trunk, lithoed shade, 12", M, A..................$200.00

Davy Crockett, lamp, chalkware figural base with scenes painted on shade, 18", VG, $100.00. (Photo courtesy Randy Inman Auctions)

Davy Crockett, lamp, electric oil lamp type w/glass shade depicting Davy & name, 12", G base/M shade, A $75.00

Davy Crockett, lamp, rotating cylinder, Econolite, 11", NM, A..................$275.00

Davy Crockett, moccasin kit, Authentic Indian Fighter, Connecticut Leather, unused, MIB, A............$115.00

Davy Crockett, moccasin kit, Old Town Crafts, complete & unused, NMIB, A......................$75.00

Davy Crockett, moccasins, leather w/image of Davy on tops, Panco, MIB, A............................$225.00

Davy Crockett, napkin set, image of Fess Parker on complete set of 30, 5" sq, MIP (unopened) $50.00

Davy Crockett, outfit, Frontiersman, girls, complete w/hat, fringed skirt, blouse & belt, Yankiboy, MIB, A........$120.00

Davy Crockett, outfit, shirt w/interchangeable pants & skirt, brn cotton w/plastic fringe, yel litho, WDP, 1950s, EX $65.00

Davy Crockett, Play Box, w/crayons, pnts, coloring book, connect-the-dots book, wallet, etc, unused, MIB, A $125.00

Davy Crockett, play horse, Pied Piper Toys, MIB, A......$125.00

Davy Crockett, Sample Kit (salesman's sample), includes plastic mug, bank & cup w/images, NM (in box w/flyer), A.$200.00

Davy Crockett, shoes, leather w/image of Davy on tops, w/leather laces, Bootcraft, unused, M (EX box), A .$175.00

Davy Crockett, soap, detailed figure holding gun, 1950s, unused, EXIB..................$75.00

Davy Crockett, stamp book, 1955, EX+ $55.00

Davy Crockett, T-shirt, w/graphics & fringe, Shirtees, 1950s, EX+ $55.00

Davy Crockett, tent, Official Fess Parker..., brn & wht litho on tan canvas, NMIB..................$150.00

Davy Crockett, towels, Kiddie Towel Set, Cannon, MIB, A.$100.00

Davy Crockett, tray, litho tin w/image of Davy fighting Indian, 12½x17", EX..................$100.00

Davy Crockett, wallet, brn vinyl w/imitation fur & color graphics, 1955, EX+IB $75.00

Davy Crockett, Western Rodeo, plastic figures, Ajax, unused, NMIB, A..................$85.00

Davy Crockett, Woodburning Set, Frontier..., ATF/USA, MIB, A $175.00

Fort Apache, Cavalry Sabre & Scabbard, plastic, Marx, 26", NMOC (featuring Captain Maddox), A $100.00

Gabby Hayes, Champion Shooting Target, Haccker/Ind, 1950s, NMIB, A..................$225.00

Gabby Hayes, doll, stuffed cloth w/fur beard & felt hat, name on belt, Etone, 1960s, 13", M $40.00

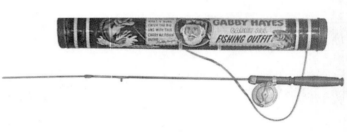

Gabby Hayes, Fishing Outfit, steel two-part rod with metal reel in tin litho cylinder, VG, A, $115.00. (Photo courtesy James D. Julia, Inc.)

Gene Autry, book bag, blk cloth w/wht trim, flip-over top w/2 buckle closures, plastic hdl, scene on front, Klick, NM+, A..................$215.00

Gene Autry, boots, blk rubber galoshes w/Gene on Champion patches, G Brown Shoe Co, unused, MIB, A $200.00

Gene Autry, doll, compo w/silk shirt & leather chaps, felt hat & boots, Terry Lee, 16", NM+, A..................$500.00

Gene Autry, flashlight, Cowboy Lariat, EXIB, A............$100.00

Gene Autry, guitar, plastic, Emenee, 32", NMIB, A.......$230.00

Gene Autry, outfit, boy's shirt & pants (not play costume), California Ranchwear, 1950s, unused, M, A $300.00

Gene Autry, Pistol Horn, Metal Products, 6½", NM+IB, A .$175.00

Gene Autry, record player, plastic with 'Flying A' decal, electric, Columbia, 13" long, VG, A, $250.00. (Photo courtesy Smith House Toys)

Gene Autry, spurs, Official Cowboy..., metal w/dk brn leather straps through silver conchos, MA Henry, NMIB, A .$220.00

Gene Autry, spurs, Official Cowboy..., metal w/gold boot straps & rawls, Leslie-Henry, EXIB, A $100.00

Gene Autry, wallet, leather w/zipper closure, image of Autry & Champion, NMIB, A $200.00

Gene Autry, wallet, plastic, image of Autry & Champion, NMIB, A...$85.00

Gunsmoke, hat, felt w/photo image of Marshal Matt Dillon, 1960s, EX...$20.00

Gunsmoke, outfit, Matt Dillon, includes metal badge, Kaynee/CBS, 1959, MIP, A $110.00

Gunsmoke, slippers, blk vinyl w/yel & red image of Matt, Chester & Doc, Columbia, 1959, unused, NM+IB, A $200.00

Have Gun Will Travel, Gold Mine playset, CBS/Multiple Products, 1959, EXIB, A $200.00

Hopalong Cassidy, autograph album, leather w/zipper closure, images of Hoppy & Topper, 5x6", NM, A...............$200.00

Hopalong Cassidy, bedspread, bl w/wht & blk image of Hoppy on Topper twirling lasso, fence & red lettering, lg, EX, A..$125.00

Hopalong Cassidy, binoculars, metal w/decals, simulated leather cb case, Sport Glass, EX+, A.....................................$100.00

Hopalong Cassidy, boots, blk rubber w/wht trim, circular color images on sides, wht rubber spurs, Goodyear, NM, A.$200.00

Hopalong Cassidy, breakfast set, 3-pc set w/cup, bowl & plate, ceramic w/Hoppy decals, W George, EXIB, A.........$250.00

Hopalong Cassidy, camera, Wm Boyd/Galter, 1940, unused, NMIB, A..$200.00

Hopalong Cassidy, chair, director's type w/fabric seat & back on wood frame, child-sz, VG, A $300.00

Hopalong Cassidy, Dr West's Dental Kit, complete w/toothpaste, brush in glass case & mirror, EXIB, A.....................$150.00

Hopalong Cassidy, figure, chalk, 1950s, 14", NM+.........$350.00

Hopalong Cassidy, Figure & Paint Set, Laurel Ann, complete, used, EXIB $265.00

Hopalong Cassidy, hat, felt w/longhorn logo, VG..........$125.00

Hopalong Cassidy, Jumbo Pencil, Writes-Erases-Sharpens, complete, 10", VG+, A $100.00

Hopalong Cassidy, Junior Chow Set (fork, knife & spoon), Imperial Knife, 1950, unused, MIB, A $210.00

Hopalong Cassidy, lamp, milk glass w/decal on bullet shape w/Hoppy & Topper on shade, Aladdin, 17½", M (EX shade), A $400.00

Hopalong Cassidy, lamp, rotating cylinder picturing Hoppy & Topper chasing stagecoach, plastic, Econolite, 10", NM+ .$500.00

Hopalong Cassidy, mask, Latex rubber, Traveler Trading Co, EXIB, A $275.00

Hopalong Cassidy, night light, figural glass gun in holster w/image of Hoppy, Aladdin, 1950, NM $350.00

Hopalong Cassidy, notebook, 2-ring leather-type binder w/litho image of Hoppy & name, zipper closure, Horn, 19", NM, A $175.00

Hopalong Cassidy, outfit, skirt & vest silk-screened w/image of Hoppy & Topper, Iskin, EXIB, A $200.00

Hopalong Cassidy, pants, bl denim w/longhorn stitching, Blue Bell, scarce, EX, A $100.00

Hopalong Cassidy, pencils, 1 doz in paper litho sleeve, scarce, M, A $120.00

Hopalong Cassidy, Picture Gun & Theatre, Stephens, complete, NMIB..$265.00

Hopalong Cassidy, playhouse, 4 lithoed panels, William Boyd/Charcook, 1950, EX+, A $650.00

Hopalong Cassidy, potato chip can, tin w/color image of Hoppy, w/lid, Kuchmann Foods, 11", EX $135.00

Hopalong Cassidy, rocking chair, vinyl seat & back on chrome-plated frame, litho wood horse head, Comfort Lines, VG+, A $650.00

Hopalong Cassidy, roller skates, complete w/jeweled leather anklets & Hoppy photo, Rollfast, 1950s, unused, NMIB.........$800.00

Hopalong Cassidy, shirt, bl denim w/longhorn stitching, Blue Bell, unused, NM, A...$160.00

Hopalong Cassidy, Crayon and Stencil Set, Transogram, 1950, complete and unused, rare, NMIB, A, $200.00. (Photo courtesy Smith House Toys)

Hopalong Cassidy, doll, rubber head, cloth clothes, gun & holster, 1950, 21", NM, A $300.00

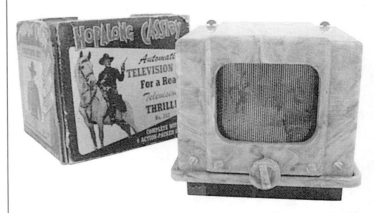

Hopalong Cassidy, TV set, plastic with pull-out knob, film strips revolve inside TV, Automatic Toy, 5x5", EXIB, A, $250.00. (Photo Randy Inman Auctions)

Hopalong Cassidy, Shooting Gallery, Automatic Toy, EXIB, A $300.00

Hopalong Cassidy, skirt, blk w/yel-fringed hem, name & 2 oval images on front, girl's sz, EX, A $90.00

Hopalong Cassidy, spurs, metal w/leather straps, incised Hopalong Cassidy Bar 20, NM+, A $200.00

Hopalong Cassidy, Stagecoach Toss bean bag target, litho tin & Masonite, Transogram, 1950s, 24x18", incomplete o/w EX .$75.00

Hopalong Cassidy, TV set, plastic, battery-op, screen lights up, More Mfg, 1950, 2¾", scarce, MIB, A $130.00

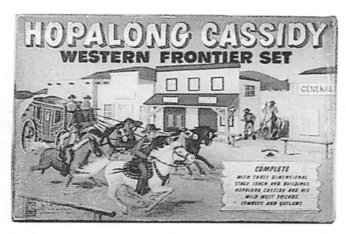

Hopalong Cassidy, Western Frontier Set, Milton Bradley, 1950, NMIB, $300.00. (Photo courtesy Smith House Toys)

Hopalong Cassidy, Woodburning Set, American Toy & Furniture Co/Wm Boyd, 1950, complete, NMIB $225.00

Hopalong Cassidy, wrist cuffs, Hoppy silk-screened on blk leather w/studs & jewels, 1950s, EX+, A, pr $250.00

Lone Ranger, guitar, Calypso Rhythm, Jefferson/American Toy Promotions/ TLR Inc., 1950s, 31", EXIB, A, 175.00. (Photo courtesy James D. Julia, Inc.)

Lone Ranger, binoculars, plastic, Harrison, EX+IB, A ...$135.00

Lone Ranger, boots, blk leather cowboy style w/wht decoration, Endicott-Johnson, EXIB, A $300.00

Lone Ranger, flashlight, tin, USA Lite, MIB, A.............$200.00

Lone Ranger, flicker ring, Lone Ranger/Captain Action, 1960s, NM...$20.00

Lone Ranger, hat, wht cloth sailor type w/bl Hi-Yo Silver! & head portrait graphic, VG+ $60.00

Lone Ranger, holster & wrist cuffs, blk litho on leather-like cb w/leather belt strap, 1930s-40s, VG+ $65.00

Lone Ranger, horseshoe set, rubber, Gardner, NMIB, A..$85.00

Lone Ranger, record player, unpnt wood case w/stamped images, Decca Lone Ranger Inc, EX $300.00

Lone Ranger, ring-toss, diecut cb, complete, Rosebud Art, MIB...$300.00

Lone Ranger, scarf & concho, silk-like w/lg bust & head images of LR & Silver, metal bull's head concho, 1950s, EX+ $65.00

Lone Ranger, target, litho tin stand-up, Marx/TLR Inc, 1938, 10" sq, EX+, A $75.00

Lone Ranger, target game, litho tin stand-up, Marx/TLR Inc, 1938, 10" sq, NMIB, A.......................................$250.00

Lone Ranger, tote bag, embossed head image on red vinyl with name and Hi-Yo Silver phrase in white, 1950s, EX, $175.00.

(Photo courtesy Lee Felbinger)

Maverick, bolo ties, Bret & Bart, w/jeweled cowboy boot & stagecoach slides, MOC, pr $100.00

Maverick, Eras-O-Picture Book, Hasbro, 1958, complete, EX $40.00

Red Ryder, gloves, Playmates, brn, red & bl cloth, tag w/premium offers, Wells Lamont Corp & SS, 1950s, NM..$30.00

Red Ryder, salesman's sample suitcase, Playmates Gloves, Mittens, Ritzee Men's Dress Gloves, Lamont, 11x15", EX $220.00

Rin-Tin-Tin, outfit, Fighting Blue Devil 101st Cavalry, shirt, leather belt, pouch w/bullets, & holster, NMIB, A .$185.00

Rin-Tin-Tin, program, Boston Garden Rodeo, personal appearance by Rinty & co-stars, 32 pgs, Oct 19, 1956, NM+ $55.00

Roy Rogers, archery set, Ben Pearson, 37", scarce, unused, NMOC, A $185.00

Roy Rogers, bank, boot shape, bronzed metal, Almar, 6", EX, C10..$75.00

Roy Rogers, bank, bronzed metal boot shape, Almar, 6", MIB, $275.00. (Photo courtesy Smith House Toys)

Roy Rogers, bank, Roy Rogers & Trigger Savings Bank, tin box w/image of Roy & Trigger framed by horseshoe, 6x8", NM+, A $225.00

Roy Rogers, bolo tie, Bustin' Bull, Putnam Prod, EX (on photo card), A $125.00

Roy Rogers, boots, blk plastic w/yel silhouette bust image of Roy & name, NM+, A...$160.00

Roy Rogers, boots, brn leather w/Roy Rogers in script above tan silhouette image of Roy on rearing Trigger, VG, A .$175.00

Roy Rogers, Branding Iron Set, EXIB.........................$75.00

Roy Rogers, chaps, full pants w/3-color silk-screened image of Roy on Trigger, 32", EX, A $130.00

Roy Rogers, Flash Camera, plastic, H. George, complete, NMIB, A, $325.00. (Photo courtesy Smith House Toys)

Roy Rogers, flashlight, Signal Siren, tin, Usalite, 7", unused, M (EX box), A $160.00

Roy Rogers, gloves, Sears, unused, MIP, A.....................$150.00

Roy Rogers, guitar, wood & pressed wood, red w/wht silhouette images, Range Rhythm Toys/Rich Toys, 31", NMIB, A.$200.00

Roy Rogers, hat, Quick Shooter, press lever & gun appears, Ideal, NMIB, A...$260.00

Roy Rogers, hat, red felt w/chin strap & red & wht RR/Roy Rogers band, RR brand silk-screened on inside, unused, NM+, A $90.00

Roy Rogers, horseshoe set, Ohio Art, MIB, A $125.00

Roy Rogers, lamp bases, plaster figures w/Roy on rearing Trigger w/fence below, Plasto Mfg, 11", EX+, pr $260.00

Roy Rogers, lariat, Lareo Co, 26", EXOC, A $100.00

Roy Rogers, modeling clay set, complete, unused, NM (in box w/image of Roy on rearing Trigger), A.....................$150.00

Roy Rogers, movie, Western Adventure Film #505-C, Hollywood Film Entertainment, 1950s, VG+ $50.00

Roy Rogers, outfit, w/shirt & chaps, Yanki Boy, EXIB, A .$150.00

Roy Rogers, outfits, w/pants, hat & vest, boys or girls, Merit/England, NMIB, A, ea...............................$115.00

Roy Rogers, paint-by-number paint set, RRE Set C/Post Sugar Crisp, 1954, used, EXIB................................$40.00

Roy Rogers, paint-by-number paint set, RRE Set C/Post Sugar Crisp, 1954, unused, MIB, A $75.00

Roy Rogers, pajamas, short-sleeved top w/lithoed fringe, lasso & image of Roy on Trigger, RR Brand on shoulders, EX, A .$65.00

Roy Rogers, pen, Tuckersharpe Products, M (M Roy Rogers Ball Pen $1.00 card), A $165.00

Roy Rogers, pull toy, horse-drawn covered wagon, paper litho on wood, removable cloth cover, NN Hill, 20", EX, A..$250.00

Roy Rogers, raincoat, yel slicker w/blk trim & images of Roy & Trigger, Buch-Baum, NM+, A.................................$190.00

Roy Rogers, Ranch Lantern, Ohio Art, 8", NM+IB, A ..$250.00

Roy Rogers, shirt, bl & wht check w/brn chest fringe, wht sleeve buttons & trim, Made in CA/JbarT, child-sz, NM, A.$125.00

Roy Rogers, slippers, 2-tone leather w/name & image of Roy on Trigger on tops, NMIB, A $225.00

Roy Rogers, spats set, Boot-Ster Mfg, 1950s, leather w/images of Roy & Trigger & signature, unused, NM+IB, A......$250.00

Roy Rogers, spurs, RR brand on conchos on leather straps, Classy, 1954, NM+IB $225.00

Roy Rogers, suspenders, Roy Rogers Braces, DH Neuman, NMOC, A $140.00

Roy Rogers, telescope, plastic, H George, 9", MIB, A $200.00

Roy Rogers, tent, miniature salesman's sample version, yel cloth w/image of Roy on Trigger, w/display base, 15", NM, A.$300.00

Roy Rogers, tie, gr silk w/image of Roy on rearing Trigger, Neumann, 1950s, MIB $75.00

Roy Rogers, tie & tie slide, DH Neuman, unused, MIB .$125.00

Roy Rogers, towel, head image of Roy & mk King of Cowboys, Cannon, 11x11", EX, A...$85.00

Roy Rogers, towel, image of Roy on rearing Trigger under ranch gate, King of Cowboys, 1950s, 40x19", EX, A $150.00

Roy Rogers, Trick Lasso/Swivel Lasso, complete, NMIP, A..$190.00

Roy Rogers, Woodburning Set, Burn-Rite, complete, EX, A..$175.00

Tom Mix, luminous arrowhead w/compass & magnifying glass, EX, C10..$35.00

Tonto, soap, figural, Castile/Kerk Guild, EXIB $50.00

Wild Bill Hickok, outfit, w/shirt, chaps, neckerchief, holster & plastic gun, Yankiboy, unused, MIB, A $125.00

Wild Bill Hickok, outfit, w/vest & chaps, blk & wht cow print & yel w/blk & wht cord trim, silk-screened image, NM, A $100.00

Wild Bill Hickok, toothbrush holder, dbl metal holsters, Tek, 1955, NMOC, A..$80.00

Wild Bill Hickok, wallet, fastens w/western buckle, NM+, C10 ....$75.00

Zorro, bolo tie, marbleized plastic disk w/name above head image on metal clasp, blk cord tie, 1950s-60s, 15", NM.........$55.00

Zorro, accessory set with mask, whip, lariat, and ring, Shimmel/WDP, M (with 24" long card picturing Guy Williams), A, $150.00. (Photo courtesy Smith House Toys)

Zorro, bowl & plate, Zorro graphics, Sun-Valley Melmac, 1950s-60s, 5" & 7¼", EX...$45.00
Zorro, hat & mask, felt, EX, C10......................................$75.00

Zorro, Magic Slate, Watkins-Strathmore/WDP, 1950s – 60s, complete, EX, $85.00. (Photo courtesy Smith House Toys)

Zorro, Oil Painting-By-Number Set, Hassenfeld Bros, 1960, complete, VGIB...$65.00
Zorro, pinwheel, plastic w/mask in center, bell rings when spinning, WDP, NM, A...$155.00
Zorro, purse, vinyl, 1993, 4x8", M, N2..............................$15.00
Zorro, Target Board w/Dart Shooting Rifle, metal, T Cohn/WDP, NMIB, A...$125.00
Zorro, Target Shoot, Lido/WDP, MIB, A...........................$225.00
Zorro, tote bag, red vinyl, EX...$275.00

Windups, Friction, and Other Mechanicals

Windup toys represent a fun and exciting field of collecting. Our fascination with them stems from their simplistic but exciting actions and brightly colored lithography, and especially the comic character or personality-related examples are greatly in demand by collectors today. Though most were made through the years of the '30s through the '50s, they carry their own weight against much earlier toys and are considered very worthwhile investments. Various types of mechanisms were used — some are key wound while others depend on lever action to tighten the mainspring and release the action of the toy. Tin and celluloid were used in their production, and although it is sometimes possible to repair a tin windup, experts advise against investing in a celluloid toy whose mechanism is not working, since the material is usually too fragile to withstand the repair.

Many of the boxes that these toys came in are almost as attractive as the toys themselves and can add considerably to their value.

Advisors: Richard Trautwein (T3); Scott Smiles (S10)

See also Aeronautical; Automobiles and Other Replica Vehicles; Boats; Chein; Lehmann; Marx; Robots and Space Toys; Strauss.

AMERICAN

American Circus, litho tin, 6", EX, A...........................$360.00
Army Car, Irwin, plastic, dk olive w/wht stenciling on door & roof, 12", MIB...$300.00
Army Tow Truck, B-Line USA #310, 1950s, plastic w/blk rubber tires, crank-activated tow line, 9", MIB, A.............$125.00
Artie the Clown in Crazy Car, Unique Art, litho tin, 7", EX $500.00
Beverly Hillbillies Car, Ideal, 1953, plastic, complete w/figures & accessories, 22½", nonworking o/w EXIB, A...........$500.00
Billiard Table w/Two Players (Mechanical Billiard Table), Ranger Steel Prod, 13½" L, NMIB $650.00
Black Boxers, Ives, Pat 1876, 2 cloth-dressed figures atop wooden box, 11", EX, A $10,450.00
Black Boy on Velocipede, Stevens & Brown, Pat 1870, cloth-dressed figure on 3-wheeled cycle, 12", EX, A......$3,080.00

Black Dancing Man, Ives/Charles Hatchkiss, 1886, 12", EX, A, $3,300.00; Black Dancing Couple, late 1800s, 11", EX, A, $4,180.00. (Photo courtesy Bertoia Auctions)

Black Double Dancers, Ives, 1890s, 2 figures in cloth dresses & wht knee socks atop wooden dovetailed box, 10", EX, A $880.00

Black Fiddler, Ives, 1880s, man w/glass eyes, cloth clothes & tin shoes seated on pnt wood box, 9½", EX, A $6,000.00

Black Preacher at the Pulpit, Ives, cloth robe, wood pulpit, 10½", redressed, EX, A $3,080.00

Black Preacher at the Pulpit, Ives, 1880s, cloth pants, stenciled wood pulpit, 10½", NMIB, A $6,600.00

Bombo (Monkey in Tree), Unique Art, litho tin, 10", EXIB..$225.00

Boss Locomotive, Fallows, pnt tin w/CI wheels, 8", Fair+, A .$275.00

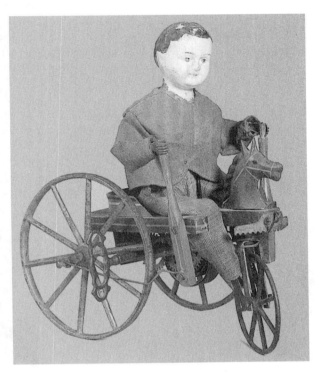

Boy on Velocipede, Ives, 1870s, 8", EX, A, $17,250.00. (Photo courtesy Skinner, Inc.)

Capitol Hill Racer, Unique Art, 1930s, litho tin, 17" L, EXIB, from $200 to $300.00

Carousel, Wolverine, litho tin, horses & planes, red, yel & bl swag & tassel motif, musical, 11" dia, NM...............$400.00

Casey the Cop, Unique Art, litho tin, 9", EXIB to NMIB, from $600 to..$1,000.00

Charlie Chaplin, B&R, litho tin, 8½", EXIB, A $1,900.00

Charlie Chaplin, Ferguson Novelty, stuffed cloth body w/pnt compo head, lead feet, Bakelite cane, 9", EX, A......$500.00

Charlie Chaplin on Bicycle, Gilbert, litho tin, gravity-powered string toy, 8", VG $75.00

Checker Cab, Courtland, litho tin w/lithoed driver, gr & yel w/blk & wht checks, 7½", VG+, A..........................$250.00

Cragstan Construction Set, 1960s, plastic, friction, 28-pc set, unused, MIB..$275.00

Dandy Jim (2 Clowns), Unique Art, litho tin, 9", EX, A .$400.00

Doin' the Howdy Doody (Howdy & Bob at Piano), Unique Art, litho tin, 8½", EX+, A $1,200.00

Doin' the Howdy Doody (Howdy & Bob at Piano), Unique Art, litho tin, 8½", NMIB, A $2,200.00

Clowns on Revolving Mules, Ives/Blakeslee, ca 1890, diecut paper litho figures on wood box, 8", EX, A, $13,200.00. (Photo courtesy Bertoia Auctions)

Donald Duck Handcar (w/Pluto in Doghouse), Lionel, 1930s, tin w/compo figures, 11", EX, A $630.00

Donald Duck Handcar (w/Pluto in Doghouse), Lionel, 1930s, tin w/compo figures, 11", NM+IB........................$1,200.00

Drum Major, Wolverine, litho tin, 13", EX....................$350.00

Duck, Clark, pnt pressed steel, friction, 9", VG.............$150.00

Elephant & Driver, Clark, elephant on 3-wheeled platform w/driver behind seated on box, pnt tin, friction, 11" L, G+, A...$200.00

Express Bus (Mystery Motor), Wolverine, litho tin, 14", NMIB, A...$200.00

Finnegan (Baggage Truck), Unique Art, litho tin, 14", NMIB $400.00

Flying Circus, Unique Art, elephant balances clown & airplane on rod, litho tin, EX $400.00

Flying Circus, Unique Art, elephant balances clown & airplane on rod, litho tin, NMIB, from $700 to................$1,000.00

Foxy Fido, Paul Jones, 1925, tin, internal flywheel action, 8", EXIB..$375.00

George Washington Holding Flag Atop Drum, Ives, ca 1870, compo head & cloth outfit, tin drum, 10", EX, A .$4,400.00

GI Joe & His Jouncing Jeep, Unique Art, 1941, litho tin, EX+IB, A...$300.00

GI Joe & His K-9 Pups, Unique Art, litho tin, 9", NM+IB..$350.00

Giant Ride Ferris Wheel, Ohio Art, litho tin w/plastic seats, 17", G, A...$175.00

Git Along Li'l Doggie Cowboy Car, Unique Art, litho tin, 7", VG $200.00

Goofy Ball (Basketball), litho cb figure, lever action, 8", EXIB, A $65.00

Groceries Delivery Van, Kingsbury, tin open C-style cab w/wht rubber tires, 8", driver & steering wheel missing, G, A.$60.00

Hobo Train, Unique Art, lithographed tin, 8", VGIB, A, $550.00. (Photo courtesy Randy Inman Auctions)

Home Run King, Selrite Mfg, litho tin, 7", VG, A.........$400.00

Horse-Drawn Carriage (Cuzner Trotter), Ives, ca 1871, cloth-dressed driver, spoke wheels, 11", EX, A..............$3,850.00

Horse-Drawn Farm Wagon, Wolverine, w/driver, 10x5", EXIB..$175.00

Hott & Tott, Unique Art, litho tin, 9", EXIB, from $1,250 to $1,400.00

Howdy Doody, see also Doin' the Howdy Doody or Pump Mobile

Howdy Doody Cart, Ny-Lint, litho tin, 9", NM, A........$425.00

Humphrey Mobile, Wyandotte, 1950, litho tin, 7", EX..$450.00

Humphrey Mobile, Wyandotte, 1950, litho tin, 7", EXIB, A $600.00

Ice Cream 5¢ Scooter, Courtland, litho tin, w/driver & bell, 6½", VGIB, A...$325.00

Jackie Gleason Bus, Wolverine, 1955, litho tin, press-down action, 14", NMIB...$900.00

Jazzbo Jim (Jigger & Fiddler), Unique Art, litho tin, 10", EX $500.00

Kiddy Cyclist, Unique Art, lithographed tin, 9", EX, $400.00. (Photo courtesy Randy Inman Auctions)

Jolly Jigger, Wolverine, litho tin, 12", EXIB..................$325.00

Jolly Jiggers (Dutch Boy & Girl), Schoenhut, clothed compo figures dance when clapboards are pressed down, EX, A $1,540.00

Jubilee Trotting Course, 1870s, EX (w/orig wood box), A $28,600.00

Jungle Pete the Mechanical Alligator, Automatic Toy, litho tin, 15", MIB $175.00

Kaufmann & Baer Special Delivery Van, Turner, 1920s, metal, spoke wheels, red & cream, w/driver, 13", A........$1,980.00

Kid Flyer, B&R, litho tin, 8", VG, A $450.00

Kiddie Fireman, Unique Art, 8½", G+, A....................$175.00

Kiddie Kampers, Sunny Andy, litho tin, gravity toy, 14" L, G, A $135.00

Kiddie-Go-Round, Unique Art, litho tin & plastic, 10", VG, A $250.00

Li'l Abner & His Dogpatch Band, Unique Art, litho tin, 6x9", EXIB..$750.00

Lincoln Tunnel, Unique Art, litho tin, 24" L, EX $400.00

Loop-A-Loop, Wolverine, litho tin, 19" track, NM $450.00

Mammy Walker, Lindstrom, litho tin, 8", EX $250.00

Man in Rowboat (Lennie), Ives, Pat 1889, cloth-dressed man w/oars in pnt-tin boat, 11", EX, A $3,850.00

Merry-Go-Round, Irwin, plastic, 4 girls seated in chairs spin around center globe, 9", MIB, A $825.00

Mickey Mouse Circus Cars, Lionel, Mickey in open front car pulling 3 circus cars, litho tin, VG, A.....................$700.00

Mickey Mouse Handcar, Lionel, Mickey & Minnie, 7½", VG+, A, $1,100.00. (Photo courtesy Bertoia Auctions)

Mickey Mouse in Race Car, litho tin w/NP side pipes, rubber tires, 4", EX, A..$500.00

Mickey Mouse on 3-Wheeled Scooter, Mavco, plastic w/movable head, ears & limbs, 6", EX, A $100.00

Monkey on Platform, very early, cloth-dressed monkey on rnd platform attached to wooden block, 11½", EX.....$1,500.00

Monkey Seated Ringing Bells, Ives, Pat 1872, plush w/cloth outfit, brass bells, 9", NMIB, A $5,500.00

Mystery Car, Wolverine, silver-pnt tin, push-down action, 13", EXIB, A $375.00

Native on Alligator, Wolverine, litho tin, 15", EX.........$400.00

Operation Airlift, Automatic Toy, litho tin w/plastic planes, 10", VG $150.00

Over & Under Toy, Wolverine, litho tin, 25" L, NMIB .$250.00

Peter Rabbit Chick Mobile, Lionel, compo figures, 9", G.$225.00

Policeman on Bicycle, AC Gilbert, litho tin, gravity-powered string toy, 8", EX $100.00

Pool Players (2 Figures), Wyandotte, litho tin, 14", VG+, A..$165.00

Popeye in Rowboat, Hoge, 1935, litho tin figure in pressed-steel boat, crank-action, 15", G, A $3,400.00

Pump Mobile, Ny-Lint, car w/Howdy Doody-type figure, litho tin, 9", NMIB, A...$500.00

Rabbit Chase No 150, Wolverine, litho tin, NMIB, A .$1,980.00

Rabbit Handcar (Happy Easter), Wyandotte, litho tin, 6", EX, A $175.00

Race Car, Irwin, 1950s, red & yel plastic, 12½", scarce, MIB .$200.00

Race Car Set, Lionel, early, 2 enameled tin cars w/rubber tires & compo drivers run on dbl-oval track, electric, EX .$1,000.00

Raggy Doodle Parachute Trooper, stuffed cloth w/pnt features, complete w/instructions, 7", VGIB, A $110.00

Red Ranger Ride 'Em Cowboy, Wyandotte, litho tin, 7", MIB $300.00

Rocking Dog w/Whirling Rope, litho tin, 6½", EXIB, A .$85.00

Rocking R Ranch, Courtland, litho tin, 18", G+, A $150.00

Rodeo Joe, Unique Art, lithographed tin, 9", VG, $300.00. (Photo courtesy James Julia, Inc.)

Santa Car (w/Mickey Mouse in Toy Bag), Lionel, WDE, 1935, litho tin & compo, 11", EX+IB, A.........................$1,925.00

Seesaw, Gibbs, pnt tin, turn-over gravity action w/2 figures descending center pole, 10½", VG+, A...................$220.00

Sherman's March, marching soldiers in wooden box w/glass window, hand-crank action, 14" L, VG $800.00

Sky Rangers, Unique Art, litho tin, rectangular base, 10", EXIB $400.00

Sky Rangers, Unique Art, litho tin, rnd base, 10", NMIB .$550.00

Soap Box Derby Speed King, Wyandotte, litho tin, 6", VG, A.$300.00

Sparkling Racer, Lupor, litho tin w/rubber tires, seated driver, 11½", NMIB, A..$200.00

Street Car #781, orange litho tin car w/cut-out windows, 9", VG $150.00

Street Sweeper, Ny-Lint, litho tin, 8", EXIB, A.............$230.00

Sunny Andy Fun Farm, Wolverine, 1930, complete, 14", EX+ $700.00

Taxi, Irwin, plastic, 12", MIB $450.00

Taxi, see also Checker Cab

Taxi, Wolverine, yel & red tin w/lithoed driver & passenger, 13", G $100.00

TC 600 Custom Cruiser, Sears, 1950s, plastic, friction, 12", NMIB $135.00

Traffic Delivery Cycle-Car, Hoge, litho tin 3-wheeled cycle w/van roof extending over driver, 11", VG+, A ...$3,740.00

Trolley, Dayton, dtd 1897, friction, pnt metal w/passengers in windows, 4 close-set spoke wheels, 15", G, A..........$250.00

Woody Woodpecker in Action, Kay-Bee Toys, 1957, pull-string action w/Woody pecking his way down pole, 19", EXIB $135.00

Zilotone, Wolverine, 7", EX, A, $725.00. (Photo courtesy Randy Inman Auctions)

ENGLISH

Big Chief Motorcycle, Mettoy, litho tin w/plastic head, 7½", NMIB, A..$1,400.00

Bus (Double-Decker), Wells, litho tin, mk Thanks For Buying British, 7", EX, A...$185.00

Clown on Motorcycle, Mettoy, litho tin, 7½", EX, from $700 to $1,000.00

Clown w/Spinning Umbrella Hat, litho tin, 8", EX........$250.00

Coupe, litho tin luxury model w/long nose, license plates on front & rear bumpers, red w/silver & blk trim, 12", VG $150.00

Donald Duck Rowing Boat, Tri-Ang Minic, 1950s, plastic boat w/rubber figure, 8", EX...$300.00

Chad Valley Delivery Van, lithographed tin, 10", MIB, $900.00. (Photo courtesy Bertoia Auctions)

Cinderella Railcar, Wells-Brimtoy, complete, EXIB, A, $1,300.00. (Photo courtesy Collectors Auctions Services)

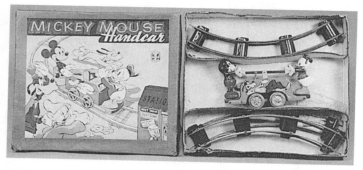

Mickey Mouse Handcar, Wells, complete, EXIB, $1,500.00. (Photo courtesy Bertoia Auctions)

Mary Had a Little Lamb, Wells, plastic, 4½", NMIB, A..$125.00
Minic Dairies Tractor Trailer, Tri-Ang Minic, red & wht w/blk rubber tires, 7", EXIB, A...$100.00
Musical Car, Tri-Ang Minic, purple, NMIB, from $200 to..$300.00
Pluto (Twirling Tail), plastic, 5½", VGIB, A.................$200.00
Police Motorcycle, Mettoy, litho tin, 7½", EX $400.00
Saloon Car, Chad Valley, litho tin, w/driver & passenger, 9", EX...$400.00
Self-Opening Garage w/Car, Mettoy, 5x8" litho tin garage w/6" plastic friction car, NMIB...$200.00
Southern Railway Delivery Truck, Tri-Ang Minic, gr w/Tri-ang Tricycles decal, 5½", EX...$100.00
Trolley Bus, Wells, mk Buy British, litho tin, EX...........$200.00

FRENCH

Advocate (Attorney at Podium), Martin, tin w/cloth outfit, 9", EX+..$1,500.00
Aeroplane Carousel, litho tin, 2 planes on center pole, 9", EXIB, from $200 to $250.00

Alfa-Romeo Racer, 22", VG+IB, A, $4,070.00. (Photo courtesy Randy Inman Auctions)

Auto Transport (Truck w/2-Wheeled Wagon), Martin, 11", EXIB $1,500.00
Barrel Man, Martin, hand-pnt tin w/cloth clothes, 7", VG, A $1,300.00
Bimbo Clown Car, litho tin, 4½", EX, A.......................$100.00
Boy Seated Backwards on Chair (mk Marque Deposee No 138-Article Francais/BTE SGDG), tin & cloth, 7x4", G, A...$1,725.00
Boy Twirling Balls, no cap, pnt tin, 8½", EX $500.00
Boy Twirling Balls, w/cap, pnt tin, 10", EX...................$900.00
Bozo the Clown (w/Umbrella), litho tin, 5", EX+IB $500.00
Bus (City), JP, litho tin w/open cab & side windows, back platform, 6 spoke wheels, w/driver, w/up, 10½", VG $675.00
Bus (Intercity Electric), litho tin w/celluloid windows, w/bell, 15", EX+, A $275.00
Cable Car Ride, 2 cable cars travel track, tin, 30", G, A .$200.00
Carpenter, Martin, woodworker w/pnt tin hands & feet, cloth outfit, tin work bench, 6" L, EX+, A $3,850.00
Cat, De Camps, wht rabbit fur body w/glass eyes, walks, tail moves, squeaks, rare, EX+, A $600.00
Diablo, Martin, pnt tin figure w/cloth suit, Diablo wand in hand, 8", EX, A $1,100.00
Dog, De Camps, chamois-covered w/glass eyes, leather collar, head moves, walks, 8x10", VG+, from $600 to........$700.00
Drunkard Holding Bottle & Cup, Martin, pnt tin w/cloth outfit, 9", EX, A $500.00
Father Francis' Pigs, Martin, pnt tin w/cloth clothes, 8", VG $1,000.00
Fisherman, Martin, pnt tin w/cloth clothes, 7", EX.....$1,800.00
Gai Violinist (Gay Violinist), Martin, pnt tin w/cloth outfit, 7½", EX, A $1,200.00

Lady w/Fan, pnt tin, 7", VG $850.00
Piano Player, Martin, pnt tin w/cloth outfit, plink-plunk music, 6", VG, from $1,200 to.........................$2,000.00
Porsche, Joustra, litho tin w/driver & passengers in windows, friction, 8½", NMIB, from $150 to $250.00
Racer #5, litho tin, red w/silver exhaust pipes, wht-wall tires, driver, 14", EX, A.........................$630.00
Renault Convertible, CIJ, pnt tin w/rubber tires, opening door, compo driver, 13", G, A.........................$675.00
Renault Coupe, CIJ, pnt tin w/rubber tires, 11½", VG, from $700 to.........................$800.00
Street Vendor, Creation Toys, CI woman pushing tin fruit cart, 6", EXIB, from $300 to.........................$500.00
Teddy Jongleur (Teddy the Juggling Clown), litho tin, 9", EX+IB, A.........................$650.00
Tiger, De Camps, real fur skin w/glass eyes, head & legs move, crouches & leaps, 5½x20", EX, from $850 to.......$1,200.00

Balloon and Toy Vendor, Distler, lithographed tin, 7", VG+, $400.00. (Photo courtesy Richard Opfer Auctioneering, Inc.)

Torpedo De Lage, Jep, lithographed tin, 13", EX+IB, A, $2,400.00. (Photo courtesy Richard Opfer Auctioneering, Inc.)

Touring Car, CR, litho tin, open w/rear luggage compartment & spare, w/driver, 15", Fair+, A.........................$800.00
VeBe Dump Truck, pnt tin w/compo driver, 12", EXIB, A.$500.00
VeBe Fire Dept Ladder Truck, pnt tin, 2 figures, 16", G+, A.$325.00
VeBe Tank Truck, pnt tin w/compo driver, 14", VGIB, A ..$850.00

GERMAN

Airplane Go Round, Distler, litho tin w/celluloid props, 2 airplanes circle tower, 7", NMIB, from $275 to $400.00
Akustico 2002, Schuco, tin w/celluloid windshield, rubber tires, 6", EXIB, from $250 to $350.00
Alpine Cable Car, Technofix, 1950s, litho tin, NMIB ...$350.00
Atom Man, see Mister Atom
Ball Player, Gely, litho tin, shoots ball into hoop on platform w/automatic return, 10", EX, A.........................$600.00
Banjo Player Seated w/Legs Crossed, Gunthermann, pnt tin, 6", Fair $900.00

Barney Google on Spark Plug, Nifty, litho tin, 7" L, VG, A.........................$800.00
Bavarian Drinker, Schuco, tin w/cloth outfit, 6½", EX, A..$450.00
Bear & Poodle Performing on 4-Wheeled Platform, pnt tin, 6", G+, A.........................$625.00
Bear Lifting Baby Bear, Schuco, fabric-covered tin w/cloth outfit, 4½", EX.........................$225.00
Billiards Player (Single Player), litho tin, 6" L, G+ $350.00
Bird in Cage, Issmayer, litho tin, chirps, 3½", no stand, VG, A.........................$100.00

Bonzo, Guntherman, lithographed tin, moving eyes and mouth, 10", VG, A, $3,080.00. (Photo courtesy Bertoia Auctions)

Bird in Cage, Issmayer, litho tin, chirps, 7", w/wire stand, VG..$200.00

Bird on Side of Tree Trunk, litho tin, pull cord to activate movements, 6", EX..$175.00

Black Minstrel w/Drum & Cymbal, pnt tin, VG.........$1,400.00

BMW Roadster, Distler, tin, rubber tires, multiple-speed transmission, 10", rstr, A...$100.00

BMW Roadster, Distler, tin, rubber tires, multiple-speed transmission, 10", VGIB, from $175 to...........................$250.00

Boy in Go Cart, Schuco #1035, 3½", EX, from $200 to.$275.00

Boy Lifting Little Girl, Schuco, tin w/cloth Bavarian outfit, 5", EX+, from $150 to...$200.00

Carousel, Gunthermann, litho tin, figures on horses & pigs on rnd base under canopy, musical, 9x10" dia, VG, A.......$1,100.00

Carousel, litho & pnt tin, 6 riders on horses, canopy w/flags & perforated base, 12" (16" to flag), VG, from $775 to....$1,000.00

Carousel, litho tin, 2 seated figures in open chairs & 2 riders on horses, w/canopy & perforated base, 8", EX+, from $400 to...$600.00

Carousel, pnt tin, dual animation w/figures on various rides under 2 canopies on rnd base, 14", EX...............$2,000.00

Cat Chasing Mouse, pnt tin, 9", VG, A..........................$525.00

Cat Trio Playing Instruments, Gunthermann, pnt tin, beveled base, 9", EX..$2,500.00

Clown Band, US Zone, litho tin, 2 clowns w/cymbals & drums on oblong base, 8" L, EX, from $350 to..................$450.00

Clown Bass Fiddler, early, pnt tin, sounds emitted, VG, A..$1,200.00

Clown Drummer, Schuco, tin w/felt outfit, 4½", NMIB, from $250 to..$350.00

Clown Juggler, Schuco, tin w/felt outfit, plastic juggling balls, 5", NMIB, from $300 to...$475.00

Clown Racing Car #2 (Oh La La), US Zone, litho tin w/rubber tires, 6½", EXIB..$875.00

Clown Riding Auto, Fischer, pnt & litho tin half-figure w/revolving head in open auto, 6" L, EX+...........$2,000.00

Clown Standing Playing Drum, pnt tin w/cloth costume, pointed hat, 9", EX+...$1,200.00

Clown Violinist, Schuco, litho tin w/cloth outfit, 4½", EXIB, from $175 to...$250.00

Clown w/Mouse, Schuco, tin w/felt outfit, 4½", VG, from $250 to...$300.00

Clown w/Suitcase, Schuco, tin w/felt outfit, tin suitcase, 4½", VG, from $300 to...$375.00

Coney Island Carnival Ride, Technofix, litho tin, 14x20", NMIB..$250.00

Convertible, Distler, 1950s, tin, long hood w/spare on curved trunk, wht-wall tires, 10½", G+IB, from $150 to....$275.00

Charlie Chaplin, Schuco, tin with cloth outfit, 6½", EX+IB, $1,000.00 to $1,200.00.

Couple Dancing the Tango, painted tin, 8½", EX, from $1,150.00 to $1,600.00. (Photo courtesy Richard Opfer Auctioneering, Inc.)

Charlie Chaplin Dancer, Krauss (?), flat tin figure on crank-op base, 6½", VG+, A.......................................$750.00

Charlie Chaplin Walker, compo head & hands w/lead feet, cloth outfit, 7½", EX, A.......................................$700.00

Cherbane, Tippco, litho tin, driver in open vehicle w/4 passenger bench seats, disk wheels w/pnt spokes, 10", EX, A.$1,100.00

Clown & Performing Dog, pnt tin, dog revolves around clown on dome base in up-&-down motion, VG, A..........$880.00

Cowboy Juggler, Schuco, tin w/cloth outfit, 5", NM, A .$725.00

Cowboy on Horse Wearing Hat & Tails w/Umbrella in Hand, early, pnt tin, EX, A...$425.00

Crawling Buttercup, Gunthermann, pnt tin, 7½", rstr, from $300 to...$400.00

Curvo 1000 Motorcycle w/Driver, litho tin, 5", NMIB, A.$1,000.00

Donald Duck, Schuco, litho tin, long-billed, 6", G+IB, A.$1,600.00

Donald Duck, Schuco, lithographed tin and plastic, newer figure, 6", NMIB, $325.00. (Photo courtesy New England Auctions Gallery)

Donald Duck, Schuco, litho tin & plastic w/felt hat & jacket, 6", EX, from $225 to $350.00
Drummer Boy, Schuco, blk shirt & cap, cloth clothes, 5", VG..$225.00
Duck Beating Drum, Schuco, tin w/felt outfit, 5", EX $700.00
Duck w/Backpack, Schuco, pnt tin w/felt jacket & backpack, 6", EX, from $300 to $400.00
Ebo Motor Limousine, HNE, litho tin, scrolled rooftop luggage rail, open-sided cab w/driver, opening doors, 11", G+, A .$1,500.00

Elephant Rolling Ball, Gunthermann, elephant in cap w/bell at end of trunk rolling litho tin ball, 8", EX, A $1,200.00
English Soldier Beating Drum, Schuco, tin w/cloth uniform & hat, 6", G+, A..$575.00
Examico 4001, Schuco, tin w/celluloid windshield, 5½", EX, from $200 to $250.00
Felix the Cat, Pat Sullivan, 1922, pnt tin, 7", overpnt, A .$400.00
Felix the Cat on Scooter, Gunthermann, 1922, litho tin, 7", EX, from $600 to $700.00
Felix the Cat on 3-Wheeled Handcar, Nifty, litho tin, 7½", EX $450.00
Ferris Wheel, Carette, pnt tin, 4 riders in open chairs in wheel w/wire frame & oblong canopy w/flag, 13", EX.......$950.00
Ferris Wheel, pnt tin, 6 riders in chairs on dbl wire attached to 3 curved columns on beveled base, 13½", EX............$500.00
Fire Ladder Truck, Bing, open cab, electric lights, disk wheels, pnt tin w/10 wooden firemen figures, 21", EX $2,750.00

Fire Ladder Truck, Carette, painted tin, 14", EX+, $6,000.00. (Photo courtesy Bertoia Auctions)

Fire Ladder Truck, Tipp & Co, litho tin, extension ladder mounted over open cab, 2 figures, 13", VG, from $200 to $400.00
Fire Ladder Truck, Tipp & Co, litho tin, extension ladder mounted over open cab, hose reel, 2 figures, 21", G, from $500 to $800.00
Flippo the Frog, Schuco, tin w/felt covering, 3", NMIB, A.$100.00
Ford Convertible, Distler, tin (various colors), rubber tires, multiple-speed transmission, 10", VG $150.00
Ford Roadster, Bing, pnt tin, w/driver, 6½", NMIB, A...$750.00
Ford Roadster, Distler, tin w/rubber tires, multiple-speed transmission, 10", EXIB...$200.00
Fox Carrying Goose Cage, Schuco, fur-head w/felt outfit, litho tin cage, 4", EX+ $900.00
Gama Tank, tin w/rubber treads, sparking gun, 6½", EX.$125.00
Garage (Fire Dept w/Hook & Ladder & Engine No 2), Bing, 2-bay, litho tin, 6x8", EX, A....................................$1,200.00
Garage w/Auto #1750, Schuco, EX (partial box), from $225 to.$300.00
Garage w/2 Autos, Bing, litho tin, 7x8", EX...................$725.00
Garage w/2 Autos, Bing, litho tin, 7x8", NM (partial box), A $1,100.00

Ferris Wheel, painted tin, 15½", EX, A, $2,400.00. (Photo courtesy Bertoia Auctions)

Gas Pump, DC, tin w/glass fill tanks, rubber hose w/nozzle, hand-crank, 8", G $225.00

General Double-Decker Bus, litho tin, seated passengers & moving ticket agent on top level, disk wheels, 8", EX..$1,750.00

Girl w/Maypole, Schuco, litho tin w/felt clothes & beret, wooden pole in hand, 5", VG, A.............................$330.00

Girl w/Stick & Bag & Two Geese, US Zone, 1950s, litho tin, 7", NMIB...$175.00

Gnome w/Gnome, Schuco, tin w/cloth outfit & leather apron, 4", VG, A..$500.00

Great Billiard Champion, KIKO, tin, player at table, 6" L, EX+IB (box also mk DRGM & Schutzmarke) $650.00

Happy Jack (Black Minstrel), WK, litho tin, crank action, 6", G, A $600.00

Hessmobile, litho tin, 2 figures, 9", VG, A $575.00

Hi-Way Henry, Fischer, litho tin, 10", G, A................$1,100.00

Horse-Drawn Fire Ladder Truck, Orobr, litho tin w/6 pnt figures on benches, 2 overhead ladders, 2 horses, 11", VG+ .$250.00

Hot Air Figure, man standing w/pack on back & valve on neck for water fill, pnt tin, 8", EX.....................$775.00

Jaguar Roadster, Distler, tin, rubber tires, top down, multiple-speed transmission, 10", EXIB, from $250 to $300.00

Jaguar Roadster, Distler, tin, rubber tires, top down, multiple-speed transmission, 10", VG, from $100 to..............$200.00

Jiggs Jazz Car, Nifty, 1924, litho tin, 7", EX, A $1,650.00

Lady Holding Garden Rake & Watering Can, Gunthermann, pnt tin, 7", VG...$850.00

Limousine, Bing, litho tin, open, NP grille, running boards, metal spoke wheels, rear spare, driver, 11", VG, from $350 to..$500.00

Limousine, Bing, litho tin 4-door w/rear opening doors, steerable front, disk wheels, no driver, 6", G, from $275 to....$350.00

Limousine, Carette, litho tin, doorless cab, railed roof, glass windows, rubber tires w/spokes, driver, 16", VG.........$2,000.00

Limousine, Carette, litho tin, doorless cab, railed roof, glass windows, rubber tires w/spokes, 4 figures, 16", EX, A..$3,300.00

Limousine, Distler, litho tin, extended front bumper, rear luggage compartment, 15½", EX $1,500.00

Limousine, Fisher, litho tin, curved roof w/railed top, open cab, metal spoke wheels, opening doors, driver, 10", VG+, A...$1,250.00

Limousine, Gunthermann, litho tin, plain roof, disk wheels, opening rear doors, driver, 11½", EX...................$1,300.00

Limousine, Gunthermann, litho tin, simulated fold-down top & divider backrest, spoke wheels, driver, 5", VG+ $950.00

Limousine, Gunthermann, lithographed tin, 12", EX+, A, $3,670.00. (Photo courtesy Bertoia Auctions)

Limousine (Model T), blk tin w/metal spoke wheels, lady driver, 6", NM, A $575.00

Mac 700 Motorcycle & Rider, Arnold, litho tin, blk version, 8", EXIB, from $850 to $1,100.00

Mac 700 Motorcycle & Rider, Arnold, litho tin, red & silver version, 8", EXIB, from $1,000 to $1,400.00

Maggie & Jiggs, Distler, litho tin figures on 4-wheeled platform, 6", EX...$1,250.00

Limousine, Carette, lithographed tin, 13", EX, A, $6,050.00.
(Photo courtesy, Bertoia Auctions)

Limousine, CC&GP Co/Bavaria, tin, 4-door w/open windows, simulated spoke wheels, electric lights, driver, 10", G $325.00

Mickey Mouse and Minnie on Dunlop Cord Motorcycle, Tipp, lithographed tin, 10" long, restored, A, $26,400.00.
(Photo courtesy Bertoia Auctions)

Magico Auto Racer, Schuco, tin, w/orig magic wand, 5½", EX, from $225 to $325.00

Man Pushing Geese in Cart, Distler, litho tin, 7", VG ...$900.00

Marta Ford Formula 1 Racer, Schuco, tin & plastic, 9½", NMIB, from $75 to $150.00

Mercedes Convertible Coupe, Distler, tin, rubber tires, rear spare, multiple-speed transmission, 10", G, A $150.00

Mercedes Micro Racer, Schuco, tin w/rubber tires, 4½", EXIB, from $150 to $250.00

Mercedes Roadster, Distler, tin w/rubber tires, multiple-speed transmission, 10", NMIB...$350.00

Mickey Mouse Hurdy Gurdy With Dancing Minnie Mouse, 1930s, lithographed tin, 6", EX, A, $8,250.00.

(Photo courtesy Bertoia Auctions)

Mickey Mouse w/Moving Eyes & Mouth, 1930s, litho tin, 9", VG, A...$16,500.00

Military Ambulance, Tipp, camo-pnt tin, opening doors, w/stretchers, 1 compo figure, 8", EX, A $575.00

Military Cannon Truck, Tipp, camo-pnt tin, compo figures, 11", VG+..$400.00

Military Cannon Truck, Tipp, gr-pnt tin, compo figures, 11", EX...$400.00

Military Searchlight Truck, Hausser, camo-pnt tin, revolving searchlight, rubber tires, 2 compo figures, 13", EX ..$800.00

Military Searchlight Truck, Tipp, camo-pnt tin, electric search-light, compo figures, 10", VG+ $400.00

Military Staff Car, Lionel, camo-pnt tin, electric lights, 3 compo figures, 10", EX, A.....................................$1,485.00

Military Tank & Cannon Set, Marklin, camo-pnt tin, rubber treads, 12", NMIB, A...$500.00

Mickey Mouse Slate Dancer, 1930s, lithographed tin, hand-crank or steam-powered flywheel, 6", EX+, A, $18,700.00.

(Photo courtesy Bertoia Auctions)

Military Truck, Tipp, camo-pnt tin, electric lights, compo figures, 12", EX, A $300.00

Military Truck, Tipp, camo-pnt tin, open bed, 8", VG+, A..$150.00

Military Truck & Cannon Set, Tipp, camo-pnt tin, compo figures, 19", VG, A..$275.00

Mirakocar, Schuco, tin, NP disk wheels, 4½", EXIB, from $125 to...$200.00

Mister Atom, Schuco, tin w/cloth outfit, 5", NM+, A.$1,350.00

Monkey (Wearing Fez) on Motorcycle, Gama, litho tin, 7", EX..$500.00

Monkey (Wearing Fez) on Motorcycle, Gama, litho tin, 7", EXIB..$650.00

Monkey Drummer, Schuco, litho tin w/cloth outfit, 4½", EX, from $100 to $150.00

Monkey Drummer in Parade Uniform w/Drumsticks, litho tin, sq clockwork box, 8", EX, A $300.00

Monkey Lifting Mouse, Schuco, litho tin w/cloth outfit, 5", EX+..$200.00

Monkey Performing on Horseback, pnt tin, 2-wheeled mecha-nism, 6½", G, A...$450.00

Monkey Standing Playing Bass Drum, pnt tin, w/bells on wire support above drum, 7", EX+ $1,430.00

Monkey Violinist, Schuco, felt-covered tin w/felt outfit, 4½", NMIB, from $225 to.......................................$300.00

Motodrill Clown, Schuco, tin figure w/cloth outfit, litho tin motorcycle, 5", VG, A..$550.00

Motorcycle Driver, Passenger & Sidecar (passenger behind dri-ver — not in sidecar), Salheimer, litho tin, VG+....$375.00

Motorbike With Cyclist, lithographed tin, 8", VG+, A, $3,520.00. (Photo courtesy Randy Inman Auctions)

Motorcycle Racer #4 (GE 258), litho tin, 7", EX, from $300 to...$400.00
Motorcycle w/Couple, Tipp, litho tin, 9½", NM.........$1,750.00
Motorcycle w/Couple (XY 176), George Levy, litho tin, 9", VG...$200.00
Motorcycle w/Couple & Child in Sidecar, Tipp, litho tin, 9", EXIB $2,000.00
Motorcycle w/Driver, Tipp, litho tin, NP luggage rack, electric headlight, full windshield, friction, 11½", EX $900.00
Motorcycle w/Driver & Covered Sidecar (T688), Tipp, litho tin, 7½", VG, A $1,200.00
Motorcycle w/German Soldier, Arnold, litho tin w/camo detail, sparkler headlight, w/rifle, 7½", EX, from $825 to ..$950.00
Motorcycle w/German Soldier (WH34), Salheimer & Strauss, litho tin, olive gr, 7", VG, A $525.00
Motorcycle w/Military Driver & Passenger, Kellerman, 2 tin figures in brn uniforms & helmets, 6", VG+.................$400.00
Mouse in Roadster #2005, Schuco, felt-covered tin, 5½", EX, A..$450.00
Mouse Lifting Baby Mouse, Schuco, felt-covered tin w/cloth pants, 4½", EX, A $175.00
Musical Doll, cloth-dressed figure atop litho tin can-shaped base w/hand crank, EX, A $500.00
Mystery Car & Garage, litho tin, 4", EXIB.....................$200.00
Oh La La Clown Racing Car, see Clown Racing Car #2
Old Sailor Walker, Gama, litho tin figure w/hands in pockets & pipe in mouth, 7", EX...$200.00
Paddy's Pride, pig pulling man in 2-wheeled cart, litho tin, 8", EX, A...$600.00
Peter Tumbling Acrobat, Schuco, tin w/cloth clothes, 5", NMIB, A..$500.00
Phaeton, Orobr, tin, open 4-door, disk wheels, driver, 6", G..$400.00
Phaeton (Double), Carette, emb litho tin vehicle w/folding cloth top, w/driver & passenger, 12", VG+, A $2,860.00

Pig Drummer, Schuco, felt-covered tin w/cloth outfit, 4½", VG+, A..$150.00
Pig Running on 3-Wheeled Mechanism, pnt tin, 5", G+, A.$275.00
Pig w/Suitcase, Schuco, tin w/cloth outfit, 5", EX+, A...$500.00
Porsche, Schuco, plastic, well detailed, 8½", EX, from $225 to $300.00
Porsche Racer #4, Schuco, plastic, silver, 11½", MIB, from $75 to $125.00
Porter Pushing Trunk on Two-Wheeled Cart, Stock, litho tin, 6½" L, VG, A $275.00
Powerful Katrinka Pushing Wheelbarrow, Nifty, litho tin, no Jimmy figure, 5½", G, from $300 to........................$450.00

Powerful Katrinka Pushing Jimmy in Wheelbarrow, Nifty, lithographed tin, 5½", VG, $950.00. (Photo courtesy Richard Opfer Auctioneering, Inc.)

Racer, Ernst Plank, pnt tin w/NP Plank emblem, w/fold horn & side spare, 10", EX+, A...$2,475.00
Racer, JDN, litho tin, bl w/yel trim, rear spare, electric lights, driver, 9½", EX, A..$1,650.00
Racer, Tipp & Co, litho tin w/lg blk rubber tires, pnt driver, 11", VG, A $275.00
Racer (Studio #1050), Schuco, 5½", EXIB, from $150 to..$250.00
Racer #4, Distler, litho tin, yel & red, w/driver, 12", EX+, A..$825.00
Racer #12 (Boattail), litho tin, silver w/gr detail, disk wheels w/red hubs, driver, 19", EX...................................$1,750.00
Racer #12 (Boattail), Tipp, litho tin, tan w/red detail, disk wheels w/red hubs, driver, 19", G, A $800.00
Radio Car, Schuco #4012, 6", NMIB, from $500 to $600.00
Rudy the Ostrich, Nifty, litho tin, 8½", G.....................$250.00
Sailor w/Binoculars, Schuco, tin w/cloth outfit, 5", VG, A...$450.00
Saloon Auto, Bing, litho tin, bl & blk w/NP grille, disk wheels, electric lights, driver, 11", EX, A..............................$925.00
Saloon Auto, Distler, litho tin, open w/simulated side vents on long hood, disk wheels, orange w/blk, driver, 10", VG, A.....$350.00
Saloon Auto, Distler, litho tin, simulated fold-down top, spoke wheels, hood lights, red w/blk, driver, 9", VG, A $350.00

Sea Captain w/Binoculars, Schuco, tin w/felt clothing & cap, 5", VG, A $275.00

Silver Mine Express, Technofix, litho tin, 22½", NM $250.00

Sky Pilot, Bing, litho tin, plane & weighted ball spirals down pylon to trestle base, 12", NMIB...........................$1,300.00

Sledding Toy, 4 compo kids on sleds on pnt-tin mountain slope w/3 trees, crank-op, 16" L, NM......................$1,750.00

Slugger Champions, US Zone, 1940s, litho tin, NM+ ...$325.00

Soldier (German) w/Staff, Schuco, litho tin, 5", EX, A .$250.00

Statue of Liberty Airplane Game, Bing, clockwork, NMIB, A $2,200.00

Storekeeper, Schuco, tin body w/celluloid head, felt vest & pants, 5", VG, from $400 to $550.00

Taxi, Karl Bub, litho tin, blk & yel w/simulated spoke wheels, electric lights, driver, 10", G, A $600.00

Tonneau No 50, Carette, litho tin w/glass windshield, rubber tires w/spoke wheels, driver, 8½", VG, A $1,200.00

Toonerville Trolley, Nifty, litho tin, disk wheels, 5", EX..$900.00

Toonerville Trolley, Nifty, litho tin, flanged wheels (scarce), 7", EX, A $2,750.00

Touring Car, Bing, 1906, pnt tin open auto w/front & back seat, rubber tires w/spoke wheels, driver, 9", EX+, A....$4,400.00

Touring Car, Bing, 1912, litho tin, open w/covered bonnet, metal spoke wheels, driver, 9½", EX, from $800 to $1,200.00

Touring Car, Carette, litho tin, open-sided w/front & back seats, 4 orig figures, 8", VG+ $3,000.00

Touring Car, Carette, litho tin, single open seat w/center steering, rubber tires w/spoke wheels, driver, 10", EX, A........$3,500.00

Touring Car, Distler, litho tin, open w/running boards & metal spoke wheels, driver & lady passenger, 8", VG, A ...$650.00

Touring Car (Vauxall), Gunthermann, litho tin, open front & back, center steering, 2 men & 2 ladies, 10", VG, A...........$3,300.00

Touring Cyclon, Greppert & Kelch, 1920s, litho tin, 3-wheeled rickshaw style w/3 spoke wheels, driver, 6½", EX, A........$2,200.00

Trolley, Bing, litho tin, w/up w/reverse mechanism, 8", EX, A...$525.00

Trolley, Gunthermann, litho tin w/glass windows, w/trolley pull & motor man, 10½", EX $1,000.00

Trolley, litho tin, opening front & rear side doors, yel w/red stripe, blk roof, 13", VG $1,100.00

Trolley, Orobr, litho tin, w/figure, 10", VG $400.00

Trolley & Auto Platform, Goso, litho tin, street scene w/2 end buildings, cop directs auto & trolley, 10", no roofs ..$350.00

Trolley #50, litho tin, 4½", VG, A..................................$275.00

Trolley #63, litho tin, battery-op lights, 9", EX, A..........$300.00

Trolley #520, litho tin w/pnt roof, glazed windows, 10", VG.$350.00

Trolley #620, litho tin, 8", EX, A $800.00

Uncle Wiggily Crazy Car, Distler, litho tin, 9½", VG.$1,400.00

Volkswagen Beetle (3 Gear Car), JNF, litho tin, silver headlights & bumpers, 7", NMIB, A $350.00

Walking Man w/Three Faces, Distler, litho tin, 8½", NMIB .$2,500.00

JAPANESE

Accordion Bear Seated on Base, MST, plush w/rubber face & hands, 10", EX, A $400.00

Air Transport Van, Daiya, 1950s, litho tin, friction, 8", NMIB $150.00

Ali & The Flying Carpet, KO, litho tin, crank action, NM.$400.00

Animal Cycle, see Rabbit on Motorcycle

Animal Express, MT, litho tin, friction, 17", EX, A..........$85.00

Astro Boy (Japanese Hero), ATD, NM+IB, A, $4,500.00.

(Photo courtesy Smith House Toys)

Atom Jet Racer #58, Yone, litho tin, rubber tires, driver, 26", VG+ $2,700.00

Atom Racer #153, Yone, litho tin, rubber tires, driver, friction, 15", EX..$1,300.00

Atom Racer #153, Yone, litho tin, rubber tires, driver, friction, 15", EXIB...$1,800.00

Atom Space Race Car #55, litho tin, lg rubber tires, driver, friction, 13", EX+, A..$825.00

Atom Star Car w/Police Motorcycle in Pursuit, Yone, litho tin, pull cycle to wind, 12" overall, EX, from $500 to $700.00

Auto Carrier, Cragstan, 1950s, litho tin, w/4 cars, friction, 9", NMIB..$100.00

Auto Transport, Sanyo, tin, w/6 cars, friction, 13", NMIB, A...$175.00

Babes in Toyland Soldier, Linemar/WDP, litho tin, 6", EXIB.$425.00

Vauxall, Guntherman, lithographed tin, with four figures, 10", VG, A, $3,300.00. (Photo courtesy Bertoia Auctions)

Baseball Catcher, Occupied Japan, celluloid figure looking up, 5½", NM+IB, A $225.00

Batman in Rocket Car, 1960s, plastic, friction, 8", scarce, EX+ $325.00

Batmobile (3-Wheeled), Ichimura, 1966, litho tin, rotating disk engine, Batman (in Japanese) on rear fenders, 6", EX .$400.00

Bear Golfer, TPS, litho tin, 8" L, EX+IB, from $225 to..$300.00

Bear in Row Boat, STE, 1950s, 10", NM+IB $275.00

Big Bad Wolf and the Three Little Pigs, Linemar, lithographed tin, 4" , EXIB, A, $650.00 each. (Photo courtesy Collectors Auction Services)

Boy Boxers on 2-Wheeled Platforms, blk & wht celluloid figures in boxing shorts, 6½", EX, A $225.00

Boy Carrying 2 Suitcases, litho tin w/celluloid head, 8", VG, A...$250.00

Boy Riding Tricycle, celluloid figure on litho tin tricycle, 6", EX..$175.00

Bulldog Truck, litho tin bulldog w/windshield eyes & open body, rubber tires, friction, 8", EXIB, A............................$200.00

Camper, Cragstan, 1950s, snub-nosed cab, friction, 8", NM .$100.00

Car & House Trailer, see Ford Auto & House Trailer

Casper Super Ghost Tank, Linemar, litho tin, 4", EXIB.$400.00

Champion Midget Racer #63, litho tin, rubber tires, driver, friction, 7", EX, A..$1,050.00

Champion Midget Racer #63, litho tin, rubber tires, driver, friction, 7", G, A..$300.00

Champion Racer #98, litho tin, rubber tires, driver, 18", NM+IB $3,000.00

Champion Racer #98, litho tin, rubber tires, driver, 18", VG.$800.00

Cheery Cook, SNK, celluloid, 5", NMIB, A...................$125.00

Chef on Roller Skates, TPS, litho tin w/cloth pants, 6", VG+, from $175 to $275.00

Child Land Ferris Wheel (Dream Land), litho tin, 10", EXIB.$225.00

Chrysler Sedan, CK, litho tin w/NP grille, full running boards, simulated spoke wheels, 7", NMIB, A $1,200.00

Circling Helicopter H-2, 1950s, litho tin, 6", EXIB $100.00

Clarabell Standing on Hands, Linemar/Kagran, 1950s, litho tin, 5", NMIB, A...$1,000.00

Clown Balancing Monkey on Chair Above Head, TPS, litho tin, 9", EX, from $400 to $450.00

Clown Violinist, TPS, stilt-like legs, cloth outfit, 9", VG, A.$120.00

Condor Motorcycle, IY Metal Toys, 1950s, litho tin, friction, 11½", EXIB, A $2,700.00

Continental Super Special Convertible, Cragstan, litho tin, celluloid windshield, compo driver, friction, 14", EXIB, A..$225.00

Continental Trailways Bus w/Observation Deck, tin, friction, 10½", EX+IB, from $150 to $250.00

Cragstan Ambulance (White Station Wagon), tin, friction, 8½", EXIB...$100.00

Cragstan Red-Mill Bank, 1950s, litho tin, coin-op, 7", NMIB..$75.00

Davidson Motorcycle & Rider, IY Metal Toys, litho tin, friction, 15", EX, A..$3,400.00

Davy Crockett Stagecoach, Linemar, litho tin, friction, 5", NM, A..$100.00

DAX 70 Honda Motorcycle, TPS, plastic, w/driver, 6x6", NMIB $100.00

DC Transit GMC Bus, ATC, litho tin w/celluloid windows, rubber tires, friction, 17", VG, A...............................$300.00

Delicious Ice Cream Truck, 1960, litho tin, w/driver & bell, friction, 8", EXIB, A..$425.00

Delicious Ice Cream Truck, 1960, litho tin, w/driver & bell, friction, 8", NM+...$300.00

Doll Buggy, see Girl Pushing Doll Buggy

Donald Duck Acrobat (Gym-Toys Acrobat), Linemar, celluloid figure, NMIB, from $300 to $400.00

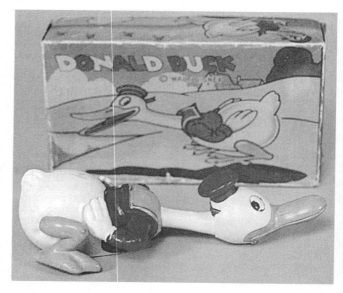

Donald Duck Crawler, Borgfeldt, prewar, painted celluloid long-billed figure, 9", NM+IB, $3,000.00. (Photo courtesy Bertoia Auctions)

Donald Duck Crawler, Borgfeldt, prewar, pnt celluloid long-billed figure, 9", EX, from $1,700 to $1,900.00

Donald Duck Flivver, Linemar, litho tin car w/celluloid figure, friction, 5½", NM..$450.00

Donald Duck Holding Closed Umbrella, Linemar/WDP, litho tin, tail spins, 5", EX, from $300 to $375.00

Donald Duck Pulling Delivery Wagon, Linemar, litho tin, friction, 6" L, EX (Poor box), A $825.00

Donald Duck Pulling Huey, Linemar, litho tin, 5½" & 2", EX, A, from $300 to $400.00

Donald Duck the Skier, Linemar, litho tin, 6", EX, A $775.00

Donald Duck the Skier, Linemar, litho tin, 6", EXIB $925.00

Donald Duck's Rocket Car, MT, litho tin car w/plastic head, friction, 13", VG, A $200.00

Dream Car, see Louis in His Dream Car

Dream Land Ferris Wheel, see Child Land Ferris Wheel

Drummer Boy Seated w/Legs Spread & Drum in Lap, litho tin w/celluloid head, 5½", G+ $375.00

Duckmobile, W Toy, litho tin car w/celluloid Donald Duck figure, friction, 6½", EXIB, from $500 to.....................$650.00

Eagle Race Car, IY Metal Toys, litho tin w/rubber tires, driver, friction, 10", G+, A $325.00

Easter on Parade, tin & celluloid, rabbit pulling chicks in cart, friction, 5½", MIB, A $125.00

Elephant Circus Truck, litho tin, elephants move back & forth in truck bed, friction, 8", NM, A $275.00

Fast Freight Continental Express Semi, Utaka, tin, friction, 12", NMIB...$150.00

Fiat 600 Auto w/Sunroof, Bandai, tin, friction, 7", EX...$100.00

Figaro the Cat (Pinocchio), Linemar, 1950s, litho tin, friction, 3", EX, A $60.00

Fire Bird Racer #3, litho tin, inflatable tires, complete w/spare pump & wrench, 14½", EXIB, A $225.00

Fire Chief Car, litho tin, friction, 8½", NMIB, A...........$110.00

Fishing Bear, TPS, litho tin, 7", EXIB, A......................$275.00

Fishing Monkey on Whales, TPS, MIB $450.00

Flintstone Pals on Dino (Fred), Linemar, litho tin, 8", EXIB..$500.00

Flintstone Turnover Tank, Linemar, 1961, litho tin, 4", MIB.$800.00

Ford Auto & House Trailer, SSS, 1950s, litho tin, friction, 15", NMIB, from $225 to...$350.00

Ford Sedan, Kosuge, prewar, litho tin, red, 7", VGIB $375.00

Gay 90's Old Timer Car, litho tin, driver, friction, 5½", EX+IB $125.00

Gay 90's Unicycle w/Bell (mk 1890), TPS, litho tin tricycle & figure w/cloth clothes, 6½", EX...............................$300.00

Girl Pushing Doll Buggy w/Umbrella, celluloid, balls hang from umbrella, 7", MIB..$125.00

Girl Roller Skater, celluloid figure on 1 skate w/wheels & high-button spats, 7½", VG..$350.00

Glide-A-Ride, 1961, friction, 9", NMIB $250.00

Go-Stop/Safety First, Alps, celluloid figure on litho tin base w/Go-Stop sign, 7½", EXIB..................................$875.00

Good Humor Ice Cream Truck, litho tin, friction, 11", G+ .$700.00

Gorilla, fur-covered w/celluloid face, 5½", EX+ $150.00

Graham Paige No 3, see Packard

Grain Hauler, 1950s, friction, 10", MIB (sealed) $125.00

Greyhound Bus, KTS, litho tin, rubber tires, friction, 15", EXIB...$200.00

Greyhound Bus, litho tin w/passengers in windows, NP bumper, friction, 12½", VG, A $300.00

Greyhound Bus, see also Magic Greyhound Bus

Greyhound Scenicruiser, litho tin w/rubber tires, friction, 23", EXIB...$400.00

Groggy Car, litho tin w/celluloid Dagwood-type figure, 4", EX, A $175.00

Ham 'N Sam (Black Jigger & Piano Player), Linemar, litho tin, 4x5", EX+IB, A $1,250.00

Happy & Sad Magic Face Clown w/Accordion, 1950s, cloth outfit, 10", NMIB...$175.00

Happy Car (Buick), Alps, 1950s, litho tin w/rubber tires, friction, 9", NM+IB, A $350.00

Happy Hippo, TPS, litho tin, 6", NMIB.........................$400.00

Happy Life, Alps, tin & celluloid, 9½", NMIB, A..........$475.00

Happy-Go-Lucky Magician, TN, litho tin, 9", EXIB......$650.00

Goofy on Tricycle, Linemar/WDP, 1950s, 7", EX, $1,000.00. (Photo courtesy Randy Inman Auctions)

Harold Lloyd One-Man Band in Cart, prewar, lithographed tin, 7", EX, A, $3,520.00. (Photo courtesy Randy Inman Auctions)

Harley-Davidson Motorcycle & Driver, IY, litho tin w/rubber tires, friction, 15", VG+ $1,900.00

Harold Lloyd Funny Face Walker, litho tin, 12", EXIB, A.$500.00

Helicopter H-2, see Circling Helicopter H-2

Helicopter on Airfield, Cragstan, litho tin, 10", EXIB ...$125.00

Henry, Porter & Brother on Trapeze, prewar, celluloid figures, wire trapeze bar, 5", EX, from $650 to $850.00

Henry & Henrietta Travelers (1934), CK, celluloid & tin, 7½", NMIB, A $6,000.00

Henry & Porter, Borgfeldt, celluloid, figures on 4-wheeled base, 6½", EX+IB $1,400.00

Henry & Porter Driver on Tricycle Cart, prewar, tin w/celluloid figures, 5", scarce, NM.................................$1,250.00

Henry & Porter on Elephant, Borgfeldt, prewar, celluloid, 8", EX, from $750 to $1,000.00

Henry & Porter on Elephant, Borgfeldt, prewar, celluloid, 8", NMIB, from $1,100 to...$1,300.00

Henry Acrobat, prewar, celluloid figure on wire trapeze, 5", EX, from $175 to $250.00

Henry Eating Ice Cream Cone, Linemar, litho tin, 5½", EX, A..$500.00

Henry Pulled By Swan, prewar, celluloid figures w/tin cart, 8", EX+..$1,400.00

Henry Pulling Little Brother, prewar, two celluloid figures, 7", NM+IB, A, $1,400.00. (Photo courtesy Randy Inman Auctions)

Highway Bus, TN, litho tin w/rubber tires, friction, 21", EXIB..$500.00

Highway Patrol Car w/Broderick Crawford, SM, litho tin, friction, 8½", NM+IB...$425.00

Highway Patrol Jeep, Daiya, 1950s, litho tin w/vinyl head, 9", NMIB..$200.00

Howdy Doody Cart, Ny-Lint, lithographed tin, 9" long, VG, from $325.00 to $425.00. (Photo courtesy Richard Opfer Auctioneering, Inc.)

Ice Cream Cycle, KO, litho tin, bump-&-go, 6", EXIB ..$300.00

Ice Cream Vendor Truck, Cragstan, litho tin, w/revolving flavor wheels, driver, friction, 10", G+ $250.00

Ice Cream Vendor Truck (Good Flavor), KO, 1950s, litho tin, friction, 7", EX+IB, A.....................................$300.00

Indianapolis 500 Racer #8, litho tin, friction, 15", VG+ .$700.00

Infants Bus, litho tin, friction, 8½", VG+IB, A..............$150.00

James Bond Astin Martin Car, 1960s, ejection switch for rooftop, 2 figures, friction, 11", EX+, from $225 to .$325.00

Japanese Dispatch Motorcycle w/Rider, prewar, celluloid figure on camouflage litho tin cycle, 5½", EX, from $450 to $600.00

Jet Racer (1955), Marusan, litho tin w/celluloid windshield, rubber tires, friction, 8", EXIB (box w/1952 Indy winner) $400.00

Jet Racer #Y53, Yonezowa, 1958, litho tin w/rubber tires, driver, friction, 11", VG..$300.00

Jiminy Cricket, Linemar/WDP, 1960s, litho tin, EX.......$425.00

Josteele FD Fire Car, SSS, 1950s, litho tin, 6½", NMIB, from $200 to...$300.00

Jumpy Rudolph, Asahi Toy, 1950s, cable action, 6", EX.$150.00

King Jet, tin, friction, 4", EX+ $50.00

King Kong, 1970s, plastic w/tin base, 7", NMIB.............$200.00

King Scooter, STS, litho tin, friction, 9", EX+IB........$3,080.00

Ladybug Family Parade, TPS, 1960s, litho tin, 13", NMIB, from $100 to...$150.00

Lazy Bones, Alps, 1960s, plush over tin, 11", NMIB $175.00

Little Italian Mouse Bouncing Racer (Topo Gigio in Car), KO, 1950s, litho tin, 5", NM+.......................................$150.00

Little Miss Automatic Ironer, MT, 1950s, litho tin, 4", NMIB...$50.00

Locomotive (Sparkling Friction #452), Marusan, litho tin, 5½", EXIB, A $130.00

Louie in His Dream Car, Linemar, litho tin w/celluloid head on figure, 5", EXIB...$650.00

Lucky Scooter Bumper Car, KO, 1950s, litho tin, 5½", NMIB...$200.00

Mach 5 Speed Racer, ASC, 1960s, friction, 11", NM.....$375.00

Magic Circus, TPS, litho tin & plastic, 6", EXIB, from $175 to...$250.00

Magic Greyhound Bus, KTS, 1950s, litho tin, friction, 10½", NMIB..$275.00

Magic Whale, litho tin, 6½", EXIB...........................$175.00

Marching Parade Boy w/Rifle, Fokuda, litho tin w/celluloid head, 9", VG...$200.00

Marionette Theatre, 2 celluloid figures on litho tin base w/canopy cover & foldable frame, 10", VG $400.00

Mary Had a Little Lamb Doll, vinyl w/cloth outfit, 5½", EXIB, A $125.00

Mercedes Benz Racing Coupe #4 (Race Car Series), Bandai, litho tin, friction, 8", NMIB, from $250 to..............$350.00

Mercury Special Racer #21, Asaki, litho tin, driver, 7", EX..$350.00

Mickey Mouse (Cowboy) on 4-Wheeled Horse, prewar, celluloid figure on wood horse, 7½", VG $1,500.00

Mickey Mouse & Donald Duck Airplane, 1950s, litho tin w/vinyl Pluto head in cockpit, friction, 9", NM $750.00

Mickey Mouse and Minnie on Rocking Bench With Bell and Whirligig, lithographed tin and celluloid, 8" long, VG, A, $5,500.00. (Photo courtesy Bertoia Auctions)

Mickey Mouse Acrobat (Gym-Toys), Linemar, plastic figure on wire apparatus, EXIB, from $350 to $400.00

Mickey Mouse in Cart Pulled by Pluto, SY, litho tin w/celluloid figures, 19", G, A..$1,100.00

Mickey Mouse in His Tin Lizzy, Linemar, litho tin car w/celluloid figure, friction, 5", scarce, NMIB, from $500 to........$700.00

Mickey Mouse on Rocking Horse, prewar, celluloid figure on wood horse, 7½", EX..$2,500.00

Mickey Mouse on Rocking Pluto, 1930s, celluloid figures, wooden rockers, complete w/lasso & reins, 8", NM, A $3,785.00

Mickey Mouse on Scooter, Linemar, litho tin, 4½", G, A .$775.00

Mickey Mouse Riding Pluto, WDP, celluloid w/tin wheeled supports, 5½x5", EX, A $1,650.00

Mickey Mouse Roller Skater, Linemar, litho tin, 6", VG, A .$625.00

Mickey Mouse Unicyclist, Linemar, litho tin w/cloth pants, 6", EXIB $1,200.00

Mickey Mouse Whirligig, Borgfeldt, prewar, celluloid, 9", rare, NMIB $3,000.00

Mickey's Delivery, Linemar, litho tin w/celluloid figure, 6" L, EX...$400.00

Mickey's Mousekemovers Truck, WDP, litho tin, friction, 13", VG+...$450.00

Midget Racer #8 (AAA), Yonezawa, litho tin, red, driver, friction, 7", nonworking o/w EX, A..............................$800.00

Military Motorcycle w/Gun in Sidecar (Passenger Behind Driver), litho tin, 4", EX...$400.00

Milk Car, Yamaichi, 1950s, litho tin, friction, 6½", EX+IB .$275.00

Minnie Mouse Knitting in Rocking Chair, Linemar, litho tin w/rubber ears, 6½", EX+..$450.00

Monkey Banana Vender, Yonezawa, litho tin, 8½", MIB, A .$100.00

Monkey Batter, litho tin, 7", NMIB, A..........................$350.00

Monkey Cycle w/Bell, Bandai, litho tin, 5", NMIB.......$225.00

Monkey Golfer, TPS, 1950s, litho tin, NMIB, from $200 to.$275.00

Moonlight Man, Bullmark, lithographed tin with movable vinyl head and cape, 9", NMIB, A, $1,770.00. (Photo courtesy New England Auctions Gallery)

Motorcycle w/Rider, Bandai, tin cycle, plastic rider w/movable head, arms & legs, friction, 12", VG $75.00

Mr Strongpup, Alps, plush & tin, 10", NMIB, A $200.00

Mystery Police Cycle, KO, litho tin, friction, 6", NMIB, from $450 to...$600.00

Ninja, CK, litho tin, pull on finger loops & Ninja climbs rope, NMIB, A..$150.00

Ninkimono Clown, MT, prewar, celluloid, 12", NMIB ..$650.00

Old Jalopy, Linemar, litho tin, 7", EX+IB $125.00

Old Smoky Fire Truck, tin, friction, 7", NMIB $50.00

Old-Timer Touring Car (1925), SSS, tin w/canvas convertible top, friction, 10", NM+IB, A..................................$75.00

Old-Timer Truck, SSS, 1950s-60s, litho tin, friction, NMIB..$60.00

Olive Oyl in Sports Car, Linemar, lithographed tin with vinyl head, friction, 8", G, A, $275.00. (Photo courtesy Bertoia Auctions)

Olive Oyl on Bell Tricycle, Linemar, litho tin, 4", EX....$500.00
Oscar the Seal, TPS, litho tin, 7", EXIB $225.00
Packard (Graham Paige #3), prewar, litho tin, 6", MIB..$450.00

Pango-Pango, TPS, litho tin, 6", NMIB, $250.00. (Photo courtesy Randy Inman Auctions)

Peacock, see Proud Peacock
Pennsylvania Locomotive, Y, litho tin, friction, 15", NMIB.$275.00
Peter Pan's Crocodile (Klimax Series), litho tin, 7", NMIB, A.$300.00
Pinocchio (Walking), Linemar, litho tin, 6", NM+IB....$450.00
Pinocchio (Walking), Linemar, litho tin, 6", VG...........$225.00
Pirate w/Peg Leg & Spy Glass, 1960s, litho tin, 7", NM+.$175.00
Pluto (Running), Linemar, litho tin, friction, 4½", VGIB,
   A $500.00
Pluto (Walking), Linemar, felt-covered w/tin eyes, 6", VG+IB,
   A $275.00
Pluto & Goofy, Linemar, litho tin, 5½", NMIB (single box for
   both figures), A $1,625.00
Pluto Acrobat (Gym-Toys), Linemar, celluloid figure on wire
   bar, 6½", EXIB, A $275.00
Pluto Horn Player, Linemar, litho tin w/rubber ears & top hat,
   6", EX, from $200 to $350.00
Pluto Pulling Delivery Wagon, Linemar, friction, 6" L, EXIB,
   A...$575.00
Pluto the Drum Major, Linemar, litho tin w/rubber ears, 6",
   NM+IB $650.00
Pluto the Unicyclist, Linemar, litho tin, EXIB, A $875.00

Police Car (1954 Ford), Marusan, litho tin, w/driver & passen-
   ger, friction, 10", EX, A $575.00
Police Patrol Car, Bandai, 1950s, litho tin, friction, 6"
   NMIB $300.00
Popeye (Tumbling), Linemar, litho tin, 4½", EX+IB......$650.00
Popeye (Tumbling), Linemar, litho tin, 4½", VG+ $350.00
Popeye & Olive Oyl Handcar, Linemar, litho tin w/'Slinky' bod-
   ies, 7" L, EX $1,200.00
Popeye & Olive Oyl Playing Ball, Linemar, litho tin, 19" L
   EXIB, A $2,300.00
Popeye Acrobat, Linemar, Popeye on rod attached to litho tin
   rocking base, EX+, A $2,400.00
Popeye Balancing Olive Oyl Seated in Chair Above His Head, Line-
   mar, litho tin, Olive w/rubber ponytail, 9½", EX $2,000.00

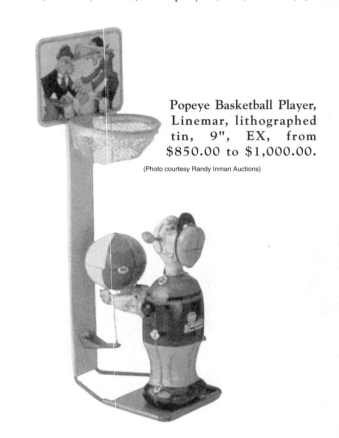

Popeye Basketball Player, Linemar, lithographed tin, 9", EX, from $850.00 to $1,000.00.

(Photo courtesy Randy Inman Auctions)

Popeye on Bell Tricycle, Linemar, litho tin & celluloid, 4½",
   VG, A $450.00
Popeye on High-wheel Bell Tricycle, Linemar, litho tin, 7", VG,
   A $600.00
Popeye Roller Skater, Linemar, litho tin w/cloth pants, 6", EXIB,
   from $1000 to $1,200.00
Popeye Roller Skater, Linemar, litho tin w/cloth pants, 6", VG+,
   A $550.00
Popeye Rollover Tank, Linemar, litho tin, 4", EX...........$375.00
Popeye w/Bobbing Head & Arms, prewar, celluloid, 9", EX,
   A $400.00
Popeye w/Squeaker, Linemar, cloth & felt figure w/punching
   action, 7½", GIB, A $550.00
Professor Ludwig Von Drake Walker, Linemar, litho tin, G+ .$325.00
Proud Peacock, Alps, litho tin, 7", EX $150.00

Proud Peacock, Alps, lithographed tin, 7", MIB, $250.00.

(Photo courtesy Bertoia Auctions)

Quick Draw McGraw, Linemar/Hanna-Barbera, litho tin, 3½", EX+, A $350.00

Rabbit on Motorcycle (Animal Cycle), 1960s, tin w/vinyl head, friction, MIB...$200.00

Racer, see also X-3 Racer

Racer #2, 1950s, litho tin, rubber tires, driver, friction, 4", NM+ $50.00

Racing Sport-O-Rama, ATC, 1950s, litho tin w/celluloid props, NMIB...$125.00

Railway Express Truck, SSS, litho tin, friction, 5", NMIB, A..$75.00

Rambler (1950s Station Wagon), Marusan, litho tin, friction, 10", EXIB, from $300 to $450.00

Refrigerator With Blinking Eyes, MT/WDP, 1950s, lithographed tin, 8", very rare, EXIB, from $400.00 to $600.00.

(Photo courtesy Smith House Toys)

Rocker Racer #54, 1950s, rubber tires, driver, friction, 7", EX+ $150.00

Royal Express, Daiya, litho tin, friction, 13½", NM+IB, A..$175.00

Sam the Strolling Skeleton, 1960s, litho tin, 5½", NMIB.$300.00

San Francisco Cable Car, 1960s, litho tin, friction, NMIB.$100.00

Santa Beating Drum, Sugimoto Tokyo, 1930s, celluloid head & arms w/compo legs, cloth jacket, 11½", NMIB, from $700 to $900.00

Santa Claus Holding Merry Christmas Sign & Bell, TN, litho tin, 7", NM+IB, A $225.00

Santa Claus Standing Behind Merry Christmas Truck, Y, cloth suit, wht fur beard & trim, 9", NMIB, from $200 to .$300.00

Santa Claus Standing Holding Bell, Alps, litho tin w/fur beard, pointed hat, 7", EXIB $150.00

Sedan, Kosuge, litho tin, long nose, running boards, 3 side windows, NP grille, metal wheels w/pnt spokes, 7", EX, A $525.00

Signal Car, MT/Occupied Japan, tin w/celluloid driver, opening trunk, 5", NMIB, A $175.00

Sioux Canoe, 1960s, friction, NMIB...........................$125.00

Sumo Wrestlers, prewar, 2 celluloid figures on cb box ring, squeeze-ball action, 4½x4½", NM+IB...............$325.00

Super Express w/Bell, litho tin, friction, 14", EXIB $150.00

Super Hero Robot, litho tin w/cartoon features, 10", G, A.$225.00

Super Highway, MT, litho tin, NMIB $300.00

Super Racer #42, lithographed tin with plastic arms, friction, 18", EX, A, $1,800.00. (Photo courtesy Richard Opfer Auctioneering, Inc.)

Superman Turnover Tank, Linemar, litho tin, 4", NM, A.$350.00

Surprise Santa Claus, see Santa Claus Standing Behind Merry Christmas Trunk

Tap Dancer By Street Sign, tin & paper figure w/celluloid head, cloth outfit, 8", EXIB, from $300 to $400.00

Terror Fish, Stingray, 1960s, opening mouth & wagging tail, litho tin, friction, 8½", NM $125.00

Thirsty Bear, Alps, 1960s, plush, 7", EXIB $75.00

Three Little Pigs, see also Big Bad Wolf & the Three Little Pigs

Three Little Pigs Acrobat, Borgfeldt, prewar, celluloid figures on wire apparatus, 11", VG, A $475.00

Three Little Pigs Acrobat, Borgfeldt, prewar, celluloid figures on wire apparatus, 11", EXIB.................................$1,000.00

Tom Tom Canoe, litho tin, friction, 9½", EXIB, A $275.00

Trailer House Set (Car Pulling Trailer Home), Y, 1950s, litho tin, friction, NMIB $450.00

Train & Jeep Race w/Rail, Marusan, 1950s, litho tin, EXIB, A..$300.00

Train Set (Engine & Coal Car), Marusan, litho tin, 8", EXIB.$175.00

Tram Car #1620, MT, litho tin, friction, 12", EX+ $350.00

Triksie Magic Dog, Alps, litho tin w/cloth outfit, 9", NMIB .$175.00
Tumbling Popeye, see Popeye (Tumbling) $700.00
Twirly Whirly Rocket Ride, Alps, litho tin, tower w/fold-out legs twirls 2 shuttles, 9x11", NMIB...............................$850.00

Walt Disney Characters Carousel, Linemar, lithographed tin with celluloid figures, 8", MIB, A, $4,000.00.

Mickey Mouse With Felix the Cat in Basket, Rogelio Sanchez, marked Isla on Shoe, lithographed tin, 6", EX, A, $8,800.00. (Photo courtesy Randy Inman Auctions)

Walt Disney Television Bank, Linemar, MIB.................$800.00
Wimpy on Bell Tricycle, Linemar, litho tin & celluloid, 4½", NM+, A..$1,225.00
Wimpy Walker, celluloid, 6½", VG+, A........................$300.00
X-3 Racer, Bandai, litho tin w/rubber tires, w/driver, friction, 7½", EX+IB $325.00
York City Water Sprayer Tank Truck, litho tin, friction, 6½", EX...$150.00

SPANISH

Bears on Motorcycle, Rico, mk RSA, litho tin, 9", EX, A .$1,600.00
Bugatti I-907, Paya, 1986, tin, 1 of 5,000 made, 19", NM, from $175 to..$225.00
Donald Duck, Guerrero, WDP, tin w/plastic figure, 10" base, NMIB, A...$150.00
Donald Duck Walking Car, litho tin car w/celluloid head, 5", NMIB, A...$275.00
Goofy Walking Car, litho tin w/celluloid figure, 5½", MIB .$500.00
Limousine, Paya, pnt tin, 2-door w/long hood, running boards, side spare, electric lights, chrome trim, 19", NM, A.$200.00
Louie Walking Car, litho tin w/celluloid figure, 5½", MIB .$250.00
Motorcyclist, Paya, litho tin, 12", EX............................$475.00
Silver Bullet Racer, Rico, silver-pnt stamped steel w/red lettering, seated driver, 10¾", EX+, A...............................$75.00

Minnie Mouse Carrying Cages With Felix the Cat, Rogelio Sanchez, lithographed tin, 7", VG, A, $22,000.00. (Photo courtesy Bertoia Auctions)

Motorcycle With Driver and Black Horn-Blowing Passenger, Paya, lithographed tin, 11", G, A, $1,500.00. (Photo courtesy Richard Opfer Auctioneering, Inc.)

Tourist, Paya, litho tin, man carrying 2 suitcases, 7", EX .$275.00
Vaquero Mareado (Rodeo Joe), Rico, litho tin, 5", rare,
NMIB..$525.00

Wyandotte

Wyandotte produced toys mostly of heavy gauge steel with a few being tin or plastic. The following listings are of vehicles and related toys from the 1920s to the 1950s. All are steel unless noted otherwise.

See also Aeronautical; Boats; Character, TV, and Movie Collectibles; Guns; Windups, Friction, and Other Mechanicals.

Allied Van Lines Semi, 1950s, diecast cab w/aluminum trailer, 25", VG, A..$150.00
Ambulance, 1940s, opening rear door, wht, 11", VG $150.00
American Airlines Airport, litho tin w/battery-powered light, pressed-steel airplane, 12x16", VG, A $300.00
Car Pulling Trailer, streamline styling, rubber tires, 26", G+, A .$465.00
Cargo Lines Semi, 1950s, litho tin cab w/pressed-steel trailer, 23", NM $325.00
Chung King Orient Express/Oriental American Foods Coast to Coast, 1950s, red diecast cab w/aluminum trailer, 25", VG, A $250.00

Circus Truck, 1940s, pressed steel with lithographed tin cages, 20", EX, A, $1,100.00. (Photo courtesy Randy Inman Auctions)

City Delivery Van, 1930s, streamline styling w/rear opening door, 11", VG, A..$185.00
Cord Fire Chief Car, 1940s, w/up, 14", Fair+, A.............$385.00
Cord Roadster, #600, friction, NP trim, rubber tires, 13", VG, A $275.00
Coupe, w/up, w/retractable roof, litho tin w/rubber tires, 12", EX..$220.00
Coupe, 1930s, electric lights, gr w/blk fenders & running boards, wht emb tires, 8", VG+, A $200.00
Delivery Truck, 1940s, streamline van body w/opening rear door, red & gr, 17½", G+, A $275.00
Dump Truck, 1930s, electric lights, 10", G, A $55.00
Dump Truck, 1930s, electric lights, 10", rstr, A $100.00
Dump Truck, 1940s, tractor-trailer w/side dump action, 17", rstr, A $75.00
Dump Truck, 1950s, front loading scoop, yel & gr w/yel & blk checked band on cab, orange dump bed, 19", G, A...$40.00
Dump Truck, 1950s, V-shaped swinging bed w/side-dump action, red w/wht, yel & blk door trim, 20", VG, A $200.00

Dump Truck, 1940s, #1002, streamline styling, 21", EX+IB, A, $400.00. (Photo courtesy Randy Inman Auctions)

Express Truck, 1940s, open U-shaped trailer, red & gr, 20", G+, A $100.00
Freight Truck, 1950s, diecast cab w/steel U-shaped open trailer w/low sides, 23", VG+, A $165.00
Fuel Truck, gr, 10½", G+, A $100.00
Garage & Cars, 4x5" litho tin garage w/2 pressed-steel streamline autos, EX, A..$210.00
Gas Pump, 1930s, pressed steel w/clear cylinder, hand crank, 9", VG+, A, from $440 to................................$470.00
Gasoline Truck, streamline styling w/opening rear door, red & silver, 21", G, A..$550.00
Great Plains Cattle Agency Truck, 1950s, semi w/stake trailer, red, yel & bl, 23", Fair, A..............................$65.00
Grey Van Lines Semi, 1940s, diecast cab w/aluminum trailer, 24", EX, A..$175.00
Hafner Union Pacific Stream Line Train, 1950s, 3-pc, EX .$250.00

Helicopter Pull Toy, 1940s, 8" wingspan, VG+IB, A, $325.00. (Photo courtesy Randy Inman Auctions)

Highway Freight Truck, 1940s, streamline trailer w/opening rear, red & bl, 20", EX $230.00
La Salle Coup, 1940s, 13", rstr, A............................$250.00
Milk Stake Truck, 1940s, wht, 4", EX, A $200.00
Moto-Fix Tow Truck, litho tin, 15", Fair+, A $80.00

Metropolitan Dept. of Public Service Garbage Truck, 1950s, 17", EX, A, $300.00. (Photo courtesy Randy Inman Auctions)

Motor Freight Lines Semi, w/open U-shaped trailer bed, 23", Fair, A...$130.00
National Bank, litho tin, 3" T, G+, A..............................$30.00
Racer, 1930s, streamline styling, electric lights, red w/wht rubber tires, 8½", EX, A..$275.00
Railway Express Agency/Nation Wide Rail-Air Service, 12", VG+, A...$250.00
Roadster, 1930s, streamline styling w/pointed hood, top down, red, V-shaped chrome-like grille, 10", VG..............$200.00
Roadster, 1930s, streamline styling w/pointed hood, top up, red & yel, V-shaped chrome-like grille, 10", NM..........$450.00
Sedan, streamline styling, electric lights, gr w/chrome-like grille, 9", EX, A...$300.00
Sedan, 1930s, wooden wheels, yel w/chrome-like grille, 9", VG+, A..$200.00
Sedan, 1940s, streamline styling, opening hood, electric lights, lt bl w/low chrome-like grille, 15½", G, A.................$500.00

Sedan, 1940s, streamline styling, non-opening hood, no electric lights, chrome trim, 15½", EXIB, A, $1,485.00. (Photo courtesy Randy Inman Auctions)

Sedan Pulling Trailer, 1930s, streamline w/Deco-style trailer, 24", rstr, A...$715.00

Shell Gas Station, lithographed tin, with accessory auto, 11x16", G, A, $300.00. (Photo courtesy Randy Inman Auctions)

Service Wrecker, 1940s, red & wht, 23", Fair+, A..........$110.00
Sportsman's Convertible, litho tin, trunk & roof open, 12½", EXIB...$300.00
Stake Truck, 1920s, electric lights, 10½", VG, A..........$130.00
Stake Truck, 1940s, cab & bed w/forward slant, red cab w/bl bed, 12", EX, A...$110.00
Stake Truck, 1950s, bl w/wht grille & wht, yel & blk door trim, red bumper & under carriage, 19", EX+IB, A..........$275.00
Super Service Garage, litho tin, 8½x8½", VG, A..........$250.00
Toy Town Estate Car, 1941 Cadillac 'woodie' w/lithoed lady driver, opening rear doors, 20", G+, A.......................$100.00
Toy Town Fire Dept, litho tin building w/plastic fire truck, 6½x8", VG+, A..$50.00
Wagon, Art Deco styling w/curved front & streamline wheel covers, 11½", G+, A...$125.00

Wyandotte Construction/Truck Lines, 1940s, streamline styling, 24", EX, A, $225.00. (Photo courtesy Randy Inman Auctions)

Wyandotte Truck Lines Semi, 1940s, streamline styling, 24", EX, A...$200.00
Wyndot (sic) Delivery Truck, litho tin, 12", G, A..........$100.00

Yo-yos

Yo-yos over the last year have taken a huge hit as far as

value, good news for collectors but bad news for dealers. Across the board most yo-yos have lost nearly 60 – 70% of value from just over a year ago. Common yo-yos have lost as much as 90% of value from just a year or two ago. Rare models have held their own but many of even the rare models have seen values drop by as much as 50%. About the only yo-yos that have held well are the rare models in near mint or mint condition. For further information we recommend *Lucky's Collector's Guide to 20th Century Yo-Yos, History and Values*, written by our advisor, Lucky J. Meisenheimer, M.D. He is listed under (M3) in the Dealer and Collector Code section.

See also other specific categories.

Alox, Flying Disc (Tournament), wood w/pnt seal, NM...$10.00
Avon, Garfield, plastic, MIP...$4.00
Cheerio, Beginners #55, wood w/foil sticker, NM............$32.00
Cheerio, Genuine Pro #99, 1950s, wood w/die stamp, M .$30.00
Cheerio, Glitter Spin, wood w/foil label & rhinestones, G.$110.00
Cheerio, Official Pro #99, wood w/foil sticker, EX...........$32.00
Dell, Big D Sleeper King, plastic, EX...............................$8.00
Dell, Big D Trickster, 1960s, plastic w/swirled colors, M...$12.00
Duncan, Beginner #44 or #1044, wood, MIP, ea..............$25.00
Duncan, Cattle Brand, late 1970s, MOC..........................$15.00
Duncan, Colorama, 1960s, plastic w/paper inserts, M $40.00
Duncan, Genuine Junior, 1930s, wood w/die stamp, VG..$12.00
Duncan, Glow Imperial, orange letters, MIP $10.00
Duncan, Imperial, Kool-Aid premium, MIP.......................$3.00
Duncan, Lil' Champ, 1980s, red w/gold raised lettering, NM..$8.00
Duncan, Little Ace, 1960s, plastic w/gold die stamp, M...$15.00
Duncan, Magic Motion, 1975, Hulk, MIP $10.00
Duncan, O-Boy, 1930s, wood, EX $20.00
Duncan, Pony #22, 1950s, clear plastic w/concentric circles, M .$30.00
Duncan, Professional, 1970s, plastic w/diamond design, M .$8.00
Duncan, Shrieking Sonic Satellite #500, MIP $25.00
Duncan, Super Heroes, 1970s, plastic, any character, M, ea .$8.00

Duncan, 8-Ball, 1960s, blk plastic, M...............................$12.00
Festival, Be a Sport Series, 1970s, MIP............................$8.00
Festival, Disney Series, Goofy, 1970s, MIP.......................$6.00
Festival, Dragonfly, 1964, plastic, M...............................$9.00
Fli-Back, #65, wood, red & bl w/gold die stamp, M $15.00
Flores, Beginner, 1920s, wood w/blk-pnt seal, M............$250.00
Goody, Joy-O-Top, 1930s, wood w/pnt seal, M $80.00
Hasbro Glo Action, 1968, MOC.....................................$10.00
Lumar, Beginner #34, 1930s, litho tin w/spiral pattern, NM.$30.00
Royal, Champion Junior, wood w/gold die stamp, M........$12.00

Royal Special (Tournament), 1950s, wood with decal seal, NM, $30.00. (Photo courtesy Lucky J. Meisenheimer)

Royal, Thunderbird, 1959, wood w/paper sticker, MIP.....$75.00
Spectra Star, Freddy Krueger, 1980s, MOC........................$5.00

Duncan Whistling Yo-yo, 1930s, lithographed tin, M, $100.00 each. (Photo courtesy Lucky J. Meisenheimer)

Dealer and Collector Codes

Most of our description lines contain a letter/number code just before the suggested price. They correspond with the names of the following collectors and dealers who sent us their current selling list to be included in this edition. If you're interested in buying a item you find listed, don't hesitate to call or write them. We only ask that you consider the differences in time zones and try to call at a convenient time. If you're corresponding, please send a self-addressed, stamped envelope for their reply. **Because our data was entered several months ago, many of the coded items will have already sold,** but our dealers tell us that they are often able to restock some of the same merchandise over and over. Some said that they had connections with other dealers around the country and might be able to locate a particular toy for you. But please bear in mind that because they may have had to pay more to restock their shelves, they may also have to charge a little more than the price quoted in their original sales list. We must stress that these people are not appraisers, so please do not ask them to price your toys.

If you have lists of toys for sale that you would like for us to use in the next edition, please send them to us at as soon as possible. We will process incoming lists as they arrive and because our space is limited, the earlier you send it, the better. Please do not ask us to include you in our Categories of Special Interest unless you contribute useable information. Not only are we limited on available space, it isn't fair to those who do. If you would like to advertise with us but cannot contribute listings, display ads are available (see page 469 for rates). We will hold a previously assigned dealer code over for you who are our contributors/advisors from year to year as long as we know you are interested in keeping it, but if we haven't heard from you by February 1, we will reassign that code to someone else. Because the post office prefers your complete nine-digit zip code, please send us that information for our files.

Direct your correspondence to: **Huxford Enterprises, Inc., 1202 7th St., Covington, IN 47932**

(A1)
Stan and Sally Alekna
732 Aspen Lane
Lebanon, PA 17042-9073
717-228-2361
fax: 717-228-2362

(A4)
Bob Armstrong
15 Monadnock Rd.
Worcester, MA 01609
508-799-0644
e-mail: RAAHNA@oldpuzzles.com
www.oldpuzzles.com

(A7)
Tatonka Toys
Matt and Lisa Adams
8155 Brooks Dr.
Jacksonville, FL 32244
904-772-6911
e-mail: beatles@bellsouth.net

(B1)
Richard Belyski
PO Box 14956
Surfside Beach, SC 29587
e-mail: peznews@juno.com
www.pezcollectorsnews.com

(B3)
Bojo
Bob Gottuso
P.O. Box 1403
Cranberry Twp., PA 16066-0403
phone/fax: 724-776-0621
e-mail: bojo@zbzoom.net

(B5)
Collection Connection
Martin and Carolyn Berens
2659 W. Kemper Rd.
Cincinnati, OH 45231-1140

(B6)
Jim Buskirk
3009 Oleander Ave.
San Marcos, CA 92069
760-599-1054

(C2)
Mark E. Chase
P.O. Box 308
Slippery Rock, PA 16057
e-mail: mark@glassnews.com
www.glassnews.com

(C3)
Ken Clee
P.O. Box 14062
Surfside Beach, SC 29581
843-650-5965
e-mail: waxntoys@aol.com
http://members.aol.com/
waxntoys/main//kidsmeal.htm

(C6)
Cotswold Collectibles
P.O. Box 716
Freeland, WA 98249
877-404-5637 (toll free)
fax: 360-331-5344
www.elitebrigade.com

(C10)
Bill Campbell
1221 Littlebrook Lane
Birmingham, AL 35235
205-853-8227
fax: 205-853-9951
e-mail: acamp10720@aol.com

(C12)
Cohen Books and Collectibles
Joel J. Cohen
P.O. Box 810310
Boca Raton, FL 33481-0310
561-487-7888
fax: 561-487-3117
e-mail: disneyana@disneycohen.com
www.disneycohen.com

(C13)
Brad Cassity
2391 Hunters Trail
Myrtle Beach, SC 29579
843-236-8697

(C16)
Howard Cherry
1275 10th St.
Cambridge, OH 43725
740-432-3364
e-mail: hccherry@cambridgeoh.com
www.hccherry.com

(D2)
Marl & B Inc.
Marl Davidson
10301 Braden Run
Bradenton, FL 34202
941-751-6275
fax: 941-751-5463
www.marlbe.com

(D7)
Saturday Heroes
Ron and Donna Donnelly
6302 Championship Dr.
Tuscaloosa, AL 35405

(F3)
Paul Fink's Fun and Games
P.O. Box 488
59 S Kent Rd.
Kent, CT 06757
860-927-4001
e-mail: PAUL@gamesandpuzzles.com
www.gamesandpuzzles.com

(F4)
Mike and Kurt Fredericks
145 Bayline Cir.
Folsom, CA 95630-8077
916-985-7986

(G1)
Gary's Trains
186 Pine Springs Camp Road
Boswell, PA 15531
814-629-9277
e-mail: gtrains@floodcity.net

(G2)
Don Goodsell
P.O. Box 48021
Los Angeles, CA 90048

(H1)
Happy Memories Collectibles
Bill Hamburg
P.O. Box 536
Woodland Hills, CA 91367
818-346-1269
fax: 818-346-0215
e-mail: WHamburg@aol.com

(H3)
George Hardy
1670 Hawkwood Ct.
Charlottesville, VA 22901
804-295-4863
fax: 804-295-4898
e-mail: georgeh@comet.net
www.comet.net/personal/georgeh/

(H8)
Homestead Collectibles
Art and Judy Turner
P.O. Box 173
Mill Hall, PA 17751
570-726-3597
e-mail: jturner@cub.kcnet.org

(H9)
C.J. Russell & The Halloween
 Queen Antiques
Pamela E. Apkarian-Russell,
The Halloween Queen
P.O. Box 499
Winchester, NH 03470
603-239-8875
e-mail: halloweenqueen@cheshire.net

(I2)
Terri's Toys and Nostalgia
Terri Ivers
114 Whitworth Ave.
Ponca City, OK 74601
580-762-8697
e-mail: toylady@cableone.net

(I3)
Dan Iannotti
212 W. Hickory Grove Rd.
Bloomfield Hills, MI 48302-1127S
248-335-5042
e-mail: modernbanks@prodigy.net

(J3)
Dana Johnson
P.O. Box 1824
Bend, OR 97709-1824
24-hour message ph: 541-318-7176
e-mail: toynutz@earthlink.net
www.toynutz.com

(J6)
June Moon
143 Vine Ave.
Park Ridge, IL 60068
e-mail: junmoonstr@aol.com
www.junemooncollectibles.com

(K1)
Simpson Mania
485 S. 12th St.
St. Helens, OR 97051

(K2)
Toy Hell
David Kolodny-Nagy
P.O. Box 75271
Los Angeles, CA 90075

(K6)
Keith and Donna Kaonis
P.O. box 344
Centerport, NY 11721
631-261-4100 (daytime)
631-351-0982 (evening)
fax: 631-261-9684

(L4)
Tom Lastrapes
P.O. Box 2444
Pinellas Park, FL 33782
727-545-2586
e-mail: tomlas1@fastmail.fm

(M2)
John McKenna
701 W. Cucharres
Colorado Springs, CO 80905
719-520-9125

(M3)
Lucky J. Meisenheimer, M.D.
7300 Sand Lake Commons Blvd.,
Suite 105
Orlando, FL 32819
407-352-2444
fax: 407-363-2869
e-mail: LuckyJ@MSN.com
www.yo-yos.net

(M7)
Judith A. Mosholder
186 Pine Springs Camp Road
Boswell, PA 15531
814-629-9277
e-mail: jlytwins@floodcity.net

(M8)
The Mouse Man Ink
P.O. Box 3195
Wakefield, MA 01880
781-246-3876
e-mail: mouse_man@msn.com
www.mouseman.com

(M9)
Steven Meltzer
1255 2nd St.
Santa Monica, CA 90401
310-656-0483
www.puppetmagic.com

(M11)
McQuillen's Collectibles
Michael and Polly McQuillen
P.O. Box 50022
Indianapolis, IN 46250-0022
317-845-1721
e-mail: michael@politicalparade.com
www.politicalparade.com

(M15)
Marcia's Fantasy
Marcia Fanta
4275 S. 33rd St. SE
Tappen, ND 58487-9411
701-327-4441
e-mail: tofantas@bektel.com

(M21)
Peter Muldavin
173 W 78th St., Apt. 5-F
New York, NY 10024
212-362-9606
e-mail: kiddie78s@aol.com

(N2)
Norman's Olde & New Store
Philip Norman
126 W Main St.
Washington, NC 27889-4944
252-946-3448

(P2)
Dawn Diaz
20460 Samual Dr.
Saugus, CA 91350-3812
661-263-8697
e-mail: jamdiaz99@earthlink.net

(P5)
Gary Pollastro
5047 84th Ave. SE
Mercer Island, WA 98040
206-232-3199

(P6)
Judy Posner
P.O. Box 2194
Englewood, FL 34295
e-mail: judyandjef@yahoo.com
www.judyposner.com

(P11)
The Phoenix Toy Soldier Co.
Bob Wilson
8912 E. Pinnacle Peak Rd.
PMB 552
Scottsdale, AZ 85255
480-699-5005
877-269-6074 (toll free)
fax: 480-699-7628
e-mail: bob@phoenixtoysoldier.com
www.phoenixtoysoldier.com

(R3)
Jim Rash
135 Alder Ave.
Egg Harbor Twp., NJ 08234-9302
609-646-4125 (evenings)

(R5)
Reynolds Toys
Charlie Reynolds
2836 Monroe St.
Falls Church, VA 22042-2007
703-533-1322
e-mail: reynoldstoys@erols.com

(S5)
Son's a Poppin' Ranch
John Rammacher
1610 Park Ave.
Orange City, FL 32763-8869
386-775-2891
e-mail: sonsapoppin@earthlink.net
www.sonsapoppin.com

(S7)
Nate Stoller
960 Reynolds Ave.
Ripon, CA 95366
209-599-5933
e-mail: multimotor@aol.com
www.maytagclub.com

(S10)
Scott Smiles
157 Yacht Club Way, Apt. #112
Hypoluxo, FL 33462-6048
561-582-6016
e-mail: ssmiles@msn.com

(S14)
Cindy Sabulis
P.O. Box 642
Shelton, CT 06484
203-926-0176
e-mail: toys4two@snet.net
www.dollsntoys.com

(S22)
Carole Smyth Antiques
Carole and Richard Smyth
P.O. Box 2068
Huntington, NY 11743

(S24)
Mark and Lynda Suozzi
P.O. Box 102
Ashfield, MA 01330
phone/fax: 413-628-3241 (9am to 5pm)
e-mail: marklyn@valinet.com
www.marklynantiques.com

(S25)
Steve Stephenson
11117 NE 164th Pl.
Bothell, WA 98011-4003
425-488-2603
fax: 425-488-2841

(T3)
Toys N Such
Richard Trautwein
437 Dawson St.
Sault Ste. Marie, MI 49783
906-635-0356
e-mail: rtraut@up.net

(V2)
Marci Van Ausdall
4532 Fertile Valley Road
Newport, WA 99156
509-292-1311
e-mail: betsymcallfanclub@
hotmail.com

(W4)
Randy Welch
27965 Peach Orchard Rd.
Easton, MD 21601-8203
410-822-5441

(W7)
Larry White
108 Central St.
Rowley, MA 01969-1317
978-948-8187
e-mail: larrydw@erols.com

(W8)
James Watson
25 Gilmore St.
Whitehall, NY 12887
518-499-0643
fax: 518-499-1759

(Y2)
Mary Young
Box 9244
Dayton, OH 45409
937-298-4838

Categories of Special Interest

If you would like to be included in this section, send us a list of your 'for sale' merchandise. These listings are complimentary to those who participate in the preparation of this guide by doing so. Please understand that the people who are listed here want to buy and sell. They are not appraisers. Read the paragraph under the title Dealer and Collector Codes for more information. If you have no catalogs or lists but would like to advertise with us, see the display ad rate sheet on page 469.

Advertising

California Raisins, M&M Toppers, and all fast-food
Ken Clee
P.O. Box 14062
Surfside Beach, SC 29581
e-mail: waxntoys@aol.com
http://members.aol.com/
waxntoys/main/kidsmeal.htm

Advertising dolls, also Dakin, and some character squeeze toys
Jim Rash
135 Alder Ave.
Egg Harbor Twp, NJ 08234-9302
609-646-4125 (evening)

Advertising Wristwatches
Sharon Iranpour
24 San Rafael Dr.
Rochester, NY 14618-3702
716-381-9467; fax: 716-383-9248
e-mail: watcher1@rochester.rr.com

Banks

Ertl; sales lists available
Homestead Collectibles
Art and Judy Turner
P.O. Box 173
Mill Hall, PA 17751
570-726-3597
e-mail: jturner@cub.kcnet.org

Modern mechanical banks: Reynolds, Sandman Designs, James Capron, Book of Knowledge, Richards, Wilton; sales lists available
Dan Iannotti
212 W. Hickory Grove Rd.
Bloomfield Hills, MI 48302-1127S
248-335-5042
e-mail: modernbanks@prodigy.net

Penny banks (limited editions): new, original, mechanical, still or figural; also bottle openers
Reynolds Toys
Charlie Reynolds
2836 Monroe St.
Falls Church, VA 22042-2007
703-533-1322
e-mail: reynoldstoys@erols.com

Antique tin and iron mechanical penny banks; no reproductions or limited editions; cast-iron architectural bank buildings in Victorian form. Buy and sell, list available upon request
Mark and Lynda Suozzi
P.O. Box 102
Ashfield, MA 01330
ph/fax: 413-628-3241 (9 am to 5 pm)
e-mail: marklyn@valinet.com
www.marklynantiques.com

Barbie and Friends

Wanted: Mackie dolls as well as vintage Barbie dolls; buying and selling ca 1959 dolls to present issues
Marl & B Inc.
Marl Davidson
10301 Braden Run
Bradenton, FL 34202
941-751-6275
fax: 941-751-5463
www.marlbe.com

Battery-Operated

Tom Lastrapes
P.O. Box 2444
Pinellas Park, FL 33782
727-545-2586
e-mail: tomlas1@fastmail.fm

Beatles Memorabilia

Buying and selling old and new memorabilia; one piece or collection
Bojo
P.O. Box 1403
Cranberry Township, PA 16066-0403
phone/fax: 724-776-0621
e-mail: bojo@zbzoom.net

Books

Specializing in Little Golden Books and look-alikes
Steve Santi
19626 Ricardo Ave.
Hayward, CA 94541
510-481-2586.
Author of *Collecting Little Golden Books, Volumes I* and *II.* Also publishes newsletter, *Poky Gazette,* primarily for Little Golden Book collectors

Breyer

Author of book, order direct
Felicia Browell
123 Hooks Lane
Cannonsburg, PA 15317
e-mail: fbrowell@nauticom.net

Bubble Bath Containers

Including foreign issues; also character collectibles, character bobbin' head nodders, and Dr. Dolittle; write for information or send SASE for Bubble Bath Bulletin
Tatonka Toys
Matt and Lisa Adams
8155 Brooks Dr.
Jacksonville, FL 32244
904-772-6911
e-mail: beatles@bellsouth.net

Building Blocks and Construction Toys

Anchor Stone Building Blocks by Richter
George Hardy
1670 Hawkwood Ct.
Charlottesville, VA 22901
804-295-4863
fax: 804-295-4898
email: georgeh@comet.net
www.comet.net/personal/georgeh/

Cast Iron

Pre-war, large-scale cast-iron toys and early American tinplate toys
John McKenna
701 W Cucharres
Colorado Springs, CO 80905
719-520-9125

Victorian bell toys, horse-drawn wagons, fire toys, carriages, penny banks, pull toys, animated coin-operated machines. Buy and sell, list available upon request, mail order and shows only
Mark and Lynda Suozzi
P.O. Box 102
Ashfield, MA 01330
ph/fax: 413-628-3241 (9 am to 5 pm)
e-mail: marklyn@valinet.com
www.marklynantiques.com

Character and Promotional Glasses

Especially fast-food and sports glasses
Mark Chase
P.O. Box 308
Slippery Rock, PA 16057
e-mail: mark@glassnews.com
www.glassnews.com

Character Clocks and Watches

Also radio premiums and decoders, P-38 airplane-related items from World War II, Captain Marvel and Hoppy items, Lone Ranger books with jackets, selected old comic books, toys and cap guns; buys and sells Hoppy and Roy items
Bill Campbell
Kirschner Medical Corp.
1221 Littlebrook Lane
Birmingham, AL 35235
205-853-8227; fax: 205-853-9951
e-mail: acamp10720@aol.com

Character Collectibles

Dolls, rock 'n roll personalities (especially the Beatles), related character items and miscellaneous toys
Bojo
Bob Gottuso
P.O. Box 1403
Cranberry Twp., PA 16066-0403
phone/fax: 724-776-0621
e-mail: bojo@zbzoom.net

Disney, books, animation art
Cohen Books and Collectibles
Joel J. Cohen
P.O. Box 810310
Boca Raton, FL 33481-0403
561-487-7888; fax: 561-487-3117
e-mail: disneyana@disneycohen.com
www.disneycohen.com

Early Disney, Gone with the Wind, Western heroes, premiums, and other related collectibles
Saturday Heroes
Ron and Donna Donnelly
6302 Championship Dr.
Tuscaloosa, AL 35405

Any and all, also Hartland figures
Terri's Toys & Nostalgia
Terri Ivers
114 Whitworth Ave.
Ponca City, OK 74601
580-762-8697
e-mail: toylady@cableone.net

Action figures, diecast, Strawberry Shortcake, Nightmare Before Christmas, Star Wars, TV & Movie Character Toys
June Moon
143 Vine Ave.
Park Ridge, IL 60068
e-mail: junmoonstr@aol.com
www.junemooncollectibles.com

Especially bendy figures and the Simpsons
Simpson Mania
485 S. 12th St.
St. Helens, OR 97051

Especially Disney; send $8 for annual subscription (6 issues) for sale catalogs
The Mouse Man Ink
P.O. Box 3195
Wakefield, MA 01880
781-246-3876
e-mail: mouse_man@msn.com
www.mouseman.com

Especially pottery, china, ceramics, salt and pepper shakers, cookie jars, tea sets and children's china; with special interest in Black Americana and Disneyana; illustrated sales lists available
Judy Posner
P.O. Box 2194
Englewood, FL 34295
e-mail: judyandjef@yahoo.com
www.judyposner.com

Especially tinplate toys and cars, battery-op toys and toy trains
Toys N Such
Richard Trautwein
437 Dawson St.
Sault Ste. Marie, MI 49783
906-635-0356
e-mail: rtraut@up.com

Cracker Jack

Larry White
108 Central St.
Rowley, MA 01969-1317
978-948-8187
e-mail: larrydw@erols.com
Author of *Cracker Jack Toys* and
*Cracker Jack, The Unauthorized
Guide to Advertising Collectibles*

Dakin

*Also advertising dolls and some char-
acter squeeze toys*
Jim Rash
135 Alder Ave.
Egg Harbor Twp., NJ 08234-9302
609-646-4125 (evening)

Diecast

*Diecast and other automotive toys;
editor of magazine*
Mr. Dana Johnson, publisher
Toy Car Collector magazine
c/o Dana Johnson Enterprises
P.O. Box 1824
Bend, OR 97709-1824 USA
541-318-7176
e-mail: toynutz@earthlink.net
www.toynutz.com

*Ertl, banks, farm, trucks, and con-
struction*
Son's a Poppin' Ranch
John Rammacher
1610 Park Ave.
Orange City, FL 32763-8869
386-775-2891
e-mail: sonsapoppin@earthlink.net
www.sonsapoppin.com

Hot Wheels
Steve Stephenson
11117 NE 164th Pl.
Bothell, WA 98011-4003
425-488-2603
fax: 425-488-2841

Dolls

*Ad dolls, Barbie and other Mattel
dolls, premiums, character memorabilia, modern dolls, related items*
Marcia's Fantasy
Marcia Fanta
4275 33rd St. SE
Tappen, ND 58487-9411
701-327-4441
e-mail: tofantas@bektel.com

*Ad dolls, also Dakin, and some char-
acter squeeze toys*
Jim Rash
135 Alder Ave.
Egg Harbor TWP, NJ 08234-9302
609-646-4125 (evening)

Betsy McCall
Marci Van Ausdall
4532 Fertile Valley Road
Newport, WA 99156
509-292-1311; e-mail:
betsymcallfanclub@hotmail.com

*Liddle Kiddles and other small dolls
from the late '60s and early '70s*
Dawn Diaz
20460 Samual Dr.
Saugus, CA 91350-3812
661-263-TOYS (8697)
e-mail: jamdiaz99@earthlink.net

*Dolls from the 1960s – 70s, includ-
ing Liddle Kiddles, Barbie, Tammy,
Tressy, etc.*
Cindy Sabulis
P.O. Box 642
Shelton, CT 06484
203-926-0176
e-mail: toys4two@snet.net
www.dollsntoys.com
Author of *Collector's Guide to Dolls
of the 1960s and 1970s*; co-author
of *The Collector's Guide to Tammy,
the Ideal Teen* (Collector Books)

Dollhouse Furniture

Renwal, Ideal, Marx, etc.
Judith A. Mosholder
186 Pine Springs Camp Road
Boswell, PA 15531
814-629-9277
e-mail: jlytwins@floodcity.net

Fisher-Price

Brad Cassity
2391 Hunters Trail
Myrtle Beach, SC 29579
843-236-8697

Games

*Victorian, cartoon, comic, TV, and
nostalgic themes*
Paul Fink's Fun & Games
P.O. Box 488
59 S Kent Rd.
Kent, CT 06757
860-927-4001
e-mail: PAUL@gamesandpuzzles.com
gamesandpuzzles.com

GI Joe

Also diecast and Star Wars
Cotswold Collectibles
P.O. Box 716
Freeland, WA 98249
877-404-5637 (toll free)
fax: 360-331-5344
www.elitebrigade.com

Guns

*Pre-WWII American spring-air BB
guns, all Red Ryder BB guns, cap
guns with emphasis on Western six-
shooters; especially wanted are pre-
WWII cast-iron six-guns*
Jim Buskirk
3009 Oleander Ave.
San Marcos, CA 92069
760-599-1054

Specializing in cap guns
Happy Memories Collectibles
Bill Hamburg
P.O. Box 536
Woodland Hills, CA 91367
818-346-1269
fax: 818-346-0215
e-mail: WHamburg@aol.com

Halloween Collectibles

Also postcards, author of books
C.J. Russell and The Halloween
Queen Antiques
Pamela E. Apkarian-Russell
P.O. Box 499
Winchester, NH 03470
603-239-8875
e-mail:
halloweenqueen@cheshire.net
The Tastes & Smells of Halloween, a
Trick or Treat Trader Publication
cookbook — Bogie book for collectors, regularly $25.00, order
from the author at $20.00 plus
shipping

Hartland

*Specializing in Hartland western fig-
ures as well as western character collectibles in general*
Howard Cherry
1275 10th St.
Cambridge, OH 43725
740-432-3364
e-mail: hccherry@cambridgeoh.com
www.hccherry.com

Specializing in Hartland sports figures
James Watson
25 Gilmore St.
Whitehall, NY 12887
518-499-0643
fax: 518-499-1772

Lunch Boxes

Norman's Olde and New Store
Philip Norman
126 W Main St.
Washington, NC 27889-4944
252-946-3448

*Also characters such as cowboys, TV
shows, cartoons, and more*
Terri's Toys
Terri Ivers
114 Whitworth Ave.
Ponca City, OK 74601
580-762-8697
e-mail: toylady@cableone.net

Marx

Figures, playsets, and character toys
G.F. Ridenour
Fun House Toy Co.
P.O. Box 444
Warrendale, PA 15086
ph/fax: 724-935-1392
e-mail: info@funhousetoy.com
www.funhousetoy.com

*Plastic figures and parts from play-
sets; also figures from about 100
other old manufacturers*
Phoenix Toy Soldier Co.
Bob Wilson
8912 E. Pinnacle Peak Rd., PMB 552
Scottsdale, AZ 85255
480-699-5005; fax: 480-699-7628
877-269-6074 (toll free)
e-mail: bob@phoenixtoysoldier.com
www.phoenixtoysoldier.com

Paper Dolls

Author of books
Mary Young
Box 9244
Dayton, OH 45409
937-298-4838

Paper Lithograph

*Antique McLoughlin games, Bliss and
Reed boats, toy wagons, Ten Pin sets,
cube blocks, puzzles and Victorian doll
houses. Buy and sell; lists available upon
request. Mail order and shows only*
Mark and Linda Suozzi
P.O. Box 102
Ashfield, MA 01330
ph/fax: 413-628-3241 (9am to 5pm)
e-mail: marklyn@valinet.com
www.marklynantiques.com

Pedal Cars

Also specializing in Maytag collectibles
Nate Stoller
960 Reynolds Ave.
Ripon, CA 95366
209-599-5933
e-mail: multimotor@aol.com
www.maytagclub.com

Pez Candy Dispensers

Richard Belyski
P.O. Box 14956
Surfside Beach, SC 29587
e-mail: peznews@juno.com
www.pezcollectorsnews.com

Plastic Figures and Playsets

*Plastic figures and parts from play-
sets; also figures from about 100
old manufacturers other than Marx*
Phoenic Toy Soldier Co.
Bob Wilson
8912 E. Pinnacle Peak Rd.
PMB 552
Scottsdale, AZ 85255
480-699-5005; 877-269-6074 (toll free)

Also GI Joe, Star Trek, and dinosaurs
Mike and Kurt Fredericks
145 Bayline Circle
Folsom, CA 95630-8077
916-985-7986

Political Toys

McQuillen's Collectibles
Michael and Polly McQuillen
P.O. Box 50022
Indianapolis, IN 46250-0022
317-845-1721
e-mail: michael@politicalparade.com
www.politicalparade.com

Puzzles

Wood jigsaw type, from before 1950
Bob Armstrong
15 Monadnock Rd.
Worcester, MA 01609
508-799-0644
e-mail: RAAHNA@oldpuzzles.com
www.oldpuzzles.com

Ramp Walkers
Specializing in ramp-walking figures, also mechanical sparklers and other plunger-type toys
Raven'tiques
Randy Welch
27965 Peach Orchard Rd.
Easton, MD 21601-8203
410-822-5441

Records
78 rpm children's records and picture disks; buys, sells, and trades records as well as makes cassette recordings for a small fee
Peter Muldavin
173 W 78th St., Apt. 5-F
New York, NY 10024
212-362-9606
kiddie78s@aol.com
http://members.aol.com/kiddie78s/

Sand Toys
Carole Smyth Antiques
Carole and Richard Smyth
P.O. Box 2068
Huntington, NY 11743
Authors of book; send $25 plus $3 for postage for a signed copy. New York residents please add 8¼% sales tax.

Schoenhut
Keith and Donna Kaonis
P.O. Box 344
Centerport, NY 11721-0344
613-261-4100 (daytime)
631-351-0982 (evening)
fax: 631-261-9864

Slot Cars
Specializing in slots and model racing from the '60s – '70s; especially complete race sets in original boxes
Gary Pollastro
5047 84th Ave. SE
Mercer Island, WA, 98040
206-232-3199

Soldiers
Barclay, Manoil, Grey Iron, other Dimestores, and accessories; also Syroco figures
Stan and Sally Alekna
732 Aspen Lane
Lebanon, PA 17042-9073
717-228-2361
fax: 717-228-2362

Also vehicles, model kits, GI Joes, games, ad figures, View-Master, non-sports cards, Star Trek, advertising, antiques, fine art, and much more (see their display ad for more information)
June Moon
Jim and Nancy Frugoli
143 Vine Ave.
Park Ridge, IL 60068
e-mail: junmoonstr@aol.com
www.junemooncollectibles.com

Trains
Lionel, American Flyer, and Plasticville
Gary's Trains
186 Pine Springs Camp Road
Boswell, PA 15531
814-629-9277
e-mail: gtrains@floodcity.net

Trains of all types; holds cataloged auctions, seeking quality collections for consignment
Stout Auctions
Greg Stout
11 West Third Street
Williamsport, IN 47993-1119
765-764-6901
fax: 765-764-1516
e-mail: stoutauctions@hotmail.com
www.stoutauctions.com

Toy Shop
Old Tyme Toystore
3914-A N. Davis Hwy
Pensacola, FL 32503
850-429-0333 or 850-429-0340
e-mail: toystore3@aol.com

Transformers
Specializing in Transformers, Robotech, Shogun Warriors, Gadaikins, and any other robot; want to buy these MIP — also selling
Toy Hell
David Kolodny-Nagy
P.O. Box 75271
Los Angeles, CA 90075
e-mail: toyhell@yahoo.com
www.angelfire.com/ca2/redpear
For copy of BotCon Transformer Comic Book, *Comic Smorgasbord Special*, send $3.00 + $1.50 for single issues, $2.50 each for 10 or more + $2.00

Windups
Also friction and battery-operated; fast-food toys, displays
Antique Toy Information Service
Send SASE, good photos (35mm preferred), and $9.95 per toy to:
Scott Smiles
157 Yacht Club Way, Apt. #112
Hypoluxo, FL 33462-6048
561-582-6016
e-mail: ssmiles@msn.com

Yo-yos
Lucky J. Meisenheimer, M.D.
7300 Sand Lake Commons Blvd.
Suite 105
Orlando, FL 32819
407-352-2444
fax: 407-363-2869
e-mail: LuckyJ@MSN.com
www.yo-yos.net
Author of book, *Lucky's Collectors Guide to 20th Century Yo-Yos*. To order call 1-877-969-6728. Cost is $29.95 + $3.20 postage.

Clubs, Newsletters, and Other Publications

There are hundreds of clubs, newsletters, and magazines available to toy collectors today. Listed here are some devoted to specific areas of interest. You can obtain a copy of many newsletters simply by requesting a sample.

We will list other organizations and publications upon request. Please send your information to us by June 1.

Akro Agate Collectors Club and
  Clarksburg Crow
Claudia and Roger Hardy
West End Antiques
97 Milford St.
Clarksburg, WV 26301
304-624-7600 (weekdays) or
10 Baily St.
Clarksburg WV 26301-2524
304-624-4523 (evenings)
www.akro-agate.com
membership: $25

The Akro Arsenal
Larry D. Wells
5411 Joyce Ave.
Fort Wayne, IN 46818
219-489-5842

Antique Advertising Association
  of America
Pastimes newsletter
P.O. Box 1121
Morton Grove, IL 60053
e-mail: aaa@aol.com
subscription: $35

*Antique & Collectors Reproduction
  News*
Antiques Coast to Coast
Mark Chervenka
P.O. Box 12130
Des Moines, IA 50312-9403
515-274-5886
800-277-05531
acrn@repronews.com
Monthly newsletter showing differences between old originals and
new reproductions.
subscription: $32 US; $42 Canada;
$59 all other foreign

Antique Doll Collector
Keith and Donna Kaonis
6 Woodside Ave., Suite 300
Northport, NY 11768
631-261-4100 (daytime)
888-800-2588 (toll free)
fax: 631-251-9684
e-mail: antiquedollcoll@aol.com
www.antiquedollcollector.com

Antique Trader Weekly
Nancy Crowley, editor
P.O. Box 1050
Dubuque, IA 52004
e-mail:collect@krause.com
www.collect.com
subscription: $38 (52 issues)
800-334-7165 (subscriptions only)

Appraisers National Association
25602 Alicia Parkway, PMB 245
Laguna Hills, CA 29653
e-mail: info@ana-appraisals.org
www.ana-appraisals.org
Free referrals to accredited appraisers for antiques and collectibles

Association of Game and Puzzle
  Collectors
197M Boston Post Road W.
Marlborough, MA 01752
e-mail: membership@agpc.org
membership: $30 per year US; $40
Canada and overseas
www.agca.com

Barbie Bazaar
5711 Eighth Ave.
Kenosha, WI 53140
262-658-1004; fax: 262-658-0433
www.barbiebazzar.com
subscription: $23.95 US; $38.95
Canada; $58.95 (foreign (for 6
issues per year)

Betsy's Fan Club (Betsy McCall)
P.O. Box 946
Quincy, CA 95971-0946
916-283-2770
e-mail: dreams@psln.com
subscription: $16 per year (quarterly)

*Beyond the Rainbow Collector's
  Exchange*
P.O. Box 31672
St. Louis, MO 63131
314-217-2727
www.jgdb.com/mfaq4.htm

Beatlefan
PO Box 33515
Decatur, GA 30033
subscription: $7 US (6 issues); $21
Canada/Mexico

Big Little Times
Big Little Book Collectors Club of
  America
Larry Lowery
P.O. Box 1242
Danville, CA 94526
925-837-2086

Bobbing Head Doll
Tim Hunter
4301 W. Hidden Valley Dr.
Reno, NV 89502
e-mail: thunter885@aol.com

Bojo
P.O. Box 1403
Cranberry Township, PA 16066-0403
724-776-0621 (9 am to 9 pm EST)
e-mail: bojo@zbzoom.net
Issues fixed price catalog containing Beatles and Rock 'n Roll memorabilia; catalog: $3

Buckeye Marble Collectors Club
Brenda Longbrake, secretary
e-mail: brenda@wcoil.com
www.buckeymarble.com

Candy Container Collectors of
  America
The Candy Gram newsletter
Betty MacDuff
2711 De La Rosa St.
e-mail:epmac27@aol.com
or
Jeff Bradfield
90 Main St.
Dayton, VA 22821
www.candycontainer.org
membership: $25

Cast Iron Toy Collectors of
  America
Paul McGinnis
1340 Market St.
Long Beach, CA 90805

Coca-Cola Collectors Club
  International
4780 Ashform Dunwoody Rd.,
Suite A
Atlanta, GA 30338
dues: $30 (US); $35 Canada; $50
overseas-airmail; $5 associates

Collector's Life
The world's foremost publication
  for Steiff enthusiasts
Beth Savino
P.O. Box 798
Holland, OH 43528
419-473-9801
800-862-TOYS (toll free)
fax: 419-473-3947
www.toystorenet.com

*Cookie Jarrin' With Joyce: The
  Cookie Jar Newsletter*
1501 Maple Ridge Rd.
Walterboro, SC 29488

Cracker Jack Collectors Association and *Prize Insider Newsletter*
Theresa Richter
5469 S. Dorchester Ave.
Chicago, IL 61615
e-mail: WaddyTMR@aol.com
www.collectoronline.com/CJCA/
subscription/membership: $20 sin-
gle; $24 family

Dionne Quints *Quint News*
Jimmy Rodolfos
P.O. Box 2527
Woburn, MA 01888
781-933-2219
e-mail: effanjay@webtv.net

Doll Castle News
P.O. Box 247
Washington, NJ 07882
908-689-7042
fax: 908-689-6320
subscription: $19.95 per year or
$37.95 for 2 years

Doll News
United Federation of Doll Clubs
10900 N. Pomona Ave.
Kansas City, MO 65153
816-891-6040
e-mail: ufdcinfo@ufdc.org
or
Elinor Champion
301-939-4689
e-mail: elinor@ufdc.org
or
Bettyanne Twigg (online club
coordinator)
e-mail: twiggtown@mindspring.com

Dollhouse Toys 'N Us
Dollhouse and Miniatures newsletter
Bob and Geraldine Scott
e-mail: Geraldine@Collector.org
www.BobScott.com/Club
membership: $25 (5 issues per
year)

Dunbar's Gallery
76 Haven St.
Milford, MA 01757
508-634-8697
508-473-5711
fax: 508-634-8698
e-mail: dunbars@mediaone.net.
Specializing in advertising, Halloween, toys, coin-operated
machines; motorcycle memorabilia. Buying and selling; holds catalog auctions

The Fisher-Price Collector's Club
The Gabby Goose newsletter
Jeanne Kennedy
1442 N. Ogden
Mesa, AZ 85205
e-mail: FPClub1@cs.com
e-mail: FPClub@aol.com
www.fpclub.org
membership: $20 ($30 for first
class mailing); $25 international

Friends of Hoppy club and *Hoppy
  Talk* newsletter
Laura Bates
6310 Friendship Dr.
New Concord, OH 43762-9708
614-826-4850
e-mail: LBates1205@cs.com
www.hopalong.com/home.asp
membership: $20 (4 newsletters
and *free* ads)

Game Times
Gene Autry Star Telegram
Gene Autry Museum
P.O. Box 67
Gene Autry, OK 73436
www.autry-museum.org

Gas Toy Collector's Association
P.O. Box 440818
Houston, TX 77244

Hello Again, Old-Time Radio
   Show Collector
Jay A. Hickerson
P.O. Box 4321
Hamden, CT 06514
203-248-2887; fax: 203-281-1322
e-mail: JayHick@aol.com
www.old-time.compponsors/
hickerson.html
subscription: $15 (sample copy
available with legal-size SASE)

Hobby News
J.L.C. Publications
Box 258
Ozone Park, NY 11416

Hopalong Cassidy Fan Club International
Laura Bates
6310 Friendship Dr.
New Concord, OH 43762
614-826-4850; e-mail
e-mail: LBates1250Acs.com
www.hopalong.com/home/asp
subscription: $20 US or $25 overseas; includes quarterly newsletter
and information on annual Cambridge, Ohio, festival

Ideal Collectors Club
Judith Izen
P.O. Box 623
Lexington, MA 02420
e-mail: jizenres@aol.com
membership: $20 per year (quar-
terly newsletter)

International Wizard of Oz Club Inc.
The Baum Bugle
P.O. Box 26249
San Francisco, CA 94126-6249
www.ozclub.org

John's Collectible Toys and Gifts catalog
John DeCicco
1323 Main St.
Lancaster, MA 01524
800-505-TOYS
www.johns-toys-store.com/store
$1 for catalog

Liddle Kiddle Konvention
Paris Langford
415 Dodge Ave.
Jefferson, LA 70121
e-mail: bbean415@aol.com
e-mail: liddlekiddlesnewsletter@
yahoo.com
www.vintageland.com/liddle_
kiddles_convention.htm

Marble Mania
Marble Collectors Society of
   America
Stanley Block
P.O. Box 222
Trumbull, CT 06611
203-261-3223
e-mail:BlockMCSA@aol.com
www.blocksite.com

Marl & B catalog (Barbie dolls)
Marl Davidson
10301 Braden Run
Bradenton, FL 34202
941-751-6275
fax: 941-751-5463
e-mail: Marlbe@aol.com
www.marlbe.com
subscription: $25 US (sample copy
$7.95); $30 Canada; $40 foreign
(sample copy $12.95)

McDonald's Collector Club
Joyce and Terry Losonsky
7506 Summer Leave Ln.
Columbia, MD 21046-2455
401-381-3358
Authors of *Illustrated Collector's*
Guide to McDonald's® Happy Meal®
Boxes, Premiums & Promotions©
($9 plus $2 postage), and *Illustrated*
Collector's Guide to McDonald's
Mccaps ($3 plus $2), both available
from the authors

McDonald's Collector's Club
(Florida Sunshine Chapter)
Bill and Pat Poe
220 Dominica Circle E.
Niceville, FL 32578-4085

850-897-4163
fax: 580-897-2606
e-mail: McPoes@aol.com
e-mail: Patpoetoys@aol.com
membership: $15 individual; $20
family/couple; $7 junior; $20 international

Model and Toy Collector Magazine
Toy Scouts, Inc.
137 Casterton Ave.
Akron, OH 44303
330-836-0668
fax: 330-869-8668
e-mail: toyscouts@toyscouts.com
www.toyscouts.com

Modern Doll Collectors' Inc.
Earl Meisinger
11 S 767 Book Rd.
Naperville, IL 60564

National Fantasy Fan Club (Disney)
Dept. AC, Box 19212
Irvine, CA 92623-9212
714-731-4705
www.nfcc.org
membership: $24 US; $30 Canada;
$40 foreign; Includes newsletters,
free ads, chapters, conventions,
etc.

Paper Collectors' Marketplace
470 Main St., P.O. Box 128
Scandinavia, WI 54977
715-467-2379
www.pcmpaper.com
e-mail:pcmpaper@gglbbs.com
subscription: $19.95 US; $34.95
Canada and Mexico

Paper Doll News
Emma Terry
P.O. Box 807
Vivian, LA 71082
subscription: $12 4 issues; $6 2
issues; $3 sample and illustrated
list

Pez Collector's News
Richard and Marianne Belyski
P.O. Box 14956
Surfside Beach, SC 29587
e-mail: peznews@juno.com
www.pezcollectorsnews.com

Playset Magazine
1240 Marlstone Place
Colorado Springs, CO, 80904
e-mail:playsetmagazine@aol.com
www.playsetmagazine.com

The Prehistoric Times
Mike and Kurt Fredericks
145 Bayline Circle
Folsom, CA 95630
916-985-7986
www.prehistorictimes.com
subscription: $28 6 issues, $7 last
edition; $5 back issue

The Prize Insider Newsletter for
    Cracker Jack collectors
Theresa Richter
5469 South Dorchester
Chicago, IL 60615
773-241-6361
e-mail: waddytmr@aol.com
www.collectoronline.com/CJCA

The Puppet Collector's Newsletter
Steven Meltzer
1255 2nd St.
Santa Monica, CA 90401
310-656-0483
e-mail: steve@puppetmagic.com
www.puppetmagic.com

The Replica
Craig Purcell, Editor
Hwys 136 & 20
Dyersville, IA 52040
319-875-2000
www.toytractorshow.com/the_
replica.htm
Marketing tool that previews
upcoming diecast releases and arti-
cles of interest to collectors;
included are Wm Britain pewter figures, Ertl diecast automotive replicas
and John Deere kits (Pre-School)

Roy Rogers-Dale Evans Collectors
    Assn.
Nancy Horsley
P.O. Box 1166
Portsmouth, OH 45662
614-353-0900

Schoenhut Collectors Club
Patricia J. Girbach
1003 W Huron St.
Ann Arbor, MI 48103-4217
e-mail: aawestie@provide.net

*Shirley Temple Collectors Conven-
    tion, Inc.*
Marge Meisinger
11 S. 767 Book Rd.
Naperville, IL 60564

The Silver Bullet
Terry and Kay Klepey
P.O. Box 553
Forks, WA 98331
360-327-3726
e-mail: slvrbllt@olypen.com
subscription: $20 per year; $5 sample issue; Back issues are available.

Snow Biz newsletter
Nancy McMichael
P.O. Box 53262
Washington, DC 20009
subscription; $10 (3 times a year)
Club has annual meeting and swap
meet.

Star Wars online newsletter
Host: Brian's Toys
http://groups.yahoo.com/brianstoys
www.brianstoys.com (sign up for
newsletter)

Still Bank Collectors Club of
    America
Larry Egelhoff
4175 Millersville Rd.
Indianapolis, IN 46205
317-846-7228
e-mail: egelhoff1@juno.com
www.stillbankclub.com
membership: $35

The Sno-Pea Trader catalog/price guide
N.F. Huber
931 Emerson St.
Thousand Oaks, CA 91362-2447
805-497-0119
subscription: $12 per year (refund-
able with purchase)

Toy Car Collector Magazine
Dana Johnson Enterprises
P.O. Box 1824
Bend, OR 97709-1824
541-318-7176
e-mail: mailto:toynutz@earthlink.net
www.toynutz.com
subscription: $29.95 US; $39.95
Canada and Mexico; $49.95 for-
eign

Toy Collector Club of America
(SpecCast toys)
P.O. Box 368
Dyersville, IA 52040
563-875-8706
fax: 563-875-8056
www.speccast.com

Toy Gun Collectors of America Newsletter
Jim Buskirk
3009 Oleander Ave.
San Marcos, CA 92069
760-599-1054
dues: $17 per year
SASA for information

Toy Shop
Mark Williams, publisher
700 E State St.
Iola, WI 54990-0001
715-445-2214
fax: 715-445-4087
www.toyshopmag.com
subscription: $33 (26 issues)

Toy Soldier Collectors of America
Charles L. DuVal
P.O. Box 179
New Ellenton, SC 29809-0179
e-mail: toysoldiercollectorsamerica
@yahoo.com
membership: $10 US and Canada;
$15 overseas

Toychest
Antique Toy Collectors of
America, Inc.
Robert R. Grew
2 Wall St., 13th Floor
New York, NY 10005
212-238-8803

Train Collectors Association/
National Toy Museum
John V. Luppino
P.O.Box 248
300 Paradise Lane
Strasburg, PA 17579-0248
717-687-8623 (business office)
717-687-8976 (Toy Museum)
fax: 717-687-0742
e-mail:toytrain@traincollectors.org
www.traincollectors.org

The Trick or Treat Trader
CJ Russell and the Halloween
Queen Antiques
P.O. Box 499
4 Lawrence St. and Rt. 10
Winchester, NH, 03470
603-239-8875
e-mail:
halloweenqueen@cheshire.net
subscription: $15 4 issues; $4 sample issue

Western & Serials Club
527 S. Front St.
Mankato, MN 56001-3718
phone/fax: 507-344-0255
e-mail: keitzer@mctcnet.net
www.angelfire.com/biz2/norman
kietzerpubs/

The Working Class Hero (Beatles
newsletter)
3311 Niagara St.
Pittsburgh, PA 15213-4223
Alternate address: 59 Crescent St.
Winsted, CT 06098
Published 3 times a year, send
SASE for information.

Yo-Yo Times
P.O. Box 1519-SCT
Herndon, VA 20172
e-mail: yoyotimes@jodiarts.com
www.yoyotimes.com
Subscription: $12 or $3 per issue

Index

A-Team...1
Action Figures................1-10,221-230,387-393
Action Jackson..1
Activity Sets....................................10-12
Addams Family..................118,134,212,325
Adventure Team Figures.....................222-223
Advertising....................................12-19
Advertising, See also Advertising Signs, Ads, and Displays; Bubble Bath Containers; Cereal Boxes; Character, TV, and Movie Collectibles; Dakins; Disney; Halloween Costumes; Pin-back Buttons; Premiums; Radios; Telephones; Western; and other specific categories
Advertising Character Watches.................117
Advertising Signs, Ads, and Displays...........19-20
Aeronautical....................................20-23
Aeronautical, See also Battery-Operated; Cast Iron, Airplanes; Model Kits; Robots and Space Toys; Windups, Friction, and Other Mechanicals
Ahi..151
Aircraft Carriers.................................63
Airline Collectibles.............................20-23
Airplanes...................................92-93,293
Al Capp...109
Alarm Clocks...............................114-115
Alice in Wonderland.............................165
All American Toy Company.....................23-24
Allen Dolls......................................33
Allied/Pyro Dollhouse Furniture................172
Alvin & the Chipmunks.........................118
American Beauties...............................301
American Character..............................182
American Flyer.............................410-411
American Metal Toys.............................366
Amos 'n Andy...................................265
AMT..277
Andy Gibb......................................352
Annie, See Little Orphan Annie
Applause, See California Raisins
Aquaman....................................137,238
Arby's..109
Arcade, See Banks; Cast Iron; Dollhouse Furniture; Housewares; Pull and Push Toys
Auburn Rubber, See Building Blocks and Construction Toys; Rubber Toys; Soldiers
Aunt Jemima.....................................12
Aurora.............................277-278,361-363
Autobot Cars....................................420

Automobiles and Other Vehicle Replicas..........24-26, 150-154
Automobiles and Other Vehicle Replicas, See also Promotional Vehicles; specific manufacturers
Baby Dolls and Other Favorites..............181-182
Bambi...165
Bamm-Bamm....................................149
Banana Splits...................................118
Bandai, See Automobiles; Battery-Operated; Boats; Model Kits; Windups, Friction, and Other Mechanicals, Japan
Banks..27-33
Banks, See also Advertising; Battery-Operated; Character, TV, and Movie Collectibles; Disney; Diecast Collector Banks; Political; Reynolds Banks; Robots, Miscellaneous; Rock 'n Roll; other specifi categories
Barbie Doll and Friends.........33-44,239,259,426
Barbie Cases.....................................38
Barbie Clothing and Accessories...............38-41
Barbie Furniture, Rooms, Houses, and Shops.....41-42
Barbie Gift Sets................................42-43
Barbie Vehicles..................................43
Barclay.....................................151,366-369
Barney Google..................................438
Bat Masterson...................................428
Batman.................1-2,81,109,118-119, 137,212,232,239,259,282,295,325
Battery-Operated Toys..........................45-50
Battery-Operated Toys, See also Aeronautical; Automobile and Other Vehicle Replicas; Boats; Marx; Robots and Battery-Operated Toys, Space Toys
Battleships.....................................63-64
Battlestar Galactica...............................2
BB Guns....................................234-235
Beanie & Cecil.................................119
Beanie Babies..................................50-59
Bears, See Teddy Bears
Beast Wars Transformers........................423
Beatles.....................................109,352-353
Bell Toys, see Pull and Push Toys
Ben (Obi-Wan) Kenobi..........................387
Best of the West..................................2
Betty Boop.....................................119
Beverly Hillbillies.........................254,433
Bicycles, Motorbikes, and Tricycles.............59-60
Big Boy.......................................12-13
Big Jim...2

Big Little Books.................................66-68
Bing...415-416
Bing, See also Aeronautica; Boats, Optical Toys; Pull and Push Toys; Steam Powered; Trains; Windups, Friction and Other Mechanicals (German)
Bionic Woman 2,119
Biplanes 21
Black Americana 60-63,434
Black Americana, See also Battery-Operated; Schoenhut; Windups, Friction, and Other Mechanicals
Black Hole 2-3
Bliss, See Boats; Dollhouse Furniture; Dollhouses; Paper-Lithographed Toys; Pull and Push Toys
Blue Box Dollhouse Furniture 172-173
Blues Brothers 119
Blythe by Kenner 183
Boats..63-66,93
Boats, See also Cast Iron, Boats; Battery-Operated; Tootsietoys; Windups, Friction, and Other Mechanicals
Boba Fett 388
Bobbin' Heads, See Character Bobbin' Heads; Political; Sporting Collectibles
Bombers...21
Bonzo...438
Book of Knowledge Banks 27-30
Books..66-73;61,385
Borden 97
Bozo the Clown 119,254,333
Brady Bunch......................................119
Bret Maverick....................................241
Breyer...73-78
Britains...369-376
Brook Shields 183
Bubble Bath Containers 78-82
Bubble Club Characters by Purex, See Bubble Bath Containers
Buck Rogers 3,119-120,135,232,308
Buddy L 82-87
Buddy L, See also Advertising; Aeronautical; Boats; Catalogs; Character, TV, and Movie Collectibles
Bugs Bunny...........................114,135,334
Building Blocks and Construction Toys 87-90
Burger King 13
Buster Brown.........................13,120,251
Cabbage Patch Kids 334
Cabin Cruisers.....................................64
California Raisins...............................90-92
CALRAB, See California Raisins
Campbell's 13,255,260
Campus Cuties 301

Candy Containers, See Halloween; other specific categories
Cap'n Crunch.....................................108
Capt. Marvel 308
Captain Action....................................3-4
Captain Kangaroo..............................120
Captain Midnight..........................308-309
Carette 416-417
Carriages 248-249
Cars..82
Case Tractors.................................200-201
Casper the Ghost 239,259,426
Cast Iron..92-95
Cast Iron, See also Banks; Dollhouse Furniture; Guns; Pull and Push Toys; Western Catalogs 105-106
Celebrity Dolls...............................183-186
Cereal Boxes and Premiums 106-108
Chad Valley......................................151
Character, TV, and Movie Collectibles..........117-132
Character, TV, and Movie Collectibles, See also Action Figures; Advertising Signs, Ads, and Displays; Battery-Operated; Books; Chein; Clocks and Watches; Coloring, Activity, and Paint Books; Dakin; Disney; Dolls, Celebrity; Fisher-Price; Games; Guns; Halloween Costumes; Lunch Boxes; Marx; Model Kits; Paper Dolls, Pin-Back Buttons; Plastic Figures; Playsets; Puppets; Puzzles; Records; Toothbrush Holders; View-Master; Western; Windups, Friction, and Other Mechanicals
Character and Promotional Drinking Glasses..108-113
Character Bobbin' Heads........................113
Character Clocks and Watches 114-117;44
Character Clocks and Watches, See also Adverting; Barbie Doll and Friends; California Raisins
Character Puzzles 331-333
Charlie Chaplin 439
Charlie McCarthy..........................120,260
Charlie Tuna................................117,334
Chatty Cathy.....................................186
Chein, See also Banks; Character, TV, and Movie; Disney; Musical Toys; Sand Toys and Pails
Cher...183,353
Chevy Coupes and Sedans.....................98
Chewbacca.......................................388
CHiPs....................4,120,239,426
Chris Dolls...36
Christie Dolls 36
Christmas 69
Cinderella..............................109,286,437
Circus Toys, See Battery-Operated; Cast Iron, Circus;

Chein; Marx; Schoenhut; Windups, Friction, and Other Mechanicals

Cisco Kid 428

Clash of the Titans 4

Cleaning and Laundry Toys 247

Clowns 294,354-355,439,445

Coca-Cola, See Advertising; Character and Promotional Drinking Glasses; Diecut Collector Banks; Radios

Colorforms, See Activity Sets; Barbie Doll and Friends; California Raisins; Character, TV, and Movie; Disney; Rock 'n Roll; Western

Coloring, Activity, and Paint Books 134-137

Columbia Bicycles 59

Comic Books 137-139,229,386

Construction Vehicles 82-83,94,314

Convoy, Highway Express, and Super Rigs 274-275

Cooking-Related Toys 247-248

Corgi 139-148

Corgitronics 146

Cracker Jack 14-15

Cragstan, See Advertising; Aeronautical; Automobiles; Battery-Operated; Boats; Robots and Space Toys; Windups, Friction, and Other Mechanicals, Japan

Creepy Crawlers 11

Crissy and Her Friends 186-187

Daisy Guns 234-235

Dakin 148-150

Dale Evans 241,428

Dam Things 424-426

Daniel Boone 426,428

Darth Vader 239,388,405

David Cassidy 353

Davy Crockett.......213,232,255,260,326,339,428-429

Dawn Dolls 187-188

Dell Fast Action Books by Whitman.................68

Dennis the Menace 120

Diana Ross 184

Dick Tracy 120;58,109,213,266,299,309,334

Diecast..150-154

Diecast, See also Corgi; Dinky; Diecast Collector Banks; Hot Wheels; Matchbox; Tootsietoys

Diecast Collector Banks 154-157

Dinky 157-165

Dinosaurs 301,399-400

Disney 165-172

Disney, See also Advertising Signs, Ads, and Displays; Battery-Operated; Books; Bubble Bath Containers; Character and Promotional Drinking Glasses;

Character Clocks and Watches; Chein; Coloring, Activity, and Paint Books; Dakins; Fisher-Price; Games; Lunch Boxes; Marx; Paper Dolls; Pez Dispensers; Pin-Back Buttons; Plastic Figures; Puppets; Puzzles; Records; View-Master and Tru-View; Western; Windups, Friction, and Other Mechanicals

Disneykins 301-302

Dollhouse Furniture 172-178

Dollhouses 178-180

Dolls and Accessories 180-200;61

Dolls and Accessories, See also Action Figures; Barbie Doll and Friends; Character, TV, and Movie Collectibles; Disney; GI Joe; other specific categories

Dolly Darlings by Hasbro 188

Donald Duck.........165-166;67,58,70,81,110,115,149, 266,296,326,336,436,439-440,445-446,451

Dr. Dolittle 120,255

Dr. Seuss 120

Drums 284

Dukes of Hazzard.....................4,120-121,255,334

Dump Trucks 85,99,264,317,320,364,402,452

Duncan...408-409,454

Electric Cars 292

Elsie the Cow 13

Elvis 184,355

Empire Strikes Back, See Star Wars

Erector Sets 88

Ertl, See Diecast; Diecast Collector Banks; Farm Toys; Model Kits

Family Affair 121

Farm Toys 200-203;94,406

Farmall Tractors..201

Farrah Fawcett-Majors 184

Felix the Cat..............................121,213,294,440

Ferdinand the Bull 166-167

Finger Puppets 325

Firefighting Vehicles ..83,94-95,250,314-316,402-403

First Gear Banks 156

Fisher-Price, See also Activity Sets; Building Blocks and Construction Toys; Catalogs; Character, TV, and Movie Collectibles; Dollhouse Furniture; Dollhouses; Dolls; Optical Toys; Puppets; other specific categories

Flash Gordon...309

Flatsys 189

Flintstones 81,110,121,149,214,255, 258,260,266,309,325,327,332,336,338,426

Flivver Delivery Trucks 85

Foghorn Leghorn...326

Ford Coupes...99
Francie Dolls 36
Gabby Hayes 429
Galoob..189,384
Games 212-219,229,237,396,409
Games, See also Advertising; Black Americana; Barbie; California Raisins; Halloween; Political; Robots and Space Toys, Miscellaneous; Sporting; Tops and Other Spinning Toys
Garfield..258,405
Gas-Powered Cars 292
Gasoline-Powered Toys............................219-220
Gendron, See Pedal Cars and Other Wheeled Goods
Gene Autry 18,72,116,135,233,286,309,429-430
General Mills..106
Gerber Babies 190
GI Joe..221-230
GI Joe, See also Games; Lunch Boxes; Puzzles; Windups, Friction, and Other Mechanicals
Gilbert 88
Gilligan's Island..122
Godzilla...282
Goofy Grams 149
Green Giant 16
Green Hornet...309,427
Green Lantern...309
Grey Iron...377-378
Greyhound Buses 99-100,446
Grizzly Adams 255
Gunboats...64
Gund..325-326
Guns..230-235
Gunsmoke..305,332,430
Hafner Trains..417
Halloween...235-238
Halloween Costumes.................................238-240
Han Solo 389
Hand Puppets...325-326
Hanna-Barbera 122-123,149-150,336
Happy Days 4,123
Happy Hooligan 355
Hartland Figures.......................................383
Hartland Plastics, Inc................................240-241
Heckle & Jeckle 123
Henry..447
Holly Hobbie 190-191,255,258
Holster Sets 235
Honey Hill Bunch.....................................191
Hopalong Cassidy................69,110,115,135-136, 214,233,255,260,266,309,325,339,340,430-41

Horse-Drawn Vehicles 95-96,393,394,435
Horses...242
Hot Wheels 242-247
Housewares 247-250
Howdy Doody..........69,123,136,325,327,332,340,447
Hubley, See Aeronautical; Banks; Battery-Operated; Cast Iron; Character, TV, and Movie Collectibles; Diecast; Guns; Optical Toys; Push and Pull Toys
Huckleberry Hound.....................79,255,325,338,340
Hulk Hogan..124
Humphrey Bogart.....................................184
Humpty Dumpty 302
Humpty Dumpty Circus Animals, Clowns, and Other Personel 357-359
Huskies (Corgi) 147
Ideal...173,404
Ideal Petite Princess.................................173-174
Ideal Young Decorator 174
Imperial Shuttles and Transports 394
Incredible Hulk 124
Indiana Jones 4-5,256,338
International Trucks...................................100
Irwin Dollhouse Furniture 174-175
Ives Trains 417
J&E Stevens 231
Jabba the Hut 394
Jack Armstrong 310
Jack-in-the Boxes 250
Jack-in-the-Boxes, See also Black Americana; Character, TV, and Movie Collectibles; Disney
Jack-o'-Lanterns 237
James Bond.........................5,124,214,283
Jawa..390
Jaydon Dollhouse Furniture 175
Jem 191-192
Jerry Mahoney..328
Jetsons...124
Jigsaw Puzzles 331-333
Jiminy Cricket...326
Jimmy Carter 307
Joe Namath...382
John Deere...202
John Wayne 184
Johnny Lightning 153
Jones Soldiers..378-379
Jungle Book 110
Keebler 16
Kellogg's..107
Kellogg's Pep Pins.....................................300
Ken Dolls 36-37

Kenner Starting Lineup Figures.....................383-384

Kenton..231

Keystone..250-251

Keystone, See also Aeronautical

Keystone Cops..355

Kiddie Car Classics..153

Kiddie Picture Disks....................................341-342

King Features..336

King Kong 124

Kingsbury, See Aeronautical; Pressed Steel; Windups, Friction, and Other Mechanicals (American)

KISS 353

Knickerbocker..325-326

Kohner..327-328

Land of the Lost 125

Lando Calrissian..390

Landspeeder...394

Lanterns...237-238

Lassie...70

Laurel & Hardy 125,185,283

Lehmann...251-253

Liddle Kiddles 192-194

Lincoln Log Soldiers...379

Lindberg Models 279-280

Linemar, See Windups, Friction, and Other Mechanicals (Japanese)

Lionel Trains...411-415

Little Golden Books.......................................68-69

Little Lulu...125

Little Orphan Annie..........118,125,215,254,258,308

Littlechaps...194-195

Locomotives, See Trains

Lone Ranger..............241;5,19,215,233,303,306,310, 332,334,338,340,431

Looney Tunes...125-126

Lost in Space..256,347

Love Boat 126

Lucille Ball 185,287

Lucotte Soldiers 379-380

Luke Skywalker..390-391

Lunch Boxes..253-260

M&M Toys 17

M*A*S*H...5-6

Mack Trucks...........................100,100,318-319

Magic Lanterns...285

Magic Sets, See Activity Sets; Character, TV, and Movie Collectibles

Magilla Gorilla 126

Major Matt Mason 6

Man From UNCLE 6,126,215,301

Manoil...153,380-382

Marbles...260-263

Marilyn Monroe 185

Marionettes..326-327

Marklin, See Aeronautica; Boats; Building Blocks and Construction Toys; Dollhouse Furniture, Steam Powered; Trains

Marklin Trains 418-419

Marvel Super Heroes...6

Marx...263-270,419

Marx, See also Advertising; Aeronautical; Banks; Character, TV, and Movie Collectibles; Dollhouses; Dollhouse Playsets, Ramp Walkers Furniture; Guns; Plastic Figrues; Playsets; other specific categories

Marx Little Hostess 175

Mary Poppins..427

Massey-Ferguson Tractors 202

Masters of the Universe 6-7

Matchbox...270-2876

Mattel..232

Mattel Talking Dolls..195

Mattel Talking Dolls, See also Character, TV, and Movie Collectibles; Disney; and other specific categories

Maverick...431

McDonald's..17

Mechanical Banks 27-30,342-344

Mego...384

Mickey Mouse.........167-170;19,68,72,79,81,110,114, 115,117,149,256,258,299,310,334,336,338, 384,405,435,441-442,448,451

Micromasters 423

Micronauts 7

Midge Dolls 37

Mighty Mouse 126,149,216,310

Mignot...382

Miller Plaster...382

Milton Bradley, See Puzzles

Minnie Mouse..170

Model Kits...276-281

Model Kits, See also Plasticville Models of Yesteryear

Monkees....................................299,325,333,354

Monogram...280

Monoplanes...22

Mork & Mindy...126

Mortimer Snerd..267

Motor Vehicles...97-104

Motorcycles...101,442-443

Movie Posters and Lobby Cards 281-284

Mr. Peanut..18,117
Mr. Potato Head..11
Munsters...127
Muppets..258
Musical Toys...284
Musical Toys, See also Character, TV, and Movie Collectibles; Disney; Rock 'n Roll; Western
NASA...348
New Zoo Revue..127
Nodders, See also Character Bobbin' Heads; Political; Rock 'n Roll; Sporting Collectibles
Noisemakers..238
Nutty Mads...303
Ocean Liners...64-65
Optical Toys...284-285
Optical Toys, See also Character, TV, and Movie Collectibles; Disney; View-Master and Tru-Vue; Western
Oscar Mayer...17
Paper Dolls...................................285-288;44,63
Paper-Lithographed Toys..............................288-289
Paper-Lithographed Toys, See also Black Americana; Boats; Circus Toys; Dollhouses; Games; Pull and Push Toys; Puzzles and Picture Books
Parker Bros., See Puzzles
Partridge Family...136
PAT Ward...110-111
Patrol Wagons...96
Peanuts...................127-128;111,113,114,256,260,325
Pedal Cars and Other Wheeled Goods...................289-293
Pencil Sharpeners, See Character, TV, and Movie Collectibles; Disney
Penny Toys...293-295
Pepsi-Cola, See Advertising; Diecast; Diecast Collector Banks; Radios
Pez Dispensers.......................................295-298
Pianos...284
Pillsbury Doughboy and Poppin' Fresh...................17-18
Pin-Back Buttons.....................................298-300
Pink Panther.................................126,149,335
Pinky Lee..128
Pinocchio.......170-171,267,283,326,327,334,340,449
PJ Dolls..37
Planet of the Apes...7
Planters Peanuts...117
Plasco...175-176
Plastic Figures......................................300-303
Plastic Toys.....................................303-304;302
Plasticville..304-305
Playmates..384-385

Playsets.........................305-307,385, 393-394
Playsets (by companies other than Marx), See Character Collectibles; Disney; and other specific categories
Pluto..171,297,449
Pocket Super Heroes.......................................7-8
Pocket Watches...115
Political..307
Pop-Up and Movable Books...............................69-70
Popeye................128-129;79,111,136,149-150,216, 233,267-268,297,310,327,336,449, 355
Porky Pig..150
Post Vehicles..108
Power of the Force, See Star Wars
Predacons..421,423
Premiums...307-312;107-108
Premiums, See also Advertising; Cereal Boxes and Premiums; Character, TV, and Movie Collectibles; Disney; Pin-Back Buttons
Pressed Steel....................................312-314;264-265
Pressed Steel, See also Aeronautical; Buddy L; Keystone; Marx; Pedal Cars; Structo; Tonka; Wyandotte
Pretender Transformers...................................422
Prince Valiant...306
Princess Diana...185
Princess Leia..391
Promotional Vehicles.................................320-322
Pull and Push Toys...................................322-325
Pull and Push Toys, See also Advertising; Character Collectibles; Disney; Fisher-Price
Puppets..325-328
Puppets, See also Advertising; Black Americana; California Raisins; Halloween; Political
Push-Button Puppets..................................327-328
Puzzles..328-333;230
Puzzles; See also Advertising; Barbie; California Raisins; Political
Quaker Cereal..107
Racers...102,268,291,443
Radios, Novelty......................................333-335
Raggedy Ann and Andy........114,129,240,256-257,339
Railway Express Line Vans.................................86
Ralstoy..154
Ramp Walkers...335-337
Records..338-342
Red Goose...18
Registering Banks...30
Renewal..176-177
Return of the Jedi, See Star Wars

Revell 281
Reynolds Banks 342-345
Ride-On Toys 83-84
Rin-Tin-Tin 306,310,333,431
Riverboats 65
Roadsters 102,291,313
Robots and Space Toys 345-352
Robots and Space Toys, See also Guns, Miscellaneous; Marx; Windups, Friction, and Other Mechanicals, Japan
Rock 'n Roll 352-354
Rock 'n Roll, See also Action Figures; Advertising Signs, Ads, and Displays; Bubble Bath Containers; Character and Promotional Drinking Glasses; Coloring, Activity, and Paint Books; Dolls, Celebrity
Rockflowers 195-196
Rocking Horses 242
Rocky & Friends 129
Rolling Stones 354
Roly Polys 254-356
Roly Polys, See also Black Americana; Character, TV and Movie Collectibles
Rosie O'Donnell 185-186
Roy Rogers 20,21,115,117,136,234,241,257, 299,303,306,310,427,431-432
Rubber Toys, See Character, TV, and Movie Collectibles; Disney; Soldiers
Russ China Trolls 425
R2-D2 392
Sabrina the Teenage Witch 129-130
Sand and Gravel Trucks 86
Sand Toys and Pails 356-357
Sandcrawler 395
Sandpeople 392
Santa Claus, See also Battery-Operated; Books; Reynolds Toys; Windups, Friction, and Other Mechanicals; other specific categories
Saturday Night Live 130
Scales 250
Schoenhut 357-359
Schoenhut, See also Building Blocks and Construction Toys; Catalogs; Character Collectibles; Disney; Musical Toys; Roly Polys
Schuco 359-360
Schuco, See also Aeronautical; Automobiles and Other Vehicle Replicas; Battery-Operated; Character, TV, and Movie Collectibles; Diecast; Disney; Windups, Friction, and Other Mechanicals
Schwinn Bicycles 60
Sedans 102,453

Sewing Machines 249
Sewing Toys 249
Sgt. Preston 310
Shadow 311
Shani 196-197
Shirley Temple 186
Shops and Single Rooms (Dollhouse) 180
Simpsons 130
Six Million Dollar Man 8,137
Skipper Dolls 37
Sky King 311
Skybusters 276
Slot Cars 360-364
Smith-Miller 364-365
Smokey the Bear 114
Smurfs 130,258
Snoopy 80,114,117,217,258,259,328
Snow White 171-172,111,257,283
Soldiers, See also Dinky (for accessory vehicles); Plastic Figures
Soldiers and Accessories 365-382
Soldiers and Accessories, See also Dinky; Plastic Figures
Solido 154
Space Patrol 311
Space Rangers 299
Space Toys, See Robots and Space Toys
Spec-Cast Banks 145-157
Speedboats 65
Spider-Man 130,325
Spinners 409
Sporting Collectibles 382-384
Sporting Collectibles, See also Cereal Boxes and Premiums; Character and Promotional Drinking Glasses; Dolls, Celebrity; Games; Pin-Back Buttons
Stake Trucks 102,317-318,319,406,453
Star Trek 384-386;339,405
Star Trek, See also Character and Promotional Drinking Glasses; Comic Books; Halloween Costumes; Lunch Boxes; Model Kits; Trading Cards
Star Wars 386-396,405
Star Wars, See also Character and Promotional Drinking Glasses; Coloring, Activity, and Paint Books; Halloween Costumes; Model Kits
Steam Engines 397-398
Steam Powered 396-398
Steam Rollers 251,398
Steam Shovels 84
Steelcraft, See Pedal Cars and Other Wheeled Goods
Steiff 398-400

Steiff, See also Character, TV, and Movie Collectibles; Disney
Still Banks..30-33,344-345
Stormtroopers...392-393
Stoves...248
Strauss...400-402
Strawberry Shortcake..........................197,339,405
Strombecker.........................177,281,363,363,364
Structo..402-403
Stunticons..421
Submarines..65
Sulphide Marbles...262-263
Sunshine Family by Mattel.............................197-198
Super Heroes...8-9,112
Super Powers..9-10
Superior Dollhouse Furniture............................177
Superman..................................81,117,130-131,
    257,258,260,268,299,311,325,333,405
Table Service..249
Tambourines...238
Tammy Dolls..198-199
Tarzan..71
Taxis..103,436
Tea Sets, See Advertising; Disney; Housewares; other specific categories
Technobots...422
Teddy Bears..........................403-404;360,398-399
Telephones...404-405
Tell-A-Tale Books by Whitman...........................70
Teresa Dolls..37-38
Thermos Bottles, See Vacuum Bottles
Thingmakers...12
Three Little Pigs..450
Three Stooges..131,137
Throttlebots...422
Thundercats..257
TIE Fighter Pilots..393
TIE Fighters...395
Tinkertoys, See Activity Sets; Building Blocks and Construction Toys; Catalogs
Tom & Jerry...131
Tom Corbett..........................234,269,311,427
Tom Mix...11,311-312
Tomy Smaller Homes.....................................177-178
Tonka...405-407
Tonto..241,303
Tootsietoys..407-409;178
Topo Gigio..114,131
Tops and Other Spinning Toys.....................408-409

Tops and Other Spinning Toys, See also Character, TV, and Movie Collectibles; Chein; Political
Touring Cars....................................103,313,444
Trains...410-419;316,324
Trains, See also Buddy L (for Outdoor Railroad); Cast Iron, Trains; Paper-Lithographed
Transformers..419-424
Tressy Dolls...199-200
Tricycles...60
Trolleys...316,444
Trolls...424-426
Trucks and Vans...84-86
Trucks and Vans, See also Pressed Steel
Tutti Dolls..38
Tyco...363
Uneeda..424-426
Universal Monsters...131
Upsy Downsys by Mattel..................................200
USS Enterprise..385
Vacuum Bottles...259-260
Vehicle Models..24-26
Velvet Dolls..187
Ventriloquist Dolls...328
View-Master and Tru-View............................426-427
Wagons...292-293
Waltons..137
Warner Bros..112,149-150
Welcome Back Kotter................131-132,333,427
Western..427-433
Western, See also Advertising Signs, Ads, and Displays; Cereal Boxes; Character and Promotional Drinking Glasses; Character Clocks and Watches; Coloring, Activity, and Paint Books; Guns; Lunch Boxes; Premiums; Puzzles and Picture Blocks; Windups, Friction, and Other Mechanicals
Whitman, See Books; Paper Dolls; Puzzles
Wild Bill Hickok.........................234,260,333,432
Windups, Friction, and Other Mechanicals...433-452
Windups, Friction, and Other Mechanicals, See also Aeronautical; Automobiles and Other Vehicle Replicas; Boats; Chein; Lehmann; Marx; Robots and Space Toys; Strauss
Winnie the Pooh..........................172,298,427
Wishniks...424-426
Wizard of Oz...10,113,132
Wolverine, See Sand Toys and Pails
Wonder Books..71
Wonder Woman............................132,260,339
Wooden Vehicles...86-87

Woodstock..114
Woody Woodpecker......................132,333,341
Wreckers..103,407
Wristwatches.....................................115-117
WWF Figures...10
Wyandotte 452-453
Wyandotte, See also Aeronautical; Boats; Character, TV, and Movie Collectibles; Guns; Windups, Friction, and Other Mechanicals
X-Wing Fighters......................................395
Yellow Cabs.......................................103-104
Yo-yos...453-454

Yo-yos, See also Advertising; Character, TV, and Movie Collectibles; Disney; Political; Sporting Collectibles; Western
Yoda...393
Yogi Bear 80,260,339
Yogi Berra...383
Zeppelins 23
Ziggy..113
Zorro 234-260,303,333,427,432-433
101 Dalmatians 333
75 Series (Matchbox) 271-272
78 rpm Picture and Non-Picture Records 339-341

We are always investigating new trends for valuable additions to our vast line-up of collectors' identification and value guides.

Knowledgeable authors are essential in maintaining our reputation as the #1 antiques and collectibles publisher.

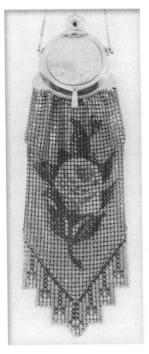

For over 30 years we have been publishing books on antiques and collectibles. Our editorial staff is highly trained and motivated to work together as a team to make your concept a reality.

Are you an authority on clocks, jewelry, watches, furniture, glass, pottery, toys, postcards, doorstops, or any other popular antiques or collectibles subject? Contact us.

We want books by passionate collectors who know their subjects inside and out. Feel free to contact us directly or visit our website for helpful information on submitting a manuscript.

CONTACT INFORMATION

Gail Ashburn, Editor
Amy Sullivan, Assistant Editor

PHONE: 1-270-898-6211
FAX: 1-270-898-8890
OFFICE HOURS 8:00 am – 4:00 pm CT

COLLECTOR BOOKS • P.O. Box 3009
Paducah, KY 42002-3009

www.collectorbooks.com

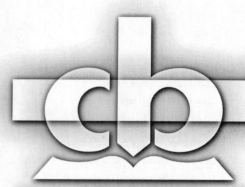

COLLECTOR BOOKS
informing today's collector

www.collectorbooks.com

For over two decades we have been keeping collectors informed on trends and values in all fields of antiques and collectibles.

DOLLS, FIGURES & TEDDY BEARS

4631	**Barbie Doll** Boom, 1986–1995, Augustyniak	$18.95
2079	**Barbie Doll** Fashion, Volume I, Eames	$24.95
4846	**Barbie Doll** Fashion, Volume II, Eames	$24.95
3957	**Barbie** Exclusives, Rana	$18.95
4632	**Barbie** Exclusives, Book II, Rana	$18.95
6022	The **Barbie Doll** Years, 5th Ed., Olds	$19.95
3810	**Chatty Cathy** Dolls, Lewis	$15.95
5352	Collector's Ency. of **Barbie** Doll Exclusives & More, 2nd Ed., Augustyniak	$24.95
4863	Collector's Encyclopedia of **Vogue Dolls**, Izen/Stover	$29.95
5904	Collector's Guide to **Celebrity Dolls**, Spurgeon	$24.95
5599	Collector's Guide to **Dolls of the 1960s and 1970s**, Sabulis	$24.95
6030	Collector's Guide to **Horsman Dolls**, Jensen	$29.95
6025	**Doll Values**, Antique to Modern, 6th Ed., Moyer	$12.95
6033	**Modern Collectible Dolls**, Volume VI, Moyer	$24.95
5689	**Nippon Dolls** & Playthings, Van Patten/Lau	$29.95
5365	**Peanuts Collectibles**, Podley/Bang	$24.95
6026	**Small Dolls** of the 40s & 50s, Stover	$29.95
5253	Story of **Barbie**, 2nd Ed., Westenhouser	$24.95
5277	**Talking Toys** of the 20th Century, Lewis	$15.95
2084	**Teddy Bears, Annalee's & Steiff** Animals, 3rd Series, Mandel	$19.95
1808	Wonder of **Barbie**, Manos	$9.95
1430	World of **Barbie** Dolls, Manos	$9.95
4880	World of **Raggedy Ann** Collectibles, Avery	$24.95

TOYS & MARBLES

2333	Antique & Collectible **Marbles**, 3rd Ed., Grist	$9.95
4559	Collectible **Action Figures**, 2nd Ed., Manos	$17.95
5900	Collector's Guide to **Battery Toys**, 2nd Edition, Hultzman	$24.95
4566	Collector's Guide to **Tootsietoys**, 2nd Ed., Richter	$19.95
5169	Collector's Guide to **TV Toys** & Memorabilia, 2nd Ed., Davis/Morgan	$24.95
5593	Grist's Big Book of **Marbles**, 2nd Ed.	$24.95
3970	Grist's Machine-Made & Contemporary **Marbles**, 2nd Ed.	$9.95
5267	**Matchbox Toys**, 1947 to 1998, 3rd Ed., Johnson	$19.95
5830	**McDonald's** Collectibles, 2nd Edition, Henriques/DuVall	$24.95
5673	Modern **Candy Containers** & Novelties, Brush/Miller	$19.95
1540	Modern **Toys** 1930–1980, Baker	$19.95
5920	**Schroeder's Collectible Toys**, Antique to Modern Price Guide, 8th Ed.	$17.95
5908	**Toy Car** Collector's Guide, Johnson	$19.95

FURNITURE

3716	American **Oak** Furniture, Book II, McNerney	$12.95
1118	Antique **Oak** Furniture, Hill	$7.95
3720	Collector's Encyclopedia of **American** Furniture, Vol. III, Swedberg	$24.95
5359	Early **American** Furniture, Obbard	$12.95
3906	**Heywood-Wakefield** Modern Furniture, Rouland	$18.95
1885	**Victorian** Furniture, Our American Heritage, McNerney	$9.95
3829	**Victorian** Furniture, Our American Heritage, Book II, McNerney	$9.95

JEWELRY, HATPINS, WATCHES & PURSES

4704	Antique & Collectible **Buttons**, Wisniewski	$19.95
1748	Antique **Purses**, Revised Second Ed., Holiner	$19.95
4850	Collectible **Costume Jewelry**, Simonds	$24.95
5675	Collectible **Silver Jewelry**, Rezazadeh	$24.95
3722	Collector's Ency. of **Compacts**, Carryalls & Face Powder Boxes, Mueller	$24.95
4940	**Costume Jewelry**, A Practical Handbook & Value Guide, Rezazadeh	$24.95
5812	Fifty Years of Collectible **Fashion Jewelry**, 1925–1975, Baker	$24.95

1424	**Hatpins** & Hatpin Holders, Baker	$9.95
5695	**Ladies' Vintage Accessories**, Bruton	$24.95
1181	100 Years of Collectible **Jewelry**, 1850–1950, Baker	$9.95
4729	**Sewing Tools** & Trinkets, Thompson	$24.95
6038	**Sewing Tools** & Trinkets, Volume 2, Thompson	$24.95
6039	Signed Beauties of **Costume Jewelry**, Brown	$24.95
5620	Unsigned Beauties of **Costume Jewelry**, Brown	$24.95
4878	Vintage & Contemporary **Purse Accessories**, Gerson	$24.95
5696	Vintage & Vogue Ladies' **Compacts**, 2nd Edition, Gerson	$29.95
5923	**Vintage Jewelry** for Investment & Casual Wear, Edeen	$24.95

INDIANS, GUNS, KNIVES, TOOLS, PRIMITIVES

6021	**Arrowheads** of the Central Great Plains, Fox	$19.95
1868	Antique **Tools**, Our American Heritage, McNerney	$9.95
5616	Big Book of **Pocket Knives**, Stewart	$19.95
4943	Field Guide to Flint **Arrowheads** & Knives of the North American Indian	$9.95
3885	**Indian Artifacts** of the Midwest, Book II, Hothem	$16.95
4870	**Indian Artifacts** of the Midwest, Book III, Hothem	$18.95
5685	**Indian Artifacts** of the Midwest, Book IV, Hothem	$19.95
6132	**Modern Guns**, Identification & Values, 14th Ed., Quertermous	$14.95
2164	**Primitives**, Our American Heritage, McNerney	$9.95
1759	**Primitives**, Our American Heritage, 2nd Series, McNerney	$14.95
6031	Standard **Knife** Collector's Guide, 4th Ed., Ritchie & Stewart	$14.95
5999	**Wilderness** Survivor's Guide, Hamper	$12.95

PAPER COLLECTIBLES & BOOKS

4633	**Big Little Books**, Jacobs	$18.95
5902	**Boys' & Girls' Book** Series	$19.95
4710	Collector's Guide to **Children's Books**, 1850 to 1950, Volume I, Jones	$18.95
5153	Collector's Guide to **Children's Books**, 1850 to 1950, Volume II, Jones	$19.95
1441	Collector's Guide to **Post Cards**, Wood	$9.95
5926	**Duck Stamps**, Chappell	$9.95
2081	Guide to Collecting **Cookbooks**, Allen	$14.95
2080	Price Guide to **Cookbooks** & Recipe Leaflets, Dickinson	$9.95
3973	**Sheet Music** Reference & Price Guide, 2nd Ed., Pafik & Guiheen	$19.95
6041	Vintage **Postcards** for the Holidays, Reed	$24.95
4733	**Whitman Juvenile Books**, Brown	$17.95

GLASSWARE

5602	Anchor Hocking's **Fire-King** & More, 2nd Ed.	$24.95
5823	Collectible **Glass Shoes**, 2nd Edition, Wheatley	$24.95
5897	Coll. **Glassware** from the 40s, 50s & 60s, 6th Ed., Florence	$19.95
1810	Collector's Encyclopedia of **American Art Glass**, Shuman	$29.95
5907	Collector's Encyclopedia of **Depression Glass**, 15th Ed., Florence	$19.95
1961	Collector's Encyclopedia of **Fry Glassware**, Fry Glass Society	$24.95
1664	Collector's Encyclopedia of **Heisey Glass**, 1925–1938, Bredehoft	$24.95
3905	Collector's Encyclopedia of **Milk Glass**, Newbound	$24.95
4936	Collector's Guide to **Candy Containers**, Dezso/Poirier	$19.95
5820	Collector's Guide to **Glass Banks**, Reynolds	$24.95
4564	**Crackle Glass**, Weitman	$19.95
4941	**Crackle Glass**, Book II, Weitman	$19.95
4714	**Czechoslovakian Glass** and Collectibles, Book II, Barta/Rose	$16.95
5528	Early American **Pattern Glass**, Metz	$17.95
6125	**Elegant Glassware** of the Depression Era, 10th Ed., Florence	$24.95
3981	Evers' Standard **Cut Glass** Value Guide	$12.95
5614	Field Guide to **Pattern Glass**, McCain	$17.95
5615	Florence's **Glassware Pattern Identification** Guide, Vol. II	$19.95

| | GLASS (continued) | | |

719 **Fostoria**, Etched, Carved & Cut Designs, Vol. II, Kerr $24.95
261 **Fostoria Tableware**, 1924 – 1943, Long/Seate.................$24.95
861 **Fostoria Tableware**, 1944 – 1986, Long/Seate.................$24.95
604 **Fostoria**, Useful & Ornamental, Long/Seate.................$29.95
399 **Glass & Ceramic Baskets**, White.................$19.95
644 **Imperial Carnival Glass**, Burns.................$18.95
327 **Kitchen Glassware** of the Depression Years, 6th Ed., Florence $24.95
500 Much More Early American **Pattern Glass**, Metz.................$17.95
915 **Northwood Carnival Glass**, 1908 – 1925, Burns.................$19.95
136 Pocket Guide to **Depression Glass**, 13th Ed., Florence $12.95
023 Standard Encyclopedia of **Carnival Glass**, 8th Ed., Edwards/Carwile.........$29.95
024 Standard **Carnival Glass** Price Guide, 13th Ed., Edwards/Carwile.........$9.95
035 Standard Encyclopedia of **Opalescent Glass**, 4th Ed., Edwards/Carwile $24.95
732 **Very Rare Glassware** of the Depression Years, 5th Series, Florence.........$24.95

POTTERY

927 **ABC Plates & Mugs**, Lindsay $24.95
929 **American Art Pottery**, Sigafoose.................$24.95
630 **American Limoges**, Limoges.................$24.95
312 **Blue & White Stoneware**, McNerney.................$9.95
959 **Blue Willow**, 2nd Ed., Gaston.................$14.95
851 Collectible **Cups & Saucers**, Harran.................$18.95
373 Collector's Encyclopedia of **American Dinnerware**, Cunningham.................$24.95
931 Collector's Encyclopedia of **Bauer Pottery**, Chipman.................$24.95
034 Collector's Encyclopedia of **California Pottery**, 2nd Ed., Chipman.................$24.95
723 Collector's Encyclopedia of **Cookie Jars**, Book II, Roerig.................$24.95
939 Collector's Encyclopedia of **Cookie Jars**, Book III, Roerig.................$24.95
748 Collector's Encyclopedia of **Fiesta**, 9th Ed., Huxford.................$24.95
961 Collector's Encyclopedia of **Early Noritake**, Alden.................$24.95
812 Collector's Encyclopedia of **Flow Blue China**, 2nd Ed., Gaston.................$24.95
431 Collector's Encyclopedia of **Homer Laughlin China**, Jasper.................$24.95
276 Collector's Encyclopedia of **Hull Pottery**, Roberts.................$19.95
962 Collector's Encyclopedia of **Lefton China**, DeLozier.................$19.95
855 Collector's Encyclopedia of **Lefton China**, Book II, DeLozier.................$19.95
609 Collector's Encyclopedia of **Limoges Porcelain**, 3rd Ed., Gaston.................$29.95
334 Collector's Encyclopedia of **Majolica Pottery**, Katz-Marks.................$19.95
358 Collector's Encyclopedia of **McCoy Pottery**, Huxford.................$19.95
677 Collector's Encyclopedia of **Niloak**, 2nd Edition, Gifford.................$29.95
837 Collector's Encyclopedia of **Nippon Porcelain**, Van Patten.................$24.95
665 Collector's Ency. of **Nippon Porcelain**, 3rd Series, Van Patten.................$24.95
053 Collector's Ency. of **Nippon Porcelain**, 5th Series, Van Patten.................$24.95
678 Collector's Ency. of **Nippon Porcelain**, 6th Series, Van Patten.................$29.95
447 Collector's Encyclopedia of **Noritake**, Van Patten.................$19.95
564 Collector's Encyclopedia of **Pickard China**, Reed.................$29.95
679 Collector's Encyclopedia of **Red Wing Art Pottery**, Dollen.................$24.95
618 Collector's Encyclopedia of **Rosemeade Pottery**, Dommel.................$24.95
841 Collector's Encyclopedia of **Roseville Pottery**, Revised, Huxford/Nickel.....$24.95
842 Collector's Encyclopedia of **Roseville Pottery**, 2nd Series, Huxford/Nickel $24.95
917 Collector's Encyclopedia of **Russel Wright**, 3rd Editon, Kerr.................$29.95
370 Collector's Encyclopedia of **Stangl Dinnerware**, Runge.................$24.95
921 Collector's Encyclopedia of **Stangl Artware**, Lamps, and Birds, Runge $29.95
314 Collector's Encyclopedia of **Van Briggle Art Pottery**, Sasicki.................$24.95
680 Collector's Guide to **Feather Edge Ware**, McAllister.................$19.95
876 Collector's Guide to **Lu-Ray Pastels**, Meehan.................$18.95
814 Collector's Guide to **Made in Japan Ceramics**, White.................$18.95
646 Collector's Guide to **Made in Japan Ceramics**, Book II, White.................$18.95
1425 **Cookie Jars**, Westfall.................$9.95
3440 **Cookie Jars**, Book II, Westfall.................$19.95
5909 **Dresden Porcelain** Studios, Harran.................$29.95
5918 Florence's Big Book of **Salt & Pepper Shakers**.................$24.95

2379 **Lehner's Ency. of U.S. Marks** on Pottery, Porcelain & China.................$24.95
4722 **McCoy Pottery**, Collector's Reference & Value Guide, Hanson/Nissen.........$19.95
5913 **McCoy Pottery**, Volume III, Hanson & Nissen.................$24.95
5691 **Post86 Fiesta**, Identification & Value Guide, Racheter.................$19.95
1670 **Red Wing Collectibles**, DePasquale.................$9.95
1440 **Red Wing Stoneware**, DePasquale.................$9.95
6037 **Rookwood Pottery**, Nicholson & Thomas.................$24.95
1632 **Salt & Pepper Shakers**, Guarnaccia.................$9.95
5091 **Salt & Pepper Shakers** II, Guarnaccia.................$18.95
3443 **Salt & Pepper Shakers** IV, Guarnaccia.................$18.95
3738 **Shawnee Pottery**, Mangus.................$24.95
4629 Turn of the Century **American Dinnerware**, 1880s–1920s, Jasper.........$24.95
3327 **Watt Pottery** – Identification & Value Guide, Morris.................$19.95
5924 **Zanesville Stoneware** Company, Rans, Ralston & Russell.................$24.95

OTHER COLLECTIBLES

5916 Advertising **Paperweights**, Holiner & Kammerman.................$24.95
5838 Advertising **Thermometers**, Merritt.................$16.95
5898 Antique & Contemporary **Advertising Memorabilia**, Summers.................$24.95
5814 Antique **Brass & Copper** Collectibles, Gaston.................$24.95
1880 Antique **Iron**, McNerney.................$9.95
3872 Antique **Tins**, Dodge.................$24.95
4845 Antique **Typewriters & Office Collectibles**, Rehr.................$19.95
5607 Antiquing and Collecting on the **Internet**, Parry.................$12.95
1128 **Bottle** Pricing Guide, 3rd Ed., Cleveland.................$7.95
3718 Collectible **Aluminum**, Grist.................$16.95
5060 Collectible **Souvenir Spoons**, Bednersh.................$19.95
5676 Collectible **Souvenir Spoons**, Book II, Bednersh.................$29.95
5666 Collector's Encyclopedia of **Granite Ware**, Book 2, Greguire.................$29.95
5836 Collector's Guide to **Antique Radios**, 5th Ed., Bunis.................$19.95
3966 Collector's Guide to **Inkwells**, Identification & Values, Badders.................$18.95
4947 Collector's Guide to **Inkwells**, Book II, Badders.................$19.95
5681 Collector's Guide to **Lunchboxes**, White.................$19.95
5621 Collector's Guide to **Online Auctions**, Hix.................$12.95
4864 Collector's Guide to **Wallace Nutting Pictures**, Ivankovich.................$18.95
5683 **Fishing Lure** Collectibles, Vol. 1, Murphy/Edmisten.................$29.95
5911 **Flea Market Trader**, 13th Ed., Huxford.................$9.95
6227 **Garage Sale** & Flea Market Annual, 11th Edition, Huxford.................$19.95
4945 **G-Men and FBI Toys** and Collectibles, Whitworth.................$18.95
3819 **General Store** Collectibles, Wilson.................$24.95
5912 The **Heddon** Legacy, A Century of Classic Lures, Roberts & Pavey.........$29.95
2216 **Kitchen Antiques**, 1790–1940, McNerney.................$14.95
5991 **Lighting Devices** & Accessories of the 17th – 19th Centuries, Hamper.......$9.95
5686 **Lighting Fixtures** of the Depression Era, Book I, Thomas.................$24.95
4950 The **Lone Ranger**, Collector's Reference & Value Guide, Felbinger.........$18.95
6028 Modern **Fishing Lure** Collectibles, Vol. 1, Lewis.................$24.95
6131 Modern **Fishing Lure** Collectibles, Vol. 2, Lewis.................$24.95
2026 **Railroad** Collectibles, 4th Ed., Baker.................$14.95
5619 **Roy Rogers and Dale Evans** Toys & Memorabilia, Coyle.................$24.95
6137 **Schroeder's Antiques** Price Guide, 21st Edition.................$14.95
5007 **Silverplated Flatware**, Revised 4th Edition, Hagan.................$18.95
6239 **Star Wars** Super Collector's Wish Book, 2nd Ed., Carlton.................$29.95
6139 **Summers' Guide to Coca-Cola**, 4th Ed.................$24.95
5905 **Summers' Pocket Guide to Coca-Cola**, 3rd Ed.................$12.95
3977 Value Guide to **Gas Station Memorabilia**, Summers & Priddy.................$24.95
4877 Vintage **Bar Ware**, Visakay.................$24.95
5925 The **Vintage Era of Golf Club Collectibles**, John.................$29.95
6010 The **Vintage Era of Golf Club Collectibles** Collector's Log, John.................$9.95
6036 Vintage **Quilts**, Aug, Newman & Roy.................$24.95
4935 The **W.F. Cody Buffalo Bill** Collector's Guide with Values.................$24.95

This is only a partial listing of the books on antiques that are available from Collector Books. All books are well illustrated and contain current values. Most of these books are available from your local bookseller, antique dealer, or public library. If you are unable to locate certain titles in your area, you may order by mail from **COLLECTOR BOOKS**, P.O. Box 3009, Paducah, KY 42002-3009. Customers with Visa, Master Card, or Discover may phone in orders from 7:00–5:00 CT, Monday–Friday, Toll Free **1-800-626-5420**, or online at **www.collectorbooks.com**. Add $3.00 for postage for the first book ordered and 50¢ for each additional book. Include item number, title, and price when ordering. Allow 14 to 21 days for delivery.

Schroeder's ANTIQUES Price Guide

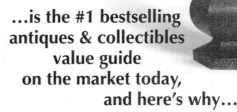

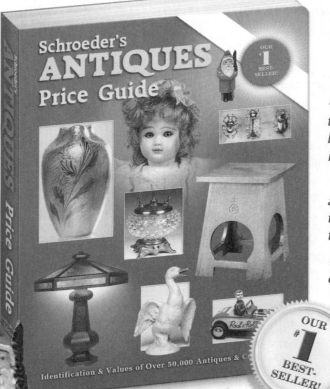

8½" x 11" • 608 pages • $14.95